new dictionary of the history of ideas

EDITORIAL BOARD

new dictionary of the history of ideas

maryanne cline horowitz, editor in chief

volume 4

Machiavellism to Phrenology

CHARLES SCRIBNER'S SONS

An imprint of Thomson Gale, a part of The Thomson Corporation

THOMSON

GALE

Detroit • New York • San Francisco • San Diego • New Haven, Conn. • Waterville, Maine • London • Munich

THOMSON
GALE

New Dictionary of the History of Ideas
Maryanne Cline Horowitz, Editor in Chief

For permission to use material from this product, submit your request via Web at http://www.gale-edit.com/permissions, or you may download our Permissions Request form and submit your request by fax or mail to:

Permissions Department
Thomson Gale
27500 Drake Road
Farmington Hills, MI 48331-3535
Permissions Hotline:
248-699-8006 or 800-877-4253, ext. 8006
Fax: 248-699-8074 or 800-762-4058

Since this page cannot legibly accommodate all copyright notices, the acknowledgments constitute an extension of the copyright notice.

While every effort has been made to ensure the reliability of the information presented in this publication, Thomson Gale does not guarantee the accuracy of the data contained herein. Thomson Gale accepts no payment for listing; and inclusion in the publication of any organization, agency, institution, publication, service, or individual does not imply endorsement of the editors or publisher. Errors brought to the attention of the publisher and verified to the satisfaction of the publisher will be corrected in future editions.

LIBRARY OF CONGRESS CATALOGING-IN-PUBLICATION DATA

New dictionary of the history of ideas / edited by Maryanne Cline Horowitz.
    p. cm.
  Includes bibliographical references and index.
  ISBN 0-684-31377-4 (set hardcover : alk. paper) — ISBN 0-684-31378-2 (v. 1) — ISBN 0-684-31379-0 (v. 2) — ISBN 0-684-31380-4 (v. 3) — ISBN 0-684-31381-2 (v. 4) — ISBN 0-684-31382-0 (v. 5) — ISBN 0-684-31383-9 (v. 6) — ISBN 0-684-31452-5 (e-book)
  1. Civilization—History—Dictionaries. 2. Intellectual life—History—Dictionaries.
  I. Horowitz, Maryanne Cline, 1945–

CB9.N49 2005
903—dc22   2004014731

This title is also available as an e-book.
ISBN 0-684-31452-5
Contact your Thomson Gale sales representative for ordering information.

Printed in the United States of America
10 9 8 7 6 5 4 3

CONTENTS

EDITORIAL AND PRODUCTION STAFF

Project Editors
Mark LaFlaur, Scot Peacock, Jennifer Wisinski

Editorial Support
Kelly Baiseley, Andrew Claps, Alja Collar, Mark Drouillard,
Kenneth Mondschein, Sarah Turner, Ken Wachsberger,
Rachel Widawsky, Christopher Verdesi

Art Editor
Scot Peacock

Chief Manuscript Editor
Georgia S. Maas

Manuscript Editors
Jonathan G. Aretakis, John Barclay, Sylvia Cannizzaro,
Melissa A. Dobson, Ted Gilley, Gretchen Gordon,
Ellen Hawley, Archibald Hobson, Elizabeth B. Inserra,
Jean Fortune Kaplan, Christine Kelley, John Krol,
Julia Penelope, Richard Rothschild, David E. Salamie,
Linda Sanders, Alan Thwaits, Jane Marie Todd

Proofreaders
Beth Fhaner, Carol Holmes, Melodie Monahan,
Laura Specht Patchkofsky, Hilary White

Cartographer
XNR Productions, Madison, Wisconsin

Caption Writer
Shannon Kelly

Indexer
Cynthia Crippen, AEIOU, Inc.

Design
Jennifer Wahi

Imaging
Dean Dauphinais, Lezlie Light, Mary Grimes

Permissions
Margaret Abendroth, Peggie Ashlevitz, Lori Hines

Compositor
GGS Information Services, York, Pennsylvania

Manager, Composition
Mary Beth Trimper

Assistant Manager, Composition
Evi Seoud

Manufacturing
Wendy Blurton

Senior Development Editor
Nathalie Duval

Editorial Director
John Fitzpatrick

Publisher
Frank Menchaca

READER'S GUIDE

This Reader's Guide was compiled by the editors to provide a systematic outline of the contents of the New Dictionary of the History of Ideas, *thereby offering teachers, scholars, and the general reader a way to organize their reading according to their preferences. The Reader's Guide is divided into four sections: Communication of Ideas, Geographical Areas, Chronological Periods, and Liberal Arts Disciplines and Professions, as indicated in the outline below.*

COMMUNICATION OF IDEAS

Introduction to History of Communication of Ideas

Communication Media

GEOGRAPHICAL AREAS

Global Entries

Africa

Asia

Europe

Middle East

North America

Latin and South America

CHRONOLOGICAL PERIODS

Ancient

Dynastic (400 C.E.–1400 C.E.)

Early Modern (1400–1800 C.E.)

Modern (1800–1945)

Contemporary

LIBERAL ARTS DISCIPLINES AND PROFESSIONS

Fine Arts

Humanities

Social Sciences

Sciences

Professions

Multidisciplinary Practices

Especially Interdisciplinary Entries

COMMUNICATION OF IDEAS

This category is the newest aspect of the *New Dictionary of the History of Ideas*; cultural studies, communications studies, and cultural history are moving the disciplines in this direction.

Introduction to History of Communication of Ideas

The following entries focus on the media humans have used to communicate with one another.

Absolute Music
Aesthetics: Asia
Architecture: Overview
Architecture: Asia
Arts: Overview
Astronomy, Pre-Columbian and Latin American
Bilingualism and Multilingualism
Borders, Borderlands, and Frontiers, Global
Calendar
Cinema
City, The: The City as a Cultural Center
City, The: The City as Political Center
Communication of Ideas: Africa and Its Influence
Communication of Ideas: Asia and Its Influence
Communication of Ideas: Europe and Its Influence
Communication of Ideas: Middle East and Abroad
Communication of Ideas: Orality and Advent of Writing
Communication of Ideas: Southeast Asia
Communication of Ideas: The Americas and Their Influence
Consumerism
Cultural Revivals
Cultural Studies
Dance
Diffusion, Cultural
Dress
Dualism
Education: Asia, Traditional and Modern
Education: Global Education
Emotions
Experiment
Garden
Gesture
Humor
Iconography
Images, Icons, and Idols
Japanese Philosophy, Japanese Thought
Language and Linguistics
Language, Linguistics, and Literacy
Learning and Memory, Contemporary Views
Mathematics
Media, History of
Metaphor
Migration: United States
Modernity: Africa
Museums
Music, Anthropology of

Communication Media

This is a listing of the types of historical evidence the author used in writing the entry. While entries in the original Dictionary of the History of Ideas were to a great extent the history of texts, the entries in the New Dictionary of the History of Ideas are generally the cultural history of ideas, making use of the records of oral communication, visual communication, and communication through practices, as well as the history of texts, in order to show the impact of the idea on a wide variety of people.

ORAL

The selective list below contains the entries that give the most coverage to historical examples of the oral transmission and transformation of ideas.

COMMUNICATION THROUGH HIGH TECHNOLOGY MEDIA (radio, television, film, computer, etc.)

VISUAL

Each of the following entries in the *NDHI* either evocatively describes ideas, includes a visual image of an idea, or provides historical examples of societies visually transmitting and transforming ideas.

PRACTICES

Most of the entries in the *NDHI* discuss how specific societies habituated people to specific ideas. This selective list includes the entries on schools of thought and practice, religions, and political movements, as well as the entries on distinctive practices.

TEXTUAL

Every entry in the *New Dictionary of the History of Ideas* used texts. The following is a list of entries that focused mainly on the history of a succession of texts. Each academic discipline has a succession of major authors with whom later practitioners of the discipline build upon and respond to creatively. The historian of a discipline—such as the history of political philosophy, literary history, or the history of science—considers the responses of thinkers and practitioners of a discipline to the major earlier texts in the discipline. In tracing the origin, development, and transformation of an idea, the historian of ideas considers thinkers' responses to texts from a variety of disciplines.

GEOGRAPHICAL AREAS

Global Entries

New Dictionary of the History of Ideas

New Dictionary of the History of Ideas

New Dictionary of the History of Ideas

New Dictionary of the History of Ideas

CHRONOLOGICAL PERIODS

This section is divided according to five periods in world history: Ancient, Dynastic, Early Modern, Modern, and Contemporary. Use this section together with the section on Geographical Areas.

Ancient (before 400 C.E.)

ENTRIES FOCUSED ON THE PERIOD

ENTRIES WITH EXAMPLES FROM BEFORE 400 C.E.

Generally the examples in this category are from the ancient Middle East, Europe, or Asia.

Modern (1800–1945)

New Dictionary of the History of Ideas

Contemporary

ENTRIES FOCUSED ON THE PERIOD

ENTRIES WITH EXAMPLES FROM THE PERIOD
SINCE 1945 (especially since the 1970s)

LIBERAL ARTS DISCIPLINES AND PROFESSIONS

This section is in accord with the university divisions of the Liberal Arts into Fine Arts, Humanities, Social Sciences, and Sciences and the graduate programs of the professions of Law, Medicine, and Engineering. The sample of Interdisciplinary Programs are listed under their most common university grouping. For example, Fine Arts includes Performance Arts; Social Sciences includes Women's Studies and Gender Studies, as well as Ethnic Studies; Sciences includes Ecology and Geology, as well as Computer Sciences; Humanities includes programs of Communication, Language, and Linguistics. Meanwhile, the growth of interdisciplinary programs reflects the increasing overlap between studies listed under the labels of Fine Arts, Humanities, Social Sciences, and Sciences. A discipline or interdisciplinary program only appears once, but an entry may appear under the several disciplines and interdisciplinary programs that influenced the scholarship of the article. Titles that appear in bold indicate entries that are especially suited as a introduction to the discipline.

Under the category Multidisciplinary Practices, there are entries on the many methods, techniques, theories, and approaches that have spread across the disciplines. The Multidisciplinary Practices help explain the contemporary trend of interdisciplinarity for which the history of ideas has long been known. At the end of this Reader's Guide is a listing of a number of entries that overlap three of the four divisions and a listing of entries that overlap all four divisions.

Fine Arts

VISUAL STUDIES

Absolute Music
Aesthetics: Africa
Aesthetics: Asia
Aesthetics: Europe and the Americas
Ambiguity
Anthropology
Architecture: Overview
Architecture: Africa
Architecture: Asia
Arts: Overview
Arts: Africa
Asceticism: Hindu and Buddhist Asceticism
Asceticism: Western Asceticism
Avant-Garde: Overview
Avant-Garde: Militancy
Aztlán
Beauty and Ugliness
Body, The
Buddhism
Change
Chinese Thought
Cinema
City, The: Latin America
City, The: The City as a Cultural Center
City, The: The Islamic and Byzantine City
Classicism
Classification of Arts and Sciences, Early Modern
Communication of Ideas: Asia and Its Influence
Composition, Musical
Consumerism
Context
Cosmopolitanism
Creativity in the Arts and Sciences
Cultural History
Dada
Death
Dream
Dress
Dystopia
Environmental Ethics
Environmental History
Everyday Life
Expressionism
Extirpation
Fascism
Fetishism: Overview
Garden
Gay Studies
Gender in Art
Genre
Geography
Geometry
Gesture
Ghetto
Globalization: Asia
Heaven and Hell (Asian Focus)
Hinduism
History, Idea of
Humanity: European Thought
Humanity in the Arts
Humor
Iconography
Ideas, History of

Images, Icons, and Idols
Imagination
Impressionism
Islamic Science
Kantianism
Knowledge
Landscape in the Arts
Life Cycle: Overview
Literary History
Literature: Overview
Maps and the Ideas They Express
Masks
Matriarchy
Media, History of
Medicine: Europe and the United States
Mestizaje
Modernism: Overview
Modernism: Latin America
Modernity: Africa
Modernity: East Asia
Monarchy: Overview
Motherhood and Maternity
Museums
Musical Performance and Audiences
Musicology
Mysticism: Chinese Mysticism
Mysticism: Christian Mysticism
Naturalism in Art and Literature
Negritude
Nude, The
Occidentalism
Organicism
Pan-Africanism
Paradise on Earth
Periodization of the Arts
Perspective
Philosophy: Historical Overview and Recent Developments
Political Protest, U.S.
Postmodernism
Pre-Columbian Civilization
Protest, Political
Psychoanalysis
Pythagoreanism
Realism
Realism: Africa
Religion: Africa
Renaissance
Representation: Mental Representation
Ritual: Public Ritual
Sacred Places
Sacred Texts: Asia
Science: East Asia
Science, History of
Science Fiction
Social History, U.S.
Sport
Surrealism
Symbolism
Syncretism
Taste
Text/Textuality
Textiles and Fiber Arts as Catalysts for Ideas
Third Cinema
Victorianism

Social Sciences

WOMEN'S STUDIES AND GENDER STUDIES

Creationism
Critical Race Theory
Death
Demography
Determinism
Development
Dystopia
Ecology
Emotions
Environmental Ethics
Environmental History
Epistemology: Early Modern
Equality: Racial Equality
Ethnohistory, U.S.
Eugenics
Evolution
Family: Modernist Anthropological Theory
Family: Family in Anthropology since 1980
Family Planning
Feminism: Overview
Game Theory
Garden
Gender: Overview
Gender: Gender in the Middle East
Gender in Art
Gender Studies: Anthropology
Genetics: Contemporary
Genetics: History of
Genocide
Gesture
Greek Science
Health and Disease
Heaven and Hell
History, Idea of
Humanism: Secular Humanism in the United States
Humanity: African Thought
Hygiene
Identity: Identity of Persons
Immortality and the Afterlife
Intentionality
Islamic Science
Jainism
Jouissance
Kinship
Learning and Memory, Contemporary Views
Life
Life Cycle: Adolescence
Life Cycle: Elders/Old Age
Lysenkoism
Machiavellism
Marriage and Fertility, European Views
Masks
Materialism in Eighteenth-Century European Thought
Mechanical Philosophy
Medicine: China
Medicine: Europe and the United States
Medicine: Islamic Medicine
Meme
Memory
Men and Masculinity
Mestizaje
Monarchy: Overview
Motherhood and Maternity
Musical Performance and Audiences
Natural History

Naturalism
Natural Theology
Nature
Naturphilosophie
Negritude
Organicism
Other, The, European Views of
Periodization of the Arts
Person, Idea of the
Perspective
Philosophies: Islamic
Philosophy of Mind: Ancient and Medieval
Phrenology
Population
Prehistory, Rise of
Probability
Progress, Idea of
Psychoanalysis
Psychology and Psychiatry
Punishment
Queer Theory
Religion: Indigenous Peoples' View, South America
Representation: Mental Representation
Science: East Asia
Science, History of
Sexuality: Overview
Sexuality: Sexual Orientation
Sociability in African Thought
Social Darwinism
Sport
State of Nature
Subjectivism
Superstition
Temperance
Terror
Text/Textuality
Totems
Untouchability: Menstrual Taboos
Utilitarianism
Victorianism
Visual Order to Organizing Collections
War and Peace in the Arts
Wildlife
Women and Femininity in U.S. Popular Culture
PHYSICAL SCIENCES
Agnosticism
Alchemy: China
Astrology: China
Astronomy, Pre-Columbian and Latin American
Calculation and Computation
Calendar
Causality
Causation
Causation in East Asian and Southeast Asian Philosophy
Change
Chemistry
Classification of Arts and Sciences, Early Modern
Computer Science
Consciousness: Overview
Consilience
Cosmology: Asia
Cosmology: Cosmology and Astronomy
Creationism
Cycles

Multidisciplinary Practices

The *New Dictionary of the History of Ideas* has many entries that discuss the methods by which scholars and researchers pursue knowledge. The entries below discuss approaches, methods, and practices that have influenced many disciplines.

ENTRIES ON MULTIDISCIPLINARY PRACTICES
THAT ORIGINATED IN ANCIENT TIMES

Especially Interdisciplinary Entries

The most interdisciplinary entries synthesized knowledge by using the methods and focusing on the topics of practitioners of several disciplines. Very few entries listed below are in only one division. Common pairs for the history of ideas are social sciences and humanities, social sciences and sciences, and humanities and sciences. In the early twenty-first century there is generally a recognition of the common overlap of the social sciences with the humanities; social scientists may take ethical and literary factors into consideration and humanists may incorporate societal contexts into their work. The presence of psychology in the sciences, as well as the quantitative nature of some social sciences work, creates an overlap of social sciences with sciences. Another interesting overlap is between humanities and sciences—topics that in antiquity were treated as philosophy or religion are now investigated by those following scientific methods.

New Dictionary of the History of Ideas

M

MACHIAVELLISM. *Machiavellism*, a word that goes back to the late sixteenth century, is a name for the theory and practice of amoral politics. In its ideal, simply abstract sense, it is not meant to coincide exactly with the views or practices of any historical individual, even Niccolò Machiavelli (1469–1527) himself. When Machiavelli praises the citizens of the ancient republic of Rome as noble and public-spirited, he is no Machiavellian. Consistent Machiavellism is unconstrained by custom, ideal, or conscience and aims only at the expedient means, lawful or not, to gain desired political ends. War is thought not only often expedient but necessary to maintain a people's vigor. The absence of moral restraint is reinforced by the fixed opinion that human beings are by nature weak, inconstant, selfish, and inclined to evil. Expositions of Machiavellism often take the form of advice for a ruler, who is regarded as indispensable to the state, and the welfare of ruler and state are considered to be identical. Aimed at practice rather than theory, the literature of Machiavellism is filled with amoral strategies to gain the ruler's ends.

Small-Scale Societies and Kingdoms

"Stateless" societies have no formal structure of government or any formal authorities. Anthropologists have made it clear that there are very few stateless societies in which violence is rare. Machiavellian deception makes its appearance wherever vengeance is taken and wars are fought. The best-known account of a violent, often deceptive people is Napoleon Chagnon's often controverted description of the Yanomamö, who live on the borderland between Brazil and Venezuela. In their chronic wars between villages, they make use of what is translated as "dastardly tricks." What was actually a raiding party once came to a village under the pretense of teaching the men of the village how to pray to a spirit that gives machetes and cooking pots. When the villagers knelt to pray to the spirit, the raiders killed them.

War, generally on Machiavellian principles, is frequent among the more organized societies called "chiefdoms." An anthropologist who studied warfare in the chiefdoms of both Oceania and North America found that it has been frequent and acute. Thus Fiji had many ruthless rulers and ruthless wars, while in North America, warfare in the form of small-scale raids seems to have been inseparable from tribal culture. In New Guinea, the surest route to leadership was by means of bold or sly killing. Some societies favored ambushing, some the destruction of property or kidnapping, and some the driving away or exterminating of the enemy. Stealthy, often treacherous raiding was usual.

In considering the Machiavellian traits of kingdoms or empires, one should at least mention those of South and Central America and Africa. The Incas justified their conquests by the claim that all other peoples had originated from them and therefore had to serve them, give them much of their wealth, and provide them—without showing any signs of grief—with children for sacrifices. The Aztecs' belief that the sun and the powers of the earth would die unless fed with human blood created a need for sacrificial victims and the wars to provide them. That Machiavellism was involved is proved by the fact that most of the victims were from other tribes, whose towns the Aztecs wrecked, whose fields they burned, and whose people they raped and murdered.

Among the African kings, the one best known for ruthlessness was Shaka (c. 1787–1828). By the conquest of many nearby peoples, he created the Zulu empire. Purposely enigmatic and frightening, and informed by a network of spies, he was as ruthless within his own country as outside it. When he gave orders to exterminate all the members of a tribe, he explained that he did so because otherwise the children would grow into possible enemies. Any relative or important person he had any reason to suspect was killed. His justification for his cruelty was that only the fear of death made it possible to hold together the many unruly clans of what would one day be a nation.

Ancient China

In Chinese tradition, Machiavellian thought and practice is associated with Legalism. Insisting on laws that apply impartially to persons of every status, Legalism provides techniques for a ruler to keep control over both officials and subjects. The first famous Legalist, Lord Shang (d. 338 B.C.E.), preached the doctrine that society could be controlled by means of penalties. When he succeeded in becoming the chief administrator of the state of Qin, he divided the population into units of five or ten persons, each responsible for the actions of all the others. Anyone failing to report an offender was to be cut in two at the waist, while someone who did report offenders was to be rewarded as if he had decapitated an enemy. Those who devoted themselves successfully to the fundamental occupations, tilling or weaving, would have their taxes remitted, but those who made socially unhelpful profits, in trade and the crafts, or were poor out of laziness would be confiscated as slaves.

A country that is strong, Shang said, can remain so only by continuing to wage war, while a country administered, as Confucians preferred, with the help of history, music, filial piety, and brotherly love, sinks into poverty or falls to its enemies.

Above all, he said, a government must promote order by means of rare but consistent rewards and frequent, consistent, severe punishments. Governed by the fear of punishment, people will obey the laws, be virtuous, and be kept happy by what they are allowed to enjoy.

The great Confucian Xunzi (c. 310–c. 215 B.C.E.) influenced the thought of the Legalists by insisting that a nation's power depends on its wealth and therefore on its inhabitants' frugality and devotion to the wealth-producing occupations, especially agriculture. He also insisted, like the Legalists, on the need for law with fixed standards of punishment and on the view, contrary to that of his Confucian predecessor Mencius, that people are by nature evil. Their nature, he says, needs to be forced into shape, so that only correct education can make them good.

Xunzi's student Han Feizi (c. 280–233 B.C.E.) argued that the ruler, out of love, should work against the natural disorderliness and self-indulgence of the people. Penalties bring order and rewards bring chaos, so penalties are the beginning of love. A state can function properly, he held, only if it has ingrained lines of command and obedience. The ruler must take many precautions to retain his rule because it is dangerous for him to trust anyone. The ruler's son, if trusted by the ruler to an incautious extreme, will be used by evil ministers to carry out their private schemes. To detect the more subtle kinds of subversion, the ruler must get the people to watch one another and be implicated in one another's crimes. To gain his own ends, the emperor should remain enigmatic and not reveal his intentions to his subordinates. Government can no longer be based on the Confucian virtues or on the model of familial relations. "The most enlightened method of governing a state is to trust measures and not men."

Li Si (c. 280–208 B.C.E.), like Han Feizi, was a student of Xunzi. Li Si was the paradigmatic Legalist because it was he who taught the king of Qin how "to swallow up the world and to rule with the title of Emperor." Appalled by his attacks on Confucian tradition, Chinese historians describe the First Emperor as a cruel, suspicious megalomaniac who by the intelligent use of force, slavery, and the conscripted labor of citizens created the great empire of China out of the motley of its many small states. In collaboration with the indefatigable First Emperor, Li Si created a unified culture, including a standardized Chinese, and a political hierarchy fully subordinate to the emperor. But Li Si is one of the greatly hated figures of Chinese history because, in order to escape criticism based on traditional standards, he tried to destroy very nearly the whole of Chinese literature and so, in effect, to destroy the tradition's moral basis and cultural continuity. To this end, in 213 B.C.E. he ordered that all books, except those on practical subjects such as medicine, divination, and agriculture, be gathered and burned. A year later, there occurred the episode—not the direct doing of Li Si—that to traditional Chinese has been the most extreme example of malignant politics: the execution of 460 scholars, who, according to Chinese tradition, were buried alive in a common grave. In the course of the later history of China, legalistic doctrines and practices were often incorporated into the ruling Confucianism.

Ancient India

Violence and treachery make a frequent appearance in the great Indian epics, the *Mahabharata* and the *Ramayana*, in which the ideal is that of a righteous king with obedient people. In the most usual Indian view, the king is related to the gods and should be revered as such. A wise man in the *Mahabharata* asks what a state without the protection of a king would be like and imagines robbers at work, women abducted, and the strong roasting the weak like fishes on a spit. The self-evident moral of such a fear is that to have no king is worse than to have to have the worst king.

The Indian science that deals explicitly with politics is Arthashastra, literally "the science that deals with *artha,* the means of subsistence." This definition turns out to be equivalent to "the science of politics." The oldest, most developed of the books dealing with the subject is the *Kautilya Arthashastra.* Its author, whose name or pseudonym, Kautilya, means "craftiness," is usually identified with Chanakya, the crafty adviser of Candragupta, who about 321 B.C.E. defeated the Nandas and created the first great Indian empire.

The *Kautilya Arthashastra* is a dryly written manual of government from the standpoint of a king's adviser. It urges the king to care for the welfare and loyalty of the farmers and of the Brahmans and priests. Religions should be respected, Kautilya says, but used for political purposes. For a successful king, he thinks, warfare is the most natural activity. Running through every subject treated in the *Arthashastra* is a concern with the safety of the king. Everyone is under suspicion, from the queen and the crown prince to the king's ministers and citizens.

To translate a pervading suspiciousness into administrative terms, Kautilya recommends an extraordinarily detailed system of domestic and foreign spying and subversion. Each agent is given a cover story, carries out the required spying, including spying on high officials, and reports back to a special station, where the report is put into code. Only a report confirmed by three spies is accepted. Spies who make mistakes are done away with quietly.

Indian literature reflects the attitudes both of Arthashastra and, more often, of those who oppose it for moral reasons. The *Arthashastra*'s cynical wisdom was exported from India by the stories of the *Panchatantra* (The five books), probably compiled by about 500 C.E. and translated into some sixty languages. By means of the *Panchatantra,* Kautilya's point of view took on the imagination and humor of folktales and taught the world at large what it implicitly always knew.

Europe

The most famous European Machiavellian was, of course, Niccolò Machiavelli, and his most famous, most Machiavellian book was *Il principe* (1513; The prince). Like his other works, it was nourished by his personal experience, especially as a diplomat, and by the literature of ancient Greece and Rome. Machiavelli must have been familiar with Thucydides's ability to report on history in an objective, amoral spirit, as in the famous dialogue in which the representatives of Athens say to those of Melos that in human affairs the question of justice enters only where there is equal power to enforce it, and that the powerful exact what they can and the weak grant what they must. Machiavelli knew Cicero's *De officiis* (On duties), which discusses the same political problems that he does, though with usually milder, more moral conclusions. Like Machiavelli, Cicero asks whether it is better for a ruler to be feared or loved—loved, Cicero concludes—and uses the image imitated by Machiavelli of the ruler as either a lion or a fox. Both Cicero and Machiavelli agree that a ruler must curb himself so as to escape hatred.

Machiavelli's Machiavellian views are that present-day human beings are incorrigibly changeable, ungrateful, and insincere; control of government therefore requires the use of force, so the ruler should be capable of leading his state in war and should be ready to abandon honesty and mercy when they interfere with effective rule. Put metaphorically, because humans act like wolves, the ruler must be the lion, and because humans do not keep their word, the ruler must also play the fox, though never openly. Knowing that humans are evil, the ruler should not be troubled by the cruelty that keeps his subjects united and loyal. But the wise ruler will keep a balance between reckless trust and the extreme distrust that unrestrained cruelty causes.

Franceso Guicciardini (1483–1540), a Florentine historian and politician and (at times) Machiavelli's friend, never became as famous as Machiavelli even though he was just as hardheadedly amoral as a political thinker, maybe even more canny, and rather more skeptical. His advice on public relations is always to deny what one does not want to be known and, regardless of even the most convincing contrary evidence, to sow doubt in people's minds by boldly stating what one wants to be believed. Mercy should be shown only when practically useful. No one who understands political life would ever show mercy when it endangers the fruit of a victory, but when it costs nothing to be merciful, mercy is politically advisable.

Guicciardini criticizes Machiavelli for reading contemporary events too often in the light of unrevealing Roman precedents. History is too mutable, he says, for us to learn much from it except not to expect any reward for good behavior or any success from the use of intelligence. The best we can do, according to him, is to maintain our dignity.

Machiavelli's *Prince* aroused interest, most of it indignant, everywhere, with the result that Machiavelli's name became a byword for evil. In Shakespeare's *Henry VI* (part 3), the future Richard III boasts that he can murder while he smiles, wet his cheeks with artificial tears, orate, deceive, conquer, change shapes, "and set the murtherous Machiavel to school." As king, in *Richard III,* this self-proposed tutor of Machiavelli is finally destroyed, like Machiavelli's hero, Cesare Borgia, by failing to control his lust for power.

A few almost contemporary philosophers praised Machiavelli's ideas. Michel de Montaigne (1533–1592) refers to him in his essay "On Presumption" and says that Machiavelli is one of those writers who prefers the good of the state to his fidelity and conscience. Almost always, says Montaigne, there is some gain in a breach of faith, as in all other wicked acts. The wretchedness of the human condition is such, Montaigne goes on, "that we are often driven to the necessity of using evil means to a good end." He sympathizes with a prince whose conscience does not allow him to do what is essential for his own preservation or the preservation of his people but doubts that such a prince will get the favor of God that he deserves ("On the Useful and the Honorable"). Though lying is to Montaigne an "accursed vice," he is ready to say that "to deprive wiliness of its rank . . . would be to misunderstand the world," and that anyone whose morals are conspicuously higher than those of his time "must either distort and blunt his rules" or "have nothing to do with us."

Francis Bacon (1561–1626), who experienced both high office and political disgrace, said that he was indebted to Machiavelli as one of those "who openly and unfeignedly declare or describe what men do, and not what they ought to do." His own aphorisms often have the disabused flavor of Machiavellism. In his essay "Of Simulation and Dissimulation," he concludes that it is best "to have openness in fame and opinion; secrecy in habit, dissimulation in seasonable use, and a power to feign if there be no remedy." Like all Machiavellians, he insists that greatness does not come to any nation that does not "directly profess arms."

Of the other philosophers close in time to Machiavelli, those most like him in their negative estimate of ordinary humans are Thomas Hobbes and Benedict de Spinoza. Hobbes (1588–1679), who does not mention Machiavelli at all, makes similar negative estimates of human behavior. But unlike Machiavelli, in *Leviathan* he belittles the idea of learning from past experience and wants his theory to be a carefully structured, syllogistic science. Spinoza (1632–1677) praises Machiavelli in his *Tractatus Politicus* (Treatise on politics) as a wise man who, because he is wise, must have had a moral purpose. He explains Machiavelli's text as probably meant to show "the folly of attempting—as many do—to remove a tyrant when the causes which make a prince a tyrant cannot be removed, but become rooted more firmly as the prince is given more reason to be afraid." Or, Spinoza says, perhaps Machiavelli wanted to show how careful a free people should be in entrusting its welfare completely to one man, who has to go in daily fear of plots and "is forced in self-defense to plot against his subjects rather than to further their interests." Rather like Machiavelli, Spinoza says that humans are by nature subject to great anger, envy, and the like and so are by nature enemies to one another. However, he adds, echoing Machiavelli's *Discourses,* it is not the inherent wickedness of the subjects of a commonwealth that leads to rebellions, wars, and contempt for the law but "the corrupt condition of the commonwealth" that has framed its laws ineptly; for "citizens are not born, but made." Spinoza also believes that a person can break his promise "by the right of nature," that is, the right of self-preservation.

Georg Wilhelm Friedrich Hegel (1770–1831) was an interestingly qualified admirer of Machiavelli. He thought that Germany, which, like Machiavelli's Italy, had difficulties in becoming a united nation, also needed Machiavelli's advice. Machiavelli, he said, had no special interest in advising a tyrant but in correcting an impossible political situation. For Machiavelli's "great and true conception produced by a genuinely political head" expresses his understanding that, under the circumstances, the "Prince" had no choice but to secure his own power as a tyrant by all the violent means that are usually considered to be crimes. The acts are justified by the vision of the sovereignty and independence of the people, the *Volk*, which depend on the destruction of the lesser local authorities. But when the tyrant's work is done, he automatically appears as a despot, and "then, it is the tyrant-slayers who are heroes."

Machiavellian Rule

The assessments of Machiavelli himself are still mixed. The more favorable ones may be exemplified by that of the twentieth-century philosopher Ernst Cassirer, who wrote that Machiavelli's accomplishment lay in not allowing his personal feelings and ideals to affect his political judgment, which was "that of a scientist and a technician of political life." But whatever the verdict on Machiavelli the person, the Machiavellism of which he wrote pales in the face of the massive attack on conventional morality by the twentieth century's great tyrants, Stalin, Hitler, and Mao.

Machiavellian behavior has been integral to the political and social life of every culture. One of the reasons why it is found everywhere is the universal need for a social system with an effective leader. When it is not clear what authority, if any, is to be obeyed, the result is uncertainty, social friction, wasted effort, dissatisfaction, and the willingness to follow any leader who promises to overcome the threat of chaos. In any case, morality proves to be easy to equate with conformity to the demands of leaders, however careless they may be of compassion and of truth. The individual conscience proves to be at its most elastic when leaders and followers assume that the cause they serve is of such surpassing importance that deception or cruelty in its behalf is in fact a moral virtue. Such a hope for a better society ordinarily requires that those who appear to be obstructing it should be identified and proclaimed to be its enemies.

See also **Political Science; Power; State, The; War.**

BIBLIOGRAPHY
Bodde, Dirk. *China's First Unifier: A Study of the Ch'in Dynasty as Seen in the Life of Li Ssu.* Leiden: Brill, 1938.
Chagnon, Napoleon A. *Yanomamö.* 5th ed. Fort Worth, Tex.: Harcourt Brace, 1997.
Ghoshal, U. N. *A History of Indian Political Ideas.* London: Oxford University Press, 1959.
Gilbert, Felix. *Machiavelli and Guicciardini.* Princeton, N.J.: Princeton University Press, 1965.
Guicciardini, Francesco. *Selected Writings.* Edited by Cecil Grayson and translated by Margaret Grayson. London: Oxford University Press, 1965.
Haas, Jonathen, ed. *The Anthropology of War.* Cambridge: Cambridge University Press, 1990.
Kautilya. *The Kautilya Arthashastra.* Translated by R. P. Kangle. 2nd ed. 3 vols. Bombay: University of Bombay, 1969.
Lewis, Mark Edward. *Sanctioned Violence in Early China.* Albany: State University of New York Press, 1990.
Machiavelli, Niccolò. *The Chief Works, and Others.* Translated by Allan Gilbert. 3 vols. Durham, N.C.: Duke University Press, 1965.
———. *The Prince.* Translated by Robert M. Adams. Rev. ed. New York: Norton, 1992.
Meinecke, Friedrich. *Machiavellism.* Translated by Douglass Scott. New Haven, Conn.: Yale University Press, 1957.
Scharfstein, Ben-Ami. *Amoral Politics: The Persistent Truth of Machiavellism.* Albany: State University of New York Press, 1995.
Spinoza, Benedict de. *The Political Works.* Translated by A. G. Wernham. Oxford: Oxford University Press, 1958.
Walter, E. V. *Terror and Resistance.* New York: Oxford University Press, 1969.

Ben-Ami Scharfstein

MACHISMO.   Machos are not born; they are made. For the same reason, the term *machismo* refers to a concept that has been invented and not to a primordial cultural trait of any particular group of people. In the United States, machismo was "discovered" by social scientists and feminists much as the New World was "discovered" by Europeans five centuries earlier: U.S. scholars and feminists noticed gender oppression in Mexico and the rest of Latin America and announced that it was a particular cultural trait among Spanish-speaking men.

Although some believe machismo has ancient roots common in all "Latin" cultures since Roman times, others argue that it is an ideology that originated uniquely in Andalusia, Spain, and was carried over the Atlantic Ocean during the Spanish Conquest. There is even an opposite theory positing that machismo was indigenous to the pre-Columbian Western Hemisphere. In fact, the term *machismo* has a very short word history dating back only a few decades in the twentieth century.

This does not mean that what scholars today call sexism is new to the Americas, or that inequality based on sexuality and gender difference—today recognized under rubrics like homophobia and misogyny—are of recent vintage. But like the expression sexism, the term machismo is new.

Perhaps the most complicated aspect of the idea of machismo stems from the fact that until fairly recently the term may have been more broadly used in the United States than in many parts of the Spanish-speaking world. Although elsewhere in the world *macho* always has had a negative connotation when referring to humans—it originates in a term that designates the male of an animal species (*hembra* being the female)—in Latin America the term has a somewhat different history. Only in the 1990s did the term come into vogue more broadly in Latin America; earlier it was mainly utilized to refer to culturally determined forms of masculinity by intellectuals and activists involved in examining and struggling against oppressive regimes grounded in ideas and relations of gender/sexuality systems in journalistic writing, social science studies, and feminist critique of the oppression of women and gays.

Pegging extreme sexism to one or another culture is a dead-end at best, and a racist subterfuge at worst. In the contemporary United States the machismo mystique is regularly employed to imply that somehow Spanish-speaking men, and especially Spanish-speaking heterosexual men, are more prone than men from other cultural backgrounds to sexist language, actions, and relationships. This is in large part a result of scholarship by U.S. academics, including anthropologists and sociologists, who have gone to Mexico and other parts of Latin America to study questions of family, kinship, and gender/sexuality and through this research have developed interpretations and paradigms consistent with hegemonic notions of studying down—that is, looking at populations that have been marginalized and oppressed (as opposed to "studying up"; that is, examining the ruling classes)—and finding political, social, and cultural fault with oppressed others.

In Latin America, the term *macho* usually must be distinguished from that of *machismo*. Macho has different meanings in different social circumstances: sometimes it refers simply to the male of a species, whether animal or plant. In other cultural contexts "to be macho" can have contradictory connotations: for older generations this may refer to something positive for men to emulate, so that a macho man is one who is responsible for the financial welfare of his family, whereas for younger men to be macho can refer to culturally stigmatized behavior like beating one's wife, and thus in order to differentiate themselves from this kind of stigmatized practice many men of these younger generations would not readily refer to themselves as macho.

The term *marianismo* was created, in almost biblical style, in machismo's image: it was not good for the macho to be alone, so in 1973 a North American academic invented *marianismo*. *Marianismo* has done damage to our understanding of gender relations and inequalities among Latin American and U.S. Latina women similar to the damage done by machismo among Latin American and U.S. Latino men. Now discredited, *marianismo* was originally an attempt to examine women's gender identities and relationships within the context of inequality, by developing a model based on a religious icon (María), the quintessential expression of submissiveness and spiritual authority. This notion of Latin American women is grounded in a culturalist essentialism that does far more than spread misinformed ideas: it ultimately promotes gender inequality. Both *marianismo* and machismo have created clichéd archetypes, fictitious and cartoonesque representations of women and men of Latin American origin. If a Mexican man, for instance, is abusive and aggressive, he will be labeled a macho. If a Mexican woman quietly endures such an abusive relationship, her behavior is automatically examined within the *marianismo* paradigm. But if a white man and a white woman display similar behavior, they are seldom analyzed in so cavalier and simplistic a fashion.

What is more, frequently these traits of machismo and *marianismo* are pegged in particular to working class men and women, as if those from the middle and upper strata were too sophisticated for their lives to be captured by such crude academic groupings. As theoretical categories, therefore, machismo and *marianismo* are not only culturally chauvinist but elitist as well. The machismo-*marianismo* paradigm represented an expression of a widespread intellectual colonial mentality in the behavioral and social sciences that remained dominant and unchallenged for far too long.

Poster by Hernando G. Villa advertising dude ranches, 1938. Although the term *machismo* is generally specific to Latin America, the concept has also spread to the United States where the connotation suggests physical toughness, masculinity, and old-fashioned family values. © Swim Ink/Corbis

As a contemporary idea, machismo has long since entered popular discourse, including among the Latino/a populations in Latin America, the United States, and elsewhere. Indeed in the twenty-first century, Latino/a cultures are commonly defined from within as inherently macho. As such machismo has become a critical aspect of Latino/a identity politics, even when, as in this case, the cultural characteristic in question is held to be a negative set of ideas and practices.

The etymology of the idea of machismo thus has roots in political and social concerns of the late twentieth century. The origin of the term is found in texts, especially journalistic, social science, and feminist dissections of Mexican men and Latinos in general in this period. The popularization of machismo as an epithet for Spanish-speaking males of the species coincided with the rise of second-wave feminism and, later, cultural identity politics in which supposedly immutable cultural traits were linked, as if genetically, to men with one or another geographic and/or class ancestry.

The origins of the term give an indication of its future as an idea: to the extent that hegemonic ideologies and ways of constructing knowledge about Latin America and Latinos remain unchallenged, including with regard to gender relations and inequalities, it will be possible to continue employing machismo in a stereotypical fashion and as an expedient label for complex social interactions. If, on the other hand, the idea of machismo and that of its even more problematic would-be opposite, *marianismo,* are recognized and discarded as antiquated paradigms invented to explain and teach about gender inequality in Latin American and Latino/a societies, then the idea of machismo could be short-lived. Machismo as a shorthand for sexism may have come into journalistic, social science, feminist, and popular vogue for a variety of reasons, including the well-intentioned desire to criticize gender inequality and oppression. The continued employment of this hackneyed term can only reflect the persistence of an elitist and racist model to understand gender inequities among women and men of Latin American origin.

See also **Feminism; Gender; Gender Studies: Anthropology.**

BIBLIOGRAPHY

de Barbieri, Teresita. "Sobre géneros, prácticas y valores: Notas acerca de posibles erosiones del machismo en México." In *Normas y prácticas: Morales y cívicas en la vida cotidiana,* edited by Juan Manuel Ramírez Sáiz, 83–106. Mexico City: Universidad Nacional Autónoma de México, 1990.

Fuller, Norma. "Reflexiones sobre el machismo en América Latina." In *Masculinidades y equidad de género en América Latina,* edited by Teresa Valdés and José Olavarría, 258–266. Santiago, Chile: FLACSO/UNFPA, 1998.

González-López, Gloria. *Erotic Journeys: Mexican Immigrants and Their Sex Lives.* Berkeley: University of California Press. Forthcoming.

Gutmann, Matthew C. *The Meanings of Macho: Being a Man in Mexico City.* Berkeley: University of California Press, 1996.

Paredes, Américo "The United States, Mexico, and *Machismo.*" In his *Folklore and Culture on the Texas-Mexican Border,* edited by Richard Bauman, 215–234. Austin: University of Texas Press, 1993.

Zinn, Maxine Baca. "Chicano Men and Masculinity." In *Men's Lives,* edited by Michael A. Messner and Michael S. Kimmel, 24–32. 5th ed. Boston: Allyn and Bacon, 2001.

Gloria González-López
Matthew C. Gutmann

MAGIC. Magic is the performance of acts or rites that are intended to influence a person, object, or event. It can also be performed to counter other magic. Magical acts or rites are usually performed with the assistance of mystical power. People who engage in the different activities magic encompasses can be called magicians, shamans, healers, sorcerers, or priests/priestesses. In some societies the knowledge required and the ability to perform magic are restricted to specialists who have undergone extensive training, while in other societies they are available to the common person and are learned as part of the enculturation process. In early-twenty-first-century anthropological discourse magic is generally considered to be a dimension of religious thought and practice and to be an aspect of culturally influenced understandings about causality, while in

popular culture magic is often associated with superstition and used to refer to ideas and practices considered to be false and inferior. Divination is frequently identified with magic. It concerns the attempt to learn or discover information that is not accessible to most human beings through acts of skilled interpretation and the use of mystical power. The information discovered can be used to inform an act of magic but divination is not itself the act of influencing people, objects, or events.

Since the early twentieth century, scholars writing on magic have been interested in a variety of issues that concern its instrumental effects, social functions, psychological functions, symbolic attributes, and the forms of thought that characterize it. Their inquiries and theories have offered a range of ways to approach the study of magic, have made important contributions to the development of the disciplines of philosophy and anthropology, and continue to raise central questions about the limitations of language and culturally influenced perception in the interpretation of less familiar ideas and practices. The study of magic presents contemporary scholarship with a rich history on which to build theories of intersubjective understanding. An analysis of the intellectual and epistemological history of Western thought about magic reveals patterns of ethnocentrism. Awareness of these constructions offers the possibility of advancing methods of cross-cultural and cross-society comparison in addition to the creation of theories that more fully address the range of ideas and practices that can be considered in magic.

Vocabularies used to describe the practitioners, outcomes, and qualities of magic seem to gain popularity for certain periods of time, evolve in ways that reflect the concerns of particular disciplines, and come to be associated with specific geographic areas of the world. Witchcraft and sorcery, for example, have been used predominantly in the social sciences to refer to harmful or destructive uses of magic. Another example is the relatively limited use of the term shamanism in anthropological literature to practitioners of magic in Northern Europe and the Americas. In addition, shamanism assumes that magical acts can have both harmful and helpful consequences. Anthropological literature that concerns practitioners of magic in Africa has often relied on the term *healing* to refer to helpful magic, and *witchcraft* to refer to harmful magic. In an attempt to develop a more universal vocabulary and to avoid some of the topical and regional associations carried by the terms *witchcraft* and *sorcery,* some scholars prefer only to use the term *magic.*

Magic, Religion, and Science

Of particular interest to intellectual history is the way that the terms magic and religion have been used in a social evolutionary framework to mark differences between the Western and non-Western, the advanced and backward, civilized and primitive cultures, and to characterize Christian and non-Christian religions. Many scholarly ideas are based on a set of assumptions about the differences between magic and religion, placing greater importance on the achievements of religion and greater value on its truth claims. These ideas bear some similarity to distinctions offered in the Old Testament and in early Christian theology. Some scholarly ideas address the difference between magic and science, where the latter is viewed in more positive terms. In the nineteenth and part of the twentieth century anthropological discussions of magic, religion, and science were heavily influenced by evolutionary theories and debates about the nature of scientific reasoning and practice. They also tended to rely on the understanding that magic involved the manipulation of mystical forces and beings, was used to achieve practical goals, and was intended to affect the natural world.

E. B. Tylor (1832–1917) and James G. Frazer (1854–1941) made some of the most important early contributions to the study of magic and religion, although both relied on ethnographic information that was limited in geographic scope and lacked extensive contextualization.

In contrast to a number of previous ideas holding that magic is an undeveloped and primitive form of thought, Tylor found that magic required a rational process of analogy based on understanding the links between cause and effect. He was also interested in its symbolic properties. He did, however, emphasize the differences between thought in magic and thought in science, for he called magic a "pseudoscience" that was incorrect and deluded. His point was that people involved in magic could not differentiate between causal relationships achieved through magic, and causal relationships that occur in nature. Although he thought that both magic and religion could exist together in any given society, he proposed that magic diminished as human institutions advanced and therefore associated scientific thought with more noteworthy human achievements.

Frazier's understanding of the relationship between magic and religion was structured according to a linear evolutionary framework composed of three forms of thought: magical, religious, and scientific. He postulated that magical thought, the earliest stage of human development, was replaced by religious thought as people observed its failures and came to believe that they could propitiate gods in order to control nature. Religious thought was then replaced by scientific thought as human beings understood natural laws.

Frazier is also noted for his insights about the thought processes that magic involves. His ideas about causality in magical thought continue to be important to arguments about differences in forms, or systems, of thought in various cultures. He observed that magic was based on two sets of assumptions about the way magic worked, which he called laws. The first was the law of similarity (characterized by homeopathic or imitative magic) and the second was the law of contact (characterized by contagious magic). In homeopathic magic he stated that "like produced like," where a thing with a property or quality similar to another thing was thought to be able to influence it. In contagious magic, a thing in physical contact with another thing was thought to be able to influence it later and at a physical distance. He observed that scientific reasoning involved a comparable thinking process, or "association of ideas," and for that reason viewed magic and science as fundamentally different from religion, which involved human beings' propitiation of superior powers.

By the turn of the century the writings of scholars with a sociological orientation increasingly became more important.

They based the distinction between magic and religion on its function and on the context of its performance. For Marcel Mauss (1872–1950), magic was private and secret, and did not contribute to group activities and organizations. Émile Durkheim (1858–1917) similarly viewed magic as an individual practice in contrast to religion, which he saw to be collective. Max Weber (1864–1920) was interested in comparing the practice of magic and religion in precapitalist and capitalist societies. He observed that magic was dominant in precapitalist societies, and was on the decline in capitalist societies along with what he called the increased "rationalization of economic life."

The Functions and Effects of Magic in Classic Anthropological Works

The early contributions of Wilhelm Wundt (1832–1920) and R. R. Marett (1866–1943) drew attention to the psychological motivations and effects of magic. Wundt, who viewed magic as a stage in the development of religion, found that the impetus to practice magic came from human beings' fear of nature and efforts to influence it. Marett saw magic as a way for humans to address emotions stemming from insecurity and to gain courage and confidence.

Beginning with the work of Bronislaw Malinowski (1884–1942) in the Trobriand Islands of Melanesia during World War I, the insights that anthropologists brought to the study of magic were based on long-term field observations and were undertaken by the writers themselves. Along with the work of his contemporary, Alfred Radcliffe-Brown (1881–1955), he greatly contributed to anthropology's developing body of thought on methods and standards for fieldwork. With extensive examples from his study, Malinowski found that magic in the Trobriand Islands addressed particular kinds of problems that were specific and practical. These he distinguished from the larger concerns of human life that he identified with religion.

For Malinowski, the many functions of magic included human beings' attempts to increase the probability of success in important activities, and increase confidence to undertake them. Magic opened up possibilities for human action. He did not view magic as a characteristic of particular kinds of societies, but thought that it could be found when human beings were confronted with a lack of knowledge or ability to control something important to their lives. Malinowski also observed that magic had social and moral functions that led to better cooperation among group members. In addition, it gave people access to what he referred to as "miracles," events that were unexpected or unlikely, thus giving them hope.

Addressing the question of the difference between magical and natural causality, Malinowski showed that the Andamanese used magic to supplement the actions of the natural world. In their horticultural and sailing activities they both relied on their own knowledge and skills, and used magic to assist them to handle unexpected events. Malinowski did not present magic, religion, and science in an evolutionary framework, but considered them as aspects of cultural systems. His approach acknowledged that the Andamanese had empirical knowledge and did not assume that magic was apart from, or a replacement for, effective activity in the world.

The work of Radcliffe-Brown among the Andamanese also provided new standards of research for the study of magic and religion. Like Malinowski, he was able to demonstrate the many social functions of magic. One of his greatest contributions was to elaborate on the term *mana*, the word for magical knowledge and power that has the potential to be both dangerous and beneficial. Objects and substances possess mana, and human beings acquire mana through their relationship with spirits.

Radcliffe-Brown observed that the Andamanese used mana as a way of distinguishing transformations in social positions. During times of transition, the dangerous aspects of mana are dominant, requiring people to observe taboos. Radcliffe-Brown stressed that the function of these ideas and the rituals associated with them was to support group collaboration and interdependence. Compared to Malinowski, he placed even greater emphasis on the social value of ritual rather than on its instrumental effects.

E. E. Evans-Pritchard (1902–1973) extended the study of the social and political context of magic. His research among the Azande of the Sudan was published in *Witchcraft, Oracles, and Magic among the Azande* (1937), a work that continues to stimulate scholarly debate and reinterpretation. His analysis of magic and witchcraft not only acknowledged their strategic uses, but permitted a more complex understanding of the relationship of witchcraft and magic to social and political institutions. He reveals that it was only men and members of the elite in Azande society who were authorized to use certain forms of magic and oracles that could identify those responsible for witchcraft. While these issues were not his central concern, his detailed and comprehensive description of Azande life allows readers to identify the implications of magic for gender relations and to support political and economic power.

One of his greatest contributions was to present magic as part of a "ritual complex" and stress their relationship rather than to focus attention on categorical distinctions. For Evans-Pritchard, magic, witchcraft, oracles, and divination worked as an integral whole and could not be understood alone. In his account of Azande ideas and practices, he showed that magic, oracles, and divination were used to address witchcraft. Oracles and divination provided information about the source of witchcraft, and magic was employed to counter it. Because the Azande used magic primarily in response to the mystical power of other human beings, and not to change nature, Evans-Pritchard did not consider the comparison of magic with science to be relevant.

One of the results of Evans-Pritchard's detailed ethnographic work was to convey the pervasive uses of magic and witchcraft in the everyday lives of the Azande. Including both the act of engaging in rituals and ways of apprehending their world, magic and witchcraft were presented as an integral part of Azande culture. Evans-Pritchard also provided information about the contents of magical acts that could be similarly compared to those in European magic. He described how the plant and animal substances used in magic were considered to be inert until activated by the verbal spells of the owner, and explained that the Azande called these substances medicines. He contested the established notion that magic was primarily used to change the natural world with his discovery that, for the

Azande, magic was used to counter the magic of others, and was therefore an activity that was largely identified with protection. He also pointed out that it was used to punish people who misused magic, a function that was considered moral.

Thought, Logic, and Rationality in Magic

Early-twenty-first-century discussions that attempt to characterize the forms, or modes of thought in different cultures, as well as their reliance on magic, often retrace debates around the work of Lucien Levy-Bruhl (1857–1939). His ideas have implications for a series of complex questions concerning the way culture can shape thought, providing an individual with either limitations or extended possibilities. Levi-Bruhl proposed that there was a major distinction between the thought of European and preliterate people, which he termed "primitive mentality." He stressed that the difference was due to the content of the ideas and causal understandings in culture, and was not the product of different mental capacity. He termed the modes of thought that characterized each as scientific and prescientific (or prelogical), respectively. He proposed that "primitive" societies tended to use mystical or supernatural explanations for unexpected occurrences. He contended that this form of thought does not permit a kind of logic that challenges or tests it. The thought process has an internal consistency and rationality, but does not follow the rules of scientific thinking and does not differentiate between what Levi-Bruhl called the natural and supernatural.

Some of Evans-Pritchard's most important contributions followed from an attempt to address Levi-Bruhl's distinction between forms of thought. Evans-Pritchard associated Azande common sense with empirical observation and science. This allowed him to contrast what he called "empirical thought" and "mystical thought," which included magic. A central point in his discussion of magic and witchcraft was that Azande thought is founded on rational processes and empirical knowledge of their world.

His ideas offered a radical departure from the preoccupation of previous literature with the dichotomy between magic and science, and between thought that either was or was not scientific. Following Levi-Bruhl's observation that the body of collective representations in cultures with prescientific thought limited possibilities for the thought system's self-critical appraisal, Evans-Pritchard used examples from his Azande material to explain how this took place. Azande responses to the failure of magic to achieve the desired result were not to question their technique or knowledge, but to question the specific acts of the magician and to assume that other magic conducted to counter theirs was stronger. These and other explanations, which Evans-Pritchard termed "secondary elaborations of belief," did not require the Azande to confront the failure of their explanation, nor the failure of their entire system of thought. This, he said, was responsible for the continuation of the belief in magic despite evidence that it was fallacious. Evans-Pritchard characterized these systems as "closed systems of thought." He observed that they were only able to operate in limited ways that did not extend beyond their own parameters. Certain forms of scientific reasoning therefore would be outside the paradigm.

Robin Horton elaborated on this issue by contrasting open and closed systems of thought. He offered that open systems had the ability to either prove or disprove particular causal relationships between acts and natural consequences. Closed systems did not encourage the verification of what was hypothesized, and the result was that the thought system continually supplied ways of accounting for particular successes or failures.

The Role of Analogy and Metaphor

Returning to the question of how thought can be similarly compared from one culture to another, and the notion that forms of thought that appear to display differences might have underlying similarities, the contributions of Claude Lévi-Strauss (b. 1908) and Stanley Tambiah (b. 1929) are particularly useful. Accepting Frazer's observation that in both magic and science relationships of cause and effect are based on analogies, Lévi-Strauss proposed that magic could be understood as a subcategory of analogical thought, and worked on the assumption that a metaphor follows natural laws. Like most early twenty-first-century scholars, he views magic, science, and religion to occupy aspects of thought and practice in all societies.

Tambiah has taken the study of magic and analogy much farther than any other scholar. Tambiah finds that analogical reasoning is a quality of both magic and science, but claims that they involve different kinds of analogies. Science, he argues, makes an analogy between known causal relationships and unknown causal relationships. Following Lévi-Strauss, he finds that magic relies on the use of a particular kind of analogy, but he emphasizes the importance of the transfer of meaning from the physical procedures in magic to a referent in the natural world. Magic offers human beings something that science does not: creative possibilities. He also observes that magic extends meaning into practical activity. The meanings produced through ideas and practices of magic are therefore central to an understanding of the workings of culture and society.

Lévi-Strauss made another important observation about the differences between magic and religion. Taking both to be categories of thought, rather than terms that referred to different contents, he proposed that the terms were used by Western thinkers to make distinctions between their own thought and what he called "outside" thought. This outside thought was designated as inferior to domestic thought. Emphasizing that neither have particular contents or meanings, and that Western thought arbitrarily provides its own subject matter, Lévi-Strauss advocated the dissolution of the category known as magic.

Magic and Modernity

Early-twenty-first-century scholarship has expanded its views on how to study magic and how to frame its object of analysis. Peter Pels (2003) observes that the practice of scholars to frame magic as the opposite of modernity has had effects that are just now being addressed. As modern discourses work to distinguish magic from the modern they also create what he calls "correspondences and nostalgias." He and other scholars such as Jean Comaroff and John Comaroff (1993) and Michael Taussig (1997) have been increasingly interested in elaborating on the specific forms that magic takes in modernity. Taussig addresses the question of how state power is experienced and understood by citizens of Columbia, where he conducted research. He finds that state power relies on different forms of magic to not only inspire awe from citizenry, but to conceal its deceits and violence.

Conclusions

A central concern in the intellectual history of magic and religion is modernity. This requires an understanding of how Western scholarship has created grand narratives that present Western societies and their political projects, notably colonialism, in a favorable light. It is clear that one of the most distinctive elements of Europe's construction or imagination of itself has been its self-designation as civilized and progressive. The simultaneous construction of other groups of people as the opposite—backward, primitive, and undeveloped—was assisted by discourses in the social sciences, philosophy, and religious studies.

The theories and assumptions about magic that scholars have used, particularly in writings prior to the work of Lévi-Strauss, demonstrate particular patterns. The ways that they chose to contrast and compare material from different cultures and societies often created an opposition between Western and non-Western, advanced and backward, and civilized and primitive cultures. When magic was contrasted with religion, it was viewed to be less comprehensive and focused on practical ends, rather than ontological or existential ones. When placed in contrast to science it was seen to be either limited or incorrect, since it did not contain a logic that could test its propositions nor question its own premises. In early-twenty-first-century analyses, magic has been compared favorably to science, and there is a general assumption that it works toward an understanding of the natural world and relies on analogical reasoning. Most scholars view magic as an aspect of religion that exists in all societies. It can be viewed as part of everyday life, guiding thought and action.

People in societies across the globe have been influenced by Western thought on magic, with its attending characterizations of culture. Magic has been present in the discourses of colonial rule, Christian conversion, educational institutions, state administrative organizations, and development policies. Whether the thought comes from popular culture or scholarly investigations, the production and reproduction of dichotomies, that according to Levi-Strauss present what is "outside" as inferior, continue to present problems for scholarship. Despite the relative lack of theoretical reflections and ethnographic works on magic prior, early-twenty-first-century scholarship is poised to extend the terrain of what can be considered to be magical and to conceptualize the new forms that magic takes in modernity.

See also **Demonology; Miracles; Superstition; Witchcraft.**

BIBLIOGRAPHY

PRIMARY SOURCES

Evans-Pritchard, E. E. *Witchcraft, Oracles and Magic among the Azande.* 2nd ed. Oxford: Clarendon, 1950.

Durkheim, Émile. *The Elementary Forms of Religious Life.* Edited and translated by Karen Fields. New York: Free Press, 1995.

Frazer, James. *The Golden Bough: A Study in Magic and Religion.* Abr. and rev. ed. Old Tappan, N.J.: Macmillan, 1985.

Levi-Bruhl, Lucien. *Primitive Mentality.* Translated by Lilian Clare. London: Macmillan, 1923.

Lévi-Strauss, Claude. *The Savage Mind.* Chicago: University of Chicago Press, 1966.

Malinowski, Bronislaw. *Magic, Science and Religion and Other Essays.* Garden City, N.Y.: Doubleday Anchor Books, 1954.

Mauss, Marcel. *A General Theory of Magic.* Translated by Robert Brain. London: Routledge and Kegan Paul. 1972.

Radcliffe-Brown, Alfred Reginald. *The Andaman Islanders: A Study in Social Anthropology.* Cambridge, U.K.: Cambridge University Press, 1922.

Tambiah, Stanley Jeyaraja. *Magic, Science, Religion, and the Scope of Rationality.* Cambridge, U.K.: Cambridge University Press, 1990.

Taussig, Michael T. *The Magic of the State.* New York: Routledge, 1997.

Thomas, Keith. *Religion and the Decline of Magic.* New York: Scribners, 1971.

Tylor, Edward Burnett. *Religion in Primitive Culture.* Vol. 2. Gloucester, Mass.: Peter Smith, 1970.

SECONDARY SOURCES

Bowie, Fiona. *The Anthropology of Religion: An Introduction.* Oxford: Blackwell, 2000.

Lehmann, Arthur C., and James E. Myers, eds. *Magic, Witchcraft, and Religion: An Anthropological Study of the Supernatural.* 4th ed. Mountain View, Calif.: Mayfield, 1997.

Morris, Brian. *Anthropological Studies of Religion: An Introductory Text.* Cambridge, U.K.: Cambridge University Press, 1987.

Pels, Peter. "Introduction: Magic and Modernity." In *Magic and Modernity: Interfaces of Revelation and Concealment,* edited by Birgit Meyer and Peter Pels. Stanford, Calif.: Stanford University Press, 2003.

Diane Ciekawy

MANICHAEISM.

Manichaeism is a now-extinct religious system characterized by dualism, asceticism, and an acute sense of worldwide mission. It originated in the teaching of Mani (216–277 C.E.), a Parthian raised in Mesopotamia in an Aramaic-speaking Jewish-Christian community known as the Elchasaites. He experienced visions in his youth that made him aware of a pantheistic presence in the world that he felt called upon to help liberate from its suffering. He broke with the Elchasaites (c. 240 C.E.), visited India, and upon his return to Mesopotamia formed his own religious community. He proselytized throughout the Persian Empire, and sent his disciples further afield to India, central Asia, and the Roman Empire. By the time of his death as a prisoner of the Persian king, Mani had succeeded in establishing a well-organized institutional structure that spread and preserved his teachings for a thousand years, despite nearly constant persecution.

Manichaeism arose in a highly cosmopolitan culture, in full awareness of antecedent west Asian religions such as Zoroastrianism, Christianity, and various pagan and Gnostic sects, as well as the Hindu, Jain, and Buddhist traditions of South Asia. According to Manichaean teaching, Mani was the last of a series of divinely inspired prophets that included Zoroaster, the Buddha, and Jesus Christ. These divine messengers were sent periodically to particular regions of the earth to reform the true message from the corruption of time, an idea found also in Islam and the Baha'i faith. Mani brought the latest restatement of truth, and took the novel precaution of committing it to writing himself, rather than trusting his disciples to hand it down correctly. The rich Manichaean literary and artistic tradition is now reduced to fragments discovered in the twentieth century in China and Egypt, precariously supplemented for the modern researcher by polemical accounts from the religion's enemies.

Doctrine

Manichaean doctrine is premised on a material and ethical dualism. The known cosmos is a mixture of two antithetical realms of being, originally separate and eternally incompatible. The realm of light is a wholly good, harmonious universe in which God, the father of greatness, dwells with innumerable light beings, which are one with him in substance and character. The realm of darkness is a wholly evil, chaotic universe dominated by a king of darkness and his female counterpart. At the beginning of time, the realm of darkness perceives and covets the realm of light and attacks it, unaware of the harm that contact with it will bring to itself. The prescient father of greatness fends off this aggression by putting forth a series of emanations to act out a strategy of containment and ultimate reseparation of light and darkness. In the primordial battle, one of these emanations enters into mixture with darkness, constraining it and forestalling a breach of the boundaries of the realm of light. This mythological background explains the evident condition of the known cosmos, in which everything is a mixture of conflicted substances and forces, engaged in a perpetual struggle for mastery. The point of Manichaean instruction is learning to identify oneself with the forces of light and goodness and striving for their ultimate reseparation from entanglement with darkness and evil.

Manichaeism is closer to Zoroastrian dualism than to Gnostic or Platonic varieties in that it avoids a spirit-matter dichotomy. Both light and darkness have material as well as spiritual properties, and even the most subtle forces are usually treated in materialistic terms. Manichaeism also shares with Zoroastrianism an activist mythology and ethic, rejecting the notion of a sinful "fall" of the soul in favor of the idea of a voluntaristic "leap" of the soul in the service of God's purposes. In other details, Manichaeism has greater affinity to Indian thinking, for example in seeing souls not only in human beings, but in all living things, even in rocks and dirt. For the Manichaeans, the soul is a collective entity, a consubstantial emanation of the deity, broken up into individuals only temporarily through mixture with evil. Humans are only one small part of a universal process of struggle and liberation of the world soul. This world soul carries with it all positive properties, such as life, growth, beauty, and brightness, whereas evil contributes to the mixture only death, decay, ugliness, and gloom. Whereas for Zoroastrians the goal is to expel evil from this world, the Manichaeans see this world as unperfectable, a temporary scene of conflict and suffering from which ultimate escape is envisioned. In this respect, Manichaeism has a common outlook with Buddhism and Jainism, as well as the more eschatological and ascetic strains of Christianity.

Based on these ideas, Manichaean practice entailed a rigorous behavioral code, designed to avoid harming the world soul in all things as much as possible, as well as ritual practices intended to aid the process of its liberation. Outbursts of anger, impatience, stupidity, greed, hatred, and violence attest to the mixture of evil with good in the human body. The evil elements must be identified for what they are, repented, resisted, and ultimately overcome by the Manichaean. Due to a number of adventitious factors, individuals have different capacities for this task, and consequently the community is divided into two grades. The first, that of the elect, was made up of those men and women willing and able to take on the most vigorous form of self-discipline, involving celibacy, poverty, and a wandering life preaching the faith. These had the ability to transmute material elements within their bodies, freeing soul fragments from the food brought to them, as well as the potential to achieve liberation at death. Those unable to adopt this life were called auditors, who remained engaged in hearth and home, but supported the elect while striving for advancement in the faith through moral growth and a better rebirth.

Later History

In the seventh century C.E., both the rise of Islam and the arrival of Manichaeism in China brought the religion into contact with new spiritual ideologies. Islam and Manichaeism had little in common doctrinally apart from minor elements of their shared west Asian heritage, which also contributed their common ritual patterns of prayer and fasting. Yet more speculative forms of Sufism and Shiism within Islam certainly drew on Manichaeism for ideas about the soul's affinity to God and transmigration. In China, Manichaean missionaries were able to draw upon, and perhaps help foster, developments within popular religion akin to Manichaean concepts. In Taoism, these included dualistic categorization of the cosmos and physiological alchemy, while in Buddhism they involved the ideas of a Pure Land (a realm of light and harmony as a goal of liberation from this world) and of Buddha Nature (an inherently pure nature in all things).

Manichaeism enjoyed a renaissance in west Asia under the tolerant Umayyad regime (661–750 C.E.), while the conversion and sponsorship of the Uygur Empire and its successor states in central Asia (c. 760–1100 C.E.) afforded secure conditions there, as well as within China, over which the Uygurs exerted strong political influence for a time. Such respites were short-lived. When public existence became untenable, Manichaeans found it convenient to take on the guise of Christians, Muslims, Buddhists, and Taoists, while maintaining their distinct doctrines and practices in secret. The suspicion of secret Manichaeans within these other religions probably far exceeded their actual number, duration, or influence. But it is possible that lingering traces of Manichaean ideas and practices in popular religion contributed to sectarian developments within Christianity, such as the Cathars of Italy and France

and the Bogomils of the Balkans, as well as within Islam, Buddhism, and Taoism. Nevertheless, the institutional structures and distinct identity of Manichaeism gradually eroded under relentless persecution, until the last remnant communities dissolved in southern China sometime in the fifteenth or sixteenth centuries.

See also **Asceticism; Christianity; Dualism; Evil; Good; Heresy and Apostasy; Jainism.**

BIBLIOGRAPHY

BeDuhn, Jason David. *The Manichaean Body: In Discipline and Ritual.* Baltimore: Johns Hopkins University Press, 2000.

Gardner, Iain, ed. *The Kephalaia of the Teacher: The Edited Coptic Manichaean Texts in Translation with Commentary.* Leiden, Netherlands: Brill, 1995.

Koenen, Ludwig, and Cornelia Römer. *Der Kölner Mani-Kodex: Über das Werden seines Leibes.* Opladen, Germany: Westdeutscher, 1988.

Lieu, Samuel N. C. *Manichaeism in the Later Roman Empire and Medieval China.* 2nd ed. Tübingen, Germany: Mohr, 1992.

Ries, Julien. *Les études manichéennes: Des controverses de la Réforme aux découvertes du XXième siècle.* Louvain-la-Neuve, Belgium: Centre d'histoire des religions, 1988.

Sundermann, Werner. *Der Sermon von der Seele (Berliner Turfantexte XIX).* Turnhout, Belgium: Brepols, 1997.

Jason David BeDuhn

MAOISM.

Maoism is not a term that is easy to define. While it is common sense that Maoism refers to the vision, ideology, and political viewpoint of Mao Zedong (1893–1976), it is difficult to pinpoint the specific contents and basic features of Mao's conceptual world in the context of the evolving course of the Chinese Communist revolution. Despite Mao's adoption of Marxist-Leninist terminology, his ways of thinking had been deeply penetrated by Chinese thought and culture. In the People's Republic of China, it is "Mao Zedong Thought," instead of Maoism, that designates Mao's ideas, strategies, and policies. During the post-Mao era, the Chinese Communist Party (CCP) leadership, in an effort to legitimize the Chinese Communist state, emphasized that Mao Zedong Thought included only those of Mao's ideas and theories that had stood the test of practice, and that the "scientific system of Mao Zedong Thought" was the product of the collective wisdom of the Party leadership, rather than Mao's sole creation. Beyond China, many radical revolutionary movements and organizations have professed loyalty to a variety of self-proclaimed versions of Maoism, even long after Mao's death.

Essential Features

This essay takes Mao's own expressions of his thoughts as the basis for defining Maoism. While the contributions of Mao's CCP comrades are acknowledged, they are not regarded as an integral part of Maoism if Mao himself did not accept or adopt them. In identifying the basic features of Maoism, moreover, it is essential to test them against the development of Mao's thoughts as a historical process. Indeed, unless Mao's own changing ideas are carefully examined, it is impossible to grasp the essence and basic features of Maoism.

Maoism as utopian vision. At its core, Maoism is first and foremost a utopian vision. Throughout Mao's political career, he fought for the ideal of universal justice and equality "all under heaven." This vision derived at one level from Mao's Sinification of Karl Marx's concept of a communist society, yet it was also compatible with the age-old Confucian ideal of a "society of great harmony." Despite the vision's central position in Mao's conceptual realm, Mao was never able to define clearly the path and the means by which it would be turned into reality. The extraordinary ambiguity of Maoism as a utopian vision provided, on the one hand, space for Mao and his comrades to develop the CCP's ideology, strategies, and policies given the changing requirements of the Chinese revolution, and, on the other, created serious internal tensions in the Maoist system—especially when Mao's ideals proved unable to stand the test of people's lived experience.

Maoism as political ideology. Maoism is also a political ideology, representing Mao's theories and methodologies about how China and the world should be transformed in revolutionary ways. Three important features distinguished Mao's concept of revolution from other revolutionary theories in the tradition of Marxism-Leninism.

First, Mao's perception of revolution was characterized by a unique notion of permanentness in time and unlimitedness in space. In particular, Mao persistently emphasized the necessity of "continuing the revolution" after the CCP seized power in 1949. However, Mao's notion of permanent revolution was by no means a simple repetition or minor alteration of earlier formulations by Marx, Lenin, or Trotsky. While adopting such Marxist discourse as the "law of historical development" to justify his revolution, Mao often used the Chinese term *tianxia* ("all under heaven") to define the space in which the revolution should occur. The *tianxia* concept had its historical/cultural origin in the long development of Chinese civilization—implying that the Chinese way of life was the most superior in the known universe. Used in connection with *tianxia* was the Chinese word *geming*—a term that in modern times would be adopted to represent the concept "revolution." The original meaning of *geming* was that violent means must be used to deprive a ruler of heaven's mandate to rule. In employing *tianxia* to define the space in which *geming* should occur, Mao, in a China-centered manner, at once attached the qualities of permanentness and unlimitedness to his perceived revolution.

Second, Mao's perception of revolution reflected the profoundly voluntaristic belief that human consciousness, rather than the material conditions of society, would determine the orientation of historical development. For Mao, an essential condition for a revolution was the consciousness and will on the part of the "great masses" to carry out revolutionary changes. In the final analysis, whether a revolution should be judged a success or a failure depended on whether it had created a new order in the hearts and minds of the people.

Third, and closely connected with the above two features, the Maoist notion of revolution put greater emphasis on destruction than on construction. Indeed, Maoism proved more ready to deal with tasks of destroying the "old" than to cope with missions of constructing the "new." Mao believed firmly that "no construction happens without destruction; only when destruction is under way does the process of construction begin." Not surprisingly, Mao's revolution was one of the most violent and destructive in history, not only during the stage of "seizing political power," but in the stage of "continuous revolution" as well.

Maoism as revolutionary strategies and tactics. Maoism also represents a series of strategies and tactics concerning how to make, enhance, and sustain the revolution. Mao certainly was a theorist and a man of ideas; but he also viewed himself as a practitioner and a man of action.

The central mission of Maoist revolutionary strategies concerned mass mobilization. In particular, Mao emphasized the importance of taking the peasants as the main force of the Chinese revolution. This clearly distinguished Maoism from the urban, working-class–centered mobilization strategies favored by orthodox Marxism-Leninism. Yet Mao's dependence on peasants drove him into a fundamental dilemma in furthering his "continuous revolution" after 1949. While adhering to the populist belief that the peasants' spontaneous "revolutionary initiatives" represented a natural source of the "revolution after revolution," Mao was simultaneously obsessed by the "petty bourgeois tendency" of the peasants in practical life. When the "socialist planning economy," which made industrial development the top priority, encountered resistance from the peasants, Mao argued that "a serious question is how to educate the peasants."

In Mao's own summary of his revolutionary strategies, he highlighted armed struggle, united front, and the Party's leadership role as the three keys that led the Chinese revolution toward victory. A firm believer in the idea that "political power grows out of the barrel of a gun" (*Selected Works,* vol. 2, p. 224), Mao invested great energy in developing strategies and tactics for waging revolutionary wars with both domestic and international aims. He summarized the basic principle of guerrilla war as "when the enemy advances we retreat to avoid him, when the enemy stops we harass him, when the enemy is tired we attack him, and when the enemy retreats we chase after him" (*Mao Zedong wenji,* vol. 1, p. 56). He also emphasized the importance of "making everyone a soldier" in waging a "people's war." The "united front" strategy was designed to "unite with all of those who can be united" in order to fight against the primary and most dangerous enemy. The adoption of this strategy in international affairs was often influenced by the traditional Chinese concept of "checking one barbarian by borrowing strength from another." In emphasizing the importance of the Party's leadership role, Mao originally embraced Lenin's "democratic centralism." However, with the deepening of his revolution he increasingly obscured the distinction between his own leadership role and that of the Party. Consequently, in his later years Mao openly celebrated the "correct personality cult," making enhancement of the cult of himself a crucial condition for the ongoing revolution.

In practice, Mao often interwove his ideas and plans with the discourse of revolutionary nationalism. Constantly appealing to the Chinese people's "victim mentality"—which was unique in the sense that it reflected the sharp contrast between the Chinese people's collective memory of their nation's glorious past and their perception of its experience of humiliation in modern times—Mao found a powerful source that continuously rendered help to legitimize his programs of transforming China and the world.

The above features of Maoism, to be sure, both persisted and evolved over the course of Mao's long career. In order to achieve a genuine understanding of these features, therefore, it is essential to undertake a historical review of the shaping of Mao's worldview, as well as of the development of Mao's thought.

Shaping of Mao's Revolutionary Worldview

Mao was born into a peasant family at Shaoshan village in Hunan Province on 26 December 1893. During his childhood Mao demonstrated a rebellious and challenge-oriented character, as reflected in his frequently conflicted relationship with his father. In his early education at the village school, he read Confucian classics (which laid the foundation of his life-long habit of using Chinese classics as a reference for strategy and policy making). But he devoted his heart and soul only to the tales of rebelling peasants fighting against the exploitative and corrupt bureaucracy (as in the popular novel *Water Margin* by Shi Nai-an). At the age of seventeen, he left home to pursue further study in Changsha, Hunan's provincial capital, where he was further exposed to the rebellion-oriented cultural environment of Hunan province. All of this helped shape Mao's belief that "rebellion is by nature legitimate."

Turning to Marxism-Leninism.
When Mao encountered the world beyond his home village, he saw a China that had been sinking into an ever-deepening national crisis in the face of incursions by the Western powers and Japan. Like many of his contemporaries, Mao was eager to find ways to save China and make the country strong. But he was never simply a nationalist. In search of means to save China, he not only pursued insights from China's own rich intellectual tradition, but also exposed himself to knowledge from the West, demonstrating a keen interest in such Western concepts as liberalism, democratic reformism, anarchism, and individualism. With the emergence of the iconoclastic "New Culture Movement" in the mid-1910s, Mao became increasingly critical of the Chinese past, contending that without thoroughly transforming Chinese culture no political and social reform could succeed. Yet he did not view wholesale Westernization as China's salvation. Unlike those of his contemporaries who traveled to Europe and Japan in order to "seek truth," Mao believed firmly that the key to solving the problems facing China must be sought in China itself.

In the wake of the anti-imperialist "May Fourth Movement" and under the influence of the Russian Bolshevik Revolution, Mao experienced the decisive intellectual turn toward Marxism-Leninism in 1919–1920. With only a vague understanding of such terms as "class struggle" and "proletarian dictatorship," Mao emphasized the "people's great unity" as a necessary condition for bringing about fundamental transformations "all under heaven." Taking the creation of universal justice and equality as a core mission, Mao envisioned that his

revolution would have to be carried out and completed by a "new human being" (*xinmin*), and that China would have to be transformed at the same time that the rest of the world was being transformed. With those ideas in mind, Mao became a founding member of the CCP in 1921.

Development of Mao's Thought to 1949

Until 1927, Mao did not rate as an outstanding leader of the CCP, and he made no original theoretical contribution to the Chinese revolution. In 1926–1927, Mao wrote a "Report on the Peasant Movement in Hunan," which represented a first step in his designation of peasants as the main force of the Chinese revolution. At the time, however, the report had little impact on the CCP's overall strategies.

Creating a rural-centered pattern of Communist revolution.
The CCP's setbacks following Jiang Jieshi's (Chiang Kai-shek; 1887–1975) bloody counterrevolutionary coup in April 1927 released Mao from the confines of old doctrines. In order to escape the purge by the Nationalist government, Mao moved to the countryside, where he organized the Red Army and waged a violent "Land Revolution." Challenging the notion that a Communist revolution would have to be carried out by urban proletarians, Mao found the necessity and possibility—within the Chinese context—of creating a rural-centered pattern of Communist revolution. Supporting this idea lay both pragmatism and romanticism. On the one hand, Mao sensed that China's conditions precluded an urban-centered Communist revolution; on the other, he perceived that China's backwardness made it easier for a revolution carried out by the peasants—the most oppressed and, therefore, the most revolutionary group in society—to succeed.

From the beginning this Maoist pattern of revolution encountered skepticism from many CCP leaders as well as from the Comintern in Moscow. Not until the mid- and late 1930s, when the Red Army had lost its base areas in southern China and barely survived the Long March, did Mao's military genius and political wisdom come to be recognized by his comrades. Following the outbreak of the Anti-Japanese War (1937–1945), Mao, in the caves of Yan'an, found both the need and the time for theoretical elaboration.

The Yan'an years: theoretical buildup.
In Maoism's development, the Yan'an years (1937–1946) represented a crucial stage. In the early Yan'an period, Mao wrote some of his most significant works, including "On Practice" and "On Contradiction." Examining the relationship between theory and practice, Mao emphasized that the former must always be tested by the latter. For Mao, this meant that Marxism should not be treated as "empty abstraction," but should be "imbued with Chinese characteristics" and "used in accordance with Chinese peculiarities." In discussing "contradiction," Mao highlighted the importance of catching the "principal contradiction" and, even more importantly, "the principal aspect of the principal contradiction." In this manner Mao virtually challenged the Marxist orthodoxy of historical materialism. He argued that, although the economic foundation generally determined the superstructure (such as politics, ideology, and culture), in specific situations—especially when the development

of the economic foundation was hindered by the superstructure—"political and cultural transformations become the principal aspect of the principal contradiction." This voluntarism in Mao's conceptual world cohered with his belief that a Communist revolution in China need not be restricted by the country's backward social and economic conditions.

In the late 1930s and early 1940s, Mao developed a more comprehensive design for the Chinese revolution, contending that it would develop in two stages: first a "new democratic revolution" and second a "socialist revolution." The mission of the first stage was to overthrow the reactionary old regime and establish a Communist-led government that would unify all patriotic social classes. The second stage of the revolution would transform state and society, resulting in China's transition to a socialist and later communist society. Mao emphasized that, without the first stage, the second stage would be impossible; and without the second stage, the first stage would be meaningless. By introducing the concept of a "new democratic revolution," Mao created broader maneuvering space for the CCP to adapt its strategies and policies to the practical situation in China. In the meantime, he made it clear that his revolution was already setting China on the path toward socialism and, eventually, communism.

The Yan'an years: making of the Yan'an Way. The Yan'an years also witnessed Maoism's further development as the CCP's dominant ideology. The "Rectification Movement" occupied a central position in this process. The movement allowed Mao to purge his opponents within the Party leadership, as well as to consolidate the CCP's independence from Moscow's control. As a result, the Mao cult entered the CCP's mainstream discourse. In 1945, the Party's constitution formally designated Mao Zedong Thought as its official ideology.

At a deeper level, the Rectification Movement offered a proving ground for Mao's grand plans of transforming Party members into "new human beings." Through carefully designed procedures of "criticism and self-criticism," Party cadres were required—even forced—to expose and eliminate the "small-self" in their innermost world. These procedures, reinforced by the egalitarian environment in Yan'an during the years of war and revolution, created the myth of the "Yan'an Way"—that the "revolutionary spirit" inspired by Mao had played and would continue to play a decisive role in enabling the Party to overcome all kinds of difficulties in order to achieve its goals.

The CCP's experience in the 1940s further solidified Maoism as the Party's dominant ideology. China's victory over Japan in 1945 was accompanied by the Party's winning political influence and military strength unprecedented in its history. In the late 1940s the CCP successfully carried out a revolutionary civil war against the Nationalist government, defeating a seemingly much stronger enemy within three short years. Mao could then claim that the path toward victory had been paved by the "Yan'an Way."

Development of Mao's Thought after 1949

When the CCP seized power in 1949, Mao announced to the whole world that "we the Chinese people have stood up." Yet he also emphasized that this was merely "the completion of the first step in the long march of the Chinese revolution," and that carrying out the "revolution after the revolution" represented an even more fundamental and challenging mission. How to prevent the revolution from losing momentum emerged as Mao's primary concern.

Mao's "post-revolution anxiety." In the mid-1950s, as the nationwide "socialist transformation" (nationalizing industry and commerce and collectivizing agriculture) neared completion, Mao sensed that many of the Party's cadres were becoming less enthusiastic about furthering the revolution. After the failure of the "Great Leap Forward" in 1958–1959, Mao realized that his revolution was losing crucial "inner support" even among the party elite. In the last decade of his life, when he pushed China into the "Great Proletarian Cultural Revolution," Mao found that a majority of the CCP elite were unable—or unwilling—to follow the development of his thinking. Mao was preoccupied by a pivotal challenge: how could he bring about transformations "all under heaven"? Facing him was a paradox deeply rooted in the challenge itself: he had to find the means for transforming the "old" world from the very "old" world that was yet to be transformed. This profound "post-revolution anxiety" played a crucial role in shaping Maoism's post-1949 development.

In search of a Chinese model of socialism. A major theoretical challenge facing Mao after 1949 was a question that he had previously had little time and opportunity to contemplate: What is socialism, and how could one build socialism in China? In Mao's initial search for answers, he paid special attention to the "Stalin model"—the only existing model of building socialism from which he could learn.

With completion of land reforms and elimination of the gentry-landlord class in 1953, Mao and the CCP immediately followed the "Stalin model" for carrying out "transition to socialism." By 1956, a highly centralized system of "planning economy" had emerged following the introduction of the First Five-Year Plan. The CCP's Eighth Congress announced in September 1956 that, with the Communist state now possessing the major means of production, class struggle no longer figured as the principle contradiction in Chinese society. Therefore, China had entered the stage of socialist construction.

While many Party cadres were excited about this "great victory of socialism," Mao sensed a decline in revolutionary vigor among his comrades. In order to create new momentum for the continuous revolution, as well as to pursue China's central position in the international Communist movement, he was determined to go beyond the "Stalin model" and to push for a more aggressive and unconventional model of socialism. In the wake of the Soviet leader Nikita Khrushchev's (1894–1971) de-Stalinization campaign and the Hungarian revolution of October 1956, Mao introduced his theory that "class struggle exists in a socialist society." He contended that the conflict between the bourgeoisie and the proletariat continued in the sphere of the superstructure even after the economic foundation had been transformed. This formed the context in which Mao turned the "Letting One Hundred Flowers Blossom" campaign into the "Anti-Rightist" movement in the summer of 1957, in which more than 300,000 intellectuals were branded as "class enemies." He also brought this "ideological struggle" to the Party leadership itself and criticized Zhou Enlai (1898–1976) for his opposition to "rash advance in socialist construction." Still with no clear definition of socialism, Mao was ready to launch in China the most radical experiments in the name of socialism and communism.

The Great Leap Forward.

The year 1958, which witnessed the dramatic "Great Leap Forward," was pivotal in Maoism's development. Early in the year, Mao formally introduced the thesis of "one revolution after another . . . being carried out uninterruptedly." In explaining why China should and must be elevated rapidly to a higher stage of social development, Mao referred to two basic conditions: the revolutionary enthusiasm of the masses and the backwardness of the Chinese economy. Revealing again the voluntarism and romanticism at the root of his conceptual world, Mao proclaimed: "China's 600 million people have two remarkable characteristics: poor and blank. That may seem like a bad thing, but it is really a good thing. Poor people want change, want to do things, want revolution. . . . The newest and most beautiful picture can be painted on a blank sheet with no blotches on it" (*Jianguo vilai Mao Zedong wengao*, vol. 7, pp. 177–178).

In the summer of 1958, Mao and the CCP leadership announced that "the realization of a Communist society in China is not far away." For the purpose of rapidly increasing China's industrial and agricultural production, Mao and the Party mobilized millions and millions of ordinary Chinese to make steel in "backyard furnaces," and to work on miscellaneous construction and irrigation projects. What excited Mao most was that tens of thousands of "people's communes" were founded throughout the country. In Mao's vision, these communes, by combining "economic, cultural, political, and military affairs" into one entity, and by practicing "compensation according to need" through a public dining system, opened the door to a communist society. At one point, Mao even raised the question of abolishing the "bourgeois right," arguing that it was time to eliminate the inequality caused by the practice of "compensation according to work."

In order to enhance popular support for his extraordinary mass mobilization efforts, Mao ordered the Chinese Communist artillery forces to bombard the Nationalist-controlled Jinmen islands in the heyday of the Great Leap Forward. Although this caused a serious international crisis between China and the United States, Mao was unafraid, arguing that international tension had a "good side of it" as it could "bring about the awakening of many people" and was therefore beneficial to the revolution.

Mao's utopian expectations collapsed with the failure of the Great Leap Forward, which caused one of the worst human tragedies in twentieth-century history. It is estimated that 20 to 30 million people starved to death in a nationwide famine during the 1959–1961 period. For the first time in Communist China's history, the myth of Mao's "eternal correctness" was called into question.

The great Sino-Soviet polemic debate.

The disastrous consequences of the Great Leap Forward resulted in a major setback in Mao's political career. With Mao relegated to the "second line" in 1960–1962, the CCP leadership adopted more moderate and flexible policies designed for economic recovery and social stability. However, Mao never intended to abandon the theory and practice of continuous revolution. When the Chinese economy began to recover in 1962, Mao called upon the Party "never to forget class struggle." This time, he was determined to turn the party and state that he himself had created and ruled into the target of his revolution.

Within this context the great Sino-Soviet debate erupted in the early 1960s. In the mid-1950s, Mao had already charged that Khrushchev, with his de-Stalinization efforts, risked discarding the banners of both Stalin and Lenin. Mao had further criticized Khrushchev's strategy of "peaceful coexistence," claiming that it obscured the fundamental distinction between revolution and counterrevolution, between communism and capitalism. Meanwhile, Mao also contended that Moscow had long carried out a policy of "great power chauvinism" toward China, characterizing Moscow as a threat to Chinese sovereignty and independence. Thus Mao effectively linked his challenge to Moscow's leading position in international communism to the theme of safeguarding China's national security interests. During the Sino-Soviet polemic of the 1960s, Mao further asserted that socialism in the Soviet Union had been gradually eroded by an emerging "bureaucratic capitalist class." With such "capitalist roaders" as Khrushchev controlling the party and state, he concluded, capitalism had been restored in Soviet society. In elaborating these "lessons of the Soviet Union," Mao emphasized that China also faced the danger of "restoration of capitalism" if its own "capitalist roaders" were not exposed and rooted out. With Mao's push, China's domestic politics and social life were again rapidly radicalized along with the escalation of the Sino-Soviet debate.

The Cultural Revolution.

Mao's efforts to instill a new social order in people's hearts and minds reached new heights when the "Great Proletarian Cultural Revolution" began in the summer of 1966. Mao initiated the Cultural Revolution for two interrelated purposes. First, he hoped that it would allow him to find new means of promoting the transformation of China's party, state, and society in accordance with his ideals. Second, he sought to use it instrumentally to enhance his much weakened authority and reputation. Both in real life and in Mao's conceptual realm, those two purposes were interwoven—for Mao believed that his preeminent leadership would best guarantee the success of his revolution.

By carrying out the Cultural Revolution, Mao easily achieved the second goal, making his power and authority absolute during the Cultural Revolution years. But the Cultural Revolution failed to bring him any closer to achieving the first goal. Although the mass movement released by the Cultural Revolution destroyed Mao's opponents and, for a period, the "old" party-state control system, it proved unable to create the new form of state power that Mao so much desired for creating a new society. When the mass practice of "fight self, criticize revisionism" turned into superficial "ritual procedures," and when Mao acted to restore and enhance the state's harsh control over society, millions of ordinary Chinese developed a profound "crisis of faith." Consequently, the economic stagnation and political cruelty prevailing in China made the people disillusioned with the ultimate benefits of Mao's ideals and plans. By Mao's own standard, the legitimacy of his continuous revolution was called into serious question as it failed the test of ordinary people's lived experience.

In the last years of his life, it became evident that Mao's revolutionary enterprise had lost the people's inner support. Even Mao himself realized this. To the visiting American journalist Edgar Snow he lamented that he was "a lone monk walking the world with a leaky umbrella."

Maoism Buried in Post-Mao China

Mao died on 9 September 1976. China has since experienced a profound derevolutionization process. The post-Mao CCP leadership discarded the Mao cult, contending that while in a general sense Mao remained a great Marxist-Leninist, he had committed mistakes throughout his career. In particular, the Party repudiated the Cultural Revolution and abandoned Mao's theory and practice of continuous revolution. Following the pragmatic "cat theory"—"white cat, black cat, so long as it catches rats, it is a good cat"—Deng Xiaoping (1905–1997) unleashed in the late 1970s a new "age of reform and opening to the outside world." Deng's gradual introduction of a "market-oriented socialist economy" brought about phenomenal economic growth in China, but it also created new divisions between rich and poor within Chinese society. Maoist egalitarianism was undermined both as an ideal and a social reality. As a result, the legitimacy of the Chinese Communist regime was further called into serious question.

Against this background, the post-Mao CCP leadership has made strenuous efforts to redefine the essence of Maoism. While claiming that Mao Zedong Thought was not merely Mao's creation but, rather, the contribution of the Party leadership's collective wisdom, the CCP discarded Mao's ideal of transforming China into a land of universal justice and equality, and abandoned Mao's practice of striving for revolutionary changes "all under heaven." In the meantime, Mao's legacy has been represented primarily in nationalistic and patriotic terms. The greatest achievements of Mao's revolution, according to the post-Mao CCP leadership, lay in the fact that it unified China, industrialized the country, and revived its greatness in world affairs. Maoism as a utopian vision, a revolutionary ideology, and a revolutionary way of transforming China and the world has effectively disappeared in post-Mao China's official discourse.

Maoism beyond China

Maoism was never exclusively a Chinese phenomenon. In the late 1940s and early 1950s, when the Chinese Communist revolution achieved nationwide victory, Communist parties in such Asian regions and countries as Indochina, Malaya, and Burma claimed to take Mao Zedong Thought as the ideological guide for their own revolutions. In the 1960s, following the great Sino-Soviet debate, the international Communist movement was divided. Some parties (such as the Albanian Labor Party) and many deviating factions within the Communist parties of different nations advocated Maoism, claiming it to

be the "third milestone" in the development of Marxism-Leninism. In most cases, those parties and factions embraced the Maoist doctrines of conducting violent revolution as the only legitimate way to overthrow capitalism's national and global dominance. They also became the CCP's allies in the "anti-revisionist struggle" against Moscow.

This situation changed drastically with the Chinese-American rapprochement in the early 1970s and, especially, after Mao's death in 1976. Mao's decision to improve relations with the "U.S. imperialists" offended many "Maoist" parties and factions elsewhere, causing them (such as Albania) to denounce Mao's China as an example of "neo-revisionism."

The post-Mao CCP leadership's virtual abandonment of Maoism further alienated China from the remaining Maoist parties and factions abroad. When the Khmer Rouge waged a war of survival in Cambodia's jungle, China supported it not because of its Maoist ideology, but because it played an important role in checking Vietnam, China's main enemy in Southeast Asia at that time. As for such Maoist revolutionary movements as the Shining Path in Peru and the Maoist guerrillas in Nepal, Beijing offered no support and paid little attention.

Does Maoism have a future? As a revolutionary ideology, Maoism has long withered in China. With the decline of such "Maoist" movements as Peru's Shining Path, it is difficult for Maoism beyond China to attract large numbers of devotees. But it seems premature to say that Mao's ideas have forever lost their influence. Some Maoist strategies—such as those concerning mass mobilization and armed struggle—will remain attractive to revolutionaries of generations to come. In a deeper sense, Maoism's most lasting legacy lies, perhaps, in its utopian vision—one concerning the necessity and possibility of achieving universal justice and equality in human society. The vision's beauty exists in its ambiguity. Because it was never clearly definable in practical political terms, the vision may have continuing appeal as long as injustice and inequality persist in human life—in China, and in other parts of the world as well.

See also **Historical and Dialectical Materialism; Marxism.**

BIBLIOGRAPHY

Barmé, Geremie R. *Shades of Mao: The Posthumous Cult of the Great Leader.* Armonk, N.Y.: M. E. Sharpe, 1996.

Breslin, S. G. *Mao: Profiles in Power.* London and New York: Longman, 1998.

Chang, Jung, and Jon Holliday. *Mao.* New York: Knopf, forthcoming (2005).

Cheek, Timothy. *Mao Zedong and China's Revolutions: A Brief History with Documents.* Boston: Bedford/St. Martin's, 2002.

Chen, Jian. *Mao's China and the Cold War.* Chapel Hill, N.C.: University of North Carolina Press, 2001.

Dirlik, Arif, Paul Healy, and Nick Knight, eds. *Critical Perspectives on Mao Zedong's Thought.* Atlantic Highlands, N.J.: Humanities Press, 1997.

Li, Zhisui. *The Private Life of Chairman Mao: The Memoirs of Mao's Personal Physician.* Translated by Tai Hung-chao. New York: Random, 1994.

MacFarquhar, Roderick, Timothy Cheek, and Eugene Wu, eds. *The Secret Speeches of Chairman Mao: From the Hundred*

Flowers to the Great Leap Forward. Cambridge, Mass.: Harvard University Press, 1989.

Mao, Zedong. *Jianguo vilai Mao Zedong wengao* (Mao Zedong's manuscripts since the founding of the People's Republic). 13 vols. Beijing: Zhongyang wenxian, 1987–1998.

———. *Mao Zedong wenji* (A collection of Mao Zedong's works). 8 vols. Beijing: Renmin, 1993.

———. *Selected Works of Mao Tse-Tung,* 5 vols. Beijing: Foreign Language Press, 1965, 1977. Available online at http://www.marx2mao.org/Mao/Index.html.

Meisner, Maurice. *Mao's China and After: A History of the People's Republic.* 3rd ed. New York: Free Press, 1999.

Schram, Stuart. *The Thought of Mao Tse-Tung.* Cambridge, U.K.: Cambridge University Press, 1989.

Schram, Stuart, ed. *Mao's Road to Power: Revolutionary Writings, 1912–1949.* 5 vols. Armonk, N.Y.: M. E. Sharpe, 1992–1999.

Schram, Stuart, ed. *Mao Zedong Unrehearsed: Talks and Letters, 1956–1971.* Harmondsworth, U.K.: Penguin, 1974.

Schwartz, Benjamin. *Chinese Communism and the Rise of Mao.* Cambridge, Mass.: Harvard University Press, 1951.

Short, Philip. *Mao: A Life.* New York: Henry Holt, 1999.

Snow, Edgar. *The Long Revolution.* New York: Random House, 1972.

———. *Red Star over China.* Rev. ed. New York: Random House, 1938.

Spence, Jonathan. *Mao Zedong.* New York: Viking, 1999.

Terrill, Ross. *Mao: A Biography.* Rev. and enlarged ed. Stanford, Calif.: Stanford University Press, 1999.

Wakeman, Frederic, Jr. *History and Will: Philosophical Perspectives of Mao Tse-tung's Thought.* Berkeley: University of California Press, 1973.

Womack, Brantly. *The Foundations of Mao Zedong's Political Thought, 1917–1935.* Honolulu: University of Hawaii Press, 1982.

Chen Jian

MAPS AND THE IDEAS THEY EXPRESS.

Cartography, the art and science of mapmaking, began before the invention of writing and continues to be fundamental to an understanding of the phenomena it represents graphically. Although typically associated with Earth, or parts of this body, its methods are applicable to the delineation of both the microcosm and the macrocosm. Thus, there is mapping of the human brain on the one hand, and the mapping of extraterrestrial space on the other. The unifying concept in mapping is the representation of spatial relationships and their interactions, and nowhere are these approaches more important than in geography. This entry will be concerned mainly with the map as it relates to physical and human geography, although some attention will be paid to extraterrestrial mapping. There will also be some references to GIS (geographical information systems); remote sensing of the environment through aerial and space imagery; and computer graphics (including animation). These are the twenty-first-century developments of more traditional forms of cartography. As Marshall McLuhan has expressed it, maps are one of a select group of media, "without which the world of science and technologies would hardly exist."

Preliterate and Early Literate Maps

The so-called Bedolina petroglyph (Fig. 1) can be used as an example to illustrate preliterate mapping. This rock carving represents a known, inhabited site in northern Italy and was carved between 2000 and 1500 B.C.E. It was made in different stages in the Bronze and Iron Ages; interestingly, the more abstract symbols (tracks and field boundaries) appear to come from the earlier period, while the more realistic symbols (animals and structures) are from the later epoch. In any case, this plan attests to the basic importance of maps to humankind from early times and illustrates symbolization and other essential map features.

Other examples of preliterate cartography could be cited, but only a small number of such early maps have survived. A much larger corpus of maps of preliterate peoples of later times exists. In Russia in the early part of the twentieth century, a collection of more than one hundred so-called "native" maps was assembled, which included examples from Asia, America, Africa, Australia, and Oceania. They were employed for widely different purposes—from oceanic navigation to ceremonial uses. Likewise, the materials used were diverse, according to those commonly within the resource base of the makers: stone, wood, animal skins, either painted with locally available pigments or carved. It is known that "primitive" societies made maps for practical uses, but also for religious and nonutilitarian purposes.

Similarly, the maps of literate peoples in antiquity are varied in terms of purpose as well as materials employed. They are also more diverse in subject matter than earlier ones: a detailed plan of a garden, c.1500 B.C.E.; a zodiacal map carved in stone, c.100 B.C.E.; and other examples from ancient Egypt. Also from this culture and period are maps on the bases of coffins, which served as "passports" to the world beyond. A very different cartographic genre was the cadastral or land ownership plan, from which it is inferred geometry arose as such property maps, made originally for taxation purposes, were used to reconstruct boundaries, erased by the flooding of the Nile.

Contemporaneous with these Egyptian maps were those from Mesopotamia, mostly using cuneiform symbols on clay tablets. This cartography, however, varied widely according to subject matter and scale: city plans; maps of the rivers Tigris and Euphrates with the surrounding Armenian mountains; and a "world" map featuring a circumfluent ocean, with distant places represented by triangles—only one of these triangles is now intact (Fig. 2). The circumfluent ocean, shown by a circle, is a reminder that the sexagesimal system of dividing this figure, the usual mode employed in mapping to this day, came to the West from Babylon by way of Greece. Babylonian maps also contain written inscriptions.

Earth as a perfect sphere and map projections.

In Greece the idea of Earth as a perfect sphere developed gradually. This concept was not, apparently, part of the culture of Egypt or of Mesopotamia, where a plane figure was used to represent the world. By contrast, once the Greeks accepted the idea of a spherical Earth, they attempted to divide the globe in different ways. They recognized parallel climate zones and antipodes, and measured the circumference of the entire globe. The most

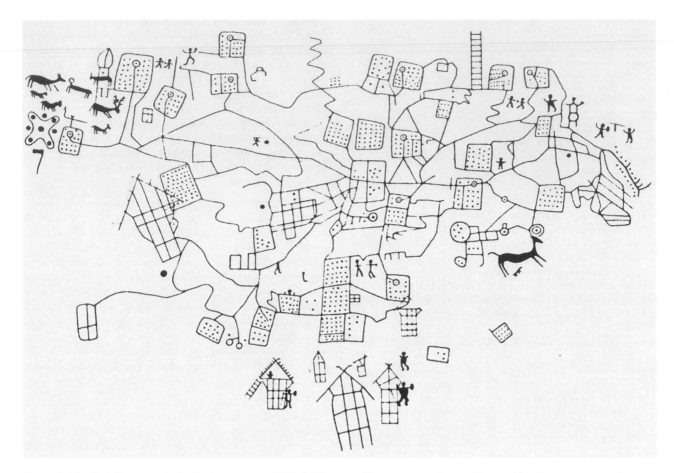

Figure 1. The Bedolina petroglyph. Rock carving, c. 2000–1500 B.C.E. COURTESY OF *IMAGO MUNDI: THE INTERNATIONAL JOURNAL FOR THE HISTORY OF CARTOGRAPHY*

successful attempt of this last was by Eratosthenes (c. 276–c. 194 B.C.E.), who, it is estimated, came within two hundred miles of the correct size of the Earth, a great triumph of antiquity. These developments made possible the invention of map projections (a systematic arrangement of the meridians and parallels of the all-side curving figure of Earth) of which two are credited to Hipparchus (2nd century B.C.E.). He espoused a smaller measure of Earth than that of Eratosthenes, and his projections, the azimuthal (radial from a point) and the stereographic (in which the circles of the Earth are represented by circles on the projection) were at first used only for astronomical purposes.

It is unfortunate that only a few examples of maps of the early Greeks have survived, because their theoretical ideas on geography (expressed in contemporaneous literature) as on many subjects, are of great importance. Apart from maps on a few early Greek coins, one must await the advances of the later Greeks, and the Romans, for visual evidence of their cartographic skills. The greatest cartographer of this later period is the Greek Claudius Ptolemy (2nd century C.E.) who worked in Alexandria and was not, presumably, related to the Egyptian dynasty of that name. Ptolemy (Ptolemaios) accepted a "corrected," shorter figure of Earth than that of Eratosthenes, which Ptolemy also used as a base for two conic-like projections he devised. It

is not certain whether Ptolemy actually made maps himself, but his list of the coordinates of some eight thousand places and his instructions for mapmaking provided the means for others to do so. In fact, the Ptolemaic corpus was transmitted via Byzantium to Renaissance Italy, where maps were compiled from this much earlier source material. Ptolemaic maps cover about a quarter of the globe, including parts of Europe, Asia, and Africa (Fig. 3). Ptolemy devised both chlamys (cloak-shaped) and simple conic-like projections for his world maps.

Some later Greeks worked under Roman masters, who generally accepted Greek ideas; but the Romans were themselves responsible for mapping some areas not part of the Greek empire, such as Gaul (France). Eminently practical, the Romans extended their rectilinear cadastral surveys (centuriation) over large areas from Britain to North Africa and made maps of their road systems. A remarkable example of the latter is the Peutinger Table (a fourth-century copy survives of this first-century C.E. itinerary map). Some of these ideas filtered down in the Middle Ages to Europeans, who were also consumed with religious iconography on their maps.

Sacred and secular maps. The most important survivor of this genre is the (East-oriented, East at the top) *Hereford*

Figure 2. Early Mesopotamian world map. Clay tablet. COPYRIGHT THE BRITISH MUSEUM

Mappa Mundi (Fig. 4). Made around 1300 C.E., this map of the world known to Europeans in the later Middle Ages combines concepts both sacred and secular and was apparently used for didactic purposes. In addition, there were maps for pilgrimage, which, like the maps of the then-known world, were products of monasteries. Contrasting with this cartography are the portolan (haven-finding) charts of the same period covering the Mediterranean and Black Seas, later extended beyond the limits of these littoral areas. Portolan charts were based on the directions of the magnetic needle, which had apparently been transmitted westward from China, via the Arabs, to the Mediterranean. There, in the later Middle Ages, it was combined with a card of the Greek system of wind directions to produce the magnetic compass. Made with the use of the magnetic compass, the portolan chart features the compass rose, emanating from which are rhumb lines to points of the compass: four, sixteen, and finally thirty-two. The North-oriented portolan charts were of great value in navigation within the Mediterranean but were of lesser use in areas where the cardinal direction of the compass varied greatly from North. The Europeans were soon to encounter such areas in their expansion to the Atlantic Ocean and beyond. Remarkably, portolan charts can be attributed to Christian, Islamic, and Jewish cartographers, sometimes working together.

China and the Arab world. From very early times there was interest in the representation of Earth in the Orient, and there are remarkable parallels between mapmaking in this region and in the Greek world and the Latin West. In the later classical period there was intermittent contact between China and Rome, and most of the then-current cartographic forms are present in both cultures, including maps of land areas and marine charts. In fact, during the European Middle Ages, China was ahead of the West (Fig. 5). Thus the most accurate map of a large geographical area was of China (c. 1100 C.E.), which utilizes a rectangular grid, and depicts the coasts and rivers of the country with great accuracy. Chinese sea charts were at least equal in quality to those of Europe at the time. In addition, map printing in China anticipates that of the West by at least three centuries. However, after 1450 C.E. when long-distance voyaging, which had taken the Chinese to the Persian Gulf and East Africa and perhaps further, was officially discouraged, Oriental mapping became extremely Sino-centric, with the rest of the world represented as peripheral to China. This influence also persisted in Korea and Japan where, however, some innovations in mapping took place especially in the delineation of urban areas and of administrative divisions.

The Arabs, especially after the rise of Islam (7th century C.E.), traveled widely from Iberia to the Orient to proselytize and trade. By sea they reached India and established settlements there and on the coasts of China; overland they controlled a large area from Spain to the Far East. They also inherited Ptolemaic cartographic (and astronomical) ideas, and improved upon them. Thus, to take one notable example, Abd-Allah Muhammad al-Sharif al-Idrisi (1100–1154) made significant contributions to cartography. Born in Morocco, Idrisi, after having traveled extensively, was invited to Sicily by its enlightened Norman king, Roger II. Under this patronage, Idrisi compiled South-oriented maps: of the world known to twelfth-century Islamic travelers, in multiple sheets; a single sheet map of Asia, Europe, and North Africa with parallels on the Greek model of "climata"; and a book of sea charts of use to sailors, "the Sons of Sindbad," and others. By astronomical observations the Arabs determined the correct length of features such as the Mediterranean Sea, but after this great flowering of mapmaking, like the Chinese of about the same time, the Arabs made no significant progress, and even retrogressed.

Printed Maps of a More Detailed Globe

Meanwhile, Europe was awakening from the long period called the Middle Ages, between classical antiquity and the Renaissance. A map that expresses medieval ideas, while heralding the new era, is the T–O map from Isidore of Seville's earlier manuscript *Etymologiarum*. (These letters refer to water bodies: the Mediterranean Sea and the Don and the Nile rivers forming the "T" within the "O," or circumfluent Ocean on these largely landcovered, east-oriented world maps.) It was published in 1472 to become the first map printed in Europe (Fig. 6). Following this, the printed map gradually replaced the manuscript map for most purposes in Europe and elsewhere.

A new approach to mapmaking arose in Europe, building upon earlier cartographic models. Greek texts of Ptolemy's

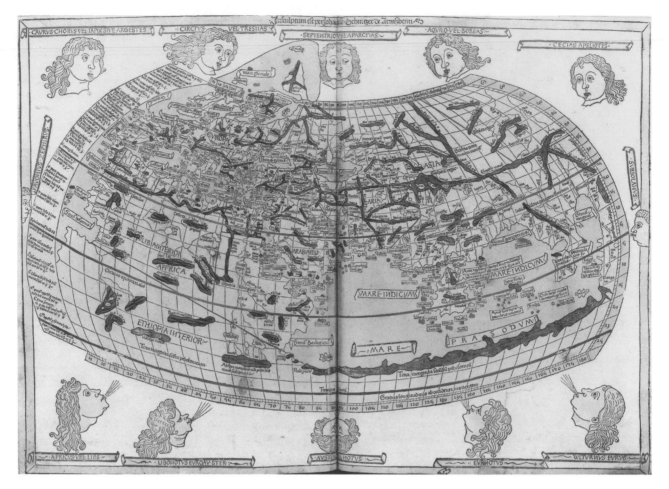

Figure 3. World map from edition of Ptolemy's *Geographia,* printed in Ulm, 1486. RARE BOOKS DIVISION, THE NEW YORK PUBLIC LIBRARY, ASTOR, LENOX, AND TILDEN FOUNDATIONS

Geographia reached Italy from Byzantium c. 1410, and were translated into Latin. Soon maps were made from these instructions, and it became the business of European cartographers to improve upon this late-classical geography, as for example in the 1427 manuscript map of Scandinavia by the Dane, Claudius Clavus. Two major developments in Europe now influenced cartography, as indeed other aspects of life: the independent invention of printing in Europe, and the spread of Europeans around the globe. The (nearly) exactly repeatable representation made possible by the printing press eventually led to a wider dissemination of geographical knowledge, while the contemporaneous discovery of half of the coasts of the world and many islands, in the fifteenth and sixteenth centuries, provided new source material for European cartographers.

The first to utilize these sources and techniques were the mapmakers of the nearly land-locked states of present-day Italy and Germany: The *Bologna Ptolemy,* 1477, twenty-six sheets printed from engraved copper plates; and the *Ulm Ptolemy,* 1486, incorporating Clavus's amendments on a single woodcut print, are examples of this cartography. After a period of coexistence, copper-plate engraving prevailed over the wood-cut method, and the Low Countries (present Netherlands, Belgium, and the lower Rhineland) became the focus of the new global cartography. The near eclipse of woodcut printing led to the virtual abandonment of color map printing in Europe for three centuries. Copper-plate engraving does not lend itself so well to color printing as does the woodblock method, of which a few examples of colored prints from the Renaissance are extant.

With their explorations along the western shores of Africa, the Portuguese from 1420 on provided a rich source of new coastal and insular information. Likewise, the Spanish provided information about the Americas, following the discoveries by Columbus, 1492–1504, and others. Although attempts were made to keep this intelligence secret, it soon became known through the dissemination of data published mostly by the other Europeans in the form of printed maps and atlases. As indicated, the cartographers of the Low Countries eventually came to dominate this lucrative trade during the sixteenth and seventeenth centuries. Although marine charts were the first products, soon other map subjects were covered: inland provinces, urban centers especially in Europe, historical topics, biblical events, and so forth.

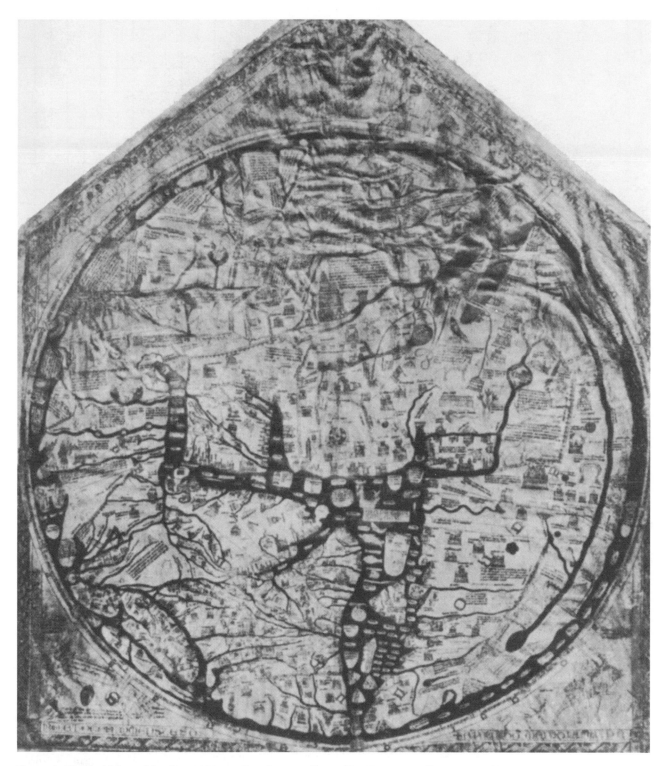

Figure 4. *Hereford Mappa Mundi,* c. 1300 C.E. Drawing on vellum. THE DEAN AND CHAPTER OF HEREFORD AND THE HEREFORD MAPPA MUNDI TRUST

Several individuals and families were involved in this map and atlas production: Abraham Ortelius, *Theatrum orbis terrarum* (1570, and later, in several languages); Gerhard Mercator, with the map projection that bears his name (1569) and *Atlas* (1595); Georg Braun (Joris Bruin) and Frans Hogenberg, *Civitates orbis terrarum* (1572, and later); Lucas Janszoon Waghenaer, *De Spieghel der Zeevaerdt* (1584), translated into English as the *Mariner's Mirrour* (1588); and others. There were

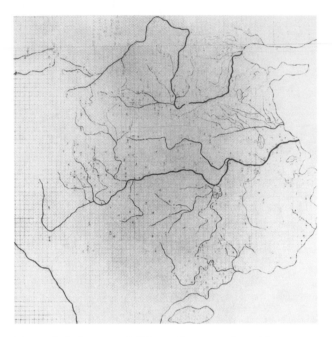

Figure 5. Early map of China with rectangular grid, c. 1137. Carved on stone. REPRINTED WITH THE PERMISSION OF CAMBRIDGE UNIVERSITY PRESS

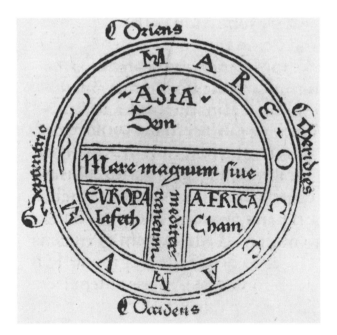

Figure 6. T-O world map from *Etymologiarum* (1472) by Isidore of Seville. BY PERMISSION OF THE BRITISH LIBRARY, IB.5438

many followers and imitators of these pioneers, and some Renaissance maps and atlases, many hand-colored prints from monotone engraved plates, became more decorative than innovative, but are prized as collector's items to this day. The greatest cartographer of the sixteenth century was Mercator, whose projection was one of a dozen new ways of expressing

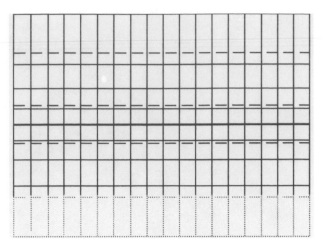

Figure 7. Mercator Projection for world map, 1569.

the graticule (lines of latitude and longitude) invented during this period. A few of these are still in use today, including the Mercator Projection (Fig. 7), on which any straight line is a correct compass direction and thus of great value to navigators, but which has been much misused for mapping Earth distributions, where correct size is important. The English mathematician Edward Wright provided an explication and details for construction of this projection (not given by Mercator) and it was popularized by Robert Dudley and others in the seventeenth century.

Early modern academies and innovative methods of representation. The Italian astronomer Giovanni Domenico Cassini (1625–1712) initiated another new approach to mapmaking when he accepted an invitation to the then recently founded Paris Observatory. Both that institution, and the observatory at Greenwich, England, were established in the middle of the seventeenth century through the sponsorship of the also newly founded Académie Royale des Sciences in France, and of the Royal Society of London, respectively. These academies were to play an important role in the development of a more scientific cartography, which characterized the mapping of the Earth during the following three centuries.

In a period of over one hundred years, four generations of the Cassini family supervised the accurate topographic mapping of France in multiple sheets. The first step was to measure the length of a degree of latitude with great accuracy, which was completed in 1670. From this base, a network of triangles was eventually extended across the whole country. The work of filling in detail, covering more than 180 sheets, was not finished until 1793. One unexpected result of this work, and measurements by French surveying expeditions at the Equator, and at high northern latitudes of Europe, was confirmation of the hypothesis of Isaac Newton that the Earth is an oblate (polar-flattened) spheroid; not a prolate spheroid, or perfect sphere, as proposed earlier. Shortly, detailed topographic surveys were undertaken in other European countries and in their overseas possessions. Thus India, under the British,

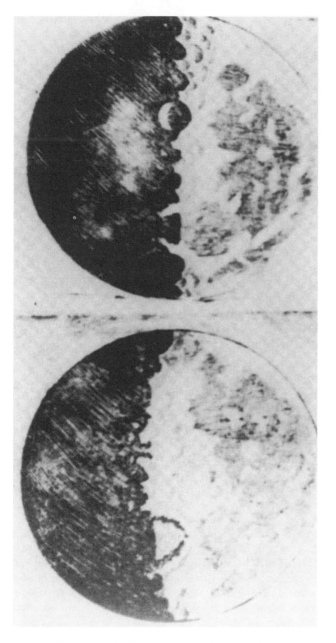

Figure 8. Lunar map by Galileo from *Sidereus nuncius* (1610).

became one of the best surveyed large countries at a fairly early date.

Other directions in which cartography developed in the seventeenth and eighteenth centuries include: astronomical mapping; thematic or special-subject mapping of Earth; the development of new representational techniques; and innovative map projections. The invention of the telescope led to the mapping of the Moon; Galileo's sketch map of 1610 was the bellwether of a large number of other lunar maps (Fig. 8). Other astronomers who made contributions to this new field of mapping include: Franciscus Fontana, Johannes Hevelius, Giambattista Riccioli, and Giovanni Demonico Cassini. Through these scientists the mapping of the side of the Moon

visible from Earth was improved and features named. Thematic mapping had existed before the scientific revolution of the seventeenth century, but a new cartography developed in this period, based on instrumental surveys: maps of wind directions and of magnetism by Edmond Halley; and isobathic (depth) mapping by Nicholas Cruquius are examples of the new scientific cartography (Fig. 9). Innovative methods of representation related to these developments included the isobath and the isogonic line, two of the earliest forms of the contour method, which was so greatly expanded in the following centuries that now there are some fifty types of isoline in use. The development of new and useful map projections also mark this period. A number of mathematicians were involved in the invention of different ways of representing the Earth on a grid or graticule (lines of latitude and longitude). In this regard particularly important were the equal-area projections of the German-Swiss Johann Lambert (1728–1777), arguably the most prolific inventor of map projections of all time. These advances continued as new overseas areas were "discovered" and mapped, facilitated by improved ships, and the solution of the problem of determining longitude at sea. The resolution of this age-old enigma in the late eighteenth century was owing to the invention of the marine chronometer, one of several devices that profoundly affected navigation and cartography.

Nineteenth Century: General and Thematic Mapping

The nineteenth century was a period of consolidation and diversification. Except for the polar regions, the main coastlands and islands of the world had been explored and charted at least at the reconnaissance level by 1800. However, much remained to be delineated, especially in the continental interiors (except Europe, which was reasonably well mapped by this date). Expeditions, mostly originating in Europe, were dispatched to all parts of the world in the nineteenth century, and small-scale general mapping became a large part of the activity of geographical societies that were founded at this time. Similarly in the Americas, interior areas were explored and mapped, at first in a provisional manner, but using instrumental surveys. Thus the world's great rivers, inland seas and lakes, mountain ranges, deserts, and so forth appeared on general sheets and atlas maps, and geography became an important school, college, and university subject.

Along with this was an interest in thematic cartography, in which distributions of phenomena hitherto little known were investigated and mapped. The beginning of regular censuses in this period in many countries provided a large body of mappable data, especially on the human population. Soon demographic maps were produced, and so-called qualities of population also received attention from cartographers—disease (as in the highly informative maps of deaths by cholera in London of Dr. John Snow), crime, poverty, and so forth. Land-use maps of crops, forest cover, and urban forms soon followed, but perhaps the most remarkable development at this time was in geologic mapping.

Geologic mapping. Great scientists turned their attention to studying the strata of the earth, as mines and canal and railroad cuts revealed the earth's substrate. Those associated with the new science of geology included James Hutton (1726–1797) in

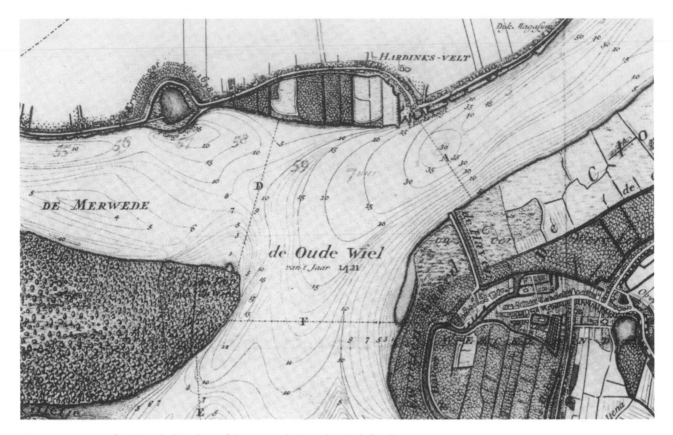

Figure 9. Section of 1729 isobathic chart of the Merwede River by Nicholas Cruquius.

Scotland, Abraham Gottlob Werner (1749–1817) in Germany, and Georges Cuvier (1769–1832) in France. But it was a contemporary of these natural philosophers, the English civil engineer William Smith (1769–1839), who is credited with successfully correlating fossils with associated strata. Smith used conventional colors and notations for rock types, based on age and lithology, and thus greatly advanced geological mapping (Fig. 10). So influential was Smith's work that when a federal, general topographical mapping agency was founded in the United States (much later, in 1879), it was named the United States Geological Survey (USGS), in contrast to the earlier, military or quasi-military topographic surveys in the Old World.

A man with vision large enough to put all of the preceding geographical knowledge into a logical framework was the Prussian Alexander von Humboldt (1769–1859) in his *Kosmos*; his fellow Prussian, Carl Ritter (1779–1859), was a great geographical educator. Both contributed original ideas to cartography: Humboldt with continental maps and profiles, and isothermal diagrams; and Ritter with the concept of altitude tints on general relief maps (this was later formalized with conventional colors for elevation in use today).

The growing United States was the beneficiary of European expertise, as when Humboldt visited Thomas Jefferson, who (like his predecessor in the U.S. presidency, George Washington) was a surveyor and cartographer. It was through Jefferson that the rectangular method of cadastral survey was applied to

the Public Domain, the most extensive example of uniform property mapping in the world. This method contrasts with irregular (metes and bounds) cadastral surveys used in the eastern United States and over most of the land area of Earth. Other Americans made signal contributions to mapping; for example, Matthew Fontaine Maury's (1806–1873) wind and current charts greatly reduced the time taken on long voyages in the period of sailing ships. Great progress was also made in land travel through the railroad, with maps used in determining the best routes and later, when the railways were built, to assist travelers in planning trips.

The traffic-flow maps of Ireland by Henry D. Harness (1804–1883) are especially innovative contributions to transportation geography. More rapid travel in an east-west or in a west-east direction necessitated the development of uniform time zones. This was accomplished in 1884 at an International Meridian Conference held in Washington D.C., when Greenwich (England) was approved as the global Prime Meridian, and the center of the first of twenty-four (one hour) time zones, which were mapped. Lithography, which eventually led to color printing of maps, was also a nineteenth-century innovation as far as cartography was concerned.

Twentieth Century: Changing Technologies

These advances continued and accelerated in the twentieth century through such developments as the airplane and

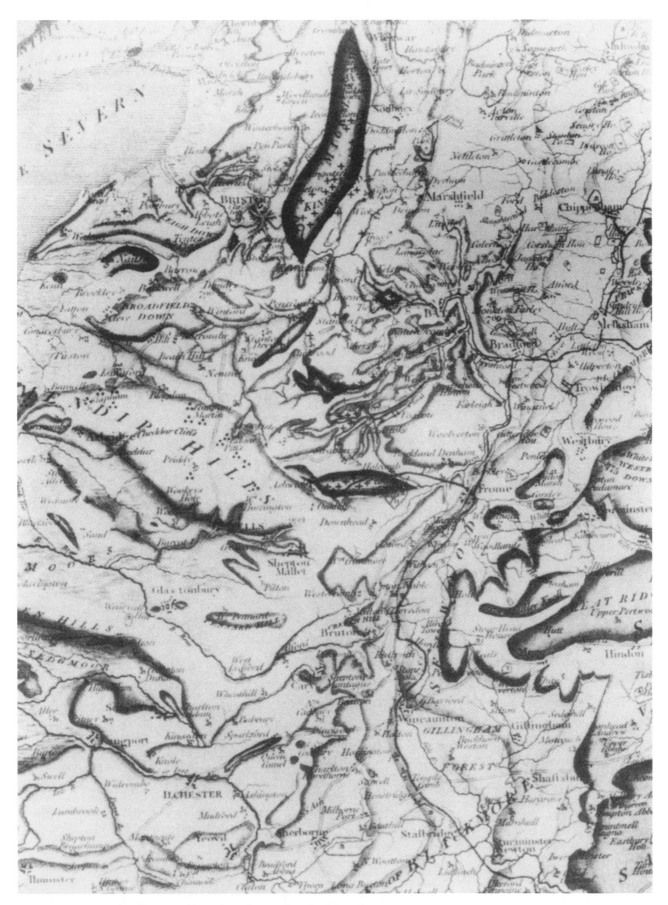

Figure 10. Section of William Smith's geological map of England (1815).

photography in the first half of the century; and space probes and more exotic imaging in the second half.

Controlled flight. Although balloons were used earlier, it was only after the development of controlled flight, through the airplane in the first decades of the twentieth century, combined with viable photography, that the new science of photogrammetry could be realized. Overlapping vertical aerial photographs could be taken at regular intervals, which, when viewed through a stereoscope, give a remarkably accurate three-dimensional view of Earth. This greatly facilitated geodetic and contour mapping, which gradually displaced other, less quantitative methods of relief representation. As photogrammetry progressed it provided a basis for mapping that was more accurate than was possible previously, and could be accomplished in much less time. It was also possible to map areas without the necessity of field work except perhaps, when feasible, for checking. Such mapping required a big capital investment, so that it became a largely national enterprise, with richer countries sometimes undertaking aerial surveys for poorer ones.

Space. In the second half of the twentieth century (partly as a result of German advances in rocketry in the first half), as well as indigenous programs in those countries, Russia and the United States became the protagonists in a "space race." But it was the more peaceful applications that advanced cartography particularly. The first science to be improved was meteorology, as weather maps produced on a daily, or an even shorter time frame, revealed patterns that had not previously been appreciated, as well as facilitating weather forecasting on a regular basis. But soon other distributions, such as land use, were imaged and monitored. This was made possible by the Landsat program of the United States, whose low-resolution imagery was made available to all countries. Remarkable Russian contributions included the first images of the previously unobserved side of the Moon. Soon the United States landed humans on this body, from which images of the whole of planet Earth were made. A great many different parts of the electromagnetic spectrum were utilized in space imaging: color, color infrared, ultraviolet, microwave, radar, and so forth, which either singly or in combination revealed remarkable patterns on Earth, and on extraterrestrial bodies. Other countries such as France concentrated on space imaging of smaller areas of Earth with higher resolution. The new science was designated "remote sensing" of the environment.

Topographical and geological mapping. From the earliest years of the twentieth century there had been a desire to have uniform map coverage of the globe. This was proposed by Albrecht Penck (1858–1945), and it became formalized as the International Map of the World (IMW) on the scale of 1:1,000,000 (one unit of the map equals one million units on the Earth). Although supervised by the League of Nations and (partly because some countries failed to cooperate) later by the United Nations, the project was never completed. However, during World War II such coverage was compiled as the World Aeronautical Chart (WAC), and the two projects combined under the supervision of the United Nations (Fig. 11).

Along with these international efforts at mapping, the nations of the world continued their own cartographical activities including, especially, the production of topographic and geological maps. But on a global basis that coverage is very uneven. The same is true for urban population and transportation mapping, which is largely the responsibility of local agencies, or even private bodies. For example, the automobile or road map, an extremely important cartographic form, is mainly undertaken by oil or tire companies, or by automobile associations in the United States, and other countries. Maps for classrooms and for other educational purposes, in most countries of the world, are likewise the concern of private map companies. This has made commercial cartography highly varied in quality, but also sometimes surprisingly innovative. It is unlikely that government-sponsored cartography alone would have produced such artistic products as the global-perspective renderings of Richard E. Harrison, the natural color relief maps of Hal Shelton, or the simulated three-dimensional isometric urban cartography of Herman Bollmann. Similarly, the statistical maps of László Lácko or the economic maps of W. William-Olsson are the product of freelance or university-based cartography. Likewise some of the most innovative projections of modern times are the work of non–government employed cartographers, including in the United States, R. Buckminster Fuller and J. Paul Goode, but such individuals are sometimes funded by government grants. The printing of maps was also advanced by color photolithography from high-speed presses at this time.

Exploration and mapping. In the twentieth century two large realms of Earth were systematically explored and mapped: the polar areas and the deep oceans. This was made possible by modern technology and, often, great human effort. Although the Northeast Passage (north of Asia) was navigated by the Baron Nils Adolf Nordenskiöld (1832–1901) in 1878–1879 in his ship *Vega,* the Northwest Passage (north of North America) was not traversed completely by ship until 1903–1906, by Roald Amundsen (1872–1928). The North Pole, or a close approximation to it, was attained over land and ice by Robert Peary (1856–1920) and the African-American Matthew Henson in 1909. These explorers were too rushed to engage in mapping, but they were later followed by aviators who had cameras and better views of the polar landscape, provided by the airplane. Nordenskiöld spent his later years collecting and studying old maps (an interest of many professional cartographers, and others).

Antarctica was little known until the twentieth century, when explorers from a number of countries made concerted efforts to explore and map the "Great White Continent." Amundsen reached the South Pole in late 1911, and Robert Scott (1868–1912) and his party died in returning from his attempt early the next year. These efforts did not lead immediately to a profound understanding of Antarctica, which was greatly advanced, however, by cartography during the International Geophysical Year (IGY) in 1958. This enhanced knowledge was made possible in part by photogrammetry, as was the 1953 conquest of Mount Everest by Edmund Hillary and the Sherpa Tenzing Norkey (1914–1986) a little earlier.

Another realm, the world's oceans, has also yielded its secrets grudgingly. Except for coastal areas, little was known of the oceans' depths until sonic sounding (from c. 1950 on) revealed the rich variety of forms of this greater part of Earth's lithosphere. The continuous trace, or profile, which is recorded

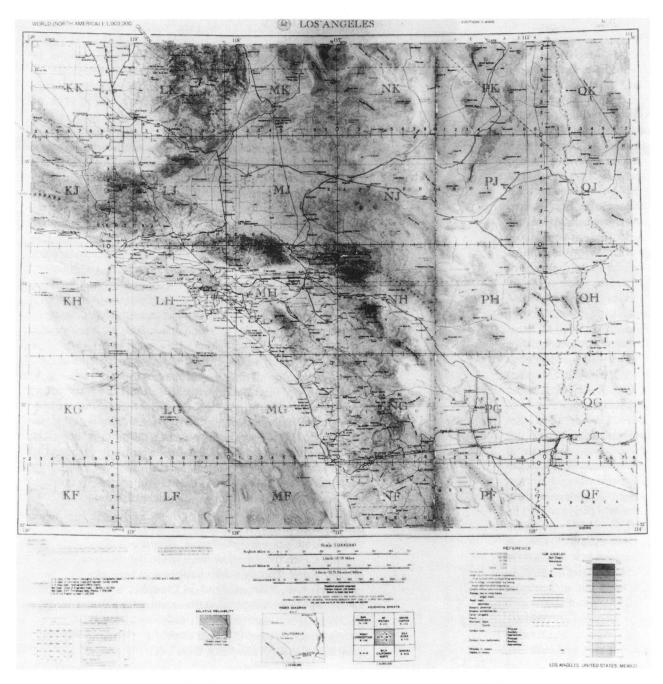

Figure 11. Map of Los Angeles, California, derived from the International Map of the World. U.S. Geological Survey

while a ship is in motion by sonar can be converted into map form revealing, for example, the profound deeps and continuous ridges of underwater areas. This cartography also confirmed the highly controversial, but now generally accepted, theory of continental drift or displacement. Cartography is so important that it can be said that a geographical discovery may not be accepted as valid until it has been authenticated by mapping.

Computer mapping. There is a close correspondence between progress in cartography and the general development of science and technology. Thus, the computer has transformed cartography since the early 1980s as much as, or more than, printing, flight, and photography did at earlier times. The computer permits manipulation of large data banks and the production of maps made without benefit of hands. Is also facilitates the making of animated maps for illustrating the dynamics of areal relationships. In this way a fourth dimension has been added to cartography—time. More maps are probably now viewed on screens, whether animated or not, than in any other medium.

This short survey of cartography has discussed how maps have conveyed ideas and represented phenomena of a wide variety of distributions. They have recorded important achievements of humankind from considerations of the shape of the earth to setting foot on the lunar surface. Preliterate as well as advanced societies have contributed to the art and science of mapping. In fact, cartography is a barometer of the progress of humankind and a reflection of changing technologies. Thus it has been advanced by inventions such as printing and flight, but also by geographical exploration and statistical methods. In the twenty-first century further dramatic developments in this ancient field of endeavor will continue and increase.

See also **Africa, Idea of; America; Europe, Idea of; Geography; Perspective; Representation.**

BIBLIOGRAPHY

Bagrow, Leo. *History of Cartography.* Revised and enlarged by R. A. Skelton. Cambridge, Mass.: Harvard University Press, 1964.

Brown, Lloyd A. *The Story of Maps.* Boston: Little, Brown, 1949.

Campbell, Tony. *The Earliest Printed Maps, 1472–1500.* Berkeley and Los Angeles: University of California Press, 1987.

Coppock, J. T., and D. W. Rhind. "The History of GIS." In *Geographical Information Systems,* 2 vols., edited by David J. Maguire, Michael F. Goodchild, and David W. Rhind. New York: Longman, 1991.

Dilke, O. A. W. *Greek and Roman Maps.* Ithaca, N.Y.: Cornell University Press, 1985.

Harley, J. B., and David Woodward, eds. *The History of Cartography.* Vol. 1. Chicago: University of Chicago Press, 1987. This is the first volume of an ongoing multivolume project.

Howse, Derek, and Michael Sanderson. *The Sea Chart.* Newton Abbot, U.K.: David and Charles, 1973.

Kain, Roger J. P., and Elizabeth Baigent. *The Cadastral Map in the Service of the State.* Chicago: University of Chicago Press, 1992.

McLuhan, Marshall. *Understanding Media.* New York: McGraw-Hill, 1964.

Parry, R. B., and C. R. Perkins. *World Mapping Today.* Boston: Butterworths, 1987.

Shirley, Rodney W. *The Mapping of the World, 1472–1700.* London: New Holland, 1993.

Skelton, R. A. *Explorers' Maps.* London: Routledge and Kegan Paul, 1958.

Snyder, John P. *Flattening the Earth: Two Thousand Years of Map Projections.* Chicago: University of Chicago Press, 1993.

Thrower, Norman J. W. *Maps and Civilization: Cartography in Culture and Society.* 2nd ed. Chicago: University of Chicago Press, 1999.

Wallis, Helen, and Arthur H. Robinson, eds. *Cartographical Innovations: An International Handbook of Mapping Terms to 1900.* Tring, U.K.: Map Collector Publications, in association with the International Cartographic Association, 1987.

Norman J. W. Thrower

MARIANISMO. *See* **Machismo.**

MARRIAGE AND FERTILITY, EUROPEAN VIEWS.

Prior to the nineteenth century, the image of the patriarchal family was a crucial component of both moral injunction (as in the Judeo-Christian fourth commandment to "honor thy father and mother") and political organization. Marriage was the keystone in the arch of social solidarities; it also signaled the creation of a new reproductive unit. For the individuals involved, marriage was at once a moment of social and personal transformation. To be married was an essential attribute of adult status. However the sexual bond at the core of these marriages was more problematic.

Judeo-Christian Tradition

Its inheritance of intertestamentary Judaism, more particularly from the radical fringes that had a fanatical devotion to self-abnegation and ritual purity, gave ancient Christianity a profoundly ambivalent attitude toward the body and sexuality. As Saint Paul wrote to the Corinthians, it was better to marry than to burn with desire (1 Cor. 7:33). Marital sexual relations were given a grudging acceptance although it was made clear that holy activity was incompatible with them: "Do not refuse each other except by mutual consent, and then only for an agreed time, to leave yourselves free for prayer" (1 Cor. 7:5). This ambivalence towards sexuality was emphasized in Saint Paul's message to fathers: "He that giveth his daughter in marriage doeth well, but he that giveth her not doeth better" (1 Cor. 7:38). The Pauline ideology of sexual austerity was later confirmed within the newly established, fourth-century Church by such powerful prince-bishops as Ambrose of Milan, who was Augustine's patron and mentor. He observed, "Marriage is honourable but celibacy is more honourable; that which is good need not be avoided, but that which is better should be chosen."

Although the continuities with its original religious milieu are striking so, too, were the changes—Christianity radically broke away from its Judaic and pagan inheritance in separating descent from reproduction. Christianity was from its beginnings a religion of revelation that believers joined by being reborn in Christ's grace. For Christians, therefore, expectations of salvation were not linked with lineage nor were the achievements of ancestors passed on to descendants. Because charisma was not transmitted, Christians were not enjoined to maintain the patriline as a religious task nor were they expected to continue the cult of the dead through physical or fictitious descendants. Its novel restrictions on the ancient practices of endogamy, adoption, and concubinage made it more difficult for the propertied classes in the Roman Empire to transfer property within the family over generations because it closed the option of creating tight, endogamous knots of restricted elementary families within which wealth could be secured in the face of demographic uncertainties.

The early modern European family system was related to the unique Christian emphasis on rebirth in Christ. This religious concept wrapped both family life and sexuality in the institutional structure of the Church. The central position of baptism in Christian society was driven by the logic of its theology that every Christian was born carnally and in sin but was then reborn spiritually in Christ's grace. Baptism was a second birth that provided a rite of entry into the Church and full citizenship in the secular world.

This holy relationship and the accompanying incest taboos found fertile soil north of the Alps where they were grafted onto Frankish kinship systems. Papal decretals, royal capitularies, episcopal statutes, canonical collections, penitentials, and sermons continuously reiterated the point that spiritual kinsmen/women were sexually off-limits to one another. In this way, the northwest European system of family formation decisively turned its back on inherited traditions of endogamy.

Puberty and Marriage

Historical demographers have provided further evidence that the early modern, northwestern European practice of deferred marriage among women was not common in earlier periods among Mediterranean populations in which few girls seem to have delayed marriage much beyond puberty. In ancient Mesopotamia, for example, teenaged girls were married to adult men in their thirties as was the case among the Jews whose intimate lives have been chronicled in the remnants of the Cairo genizah. One gains some appreciation of the rabbinical injunction to early marriage for women from the following extract from the Mesopotamian Talmud: "Concerning the man who loves his wife as himself, who honors her more than himself, who guides his sons and daughters in the right path, and arranges for them to be married around the period of puberty, of him it is written: *Thou shalt know that thy tent is at peace.*"

Among the Romans—or at least the elite—there was a pronounced inequality in spousal marriage ages. Girls who had just reached menarche were frequently married to men in their mid-twenties. Similar findings—based on Inquisition registers, Renaissance taxation records, marriage contracts from the Toulouse area, and fourteenth-century Macedonian documents—have all described a situation in which teenaged girls were married to men ten years their senior. Early ages at first marriage for women continued to be a characteristic of eastern Europe and many parts of the Mediterranean basin as late as 1900.

Consensual Unions

The emergence of the discrete, single-family household was a landmark, which coincided with the Church's insistence on consensual unions. It separated the couple from its wider networks of clan and lineage thereby making the reproduction of families into an affair of two individuals although for most propertied peasants this was more a matter of ideology than everyday life. But because the vast majority of the peasantry was neither sufficiently well endowed with land nor likely to be subject to the same manorial controls, a treatment of the solid core of the customary tenants must be balanced with an even-handed consideration of those who were marginal, downwardly mobile, and often free.

There is little evidence to suggest that seignorial authorities arranged the peasantry's marriages or intervened in their family formations. If anything, in fact, the opposite appears closer to the mark. The peasantry may have been valued because of their ability to breed but the choice of partner seems

to have usually been their own concern. The lord's concern was to make sure that extramanorial marriages did not deplete his landed estate by draining it of present and future labor power and revenue sources. In this way, the marital horizons for the customary tenantry were limited by the political framework of feudalism, which bore down with unequal pressure on sons and daughters, and much more heavily on the firstborn than on younger siblings. It was not enough to discover an attractive match; it was also necessary to find a suitable match. Marriage negotiations involved a four-sided decision-making process—two individuals and two sets of parents—in which no one player had veto-power: It was probably as difficult for a young woman to resist the imprecations of her parents as it was for a young man to sway his. If all these conditions were met, then courtship would lead to marriage; and marriage would lead to the creation of a new family unit.

Oddly the personal, sexual, and marital freedom of noninheriting younger siblings must have acted as a solvent on the restrictive powers of the older generation. Their sociability, seemingly characterized by flirtatious behavior and a casual attitude toward premarital sex and illegitimacy, was the concern of moralists and the fear of parents. The generational battle in the homes of the peasant patriarchs could not have been uninfluenced by this social milieu—sons and daughters had in their disposition over themselves a card of their own to play. Moreover this youthful card was enhanced by the Church's rules of consensual marriage, which sanctioned clandestine unions. Because a troth (promise) made a binding marriage in the eyes of the Church, the best-laid plans of a peasant patriarch could come unstuck if he was blind to the urges of his son or his daughter. This suggests that the culture of maypoles, youth guilds, dancing, festivals, games, and even the solemnities of the Church's ritual calendar all gave a measure of bargaining power to those who had reached puberty. It further suggests that parental power was not absolute, even if it was backed by the threat of disinheritance.

Having entered the marriage market and picked an appropriate partner, the courtship process slid into a familiar sequence of customary conventions.

> After the hand fasting & makyng of the contracte, the church goyng & weddyng shulde not be deffered to long, lest the wicked sowe hys vngracious sede in the mene season. . . . For in some places ther is such a maner, wel worthy to be rebuked, that at the hand fastynge there is made a great feast & superfluous bancket, & even the same night are the two hand fasted persones brought & layd together, yea certayne wekes afore they go to the church. (Howard, p. 349)

In cases where property was a paramount concern, marriage contracts were drawn up and earnest money was exchanged. These details were often recorded in the full publicity of the manor court. Occasionally eager peasant patriarchs enlisted the court's services while their children were still infants. But such instances are exceptional—the Church forbade child marriage since it was considered impossible for a minor to give his/her informed consent.

Marriage Covenant

The couple's marriage covenant had several dimensions—first there was the settlement of material goods and landed property; second there was the public trothplight by which the couple announced their intentions; and third there was the wedding in the Church and the ring ceremony. In most cases, these three stages followed one another in an orderly succession. However there was no need for a settlement, a *public* trothplight, or a clerically sanctioned wedding. In terms of both the common law and the Church, a *private* agreement between the two partners was sufficient to constitute a legal, Christian marriage.

Why, then, did publicity surround each and every one of the three stages? First marriage was a rite of passage—from dependency to adulthood in the eyes of the couple's family and the wider community; second publicity sanctioned the match and was a means of granting approval to it; third publicity eliminated hidden impediments to a successful marriage, such as previous agreements and duplicitous scheming, by bringing the agreement into full view; fourth publicity and approval gave the match both legal and moral standing before the law and the Church; fifth publicity legitimated all subsequent children of their union; and sixth publicity and communal approval enabled the servile population to enlist the Church on their side in the event that seignorial authorities tried to thwart their choice of marriage partners.

It is stretching matters to suggest that peasant marriages were characterized by "rough equality" (Power, p 75). The peasants' marital economy was a "partnership in which each person contribute[d] a specialized skill that complements the other" (Hanawalt, p. 17). These women were expected to do a double day of labor and were without independent civil rights within the peasant community. It was, for all intents and purposes, impossible for women to act in the public sphere. If this was a "partnership," then it was an unequal one. The expectation of "partnership" played a significant role in joining together men and women of roughly similar ages. And, most likely, this expectation was a crucial ingredient in making consent on the part of the prospective husband and wife something more than lip service. Bad as it was, gendered inequality in feudal society was still an improvement for women compared to the earlier situation in pre-Christian antiquity when monogamy was uncommon, adultery was frequent, and divorce was routine. Furthermore for the unfree, marital breakup was subject to the impulse of the spouses' masters, while the servile population surrendered humiliating payments for "wife-rent" to their lords.

Later Marriage

Prior to the advent of parish registers in the sixteenth century, very little is known about ages at first marriage for either men or women. Surveying the published statistical evidence from fifty-four studies, Michael Flinn describes an early modern northwestern, Europe family system in which the average age at first marriage for women fluctuated around twenty-five. Flinn does not provide measurements to assess the spread of the distribution around this midpoint, but other studies have determined the standard deviation to be about six years meaning that about two-thirds of all northwest European women married for the first time between twenty-two and twenty-eight. A few teenaged brides were counterbalanced, as it were, by a

similar number of women who married in their thirties. Perhaps one woman in ten never married. In the demographer's jargon, that tenth woman was permanently celibate. This unique marriage strategy was vitally important for two reasons: First it provided a "safety valve"—or margin for error—in the ongoing adjustment between population and resources that characterized the reproduction of generations and social formations; and second it meant that the role of women was less dependent and vulnerable insofar as they were marrying as young adults, not older children.

The Demographic Revolution of the eighteenth century produced a declining age at first marriage for women and a tremendous drop in the number who were "permanently celibate." In the preindustrial, demo-economic system of reproduction, about three-fifths of all families were likely to have had an inheriting son while another fifth would have had an inheriting daughter. Thus about one-fifth of all niches in the landed economy became vacant in each generation. In the seventeenth century, infrequent, late marriage was connected with low levels of illegitimacy whereas in the post-1750 period, frequent, early marriage was associated with skyrocketing levels of illegitimacy and bridal pregnancy. The demographic implications of cottage industrialization were as much the result of more frequent marriages, by more people, as of earlier and more fertile ones. In addition rural industrialization permitted married couples to stay together, while previously marriages were fragmented—and wives and children deserted—because the plebeian family's economic base was weak and subject to cyclical strains. Industrialization permitted cottagers, who formed the backbone of many handicraft industries, to move into new zones of economic and social freedom, which translated into stabilization of their marriages.

There were other effects that resulted from independent shifts in the mortality schedule; not the least being the changing configuration of the age-pyramid, which rapidly broadened at its base. Better chances of child survival combined with the diminishing chance of marital breakup to swell the lower age groups at the end of the eighteenth century. Generations followed one another more quickly. This factor played no small role in contributing to the maintenance of high fertility rates.

Domesticity versus Men's Work

The family production unit's reliance on its own labor power merely served to expose it, nakedly, when the terms of trade swung violently against it after the mid-nineteenth century. Simple, repetitive tasks by which women and children had contributed significantly to the domestic economy of the peasant household inexorably declined in the face of competition from, first, specialized producers and, next, factory-based manufacturering. One of the most significant additions to the domestic economy was provided by spinning—an activity of women and children; the mechanization of spinning in the last decade of the eighteenth century effectively demolished this cottage industry at the moment when population growth was creating increasing stress on the income of the semi-proletarian households. The birth pangs of industrial society sent shock waves into the very core of the cottagers' lives; the family work unit was inexorably superseded.

Women and children were doubly marginalized from the world of work. Gendered roles and age-stratified activities replaced the mutuality of the cottage. The ideology of domesticity provided the key entry-point for the new culture of bread-winning respectability.

> Not only does it (i.e., agricultural labour) almost unsex a woman in dress, gait, manners, character, making her rough coarse, clumsy and masculine; but it generates a further very pregnant mischief by infitting or indisposing her for a woman's proper duties at home.

This quotation from the "Report on the Employment of Children, Young Persons and Women in Agriculture" (1867), a British document, resonates in the reader's ears. At the heart of the writers' concerns is a worry that the supposed "natural" character of rural, proletarian women was threatened by "masculine" work. Such women would not only be "unsexed" but also socially deranged since they would be indisposed to "a woman's proper duties at home." Powerful as this prescription might have been, it was essentially beside the point because such working women had never conformed to bourgeois expectations nor did they give "femininity" more importance than family subsistence needs, which were always their primary focus.

In contrast to the rough-and-ready morality of the field and street, female mentalities were reeducated to make the cozy hearth a proper home. Work was reclassified as a masculine endeavor; masculinity was tested in the labor process and judged by the harmony of domestic discipline and its respectable independence. Propriety was to be the moral property of women who were reformulated as model wives and mothers. The vice of the bad home, and the virtue of the good home, could be just as easily translated to descriptions of the good and bad wife: one was chaotic, promiscuous, unsettled, sensual, dirty, and unhealthy; the other was orderly, modest, stable, rational, clean, and well. And what was true of the wife in her home determined the family also.

In French towns of Lille, Mulhouse, Rouen, and Saint Chamond—as in the English coal-mining region of County Durham—the proliferation of proletarians disturbed social policy makers. Nineteenth-century social reformers regarded the menacing features of urban, industrial society to reside in a realm of human behavior removed from the public theaters in which working-class challenges to the status quo usually took place. Malthusian social policy has ever since been based on the understanding that the disorderly family was the problem while the ordered married family was the solution to the population question. The personal was politicized. The working-class family's profligacy—its population power—was thus the outer/public face of its inner/private lack of control.

Reduction in Family Size

The organization of national social systems of education and welfare during the last decades of the nineteenth century combined with the spread of public health measures, which radically changed children's chances of survival, to provide the historical context in which the ongoing revolution in the family was keynoted by the decline in fertility. The average English woman

marrying in the 1860s had 6.16 children; her daughters, marrying in the 1890s, had an average of 4.13 children; her granddaughters, marrying in the 1920s, had on average 2.31 children. The decline of marital fertility was both an innovation and an adjustment; it not only responded to macrolevel changes in social organization but also represented one of the primary ways in which individual men and women acted to make their own history. Not only were the numbers of children dropping dramatically—and almost all of these children surviving infancy—but the period of the family cycle devoted to child-raising was likewise abridged. The very nature of married life changed in response to these demographic innovations.

Some demographers have explained this phenomenon in terms of a shift from "quantity to quality" in relation to the time, energy, and resources devoted to each individual child; but something else was at work. A Manchester woman's 1945 observation weaves together several threads into something like a whole cloth: "People wish to have a small family on account of public opinion which has now hardened into custom. It is customary—and has been so during the last twenty-five years or so—to have two children and no more if you can avoid it. A family of five or six children loses in prestige and, some think, in respectability. It is on behalf of their children that parents feel this most keenly" (Mass-Observation, pp. 74–75). She captures, first the temporality of change ("During the past twenty-five years or so"—namely, since the end of World War I); second the reconstruction of mentalities that have "now hardened into custom"; third the interpenetration of the public and the private, neatly encapsulated by the use of those notoriously elastic terms "public opinion" and "respectability"; fourth "on behalf of their children" joins the sentimentalization of childhood together with the exigencies of human-capital formation; and fifth that it is both "parents"—the respectable husband and his Malthusian wife—who decide together to control their fertility within marriage.

Fertility control was possible without the active involvement of both husbands and wives—the widespread prevalence of abortion stands in testimony to the studied indifference of many men—but the sentimentalization of the family made it more likely that methods of control would come within the parameters of conjugal agreement. Because most of the decline in marital fertility was the product of two ancient practices—coitus interruptus and abstinence—it is clearly important to pay close attention to the changing temper of communication between husbands and wives. Cultural forces, especially the "regendering" of the marital union, both narrowed the scope of the marital union and intensified its internal dynamics. The texture of the intimate relationship within marriage was not just important in its own right but also of crucial significance in reconstructing attitudes to the quality of married life, particularly in relation to the importance of parenting. In contrast to older images that emphasized the importance of work and kinship alliance, modern marriage was portrayed as the romantic union of two individuals. The modern family of "mom, dad, and the kids" was based on the idea that romance was not inimical to marriage and the experience of childhood was massively reimagined by this transition to privacy, domesticity, and, above all, child-centeredness.

New Status to Wedding

Indeed in the course of modernization—roughly coinciding with urbanization, industrialization, and the rise of the modern state, that is, from about 1750, and with increasing intensity after 1870—there was a gradual elevation in the importance of the wedding. In the earlier social formations, the wedding was the final stage in a marriage process by which two people pledged themselves to one another in the full view of family, friends, and community. The rise of mass society had the curious effect of denying publicity to the marriage while creating a need for it. In the urban world, the newly independent couple re-created the big wedding that had characterized village life. "Stag parties," "hen parties," and "showers" became common and, among an increasingly secular population, the church wedding became an important festivity in the course of the twentieth century. Most women were profoundly influenced by this invented custom that has had a powerful impact on popular consciousness. Mass media—magazines and, above all, movies—glorified the white wedding to make it into a social ideal, not only a right of passage but also a statement of social and individual respectability. This respectability was, of course, deeply gendered as those women who became "brides" were decked out in a glossy, flowing white satin dress and veiled in lace; their outward appearance emphasized purity and innocence upon entering the married state.

Different Family Arrangements

Yet just as the image of the white wedding was at its zenith, in the third quarter of the twentieth century, other forces were at work redefining the culture of marriage. The modern sentimental marriage is, in the early twenty-first century, widely perceived to be in crisis. Since the late-twentieth century, society seems to be in the process of making a different social system in a global world, one whose ripples can be felt in the most personal organization of private experience. In the world past, pluralism was the product of uncontrollable demography abetted by the rigidity of social hierarchies; in the world of the early-twenty-first century, by way of contrast, familial pluralism appears to be the product of centrifugal forces of individualism that castigate the traditional marriage as being both repressive and antisocial.

If, as Jean-Louis Flandrin suggests, the early modern state pivoted on the "government of families," and if, as Jacques Donzelot relates, the modern state practices "government through the family," then it can be argued that in the early twenty-first century the evolution is towards another configuration—government without the married family. The language of the sentimental family, as well as the invented custom of public weddings, has been borrowed indiscriminately by people whose private lives were cloaked in this time-honored disguise. Even though the majority of both males and females regard the nuclear family as the sentimental site for parenting, one in four births takes place out of wedlock. Single-parent households (usually headed by women) have become so prevalent that as many as 50 percent of children may live apart from their fathers at some time in their lives. More marriages are terminated by divorce than by death. A sociological discussion estimated that there are as many as 200 different "family"

arrangements recognized by Americans and Europeans. (Bernardes, p. 192–195). In the early twenty-first century, American religious and political leaders are also grappling with demands for same-sex marriage, yet another indication of the transformation of the institution. Indeed the debate itself, which has raised issues of inheritance, parenting, care for the sick and dying, immigration and citizenship, romance, love, and the desire for weddings as rites of passage and public events, reveals the contradictory definitions of marriage and the many purposes that this institution continues to fulfill.

At the beginning of the twenty-first century, then, the loss of prescriptive unanimity is thus a matter of fact. Those who mourn that loss cannot forget the sentimental family; yet the cost exacted by modern memory is that socially nostalgic conservatives have mistaken the image of the sentimental family for the continuity and contradictions of past realities.

See also **Childhood and Child Rearing; Demography; Family; Gay Studies; Love, Western Notions of.**

BIBLIOGRAPHY

Bernardes, Jan. "Do We Really Know What "The Family" Is?" In *Family and Economy in Modern Society,* edited by Paul Close and Rosemary Collins. Basingstoke, U.K.: Macmillan, 1985.

Brown, Peter. *The Body and Society.* New York: Columbia University Press, 1988.

Donzelot, Jacques. *The Policing of Families.* New York: Pantheon Books, 1979.

Duby, Georges. *The Knight, the Lady, and the Priest: The Making of Modern Marriage in Medieval France.* Translated by Barbara Bray. New York: Pantheon Books, 1983.

Flinn, Michael W. *The European Demographic System, 1500-1820.* Baltimore, Md.: Johns Hopkins University Press, 1981.

Flandrin, Jean-Louis. *Families in Former Times: Kinship, Household and Sexuality.* Translated by Richard Southern. Cambridge, U.K.: Cambridge University Press, 1979.

Foucault, Michel. *The Care of the Self.* Vol. 3 of his *History of Sexuality.* Translated by Robert Hurley. New York: Vintage Books, 1986.

Gillis, John. *For Better, For Worse: British Marriages, 1600–Present.* New York: Oxford University Press, 1985.

Goitein, Shelomo D. *The Family.* Vol. 3 of his *A Mediterranean Society.* Berkeley: University of California Press, 1978.

Goldberg, Peter Jeremy Piers. *Women, Work, and Life Cycle in a Medieval Economy.* Oxford: Clarendon, 1992.

Goody, Jack. *The Development of Marriage and the Family in Europe.* Cambridge, U.K.: Cambridge University Press, 1983.

Hanawalt, Barbara. *The Ties that Bound: Peasant Families in Medieval England.* New York: Oxford University Press: 1986.

Herlihy, David, and Christiane Klapisch-Zuber. *Tuscans and their Families: A Study of the Florentine Catasto of 1427.* New Haven, Conn.: Yale University Press, 1985.

Hopkins, Keith. "The Age of Roman Girls at Marriage." *Population Studies* 18 (1965): 309–327.

Howard, George Elliott. *A History of Matrimonial Institutions.* Vol. I. Chicago: University of Chicago Press, 1904.

Ladurie, Emmanuel Le Roy. *Montaillou: Cathars and Catholics in a French Village, 1294–1324.* Translated by Barbara Bray. London: Scolar Press, 1978.

Laiou-Thomadakis, Angeliki E. *Peasant Society in the Late Byzantine Empire: A Social and Demographic Study.* Princeton, N.J.: Princeton University Press, 1977.

Laqueur, Thomas. *Making Sex: Body and Gender from the Greeks to Freud.* Cambridge, Mass.: Harvard University Press, 1990.

Laribiere, G. "Le mariage a Toulouse aux XIVe et Xve siècles." *Annales du Midi* 79 (1967): 334–361.

Lee, James, and Wang Feng. *One Quarter of Humanity: Malthusian Mythology and Chinese Realities.* Cambridge, Mass.: Harvard University Press, 1999.

Mass-Observation. *Britain and Her Birth-Rate.* London: J. Murray, 1945.

Mitterauer, Michael. "Christianity and Endogamy." *Continuity and Change* 6 (1991): 295–333.

Power, Eileen. *Medieval Women.* Cambridge, U.K.: Cambridge University Press, 1975.

Roth, Martha. "Age at Marriage and the Household: A Study of Neo-Babylonian and Neo-Assyrian Forms." *Comparative Studies in Society and History* 29, no. 4 (1987): 715–747.

Saller, Richard. "European Family History and Roman Law." *Continuity and Change* 6 (1991): 335–346.

Scammell, Jean. "Freedom and Marriage in Medieval England." *Economic History Review,* 2nd ser. 27 (1974): 523–537.

Smith, Richard. "The People of Tuscany and Their Families: Medieval or Mediterranean?" *Journal of Family History,* 6 (1981): 107–128.

Smith, Thomas C. *Nakahara. Family Farming and Population in a Japanese Village, 1717–1830.* Stanford: Stanford University Press, 1977.

David Levine

MARXISM.

This entry includes three subentries:

Overview

Asia

Latin America

OVERVIEW

Few sets of ideas are richer and more conflicted than those that have been put forward under the heading of Marxism. Marxism's founder, the German philosopher Karl Marx (1818–1883), had a wide-ranging curiosity about many aspects of humankind and a stamina matching his curiosity. But as the American philosopher Sidney Hook pointed out in his article on Marxism in the 1973 edition of the *Dictionary of the History of Ideas,* Marxism is more than simply "the ideas of Karl Marx" (vol. 3, p. 146); it also includes a vast array of thinking that took its point of departure from Marx. Indeed, Hook suggested that what Marx (and his friend, Friedrich Engels [1820–1895]) really meant is "by far not as significant as what they have been *taken* to mean" (p. 147). However, it seems clear that an understanding of both the original and the derived ideas is needed for an adequate understanding of Marxism.

The Critical Project of Karl Marx

Marx fits within a wider group of Western thinkers who, beginning in the seventeenth century, offered new, secularized answers to the old questions, What is the good life for human beings? and, How is that life to be attained? In part, Marx was a laughing heir of the eighteenth-century Enlightenment—a thinker far more optimistic about human prospects than almost all his predecessors. Yet there is also a basso profundo in his thinking, a sense of the immensity of pain and suffering that will be needed before humans can hope to become the free, autonomous, rational, loving, creative, communal beings that he hoped would eventually make their way on the earth.

Among major predecessors of Marx's social theory are Thomas Hobbes (1588–1679), John Locke (1632–1704), Jean-Jacques Rousseau (1712–1778), and Adam Smith (1723–1790). Marx was also influenced by conceptions of the self associated with the German Romantic tradition. Many intellectual tendencies found their way into his thinking through the philosopher Georg Wilhelm Friedrich Hegel (1770–1831), whose lectures (published shortly after his death) and books sought to cover the entire range of human culture. Further, although Marx's orientation was relentlessly secular, there are residues in his thinking of some religious conceptions. He continued, in a secular and universalized form, Christian conceptions of perfection. Further, as Warren Breckman has shown, his notion of humanity emerged from a theological debate concerning the personality of God.

Marx was born in Trier in the Rhineland region, which after the defeat of Napoléon in 1815 was ruled by conservative Prussia. Marx's father was obliged to convert from Judaism to Lutheranism in order to keep his position as a lawyer in the local court system. In 1835 Karl went to university—first to Bonn, the next year to Berlin. Although for career reasons his father wanted Marx to study law, Karl quickly gravitated to philosophy. He found the law too limiting, and he also believed for a time that, by pointing out inadequacies in existing institutions, philosophy could help bring about progressive change in Germany.

Hegel. From 1837 onward Marx absorbed from Hegel's writings, as well as from the generalized Newtonianism then dominant, a particular understanding of what a properly rational, scientific knowledge of the world requires (Megill, chap. 1). Such an understanding, Marx held, must be universal in form and must generate necessary rather than merely probable knowledge. Further, Hegel regarded human history as a rational process of intellectual and cultural advance, analogous to the progress of knowledge that he saw in the history of philosophy, and Marx adopted this view also. Hegel held that philosophy advances by means of rational debate (called "dialectic" in Greek). Sharpening Hegel, Marx interpreted dialectic as requiring critique of the existing order.

After finishing his doctoral dissertation, on ancient philosophy, in 1841, Marx became an oppositional journalist. In October 1843 he moved to Paris, which was the center of European radicalism and the largest city on the European continent. Here he coedited a critical journal that was to be smuggled into Germany. He also intended to complete a critique of

Hegel's political theory and to write a political history of revolutionary France. Meanwhile, in the streets, bars, cafés, and meeting rooms of Paris he discovered the revolutionary agent that he concluded would overthrow the existing order—the working class or, as he called it, the proletariat.

Estrangement (alienation).

By July 1844 Marx had abandoned political theory and political history (although he never abandoned political activism, to which he devoted intense time and energy). Instead he turned to a critique of economics. In his "Economic and Philosophical Manuscripts" (May/June–August 1844; published 1932) and in related manuscripts, Marx analyzed the claims of such economists as David Ricardo (1772–1823) and James Mill (1773–1836). Notably, he criticized them for ignoring the "estrangement" (or alienation) that he saw workers as subjected to in a private-property-based economic system. Workers do not find either gratification or the possibility of self-development in their work. The products of their labor become a means for oppressing them. They become estranged from each other.

Marx borrowed the notion of estrangement from the critical theologian Ludwig Feuerbach (1804–1872). In his *Essence of Christianity* (1841), Feuerbach had argued that religion estranges human beings from their best qualities, which are attributed to God, Christ, and so on. Religion therefore needs to be superseded by a this-worldly humanism. Marx's innovation was to apply Feuerbach's critique of religion to economic theory and economic life.

Marx also contended, although elliptically, that the system of private property and exchange (buying and selling) is irrational: it is unplanned, it results in an unpredictable rise and fall of prices, and it has no intelligible historical progression.

History of production and needs.

In January 1845 Marx moved to Brussels. In collaboration with the young businessman Engels, who had recently become his friend, he wrote *The German Ideology* (1845–1846; published 1932). Part 1, mostly Marx's work, sketches out a rational history of humankind, focused not on philosophy but on humans' actions to wrest a living from the material world. Using their intelligence, human beings develop their "productive forces," which improve over time. More advanced productive forces continually come into conflict with the retrograde forms by which society and production are organized (later, Marx and Engels would call these forms "relations of production"). History up to now, Marx and Engels held, has been dominated by class conflict: famously, they declared in their revolutionary pamphlet *The Communist Manifesto* (1848) that "the history of all hitherto existing society is the history of class struggles." In their view, these struggles are all ultimately rooted in conflict between forces and relations of production.

Marx (and Engels) also asserted that history would culminate in a socialist society that would function without a political state and without private property and exchange. However, they offered only sketchy accounts as to how this society would actually operate.

The revolutions of 1848 and an analysis of capitalism.

The revolutions of 1848 disappointed Marx, for the established order proved remarkably successful in thwarting political—let alone social—reform. Marx responded to the disappointment by turning to a serious analysis of "the capitalist mode of production." Now living in London, he began in 1851 to study the economy systematically. After a massive effort of research, he published *Capital* (*Das Kapital*), volume 1, in 1867. Although never finished, *Capital* is rightly regarded as Marx's most important work. In it, he attempted to penetrate beneath the arbitrary, merely surface phenomena of economic life to what he saw as capitalism's deep structure.

Adding to his earlier claims about estrangement, Marx in *Capital* focused to a greater degree than earlier on what he saw as the irrational and exploitative aspects of capitalism. Under capitalism, he held, workers are necessarily exploited—that is, they are deprived of the "surplus value" that their labor creates. Exploitation, he contended, is unavoidable as long as the capitalist system (oriented to private property and the market) exists.

Most subsequent economists rejected Marx's claim that labor is the sole creator of value, as well as his related assumption that the value of a commodity somehow exists objectively in the commodity. However, two of Marx's general contentions have not yet been proved false. First, he was persuaded that capitalism has a built-in dynamism, a tendency to transform its own conditions of production. Indeed, in *The Communist Manifesto* he and Engels were perhaps the first to sketch out the process of worldwide capitalist expansion and transformation that we now call "globalization." Second, he held that exploitation under capitalism does not arise from the good or bad intentions of individuals, but is systemic. Position in the system, not greater intelligence or harder work, is the most likely explanation for why the coffee futures trader in New York makes vastly more money than the small coffee producer in Central America.

Necessity of revolution.

The convinced, root-and-branch Marxist claims that capitalism must be destroyed because it necessarily brings with it estrangement, exploitation, and a disorderly irrationality (overproduction, underconsumption, boom-and-bust economic cycles). The root-and-branch Marxist holds that piecemeal reform of the system is insufficient to solve these problems. He or she also holds that capitalism will be destroyed—it is doomed to collapse.

Insistence that capitalism cannot be reformed and that the proletariat (the industrial working class) is the revolutionary class that will destroy it were the two touchstones of Marx's thinking from 1843–1844 onward. To be sure, in his later years Marx suggested that in some countries revolution might occur by electoral rather than by solely violent means, and Engels shared this view. But this was not a rejection of revolution, which in Marx's lexicon equates not to violence, but to a radical transformation of the dominant economic and social system however achieved.

A conceptual treasure-trove.

Marx wrote interestingly on more topics than the ones noted above. His letters, published works, and manuscripts contain many false starts, curiosity-driven meanderings, pregnant suggestions, intelligent analyses, incipient but never fully developed theories, and journalistic commentaries on current events, as well as reservations concerning some of his own views. He was often insistently dogmatic, and yet at other times surprisingly flexible. Toward the end of his life, he rebelled against a dogmatic tendency that he detected among some of his followers, declaring "I am not a Marxist."

Doctrinal Marxism

During the 1880s and 1890s Marxism became doctrine in many European labor and working-class political organizations. Its scientism accorded with the spirit of the age. Its prediction that capitalism cannot escape economic crisis seemed congruent with the so-called Great Depression of 1873–1896. Marxism spread through the German Social Democratic Party after the chancellor, Otto von Bismarck, instituted the antisocialist laws (1878), and in the wake of the party's legalization (1890) became its official ideology (1891). Although in other countries Marxism was less prominent, by around 1900 it was certainly the most influential left-wing ideology in Europe.

The main intellectual basis of doctrinal Marxism was Engels's version of Marx. Engels embedded Marx's analysis and critique of capitalism in a general view of history, which he in turn embedded in an ontological theory. As a theorist, Marx himself was mainly concerned with understanding the "economic law of motion of modern society" (*Capital,* 1st ed. preface), and after 1845 he rarely thought in more general terms. But in *Socialism: Utopian and Scientific* (1880) and other writings, Engels portrayed Marx as the discoverer of a general theory of history, which Engels called "the materialist conception of history" or "historical materialism" (terms never used by Marx). Engels also contended that "scientific socialism" includes a theory of reality in general, according to which reality is material and dialectical (conflict-driven). Marx himself never put forward such a theory.

In Engels's version, Marxism claimed to be an all-embracing science. Whereas other socialisms are utopian, Marxism has the measure of the world as it is. In his 1883 "Speech at Marx's Graveside," Engels declared that Marx had discovered "the law of development of human history," just as Darwin had (allegedly) discovered the law of development of organic nature. In an age enamored of natural science, such claims were the way to popularity. But the result was to downplay Marx's early concern with human activity or praxis and his critique of estrangement. Relatedly, Engels misrepresented Marx's relation to Hegel.

Doctrinal Marxism to 1914

Leszek Kolakowski has referred to 1889–1914, the period of the second Socialist International, as "the golden age" of Marxism. The Socialist International was an organization, founded at a congress in Paris in 1889, that aimed to encourage cooperation among the socialist parties of the different European countries. Admittedly, in this period Marxism began to acquire something of the rigid and schematic character of a catechism, but among both Marxists and people who were just interested in Marxism, serious discussion of unclear points nonetheless took place. These included such questions as the

following: If there is a law of development of human history, how does it operate? Does an explicitly normative or ethical dimension need to be added to "scientific socialism"? How is the economic "base" related to the legal, political, and cultural "superstructure"? Is socialism the inevitable outcome of capitalist development, or is it only one possibility? Is reform a worthy goal, or should Marxists focus entirely on revolution? Should socialist parties form alliances with non-socialist parties? How violent will the revolution be? Can a socialist worldview legitimately make use of non-Marxian resources?

Most (perhaps all) exponents of Marxism agreed that the goal of human history is some sort of exploitation-free society without class or other kinds of divisions, with a full development of science and technology and true freedom. The disagreements were about how this goal was to be achieved.

Revisionism and antirevisionism. Marx predicted that capitalism would collapse under the combined weight of its economic difficulties and the proletariat's uprising against it. But by the late nineteenth century it was clear that economic upswing and actual or anticipated gains from trade unions and socialist parties were keeping revolution on the back burner. Few workers were revolutionary. In spite of its official Marxism after 1891, the actual orientation of German Social Democracy was deeply reformist. In response to this reality, the party activist and journalist Eduard Bernstein (1850–1932) argued in *Die Voraussetzungen des Sozialismus und die Aufgaben der Sozialdemokratie* (1899; translated as *Evolutionary Socialism* [1909]) that the collapse of capitalism is neither imminent nor inevitable, that the number of property owners is increasing, and that socialism is more likely to be achieved by gradual reform within capitalism than by revolution. Although a large minority of German Social Democrats agreed with Bernstein, such party leaders as Karl Kautsky (1854–1938) and August Bebel (1840–1913), as well as theorists outside Germany, excoriated Bernstein's "revisionism." Bernstein's opponents rightly saw that revolution was central for Marx. They were anxious to maintain unity and commitment in the socialist movement. And Bernstein's claims did not have anything like apodictic certainty. Even much later than 1899 it remained plausible to believe that capitalism was doomed, as the flourishing of Marxism during the 1930s depression shows.

Marxist theorists and party leaders, as well as other interested observers, responded to Bernstein in various ways. Kautsky repeated the increasingly hackneyed claim that the necessary development of the historical process will lead to revolution, a position that relieved Social Democrats of any need to act to bring the revolution about. The French social theorist Georges Sorel (1847–1922) scorned both Bernstein and orthodox Marxists like Kautsky and contended for a revolutionary movement committed to what Sorel called "the myth of the general strike," that would see its goal as a total, apocalyptic transformation of the world. The Russian revolutionary V. I. Lenin (1870–1924) opted for a centralized, vanguard party that would guide the too-hesitant proletariat toward revolution. The German (also Jewish-Polish) Social Democrat Rosa Luxemburg (1870–1919) polemicized against party bureaucracy and against Leninist top-down centralism, and in the face of massive contrary evidence put her faith in spontaneous revolt by the proletariat. The French socialist leader Jean Jaurès (1859–1914) supported Kautsky against Bernstein, and held that socialism would come about by revolution. But at the same time he was a natural conciliator and a moralist, having none of the characteristics of a revolutionary.

Kantian Marxism. Another type of Marxism in this period modified or even abandoned Marxist (actually Engelsian) historical theory. The Italian philosopher Antonio Labriola (1843–1904) anticipated a heterodox strand in post-1917 Marxism in his attempt to show that Marxism takes its point of departure from human praxis, or action, which he saw as including all aspects of human life, including intellectual activity. Other Marxist thinkers insisted (contra both Engels and Marx himself) that Marxism needs a normative dimension, the movement of history being irrelevant to what human beings *ought* to desire. The influential school of "Austro-Marxists," involving such figures as Max Adler (1873–1937), Otto Bauer (1881–1938), and Rudolf Hilferding (1877–1941), adopted this position.

The Austro-Marxists also argued against the Leninist tendency to reduce theoretical ideas to mere weapons in the class struggle: instead, they held that Marxist theory ought to appeal to all rational minds. They likewise linked Marxism to a Kantian moral universalism. Like other Kant-inclined Marxists elsewhere, they held that socialism and the Kantian ideal of a "kingdom of ends" are congruent. Individual human beings should never be treated as mere means toward the development of some higher good. Such views were far distant from the theory and practice of Leninism.

After 1914: Leninism and Marxism-Leninism

The rise of Leninism dramatically changed the complexion of Marxism. As Neil Harding has argued, Marxism in its guise as "a theory and practice of revolutionary transformation" was virtually dead by 1914 (p. 114). Although many Marxists still made use of revolutionary rhetoric, the advance of political democracy, economic improvement, and the failure of class polarization to occur militated against revolutionary action. But in August 1914, World War I began, and all the national parties in the Socialist International supported their respective governments in the war crisis, although they had sworn not to do so. Lenin, head of the revolutionary Bolshevik wing of the Russian Social Democratic Party, was enraged at the apostasy of virtually all "orthodox" Marxists. More than this, he quickly came to see the war as marking the total bankruptcy of capitalist civilization, which in his view had forfeited its right to exist.

In response to the crisis of 1914, Lenin, living in exile in Switzerland, formulated a distinctive version of Marxism, which first took shape in his pamphlet *Imperialism, the Highest Stage of Capitalism,* written in Zurich in 1915–1916 and published in Russia in April 1917, after he had returned there in the wake of the February Revolution. By a combination of intelligence, a focus on essentials, brilliant organization, ruthlessness, and luck, Lenin and his colleagues, notably Leon Trotsky (1879–1940), seized power in the October 1917 revolution (actually, more a coup d'état than a revolution), and held onto

it. The regime that they established in the former Russian Empire (reconstituted as the Union of Soviet Socialist Republics [USSR] in 1922) promoted the Leninist interpretation of Marxism as the authoritative version. Later, under the auspices of Joseph Stalin (1879–1953), the authoritative version came to be known as "Marxism-Leninism."

In the period of the Cold War, the world was dominated by a bipolar conflict between "the West" and "the Communist world." Communist regimes claimed to take their inspiration from the so-called "classic writers of Marxism-Leninism." At a minimum these included Marx himself, Engels, and Lenin. (Other figures also achieved canonical authority where they had the power to impose it, notably Stalin and Mao Zedong [1893–1976].) For much of the twentieth century it was overwhelmingly Marxism-Leninism that defined Marxism, and the fate of Marxism-Leninism was closely tied to the fate of the USSR. Even now the popular image of Marxism most often simply reproduces the Marxist-Leninist version. There are even theorists who claim that there is no "authentic Marx" apart from Lenin.

Lenin before Leninism. The central problem that faced Lenin before 1914 was the problem of how socialist revolution was to be brought about in Russia, where industry, by 1900, had barely developed and where most of the population were illiterate peasants of diverse nationalities. In the face of this problem and in response to disagreements within the Russian Social Democratic Party, Lenin, in his 1902 pamphlet *What Is to Be Done?,* laid great emphasis on party organization. Attacking Russian colleagues who celebrated a "spontaneous" awakening of the proletariat and who denigrated "theory" and "method," he argued that workers left to their own resources cannot go beyond a "trade union consciousness." Only with guidance from a centrally organized party of professional revolutionaries in possession of the right (Marxist) theory can the proletariat rise up to revolutionary consciousness and action.

Some commentators have seen Lenin's position as involving a kind of conspiratorial Jacobinism or Blanquism foreign to the spirit of Marx himself. (Blanquism was so named after the French activist Louis Auguste Blanqui [1805–1881], an advocate of the forcible seizure of political power by professional revolutionaries.) But this criticism is mistaken. First, in 1902 and even much later, Lenin held that the success of revolution in Russia depended on socialist revolution also breaking out in the more advanced countries to Russia's west. Second, Marx himself faced, in his early years, the problem of how revolution was to come to Germany, which at that time was economically backward in comparison to France, Belgium, and England. In the same essay in which he announced his "discovery" of the proletariat, he also asserted emphatically that revolution will come to Germany when philosophy (theory) allies itself with the oppressed proletariat's practical experience. Marx did not claim that the oppressed weavers of Silesia would become conscious of their situation on their own (Marx, "Introduction" to *A Contribution to the Critique of Hegel's "Philosophy of Right,"* published February 1844). In short, only the intelligentsia is capable of revealing to the proletariat the true meaning of its own experience.

Capitalism and imperialism. Lenin's immediate reaction to the outbreak of World War I was to engage in "a doctrinaire restatement of the fundamentals of Marxism" (Harding, p. 77). He then turned to an attempt to reconstruct the deep roots of Marxism in Hegel's thought, which led him to conclude that his fellow Marxists had failed to understand Marx's dialectical method, which always looks to find contradictions in existing reality.

Lenin also concluded that other Marxists had failed to understand the actual situation of capitalism in its contemporary guise. In Lenin's view, capitalism had now entered into the stage of state-directed violence. Its economic contradictions were such that they could only be overcome, temporarily, by an imperialist expansion enabling the extraction of super-profits from less-developed countries. Capitalism now constituted a world system, and Lenin argued that the system was destined to break at its weakest link, which was most likely to be at the periphery—for example, Russia. Thus, on returning to Russia in April 1917, Lenin felt justified in proclaiming that a socialist—and not just a bourgeois—revolution was underway.

Leninism and science. Lenin's views altered to some extent in the difficult years from 1917 to his death in 1924. The complexities must be left aside here. The central point is that notions of open discussion and mass participation quickly disappeared from the horizon of the regime. Rather, the party, and in particular its highest leaders, came to substitute for the proletariat, which itself amounted to only a small part of the population of the USSR.

The theoretical justification for this development was to be found ultimately in Marx's commitment to science. It is not for nothing that in December 1920 Lenin announced that "Communism is Soviet power plus electrification of the whole country" ("Soviet [worker-council] power" quickly faded, however). In theory, all decisions were to be made on the basis of expert, scientific knowledge, and politics was to fade from view. In practice, the attempt to impose decisions on the country—to make the country conform to the theory—was undoubtedly an important reason why the USSR under Stalin became a tyranny the likes of which had never before been seen.

In the canonical form that it acquired by the late 1930s, Marxism-Leninism claimed to offer the explanatory key to all of reality. The term associated with this monism was "dialectical materialism" (coined by the Russian Marxist G. V. Plekhanov [1857–1918] in 1890). Unimportant before 1917, in the Soviet period dialectical materialism became a widely used shorthand term for Marxism, in large measure as a result of Stalin's efforts. According to dialectical materialism, an inexorable developmental process permeates all of reality. The struggles that occur in human history are merely one manifestation of this process. We are thus in a position to know that history will lead, with utter inevitability, through the travails of the present to the sunny uplands of socialism.

It is often assumed that Marx himself was a "dialectical materialist." The theory of dialectical materialism was originated by Engels. It is not articulated in any of Marx's own writings. Both Marx and Engels claimed that Marxian socialism was

scientific, but it was Engels who intuited that many potential adherents of Marxism were looking for an all-embracing worldview. Purporting to explain everything, dialectical materialism aimed to displace all competing worldviews, notably religion. To its adherents, it offered a sense of certainty. In Stalin's calculation, this sense of certainty served the interests of the bureaucratic tyranny that he established over the USSR.

Advance and retreat of Marxism-Leninism. Marxism-Leninism prescribed a way out of backwardness through revolution, science, and rationality that many intellectuals in Asia, Africa, and Latin America found appealing. For over half a century it had a significant following in the "underdeveloped" world. However, few Marxist-Leninist regimes came into being independently of the direct application of military force by the USSR. In order to succeed, revolutionary movements needed a favorable concatenation of circumstances and an indigenous cadre of militants willing to adjust their message to suit the audience. This did happen in China. In 1926 urban workers made up only 0.5 percent of the Chinese population. As Mao Zedong saw in his prescient "Report on the Peasant Movement in Hunan" (1927), the party had to appeal to the peasantry. The People's Republic of China came into being in 1949 as a result of a successful mobilizing of a revolutionary peasantry. Meanwhile, in the wake of World War II the Soviet Union and its victorious army imposed Marxism-Leninism on Eastern Europe.

At the beginning of the twenty-first century, the fundamental fact confronting doctrinal Marxism was the all but total disappearance of Marxist-Leninist regimes and movements. Over the course of a generation and more, the Soviet Union became more and more sclerotic and then, in 1991, collapsed, having already lost its Eastern European satellites in 1989. Meanwhile, the People's Republic of China turned toward participation in the market following the "Reform and Opening" process initiated by Deng Xiaoping in the late 1970s. By 2004, only a few countries, notably Cuba and North Korea, were still claiming to be built on Marxist-Leninist principles.

As for large-scale Marxist or Marxist-Leninist political movements, by 2004 none existed. When the Leninist regime in the USSR was being consolidated, some elements of European social democracy set themselves up as the avowedly democratic wing of Marxism in opposition to Leninism. But social democracy's Marxism became attenuated over time, eventually disappearing into a generalized commitment to social welfare and to some measure of social and economic egalitarianism.

Marxism beyond Doctrinal Marxism

A large body of Marxian writing and reflection lies beyond the framework of doctrinal Marxism. Until World War II almost all of this "independent Marxism"—as we might call it—emerged within the framework of, or at least in close dialogue with, doctrinal Marxism. After World War II, this changed, for much Marxian reflection was carried out in essential independence from both official Marxism-Leninism and from whatever Marxist residues remained in the social democratic movement. In addition to independent Marxists, there were many scholars and intellectuals who deployed Marxian perspectives without accepting Marxism as a whole and usually without even considering themselves Marxists. This is a tradition that goes back to the early twentieth century. By the end of the twentieth century it was certainly the dominant mode of serious intellectual work and reflection in a Marxian register. Of course, one encounters a difficulty here, for at this point one reaches the boundary of what can legitimately be called Marxism.

Existential Marxism. Another difficulty is that of characterizing in a general way the Marxisms that diverge from doctrinal Marxism. Beyond social-democratic and Marxist-Leninist Marxisms, Hook identified a third, post-1945 variant: existential Marxism. In doing so he inflated the significance of a relatively minor school of mainly French Marxists. Still, Hook's category does point in the direction of at least two significant developments in post-1945 Marxism. First, after about 1950, much effort went into reinterpreting Marx in the light of the "Economic and Philosophical Manuscripts," which revealed a "humanist" Marx different from the Marx of Marxism-Leninism. While Marx was no existentialist, his early interest in estrangement and in activity do reveal affinities with existentialism. Second, an important development since World War II among persons sympathetic to Marxism has been the impulse to work in the mode of "Marxism and . . . "—combining Marxism with something else, whether method, school, commitment, or discipline. In offering an existentially inflected Marxism in his *Critique of Dialectical Reason* (1960), the French philosopher Jean-Paul Sartre (1905–1980) was operating in just this sort of combinatory mode. A German-Jewish refugee to the United States, Herbert Marcuse (1898–1979), engaged in a similar effort, variously combining a Marxian perspective with Freud (*Eros and Civilization,* 1955) and with vaguely Heideggerian notions of an oppressive modernity (*One-Dimensional Man,* 1964). Other combinations involved less an attempt to combine Marxism with some other perspective than an attempt to apply Marxism to an implied object of study. It was a potentially unending intellectual game, for one could pair Marx with other partners virtually at will: a short list includes feminism, structuralism, psychoanalysis, ecology, anthropology, history, literary criticism, literary theory, film studies, and cultural studies. Although it involves much question-begging, the game still continues.

Western Marxism. Other commentators have identified a tradition of "Western Marxism." "Western Marxism" is largely a post hoc imposition. Still, the category can help us to see common features in a large body of Marxist theory that first emerged as a challenge to Engelsian and Leninist versions of Marxism. The unintending founder of Western Marxism was György Lukács (1885–1971), whose *History and Class Consciousness: Studies in Marxist Dialectics* (1923) was actually written in defense of "orthodox Marxism." But in the midst of defending orthodox Marxism, Lukács emphasized two concepts that were to be important for Western Marxism. One was estrangement (which he intuited in Marx without having read the then-unavailable "Economic and Philosophical Manuscripts"). The other was totality. The gist of this latter concept is the claim that the correct understanding of any reality requires that one first understand it as a *whole* (which among other things, involves understanding its place within the historical process),

rather than arriving at conclusions about it solely by induction from particulars. Lukács held that bourgeois empiricists, as well as some Marxists, had failed to understand this point. A second theorist often seen as a founder of Western Marxism was Karl Korsch (1886–1961), who in Marxism and Philosophy (1923) and other writings emphasized that Marxism is primarily concerned with human practice (praxis) and, like Lukács, criticized positivist or empiricist versions of Marxism.

Other theorists commonly associated with so-called Western Marxism include Karl Korsch (1886–1961), Antonio Gramsci (1891–1937), Ernst Bloch (1885–1977), Herbert Marcuse, Henri Lefebvre (1905–1991), Sartre, Maurice Merleau-Ponty (1908–1961), and the "Frankfurt School" theorists Walter Benjamin (1892–1940), Max Horkheimer (1895–1973), and Theodor Adorno (1903–1969). What is most striking about the "Western Marxists" is that none of them focused on Marxism's basic socioeconomic claims. They either directly assert or implicitly assume the truth of these claims, but they never see the need to show that they are true in fact. For example, Lukács emphatically saw the proletariat as the "identical subject-object" of history, but he never did the work to show how this must be so. The omission was made easier by the fact that Western Marxists focused overwhelmingly on culture, social consciousness, and ideology rather than on economics. For example, Gramsci is best known for his notion of hegemony, a kind of updated notion of ideology; Benjamin was a brilliant cultural and literary critic; and Adorno offered a cutting analysis of "the culture industry."

One historian of Western Marxism, Martin Jay, has noted that a loss of confidence in the validity and usefulness of Western Marxism occurred by the late 1970s, after a brief period in which it had attracted some young, leftist, mainly American academics. The reasons for this deflation are no doubt complex, as are the reasons for the decline of Marxism generally. One crucial consideration is that thinking persons can hardly go on begging the question as to the truth of a theory's basic claims for long before doubts need to be addressed. It is "no accident," as a Marxist might say, that such figures as Jürgen Habermas (b. 1929), scion of the Frankfurt School, and Agnes Heller (b. 1929), Lukács's most distinguished student, took issue, sooner or later, with Marxism.

By the 1970s, commitment to Marxism was not easy to maintain, for there had been too much experience contrary to Marx's hopes and predictions. Marx's claim that capitalism was doomed to collapse in a proletarian revolution had to face both the failure of any unified proletariat to appear and the fact that the institutions of capitalist society had managed to muddle through again and again. Marx's claim that socialism would be better than capitalism had to face both the experiential disconfirmation offered by actually existing communist states, and a serious argument, first articulated by Ludwig von Mises in 1920, to the effect that a complex nonmarket economy cannot operate efficiently, because markets are indispensable information-gathering mechanisms (see Steele).

Analytical Marxism. Although various claims central to Marxism no longer seem tenable, Marxism has a legitimate survival in at least two respects. First, Marxism exists as a set of suggestions for research, for Marx offered many specific claims and suggestions concerning modern society and politics. Some of these are false, as Richard Hamilton has shown. But others, particularly when reformulated as abstract theoretical claims to be tested in specific present-day contexts, remain alive in current social science. For example, Marxism has been influential in recent thinking about international political economy—hardly surprising, in the light of Marx and Engels's early insistence on capitalism's global character. It has influenced thinking about state power, a theme emphasized by the Marxist political theorists Ralph Miliband (1924–1994) and Nicos Poulantzas (1936–1979) and picked up by others subsequently (see Aronowitz and Bratsis). It has influenced thinking about democratization—in particular, the thinking of those political scientists concerned with the relation between class structure and democracy. Finally, it has helped to inspire empirical research into the workings of class in modern society.

A question that arises in relation to such studies is: How Marxist are they? Clearly, they are not Marxist by the standards of revolutionary Marxism, since they are academic studies and not attempts to promote the revolution (at most, such researchers hope to encourage reform). But since in 2004 there exist virtually no active Marxian revolutionaries apart from the small circle of Nepalese Maoists, this is a high standard. By less stringent standards, such studies may well be Marxist in a looser sense—in the sense of taking Marx seriously, working within a tradition of Marxism, using Marxian language, and maintaining a normative commitment to the values of freedom, equality, and human dignity. Certainly, in the late 1970s a small but lively group of Anglo-American academics began to identify themselves as "analytical" or "rational choice" Marxists (see Roemer, Wright, and Wright et al.). However, insofar as their investigations were integrated into fields or subfields in political science, economics, sociology, and so on, these tended to become "research" rather than "Marxist research."

Thus one meets again a boundary, where what is valid in Marxism passes over into an intellectual territory that is no longer Marxist. Some writers, notably Ernesto Laclau (b. 1935) and Chantal Mouffe (b. 1943) have called this territory "post-Marxism" (see Sim). In the eyes of such writers, post-Marxism involves a reformulation of Marxism in order to accommodate such "movements" as poststructuralism, postmodernism, and second-wave feminism. Here Marxism appears, not as a set of analyzable propositions, but, in a much more attenuated guise, as a form of critique and of hope from which almost all specifically Marxian claims have disappeared. This is the second way in which Marxism continues to have a legitimate survival in the twenty-first century.

See also **Capitalism; Communism; Economics; Hegelianism; Kantianism; Maoism; Revolution; Socialism.**

BIBLIOGRAPHY

PRIMARY SOURCES

Lenin, V. I. *The Lenin Anthology.* Edited by Robert C. Tucker. New York: Norton, 1975. Possibly the best one-volume anthology.

Marx, Karl, and Friedrich Engels. *Collected Works.* 50 vols. New York: International Publishers, 1975–2004. Imperfectly edited and omits some manuscript writings, but indispensable for English-readers.

———. *Karl Marx, Friedrich Engels Gesamtausgabe (MEGA).* Berlin: Dietz, 1972–1999. Berlin: akademie-Verlag, 1999–. Meticulously edited; will make all previous editions obsolete. Eventually 114 vols. Not to be confused with the "Old *MEGA*" (1927–1935).

———. *The Marx-Engels Reader.* Edited by Robert C. Tucker. 2nd ed. New York: Norton, 1978. Possibly the best one-volume anthology.

www.marxists.org. Makes freely available a large collection of works by many authors, beginning with Marx and Engels.

SECONDARY SOURCES

Aronowitz, Stanley, and Peter Bratsis, eds. *Paradigm Lost: State Theory Reconsidered.* Minneapolis: University of Minnesota Press, 2002. Marx's theory of the state, updated.

Avineri, Shlomo, *The Social and Political Thought of Karl Marx.* London: Cambridge University Press, 1968. Slightly outdated but still useful.

Bottomore, Tom, ed. *A Dictionary of Marxist Thought.* 2nd ed. Oxford and Cambridge, Mass.: Blackwell, 1991. Articles on major topics in Marxism.

Breckman, Warren. *Marx, the Young Hegelians, and the Origins of Radical Social Theory: Dethroning the Self.* New York: Cambridge University Press, 1999. Shows connections between theological and sociopolitical concerns in the background to Marx.

Carver, Terrell, ed. *The Cambridge Companion to Marx.* Cambridge, U.K.: Cambridge University Press, 1991. Articles on various aspects of Marx's theoretical project.

Draper, Hal. *The Marx-Engels Cyclopedia.* Vol. 1: *The Marx-Engels Chronicle: A Day-by-Day Chronology of Marx and Engels's Life and Activity.* Vol. 2: *The Marx-Engels Register: A Complete Bibliography of Marx and Engels' Individual Writings.* Vol. 3: *The Marx-Engels Glossary: Glossary to the Chronicle and Register, and Index to the Glossary.* New York: Schocken, 1985–1986. Indispensable for serious research on Marx.

Fehér, Ferenc, Agnes Heller, and György Márkus. *Dictatorship over Needs.* Oxford: Basil Blackwell, 1983. Critical analysis of the "command" society that was Soviet-style socialism.

Hamilton, Richard. *The Bourgeois Epoch: Marx and Engels on Britain, France, and Germany.* Chapel Hill: University of North Carolina Press, 1991. Attacks Marx and Engels's historical claims.

Harding, Neil. *Leninism.* Durham, N.C.: Duke University Press, 1996. Succinct, highly critical account.

Hook, Sidney. "Marxism." *Dictionary of the History of Ideas.* 5 vols. New York: Scribners, 1973-1974. Vol 3, pp.146–161. A clear account, reacting against Stalinism. Can also be accessed at www.historyofideas.org.

Jay, Martin. *Marxism and Totality: The Adventures of a Concept from Lukács to Habermas.* Berkeley: University of California Press, 1984. Charts a course through "Western Marxism."

Kolakowski, Leszek. *Main Currents of Marxism: Its Rise, Growth, and Dissolution.* Vol. 1: *The Founders.* Vol. 2: *The Golden Age.* Vol. 3. *The Breakdown.* Translated by P. S. Falla. Oxford: Oxford University Press, 1981. A critical account. Vol. 2 is the best volume; its coverage is unduplicated elsewhere.

McLellan, David. *The Thought of Karl Marx: An Introduction.* 3rd ed. Edited by David McLellan. London: Macmillan, 1995. Discusses major themes in Marx's thinking, with illustrative

Marx texts; also links writings to Marx's biography. Convenient, succinct.

Megill, Allan. *Karl Marx: The Burden of Reason (Why Marx Rejected Politics and the Market)*. Lanham, Md.: Rowman and Littlefield, 2002. Impact of Hegelian philosophy on Marx.

Roemer, John, ed. *Analytical Marxism*. Cambridge, U.K., and New York: Cambridge University Press, 1986. Essays by G. A. Cohen, Jon Elster, and others.

Sassoon, Donald. *One Hundred Years of Socialism: The West European Left in the Twentieth Century*. New York: New Press, 1996. Socialism, Marxist and not, in twentieth-century Western Europe.

Siegel, Jerrold E. *Marx's Fate: The Shape of a Life*. 1978. Reprint, University Park: Pennsylvania State University Press, 1993. The most intellectually serious biography.

Sim, Stuart. *Post-Marxism: An Intellectual History*. London and New York: Routledge, 2000. Residues of Marxism after the collapse.

Steele, David Ramsay. *From Marx to Mises: Post-Capitalist Society and the Challenge of Economic Calculation*. La Salle, Ill.: Open Court, 1992. Implications of von Mises's argument against non-market socialism.

Wright, Erik Olin. "What Is Analytical Marxism?" In *Rational Choice Marxism*, edited by Terrell Carver and Paul Thomas, 11–30. University Park: Pennsylvania State University Press, 1995. Definition and defense of analytical Marxism.

Wright, Erik Olin, Andrew Levine, and Elliott Sober. *Reconstructing Marxism: Essays on Explanation and the Theory of History*. London and New York: Verso, 1992. Analytical reconstruction of Marxism.

Young, Robert J. C. *Postcolonialism: An Historical Introduction*. Oxford, and Malden, Mass.: Blackwell, 2001. Discusses role of Marxism in anticolonial struggles.

Allan Megill

ASIA

The writings of Karl Marx offer both a critique and a celebration of modern capitalism. On the one hand, Marx presented a devastating moral indictment of the capitalist exploitation of labor and the drowning of all human relationships in "the icy waters of egotistical calculation." On the other, Marx saw capitalism as a necessary and progressive phase of historical development, yielding the essential material and social prerequisites for socialism—modern industry and the proletariat.

The proposition that socialism presupposes capitalism was seen as universally valid. "The bourgeoisie, by the rapid improvement of all instruments of production," Marx wrote in *The Manifesto of the Communist Party* (1848), "batters down all Chinese walls. . . . It compels all nations on pain of extinction, to adopt the bourgeois mode of production. In one word, it creates a world after its own image."

In this mid-nineteenth-century anticipation of the late-twentieth-century phenomenon of "globalization," Marx assumed that the precapitalist countries of Asia were destined to follow the Western capitalist path of development. They would do so under the universalistic pressure of Western imperialism. While imperialism was morally detestable, it was historically progressive, breaking apart stagnant "Asiatic" societies

unable to move into modern history on their own. In universalizing capitalism, imperialism was laying the basis for an international socialist future.

Japan

It was entirely logical that Japan should have been the first Asian country where Marxism took root. Japan was the earliest Asian land to embark on a program of capitalist development. In the 1890s, in response to the social tensions of Meiji modernization, Japanese intellectuals imported Marxism along with a variety of other proscribed Western socialist theories. By the time of the Russo-Japanese War of 1904–1905, Marxism established itself as the dominant socialist theory. And the preeminent version of Marxism was the economically deterministic doctrine of Karl Kautsky (1854–1938).

The early Japanese Marxists often intermingled anarchist and utopian socialist ideas with their Marxian beliefs. It was not until the Russian Revolution of 1917 that Marxism found coherent political and intellectual expression. The Japanese Communist Party (JCP), founded in 1922, became the carrier of the Leninist version of Marxism while the Japanese Socialist Party largely based itself (in its various incarnations) on the more orthodox Marxist teachings of Kautsky. But Japanese Marxism in the 1920s and 1930s, partly because of severe state repression, was less influential as a political than an intellectual movement. By the late 1920s, Marxist influences were dominant in the economics departments of elite Japanese universities. The celebrated 1927–1937 debate on the nature of Japanese capitalism was a major contribution to international Marxist scholarship.

The rise of militarism and fascism in the 1930s led to the wholesale jailing of Marxists and the virtual total suppression of Marxian ideas. With the defeat of the fascist regime in 1945, Marxist intellectual and political life revived under the American occupation. Marxist theory became highly influential in economic and historical scholarship. Marxism found vigorous political expression in the small but influential Communist Party and also in the much larger Japanese Socialist Party (JSP). The JSP, which gained substantial electoral support, was hindered in its bid for power by a long-standing division between Marxist-Leninists and social democrats. A further political obstacle was the general prosperity yielded by Japan's phenomenal economic growth, which eroded Marxist influence. However, the stagnation of Japanese capitalism since 1990 perhaps augurs well for the reinvigoration of Japanese Marxism.

China

It was primarily in Japan that Chinese students and political exiles learned about Western socialism. In the first decade of the twentieth century, young Chinese intellectuals were attracted to a wide range of socialist ideologies, especially to the anarchist ideas of Pyotr Kropotkin (1842–1921) and Mikhail Bakunin (1814–1876), but also to various forms of "utopian socialism." There was some intellectual interest in Marxism, and fragments of the writings of Karl Marx and Friedrich Engels were translated into Chinese as early as 1907. But while there were many Chinese anarchists, there were no Chinese converts to Marxism prior to the Russian Revolution of 1917.

It is not difficult to understand why Marx struck few responsive chords among Chinese intellectuals who were increasingly attracted to Western socialist doctrines. Marxist theory, in its orthodox form, taught that a well-developed capitalist economy was an essential prerequisite for socialism. But China was an overwhelmingly agrarian land with little modern industry and only a tiny urban working class. What Marxism conveyed to nationalistic Chinese intellectuals, increasingly alienated from traditional culture and attracted to Western socialist visions, was the disheartening message that they could only wait patiently on the political sidelines while capitalist forces of production did their historical work.

Marxism gained its first substantial appeal in China under the twin impact of the 1917 Bolshevik Revolution and China's May Fourth Movement of 1919. The messianic appeals of the Russian Revolution did not strike the Chinese intellectual world as a "thunderbolt," as Mao Zedong later claimed, but it did arouse sympathetic interest, not least of all because Chinese intellectuals had felt a certain kinship with backward Russia since 1905. It also produced China's first Marxists, including Li Dazhao at Beijing University, soon to be a cofounder of the Chinese Communist Party.

The Bolshevik Revolution also brought to China the Leninist version of Marxism, which made the doctrine far more relevant to an economically backward land than orthodox Marxian teachings. The Leninist theory of imperialism provided a place for economically backward lands in the world revolutionary process, thus helping to satisfy nationalist and politically activistic impulses. It provided an important revolutionary role for peasants in an overwhelmingly agrarian society. And the concept of the "vanguard" party, which assigned a decisive historical role to the "consciousness" of the intelligentsia, had enormous appeal.

Yet the Russian Revolution and Leninism would have had a much more limited appeal had it not been for the westernizing May Fourth Movement (c. 1915–1921), which burst into political activism shortly after World War I. The cynical betrayal of Chinese interests (in favor of Japanese imperialism) at the Versailles Peace Conference of 1919 led to widespread disillusionment with Western liberalism, opening the way for Marxian influences. Marxism received its main political expression in the Chinese Communist Party (CCP), formally established in 1921, although Marxism also significantly influenced the Nationalist Party of Sun Yat-sen and politically independent Chinese scholars.

There was little distinctive about Chinese Marxism in the early history of the CCP (1921–1927). The official ideology was Marxism-Leninism, as interpreted in Moscow and conveyed by the Comintern. In accordance with official ideology, the CCP found its main base in the urban proletariat and pursued a "two-stage" revolutionary policy, with a "bourgeois-democratic" phase preceding the socialist phase. In the first stage, the CCP was the junior partner in a Comintern-arranged tripartite alliance with the Nationalist Party of Sun Yat-sen and the Soviet Union. But the mass movement of workers and peasants proved too socially radical for the limited nationalist aims of the alliance, which were confined to national unification and

independence. The result was that the Nationalists, now led by Chiang Kai-shek, turned their Soviet-built army against their Communist allies in 1927, violently crushing the popular movement of workers and peasants. The Communists who survived the carnage fled to the more remote areas of the countryside. The suppression of Communist organizations in the cities in 1927 opened the way for the emergence of "Maoism" as a rural-based Marxian revolutionary strategy.

What came to be celebrated as "The Thought of Mao Zedong" was a doctrine that evolved over two decades of rural revolutionary warfare, culminating in the establishment of the People's Republic in 1949. Maoism, far from being "orthodox" or "hardline" Marxism as frequently characterized in the West, was marked by its departures from the premises of both original Marxism and Leninism. First, Maoism was based on the belief that the peasantry is the principal revolutionary class, even though lip service was ambiguously paid to the principle of "proletarian leadership." This was logically accompanied by a celebration of the virtues of rural life and a suspicion that cities were the breeding grounds of political conservatism and moral corruption. Maoism, thus, inverted the Marxist (and Leninist) conception of the relationship between town and countryside in the making of modern history.

Maoism not only strayed from Marxism in turning to the countryside but was also profoundly non-Leninist in celebrating the spontaneity of peasant revolt. While Mao appreciated the efficacy of Leninist principles of organization, he never accepted the intellectual basis of Lenin's "vanguard party"—the insistence that the "consciousness" of the intelligentsia had to be imposed on the "spontaneous" movement of the masses.

Mao's unique strategy of revolution was profoundly non-Marxist not only in the belief that the truly revolutionary class was the peasantry, but also in its conception that the revolution would take the form of a military struggle. Rather than the seizure of state power, the Maoist notions of "people's war" and "protracted warfare" envisioned that the expansion of the Red Army would permit the gradual building of nuclei of revolutionary political power in the rural areas. Ultimately, Maoists envisioned that the forces of revolt in the countryside would "surround and overwhelm" the conservative cities.

One of the pervasive features of Maoism was its voluntarist belief that human consciousness was the decisive factor in history. The Maoist maxim that "men are more important than machines" betrayed a striking lack of confidence in the "objective laws" of history proclaimed in Marxist theory, although the latter were ritualistically repeated in official texts. But the actual belief was that socialism was not dependent on any Marxian-defined level of economic development; rather, the historical outcome would be determined by the spiritual qualities of the people and their leaders.

The incorporation of Chinese nationalism into the Chinese version of Marxism enabled Mao to harness popular patriotic sentiments to the Communist cause during the decisive Yenan phase of the revolution, which coincided with the Japanese invasion of China (1937–1945). It made the Chinese Communist Revolution as much a war of national liberation as a social revolution.

Perhaps the most profound Maoist departure from the logic of Marxism was a pervasive populist-type belief in the advantages of backwardness. China's alleged condition of being "poor and blank," Mao believed, was a source of great moral purity and revolutionary energy that foreshadowed China's imminent leap to a socialist utopia. It was a totalistic rejection of the Marxist (and Leninist) insistence that socialism must be based on the material and cultural accomplishments of capitalism.

Such Maoist revisions of the inherited body of Marxist-Leninist theory, which were celebrated as the "Sinification of Marxism," were ideological preconditions for the peasant-based revolution that brought the Communists to power in 1949. But they left only tenuous intellectual ties between Maoism and Marxism.

In the end, Maoism sowed the seeds of its own demise. Maoist political methods and values, which continued to bear the birthmarks of its backward rural environment, became increasingly anachronistic in a rapidly industrializing society. It was thus inevitable that Mao's successors would purge Chinese Marxism of its more radical and utopian elements. They first returned to a more orthodox Marxist emphasis on the determining role of economic forces in history. What followed was the ritualization of Maoism, whose vocabulary was retained—but only in the form of nationalistic slogans severed from the actual policies that have generated a capitalist-type economy. The final chapter in the history of Maoism has seen its reduction to a nostalgic pop culture phenomenon—such as the opening of expensive Mao-themed restaurants and the sale (over the Internet) of old Mao badges and other memorabilia of the Cultural Revolution.

Yet if Maoism is exhausted, this is not necessarily the case for other forms of Marxism. The rapid development of capitalism in recent decades has yielded a massive industrial working class and an equally large *Lumpenproletariat* of migrant laborers. Many of the illegal trade unions that have attempted to speak on behalf of these highly exploited groups have done so in classic Marxist terms. It would be a grand irony of modern history if the greatest challenge to the Communist state appears in the form of a working-class movement proceeding under a Marxist banner.

Vietnam and Southeast Asia

In Southeast Asia, Marxism found its main political expression in Vietnam and, abortively, in Indonesia. Vietnamese Marxism was bound up with nationalism from the outset. In the early post–World War I years, Ho Chi Minh (1890–1969), the preeminent figure in the history of the movement who was initially attracted by the nationalist appeals of the Leninist theory of imperialism, became a founding member of the French Communist Party. Ho united several small Vietnamese Marxian-oriented parties into the Indochina Communist Party in 1930, but the party (and Marxism in general) were suppressed by the French colonial administration, forcing Ho to operate largely from abroad until World War II.

In 1941, the Vichy-controlled French colonial regime in Vietnam began active collaboration with the Japanese army.

The conditions were thus created for the ICP to emerge as the organizer of nationalist resistance to foreign domination—in the form of the Viet Minh, established in 1941 as an antifascist united front that took on an increasingly military character. While the Viet Minh was broadly based, it was Communist controlled—and its leader Ho Chi Minh became the symbol of Vietnamese nationalism. Adopting guerilla warfare tactics, Communist-led military forces successively fought the Vichy French colonial regime, the Japanese army in 1945, the postwar French colonial administration, and eventually the United States in a war that lasted more than three decades. The Communist victory in 1975 was essentially the triumph of Vietnamese nationalism. Marxism-Leninism, the official ideology, lent a social revolutionary dimension to the movement. But nationalism was always at the heart of its goals and appeals.

The Communist success in Indochina was not replicated elsewhere in Southeast Asia. Indonesia offers a particularly striking contrast. The Indonesian Communist Party, organized under the influence of Dutch Marxists in the 1920s, was among the earliest and largest Marxist parties in Asia. But the party's identification with ethnically Chinese Indonesians, its pro-Beijing sympathies, and its hostility to Islam undermined its nationalist credentials. Thus, the Communist bid for power in 1965 was crushed by the Indonesian army operating under nationalist and Islamic banners. Neither Indonesian Marxism nor Communism survived the bloodbath that took an estimated half-million lives, mostly ethnic Chinese.

Elsewhere in Southeast Asia, the main political manifestations of Marxism took the form of abortive Communist-led guerrilla insurgencies. Hostility to ethnic Chinese, as well as to China, was a major factor in the failure of Communist movements in Malaysia, Thailand, and Burma. Only in the Philippines, where Chinese migrants are socially well-integrated, does a Communist insurgency continue to simmer.

India

The diverse political implications of Marxism in Asia are suggested by comparing India with China. The two are countries of similar size and population, and both were impoverished agrarian lands in the mid-twentieth century. Yet while a Marxian-based political movement came to power in China and carried out the most massive of modern social revolutions, Marxian-oriented parties have been of marginal significance in India.

The difference cannot be attributed to a better understanding of Marxist theory by Chinese intellectuals. Propelled by the nationalist appeals of the Leninist theory of imperialism, Marxist ideas spread widely among Indian intellectuals in the wake of World War I, at the same time they did in China. Indeed, Marxism probably had a broader and deeper intellectual impact in India than in China because of the accessibility of English Marxist sources.

Although the Indian Communist Party was not formally established until 1926, radical Marxist groups flourished in the major cities from the early 1920s. However, the ICP was banned by the British colonial regime and its leaders were often jailed. Marxist and Communist influences were covertly expressed through the Indian National Congress of Mahatma Gandhi (1869–1948) and Jawaharlal Nehru (1889–1964), which monopolized Indian nationalist resistance to British rule, winning the support of the peasantry as well as most urban social groups.

The failure of the ICP to emerge as a serious nationalist force relegated it to a relatively minor role in India's political life. Communist support of the British during World War II, demanded by the Comintern's antifascist united front policies, underscored the Indian party's lack of nationalist credentials. Nor were the ICP's prospects enhanced by the factionalism that plagued the Marxian movement in the post-independence period. The main (but not the only) division was between pro-Moscow and pro-Beijing parties following the Sino-Soviet split of 1958. The factional cleavage between "Marxist-Leninists" and "Maoists" highlighted the failure of the ICP to develop a distinctive form of Marxism suited to specifically Indian social conditions and cultural traditions. This failure, in turn, confined the various Marxian parties to a combined total of less than 10 percent of the electoral vote, although the Communists were able to win sufficient support to lead reformist coalition governments in the states of Kerala and West Bengal. In all, however, while Marxism has had a significant impact on Indian intellectual life, its political expression has been feeble.

Conclusion

It would be futile to generalize about the role of Marxism in the several dozen historically and culturally distinct countries of Asia. However, two brief observations might be ventured. First, Marxian-inspired movements in Asia have been politically successful only where they have come to express popular nationalist feelings and aspirations, as has been the case in China and Vietnam. This does not mean that Marxian Communism in Asia can be reduced to a species of nationalism, but a genuine nationalist content and appeal clearly has been an essential precondition for political success. In view of the original doctrine's internationalist message, this is one of the great ironies of the history of Marxism in the modern world.

Second, where Communists have come to power, Marxism, essentially a critique of capitalism, paradoxically has functioned as an ideology of economic development whose social outcome is a capitalist-type economy. This is clearly the case in China, and appears to be the likely fate of Vietnam.

See also **Capitalism; Communism; Historical and Dialectical Materialism; Marxism: Overview.**

BIBLIOGRAPHY

Bernstein, Gail Lee. *Japanese Marxist: A Portrait of Kawakami Hajime, 1876–1946.* Cambridge, Mass.: Harvard University Press, 1976.

Carrère d'Encausse, Héléne, and Stuart R. Schram. *Marxism and Asia: An Introduction with Readings.* London: Allen Lane, 1969.

Duus, Peter, and Irwin Scheiner. "Socialism, Liberalism, and Marxism, 1901–31." Vol. 6, chap. 13, *The Cambridge History of Japan,* edited by Peter Duus. Cambridge, U.K.: Cambridge University Press, 1988.

Hammer, Ellen J. *The Struggle for IndoChina.* Stanford, Calif.: Stanford University Press, 1954.

Meisner, Maurice. *Li Ta-chao and the Origins of Chinese Marxism.* Cambridge, Mass.: Harvard University Press, 1967.

———. *Marxism, Maoism, and Utopianism: Eight Essays.* Madison: University of Wisconsin Press, 1982.

Overstreet, Gene D., and Marshall Windmiller. *Communism in India.* Berkeley: University of California Press, 1960.

Scalapino, Robert A. *The Japanese Communist Movement, 1920–66.* Berkeley: University of California Press, 1967.

Scalapino, Robert A., and Dalchoong Kim. *Asian Communism: Continuity and Transition.* Berkeley: University of California Press, 1988.

Schram, Stuart R. *Mao Tse-tung.* New York: Simon and Schuster, 1967.

Schwartz, Benjamin. *Chinese Communism and the Rise of Mao.* Cambridge, Mass.: Harvard University Press, 1951.

———. *Communism and China: Ideology in Flux.* Cambridge, Mass.: Harvard University Press, 1968.

van der Kroef, Justus M. *Communism in South-east Asia.* London: Macmillan, 1981.

Young, Marilyn B. *The Vietnam Wars, 1945–1990.* New York: HarperCollins, 1991.

Maurice Meisner

LATIN AMERICA

Throughout the twentieth century, Latin Americans wrestled with the enduring problems of foreign domination, social inequality, and poverty. Marxist popular movements, political parties, and intellectuals were often key players in these struggles, forming an important basis for trenchant social critique, mass social movement, and revolutionary organization. Even in countries where Marxist ideas, parties, and organizations never developed a mass following or consistent electoral presence, they exercised a broad influence on social movements, politics, and culture. Latin American Marxism cannot be abstracted from this broader social, political, and intellectual ferment. Despite the insistence of many Marxist political parties and regimes on ideological unity, the history of Latin American Marxism has been characterized by creative engagement, partisan debate, and heterodoxy.

Antecedents and Origins

This ferment is reflected in how Latin American Marxists tell their own history. Although Marxist parties and popular organizations, *strictu sensu,* did not exist until the 1920s, many of the popular icons of latter-day Marxist movements have been drawn from earlier generations and other traditions of social struggle. Heterodox Marxist intellectuals have tended to echo radical currents in nineteenth-century liberalism, which suggested that village and ethnic communitarian traditions might be a foundation for radical social transformation. To some extent, these Jacobin intellectuals merely ratified a kind of organic popular liberalism, in which local and regional parties and militias sought to parlay their defense of community into broader visions of national transformation (and sometimes into effective guerrilla resistance to foreign invasions); the degree of contact and mutual influence between popular liberals and urban Jacobins is still an open question. The late nineteenth and early twentieth centuries also saw the beginnings of a strong anarchosyndicalist and socialist movements in Latin America's nascent urban working classes, which were the foundation for many early communist parties in the 1920s.

The first communist parties in Latin America were founded in the wake of the Russian Revolution of 1917, but they maintained a strong bent toward ideological heterodoxy. In Brazil, for example, former anarchists formed a communist party in 1922, although many of their delegates were vetoed at Comintern congresses. The Mexican Communist Party, the first Comintern section in Latin America (and the first communist party outside Russia), became a de facto training ground for activists in the ruling Partido Revolucionario Institucional; murals by Communist Party members Davíd Alfaro Siquieros and Diego Rivera still adorn government buildings. In 1928 the prominent Marxist theorist José Carlos Mariátegui founded the Partido Socialista del Perú (PSP). Mariátegui insisted that Marxist ideas needed to be adapted to the distinctive reality of Latin America, particularly its indigenous traditions, and he rejected Leninist notions of party centralism. The PSP affiliated with the Comintern only after Mariátegui's death.

One of the most original Marxist thinkers in Latin America, Mariátegui gave a distinctive Marxist cast to the broadbased political movement known as *indigenismo,* which sought to ensure the rights of contemporary Native American peoples and to vindicate Latin America's indigenous past. Mariátegui initially worked with the Alianza Popular Revolucionaria Americana (APRA) of Haya de la Torre and shared the APRA's characterization of the "Indian problem" as a social and political issue rather than a moral or racial one. But Mariátegui also insisted on working-class agency and insisted that socialism was not alien to Peru's indigenous peoples, viewing the pre-Hispanic Inca empire as a form of primitive communism. Anticipating many of Chairman Mao Tse-tung's ideas, he insisted that socialist revolution would result from a long "accumulation" of forces. Indeed, in the 1980s and 1990s the Maoist Sendero Luminoso claimed Mariátegui as a founding ancestor, although this legacy continues to be contested vigorously by other left opposition movements and intellectuals.

1929–1959: International Crises and the Search for Common Ground

Despite the independence of many Latin American Marxist thinkers, international developments also continued to shape Marxist ideas in Latin America. The global economic crash of 1929 reinforced the Comintern's turn toward ultraleftism, and in many countries communist parties broke with allies in reformist unions and organizations, established rival organizations, and vigorously contested the state. The resulting repression drove many of these parties into semiclandestine status; an attempted insurrection in El Salvador ended in catastrophe, with more than ten thousand killed. In 1935 the rise of fascism prompted the Comintern to call for a "popular front" of proletarian parties and the antifascist bourgeoisie. During World War II, Latin American communist parties also abandoned their earlier anti-imperialism in favor of a broad international alliance against fascism. They also built alliances with right-wing groups and local dictators such as Batista in Cuba and Somoza in Nicaragua. In Chile, the Popular Front of communist, socialist, and radical parties won the presidency in 1938 and pursued a program of moderate reform. In many other countries, however, communist parties lost ground to populist regimes or other left opposition movements.

The wholesale repression of communist parties—and the aggressive intervention of the United States—encouraged Latin American communists to continue alliances with liberal and democratic parties in the postwar years. Marxist intellectuals embraced Latin American liberals' age-old enthusiasm for national "development," combining sophisticated critiques of global political economy with vague tropes of modernity. Latin American poverty, they held, stemmed from its economic dependency on the United States, whereby Latin American economies exchanged raw materials for manufactured goods at disadvantageous terms. They tended to view the development of a capitalist industrial economy and urbanized society as a prerequisite for socialist revolution. In some instances, Marxist intellectuals revived Simón Bolívar's dream of a broad alliance of Latin American nations, which would permit the development of economies of scale and the political strength to stand up to an aggressive United States.

Other Marxist intellectuals, particularly in the Caribbean, emphasized connections with anticolonial struggles in other parts of the world as well as the struggle for racial justice in the United States. This trend was exemplified by C. L. R. James, whose work remains important in both international Marxist theory and cultural studies. Born in the then-English colony of Trinidad, C. L. R. James's initial focus was on his native Caribbean, and his early work included social-realist fiction set in West Indian slums as well as his classic study of the 1793 slave revolt in Saint Domingue (Haiti), *The Black Jacobins* (1938). He also wrote two key works on Marxist theory and practice, *Notes on Dialectics* (1948) and *State Capitalism and World Revolution* (1950). His *Mariners, Renegades, and Castaways* (1953) analyzed the relations among *Moby Dick*'s narrator, the ship's captain, and its expert "Third World" crew. *Mariners* anticipated James's involvement in revolutionary decolonization movements in Africa, the Caribbean, and Latin America, as well as among African Americans in the United States. It also presaged the broader internationalism of Latin-American Marxists following the Cuban Revolution.

Foquismo

Latin American communist parties tended to remain chary of insurrectionary strategies and labor radicalism in the postwar years. Indeed, the most militant opposition often came from other left dissidents. In Cuba, where the Communist Party had initially collaborated with the U.S.-backed military regime of Fulgencio Batista, the leadership of a nascent revolutionary movement emerged from the populist Ortodoxo Party (Partido del Pueblo Ortodoxo), and it was inspired as much by the romantic ideal of the revolutionary *atentat* (a spectacular act of revolutionary violence that was meant to inspire mass insurrection) as by Leninist notions of party organization. The movement's victory in 1956 was a puzzle for many Latin American Marxists as much as for U.S. cold warriors, as was the subsequent radicalization of the Cuban revolutionary regime. In the face of U.S. economic blockade and a CIA-sponsored invasion attempt, the revolutionary government in Cuba proclaimed its Marxist-Leninist orientation and accepted the Soviet Union's political support, military protection, and economic backing. Despite the Soviet Union's increased leverage, however, the revolution's leadership continued to depart from Marxist-Leninist orthodoxy.

In the years following the revolution, the revolutionary *comandante* Ernesto "Ché" Guevara elaborated a new theory of revolution known as foquismo, in which the revolutionary *foco*, a small cell of guerrillas in the countryside, replaced the vanguard party. Ché's theory contained an implicit criticism of most Latin American communist parties, which had all but abandoned revolutionary violence. Latin American revolution was not simply a possibility, *foco* theory held, but also a moral imperative. Revolutionaries must create "subjective" conditions for revolution rather than awaiting the proper objective conditions. The rural peasantry, rather than the urban proletariat, was the seedbed of socialist revolution. Similarly, a socialist, anti-imperialist revolution was a prerequisite for national economic development, rather than the other way around. In Ché's view, the Cuban Revolution was a beachhead for a broader Latin American revolution; the Andes would become the Sierra Maestra of South America.

Ché is conventionally portrayed as a romantic counterpoint to the authoritarian turn of the Cuban Revolution and the Soviet Union. Indeed, in his final years Ché did publicly clash with the Soviet Union and—less publicly—with Fidel Castro, and *foquista* guerrillas elsewhere in Latin America often clashed with mainline communist parties. But Ché's insistence on the centrality of the revolutionary *foco* also helped underwrite the exclusion of other groups that had been instrumental in Batista's overthrow and a rigid intolerance of political heterodoxy. Inspired by Ché's writings and example, a generation of young revolutionaries sought to establish guerrilla *focos* throughout Latin America, often without any advance political work, local ties, or knowledge of the terrain. Almost all of these expeditions ended in ignominious defeat—most notoriously Ché's own expedition to Bolivia—and later rural guerrilla movements, including the *foquista* movements that had survived the repression of the late 1960s and 1970s, tended to abjure Guevara's insurrectionary strategy in favor of a "prolonged people's war" like those waged in Vietnam and China.

One of the most severe critiques of *foquismo* came from Abraham Guillén, a Spanish Civil War veteran living in Argentina and Uruguay. In his *Estrategia de la guerrilla urbana* (1966), Guillén echoed Ché's call for popular insurrection and Latin American liberation on a continental scale, but he also insisted that the movement would be led by urban proletariat rather than the rural peasantry. During the 1960s and 1970s, urban guerrilla movements emerged throughout Latin America, most famously the Argentine Montoneros and the Uruguayan Tupamaros. None of these movements were strictly Marxist in orientation, and they often drew their leadership from the left wing of national populist movements as well as communist dissidents. Indeed, like *foquista* guerrillas, they tended to clash with mainline communist parties, which often viewed voluntarist and insurrectionary strategies as little more than

dangerous adventures. After Ché's death at the hands of CIA-backed counterinsurgency forces—and under pressure from the Soviet Union—the Cuban government, too, abandoned its earlier support of revolutionary *focos* and sought a rapprochement with other Latin-American governments.

The 1970s and After: New Heterodoxies

Where possible, mainline communist parties tended to support a moderate strategy of trade unionism and broad electoral alliances. In 1970 the Chilean Marxist Salvador Allende was elected president at the head of a shaky coalition of radical, socialist, and communist parties. The Chilean Unidad Popular (UP) embarked on a modest program of social reforms within a constitutional framework. Strategic industries such as coal and steel were nationalized. With the government's sometimes reluctant backing, workers began seizing factories and transforming them into social property, including properties of U.S.-based multinationals such as Ford and ITT. The government also embarked on a far-reaching agrarian reform; by 1973, 60 percent of Chile's agricultural land had been expropriated and distributed to peasants. Nonetheless, the opposition maintained control of the Chilean congress, and the UP itself was deeply divided. United States economic sanctions and sabotage by producers, landowners, and merchants led to inflation and shortages, undermining the UP's support from an already skittish middle class. From the beginning the United States worked for Allende's overthrow, and on 11 September 1973, his government was toppled in a CIA-sponsored military coup.

One of the more novel movements of the 1970s was the marriage of older traditions of social Catholicism and popular religiosity with Marxist ideas and political organization. In what has become a foundational text of this "liberation theology," the Peruvian priest Gustavo Gutiérrez founded a new reading of biblical and church writings in Marxist dependency theory. Other religious activists—most famously the Colombian priest Camilo Torres and the Nicaraguan *padre* Ernesto Cardenal—embraced an insurrectionary strategy and participated in armed revolutionary movements. Many other priests and pastoral lay workers helped members of marginal *barrios* and villages form affinity groups known as *comunidades eclesiales de base* (CEBs), viewing popular communitarian ideals as a revindication of the primitive church. Founding their work in a process of participatory education known as *concientización* (roughly, "consciousness-raising" or "conscience-raising"), radical religious activists encouraged CEB members to apply biblical writings to their own concrete social reality.

Other communitarian traditions continued to be instrumental in Marxist ideas and movements in the final decades of the twentieth century. In Nicaragua, the Frente Sandinista de Liberación Nacional (FSLN), a broad, if shaky, coalition of Marxist guerrilla movements and liberal dissidents, overthrew the brutally repressive Somoza dictatorship in 1979. The movement's heterogeneity, its deep roots in autochthonous liberal and communitarian traditions, and the somewhat lukewarm support of Cuba and the Soviet Union meant that the Sandinista government tended to abjure Leninist party organization in favor of liberal principles of electoral democracy. It also engaged in a moderate program of land reform (generally along cooperative rather than collectivist lines), improved education and other public services, and enacted progressive social legislation. The Sandinista government survived an eleven-year CIA-sponsored campaign of intimidation, assassination, and sabotage that cost Nicaragua more than thirty thousand lives, and in 1990 it peacefully ceded power to the liberal opposition following an internationally supervised democratic election.

The years following the disintegration of the Soviet Union were a period of retrenchment in Latin America's Marxist left. The fall of the Soviet Union, the aging of the revolutionary elite, and the coming of age of a postrevolutionary generation forced the Cuban government to adopt a program of economic flexibility and Guevarist moral incentives, opening limited spaces for private entrepreneurs and developing ties with European social democracies. In much of the rest of Latin America, the economic crises at the end of the twentieth century and beginning of the twenty-first changed the profile of the Marxist left's social bases, displacing much of the rural poor, impoverishing the urban working class, and weakening the middle class. At the same time, the transnational movement of people, information, capital, and commodities—and the negotiation of bilateral and multilateral trade agreements—spurred a new transnational focus in the Marxist left.

On 1 January 1994, the same day the so-called North American Free Trade Agreement went into effect, the Ejército Zapatista de Liberación (EZLN) captured four municipalities in the southern Mexican state of Chiapas—and captured, too, the world's imagination through its creative use of political theater, mass media, and the Internet. Founded some eleven years earlier, the EZLN's founders had adopted the classic Maoist strategy of "prolonged people's war," forming ties with communities in the Chiapas highlands and learning the local Tzotzil language. Unlike Peru's Sendero Luminoso, however, which shared the EZLN's focus on an indigenous social base and initial Maoist strategy, the EZLN abandoned Marxist schemes of revolutionary organization, adopting a democratic decision-making process and turning leadership over to indigenous communities. Like many other Latin American popular movements in the 1980s and 1990s, the EZLN foreswore armed seizure of power in favor of "armed negotiation," seeking a democratic opening in Mexico's political system and legal protections for its indigenous communities. In this regard it was perhaps inspired by recent Latin American guerrilla movements, which during the 1990s were able to negotiate democratic openings in their respective countries.

The EZLN shared with other contemporary Marxist-influenced popular movements and Marxist thought an outspoken opposition to the neoliberal hegemony in Latin America and around the world. These movements continued to draw from other popular traditions of community and protest as well as recent analyses of imperialism and modernity. Despite the near-disappearance of Latin American communist parties by the start of the twenty-first century, Marxist critiques of poverty, inequality, and foreign domination—and Marxist-inspired social movements—remained powerful influences in Latin American scholarly debates and political struggles.

See also **Communism: Latin America; Dictatorship in Latin America; Marxism: Overview.**

BIBLIOGRAPHY

Allende Gossens, Salvador. *Chile's Road to Socialism.* Edited by Joan E. Garces, translated by J. Darling, introduction by Richard Gott. Baltimore, Md.: Penguin, 1973.

Angell, Alan. "The Left in Latin America since c. 1920." In *Latin America since 1930: Economy, Society, and Politics.* Vol. 6 of *Cambridge History of Latin America,* edited by Leslie Bethell. New York: Cambridge University Press, 1984.

Carr, Barry, and Steve Ellner, eds. *The Latin American Left: From the Fall of Allende to Perestroika.* Boulder, Colo.: Westview Press, 1993.

Castañeda, Jorge G. *Utopia Unarmed: The Latin American Left after the Cold War.* New York: Knopf, 1993.

Chomsky, Aviva, Barry Carr, and Pamela Maria Smorkaloff, eds. *The Cuba Reader: History, Culture, and Politics.* Durham, N.C.: Duke University Press, 2003.

Guevara, Ernesto Ché. *Guerrilla Warfare.* Introduction to the Bison Books edition by Marc Becker. Lincoln: University of Nebraska Press, 1998.

Guillén, Abraham. *Philosophy of the Urban Guerrilla: The Revolutionary Writings of Abraham Guillén.* Translated and edited with an introduction by Donald C. Hodges. New York: Morrow, 1973.

Gutiérrez, Gustavo. *A Theology of Liberation: History, Politics, and Salvation.* Translated and edited by Sister Caridad Inda and John Eagleson. Maryknoll, N.Y.: Orbis Books, 1988.

James, C. L. R. (Cyril Lionel Robert). *The C. L. R. James Reader,* edited and with an introduction by Anna Grimshaw. Cambridge, Mass., and Oxford: Blackwell, 1992.

Löwy, Michael. *Marxism in Latin America from 1909 to the Present: An Anthology,* edited and with an introduction by Michael Löwy; translated from Spanish, Portuguese, and French by Michael Pearlman. Atlantic Highlands, N.J.: Humanities Press, 1992.

Marcos, Subcomandante. *Shadows of Tender Fury: The Letters and Communiqués of Subcomandante Marcos and the Zapatista Army of National Liberation.* Translated by Frank Bardacke, Leslie López, and the Watsonville Human Rights Committee, California; introduction by John Ross; afterword by Frank Bardacke. New York: Monthly Review Press, 1995.

Mariátegui, José Carlos. *Seven Interpretive Essays on Peruvian Reality.* Translated by Marjory Urquidi; introduction by Jorge Basadre. Austin: University of Texas Press, 1971.

Michael Werner

MASKS. The Western term for an object that transforms a face, *mask,* derives from the Arabic word *maskhara,* "to transform into an animal or monster." This term was derived from the term *msk,* used in the middle Egyptian period to denote "second skin." In Arabic, it became *msr,* which meant "to Egyptianize," referring to the ubiquitous practice among Egyptians of masquerading, as the Arabs noted (Nunley and McCarty, p. 15). Masks, however, were an integral component in the development of human culture and social evolution long before the term *mask* ever existed. A lion-headed human figure carved from mammoth ivory found in France has been dated to at least 30,000 B.C.E., from the later Aurignacian (Upper Paleolithic) period. Moreover, masked images of humans have been found on Mimbres pottery (ninth to thirteenth centuries) in the American Southwest and in painted images on rock surfaces in Australia, Africa, and Siberia.

Origins

Given that masks and the performance complex of masking, known as the masquerade, are found in practically all cultures at one time or another, there must be some fundamental reasons for the emergence of such a cultural practice. The development of shamanism seems to go hand in hand with masking and masquerading. As humans began to observe nature empirically, including their own behavior, parts of the puzzle explaining reality appeared to be missing. Explanations for disease, drought, floods, lightning strikes, and aberrant human behavior were sought in the invisible world where the actions and forces of spirits, like subatomic particles, figured prominently in the phenomena of the visible world.

The development of the abstract concept of spirit may have many sources. One plausible hypothesis suggests that, as humans began to recognize themselves and other animals in temporary reflections, they concluded that such appearing and disappearing images were the counterparts of beings existing in an invisible world and that everything in the visible world had a spiritual counterpart in the invisible world. A bison, for example, had a spirit force that remained active in the invisible world after the animal was hunted down and killed. These early peoples believed that the bison's spirit had returned to this world and been reborn in the flesh. An incipient shamanic cosmology eventually mapped the perceived universe with the salient domains being the sky, earth, and water. Food, weather, fertility, and life itself depended on these realms.

Humans associated particular animals with the realms each inhabited. An eagle was associated with the sky and sun, a jaguar with the earth and darkness, and a salmon with water and life. They also observed transformations along the path of the sun, which produced day and then night as that star passed to the invisible world. The motion of the sun also produced the seasons and, by extension, the "seasons" of humans. Birth was equated with spring, maturity with summer, old age with fall, and death with winter. These transformations were believed to be controlled by invisible forces.

How did humans connect masking and the masquerade to these unseen forces? The answer is partly found in the development of human cognition during ancient times, which found a way of accounting for real-world events that continues in some traditional societies. As hunters and gatherers, humans were an integral part of the "natural environment." They carefully observed the behavior of all animals. People as well as groups of people, such as clans, assumed the attributes of these animals (totemism). Some people moved like deer, looked stocky like bears, or were mean-spirited like swans. Some were bullish (as described by Sean StandingBear, Osage oral historian and artist). Other people, however, shared the traits of many creatures and were thought to be

African costume designed by Wallace Alexander for CARIBANA Festival, Toronto, Ontario, 1986. Masks are an integral part of dress for festivals and special occasions around the world. Masquerades serve many functions, such as marking seasonal changes, celebrating rites of passage, and paying homage to ancestral ties. COURTESY OF JOHN NUNLEY

capable of shape-shifting. As people allied themselves with certain animals, their totems, they had the right to wear masks and perform as those animals. By wearing the mask of a jaguar, for example, a clan could enter the invisible underworld and communicate with the jaguar's forces in order to prepare for war. Another person might perform in a whale mask and enter the invisible world in the depths of the ocean to ask the whales to give up some of their own in order for humans to have a safe and successful whale hunt. The tensions humans felt between the invisible and visible domains could be resolved for a while in the masquerade performance and its associated rituals.

By creating different constellations of masking, communities created their own social identity. When a person or group commits to a masking identity, one is transformed; "I am not myself," as the African art historian Herbert Cole (1995) has phrased it. When everyone involved in the masquerade adopts this belief we, as humans, have reinvented who we were and are. Thus, reinvention through the masquerade became a principle vehicle for creating culture and social identity.

While other animals often seem unaware of their reflected image, for example, when they drink from a lake or pond, humans have long observed their image, particularly the face in reflective surfaces, including water and shiny hard surfaces. By manipulating their image with paint, feathers, body scarification, and tattoos, people consciously reinvent who they are in order to strengthen social bonding and group identity, both crucial to survival. Interestingly, human facial expressions, controlled by the competing voluntary and involuntary parts of the brain, also affect social bonding. The involuntary part of the brain lies in the older "primitive" portion, where it competes with the voluntary portion. This tug-of-war is often visible in the way human facial expressions suddenly change. For example, when hearing that someone secretly hated has fallen on hard times, one's voluntary facial expression—the aspect that can be controlled—may communicate, "That's too bad. I'm so sorry." But, toward the end of that expression, the involuntary part of the brain takes over and an incipient smile becomes apparent.

Lying is simply a manipulation of facial expressions, voice modulation, and body language to ensure social bonding in both the long and short terms. Similarly, the use of a mask freezes the facial expression and eliminates this kind of ambivalence. Thus, a person wearing a mask while circumcising a young boy is protected by the steady gaze of the mask, which hides his true expression at an emotionally volatile time. The masks worn by executioners perform the same function.

Gender also adds to the understanding of the origins of masks and masquerades. In ancient times, men invented masks as decoys to take advantage of an animal and to become the animal in order to communicate with its spirit for cooperation in the hunt. Moreover, the entire masquerade complex includes men making masks, dancing as the masqueraders, sacrificing blood to the masks, and the symbolically violent act of drumming, which is for a man to strike with his hand or club the skin of an animal stretched over a wood cylinder. These active behaviors, so prevalent in traditional societies and in some contemporary ones, are regarded as men's work. Women, on the other hand, are expected to perform long-term nurturing tasks, patiently and less obviously, compared to men's actions.

The Functions of Masking

Masquerades have many functions, yet they appear to cluster into particular categories. There are masks associated with rites of passage such as adolescents' initiations, other age-related ceremonies, and death. Masking in seasonal festivals and renewal rituals is associated with the earth's fertility and the path of the sun as it appears to us from Earth. In other masquerades, men play women, generally as the maiden, mother, and crone. Masks also evolved into theater as, for example, in ancient Greece or the Noh drama of Japan. In some sports and in hazardous occupations, masks are worn to protective the face.

As people change physically, especially at adolescence, old age, and death, masking rituals are performed to mark the transition and make it safe. Adolescent energy, for example, can be dangerous and destabilizing to society. To insure a safe transition, groups of young boys, for example, may be gathered

and kept away from their village for long periods of time while they are taught the ways of masculine adulthood. Masquerades are performed in order to teach the adolescents and to communicate to the village that the transition has been blessed by the appropriate spirits in the invisible world and is a success. Frequently, masks that accompany the dead in burial are placed over the face or head, thus assuring their safe journey or passage through the underworld and to a place where their spirits can assist, not hinder, their people in the visible world.

Other masquerades celebrate the changes of the seasons, which are associated with renewal and fertility. The Corpus Christi masking festivals of Ecuador celebrate the fertility of Christ's body and its positive impact on the fertility of crops and the harvest. Musical bands play as the processions of masqueraders move through the streets of Pujilí. The many plastic dolls on the mask superstructures serve as metaphors for fertility. The mirrors reflect the powerful light of the sun, which makes all life possible. Urban festivals, such as Carnival and its pre-Lenten celebrations, were all at one time associated with fertility.

In Bulgaria, masquerades are intimately associated with agriculture and human fertility, while in Basel, Switzerland, and Trinidad and Tobago there is far less emphasis on fecundity and more interest in the renewal of social and individual identities. These festivals often address local political, health, and economic issues, as well as global themes concerning war and other events reported in the popular media.

Within most masquerade festivals, only men play the roles of women, which fall into three categories: the maiden, mother, and crone. In general, men play women's roles, first because men monopolize the masking process, and second, in order to communicate to both sexes the kinds of behavior they believe are appropriate for women. Maringuila maidens in the masquerades in Michoacán, Mexico, represent idealized beauty and how young women should conduct themselves in public.

Among the Yoruba Gelede of West Africa and in some Latin American countries, men dress as mothers and convey, through the round forms of their costumes and masks, women's promise of fertility and ability to bring stability to society. The two-faced Gelede mask reminds participants that each person has an inner and outer self, and that it is the inner face that keeps the outer appearing cool and collected during stressful times (Nunley, 1996, p. 1782).

Men have always feared old women, most likely because the latter cannot give birth and are no longer sexually desirable. Old women might, from the men's point of view, pose a threat to society, as they are often accused of witchcraft. Thus males play the crone to neutralize the potential destructive force they fear.

Masks are also associated with physical and spiritual dangers, in other words offense and defense. Shamans in full ritual dress, including masks, enter the invisible world on behalf of clients or even an entire community to eliminate dangers posed by disease, weather, particular people, or enemy communities. A Siberian shaman once wore such ritual dress while dancing to the rhythm of a drum and the rattling sound of his medicines and metal objects attached to his garment. While spinning and mimicking the flight of birds, he once traveled in the invisible world and dealt effectively with both good and bad spiritual forces, thus protecting his clients. Likewise, an Oku sorcerer's ritual dress, complete with a hooded bird mask, fulfilled the same function.

In industrial societies space suits and helmets (masks) are used to protect astronauts on their flights into space. Like the shaman, who could look back on the visible world from his spiritual space, the astronauts looked back from the moon and showed the world from a new perspective. Looking back at the world from the moon, people learned how small and interconnected the world is and, as well, its vulnerability. The environmental movement was inspired by this realization.

Masks are also used in theater and in films. Greek theater masks, which evolved from the old Dionysian cults, were concerned with death, rebirth, and fecundity. They were worn by actors who played specific roles in the tragedies. In Asia, masks are frequently found in live theater in the great epics about Hindu deities, Japanese Noh theater, Chinese New Year pageants, and in Balinese street theater celebrating the exploits of the forceful crone known as Rangda. In Western films such as *Star Wars* or the popular television series *Star Trek,* masks cover the faces of beings from other galaxies as well as cyborgs, characters that are both biological and mechanical.

Masks and masquerades are inextricably linked to the development of culture and human identity. In the ludic performances of masks, social bonding occurs and roles are defined on many levels, including gender. Masks play to the spirits of the invisible world; they are the "x" commodity in the equations of the many worldviews invented by humans. Masks have existed from ancient times to space explorations. While masquerades were and are integral components of traditional societies, they have found new meanings and purposes in film, sports, and modern warfare. I am a soldier, I am a hockey goalie, I am Darth Vader, I am the spirit of the bison: in other words, "I am not myself," a conceptual tool that has led to individual and social reinvention, the essence of being human.

See also **Animism; Dress; Gender Studies: Anthropology; Gesture; Identity: Personal and Social Identity; Religion; Ritual; Theater and Performance; Totems; Tragedy and Comedy.**

BIBLIOGRAPHY

Brockett, Oscar G. *History of the Theatre.* Boston: Allyn and Bacon, 1995.

Bullough, Vern L., and Bonnie Bullough. *Cross-Dressing, Sex, and Gender.* Philadelphia: University of Pennsylvania Press, 1993.

Burch, Jr., Ernest S. "War and Trade." In *Crossroads of Continents: Cultures of Siberia and Alaska,* edited by William W. Fitzhugh and Aron Crowell, 227–240. Washington, D.C.: Smithsonian Institution Press, 1988.

Coe, Michael D. *The Jaguar's Children: Pre-Classic Central Mexico.* New York: The Museum of Primitive Art, 1965.

Cole, Herbert M., ed. *I Am Not Myself: The Art of African Masquerade.* Los Angeles: Museum of Cultural History, University of California at Los Angeles, 1985.

DeMott, Barbara. *Dogon Masks: A Structural Study of Form and Meaning.* Ann Arbor, Mich.: UMI Research Press, 1980.

Drewal, Henry John, and Margaret Thompson Drewal. *Gelede: Art and Female Power among the Yoruba.* Bloomington: Indiana University Press, 1983.

Duchartre, Pierre-Louis. *The Italian Comedy.* Translated by Randolph T. Weaver. New York: Dover Publications, 1966.

Eliade, Mircea. *Shamanism: Archaic Techniques of Ecstasy.* Translated by Willard R. Trask. Princeton, N.J.: Princeton University Press, 1964.

Esser, Janet Brody, ed. *Behind the Mask in Mexico.* Santa Fe: Musuem of New Mexico Press, 1988.

Ferris, Lesley. *Acting Women: Images of Women in Theatre.* New York: New York University Press, 1989.

Gennep, Arnold van. *Rites of Passage.* Translated by Monika B. Vizedom and Gabrielle L. Caffe. Chicago: University of Chicago Press, 1961.

Hammoudi, Abdellah. *The Victim and Its Masks: An Essay on Sacrifice and Masquerade in the Maghreb.* Translated by Paula Wissing. Chicago: University of Chicago Press, 1993.

Ivanov, S., and V. Stukalov. *Ancient Masks of Siberian Peoples.* Text in English and Russian. Leningrad: Aurora Art Publishers, 1975.

James, Edwin Oliver. *Seasonal Feasts and Festivals.* New York: Barnes and Noble, 1961.

King, Barbara J. *The Information Continuum: Evolution of Social Information Transfer in Monkeys, Apes, and Hominids.* Santa Fe: SAR Press; distributed by the University of Washington Press, 1994.

Lévi-Strauss, Claude. *The Way of the Masks.* Translated by Sylvia Modelski. Seattle: University of Washington Press, 1982.

Marshack, Alexander. *The Roots of Civilization: The Cognitive Beginnings of Man's First Art, Symbol and Notation.* Mount Kisco, N.Y.: Moyer Bell, 1991.

McCarty, Cara. *Modern Masks and Helmets.* Pamphlet. New York: Museum of Modern Art, 1991.

Napier, A. David. *Masks, Transformation, and Paradox.* Berkeley: University of California Press, 1986.

Nunley, John W. "Cover Story." *Journal of the American Medical Association* 276, no. 22 (December 11, 1996): 1782.

———. *Moving with the Face of the Devil: Art and Politics in Urban West Africa.* Urbana: University of Illinois Press, 1987.

Nunley, John W., and Cara McCarty. *Masks: Faces of Culture.* St. Louis, Mo.: St. Louis Art Museum and Abrams Publishing, 1999.

Nunley, John W., and Judith Bettelheim. *Caribbean Festival Arts: Each and Every Bit of Difference.* St. Louis, Mo., and Seattle: The Saint Louis Art Museum and University of Washington Press, 1988.

Oliver, Douglas L. *Oceania: The Native Cultures of Australia and the Pacific Islands.* Vol. 1. Honolulu: University of Hawai'i Press, 1989.

Pani, Jiwan. *World of Other Faces: Indian Masks.* New Delhi, India: Ministry of Information and Broadcasting, 1986.

Phelan, Peggy. "Crisscrossing Cultures." In *Crossing the Stage: Controversies on Cross-dressing,* edited by Lesley Ferris, 155–170. London and New York: Routledge, 1994.

Sarachchandra, E. R. *The Folk Drama of Ceylon.* 2nd ed. Colombo, Ceylon: Department of Cultural Affairs, 1966.

Slattum, Judith. *Balinese Masks: Spirits of an Ancient Drama.* San Francisco: Chronicle Books, 1992.

Thackeray, J. F. "New Directions in the Study of Southern African Rock Art." *African Arts* 26, no. 1 (January 1993): research note.

Turner, Victor W. *The Ritual Process: Structure and Anti-Structure.* Chicago: Aldine Publishing, 1969.

Walker, Barbara. *The Crone: Woman of Age, Wisdom, and Power.* New York: Harper and Row, 1985.

John Nunley

MATERIALISM IN EIGHTEENTH-CENTURY EUROPEAN THOUGHT.

Materialism is the generic name of a variety of doctrines that deny the existence of non-material substances. Materialism may be either a metaphysical or a methodological concept. In its most coherent and radical form, it is a type of *monism,* the metaphysical position stating that there is only one principle—matter and its properties—in terms of which all reality is to be explained.

In the eighteenth century, materialism developed into a philosophy and gained a following that continues into the present day. Some eighteenth-century materialist philosophers were downright atheists. A few philosophers, such as the Stoics or Thomas Hobbes, while not atheists, held that God is corporeal. Others preferred some form of *deism,* the idea that a transcendent, noninterventionist God rules the world through constitutive laws of nature. For them, materialism was a methodology to follow when inquiring about the natural world, rather than a complete metaphysical commitment.

Materialism should not simply be identified with the Enlightenment, the eighteenth-century cultural movement that endorsed an understanding of the natural world, including humankind, based exclusively on reason, with no possibility of appeal to the supernatural. The Enlightenment included a secular interpretation of ethics and politics. While materialistic trends were an important part of the Enlightenment, its scope and philosophical commitments were far broader and more varied, involving an agenda that was political as well as philosophical including, in the case of several important thinkers, a straightforward belief in a God who acts in the world.

Seventeenth-Century Background

Eighteenth-century materialism in a sense is an extension of the seventeenth-century mechanical philosophy that was the hallmark of the scientific revolution. The mechanical philosophy offered a worldview in which matter and the natural laws of motions were supposed to explain all phenomena. In the seventeenth century, only Thomas Hobbes (1588–1679), in *Leviathan* (1651) and other works, and (in a much more problematic way) Baruch Spinoza (1632–1677) went so far as to argue that the mechanical philosophy could explain all the aspects of mental life. Later in the century, such monistic views, as well as trends that were inherent in the philosophy of René Descartes (1596–1650), such as the reduction of nonhuman forms of life to automata, developed the form of materialism that was characteristic of the eighteenth century.

Despite the coherence of Hobbes's materialism, the authors who were most fundamental to the passage from seventeenth-century mechanical philosophy to eighteenth-century materialism were Isaac Newton (1642–1727) and John Locke

(1632–1704). Isaac Newton was a multifaceted, iconoclastic figure. He can hardly be called a materialist in any metaphysical sense. However, the impressive results he achieved in physics gave an impulse to methodological materialism in science and well beyond. John Locke's *Essay concerning Human Understanding* (1690; 4th edition published in 1700) developed a sensationalist psychology, based on the idea that sense perception and mental mechanisms of reason, usually in the form of calculation and association, explain all mental life without the need to postulate any nonmaterial substance. Locke famously debated whether material things (such as rocks) could think. He concluded that God could have created thinking matter and was opposed by Bishop Edward Stillingfleet (1635–1699). Locke's position was later then taken up by Anthony Collins (1676–1729) against Samuel Clarke (1675–1729). A follower of Newton, Clarke is well known because of his controversy with Gottfried Wilhelm von Leibniz (1646–1716).

Another relevant source of ideas came from the French-based seventeenth-century movement of the libertines, or freethinkers (not meant as a compliment), who opposed religious oppression, and who, often in anonymous publications, defended the free use of reason against the suffocating Catholic Counter-Reformation. Libertines challenged religious authority in morals and politics, using ideas inspired mainly by the materialism of the ancient atomistic, Epicurean, and skeptical traditions. To this movement belong authors as different as Pierre Gassendi (1592–1655) and Cyrano de Bergerac (1619–1655). The anonymous *Theophrastus redivivus,* published around 1660, espoused the most radical theses of libertinism, such as atheism, materialism, and a form of ethical Epicurean hedonism.

The Eighteenth Century

The eighteenth century was an age of prodigious scientific learning. While the seventeenth century's philosophical milieu was influenced mainly by physics (mechanics and cosmology), the eighteenth century became especially fascinated with chemistry, or the constitution of matter, and by the phenomenon of life and its forms of organization. In this sense, materialist philosophers and scientists were strongly motivated to explain the complexities and diversities of life without reference to divine intervention.

The diversity of life had been unprecedentedly systematized by Carolus Linnaeus (1707–1778), whose *Systema naturae* (System of nature) was published in 1735; however, biological diversity was well known long before the eighteenth century, and the discoveries explorers made around the world drew the attention of many scientists. The ideas of evolution and adaptation had begun to gain momentum, championed in different forms by Buffon and by Diderot. Between the end of the eighteenth century and the beginning of the nineteenth, evolution of species was a concept that, though rejected by most, was part of the scientific debate with the works of Jean-Baptiste Lamarck (1744–1829) and Erasmus Darwin (1731–1802). They both struggled with an account of life and diversity based on adaptation to a changing environment and competition for resources.

Another major scientific figure was Antoine-Laurent Lavoisier (1743–1794). Known as the scientist who began the chemical revolution by changing the concept of *chemical element* and discovering *oxygen,* which term he coined, Lavoisier developed a new physicochemical nomenclature that stressed the quantitative aspects of combining chemical elements. While Lavoisier was not particularly philosophical, his revisions of the structure of chemical knowledge, and thus of matter theory, brought about a change in the understanding of matter and the mechanisms by which it worked. In this sense, Lavoisier was like many other scientists in the eighteenth century: while maybe not metaphysical materialists themselves, they helped develop a scientific methodological materialism that could support a metaphysical alternative to religion and traditional dualism. Lavoisier, who was a tax collector for the royal government, was guillotined in 1794 during the French Revolution.

French Materialism

François Marie Arouet, better known as Voltaire (1694–1778), endorsed Locke's sensationalism and argued against Spinoza and Nicolas Malebranche (1638–1715) in his *Dictionnaire philosophique* (1764; Philosophical dictionary) and *Lettres anglaises ou philosophiques* (1734; English or philosophical letters). He also became very popular as an apologist for Newton, with his *Éléments de la philosophie de Newton* (1738; Elements of Newton's philosphy). Voltaire opposed institutionalized religion and intolerance based on superstition, and, although not an atheist, he supported the rationalistic deism. His famous *Candide* (1759) is a witty and ironic, though simplistic, lampoon of Leibniz's metaphysics of the best of all possible worlds.

His mistress and patron of the great French salon, Madame Émilie du Châtelet, who, with his aid, translated Newton's *Principia mathematica* into French, was also a prominent supporter of Newtonianism and did much to publicize these new scientific views. They were both forced to flee Paris in 1747. Once in Berlin, Voltaire entered a dispute with his old friend and protégé Pierre-Louis Moreau de Maupertuis (1698–1759), the president of the Berlin Academy and author of *Venus physique* (1745; The physical Venus) and *Système de la nature* (1751; System of nature).

Paul-Henri-Dietrich d'Holbach's (1723–1789) most famous book, *Système de la nature, ou des loix du monde physique et du monde moral* (1770; The system of nature, or the laws of the physical and moral world), was published under the name of J. B. Mirabaud. Following the tenets of Epicurean atomism, the book derided religion and espoused an atheistic, deterministic materialism: all causation was reduced to patterns of motion, man became a machine devoid of free will, and religion was excoriated as not just untrue, but dangerous. *Système social* (1773; Social system) placed morality and politics in a utilitarian framework: duty was reduced to prudent self-interest. D'Holbach used his inherited fortune to support Diderot's *Encyclopédie* project, writing many articles for these volumes himself and translating from German.

George Louis Leclerc, comte de Buffon (1707–1788) was appointed to the French Academy of Science in 1734; in 1739 he became superintendent of the Royal Botanical Garden (Jardin du Roi; present-day Jardin des Plantes). Buffon was given the task of completing a catalog of the royal collections in natural

history, which he transformed into a project to produce an account of the whole of nature. This became his great work, *Histoire naturelle, générale et particulière* (1749–1804; General and particular natural history), which was the first modern attempt to systematically present all existing knowledge in the fields of natural history, geology, and anthropology in a single publication. Buffon criticized the Swedish naturalist Linnaeus for the artificiality of his taxonomy of plants and animals. Buffon opposed metaphysics in science, denied divine intervention in nature, and was Newtonian in believing that knowledge should be derived from observations of natural phenomena. He held that what separated humans from animals was reason alone, through their use of language. He was the first to reconstruct a geological history, including a discussion of nature and a theory of the age of the earth, in a series of stages in *Histoire et théorie de la terre* (1749; History and theory of the Earth), and in *Époques de la nature* (1778; Epochs of nature), he proposed the theory that the planets had been created in a collision between the sun and a comet. His theory of the age of the Earth incensed religious opponents. Buffon divided matter into vital and nonvital, balancing an overall Newtonian physical framework with vitalistic tendencies (though rejecting nonmaterial substances). So, he opposed the idea that life was a form of organization of matter. On the other hand, life being a property of matter (of "organic molecules"), it does not require any explanatory principle external to matter. Buffon believed in spontaneous generation as resulting from aggregation of organic molecules present in the environment; his theory was criticized by Lazzaro Spallanzani (1729–1799), whose experiments confirmed Francesco Redi's (1626–1697) rejection of spontaneous generation.

The outcry following publication of Julien Offroy de La Mettrie's (1709–1751) materialistic views in *Histoire naturelle de l'âme* (1745; Natural history of the soul) forced his departure from Paris. In Holland, in 1747, he published *L'homme machine* (The man-machine), which was publicly burned, even in that notoriously liberal environment. La Mettrie then fled to Berlin to ask for the protection of Frederick II of Prussia (r. 1740–1786). La Mettrie, in opposition to Descartes, held that matter was not only extended, but also endowed with an inherent principle of motion and that it could have sensations. Humans were infinitely more complex than lower machines, yet they were still machines. La Mettrie suggested that atheism and an ethics of hedonism were the only proper paths toward human happiness.

Claude Adrien Helvétius (1715–1771) in his *De l'esprit* (1758; On the spirit) explains all of human reason as being based on sensation (like Locke and Condillac). Like La Mettrie, Helvétius placed humans on a continuum with animals. Helvétius also adumbrated a somewhat Epicurean ethical system based on self-interest, pleasure, and pain. His book provoked an outraged reaction both in the court and in the schools; both the Sorbonne and the Parlement of Paris condemned it. Despite Helvétius's public recantation, it was burned publicly (along with the works of other philosophes like Voltaire). Helvétius, like La Mettrie, was welcomed at the Prussian court in Berlin.

Étienne Bonnot de Condillac (1715–1780) maintained an empirical sensationalism based on the principle that observations made by sense perception are the foundation for all human knowledge. The ideas of his *L'essai sur l'origine des connaissances humaines* (1746; Essay on the origins of human knowledge) are close to Locke's, though on certain points, as in rejecting what he took to be Locke's innate ideas of reflection, Condillac modified Locke's position. In his most significant work, the *Traité des sensations* (1754; Treatise on sensations), Condillac denied, for example, that the human mind makes inferences about the shapes, sizes, positions, and distances of objects. Examining each sense separately and the knowledge thereby obtained, he concluded that all human knowledge is sensation transformed by language. Modeled on algebra, language was the underlying principle used to form all higher cognition. In this work he famously analogized man to a statue who gains complex reasoning from its underlying sensations. The importance of language to thought and rational progress is one of the major themes of the Enlightenment. Despite Condillac's materialistic psychology, he believed his views about the nature of religion, especially the reality of the soul, to be consistent with his sensationalism. Condillac's own brand of sensationalism had many followers in Italy. In particular, the jurists Giandomenico Romagnosi (1761–1835), Cesare Beccaria (1738–1794), and Melchiorre Gioia (1767–1829) used his epistemology as a basis for a rationalistic study of jurisprudence and political and social theory.

In 1745 the publisher André Le Breton (1708–1779) approached Denis Diderot (1713–1784) with a proposal to produce a French translation of Ephraim Chambers's *Cyclopaedia,* (first edition, 1728). Together with the mathematician and philosopher Jean Le Rond d'Alembert, Diderot transformed the project into the great *Encyclopédie.* By adhering to strictly rationalistic and materialistic principles, Diderot and d'Alembert saw themselves as forging a weapon against the hold of religion on science and human knowledge. In 1749, Diderot published the *Lettre sur les aveugles à la usage de ceux qui voient* (An essay on the blind for those who can see), remarkable for introducing the first sketch of Diderot's "evolutionary theory" of survival by adaptation. The existence of diversity and monstrosities in nature is explained by a theory of evolution from chaos; the apparent order and adaptation is explained with a probabilistic argument, since nature has time for innumerable trials that lead to growth, increased complexity, and specialization. Only the organisms that became adapted to their environment could survive. Diderot held that our sensory organs, not ideas about essences, should determine our metaphysics. This open endorsement of radical materialism was condemned and, in 1749, led to Diderot's being incarcerated for three months.

Another ugly moment for Diderot came when Helvétius's *De l'esprit,* was condemned to be burned by the Parlement of Paris in 1758, and the *Encyclopédie* itself was formally suppressed. Diderot published the remaining volumes semiclandestinely. Among his philosophical works, special mention may be made of *L'entretien entre d'Alembert et Diderot* (written 1769, published 1830; Conversation between d'Alembert and Diderot), *Le rêve de d'Alembert* (written 1769, published 1830; D'Alembert's dream), and the *Éléments de physiologie* (1774–1780; Elements of physiology). In these works Diderot developed his materialist philosophy and concluded that

simple, reductive mechanical explanations are not sufficient to explain sentient life, without assuming that all matter is potentially sentient and that life and sentiency are specialized functions that arise from a higher level of complexity. In *Jacques le fataliste* (1771; Jacques, the fatalist) Diderot gave a common sense solution of the problem of free will: while there are no rational arguments to support free will, he argued that extreme determinism is ultimately self-defeating.

Jean Le Rond d'Alembert (1717–1783) attended a prestigious Jansenist school where he developed a lifelong distaste for religion. After studying law for two years and medicine for one, he finally discovered his passion for mathematics, which he mainly taught himself. In 1739 he read his first paper to the French Academy of Sciences, of which he became a member in 1741. In 1743 he published his *Traité de dynamique* (A treatise on dynamics), containing the famous "d'Alembert's principle," stating that Newton's third law of motion (for every action there is an equal and opposite reaction) is true for both freely moving and fixed bodies. Other mathematical works followed; in particular the development of partial differential equations. In 1745, d'Alembert joined Diderot in the *Encyclopédie* project as editor of the mathematical and scientific sections. In fact, his contribution went much further, including the *Discours préliminaire* (Preliminary discourse) that introduced the first volume in 1751. The introduction endorsed a view of science as a unified and rational enterprise.

Besides the authors mentioned above, it is useful to recall that there was a clandestine literature that offered materialistic responses to Descartes and that most likely contributed to the philosophical educations of the authors listed. Of particular interest, a collection of manuscripts at the Douai library (ms. 702), on which appears the date 1723, and contains, among others, a *Dissertation sur le sentiment des bêtes, l'instinct et la raison, contre les Cartésiens* (Essay on the feelings of animals, instincts and reasons, against Cartesians); *L'essai philosophique sur l'âme des bêtes* (Amsterdam, 1732; Philosophical essay on the soul of animals); and *Principes physiques de la raison et des passions des hommes* (1709; Physical principles of reason and passions of men) by a Dr. Maubec. Most of this literature, while it circulated widely in its day, is still available only in manuscript.

A late-eighteenth-century figure, Pierre-Jean-Georges Cabanis (1757–1808), was a French philosopher, physician, and physiologist who published *Rapports du physique et du moral de l'homme* (1802; Relations of the physical and moral of man). Cabanis, opposing Condillac's sensationalism, explained all of reality, including the mind-body relations in man, in terms of a mechanistic materialism built on the organic needs of an organism and its automatic responses (the irritable properties of tissues). For Cabanis, life was merely an organization of physical forces; "secretions" in the brain, analogous to the liver's secretion of bile, produced thoughts. The concept of *soul* was superfluous, since consciousness was merely an effect of mechanistic processes, and sensibility, the source of intelligence, was a property of the nervous system. Cabanis is best known, however, as a medical reformer who brought new ways of health care and medical education to France.

English Materialism

John Toland (1670–1722) was born Catholic, though he converted to Protestantism and later endorsed Socinianism, which, like Unitarianism, denied the doctrine of the Trinity. He wrote several texts in which he supported a naturalized and historical interpretation of the holy texts and of miracles. In *Christianity not Mysterious* (1696) he claimed that reason is sufficient to explain all religious "mysteries." In *Letters to Serena* (1704) and *Pantheisticon* (1720), he endorsed a form of pantheism in which God-soul is identical with the material universe. He defended Giordano Bruno (1548–1600), whose pantheistic and materialistic philosophy obviously influenced him. Pantheism was the doctrine that God was everywhere and was all things.

Anthony Collins (1676–1729) was a provocative author who argued, in his *Discourse of Free-thinking* (1713, published anonymously), that free and rational inquiry is the best defense for religion against atheism. In *Inquiry concerning Human Liberty and Necessity* (1715) and *Liberty and Necessity* (1729), he denied free will and defended determinism on the grounds of the necessity of a cause-and-effect relationship between events. He wrote *A Letter to Mr. Dodwell* (1707), to which Samuel Clarke, Newton's disciple, responded. This led to a two-year correspondence (1706–1708) in which Toland defended the idea that all life and consciousness arises from emergent properties of systems of material particles.

David Hartley (1705–1757) saw himself as carrying out Newton's scientific project for the human being and offered a physiological explanation for the association of ideas in materialistic terms in his *Observations on Man: His Frame, His Duty, and His Expectations* (1749). Hartley used Newton's theory of vibrating corpuscular matter and forces of attraction and repulsion as a metaphysical basis for Locke's associationist psychology. He explained mental life in terms of associations and inhibitions, which themselves were to be explained by attraction and repulsion in the nervous system and the brain. Hartley, however, was a deeply religious thinker who believed that "theopathy," the love of God, was a natural emotion, and whose depiction of salvation bordered on mysticism.

Joseph Priestley (1733–1804) was a freethinker who formally rejected Calvinism to enter the Unitarian denomination. Priestley is known mainly for his work in physics and chemistry. He consistently pursued science as a rational enterprise based on facts and experimentation, rather than on dogmatic principles. His view of nature was informed by his belief in a benevolent God who operates through laws of nature that become accessible through careful observation. While this belief in God somehow influenced Priestley's heuristics, his work in chemistry and physics and his political and economic theories were informed by a methodological materialism in which only matter and natural laws were relevant. Between 1772 and 1790, he published six volumes of *Experiments and Observations on Different Kinds of Air* and several papers in the *Philosophical Transactions of the Royal Society*, of which he was a member. He is well known for his contributions to the chemistry of gases, and for his development of a theory of phlogisticated air (which was opposed to Lavoisier's, who repeated Priestley's experiments, and rejected the phlogiston theory in favor of his new oxygen theory).

Conclusion

While it is difficult to find philosophically important individual (materialist) thinkers in other European countries, the materialistic current of the Enlightenment and its belief in the virtues of science swept through Europe, influencing, more or less directly, the political life in every country, with the endorsement of various forms of scientific progress and "enlightened" government. The application of science and the scientific method, mostly based on methodological materialist doctrines, became the hallmark of progress (itself an early-eighteenth-century notion). These beliefs brought important changes in urban development, public health, and industry thoughout Europe.

The influence of European political and social thought, especially concerning tolerance and education, was also felt by American writers and had a fundamental role in the American Revolution and the writing of the U.S. Constitution. However, no movement endorsing materialism, methodological or metaphysical, can be traced.

See also **Cartesianism; Deism; Enlightenment; Mechanical Philosophy; Monism; Scientific Revolution.**

BIBLIOGRAPHY

Allen, Richard C. *David Hartley on Human Nature.* Albany: State University of New York Press, 1999.

Bloch, Olivier, ed. *Le matérialisme du XVIIIᵉ siècle et la littérature clandestine.* Paris, Vrin, 1982.

Bremner, Geoffrey: *Order and Chance: The Pattern of Diderot's Thought.* New York: Cambridge University Press, 1983.

Buchwald, Jed Z., and I. Bernard Cohen. *Isaac Newton's Natural Philosophy.* Cambridge, Mass.: MIT Press, 2001.

Cassirer, Ernst. *The Philosophy of the Enlightenment.* Translated by Fritz C. A. Koelln and James P. Pettegrove. Boston: Beacon, 1955.

Corsi, Pietro: *The Age of Lamarck : Evolutionary Theories in France, 1790–1830.* Translated by Jonathan Mandelbaum. Rev. and updated. Berkeley: University of California Press, 1988.

Evans, Robert Rees. *Pantheisticon: The Career of John Toland.* New York: Lang, 1991.

Ferrone, Vincenzo. *The Intellectual Roots of the Italian Enlightenmen : Newtonian Science, Religion, and Politics in the Early Eighteenth Century.* Translated by Sue Brotherton. Atlantic Highlands, N.J.: Humanities, 1995.

Jacob, Margaret. *The Radical Enlightenment: Pantheists, Freemasons, and Republicans.* Boston: Allen and Unwin, 1981.

Lennon, Thomas. *The Battle of the Gods and Giants: The Legacies of Descartes and Gassendi, 1655–1715.* Princeton, N.J.: Princeton University Press, 1993.

McNeil, Maureen. *Under the Banner of Science: Erasmus Darwin and His Age.* Wolfeboro, N.H.: Manchester University Press, 1987.

Reill, Peter Hanns, consulting editor, and Ellen Judy Wilson, principal author. *Encyclopedia of the Enlightenment.* New York: Facts on File, 1996.

Vartanian, Aram. *Diderot and Descartes: A Study of Scientific Naturalism in the Enlightenment.* Westport, Conn.: Greenwood, 1975.

———. *Science and Humanism in the French Enlightenment.* Charlottesville, Va.: Rookwood, 1999.

Yolton. John W. *Locke and French Materialism.* New York : Oxford University Press, 1991.

———. *Thinking Matter: Materialism in Eighteenth-Century Britain.* Minneapolis: University of Minnesota Press, 1983.

Peter Machamer
Francesca di Poppa

MATHEMATICS. This article comprises a compact survey of the development of mathematics from ancient times until the early twentieth century. The treatment is broadly chronological, and most of it is concerned with Europe.

Unknown Origins

It seems unavoidable that mathematical thinking played a role in human theorizing from the start of the race, and in various ways. Arithmetic (as the later branch of mathematics became known) would have been one of them, motivated initially by forming integers in connection with counting. But other branches surely include geometry, linked to the appreciation of line, surface, and space; trigonometry, inspired by awareness of angles; mechanics, related to the motion of bodies large and small and the (in)stability of structures; part-whole theory, from consideration of collections of things; and probability, coming from judging and guessing about situations. In all cases the thinking would have started out as very intuitive, gradually becoming more explicit and less particular.

Some of the associated contexts would have been provided by study of the environment (such as days) and the heavens (such as new and full moons), which was a major concern of ancient cultures in all parts of the world; in those times mathematics and astronomy were linked closely. For example, the oldest recognized artifact is a bone from Africa, thought to be about thirty-seven thousand years old, upon which phases of the moon seem to have been recorded.

Among the various ancient cultures, the Babylonians have left the earliest extant evidence of their mathematical practice. They counted with tokens from the eighth millennium; and from the late fourth millennium they expressed numbers and properties of arithmetic in a numeral system to base 10 and handled fractions in expansions of powers of 1/60. Many surviving artifacts seem to relate to education—for example, exercises requiring calculations of unknown quantities, which correspond to the solution of equations but are not to be so identified. They also developed geometry, largely for terrestrial purposes. The Egyptians pursued similar studies, even also finding a formula (not the same one) for the volume of the rectangular base of a pyramid of given sides. They also took up the interesting mathematical problem of representing a fraction as the sum of reciprocals.

A major mathematical question for these cultures concerned the relationship between circles and spheres and rectilinear objects such as lines and cubes. They involve the quantity that we symbolize by π, and ancient evidence survives of methods of approximating to its value. But it is not clear that these cultures knew that the same quantity occurs in all the relationships.

On Greek Mathematics

The refinement of mathematics was effected especially by the ancient Greeks, who flourished for about a millennium from the sixth century B.C.E. Pythagoras and his clan are credited with many things, starting with their later compatriots: the eternality of integers; the connection between ratios of integers and musical intervals; the theorem relating the sides of a right-angled triangle; and so on. Their contemporary Thales (c. 625–c. 547 B.C.E.) is said to have launched trigonometry with his appreciation of the angle. However, nothing survives directly from either man.

A much luckier figure concerning survival is Euclid (fl. c. 300 B.C.E.), especially with his *Elements*. While no explanatory preface survives, it appears that most of the mathematics presented was his rendition of predecessors' work, but that (some of) the systematic organization that won him so many later admirers might be his. He stated explicitly the axioms and assumptions that he noticed; one of them, the parallel axiom, lacked the intuitive clarity of the others, and so was to receive much attention in later cultures.

The *Elements* comprised thirteen Books: Books 7–9 dealt with arithmetic, and the others presented basic plane (Books 1–6) and solid (Books 11–13) geometry of rectilinear and circular figures. The extraordinary Book 10 explored properties of ratios of smaller to longer lines, akin to a theory of irrational numbers but again not to be so identified. A notable feature is that Euclid confined the role of arithmetic within geometry to multiples of lines (say, "twice this line is . . . "), to a role in stating ratios, and to using reciprocals (such as 1/5); he was not concerned with lengths—that is, lines measured arithmetically. Thus, he said nothing about the value of π, for it relates to measurement.

The Greeks were aware of the limitations of straight line and circle. In particular, they found many properties and applications of the "conic sections": parabola, hyperbola, and ellipse. Hippocrates of Chios (fl. c. 600 B.C.E.) is credited with three "classical problems" (a later name) that his compatriots (rightly) suspected could not be solved by ruler and compass alone: (1) construct a square equal in area to a given circle; (2) divide any angle into three equal parts; and (3) construct a cube twice the volume of a given one. The solutions that they did find enlarged their repertoire of curves.

Among later Greeks, Archimedes (c. 287–212 B.C.E.) stands out for the range and depth of his work. His work on circular and spherical geometry shows that he knew all four roles for π; but he also wrote extensively on mechanics, including floating bodies (the "eureka!" tale) and balancing the lever, and focusing parabolic mirrors. Other figures developed astronomy, partly as applied trigonometry, both planar and spherical; in particular, Ptolemy (late second century) "compiled" much knowledge in his *Almgest,* dealing with both the orbits and the distances of the heavenly bodies from the central and stationary Earth.

Traditions Elsewhere

Mathematics developed well from antiquity also in the Far East, with distinct traditions in India, China, Japan, Korea, and Vietnam. Arithmetic, geometry, and mechanics were again prominent; special features include a powerful Chinese method equivalent to solving a system of linear equations, a pretty theory of touching circles in Japanese "temple geometry," and pioneering work on number theory by the Indians. They also introduced the place-value system of numerals to base 10, of which we use a descendant that developed after several changes in adopted symbols.

This system of numerals was mediated into Europe by mathematicians working in medieval Islamic civilization, often though not always writing in Arabic. They became the dominant culture in mathematics from the ninth century and continued strongly until the fourteenth. They assimilated much Greek mathematics; indeed, they are our only source for some of it.

The first major author was al-Khwarizmi (fl. c. 800–847), who laid the foundations of algebra, especially the solution of equations. He and his followers launched the theory using words rather than special symbols to mark unknowns and operations. Other interests in geometry included attempts to prove Euclid's parallel axiom and applications to optics and trigonometry; an important case of the latter was determining the *qibla* (that is, the direction of Mecca) for any time and place at times of Muslim prayer. Their massive contributions to astronomy included theory and manufacture of astrolabes.

The Wakening Europe from the Twelfth Century
From the decline of the Roman Empire (including Greece) Euclid was quiescent mathematically, though the Carolingian kingdom inspired some work, at least in education. The revival dates from around the late twelfth century, when universities also began to be formed. The major source for mathematics was Latin translations of Greek and Arabic writings (and re-editions of Roman writers, especially Boethius). In addition, the Italian Leonardo Fibonacci (c. 1170–c. 1240) produced a lengthy *Liber Abbaci* in 1202 that reported in Latin many parts of Arabic arithmetic and algebra (including the Indian numerals); his book was influential, though perhaps less than is commonly thought. The Italian peninsula was then the most powerful region of Europe, and much commercial and "research" mathematics was produced there; the German states and the British Isles also came to boast some eminent figures. In addition, a somewhat distinct Hebrew tradition arose—for example, in probability theory.

A competition developed between two different methods of reckoning. The tradition was to represent numbers by placing pebbles (in Latin, *calculi*) in determined positions on a flat surface (in Latin, *abacus*, with one *b*), and to add and subtract by moving the pebbles according to given rules. However, with the new numerals came a rival procedure of calculating on paper, which gradually supervened; for, as well as also allowing multiplication and division, the practitioner could show and check his working, an important facility unavailable to movers of pebbles.

Mathematics rapidly profited from the invention of printing in the late fifteenth century; not only were there printed Euclids, but also many reckoning books. Trigonometry became a major branch in the fifteenth and sixteenth centuries, not only for astronomy but also, as European imperialism developed, for

cartography, and the needs of navigation and astronomy made the spherical branch more significant than the planar. Geometry was applied also to art, with careful studies of perspective; Piero della Francesca (c. 1420–1492) and Albrecht Dürer (1471–1528) were known not only as great artists but also as significant mathematicians.

Numerical calculation benefited greatly from the development of logarithms in the early seventeenth century by John Napier (1550–1617) and others, for then multiplication and division could be reduced to addition and subtraction. Logarithms superseded a clumsier method called "prosthaphairesis" that used certain trigonometrical formulas.

In algebra the use of special symbols gradually increased, until in his *Géométrie* (1637), René Descartes (1596–1650) introduced (more or less) the notations that we still use, and also analytic geometry. His compatriot Pierre de Fermat (1601–1665) also worked in these areas and contributed some theorems and conjectures to number theory. In addition, he corresponded with Blaise Pascal (1623–1662) on games of chance, thereby promoting parts of probability theory.

In mechanics a notable school at Merton College, Oxford, had formed in the twelfth century to study various kinds of terrestrial and celestial motion. The main event in celestial mechanics was Nicolaus Copernicus's (1473–1543) *De revolutionibus* (1453; On the revolutions), where rest was transferred from the Earth to the sun (though otherwise the dynamics of circular and epicyclical motions was not greatly altered). In the early seventeenth century the next stages lay especially with Johannes Kepler's (1571–1630) abandonment of circular orbits for the planets and Galileo Galilei's (1564–1642) analysis of (locally) horizontal and vertical motions of bodies.

The Epoch of Newton and Leibniz
By the mid-seventeenth century, science had become professionalized enough for some national societies to be instituted, especially the Royal Society of London and the Paris Académie des Sciences. At that time two major mathematicians emerged: Isaac Newton (1642–1727) in Cambridge and Gottfried Wilhelm von Leibniz (1646–1716) in Hanover. Each man invented a version of the differential and integral calculus, Newton first in creation but Leibniz first in print. The use here of Leibniz's adjectives recognizes the superior development of his version. During the early 1700s Newton became so furious (or envious?) that he promoted a charge of plagiarism against Leibniz, complete with impartial committee at the Royal Society. It was a disaster for Britain: Newton's followers stuck with their master's theory of "fluxions" and "fluents," while the Continentals developed "differentials" and "integrals," with greater success. The accusation was also mathematically stupid, for conceptually the two calculi were quite different: Newton's was based upon (abstract) time and unclearly grounded upon the notion of limit, while Leibniz's used infinitesimal increments on variables, explicitly avoiding limits. So even if Leibniz had known of Newton's theory (of which the committee found no impartial evidence), he rethought it entirely.

Leibniz's initial guard was largely Swiss: brothers Jakob (1654–1705) and Johann Bernoulli (1667–1748) from the

1680s, then from the 1720s Johann's son Daniel (1700–1782) and their compatriot Leonhard Euler (1707–1783), who was to be the greatest of the lot. During the eighteenth century they and other mathematicians (especially in Paris) expanded calculus into a vast territory of ordinary and then partial differential equations and studied many related series and functions. The Newtonians kept up quite well until Colin Maclaurin (1698–1746) in the 1740s, but then faded badly.

The main motivation for this vast development came from applications, especially to mechanics. Here Newton and Leibniz differed again. In his *Principia mathematica* (1687) Newton announced the laws that came to carry his name: (1) a body stays in equilibrium or in uniform motion unless disturbed by a force; (2) the ratio of the magnitude of the force and the mass of the body determines its acceleration; and (3) to any force of action there is one of reaction, equal in measure and opposite in sense. In addition, for both celestial and terrestrial mechanics, which he novelly united, the force between two objects lies along the straight line joining them, and varies as the inverse square of its length.

With these principles Newton could cover a good range of mechanical phenomena. His prediction that the Earth was flattened at the poles, corroborated by an expedition undertaken in the 1740s, was a notable success. He also had a splendid idea about why the planets did not exactly follow the elliptical orbits around the sun that the inverse square law suggested: they were "perturbed" from them by interacting with each other. The study of perturbations became a prime topic in the eighteenth century, with Euler's work being particularly significant. Euler also showed that law 2 could be applied to any direction in a mechanical situation, thus greatly increasing its utility. He and others made important contributions to the mechanics of continuous media, especially fluid mechanics and elasticity theory, where Newton had been somewhat sketchy.

Mathematics in the Eighteenth Century: The Place of Lagrange

However, Newton's theory was not alone in mechanics. Leibniz and others developed an alternative approach, partly inspired by Descartes, in which the "living forces" (roughly, kinetic energy) of bodies were related to their positions. Gradually this became a theory of living forces converted into "work" (a later term), specified as (force x traversed distance). Engineers became keen on it for its utility in their concerns, especially when impact between bodies was involved; from the 1780s Lazare Carnot (1753–1823) urged it as a general approach for mechanics.

Carnot thereby challenged Newton's theory, but his main target was a recent new tradition partly launched by Jean d'Alembert (1718–1783) in midcentury and developed further by Joseph-Louis Lagrange (1736–1813). Suspicious of the notion of force, d'Alembert had proposed that it be defined by Newton's law 2, which he replaced by one stating how systems of bodies moved when disturbed from equilibrium. At that time Euler and others proposed a "principle of least action," which asserted that the action (a mechanical notion defined by an integral) of a mechanical system took its optimal value when equilibrium was achieved. Lagrange elaborated upon these principles to create *Méchanique analitique* (1788), in which he challenged the other two traditions; in particular, dynamics was reduced mathematically to statics. For him a large advantage of his principles was that they were formulated exclusively in algebraic terms; as he proclaimed in the preface of his book, there were no diagrams, and no need for them. A main achievement was a superb though inconclusive attempt to prove that the system of planets was stable; predecessors such as Newton and Euler had left that matter to God.

Lagrange formulated mechanics this way in order to make it (more) rigorous. Similarly, he algebraized the calculus by assuming that any mathematical function could be expressed in an infinite power series (the so-called Taylor series), and that the basic notions of derivative (his word) and integral could be determined solely by algebraic manipulations. He also greatly expanded the calculus of variations, a key notion in the principle of least action.

As in mechanics, Lagrange's calculus challenged the earlier ones, Newton's and Leibniz's, and as there, reaction was cautious. A good example for both contexts was Pierre-Simon Laplace (1749–1827), a major figure from 1770. While strongly influenced by Lagrange, he did not confine himself to the constraints of Lagrange's book when writing his own four-volume *Traité de mécanique céleste* (1799–1805; Treatise on celestial mechanics). His exposition of celestial and planetary mechanics used many differential equations, series, and functions.

The French Revolution and a New Professionalization

Laplace published his large book in a new professional and economic situation for science. After the Revolution of 1789 in France, higher education and its institutions there were reformed, with a special emphasis upon engineering. In particular, a new school was created, the École Polytechnique (1794), with leading figures as professors (such as Lagrange) and as examiners (Laplace), and with enrollment of students determined by talent, not birth. A new class of scientists and engineers emerged, with mathematics taught, learned, researched, and published on a scale hitherto unknown.

Of this mass of work only a few main cases can be summarized here. Joseph Fourier (1768–1830) is noteworthy for his mathematical analysis of heat diffusion, both the differential equation to represent it (the first important such equation found outside mechanics) and solutions by certain infinite series and by integrals that both now bear his name. From the 1820s they attracted much attention, not only for their use in heat theory but especially for the "pure" task of establishing conditions for their truth. New techniques for rigor had just become available, mainly from Augustin-Louis Cauchy (1789–1857), graduate of the École Polytechnique and now professor there. He taught a fourth approach to the calculus (and also function and series), based like Newton's upon limits but now fortified by a careful theory of them; although rather unintuitive, its mathematical merits gradually led worldwide to its preference over the other three approaches.

Ironically, Cauchy's own analysis of Fourier series failed, but a beautiful treatment following his approach came in 1829 from

J. P. G. Dirichlet (1805–1859)—a French-sounding name of a young German who had studied with the masters in Paris. Dirichlet also exemplifies a novelty of that time: other countries producing major mathematicians. Another contemporary example lies in elliptic functions, which Carl Jacobi (1804–1851) and the young Norwegian Niels Henrik Abel (1802–1829) invented independently following much pioneering work on the inverse function by A. M. Legendre (1752–1833).

Jacobi and Abel drew upon a further major contribution to mathematics made by Cauchy when, by analogy with the calculus, he developed a theory of functions of the complex variable x + √−1y (x and y real), complete with an integral. His progress was fitful, from the 1810s to the 1840s; after that, however, his theory became recognized as a major branch of mathematics, with later steps taken especially by the Germans.

Between 1810 and 1830 the French initiated other parts of mathematical physics in addition to Fourier on heat: Siméon-Denis Poisson (1781–1840) on magnetism and electrostatics; André-Marie Ampère (1775–1836) on electrodynamics; and Augustin Jean Fresnel (1788–1827) on optics with his wave theory. Mathematics played major roles: many analogies were taken from mechanics, which itself developed massively, with Carnot's energy approach elaborated by engineers such as Gaspard-Gustave Coriolis (1792–1843), and continuum mechanics extended, especially by Cauchy.

Geometry was also taught and studied widely. Gaspard Monge (1746–1818) sought to develop "descriptive geometry" into a geniune branch of mathematics and gave it prominence in the first curriculum of the École Polytechnique; however, this useful theory of engineering drawing could not carry such importance, and Laplace had its teaching reduced. But former student Jean Victor Poncelet (1788–1867) was partly inspired by it to develop "the projective properties of figures" (*Traité des propries projectives de figures*, 1822), where he studied characteristics independent of measure, such as the order of points on a line.

The main mathematician outside France at this time was C. F. Gauss (1777–1855), director of the Göttingen University Observatory. Arguably he was the greatest of all, with major work published in number theory, celestial mechanics, and aspects of analysis and probability theory. But he was not socially active, and he left many key insights in his manuscripts (for example, on elliptic functions).

Other major contributors outside France include George Green (1793–1841), who, in *An Essay on the Application of Mathematical Analysis to the Theories of Electricity and Magnetism* (1828), produced a wonderful theorem in potential (his word) theory that related the state of affairs inside an extended body to that on its surface. But he published his book very obscurely, and it became well-known only on the reprint during the 1850s initiated by William Thomson (later Lord Kelvin), who was making notable contributions of his own to the theory.

Midcentury Internationalism
By the 1840s Britain and the Italian and German states were producing quality mathematicians to complement and even rival the French, and new posts were available in universities and engineering colleges everywhere. Among the Germans, two figures stand out.

From around 1860 Karl Weierstrass (1815–1897) gave lecture courses on many aspects of real- and complex-variable analysis and parts of mechanics at Berlin University, attended by students from many countries who then went home and taught likewise. Meanwhile at Göttingen, Bernhard Riemann (1826–1866) rethought complex-variable analysis and revolutionized the understanding of both Fourier series and the foundations of geometry. Much of this work was published only after his early death in 1866, but it soon made a great impact. The work on Fourier series led Georg Cantor (1845–1918) to develop set theory from the 1870s. On geometry Riemann showed that the Euclidean was only one of many possible geometries, and that each of them could be defined independently of any embedding space. The possibility of non-Euclidian geometries, using alternatives to the parallel axiom, had been exhibited around 1830 in little-recognized work by Janos Bolyai (1802–1860) and Nicolai Lobachevsky (1793–1856) (and, in manuscript, Gauss); Riemann, however, went much further and brought us proper understanding of the plurality of geometries.

Weierstrass emulated and indeed enhanced Cauchy-style rigor, carefully formulating definitions and distinctions and presenting proofs in great detail. By contrast, Riemann worked intuitively, offering wonderful but often proof-free insights grounded upon some "geometric fantasy," as Weierstrass described it. A good example is their revisions of Cauchy's complex variable analysis: Weierstrass relied solely on power series expansions of the functions, whereas Riemann invented surfaces now named after him that were slit in many remarkable ways. Among many consequences of the latter, the German Felix Klein (1849–1925) and the Frenchman Henri Poincaré (1854–1912) in the early 1880s found beautiful properties of functions defined on these surfaces, which they related to group theory as part of the rise of abstract algebras.

Another example of the gap between Riemann and Weierstrass is provided by potential theory. Riemann used a principle employed by his mentor Dirichlet (and also envisaged by Green) to solve problems in potential theory, but in 1870 Weierstrass exposed its fallibility by a counterexample, and so methods became far more complicated.

Better news for potential theory had come at midcentury with the "energetics" physics of Thomson, Hermann von Helmholtz (1821–1894), and others. The work expression of engineering mechanics was extended into the admission of potentials, which now covered all physical factors (such as heat) and not just the mechanical ones that had split Carnot from Lagrange. The latter's algebraic tradition in mechanics had been elaborated by Jacobi and by the Irishman William Rowan Hamilton (1805–1865), who also introduced his algebra of quaternions.

Among further related developments, the Scot James Clerk Maxwell (1831–1879) set out theories of electricity and magnetism (including, for him, optics) in his *Treatise on Electricity and Magnetism* (1873). Starting out from the electric and magnetic potentials as disturbances of the ether rather than Newton-like forces acting at a distance through it, he presented relationships between his basic notions as differential equations (expressed in quaternion form). A critical follower was the Englishman Oliver Heaviside, who also analyzed electrical networks by means of a remarkable but mysterious operator algebra. Other "Maxwellians" preferred to replace dependence upon fields with talk about "things," such as electrons and ions; the relationship between ether and matter (J. J. Larmor, *Aether and Matter,* 1900) was a major issue in mathematical physics at century's end.

The Early Twentieth Century

A new leader emerged: the German David Hilbert (1862–1943). Work on abstract algebras and the foundations of geometry led him to emphasize the importance of axiomatizing mathematical theories (including the axioms of Euclidean geometry that Euclid had not noticed) and to study their foundations metamathematically. But his mathematical knowledge was vast enough for him to propose twenty-three problems for the new century; while a personal choice, it exercised considerable influence upon the community. He presented it at the International Congress of Mathematicians, held in Paris in 1900 as the second of a series that manifested the growing sense of international collaboration in mathematics that still continues.

One of Hilbert's problems concerned the foundations of physics, which he was to study intensively. In physics Albert Einstein (1879–1955) proposed his special theory of relativity in 1905 and a general theory ten years later; according to both, the ether was not needed. Mathematically, the general theory both deployed and advanced tensor calculus, which had developed partly out of Riemann's interpretation of geometry.

Another main topic in physics was quantum mechanics, which drew upon partial differential equations and vector and matrix theory. One of its controversies concerned Werner Heisenberg's principle of the uncertainty of observation: should it be interpreted statistically or not? The occurrence of this debate, which started in the mid-1920s, was helped by the increasing presence of mathematical statistics. Although probability must have had an early origin in mathematical thinking, both it and mathematical statistics had developed very slowly in the nineteenth century—in strange contrast to the mania for collecting data of all kinds. Laplace and Gauss had made important contributions in the 1810s, for example, over the method of least-squares regression, and Pafnuty Chebyshev (1821–1894) was significant from the 1860s in Saint Petersburg (thus raising the status of Russian mathematics). But only from around 1900 did theorizing in statistics develop strongly, and the main figure was Karl Pearson (1857–1936) at University College, London, and his students and followers. Largely to them we owe the definition and theory of basic notions such as standard deviation and correlation coefficient, basic theorems concerning sampling and ranking, and tests of significance.

Elsewhere, Cantor's set theory and abstract algebras were applied to many parts of mathematics and other sciences

in the new century. A major beneficiary was topology, the mathematics of location and place. A few cases had emerged in the nineteenth century, such as the "Möbius strip" with only one side and one edge, Riemann's fantastical surfaces, and above all a remarkable classification of deformable manifolds by Poincaré; most of the main developments, however, date from the 1920s. General theories were developed of covering, connecting, orientating, and deforming manifolds and surfaces, along with many other topics. A new theory of dimensions was also proposed because Cantor had refuted the traditional understanding by mapping one-one all the points in a square onto all the points on any of its sides. German mathematicians were prominent; so were Americans in a country that had risen rapidly in mathematical importance from the 1890s.

Some Reflections

The amount of mathematical activity has usually increased steadily or even exponentially, and the growth from the mid-twentieth century has been particularly great. For example, the German reviewing journal *Zentralblatt Math* published at the beginning of the twenty-first century a six-hundred-page quarto volume every two weeks, using a classification of mathematics into sixty-three numbered sections. To suggest the rate of increase, the other reviewing journal, the U.S. periodical *Mathematical Reviews,* published 3,800 octavo pages in 1980, 7,500 pages a decade later, and 9,800 pages in 2003. It would be impossible to summarize this mountain of work, even up to 1970; instead, some main points are noted relating to the previous sections and to the companion articles on algebras and on logic.

Not only has the amount increased; the variety of theories has also greatly expanded. All the topics and branches mentioned above continue to develop (and also many more that were not noted), and new topics emerge and fresh applications are found. For example, beginning with the 1940s mathematics became widely utilized in the life sciences and medicine and has expanded greatly in economics and other social sciences relative to previous practice.

Much of that work lies in statistics, which after its very slow arrival has developed a huge community of practitioners in its own right. Often it functions rather separately from mathematics, with its own departments in universities.

Another enormous change has been the advent of computing, again particularly since World War II and indeed much stimulated by war work as on cryptography and the calculation of parameters in large technological artifacts. Mathematics plays a role both in the design, function, and programming of computers themselves and in the formulation of many mathematical theories. An important case is in numerical mathematics, where approximations are required and efficient algorithms sought to effect them. This kind of mathematics has been practiced continuously from ancient times, especially in connection with all sorts of applications. Quite often algorithms were found to be too slow or mathematically cumbersome to be practicable; but now computer power makes many of them feasible in "number crunching" (to quote a popular oversimplification of such techniques).

A feature of many mathematical theories is linearity, in which equations or expressions of the form

(A =) ax + by + cz + . . . and so on finitely or even infinitely

make sense, in a very wide range of interpretations of the letters, not necessarily within an algebra itself (for example, Fourier series shows it). But a dilemma arises for many applications, for the world is not a linear place, and in recent decades nonlinear theories have gained higher status, partly again helped by computing. The much-publicized theory of fractals falls into this category.

From the Greeks onward, mathematicians have often been fascinated by major unsolved problems and by the means of solving them. In the late 1970s a proof was produced of the four-color theorem, stating that any map drawn upon a surface can be colored with four colors such that bounding regions do not share the same color. The proof was controversial, for a computer was used to check thousands of special cases, a task too large for people. Another example is "Fermat's last theorem," that the sum of the nth powers of two positive integers is never equal to the nth power of another integer when n>2. The name is a misnomer, in that Fermat only claimed a proof but did not reveal it; the modern version (1994) uses modern techniques far beyond his ken.

This article has focused upon the main world cultures, but every society has produced mathematics. The "fringe" developments are studied using approaches collectively known as ethnomathematics. While the cultures involved developed versions of arithmetic and geometry and also some other branches, several of them also followed their own concerns; some examples, among many, are intricate African drawings made in one unbroken line, Celtic knitting patterns, and sophisticated rows of knotted strings called *quipus* used in Mexico to maintain accounts.

A thread running from antiquity in all cultures, fringe or central, is recreational mathematics. Unfortunately, the variety is far too great even for summary here. Often it consists of exercises, perhaps posed for educational use, or perhaps just for fun; an early collection is attributed to Alcuin in the ninth century, for use in the Carolingian Empire. Solutions sometimes involve intuitive probability, or combinatorics to work out all options; with games such as chess and bridge, however, the analysis is much more sophisticated. Several puzzles appear in slightly variant forms in different cultures, suggesting transmission. Some are puzzles in logic or reasoning rather than mathematics as such, and it is striking that for some games the notion of decidability was recognized (that is, is there a strategy that guarantees victory?) long before it was studied metamathematically in the foundations of mainstream mathematics.

Lastly, since the early 1970s interest in the history of mathematics has increased considerably. There are now several journals in the field along with a variety of books and editions, collectively covering all main cultures and periods. One main motive for people to take up historical research was their dislike of the normal unmotivated way in which mathematics was (and is) taught and learned; thus, the links between history and mathematics education are strong. For, despite many appearances to the contrary, mathematics is a human activity.

See also **Algebras; Astronomy, Pre-Columbian and Latin American; Calculation and Computation; Geometry; Logic; Logic and Philosophy of Mathematics, Modern.**

BIBLIOGRAPHY

Bottazzini, Umberto. *Il flauto di Hilbert.* Turin: UTET, 1990.

Cajori, Florian. *A History of Mathematical Notations.* 2 vols. La Salle, Ill., and Chicago: Open Court, 1928–1929.

Cantor, Moritz. *Vorlesungen über Geschichte der Mathematik.* 4 vols. Leipzig, Germany: Teubner, 1899–1908. Classic source of the history of mathematics to 1799.

Chabert, Jean-Luc, et al., eds. *A History of Algorithms: From the Pebble to the Microchip.* Translated by Chris Weeks. Berlin and New York: Springer, 1999. French original, 1994.

Cooke, Roger. *The History of Mathematics: A Brief Course.* New York: Wiley, 1997.

Dauben, Joseph W., ed. *The History of Mathematics from Antiquity to the Present: A Selective Bibliography.* Rev. ed. New York: Garland, 1985. Lewis, Albert, ed. *The History of Mathematics: A Selective Bibliography.* Providence, R.I.: American Mathematical Society, 2000. In CD ROM format.

Dauben, Joseph W., and Scriba J. Christoph, eds. *Writing the History of Mathematics: Its Historical Development.* Basel, Switzerland, and Boston: Birkhaüser, 2002.

Dieudonné, Jean, ed. *Abrégé d'histoire des mathématiques 1700–1900.* 2 vols. Paris: Hermann, 1978. Includes a few parts on pure mathematics.

Dold, Yvonne, et al., eds. *From China to Paris: 2000 Years Transmission of Mathematical Ideas.* Stuttgart: Franz Steiner, 2002.

Folkerts, Menso, Eberhard Knobloch, and Karin Reich. *Mass, Zahl, und Gewicht.* 2nd ed. Wiesbaden: Harrassowitz, 2001. Much elaborated exhibition catalog.

Goldstein, Catherine, Jeremy Gray, and Jim Ritter, eds. *L'Europe mathématique: histoires, mythes, identités.* Paris: Editions de la Maison des Sciences de l'Homme, 1996.

Gottwald, Siegfried, Hans-Joachim Ilgands, and Karl-Heinz Schlote, eds. *Lexikon bedeutender Mathematiker.* Leipzig: Bibliographisches Institut, 1990. Many short biographies.

Grattan-Guinness, I., ed. *Companion Encyclopedia of the History and Philosophy of the Mathematical Sciences.* 2 vols. London and New York: Routledge, 1994. Reprint, Baltimore: Johns Hopkins University Press, 2003. Material up to the 1930s.

———. *The Norton History of the Mathematical Sciences: The Rainbow of Mathematics.* New York: Norton, 1998. Coverage until World War I.

Historia mathematica (1974–). The best single source for new historical writings.

Klein, Felix, et al., eds. *Encyklopädie der mathematischen Wissenschaften.* 23 vols. Leipzig, Germany: Teubner, 1898–1935.

Kline, Morris. *Mathematical Thought from Ancient to Modern Times.* New York: Oxford University Press, 1972.

Kramer, Edna E. *The Nature and Growth of Modern Mathematics.* New York: Hawthorn, 1970.

May, Kenneth O. *Bibliography and Research Manual of the History of Mathematics.* Toronto: University of Toronto Press, 1973.

Montucla, Jerome E. *Histoire des mathématiques.* 2nd ed. 4 vols. Vols. 3–4 edited by J. J. Lalande. Paris: Agasse, 1799–1802. Reprint, Paris: Blanchard, 1968.

Pier, Jean-Paul, ed. *Development of Mathematics 1900–1950.* Basel, Switzerland, and Boston: Birkhäuser, 1994. This and the follow-up volume focus mostly on pure mathematics.

———. *Development of Mathematics 1950–2000.* Basel, Switzerland, and Boston: Birkhäuser, 2000.

Roche, John J. *The Mathematics of Measurement: A Critical History.* London: Athlone Press, 1998.

Scriba, C. J., and P. Schreiber. *5000 Jahre Geometrie. Geschichte, Kulturen, Menschen.* Berlin and New York: Springer, 2000.

I. Grattan-Guinness

MATRIARCHY.

Matriarchy is usually defined as a political system in which women are the dominant political actors, as opposed to patriarchy, in which men are the exclusive or primary heads of families, social groups, or political states. But matriarchy has always been a controversial term, since whenever it is mentioned, there are debates about whether matriarchies are imagined utopias or real societies, whether they existed at some time in the distant past or could be re-created in a possible future, and how the definitions of gendered power themselves might have shifted in relation to varying social and historical contexts. The idea of matriarchy has served to inspire a whole series of legends and myths, experiments in alternative lifestyles, feminist spirituality, and woman-centered collectives, but it has long been rejected within mainstream anthropology. In the early twenty-first century new field research in Indonesia, Melanesia, and China has raised new questions about the definition of the term itself, and reinvigorated debates about when—if ever—it can be used responsibly.

Nineteenth-Century Evolutionary Theory

J. J. Bachofen began the modern debate about matriarchy with his 1861 book on "mother right," in which he argued that one early social formation was a family which traced descent through the mother, and in which "government of the state was also entrusted to the women" (p. 156). Bachofen developed a three-stage model: In the barbaric or hetaeristic stage (from the Greek *hetero,* meaning both), neither men nor women had control, and people engaged in indiscriminate sexual activity, worshiping Aphrodite and valuing the erotic above all else. Then women tired of this system and banded together for their own defense, creating a matriarchy in which Artemis and Athena emerged as the main deities. Agriculture was developed during this period, and so were the stories of Amazons and Furies. Bachofen argued that "matriarchal people feel the unity of all life, the harmony of the universe" (p. 79), and embraced a philosophy of "regulated naturalism" in which maternal love was the basis of all social ties. In the final stage of the development of civilization, men seized control from women, and their struggle to assert their domination was reflected in stories of Zeus triumphing over the Titans, Hades raping Persephone, Perseus slaying the Medusa, and Oedipus killing the Sphinx. Bachofen interpreted mythical accounts of sexual conflict as evidence for a historical transition from matriarchy to patriarchy.

Friedrich Engels developed a materialist version of this theme in *The Origin of the Family, Private Property and the State* (1884), arguing that matriarchy developed from a situation of group marriage, in which paternity was uncertain so only female blood lines could be traced reliably. Early human societies were presumed to have been egalitarian, and various forms of inequality were introduced in conjunction with the emergence of private property. When property rights came to be invested in men, the development of patriarchy was tied to the birth of capitalism, in which laborers were no longer the owners of the products of their labor.

Anthropologists working on comparative evidence from a number of societies tried to develop a more rigorous definition of matriarchy. E. B. Tylor grouped matrilineal descent with postmarital residence in the wife's household and evidence that "the wives are the masters" in the family (p. 89), and described the Minangkabau of Indonesia as one possible matriarchy. He later reconsidered this position and decided that the term maternal family would be preferable to matriarchy, since "it takes too much for granted that the women govern the family" (p. 90). Lewis Henry Morgan's intensive studies of the Iroquois documented political institutions in which women played important roles, and his *Ancient Society* (1877) formed the basis of Engel's speculations. But as more field studies of matrilineal societies were completed, few of them seemed to have anything approaching female rule over men, and by 1921 Robert Lowie's *Primitive Society* concluded that there was no evidence that women had ever governed the primitive equivalent of the state.

Twentieth-Century Gender and Kinship Studies

In *Matrilineal Kinship* (1961), David Schneider reexamined several decades of scholarship on the subject and concluded that "the generalized authority of women over men, imagined by Bachofen, was never observed in known matrilineal societies, but only recorded in legends and myths. Thus the whole notion of matriarchy fell rapidly into disuse in anthropological work" (p. viii).

The possibility of matriarchy was also denied in one of the founding texts of feminist anthropology, Michelle Rosaldo and Louise Lamphere's *Women, Culture and Society* (1974), which started with an infamous (and later retracted) assertion of the universality of male dominance: "It seems fair to say, then, that all contemporary societies are to some extent male-dominated, and although the degree and expression of female subordination vary greatly, sexual asymmetry is presently a universal fact of human and social life" (p. 3).

Twenty years after that statement was published, several contributors to the Rosaldo and Lamphere book specifically recanted this assertion, but none of them went so far as to embrace the idea of matriarchy. Sherry Ortner writes that in the early 1970s, when interest in feminist anthropology began to grow, she and many other anthropologists were asked about matriarchies: "Was it not the case, people wanted to know, that there were societies in which women had the kind of powers and authority men have in our own society? With a reasonable degree of unanimity, anthropologists said no. Well, then, continued the questioners, weren't there matriarchies in the past? Here there was somewhat less unanimity among the anthropologists, but by and large no professional scholar in the field was willing to make a strong claim for any past matriarchies either" (p. 139). But she noted that the anthropological consensus fell apart completely when the issue of egalitarian societies was raised. Revisiting her own argument that women's closeness to nature was used as a universal structural principle to justify their subjugation, she later explained that gender egalitarian societies may indeed exist, but "the egalitarianism is complex, inconsistent, and—to some extent—fragile" (p. 175).

Ortner's later position is nuanced in relation to late twentieth-century terminology, which distinguishes between cultural ideologies and cultural practices, and looks at "gender hegemonies" rather than gender dominance. A belief that men are superior to women may be posited in mythology or even institutionalized in the formal ranking of social groups, but it is never total. In many cultures, women have a great deal of power that actually counterbalances claims of male prestige, and notions of charisma and social value are always subject to individual adjustments and reevaluations. Women can in fact have significant amounts of power, authority, autonomy, and prestige in systems where men are the formal leaders, and systems that appear "hegemonically egalitarian" may also contain subtle ways to give men the edge over women in a number of informal contexts.

Joan Bamberger's contribution to *Women, Culture, and Society* argued specifically that myths and legends about female rule were told not because they reflected a previous history of matriarchy (as Bachofen believed) but instead as "social charters" for male dominance. Looking in some detail at a series of myths about the rule of women in Amazonian societies, she found that the myths themselves justify the rule of men "through the evocation of a vision of a catastrophic alternative—a society dominated by women. The myth, in its reiteration that women did not know how to handle power when in possession of it, reaffirms dogmatically the inferiority of their present position" (p. 279). Men stole the sacred objects that gave women supernatural power, and women have since been "forever the subjects of male terrorism," so that these "myths of matriarchy" are in fact arguments for patriarchy.

It is possible that Bamberger's interpretation of myths of matriarchy is a more astute reading of Western mythmakers than of indigenous traditions. The myths and legends that Bachofen surveyed were indeed told in patriarchal Rome and Greece in order to justify the abandonment of matrilineal kinship and certain female-centered cults. But the idea of a simple reversal of gender roles within a similar system of domination and control may obscure other possibilities, which are not so easily reducible to a looking glass inversion of male domination and female subjugation.

Virginia Woolf echoed Bamberger's argument when she wrote in *A Room of her Own*:

Women have served all these centuries as looking glasses possessing the magic and delicious power of reflecting the figure of men at twice its natural size. . . .Whatever may be their use in civilized societies, mirrors are essential to all violent and heroic action. That is why Napoleon and Mussolini both insisted so emphatically on the inferiority

of women, for if they were not inferior, they would cease to enlarge. That serves to explain in part the necessity that women so often are to men." (p. 37)

Early-twenty-first-century research suggests that there is a much wider range of social alternatives than the simple binarism invoked by the terms matriarchy and patriarchy. Looking for a chimeric inversion of Western forms of male domination—which are, as Woolf notes, accentuated in the specific contexts of fascism and imperial conquest—is too limiting, since not all societies treat male/female relations in terms of colonization or domestication. Inequality can be constructed through sexual difference, but when this happens it is useful to recall Marilyn Strathern's argument that gender appears not as an immutable construct, but as a transactable one: "The difference between men and women becomes a vehicle for the creation of value, for evaluating one set of powers by reference to another" (p. 210).

Examined from this perspective, gender as a principle of contrast for social classification does not carry a consistent positive or negative valuation as part of its conceptual baggage. As Third World women and "native anthropologists" become more involved in academic discussions of gender equality, many of them criticize what they call the "false utopias" of the search by European-American feminists for hope and inspiration from exotic others. As Shanshan Du argues: "Ironically, by projecting diverse utopian ideals into cross-cultural studies, the declaration of the non-existence of gender-egalitarian societies became a self-fulfilling prophecy. After all, there is always an unbridgeable gap between a utopian fantasy and a real society because the latter never operates on seamlessly coherent principles" (p. 4). She notes the example of the Crow Indians, who have many egalitarian institutions and ideologies, and where women are at least as prominent as men in many significant rituals. However Western anthropologists described the Crow as "male dominant" because of the existence of a menstrual taboo, although later studies have shown that menstrual taboos are complex and can also serve to empower women and grant them access to certain spiritual powers. Du calls this a "Eurocentric bias" which sets its own standards for sexual "political correctness" and is not sensitive to contextual meanings and configurations.

Alternatives to Matriarchy: Matrism, Gender Egalitarianism, and Diarchy

In order to expand the conceptual tool kit of anthropologists for understanding gender relations in other societies, several writers have proposed alternative terms designed to avoid the simplifications implied by matriarchy. Riane Eisler argues in *The Chalice and the Blade* (1987) that patriarchy and matriarchy are "two sides of the same coin," because both of them involve "the ranking of one half of humanity over the other" (p. xvii). She prefers a partnership model that is "primarily based on the principle of linkage rather than ranking," so that gender differences between men and women can be spoken of in ways that do not equate them with either inferiority or superiority. Instead of matriarchy and patriarchy, Eisler proposes the term *gylany* for societies where gender relations follow the partnership model, and *androcracy* for others characterized by male dominance and ranking relations. Her title derives from symbols for these two paradigms: the chalice, symbolizing life begetting, community, and sharing; and the blade, symbolizing the power to take rather than give life—the militaristic ideal to establish and enforce domination. She represents the Neolothic as an era of peace when people worshipped the goddess, which was then destroyed by the invasion of Hebrews and "Kurgans." The blade came to displace the chalice, and men came to displace women as the central power in the society.

These terms have not been widely adopted, and they are based on the work of Marija Gimbutas, who has excavated hundreds of female figurines from the period 7000 to 3500 B.C.E., which she interprets as mother goddesses. Several archaeologists, such as Ruth Tringham and Margaret Conkey, have argued that her interpretations are highly speculative, but they have had tremendous popular appeal, and her ideal of an early cult of a fertility deity represented as a large, possibly pregnant, woman has been widely disseminated. Gimbutas writes critically of the "indolent assumption" that ancient societies must have resembled those of the present, and presents her own theory that these figurines were produced by groups of people whose social forms she describes as "matristic":

> Indeed we do not find in Old Europe, nor in all of the old world, a system of autocratic rule by women with an equivalent suppression of men. Rather, we find a structure in which the sexes are more or less on equal footing. . . . [T]he sexes are "linked" rather than hierarchically "ranked." I use the term matristic simply to avoid the term matriarchy, with the understanding that it incorporates matriliny. (p. 324)

Gimbutas's work provides an archaeological argument for ideas about the importance of goddesses in early Europe that have also been developed by Robert Graves (1946), and many contemporary neopagans (Adler; Pike). Graves argued that goddess worship coincided with the time when calendars were primarily determined by the moon, and noted the correspondence of the lunar and menstrual cycles, and that the Earth Mother was associated with the Moon Goddess. He traced the changeover to patriarchy with the changeover to the solar calendar and the worship of a solar deity. His work is more a poetic vision of artistic inspiration than a work of scholarship, and has been widely discredited.

Eisler and Gimbutas consider themselves "revisionist" historians who have brought together neglected evidence of a nurturant, female-centered society, but they (like the nineteenth-century evolutionary theorists) base this universalist theory solely on evidence from Europe and the Middle East. Even within that area, their scholarship has been widely criticized as biased, selective, and unscientific, and most anthropologists consider their work to present a view of the "matrist" past as unlikely as their utopian vision of a partnership future. The phenomenon of these revisionist feminist visions is itself of great interest, however, and has proved important in inspiring the neopagan movement, Wicca, and best sellers such as *The DaVinci Code.*

Anthropologists have invoked a number of other terms that are close to matriarchy but not exact equivalents: David Hicks describes the patrilineal Tetum of Viqueque, East Timor as having "a maternal religion," in which men dominate the affairs of the upperworld, but women play a central role in rituals of death, birth, and regeneration. Annette Weiner (1976) describes the Trobrianders of Papua New Guinea as giving value and autonomy to women through their matrilineal institutions, while men travel from island to island to seek renown and political positions of power. She has specifically argued that Bronislaw Malinowski failed to pay attention to certain crucial ways in which Trobriand women played important roles in their society because he focused too exclusively on a male-dominated politics:

> The discovery that Trobriand women have power and that women enact roles which are symbolically, structurally, and functionally significant to the ordering of Trobriand society, and to the roles that men play, should give us, as anthropologists, cause for concern. . . . We have allowed 'politics by men' to structure our thinking about other societies; we have let ourselves believe that, if women are not dominant in the political sphere of interaction, their power remains at best peripheral." (227–228)

Others have been more assertive in presenting case studies that directly counter ideas of pervasive inequality. Maria Lepowsky claims to have discovered on Sudest Island "a sexually egalitarian society that challenges the concept of the universality of male dominance and contests the assumption that the subjugation of women is inevitable" (p. vii). The example of the Vanatinai shows, she argues, that gender equality is possible when there is little emphasis on class, rank, age grades, or other forms of social stratification. The decentralization of political power allows for the equal treatment of all categories of individuals, allowing for a much greater sense of personal autonomy for both women and men, and little formal authority of any one person over another. Strength, wisdom, and magical power are valued as characteristics that enhance communal solidarity, and individuals who have these may become "big women" or "big men" without gender bias. Descent is matrilineal, but its influence is buttressed by gender blind institutions like a bilocal pattern of postmarital residence, in which married couples live alternately with their two natal families for many years. So this egalitarianism is defined more by a respect for idiosyncrasy and the absence of formal structure than by a positive value attached to women.

Studies of bilateral societies in Indonesia where gender receives relatively little emphasis, such as the Wana of Sulawesi (Atkinson) or the Meratus of Kalimantan (Tsing), also document a lack of any formal ideology about male supremacy, and ideas of gender crossing (male "pregnancy," female shamans speaking in male voices) that suggest gender is not conceptualized as fixed. Ortner (1996) compares these to the example of the Andaman Islanders, who had a clear but balanced division of labor (men hunted, women gathered), and a spiritual world in which supernatural beings of both sexes played significant, generally complementary, and sometimes reversible roles, with one deity of variable—but usually female—gender who seemed to represent fertility. All of these societies can be described as gender balanced and flexible, in which men and women were allowed to participate equally in all forms of social relations, but men nevertheless tended to emerge as leaders in some of these domains.

Feminist scholars such as Ortner, Atkinson, and Tsing stress religion and ideology in their portraits, while scholars in the Marxist tradition build on the work of Engels to argue that nonstratified societies in which both sexes have control over the means of production and their own labors are gender egalitarian. Eleanor Leacock (1978) argues that many precapitalist societies were egalitarian, and Karen Sacks (1979) suggests that, when relating to each other as siblings rather than spouses, men and women can be institutionally equal even in patrilineal, patrilocal societies.

Two early-twenty-first-century ethnographies by Chinese scholars bring together Marxist and symbolic approaches to argue that gender equality is possible and often found in the minority groups of the Chinese highlands. Shanshan Du's *"Chopsticks Only Work in Pairs"* (2001) stresses complementarity among the Lahu people in Yunnan and the importance of the husband-wife dyad in kinship, labor, and social leadership. She argues that mythology and religion reflect a "dyadic world view," based on cooperation between men and women, since "a single chopstick cannot pick up food" (p. 30). Lahu origin myths feature cross-sex twins who combine male and female attributes in an image of overarching power. While her account places heavy value on the marital unit, Cai Hua's *A Society without Fathers or Husbands: The Na of China* (2003) looks at another group near the Burmese border where brothers and sisters live their whole lives together, raising the sister's children, and reproduce through short term "visits" which are never socially sanctioned as marriage. This arrangement does give women greater autonomy than the traditional Confucian family, and also challenges the usual anthropological orthodoxy about the universality of male-female pair bonding. Hua argues that in this society "sexuality is not a piece of merchandise but a purely sentimental and amorous matter that implies no mutual constraints" (Hua, p. 181). The Na, like the famous Nayar of India studied by Kathleen Gough (Schneider and Gough), are matrilineal, and have resisted communist efforts to bring then into mainstream values. The sibling relationship defines the household completely, and visiting lovers have no connection with the family, have no responsibilities, and do not acknowledge their fatherhood; the children, in turn, do not know their fathers.

Another alternative to matriarchy that works with dyads and sibling symbolism is diarchy, which some scholars grouped with egalitarian structures as a form of "partnership societies." Diarchic societies are marked by a pervasive system of symbolic gender dualisms, "an ideology of balanced powers" in which the members of the male/female pair are ordered by difference and interdependence, rather than dominance and subjugation (Hoskins, 1988, p. 51). A doctrine of mutuality and shared concerns is expressed in ideas of delegation and oscillating rule.

European travelers to the Amazonian jungle and the New Guinea highlands encountered "myths of matriarchy" that presented an apparent confirmation of their own fantasies of Amazon warrior princesses and Melanesian "free love." But travelers in the Indonesian archipelago who visited the islands of Sumba, Flores, Timor, and Savu found a mixture of matrilineal and patrilineal groups who shared an ideology of dual governance often express as a "male ruler" and "female ruler," or—even more paradoxically—a man specifically referred to as a woman who held a position of sovereignty. This pattern had first been documented in Indian kinship, where Georges Dumezil described the idea that "sovereignty aligns itself in two planes, at once antithetical and complementary," and it is also found in Chinese and Vietnamese popular religion. The division between spiritual authority and temporal power was predicated on the conceptual opposition between female and male, in a pattern also familiar in Polynesia.

The complementarity of diarchic systems operates with the principles of male and female as abstract entities, and associates them with ideas of a proper balance of action and passivity. Women are typically associated with origins, fertility of the earth, and human reproduction, while men are associated with military and executive power, differentiation, and rank. Diarchic divisions assign to the female principle an equal role in the creation of the world, but at times the passivity of their role as Earth Mother may seem to place real women at a disadvantage, bound by the restrictions inherent to their ritual prominence. Among the Kodi of Sumba, for instance, the conceptually female priestess of the Sea Worms is secluded for several months before the rice harvest to protect the crop. In the early-twenty-first-century, a man, who is both empowered and restricted by the central symbolic role he plays, is cast as the priestess.

Gender dualism, which can be defined for comparative purposes by the formal requirement that a female and male component be included in each unifying hierarchical entity, is found throughout Eastern Indonesia. It occurs in patrilineal as well as matrilineal societies, and coexists with polygyny, occasional violence against women, and male leadership, so it is not necessarily a vision of gender equality, but it does highlight interdependence and complementarity. The importance of opposite sex couples, portrayed as parents, siblings, or ancestors, in Eastern Indonesian sexual imagery is an index of the value given to heterosexual relations, and what can only be called a vision of sexual union—the bringing together of male and female in an act of pleasure, release, and potential reproduction.

Are the Minangkabau a Modern Matriarchy?

In 2002 Peggy Sanday revived controversies about the anthropological use of the term matriarchy by titling her study of Minagkabau gender relations *Women at the Center: Life in a Modern Matriarchy*. Well aware that the term had been rejected by serious scholars for about a century, she provocatively decided to challenge this usage with an argument that matriarchy should be redefined to correspond to the usage of a Dutch-Indonesian term (*adat matriarchaal*) used by roughly 8 million Minangkabau to describe their own customs. The Minangkabau are one of the world's largest matrilineal societies, and they are also almost all committed Muslims in the nation with the largest Islamic population in the world. While Sanday describes the term as an "indigenous category," its early-twenty-first-century use is obviously the hybrid result of several centuries of dialogue with European traders, scholars, and administrators, who have long been intrigued by the mixture of matriliny and Muslim piety found in the Minang homeland in Sumatra, Indonesia.

Sanday argues that

the definition of matriarchy as the control of political power by women should be abandoned in favor of a definition emphasizing the role of maternal symbols in webs of cultural significance. The focus should be on the structure and content of dominant gender symbols, not just the linked relationship between the sexes as Eisler suggests. The partnership is important, but it alone does not define matriarchy because there are at least three types of symbolic structures representing gender in partnership societies: egalitarian, diarchic and matiarchic. Egalitarian structures are those in which gender differences are not symbolically marked, although sex differences may play a role in the division of labor. Diarchic societies are marked by a pervasive system of symbolic gender dualisms, Matriarchic structures, like those of the Minangkabau, are based on a maternal model. In all three, although the content of the symbols differ, male and female function as two equal halves of the larger whole and neither dominates the other. (p. 236)

The Minangkabau have been the focus of many anthropological and historical studies, but no other contemporary scholar has chosen to describe them as matriarchic. While Sanday's claims are based on long-term ethnographic research, her colleagues have not for the most part been convinced that such a change in terminology is needed or helpful.

Sanday notes that her usage is in some ways a return to the original Greek meaning of the term. The root *matri,* from the Latin *mater,* means "mother, nurse, origin, source," while the suffix *archy,* from the Greek *arche,* refers to "beginning, foundation, source of action, first principle," and also the idea of "political power, rule, control of the state" (p. 237). Sanday says Mingkabau customs correspond to the first meaning, while they do not fulfill the conditions of the second. She calls for a new cross-cultural definition of matriarchy as "cultural symbols and practices associating the maternal with origin and center of the growth processes necessary for social and individual life" (p. 237). According to this definition, many of the societies studied by gender researchers—the Trobriand Islanders, the Vanatinai of Sudest Island, the Crow Indians, the Lahu and Na of southern China, and the Tetum of Vicenque, Timor—might qualify as matriarchies, since they do emphasize maternal symbols and nurturance, although in many other ways they are quite different from each other.

The use of matriarchy as an umbrella term for societies that value women's reproductive and nurturing powers seems too broad to be of much use for comparative purposes. What

Sanday wants to call matriarchic has been described by Annette Weiner as "woman focused" (1976), by Sherry Ortner as an "egalitarian hegemony," by Karen Sacks as a "sister-based society," and by Eleanor Leacock as a "precapitalist form of sexual equality." It is also close to the sacred ideals of the Okinawans of Japan (Sered), the dualistic Kodi of Sumba (Hoskins, 1993, 1998), and the highland Wana and Meratus of the Indonesian islands of Sulawesi and Kalimantan (Atkinson; Tsing). All of these examples provide evidence for diversity of gender relations that cannot be reduced to a simple stereotype of male supremacy, but which are also stubbornly idiosyncratic and unlike each other in important ways. Anthropology has long been a celebration of difference, and while it does need a comparative vocabulary, this vocabulary is only helpful if it is very rigorously defined. Expanding the notion of matriarchy beyond its largely discredited nineteenth-century significance does not seem to advance this process.

See also **Family; Feminism; Gender; Kinship; Motherhood and Maternity; Womanism.**

BIBLIOGRAPHY

Atkinson, Jane. "How Gender Makes a Difference in Wana Society." In *Power and Difference: Gender in Island Southeast Asia,* edited by Jane Atkinson, and Shelly Errington, 59–94. Stanford, Calif.: Stanford University Press, 1990.

Bachofen, J. J. *Myth, Religion and Mother Right: Selected Writings of J. J. Bachofen.* Translated by Ralph Manheim. Princeton, N.J.: Princeton University Press, 1967.

Bamberger, Joan. "The Myth of Matriarchy: Why Men Rule in Primitive Society." In *Women, Culture, and Society,* edited by Michelle Rosaldo, and Louise Lamphere, 263–280. Stanford, Calif.: Stanford University Press, 1974.

Buckley, Thomas, and Alma Gottlieb, eds. *Blood Magic: The Anthropology of Menstruation.* Berkeley: University of California Press, 1988.

Du, Shanshan. *"Chopsticks Only Work In Pairs": Gender Unity and Gender Equality among the Lahu of Southwest China.* New York: Columbia University Press, 2002.

Engels, Friedrich. *The Origin of the Family, Private Property and the State.* 1884. Reprint, with an introduction and notes by Eleanor Leacock. Translated by Alan West. New York: International Publishers, 1972.

Eisler, Riane. *The Chalice and the Blade: Our History.* Cambridge, Mass.: Harper and Row, 1987.

Gewertz, Deborah, ed. *Myths of Matriarchy Reconsidered.* Oceania Monographs. Sydney, Australia: University of Sydney, 1988.

Gimbutas, Marija. *The Civilization of the Goddess: The World of Old Europe.* San Francisco: HarperSanFrancisco, 1991.

Graves, Robert. *The White Goddess: A Historical Grammar of Poetic Myth.* London: Creative Age Press, 1948.

Hicks, David. *A Maternal Religion: The Role of Women in Tetun Myth and Ritual.* Special report no. 22. DeKalb, Ill., and Detroit, Mich.: Northern Illinois University, Center for Southeast Asian Studies, 1984.

Hoskins, Janet. *Biographical Objects: How Things Tell the Story of People's Lives.* Routledge Press, 1998.

———. *Blood Mysteries: Beyond Menstruation as Pollution.* Special issue of *Ethnology* XLI, no. 4 (2002).

———. "Matriarchy and Diarchy: Indonesian Variations on the Domestication of the Savage Woman." In *Myths of Matriarchy Re-*

considered, edited by Deborah Gewertz, 34–57. Oceania Monographs. Sydney, Australia: University of Sydney Press, 1988.

———. *The Play of Time: Kodi Perspectives on Calendars, History, and Exchange.* Berkeley: University of California Press, 1993.

Hua, Cai. *A Society Without Fathers or Husbands: The Na of China.* Translated from the French by Asti Hustvedt. New York: Zone Books, distributed by MIT Press, 2001.

Leacock, Eleanor. "Interpreting the Origins of Gender Inequality: Conceptual and Historical Problems." *Dialectical Anthropology* 7 (1983): 263–284.

Lepowsky, Maria. *Fruit of the Motherland: Gender in an Egalitarian Society.* New York: Columbia University Press, 1993.

Morgan, Lewis Henry. *Ancient Society.* 1877. Reprint, edited and with an introduction by Lesley White. Cambridge, Mass.: Belknap Press of Harvard University Press, 1964.

Ortner, Sherry. *Making Gender: The Politics and Erotics of Culture.* Boston: Beacon Press, 1996.

Pike, Sarah. *Earthly Bodies, Magical Selves: Contemporary Pagans and The Search for Community.* Berkeley: University of California Press, 2001.

Rosaldo, Michelle, and Louise Lamphere. "Introduction." In *Women, Culture and Society,* edited by Michelle Rosaldo and Louise Lamphere, 3–15. Stanford, Calif.: Stanford University Press, 1974.

Sacks, Karen. *Sisters and Wives: The Past and Future of Sexual Equality.* Westport, Conn.: Greenwood Press, 1979.

Sanday, Peggy Reeves. *Women at the Center: Life in a Modern Matriarchy.* Ithaca, N.Y.: Cornell University, 2002.

Schneider, David. "Introduction: The Distinctive Features of Matrilineal Descent Groups." In *Matrilineal Kinship,* edited by David Schneider and Kathleen Gough, 1–29. Berkeley: University of California Press, 1961.

Strathern, Marilyn. "Conclusions." In *Dealing with Inequality: Analysing Gender Relations in Melanesia and Beyond,* edited by Marilyn Strathern. Cambridge, U.K.: Cambridge University Press, 1987.

Tringham, Ruth, and Margaret Conkey. "Rethinking Figurines: A Critical View from Archaeology of Gimbutas, the 'Goddess' and Popular Culture." In *Ancient Goddesses: The Myths and the Evidence,* edited by Lucy Goodison, and Christine Morris, 22–45. Madison: University of Wisconsin Press, 1999.

Tsing, Anna Lowenhaupt. "Gender and Performance in Meratus Dispute Settlement." In J. Atkinson and S. Errington, eds. *Power and Difference: Gender in Island Southeast Asia,* edited by Jane Atkinson, and Shelly Errington. Stanford: Stanford University Press, 1990.

Tylor, E. B. The Matriarchal Family System. *Nineteenth Century* 40 (1896): 81–96.

Weiner, Annette B. *Women of Value, Men of Renown: New Perspectives in Trobriand Exchange.* Austin: University of Texas Press, 1976.

Janet Hoskins

MATTER AND FORMS OF MATTER. *See* **Physics.**

MECHANICAL PHILOSOPHY. The mechanical philosophy was a philosophy of nature, popular in the seventeenth century, that sought to explain all natural phenomena in terms of matter and motion without recourse to any kind of action at a distance (cause and effect without any physical contact). During the sixteenth and seventeenth centuries, many natural philosophers rejected Aristotelianism, which had provided the form of and foundations for natural philosophy at least since the thirteenth century. The mechanical philosophy, which was rooted in ancient Greek atomism, was one candidate for a new philosophy. Atomism was the theory that everything in the material world consists of imperceptible, solid, indivisible bits of matter—atoms—that move about in empty space. Not all mechanical philosophers were strict atomists, but they attempted to explain all natural phenomena in terms of the configurations, motions, and collisions of small, unobservable particles of matter. A central doctrine of the mechanical philosophy was the theory of primary and secondary qualities, according to which matter is really endowed with only a few primary qualities and all others (such as color, taste, or odor) are the result of the impact of the primary qualities on human sense organs. Nature was thus mechanized and most qualities were considered subjective.

Background

The mechanical philosophy derived from the views of the Greek philosopher Epicurus (341–271 B.C.E.), who sought the key to the good life. He considered the good life to be one that maximizes pleasure and minimizes pain. Epicurus believed that the greatest sources of human unhappiness, apart from bodily pain, are fear of the gods and anxiety about punishment after death. To eliminate these causes of distress, he sought to explain all natural phenomena in naturalistic terms—the chance collisions of material atoms in empty space (his version of atomism), thus eliminating the gods' interference in human lives. He claimed that the human soul is material, composed of atoms that are exceedingly small and swift. The Epicurean soul did not survive death. Thus there is no reason to fear punishment in the afterlife. Epicurus believed that the atoms have always existed and that they are infinite in number. Epicureanism, while not strictly atheistic, denied that the gods play a role in the natural or human worlds, thus ruling out any kind of divine intervention in human life or providence in the world. Because of its reputation as atheistic and materialistic, Epicureanism fell into disrepute during the Christian Middle Ages. The writings of Epicurus and his Roman disciple Lucretius (c. 96–c. 55 B.C.E.) were recovered and published during the Renaissance, which began in fourteenth-century Italy.

Following the development of heliocentric astronomy in the late sixteenth and early seventeenth centuries, many natural philosophers believed that Aristotelianism, which rests on geocentric assumptions, could no longer provide adequate foundations for natural philosophy. Among the many ancient philosophies that were recovered by Renaissance humanists, Epicurean atomism seemed particularly compatible with the spirit of the new astronomy and physics. Early advocates of the mechanical philosophy included David van Goorle (1591–1612), Sebastian Basso (fl. 1550–1600), Galileo Galilei (1564–1642), and various members of the Northumberland Circle of which Walter Warner (c. 1557–c. 1642), Thomas Harriot (1560–1621), and Nicholas Hill (c. 1570–1610) were members. Although each of these men favored some version of atomism, none of them developed a systematic philosophy. Isaac Beeckman (1588–1637), a Dutch schoolmaster, advocated a mechanical view of nature and wrote about it extensively in his private journal, which was not published until the twentieth century. Beeckman's personal influence was enormous, however, and he was instrumental in encouraging a pair of French natural philosophers, Pierre Gassendi (1592–1655) and René Descartes (1596–1650), to adopt the mechanical philosophy.

Major Advocates of the Mechanical Philosophy

Gassendi and Descartes published the first systematic and the most influential accounts of the mechanical philosophy. Their treatises spelled out the fundamental terms of the mechanical philosophy and functioned as programmatic statements, describing what such a philosophy would look like in practice. Although both men agreed that all physical phenomena should be explained in terms of matter and motion, they differed about the details.

Gassendi believed that God had created indivisible atoms and endowed them with motion. The atoms, colliding in empty space (the void), are the constituents of the physical world. In his massive *Syntagma philosophicum* (published posthumously in 1658; Philosophical treatise), Gassendi set out to explain all the qualities of matter and all the phenomena in the world in terms of atoms and the void. He argued for the existence of the void—a controversial claim at the time—on both conceptual and empirical grounds, appealing to recent barometric experiments of Evangelista Torricelli (1608–1647) and Blaise Pascal (1623–1662). The primary qualities of Gassendi's atoms were size, shape, and mass. He attempted to explain all the qualities of bodies—light, color, sound, taste, smell, heaviness, and lightness—in atomic terms. Among the qualities he included were the so-called occult qualities, which seemed to involve action at a distance and had generally resisted explanation in mechanical terms. After laying the foundations for his philosophy, Gassendi gave an account of the entire creation: the heavens, the inanimate world, the animate world, and the human soul.

Writing in the manner of a Renaissance humanist, Gassendi saw himself as the restorer of the philosophy of Epicurus. Deeply concerned with Epicurus's heterodox ideas, Gassendi, a Catholic priest, sought to modify ancient atomism so that it would be acceptable to seventeenth-century Christians. Accordingly, he insisted on God's creation of a finite number of atoms, on God's continuing providential relationship to the creation, on free will (both human and divine), and on the existence of an immaterial, immortal human soul that, he claimed, God infuses into each individual at the moment of conception.

Gassendi was not a materialist. He argued for the existence of an incorporeal, immortal soul and also believed in the existence of incorporeal angels and demons. In addition to the immaterial, immortal soul, Gassendi claimed that there exists a material, sensible soul, composed of very fine and swiftly moving particles. This material soul (which animals also possess) is responsible for vitality, perception, and the less abstract aspects of understanding. The material soul is transmitted from one generation to the next in the process of biological reproduction. Gassendi's ideas were brought to England by Walter Charleton (1620–1707) and popularized in France by François Bernier (1620–1688).

Although Descartes also articulated a full-fledged mechanical philosophy in his *Principia philosophiae* (1644; Principles of philosophy), his ideas were quite different from Epicurean atomism. Impressed by the rigor of mathematical reasoning and Galileo's mathematization of physics, Descartes wanted to develop a mathematical approach to the mechanical philosophy. In contrast to Gassendi's atomism, Descartes was a plenist, claiming that matter fills all space. He claimed tht matter is infinitely divisible, thus denying the existence of both atoms and the void. He believed that matter possesses only one primary quality, geometrical extension. This belief provided foundations for his attempted mathematization of nature. Descartes drew a sharp distinction between matter and mind, considering thinking to be the essential characteristic of the mind. Like Gassendi's doctrine of the immortal soul, Descartes's concept of mind established the boundaries of mechanization in the world.

Descartes attempted to deduce the laws of motion—the conservation of motion and the principle of inertia—from first principles. From the laws of motion, he attempted to derive mathematical laws of impact. Although these laws were inadequate, even in seventeenth-century terms, their prominent place in his system reflects their importance in a mechanical philosophy, according to which contact and impact are the only causes in the physical world. Having established the physics that he considered fundamental to his system, Descartes proceeded to give mechanical explanations of all the phenomena in the world, including cosmology, light, the qualities of material things, and even the human body.

Like Gassendi, Descartes intended his philosophy to replace Aristotelianism. He hoped that the Jesuit colleges would adopt the *Principia philosophiae* as a physics textbook in place of the Aristotelian texts still in use. His hopes were dashed posthumously, however, when the Roman Catholic Church condemned his book in 1662 and then placed it on the Index of prohibited books one year later, in response to his attempt to give a mechanical explanation of Real Presence (the doctrine holding that Christ is actually present in the Eucharist).

William Harvey (1578–1657), a medical practitioner and teacher, inspired Descartes's mechanical philosophy by his experimental proof of the circulation of the blood, published in *Exercitationes Anatomica de Motu Cordis et Sanduinis in Animalibus* (1628). Harvey's natural philosophy was actually more Aristotelian than mechanical, a point manifest in his work on embryology, in which he adopted an Aristotelian explanation of generation—epigenesis, according to which the embryo is formed from the fluids contributed by both parents in the process of reproduction. Nevertheless, impressed by Harvey's use of mechanical analogies to describe the flow of blood, Descartes attempted to develop a complete physiology based on his own mechanical principles. Gassendi was not convinced by Harvey's evidence and rejected the circulation of the blood.

Another mechanical philosopher, Thomas Hobbes (1588–1679), was the specter haunting more orthodox natural philosophers. Hobbes's philosophy seemed—to the seventeenth-century reader—to be materialistic, deterministic, and possibly even atheistic. In *The Elements of Philosophy* (1642–1658), Hobbes propounded a complete philosophy—of matter, of man, and of the state—according to mechanistic principles. Although the details of his mechanical philosophy were not very influential among natural philosophers, his mechanical account of the human soul and his thoroughly deterministic account of the natural world alarmed the more orthodox thinkers of his day. His claims underscored their fears that the mechanical philosophy would lead to materialism, deism, and even atheism.

Later Developments

Gassendi and Descartes set the agenda for the next generation of natural philosophers, who accepted mechanical principles in general, believing that they had to choose between Gassendi's atomism and Descartes's plenism. Robert Boyle (1627–1691), Christiaan Huygens (1629–1695), and Isaac Newton (1642–1727), among the most prominent natural philosophers of the second half of the seventeenth century, developed their philosophies of nature in this context.

Boyle is best known for his attempt to incorporate chemistry within a mechanical framework. His corpuscular philosophy—which remained noncommittal on the question of whether matter is infinitely divisible or composed of indivisible atoms—was founded on a mechanical conception of matter. His reluctance to commit himself about the ultimate nature of matter reflected his concern about the atheism still associated with Epicureanism as well as his recognition that some questions lie beyond the ability of human reason to resolve. Material bodies are, according to Boyle, composed of extremely small particles, which combine to form clusters of various sizes and configurations. The configurations, motions, and collisions of these clusters produce secondary qualities, including the chemical properties of matter. Boyle conducted many observations and experiments aiming to demonstrate that various chemical properties can be explained mechanically. He performed an extensive series of experiments with the newly fabricated air pump to prove that the properties of air—most notably its "spring"—could be explained in mechanical terms.

Huygens followed Descartes in attempting to mathematize physics and the mechanical philosophy. He applied this approach to create a wave theory of light, a mathematical analysis of centrifugal force, and an improved theory of impact. He applied mathematics to physical problems far more successfully than had Descartes.

Newton, whose reputation rests on his achievements in mathematical physics and optics, accepted the mechanical philosophy from his student days at Cambridge University. A notebook written in the mid-1660s shows him thinking about natural phenomena in mechanical terms and designing thought experiments for choosing between Cartesian and Gassendist explanations of particular phenomena. A number of phenomena—including gravitation, the reflection and refraction of light, surface tension, capillary action, and certain chemical reactions—persistently resisted explanation in purely mechanical terms. Failing in the attempt to explain them by appeal to hypotheses about submicroscopic "aethers," Newton was led to the view that there exist attractive and repulsive forces between the particles composing bodies. This idea came to him from his alchemical studies. Newton's most notable discovery, the principle of universal gravitation, which provided a unified foundation for both terrestrial and celestial mechanics and which marks the culmination of developments started by Nicolaus Copernicus in the mid-sixteenth century, demanded a concept of attractive force. The concept of force, which seemed to some contemporaries to be a return to older theories of action at a distance that had been banished by the mechanical philosophy, enabled Newton to accomplish his stunning mathematization of physics and thereby fulfill the primary goal of the mechanical philosophy.

In the decades after Newton's death, the worst fears of the Christian mechanical philosophers of the seventeenth century came true. John Locke (1632–1704) argued for the reasonableness of Christianity, and his environmentalist analysis of the human mind—which grew directly from the ideas of the mechanical philosophers—implied the denial of the Christian doctrine of original sin. Deism and natural religion flourished both in England and on the Continent.

Debates about theories of generation became inextricably connected to philosophical and theological implications of the mechanical philosophy. While advocates of epigenesis tended to adopt vitalistic theories of life, theories that invoked some kind of nonmechanical entity to explain the properties of living things, another theory of generation, known as preformationism, seemed to be more compatible with the mechanical philosophy. Preformationism maintained that all living things existed within their ancestors, created by God at the beginning of life with a precise moment established for each one to emerge and become alive. Although preformationism was compatible with both divine providence and the doctrine of original sin, it also raised the specter of materialism that haunted the mechanical philosophy.

Some of the French philosophes, notably Julien Offroy de La Mettrie (1709–1751) and Paul-Henri-Dietrich d'Holbach (1723–1789), espoused atheistic materialism and also adopted vigorously anticlerical and antiecclesiastical views. David Hume (1711–1776) undermined the possibility of natural religion and a providential understanding of the world by demonstrating the invalidity of the standard arguments for the existence of God, particularly the argument from design that had played such a crucial role for the seventeenth-century mechanical philosophers. Newtonian mechanics rose to great heights, having shed the theological preoccupations of its creator. These developments culminated in the work of Pierre Simon Laplace (1749–1827), who articulated a clear statement of classical determinism and was able to demonstrate that the solar system is a gravitationally stable Newtonian system. When asked by Napoléon Bonaparte what role God played in his system, Laplace is reputed to have replied, "I have no need for that hypothesis."

See also **Aristotelianism; Cartesianism; Humanism; Newtonianism.**

BIBLIOGRAPHY

Dobbs, Betty Jo Teeter. *The Janus Faces of Genius: The Role of Alchemy in Newton's Thought.* Cambridge, U.K.: Cambridge University Press, 1991.

French, Roger. *William Harvey's Natural Philosophy.* Cambridge, U.K.: Cambridge University Press, 1994.

Garber, Daniel. *Descartes' Metaphysical Physics.* Chicago: University of Chicago Press, 1992.

Hutchison, Keith. "What Happened to Occult Qualities in the Scientific Revolution?" *Isis* 73, no. 2 (1982): 233–253.

Kargon, Robert Hugh. *Atomism in England from Hariot to Newton.* Oxford: Clarendon Press, 1966.

Lüthy, Christoph, John E. Murdoch, and William R. Newman, eds. *Late Medieval and Early Modern Corpuscular Matter Theory.* Leiden, Netherlands: Brill, 2001.

Mintz, Samuel I. *The Hunting of Leviathan: Seventeenth-Century Reactions to the Materialism and Moral Philosophy of Thomas Hobbes.* Cambridge, U.K.: Cambridge University Press, 1962.

Osler, Margaret J. *Divine Will and the Mechanical Philosophy: Gassendi and Descartes on Contingency and Necessity in the Created World.* Cambridge, U.K.: Cambridge University Press, 1994.

Westfall, Richard S. *The Construction of Modern Science: Mechanisms and Mechanics.* New York: Wiley, 1971.

———. *Never at Rest: A Biography of Isaac Newton.* Cambridge, U.K.: Cambridge University Press, 1980.

Margaret J. Osler

MEDIA, HISTORY OF.

MEDIA, HISTORY OF. The term *media history* is almost a tautology when the historic is distinguished from the prehistoric by the presence of recording media. History is always already mediated. A distinct domain of historiography whose object is human communication technologies will to this extent always be tempted to assimilate all human history to itself. Among late-twentieth- and early-twenty-first-century media historians, this principle has advanced to the stage at which alternative programs for understanding human activity—terms such as society, culture, economy, and power—appear as either abstractions lacking the empirical bases of media and mediation, or as derivatives of them. Media history, it can be argued, explains society, culture, and politics better than those concepts explain media.

Periodization

The most common periodization employed distinguishes at the minimum oral and literate phases, indicating that oral communication (along with gesture, dance, potlatch, and other features of orality) are to be included as media. Aristotle's definition of the human being as the *zoon politikon* clearly regards humans as properly belonging to a polis or community, but also indicates that humans are distinguished by communication since, as Claude Lévi-Strauss was at pains to demonstrate, and as the Latin etymologies suggest, there can be no conception of a community without communication, and vice versa. To this extent media history must be one of the central disciplines of the human sciences, embracing not only literary and linguistic studies, but sociology, political science, economics, and the discipline of history itself.

The story of media history is the tale of the long struggle for existence of a materialist understanding of human interaction. The central challenge has been (and remains) the task of shedding idealist conceptualizations like society and culture in favor of tracing the embodied forms in which they are constructed and lived. However, this project is hampered by the sheer scope of the enterprise. The practice of media history takes two major forms: the macroscopic address to the vast accumulation of human media artifacts on the one hand, and detailed investigations of specific conjunctures in the history of specific media on the other. The former is constantly plagued by the temptation of vast generalization, the latter constrained to merely local findings whose contribution to a general theory of media history is therefore rarely clear.

Like that of all historiography, the objective of media history is to understand historical process. The majority of media historians are explicit in adding that the reason for undertaking this task is to guide the emergence of future media or to warn against the outcomes of long- or short-term trends, a linear model with associations to teleologies of both progress and apocalypse. Umberto Eco distinguishes between apocalyptic and "integrated" scholars of the media. The former blame not individual media texts but whole media technologies for the loss or destruction of older values; the latter embrace everything new as proof of progress toward some ultimate good. In the work of the best-known among media historians, Marshall McLuhan (1911–1980), the narrative of evolution has an interestingly spiral dimension, returning in heightened form to its oral origin in the figure of the electronic "global village" (pp. 166–167). A noted Joyce scholar, McLuhan may have derived the spiral form of history from Joyce's source, Giambattista Vico (1688–1744). Be that as it may, he shares with other teleological media historians a mystical belief in eternal return or in millenarian thought that responds to a heartfelt longing for historical symmetry.

McLuhan's spiral might be seen as syncretic, even atavistic. His teacher, Harold Innis, perhaps as a result of his experience of trench warfare in Europe, had a far simpler and more immediately political teleology. Innis divided media into heavy, durable media like stone tablets, suited to carrying ideas through time, and light, ephemeral media like parchment, more suited to spatial dissemination. Though the oral tradition had a strongly conservative function before the invention of writing, afterwards its role became one of swift adaptation. Concluding his study *Empire and Communications,* Innis calls for "determined efforts to recapture the vitality of the oral tradition" (p. 170), appealing to the traditions of common law to equilibrate what, in 1950, appeared as the triumph of spatial over temporal media. Integrated critics are rarely so openly committed to utopian political projects for reform or remaking of the media. An avowed belief in the inevitability of progress is once again a widespread phenomenon, not only in the pages of hip corporate culture magazines like *Wired* but especially among respected scholars of digital media, most of all those who, like Roy Ascott, are also committed teachers and creative activists.

Technology and the "General Accident"

Even less convinced of the need for or efficacy of planning and action are the apocalyptic critics, foremost among them today Jean Baudrillard and, increasingly, Paul Virilio. Baudrillard traces media history in four phases: (1) it is the reflection of a profound reality; (2) it masks and denatures a profound reality; (3) it masks the absence of a profound reality; (4) it has no relation to any reality whatsoever: it is its own pure simulacrum (Baudrillard, 1994, p. 6 and 1983, p. 11). In later writing Baudrillard, like Debord, suggests that, far from integration, we are doomed to the disintegration of media and world alike. Since Baudrillard concentrates only on the representational functions of the media, he is blind to their communicative roles and is determinedly centered on the industrialized world. Widely read when television was still the dominant medium, his work has been eclipsed in the rise of telecommunication toward hegemony among media in the early twenty-first century. More persuasive, perhaps because less nihilistic, Paul Virilio argues that the invention of railways was also the invention of the train wreck, that of automobiles of the car crash, and that the assimilation of all our media into a unified digital circulation leads inexorably to what he calls the rapidly approaching "general accident." Prefigured by the atom bomb and the information bomb, the genetic bomb is the latest cataclysm waiting to occur, all of them motivated by and dependent upon the mass mediation of speed and the concomitant abolition of time. The proximity of Virilio's conclusions to those of Innis is deceptive: where Innis saw the grounds for active engagement in the reconstruction of contemporary media, Virilio sees an unavoidable Armageddon.

Innis and McLuhan are not the only figures who ground contemporary media history. Unwelcome because of his Nazi heritage, Martin Heidegger (1889–1976) is nonetheless the silent foundation of much continental media history. In his 1954 essay on "The Question Concerning Technology," technology figures on the one hand as an ordering of materials, an instrumental relation to the world that blocks our understanding of it. On the other hand, as a collection of devices that ensure survival, technology is ultimately in the service of humankind becoming the one species in whom the coming-to-being of the world can be realized.

Technology at its best thus serves its own ultimate overcoming (a conclusion distressingly close to Heidegger's ideological consorts in the Nazi Party). In Virilio's terms, the data crash is the necessary precondition for the self-realization of the world. In another essay, Heidegger prefigures Virilio's critique of the sedentarization of Western society, blaming television for "the abolition of every possible remoteness" (1971, p. 165). The industrialization of media in the form of standard delivery systems (an unchanging receiver frames all the changing content of television), unlimited replicability, and instantaneous broadcast appear to apocalyptics as signals of a collapse, of reality or humanity or both, into an undifferentiated and unchanging sameness. A similar thought undergirds some theories of cultural imperialism and globalization. The apparent novelty of the position is undermined by a reading of Plato's *Phaedrus,* where Socrates tells the story of Thamus's indignant critique of writing when the new technology was

brought to him by Theuth: "What you have discovered is a receipt for recollection, not for memory. And as for wisdom, your pupils will have the reputation for it without the reality" (p. 184). Like Plato, Heidegger appears to believe in some form of original sin inhering in the medium he critiques. This thought is more nearly explicit in Heidegger's pupil Hans-Georg Gadamer, who notes, for example, that "Literary art can be understood only from the ontology of the work of art, and not from the aesthetic experiences that occur in the course of the reading" (p. 161). This holds true not only of a text that retains its integrity regardless of the form in which it is read or performed, but of the written medium from the beginning.

Historical and Technological Media

A more subtle strand of media history than this blunt confrontation of integrated and apocalyptic critics arises in the work of the Frankfurt School, the most influential essay here being Walter Benjamin's "Work of Art in the Age of Mechanical Reproduction" (1969). Benjamin's periodization does not concern the transition from oral to literate but from the unique object to serial production, and his concern is with the consequent loss of "aura," of sanctity and intrinsic value, which media artifacts undergo as a result. Confronting the rise of fascism and contesting the Stalinization of Popular Front cultural policy in the 1930s, Benjamin argues for both the utopian capacities of popular media and the necessity to engage with them as vanguard arenas of creative endeavor. Perhaps the most significant response appears in a letter responding to the draft manuscript written by Theodor Adorno, arguing that popular and avant-garde are "torn halves of an integral freedom to which, however, they do not add up" (1977, p. 123). In his joint work with Max Horkheimer and in other later writings, Adorno elaborates and develops this insight into media history, concluding in 1953 that under contemporary conditions, "people become welded to the unavoidable . . . television makes once again into what they already are, only more so" (1998, p. 50). This vision of industrial and technological media in the service of the status quo is more thoroughly historicized in Jürgen Habermas's influential account of the formation and deformation of the public sphere, created at the time of the European Enlightenment through the power of the printing press, and distorted into mere opinion polling in the age of mass circulation newsprint, radio, and television. A similar thesis, inspired more specifically by the analysis of reification in Georg Lukacs, is expressed by the French situationist Guy Debord, for whom the age of commodity production had, between the Wall Street crash of 1929 and the late 1960s, given way to an age of spectacle. Where earlier media formations had served to gather people into communities, to conserve traditions, and to propagandize new ways of living, spectacular media serve to promote an endless round of imaginary desires that in turn maintain endless overconsumption through which the overproduction required for the survival of capitalism can be regulated. Unlike Baudrillard, Debord—a convinced Hegelian—believed in the necessity of a dialectical resolution to this sham culture.

Ubiquitous Media

Such macroscopic accounts of media history must be balanced against the increasing amount of scholarship devoted to unearthing and revaluing the histories of specific moments in the history of media. Many textbooks and most popular print, online, and televisual accounts of media history share the linear model of progress (for example, color is an advance on black and white, sound an advance on silent cinema) and a focus on individual contributions. Historians engaged in revaluing the evolution of specific technologies like cinema sound (Crafton) and widescreen technologies (Belton) have made clear the nonlinear evolution of media technologies and techniques, while individual careers have been revalued in the context of publicity campaigns and the emergence of research and development as a core activity of communications industries since the late nineteenth century.

Increasingly, major corporations have been seen as agents of historical change (see, for example, Sanjek and Sanjek), and companies like the BBC and Disney have both official and unofficial historians publishing on them. The digital media have spawned a publishing industry devoted to histories of companies, sectors, software, infrastructure, components, and research institutes. The United Kingdom was the first country to produce a multivolume history of its cinema industry, begun by Rachel Low in 1948. Similar projects now exist or are in progress for many other countries, including France, Germany, and the United States, while loose groupings of researchers are advancing parallel projects on print and electronic media in a number of countries around the world.

The history of print media has been revolutionized by the work of Lucien Febvre and Henri-Jean Martin, Roger Chartier, and Elizabeth Eisenstein, among others, and the role of print in the colonizing and decolorizing processes has attracted especially significant work. Less obvious media formations such as news agencies have also attracted both company and sector histories. Much work has been done to refocus the broad-brush approach to the transition from oral to literary cultures in Europe, Latin America, Africa, and Polynesia, and major work has been undertaken on the links between media, the relations between media and transport technologies, and shared infrastructures like libraries. Such patient and passionate archival research has made it far more difficult to generalize or to repeat unexamined truisms. This has been particularly important to activists and scholars of the globalization process and the transitions from state-run to commercial models of print and broadcasting.

Current Studies in Media History

Two scholars, both of whose careers bridge Latin American politics and French academia, have made sterling progress toward bridging the gap between the macro and micro scales of media history. Régis Debray, best known perhaps for his account of guerrilla war with Che Guevara, has proposed a mediological analysis that, while repeating the linear model first outlined by McLuhan, does so in the context of a materialist philosophy that both derives from and critiques Marxism. Debray argues for a practice that concentrates on the infrastructures and materials of communication. Rather than study the literary style of a correspondence, for example, he points toward the pens, paper mills, postal delivery system, even the rearing of horses on which the delivery of mail depended,

arguing that Voltaire's letters are unthinkable outside a centralized and militarized state. In a series of books published during the 1990s, Debray draws together an eclectic if rather Eurocentric collection of detailed cases in support of a general thesis critical of both idea- and individual-centered historiography. In their place he suggests a multiply overlapping formation of different media usages associated with material practices like the organization of political parties or compulsory schooling. The practice of law and parliamentary democracy require specific media formations that guide and shape their capacities. Epochal changes, however, do not eradicate earlier forms. Like Jay David Bolter and Richard Grusin, Debray argues for the remediation of old media form and content by new technologies. Like Gadamer, he argues that mediation abides in objects, not in their relations; like Friedrich Kittler he sees particular media practices as the basis of the defining discourse networks of particular periods; and like Raymond Williams he believes that Marxism's "superstructure" of ideas is entirely material. His achievement is to have synthesized these earlier arguments into a practice with a powerful political project ahead of it.

Media history also includes critical reflection on its own past. In some ways more radical than Debray, the work of the Chilean exile Armand Mattelart has been instrumental both in accounting for the movement of thought about the media and in the materialization of such thinking in media practice and policy. Like Virilio, Mattelart is convinced of the interrelation of transport, military, and media technologies and is highly critical of the intellectual traditions that have severed media communication from the communication of goods and people. Far less exclusively bound than Debray to the history of Western media, Mattelart has made major contributions to the study of global media over thirty years and has provided radical revaluations of earlier historiography and theoretical accounts, crucially in arguing for a more integral approach to understanding the networks of interaction between transport, production, and communication. Debray and Mattelart suggest ways of rejoining the meticulous assessment of specific moments with the large-scale analysis of historical processes that in some ways echo an earlier tradition in technology and design history marked by the names of Lewis Mumford and Siegfried Giedion. Mattelart is explicit in drawing inspiration from the former. The latter, well known in industrial design circles, has much to tell contemporary scholars about historical methods appropriate to the field. Part of the challenge of media history is to recover from obscurity the work of earlier generations and to revalue the work of cultural historians like E. P. Thompson and George Rudé in the light of the new object of media history.

Popular and occasionally academic histories of the "social impacts" of media, whether of whole media technologies or of specific media artifacts and genres, suffer from the lack of any known society without media. Moreover, any new medium is always mediated by other media and is held by many historians to have older media for its initial content. Polemics blaming media have been rife since Shakespeare's time, when ballads and broadsheets were blamed for apprentice riots. Rock and roll, comic books, video, and video games have been more recent targets in the West, and television, radio, music, fashion, and Western technological media generally have been blamed in Islam. Norbert Elias suggests a more subtly functionalist approach, writing of popular songs that "the emotional need behind them, born of the impossibility of finding in scanty leisure time the relationships which working life precludes, is absolutely genuine" (p. 34). The attribution of values to specific media is a significant element of media history. It is unclear whether prestigious media like oil painting became male preserves due to their prestige, or whether women's media like watercolors lost prestige because of their femininity. Both processes probably occurred. Mass culture, in the sense of industrially produced media, has a history of identification with femininity. Novel reading, television, and telephony are among the domestic and private consumer forms that have been strongly feminized. On the other hand, Sadie Plant argues that network computing and mobile telephony correspond respectively to weaving and knitting, women's media par excellence, explaining women's high levels of participation in Internet and wireless telecoms. A key task for media history remains that of explaining why human communication, ostensibly the vehicle of democracy and evolution, has so often been restrictive, oppressive, exploitative, and exclusive.

It would appear from the oldest creation myths that keeping secrets and lying have been features of communication since the beginning. Elias proposes the rise of priestly hierarchies as a source of privileged access to key media such as writing and architecture. Jared Diamond adds the proposal that even before recorded history, possession of writing technology was a source of power for would-be conquerors, and that successful enemies adopted the technology for their own. Certainly differential access to specific media was an intrinsic element of rule in India where, as Homi Bhabha points out, the colony was governed by writing, while the United Kingdom's Parliament ran on speech. Both print and broadcast media have been explicitly deployed in the interests of nation-building from Hitler's Germany to Jawaharlal Nehru's and Indira Gandhi's India, just as standardization of dialects and eradication of minor languages had been a routine activity of nationalist revolutions throughout Europe in the eighteenth and nineteenth centuries. Since communication appears to be an inalienable quality of human societies, and given the lengthy history of intercultural communication at least in the Old World, it seems most likely that media historians must investigate the blockages, delays, and destructions of media flows as much as their origination and propagation.

Among the specific areas where this work might be undertaken are the fields of advertising, marketing, public relations, and propaganda. As an indication of the difficulty of these terms, however, it is important to recall the etymology of *propaganda:* the Vatican office devoted to the propagation of the faith. The modern term has little meaning before the age of mass literacy and broadcast media, even though José Antonio Maravall argues for its relevance to the Spanish Baroque and John Beverley to the colonial period in Latin America. But although there is archeological evidence of street signs among the ruins of Pompeii, it is misleading to understand them as advertising or public relations in any recognizable sense. Such practices evolved in step

with the emergence of mass consumption in the nineteenth century and are deeply grounded in contemporary information-gathering devices. The emergence of contemporary bureaucracies, distinguished from the Baroque clerisy precisely by their modern media (filing cabinets, adding machines, typewriters), is in turn integral to the conception of the public as a body of consumers to whom both political and commercial messages can be delivered. The radical expansion of the commodity form into leisure activities in the later nineteenth century, a process ongoing in the opening up of the People's Republic of China in the early twenty-first century, required not only mass manufacture and mass literacy but the mass distribution of a repertoire of shared codes, conventions, and desires stemming from the managerial mode of bureaucracy emergent in such communication sectors as the railways and the department store. Certainly the industrialized media deployed techniques derived from the ancients: rhetoric, spectacle, shock, sensuality. The application of concepts of efficiency to communications, however, seems to date no earlier than the Counter-Reformation in Europe, though a case can be made for its significance in the far earlier Confucian bureaucracy in China, where the difficulty of the writing system and the exclusive nature of education were used to limit radically all access to communications systems, including the mails and navigable rivers. It is this admixture of efficiency that characterizes the contemporary industrial communications sector as, in Horkheimer's terms, instrumental.

At the same time, when even as sophisticated a thinker as Félix Guattari can assert that "domestic life is being poisoned by the gangrene of mass-media consumption" (p. 27), it is important to consider the role of media not only in constructing concepts of domesticity, but in their subversion. Media are not single, nor exclusively industrialized and instrumental. Critics of globalized media, including Ulf Hannerz, Dayan Thussu, Arjun Appadurai, David Morley and Kevin Robins, and Annabelle Sreberny-Mohammedi and her colleagues emphasize that media not only inform contemporary audiences on issues as large as global warming and as particular as human rights abuse; they also provide vehicles, however limited, for democratic participation and creativity, and globalized industrial media are counterbalanced by diasporan cycles of music, stories, art forms, and political messages operating as informal marginalia to the corporate music business, the Internet, fashion, and the postal service. Even where instrumental media are concerned, the history of audiences indicates a complex work of attention and signification undertaken by viewers, readers, listeners, and participants perpetually ready to convert the proclamations of power into carnival, satire, and rebellion. The significant rise in both the numbers of global organizations and participation in them likewise suggests that media processes remain at least as complex as in former epochs, and therefore can be considered to continue to exist as historical processes.

In conferences during 2000, film archivist Paolo Cherchi Usai estimated that nine billion hours of moving image media were being generated annually. Add to this photographs, print, Web sites, e-mails, let alone conversation, and the information produced in any one year is beyond the reach not just of any one scholar, but of the whole community of media historians. Seen from this standpoint, "the media" as object of study

VILÉM FLUSSER

The work of Vilém Flusser, which has begun to be translated into English in the last decade, is destined to have a major impact on media history. Exiled from his native Prague in 1939, Flusser turned his exile in Brazil and later in France into the grounds of a radical philosophy of freedom. Linking information theory with phenomenology, Flusser argues that pre-history's image-based media were mythic in tone and magical in orientation. They intended to control the world by picturing it. The invention of the alphabet created a new mode of control: lineal, causal, and ultimately scientific. In the invention of photography, he sees the return of the mythic image, but this time an image not of the world but of texts. Rather than image the world, film, television, photography, and computer-generated imaging depict scientific knowledge, philosophical arguments, political beliefs, and commercial messages.

Since writing marks the beginning of history, the technical image marks its end. The post-historical image is programmed by the texts that precede it, and in turn programs its end users. Every new image is a step toward the exhaustion of information, understood as the improbability of a given message in a particular system. Every new photograph both exhausts the stock of possible photographs still to be taken and adds to the assimilative power of the photographic apparatus. The task of photographers, and by extension all who work in the technical media, is to work at the level of information, program, code, and apparatus to increase the level of improbability. As writing loses its centrality, humanity loses the historical consciousness of linear causality. The resultant universe is entropic in information theory and absurd in phenomenological thought. The task, then, of experimentation in media and of media history alike is to create meaning in the face of randomness and freedom in the face of its necessity.

---

appear impossibly huge. At the same time, media history, and media theory and criticism, with honorable exceptions, have failed to address some key areas, notably amateur media, consisting of diaries, photo albums, letter writing, and Web sites, and workplace media, including bookkeeping, filing, cash registers and adding machines, cartography, and professional software. Equally, again with honorable exceptions, the focus has been largely on the developed world seen from Eurocentric positions. Acquainted as they are with the irreparable loss of much if not most early film, radio, and television, archivists are painfully aware that their inevitable sampling must respond not only to current but to future research agendas, and that in addition to content, it is increasingly necessary to archive hardware and documentation. The study of humans as the communicative species becomes both more materially feasible and more challenging, the richer and more archivable our communications become.

See also **Authority; Cinema; Communication of Ideas; Globalization; Representation: Political Representation; Technology; Third Cinema.**

BIBLIOGRAPHY

Adorno, Theodor W. *Critical Models: Interventions and Catchwords.* Translated by Henry W. Pickford. New York: Columbia University Press, 1998.

———. "Letters to Walter Benjamin," 18 March 1936, in *Aesthetics and Politics,* by Ernst Bloch et al., 120–126. London: New Left Books, 1977.

Baudrillard, Jean. *Simulacra and Simulation.* Translated by Sheila Faria Glaser. Ann Arbor: University of Michigan Press, 1994.

———. *Simulations.* Translated by Paul Foss, Paul Patton, and Philip Beitchman. New York: Semiotexte, 1983.

Benjamin, Walter. "The Work of Art in the Age of Mechanical Reproduction," in his *Illuminations,* 217–251. Edited by Hannah Arendt. Translated by Harry Zohn. New York: Schocken, 1969.

Briggs, Asa, and Peter Burke. *A Social History of the Media: From Gutenberg to the Internet.* Cambridge: Polity, 2002. Contains a valuable bibliography.

Debord, Guy. *The Society of the Spectacle.* Rev. ed. Detroit: Black and Red, 1977.

Debray, Régis. *Cours de médiologie générale.* Paris: Gallimard, 1991.

Elias, Norbert. "The Kitsch Style and the Age of Kitsch," in *The Norbert Elias Reader: A Biographical Selection,* edited by Johan Goudsblom and Stephen Mennell, 26–35. Oxford and Malden, Mass.: Blackwell, 1998.

———. *The Symbol Theory.* London: Sage, 1991.

Flusser, Vilém. *Towards a Philosophy of Photography.* Translated by Anthony Matthews. London: Reaktion, 2000.

Gadamer, Hans-Georg. *Truth and Method.* 2nd rev. ed. Translation revised by Joel Weinsheimer and Donald G. Marshall. London: Sheed and Ward, 1989.

Guattari, Félix. *The Three Ecologies.* Translated by Ian Pindar and Paul Sutton. London and New Brunswick, N.J.: Athlone, 2000.

Heidegger, Martin. *Poetry, Language, Thought.* Translated by Albert Hofstadter. New York: Harper and Row, 1971.

Innis, Harold A. *Empire and Communications.* Revised by Mary Q. Innis. Toronto: University of Toronto Press, 1972.

Mattelart, Armand. *The Invention of Communication.* Translated by Susan Emanuel. Minneapolis: University of Minnesota Press, 1996.

McLuhan, Marshall, and Quentin Fiore. *The Medium Is the Massage: An Inventory of Effects.* Harmondsworth, U.K.: Penguin, 1967.

Plato. "Phaedrus," in *The Essential Plato,* translated by Benjamin Jowett. New York: Book of the Month Club, 1991.

Sanjek, Russell, and David Sanjek. *American Popular Music Business in the 20th Century.* Oxford and New York: Oxford University Press, 1991.

Winston, Brian. *Media, Technology, and Society, a History: From the Telegraph to the Internet.* London: Routledge, 1998. Contains a valuable bibliography.

Sean Cubitt

MEDICINE.

This entry includes four subentries:

China
Europe and the United States
India
Islamic Medicine

CHINA

"Classical Chinese medicine" refers to the cumulative practices and abstract doctrines passed down by a small literate minority in China beginning in the first century B.C.E. As in any traditional society, this elite knowledge has made up only a small part of China's health care practices, which include self-therapy, family therapy, and ritual and religious curing. Since 1949, as these elements have changed and their balance has shifted, state-regulated medical practice has come gradually to be divided between biomedicine and a greatly modernized form of the classical art generally called traditional Chinese medicine, or TCM, and hybrids of the two.

Literature

More than ten thousand medical books survive from imperial China (221 B.C.E.–1911 C.E.). These include a small number of doctrinal works with a large accumulation of commentaries and scholarly studies; works on nosology and diagnosis; a great many formularies, most of which systematically set out therapeutic methods; collections of materia medica, which over the last millennium tended to incorporate compound drug formulas; collections of the medical case records of physicians; as well as more or less distinct genres for gynecology, pediatrics, and external medicine. Since the 1950s, scholars in China have edited, annotated, and reprinted many significant early works, and have translated some of the most important into the modern vernacular. Scholars in Asia and elsewhere have used this literature to throw light on a wide range of Chinese ideas, ranging from ethics to gender.

Doctrines

In most of early medieval Europe, only a few classical medical treatises survived, primarily in the libraries of monastic institutions, and most medical practitioners had little education. The outcome was a split between theory and practice. In China there was no such split. Almost all of the literature, including works on doctrinal foundations, was written by practitioners.

Excavated writings on medical divination (from c. 316 B.C.E.) and on medicine (from c. 205 B.C.E.) show traces of a gradual separation of both from popular ritual healing, which had a strong occult component. The first collection of mature classical writings is the *Yellow Emperor's Inner Canon (Huangdi nei jing,* c. first century B.C.E.). It was one of a number of foundational works but the others of the same period have been lost. Although physicians through history considered the *Inner Canon* a coherent two-part treatise, David Keegan has shown that it incorporates many separate texts from different sources, some of which comment on, elaborate on, or disagree with others. The various understandings of the body, health, illness, and therapy contained in the work are inconsistent in many respects. Still, all its component text understand the body to be an ensemble of processes that, in health, remain in harmony with those of the cosmos. Reconciling the discrepancies in this most authoritative of classics in order to present a single picture was the goal of several doctrinal works over the next two centuries.

The *Inner Canon* defined what remained the chief characteristics of medicine: It was process-oriented and relational. Medicine treated a complex ensemble of life processes. Diagnosis was generally a matter of identifying abnormal states of the body as a whole (although, given the diversity of practitioners, the training of many allowed no more than proceeding from a list of symptoms to the name of a disorder). Even physicians who treated particular local symptoms did so from the viewpoint of the whole. Wounds were disorders in the same sense as fevers; they affected not only the lesion but all body processes. Body and mind, complementary aspects of a single organism, were bound to affect each other. Because a disease was a process, doctors had to determine its stage and anticipate its evolution. Medical thinkers defined concepts in relation to others; yang was never an absolute property, but implied a relationship to something else that, in the particular pair, was yin. A young woman might be yin in a discussion of gender relations that compares her with a male, but yang in comparison with an aged man who lacks her vitality.

The conviction that both the state and the body are microcosms that partake in the dynamic order of the universe emerged in political theory, moral philosophy, and medical thought over the last three centuries B.C.E. Intellectuals built these doctrines on the concept of *qi,* which was both the basic material that filled the universe and formed individual things, and the vitality that maintained body states and brought about change. The *Inner Canon* integrated this notion with that of yin and yang and the five phases *(wuxing).* It interpreted the former as paired, opposed, but complementary aspects of *qi,* and the latter as five aspects of it, permitting a finer analysis of interaction in cyclic change. This synthesis became ubiquitous in the history of Chinese ideas. Within medicine, additional analytic categories, especially threefold and sixfold ones, made possible a sophisticated organization of knowledge.

Authors built up a model of fivefold and sixfold systems of vital function that stored and circulated *qi* throughout the body. The supply of *qi* was partly inborn and partly metabolized from air (i.e., ambient *qi*) and food. These systems were named for the main viscera. Unlike in the European understanding, organs were not considered processing stations, but rather bureaucratic offices responsible for order and control of spontaneous processes.

The main principle of health was the unimpeded circulation of *qi*; blockages and stases led to pain and dysfunction. The normal body's relation to its environment was equally important; it had to be open to air and food, but closed to pathogens, and it had to excrete what it could not assimilate without allowing leakage of the body's own *qi*. Medicine from the earliest times also incorporated the value of moderation, not only in conduct but in thought. Just as sensual indulgence could open the way to invasion by pathogens, jealousy or longing could generate medical disorders.

Therapy

Physicians largely depended on opposition therapy, but could modulate it in sophisticated ways. Once the practitioner knew the character of the disorder, he chose therapies to oppose and overcome the imbalance by strengthening the body's functions or attacking the pathogenic agent. The physician's tools included modifications of diet and exercise, massage and manipulation, and a great variety of drugs (over eighteen hundred, mineral and animal as well as botanical, in the great *Bencao gangmu* [1596; *Systematic materia medica*]), as well as acupuncture (inserting needles at certain locations on the circulation pathways to adjust the movement of *qi*) and moxibustion (burning cones of leaf pulp to stimulate these locations more intensely).

Modernization

Biomedicine had little influence on health care in China until after 1949. At that point there were too few qualified personnel to provide basic medical care for the whole population. The government of the People's Republic organized a network of schools to train doctors of traditional Chinese medicine (*Zhongyi*) and a system of modern medical schools. Both trained secondary-school graduates. The Cultural Revolution, from the mid-1960s to the mid-1970s, brought the two closer as those in power demanded that physicians in each sector be trained more than negligibly in the other. This demand also incorporated in the curricula of the TCM schools modern subjects such as anatomy and biochemistry. The government's policy of pushing for synthesis led to textbook interpretations of the old functional discourse in new frameworks close to Western anatomical, lesion-centered views.

The basic education of physicians in imperial China was a matter of memorizing, and learning to apply the methods of reasoning and treatment in classical writings. But by 1980, few secondary-school graduates learned to read classical Chinese. The classics necessarily played a small part in their medical courses, and their confidence in the use of such traditional concepts as *qi*, yin and yang, and the five phases lessened. By 1980 symptom-based diagnosis that drew on biomedical concepts had become common among young practitioners. Therapy increasingly added to traditional remedies both standard packaged formulas and biomedical drugs. By 2000, medical-school teachers and their pupils were using many styles of synthesis involving traditional and modern medicine—recapitulating the diversity of medical reasoning and practice in previous centuries.

See also **Medicine: India; Science: East Asia; Yin and Yang.**

BIBLIOGRAPHY

Furth, Charlotte. *A Flourishing Yin: Gender in China's Medical History, 960–1665.* Berkeley: University of California Press, 1999. On medical care for women and childbirth, with a chapter on women as healers.

Keegan, David. "*Huang-ti nei-ching:* The Structure of the Compilation, the Significance of the Structure." Ph.D. diss., University of California, Berkeley, 1988.

Lloyd, Geoffrey, and Nathan Sivin. *The Way and the Word: Science and Medicine in Early China and Greece.* New Haven, Conn.: Yale University Press, 2002.

Scheid, Volker. *Chinese Medicine in Contemporary China: Plurality and Synthesis.* Durham, N.C.: Duke University Press, 2002. Important, well-informed study.

Sivin, Nathan. *Traditional Medicine in Contemporary China: A Partial Translation of Revised Outline of Chinese Medicine (1972); with an Introductory Study on Change in Present-day and Early Medicine.* Ann Arbor: University of Michigan, Center for Chinese Studies, 1987.

Nathan Sivin

EUROPE AND THE UNITED STATES

Organized societies such as Babylon and ancient Egypt supported the practice of professional medicine, including surgery, but it was in Greece that European or, more cosmically, Western medicine first emerged after the fifth century B.C.E., when the classic texts began to appear.

Ancient Greece and Rome

The ancient Greeks had many ways of healing the sick. Plant gatherers and drug sellers, especially of herbal medicines, were the key people in the establishment of the vast Greek pharmacopoeia. Women healers had their own special categorization. And there were two groups making up a motley crew specializing in diagnosis and treatment calling on the gods and their evil relatives. One constant in Greek medicine was the existence of religious medicine, practiced in the sanctuaries of Asclepius, the Greco-Roman god of medicine. The heritage of Asclepius continues to survive in his professional symbol, the caduceus (one snake only). The medicine of the gods used declamation, singing, and music to speed up the healing process. Ancient Greeks, heavily invested in the "irrational," had more in common with Catholics who go to Lourdes for cures than with rationalist skeptics.

Hippocratic medicine. The most famous document in medical history, the Hippocratic Oath (c. 400 B.C.E.), which established a model of ethical and professional behavior for healers, invoked all the gods, beginning with Apollo. When did the epistemological rupture between mythical thinking and the sort of thinking flattered as scientific, implying a rupture between sacred and scientific healing, take place? The traditional answer is that the change occurred or at least is evident in the Hippocratic corpus, a diverse collection of sixty-odd works by different authors beginning in the sixth century B.C.E., cobbled together about 250 B.C.E. in the library at Alexandria. (A scholarly industry keeps changing the dates of composition of the works and squabbling about textual authenticity.) In the ongoing creation of the Western medical myth it is Hippocrates (the mythic father, also a real person living c. 460–370 B.C.E.) and his followers, who are given credit for establishing the rationalistic basis of scientific medicine. The text *On the Sacred Disease* (c. 410 B.C.E.) denies that epilepsy is a sacred disease, assigning it a natural etiology within the humoral paradigm based on the four body fluids: phlegm, yellow bile, black bile, and blood. (Epilepsy was caused by phlegm convulsing the body as it struggled to free itself from being blocked in the air passages.)

This Hippocratic corpus is notorious for having developed the theory of humors (*chymoi*), which provided a grid for many medical systems over the centuries. *On the Nature of Man,* an anatomical and physiological treatise, went farthest among the Hippocratic writings in the acceptance of the theory of the four humors. According to humoralism, a person's physical and mental qualities are determined by the four chief fluids of the body, thus making it possible to explain health and disease in humoral terms, with health being an overall balance of the four humors. An upset in this balance, with too much or too little of a humor or two, produces disease. The grid of the system was composed of the humors associated with four organs and the qualities or nature of their products. The heart is associated with blood, warm and moist; the brain with phlegm, cold and moist; the liver with yellow bile, warm and dry; and the spleen with black bile, cold and dry. A sick person could correct an imbalance by taking substances characterized by the opposite qualities. In this scheme both people and medicinal substances had complexions and temperaments, that is, a defining humoral composition. The qualities of the humors were thought to correspond to the qualities of the basic elements of the universe: air, water, fire, and earth. This unified theory of humanity in the universe proved so satisfactory to the Western mind that the medical part of the theory was accepted, though much mangled, up through the eighteenth century. The theory "provided the 'reasons' for techniques of evacuation . . . such as venesection [blood-letting], cupping, cathartics, emetics, sneezing, sweating, [and] urination and so on" (Ackerknecht, p. 53). In the flexible Hippocratic humoral grammar the number of humors varied from one text to another. These humors also existed in a healthy person, though invisible to the medical gaze in this case.

The Hippocratic treatise *On Regimen* gave a great deal of attention to diet in the context of an active, well-regulated life.

People absorb food and air, which become part of them and are also the main cause of internal diseases. Wine, which Louis Pasteur later classified as a food, was also an ideal item of medication, for it could be prescribed in many forms and was the best of excipients for the many herbs at the doctor's disposal. Taken pure or mixed with other ingredients, wine could be tailored to individual constitutions. The text *Affections* praised wine and honey for both sick and healthy people. Wine could be mixed with honey or even milk. Greek civilization generally required that wine be cut with two or three parts water to one part wine, but the medical canon permitted the doctor to prescribe it pure or in a variety of mixtures, according to the seasons. In winter the heat and dryness of a small amount of pure wine could counter the baleful effects of humidity and cold. Sometimes doses were quantified, sometimes not.

Galen. By the third century B.C.E., Greek civilization had spread through the Mediterranean basin, blossoming brilliantly in Alexandria, where Ptolemy I ruled from 323 to 285 B.C.E. Hellenistic or Alexandrian medicine placed much emphasis on anatomy and physiology, with Herophilus of Chalcedon (c. 330–c. 260 B.C.E.) and Erasistratus of Chios (fl. 330–250 B.C.E.) providing a mechanistic description of the organs of the human body; humoral theory played only a minor role. Dissection became an important tool in the advancement of medical knowledge, leading to the discovery of new organs such as the prostate and establishing the importance of the brain within the newly represented nervous system. Both theories and sects pullulated in Greek medicine, including groups now classified as empiricists, rationalists, and methodists. Healers became more clearly professional, though they were still trained privately rather than institutionally. By the time Rome conquered the Greek world in the second century B.C.E., Greek medicine was already leavening the simpler medical thought of the conqueror. Greek was a technical language designating diseases, remedies, and instruments for which words had not yet been invented in Latin, but sometimes with the arrival of new works in medicine and in botany Greek terms drove out Latin words in professional discourse. Many of the Roman healers were not citizens, and some were even slaves without civil rights, thus ensuring low social status for most physicians.

The most famous doctor in the history of medicine between Hippocrates and Sigmund Freud was a Greek practicing in the Roman Empire. Other names (Aretaeus of Cappadocia and Soranus and Rufus of Ephesus, for example) earn a paragraph or so in medical history books but only in the shadow of Galen (129–216 C.E.). After arriving in Rome in 161 he gained a reputation in treating upper-class patients, became physician to the imperial family, and pioneered in sports medicine as official physician to the gladiatorial school. He was one of the greatest scribblers in the history of medicine; the classical philologist Ulrich von Wilamowitz-Moellendorff (1848–1931) called him a windbag. He produced works running the gamut from *On Bones for Beginners* to his more philosophical work, *On the Therapeutic Method.* Much was just lifted wholesale from other authors. Galen believed that the physician is a philosopher as well as a healer. A good case can be made for Galen's being "the central figure in the development of the Western tradition of medicine," as Vivian Nutton points out, especially in his transmission of a Galenized Hippocratic gospel to posterity (p. 58). The great clinician, perpetuator of the tradition of bedside medicine, at least for his wealthy clients, stands out also for his discoveries through experiments on animals and for diagnosis and surgery. Dissection of human corpses and, possibly, vivisection of living criminals had gone out of style, with animals replacing the cadavers and victims. Galen left significant errors for other great minds to correct—in clinical medicine as well as in physiology and anatomy. His legacy was eclipsed by the breakup of the empire accompanied by economic and urban decline.

The Medieval World

With the rise of Christianity in late antiquity, medicine gave a greater role to religion; miracles became more important than enemas. Earlier medieval Christianity did preserve a certain amount of learned medicine in encyclopedias, and the creation of "great texts" gave a coherence and canonic orthodoxy to an ossified Galenism that survived into the seventeenth century. Folk or popular medicine was also incorporated into medical literature, though it is doubtful that it was practiced more widely than in antiquity. In terms of remedies, there was a great deal of overlap between popular and professional medicine. The *Liber simplicis medicinae* (Book of simple medicine, c. 1150–1160) by the famous healer Hildegard von Bingen provided an encyclopedia of these traditional remedies, many herbal and some fantastic, for numerous ailments.

Arabic-Islamic medicine. During the Middle Ages the most dynamic and learned European medicine was Arabic or Arabic-Islamic, though there is little in the Koran about medicine. Arabic medicine down to the eighth century was based on popular practices using a *materia medica* of natural items, organic and inorganic, including camel urine as a general tonic. Urine (along with feces) was also an important ingredient of European *Dreckapotheke* (filth pharmacy). Greek humoral medicine, based on a secular culture, probably survived among the elite in cities of the eastern part of the Roman Empire, even after the Arab conquests. Greek medicine revived in ninth-century Baghdad, chiefly as a result of a the translation of Greek texts into Arabic. The works of Galen, the medical culture hero, became the vehicle of Hippocratic medicine in the Eastern and Western caliphates, especially in Muslim Spain.

By the eleventh century, a vast body of translations with commentaries was augmented by an original medical literature in Arabic. Arab-Islamic medicine produced remarkable summas based on a wide range of sources. As in the written history of Western medicine, historiography tends to emphasize the importance of great physicians, both for their clinical acumen and for the famous works they spawned. Among the great Persians were the philosopher-physician al-Razi (c. 865–925), a critical disciple of Galen; the prolific Avicenna, (Ibn Sina; 980–1037), author of the *Canon* or the medical code, a million-word everything-you-need-to-know for doctors; al-Zahrawi, who wrote a classic text on surgery (mostly cautery in Arab-Islamic medicine); Averroës (Ibn Rushd; 1126–1198); and Moses ben Maimon (Maimonides; 1135–1204), who ended up in Cairo as court physician to Saladin (1138–1193). Razi's work *On Measles and Smallpox* was still useful enough

to be published in English by the Sydenham Society in 1848. Spread over a vast empire, Arab-Islamic medicine vastly expanded the healer's pharmacological arsenal with drugs and remedies from Persian and Indian sources, created the first pharmacies, and laid the chemical (alchemical) foundations of modern pharmacy. The vocabulary of European languages was considerably enriched by this activity and by the creation of medical discourse. Medical education was still mostly a private affair, except in the hospital, an important fixture in cities. Roman hospitals had been restricted to soldiers and slaves; Islamic hospitals open to all (a pious hope) were real medical institutions. In 1365 Granada established the first European mental hospital, following the pioneering institutions in other Islamic countries. It looked as if Greek medical glories had been restored and improved.

How it all came to an end is open to debate. Erwin Ackerknecht explained the decline of Arab-Islamic medicine in Gibbonian terms: early Arab tolerance was submerged in Islamic fanaticism. Just add the triumph of the barbarians and one has a crude version of Edward Gibbon's (1737–1794) model of the decline and fall of the Roman Empire. Christians conquered Cordova in 1236; the Mongols sacked Baghdad in 1258; the Ottoman Turks conquered the Levant—Constantinople fell in 1453—and swept into the Balkans and the Mediterranean. Arab civilization declined after the thirteenth century, but the old medical system survived, especially in the Ottoman Empire, until the nineteenth century and continues to survive in a form known as Yunani medicine (*Unani tibb,* Greek medicine) on the Indian subcontinent. What influence Arab-Islamic medicine had on the rise of the medical profession in medieval Europe is open to speculation, but it is clear that Arab medicine exercised a powerful intellectual influence on the revival of Greek medicine in the early medieval period.

Medieval physic. This revival of formal medicine in the West began in the southern Italian town of Salerno, a dynamic, multiethnic place under Norman power; the town is a hundred miles south of the great monastery of Monte Cassino, whose library held a collection of medical texts, and which stimulated an interaction with Salerno. The teachers at the medical school in Salerno developed a good curriculum, founded on their translations of the great texts of Greek (from Arabic) and on Arab medicine. Constantine the African (Constantinus Africanus; c. 1020–1087) was instrumental in transmitting a Galenized Hippocrates to the Latin world with its new concepts, couched in a new technical vocabulary, in anatomy and physiology. By the thirteenth century, an enriched Arabic-tinted medical Latin identified medicine as a separate and elite discipline—and a few centuries later provided medical discourse for Molière. The new medical canon, flattered as the *Little Art of Medicine* (Articella) in the sixteenth century, was based on a group of translated works, especially Constantine's version of the *Liber ysagogarum* (Medical questions) or introduction of *Hunayn ibn Ishaq al ibadi* (Johannicius). This work became the basis for the medical teaching of the difficult art of diagnosis and of the gamble of therapy—Constantine's book on drugs, the *Antidotarium,* expanded the therapeutic repertoire. This introductory book emphasized the therapeutic need to regulate

Galen's "six nonnaturals" (food and drink; sleep and waking; environment; evacuation, including sexual; exercise; and mental state) in order to preserve the natural humoral balance in the body, thus avoiding illness, or to restore balance, thus curing an illness. This emphasis on regimen or lifestyle was made famous in the popular *Regimen sanitatis salernitanum,* a book of verses perhaps concocted by Arnau de Villanova (c. 1235–1312), physician to the high and mighty (popes and kings) and professor at the University of Montpellier. Many popular works adopted this holistic framework in giving advice to the sick and those trying to stay healthy.

With the economic revival of Europe in the period 1200–1350, there appeared an age of construction in hospitals and universities as society invested in the care of the sick and the production of clergy, lawyers, teachers, and doctors. Medical education, when it was organized in places such as Bologna and Montpellier, was a long, tedious affair (about ten years) attempted by few. Padua, degree mill of the age, granted nine medical and surgical degrees in 1450; it had a large faculty of sixteen. Europe probably produced enough physicians to treat elite patients and to discourse with them in the Aristotelian lingo they both had ingested in the faculties. The rest of the population cured themselves or depended on charlatans (not necessarily a pejorative designation) or empirics of varying degrees of ignorance and skill. Neither doctor nor empiric could do much in dealing with smallpox, influenza, insanity, leprosy (a popular diagnosis in the eleventh and twelfth centuries), and the Bubonic plague (1347–1351), which killed off about a quarter of the European population. The wise doctor limited himself to dietetics, according to the Galenic gospel of the "nonnaturals," some drugs, and a bit of minor surgery. With a degree and well-heeled patients, he could become rich. There was not much competition. In 1454 Vienna, with a population of fifty thousand, had eleven M.D.s.

Medieval surgery. Surgery, often identified as a craft, has sometimes been promoted to the status of an intellectual adventure. It was certainly a dangerous though not necessarily fatal adventure to have surgery in pre-Listerian times. Roman surgery can appear "remarkably modern," meaning comparable to the surgery of the 1970s (Nutton, p. 57). Great surgeons such as John Bradmore (d. 1402), John of Arderne (c. 1307–1370, and Henri de Mondeville (c. 1260–1320) were remarkably successful in carrying out dangerous operations, some on the battlefield, often improving on ancient techniques. It is not surprising that mortality rates were high; what is surprising is the survival of a patient exposed to massive infection. The ancient technique of using wine to irrigate wounds and incisions is probably one part of the explanation. Surgeons liked to write as well as cut. The leading surgeons produced classic texts, thus following in the literary Hippocratic-Galenic tradition. Outside Italy surgery may not have been a respectable part of the curriculum, but from the twelfth century on, leading surgeons were closer to physicians than to barber-surgeons and empirics; in some towns cooperation between all groups was more striking than clashes. Even snarling Parisian surgeons and physicians could come to a limited agreement in 1210 over dissections. While the doctor envied the surgeon's skill, the surgeon lusted after the doctor's cultural capital and academic baggage. The social status of surgery was helped by the official role of the surgeon in autopsies for investigations of homicide and in the public dissection of criminals. The growing importance of anatomy (including the dissection of human corpses) in medical education during the fourteenth century also promoted the surgeon. Medicine and surgery had become part of society in an unprecedented way as a result of the new governmental function of practitioners and the related development of institutions.

Renaissance Medicine

In the sixteenth century, Greek medicine was reborn yet again but with a difference. The upside of the fall of Constantinople was an influx of Greek scholars and manuscripts into Italy. A scholarly industry soon developed for the study of ancient Greece and for the publication of the works forming the basis of Western civilization, including medicine. In 1525 the Aldine Press in Venice published Galen's complete works in Greek. (In the sixteenth century 590 different editions of Galen were published.) The next year Aldine also published the Hippocratic corpus. New Latin translations soon appeared for the Greekless. Medical humanism was on a solid footing; what the return to a true Galenism meant for the practitioner and patient is not clear, except for a new emphasis on the etiology of disease and the tailoring of therapy to a profile of the individual patient. Clinical bedside teaching—its origins are piously traced back to Hippocrates—was integrated into medical education at Padua in 1578 by Giambatista da Monte (1498–1552), who was also keen on method as the key to knowledge and practice. Galen's *Method of Healing,* brought up to date by the professors, could put doctors on an infallible path to correct diagnosis and treatment. All they had to do was look in a *practica,* or crude physician's handbook, whose professorial prolixity often reduced its usefulness.

The new anatomy. Historians agree on the main developments in Renaissance medicine: first, the revival of a modestly revised Galenism; second, the related renewal of anatomy, which was linked to the flourishing artistic culture in Italy. Artists used the knowledge from dissection as the conceptual foundation of the new art. Anatomical texts illustrated by artists displayed a representational, natural body rather than the pedagogical schematic model of medieval texts. Michelangelo collaborated with Realdo Colombo (1516?–?1559), who in 1548 became professor of anatomy at the Papal University in Rome. A great deal of the new work in anatomy was concerned with modifying Galen, who had sometimes extrapolated from animal to human anatomy, as in the case of the five-lobed liver. The major demolition job on Galen was done by one of his most fervent disciples, Andreas Vesalius (1514–1564), who in 1537 moved to Padua, took his degree and, though an academic physician, became lecturer in anatomy and surgery. Influenced by the Bolognese model, Vesalius increased his dissecting activity—a sympathetic judge increased his supply of cadavers of executed criminals—and by lecturing while dissecting, he integrated physician, anatomist, and surgeon and gave a coherence to the subject. In 1543 Vesalius published *De humani corporis fabrica* (On the fabric of the human body), a great classic of descriptive anatomy. This book

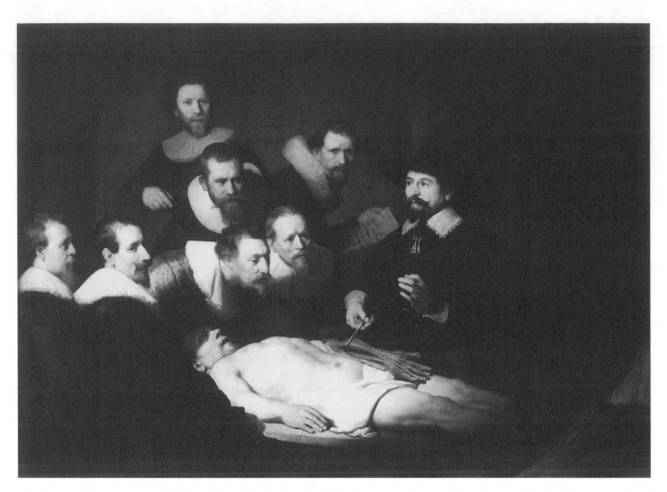

The Anatomy Lecture of Dr. Nicolaes Tulp (1632) **by Rembrandt. Oil on canvas.** The study of anatomy dates back as early as 1600
B.C.E. In the fifth century B.C.E., the Greek physicians Herophilus and Erasistratus made the first substantial progress in the field by
confirming many bodily functions through dissection. © FRANCIS G. MAYER/CORBIS

was "the first proper account of *human* anatomy" (Wear,
p. 275); the artistic but scientifically precise illustrations were
a key part of the text. By his teaching and book, Vesalius eventually changed the way doctors understood the human body,
ensured the triumph of an anatomical method based on dissection and observation, and left future investigators plenty of
problems to solve within the emerging physiological paradigm.
Galenic views on the blood and the heart, or his cardiovascular system, came to be recognized as seriously flawed. The new
model was completed *grosso modo* in 1628, when William
Harvey (1578–1657) published *An Anatomical Essay Concerning the Movement of the Heart and Blood in Animals* (*De
motu cordis*).

The Harveian Revolution (Seventeenth Century)

Until the seventeenth century, medicine operated within the context of the Galenic blood system, or rather, two blood systems.
Using chyle (concocted in the stomach from food), the liver produced venous blood, which moved through the veins to various
parts of the body to provide for nourishment and growth. The
heart was the source of arterial blood, a concoction of venous
blood, and pneuma (vital air, the stuff of life), which also moved

through the body as needed. The venous blood seeped from the
right side to the left side of the heart through invisible pores in
the interventricular septum. The air came from the lungs via the
venal artery (today's pulmonary vein). Blood did not return to
the heart but was consumed: no circulation. This coherent, rational system, concordant with major therapies, also explained
mental functions by diverting a little arterial blood for conversion into animal spirits (highly refined spirituous air) to flow
though the nervous system.

Movement of the heart and blood. Harvey was a Cambridge man who took his medical degree at Padua, where he
worked under Girolamo Fabrici (Fabricius ab Aquapendente;
c. 1533–1619), the first anatomist to discuss the venous valves
(*De venarum ostiolis;* 1603). By the time Harvey arrived in
Padua, Galen's model had been seriously damaged, though no
one had thrown Galen's works into a bonfire, as Paracelsus
had supposedly done with Avicenna's *Canon* in 1527. Vesalius had denied the origin of the vena cava in the liver and, in
the second edition of *De humani corporis fabrica,* the theory
of the porous septum in the heart. After some vivisectionist
experiments, Columbo argued for the pulmonary transit, or

movement of blood though the lungs, and also described accurately the action of the heart in systole and diastole. Other anatomists confirmed these discoveries.

On his return to England, Harvey practiced in London, becoming one of the city's most famous doctors and after 1618 one of the royal physicians. *De motu cordis* does not introduce its great novelty, the circulation of the blood, until chapter eight, and then only apologetically in an Aristotelian, vitalistic framework. Unlike René Descartes (1596–1650), Harvey was not a mechanist. His work was based on dissection, vivisection, and a famous quantitative experiment in which he measured the amount of blood passing thorough the heart in a given time, thus showing that the system had to circulate the same blood or explode. Of course Harvey's argument on circulation was incomplete because he could not see the capillaries, though he inferred their existence; Marcello Malphighi (1628–1694) used a microscope to discover them in a frog's lungs (*On the Lungs*, 1661). Robert Hooke (1635–1703) as well as an Oxford group pinpointed the importance of the mixing of air and blood in the lungs. (An explanation of respiration, completing the system, was not possible before the chemical revolution of the late eighteenth century.) Galenic physiology, with the liver as a blood-making organ, became untenable, as Jean Riolan the Younger (1580–1657) recognized in a weak scientific attack on Harvey, who had little trouble in showing it to be nonobservational nonsense. Physicians were too conservative to abandon the Galenic practice of venesection, and this points to a problem of new medical science: the development of a related therapy is usually in the future, leaving doctor and patient both victims of the old science with its traditional therapeutics.

Paracelsus: Crude chemotherapy.
The end of Galen's iconic status was balanced by a revival of Hippocrates, the perfect cover for an attack on orthodoxy. Paracelsus (Bombast von Hohenheim; 1493–1541) denounced learned medicine but praised Hippocrates, a curious patron for his brand of medicine based on the Christian religion, magic, astrology, observation, and personal experience. Ackerknecht called him a "medical Doctor Faustus" (p. 108). Paracelsus's cosmic "doctrine of signatures" identified the curative power of plants according to their resemblance to the organ affected; this was a pretty standard belief in popular medicine as well. In his natural philosophy, the Aristotelian-Galenic system of qualities, elements, and humors was replaced by a chemical fantasy associating substances with principles of solidity (salt), inflammability (sulfur), and spirituousness (mercury). Specific remedies of this chemical therapy cured specific diseases, whose agents might be poisons from the stars or from minerals on earth. Paradoxically, the advocate of the idea of a chemical etiology of and cure for diseases is the culture hero of alternative medicine. He was antiestablishment. Reading deeply into the book of nature, he concluded that therapy should be based on the principle of "like cures like": applying what is suitable to the affected part, rather than following Galenic therapeutics based on the principle of opposition. Paracelsus had many followers, the most famous being Jan Baptista van Helmont (1579–1644), master of medical chemistry (iatrochemistry) and defender of the ontological concept of disease, meaning

that every disease has its own unique principle and therefore a specific treatment. The theory was useful in attacking bloodletting as a debilitating practice based on the erroneous idea that plethora causes disease. But like its Galenic enemy, Paracelsan iatrochemistry declined in the second half of the seventeenth century. The choleric Harvey, no friend of chemistry, regarded the Paracelsans as "shitt-breeches."

Sydenham: Bedside medicine.
Unlike Harvey, Thomas Sydenham (1624–1689) was on the winning side in the English Civil War. Unlike Harvey, he did not have any scientific manuscripts for soldiers to destroy. Sydenham, an Oxford man scornful of learned medicine, advocated observation and the bedside tradition. His hero was Hippocrates, reinvented as an inspiring clinical spirit at the bedside. The "English Hippocrates" believed in specific remedies for diseases; cinchona bark against the ague (benign tertian malaria), for example. Unlike Harvey, Sydenham, accepting Francis Bacon's (1561–1626) philosophy of science, was interested in classifying diseases, epidemic fevers in particular; the botanical model was useful here in his attempt to develop a clinical medicine for the London masses who suffered from the ague from March to July. In the midst of these conceptual upheavals on the functioning of the body and the nature of diseases, therapeutics changed little, except that a "new" disease like syphilis might require a "new" and horrible treatment (mercury). Herbal remedies continued in both popular and professional use. The old humoral procedures of bleeding, purging, induced vomiting, blistering, and cupping survived in the medical repertory. No wonder Sydenham admitted that without opium, medicine was a cripple. (Sydenham's laudanum contained 200 grams of opium, 100 grams of saffron, and 15 grams each of cinnamon and of cloves in 100 grams of Malaga wine.) Sydenham doubted that using the microscope or studying anatomy would advance medicine. Prophecy should be left to the prophets.

From Enlightened to Clinical Medicine
The age of Enlightenment (and revolution), even in medicine, is how historians conceive of the eighteenth century. Centers of new or innovative medicine shifted over the centuries: ancient Athens and Rome, Salerno, Montpellier, Edinburgh, Leiden, Vienna, London, Paris, New York, and so forth. After the medieval creation of universities, learned or academic medicine, often connected to a clinic or a hospital, played a major role in reorienting medicine in theory and sometimes in practice. In spite of the profession's hero worship of Hippocrates, what was going on in faculties of medicine by the late seventeenth century had little to do with classical medicine. At Leiden, then "the medical center of the world" (Ackerknecht, p. 130), teaching was organized on the basis of subjects rather than the teachings of the great doctors; bedside teaching and the dissection of corpses had also become important. Hermann Boerhaave (1668–1738) was at the center of the new dispensation. His students included the founders of the great centers of clinical medicine in Edinburgh and Vienna. Boerhaave, inspired by experimental natural philosophy, concocted a hydraulic model of the body with a corresponding mechanistic explanation of disease. His mighty text

Illustration of physician Réné-Théophile-Hyacinthe Laënnec (1781–1826) tending to a patient, after 1816 painting by Theobold Chartran. During the late eighteenth century, medicine began to progress into an institutionalized occupation, rather than just a societal system, and accredited doctors began to rise in prestige.

The Institutes of Medicine (1708) ran through ten editions and endured a few translations into vernacular tongues. In 1724 Boerhaave wrote up a famous case history of a male who had died of a ruptured esophagus. It can been argued that this was the first modern form of this literary genre, covering the patient's history, a physical examination, a diagnosis, the course of disease, and an autopsy. Boerhaave developed a modern medical curriculum with a sequence of natural science, anatomy, physiology, and pathology, complemented by clinical instruction in a twelve-bed ward. This looks like the birth of that elusive entity the clinic; Michel Foucault insists that it was a protoclinic, for Boerhaave still struggled in the "old age of the clinic" (Foucault, ch. 4).

Pathological anatomy.

It had become clear that death could give insight into disease, possibly even establish its cause. Though tedious to use because of its two correlating indexes, the prolix work *On the Sites and Causes of Disease* (1761), by the Paduan anatomist Giovanni Battista Morgagni (1682–1771), achieved part of its noble aim of establishing a connection between the patient's symptoms and the lesions of the diseased organ in the corpse. Morgagni logged in some seven hundred autopsies. A new etiology of disease shifted it from a general theory to a specific organ, a site, where lesions

produced by morbid changes in the organ could be matched with symptoms of disease in the patient. The London doctor Matthew Baillie (1761–1823) carried this anatomo-pathology further in a famous work on *Morbid Anatomy . . .* (1793), which provided classic textbook descriptions of diseases, including cirrhosis of the liver and emphysema.

In Paris the hospital came to dominate medicine through surgery and teaching. At the gigantic Hôtel-Dieu, Xavier Bichat (1771–1802) did six hundred autopsies as a basis for his *Treatise on Membranes* and his book *General Anatomy applied to Physiology and Medicine* (3 vols., 1801). Bichat's famous, complex theory of tissues, or membranes, shifted the etiology of localized disease from the organ to lesions of specific tissues. This shift allowed a lesion to be more precisely identified according to the particular tissue affected rather than the whole organ: inflammation of the heart was replaced by identification of inflammation of membranes or the muscle itself. "Life, disease and death now form[ed] a technical and conceptual trinity," as Michel Foucault put it in consecrating "death [as] the great analyst" (p. 144). Death, formerly the domain of the priest, had become part of medicine, and, along with life and disease, integrated into the medical gaze. Or, as Roy Porter puts it in ordinary discourse, Bichat's "work laid the foundations for nineteenth-century patho[logical] anatomy" (p. 265). Medicine could become a science enabling diagnosis to be more precise. The tool was the modern physical examination (still the doctor's best diagnostic tool), which consecrated the techniques of inspection, palpation, percussion, and auscultation. The patient's symptoms and the signs detected by the doctor could be related to the lesions that had been observed in diseased organs. With a galaxy of stars—Jean-Nicolas Corvisart des Marets (1755–1821), René Laennec (1781–1826), and Pierre Louis (1787–1872) prominent among them—Parisian hospital medicine enjoyed its day in the sun as a model having considerable influence on medical thought and education.

The clinic.

What was the clinic? The teaching clinic meant different things in different countries. In France clinical medicine put an emphasis on surgery, chiefly in large city hospitals. Military demand was a powerful stimulus to medical growth in the eighteenth century, and the need for army doctors rose during the French Revolutionary and Napoleonic wars. British clinical education was also mainly an affair of London institutions and provincial hospitals; Edinburgh and Glasgow resembled more the German model. In the German states small university-affiliated clinics and infirmaries provided practical education. The public hospitals of Paris had twenty thousand beds in which to stack, examine, and perhaps cure—an autopsy was more frequent—the city's vast diseased population. Medicine in Paris distinguished itself by the accessibility of public hospitals to students wanting instruction from great men like Laennec and experience in bedside medicine and dissection. Lots of corpses were available, for mortality at the Hôtel-Dieu was about 25 percent, two and one half times that of most English hospitals. Foreign students and doctors found Restoration Paris a profitable place in which to learn the latest French medical fashion; on returning home, they carried versions of the French model with them to many cities, including Vienna, Boston, and even London. London, whose population reached a million and a half by 1831, developed large teaching hospitals. Paris, whose population did not reach a million until 1846, was notorious for its concentration of patients and after the 1830s the development of medical specialization. The bedside tradition foundered when dozens or even many more students crowded round the patient's bed to receive the master's instruction. More profitable instruction was to be had from private courses organized by Parisian doctors. Limits on numbers were also imposed through elite selection in intern and extern examinations. The lecture shifted to the amphitheater. In spite of the fame of Paris hospital medicine, a student got a better education in private instruction by a great man, perhaps even Laennec, who gave a private course in the small ward of a big hospital, thus providing the advantages of both pedagogical worlds.

From Clinical to Laboratory Medicine

Medicine was transformed institutionally, practically, and intellectually in the century after the 1750s. Medicine evolved from a cultural system to an occupation, as the practitioners of professional medicine grew in prestige and began to dominate their rivals, the charlatans or empirics of popular medicine.

Physiology. One of the striking intellectual developments of this period was the emergence of physiology as an autonomous experimental science, probably first in France through the work of Bichat, François Magendie (1783–1855), and Claude Bernard (1813–1878). Physiology distinguished itself by the use of operative or experimental surgery, which might be seen as a mutation of an ancient tradition running from the Alexandrian school through Galen to the Italian schools and Harvey. Much knowledge was gained; many animals were sacrificed. With the advent of Bernard, the historian passes into a different conceptualization of the development of medicine: from pathological anatomy in the hospital to medicine in the laboratory. Medicine seemed in danger of becoming obsessed with the pathological, always a danger in the doctor's world of disease. Bernard's physiological medicine showed how essential it was to understand the normal as well as the pathological, indeed, that there is only a narrow divide between them. Understanding the functions of an organ became central to understanding a disease. For example, Bernard's experimental demonstration of the role of the liver in making glycogen and in regulating glucose levels in the blood provided the basis for understanding diabetes—an alteration or disorder in a normal function produced the lesion or disease. (The new world of internal secretions later gave rise to the science of endocrinology.) Such discoveries could only occur in a controlled laboratory experiment on an animal. Bernard's view was similar to that of Rudolf Virchow (1821–1902): "Disease is nothing but life under altered circumstances." Imitating Virchow, Canguilhem (p. 100) made a brilliant diagnosis: "Diseases are new ways of life."

Medical science in Germany. In the middle of the nineteenth century the center of medical excitement and interest began to shift from Paris to German centers, where heavy investment in higher education had begun to pay large research dividends. The history of medicine at this point becomes of necessity rather Whiggish as discovery after discovery has to be cataloged, and the practice of medicine itself seems to have improved. Some of the progress was driven by instruments, especially the microscope, which had been of no interest to Bichat but was indispensable to Virchow, pathologist and Progressive politician. The great unifier of physiology and pathology, Virchow developed the medical implications of cell theory. To understand diseases, one had to understand the cell. From Morgagni's emphasis on the organ to Bichat's concentration on tissues to Virchow's consecration of the cell (*Cellular Pathology,* 1858), medicine, like the other sciences, turned increasingly microscopic. The whole patient would soon be hard to find, but the German model of medical science became universally admired and imitated, especially in a few select American institutions (Johns Hopkins, Harvard, and the Universities of Pennsylvania and of Michigan). Of course it would be a while before the chasm between laboratory and hospital (and physician) would be bridged and the hospital would begin "to resemble a factory" (Porter, p. 347).

The immediate influence that experimental physiology had on the practicing physician is not easy to assess; the impact of sciences such as chemistry (in anesthesiology), microscopy, and bacteriology was much clearer by the end of the nineteenth century. Over the long haul no doubt physicians came to place considerable reliance on various physiological instruments to record and analyze data. Most of these instruments, like the kymograph, were invented and developed in the German states. The stethoscope replaced the urinal as the symbol of the profession. A much-improved microscope became indispensable to medical and biological research in the second half of the nineteenth century and, with the white coat, the accessory of the successful doctor. Wilhelm Conrad Roentgen discovered X-rays in 1895, and by the 1920s diagnostic medicine embraced X-rays for large masses of people. Physics was becoming an essential part of medicine, which by the early 2000s was integrated into the world of engineering and physics through CAT and PET scans and magnetic resonance imaging in order to model the structure and functioning of the body.

Women doctors. The autonomous and monopolistic organization of the medical profession under governmental protection is a late development in the history of medicine, essentially post-Revolutionary (1789). Universities assumed the primary role in medical education, though private schools or institutes and, above all, hospitals played major roles in Britain and France. Medical history teems with women healers, but they were not admitted to medical schools until the late nineteenth century, with resistance holding out until the early twentieth century in Germany. Fortunately for Russian Jewish women, Switzerland's facilities were open, beginning with the University of Zurich in 1864. The mobilization and slaughter of male doctors in both world wars helped increase the number of women doctors, though Nazi Germany dealt a blow to the movement that had made one-fifth of the German medical profession female by 1933. After World War II, female enrollments in medical schools rose and continued to rise to near equality of the sexes (in numbers only) in the profession by the early twenty-first century. Not welcome in certain specialities such as surgery, women tended to go into

> [After recalling his agreements with Galen and Colombo, Harvey declares his belief in the circular movement of the blood, views so] novel . . . that in speaking of them, I . . . dread lest all men turn against me. . . . However, the die has now been cast, and my hope lies in the love of truth and the clear-sightedness of the trained mind. . . .
>
> We have as much right to call this movement of the blood circular as Aristotle had to say that the air and rain emulate the circular movement of the heavenly bodies.
>
> This organ [the heart] deserves to be styled the starting point of life and the sun of our microcosm just as the sun deserves to be styled the heart of the world. For it is by the heart's vigorous beat that the blood is moved, perfected, activated, and protected from injury and coagulation. The heart is the tutelary deity of the body, the basis of life, the source of all things, carrying out its function of nourishing, warming, and activating the body as a whole.
>
> SOURCE: William Harvey, *The Circulation of the Blood and Other Writings,* trans. Kenneth J. Franklin, with an introduction by Andrew Wear (London: J. M. Dent and Sons, 1963), pp. 46–47.

general practice and areas of specialization such as bacteriology, anaesthesia, pediatrics, neuropsychiatry, dermatology, and nonsurgical gynecology.

The rise of psychiatry. An enormous number of drugs were available to healers from Hippocrates to Magendie, whose *Formulary* of 1821 introduced the notion of chemical purity into the pharmacopoeia. In the *materia medica* in use before the 1950s there is a striking absence of psychotropic drugs; the first, lithium, used to treat manic depression, dates from 1949. (Phenobarbital had been found effective against epileptic seizures in 1912.) So how did doctors treat mental disease? The answer is that they did nothing for most of medical history. "Madness" was generally not the province of the doctor, but of the churches and the family. "Madhouses" were generally charitable or religious institutions with medical connections until the nineteenth century, when the treatment of the insane evolved into a specialized branch of medicine. The development of psychiatry was accompanied by the rise of the "new" asylum—new because of its practice of a humane treatment of the mentally ill. Politicians in the late-eighteenth-century French state, converted to the scientific gospel, became convinced that madness could be cured, with the hospital functioning as a healing machine. Ideologue doctors such as Pierre-Jean-Georges Cabanis (1757–1808) provided epistemological (that is, scientific) respectability for medicine by emphasizing its roots in classification and a content related to sensationalist psychology.

The moral treatment, made famous by Philippe Pinel (1745–1826) at Bicêtre, the Salpêtrière, and Charenton, indulged in sympathetic but firm handling and even theatrical performances by the actor-inmates. "A historic transformation . . . in Paris" (Weiner, p. 275): the mentally ill were recognized as human beings with natural rights, and mental illness was classified as a curable disease. Doctors soon invented new categories of disease out of the old simple divisions of insanity; perhaps the most notorious new disease was Jean-Etienne Esquirol's (1772–1840) concoction of monomania. Esquirol's work *Mental Illnesses,* a classic text, was published in 1838, the year the government voted to create a national asylum system. The treatment of the insane became a matter of a scientific management of the mind and emotions rather than the traditional bleeding and purging of the body. Psychiatry arrived in the faculty of medicine in Paris in 1882, when the neurologist Jean-Martin Charcot (1825–1893) was appointed professor of diseases of the nervous system. There is no evidence that all this science and institutional growth contributed to a higher cure rate for patients suffering from the old mental diseases or even the new ones such as neurasthenia and hysteria, which some doctors attributed to industrial civilization. A desperate Western psychiatry indulged in thousands of lobotomies between 1935 and 1950.

As with clinical medicine, psychiatry in Germany (and Austria) differed from psychiatry in France and Britain in being connected directly with research-related university medicine, particularly neurology. Wilhelm Griesinger (1817–1868), professor of psychiatry and neurology in Berlin, developed a department for the study of mental disorders and founded the *Archiv für Psychiatrie und Nervenkrankheiten* (1868). Sigmund Freud (1856–1939) specialized in clinical neurology, but he

A physiological laboratory, therefore, should now be the culminating goal of any scientific physicians' studies. . . . Hospitals, or rather hospital wards, are not physicians' laboratories, as is often believed; . . . these are only fields for observation; there must be what we call clinics, since they determine and define the object of medicine, i.e., the medical problem; but while they are the physician's first study, clinics are not the foundation of scientific medicine; physiology is the foundation of scientific medicine because it must yield the explanation of morbid phenomena by showing their relations to the normal state. We shall never have a science of medicine as long as we separate the explanation of pathological from the explanation of normal, vital phenomena.

. . . In leaving the hospital, a physician . . . must go into his laboratory; and there by experiments on animals, he will seek to account for what he has observed in his patients, whether about the action of drugs or about the origin of morbid lesions in organs or tissues. There . . . he will achieve true medical science. Every scientific physician should, therefore, have a physiological laboratory. . . . The principles of experimental medicine . . . [are] simply the principles of experimental analysis applied to the phenomena of life in its healthy and its morbid states.

SOURCE: Claude Bernard, *An Introduction to the Study of Experimental Medicine,* trans. Henry Copley Greene, with an introduction by Lawrence J. Henderson (New York: Collier Books, 1961), pp. 174–175.

recognized the bankruptcy of the old organic psychiatry, which attributed mental disorders to structural disease in the brain. Pinel had similarly become disillusioned with the hope of finding lesions in the brains of the mentally diseased. Freud's new dynamic psychiatry with its radical views of the human personality is probably the most influential and most controversial medical paradigm in the history of Western civilization and its discontents. The success of the "talking cure," or psychoanalysis, in treating mental disorders provided the basis for modern psychotherapy, but much of psychiatry has since followed the biochemical path to Prozac and other psychotropic drugs. The ideology of most German (and French) psychiatrists was scientific materialism, with their medical science being basically neurological and neuropathological. Medicine loves classification: German psychiatry was obsessed by it. The twenty-first century's bible of the profession, the *Diagnostic and Statistical Manual of Mental Disorders* (DSM-IV; 4th edition, 1994) has its origin in the classification of mental disorders done by Emil Kraepelin (1856–1926), who drew on the work of several other men of method. To venture beyond the current DSM paradigm and DSM-IV framework, the powers in mental health issued *A Research Agenda for DSM-V* in 2002.

Did science matter?   Concluding his book on nineteenth-century scientific medicine, W. F. Bynum asked "Did science matter?" The answer is yes. Consider surgery. No branch of medicine changed more radically than surgery during the second half of the nineteenth century. Surgery itself had been socially and cognitively (through the study of anatomy) transformed by 1790. Surgery joined medicine as a liberal profession, that is, a group in possession of scientific or esoteric knowledge, transmitted through institutions; recognized by the state, the profession also controlled admission to its ranks and tried to control the practice of medicine within certain areas. The French doctorate in surgery, introduced in 1749, required a thesis in Latin, which nicely hid professional secrets from the *polloi*. Reform of French medical education in 1794 integrated surgery into the regular training of doctors.

With the growing importance of the hospital and the increasing prestige of pathological anatomy, the professional status of surgeons soon equaled that of physicians. Whether chloroform did "a lot of mischief" by enabling "every fool to become a surgeon" (Sir Patrick Cullen, in Bernard Shaw's *Doctor's Dilemma,* 1906) is open to question. But it is certain that the cult of the surgeon could not have emerged at the end of the nineteenth century without anesthesiology. In 1846 the first amputation with a patient under ether was done in Boston; the next year James Y. Simpson (1811–1870), professor of obstetrics, first administered chloroform at the Infirmary in Edinburgh. The incorporation of bacteriology into surgical practice was equally important to the cult.

> The wish-fulfillment can be detected . . . easily in . . . dreams. . . . A friend of mine . . . said to me one day: "My wife has asked me to tell you that she had a dream yesterday that she was having her period. You can guess what that means." The fact that this young married woman dreamt that she was having her period meant that she had missed her period. I could well believe that she would have been glad to go on enjoying her freedom a bit longer before shouldering the burden of motherhood. It was a neat way of announcing her pregnancy.
>
> SOURCE: Sigmund Freud, *The Interpretation of Dreams,* trans. James Strachey (New York: Avon Books, 1965), p. 159.

Germ theory. The medical acceptance of germ theory is a complex story. Since disease killed more soldiers than bullets, army doctors, desperate for an etiology and a therapy, were among the first to embrace the gospel of germs. The antiseptic, then aseptic practices of Joseph Lister (1827–1912)—Lister's system—was inspired by his reading a paper on fermentation by Louis Pasteur (1822–1895). Listerism was accepted most enthusiastically in German-speaking areas, where there was also a striking development of surgery of the abdominal, thoracic, and cranial cavities, and, more controversial, the female reproductive system. Pasteur, accepting the idea that fermentation, putrefaction, and infection are related, developed a germ theory of infection. What distinguished his theory was a set of brilliant if controversial experiments on wine diseases, chicken cholera, anthrax, and rabies. Without understanding the immune system—researchers are still investigating how it works—Pasteur and his colleagues developed vaccines to prevent disease. Development of immunization against rabies (such as Creutzfeldt-Jacob disease, a frightening but minor killer) made it possible for Pasteur to collect enough funds to establish the Institut Pasteur (1888).

Bacteriology was largely a German creation. Robert Koch (1843–1910) identified major killers such as the tuberculosis and cholera bacilli and codified a method for investigating the etiology of infections. His students went on to identify the microorganisms causing a large number of diseases (diphtheria, typhoid, gonorrhea, and syphilis, among others) Koch spent the period from 1896 to 1907 in Africa studying its diseases; partly as a result of European invasions that displaced populations, millions of Africans suffered from helminth (intestinal worm) infections, in addition to germ and viral diseases. Many other medical researchers of the imperial powers also spent time in areas where tropical diseases presented a challenge not to be found in Europe. The germ-theory model of disease with its simple etiology did not work for diseases such as yellow fever and malaria; the parasitological model required the concept of a vector such as the mosquito. If the prion, which has no nucleic acids (DNA and RNA), causes bovine spongiform encephalopathy (BSE, popularly known as "mad cow disease") and its human form, the "new" Creutzfeld-Jacob disease, then a new model of infection will appear in medicine.

With four institutes named after him, the imperious Koch went on to glory, though not so great as that of Pasteur, with whom he squabbled over the great germs of the day. Supported by well-developed chemical and pharmaceutical industries, German scientists were able to pioneer in serum therapy (antitoxins) and chemotherapy, whose most famous product might have been the arsenical compound salvarsan (not a magic bullet) for treating syphilis. More useful drugs to come out of Germany included chloral hydrate, aspirin, and phenobarbital. But no drug has ever been more useful or cheaper than quinine, the extract of the bark of the cinchona tree, used in fighting malaria, still one of the great killer diseases.

Public health. So what was the effect of all this progress in medical science on public health? Mortality did decline in the second half of the nineteenth century, particularly deaths from tuberculosis, scarlet fever, diphtheria, typhus, typhoid, cholera, and smallpox (mostly before 1850 in this case). The decline started before effective medical means could combat these diseases. Nonmedical factors seem to explain why people lived longer: first, improved nutrition, which made people more resistant to diseases such as tuberculosis; second, the attenuated virulence of some microbes, such as the diphtheria bacillus; third, effective public health measures such as supplying towns and cities with safe water, installing sewage systems, and clearing slums. The effect of the Malthusian check of infectious disease on population growth was severely reduced if not eliminated. The introduction of antibiotics lowered mortality even further. Sulfa drugs, the first effective step toward the control of bacterial diseases, became widely available only in the early1940s and penicillin shortly after.

The Twentieth Century: Science, State, and Business

Whiggish authors justifiably rave about the "stupendous progress" of medicine in the twentieth century; it was also the century that witnessed the greatest medical crimes in history.

Medical murder and human experimentation. Enthusiastically serving scientifically deluded politicians and bureaucrats, a large number of doctors turned medical research into a large-scale immoral and deadly science in the Japanese empire,

---

KOCH'S POSTULATES (FORMALIZED IN 1882)

That the organism could be discoverable in every instance of the disease;

That, extracted from the body, the germ could be produced in a pure culture, maintainable over several microbial generations;

That the disease could be reproduced in experimental animals through a pure culture removed by numerous generations from the organisms initially isolated;

That the organism could be retrieved from the inoculated animal and cultured anew.

SOURCE: Roy Porter, *The Greatest Benefit to Mankind: A Medical History of Humanity,* (New York and London: Harper Collins, 1997), p. 436.

---

the United States, and, above all, in Nazi Germany. Adopting eugenic policies, Nazi doctors and their collaborators sterilized hundreds of thousands of mentally handicapped and sick persons, epileptics, and alcoholics. Other countries—Sweden and the United States, for example—also pursued sterilization policies. Patients in mental hospitals were starved and, during World War II, gassed. A racial agenda supported cost-effective medicine. Human experimentation carried out by doctors flourished in certain death camps. Beginning with the postwar Nuremberg Code, international declarations have outlawed such medical horrors. A nonethical medicine has a murderous potential; so it is back to Hippocrates, the phoenix of Western medicine, who was also Heinrich Himmler's medical hero.

Medical progress. By the end of the twentieth century, European medicine was remarkably similar to but not identical with American medicine in terms of clinical science, medical research, and surgery; it was different in its relations with the market economy, in the state's provision of universal primary medical care as a basic service, and in its cultural values. For considerably less cost, Europeans were just as healthy and, in many groups, enjoyed greater longevity than Americans. "Big medicine," which includes giant hospitals, often including extensive imaging and laboratory facilities, enormous bureaucracies, global drug companies, and large medical schools, was of course just as much a feature of the European as the American scene. Nowhere is this clearer than in the "war on cancer," the most useful of diseases in the promotion of the modernization of medicine; cancerology became the growth model of big medicine. The conceptual basis of medicine has changed radically since the eighteenth century. The changes can all be blamed on discoveries in genetics, immunology, neurology, endocrinology, pharmacology, and, the stepchild of medical education, nutritional science.

Still, science cannot escape being part of culture. Even in the new surgical fields that have opened up in organ transplantation and in cardiology, certain cultural differences distinguish medical practice in different countries. German doctors, loving the heart above all other organs, are much more inclined to use drugs than surgery in treating cardiovascular diseases. The number of coronary bypass operations per 100,000 people in 1998 was 202 for the United States, 90 for Germany, and 35 for the United Kingdom; the last figure probably reflected a generally bad state of cardiovascular care. French doctors seem much more concerned with the functioning of the liver than doctors in other cultures; they are also much more conservative in n recommending hysterectomies. French doctors are too generous with the use of ionizing radiation—825 procedures per 1,000 inhabitants—nearly twice as many procedures as in Britain. Wherever one looks, health is a major European growth industry. There is no shortage of disease, including hypochondria. Every age seems to have its "epidemic"—in the early twenty-first century, it is HIV-AIDS. And with the doctor accepting the modern idea that a well person is only an insufficiently diagnosed patient, and genetic medicine aiming to define genetically determined disease susceptibility in individual patients, the normal may become, as in Jules Roman's famous play *Knock,* the profitable pathological.

See also **Alchemy; Biology; Health and Disease; Psychology and Psychiatry; Science.**

BIBLIOGRAPHY

Ackerknecht, Erwin H. *A Short History of Medicine.* Baltimore, Md.: Johns Hopkins University Press, 1982. Whiggish and opinionated; students like its brevity.

Bonner, Thomas Neville. *Becoming a Physician: Medical Education in Britain, France, Germany, and the United States, 1750–1945.* New York: Oxford University Press, 1995.

Bynum, W. F. *Science and the Practice of Medicine in the Nineteenth Century.* Cambridge, U.K.: Cambridge University Press, 1994. An essential book on the nineteenth century.

Canguilhem, Georges. *The Normal and the Pathological.* Translated by Carolyn R. Fawcett. New York: Zone Books, 1991. Published in French, 1996.

Cantor, David, ed. *Reinventing Hippocrates.* Aldershot, U.K.: Ashgate, 2002.

Conrad, Lawrence I., et al. *The Western Medical Tradition, 800 B.C. to 1800 A.D.* Cambridge, U.K.: Cambridge University Press, 1995.

Dally, Ann. *Women under the Knife: A History of Surgery.* New York: Routledge, 1992.

Debus, Allen. *The French Paracelsians: The Chemical Challenge to Medical and Scientific Tradition in Early Modern France.* Cambridge, U.K.: Cambridge University Press, 1991.

Evans, Richard J. *Death in Hamburg: Society and Politics in the Cholera Years, 1830–1910.* Oxford: Clarendon, 1987.

Foucault, Michel. *The Birth of the Clinic: An Archeology of Medical Perception.* Translated by A. M. Sheridan Smith. London: Tavistock, 1973. Published in French, 1963.

Gay, Peter. *Freud: A Life for Our Time.* New York: Norton, 1988.

Geison, Gerald L. *The Private Science of Louis Pasteur.* Princeton, N.J.: Princeton University Press, 1995.

Gelfand, Toby. *Professionalizing Modern Medicine: Paris Surgeons and Medical Science and Institutions in the Eighteenth Century.* Westport, Conn.: Greenwood, 1980.

Goldstein, Jan E. *Console and Classify: The French Psychiatric Profession in the Nineteenth Century.* 2nd ed. Chicago: University of Chicago Press, 2001.

Hannaway, Caroline, and Ann La Berge, eds. *Constructing Paris Medicine.* Atlanta: Rodopi, 1999.

Kevles, Bettyann Holtzmann. *Naked to the Bone: Medical Imaging in the Twentieth Century.* New Brunswick, N.J.: Rutgers University Press, 1997.

Kiple, Kenneth F., ed. *The Cambridge World History of Human Disease.* Cambridge, U.K.: Cambridge University Press, 1993.

Lesky, Erna. *The Vienna Medical School of the Nineteenth Century.* Translated by L. Williams and I. S. Levij. Baltimore, Md.: The Johns Hopkins University Press, 1976.

Nutton, Vivian. "Roman Medicine, 250 BC to AD 200." In *The Western Medical Tradition, 800 BC to AD 1800,* by Lawrence I. Conrad et al., 39–70. Cambridge, U.K.: Cambridge University Press.

Payer, Lynn. *Medicine and Culture: Varieties of Treatment in the United States, England, West Germany, and France.* New York: Holt, 1996. Amusing and incisive analysis of the cultural foibles of medicine.

Porter, Roy. *The Greatest Benefit to Mankind: A Medical History of Humanity.* New York: W. W. Norton, 1998. For a survey of the field.

Ramsey, Matthew. *Professional and Popular Medicine in France, 1770–1830: The Social World of Medical Practice.* Cambridge, U.K.: Cambridge University Press, 1988.

Risse, Guenter B. *Mending Bodies, Saving Souls: A History of Hospitals.* New York: Oxford University Press, 1999.

Romain, Jules. *Knock ou le triomphe de la médecine.* Paris: n.p., 1924. This play (1923), made famous by Louis Jouvet in the role of Knock, enjoyed a revival on the Paris stage in the early 2000s with Fabrice Lucchini as Knock.

Weiner, Dora B. *The Citizen-Patient in Revolutionary and Imperial Paris.* Baltimore: Johns Hopkins University Press, 1993.

Harry W. Paul

INDIA

The historical record for Indian civilization begins in the third millennium B.C.E., with the Indus Valley culture, but beyond evidence of a good knowledge of the plant and animal environment, little information can be recovered concerning the healing traditions of this time. Simple ideas related to disease and healing can be found in greater abundance in the corpus of religious hymns called the Vedas, composed originally in an old form of Sanskrit during the early to mid-second millennium B.C.E. These ideas have much in common with religious materials worldwide: a concern with hostile demons, curses, and poisoning, and a detailed awareness of the plant world as a source of healing herbs. Outside the metropolis in India today, such ideas continue to form a prominent part of health-related beliefs and activities. Considering health as, in Georges Canguilhem's words, "a margin of tolerance for the inconsistencies of the environment," such practices and ideas can be seen as a perfectly reasonable and indeed rational extension of the use of a continuum of efforts—from prayer to warfare—as means for creating an acceptable environment in which to live.

Systematic Medicine

Structured systematic thought about medicine in India can first clearly be detected in sayings of the Buddha. In the *Samyuttanikaya* (4.230–231), part of the Buddhist canon (c. 250 B.C.E.), the Buddha is represented as contradicting the view that suffering is caused only by the effects of bad karma. He says that it is caused by eight factors: bile, phlegm, wind, and their pathological combination, changes of the seasons, the stress of unusual activities, external agency, as well as the ripening bad karma. This is the first moment in documented Indian history that these medical categories and explanations are combined in a clearly systematic manner, and it is these very factors that later became the cornerstone of classical Indian medical theory, or ayurveda (Sanskrit, "the knowledge for long life"). Great encyclopedias of medicine were composed in India during the centuries before and after the time of Christ, and these works brought together not only treatises on anatomy, including embryology, diagnosis, surgery, epidemics, pharmacology, and so forth, but many reflective philosophical passages discussing, for example, the origin of the human being, the rules of medical debate, methods for the interpretation of technical terminology and scientific expression, and so forth.

The two best-known compendia to survive from this era go under the names of their editors, Sushruta and Caraka. All this work was synthesized in the early seventh century C.E. into the great work *The Heart of Medicine* by the Sindhi author Vagbhata. This work became the textbook par excellence for ayurveda, the Sanskrit equivalent of Avicenna's *Canon,* and every bit as influential as that work. The later history of Sanskrit medical literature is a mixture of further works of grand synthesis and the proliferation of works on specialized topics and manuals for the working physician. Innovation took place both in the content and the form of the medical literature. By the nineteenth century, when European medical education and practice began to have a decisive impact in South Asia, Indian students who chose to specialize in medical studies were being exposed to a tradition of sophisticated medical reasoning and theory almost two thousand years old. This tradition was embodied in its practitioners and the literature they preserved through energetic and wide-ranging manuscript copying, which included multilingual dictionaries of materia medica, allegorical medical dramas, toxicological manuals, and veterinary texts, in addition to more predictable reference and teaching works. Hindu and Muslim physicians sometimes worked side by side, though their practices remained distinct.

Medical Concepts and Therapies

The systematic doctrines of ayurvedic medicine included a humoral theory somewhat akin to that of Hippocrates and Galen. Indian medicine admitted three humoral substances, namely, wind, bile, and phlegm. However, a certain indecision is visible within the tradition as to the status of blood, which shared with the humors the critical feature of being able to cause illness through becoming corrupt, and blood is sometimes implicitly included as a fourth humor. Disease was classified in several interesting and useful ways, and a system of triage was developed that guided the physician to focus on treatable and curable cases, while discouraging involvement with patients who were clearly in the grip of terminal conditions. Several thousand plants were known for their medicinal values, and described in terms of a pharmacological typology based on flavors (six types), potency (usually two: hot and cold), postdigestive flavorings (usually three), and pragmatic efficacy (used when the effect of a medicine is not adequately defined by the earlier categories). This typology formed a system of interlocking correspondences and antipathies with the system of humors and other physiological categories as expressed through the vocabulary of pathology.

Sanskrit medical treatises recommended a wide range of therapeutic techniques, including herbal drugs, massage, sauna, exercise, diet (including the use of meat broths and other nonvegetarian tonics), bloodletting (including leeching), simple psychotherapy, and surgery. One important group of five specific therapies became established early. According to Caraka, these were: emetics, purgation, two types of enema, and nasal catharsis. Sushruta replaced one of the enema treatments with bloodletting. Other authors added sweating and massage, as well as other therapies, into what became historically an increasingly important and elaborate complex of treatments. This "five therapies" treatment is still popular and important today. The theories and techniques described in this tradition were widely known and practiced by learned physicians and their staffs and students all over India. Of course, as in all parts of the world, there were many quacks and charlatans, a problem explicitly discussed in the very earliest Sanskrit medical writings.

Surgery

Surgery had a different history from the other parts of traditional medicine. The compendium of Sushruta includes many chapters on the training and practice of surgeons. The early date of this treatise and the great accuracy, insight, and detail of the surgical descriptions are most impressive. One can infer that the surgical profession had developed over several generations at least and had arrived at an advanced stage. Surgeons were thought of as a separate group of practitioners from the more normative herbal healers, yet for some unknown reason, their tradition was recorded in the Sanskrit language and integrated into the medical corpus. This legacy was then passed

down the centuries as part of ayurveda. However, the actual practice of surgery did not survive in the same way. The early and medieval historical sources of India gives us almost no evidence of advanced surgery being practiced. By the time foreign observers from China, and later Afghanistan and Europe, begin to describe India, Sushruta's surgery had all but vanished. A few barber-surgeon practitioners preserved limited skills in couching for cataract and bone-setting, and even in types of plastic surgery, but these were no longer integrated into the learned practice of classical Indian medicine. Early European surgeons were in much demand in India from their arrival in the sixteenth century onward, although by contrast European physicians were not sought after, and the flow of knowledge about simples and drugs was from East to West.

Modernization and Globalization

Under first the Moghul and then the British colonial powers, indigenous Indian medicine survived as it always had, mainly through support from patients and the community, but with occasional patronage from the state, with education and practice being devolved and decentralized, often taking place at the family level. During the twentieth century, ayurveda assumed an important role as an icon of national identity during the independence struggle. After independence, the government of India adopted the traditional systems of Indian medicine, including ayurveda, Islamic Unani medicine, yoga, and the South Indian Siddha tradition and provided a state-sponsored structure of education and practice on the model of Western medicine. To these indigenous traditions were also added homeopathy and naturopathy, both adopted and tightly integrated as part of "Indian" health care and administered by the same department within the Ministry of Health and Family Welfare. At the start of the third millennium, a process of globalization—similar to that which took place earlier with yoga—has begun to occur also with ayurveda. In diaspora ayurveda is changing and adapting, as it moves from its premodern role in India to a new position as one part of a portfolio of alternative and complementary therapies offered alongside modern biomedicine.

See also **Medicine: China; Yoga.**

BIBLIOGRAPHY

Dash, Vaidya Bhagwan. *Fundamentals of Āyurvedic Medicine.* Vol. 85, Indian Medical Science series. Rev. and enlarged. Delhi: Sri Satguru Publications, 1999.

Government of India, Ministry of Health & Family Welfare. "Indian Systems of Medicine and Homoeopathy: A Gateway for Information." Available on the Internet at http://indianmedicine.nic.in/.

Jolly, Julius. *Indian Medicine* (1951). Translated by C. G. Kashikar. 3rd ed. New Delhi: Munshiram Manoharlal, 1994.

Langford, Jean M. *Fluent Bodies: Ayurvedic Remedies for Postcolonial Imbalance.* Durham, N.C.: Duke University Press, 2002.

Meulenbeld, Gerrit Jan. *A History of Indian Medical Literature.* 5 vols. Groningen: E. Forsten, 1999–2002.

Mukhopadhyay, Alok, ed. *State of India's Health.* New Delhi: Voluntary Health Association of India, 1992.

Sharma, Priya Vrat. *Caraka-Samhita: Agnivesa's Treatise Refined and Annotated by Caraka and Redacted by Drdhabala (text with*

English translation). 4 vols. Varanasi, Delhi: Chaukhambha Orientalia, 1999–2001.

———. *Suśruta-Samhitā, with English Translation of Text and Dalhana's Commentary Alongwith [sic] Critical Notes.* 3 vols. Vol. 9, Haridas Ayurveda series. Varanasi, India: Chaukhambha Visvabharati, 1999–2001

van Alphen, Jan, and Anthony Aris, eds. *Oriental Medicine: An Illustrated Guide to the Asian Arts of Healing.* London: Serindia, 1995.

Wujastyk, Dominik. *The Roots of Āyurveda: Selections from Sanskrit Medical Writings.* 3rd ed. London and New York: Penguin, 2003.

Zysk, Kenneth G. *Asceticism and Healing in Ancient India: Medicine in the Buddhist Monastery.* 2nd ed. Vol. 2, *Indian Medical Tradition.* Delhi: Motilal Banarsidass, 1998.

Dominik Wujastyk

ISLAMIC MEDICINE

Islamic medicine refers to the range of health-promoting beliefs common to and actions taken in Muslim societies, whether by Muslims or others. As with other traditional medical systems, Muslim medicine was composed of several subsystems, each involving a unique etiology and practice and each enjoying a different legitimacy. These subsystems were not independent of each other and none enjoyed complete hegemony. In the Muslim context this means that humoralism, folklore, and prophetic medicines were all present in the medical therapeutic scene.

Theories Composing Muslim Medicine

Popular medicine was sanctioned by custom, a wide consensus from below, not by any religious, judicial, or scientific authority. This medical folklore in itself took many forms and was the outcome of diverse pre-Muslim cultural traditions (such as those of Arabs, Greeks, Persians, and Berbers) and differing ecological environments with their distinctive medical problems as well as flora and fauna from which medication was prepared.

By contrast, what Muslims call prophetic medicine (*al-Tibb al-Nabawi*) does not rely on custom. Instead it originated from (and therefore is sanctioned by) the sayings of the Prophet Muhammad. These sayings, in which Muhammad gave his opinions on medical practices, constituted the basis for a distinctive medical system from the ninth century onward. The Shiites entrust the imams, the descendants of Muhammad's family and therefore the spiritual leaders of the community, with extraordinary healing abilities as part of their supernatural attributes; thus in Shiism the role of Muhammad as healer is downplayed. But in general the field of prophetic medicine engaged many of the most renowned scholars of their time (for example, the Egyptian Jalal al-Din al-Suyuti, d. 1505). Among the population at large, medical rites and practices were connected with live and dead saints. Certain individuals were (and still are) believed to possess extraordinary healing powers, so that visiting them or their graves was believed to be medically beneficial.

Mechanical medicine, based on the humoralism inherited from Greek antiquity, constitutes the third tradition. This medicine is based on the well-known idea of four elements: a physical and philosophical metatheory according to which everything in nature is a mixture of fire, earth, air, and water. Each element embodies two of the four qualities of hot, cold, dry, and moist. The human body was understood to correspond with this model, because it is a microcosmos of nature. The body consists therefore of four humors, or fluids, the physiological blocks of the body: blood (air), phlegm (water), black bile (earth), and yellow bile (fire). In case of illness, which is a state of imbalance in the body, it was up to the humoralist physician to diagnose which of the four humors was in excess or deficient. The physician then proceeded to recommend a course of treatment, usually by diet, to correct or counterbalance the offending humor. Excess in black bile, for example, known to be cold and dry, necessitated adding warmth and moisture artificially. This tradition asserted its legitimacy by drawing on scientific treatises of the sages of antiquity, as mediated through the intellectual and literary discourses of famous Muslim medical figures.

Hospitals

One of the unique features of Muslim medicine was the use and development of hospitals (*bimarsitans* or *dar al-shifas*). Hospitals were founded in most major Muslim cities, starting in Baghdad, the capital of the Muslim empire, in the ninth century, and reached an especially high standard during Mamluk and Ottoman periods (from the thirteenth century). Muslim hospitals were urban charitable institutions funded by endowments (*waqfs*) that offered free treatment to the sick by an expert medical staff. In contrast to their European counterparts, Muslim hospitals were "true" hospitals in that they were designed to offer the sick expert medical treatment by professionals, whereas many premodern European hospitals (mainly in the medieval Latin West) usually restricted themselves to spiritual aid and substance to exhausted and convalescent people.

Ages of Translations

Muslim medicine has always been in contact with other medical systems through translations of medical treatises. The translation movement has worked in both directions; that is, both to and from Muslim languages. Muslim Galenic medicine owed much of its origin to a massive move to translate from Greek to Arabic in the ninth century. This was part of the general introduction of Hellenic culture and science into the Muslim world. Most of the translations were done via mediator languages, mostly Syriac and to some extent Persian. Translators, many of whom were Christians (such as the famous Husayn ibn Ishaq), enjoyed caliphal patronage. Al-Ma'mun (reigned 813–833) should be given special mention for sponsoring the great library of Baghdad, *Bayt al-Hikma* (literally, "House of Wisdom"), which was the center of intellectual activity at the time. Although we associate the Age of Translation with Hellenic medicine, during the ninth century traditional Indian medicine (Ayurveda) was translated into Arabic as well, either directly from Sanskrit or by way of Persian. In the long run, however, it was Hellenic medicine that became dominant in the caliphal court.

Muslim doctors were the custodians of Hellenic medicine, which they expanded, corrected, systemized, and summarized (for example, in the fields of pharmacology, ophthalmology, pathology, and many others). In anatomy, for example, Ibn al-Nafis (d. 1288) is credited with describing the circulation of blood in the lungs for the first time. He formulated this description through logical deduction rather than clinical observation. Many Muslim medical texts were translated into European languages during the later Middle Ages. Thus many Muslim physicians became known to Europe, as well as otherwise "lost" texts from antiquity. Figures like Abu Bakr Muhammad ibn Zakariya al-Razi (d. 925), Abu Qasim al-Zahrawi (d. 1013), and Ibn Sina (d. 1037) were famous in Europe by the Latinized form of their names (Rhazes, Albucasis, and Avicenna, respectively), and their treatises became standard medical texts well into the eighteenth century.

In the early modern period another move to translate medical texts occurred, again from European to Muslim languages. This time nonhumoral concepts were introduced to Muslim medicine. A prime example of a physician who applied the concepts of European medicine is Salih ibn Sallum, from Aleppo (d. 1670), the head physician of the Ottoman Empire, who was influenced by Paracelsus (d. 1541), the German-speaking physician who was the first to treat patients with chemical rather than botanic or natural medications. Ibn Sallum's work in Arabic was soon translated into Ottoman Turkish. Translation of European texts accelerated in the following centuries, especially during the nineteenth century, when many European texts were translated into Muslim languages as part of the move from traditional medicine to Western biomedicine.

Changes from the Nineteenth Century Onward

Beginning with the late eighteenth century, major political and socioeconomic transformations have occurred in the Muslim world that profoundly changed medicine and public health. European medicine was introduced on a much larger scale in various ways. Students were sent to universities in Europe to learn medicine. In addition, medical schools were shaped according to the Western model, at which European professors taught European medicine in French, were founded in all major capitals of the Middle East during the first half of the nineteenth century. The first was established in 1827 near Cairo, followed shortly by a military medical school in Istanbul. The third, another military medical school, was included in a polytechnic school founded in Tehran in 1850–1851.

Despite the profound Westernization of medical theory and the medical establishment in the Muslim world, traditional Muslim medicine is still being practiced. It is not found in the state-run hospitals or in universities, but it is present at the popular level. Religious circles promote prophetic medicine, and in recent years many traditional texts have been reprinted and Internet websites devoted to this subject have been set up.

See also **Islamic Science; Medicine: China; Medicine: Europe and the United States; Medicine: India.**

BIBLIOGRAPHY
Adivar [Adnan], Abdülhâk. *La Science chez les Turcs Ottomans.* Paris, 1939. More recent editions exist in Turkish, such as *Osmanlı Türklerinde İ lim.* 5. basım. Istanbul: Remzi Kitabevi, 1991.

Conrad, Lawrence I. "Arab-Islamic Medical Tradition." In *The Western Medical Tradition 800 BC to AD 1800,* edited by Lawrence I. Conrad et al. Cambridge, U.K.: Cambridge University Press, 1995. A good introduction that renders the classic by Manfred Ullman up to date.

Dols, Michael W. *Medieval Islamic Medicine: Ibn Ridwan's Treatise "On the Prevention of Bodily Ills in Egypt."* Berkeley: University of California Press, 1984. A translation of an eleventh-century medical treatise by an Egyptian physician that reflects Muslim humoral medical knowledge of the period.

———. *Majnūn: The Madman in Medieval Islamic Society.* Oxford: Clarendon, 1992. A study of madness in Muslim society that also includes the medical aspects of this social and cultural phenomenon.

Elgood, Cyril. *A Medical History of Persia and the Eastern Caliphate from the Earliest Times until the Year A.D. 1932.* Cambridge, U.K.: Cambridge University Press, 1951.

———. *Safavid Medical Practice or the Practice of Medicine, Surgery and Gynaecology in Persia between 1500 A.D. and 1750 A.D.* London: Luzac, 1970.

Ullman, Manfred. *Islamic Medicine.* Edinburgh: Edinburgh University Press, 1978.

Miri Shefer

MEDITATION, EASTERN. Many religious traditions have practices that could possibly be labeled *meditation.* In Judaism, Christianity, and Islam, these practices are usually associated with prayer, contemplation, or recitation of sacred texts. In the religious traditions of the Native Americans, Australian aboriginals, Siberian peoples, and many others, what could be identified as meditation techniques are incorporated within the larger rubric of shamanism. It is, however, in the religions of Asia that meditation has been most developed as a religious method. Meditation has played an important role in the ancient yogic traditions of Hinduism and also in more recent Hindu-based new religious movements such as Maharishi Mahesh Yogi's Transcendental Meditation program. But it is most especially in the monastic or "elite" forms of the various traditions of Buddhism (Theravada, Tibetan/Vajrayana, and Ch'an/Zen) that meditation techniques have taken center stage and have been developed to the highest degree of sophistication and complexity.

Meditation can be loosely defined as a mental regimen or discipline designed to promote concentration and the capacity for what is called "one-pointedness" (*ekagrata*) of mind. There are many different meditation methods and many different recommended objects on which to meditate. Some traditions emphasize breathing exercises that focus the mind on inhalation and exhalation; others instruct the practitioner to meditate on the subtle workings of his or her own mind. Still others emphasize concentration on certain symbols (such as cosmic representations known as *mandalas* or *yantras*) or on sacred sounds called mantras. In some traditions it is God or one of the gods (or one of the Buddhas or bodhisattvas) upon which one meditates, while in others it is a problem or puzzle (the Zen *koan*) or a topic of an analysis such as death or attachment to the physical body. In yet other meditations it is a virtuous emotion or quality such as renunciation, compassion, or loving-kindness upon which one meditates, and in still others it is simple mindfulness or awareness (the constant watchfulness entailing "being here, now") that is emphasized.

But fundamentally all forms of meditation have as their goal the ability to concentrate for long periods of time single-pointedly and intensely on the object of meditation. The mind is sometimes likened to a pool of water that is muddy and turbulent; the goal of meditation is to calm the mind so as to be able to see its true nature clearly. Alternatively, the goal of meditation is said to be the suspension of ordinary discursive thought and the attainment of a state whereby all dualities are transcended—especially the distinction between the perceiving and thinking subject and the object of perception or thought. In any event, Hindu and Buddhist texts alike claim that the perfection of the ability to meditate well and for long periods of time will help produce in the practitioner high spiritual states of awareness, supernatural powers, wisdom and insight into the true nature of reality, and finally, salvation itself (*moksha* or nirvana, both of which entail liberation from ignorance, suffering, and rebirth).

The practice of meditation in India goes back to at least the middle of the first millennium B.C.E. and probably much earlier. The ancient Hindu mystical and philosophical texts called the Upanishads refer to meditation, and the early texts of Buddhism assume its existence as a technique taught by a wide variety of religious teachers. By the time of the turn of the Common Era, if not centuries before, meditation had become highly systematized in both Hindu and Buddhist traditions.

In all the meditation traditions originating in ancient India, emphasis is placed on finding a quiet, solitary place (the wilderness, a monastery, or an ashram or retreat) and assuming a sitting posture that will be conducive to meditation. The most famous of these postures, or *asanas,* is the "lotus position," whereby the meditator sits with legs folded and feet resting on the thigh or knees. The hands are kept folded in the lap or in a special gesture called a *mudra,* and the eyes are kept closed or slightly open in an unfocused, downward-looking gaze. The back is kept straight to enhance alertness and to help the "inner channels" of the mystical body open up and run smoothly.

In Hinduism, meditation is most frequently encountered as part of a more general practice of yoga. In the *Yoga Sutras* of Patanjali, the classical source on ancient Indian yoga dating to around 200 or 300 C.E. and perhaps earlier, meditation techniques are basically indistinguishable from the practice of yoga. For Patanjali, one might say, yoga *is* meditation. Yoga is defined as the "cessation of the turnings of thought" (*Yoga Sutras* 1.2), implying the ability to control even the subtlest example of the mind's activity.

Patanjali organizes the practice of yoga into eight "limbs" or parts (*ashtanga*). The first two limbs of yoga entail living a life guided by moral principles and personal observances. The third limb of yoga encompasses the physical postures, which have as their purpose to prepare the body for the meditation

techniques that follow. The fourth limb is control of the breath, which "makes the mind fit for concentration" (*Yoga Sutras* 2.53). The regulation of the breath is followed by "withdrawal of the senses," the disengagement of the sense organs with their objects and the turning inward of thought. This allows the yogin to develop the final three limbs or stages: concentration ("binding thought in one place"), meditation (unwavering attention on an object), and pure contemplation or *samadhi,* defined as "meditation that illumines the object alone, as if the subject were devoid of intrinsic form" (*Yoga Sutras* 3.1–3). These last and culminating stages of the yogic practice are "internal" (as opposed to the "external" limbs that came before) and when they are "focused on a single object constitute perfect discipline" (*Yoga Sutras* 3.4, 7).

Various techniques for "fixing" the attention (*trataka*) were developed in later esoteric Hindu traditions, all of which were meant to induce the trance state called *samadhi.* In some cases the practitioner was instructed to fix his or her attention on certain places in the body—the crown of the head, the spot between the eyebrows, the tip of the nose, the navel, and so on—in order to gather one's mental energy at a single point. In other instances, the practitioner was instructed to focus on a small object such as a speck on the wall or a mustard seed, or to stare at a distant object to the exclusion of all others in one's purview, or to focus on one or another of the Sanskrit letters or some other image. Meditation on those powerful, sacred sounds known as *mantras* (the most famous of which is "*om*") was especially common. In the theistic sects, the object of meditation was often the deity. In the Bhagavad Gita, for example, the practitioner is advised to sit quietly, fix one's sight on the tip of the nose, and meditate on Krishna.

But it is especially in the Buddhist traditions that stem from India (and were then spread throughout Asia) that meditation becomes absolutely central. Gautama Buddha was said to have achieved his enlightenment through the method of meditation, and ever since, meditative concentration, together with ethics and wisdom or insight, has been the pivot of Buddhist practice. Early Buddhist texts list a set of forty possible topics of meditation (in Pali, *kammatthana*). Some are labeled "devices" (meditation on the elements, or on shapes or colors) that help the meditator fix his or her concentration on a particular image. Another topic is designated "recollections," whereby the meditator recalls the virtues of the Buddha, the dharma (the teachings of the Buddha), or the *sangha* (the Buddhist community) or is reminded of his or her own mortality through a meditation on death's inevitability.

Yet another set of meditation topics is designed to wean the meditator from attachment to the physical body. He or she is encouraged to concentrate on the repulsive and impermanent characteristics of the body or of food (and what happens to it as it is digested), or is urged to focus on various aspects of a decomposing corpse. Still another kind of meditation recommended in the early texts of Buddhism concerns what are known as the "four stations of Brahma" or the "four immeasurables": friendliness or loving-kindness, compassion, empathetic joy, and equanimity or even-mindedness. These meditation topics are sometimes recommended to meditators of different personalities or proclivities. For a devotional type of person, for example, meditation on the Buddha or the Sangha might be most appropriate, whereas for a sensual type of mediator the most effective topic might be the disgusting nature of the human body.

Buddhist traditions analyze the results of meditation into eight stages of increasingly subtle states of consciousness called the "absorptions" or "trance" states of higher consciousness (in Pali, *jhana;* in Sanskrit, *dhyana*). These are, it is said, the states of mind the Buddha passed through in deep meditation on his way to enlightenment. The first is described as a mental state of detachment from sensual pleasures and craving, in which, however, the discursive intellect is still active. In the second state, the mind grows more still, concentration increases, discursive thought ends, and great joy and peace arise. The third stage is characterized by the transcendence of sensual joy itself and the attainment of equanimity, which brings about a higher form of bliss, and by the diminishing of the sense of self as the subject of this experience. The fourth trance state is where consciousness of all duality abates and one achieves the "utter purity of mindfulness," which lies beyond all words. The second set of four even subtler states of mind are called the "formless" *jhanas* because they are based on contemplation of formless subjects: the infinity of space, the infinity of consciousness, nothingness, and "neither perception nor nonperception." The last of these is where subject and object are nearly indistinguishable and all pairs of opposites are totally transcended.

Such deep states of concentration are to be linked, however, with "insight" (in Pali, *vipassana;* in Sanskrit, *vipashyana*) into the true nature of reality in order to produce the state of liberation the Buddhist meditator seeks. When combined with the ability to focus deeply on the object of meditation, the analysis of reality reveals it to be impermanent, without essence or "self," and thoroughly bound up in suffering. It is these deep insights into the true nature of reality, gained through the ability to concentrate in meditation, that will lead the seeker to "release," or the "extinguishing" of ignorance and suffering (nirvana), just as such techniques brought the Buddha to his enlightenment.

The Mahayana traditions equally emphasize the importance of meditation and most especially the combination of the ability to focus the mind one-pointedly (what is sometimes here called "calm abiding" or *shamatha*) and the penetration or insight into the true nature of reality termed *vipashyana.* Such a potent synthesis is said to lead the meditator to a realization of the "emptiness" (*shunyata*) of intrinsic existence of all things. Nothing, according to this view, has existence independently or has a self-nature; everything exists only dependently or nominally. Such a realization of emptiness in deep meditation becomes the impetus for the meditator's own enlightenment.

In the various Mahayana traditions, meditations designed to attain the realization of emptiness range from attempts to empty the mind completely of all conceptual thought, to the stripping away of all conceptual imputations of reality and then analyzing what is left, to even more radical techniques to shock the discursive mind out of its complacency so as to recognize its true, innate, and intuitive "Buddha nature." Among the most famous of these latter meditative tools is the *koan* used

in the Ch'an/Zen schools of Buddhism. The *koan* is a kind of a riddle or puzzle designed to break down ordinary ways of thinking and jolt the meditator into the wholly different mindset of "enlightenment" (Japanese *satori*).

Other Mahayana traditions are more devotional in their emphasis. Here, meditation takes the form of fixing the mind on the Buddha or bodhisattva to whom one is devoted and whom one asks for help. In these traditions, prayers or *mantras* become the centerpiece of meditation practice, or the name of one of the Buddhas or bodhisattvas is invoked repeatedly. The recitation of the phrase *namu amida butsu* ("Homage to Amida Buddha") in the Japanese Pure Land sects is an example of this kind of meditation. In some of these devotional Buddhist traditions, certain Sutras or sacred texts are thought to have such salvific power that the mere repetition of the text or even just chanting the condensed verbal essence or title of the Sutra will produce efficacious results in the meditator. In the Pure Land sects of Buddhism, meditation sometimes revolves around complex visualizations of one or another of the "paradises" or "pure lands" of the Buddhas and bodhisattvas in the hopes of attaining a rebirth there.

Meditation, a feature of many traditional religions, is becoming part of secular life in the modern world. Meditation techniques seem to produce states of mind that Western scientists are beginning to think may very well have measurable effects on the mental and physical health of the meditator. Sports trainers, coaches, and psychologists utilize visualization techniques to help professional athletes perform better. The reduction of anxiety that comes from the ability to focus and calm the mind in meditation is now generally recognized, and meditation is sometimes integrated into the workplace to help workers deal with stress. Neuroscientists and doctors are finding not only that accomplished meditators can achieve states of focused attention and concentration far beyond what scientists previously thought was possible but also that meditation seems to have a positive effect on the nervous, immune, and endocrine systems. Meditation, for centuries practiced primarily by monks and ascetics in Asia, is increasingly being mainstreamed in the West as a technique that promotes relaxation, better attention and concentration, the reduction of stress, and general good health.

See also **Asceticism: Hindu and Buddhist Asceticism; Buddhism; Hinduism; Yoga.**

BIBLIOGRAPHY

Conze, Edward. *Buddhist Meditation.* New York: Allen and Unwin, 1956.

The Dalai Lama. *Stages of Meditation.* Root text by Kamalashila; translated by Geshe Lobsang Jordhen, Losang Choephel Ganchenpa, and Jeremy Russell. Ithaca, N.Y.: Snow Lion, 2003.

Humphreys, Christmas. *Concentration and Meditation: A Manual of Mind Development.* Baltimore: Penguin Books, 1968.

King, Winston L. *Theravāda Meditation: The Buddhist Transformation of Yoga.* University Park: Pennsylvania State University Press, 1980.

Thera, Nyanaponika. *The Heart of Buddhist Meditation (Satipattāna): A Handbook of Mental Training based on the*

Buddha's Way of Mindfulness, with an Anthology of Relevant Texts Translated from the Pali and Sanskrit. 1st U.S. ed. New York: Citadel, 1969.

Wallace, B. Alan. *The Bridge of Quiescence: Experiencing Tibetan Buddhist Meditation.* Foreword by H.H. the Dalai Lama. Chicago: Open Court, 1998.

Wayman, Alex, trans. *Calming the Mind and Discerning the Real: Buddhist Meditation and the Middle View, from the Lam rim chen mo Tson-kha-pa.* New York: Columbia University Press, 1978.

Zahler, Leah, ed. *Meditative States in Tibetan Buddhism: The Concentrations and Formless Absorptions.* London: Wisdom, 1983.

Brian Smith

MEME.

Meme is indeed an interesting and apt subject to include in a dictionary of the history of ideas, for it is nothing less than a meta-concept for describing the transmission of knowledge among persons and cultures. Memetics—the study of memes—is, briefly stated, evolutionary theory applied to ideas. The word itself was coined by the British biologist Richard Dawkins in his 1976 book *The Selfish Gene* as a neologism derived from *mimeme* (that which is imitated) and *gene*. However, Dawkins's insight was presaged by William S. Burroughs's observation that "language is a virus from outer space" and by the work of thinkers ranging from the dadaists to Jacques Derrida, who, in seeking to transcend language and textuality, recognized the role that language and ideas play in controlling human behavior. In the late twentieth century and early twenty-first century, however, memetics has drawn its strongest supporters from the rather more literally minded camp of computer scientists and devotees of Internet culture—not only because the memetic model of human intelligence is similar to the programming of a computer but because memes are a useful metaphor for describing certain phenomena that occur in the online world.

Cultures, Dawkins observed, evolve much as organisms do, and he conceptualized memes as ideas that guide human behavior just as a snippet of genetic code can guide instinctual mating or dominance behaviors. Much like genes, memes arise in response to a new stressor in the environment and evolve in response to changing conditions:

> all life evolves by the differential survival of replicating entities. . . . I think that a new kind of replicator has recently emerged. . . . It is still in its infancy, still drifting clumsily about in its primeval soup, but already it is achieving evolutionary change at a rate that leaves the old gene panting far behind. The new soup is the soup of human culture. (Dawkins, pp. 191–192)

A meme can be a concrete technology, such as a technique for making a stone spearhead, or an entirely abstract idea, such as "kingship" or "jihad." Examples of memes range from methods of making pottery and building arches to songs and stories, to tastes in clothing and fashion, to even more sophisticated behaviors, such as manufacturing hydrogen bombs, which require a "meme complex" or group of mutually reinforcing memes—in this case, the concepts of metalworking, atomic theory, and explosives.

As the result of natural selection, some memes become rare or are altogether eliminated from the "meme pool," the collective sum of a society's knowledge; they can also be overwritten by an invading group's memes. For instance, few twenty-first-century Native Americans know techniques that were indispensable to their pre-Columbian ancestors, such as flint-knapping or making a fire with the bow-and-drill method. Some memes (such as "cooking") survive because they are generally useful; others (such as "sports cars") trigger hardwired evolutionary imperatives, such as "food" or "sex" or "danger"; still others use more insidious means to ensure their own survival. For instance, chain letters, though intrinsically useless, have managed to be successfully passed on for decades because they contain instructions for their own reproduction and because they successfully exploit the human desire to get something for nothing, while evangelical religions (to give another example of a self-perpetuating meme) emphasize the virtues of proselytizing.

These latter cases serve to illustrate an important point of Dawkins's conceptualization, namely, the parasitic quality of memes. Lacking any physical way of reproducing themselves, memes survive and grow by imitation or by transmission from mind to mind. The transmission may occur through the observation and copying of a certain behavior or technique; it may occur as a craft is taught to an apprentice or as a farmer shows his or her son how to shear sheep; or it may be verbal, as by a professor's lecturing or assigning reading to her or his students. The participants need not speak the same language, as was the case with American GIs learning judo in occupied Japan. The transmission may be by force, such as the spread of the meme complexes of Islam and Christianity by conquest; or it can be by trade and indirect influence, such as the spread of classical Greek and Chinese ideas and motifs through the ancient Mediterranean and East Asia, respectively. Certain ideas are more easily imitated, or more contagious, than others; these are the memes that tend to be selected for survival, irrespective of the benefits to the individual they infect; in fact certain memes (such as celibacy or kamikaze missions) may be detrimental to the host's genetic survival but are nonetheless highly successful at reproducing themselves. Thus a viral contagion is a more apt metaphor to describe the meme than is sexual reproduction—a comparison Dawkins also used to describe the genetic code itself. To extend the metaphor, one is "infected" by an idea as a cell is by a pathogen, and one is compelled to carry the idea to others so that it may reproduce itself. Much like a computer virus, information begets information.

The Selfish Meme

Even memes like "celibacy" and "kamikaze mission," while detrimental for their individual hosts, may nonetheless be beneficial for the meme pool at large. As Matt Ridley so eloquently explains in his 1996 book *The Origins of Virtue,* magnanimous social behavior is nonetheless often guided by the self-interest of all involved. Like ants, human beings seem to have evolved to be genetically hardwired to cooperate. Successful memes can build on this tendency. For instance, few animals, including humans, are munificent to those outside their immediate group or tribe, but the "patriotism" meme, by giving us a way to conceptualize an entire nation as an extended tribe, is one way of explaining the phenomenon of the growth of nation-states—or "imagined communities," as Benedict Anderson put it in his 1983 book of the same title. Thus even memes that are detrimental to the individual can confer an evolutionary advantage; to build on the example of patriotism, groups with memes that promote extensive cooperation (such as Caesar's Roman legions) will tend to outcompete groups who do not (such as the tribes of Gaul). *Dulce et decorum est pro patria mori* (It is sweet and proper to die for one's country).

One of the most philosophically depressing implications of memetic theory is that it is our memes, not human genius and creativity, that are the guiding force in history. Just as Dawkins reduced biological organisms to a vehicle for the self-perpetuation of genetic material, so it is with memes. Our various behaviors, from building cathedrals to writing novels, can be viewed as nothing more than our memes attempting to survive and grow. "Memes might come to be viewed explicitly as the primary actors in the drama of human history, exerting an iron-fisted control precisely analogous to that of Richard Dawkins's 'selfish genes' in the pageant of biological evolution," as James Gardner put it in his article "Memetic Engineering" in the May 1996 issue of *Wired* magazine. Such an idea is tremendously troubling for notions of free will. Gardner continued:

> A meme-focused vision of culture and consciousness acknowledges forthrightly that memes are not mere random effluvia of the human experience but powerful control mechanisms that impose a largely invisible deep structure on a wide range of complex phenomena—language, scientific thinking, political behavior, productive work, religion, philosophical discourse, even history itself.

Memetic Engineering

To add to the confusion, the modern world has seen an unprecedented multiplication and proliferation of memes, with mass media being the preeminent transmission vector. Some of these memes are devised with rational ends, such as advertising consumer products; others are devised solely as play; others are "junk" memes. Hula hoops, the Burma Shave billboards of the 1950s, the slogan "There's always room for Jell-O," the synthesizer intro to the 1984 song "Jump" by Van Halen, or the three-note "by Men-nen" jingle, while of no use to those they infect, are excellent examples. The Internet in particular is a virtual memetic petri dish, with examples such as the non-sensical phrase "all your base are belong to us" (from a badly translated 1988 Japanese video game called Zero Wing) spontaneously arising on message boards in 2000, spreading from mind to mind via the ether and then dissipating, not unlike a particularly virulent disease burning its way through the population.

Thus the idea of memetic engineering consists not only in choosing which memes to be influenced by but also in counterpropaganda and countersloganeering designed to purge from the meme pool those ideas deemed deleterious to society at large. The essential component in memetic engineering is faith in human reason to discern the most advantageous memes. Dawkins himself expressed a secular humanist optimism when he wrote, "We, alone on Earth, can rebel against the tyranny of the selfish replicators" (p. 201). (Of course, from another perspective, this could be seen as just another Darwinian struggle, with the meme for "secular humanism" trying to crush its competitor for mindshare, the meme for "theocracy.")

One example of the deployment of this idea is the activist Andrew Boyd's Billionaires for Bush (or Gore) campaign, which used the ironic, parodical image of the superwealthy taking to the streets in support of their candidates in order to "piggyback" on mainstream media coverage of the 2000 U.S. presidential election and thus call attention to social issues neglected by the candidates. The idea of memetic engineering was both popularized and taken to its logical end by the 1992 science fiction novel *Snow Crash* by Neal Stephenson. Though the actual word *meme* never occurs in the book, the plot makes clear reference to Dawkins's work. The title, for instance, refers to a key element in the book's plot, a literal "mind virus" modeled after a computer virus that is capable of destroying a user's mind through merely being seen on a computer screen. The resolution involves a clay tablet from ancient Mesopotamia, on which are recorded syllables in an ancestral ur-language (reminiscent of ideas of the "deep structure" of language popularized by Noam Chomsky and others) that can program human beings, like robots, into performing tasks for those who know how to wield the power. *Snow Crash* is frequently cited in meme circles as an example of the power of memes taken to the nth degree.

Criticism of Memetic Theory

Despite the cult popularity of the idea, memetic theory is hardly discussed in recent texts on evolutionary psychology and linguistics. The prevailing consensus seems to be that the meme is a nice metaphor but one that has perhaps been taken too far. Memes, after all, are hard to define, quantify, and measure; their very existence is somewhat nebulous, inferable but not scientifically verifiable.

Some have also assailed memes not only as bad science but as reactionary politics. The complexity of human development is overly reduced into nonmaterialist, quasi-mystical, pseudo-scientific terms, which in turn are only a new Kabbalah, a recasting of age-old ideas of angels and demons and magic words that can control reality. Many also question the memetics community's frequent, almost reflexive, assaults on religion, which they characterize as nothing more than preprogrammed, irrational memetic replication. Moreover the idea of human behavior as nothing but the programming of snippets of information is troubling to many—and not only those who still maintain a belief in free will. To hold with a radical memetic view of human behavior is to ignore the factors of economics, environment, and politics in history. As such, memetics is a fascinating and promising protoscience but further research and experimentation is needed before it can become a full-fledged discipline in its own right.

See also **Computer Science; Genetics; Ideas, History of.**

BIBLIOGRAPHY

Aunger, Robert. *The Electric Meme: A New Theory of How We Think.* New York: Free Press, 2002.

Blackmore, Susan. *The Meme Machine.* New York and Oxford: Oxford University Press, 1999.

Boyd, Andrew. "Truth Is a Virus: Meme Warfare and the Billionaires for Bush (or Gore)." In *The Cultural Resistance Reader,* edited by Stephen Duncombe. New York: Verso, 2002.

Dawkins, Richard. *The Selfish Gene.* New ed. Oxford and New York: Oxford University Press, 1989. Originally published in 1976.

Gardner, James. "Memetic Engineering." *Wired* 4.05 (May 1996). Available at http://www.wired.com/wired/archive/4.05/memetic .htm.

Journal of Memetics. Available at http://jom-emit.cfpm.org/.

Ridley, Matt. *The Origins of Virtue.* New York: Penguin Books, 1996.

Stephenson, Neal. *Snow Crash.* New York: Bantam, 1992.

Kenneth Mondschein

MEMORY. The history of the idea of memory is associated with the cultural uses of two kinds of memory, episodic and semantic. Episodic memory concerns the conscious recall of particular events. Interest in its nature dates from antiquity, and mnemonic techniques for strengthening memory's resources, known as the "art of memory," were developed as rhetorical skills. Semantic memory deals in tacit understandings—habits of mind and implicit knowledge on the boundary between the conscious and the unconscious. In modern times, scholars have treated it as a realm apart from episodic memory in light of a newly discovered awareness of the significance of the social contexts of collective memory.

The Ancient Art of Memory

In ancient Greek mythology, Mnemosyne, the goddess of memory, was revered as mother of the Muses of the arts and sciences. Ever since, students of memory have acknowledged memory's creative power to evoke the imaginative forms through which humankind represents the reality of its experience. The ancient idea of memory was grounded in the concept of mimesis, according to which memory and imagination are reverse sides of the creative act of "imitating nature." In the primarily oral culture of ancient Greece, the rhapsodes were renowned for their prodigious powers of memory, which allowed them to sing the Homeric epics, the repositories of the Greek heritage and the foundation of Greek cultural identity. But the use of memory in oral tradition was uncritical, and scholars have made much of the differences between the intuitive poetic storytelling of rhapsodes and the studied analytical use of memory among the literate rhetoricians of an incipient manuscript culture.

A changing conception of memory, therefore, is coeval with the passage from primary orality to manuscript literacy (beginning about the seventh century B.C.E.), which permitted a newfound critical perspective on memory's nature. By late antiquity, the idea of memory as remembered episode had come to be closely associated with the art of memory, a rhetorical technique of displacement for accurately recalling facts and stories worthy of remembrance. The art located data difficult to remember within easily remembered imaginary structures of places and images. The discovery of this method for associating the unfamiliar with the familiar is attributed to the Greek poet Simonides of Ceos (556–468 B.C.E.) and was developed especially by Roman rhetoricians. The *Rhetorica ad Herennium* (82 B.C.E.), attributed by some to Cicero, is the oldest such manual to have survived from antiquity. Throughout the Middle Ages and Renaissance, the art found expression in ever more complex mnemonic schemes, until it was marginalized by new encyclopedic reference books for storing knowledge in the emerging print culture of the Enlightenment.

The English historian Frances A. Yates (1899–1981) was the first modern scholar to analyze the history of the intellectual uses of mnemonic technique. She grounds this critical perspective in two seminal conceptions of memory derived from ancient Greek philosophy, one formulated by Plato (c. 428–348 or 347 B.C.E.), the other by Aristotle (384–322 B.C.E.). Plato emphasized the power of memory to open pathways to the archetypes of transcendental knowledge. Aristotle presented a down-to-earth analysis of memory's powers of recognition and recall and described mnemonics as a guarantor of the capacity of a well-ordered mind to hold fast to its learning. Yates was especially interested in the ambition the Neoplatonist rhetoricians of the Renaissance had to construct imaginary memory palaces whose architectural structures were purported to mirror those of an ideal universe and so to provide hermetic keys to correspondences between earthly and transcendental realities. But the rise of empirical science in the seventeenth century undercut the art of memory's idealist presuppositions, and while the art remained an elegant technique for the rhetorical display of erudition, it was soon acknowledged that its methods led only to a philosophical dead end.

Modern Memory and Personal Identity

The spread of print literacy by the eighteenth century transformed the cultural understanding of episodic memory. In print culture, collective knowledge could be easily preserved in readily accessible, alphabetically indexed reference books, rendering obsolete the practical applications of the art of memory in information retrieval. The psychological effect was to free memory for personal reflection on formative life experience, particularly that of childhood. The idea of memory thenceforth came to be closely allied with autobiographical soul-searching. The prototypes for this genre of self-analysis were the *Confessions* (1762) by the French philosopher Jean-Jacques Rousseau (1712–1778) and the *Prelude* (1805) by the English poet William Wordsworth (1770–1850). But for early twentieth-century readers, the most poignant introspective evocation of the past was that of the French writer Marcel Proust (1871–1922), who, in his multivolume novel *In Search of Lost Time* (1913–1927), marveled at the way an impromptu experience of sensory recall could spontaneously awaken the brilliant immediacy of an entirely forgotten cultural world. For the literati of the modern age, recovered memory was perceived to be the surest route to the discovery of the deep sources of personal identity.

Memory reconceived as the search for self was given a scientific foundation by the Austrian physician Sigmund Freud (1856–1939). Just as Plato had recourse to memory as a means for lifting the soul to an awareness of an ideal world, so Freud aspired to employ memory to open passageways leading to truths hidden in the unconscious. He invented psychoanalysis as a therapeutic technique for helping his patients cope with their neuroses, which he attributed to repressed memories of trauma earlier in their lives. Freud thought of the unconscious psyche as a subterranean archive where forgotten memories of unresolved issues pressed their unanswered claims on the conscious mind in ways that impaired its capacity to deal with present realities. In recovering repressed memories, patients would come to recognize the sources of their inner conflicts and so gain self-knowledge that would enable them to act more effectively in their present endeavors. Like the art of memory, Freud's psychoanalytic technique used the principle of displacement. Seemingly innocuous dreams, "screen memories," and slips of the tongue were often place markers for trauma in an individual's life history, providing clues to more troubling memories buried in the unconscious. The skilled psychoanalyst could help patients recover them.

The Social Frameworks of Collective Memory

In the early twentieth century, near the time when Freud's findings were being popularized, sociologists began to inquire into the nature of semantic memory as a realm of remembrance of a different order—socially conditioned memory, often tacitly understood. Here the memory was considered in its social context, as subject to social and cultural influences. The French philosopher Henri Bergson (1859–1941) prepared the way at the turn of the twentieth century by pointing out the difference between the memory of specific events and the memory of enduring attitudes, a distinction he correlated with that between the moment and duration. The French sociologist Maurice Halbwachs (1877–1945) elaborated a more complete theory of collective memory during the 1920s. For him, collective memory is a function of social power, and its expression varies with the social settings in which we find ourselves. We localize images of the past within imaginary frameworks that conform to our social understanding. For that reason, collective memory is provisional until it is evoked within specific social contexts, and its form and strength is relative to the social forces that impinge on our present circumstances. Without such social props, collective memory cannot survive. Halbwachs was especially insightful about how commemorative practices assimilate specific images of episodic memory into the idealized structures of semantic memory. As for its place in the history of ideas, Halbwachs's theory draws on the method of the art of memory to demonstrate how the strategic mobilization of commemorative monuments in mnemonic landscapes reinforces officially sanctioned collective memory.

The Fragility of Memory in a Postmodern Age

In the twenty-first century, we know more about memory than ever before, but trust its resources less. The idea of memory, conceived as the keystone of identity for the nineteenth century, has been reconceived as the debris of lost identities, the freestones of aging memory palaces that have fallen into ruins. Since the last quarter of the twentieth century, the topic has inspired intense interest among historians, literary critics, folklorists, sociologists, anthropologists, psychologists, and neurobiologists. Across the curriculum, scholars are as one in noting that memory is easily and often remodeled, almost always distorted, and hence unreliable as a guide to the realities of the past. The idea of memory, therefore, is noteworthy for its fragility, vulnerable as it is not only to the vagaries of the mind but also to social, political, and cultural forces that would alter or obliterate it.

On the edge of fragile memory lies nostalgia, the most elusive of memory's protean forms and one beginning to receive critical attention. An admixture of sweetness and sorrow, it expresses a longing for a vanishing past often more imaginary than real in its idealized remembrance. Nostalgia exercised a powerful appeal in the Romantic sentiments of the nineteenth century, tied as it was to regret over the passing of ways of life eroded by economic and social change, a generalized popular enthusiasm for innovation, and rising expectations about what the future might hold. Nostalgia was the shadow side of progress. Chastened by the disappointments of the twentieth century, however, the idea of progress has fallen on hard times, and nostalgia presents itself as an even more diffuse longing for a fantasy world that never existed (for example, the classless society in Communist propaganda). So reconceived, nostalgia has come to be criticized as a dangerous surrender to anarchistic illusion that contributes to memory's vulnerability to exploitation and misuse.

Situated at an interdisciplinary crossroads, the idea of memory has yet to promote an exchange between humanists and scientists, though they make their way along converging avenues of research. Scientists have moved away from Freud's claim about the integrity of memory's images. Steady research in psychology over the course of the twentieth century exposed the intricacies of the mental process of remembering, which involves complex transactions among various regions of the brain. For psychologists, remembering is conceived as a dynamic act of remodeling the brachial pathways along which neurons travel as they respond to sensory stimuli. The images of memory are encoded in neural networks, some in short-term and some in long-term configurations, and so are mobilized as conscious memories in multifold and continually changing ways. Memory resides in these ephemeral expressions, and its images are constantly subject to revision in the interplay of well-established patterns and chance circumstances that governs recall.

Some neuroscientists propose that memory is an adaptive strategy in the biological life process. Drawing on Charles Darwin's theory of natural selection, the American neuroscientist Gerald Edelman (1929–) argues that there is a selective process by which memory cells cluster in the neuronal groups that map neural pathways. He identifies two repertoires of such clusters in the gestation of the brain, one, primarily genetic, in embryo, and the other, primarily adaptive, after birth. They establish the categories of recognition through which the brain thenceforth processes external stimuli, though these categories are continually modified as the brain adapts to new life experience. In this sense, each act of recollection is a creative process that entails a reconfiguration of synaptic connections. There is an intriguing analogy between Edelman's two stages of memory cell formation and the mnemonist's two-step reinforcement of memory in repertoires of places and images. There is a resonance as well between Edelman's notion of the brain's mapping of neural pathways and Halbwachs's conception of the topographical localization of social memory. Both affirm the constructive nature of the act of memory in the interplay of recognition and context.

Cultural Contexts of Memory in the Twenty-First Century

Among contexts contributing to the idea of memory's fragility in the twenty-first century, one might highlight the following:

The one-way transit to amnesia in the pathologies of dementia. The degree to which the workings of memory elude research in the biological sciences is dramatized by the difficulties of understanding the perplexing diseases that lead to the deterioration of memory in old age. Freud's faith in the prospect of memory retrieval is difficult to reconcile with the insurmountable barriers erected by the ravages of dementia. An unfortunate by-product of longevity in the affluent Western world has been an increasing susceptibility to the maladies of memory impairment with advancing years. Alzheimer's disease is the most dreaded among an array of forms of dementia that rob victims of their memories and by consequence of their identities. Here there can be no recall of the past from the oblivion imposed by neurological degeneration. Alzheimer's disease has come to serve as a cultural metaphor for twenty-first century fears of trends that promote not only personal but also social amnesia.

Media and the eclipse of tradition in mass culture. The twenty-first century is characterized by its present-mindedness, but ironically has little regard for the presence of the past. We live in a consumer society whose interest lies in using and then discarding the resources of the present, not conserving them for future generations. Tradition, once valued as the bequest of the wisdom of past generations to the present one, is dismissed as trivial to the manufactured pursuit of immediate gratification in which the hallmarks of tradition are redeployed as the kitsch of consumerism, divested of the social and cultural frameworks that once defined social identity.

The media work their pervasive influence thanks to a revolution in the technologies of communication in the late twentieth century. The invention of new forms of electronic communication—notably the personal computer, linked by the Internet to a worldwide web of memory banks in cyberspace—so vastly expanded the capacity and facilitated the ease of information retrieval that it reshaped both perception and learning in ways analogous to those that accompanied the transition from orality to literacy (during which the art of memory was invented), and then from manuscript to print culture (when the interconnection of memory and personal identity was established). In this respect, the organization of knowledge on computer screens and Internet Web pages departs from its linear organization in print culture, to be reconfigured spatially on Web sites and in icons reminiscent of the places and images of the art of memory. Temporal models (timelines) are replaced by spatial ones (hyperlinks among Web sites).

The revolution in media communication accelerated the fraying of older forms of social and cultural identity. The media mold images in pervasive and homogeneous ways by virtue of their expanded control of the networks of communication, and favor tendentious publicity over deliberation. The media deepen present-mindedness, since their imperative is to publicize images of recent events as quickly as possible before moving on to others even more recent and enticing in their prurient interest. They evoke a sense of immediacy in which the past is glossed over and the future reduced to idle speculation. The mnemonic power of forms of publicity to incite interest prevails over the force of ideas, undermining the value of cultural traditions that once provided sure reference points of collective identity.

A reluctance to mourn. In the late twentieth century, historians too turned avidly to research on memory, more specifically to the relationship between memory and the dissolving cultural identities of the postmodern age. Whereas scholars of the nineteenth century had looked to formative beginnings, those of the late twentieth century were more interested in irresolute endings. During the 1970s, social historians such as Philippe Ariès, Pierre Chaunu, and Michel Vovelle launched studies of changing attitudes toward death and mourning across several centuries, in some sense as a response to the denial of death and the difficulties of mourning common in the late twentieth century. For comparison, Ariès portrayed the nineteenth century as a golden age of mourning. He noted newly intense expressions of personal mourning, made manifest in lavish funeral rituals and ornate commemorative monuments in cemeteries reconceived as gardens for meditation. Mourning in the nineteenth century confirmed personal identity by integrating the rituals of private mourning into well-established public traditions. The twentieth century, he claimed, was conspicuous for its reluctance to face death's realities and its diminished capacity to devote time and intensity to the process of coming to terms with the loss of loved ones.

The politics of memory. Historians soon extended their inquiry to encompass public commemoration—what the U.S. psychologist Peter Homans has characterized as the mourning of symbolic loss. During the 1980s, historical scholarship addressed the politics of memory, especially as it was displayed in the nineteenth-century commemorative practices that solemnized the building of nation-states in their use of icons of sacred moments (for example, national holidays) and avatars of patriotism (such as "founding fathers"). Given the challenges facing the nation-state in an age more acutely aware of the need for global perspectives on humankind, the historians' perspective on the making of national memory tended to dwell on its present-minded politics and geographical parochialism. Such research drew heavily on Halbwachs's theory of collective memory, as historians sought to rein in memory's claims on the past. In parallel with the efforts of philosophers and literary critics to deconstruct the forms of cultural discourse, historians sought to expose the building blocks from which practices of public commemoration had been constructed. They juxtaposed and to some degree reduced the reverential task of commemoration to its efficacious use in consolidating political allegiances.

Eric Hobsbawm and Terence Ranger's *The Invention of Tradition* (1983) and Pierre Nora's *Les lieux de mémoire* (1984–1992) stand out as pioneering studies in this field. Both seek to expose memory's role in the making of political identities that have become suspect in their biases and whose appeal at the turn of the twenty-first century began to wane. Nora's book on the making of the French national memory provided a method for digging through the accumulating layers of mementos that contributed to the making of political identity over long periods of time. It inspired a host of studies dealing with like political uses of memory in countries around the world.

Traumatic memories of atrocities. The twentieth century witnessed episodes of genocide and mass destruction on a scale that traumatized entire populations into collective repression. Reckoning with these unhappy memories demanded a new approach. Concerned that the worst atrocities might be glossed over and forgotten, historians undertook an inquiry into a relationship of a different order between memory and history. These investigations reiterated Freud's thesis about the necessity of "working through" the trauma of repressed memory to uncover harsh and painful truths about crimes against humanity. They concluded that some memories cannot be easily tamed by history, and that they maintain their singularity at the limits of history's powers of representation. Memories of the Holocaust of European Jewry are the most studied among them.

The problems involved in historicizing the memory of the Holocaust was the subject of the much-publicized "historians' controversy" in Germany during the 1980s. One group of historians contended that it was time to place the Holocaust in historical context. Another countered that no extant conceptual framework is adequate for doing so. It argued for the importance of the preliminary task of gathering testimony from Holocaust survivors still struggling to come to terms with their painful memories. Meditating on the differences between memory and history, the Israeli historian Saul Friedländer (b. 1932) wondered whether history could ever do justice to the existential meaning the Holocaust held for its victims. His question is whether the immediacy of memory can ever be reduced to the selective perspectives and conceptual abstractions of historical interpretation. He suggests that traumatic memory may be a realm of human understanding whose meaning is to some degree incommensurable with historical explanation. The conversation among historians about the limits of history's claims on traumatic memory lingered into the 1990s, and the European Holocaust served as a point of departure for studies of other instances of genocide in the late twentieth century, the memory of which presented obstacles to adequate historical interpretation.

History's Claims on Memory: A Remedy or a Poison?

The dispute about the relationship between memory and history was put in philosophical perspective by the French phenomenologist Paul Ricoeur (b. 1913). After reviewing the many routes of scholarly inquiry into the idea of memory at the turn of the twenty-first century, he closes his analysis with a meditation on the concerns of the historians of the Holocaust about history's premature claims on memory. In considering why history must first beg pardon of memory, he guides our attention to Plato's philosophical dialogue *Phaedrus,* an evocation of the debate among the ancients about differences between the remembered and the written word that provides an analogy with the current debate about memory's relationship to history. In this dialogue,

Plato's teacher Socrates ruminates on whether efforts to tame memory to the critical perspectives of writing have merit. He poses the question: Is writing as an aid to memory a remedy or a poison? The written word can be a remedy in the sense that it secures knowledge in an enduring form. But it does so by setting limits on the depiction of the past and so discards with a certain finality alternate ways of evoking its presence. Memory, by contrast, may at any moment rescue the past from oblivion. Its uses reside not only in its resources for preservation but also in those for creation. Its virtue lies in its ontological claim to body forth the imaginative forms that make conscious knowledge of human experience possible. History at its best deepens human understanding in its accurate reporting and intelligent interpretation of the past, and it strives to be conclusive. But memory's fidelity to the experience of the past is the basis of its openness toward the future, and it resists closure. Memory stands "as a little miracle" in its distinctive capacity to trigger the creative imagination in a way no other faculty of mind can.

The U.S. intellectual historian David Gross (b. 1940) adapts that insight to consider the status of memory in the twenty-first century. He notes the readiness of society to consign to oblivion all that stands in the way of present-minded expectations. He sorts out the intellectuals of late modernity into those who would discard and those who would value the past remembered. He highlights modern "rememberers" who have argued persuasively for the importance of the past to their present concerns—among them Proust and Freud, but also the nineteenth-century German philosopher Friedrich Nietzsche (1844–1900) and the twentieth-century German literary critic Walter Benjamin (1892–1940).

Benjamin in particular fascinated scholars because of his aphoristic insight into memory's remedy for the deficiencies of the timeworn claims of the modern vision of history on the contemporary age. Especially provocative is his interpretation of the painting *Angelus Novus* (1920) by the surrealist artist Paul Klee, a tableau of the angel of history looking back sadly on the events of the modern age, not as milestones of civilization's advance but rather as remnants of its failed projects and endless disappointments. A disillusioned socialist nostalgic for the heroics of the nineteenth-century revolutionary tradition, Benjamin longed for memory's spark to jump-start an alternative future. Neglected memories, he maintained, respond to our imaginative gaze like heliotropes opening to the sun.

Although assailed by all the pressures of present-minded perspectives that deny the importance of recollecting the past, the rememberers appeal to the present age by calling to mind the striking diversity and rich complexity of past human experience, and so deepen understanding of the timefulness of the human condition in its manifold meanings. Memory's claim on the past, they argue, lies in its creative capacity to resurrect lost worlds worthy of our consideration. Their insight recalls the ancients' reverence for the goddess Mnemosyne, who out of the eons of humankind's lost primordial past brought into consciousness the imaginative forms from which all the arts and sciences would spring.

See also **Autobiography; Death; Ritual: Public Ritual; Tradition.**

BIBLIOGRAPHY

Ariès, Philippe. *The Hour of Our Death.* Translated by Helen Weaver. Oxford: Oxford University Press, 1991.

Boym, Svetlana. *The Future of Nostalgia.* New York: Basic Books, 2001.

Edelman, Gerald M. *Neural Darwinism: The Theory of Neuronal Group Selection.* New York: Basic Books, 1987.

Gillis, John R., ed. *Commemorations: The Politics of National Identity.* Princeton, N.J.: Princeton University Press, 1994.

Gross, David. *Lost Time: On Remembering and Forgetting in Late Modern Culture.* Amherst: University of Massachusetts Press, 2000.

Havelock, Eric. *Preface to Plato.* Cambridge, Mass.: Harvard University Press, 1963.

Hobsbawm, Eric, and Terence Ranger, eds. *The Invention of Tradition.* Cambridge, U.K.: Cambridge University Press, 1983.

Homans, Peter, ed. *Symbolic Loss: The Ambiguity of Mourning and Memory at Century's End.* Charlottesville: University Press of Virginia, 2000.

Hutton, Patrick H. *History as an Art of Memory.* Hanover, N.H.: University Press of New England, 1993.

Matsuda, Matt K. *The Memory of the Modern.* New York: Oxford University Press, 1996.

Nora, Pierre, ed. *Les lieux de mémoire.* 3 vols. Paris: Gallimard, 1984–1992.

Olney, James. *Memory and Narrative: The Weave of Life-Writing.* Chicago: University of Chicago Press, 1998.

Ricoeur, Paul. *La mémoire, l'histoire, l'oubli.* Paris: Editions du Seuil, 2000.

Rosenfield, Israel. *The Invention of Memory: A New View of the Brain.* New York: Basic Books, 1988.

Roth, Michael, and Charles Salas, eds. *Disturbing Remains: Memory, History, and Crisis in the Twentieth Century.* Los Angeles: Getty Research Institute, 2001.

Schacter, Daniel L. *Searching for Memory: The Brain, the Mind, and the Past.* New York: Basic Books, 1996.

Yates, Frances A. *The Art of Memory.* Chicago: University of Chicago Press, 1966.

Patrick H. Hutton

MEN AND MASCULINITY.

Most human cultures, perhaps all, have accounts of gender relations, explaining and illustrating what it is to be a woman or a man, and how women and men are interrelated. The forms taken by these accounts vary greatly—ancestor myths, moral exhortation, exemplary narratives, drama, social science, philosophical speculation, and visual imagery. In many, there is a specific account of the domain of men, the characteristic activities of men, and the psychological traits of manhood.

Stories of Men

The earliest surviving text of classical Greek civilization centers on the deeds of ruling-class men, informed by a conflict over men's rights to women. Homer's *Iliad* presents a vivid picture of a military encampment and a besieged city, with warrior-heroes roaming the countryside, carrying off women and occasionally massacring the population of a captured town. War is undoubtedly men's affair, and both courage and military skill are tests of manhood. The business of men in these stories is to rule, cultivate land, found cities, and fight. Greek legend includes warrior women, but they are exotic figures. The central women in Homer's tales are Helen, the wandering queen who was fought over by the men, and Andromache and Penelope, archetypes of domestic faithfulness.

Yet Homer is no admirer of pure brawn. The mighty but slow-witted Ajax is of limited interest in the *Iliad* and becomes almost a comic figure in later Greek literature. The hero Achilles is an invincible fighter but is at the center of the story precisely because he is also highly emotional, takes offense, and refuses to fight. The hero of the *Odyssey* is perfectly capable of slaughter—Penelope's suitors ultimately get the same treatment as Helen's. But Odysseus is far more famous for his quick wit and his ability to talk his way out of trouble.

Attic drama of the fifth century B.C.E. tells a string of stories about men, power, and violence. They include the conscience-stricken Oedipus, the proud and rigid Creon, the vengeful Orestes, the prying Pentheus, and the faithless Jason. Classical Hellenic literature thus presents a spectrum of images of men. The texts complicate, and often call into question, the central image of the warrior-prince, which nevertheless remains an ideal, a point of reference.

It was the uncomplicated image of the warrior-prince that passed down into modern European tradition as an ideal of masculinity, reshaped by feudalism. In Sir Thomas Malory's fifteenth-century reworking of the Arthurian legends, for instance, the presumed context is always one of fighting or preparation for fighting. Although Malory's *Morte D'Arthur* presents variations in the style of warriorhood—some of the knights are cool and others are hot-blooded, some are painfully honest and others treacherous—skill in battle is always the vital test of the "worshipful" knight. Yeomen and villeins are another question to Malory, but among his elite, there is only one male character who is not part of the armed competition for "worship"—the unaccountable prophet/witch Merlin. Arthur himself, it is easily forgotten, was a bastard even in the mainstream legend, and pulling a sword from an anvil was hardly an established form of royal election. He had to establish his claim to kingship by mass killings—"passynge grete slaughtir," in Malory's phrase—in a protracted civil war.

Historic images of warrior-heroes were handed down, and reworked as somewhat more widely available ideals, in European modernity. The point is made in a British popular song of the eighteenth or nineteenth century:

> Some talk of Alexander, and some of Hercules,
> Of Hector and Lysander, and such great names as these,
> But of all the world's brave heroes, there's none that can compare,
> With a tow row row, with a tow row row, to the British Grenadier.

So it had already been in Shakespeare, with his archetype-soldier,

> Full of strange oaths, and bearded like the pard,
> Jealous in honour, sudden and quick in quarrel,

Seeking the bubble reputation
Even in the cannon's mouth. (*As You Like It*, 2.7.150–153)

Questioning Masculinity

The word *masculine* (as a synonym for *male*) is a very old word in English. It was used by Chaucer in the fourteenth century. However, the terms *masculinity, masculinize,* and *masculinism* came into common use in English only in the late nineteenth century. This change in language signaled a rather different way of looking at men and their position in the world.

This change was part of the cultural response made, in the bourgeois society of the industrialized countries, to the women's suffrage movement, and to the broad challenge by first-wave feminism to Victorian-era patriarchy. The bourgeois society of imperial Europe (and its offshoots in colonies, notably in the United States) had taken the separation of men's and women's spheres to an extreme. It defined not only war as men's business but also property, knowledge, government, and, in many contexts, even waged work as such. In this context the concept of masculinity had a slightly conservative flavor, suggesting that social inequalities were rooted in permanent differences of the character of men and women. Many thinkers of the time assumed that these were based in the imperatives of biological evolution.

The term *masculinity* not only had antifeminist overtones, it had a clinical flavor as well. Femininity in men was seen as a source of sexual crime, especially (though not exclusively) homosexuality. Masculinity in women was also seen as a kind of pathology, especially threatening to their capacity to bear children.

From the start, however, this idea was contested. Not only women of the suffrage movement, but also men like John Stuart Mill (1806–1873) and Lester Ward (1841–1913) supported equality between women and men, convinced that social progress would iron out most of the differences between men's and women's lives (see the documentary history by Kimmel and Mosmiller).

Vaerting

In the next generation, the pioneering German educator Mathilde Vaerting (1884–1977) produced in *The Dominant Sex* (1923) perhaps the most revolutionary theory of gender ever written. She argued that masculinity and femininity were not fixed characteristics but reflected the fact that we lived in a male-dominated society—a *Männerstaat* (men's state). In societies where women held power, she argued, men showed the very characteristics that Western bourgeois society saw as quintessentially feminine. Masculinity or masculine characteristics, to Vaerting, were thus not expressions of the male body, and had nothing whatever to do with evolutionary forces. They were the consequences of social power structure and of this alone.

Vaerting based her arguments on a social learning theory, common among progressive educators at the time. She traced gender patterns in institutions such as the legal system (anticipating a later generation of sociological research on gender). Among other consequences of her perspective was a remarkable

prediction of the men's liberation movement, which appeared fifty years later.

Vaerting's ideas did attract some attention in the 1920s. But first-wave feminism was in decline, Vaerting lost her academic position when fascism came to power in Germany, and it was in other currents of thought that the questioning of masculinity was carried forward.

Freud

It was the work of the Austrian physician Sigmund Freud (1856–1939), more than anything else, that disrupted the apparently natural object "masculinity" and made an enquiry into the process of its construction possible.

Freud's ideas about masculinity developed in three steps. The first came in his initial statements of psychoanalytic principles: the idea of continuity between normal and neurotic mental life, the concepts of repression and the unconscious, and the method that allowed unconscious mental processes to be read through dreams, jokes, slips of the tongue, and symptoms. Freud understood that adult sexuality and gender were not fixed by nature but were constructed through a long and conflict-ridden process. The Oedipus complex, an emotional tangle of middle childhood involving desire for one parent and hatred for the other, was the key moment in this development. What precipitated the oedipal crisis, for boys, was rivalry with the father and terror of castration. Here Freud identified a formative moment in masculinity and pictured the dynamics of a formative relationship.

In his theoretical writing, Freud complicated this picture. Homosexuality, he argued, is not a simple gender switch, and "a large proportion of male inverts retain the mental quality of masculinity." Freud suggested that masculine and feminine currents coexist in everyone. Adult masculinity was a complex, and in some ways precarious, construction. In his longest case history, the "Wolf Man," Freud pushed behind the Oedipus complex to find a pre-oedipal, narcissistic masculinity that underpinned castration anxiety.

In a final stage, Freud developed his account of the structure of personality, in particular the concept of the superego, the unconscious agency that judges, censors, and presents ideals. The superego is formed, in the aftermath of the Oedipus complex, by internalized prohibitions from the parents. Freud gradually came to see it as having a gendered character, being crucially a product of the child's relationship with the father, and more distinct in the case of boys than of girls. This provided the germ of a theory of the patriarchal organization of culture, transmitted from one generation to the next through the construction of masculinity.

Adler

The potential in Freud's work for a radical critique of masculinity was apparent very early. It was taken up by Alfred Adler (1870–1937), a socialist psychiatrist convinced of the importance of social factors in disease. He was one of Freud's first and most important professional supporters but broke with him in 1911, partly over the analysis of masculinity.

Adler's argument started from the familiar polarity between masculinity and femininity but immediately emphasized the feminist point that one side of the polarity is devalued in culture and associated with weakness. Children of both sexes, being weak vis-à-vis adults, are thus forced to inhabit the feminine position. Submission and striving for independence occur together in a child's life, setting up an internal contradiction between masculinity and femininity. In normal development, some kind of balance is struck. But if there is weakness, there will be anxiety that motivates an exaggerated emphasis on the masculine side of things. This "masculine protest," in Adler's famous phrase, is central to neurosis, resulting in overcompensation in the direction of aggression and a restless striving for triumphs.

Adler considered the masculine protest to be active in both normal and neurotic mental life. The masculine protest was a feature of women's psychology as well as men's but was overdetermined by women's social subordination. In men it could become a public menace. Adler took a highly critical view of dominating masculinities, commenting on "the arch evil of our culture, the excessive pre-eminence of manliness."

World War I left Adler in no doubt about the connections between masculinity, power, and public violence. His 1927 book, *Understanding Human Nature,* made a clearer statement of a psychoanalytic case for gender equality than was found anywhere else until the 1970s.

Other Psychoanalysts

Other psychoanalysts contributed to the argument about femininity and masculinity, though none gave the issue so central a place. Karen Horney (1885–1952) pointed to the importance of "the dread of woman," originating in fear of the mother, in the depth psychology of men. Carl Jung (1875–1961) speculated in *The Relations Between the Ego and the Unconscious* that masculinity and femininity functioned as opposites within personality, in a kind of balance: "The repression of feminine traits and inclinations causes these contrasexual demands to accumulate in the unconscious" (p. 187). This idea, filtered through Jung's later theory of archetypes, resurfaced in the 1980s and became the key theme of a popular therapeutic movement in the United States.

After the 1920s, psychoanalysis moved far to the right on most issues, and discussion of the theory of gender was no exception. When psychoanalysts became popular writers on gender issues in the 1950s, their message identified mental health with gender orthodoxy. The course toward adult heterosexuality, which Freud had seen as a complex and fragile construction, was increasingly presented as a nonproblematic, natural path of development. Anything else was seen as a sign of pathology, especially homosexuality, which was declared inherently pathological, the product of disturbed parent–child relationships. Psychoanalysis as a practice became increasingly a technique of normalization and attempted to adjust its patients to the existing gender order—as is shown in Kenneth Lewes's excellent history of psychoanalytic ideas about male homosexuality. It was only after the impact of feminism in the 1970s that the critical potential in psychoanalytic ideas about gender was rediscovered.

Sex Differences and Ethnography

The first important attempt to create a social science of masculinity centered on the idea of a male sex role. Its origins go back to late-nineteenth-century debates about sex difference,

when resistance to women's emancipation was bolstered by a scientific doctrine of innate sex difference. The first generation of women who entered U.S. research universities not only violated the doctrine of female mental inferiority, they also questioned its presuppositions by researching the differences in mental capacities between men and women. They found very few.

This scandalous result triggered an enormous volume of follow-up research, which has flowed from the 1890s to the present and covered not only mental abilities but also emotions, attitudes, personality traits, interests—indeed, everything that psychologists thought they could measure. The main results have not changed. Sex differences, on almost every psychological trait measured, are either nonexistent or fairly small. When groups of studies are aggregated by the statistical technique of meta-analysis, it is more likely to be concluded that some sex differences in psychological characteristics do exist. These, however, are often influenced by social circumstances.

The idea of a social interpretation of sex differences came principally from anthropology. This new discipline was, after psychoanalysis, the main intellectual force that relativized Western concepts of masculinity and femininity. Ethnographers such as Bronislaw Malinowski (1884–1942) and Margaret Mead (1901–1978) published detailed accounts of non-Western societies that were very widely read in the 1920s and 1930s. In these cultures, men and women were seen to behave in ways that were intelligible and consistent, yet very different from the patterns familiar in metropolitan bourgeois society. Mead's *Sex and Temperament in Three Primitive Societies* (1935), in particular, showed men following radically different ideals of conduct in different cultural contexts. The models of heroic masculinity familiar in Western literature were, it seemed, specific to the West.

From anthropology, also, came the idea of the functional interrelatedness of a society and the idea of a social role within it. In the 1940s and 1950s these ideas were applied to sex difference research and gave birth to the term "sex role," which in time passed into everyday speech.

The Male Sex Role

The usual conception of "sex role" is that a man or a woman enacts a general set of expectations attached to their sex. There are always two sex roles in any cultural context, one male and the other female. Masculinity and femininity are quite easily interpreted as internalized sex roles, the products of socialization. The reason why this socialization occurs, according to structural-functionalist sociology and anthropology, is that it is necessary for the stability or reproduction of the society as a whole. Sex differences in behavior (which are persistently exaggerated in the sex role literature) are thus explained on the small scale by social learning, on the large scale by the functioning of society.

Most often, sex roles are seen as the cultural elaboration of underlying biological sex differences. But the idea of a biological base can be dispensed with. The most sophisticated statement of sex role theory was made in the mid-1950s by Talcott Parsons, the leading sociological theorist of the time. In Parsons's argument, the distinction between male and female sex roles is treated as a distinction between "instrumental" and "expressive" roles in the family (when considered as a small group).

The idea that masculinity is the internalized male sex role allows for social change. Change was a central theme in the first detailed discussions of the male sex role that appeared in U.S. social science journals in the 1950s. The most notable was a paper by Helen Hacker called "The New Burdens of Masculinity," which suggested that expressive functions were now being added to instrumental functions. Men were thus expected to show interpersonal skills as well as being "sturdy oaks." For the most part, however, the first generation of sex role theorists assumed that the roles were well-defined, that socialization went ahead harmoniously, and that sex role learning was a thoroughly good thing. Successful internalization of sex role norms contributed to social stability, mental health, and the performance of necessary social functions.

Men's Liberation and the Critique of Sex Roles

The new feminism in the 1970s did not abandon the concept of sex roles, but it reevaluated their meaning. It was argued that the female sex role was inherently oppressive and that role internalization was a means of fixing girls and women in a subordinate position. Almost immediately, a parallel analysis of the male sex role appeared. By the mid-1970s there was a small but much-discussed men's liberation movement in the United States, and a small network of men's consciousness-raising groups in other developed countries as well. A minor publishing boom developed in books about the "problem" of men and also in papers in counseling and social science journals. Their flavor is indicated by one title: "Warning: The Male Sex Role May Be Dangerous to Your Health."

The picture of the male sex role in most of this literature was conventional and typically middle class, emphasizing traits such as inexpressiveness, orientation to careers, and competitiveness. Authors pointed to the role of commercial sports, such as football, in creating popular images of competitive, aggressive masculinity. They pointed to highly stereotyped representations of men in film and television genres such as the western, the war movie, the gangster movie, and the cop serial, not to mention advertisements such as the famous "Marlboro Man" campaign.

There was some attempt to outline a process of change. The American psychologist Joseph Pleck, one of the most prolific writers in this field, contrasted a traditional with a modern male role. Much of the writing in the United States in the 1970s encouraged men toward the modern version, recommending therapy, consciousness-raising groups, political discussion, role-sharing in marriage, or self-help.

By the 1980s, intellectual weaknesses in the sex role concept were acknowledged, and political divisions in the men's movement had become wide. The antisexist and profeminist tendency of the early men's liberation groups were contested by men's rights groups who were antagonistic to feminism and by a therapeutic movement that took a very different view of masculinity, partly based on a late revival of Jung. Political ambivalence was inherent in the framework of sex roles. There is a basic tendency in sex role theory to understand men's and women's positions as consensual and complementary—a point made explicit by Parsons's theory of instrumental (masculine)

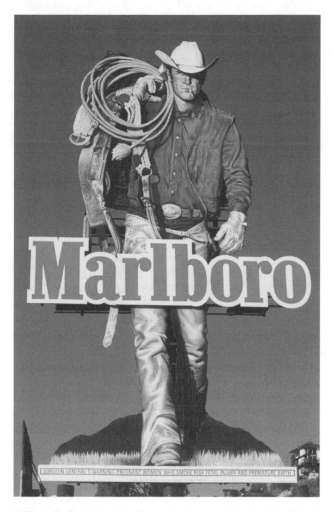

Billboard advertising Marlboro cigarettes, 1988. In the United States during the 1970s, a small movement sprang up to protest stereotypical male role models in society. Marlboro's advertising campaign, which featured masculine, rugged cowboys was singled out as an offender. © CARL & ANN PURCELL/CORBIS

and expressive (feminine) orientations. Attempts by Pleck and others to create a nonnormative sex role theory proved unsuccessful in the long run.

Gay Liberation and Queer Theory

The most effective political mobilization among men around gender and sexual politics was the gay liberation movement that took shape around 1968–1970 in the United States and eventually became worldwide. Gay men mobilizing for civil rights, personal safety, and cultural space have acted on the basis of a long experience of oppression by heterosexual men. The term *homophobia* was coined around 1970 to describe this experience. A central insight of gay liberation is the depth and pervasiveness of homophobia, closely connected with dominant forms of masculinity.

Straight men's homophobia involves real social practices, ranging from job discrimination to media vilification to imprisonment, and sometimes to murder. These practices draw social boundaries, defining approved masculinity by its difference from the rejected. Theorists such as Dennis Altman in *Homosexual: Oppression and Liberation* (1972) regarded the oppression of homosexuals as part of a larger enterprise of maintaining an authoritarian social order and often saw it as connected to the oppression of women. Yet gay men have also noticed a certain fascination with homosexuality on the part of straight men. This knowledge was behind the slogan "Every straight man is a target for gay liberation!"

Gay liberation coincided with the emergence of visible gay communities in many cities of the developed world. From the 1970s on, these communities have been the sites of public manifestations of gay identity, ranging from the election of gay politicians to street parties and gay pride marches. For example, by the 1990s the annual lesbian and gay Mardi Gras parade had become the most popular street event in the social life of Sydney, attracting a huge straight audience. Styles of self-presentation in gay communities have shifted with time, from traditional "camp" behavior to the parodic butch masculinity of the late-1970s "clones," changing again with the impact of the HIV/AIDS epidemic in the 1980s, the diversification of sexual subcultures, and the rise of "queer" sensibility in the 1990s.

Gay liberation, both in theory and practice, made a crucial difference to contemporary thought about masculinity. Gay culture makes visible alternative ways of being a man. Gay politics responds to, and thus makes visible, oppressive gender relations between groups of men. Gay men's collective knowledge includes gender ambiguity, tension between bodies and identities, and contradictions in and around masculinity.

Many of these themes were picked up in queer theory, a new style of lesbian and gay theorizing that emerged under the influence of poststructuralism in the 1990s. In a diverse trend of thought rather than a formal body of doctrines, queer theorists have challenged the notion of fixed gender or sexual identities, thus challenging the basis of gay community politics. They have identified homoerotic subtexts throughout Western culture and have criticized feminist gender theory as being based on an unexamined heterosexism. Applied to men and masculinity, in texts such as David Buchbinder's *Performance Anxieties* (1998), queer theory questions the naturalness of the category "men" and sees masculine identity not as the settled foundation of behavior but as something always insecure, constantly being created in performance.

Social Construction

The contemporary field of masculinity research, alternatively known as men's studies or critical studies of men, was created when several impulses in the 1980s moved discussions decisively beyond the sex role framework. One was the continuing development of theories of gender, both structuralist and poststructuralist, which provided more sophisticated models of the gender relations in which men are located and masculinity is constituted.

A second impulse was provided when the coexistence of multiple masculinities was recognized—a move strongly influenced by gay thought. A third impulse was a new wave of empirical research in sociology, history, and cultural studies. This research

has been very diverse in subject matter but has generally had a local character. Its main focus has been the construction of masculinity in a particular milieu or moment: a printing shop in Great Britain, a professional sports career in the United States, a group of colonial schools in South Africa, drinking groups in Australian bars, a working-class suburb in Brazil, or the marriage plans of young middle-class men in urban Japan. Its characteristic research style has been ethnographic, making use of participant observation, open-ended interviewing, or discursive analysis of texts in popular culture. The primary research task has been to give close descriptions of processes and outcomes in the local site. This body of research was systematized in the mid-1990s in R. W. Connell's *Masculinities*.

This "ethnographic moment" in masculinity research developed first in the English-speaking world, mainly in Australia, the United States, and Great Britain. In central and northern Europe, where feminist and gay research had also taken an early interest in the gender practices of men, there was more emphasis on survey research, such as the well-known "Brigitte study," based on a national survey in Germany in 1984–1985, sponsored by a women's magazine and conducted by feminist sociologists Sigrid Metz-Göckel and Ursula Mueller. There was also a focus on the ways men are positioned in relation to gender equity policies, a concern that has continued in Scandinavia to the present. The results of this great social experiment have recently been drawn together by the Norwegian sociologist Oeystein Holter, emphasizing that in favorable circumstances men can and do change their gender practices. In the same region, an interest developed in using masculinity research to uncover the roots of violence, which in recent years has become one of the most important fields of application of masculinity research internationally.

The picture that emerged from this research differed significantly from older ideas of the male sex role and even more from conceptions of "natural" masculinity. One of the key achievements of this research was to document the diversity of masculinities. There is not just one pattern of masculinity, good in all times and places. Different cultures vary, some being much more peaceable than others. Within a single society—even within a single community or institution—there will be different patterns of masculinity, different recognizable ways of "being a man." Just as we now recognize the diversity of family forms, so we also now recognize that there are likely to be different constructions of masculinity in different social class settings, different ethnic communities, and different regions.

Hegemonic Masculinity

But different masculinities do not sit side by side as alternative lifestyles that men can freely choose. There are definite relationships between different masculinities. Most importantly, there are relationships of hierarchy and exclusion. In most communities there is a specific pattern of masculinity that is more respected than others. The hegemonic pattern of masculinity is often associated with national identity, celebrated in popular films and sports, presented as an ideal to the young, and constantly used as a basis of advertising. Other patterns of masculinity exist but do not attract the same respect—indeed, some forms of masculinity are actively stigmatized.

A good deal of debate has surrounded the concept of "hegemonic" masculinity. In some usages, it has turned into the concept of a fixed identity or stereotype, not very different from the old model of the male sex role. In others, however, it is recognized that only a minority of men actually embody a hegemonic model. Yet the hierarchy around this version of masculinity can be an important source of conflict and violence among men.

Recent social research also stresses that masculinity exists not only as a pattern of personal life, but also impersonally in communities, institutions, and cultures. Collective definitions of manhood are generated in community life, and are likely to be contested—and change—as the situation of a community changes, for instance with the decline of industrial employment or changing definitions of marriage, such as attempts in the early years of the twenty-first century to include same-sex domestic partnerships or gay marriage within the legal systems of some of the developed countries. Organizations such as armies and corporations embed particular hegemonic patterns in their organizational cultures, and mass media circulate particular icons of masculinity while discrediting others.

Historical and sociological research has produced convincing evidence that masculinities change over time. Men's patterns of conduct, and beliefs about gender issues, do not change with dramatic speed. But research has shown significant generational shifts, for instance in sexual behavior, and in beliefs about men's and women's roles in society.

Change is to be expected because of the contradictions and tensions in gender relations. These give rise to a complex field of masculinity politics—mobilizations among different groups of men, some of them challenging for the hegemonic position in the local gender order, some defending more limited agendas. This conception is crystallized by Michael Messner in *The Politics of Masculinities* (1997).

Global Perspectives

Until recently, most of the research on, and debate about, masculinity has been about men in First World countries. We need to think beyond this context; and even within it, we need to consider the situation of local masculinities in a global context. Global history and contemporary globalization must be part of our understanding of masculinities. Individual lives are powerfully influenced by geopolitical struggles, imperialism and colonialism, global markets, multinational corporations, labor migration, and transnational media. Not only ethnographic but postcolonial studies are important for understanding the cultural dynamics of contemporary masculinities.

There has been some research on immigrant men in First World contexts. However, up to the 1980s little research was carried out on masculinities in Third World and/or postcolonial countries, and what was done was affected by Eurocentrism. In his excellent ethnographic study of men in Mexico City, *The Meanings of Macho* (1996), Matthew Gutmann criticizes the tendency of Anglo researchers to characterize Latino men as "macho." More recent studies have acknowledged the great variety of masculinities throughout the Latin American world. For example, a remarkable series of studies coordinated

by José Olavarría, focused in Chile but involving researchers in other countries, has documented diversity in relation to identity, fatherhood, violence, and sexuality. Olavarría's exploration of the dilemmas of Chilean youth as they attempt to construct a path toward fatherhood in a country undergoing globalization is particularly important.

More work is now being done in other regions outside the metropole—for example, by Japanese and Middle Eastern scholars. The importance of race and class in shaping gender patterns is strikingly shown in southern Africa. By the late 1990s, South Africa had the highest rates of violent death and rape in the world, the second highest number of gun-related homicides, and one of the world's highest rates of HIV infection. These are connected with a turbulent gender politics in which different patriarchies contest, and different agendas for reform are found. South African masculinities, as shown by Robert Morrell's collection, *Changing Men in Southern Africa* (2001), are both diverse and contested.

In the contexts of the developing world, as Morrell points out, gender work on men and masculinities must focus on very different issues from those in the developed world. For this reason, researchers in postcolonial contexts do not necessarily adopt theories of hegemonic masculinity or of new masculinities on the Western model. The idea of the "new man" popular in First World media has little relevance beyond the lives of such white, middle-class, urban men. How to make use of the new research is still uncertain. A controversy has developed about how men ought to be included in research and policy about gender and development. As Sarah White shows in a recent review of the argument, complex political issues arise here in a field that has sought, with some recent success, to place women's interests on the agenda of development agencies.

Attention is now being turned to the patterns of masculinity in transnational agencies and institutions. There is some reason to think that older models of bourgeois masculinity, embedded in local ruling classes and conservative cultures, are being replaced by a transnational business masculinity. Compared with older hegemonic masculinities, the new model is more individualist, liberal in relation to sexuality and social attitudes, and oriented to power through markets rather than through bureaucratic domination. This model has been criticized, and plainly the interplay of masculinity with globalization needs much more investigation.

At the same time, as the return to military intervention abroad by the U.S. government suggests, there is cultural and political space for a reassertion of "hard" masculinities. The unevenness and relentlessness of change on a world scale are well captured in the 2001 volume *A Man's World? Changing Men's Practices in a Globalized World*, edited by Bob Pease and Keith Pringle. The issues reviewed in this article are currently the subject of active debate and research, with global issues an important focus.

See also **Anthropology; Character; Cultural Studies; Equality; Gender; Identity: Personal and Social Identity; Machismo; Natural Law; Queer Theory.**

BIBLIOGRAPHY

Adler, Alfred. *Understanding Human Nature.* 1927. Translated by C. Brett. Oxford: Oneworld, 1992.

Altman, Dennis. *Homosexual: Oppression and Liberation.* London: Lane, 1974.

Buchbinder, David. *Performance Anxieties: Re-producing Masculinity.* Sydney: Allen and Unwin, 1998.

Connell, R. W. *Masculinities.* Berkeley: University of California Press, 1995.

Freud, Sigmund. *The Case of the Wolf-Man: From the History of an Infantile Neurosis.* San Francisco: Arion, 1993. Reprinted from the standard edition of the *Complete Psychological Works of Sigmund Freud,* v. 17. London: Hogarth, 1917.

Gutmann, Matthew. *The Meanings of Macho: Being a Man in Mexico City.* Berkeley: University of California Press, 1996.

Hacker, Helen Mayer. "The New Burdens of Masculinity." *Marriage and Family Living* 19 (August 1957): 227–233.

Holter, Oeystein Gullvag. *Can Men Do It? Men and Gender Equality: The Nordic Experience.* Copenhagen: Nordic Council of Ministers, 2003.

Homer. *The Iliad.* Translated by Michael Reck. New York: IconEditions, 1994.

Jung, Carl G. "The Relations Between the Ego and the Unconscious." In *Collected Works.* Vol. 7. London: Routledge and Kegan Paul, 1953.

Kimmel, Michael S., and Thomas E. Mosmiller, eds. *Against the Tide: Pro-Feminist Men in the United States, 1776–1990, a Documentary History.* Boston: Beacon, 1992.

Lewes, Kenneth. *The Psychoanalytic Theory of Male Homosexuality.* New York: Simon and Schuster, 1988.

Malory, Thomas. *Works.* Edited by E. Vinaver. Oxford: Oxford University Press, 1971.

Mead, Margaret. *Sex and Temperament in Three Primitive Societies.* 1935. New York: William Morrow, 1963.

Messner, Michael A. *The Politics of Masculinities: Men in Movements.* Thousand Oaks, Calif.: Sage, 1997.

Metz-Göckel, Sigrid, and Ursula Mueller. *Der Mann: Die Brigitte-Studie.* Weinheim: Beltz, 1986.

Morrell, Robert, ed. *Changing Men in Southern Africa.* London: Zed, 2001.

Olavarría, José. *Y todos querian ser (buenos) padres: varones de Santiago de Chile en conflicto.* Santiago: FLACSO-Chile, 2001.

Parsons, Talcott, and Robert F. Bales. *Family, Socialization and Interaction Process.* London: Routledge and Kegan Paul, 1956.

Pease, Bob, and Keith Pringle. *A Man's World? Changing Men's Practices in a Globalized World.* London: Zed, 2001.

Pleck, Joseph H. *The Myth of Masculinity.* Cambridge, Mass.: MIT Press, 1981.

Vaerting, Mathilde. *The Dominant Sex: A Study in the Sociology of Sex Differentiation.* 1921. Westport, Conn.: Hyperion, 1980.

White, Sarah C. "'Did the Earth Move?' The Hazards of Bringing Men and Masculinities into Gender and Development." *IDS Bulletin* 31, no. 2 (April 2000): 33–41.

R. W. Connell

MESTIZAJE. The concept of *mestizaje* expresses the tensions, contradictions, and ambiguities of its birth in the New World. More important, it is a concept that continues to have spiritual and aesthetic dimensions. *Mestizaje* refers to racial and/or cultural mixing of Amerindians with Europeans, but the literal connotation of the word does not illuminate its theoretical applications and its more recent transformations. Since its inception in the New World and during those moments when race was a significant factor in social standing, *mestizaje* has been invoked to remedy social inequality and the misfiring of democracy.

Origins

In 1925 José Vasconcelos, the Mexican philosopher and educator, wrote *La raza cósmica* both to challenge Western theories of racial superiority and purity and to offer a new view about the mixing of African, European, and indigenous peoples in Mexico and throughout Latin America. The essay was an effort to undercut the maligned position of indigenous people and their material domination since the conquest, but it was unable to break completely from the civilizing motives of New Spain. *Mestizaje* was the political ideology of modern national identity, unity, and social progress. Yet Vasconcelos's vision pointed to Iberian culture, particularly Christianity, as the source for modernization and progress. Mexican nationalism has continued to construct its citizens as mestizos.

The material and ideological weight of the conquest was also difficult to shake in earlier formations of *mestizaje.* Even while under Spanish rule, criollos exalted the Aztec or Inca past and condemned the conquest, but their celebration of *mestizaje* did not include the elimination of economic domination, political disempowerment, and cultural genocide of indigenous populations. Throughout New Spain, claims of *mestizaje* were meant to indicate a bond against the *peninsulares,* the Spanish settlers with exclusive rights to high political office, and to legitimate creole equality with *peninsulares* at home and in Europe. Other classifications of mixture in the caste system were not exalted, and the status of mulattos and others was not reconsidered. Historians agree that during the colonial, independence, and revolutionary periods, *mestizaje* functioned to reduce cultural, linguistic, and political diversity in Mexico and to authorize the privileged status of ruling elites. In short, the original concept emphasized the assimilation and appropriation of indigenous cultures and the promise of progress and justice through Europe. As such, hybridity was cloaked under the banner of national unity. For the Mexican philosopher Octavio Paz (1914–1998), however, the trauma of *mestizaje* serves as a symbol of illegitimacy, a concept he develops in *Labyrinth of Solitude* (1961) and a foundation of his argument on Mexican national character.

Chicanos and *Mestizaje*

In contrast, contemporary expressions of *mestizaje* emphasize hybrid cultural experiences and the relations of power. The social position of contemporary thinkers somewhat explains the late-twentieth-century formulations of *mestizaje.* Whereas Mexican philosophers were members of the dominant sectors of society, Chicana and Chicano social critics, artists, and creative writers who reformulated *mestizaje* beginning in the late 1960s did not enjoy such a place in the United States or Latin America. In multiple genres, the earliest Chicano articulations of *mestizaje* were a strategy of affirmation, liberation, and identity.

Mexican Americans join three historical moments and expand the original concept of *mestizaje.* The first event occurred in 1521 with the Spanish conquest of the Aztec Empire; *el segundo mestizaje* (the second cultural mixing) occurred at the end of the Mexican-American War (1846–1848), in which the United States annexed over half of Mexico's territory; and the third event is the contemporary cultural interchange among Chicanos and European Americans. All three moments originate in disempowerment and suggest a rebirth. Particularly since the second historical moment, Chicanos and Chicanas have positioned *mestizaje* as an alternative to the social contract of assimilation. In making parallel the historical legacies of the seventeenth and nineteenth centuries, *mestizaje* no longer serves a pluralist agenda. In the United States, it functions as an antidote to modern anti-Indian and anti-Mexican sentiments, and although alliances with Native American populations in the American Southwest have been formed, they do not continue to anchor Chicano thought in the same way that Mexico's indigenous and pre-Columbian civilizations inform Chicano and Chicana *mestizaje.*

Chicano *mestizaje* enacts a void and a congested condition. For example, the poem "I Am Joaquin" (1967) by Rodolfo "Corky" Gonzales expresses a fusion of two opposites, Mexico and the United States, which are blended to form a third cultural experience: Chicano. The hybrid Chicano is neither Mexican nor American. Artists such as Amado Peña (with "Mestizo," silkscreen, 1974) and Emanuel Martinez (with "Mestizo Banner," silkscreen on canvas, 1967) produced the fusion in graphic form with a mestizo tripartite head in which two profiles faced left and right and were united in the third face in frontal position. Other artistic and scholarly proposals overdetermined a gendered *mestizaje,* emphasizing select indigenous characteristics and a masculine repertoire.

Critique and Reformulation

While social analysts agree that *mestizaje* has recuperative properties for Mexican Americans and that it successfully challenges Paz's diagnosis of a mixed nation as pathological, the neoindigenous emphasis can be ironically similar to Western distortions of native peoples, as both rely on a timeless, primordial culture. Chicano/a social critics such as Norma Alarcón and Chon A. Noriega point out that this use of *mestizaje* constructs a "pure" origin and relies on a static and unchanging past. The essentialist disposition of *mestizaje,* particularly the romantic neoindigenous perspective, clashes with the reality of Native American experiences as well as indigenous social and political struggles throughout the Americas. Furthermore, as Chicana feminists point out, an essentialist view of Mexican-origin people in the United States also distorts differences and inequalities within said communities. Chicana feminist challenges to patriarchy and homophobia helped to develop the critique of essentialism, and this had a lasting effect on the contemporary notion of *mestizaje.*

In her foundational book, *Borderlands/La Frontera: The New Mestiza* (1987), Gloria Anzaldúa fleshes out and complicates *mestizaje.* Performing a postmodern style that mixes autobiography, poetry, mythology, historical document, and documentation into theoretical proclamation, she problematizes conventions of race, nation, sexuality, and gender, drawing attention to fluidity within identity rather than a singular subject position. According to Anzaldúa, *mestizaje* is the demystification of social boundaries

and territorial borders. Thus conceived, the spaces between cultures and nations are porous and flexible. However, it is not just her acknowledgment of internal complexities that makes a mestiza consciousness significant. Anzaldúa does not imagine distinctions in opposition to each other but acknowledges concurrent identities, shifting strategies, and capacities for change.

The reformulated concept is more successful at challenging the premise of white racial superiority, purity, and essentialism. *Mestizaje* is a source of creativity, survival, and triumph. Unlike Mexican and Chicano cultural-nationalist formulations of *mestizaje,* Anzaldúa acknowledges all combinations and the places of contradiction that can result. Always synthesizing, *mestizaje* is a force of movement, combination, and transformation. Her own thinking about *mestizaje* fuses with the Nahuatl concept of *nepantla* (middle place or place of passage), thereby adding the potential for agency within the concept.

Spread and Influence

Nonlinear thought and unfixed identities have intellectual and political appeal for numerous fields, especially those also influenced by poststructural and postmodern schools of thought. Because of the liberatory dimensions of the concept of *mestizaje,* it is widely used in postcolonial, ethnic, and feminist studies and Latino theology. Most credit Anzaldúa with creating the aperture for understanding and theorizing about the ability to have multiple social perspectives and positions with concrete material forms of oppression or privilege.

The scholars Chela Sandoval and Emma Pérez, as well as the Latino theologian Virgilio Elizondo, explore the implications of mestiza consciousness for U.S. Third World feminists, including Chicana feminists and Latino Catholic congregations, respectively. For Elizondo, *mestizaje* is divine grace, which elevates the spiritual qualities of *mestizaje* as articulated by Vasconcelos but without the Eurocentric imperative. *Mestizaje* becomes the existence that resurrects humanity, and all have the potential for salvation since Elizondo ultimately describes all cross-cultural contacts as *mestizaje.* Expansions of the concept by Elizondo and others have been met by intense criticism. Most Latino theologians, such as María Pilar Aquino and Gloria Inés Loya, present its historical specificity as an important term of its experience and path to salvation. The recuperative properties of *mestizaje* are significant for postcolonial scholars. Both Chicana feminists Pérez and Sandoval reveal how the new *mestizaje* offers a political method or compass for mobilizing oppositional forms of consciousness that will produce equity. It is a method that develops and exceeds the modes of assimilation, revolution, supremacy, and separatism, each of which is a strategy unable to reconcile or allow for the multiple social positions and perspectives as delineated by Anzaldúa.

By the early twenty-first century, the concept of hybridity and cross-cultural contact had permeated social science and humanities scholarship. It also continued to travel North, and French-Canadian scholars relate it to *métissage* (French; "mixed blood"). Whether universal or not, the contemporary reconfiguration explores sites of convergence and disjuncture with attention to the pressure of power, and its meaning can be used to assess the distance between *mestizaje* and *métissage.* Nevertheless, reformulations of *mestizaje* have recuperative power for those maligned by nation and empire, sexism and homophobia, material and political displacement. If the analysis of intercultural exchange includes attention to ambiguity and contradiction, *mestizaje* can continue to offer a strategy of resistance and liberation in the twenty-first century.

See also **Creolization, Caribbean; Ethnicity and Race; Identity, Multiple.**

BIBLIOGRAPHY

Alarcón, Norma. "Chicana Feminism: In the Tracks of 'the' Native Woman." In *Living Chicana Theory,* edited by Carla Trujillo, 371–382. Berkeley, Calif.: Third Woman Press, 1998.

Anzaldúa, Gloria. *Borderlands/La Frontera: The New Mestiza.* San Francisco: Spinsters/Aunt Lute, 1987.

Aquino, María Pilar, Daisy L. Machado, and Jeanette Rodríguez. *A Reader in Latina Feminist Theology: Religion and Justice.* Austin: University of Texas Press, 2002.

Elizondo, Virgilio. *The Future Is Mestizo: Life Where Cultures Meet.* Rev. ed. with a new foreword by Sandra Cisneros and introduction by Davíd Carrasco. Boulder: University Press of Colorado, 2000.

Gonzales, Rodolfo "Corky." "I Am Joaquin." In *Latino/a Thought: Culture, Politics, and Society,* edited by Francisco H. Vázquez and Rodolfo D. Torres, 75–87. Lanham, Md.: Rowman and Littlefield, 2003.

Noriega, Chon A. "Between a Weapon and a Formula: Chicano Cinema and Its Contexts." In *Chicanos and Film: Representation and Resistance,* edited by Chon A. Noriega. Minneapolis: University of Minnesota Press, 1992.

Loya, Gloria Inés. "Pathways to a Mestiza Feminist Theology." In *A Reader in Latina Feminist Theology: Religion and Justice,* edited by María Pilar Aquino, Daisy L. Machado, and Jeanette Rodríguez, 217–240. Austin: University of Texas Press, 2002.

Paz, Octavio. *The Labyrinth of Solitude: Life and Thought in Mexico.* Translated by Lysander Kemp. New York: Grove Press, 1961.

Pérez, Emma. *The Decolonial Imaginary: Writing Chicanas into History.* Bloomington: Indiana University Press, 1999.

Sandoval, Chela. "*Mestizaje* as Method: Feminists-of-Color Challenge the Canon." In *Living Chicana Theory,* edited by Carla Trujillo, 352–370. Berkeley, Calif.: Third Woman Press, 1998.

Vasconcelos, José. *The Cosmic Race: A Bilingual Edition.* Translated and annotated by Didier T. Jaén; afterword by Joseba Gabilondo. Reprint, Baltimore: Johns Hopkins University Press, 1997.

Karen Mary Davalos

METAPHOR. Metaphor, traditionally defined as the transference of meaning from one word to another, is perhaps the most intensely and variously studied instance of figurative language. This is so because metaphor enjoys two distinct primary aspects, presenting itself as (1) a form (a discrete, replicable linguistic structure, conceivable as extrinsic to thought) and (2) a power (a cognitive operation issuing from an intrinsic and inherently creative mental faculty). Aristotle (384–322 B.C.E.), who begins the Western tradition's systematic investigation of metaphor, is the first to address the trope's double nature. On the one hand, he treats metaphor in the context of style (implicitly rendering it secondary to invention, the first of the five parts of rhetoric), as deviation from the ostensible clarity of everyday language that is subject to rules of propriety. On the other, he calls metaphor "a kind of enigma" and claims that for the verbal artist "the greatest thing by far is to have a command of metaphor" because "this alone cannot be imparted by another; it is the mark of genius, for to make good metaphors implies an eye for resemblances" (1961, p. 104).

The dominant Aristotelian idea of metaphor is not, however, either a balanced opposition or mixture of metaphor's two primary aspects. Of the two, Aristotle chooses to emphasize the formal view—perhaps because it confirms the primacy of reason and cooperates with his systematic and pedagogical motives. The philosophical and cultural consequences of Aristotle's formal emphasis are substantial and lasting: along with cultural and intellectual traditionalism, this emphasis holds that the office of language is mimetic, that of representing the world. From such a notion of language follows the implication that the truth and value of verbal art is measured by its fidelity to an unchanging, external, and therefore communally explicable reality.

The Classical System

The Aristotelian privileging of metaphor's formal aspect and its attendant assumptions, emphases, and procedures are together amplified and reified by his classical inheritors. In this tradition, metaphor's creative aspect tends to be viewed with suspicion. For instance, in *De oratore* (55 B.C.E.; On oratory), through a fabular comparison between metaphor and clothing, Cicero (106–43 B.C.E.) articulates a view of language as a form of ethical conduct that must not stoop to don the potentially corruptive finery of metaphor: "For just as clothes were first invented to protect us against cold and afterwards began to be used for the sake of adornment and dignity as well, so the metaphorical employment of words was begun because of poverty, but was brought into common use for the sake of entertainment." Cicero uses his comparison to caution us against "borrowing" fancy metaphors because they suggest "poverty" of thought and expression (p. 121–123). But it is largely through Cicero's precise, nuanced discussion of the proper and improper forms and uses of intentionally shaped language that his motive to civilize the power of metaphor is transmitted, inspiring the anonymous author of the *Rhetorica ad Herennium* (first century B.C.E., Rhetoric to Herennius) and Quintilian (c. 35–95/6 C.E.), author of *Institutio oratoria* (first century C.E.; Institutes of oratory).

Quintilian's terminological and conceptual precision expands the formal context within which metaphor may be understood. Because his primary interest is pedagogically useful classification, Quintilian chooses to treat metaphor as a member of the tropes, which involve "the artistic alteration of a word or phrase from its proper meaning to another" (p. 301). Treating metaphor as a member of a class of similar forms allows Quintilian to note metaphor's uniqueness without committing himself to an equal exploration of both its aspects. For example, while he allows that metaphor is the "commonest and by far the most beautiful of tropes," and praises it for "accomplishing the supremely difficult task of providing a name for anything" (p. 303), he restricts an attribution of cognitive agency to the tropes as a class: "The changes involved [in the use of tropes] concern not merely individual words, but also our thoughts and the structure of our sentences" (p. 301–303). It is noteworthy that here, in the midst of explicating a system whose formal emphasis diminishes metaphor's creative aspect, Quintilian states that tropes *in themselves* can play a serious role in thinking. Though muted, this connection between figured language and cognition anticipates the ground from which springs the Middle Age's most important contribution to ideas about metaphor: the notion that, when interpreted correctly, the ambiguities and excesses of figured language involve human understanding with a superior order of knowledge and being.

The Middle Ages

The institutionalization of Christianity required the preservation of classical learning, including Greco-Roman ideas of metaphor. However as Erich Auerbach points out in *Mimesis: The Representation of Reality in Western Literature* (1968), the passage from classical to Christian civilization involved a radical change in the context within which figured language was understood. Because the classical system depended upon a precise delineation and separation of elements, Auerbach sums up its emphasis as "aesthetico-stylistic." In contrast, the Christian "ethico-theological" emphasis assumes the merging of hitherto distinct styles and foregrounds a decidedly un-Roman urgency concerning interpretation. To the early Christian fathers, figured language represented a formidable theological problem. The scriptures contain many figures and ambiguities, and Christ often chooses to teach through metaphor and parables—but the classical technology of eloquence (particularly how it defines and achieves the high style, language that moves the audience to action) is pagan and elite, neither holy nor humble.

In line with the classical tradition, which he resourcefully defends throughout *De doctrina christiana* (396–426; On Christian doctrine) as being essential for proper scriptural interpretation, Augustine (354–430) discusses metaphor as a trope. It is, however, how he defines a sign that clearly indicates the Christian break from the past: "A sign is a thing which, over and above the impression it makes on the senses, causes something else to come into the mind as a consequence of itself" (p. 535). For Augustine, words (the most important human signs) have an intrinsic power that may exceed the limits erected by the classical doctrine of mimetic fidelity and enforced by the Greco-Roman insistence on decorum. Augustine's view of words as signs helps him to renew and meld the two aspects of metaphor that Aristotle delineated and his classical inheritors further isolated from each other.

The Renaissance

In step with sweeping material and social changes, including the Reformation and a gathering intellectual consensus that the universe and the mind similarly follow the laws of logic, a new context for understanding the relationship between thought and language was developing. Peter Ramus's (1515–1572) challenge to the Scholastic status quo represented this new context and prepared the way for the Enlightenment's cult of reason and pursuit of a language free from the excesses and ambiguities of figured language. Ramus replaces the transcendent Augustinian sign with stark syllogism and calls for a thorough

reorganization of the rhetorical system. As pertains to metaphor, Ramism's most consequential features are the tightly related assumptions that (1) thought follows the rules of logic and (2) language, because of its vital role in thinking, must be plain and clear. From the Ramist perspective, metaphor has no place in serious discourse and, thus, the nature and tension between its two aspects is rendered moot. However, despite its antimetaphorical outlook, Ramism did not stifle either the flowering of Renaissance rhetoric or subsequent investigations of metaphor. Because the culture of early modern Europe was, in many respects, as medieval (traditional and collectively minded) as it was modern, oratory and poetry were highly respected and widely practiced. Thus Elizabethan and metaphysical metaphors, such as those invented by Shakespeare and Donne, tend to strike an organic balance among three elements: tradition, the age's increasing emphasis on logic as a basis for artistic invention, and its discovery of a new model of subjectivity distinguished by a personal struggle for self-knowledge and self-determination.

Similar to Ramus, Francis Bacon (1561–1626) was an enemy of Scholasticism and a champion of reason and an unadorned language capable of serving it. In contrast to Ramus, however, Bacon was skeptical of the syllogistic process because, as he writes in *The New Organon* (1620), "the syllogism consists of propositions, propositions consist of words, words are symbols of notions." "Our only hope" of knowing nature, the truth of things and ourselves, Bacon asserts, "lies in . . . true induction" (p. 41). The foundations of his method—which inspired the British Royal Society's call for a scientific plain style in language and influenced a range of later philosophers, including Giambattista Vico (1688–1744)—is rooted in the principle that true knowledge comes of what one has "observed in fact or in thought of the course of nature. Beyond this he neither knows anything nor can do anything" (Bacon, p. 39). To Bacon, then, the knowledge that comes of metaphor and other figures of speech number among the "Idols" that confuse human kind, leading us into error. It is Bacon's dream of a scientific language, one enabling the direct perception and undistorted discussion of reality through the control and exclusion of tropes and figures, that predicts and helps lay the ground for the Enlightenment's general perspective of metaphor.

The Enlightenment

John Locke (1632–1704), one of the Enlightenment's most representative thinkers, born into a culture increasingly defined by a belief in the verity of empirical science and its procedures, solves the problem of metaphor by rejecting both of its aspects. In *An Essay Concerning Human Understanding* (1690), Locke holds that the foundations of thought are simple ideas, which are obtained through direct sense impressions. From this perspective, words should refer to things and the most that may be expected of language is that it further discursive "Order and Clearness." As for metaphor and "all the [other] artificial and figurative application of Words Eloquence hath invented, [these] are for nothing else but to insinuate wrong *Ideas,* move the Passions, and thereby mislead the Judgment" (Locke, p. 508). In order to get at the "true ideas upon which the inference depends," Locke advises that from language one should "strip" the "superfluous ideas" evoked by tropes and figures, and then "lay the naked *Ideas* on which the force of the argumentation depends, in their due order." Thus confronted with "true ideas" in their natural order, the mind easily perceives the truth of things and their relations (Locke, p. 676).

To Locke, metaphor's enigmatic power to create images and ideas is so corrupting of thought that he entirely exiles it from his model of consciousness and (correct) philosophical process. Of course, neoclassical thinkers, such as Voltaire (1694–1778) and Samuel Johnson (1709–1784), continued to use and productively discuss figured language—but in a context whose emphases denied relativism and forestalled the exploration of categories such as the primitive and the irrational.

Giambattista Vico's (1668–1744) views are a notable exception to the late-Enlightenment outlook and its limited and generally dismissive idea of metaphor. Although not influential in his lifetime, Vico's ideas clearly anticipate aspects of the Romantics' intense interest in and philosophical linking of poetic language, primitivism, and psychological and historical relativism. Vico's thought thus demonstrates both the continuities and differences between Enlightenment and Romantic thinking about metaphor.

Romanticism

As reflected in *La scienza nuova* (1725; The new science), Vico sees language as a social construction intimately involved with cognitive development and epistemology. Because society has changed—moving from an original theological stage, through a heroic epoch, to a present-day civilized, humanistic order—so, too, have language and human nature altered. Articulating ideas similar to those espoused by later, Romantic philosophers, such as Jean Jacques Rousseau (1712–1778) and Johann Gottfried von Herder (1744–1803), Vico postulates that, during the theological epoch (which has its analog in individual cognitive development), humans shared a primitive, metaphorically rich language, which was later complicated and variegated through cultural pressures and the advance of rational thinking. Rather than the opposite or absence of thought, figurative language demonstrates an elemental mode of thinking that Vico calls "poetic logic."

Samuel Taylor Coleridge (1772–1834) serves as a particularly influential specimen of Romantic thinking about metaphor. Neoplatonic in inclination and influenced by Vico, Rousseau, and the German Romantics, Coleridge famously distinguishes between imagination and what to him is the inferior mode of fancy, thereby clarifying his age's impatience with the limits of empirical knowledge. To Coleridge, imagination is a creative, connective power that unites nature and the poet, whose genius is realized through "organic," original form rather than "mechanic," derivative form. Coleridge defines poetry—and thus the exercise of its modes, such as metaphor—as a self-expressive activity whose object (pleasure) is opposed to that of science (truth).

Although Coleridge maintains that poetry enables a view of nature superior to that obtained through scientific inquiry, his system effectively treats poetry and science as complementary opposites: each (paradoxically) capable of discovering, through its specific symbolic activity, aspects of the reality that simultaneously undergirds and lies beyond symbols. Coleridge's Neoplatonic view of nature and its potential accessibility through human inquiry were not, however, shared by all Romantic thinkers. In particular, Friedrich Nietzsche (1844–1900) unequivocally states that human beings are "indifferent" and even hostile to "pure knowledge," to the "thing in itself." More important, Nietzsche denies that language—and by way of extension, any symbolic activity—is capable of revealing any meaning beyond that which it constructs. From this anti-essentialist perspective, the truths obtained through language are "illusions," members of a "worn out" "army of metaphors." Nietzsche is not, however, recycling a Ramist or Baconian position: To him a metaphor-free language is as impossible as a value-free science. In Nietzsche's opinion, metaphor and reality are so entwined as to be synonymous.

The Twentieth Century

With few exceptions, the twentieth century's consequential ideas of metaphor may be classified as Romantic because: (1) the trope is held to be cognitively and linguistically essential; and (2) its form and power are treated as an organically related unit. One crucial distinction between Romantic and twentieth-century ideas of metaphor, however, is that the latter summarily rejects transcendence, the notion that symbolic activity gives human beings access to supernatural knowledge and being. The origins of this rejection are manifold, but its primary engine and context is modern, disciplinary science. In this particular context, metaphor strongly tends to be viewed as an embedded phenomenon, as functioning within a cognitive, linguistic, or social system of such complexity that its elements and operations are generally accessible only to specialists—thus the contentious variety and intellectual weight of most contemporary ideas of metaphor.

Sigmund Freud (1856–1939) and Roman Jakobson (1896–1982) helped found and define structuralism, which, despite challenges mounted by poststructuralist thinkers beginning in the 1960s, continues to dominate contemporary theories of metaphor. Freud, best known as the founder of psychoanalysis, sees metaphor as a verbal elaboration and symptom of the elemental psychological process of condensation. Jakobson, drawing upon the theories of Ferdinand de Saussure (1857–1913) and through his work with persons suffering from aphasic disorders, proposes a functional synonymy between metaphor and the associative process, in his view one of the two basic operations used by the mind to construct language.

The structuralist approach to metaphor is not, however, exclusive to Freud, Jakobson, and their direct inheritors, thinkers as diverse in outlook as Jacques Lacan (1901–1981), Claude Lévi-Strauss (b. 1980), and Julia Kristeva (b. 1941). An alternative current of structural attention to metaphor is represented by the work of Stephen C. Pepper (1891–1972) and a set of like-minded scholars who constitute what may be called the "Vicoian school." Rather than embedding metaphor in a psycholinguistic system, in *World Hypotheses: A Study in Evidence* (1942), Pepper projects metaphor onto the history of thought, which he views as a series of distinct "world hypothesis," each "determined by its root metaphor" (p. 96). The philosopher and historiographer Hayden White (b. 1928) similarly embeds metaphor in the social fabric, considering the metaphorical process as the ground for one of four modes of historical understanding. A related understanding of metaphor is offered by Thomas Kuhn (1922–1996), who proposes the concepts of the "paradigm" and the "paradigm shift" as instruments for illuminating the relationship between changes in worldview and the process of scientific discovery.

Because structuralist argumentation, like that of traditional philosophy and science, generally presupposes a separation between the object of study and the dyad of investigator and method, it tends toward universalizing claims. Thus structuralism has helped stimulate the growth of a sophisticated alternative context for thinking about metaphor, one directly inspired by Nietzsche's militant rejection of objectivity, consistency, and unexamined systematic thinking. Jacques Derrida (b. 1930), the architect of deconstruction and a primary disseminator of poststructuralism, cautions against the abstractions produced by and upon which metaphysical systems are built. In the essay "White Mythology" (1972), Derrida holds that metaphor is a "metaphysical concept" created when "primitive" meanings are renamed and "circulated" in philosophical discourse. Hence his claims that "philosophy . . . is a . . . process of metaphorization" whose verity depends upon effacing its metaphorical roots (p. 210–211).

The formulation and widespread dissemination of poststructuralist ideas signals a broad and definite movement away from the traditional view of language as mimetic and the consequent treatment of intentional figuration as supplementary to thought and expression. For instance, through an interdisciplinary blend of philosophy, linguistics, cognitive science, and intercultural comparison, George Lakoff and Mark Johnson have moved the metaphorical function beyond language and, thus, beyond questions of representation. To these thinkers, "our ordinary conceptual system . . . is fundamentally metaphorical in nature" (p. 3), grounded in the universal and yet particular facts of the body.

Working within (and beyond) the discipline of anthropology, James W. Fernandez offers an approach to metaphor that, similar to Lakoff and Johnson's, assumes the trope's embedment and the intellectual obligation to foreground principles of cultural relativism. To Fernandez, metaphor is a "strategic predication" of identity that "leads to performance." Rather than identifying metaphor as either a cognitive, linguistic, or structural abstraction (classifications that similarly encourage metaphor's division into two aspects), Fernandez understands metaphor in much the same way that Henry Louis Gates Jr. (b. 1950) conceives the practice of "signifyin(g)" in African-American culture. Like "signifyin(g)," metaphor is a lived strategy, one that plays a key, mediating role in the mutual construction of identity, emotions, and the immediate social matrix. While it is impossible to predict the larger consequences of the ongoing shift in ideas of metaphor, the work of comparativists like Earl Miner (1927–2004) suggests that future understandings of metaphor will be all the richer because they will spring from and advance dialogue between heretofore intellectually separated traditions and cultures.

See also **Genre; Literature; Narrative; Rhetoric.**

BIBLIOGRAPHY

Aristotle. *Aristotle's Poetics.* Translated by Samuel H. Butcher. New York: Hill and Wang, 1961.

———. *The Rhetoric of Aristotle.* Translated by Lane Cooper. Englewood Cliffs, N.J.: Prentice-Hall, 1988.

Auerbach, Erich. *Mimesis: The Representation of Reality in Western Literature.* Translated by Willard R. Trask. Princeton, N.J.: Princeton University Press, 1968.

Augustine. "On Christian Doctrine." Translated by J. F. Shaw. In *A Select Library of the Nicene and Post-Nicene Fathers,* 1st series, edited by Philip Schaff. Vol. 2 of *St. Augustine.* Grand Rapids, Mich.: Eerdmans, 1956, reprint.1983. Originally published in 1887.

Bacon, Francis. *The New Organon.* In *The New Organon and Related Writings.* Edited with an introduction by Fulton H. Anderson. New York: Liberal Arts Press, 1960.

Cicero. *De oratore.* 2 vol. Translated by Edward W. Sutton and Harris Rackham. Cambridge, Mass.: Harvard University Press, 1942.

Coleridge, Samuel Taylor. *Biographia Literaria: or Biographical Sketches of My Literary Life and Opinions.* Edited by George Watson. Rutland, Vt.: Charles E. Tuttle, 1991.

Derrida, Jacques. "White Mythology: Metaphor in the Text of Philosophy." In his *Margins of Philosophy,* translated by Alan Bass. Chicago: University of Chicago Press, 1982.

Fernandez, James W. *Persuasions and Performances: The Play of Tropes in Culture.* Bloomington: Indiana University Press, 1986.

Gates, Henry Louis, Jr. *The Signifying Monkey: A Theory of African-American Literary Criticism.* New York: Oxford University Press, 1989.

Hawkes, Terence. *Metaphor.* London: Methuen, 1972.

Kristeva, Julia. "Freud and Love: Treatment and Its Discontents." Translated by Léon S. Roudiez. In *The Kristeva Reader,* edited by Toril Moi. New York: Columbia University Press, 1986.

Lakoff, George, and Mark Johnson. *Metaphors We Live By.* Chicago: University of Chicago Press, 1980.

Locke, John. *An Essay concerning Human Understanding.* Edited by Peter H. Nidditch. New York: Oxford University Press, 1979.

Nietzsche, Friedrich. "On Truth and Lie in an Extra-Moral Sense." In *The Portable Nietzsche,* translated by Walter Kaufman. New York: Penguin, 1982.

Ong, Walter J. *Ramus, Method and the Decay of Dialogue: From the Art of Discourse to the Art of Reason.* Cambridge, Mass.: Harvard University Press, 1983.

Ortony, Andrew, ed. *Metaphor and Thought.* 2nd ed. New York: Cambridge University Press, 1993.

Pepper, Stephen C. *World Hypotheses: A Study in Evidence.* Berkeley: University of California Press, 1942.

Quintilian. *Institutio oratoria.* 4 vols. Translated by Harold E. Butler. Cambridge, Mass.: Harvard University Press, 1996.

Ricoeur, Paul. *The Rule of Metaphor: Multi-disciplinary Studies of the Creation of Meaning in Language.* Translated by Robert Czerny with Kathleen McLaughlin and John Costello. Toronto: University of Toronto Press, 1977.

Vico, Giambattista. *The New Science of Giambattista Vico.* Rev. and abr. ed. Translated by Thomas Goddard Bergin and Max Harold Fisch. Ithaca, N.Y.: Cornell University Press, 1968.

Cristophor Hollingsworth

METAPHYSICS.

This entry includes two subentries:

Ancient and Medieval
Renaissance to the Present

ANCIENT AND MEDIEVAL

In the early twenty-first century *metaphysics* is a term used fairly loosely to describe philosophical investigation of the fundamental constituents of reality. But, in the Middle Ages, there was great debate about what was the subject of metaphysics, and that controversy had ancient roots.

What Is Metaphysics?

The word *metaphysics* is taken from the title, given by an editor in antiquity, to a treatise (or, rather, a set of material, not all of which belongs together) by Aristotle (384–322 B.C.E.): the word may have been chosen just because the work was placed after (*meta*) the physics, or it may have meant that the work deals with things beyond the physical. Aristotle does, in most of the *Metaphysics,* seem to believe that he is engaged in a single, distinctive enterprise of "first philosophy"—but he characterizes its aim in a number of different, and arguably incompatible, ways: it is the study of first principles, or of being qua being, or the investigation of substance, or its main concern is with immovable substances, that is to say, with the gods. This final, theological aspect led many later ancient philosophers to envisage the *Metaphysics* as an investigation, not of being in general, but of the highest sort of supra-sensible being—an approach that fitted the overwhelming concern of late antique philosophers with the intelligible world and the general wish to syncretize Aristotle and Plato.

In the Middle Ages, the question of the subject-matter of metaphysics became more problematic. The two greatest medieval Islamic philosophers, Avicenna (Ibn Sina; 980–1037) and Averroës (Ibn Rushd; 1126–1198), knew Aristotle's *Metaphysics* well. Avicenna held that God could not be the subject of metaphysics, because it is in metaphysics that the existence of God is demonstrated, and no science can demonstrate the existence of its own subject. Metaphysics, therefore, has as its subject being qua being. Averroës disagreed. He held that the existence of God is demonstrated in physics, and so metaphysics can be regarded as the study of the first being, the separate substance that, as final cause, is the mover of all things.

Avicenna's view predominated among the Christian Scholastics, who saw metaphysics primarily as the study of being in general (*ens commune*) rather than of a particular, special being. But Duns Scotus (c. 1266–1308), at least, was willing to say that God is a sort of being, and so is considered in metaphysics along with all other beings. Thomas Aquinas's (c. 1224–1274) position had been, perhaps, more nuanced. God is not, he thought, contained under the notion of being in general, but he is included within metaphysics in that he is the cause of being in general, which the subject studies.

Form in Metaphysics

One central notion in metaphysics (understood in a broad sense, and going back to before the word was invented) is that of form. Plato (c. 428–348/7 B.C.E.) reasoned that there could be no knowledge of the objects of everyday experience, but merely opinion about them, because they are constantly changing and cannot be said to be, but merely to become. The objects of knowledge, he thought, must be unchanging things—what he called "Forms" or "Ideas." Although Platonic Forms can be grasped only through the powers of the intellect, not by the senses, they are by no means merely mental entities, but independently existing realities, as a result of participation in which the objects of sense perception have the characteristics they do—so, for example, beautiful things are beautiful by virtue of participating in the Form of Beauty (or, as Plato sometimes says, in Beauty Itself). Beyond this, Plato gives rather different accounts of the Forms from dialogue to dialogue, and even within the same dialogue. In perhaps his most famous discussion of them, in the central books of the *Republic,* he presents a supreme Form, the Form of the Good, which is understood only after years of intellectual training. The other Forms, Plato says, depend on the Form of the Good and are grasped properly only once the Form of the Good is grasped. In the *Timaeus,* Plato shows the universe being constructed as an ensouled living thing, according to the pattern of the Ideas.

Aristotle's account in his *Metaphysics* of how things are constituted also uses the notion of Form, but it is treated very differently. The Forms Aristotle discusses are those of types of natural things, divided according to natural kinds. For instance, one natural kind is Man, another is Horse. According to this hylomorphic account, each man is a man by virtue of the Form of humanity, and each horse a horse by virtue of the Form of equinity. These Aristotelian Forms are not, like Plato's Forms, independent single entities in which many particular sensible things participate. Rather, a particular member of a natural kind—this man, for instance—is a concrete whole composed of matter and Form. Yet the Form that makes him a man is the same as the Form by which any other man is a man. By grasping this Form with our intellects, we have a universal notion of Man, which we are able to use in formulating scientific truths, not about this or that man, but about Man in general.

In the Middle Ages, Plato's Theory of Forms in its pure state had very few adherents. But an adapted version of it, which goes back to Philo (c. 13 B.C.E.–45/50 C.E.), the Hellenistic Jewish thinker, was extremely popular: the Forms are said to be in the mind of God. Thinkers as diverse as Augustine, Eriugena, Abelard, and Aquinas used this idea as one of the ways of describing God's relation to created things. It was not until William of Ockham (c. 1285–?1349), in the early fourteenth century, that this picture was seriously questioned. Adoption of this version of Platonic Ideas still left Aristotelian hylomorphism as the main way of explaining the constitution of concrete things, and there was a vigorous debate in the twelfth century about whether (on the basis of the version of Aristotle's theory proposed in his *Categories*) Forms in reality are really universal, or are universal merely in the way they are used in human thought and language. In the thirteenth and fourteenth centuries, hylomorphism was the basis (following Aristotle's *On the Soul*) for the theory of intellectual cognition. The Form that makes, for example, a horse a horse informs the matter-like potential intellect of the person who intellectually grasps the notion of horse.

Two Main Questions of Medieval Metaphysics

Another important debate in later medieval metaphysics was about whether essence—the sort of thing something is—and existence (*esse*)—the fact of the thing's actually existing—are really distinct. Aquinas held that they are, and that in everything except God there is a real composition between them. This theory allows Aquinas, who does not believe that every creature is a composite of matter and form, to identify one sense in which nevertheless God alone is noncomposite. Not many of his successors followed him, however, in this insistence that the distinction between essence and existence is real. Some, such as Duns Scotus, held the distinction to be more than mental, but less than real, while Ockham argues that "essence" and *esse* mean the same thing.

The same thinkers also considered whether "being" in a general sense is a notion under which fall both God and his creatures. Aquinas insisted that the notion applies only analogically (and so equivocally) to God, on the one hand, and created things on the other. Scotus (followed by many fourteenth-century thinkers) argued for a subtle form of univocal predication of "being," although he fully acknowledged that God's infinite way of being is unlike that of any creature.

See also **Aristotelianism; Form, Metaphysical, in Ancient and Medieval Thought; Metaphysics: Renaissance to the Present.**

BIBLIOGRAPHY

PRIMARY SOURCES

Aristotle. *Metaphysics.* In *The Complete Works of Aristotle,* edited by Jonathan Barnes. Vol. 2. Princeton, N.J.: Princeton University Press, 1985. Translations with extensive philosophical annotation of individual books of the *Metaphysics* can be found in the Clarendon Aristotle Series, published by Oxford University Press.

Plato. *Dialogues.* Various translations are available.

Aquinas, Thomas. *Selected Philosophical Writings.* Edited and translated by Timothy McDermott. Oxford and New York: Oxford University Press, 1993. Contains a number of passages central to Aquinas's metaphysics, including the whole of *De ente et essentia,* 90–113.

SECONDARY SOURCES

Barnes, Jonathan. "Metaphysics." In *The Cambridge Companion to Aristotle,* edited by Jonathan Barnes, 66–108. Cambridge, U.K., and New York: Cambridge University Press, 1995.

Dumont, S. "Henry of Ghent and Duns Scotus." In *The Routledge History of Philosophy,* Vol. 3: *Medieval Philosophy,* edited by John Marenbon, 291–328. London and New York: Routledge, 1998. The chapter is almost entirely on their metaphysics.

White, Nicholas P. "Plato's Metaphysical Epistemology." In *The Cambridge Companion to Plato,* edited by Richard Kraut, 277–310. Cambridge, U.K.: Cambridge University Press, 1992.

Wippel, John F. "Essence and Existence." In *Cambridge History of Later Medieval Philosophy: From the Rediscovery of Aristotle to the Disintegration of Scholasticism, 1100–1600,* edited by Norman Kretzmann, Anthony Kenny, and Jan Pinborg, 385–410. Cambridge, U.K., and New York: Cambridge University Press, 1982.

John Marenbon

RENAISSANCE TO THE PRESENT

Metaphysics, in its most basic sense, is an account of what exists. It may include accounts of what sorts of things exist; of what really exists as opposed to what merely appears to exist; of what exists necessarily rather than by accident; of what it is that underlies everything else; or of the most general laws governing existing things. This article will describe some of the most important metaphysical positions that have appeared since the Renaissance and, where space permits, some of the reasons that have motivated the philosophers who hold them. The dates given for different eras are particular to this discussion. They name the year of birth of the earliest philosopher covered in each section and the year of death of the latest.

The Renaissance (1433–1617)

Better and more widely available texts of the writings of Plato mark the Renaissance. The new, widespread distribution of Platonic and Neoplatonic works, due in large part to the work of Marsilio Ficino (1433–1499) led to a major revival of those views. One of Ficino's most influential views is his account of a hierarchy of perfection among existing things in which the highest thing, God, possesses the most perfection and the lowest thing, the body, the least.

The philosophy of the Renaissance remained, however, generally Scholastic. That is, it was dominated by Aristotelian views as codified by medieval commentators. Among Scholastics, Francisco Suárez (1548–1617) is notable for offering a definition of metaphysics as the science of being qua being, which distinguishes metaphysics from less lofty accounts of accidental features of existing things and focuses inquiry on the nature of being itself. Suárez's seminal work, *Disputationes metaphysicae* (1597), also offered an original account of the metaphysical status of universals, in which it is true that only individual things exist but contrary to nominalism—the view that universal terms are merely labels for arbitrary collections of individuals—it is also true that universals are abstractions from nonconventional similarities among individuals.

The Early Modern Period (1561–1753)

Early modern metaphysics is in large part a response to the challenges that dramatic advances in physics and astronomy presented for theology and Aristotelian philosophy. Francis Bacon (1561–1626) is the figure who perhaps best marks the transition between Renaissance and early modern philosophy. Bacon's major work, *The New Organon,* as its title suggests, was an attempt to supplant Aristotle's authority. Two doctrines of that work form the basis of many of the period's debates. First, Bacon asserted that a traditional part of metaphysics, the inquiry into the final causes, or purposes, of nature, is barren, thereby divesting natural science of an important theological element. Second, Bacon denied that forms,

FINAL CAUSES

[The mind] falls back on things that are more familiar, namely final causes, which are plainly derived from the nature of man rather than of the universe, and from this origin have wonderfully corrupted philosophy. (Bacon, 1620, p. 44)

When dealing with natural things we will, then, never derive any explanations from the purposes which God or nature may have had in view when creating them and we shall entirely banish from our philosophy the search for final causes. (Descartes, 1647, vol. 1, p. 202)

Nature has no end set before it, and . . . all final causes are nothing but human fictions. (Spinoza, 1660s? *Ethics* I Appendix)

Whatever Descartes may have said, not only efficient causes, but also final causes, are to be treated in physics, just as a house would be badly explained if we were to describe only the arrangement of its parts, but not its use. (Leibniz, 1702, pp. 254–255)

May I regard purpose-like orderings as intentions. . . ? Yes, but . . . it must not matter at all whether you say, "God has wisely willed it so" or "Nature has wisely so ordered it." (Kant, 1781, p. 620)

[Spirit] is in itself the movement which is cognition—the transforming of the in-itself in that which is for-itself, of substance into subject. (Hegel, 1807, p. 488)

understood as abstract natural kinds, are principally what exists. Metaphysics, on Bacon's view, is the study of first and formal causes in nature. It is, in short, the study of the most general laws or reasons by which natural events may be understood.

René Descartes (1596–1650) followed Bacon in denying that explanations in terms of final causes are appropriate in the sciences. He defended the existence and perfection of God but focused his metaphysics, as Bacon did, on providing an account of the natural world. In his most important philosophical works, *Meditations on First Philosophy* (1641) and *Principles of Philosophy* (1644), he argued that there are two basic kinds of substances or things with independent existence: minds and bodies. Any substance is characterized by a property necessary for its existence, which Descartes called in different places its nature, essence, or attribute. The nature of mind is thought; of body, extension. Substances have, in addition, properties that are not essential to them and that they can gain or lose without themselves going out of existence. Such properties are called modes or affections.

Descartes's metaphysics is best known for one argument and a problem that the argument generates. He argued that

the existence of the self can be known for certain just because, at the very time one doubts the proposition "I exist," one is at the same time thinking and therefore existing (Descartes, vol. 1, pp. 194–195). From this argument, often referred to as "the cogito," Descartes eventually concluded that the essence of mind—and so perhaps of the person—is thought. However, it is clear that people have and are intimately aware of their own bodies. The mind-body problem arises from an attempt to give an account of human nature. Are people essentially, minds, bodies, or both? Moreover, if people are both, the relationship between mind and body needs to be explained. For Descartes, this latter problem was especially difficult. He endorsed a view of perfection in the world much like that of Ficino, in which minds are much more perfect than bodies, so he had to explain in his theory of perception how something less perfect apparently causes changes in something more perfect.

Benedictus, or Baruch, de Spinoza (1632–1677) published during his lifetime a well-received commentary on Cartesian philosophy. Many of his best-known metaphysical positions, which are found in their most mature form in his posthumously published *Ethics,* can be understood as reactions to Cartesianism. Spinoza identified God with Nature and defended against Cartesian dualism a substance monism in which God is the only substance (EIp14) and possesses all attributes (Spinoza, EId6), including both extension and thought. Spinoza rejected any purpose in nature. (Spinoza is cited here in the customary fashion. For example, EIIp7 means *Ethics,* Part II, proposition 7.) He defended, largely against Descartes, necessitarianism (EIp33), the view that things could not have been any other way than the way they are, and universal determinism (EIp28–Ip29), in which every existing mode is the effect of some efficient cause. Spinoza addressed the mind-body problem by means of the doctrine known as parallelism, in which mind and body do not interact (EIIp7). Instead, the chain of causes and effects may be understood equally well as a chain of exclusively mental or exclusively physical events.

John Locke (1632–1704), whose philosophy is, much like Bacon's, an attempt to vindicate mechanistic science, adopted a slightly different notion of substance. For Locke, substances are much the same things as Cartesian substances—persons, God, angels, and ordinary material objects. Substances are so designated, however, not because of their independent existence but because they form a substratum for clusters of properties in which those properties inhere and which can survive change in those properties. Although Locke, like his predecessors, described modes at length, he considered them properly ideas rather than properties of substance. The important, knowable properties of substance, in his view, are qualities. In his *Essay concerning Human Understanding,* Locke famously (or notoriously) defended Robert Boyle's (1627–1691) distinction between primary qualities, such as extension, which really are in substances, and secondary qualities, such as white, which are mere powers to produce certain sensations in people (Locke, 2.8.12–13). This doctrine may be a result of Locke's attempt to ground corpuscularian physical theories, in which extension and other primary qualities were supposed to explain color perceptions and other secondary qualities.

Gottfried Leibniz (1646–1716) was perhaps the most sophisticated metaphysician of the early modern period. He read his predecessors and contemporaries widely and engaged with their views in a variety of contexts. Leibniz was by temperament conciliatory, and his sympathy toward Scholasticism emerges most clearly in his attempt to reintegrate final causes into metaphysics, both at the level of scientific explanation and at the very general level (pp. 52–55). Leibniz's fundamental metaphysical principle, the Principle of Sufficient Reason, is the doctrine that there is reason for every state of affairs. At the most general level, this reason must be in terms of God's purposes: God chooses that the world be this world rather than other possible worlds because this one is the best of all possible worlds (pp. 96–97). The Principle of Sufficient Reason formed the basis for some powerful criticisms of Newtonian physics. It is also the principal target of Voltaire's satire, *Candide.*

From at least the 1680s, Leibniz understood substances in grammatical terms, as subjects of predication that cannot themselves be predicated of something else. For example, "a king" can be either the subject or predicate of a proposition, so it is not substance; "Alexander," however, can only be a subject, so Alexander is a genuine substance (pp. 41–42). Because Leibniz

---

KANT'S "COPERNICAN REVOLUTION" IN METAPHYSICS

Up to now it has been assumed that all our cognition must conform to the objects; but all attempts to find out something about them a priori through concepts that would extend our cognition have, on this presupposition, come to nothing. Hence let us once try whether we do not get farther with the problems of metaphysics by assuming that objects must conform to our cognition, which would agree better with the requested possibility of an a priori cognition of them, which is to establish something about objects before they are given to us. (B xvi, p. 110)

---

conceived of each substance as a complete concept or a subject with a comprehensive list of true predications of it, he denied that substances change. So he denied, at the strictly metaphysical level, causal interaction among substances (p. 47). His grammatical conception of substance caused him to endorse a version of idealism, the view that substances cannot be material (p. 79) and in 1714 the theory of monads, his mature metaphysics in which all things either are or are composed of simple, indivisible, inalterable, indestructible, perceiving things.

George Berkeley (1685–1753) formulated an influential version of idealism. He was influenced by Leibniz's views on material objects and also by the Cartesian Nicolas Malebranche's (1638–1715) criticisms of accounts of causal influence among bodies. His most explicit target, however, was Locke's version of the distinction between primary and secondary qualities. Berkeley argued that Locke was right to think that sensations such as pain and white that are caused in people do not resemble their objects but that Locke had no reason for thinking that the perception of extension and other purported primary qualities is different. In either sort of case, one has access only to one's sensations, and these are certainly ideas. Berkeley identified ordinary objects and the physics of ordinary objects, then, as concerning ideas rather than their cause, which can only be God.

David Hume (1711–1776) followed Berkeley in construing ordinary objects as ideas (1.2.6). He was, however, skeptical about the causes of ideas and indeed is best known for his skepticism about causality generally. Hume denied that any sort of necessary connection could be known through experience and so denied all causal connections of the sort asserted by many of his predecessors. He redescribed causal relations as laws concerning the causal conjunction of events of one sort with events of the other. Hume has traditionally been understood as moving from causal language in the description of nature, in which

---

THE REJECTION OF METAPHYSICS

[Pragmatism] will serve to show that almost every proposition of onto-logical metaphysics is either meaningless gibberish,—one word being defined by other words, and they by still others, without any real conception ever being reached,—or else is downright absurd. (Peirce, "What Pragmatism Is")

The fundamental faith of the metaphysicians is the faith in opposite values. . . . one may doubt, first, whether there are any opposites at all, and secondly whether these . . . opposite values . . . are not perhaps merely foreground estimates, only provisional perspectives, perhaps even from some nook, perhaps from below. (Nietzsche, section 2)

The non-theoretical character of metaphysics would not be in itself a defect. . . . the danger lies in the deceptive character of metaphysics; it gives the illusion of knowledge without actually giving any knowledge. This is why we reject it. (Carnap, "The Rejection of Metaphysics," from *Philosophy and Logical Syntax,* 1934, section 5)

---

events of one sort are said to cause events of another sort, to the language of laws, in which, more modestly, events of one sort are said to follow events of another sort with lawlike regularity.

German Idealism (1724–1831)

German idealists attempted to preserve causal laws and other necessary truths about objects by emphasizing the role of the self in understanding objects. As the movement developed, figures such as Gottlieb Fichte (1762–1814) went further, arguing that, in a sense, the self creates objects.

Immanuel Kant (1724–1804), in his *Critique of Pure Reason,* defended the view, largely against Hume, that there are basic a priori laws, including causal laws, governing all objects of experience. Kant's "Copernican Revolution" in metaphysics changed the focus of metaphysical inquiry from nature exclusively to the thinking self as it understands nature. He argued that there are concepts—Categories—and space and time—Forms of Sensible Intuition—by which one understands and experiences things. Because one cannot but think things under these Categories and Forms, they are a priori conditions of different kinds of thought and therefore form the basis for judgments of necessity. Kant described his view as "transcendental idealism" because, although the Categories and Forms make possible objectively valid and necessary laws governing objects of experience, they cannot be ascribed to objects except insofar as those objects are experienced.

In experience, Kant rescued the traditional metaphysical distinction between form and matter: form is the a priori aspect of experience that mind imposes on matter in cognition. The inquiry into the nature of objects independent of experience by means of concepts, however, which Kant understood as the

project of traditional metaphysics, cannot produce knowledge. However, Kant allowed that such inquiry, which he called "dialectic," is founded upon important human interests, such as the quest to understand practical freedom or to find purposiveness or systematic unity in nature.

Georg Hegel (1770–1831) held that ultimately only spirit is real. Hegel argued that history, in particular the history of human society, is a history of dialectical thought. Hegel, then, moved mind out of the individual altogether and eventually into an account of stages of human consciousness that are at once a kind of progression of reasoning, steps of psychological development, and social structures. *Dialectic* had a very different meaning for Hegel from that which Kant gave it. Hegel retained a focus on the process of reasoning that characterized Kant's dialectic and continued to consider the question of the invalidity of particular applications of a concept. The invalidity of a particular kind of reasoning is, however, of interest principally not because it makes a category mistake in applying concepts inappropriately but as itself a flawed way of being or experiencing objects in the world, which, because of its flaws, leads also to a particular new way of being.

The End of Metaphysics (1839–1980)

Kant himself rejected metaphysics, considered as an attempt to know objects outside experience. Forms of that position characterized three major recent philosophical movements that drew on his emphasis on the thinking self and his devotion to empiricism.

American Pragmatism. This movement emphasized, following Kant and in some cases Hegel, the role of concepts in experience. John Dewey (1859–1952) argued that concepts distort our understanding of the unity of nature. Charles Peirce

---

(1839–1914) similarly took conceptual analysis to demonstrate that the propositions of traditional metaphysics are nonsensical. William James (1842–1910) defended the use of concepts and took metaphysics to be the task of understanding why people organize experience the way they do. Some traditional metaphysical notions remained in American Pragmatism. Peirce, for example, defended an account of generals, a theory of natural kinds. However, the movement was generally critical of traditional, a priori metaphysics.

Phenomenology and existentialism. These movements, which started perhaps with the works of Nietzsche, emphasized the importance of perspective for undermining or perhaps reassessing metaphysics.

Phenomenology is the study of things as one experiences them. In *Ideas,* Edmund Husserl (1859–1938) argued that this project requires setting aside questions of existence, which amounts to making questions of metaphysics secondary to questions of experience. Martin Heidegger (1889–1976), slightly differently, made questions of existence, or being, just questions of experience. The study of being is not, for Heidegger, then, the study of the being of fundamental things in the universe that are independent of experience but instead the study of the being of things as they are experienced and, perhaps more important, formed and conceived by the thinker. Existentialism, perhaps best known from the works of Jean-Paul Sartre (1905–1980), in the most general terms is the conclusion, from either of these positions, that there are no metaphysical facts about the world, with the result that if one really needs such facts, as Kant suggested, one must either create them or insist upon what one has no claim to know.

Logical positivism. Ludwig Wittgenstein (1889–1951) and Rudolf Carnap (1891–1970) derived, largely from Kant, the view that knowledge is only of objects of experience. Logical positivists held, furthermore, that as terms apply meaningfully only to objects of experience, metaphysical claims are not merely false or mistaken but nonsensical. The movement was largely responsible for making language and its meaning the focus of a great deal of recent philosophical inquiry in metaphysics and also in epistemology and ethics.

Twenty-First-Century Developments

It is difficult to predict the debates and positions for which the early twenty-first century era will be remembered. A result of the focus on language and meaning produced by logical positivism is perhaps that many important metaphysical debates at the beginning of the twenty-first century have centered not on the question of what existence is or is like generally but on the question of whether particular sorts of things exist. A response to the positivist challenge to ethics, for example, has been to claim that terms in ethics are meaningful in the sense that they refer to real, existing things in the world, good and evil. In modal metaphysics, questions about the meaningfulness of possibility have produced debates over the metaphysical status of possible worlds: are possibilities real, and if so, how are they different from actual existents? Finally, the mind-body problem, now recast as the question of the relationship between the mind and the brain, and the existence

of general or natural kinds, often a problem for set theory, have remained hotly debated matters.

The tradition of phenomenology and existentialism has given way to the movements of structuralism and deconstructionism. Proponents of these methods might, like many phenomenologists, deny that they study anything like traditional metaphysics. Structuralists abstract from the genesis and subject of a particular kind of world or experience and analyze it as a product of thought, or text, without a thinker, who, it is argued, is irrelevant to meaning. Deconstructionism is the view that largely as a result of the fact that texts are created by thinkers, the relevant structures are binary and can be understood in terms of opposition within the structure. The aim of deconstruction is to show how, like the self and the world for Fichte, the opposed units in the structures depend upon one another.

See also **Knowledge; Philosophy; Pragmatism.**

BIBLIOGRAPHY

Bacon, Francis. *The New Organon.* Edited by Lisa Jardine and Michael Silverthorne. Cambridge, U.K.: Cambridge University Press, 2000.

Carnap, Rudolf. *Philosophy and Logical Syntax.* Bristol, U.K.: Thoemmes Press, 1996. This most recent edition is out of print. The work is widely available online.

Descartes, René. *The Philosophical Writings of Descartes.* 3 vols. Translated by John Cottingham, Robert Stoothoff, Dugald Murdoch, and Anthony Kenny. Cambridge, U.K.: Cambridge University Press, 1991.

Hegel, Georg. *Phenomenology of Spirit.* Translated by A. V. Miller. Oxford: Clarendon Press, 1977.

Husserl, Edmund. *Ideas Pertaining to a Pure Phenomenology and to a Phenomenological Philosophy. First Book: General Introduction to a Pure Phenomenology.* Translated by D. Cairns. Dordrecht: Kluwer, 1988.

Kant, Immanuel. *Critique of Pure Reason.* Translated and edited by Paul Guyer and Allen W. Wood. Cambridge, U.K.: Cambridge University Press, 1998.

Leibniz, Gottfried. *Philosophical Essays.* Edited and translated by Roger Ariew and Daniel Garber. Indianapolis: Hackett, 1989.

Locke, John. *An Essay concerning Human Understanding.* Edited by Peter Nidditch. Oxford: Clarendon, 1975.

Nietzsche, Friedrich. *Beyond Good and Evil.* Translated by Walter Kaufman. New York: Vintage Books, 1966.

Peirce, C. S. "What Pragmatism Is." *Monist* 15, no. 2 (1905): 161–181.

Spinoza, Benedictus de. *The Collected Works of Spinoza.* Vol. 1. Edited and translated by Edwin Curley. Princeton, N.J.: Princeton University Press, 1985.

Michael LeBuffe

MICROCOSM AND MACROCOSM.

Microcosm and macrocosm are two aspects of a theory developed by ancient Greek philosophers to describe human beings and their place in the universe. These early thinkers viewed the individual human being as a little world (*mikros kosmos*) whose composition and structure correspond to that of the universe, or great world (*makros kosmos,* or *megas kosmos*). *Kosmos* at this time meant "order" in a general sense and implied a harmonious, and therefore beautiful, arrangement of parts in any organic system; hence it also referred to order in human societies, reflected in good government. Comparisons between society and the human being, as well as society and the universe, were varieties of microcosmic theory. These analogies enjoyed a long life, first in the Mediterranean region during antiquity and later throughout Europe during the Middle Ages. The ideas were commonplace during the Renaissance and early modern times but lost their plausibility when a mechanistic model of the universe became dominant in the seventeenth and eighteenth centuries.

Origins

The most fully developed version of the idea in antiquity was made by Plato (427?–347 B.C.E.), but fragmentary evidence indicates that philosophers before him articulated some version of it. The idea may have begun as an archetypal theme of mythology that the pre-Socratic philosophers reworked into a more systematic form. Unfortunately, it is impossible to reconstruct their thinking in much detail, and clear references attributing the doctrine to Democritus (c. 460–c. 370 B.C.E.) and Pythagoras (c. 582–c. 507 B.C.E.) are quite late, dating to the fifth and ninth centuries C.E., respectively. Some form of the idea seems to have been common among most ancient cultures. Since comparisons of human beings and the universe were made in India and China, the concept may ultimately be of Asian origin; but the available sources do not indicate that the theory in Greece was the result of cultural diffusion. Among extant Greek texts, the term first appears in the *Physics* of Aristotle (384–322 B.C.E.), where it occurs in an incidental remark (*Physics* 8.2, 252b). Plato did not use the terminology when he developed the idea.

Plato

In the *Philebus* (28d–30d), Plato argued that human beings and the universe are both composed of an elemental body and a rational soul, and that just as the human body derives from the universe's body, the human soul must derive from the universe's soul. The universe is, therefore, not only an orderly system but an intelligent organism as well. Plato expounded this theme at greater length in the *Timaeus* (29d–47e), where he explained how the structure of the human being parallels that of the universe through certain correspondences in body and soul. Just as the body of the universe is spherical, and its soul is composed of orbits along which the planets wander, so too the soul of the human being is composed of orbits along which its emotions rove, and it inhabits the head, which is spherical. The rest of the human body exists merely to serve the head.

Unlike the macrocosm, which contains all things and is immortal, and hence has no need of sensory or digestive organs or limbs for locomotion, the microcosm is only a part of the whole, and its existence is threatened by the surrounding elements, so that it needs such additional parts to perceive and avoid danger and to replenish the nutrients it loses. Furthermore, the external disturbances that threaten the microcosm cause the orbits of its soul to be disrupted, throwing its

emotions into disarray. Yet when the disordered microcosm observes the heavens, it sees there the orderly motions of the planets following the orbits of the macrocosmic soul. With the aid of philosophical study, it becomes aware of the correspondence between itself and its great counterpart. Having attained this insight, the microcosm realizes that just as the universe employs reason to govern the planets, it too should employ reason to govern its emotions. In this way the microcosm overcomes its inner discord and prepares its soul for a return to the heavens from which it came.

The Body Politic

In the *Republic* (Book 4), Plato united the microcosmic theme with the pre-Socratic tendency to view cosmology in political terms when he discussed his model of an ideal city-state in order to explore the nature of the human soul. The structure of each is tripartite and hierarchical. The class of philosopher-kings corresponds to reason (located in the head), the warrior class corresponds to irascibility (located in the breast), and the worker class corresponds to appetite (located in the belly). If the city or the soul is to function in harmony, the lower parts must obey the higher, and the higher must guide prudently. This organic notion of the body politic exerted an extraordinary appeal. St. Paul of Tarsus used it to describe the church as the mystical body of Christ (1 Corinthians 12, et al.), and medieval thinkers such as John of Salisbury (c. 1110–1180), in the *Polycraticus,* and Marsilius of Padua (c. 1270–c. 1342), in the *Defensor pacis,* presented their political ideas within its framework. Theories of the body politic remained strong in early modern times, even inspiring the *Leviathan* of Thomas Hobbes (1588–1679).

The common contemporary use of organic analogies to describe the nation or the country is, therefore, an inheritance from earlier macrocosmic metaphors. This way of thinking was not confined to the West. It was, for example, reflected in the Indian Vedas, which explained the caste system by way of an anatomical analogy according to which each level of the social order sprang from a bodily part of Brahma, the Hindu creator-god.

Hellenism and Late Antiquity

Among the Hellenistic philosophers, the Stoics preserved the idea of the universe as a living organism, but the human being as a miniature image of it did not, apparently, interest them as much. The Middle Platonists also accepted the existence of a world-soul and, like the Stoics, considered it divine. The Neoplatonist Plotinus (205–270 C.E.) refined this idea and called the human being "an intelligible world" (*Enneads* 3.4.3) who, like the universe, is an intellect that governs a soul that animates a material body. Later Neoplatonists, believing that the correspondences between microcosm and macrocosm, if properly invoked, would allow them to draw upon hidden reserves of psychic energy immanent in the living universe, employed a form of ritual magic called "theurgy" to assist them in their spiritual aspirations. Others less spiritually inclined, however, hoped to use these cosmic sympathies to manipulate the world for material benefit or to predict the course of future events. Astrologers employed the theory of melothesia—that each sign of the Zodiac corresponds to a specific part of the human body—in the practice of medicine.

The broad appeal of the microcosm is reflected in its adoption by Jews, Christians, Gnostics, Manichaeans, and the authors of the Hermetic corpus (attributed to Hermes Trismegistus). The Jewish philosopher Philo of Alexandria (c. 20 B.C.E.–c. 50 C.E.) somewhat anticipated Plotinus by calling man "a miniature heaven" (*On the Creation* 27.82). He preferred, however, to compare the human being with God, since Scripture taught that man and woman were made in God's image and likeness (Genesis 1:26–27); he reasoned, therefore, that human souls govern their bodies in much the way that God governs the physical world (*On the Creation* 23.69). Philo employed unusual terminology, substituting for *mikros kosmos* the expression *brachys kosmos,* or "short world," which appeared later as *brevis mundus* in the Latin works of Calcidius (*Commentary on Plato's Timaeus,* 202; third or fourth century C.E.) and Macrobius (*Commentary on Cicero's Dream of Scipio,* 2.12; fl. c. 430 C.E.).

Jewish and Muslim Theories in the Middle Ages

Medieval theories of the microcosm developed separately in the three religious traditions, but there were some points of contact between Jews and Muslims. The Talmud and the Midrash included a few microcosmic references, and the theory was very prominent in the mystical tradition known as the Kabbalah. The earliest kabbalistic text, the *Book of Creation* (*Sefer Yezirah;* perhaps composed between the third and sixth centuries C.E.), observed correspondences between the letters of the Hebrew alphabet, features of the physical world, and the human body. The thirteenth-century *Book of Splendor* (*Zohar*) taught that the first emanation in the creative process is the cosmic man (Adam Kadmon), through whom the rest of creation emanates, so that terrestrial human beings are modeled on an ideal form that provides the pattern for all of creation.

Arabic influence may have inspired two Jewish philosophers, Ibn Gabirol (Avicebron, c. 1021–c. 1058) in his *Fountain of Life,* and Ibn Saddiq (1075–1149) in his *Microcosm,* to combine microcosmic speculation with the Delphic maxim, "Know thyself"; both demonstrated how self-knowledge leads to knowledge about the universe. Although Maimonides (1135–1204) found fault with certain aspects of microcosmic theory in his *Guide for the Perplexed* (1.72), he nevertheless accepted much of it.

The most remarkable development of the microcosm among the Muslims appeared in the encyclopedia known as the *Epistles* (*Rasa'il*) of the Brethren of Purity (*Ikhwan-al-Safa*) in the city of Basra during the tenth and eleventh centuries. While two of its fifty-two treatises are devoted to microcosm and macrocosm, correspondences between the two worlds are noted throughout the work as it traces the procession of creatures from God and their mystical return to God through human understanding. Al-Biruni (973–c. 1051) accepted the microcosmic model, while Ibn Sina (Avicenna, 980–1037) made it the foundation of his theory of medicine.

Greek Christian Theories

Although the ancient idea of the microcosm appealed to many Christian thinkers, their view of the macrocosm as an inanimate structure created by God *ex nihilo* at the beginning of time led to major alterations of the ancient theory. Most conspicuously, the world-soul was omitted or interpreted allegorically as a reference to God's providential care for the created world. Although Greek Christians, unlike the Latins, had direct access to the ancient sources, they were ambivalent about the pagan philosophical heritage.

Gregory of Nyssa (c. 335–c. 394) criticized the comparison of humanity with the universe (*De hominis opificio,* 17), stressing, like Philo, that it was more appropriate to compare humanity with God; but he nevertheless retained a modified version of the theory. Cosmas Indicopleustes, a sixth-century Greek from Alexandria in Egypt, rejected the idea of a spherical world in his *Christian Topography,* since he considered Moses' tabernacle a symbolic representation of the universe. He nevertheless accepted the idea that humanity contains the universe within itself and therefore thought the pagans were right to have called man a microcosm (Book 7).

Greek theologians tended to view humanity as a mediator who united the material and spiritual worlds by virtue of being the only creature to possess both a body and a rational soul; at this critical juncture in the chain of being, humanity shared some characteristic with every kind of creature and thus represented the entire universe. The Greek fathers influenced the anthropology of the Irish Neoplatonist, John Scot Eriugena (c. 800–c. 877), but the idea of the microcosm in the Latin West was received mainly through Calcidius and Macrobius, and disseminated by the encyclopedist Isidore of Seville (c. 560–636; *De natura rerum,* 9.2) and the Venerable Bede (673?–735; *De temporum ratione,* 35).

Latin Christian Theories

Latin terminology generally assumed comparative forms—"lesser world" (*minor mundus*) and "greater world" (*maior mundus*)—although it also adopted the Greek loanwords *microcosmus* and *macrocosmus* (or more commonly *megacosmus*). Latin treatments of the microcosm were generally superficial until the twelfth century, but certain distinctive features did appear before then. Although Augustine of Hippo (354–430) preferred the comparison of humanity to God, he developed a theory of the seven ages of man and the world, which was a projection of the seven days of creation and the seven stages of the human life cycle onto history (*De Genesi contra Manichaeos,* 1.22.33–1.23.41). Pope Gregory the Great (c. 540–604) offered a concise and oft-repeated formula that combined the microcosm with the concept of the Chain of Being, whereby humanity was thought to contain all of creation because it shares simple existence with stones, life with plants, sensation with beasts, and reason with angels (*Homiliae in Evangelium,* 29).

Under Gregory's influence, Jesus' injunction to preach to "all creation" (Mark 16:15) was commonly interpreted as a reference to the human race in its status as an epitome of the created world. Robert Grosseteste (c. 1175–1253) later suggested in several works that the Incarnation not only fulfilled a redemptive role but also reconciled the creator to all creatures, since God became the creature who embodies all creation. This cosmological role of the Incarnation was restated by Nicholas of Cusa (1401–1464) in *Learned Ignorance* (*De docta ignorantia*, 3.3).

The microcosm received special attention in the Latin West during the twelfth century, when a revival of Platonism coincided with a keen interest in the natural world and new confidence in the power of human reason. The most extraordinary product of this fusion was the *Cosmographia* of Bernardus Silvestris, written about 1147 in two books entitled *Megacosmus* and *Microcosmus,* which depict the creation of the two worlds by Neoplatonic emanations, personified as characters in a mythological drama. The intellectual atmosphere that fostered such creative approaches to old ideas also influenced spiritual meditation, which is evident in Hildegard of Bingen's (1098–1179) *Book of Divine Works* and in the allegorical commentary on Genesis by Godfrey of Saint-Victor (c. 1125–1194). Microcosmic thinking had always been implicit in monastic studies of Genesis that compared the human soul to the physical world by viewing God's work during the six days of creation figuratively, as stages of spiritual progress that the monk should pursue. Godfrey noted the similarity between the ancient theory and the medieval hermeneutical method and made the connection explicit by entitling his book *Microcosmus.*

Early Modern Theories and Aftermath

The scholasticism of the thirteenth and fourteenth centuries had little use for highly malleable metaphors, and it was not until the Platonic revival of the Renaissance that the microcosm again received substantial attention. Although Ernst Cassirer argued that Renaissance thinkers significantly redefined the microcosm (*The Individual and the Cosmos in Renaissance Philosophy,* trans. 1964), one must acknowledge that the fifteenth-century philosophers actually owed more of a debt to medieval conceptions than Cassirer supposed, as observed by Bernard McGinn (*The Golden Chain,* 1972). For instance, Nicholas of Cusa's christological use of the microcosm had already been outlined by Robert Grosseteste (as noted above), and although Giovanni Pico della Mirandola (1463–1494) offered a sustained discussion of the microcosm in his *Heptaplus* (a commentary on the creation-account in Genesis), much of his contribution in that work consisted of bringing together different currents of microcosmic theory (a testament to his wide reading and powers of synthesis). Although a new application of the ancient theory was made by Paracelsus (1493?–1541), his innovation promoted an alchemical theory of medicine rather than philosophical conceptions of the self.

Despite a surge of interest in the microcosm during the early modern period, reflected in a wide range of disciplines, the theory did not lead to new discoveries and it was gradually relegated to the margins of science and philosophy along with the "occult" disciplines that maintained an affinity to it. One of the last major statements of the theory on the verge of its abandonment by most philosophers and scientists was Robert Fludd's (1574–1637) impressively illustrated *History of the Macrocosm and Microcosm* (*Utriusque cosmi, maioris scilicet et minoris ...historia,* 1617–1621); it is significant that Fludd's grand synthesis was regarded as a bible of Rosicrucianism, a mysterious movement associated with occultism.

The microcosm continued to inspire esoteric thinkers and opponents of modern materialism, such as the theosophist H. P. Blavatsky (1831–1891), who combined the microcosm with evolution in *The Secret Doctrine* (1888), and the anthroposophist Rudolf Steiner (1861–1925), whose lectures on the two worlds, delivered in 1910, were later published as *Makrokosmos und Mikrokosmos* (1933). Although the idea of the microcosm as a synonym for humanity became untenable among mainstream thinkers by the eighteenth century, the word itself was retained as a reference to any subsystem, in which sense it is commonly used today.

See also **Christianity; Neoplatonism; Organicism; Platonism.**

BIBLIOGRAPHY

PRIMARY SOURCES

Bernardus Silvestris. *The Cosmographia of Bernardus Silvestris.* Translated by Winthrop Wetherbee. New York: Columbia University Press, 1973.

Hildegard of Bingen. *Hildegard of Bingen's Book of Divine Works, with Letters and Songs.* Edited by Matthew Fox. Santa Fe, N.M.: Bear and Company, 1987.

Ibn Saddiq, Joseph. *The Microcosm of Joseph Ibn Saddiq.* Critically edited by Saul Horovitz; translated by Jacob Haberman. Madison, N.J.: Fairleigh Dickinson University Press, 2003.

Pico della Mirandola, Giovanni. *On the Dignity of Man, On Being and the One, Heptaplus.* Translated by Charles Glenn Wallis, Paul J. W. Miller, and Douglas Carmichael. Indianapolis: Bobbs-Merrill, 1965.

SECONDARY SOURCES

Allers, Rudolf. "Microcosmus: From Anaximandros to Paracelsus." *Traditio* 2 (1944): 319–407.

Altmann, Alexander. "The Delphic Maxim in Medieval Islam and Judaism." In *Biblical and Other Studies,* edited by Alexander Altmann, 196–232. Cambridge, Mass.: Harvard University Press, 1963.

Boas, George. "The Microcosm." In *The History of Ideas: An Introduction,* 212–238. New York: Scribners, 1969.

Conger, George Perrigo. "Cosmic Persons and Human Universes in Indian Philosophy." *Journal and Proceedings of the Asiatic Society of Bengal* New Series, 29 (1933): 255–270.

———. *Theories of Macrocosms and Microcosms in the History of Philosophy.* New York: Russell and Russell, 1967. Reprint of a Columbia University dissertation from 1922.

Dales, Richard C. "A Medieval View of Human Dignity." *Journal of the History of Ideas* 38 (1977): 557–572.

Finckh, Ruth. *Minor Mundus Homo: Studien zur Mikrokosmos-Idee in der mittelalterlichen Literatur.* Göttingen: Vandenhoeck and Ruprecht, 1999.

Guthrie, W. K. C. "Man's Role in the Cosmos. Man the Microcosm: the Idea in Greek Thought and its Legacy to Europe." In *The Living Heritage of Greek Antiquity,* 56–73. European Cultural Foundation. The Hague: Mouton, 1967.

McGinn, Bernard. *The Golden Chain: A Study in the Theological Anthropology of Isaac of Stella.* Washington, D.C.: Cistercian Publications, 1972.

Nasr, Seyyed Hossein. *An Introduction to Islamic Cosmological Doctrines: Conceptions of Nature and Methods Used for Its Study by the Ikhwan-al-Safa, al-Biruni, and Ibn Sina.* Albany: State University of New York Press, 1993.

Norford, Don Parry. "Microcosm and Macrocosm in Seventeenth-Century Literature." *Journal of the History of Ideas* 38 (1977): 409–428.

Saxl, F. "Macrocosm and Microcosm in Mediaeval Pictures." In *Lectures,* Vol. 1, 58–72. London: Warburg Institute, 1957.

Robert Ziomkowski

MIGRATION.

This entry includes three subentries:

Africa
Migration in World History
United States

AFRICA

Historically, migration has been a way of life in Africa. Over the generations African people have migrated in response to demographic, economic, political, and other factors, including environmental disasters and conflicts. The histories of many African communities record their migratory movements from one area to another or the incursions of more powerful migrant groups who conquered and reorganized their societies. These large movements across the continent have accounted for the rapidity of the spread of new ideas and changes in culture.

Migration in Africa has been of three types: intra- and inter-country (internal) movements of people *within* the continent; movement from outside *into* the continent; and movement *from* the continent outward.

Internal Migration

Although the most prominent movement within the continent in historic times probably was that of the Bantu-speaking peoples, there have been many different movements of peoples from one region of the continent to another and over many centuries. Because of a population explosion that is yet to be fully understood, Bantu-speaking peoples have spread over most of the continent south of the equator. Bantu migrations were reflected in the expansion of Bantu languages in several parts of East, Central, and Southern Africa. Other examples of major intracontinental migration include that of the nomadic Bedouin Arab peoples, the Banu Hilal and the Banu Sulaym, into the Maghreb beginning from the second half of the eleventh century. They initiated a massive movement, infiltrating the cultivated lands while spreading westward from Tunisia to Morocco. The arrival of the Bedouin Arabs provoked a rapid Arabization of the Maghreb region. A high proportion of the Berbers were assimilated to the Arabs through intermarriage, and Arabic became the lingua franca for most of the population. In the mountainous areas, including the Atlas range in Morocco and the Kabylie mountains of Algeria, however, the Berbers maintained their language and culture, together with a fierce spirit of independence.

Intraregional migration also took place in West Africa. Hausaland, for example, was a major recipient of large-scale migration, with peoples and groups coming from different directions and at different times for different purposes. Sources of migration into the Hausa country were the Sahel in the north, Bornu in the east, and the regions of the late Mali and Songhay empires in the west. The Fulani, who reached Hausaland from the west, were the most prominent immigrants into the region. The vast majority of Fulani immigrants were nomadic pastoralists in search of new and better grazing for their cattle, although there were also some Muslim clerics among them. Other migrant groups included the Tuareg, who were mostly pastoralists and who showed little interest in territorial occupation and settlement. Migrants from Bornu included refugees, aristocrats, merchants, and scholars who settled in all parts of Hausaland. Other immigrants were the Wangara/Dioula; the Songhay fishermen, who settled in the Lower Rima River Valley; and the Arab and Berber merchants and scholars who came from North Africa and the Timbuktu area and began entering the region in the second half of the fifteenth century, about the same time as the Fulani. The influx into the region was connected with the growing prosperity of the Hausa states and the adoption of Islam by further groups and strata of the urban population.

The dominant trend in internal migration in more recent times has been the movement from rural to urban areas. Contact with Western Europe facilitated the emergence of new towns and other urban centers that served as colonial administrative centers or as economic or industrial centers. Many capital cities of West African countries developed as artificial ports built on vacant or sparsely populated sites. These administrative, industrial, and commercial centers all experienced rapid growth during the years of colonial rule, with implications for migration. The new towns developed certain characteristics that contrasted sharply with the traditional culture. An improved physical environment—sanitary facilities, roads, street lighting, health services—combined with other rudiments of urbanism to provide the background to the rural-to-urban migration that was a hallmark of the colonial period. This prompted the "bright lights" theory of migration (that is, that rural-to-urban migrants tended to be attracted by the new facilities in the towns). However, empirical studies—such as the one on Tukulor migration to Dakar (Diop)—confirm that rural-to-urban migration was neither the outcome of an attraction to the city nor youthful rejection of traditional values. Rather, it resulted from serious and persistent underdevelopment in the communities of origin of the migrants. In the case of Tukulor migration from the Senegal River Valley, money sent back to the village by the new city dwellers was crucial to maintaining a minimum standard of living in the valley.

But regional economic disparities were not the only factors that prompted internal migration, particularly in the colonial times and after. The transformation of agriculture during this period that resulted from the creation of large plantations by the colonizers in certain regions of the continent was a major factor. The new plantations required a substantial labor force that was not always available locally. The required movement of population was often achieved by force. Colonial intervention in the mining sector prompted similar forceful movement of the people, achieved through policies designed to drive peasants from their land and attract them to the mining areas. Moreover, colonial fiscal measures, particularly the introduction of the head tax payable in cash, also gave rise to migration. It was impossible for most rural families to raise the necessary sums from the village, and this necessitated the migration of one or more members of a household to the city. In other instances, villagers fled the tax by migrating to neighboring territories.

Intra- and intercountry migrations remain a prominent feature of African life. The persistence is partly the outcome of the fact that migrants have always considered the various subregions as single economic units within which trade in goods and services flowed. But more important, intraregional migration has been sustained by the persistence and intensification of widespread poverty, the deteriorating economic situation, and the consequences of the various macroeconomic adjustment measures. In addition, conflicts and environmental degradation, particularly in the Sahel regions, desertification, and cyclical famines have further aggravated the pressure for migration from poorer to relatively prosperous regions of the continent. The deteriorating economic situation and pressures have also affected in recent times the traditional labor-importing countries, including Gabon, Côte d'Ivoire, Zimbabwe, and Nigeria. The inability of their economies to continue accommodating clandestine labor migrants was at the root of the various expulsion measures directed at foreign nationals at different times. On the other hand, the violent conflicts that have plagued the political landscape of many African countries—Burundi, Rwanda, Liberia, Sierra Leone, and recently, Côte d'Ivoire—as well as the Horn of Africa have produced massive waves of refugees who sought sanctuary in neighboring African countries. Many have chosen to remain as migrants in the countries of their sanctuary even after conflicts have ceased in their homelands.

Immigration into Africa

In modern times, the major movements into the continent have been of European settlers into northern Africa and of European and Asian settlers in Southern and East Africa. The Dutch migrations into Southern Africa began in 1652, when a European settlement was established by the Dutch East India Company at the Cape of Good Hope. The colony was intended to serve merely as a refreshment station for the company's ships on their way to India and was originally peopled by the company's servants. But with the decision to allow some of these people to settle as free citizens owning their own farmlands, the Dutch (Boer) population in the region began to swell, and soon a deliberate policy of increasing the settler population was instituted to strengthen it against possible attacks. More Dutchmen arrived as well as a party of French Protestant Huguenots fleeing religious persecution in France. The French refugees lost their language and became absorbed into the predominantly Dutch population. As most were farmers, this meant that more land was needed as the population increased. From the coast, the settlers later moved inland to the Highveld region, where, in the nineteenth century, a series of military conflicts occurred between them and the Bantu speakers. The Dutch—and the absorbed French refugees—constituted about one-third of the European population and were the ancestors of many modern white South African families. Other major European settlements took place in the nineteenth century: the British were dominant in modern-day KwaZulu/Natal Province of South Africa as well as in Zambia, Zimbabwe, and the East African highlands; the Germans were predominant in modern Namibia; and the Portuguese were in Angola and Mozambique.

When the European colonies were first founded, there was no conscious policy of introducing racial discrimination and settler rule. However, the presence of large settler populations later affected the pace of political developments in these territories, and the achievement of self-government and independence by the African peoples of South Africa, Namibia, Zimbabwe, Angola, and Mozambique was delayed. The struggles for independence and majority rule became the source of much bitterness and violence between races in Southern Africa. On the other hand, the growth of Arab nationalism and the emergence of Morocco, Algeria, and Tunisia—North African countries with vast European settler populations—as independent states led to the return of between one and two million colonists to their European homelands in the late 1950s and early 1960s.

Emigration from Africa

Probably the greatest outward regional movement of people in human history was that of Africans to the Americas and the Caribbean during the period of the slave trade from the sixteenth to the nineteenth century. Estimated figures of Africans forcibly uprooted from their homelands, largely from West Africa and to a lesser extent from Angola, range from fifteen to twenty million. Substantial numbers of these died in the appalling conditions of the trans-Atlantic passage. The slave trade was also active on the east coast of Africa, particularly on the island of Zanzibar. Although the composite effect of the loss of this considerable size of manpower is yet to be fully quantified and appreciated, there is no doubt that it retarded the African continent's development. At the same time, these forced migrants made substantial contributions to the development of the New World.

In recent years a combination of factors, including the worsening economic situation of most African countries, perennial conflicts, and environmental degradation, have provoked a new outward movement of Africans from the continent. The stressful socioeconomic environment created by the retrenchment of public sector workers in states across the continent implementing diverse programs of structural adjustment, the decline in real incomes, and the hostile political environment occasioned by the consolidation of autocratic regimes in several states have combined to generate and sustain pressures that trigger the outflow of professional and skilled persons on a scale hitherto not experienced. This migration has been to Europe, North America (United States and Canada), and the Gulf states. Some Africans have also found their way to Asian and Pacific countries. This phenomenon has come to be described in the literature and general discourse as the *brain drain*. Thousands of highly skilled migrants, including doctors, nurses, lecturers, teachers, engineers, scientists, technologists, and other professionals, have moved from a number of African countries to the destination states attracted by relatively higher salaries and better working and living conditions. This is in addition to movements from poorer to relatively richer regions of the continent. Also, many students in various disciplines failed to return to their home countries from these richer countries at the end of their training.

The stressful socioeconomic environment has produced other survival strategies that affect contemporary migration patterns and gender roles in the continent. Clandestine migration, an age-old phenomenon, has reached new proportions as young migrants are adopting more sophisticated, daring, and evasive methods to enter the countries of the North— even as these destination states continue to tighten their border controls. Many clandestine migrants enter the host states as tourists or students and later work and live there without officially changing their status. Others travel via intermediary countries, where they obtain false documentation for a fee. Another phenomenon is autonomous female migration, which is equally a response to deepening poverty in the subregion. With several families forced to adopt migration as a coping mechanism of the last resort, the traditional male-dominated, long-term, and long-distance migratory streams are becoming increasingly feminized. A significant proportion of females now migrate independently to fulfill their own economic needs rather than simply joining a husband or other family members. Higher educational attainment among females has also enhanced their mobility and their propensity to migrate both locally and internationally.

Explaining African Migration

Although the most common explanations are those focusing on the economic dimensions, a general survey of the literature on demographic mobility reveals numerous economic, sociological, and demographic attempts to explain the initiation of internal and international migration. Migration is seen as a response to both endogenous and exogenous variables. These variables are, in sum, the overall effects of sociocultural, economic, political, and psychological conditions on the migrant. The decision to migrate is thus a response to one or many of the variables and the location of such variables. The sociologist describes migration in relation to the nature and magnitude of its social and cultural dimensions, the destination, and the sending area. The economist, on the other hand, reflects on the occupational and employment status, pressure of demand and supply, and relationships among wage, income, and price levels. Demographic explanations relate all the variables to the prospect of measurement and control of migration and its effect on growth and development.

Given Africa's cultural, linguistic, and economic variegations, and its vast country-to-country differences, a systematic analysis of any aspect of its social behavior can be a difficult enterprise. Analysis of its migration behavior is no less challenging. When applied to the African situation, accepted theories of migration reveal the need for the development of models that distinguish between developed and developing countries. Indeed, a number of explanatory models have been developed in the literature seeking to explain internal and international migration of labor in undeveloped countries. Three of these are especially suited to the African situation. These are the Todaro's, Mabogunje's, and Byerlee's models.

Todaro's model is a modification of the neoclassical economic (human capital) theory of migration. The theory posits that migration is the consequence of individual cost-benefit calculation. Todaro proceeds by affirming that migration is based on rational economic calculations and argues that the decision of the individual to migrate is usually a response to rural-urban differentials in expected rather than actual income earnings. This model assumes that the potential migrant selects a location that maximizes expected gains from migration. This was the first explanatory attempt emphasizing that potential migrants should base the decision to move on rational calculation of differences in expected earnings.

Mabogunje's model constitutes the second approach at explaining migration in Africa. The model is a creative adaptation of the world systems model in which Mabogunje asserts that rural-urban migration in Africa is controlled by systematic interrelationships of rural-urban control systems, rural-urban adjustment mechanisms, and the positive or negative flow of information about migration. The model identifies the *push* and the *pull* sides of migration. Local economic conditions that affect the pool of migrants constitute the push side. The size of this pool is affected by social practices, customs, community organization, and inheritance laws in the sending community. Wage rates and job opportunities emanating from the urban system constitute the pull side of migration, and these determine whether individuals in the pool of potential migrants would migrate.

In a modification of the human capital approach, Byerlee adopts a cost-benefit economic model in which he considers migration as the outcome of a cost-return calculation. Byerlee posits that the decision to migrate will be made when the perceived returns of migration exceed the perceived costs. The model goes beyond the conventional cost-return analysis of the human capital approach as it includes elements of the social system. It also explicitly identifies determinants of rural and urban incomes and introduces risks and other psychic costs into the migration decision-making process.

All three approaches have made significant contributions to a conceptual understanding of the migration process in Africa. Todaro's model provides a good explanation for labor migration in Africa, as it recognizes the unequal and uneven distribution of economic and social development between regions of the same country and among countries as a primary determinant of migration. The strength of Mabogunje's approach lies in its macrosystem emphasis, given its recognition of the economic, cultural, and social relationships between rural and urban areas. Mabogunje's model is particularly helpful in understanding the impact of family and community organization on migration. Byerlee's conceptualization of the motivation for migration in Africa has also contributed significantly to a conceptual understanding of migration in the region.

Despite their theoretical contributions, all three models fail to deal adequately with several elements of migration, including forced migration. With regard to historically more recent migration patterns, the models fail to deal with non-wage urban income, which accounts for an increasing proportion of urban employment.

One element of migration that has assumed increasing importance in recent years is the large-scale international migration of skilled persons from Africa to relatively more developed regions of the world. Attempts to provide explanatory models for understanding the motivation for this phenomenon confirm that the behavior of the so-called highly trained migrants, including scientists, engineers, artists, and intellectuals, is fundamentally determined by the same kind of motivations and market forces as those of less highly trained migrants. However, interpretations of the effect of the migration of highly skilled workers on the developing sending countries differ. Most economists are agreed that although some degree of mobility is necessary if developing countries are to integrate into the global economy, large-scale losses of skilled workers are detrimental to developing countries and pose the threat of a brain drain.

Neoclassical models of economic development hold that brain drain has adverse effects on the development of the sending country, slowing down the GDP growth rates and adversely affecting those who remain. Consequently, poverty and inequality are likely to increase. More recent economic theory—the endogenous growth theory—also predicts that emigration of highly skilled workers reduces economic growth rates. In contradistinction, another theoretical variant holds that at some optimal level of emigration (greater than none but not too much), sending countries actually benefit. It is argued that the possibility of emigrating to higher-wage countries may stimulate individuals to pursue higher education in anticipation of migrating to secure, better-paid work abroad. The consequence is the development of a large pool of better-trained human capital in the sending country. The implication is that there may be an "optimal level of emigration" or a "beneficial brain drain." Empirical analysis offers some support for the various theoretical expectations.

Conclusion

Human migrations in historic times have transformed the entire aspects of lands and continents and the racial, ethnic, and linguistic composition of their populations. Migration in Africa has had similar consequences. The peopling of the continent and the consolidation of its racial, ethnic, and linguistic landscape certainly cannot be totally separated from the consequences of the various migratory movements.

See also **Diasporas: African Diaspora; Migration: Migration in World History.**

BIBLIOGRAPHY

Adepoju, Aderanti. "Fostering Free Movement of Persons in West Africa: Achievements, Constraints, and Prospects for Intraregional Migration." *International Migration* 40 (2002).
———. *New Conceptual Approaches to Migration in the Context of Urbanization: Case of Africa South of the Sahara.* Liège, Belgium: IUSSP, 1978.

Afigbo, A. E., et al. *The Making of Modern Africa: The Nineteenth Century.* Vol. 1. Essex, U.K.: Longman, 1986.
Allen, Chris, and Gavin Williams, eds. *Sociology of Developing Countries in Sub-Saharan Africa.* London: Macmillan, 1982.
Amin, Samir, ed. *Modern Migrations in Western Africa.* New York: Oxford University Press, 1974.
Arthur, John A. "International Labor Migration Patterns in West Africa." *African Studies Review* 34 (1991): 65–87.
Byerlee, D. "Rural-Urban Migration in Africa: Theory, Policy and Research Implications." *International Migration Review* 8 (1974): 543–566.
Caldwell, J. C. *African Rural-Urban Migration: The Movement to Ghana's Towns.* New York: Columbia University Press, 1969.
DeJong, G., and Robert W. Gardner, eds. *Migration Decision Making.* New York: Pergamon, 1981.
Diop, A. A. B. "Enquête sur la Migration Toucouleur à Dakar." *Bulletin de l'IFAN.* Ser. B., no. 22 (1960): 393–418.
Gaude, J. *Causes and Repercussions of Migration: A Critical Analysis.* Geneva: International Labour Office, 1976.
Harris, J., and M. Todaro. "Migration, Unemployment and Development: A Two-Sector Analysis." *American Economic Review* (March 1970): 126–142.
Jackson, J. A. *Migration.* Cambridge, U.K.: Cambridge University Press, 1969.
Jansen, C. J., ed. *Readings in the Sociology of Migration.* Oxford: Pergamon Press, 1970.
Lowell, B. Lindsay, and A. Findlay. *Migration of Highly Skilled Persons from Developing Countries: Impact and Policy Responses—Synthesis Report.* International Migration Papers 44. Geneva: International Labour Office, 2002.
Mabogunje, A. L. "Historical Geography: Economic Aspects." In *UNESCO: General History of Africa: Methodology and African Prehistory*, vol. 1, edited by J. Ki-Zerbo. Berkeley: University of California Press, 1981.
———. "Systems Approach to a Theory of Rural-Urban Migration." *Geographical Analysis* 2 (1970): 1–17.
Murdock, G. P. *Africa: Its Peoples and Their Culture History.* New York: McGraw-Hill, 1959.
Ricca, S. *International Migration in Africa.* Geneva: International Labour Office, 1989.
Sjaastad, L. A. "The Costs and Returns of Human Migration." *Journal of Political Economy* 70 (1962): 80–93.
Swindell, K. "Labour Migration in Underdeveloped Countries: The Case of Sub-Saharan Africa." *Progress in Human Geography* 3 (1979): 239–257.
Todaro, M. "A Model of Labour Migration and Urban Unemployment in Less Developed Countries." *American Economic Review* 59 (1969): 138–148.
Wallerstein, I. "Migration in West Africa: The Political Perspective." In *Urbanization and Migration in West Africa*, edited by H. Kuper. Berkeley: University of California Press, 1965.
Zachariah, K. C., and J. Condé. *Migration in West Africa: Demographic Aspects.* New York: Oxford University Press, 1981.

Sola Akinrinade

MIGRATION IN WORLD HISTORY

Migration is a central aspect of human existence. This is evident from the debate about the origins of the human species, which spread, according to the evidence, from Africa across all continents. On the level of ideas and prejudices, this has resulted in racialized debates about white distinctiveness and Afrocentrism. In prehistoric times, some thirty to forty thousand years ago, human beings migrated from the tricontinental Eurasia-Africa across a land bridge into the Americas and across the seas to Australia. Migration meant diversification of cultures and physical features. Whole peoples, but also clans and groups, continued to migrate throughout the millennia. While Asia's population was settled some sixty-five hundred years ago, in Europe whole peoples continued to migrate until some twelve hundred years ago, often moving from east to west. In Africa, the southward spread of sub-Saharan Bantu-speaking peoples continued to even more recent times.

Once the movement of whole peoples came to an end, migration of members of ethnocultural groups and individuals led to genetic and cultural mixing: Manchu moved southward into China; Norsemen (and -women) moved from Scandinavia eastward along the rivers to the Moskva region where they formed the society of the Rus, and westward along the coasts where they settled in Normandy, in parts of the isles later called "British," and, further southward, in Sicily and Palestine; Slavic and Germanic peoples interacted in central Europe; in the Americas the southward movement of First Peoples resulted in a differentiation into major cultural regions and language groups; in the southeast Asian islands, exchanges of population involved sophisticated sea voyaging; and in Africa pastoralists moved into areas of agriculturalists. In customary male-centered thought, such movements have often been interpreted as the expansion of warrior males and subjugation of "lesser"—more correctly, less armed—peoples. Recent genetic scholarship has revised this imagery: Arriving men, dominant as oppressors, had children with local women, and both genetically and culturally women became dominant. In the case of the Anglo-Saxon conquest of the Celtic-settled (British) islands, the Celtic women's genetic heritage and cultural practices have had a stronger impact than the lore of strong Anglo-Saxon men, as later British historians had believed.

Patterns of Migration

Until recently, no worldwide periodization of migration since Mediterranean antiquity had been attempted, though specific movements were well-studied. The composition and character of migration was influenced by cultural practices in the society and religious creed of origin. Greek migration in the Mediterranean world was one of artisans, traders, and cultural elites resulting in a process of Hellenization. The Roman Empire's expansion was one of soldiers and the imposition of rule; it brought South European and North African men to northern Europe. One of its military officers, a man from sub-Saharan Africa, became Christian Europe's Saint Mauritius (also called Saint Maurice, d. c. 286). The spread of Islam occurred through traveling merchants and, to some degree, through military action. These migrant Arabs and their religious culture equalized social relations among Hindu Indians because they knew no castes, but they hierarchized gender relations because women's status was lower in Islamic societies than in Hindu societies. In China migrating agriculturalists, as if forming a distinct ethnocultural group, were designated as "Han." Their regions of settlement were interspersed with those of long-settled cultural groups. In Africa, major east–west movements of people in the Sahel zone resulted in the formation of states, empires, and urban cultures. In Australia, multiple societies, later generically termed *Aboriginal,* emerged by separation rather than overlay or penetration. In the Americas some societies developed agricultural practices and became geographically stable, while others pursued hunting and remained mobile. All were connected through long-distance trading and some, seemingly, through exchange of spiritual concepts and scientific observation of celestial phenomena.

In the Eurasian-African world, patterns of migration changed in the period from the mid-fifteenth to mid-sixteenth century. By the 1440s populations had recovered from the demographic shrinkage imposed by the great plagues of the latter 1340s. In imperial China, the bureaucracy decreed an end to overseas contacts. To 1435, fleets of ships, vastly superior to European vessels, had carried expeditions of up to about thirty thousand men (and women) along the coasts of the South Asian subcontinent and to the East African ports. In the social hierarchy of Chinese society, merchants ranked low, and those who, from the southern provinces distant from the court, continued to trade overseas developed a Southeast Asian diaspora that lacked state support. In contrast, the Iberian Portuguese court provided financial and military backing to sailors and merchants who sent trading expeditions to the northwest African coast. They and, later, other Europeans developed fortified trading posts, "forts," wherever they gained a bridgehead. By the 1440s, the first enslaved Africans were brought to Portugal. Underemployed seafarers of the declining Italian port cities, Cristoforo Colombo (Christopher Columbus) and Giovanni Caboto (John Cabot) among them, migrated to the Atlantic coast. Relying on lore and knowledge of Breton, Basque, Bristol, and Icelandic sailors, and encouraged by the changing view of the earth as a globe rather than a disk, they explored westward routes aiming to reach the riches of Asia, whether China or India. Thus, a barrier on this route, the Americas, became part of the European's mental maps. In North European annals the existence of a Vinland had been chronicled since the time of the Norse voyages. Only Australia was still absent from this view of the world.

From 1550, the wealth of some of the Asian and Central and South American societies, the political-military power of the somewhat economically marginal European societies, and the transfer of germs from Eurasia to the Americas resulted in vast demographic changes: (1) the near genocide of many peoples of the Americas and the resettling of that region with immigrants from many European societies; (2) the usage of men and women from many cultures of sub-Saharan Africa as enslaved labor by European-origin investors in the process of establishing the subtropical plantation belt; and (3) the European military-commercial exploitation of the peoples of the Indian Ocean region and, subsequently, those of East Asia. As a result, several hemispheric and near-global migration systems emerged. From Europe, merchants and military as well as administrative personnel migrated outward. Their arms and purchasing power induced migration of producers and common laborers. Where they established mines or plantations—also called "factories in the fields" (Wolf)—they needed large numbers of workers but were not willing to pay wages or provide working conditions acceptable to local populations. In densely populated Asia, they forced men and women to work the fields. In Latin America they immobilized surviving earlier populations as agricultural worker families under the *encomienda* labor distribution system or forced them to migrate hundreds of miles to labor in the silver mines under the *mita* system.

Through the postcontact epidemics and wars of annihilation, however, the peoples of the Americas had been decimated, and thus traders from most European coastal states initiated a mass importation of enslaved laborers from Africa with the help of slave-catching coastal societies in West and, to a lesser degree, East Africa. Through investment and superior armament the European colonizer migrants established the South Atlantic African-American forced slave migration system. To fill the demand for tropical produce they transported some 9.8 million men and women to the Americas from about 1500 to the 1870s. This is a downward revision from earlier estimates of fifteen million. Another two million died during the so-called transatlantic middle passage. Additional millions perished during capture and on the routes to the African coast. This trafficking in human beings depleted the population base in West and Central Africa. In addition to the chattel slavery in the Atlantic world, societies of the Indian Ocean also used slaves for services and in commerce. Figures are difficult to ascertain.

The mixing between European colonizer men and Asian, Latin American, and Afro-American women, frequently through rape but more often through hierarchical consensual unions, led to the emergence of new peoples in the Americas and of smaller groups in Africa and Asia (in a process known as ethnogenesis). Conceptualizing these new peoples was difficult. In European thought of the times, those born in the colonies were "creoles" and inferior to "pure" European-born people. In the minds of European colonials, however, those born of European-origin parents considered themselves European and preferred to apply the term *creole* to people born of culturally mixed backgrounds and with shades of skin construed as "dark" or "black"—similar to the use of such terms as *mestizo* or *mulatto*. Whereas religion and craft had served to define identities before the beginning of colonization, the ideologues of Christianity and of exploitation increasingly made color of skin (race) and genetically defined ethnic groups the marker of belonging. "Race," however, was lived differently in Anglo and Latin colonial societies: strict racial separation ruled in the former, intermixing and hierarchization of shades of skin color in the latter.

In the nineteenth century, when the Afro-Atlantic forced migration system came to an end, the demand for labor was filled by an Asian contract labor system and by a transatlantic proletarian mass migration from Europe. Mainly Indians and Chinese were brought to plantations and mines under five-year contracts, in a system that has been called "a second slavery" (Tinker). This system lasted until the early twentieth century. Simultaneously, free Chinese and other Asian migrants developed a transpacific migration system from the late 1840s on. The largest of these systems, the European–Atlantic one, at first encompassed two routes, from southern Europe to Latin America and from western, northern, and, later, eastern Europe to

North America. Italian labor migrants integrated the routes in the 1880s. From 1815 to the 1930s some fifty-five million men and women moved westward, some seven million returning to their cultures of origin. In addition, the agricultural migration from European Russia to the southern belt of Siberia and the labor migration within European Russia coalesced into a Russo-Siberian migration system, in which some ten million men and women moved eastward and even larger numbers moved to the industrializing cities. While the nineteenth century is considered the century of proletarian mass migrations, the rate of migration per thousand people was higher in seventeenth-century industrializing societies such as the Netherlands and Sweden. Contrary to widespread ideas, even peasant societies have never been sedentary; in each generation, sons and daughters who could no longer be fed on the parental land had to move elsewhere to eke out a living in marginal agriculture or in urban wage labor. The farmers of the nineteenth-century migrations cultivated new fertile plains in North America, southern Russia, Argentina, and Australia, and their mass production of grain led to a collapse of world market prices and, consequently, to a worldwide agricultural crisis that forced millions more to leave the land for urban jobs.

In the twentieth century, wars and the depression after 1929 reduced labor migrations. Warfare and fascism in Europe generated huge numbers of refugees. From the 1950s on, the politically decolonizing but economically dependent societies of the southern hemisphere became refugee-generating states. Exclusion and border controls in the advanced industrial (and white) societies of the northern hemisphere as well as discriminatory terms of trade led to "global apartheid" (Richmond). Labor needs of the northern economies were filled by south–north migrations from both the Mediterranean and Caribbean basins. The search for more options and better lives led nonwhite people to migrate toward the industrial and social security states of the north, if necessary without documents or, from the point of view of the receiving societies, as "illegals." To such migrations the North American societies have responded more openly, proving more willing to grant amnesties than European societies (derided in some circles as "fortress Europe"). In other parts of the world, regional systems of migration emerged: internally in China, to the oil-producing states of the Persian Gulf, in West Africa, and elsewhere. By the beginning of the twenty-first century, migration systems had become even more multifocal than in the past.

Throughout history women's options to migrate were restrained by male-imposed concepts of gender roles. With permanent settlement, however, communities of migrants demanded and continue to demand the presence of women for family formation and the building of networks. Women have always been part of migrations; from the 1930s on they even formed a slight majority of those heading for North American societies. Both refugee migration and the demand for service labor led to a feminization of migration in the last decades of the twentieth century.

Governmental Policies

Governmental policies on migration have evolved in stages. Before the coming of colonialism, merchants, small producers, dockworkers, and sailors were free to migrate between the ports of the trade emporia of the Indian Ocean, and cultural communities of migrants were often granted self-administration. In European societies, the shift from dynastic systems to nation-states resulted in a massive deterioration of migrants' status. In dynastic systems, incoming migrants negotiated their status with the ruler and were usually free to practice distinct customs and use their own language, provided they promised loyalty. The Protestant French Huguenots of the sixteenth and seventeenth centuries are the best example. Nation-states, however, postulated unity or even uniformity of culture and demanded that incoming migrants renounce their own culture, religion, and language—or, in short, assimilate. The elevated position of the "nationals" over resident "minorities" and immigrant "ethnics" stood juxtaposed to the republican ideal of equality before the law. Passports, a late-nineteenth-century invention of nation-states, along with border controls and immigration legislation, excluded ever-larger categories of potential migrants from entering a society. Racial thought contributed to exclusion, and fear of class struggles led to increased control over labor migrations. Through the early twenty-first century, nation-states have still not overcome this "otherizing" of newcomers. Rather than being admitted to citizenship, newcomers are labeled "aliens," "foreigners," temporary laborers, or, euphemistically, guest workers. The common notion of "guests" does not imply using them as cheap workers, to be sent home whenever an economic downswing results in a diminished need for labor. Such practices have also been adopted by West African societies, especially Ghana and Nigeria, as well as by the oil-producing states of the Middle East.

Public opinion has classified newcomers according to religion, power, economic pursuit, and, only recently, color of skin. In many-cultured societies—the Ottoman Empire being the best example—cultural groups of peoples governed themselves through their religious rulers, and newcomers, such as the Jews, who were expelled from the Iberian societies after 1492, were incorporated under these principles. In China, imperial officials from afar provided but a thin overlay of resident populations, and people lived according to their own customs. In the nineteenth-century Habsburg "monarchy of many peoples," nationalizing tendencies and investment strategies reduced such self-determination of cultural groups. While conflicts have always occurred, the marginalization and otherizing practices of the late nineteenth and twentieth centuries paralleled the nation-states' cultural homogenization policies.

Global versus Nationalist Perspectives

Research has only recently achieved a global perspective on migration. Into the 1970s, nationalist historians assumed that *emigrants* depart from a nation-state and arrive as *immigrants* in ethnic enclaves of the receiving nation-state. Since then, this dichotomous perspective and terminology has been replaced by the neutral term *migrant:* People may move over short distances, for example, from rural to urban environments; or seasonally, as harvest laborers, from infertile hilly regions to farms in fertile valleys and plains; or to urban positions as female domestics, apprentices, or day laborers. People migrate over medium distances to specific segments of labor markets or to

available agricultural lands within a state (internal migration), in borderlands (intercultural migration, for example, from China to Mongolia), or across international borders. Because nation-states counted migrants only at such borders, international migration caught the attention of nation-state socialized scholars much more so than the less documented internal migration. The latter, however, included the whole process of urbanization, marriage migration, and industrialization and has been far more voluminous. Population registers of cities, parish records, and marriage lists provide the evidence.

The emigration–immigration dichotomy also assumed one-directional, one-time moves. Migrants, however, may move seasonally, for several years or for their working life. They may return regularly or occasionally. They may repeat the process of migration several times. Some migrations, such as those of early modern European artisans, Chinese transport laborers, and women earning money for a dowry, are circular: the migrants traverse short or long distances but finally return to their community of origin. Some migrations occur in stages, with a part of the intended trajectory undertaken at a time, for example, first to a nearby market city, then, with new wage earnings, to a port city, and finally to an overseas destination. Given that migration is costly, not only because of the cost of transport but also because during the voyage no income can be earned, many families decide to send one member with high earning capacity first. Then, in sequential or chain migration, other family members or friends follow whenever the "first-comer" is able to send money for travel or, at least, provide temporary shelter and access to a job. Such "free" migrations occur within economic and social constraints in the society of origin. Migrants pursue better options in their selected receiving society; for women this often involves less restrained gender roles.

Forced migrations, which encompass slavery, contract labor, and forced labor on the one hand and refugee migration on the other, have been studied separately. The distinction is both justified and misleading. Forced migrants have few opportunities to acculturate according to their own interests, whether within the slavery system in the Americas or in twentieth-century German, Russian, and Japanese labor camps. But in order to survive forced labor regimes, they have to develop strategies to make conditions physically and spiritually bearable. Refugees are "unwilling" migrants and often look back to the expelling society in hopes that changes will occur permitting their return. Because they are often not welcome in receiving societies and frequently receive no material support, they—like voluntary migrants—have to insert themselves into the receiving economy.

A further fallacy of the nationalist approach to migration has been the assumption that people are essentially monocultural. Such scholars have considered migrants to be uprooted, in limbo between cultures, and incapable of adjusting to their new sociocultural environment. Since the 1980s, however, sociological and historic research has shown that while involuntary migrants may be uprooted, voluntary ones develop individual and social capital and act in supportive networks that permit continuity as well as change. They live transculturally rather than ensconced in ethnic ghettos; they need the ability to function in more than one society.

Thus, many societies across the ages have sought migrants as innovators, connectors, or simply additional human capital. Many migrants, in turn, have sought independence from parents, constraining social norms, and dire economic circumstances by moving between one state or society to another.

See also **Asian-American Ideas (Cultural Migration); Borders, Borderlands, and Frontiers, Global; Creolization, Caribbean; Diasporas; Ethnicity and Race; Slavery; State, The.**

BIBLIOGRAPHY

Appleyard, Reginald T., ed. *International Migration Today*. 2 vols. Paris: Unesco, 1988.

Bade, Klaus J. *Migration in European History*. Translated by Allison Brown. Oxford: Blackwell, 2003.

Cohen, Robin, ed. *The Cambridge Survey of World Migration*. Cambridge, U.K.: Cambridge University Press, 1995.

Curtin, Philip D. *Cross-Cultural Trade in World History*. Cambridge, U.K.: Cambridge University Press, 1984.

Fawcett, James T., and Benjamin V. Cariño, eds. *Pacific Bridges: The New Immigration from Asia and the Pacific Islands*. Staten Island, N.Y.: Center for Migration Studies, 1987.

Gungwu, Wang, ed. *Global History and Migrations*. Boulder, Colo.: Westview Press, 1997.

Hoerder, Dirk. *Cultures in Contact: World Migrations in the Second Millennium*. Durham, N.C.: Duke University Press, 2002.

———. "From Migrants to Ethnics: Acculturation in a Societal Framework." In *European Migrants: Global and Local Perspectives*, edited by Dirk Hoerder and Leslie Page Moch, 211–262. Boston: Northeastern University Press, 1996.

Isajiw, Wsevolod W. *Understanding Diversity: Ethnicity and Race in the Canadian Context*. Toronto: Thompson Educational, 1999.

Kritz, Mary M., Lin Lean Lim, and Hania Zlotnik, eds. *International Migration Systems: A Global Approach*. Oxford: Clarendon, 1992.

Massey, Douglas S., et al. "Theories of International Migration: A Review and Appraisal." *Population and Development Review* 19, no. 3 (1993): 431–465.

Moch, Leslie Page. *Moving Europeans: Migration in Western Europe since 1650*. 2nd ed. Bloomington: Indiana University Press, 2003.

Pan, Lynn, ed. *The Encyclopedia of the Chinese Overseas*. Richmond, U.K.: Curzon Press, 1999.

Parnwell, Mike. *Population Movements and the Third World*. London: Routledge, 1993.

Richmond, Anthony H. *Global Apartheid: Refugees, Racism, and the New World Order*. Toronto: Oxford University Press, 1994.

Tanner, Helen Hornbeck, ed. *The Settling of North America: The Atlas of the Great Migrations into North America from the Ice Age to the Present*. New York: Macmillan, 1995.

Wolf, Eric R. *Europe and the People without History*. Berkeley: University of California Press, 1982.

Tinker, Hugh. *A New System of Slavery: The Export of Indian Labour Overseas, 1830–1920*. London: Oxford University Press, 1974.

Dirk Hoerder

UNITED STATES

Amerindians, Pilgrim fathers, immigrants, slaves, Asian–Americans, Hispanics—all denote historical population groups in the United States and in the Americas, but each group is placed in a different frame of reference. All of them arrived as migrants with norms, values, and belief systems of their ancestors and premigration society as a whole. Before immigrating they also had experienced culture-specific material ways of life. They arrived at particular historic conjunctions and developed lifeways specific to the region or city in which they settled.

First Americans

Some thirty to fifty thousand years ago, peoples from Asia migrated across a land bridge, today's Bering Strait, into North America and beyond. Distinct linguistic groups and several complex cultures emerged, such as Hohokam farming and Pueblo culture in the southwestern mesas and a mound-building culture in the Ohio Valley. After 1492 the native populations of the Americas were gradually decimated by a combination of Eurasian germs and Old World arms. By the 1830s Amerindians had been forced to vacate all lands east of the Mississippi, and the U.S. Supreme Court had designated them as *domestic dependent* nations without sovereignty. By the 1870s white Americans had begun to speak of a "vanishing race," imagining Amerindians as the generic horse-mounted Plains "Indian." Though Helen Hunt Jackson's *A Century of Dishonor* (1881) initiated a public debate about the denigration of native peoples' cultures, the Dawes General Allotment Act (1887) dissolved tribes—a term for cultural groups that suggests a primitive stage of development—based on the notion (implemented in 1924) that citizenship could only be conferred on individuals. Native Americans were confined to reservations, denied self-government, and deprived of their cultural practices. European-Americans developed the idea that "Indians" were dependent on government handouts. Over the next century, however, migration to the cities by native people and resistance by the American Indian Movement led to a slow reversal of government policies by the 1970s. Armed struggle, legal action, and self-organization by and on behalf of Native Americans forced U.S. governmental institutions and public opinion to revise their notions of "Indians" and to accept varying degrees of Native American self-determination.

Old World Migrants

Europeans from Scandinavia reached North America around 1000, and transpacific contacts probably also occurred early. Lasting European contact seems to have begun with the establishment of Basque, English, and Portuguese fisheries off the Newfoundland shores. In the mid-sixteenth century invasion forces as well as settlers from New Spain had reached present-day New Mexico. The territories of the north, known for their fur economies, were targeted by numerous large European mercantile companies and dynasties. The gentlemen adventurers in Virginia and the religious colonizers in New England would eventually provide a profitable return on the investments of such companies that financed their voyages. Since demand for male and female laborers exceeded the available migrants, several European states established a system of indentured servitude by which poor men and women sold their labor for a number of years in return for passage to North

American or Caribbean colonies. Such redemptioners were free after serving for a period of between three and seven years. This system of bound white labor ended in the 1820s, although "free" departure under severe economic constraints lasted.

Racial and Religious Hierarchy

To increase the labor supply in the southern colonies of North America and in the Caribbean colonies, men and women from Africa were transported to the Americas and sold as slaves. To the 1830s more Africans than Europeans arrived in the Americas. The forced migration of African people occurred in stages, thus preventing them from reestablishing their lives in terms of ethnocultural groups. African Americans were relegated to a status as *domestic dependents*. The American concept of e pluribus unum applied only to freeborn white Europeans, who were the model of Michel Crèvecoeur's new American man (*Letters from an American Farmer,* 1782). Twentieth-century scholarship reconceptualized the process of the (re)peopling of the Americas, examining not just the history of free migration but that of involuntary (economically induced) migration, forced migration, and destruction of the Amerindians.

Migration to the United States during the nineteenth century, from the end of the Napoleonic Wars in 1815 to the beginning of World War I in 1914, has traditionally been divided into two stages that involved two different regions of origin and thus two different "racial" groups: an early agrarian "old" immigration from west-central and northern Europe and an urban "new" immigration from eastern and southern Europe starting in the mid-1880s. The distinction dates from the late nineteenth century, when the darker-complected "new immigrants" were considered racially inferior. The Eurocentric perspective covers the vast majority of newcomers, but importation of enslaved Africans, outlawed in 1808, continued illegally. Chinese of several cultural groups from the empire's southern provinces and other migrants from Asia arrived from the mid-1840s in Pacific Coast cities as merchants, prospectors, and credit-ticket laborers. The racial hierarchy of white America was extended to Mexican-Americans following territorial gains of the Treaty of Guadeloupe Hidalgo. The process of hierarchization included religion along with race, placing non-Christian Africans, "heathen" Chinese, and Roman Catholic "papists" in categories below that of white Anglo Protestants.

Only one-third of the migrants to the United States in the 1840s were agriculturalists. Eastern European farming families first arrived in the 1840s, while the northern European industrial laborers came after the 1880s. On average the male-female ratio stood at 60 to 40. The new states in the West sought to increase their economic potential and revenues, and the fast-growing industries in the East actively recruited newcomers from Europe. Railroad construction companies did the same in Asia. An anti-immigrant or nativist movement emerged in the 1850s; exclusion of "the Chinese"—a summary term for people from different cultures and dialects from the empire's southern provinces—which was first attempted in 1879, became law in 1882. The designation *immigrant,* once reserved for newcomers from Europe and contrasted to *sojourners* from Asia, reveals a dichotomy, with *emigrants* as the complementary term used in Europe. Agrarian settler families, who sold their possessions before departing for America, could hardly return to their native lands, but labor migrants often came as temporary workers. Return migrants, estimated at 7 million from the 1820s to the 1930s, were not counted by the U.S. Bureau of Statistics before 1907: The image of "immigration country" captured statisticians' minds and prevented them from even looking for returnees. The emigrant–immigrant dichotomy also hides internal migrants: Europe's societies of origin experienced far more internal migration than emigration; like the North American societies, most were labor-importing ones. U.S. internal migration, rather than being merely a westward colonization and mining movement, involved west-east rural-to-urban migration, the so-called Great Migration of African–Americans from southern agriculture to northern industries, as well as numerous other smaller moves.

Twentieth Century

Similarly problematic is the cultural classification of European migrants into "ethnic groups," a differentiation denied "Asians," "Indians," or "Negroes." European migrants were regionally diverse, nation-states having only come into being in the nineteenth century. Thus the nation-to-ethnic-enclave paradigm constituted an ahistoric simplification. At the end of the century biological-racist classifications (scientific racism) were increasingly applied to European newcomers from eastern Europe ("dark"), from Italy ("olive"), or of Jewish faith and excluded nonwhite populations from other continents altogether. While U.S. gatekeeper elites demanded Anglo conformity or assimilation, newcomers suggested a "melting pot" concept, a term that became popular after Israel Zangwill's play of that title of 1908. The prescription for Anglo conformity excluded by definition peoples from Europe's peripheries. Conceptual exclusion was paralleled by legal exclusion. Congress enacted restrictions on the open-door policy of admission to the United States starting in the 1880s. Further restrictions were legislated in 1917 and 1924. To access other labor reserves, men from Mexico were admitted under specific provisions covering temporary labor. With the closing of the front door facing the Atlantic, a back door on the Rio Grande was opened. The Pacific door was left ajar for merchants and students, in the interest of trade and cultural expansion. When scientific racism subsided, the paradigm of uprootedness emerged as a new hierarchization. While immigrants were recognized as "making the American people" (Handlin), immigrants in general and the Irish in particular were considered as suspended between cultures and thus in need of help with assimilation. Many European immigrants of the late 1940s and 1950s had in fact been uprooted but by war and forced labor camps—earning status as displaced persons—rather than by migration.

The 1965 Immigration and Nationality (Hart-Celler) Act intended to end discrimination of migrants based on skin color or cultural origin. A merit-based point system favored skilled, professional, and highly educated men and women in order to boost U.S. economic performance. The underlying assumption that Europeans could meet the new immigration criteria was wrong, and the composition of migration to the United States changed totally. Transatlantic migration subsided after Europe's recovery from the devastations of World War II with the exception of departures from southern European societies and refugees from the socialist countries. In contrast, transpacific migration from developed societies in Asia with high educational performance increased and surpassed transatlantic migration by the 1970s. Wage differentials—sometimes offset by cost-of-living levels—attracted men and women from low-wage societies in Asia. A humanitarian aspect of the point system and the citizenship legislation permitted highly qualified migrants to bring relatives regardless of their levels of qualification and English-language skills. U.S. soldiers stationed in Southeast Asia during the Vietnam War led to the first "war bride" migration, and in the aftermath of Vietnam large numbers of refugees arrived in the United States in the mid-1970s. A further, but temporary, incentive for Chinese to migrate to the United States was the return of Hong Kong to the People's Republic of China in 1997.

Intracontinental northbound migration from Mexico and the Caribbean as well as from other Latin American states surpassed transpacific migration in the 1980s. Mexican laborers and laboring families continued to be recruited seasonally or without legal work documents. Puerto Rican (internal) and other Caribbean (external) migrants arrived in large numbers; Cuban exiles were hosted, while Haitian refugees were rejected. U.S. governmental support for right-wing regimes in several Latin American states resulted in an exodus of political refugees. While Asian-Americans, Mexican-Americans, and Hispanics in general created civil rights movements, advocates of "whiteness" initiated another racial debate about "the browning" of the United States and generated new calls for conformity. Undocumented migrants, upon whom certain economic sectors relied, were offered legitimization, that is, were given legal status. From the mid-1960s on scholarship on the subject of migration departed from the ethnic-group and migrant-dislocation paradigms. Scholars observed the ability of migrants to function and negotiate in two cultures, to create relations between cultural groups, to fuse multiple elements into multicultural lives and hybrid forms of expression. The perspective of women's studies brought inclusion of migrant women—since the 1930s about one-half of all migrants to the United States—into the historical narrative (Gabaccia). However, race and culture continued to be reflected in scholarship. The experiences of African-Americans were studied separately under the heading of slavery, while research on Asian or Hispanic migrants utilized the model of European experience. Migrant origins, once nationalized, both as regards communities of origin and destinations, were regionalized as well as integrated into continental, hemispheric, or global migration systems (Gilroy; Hoerder; Ruíz; Takaki). Nation- or multicultural-state superstructures lost centrality of position in the analysis but remain important in establishing legal and institutional frames for admission (or rejection) and inclusion (or exclusion). Emphasis on exchange between cultural groups and on negotiating identities is reflected in concepts of diasporic belongings and societal embeddedness as well as in transnational or transcultural capabilities to chart life projects and develop ways of everyday life under conditions of high mobility (Portes; Rumbaut; Foner).

See also **America; Assimilation; Black Atlantic; Diasporas; Slavery.**

BIBLIOGRAPHY

Berkhofer, Robert F., Jr. *The White Man's Indian: Images of the American Indian, from Columbus to the Present.* New York: Vintage, 1979.

Conniff, Michael L., and Thomas J. Davis. *Africans in the Americas: A History of the Black Diaspora.* New York: St. Martin's Press, 1994.

Delgado, Richard, and Jean Stefancic, eds. *The Latino/a Condition: A Critical Reader.* New York: New York University Press, 1998.

Foner, Nancy. *From Ellis Island to JFK: New York's Two Great Waves of Immigration.* New Haven: Yale University Press, 2000.

Gabaccia, Donna. *From the Other Side: Women, Gender, and Immigrant Life in the U.S., 1820–1990.* Bloomington: Indiana University Press, 1994.

Gilroy, Paul. *The Black Atlantic: Modernity and Double Consciousness.* Cambridge, Mass.: Harvard University Press, 1993.

Handlin, Oscar. *The Uprooted.* New York: Grosset and Dunlap, 1951.

Hing, Bill Ong. *Making and Remaking Asian America through Immigration Policy, 1850–1990.* Stanford, Calif.: Stanford University Press, 1993.

Hoerder, Dirk, ed. *Labor Migration in the Atlantic Economies: The European and North American Working Classes during the Period of Industrialization.* Westport, Conn.: Greenwood Press, 1985.

Jackson, James H., Jr., and Leslie Page Moch. "Migration and the Social History of Modern Europe." In *European Migrants: Global and Local Perspectives,* edited by Dirk Hoerder and Leslie Page Moch. Boston: Northeastern University Press, 1996.

Kelley, Robin D. G., and Earl Lewis, eds. *To Make Our World Anew: A History of African Americans.* New York: Oxford University Press, 2000.

Portes, Alejandro, and Rubén G. Rumbaut. *Legacies: The Story of Immigrant Second Generation.* Berkeley: University of California Press, 2001.

Ruíz, Vicki L. *From Out of the Shadows: Mexican Women in Twentieth-Century America.* New York: Oxford University Press, 1998.

Rumbaut, Rubén G., and Alejandro Portes. *Ethnicities: Children of Immigrants in America.* Berkeley: University of California Press, 2001.

Takaki, Ronald T. *Strangers from a Different Shore: A History of Asian Americans.* Boston: Little, Brown, 1989.

Thernstrom, Stephan, ed. *Harvard Encyclopedia of American Ethnic Groups.* Cambridge, Mass.: Belknap Press of Harvard University, 1980.

Zhou, Min, and James V. Gatewood, eds. *Contemporary Asian America: A Multidisciplinary Reader.* New York: New York University Press, 2000.

Dirk Hoerder

MILLENARIANISM.

This entry includes three subentries:

Overview
Islamic
Latin America and Native North America

OVERVIEW

Millenarianism refers to religious beliefs about a thousand-year period at the end of the world. This period, the millennium (from two Latin words, *mille,* thousand, and *annum,* year), is described in the Bible's Book of Revelation (20:1–6). Millenarians, while believing that Christ's Second Coming will usher in this earthly kingdom for the faithful, differ on the timing of the millennium. Some (premillennialists) believe Christ will return before the perfect age, while others (postmillennialists) expect that Christ will return after the elect have established the millennium either by preaching the gospel or by fire and sword. Millenarianism is synonymous with millennialism. A closely related term, *chiliasm,* (based on the Greek word for a thousand) is similar in meaning but sometimes has the association of the violence needed to bring about this thousand-year period. While individuals may quietly embrace millenarian beliefs, characteristically it has been through larger movements that millenarian hopes get expressed most dramatically.

Origins of Millenarianism

The roots of millenarianism are in apocalyptic literature. Ancient Near Eastern myths depict a great battle between good and evil, but explicit apocalyptic literature first appears in both the Jewish and Christian Scriptures of the Hellenistic period, from approximately 200 B.C.E. to approximately 100 C.E. The Book of Revelation (its Greek name, Apocalypse, means unveiling or revelation and provides the generic term for consolation literature and supplies much of the imagery of millenarianism) was written in 92–96 C.E. Apocalyptic writings, such as Second Isaiah (chapters 40–55), Isaiah (24–27), and Daniel (2:13–45, chapters 7–12), sought to comfort believers in times of difficulty and to put contemporary suffering in perspective. God would enable his suffering faithful, his elect ones, to triumph and have dominion over their enemies.

The earliest Christian communities arose amid Jewish apocalyptic thinking and Jewish renewal movements such as the Maccabees and Zealots. The earliest Christian literature reflects this eschatological expectation. St. Paul repeatedly refers to the Parousia, the Lord's Second Coming (1 Thess. 2:19, 3:13, 4:15, 5:23). The synoptic Gospels (Matthew, Mark, and Luke) similarly reflect the concerns of the first generation of Christians, for example, recalling how Jesus began his ministry with an urgent proclamation of the imminence of the end times and the coming of the Kingdom: "The time is fulfilled, and the kingdom of God is at hand" (Mark 1:15). Early Christians were convinced the Second Coming would occur in their lifetime.

The Book of Revelation, written in response to the unexpected persecution of Christians as well as the nonappearance of the Parousia, uses mysterious symbols, striking images, and visions to provide for suffering believers assurance of the Lord's imminent return, restoration of order in the cosmos, and a final victory with a new creation. Satan would be bound and the saints would reign with Christ for a thousand years (20:1–6).

Millenarian Movements

The first major millenarian movement after the early Christian communities was Montanism. Montanus, its founder, sought to restore the enthusiasm of the early period of the church. Montanus's movement began about 172 C.E. He expected the Lord to return to Pepuza and Tymion, two small towns in Asia Minor. The New Jerusalem would soon descend to earth and the thousand-year reign of Christ would begin. Montanus encouraged his followers to live in strict asceticism to prepare for this Second Coming. The church turned against Montanus because millenarianism was not central in Christian doctrine and because ecstatic prophecy and private interpretation undermined church discipline.

St. Augustine of Hippo (354–430) effectively closed the door on millenarian speculation for centuries by writing against the kind of literal interpretation of Scriptures that promised a physical paradise on earth. But early in the Middle Ages Joachim of Fiore (1130 or 1135–1201 or 1202) reopened the door for many apocalyptic and renewal movements, such as the Spiritual Franciscans and the Fraticelli. Joachim believed his own age was in crisis and preached that human agency would contribute to bringing the church through to the final stage of history, the age of the Holy Spirit.

In many instances millenarian hopes and expectations became intertwined with political and social aspirations and resulted in a violent mix—especially when reform efforts, blocked by rigid church and secular authorities, became radical and extreme. Such a situation occurred, for instance, in the fifteenth century in Bohemia and Moravia, when the Hussite reform movement, blended with inchoate nationalistic feelings and social tensions, became the Hussite Revolution, which in turn spawned the radical millenarian movement of the Taborites. Using religious images and millenarian beliefs, Taborites created a short-lived millenarian society that fought violently against the forces sent to crush it.

In sixteenth-century Germany Lutheran reforms triggered a sense of liberation as well as disorientation amid social and religious changes. Just as Martin Luther used apocalyptic imagery to portray the pope as the Antichrist, Thomas Müntzer portrayed Luther as the Beast of the Apocalypse because Luther was countering Müntzer's reformist efforts. Müntzer committed himself to social and religious revolution, believing any who opposed this process of the last days must be violently annihilated. Anabaptist groups channeled reform hopes into efforts to establish a new golden age. Some groups preached a nonviolent awaiting for the end times, while other segments developed a fanatical millenarianism as authorities opposed them. In Münster the Anabaptists set up the new Kingdom of Zion, which came to a violent and bloody end in 1535.

At the end of the sixteenth century and early in the seventeenth, the political and religious conditions in England prompted a wave of millenarian interest and excitement. English Puritans increasingly interpreted biblical prophecies about calamities and the Second Coming as referring to contemporary situations. Learned men tried to decipher from Scripture the date when the end of the world might arrive. The most radical of English millenarians were known as the Fifth Monarchy Men (from the vision recounted in the Book of Daniel, chapter 7). In the early eighteenth century France's Camisards or "French Prophets" sought from the Catholic king some tolerance for their Protestant culture and practices. The Camisards believed their sufferings were part of God's plan for the coming of the millennium. Lay prophets, including many children, amid physical manifestations of shaking and convulsions, revealed that the Judgment Day was soon approaching, that the reign of the Beast of the Apocalypse would soon end.

Millenarianism in North America

North America was especially fertile soil for the growth of millenarian movements and ideas. English Puritans brought millenarianism with them to American shores with the apocalyptic vision of being God's instruments in establishing the New Kingdom. John Winthrop, the governor of Massachusetts Bay Colony, expressed the Puritan aspiration of building a revolutionary city, a New Jerusalem, "coming down out of heaven from God" (Rev. 21:10). Early Puritan divines such as Joseph Cotton and Increase Mather continued the tradition of learned speculation about the date the millennium would begin and how the conversion of the Jews must precede the Second Advent of Christ. A not-inconsiderable part of American optimism and expansionism rested on beliefs about being God's elect and about the qualities of the earthly paradise.

William Miller, born in 1782 in Massachusetts, scrutinized the Scriptures and reconfigured biblical chronology. If the world began in 4004 B.C.E. and lasted 6,000 years, Miller concluded that "sometime" between 1843 and 1844 would be the end of the world. His pamphlet about the Second Coming of Christ and his reign convinced upwards of fifty thousand Americans that time would run out in 1844.

Of course, the world did not end, and the Great Disappointment of 1844 fragmented the Millerite movement. The diversity of responses to the nonappearance of the end included efforts to recalculate and "adjust" the prophetic dates of Jesus's Second Coming. Seventh Day Adventists and Jehovah's Witnesses evolved from the discouragement and divisions of Millerism. They, along with the Mormons, another fast-growing American religion, have explicit millenarian expectations, implying the lasting appeal of millenarian hopes.

Although most millenarian terms, images, and ideas originated within ancient Judaism and early Christianity, millenarianism has echoes in other religions and in cults. At its core, millenarianism offers the idea of history as progressing toward a transformed world. This nourishes the ever green yearning for an end of suffering and oppression and hardship. It is not surprising, then, that anxious and "deprived" people continue to look for signs that a new age is dawning. This human aspiration for a transformed world can then be discerned not only behind a variety of utopias and ideas about society, including those of Karl Marx or Hitler's Thousand Year Reich, but also in such contemporary millenarian cults as the People's Temple, the Branch Davidians, Heaven's Gate, and AUM Shinrikyo.

See also **Christianity; Eschatology; Judaism; Puritanism; Utopia.**

BIBLIOGRAPHY

Baumgartner, Frederic J. *Longing for the End: A History of Millennialism in Western Civilization.* New York: St. Martin's, 1999.

Barkun, Michael. *Crucible of the Millennium: The Burned-Over District of New York in the 1840s.* Syracuse, N.Y.: Syracuse University Press, 1986.

Kaminsky, Howard. *A History of the Hussite Revolution.* Berkley and Los Angeles: University of California Press, 1967.

Landes, Richard A., ed. *Encyclopedia of Millennialism and Millennial Movements.* New York: Routledge, 2000.

Laursen, John Christian, and Richard H. Popkin, eds. *Millenarianism and Messianism in Early Modern European Culture.* Vol. 4: *Continental Millenarians: Protestants, Catholics, Heretics.* Boston: Kluwer, 2001.

McGinn, Bernard, ed. *The Encyclopedia of Apocalypticism.* Vol. 2: *Apocalypticism in Western History and Culture.* New York: Continuum, 1998.

St. Clair, Michael. *Millenarian Movements in Historical Context.* New York: Garland, 1992.

Wessinger, Catherine Lowman. *How the Millennium Comes Violently: From Jonestown to Heaven's Gate.* New York: Seven Bridges, 2000.

Michael St. Clair

ISLAMIC

Millenarianism in Islam is a major theme that runs through the entire gamut of classical Islamic civilization. Although the Koran itself does not propose a millenarianism, as its major theme is eschatological and otherworldly, starting from the end of the seventh century C.E., the tradition literature (*hadith*) contains visions of a messiah and of a messianic age. The earliest messianic figure in Islam was probably Jesus, who was taken up to heaven by God—rather than crucified (Koran 3:55) as in Christianity—with the understanding that he would return at the end of the world; the more prevalent figure, however, was that of the Mahdi, the rightly guided one. This title began to appear attached to prominent political and religious figures by the middle of the seventh century, but the predictions concerning him received their present form during the period of the Abbasid revolution (740–749): the Mahdi will arise in the east, in the region of Khorasan (today eastern Iran and Afghanistan), raise an army, march through the Iranian plateau to Iraq and establish his messianic kingdom there after purifying the Muslim world of evil. This scenario mirrored the Abbasid rise to power closely and served to legitimize their revolution. By contrast, the figure of Jesus remained in Muslim apocalyptic beliefs primarily to fight and slay the Dajjal (the Antichrist), who will appear prior to the messianic kingdom and test the Muslims. Jesus will return from heaven at the advent of the messianic age, slay the Dajjal near Jerusalem, and then pray behind the Mahdi.

By contrast, the Shiite messianic vision was based upon the return of the Twelfth Imam (descended from the Prophet Muhammad), who went into occultation in 874. The Twelfth Imam will arise either in the east, as in the Sunni version, or in Mecca in some other versions and will similarly purify the Muslim world and take vengeance upon those who have oppressed the Shiites. However, in both the Sunni and the Shiite versions, the messianic age is not an extensive one; Sunnis believe that it will last between five and nine years, while Shiites allow for the possibility of twenty to forty years and, in some versions, up to three hundred years. For the most part, this period is characterized by the messianic tradition, "He will fill the earth with righteousness and justice just as it has been filled with unrighteousness and injustice" (Cook, 2003, p. 137). The specifics of this tradition are not fleshed out, however, and its powerful message remains available for any movement to use.

Starting with the Abbasids (747–1258), a wide range of both Sunni and Shiite Muslim dynasties and rulers have used messianic or millenarian slogans or visions to justify their rule. The first seven Abbasid rulers all took messianic titles for their regnal names and spread the idea that their rule was the promised messianic kingdom. As the Abbasid dynasty lost power through the ninth century, other rulers appropriated or manipulated these beliefs. Many rulers gained legitimacy through the tradition that "at the turn of every one hundred years God sends a renewer to renew His religion." This renewer, the *mujaddid*, was for the most part a religious figure, but the renewal movements spawned by his activities often had political ramifications as well.

In 899 the sevener Shiites (those who accepted seven imams descended from the Prophet Muhammad), also known as the Ismailis, proclaimed their messianic kingdom in North Africa. The dynasty they produced, the Fatimids, eventually moved to Egypt, where they founded Cairo in 969 and for a time provided serious competition with the Abbasids for primacy in the Muslim world. Like most Muslim dynasties founded on messianic claims, there was a transition after the first couple of rulers to a nonmessianic form of legitimacy. After the fall of the Abbasids in 1258 at the hand of the Mongols, Muslim dynasties all over the Middle East used messianic legitimacy to found their rule. This took several forms, the first of which was the traditional messianic religious form, conforming closely (or at least as closely as possible) to the traditions. A good example of this is the Safavid dynasty of Persia (1499–1736), which converted the Persian people (for the most part) to Shiism. This dynasty reached its peak in a wave of expectation keyed to the Muslim year 1000 (1591–1592 C.E.). Immediately after the passing of this date, the Safavids brutally suppressed their extremist followers, the Kizilbash, and thereafter ruled without recourse to messianic themes.

Another paradigm employed more secular messianic themes, such as universal justice (also present in Islam) and stability. The best example of this trend was the Ottoman dynasty (c. 1300–1918), especially under Sulayman the Magnificent (1520–1566), who was known as Sulayman the Law-Giver (Fleischer, 1992). Yet other rulers more marginally Muslim, such as Timur (Tamerlane; c. 1336–1405), employed millenarian themes taken from the world of astrological calculations and called themselves *Sahib-i Qiran* (the Lord of the Auspicious Conjunction). This term and its cognates implied that the world of the stars (governed, of course, by God) had conferred special favor upon Tamerlane and other Turkish and Persian rulers who used it and thereby had the "mandate of heaven" for their rule.

Not all millenarians were successful, and some of the more prominent failures left very conspicuous marks on Muslim history. The messianic revolt of Muhammad al-Nafs al-Zakiyya,

a descendent of the Prophet Muhammad, in Medina in 762, for example had a profound influence upon the shaping of the tradition of the appearance of the Mahdi despite the fact that the revolt itself was a failure. Many other movements were characterized by outlandish or exaggerated predictions or, while occasionally serving to vent popular frustrations, fizzled politically. A good example of this type of movement was the Syrian belief in the Sufyani, a descendent of the early caliph Mu'awiya bin Abi Sufyan (602–680), who was supposed to appear and liberate the Syrians. No less than fourteen different appearances of people claiming to be the Sufyani can be documented from history, all of them ending tragically.

Millenarianism in Islam is far from dead. The messianic ideals surrounding the Mahdi, the religious renewal of the *mujaddid* and the fear engendered by the Dajjal are quite common in contemporary Muslim apocalyptic literature. A great deal of apocalyptic speculation was attached to the year 1400 (1978–1979 C.E.), when major upheavals occurred around the Muslim world, including the messianic revolt of Muhammad al-Qahtani and Juhayman al-'Utaybi at the Holy Mosque in Mecca and the Islamic Revolution in Iran. According to the authoritative treatise of Jalal al-Din al-Suyuti (d. 1505), *al-Kashf 'an mujawizat hadhihi al-umma al-alf* (Revelation of this Community's Passing of the Thousand-Year Mark), the end of the world should be expected around the year 1500 (2076 C.E.). Most early twenty-first-century apocalyptic tracts feature scenarios and dates that are built around his prediction. Mahdi figures continue to appear with regularity, and contemporary radical Islam includes messianic expectations for a proposed revival of the caliphate and a united Muslim state.

Scholarship on the subject of Islamic millenarianism has been primarily confined to Shiite movements. One important work is Abdelaziz Sachedina's *Islamic Messianism*, which examines early Shiite ideals and beliefs. Wilferd Madelung has published a number of studies on the subject of Sunni and Shiite apocalyptic and messianic traditions, primarily building upon the early work of Nu'aym bin Hammad al-Marwazi (d. 844). Messianic themes among dynasties are usually to be found in historical works and have yet to be studied as a whole. David Cook's *Studies in Muslim Apocalyptic* covers many of the basic themes of Muslim apocalyptic and messianic belief; his 2003 work, *Contemporary Muslim Apocalyptic Literature*, presents the literature current at the turn of the twenty-first century.

See also **Islam; Millenarianism: Latin America and Native North America; Millenarianism: Overview; Mysticism.**

BIBLIOGRAPHY

Cook, David. *Contemporary Muslim Apocalyptic Literature*. Syracuse, N.Y.: Syracuse University Press, 2003.

——. *Studies in Muslim Apocalyptic*. Princeton, N.J.: Darwin Press, 2002.

Fleischer, Cornell, "The Law-Giver as Messiah: The Making of the Imperial Image in the Reign of Suleyman." In *Suleyman the Magnificent and His Time: Acts of the Parisian Conference Galeries Nationales du Grand Palais 7–10 March 1990*, edited by Gilles Veinstein, 159–177. Paris: École des Hautes Études en Sciences Sociales, 1992.

Madelung, Wilferd. "Apocalyptic Prophecies in Hims during the Umayyad Age," *Journal of Semitic Studies* 31 (1986): 141–185.

Sachedina, Abdulaziz Abdulhussein. *Islamic Messianism: The Idea of Mahdi' in Twelver Shī'ism.* Albany: State University of New York Press, 1981.

al-Suyuti, Jalal al-Din. *al-Kashf 'an mujawizat hadhihi al-umma al-alf.* In his *al-Hawi li-1 -Fatawa.* Beirut: Dar al-Fikr, n.d.

David Cook

LATIN AMERICA AND NATIVE NORTH AMERICA

The history of humankind is replete with the desire for better times, a more just order, and leaders who can bring their people into a better world, often having to defeat or destroy a world that is viewed as unjust and inequitable. These desires have frequently been fueled by faith or have taken specifically religious forms; and in addition have often been organized around or contained elements of ethnicity, identity, and race.

Old World Origins

In the area stretching from Asia Minor through Europe and into regions colonized by political and religious powers emanating from these areas—such as the New World—these desires have often been linked to the Judeo-Christian tradition. These beliefs and desires and the movements they have generated have become popularly known as millenarianism or chiliasm (a word of Greek origin). However, as one of the most noted scholars of the subject, Norman Cohn, has pointed out, "These movements have varied in tone from the most violent aggressiveness to the mildest pacifism and in aim from the most ethereal spirituality to the most earthbound materialism; there is no counting the possible ways of imagining the Millennium and the route to it" (p. xiv).

The term *millenarianism* comes from the belief by some Christians that Christ will return to earth and establish a kingdom in which he will reign over a society that is blessed spiritually and materially and in which the enemies of this Christian fold will be defeated. This rule, it is believed, will last for a thousand years—a millennium—before the faithful or Saints will ascend to heaven while those who are seen as evildoers will suffer eternal damnation. Hence the belief in the coming millennial earthly paradise of Christ became known as millenarianism. The actual concept of millenarianism, however, predates Christ. Long before Christians separated from Jews, the idea of a prophet or Messiah—a powerful, wise, and just ruler of the faith—was a part of Jewish belief in the coming of a world where the longed-for order was restored.

While a belief in the coming of the Messiah alone is not necessarily millenarian, when it is attached to persecution or the desire to attain a proper and just order, it can become millenarian. Hence during the centuries and decades before and after the birth of Christ, when Jews were suffering persecutions, were not self-governing, or were divided by class and other interests, numerous millenarian movements and leaders emerged. For instance, in the second century B.C.E., a time of crisis for Jews, the Book of Daniel was written in which Daniel dreams that the enemies of the Jews are destroyed and an everlasting kingdom is established with dominion over all.

While millenarian movements enjoyed some popularity within the early Christian Church in the first three or four centuries C.E., these movements, in both the Greek and Western churches, were eventually considered heretical. This was especially true after the official church became more tied to the state. In the early Christian world, many people led difficult lives and were strongly influenced by accounts such as those in the New Testament Book of Revelation, in which an angel descends to earth, seizes the Devil, and binds him for a thousand years: "Also I saw the souls of those who had been beheaded for their testimony to Jesus and for the word of God, and who had not worshiped the beast or its image. . . . They came to life again, and reigned with Christ a thousand years" (Rev. 20:4).

From the late eleventh century to the sixteenth century, millenarianism became a more common phenomenon in certain regions of Europe that were experiencing change in the traditional order. Norman Cohn argues, "The areas in which the age-old prophecies about the Last Days took on a new, revolutionary meaning and a new, explosive force were the areas of rapid social change—and not simply change but expansion: areas where trade and industry were developing and where the population was rapidly increasing" (p. 22). In this world of growing disorder, complexity, and insecurity, millenarian ideas were often blended with antagonisms of class, religion, and identity that imbued these movements with a revolutionary character that could appear threatening or hopeful, depending on one's position in society and relationship to the movement.

Movements such as the People's Crusade and the Shepherd's Crusade witnessed the rising of poor and marginalized people against elites and Jews. The Calabrian abbot Joachim de Fiore used biblical study, especially of the Book of Revelation, to develop a model for understanding history and for creating a vision of the final period of life on earth. These Judgment Days, or Last Days, involved a world where social classes had been leveled, governing structures and church did not exist, and people led a "spiritual" existence that freed them from work because in this spiritual form they did not require food. Surprisingly, the church did not repress this movement even though Christ was not at the center of this new interpretation. Hence from at least the thirteenth century on, even in the Christian tradition, millennial views existed without Christ.

It is in this tradition that scholars in the modern period have increasingly used millenarianism as a tool to study and explain movements that seek to redeem societies and rescue them from rapid social change, colonial incursions, and loss of traditional meaning; this tool also helps in understanding millenarian movements such as the Anabaptists, the Ranters, and others in Europe. While in the modern period Norman Cohn saw certain medieval and early modern millennial movements in Europe as the deep roots of modern communism and Nazism through movements such as that of Thomas Müntzer and the Shepherd's Crusade, studies of the New World have focused on millenarian movements of the poor and oppressed seeking a measure of control, hope, and dignity in their lives and cultures.

Importance in Latin America and Native North America

These movements and interpretations of them are especially prominent among the native peoples of the Americas and those who study them. In the late-eighteenth- and early-nineteenth-century United States, Tecumseh, a leader of the Shawnee nation, and his brother Tenskwautawa, known as "The Prophet," organized Shawnee and other tribes of the Midwest in a movement to reject European ways, return to their old traditions, and end warfare between native peoples. This was part of their effort to drive out nonindigenous peoples and restore a new indigenous order based on the old ways. Tecumseh, who had studied the Bible, even injected European religion into the fray when he asked how white people could be trusted when they had nailed Jesus Christ to a cross.

The Ghost Dances of the U.S. West in the late nineteenth century represented another form of millenarianism. Indigenous peoples of the western plains, who had been severely battered by waves of settlers, the Indian wars fought by the U.S. government, and the destruction of the buffalo herds, called upon their gods to restore power to them. Often overcome with a spirit, these peoples felt imbued with the power to defeat their enemies and redeem their world.

Latin America has also been the source of important millennial movements, including those in which native peoples challenged the European-dominated order. In Peru, in the wake of massive deaths due to European diseases and the encounter with European colonialism, the Taki Onqoy (Dancing Sickness) movement of the 1560s saw the reemergence of old regional gods such as those that lived in mountains, rocks, and in water, but not the gods or leaders of Inca imperialism. These older regional leaders and gods promised salvation to those who were taken by the spirit, but the name Taki Onqoy, or Dancing Sickness, was given to the movement by those who observed its impact on the behavior of those imbued with the spirit who wished to renounce everything that was European and drive out the Europeans as well as other people and things not native to the Andes.

In Chiapas, Mexico, in the early 1700s a millenarian movement arose among the Tzeltal people in response to a vision of the Virgin, who appeared and told them to drive out all nonnative peoples. Some of these highland Maya even proclaimed themselves to be the true Christians while referring to the Europeans as Jews, thus putting the Europeans outside the realm of those protected by the Christian God.

Perhaps the greatest of New World millenarian movements, and one which may still be ongoing, is that of Inkarrí. According to this belief, which was important in validating the revolutionary upheaval of Túpac Amaru in the 1780s, the Inca was to be reborn from the buried but regenerating head (symbolic or real) of an earlier Inca. When the time is right, the Inca will reemerge to lead the indigenous people of the Andes (who are sometimes also referred to as Incas) in the restoration of a more just and equitable social order. The Inkarrí movement is still culturally alive and people are still waiting.

See also **Millenarianism: Islamic; Mysticism; Religion; Sacred Texts.**

BIBLIOGRAPHY

Cohn, Norman. *The Pursuit of the Millennium.* 2nd ed. New York: Harper and Row, 1961.

Flores Galindo, Alberto. *Buscando un Inca.* Lima, Peru: Instituto de Apoyo Agrario, 1987.

Gosner, Kevin. *Soldiers of the Virgin: The Moral Economy of a Colonial Maya Rebellion.* Tucson: University of Arizona Press, 1992.

Stavig, Ward. "Túpac Amaru, the Body Politic, and the Embodiment of Hope: Inca Heritage and Social Justice in the Andes." In *Death, Dismemberment, and Memory: Body Politics in Latin America,* edited by Lyman Johnson. Albuquerque: University of New Mexico Press, 2004.

———. *The World of Túpac Amaru: Conflict, Community, and Identity in Colonial Peru.* Lincoln: University of Nebraska Press, 1999.

Szeminski, Jan. *La utopía tupamarista.* Lima: Fondo Editorial de la Pontificia Universidad Católica del Peru, 1984.

Thornton, Russell. *We Shall Live Again: The 1870 and 1890 Ghost Dance Movements as Demographic Revitalization.* Cambridge, U.K.: Cambridge University Press, 1986.

Wright, Ronald. *Stolen Continents.* Boston: Houghton Mifflin, 1992.

Ward Stavig

MIND. The science of mind is the empirical and theoretical search for the foundations of our mental lives. Unlike other subjects of scientific investigation, such as stars or rocks, human mental lives defy easy definition. Yet few would dispute that such a definition would have to encompass consciousness, emotions, reasoning, language, memory, and perception. As far back as ancient Greece, one can find accounts of how these faculties are produced by the body or the soul. But it was only in the seventeenth century that they became subjects of modern scientific investigation. In the subsequent centuries, scientists have sought to dissect the mind into its components, and to assign those components to different structures of the brain. While a full history of the science of mind would demand thousands of pages, a survey of a few key topics can give a sense of its development.

The Mind Before Neurology

To many readers, the relationship between the brain and mind may be obvious, but that has not always been the case. In 1652, for example, the philosopher Henry More (1614–1687) declared that the brain "is no more capable of thought than a cake of suet or a bowl of curds" (Zimmer, p. 5).

Medieval and Renaissance physicians sought to understand the mind with a mix of Christian theology and Greek philosophy. They believed the body, for example, was divided into three anatomical regions, each designed for its own soul. The vegetative soul in the liver was responsible for desires and appetites. The heart housed the vital soul, which produced passions and action.

The rational soul, not surprisingly, was a more complicated matter. Since it was immaterial and immortal, it could not reside in one specific place in the body. But its faculties—such as reason, memory, and imagination—were believed to be carried out by "animal spirits" that supposedly swirled within three hollow chambers in the head known as the ventricles.

Anatomy, then, was the study of the houses of the souls. But anatomy alone was not enough to account for the life of the mind. Physicians also had to understand the fluids that coursed through the body. Known as the four humors (black bile, yellow bile, blood, and phlegm), these humors needed to be balanced for good health; if they fell out of equilibrium, they brought disease. Humors also gave each individual his or her temperament, be it the sad detachment of melancholy or the swift rage of choler. As the humors became corrupted or moved to the wrong place in the body, they could cause epilepsy or alter the temperament, even leading to madness. Physicians sought to cure many psychological disorders by bringing the humors back in balance, typically with bleeding and purging, or by applying herbs.

During the Renaissance, these theories of souls and humors were vigorously debated. And yet in all these arguments, the brain was strangely absent. The substance of the brain—now recognized as consisting of billions of neurons trading complex signals—was seen as nothing more than phlegm. This is understandable when one considers how delicate the brain is. Without preservatives or refrigeration, a brain quickly decays after death, while muscles and bones remain available for further study.

Descartes's Ambiguous Legacy

This "pre-cerebral" view of the mind disappeared in the 1600s, in the wake of advances in physics, anatomy, and chemistry. Galileo Galilei (1564–1642) and other natural philosophers challenged the physics of Aristotle (384–322 B.C.E.), replacing it with a new "mechanical philosophy" in which mechanical forces acting on atoms or other small particles produced all physical change. In the 1630s the French philosopher René Descartes (1596–1650) used the new mechanical philosophy to offer a novel description of the body. He no longer relied on vegetative or vital souls to produce the body's functions. Instead, he proposed that the body was made of particles that obeyed the laws of physics. A body was no different from a mechanical doll: neither needed a soul to drive its movements. Instead, Descartes envisioned nerves as a system of cords and inflating tubes that mechanically produced involuntary movements.

Descartes managed to take a crucial step towards a science of the nervous system, despite the fact that he was woefully confused about the brain. He accepted the medieval notion of spirits flowing through the ventricles. He even used it to determine where the rational soul was located. For Descartes, it was obvious that the pineal gland, which was believed to dangle over the ventricles, had to be where the rational soul influenced the spirits, steering them toward different nerves in order to produce voluntary movements.

This scenario, as strange as it may seem to the modern reader, accorded with Descartes's overall philosophy. He believed that nature, including the human body, was composed solely of passive matter. The human mind, on the other hand, was completely immaterial and not subject to the laws of nature. Thus Descartes required a site where the immaterial and material could intersect. The pineal gland fit all of these requirements. It would take a separate revolution in anatomy before the brain could be appreciated as more than a bowl of curds.

Thomas Willis and the Birth of Neurology

The modern study of the body's functions began with the work of the English physician William Harvey (1578–1657). Harvey trained at the University of Padua, where he learned Aristotle's methods of comparative zoology and functional anatomy. He returned to England and eventually became a royal physician to James I and Charles I, during which time he discovered the circulation of the blood.

As important as this discovery was, however, Harvey's methods were even more significant. He did not rely solely on Galen (129–c. 199 C.E.) or some other ancient source. Rather, he searched for confirmation of his hypothesis in comparative studies on animals and through experiments. By the 1650s, young natural philosophers were emulating Harvey, not Aristotle, as they studied the liver, lungs, and other organs of the body. And in the early 1660s, a group of Harvey's disciples applied his methods to the brain.

These natural philosophers were led by an Oxford physician named Thomas Willis (1621–1675). A royalist soldier during the English Civil War, Willis had been rewarded at the Restoration with an appointment as professor of natural philosophy at Oxford. He used the new position to embark on a bold project—to seek out the hiding place of the mind. Based on a decade of previous research, including dissections, chemical experiments, and medical observations, Willis decided that the most promising way to study the mind was to make a careful study of the brain.

Willis enlisted a number of colleagues, including his junior medical partner Richard Lower (1631–1691) and his young friend Christopher Wren (1632–1723). They dissected brains of humans, dogs, sheep, and other animals, and Willis recorded their work in his 1664 book *The Anatomy of the Brain,* the first major work on the brain ever written. Over the next eight years he would rely on both his anatomical discoveries and his careful bedside observations to write *Pathologiae Cerebri* (Cerebral pathology), a book on convulsive disorders, and *Two Discourses Concerning the Soul of Brutes,* on neurological and psychological disorders.

Together, this trilogy stands as a defining moment in neuroscience. (Indeed, Willis even coined the word *neurology.*) Willis dismissed Descartes's notions of the pineal gland and ventricles, demonstrating that these chambers could not possibly house the spirits. The brain itself was the site of mental functions, Willis argued, and he carried out experiments to show that different functions were localized in different regions. Instead of Descartes's speculative sketch of involuntary movements, he offered a far more accurate account of reflexes.

Willis also added chemistry to Descartes's mechanical nervous system. As a young physician, Willis had been strongly influenced by the work of alchemist-physicians such as Paracelsus (1493–1541) and Jan Baptista Van Helmont; he also worked with the Irish chemist Robert Boyle (1627–1691) in 1650s Oxford. Willis envisioned the brain as an alembic (an apparatus alchemists used to distill substances), and he conceived of the brain's disorders as disorders of chemistry. He saw epilepsy, for example, not as demonic possession, but as uncontrolled explosive reactions in the brain and nerves.

In the decades around the turn of the twenty-first century, neuroscientists looked back at Willis's work with growing admiration. He has even been called the Harvey of the nervous system. Not only did Willis create a masterful theory of the brain, but in his writings scientists can see the first clinical descriptions of a wide range of neurological conditions, ranging from myasthenia gravis to narcolepsy. By the late seventeenth century, the work of Willis and continental anatomists such as Nicolaus Steno (1638–1686) and Franciscus dele Bo Sylvius (1614–1672) had led most physicians to accept the basic tenets of neurology.

Nineteenth Century Investigation: Broca and Donders

Neurology advanced during the 1700s and early 1800s, as researchers discovered electricity's role in the nervous system and mapped out reflex pathways between the spine and limbs. But Willis's most ambitious project—to work out the foundations of the mind—did not see major advances until the mid-1800s. The huge technical challenge of studying many aspects of human cognition certainly was responsible for some of the delay. But the Cartesian dualism that lingered into the nineteenth century also acted as a brake on progress. Many researchers continued to believe that the mind was a unitary, immaterial entity. It was therefore impossible to discover its components, as had been done with the heart or the lungs. According to one prominent French neurologist in the 1800s, to divide the soul was to deny it.

A growing number of scientists rejected this claim during the nineteenth century. The concept that humans were the product of evolution—first broached in the 1700s and brought to fruition by Charles Darwin (1809–1882) in the following century—implied that the faculties of the mind were the product of evolution as well. Scientists began to divide the soul, as it were, and in the process they established the foundations of cognitive neuroscience. The work of two researchers in particular, Pierre-Paul Broca (1824–1880) and Frans Cornelius Donders (1818–1889), illuminate the scientific shift that occurred in the mid-1800s.

In 1861, the French physician Broca treated a man who suffered a stroke. The patient could understand language but could not speak, except for one sound, "tan." (The patient became known as Tan.) After Tan's death, Broca followed Willis's example and autopsied his patient's brain. Tan's brain was damaged in the left frontal lobe. Other patients with the same difficulty in speaking exhibited damage in the same place. Broca demonstrated that a restricted part of the brain was responsible for a restricted aspect of human mental life—specifically, the ability to produce speech.

At the same time that Broca was doing this work, the German ophthalmologist Donders was dissecting the mind in a radically different—yet complementary—way. In the early 1800s, physiologists and physicists began to study the performance of people in simple tasks, such as recognizing colors and shapes. These tests, the researchers hoped, would reveal the inner workings of the mind without any recourse to anatomical details. In the 1860s Donders performed one of the most elegant of these tests. He first measured how long it took for people to react to seeing a light come on. In his second experiment, one of two differently colored lights could turn on, and his subjects had to indicate which color had come on. He found that it consistently took 50 milliseconds longer to discriminate colors than to perceive the presence of a light. Essentially, Donders was doing in time what Broca was doing in space: He was isolating and studying a specific mental function.

In the twenty-first century, cognitive neuroscientists continue to employ the methods of Broca and Donders, albeit with more sophisticated technology.

Cognitive Neuroscience

Cognitive neuroscience, which focuses on how the mind emerges from the brain, first developed as a discipline in the 1960s. Unlike Willis or Broca, contemporary cognitive neuroscientists can build on the extraordinary advances in the understanding of the brain that took place in the late nineteenth and twentieth centuries. For example, it is now accepted that the brain is composed of several billion neurons, which project a trillion branches to contact other neurons. Neurons carry information as electrical impulses, and communicate with other neurons by releasing a variety of chemicals known as neurotransmitters.

Cognitive neuroscience has also gained great strength from new technologies that provide high-resolution information about brain activity. Consider one technology known as functional magnetic resonance imaging (fMRI). fMRI represents a modern twist on the investigative methods of Willis, Broca, and Donders. A human subject lies with head surrounded by a large, doughnut-shaped magnet. The magnet's powerful field causes some molecules in the subject's brain to release radio waves. Detectors pick up these signals, which a computer uses to reconstruct the structure of the brain. Additional analysis of this data can reveal movements of blood in the brain, which reliably indicate highly active regions of the brain.

A complex cognitive task, such as reading or recalling a person's face, involves many regions of the brain. In order to isolate components specific to these tasks, scientists borrow Donders's subtraction method. They scan the brains of their subjects as they perform one task, and then have them perform second task that is almost—but not quite—identical to the first. The scientists then study the fMRI scans for brain activity produced by the second task that are not produced by the first task as well.

Consider, for example, the ability to understand other people's thoughts and intentions (known as *mentalizing*). Psychologists and neuroscientists are fascinated by this ability because it appears to be unique to humans and may therefore represent a crucial innovation in the social evolution of the human species. Psychologists have also demonstrated that autistic people do a poor job of mentalizing. Yet despite this deficit, they can still develop other skills such as mathematics and music. This pattern suggests that mentalizing is not the result of a general-purpose intelligence, but is instead a distinct, modular function of the brain that can be selectively disabled.

In 2001, British researchers found support for this hypothesis with the help of fMRI. They designed an experiment based on the game of "rock, scissors, paper." In each round, two players simultaneously choose one object. Rock beats scissors, scissors beat paper, and paper beats rock. The subjects lay in a brain scanner and played the game on a computer screen. In some cases, they were told they were playing against a computer; in other cases, they thought their opponent was a person. In fact, the researchers generated a random sequence of choices. The only difference lay in the attitude of the subjects. As the researchers confirmed in interviews after the study, when subjects thought they were playing against a person, they tried to figure out their opponent's strategy.

Scans revealed some regions that became active in both versions of the game. But the researchers also found a handful of small regions in the brain that were only active when the subjects thought they were playing against a person. One region has been shown in other studies to integrate information from face and hand movements. Another region is active during emotional experiences, and a third distinguishes self from non-self.

These results illuminate a general lesson of cognitive neuroscience: Most complex functions of the mind, such as mentalizing, are not carried out in a single region of the brain. Instead, a network of regions works together, integrating their activities. This realization has immediate practical implications. The deficit in mentalizing found in autistic people, for example, may not be the result of a lesion to a particular region of the brain. Instead, it may result from damage to the connections between the components of the mentalizing network.

Aspects of Mind

Contemporary cognitive neuroscience has made important strides in analyzing the mind. Three areas of particularly intense research are perception, emotion, and consciousness.

Perception. Contemporary cognitive neuroscience focuses on aspects of mind that are both important and scientifically tractable. A vast amount of research has been carried out on perception, and in particular, on vision. Researchers have repeatedly demonstrated that the mind does not simply perceive a photograph-like representation of the world. That would demand far more information than the brain can handle. Even if the mind could cope with such a torrent of data, it would probably miss the most important aspects of what is seen—for example, a carelessly driven car lurching onto the road.

Instead, the visual perception system searches for certain patterns. If one sees a few fragmentary lines aligned together, the lines are automatically perceived as a single edge. Different parts of the visual system are tuned to different patterns; some neurons are most sensitive to movement, for example, while others are sensitive to contrasts. These regions are arranged in a pathway, with the first regions along the pathway handling simple processing and then passing on information to regions that can recognize more abstract information, such as faces.

Emotion. Among the investigations of the mind, emotions have posed a particularly difficult challenge. Medieval European thinkers ascribed many of the states called emotions to souls residing in the heart and liver, or to the four humors. Descartes helped to render these explanations obsolete, but his dualism posed problems of its own. Having divided the human being into two distinct substances—body and mind—he had to struggle to find an explanation for emotions. Emotions clearly affect the body, raising heart rate, causing one to blush, and so on. And yet humans also generally used their powers of reason to reach goals, which can be motivated by emotions. Fear of a fire, for example, might spur someone to figure out the fastest way out of a burning building. So somehow emotions must be able to influence the soul, despite the soul being made of a separate substance than the body.

Descartes envisioned passions as purely physical phenomena that could influence the mind by acting on the pineal gland, the soul's intersection with the body. The function of the passions, Descartes argued, was to dispose the soul to want the things that are useful, and to dispose the body to make the movements that would help to acquire those things. But he also argued that passions can cause suffering and thus need to be mastered by the soul. Descartes defined this mastery as wisdom.

Contemporary neuroscientists are weaning themselves from Descartes's dualism in their studies of emotions. They recognize human emotions as having a long evolutionary history. Emotions originated hundreds of millions of years ago as adaptive responses that simpler animals produced in response to a changing environment. Signs of danger, for example, triggered releases of hormones that prepared animals to fight or flee. Signs of potential reward (such as food or a mate) triggered release of neurotransmitters that caused feelings of anticipation and heightened attention.

While human emotions share a common ancestry with reactions in other animals, they are modified for the peculiarities of the human species. Fear is a case in point. Humans and other vertebrates rely on a region of the brain known as the amygdala to produce a sense of fear and vigilance. Rats learn to fear a flash of light if it reliably precedes an electric shock; remove their amygdala, and they never make the association. Humans with lesions in the amygdala also fail this test. But brain imaging shows that the human amygdala is also extremely sensitive to facial expressions. It takes only a few hundredths of a second for the amygdala to respond to an angry face, long before one becomes consciously aware of perceiving it. This is not surprising, given that humans are an intensely social species.

Emotions are also intimately involved in the most abstract thinking of which humans are capable. For example, Antonio Damasio (b. 1944) of the University of Iowa has shown that lesions to an emotion-associated region called the orbitofrontal cortex can lead to poor decision making. Damasio hypothesizes that normally people are guided by emotional reactions to memories of relevant experiences in the past.

Consciousness. While cognitive neuroscientists have made great strides in identifying the components of the mind, they have much left to learn about their integration. Perhaps the most powerful example of this challenge is consciousness. Neuroscientists long shied away from the question of consciousness, feeling that it was impossible to formulate a scientific program to study it. At the close of the twentieth century, though, they began to overcome their reticence and began making serious attempts to solve this mystery.

Consciousness refers to people's awareness of themselves and of their own experiences. At the same time, philosophers also see in consciousness a feature known as qualia: the subjective experience generated in each person's brain. To appreciate the difficulty of studying qualia, imagine a neuroscientist who lacks color vision, seeing the world only in black and white. Imagine that she succeeds in learning everything there is to know about how the retina transfers information about different frequencies of light to the brain, and how the brain processes that information. But she does not know what it is like to experience the sight of red, or any other color. These qualia remain beyond her reach.

Despite these conceptual obstacles, neuroscientists are beginning to study consciousness. Some are using fMRI to compare the human brain in different states of consciousness. For example, scientists can measure the differences in the brain before it is aware of seeing an object and afterwards. They can also compare unconscious processing of sensory information versus conscious processing. In another line of research, scientists place electrodes on a subject's scalp in order to take high-resolution recordings of brain waves, looking for changes in frequencies that might represent signatures of consciousness.

Such studies do not pinpoint a "consciousness organ" in the brain. Rather, they offer an increasingly detailed picture of neural activity that correlate with conscious experiences. In one model that has emerged from this work, brain waves produced in different parts of the brain become synchronized during consciousness, producing a "global workspace" in which the processes going on in different parts of the brain are united.

There are a number of other models that are being explored, however, and none has emerged as a clear favorite over the others. Some researchers have suggested that the study of consciousness in the twenty-first century is like the study of hurricanes in the 1800s. Nineteenth-century meteorologists could collect very little data in order to understand and predict hurricanes. They could take readings of air pressure, winds, and rainfall at a few weather stations, and then try to extrapolate those results. Only when weather satellites were launched into orbit were meteorologists able to see an entire hurricane and track it across the Atlantic. In order to produce a satisfying theory of consciousness, scientists may have to wait for the arrival of satellites for the mind.

See also **Behaviorism; Biology; Body, The; Cartesianism; Determinism; Dream; Dualism; Genius; Humanity;** *Imagination; Knowledge; Medicine; Person, Idea of the; Psychology and Psychiatry.*

BIBLIOGRAPHY

Albright, Thomas D., et al. "Neural Science: A Century of Progress and the Mysteries That Remain." *Cell* 100 Supplement (2000): S1–55.

Brazier, Mary Agnes Burniston. *A History of Neurophysiology in the 19th Century.* New York: Raven Press, 1988.

Churchland, Patricia Smith. *Neurophilosophy: Toward a Unified Science of the Mind-Brain.* Cambridge, Mass.: MIT Press, 1986.

Damasio, Antonio. *The Feeling of What Happens: Body and Emotion in the Making of Consciousness.* New York: Harcourt Brace, 1999.

Descartes, René. *The Passions of the Soul.* Translated and annotated by Stephen Voss. Indianapolis: Hackett, 1989.

Finger, Stanley. *The Minds Behind the Brain: A History of the Pioneers and Their Discoveries.* Oxford: Oxford University Press, 2000.

French, Robert K. *Dissection and Vivisection in the European Renaissance.* Aldershot, U.K.: Ashgate, 1999.

Gallagher, Helen, and Chris D. Frith. "Functional Imaging of 'Theory of Mind.'" *Trends in Cognitive Sciences* 7(2003): 77–83.

Gaukroger, Stephen. *Descartes: An Intellectual Biography.* Oxford: Clarendon, 1995.

Gazzaniga, Michael, Richard B. Ivry, and George R. Mangun, eds. *Cognitive Neuroscience.* 2nd edition. New York: Norton, 2002.

Koch, Christof. *The Quest for Consciousness: A Neurobiological Approach.* New York: Roberts, 2004.

Martensen, Robert L. *The Brain Takes Shape: An Early History.* Oxford: Oxford University Press, 2004.

Pinker, Steven. *How The Mind Works.* New York: Norton, 1997.

Young, Robert M. *Mind, Brain, and Adaptation in the Nineteenth Century: Cerebral Localization and its Biological Context from Gall to Ferrier.* Oxford: Clarendon, 1970.

Zimmer, Carl. *Soul Made Flesh: The Discovery of the Brain—And How It Changed the World.* New York: Free Press, 2004.

Carl Zimmer

MINORITY. The term *minority group* and its opposite, *majority group,* have been widely used both among social scientists and the general public in recent decades. In social scientific (and often popular) use of these terms, they do not usually refer per se to a numerical minority or majority. Rather, the social-scientific meaning of a minority group is a group that is assigned an inferior status in society, one that enjoys less than its proportionate share of scarce resources. Frequently, minority group members are discriminated against, and in some cases they are severely and systematically exploited for economic gain by the majority group, as illustrated in U.S. history by enslavement of African-Americans and by the taking of land from American Indians and from Mexicans who settled in what became the U.S. Southwest.

Usually, a minority group is defined on the basis of a relatively permanent and unchanging status and on the basis of being different—often visibly—from the majority group. This definition includes minorities based on ascribed statuses such as race, ethnicity, and gender and other statuses that are difficult or impossible to change, such as sexual orientation and disability. It also includes groups with common identities that are deeply held and relatively unlikely to change, most commonly religious or linguistic groups. When minority status is assigned on the basis of race or ethnicity, it often involves groups that have been conquered or colonized in the past, as is the case, in the United States, of African-Americans, Mexican-Americans and Puerto Ricans, and American Indians. In these instances, the degree of subordination experienced by the groups tends to be particularly intense. It is notable, for example, that the present and historic status of the four aforementioned groups is significantly more disadvantaged than that of most immigrant groups in the United States. For all types of minority groups, it is typically true that (1) the group is different in some way that is regarded as socially significant from those who hold the dominant influence in society, and (2) on the basis of that difference the group is assigned to a subordinate or disadvantaged status.

Widening the Definition

The concept of minorities has existed for over a century, and until the 1960s and 1970s the term generally referred to national or ethnic minorities in heterogeneous nation-states. In the 1960s and 1970s, the range of characteristics used to identify minority groups widened (e.g., gender, disability, sexual orientation), and the practice of defining minority groups primarily on the basis of power and status disadvantages became common. The focus on disadvantages is evident in the writings of Schermerhorn (1970), who argued that minority groups should be defined on the basis of relative size and power. A group disadvantaged with respect to both size and power, in Schermerhorn's definition, was a minority group, while a group advantaged in both regards was a majority group. A large group without power was referred to as *mass subjects,* while a small group with power was called an *elite.* In common usage, however, the term *mass subjects* is rarely used in the early twenty-first century. While *elite* is more widely used, it is usually employed in an economic and political sense without a direct tie to race, ethnicity, religion, language, or other characteristics commonly associated with minority and majority groups. It is, however, usually true that elites, as referred to in this sense, are members of dominant or advantaged racial, ethnic, religious, and linguistic groups.

While it is usually true that minority groups are numerical minorities, this is not always the case, as is illustrated by the subordinate status of women in the United States and, until recently, blacks in South Africa. Although Schermerhorn's term *mass subjects* might be a more appropriate label for such groups, they are more commonly referred to as having a minority status, referring to their subordinated position with regard to power, status, and economic opportunities. Although over 80 percent of the South African population is black, the political system was, until the mid-1990s, completely under the control of a small white numerical minority (but a majority group in the social-scientific sense) since the country was created in 1949. Racial separation and discrimination were written into the laws

at that time, and these laws remained in effect for forty years. In the early twenty-first century South Africa is a representative democracy, and the black numerical majority is in political control. Yet, in another sense, blacks still remain a minority group in South Africa, since the economic wealth of the country remains largely controlled by whites.

Another instance of a numerical majority that is a sociological minority group is women in the United States. Women make up slightly over half of the U.S. population but relatively few hold offices in the nation's higher political governing bodies (such as the U.S. Congress). Even at the start of the twenty-first century, full-time working women are paid only about 76 percent of the wages of similarly educated working men (U.S. Census Bureau, 2003). Thus, even though they are a numerical majority, women have in many ways been relegated to a subordinate role in American society. Accordingly, they can be regarded as a minority group in the social-scientific sense.

A helpful way to think about minority and majority groups, suggested by Norman Yetman (1991, p. 11), is to consider minority as a synonym for *subordinate,* and majority as a synonym for *dominant.*

Minority Status and the Individual

Discussion thus far has focused on groups because minority or majority status is defined on the basis of belonging to an identifiable group in society. An individual may be black, or Muslim, or female, or gay, or a non-English speaker, or have a disability. In each case, such an identity or social characteristic will identify that individual as belonging to a group with a collective disadvantage or a group that is the object of collective discrimination, exploitation, or stigma. However, although minorities are defined on the basis of groups, the consequences are very real for individuals (Goldman, 2001). It is individual human beings who are denied employment, schooling, or housing because of their race, disability, or sexual orientation, persecuted because of their religious beliefs, ridiculed because of their language, or underpaid because of their sex.

In the early twenty-first century, there has been some criticism of the term *minority* (Wilkinson, 2002). A number of objections have been raised, including the following: (1) since such status is not defined on the basis of numbers, *minority* is not a correct term; (2) the term *minority* can be a negative label and defines the groups so labeled from the standpoint of the dominant group; (3) groups with little in common, such as African-Americans and white women, are lumped together under one rather meaningless label; (4) the criteria used to define minorities are ambiguous and inconsistent; (5) the statuses that form the basis of defining minority groups include both true ascribed statuses and statuses that involve an element of choice (e.g., religious belief); and (6) the term *minority* obscures the very real impacts of racial, gender, and other forms of discrimination, using an ill-defined term to focus on groups rather than on systemic discrimination. Despite these genuine difficulties with the term, it continues to be used widely, both in social science and in popular terminology. A search of the EBSCO Academic Search Elite database in May 2003 yielded 11,822 hits on the term *minorities.* One reason for this common use (though also a point of objection from critics of its scientific validity) is that it has been reified through governmental protections for a wide range of groups labeled as "minorities." In addition—at least in the social sciences—there is general agreement on the experiences that lead a group to be considered a minority group. These experiences include victimization, discrimination, exploitation, and political and economic disadvantage. While each group considered a minority experiences these processes in a unique way, all such groups experience them to a greater or lesser degree. Moreover, possible alternative terms also pose problems: it is not clear, for example, that *subordinate* conveys a more positive image than *minority.* The purpose, if not always the consequence, in using such terms in social science is not to convey negative connotations, but rather to describe a similar situation—minority or subordinate status—that is experienced by a number of different groups.

See also **Discrimination; Ethnicity and Race; Identity; Prejudice.**

BIBLIOGRAPHY

Blauner, Robert. *Racial Oppression in America.* New York: Harper and Row, 1972.

Goldmann, Gustave. "Defining and Observing Minorities: An Objective Assessment." *Statistical Journal of the UN Economic Commission for Europe* 18, nos. 2/3 (2001): 205–216.

Killian, Lewis M. "What or Who Is a 'Minority'?" *Michigan Sociological Review* 10 (1996): 18–31.

Schermerhorn, Richard A. *Comparative Ethnic Relations: A Framework for Theory and Research.* New York: Random House, 1970.

U.S. Census Bureau. "Current Population Survey—Annual Demographic Survey. Table PINC-05. Work Experience in 2001—People 15 Years Old and Over by Total Money Earnings in 2001, Age, Race, Hispanic Origin and Sex." Available on the World Wide Web at http://ferret.bls.census.gov/macro/032002.

Wilkinson, Doris. "The Clinical Irrelevance and Scientific Invalidity of the 'Minority Notion': Deleting It from the Social Science Vocabulary." *Journal of Sociology and Social Welfare* 29, no. 2 (2002): 21–34.

Yetman, Norman R. *Majority and Minority: The Dynamics of Race and Ethnicity in American Life.* 5th ed. Boston: Allyn and Bacon, 1991.

John E. Farley

MIRACLES. Miracles, miracle workers, and their stories are found in the life and literature of all ancient societies and are not limited to religious texts. In ancient Greece figures like Epimenides, Pythagoras, and Apollonius of Tyana were all renowned for working miracles. To this day, healing remains the form that most claimed miracles take, and many of these miracles are associated with visitations to the shrines of saints. In Africa, India, parts of Asia, and Latin America, miracles remain an important and powerful dimension of "primal" religions and cults. Indeed, miraculous healings and exorcisms are the characteristic features of the world's fastest-growing form of

Christianity: Pentecostalism. Contrary to secularization theorists, belief in God—and in miracles—have not disappeared with the advance of science and the rationalization of Western societies. For example, opinion polls at the close of the second millennium showed that nearly 90 percent of Americans believed in God, 84 percent believed in miracles, and nearly half (48 percent) said they had experienced a miracle in their own lives or in the life of someone else (*Newsweek,* 1 May 2000, p. 57).

Viewed historically, miracles and their stories were recognized and accepted long before systematic efforts to define what a miracle is. This is not surprising since the cultures that produced the scriptures sacred to the world's major religions—in this entry, Hinduism, Buddhism, Judaism, Christianity, and Islam—did not regard nature as a closed system operating according to its own laws and therefore impervious to the action of God or the gods. Nonetheless, they recognized miracles as extraordinary occurrences. Thus, one classic definition, from Thomas Aquinas in the thirteenth century, holds that "those things are properly called miracles which are done by divine agency beyond the order commonly observed in nature." The medieval Jewish scholar Moses Maimonides (1135–1204) thought that miracles—especially those in the Bible—were designed by the creator for very specific purposes and, though contrary to the observable laws of nature, were instituted at the beginning of creation as part of God's divine plan. For Deists and other Enlightenment thinkers of the eighteenth century, nature was considered to be subject to immutable laws that even God cannot abrogate. As Voltaire famously put it: "It is impossible that the infinitely wise Being has made laws in order to violate them. He has made this machine [the universe] as good as he could." Still influential is David Hume's argument that not only are miracles impossible, but also that "No testimony is sufficient to establish" that a miracle has occurred.

Miracles as Narrative Constructions

But "nature" and its "laws" are notoriously loose, historically conditioned concepts, and the constructs of contemporary sciences correspond to no one's sense of "the order commonly observed in nature." Far more useful and descriptive in any cultural context is the biblical understanding of miracles as "signs and wonders" (Hebrew, *otot u-mofetim*). Viewed this way, a miracle (from the Latin *miraculum*) is an event that astonishes beholders (wonder) and at the same time conveys meaning (sign). Absent the sign factor, it is impossible to distinguish miracle from mere coincidence. Since signs are always signs of something, we can say that a miracle is an unusual event that discloses the meaning and power of the transcendent within the world of time and space.

From this definition it follows that miracles are always narratively constructed. To take a common example: if a terminally ill patient is suddenly cured and attendant physicians can find no cause in medicine or science to explain the cure, the patient or others may claim that the patient's sudden restoration to health is the result of prayer to God for a miracle. That is, they explain the otherwise inexplicable by fashioning a story. This is precisely what happens within the Vatican's Congregation for the Causes of Saints, the most rigorously methodological source of contemporary miracles and their stories. Once church officials are satisfied that a candidate for sainthood exhibited extraordinary virtue, they require two posthumous miracles attributed to the intercession of the candidate as a sign from God that the deceased candidate truly is now with God in the afterlife. Only after a board of physicians concludes that an unexpected healing has no known scientific cause does a board of theologians consider whether the healing is also a "divine sign."

Miracles in Sacred Scriptures

The best-known miracles are those found in the scriptures of the major world religions, and in the sacred biographies of the saints, sages, and spiritual masters who embody and extend scriptural precedents. When experienced as events embedded in religious traditions, miracles tend to define themselves as stories that in some way repeat or echo previous miracles within the same tradition. For example, the Hebrew Scriptures (for Christians, the Old Testament) contains so many and various kinds of miracles—divine rescues, healings, feedings, punishments and blessings, even raisings of the dead and one ascension (of Elijah) into heaven—that it can fairly be regarded as the repository of most of the forms that miracles take in the later Jewish, Christian, and Muslim traditions.

Within the Hebrew Scriptures themselves, later books deliberately recall earlier miracle stories. For example, there are 120 repetitions and allusions to the ancient Israelites' divinely provided crossing of the sea of reeds, the great deliverance miracle in the Book of Exodus. When the prophet Elisha picks up the mantel of his predecessor, Elijah, the power to produce similar miracles passes with it. When Jesus heals the sick and raises the dead, these miracle stories echo the miracles of Elijah and Elisha, though Jesus does them on his own authority. Likewise in the Book of Acts, the apostles Peter and Paul work the same kind of miracles that Jesus did, but they do so in his name and through the power of the Holy Spirit. Although in the Koran the prophet Muhammad notably refuses to work miracles, the story of his ascension (*mi'raj*) into heaven, a narrative developed out of a Koranic verse (Q. 17:1), replicates and surpasses the ascensions of Elijah and Jesus. This same story also provides the model of the mystical path followed by later Muslim mystics who are the chief miracle-workers in Muslim tradition.

In Buddhism, miracle stories are tied directly to Buddhist teachings as manifestations of their power to liberate. Thus the Buddha's first disciples collectively repeat the miracles of the master as they progress along the path to perfect enlightenment. In the Puranas ("ancient tales"), a vast and very popular collectin of sectarian scriptures composed and edited between the second and seventeenth centuries C.E., the miracles of Lord Krishna not only echo previous stories of earlier Vedic gods but also have the power to establish in his devotees the ability to replicate the experiences of Krishna, in some cases by becoming Krishna himself.

From this it can be seen that miracles achieve their meaning as signs through specific narrative traditions. Conversely, narrative traditions—to a large extent—determine which kinds of extraordinary events are recognized as miracles and which are not. Thus, in order to understand the significance of many scriptural

miracles, one most know what previous miracles are being replicated, echoed, or superceded. But there are important exceptions in Islam. In the Koran, Muhammad says "the signs [*aya*, meaning miracles] are with God alone;" the greatest sign is the Koran itself, every Arabic verse (sura) of which Muslims regard as the actual words of Allah. But the miracles attributed to Muhammad (*mu'jizat*) are all found elsewhere, chiefly in the hadith (roughly, "the traditions") of the Prophet, considered second only to the Koran in importance. However, in the various authoritative collections of the hadith, Muhammad's miracles tend to be merely listed apart from any interpretive narrative context. This arrangement suggests that miracles were incidental to the life and importance of the Prophet and may have been included in the hadith for the apologetic purpose of demonstrating that Muhammad, like Jesus, Moses, and other prophets of Allah before him, possessed the power to work miracles. Thus, among the three monotheistic traditions, Islam makes a formal and linguistic distinction between the miracles produced as signs by God and the miracles attributed to the prophets, whereas in Judaism and Christianity the distinction is informal: in the Bible, the power to work miracles belongs to God as the creator and sustainer of the world, but beginning with Moses that power passes to the prophets. In the New Testament, Jesus not only heals and raises the dead, like earlier Jewish prophets, but also exercises power over nature (as in calming storms and walking on water), a sign of his divinity since the power to control nature belongs to God alone.

In the various religious and philosophical traditions collectively known as Hinduism, miracles are usually understood as manifestations of innate divine power. Here we must distinguish between the miracles of God or gods, principally Shiva, Vishnu, and the latter's many avatars (especially Krishna and Rama) and the miracles of the saints or renunciates in a long line of ascetics reaching back to the fabled sages (*rishi*) of the Vedic period (1500–500 B.C.E.) Stories of the gods and their avatars belong to the great and complex tapestry of Hindu mythology and need not concern us here. Far more relevant to the Hindu understanding of miracles are the stories told of the saints.

Just as the Hindu deities can descend in human forms (avatars), so the Hindu saints can, through the practice of asceticism (*tapas*), rise to godlike status. Thus the saint is often understood to be a "god-man" or a "goddess woman" by virtue of having "realized" the divinity innate in all human beings. In this context, a miracle is a manifestation of supernormal powers (*siddhi*) acquired as a function of attaining ever purer forms of consciousness (*samadhi*) through meditation and physical austerities. A classic treatment of the *siddhi* is the Yoga Sutra of Pantanjali, where the list of supernormal powers includes knowledge of previous lives; clairvoyance; knowledge of the moment when one will die; control over and thus freedom from one's bodily systems; the ability to levitate and transverse great distances in a moment's time; the power to expand or shrink one's body; and so forth.

Although the Buddha rejected the traditional practices of Indian ascetics, Buddhism incorporates the same understanding of miracles as supernormal powers that Pantanjali outlined.

The main difference is that there is no "self" to be realized in Buddhist teachings—it is the last and greatest of illusions—which is why the Buddha taught his disciples not to display their acquired powers before the laity: to do so would manifest pride and so trap them in yet another form of attachment to self. Yet after his own enlightenment the Buddha did perform many miracles, some of them more fantastic than any attributed to Hindu god-men. But he did so for evangelistic purposes, secure in the knowledge that he had liberated himself from all attachments.

Although miracles are found in all religions, in none of them are they considered a substitute for faith or commitment to a spiritual path. As signs, they point to different meanings according to traditions, and so may be seen as boundary stories separating one religious tradition from another. As wonders, miracles continue to elicit curiosity, if not always belief. An old Hasidic saying nicely captures the ambivalence that has always attended miracles and their stories: "He who believes all these tales is a fool, but anyone who cannot believe them is a heretic."

See also **Mysticism; Religion; Sacred Texts.**

BIBLIOGRAPHY

Aquinas, Thomas. *The Summa Contra Gentiles of Saint Thomas Aquinas.* Translated by the English Dominican Fathers from the latest Leonine edition. Book 3. London: Burns, Oates and Washburn, 1923–1929.

Gallup, George, Jr., and Jim Castelli. *The People's Religion: American Faith in the 90's.* New York: Macmillan, 1989.

Hume, David. "Of Miracles." In *Enquiries Concerning Human Understanding and Concerning the Principles of Morals,* edited by L. A. Selby-Bigge. 3rd ed. Oxford: Clarendon Press, 1975.

Meier, John P. "Miracles and Modern Minds." In *A Marginal Jew: Rethinking The Historical Jesus.* Vol. 2: *Mentor, Message, And Miracles.* New York: Doubleday, 1994.

Voltaire. *Philosophical Dictionary.* Translated and edited by Peter Gay. New York: Basic Books, 1962.

Woodward, Kenneth L. *The Book of Miracles: The Meaning of the Miracle Stories in Christianity, Judaism, Buddhism, Hinduism, Islam.* New York: Simon and Schuster, 2000.

———. "The Science of Miracles and the Miracles of Science." In his *Making Saints: How the Catholic Church Determines Who Becomes a Saint, Who Doesn't, and Why.* New York: Simon and Schuster, 1996.

Kenneth L. Woodward

MODERNISM.

This entry includes two subentries:

Overview
Latin America

OVERVIEW

A movement of indeterminate origin and span, modernism nevertheless retains the distinctiveness of a major episode in the history of culture. Its most renowned manifestations performed a radical break with the dominant arts of the nineteenth century. They were direct provocations to prevailing norms: norms of beauty, of the representational integrity of the human body, of the continuity of forms, of the consolations of progress, of secure reception by an audience. Despite striking differences, these artifacts were quickly recognized as part of a broad cultural transformation. They incited popular outrage, putting the category of "art" into question and forcing the issue of "difficulty." The emergence of modernism is inseparable from the active controversy that was an inescapable aspect of its development.

Distinctions among modernization, modernity, and modernism remain indispensable: modernization as the condition of social, economic, and technological change; modernity as the lived social experience of these transforming conditions; and modernism as the cultural activity situated within and alongside these other dimensions. That no secure origin of modernism can be offered is a reflection of its complex relations. The process of modernization—uneven industrialization, the widening of empire, the spread of technologies, the emergence of class society, the struggle for the rights of women—has no fixed starting point, nor does the experience of modernity, the sensation of being unmoored from a continuous past or uprooted from an organic community.

Despite the indeterminacy at its limits, the period known as high modernism, roughly bound by the years 1890 through 1930, achieves historical definition. It does so through the magnitude and extremity of artistic experiment, the proliferation of public gestures (such as exhibitions and manifestos), the attentions of the press, the growing international circulation of experimental texts and ideas, and the widening consciousness of cultural and social change. Any single characteristic of modernism can be traced far back in cultural history. What distinguishes the movement is the convergence of multiple tendencies, including the exploration of such negative states as violence, irrationality, and nihilism alongside the affirmation of art as a redemptive possibility.

Immediate antecedents of high modernism are many and diverse. Charles Baudelaire (1821–1867), in the poems of *Les Fleurs du mal* (1857) as well as in his essays, introduced preoccupations taken up repeatedly over subsequent decades: a fascination with and revulsion from the modern city, an encounter with transgressive eroticism, an acceptance of evil, a delight in artifice (especially through the figure of the dandy), and a commitment to the craft of lyric poetry and the power of the Symbol. Whereas Baudelaire enacted his encounter with modernity in compact poetic forms, Richard Wagner (1813–1883) promoted radical transformation on the grand scale. He aimed for a complete reconstruction of nineteenth-century opera, based on his vision of the *Gesamtkunstwerk,* the "total work of art" that combines drama, music, dance, and stage-setting. Wagner's demand for spectacular dramatic gesture, his investment in large mythic narrative, and his creation of the Bayreuth festival represent efforts to renovate culture through the public force of art.

The symbolic and mythic projects of Baudelaire and Wagner developed in parallel to a newly austere realism that often looked to experimental science as a model. The paintings of Gustave Courbet (1819–1877), including *The Stone Breakers* (1849) and *The Burial at Ornans* (1850), refused pictorial idealism, representing workers and common citizens in ordinary dress and everyday poses. Gustave Flaubert (1821–1880), whose *Madame Bovary* (1857) epitomized the new realism, wrote that art "must rise above personal emotions and nervous susceptibilities. It is time to endow it with pitiless method, with the exactness of the physical sciences" (p. 195). Beginning in the 1870s, Henrik Ibsen (1828–1906) composed a series of plays—*A Doll's House, Ghosts, The Pillars of Society*—that insisted on a "realist" analysis of middle-class ideals and that generated uproar throughout Europe. In their methods as their subjects, Courbet, Flaubert, and Ibsen pursued the unmasking of illusion and the hard-won claims of truthful fiction.

Although these figures differed in their work and their legacies, each prepared for the advent of high modernism. The decisive event was the emergence of an oppositional culture. It was only when singular provocations became related to one another, sometimes loosely, sometimes closely, that modernity recognized modernism and modernists became conscious of their historical possibility. There was no modernism without individually audacious artifacts, but equally no modernism without exchanges among artists and relationships among their works.

Impressionism, Symbolism, Oppositional Culture

Impressionism became a visible and contentious movement in the 1870s when a group of young French painters, including Claude Monet, Camille Pissarro, Berthe Morisot, Alfred Sisley, and Jean Renoir, gave several controversial exhibitions in Paris. Their break with academic painting and their commitment to everyday life followed Courbet, but they went further in the attempt to render the visible world as they experienced it subjectively: unstable, evanescent, and elusive. As significant as the new pictorial style was the collective aspect of Impressionism. Like the short-lived Pre-Raphaelite Brotherhood that had appeared in London in the 1850s, Impressionism generated hostility in part because the alliance among artists suggested a viable alternative to cultural orthodoxy.

A second French movement, more significant and sustained, was symbolism, which emerged in the 1880s. Stéphane Mallarmé (1842–1898) and Paul Verlaine (1844–1896) were presiding figures, and Arthur Rimbaud (1854–1891) was the legendary seer who had disappeared from France. The symbolists looked back to Baudelaire and resisted the dominance of realism, especially in its more extreme manifestation in the naturalist novels of Émile Zola (1844–1896) and the Goncourts (Edmond [1822–1896] and Jules [1830–1870]). Symbolism offered the rituals of the poetic enigma: evocative music, not descriptive reference. "To *name* the object," wrote Mallarmé, "is to destroy three-quarters of the enjoyment of the poem" (p. 869). The poetic Symbol could be a sound, a scent, or a memory incarnating the invisible meanings of the world or intimating a mystery beyond the senses. Much symbolist polemic was a refusal of modernization (science, urbanism, mass politics, and the dislocations of individual experience). Apart from the success of individual poems, such as Mallarmé's *L'Après-midi d'un faune* or Rimbaud's *Le Bateau*

ivre, the importance of symbolism was that it offered an aesthetic counterworld. It was at once an artistic program and a social formation.

In Britain a critical lineage stretching from John Ruskin and Matthew Arnold to Walter Pater brought the idea of "culture" close to the symbolist vision of an alternative universe of value. A disciple of Pater, Arthur Symons (1865–1945) helped to introduce symbolism to the English-speaking world, presenting it as a fulfillment of literature's highest responsibilities: "for in speaking to us so intimately, so solemnly, as only religion had hitherto spoken to us, it becomes itself a kind of religion, with all the duties and responsibilities of the sacred ritual" (p. 9). He introduced Mallarmé to W. B. Yeats (1865–1939), who also imagined a literature imbued with the force of religion and resistant to a mechanized social world and materialist philosophy. Yeats looked to magic and the occult, as well to the folklore and fairy tales of Ireland. His responsiveness to such a range of countertraditions suggests the extent of the division between the new literary movements and the modernizing social world around them.

Nineteenth-century cultural movements emerged within the broader context of modernity: in particular, the recognition of class conflict in postrevolutionary Europe. The European-wide revolutions of 1848 established modern society as a struggle between competing groups. It is often noted that the term *avant-garde* began with political and military meanings and only transferred its reference to the arts in the nineteenth century. Many artists had joined the revolutionary struggles, not only in 1848 but also in the Paris Commune of 1871. The turn away from politics is a striking feature of much late-century culture, with symbolism as a defining example; yet the political struggle generated possibilities for historical change that affected even those artists who refused the call of politics.

The Assertion of Modernism, 1890–1914

The reaction against symbolism began early, and even as its influence was passing to other national cultures, it attracted stringent critique. In the 1890s symbolism often became identified with decadence, in which the austere experiments of Mallarmé gave way to easier rhythms of yearning and escape. The tableau of the weary poet cultivating the sensations of dream became a European-wide image, vulnerable to caricature and dismissal. J. K. Huysmans's *À Rebours* (1884) helped to inspire Oscar Wilde's *The Picture of Dorian Gray* (1891), which dramatized but also ironized the languid life of decadence, the vocation of the senses. Wilde is a decisive figure, one who in his life and work carried Decadence into the public world and who detached himself from it through wit, irony, and paradox. When Wilde went to trial in 1895, the encounter between oppositional culture and the canons of respectability became vivid and painful. His conviction, imprisonment, and early death revealed the entanglements of modernism within the social world it refused.

The turn of the century brought a perceptible change in artistic and literary movements. The symbolist poet, committed to ritual incantations of the suggestive word, gave way to the young, assertive artist, eager to contend with aesthetic convention and social orthodoxy. When Pablo Picasso (1881–1973) painted a brothel tableau in *Les Demoiselles d'Avignon* (1907), with its harsh forms, its sexual brazenness, its direct encounter with the eyes of the viewer, he enacted the turn from weariness to confrontation. In *A Portrait of the Artist as a Young Man,* James Joyce's Stephen Dedalus sets himself as the antagonist of a sluggish culture, daring to echo Satan's "Non Serviam." Arnold Schoenberg's *Pierrot Lunaire* (1912) conveyed the shock of atonality to Western music, attracting tones of outrage to match its experiment in dissonance. In his first Futurist manifesto (1909) Filippo Tommaso Marinetti asserted, "No work without an aggressive character can be a masterpiece" (p. 41). He toured Europe, celebrating an escape from the exhausted past into the speed and violence of modern technology.

There had been precursors of this emphatic confrontalism too. Rimbaud had made scorn for mediocrity a founding principle of his verse. Vincent Van Gogh (1853–1890) released the intensity of color to create intensities of affective assault. But the context that prepared for high modernism was wider than literature and the arts. The unsettled life at the end of the nineteenth century was not simply the background of high modernism; it became an ongoing concern for an intellectually self-conscious movement intent to reengage the world. Major influences included the revolutionary theory of Karl Marx transmitted through post-Marxist theorists in Europe; Friedrich Nietzsche's critique of Christianity in favor of the "overman" and the will to power; Sigmund Freud's psychoanalytic exposition of the unconscious, dreams, bisexuality, and neurosis; James George Frazer's comparison of pagan rituals and modern life in *The Golden Bough;* and Henri Bergson's arguments for an experience of pure duration available only to the deep self. These ambitious theories conflicted on many points: Marx's social vision against Freud's pessimistic view of instinctual conflict and Bergson's strictly philosophic approach, Frazer's scholarly assimilation of primitive and modern attitudes in contrast to Nietzsche's tense demand for a transvaluation of all values. What they shared was a sense of radical transformation. High modernism participated in this active theoretical milieu, in which it seemed that every basis for human self-understanding was under reconsideration. Intellectual life was often an essential element in the art, and the centrality of manifestos in high modernism is another register of the intellectual character of the movement. New artifacts did not appear as isolated provocations; they arrived within a dense context of essays, reviews, and manifestos that connected the making of modernist artifacts to the unfolding of modern theory.

Outside the realm of theoretical writing stood the power of social events. The development of a large reading public and mass democracy incited a modernist anxiety over popular culture recurrent through the period. The conflict between the sexes, including the image of the New Woman and the militant demand for female suffrage, challenged the representation of sexuality in the visual arts, the structure of the marriage plot, and poetic lyricism. This was also the new age of European imperialism, and whether empire became part of the focal subject matter, as with Joseph Conrad and E. M. Forster, or remained unacknowledged, it formed an inescapable cultural context. The political environment sometimes inspired arts to

social engagement, as in the feminist writings of Virginia Woolf or in the political theater of Vsevolod Meyerhold and Bertolt Brecht; just as often it created styles of resistance or right-wing reaction, as in the later works of T. S. Eliot, Ezra Pound, or Wyndham Lewis. In either case, the success of left-wing parties, the threat of revolution in Germany, and its success in Russia meant that experimental artists worked within a milieu of political hopes and fears.

High Modernism and the Avant-Garde, 1914–1930

The devastations of World War I created a social trauma that lasted a generation and intensified the ambitions of the arts. Beginning shortly before the war and continuing through the following decade, an astonishing variety of technically audacious works appeared. A community of artists, readers, viewers, editors, and curators created a receptive context encouraging ever more experimental work, including the move to abstraction in the fine arts (Wassily Kandinsky in painting, Henri Gaudier-Brzeska and Vladimir Tatlin in sculpture); the development of new cinematic styles (Sergei Eisenstein, Fritz Lang, Dziga Vertov); the architectural revolution of Le Corbusier (modern materials in abstract forms); the theatrical extravagance of the *Ballets Russes* accompanied by the music of Igor Stravinsky; the twelve-tone technique of Schoenberg; and the experiments in narrative consciousness of Marcel Proust, James Joyce, Virginia Woolf, and William Faulkner. This profusion has been called the "the last *literary season* of Western culture" (Moretti, p. 209). A claim of modernism to historical distinctiveness rests first of all on the sheer abundance of formally provocative art and the wide attentiveness to it.

A frequently noted aspect of modernist form is its fragmentation: the dissolution of continuity in speech, wholeness in the body, consecutiveness in narrative. The one- or two-lined lyrics of imagism, the abrupt focal shifts in the work of Gertrude Stein, the disintegration of the face in analytic cubism, the rapid editing in the cinema of Sergei Eisenstein and Dziga Vertov, all present decomposing forms shorn of the usual contexts of meaning. "Image," "vortex," "moment," "epiphany" were some of the names given to these radiant fragments. A prominent concern then became the passage from these shorter forms, however resonant, toward more encompassing structures: longer poems, more capacious novels, larger paintings, more ambitious films and music. The later phase of modernism, which contains some of its most striking artifacts (Eliot's *The Waste Land,* Picasso's *Three Musicians,* Joyce's *Ulysses,* Eisenstein's *October,* Schoenberg's unfinished *Moses und Aron*), turns toward synthetic forms that might arrange fragments into broader patterns. The use of myth was a dominant resource for Joyce, Eliot, and Stravinsky; in Eliot's formulation, the mythic method gave a form of order that made "the modern world possible for art." Eisenstein's development of cinematic montage, the conceptual and metaphoric linking of separate images, was another manifestation of synthesis.

Was high modernism then a new aesthetic order or a new antiorder? This question circulated among artists and their critics. Despite the theoretical justifications brought forward to explain the difficult art, it is clear that modernist masterworks contained much that was contingent and resistant to explanation. The sheer eruptive energies, the sense of play, the pleasure in accident, and the linguistic and visual anarchy cannot be safely ordered as examples of a new "method." The implications of this disruptive aesthetics were most fully drawn by the avant-garde groups that developed during and after the war, especially expressionism, dadaism, and surrealism. These groups differed significantly, but they shared a commitment to aesthetic radicalism and direct public challenge. In Germany a group of poets, painters, and filmmakers began to work under the heading *expressionism*, aiming not to receive the world's impressions but to express irrational and intuitive states of mind. They opened the visual world to exaggeration, heightened gesture and emotion, and deformed space and time in their refusal of a corrupt social order. Beginning in Switzerland and spreading quickly to France and Germany, dadaism saw the war as marking the failure of civilization and developed the practice of antiart as a gesture of defiance. In 1916 Hugo Ball opened the Cabaret Voltaire in Zurich, where performances included cacophonous music, nonsense poetry, comic recitation, and costumed theatricality. Dada put in question the most central assumptions of Western art: its seriousness, its coherence as an artifact, its separation from the everyday social world. The dissolution of dada in the early 1920s led some of its members to join André Breton's surrealism, which emphasized the recovery of repressed sources of the imagination and their release into arational art. Rimbaud's call for a derangement of the senses was one major influence; Freud's theory of the unconscious was another. Automatic writing, hallucination, and dreams were seen as instruments of liberation from a constrained and destructive reality. Many of the surrealists, like many of the Dadaists, understood their place within the avant-garde as part of a more general program of political and cultural revolution.

Useful distinctions have often been made between the high modernism of Yeats, Eliot, Rilke, Joyce, Proust, and Mann, deeply committed to the integrity of the artifact, and the "historical avant-garde" constituted by these socially active movements that questioned the coherence of art and its withdrawal from social life. Historically attentive scholarship has shown, however, that these are not rival camps or opposing sides of a cultural dyad. Within high modernism one finds both signs of radical indeterminacy in form and strong statements of social engagement. Ezra Pound's assertion that "the artists were the antennae of the race" (p. 67) represents a characteristic modernist demand, sometimes from the political right and sometimes from the left, for social change founded on the basis of revolutionary art. Similarly, within the avant-garde, one finds scenes of consolidation, where the discord resolves into determinate artifacts. The "avant-garde" and "high modernism" are best seen as moments within the conditions of cultural modernity: an ongoing dialectic between openness and indecidability, on the one hand, and formal integrity, on the other.

Modernism after High Modernism

The later history of the movement involved its circulation into new cultural settings around the world, where it met other forms of modernity and became at once an influence and an object of resistance. The Harlem Renaissance, an efflorescence of African-American literature after World War I, emerged out of local and national contexts—specifically, the consolidation of cultural possibility in New York after the Great Migration northward. It generated experimental forms (for instance, in Jean Toomer's *Cane*), but it also accommodated traditional styles, as in sonnets of Claude McKay. The Harlem Renaissance was not a product of high modernism; rather, it was a parallel movement, intersecting and diverging, that obliges us to recognize a wider, more differentiated history of cultural modernity.

Late-twentieth- and early-twenty-first-century scholarship has shown how modernism played a double-sided role in the national independence movements before and after World War II. The European provenance of celebrated masterworks could make them appear distant and oppressive, tainted by the imperial past. But within the context of the traditional curriculum of the colonial schools, Modernism was also taken as a force of resistance to a canon still derived from nineteenth-century achievement. In the work of Chinua Achebe in Nigeria or Ngugi wa Thiong'o in Kenya complicated double inheritance appears: modernism is at once acknowledged and appropriated, but it has no special privilege alongside other literary aims. It combines with storytelling traditions and national aspirations (Gikandi, 1987). Other studies have shown that in the Caribbean the formal techniques refined by modernism converged with styles of experiment associated with the hybrid history of the islands (Gikandi, 1992). The "creolization" of everyday speech created regional contexts for modernist art, and the conditions of social conflict brought resistance to the elite prestige of European high modernism.

Modernism came to no definite end. The call to "make it new," the use of formal discontinuity, the willingness to compose and present difficult works of art, all continued through the end of the twentieth century. But in the last half of that century, the assimilative power of culture diminished the challenge of such work. A movement that had offered an oppositional principle and a call for transformation found itself part of the routine of shock, celebrity, and fashion.

See also **Avant-Garde; Dada; Expressionism; Impressionism; Naturalism in Art and Literature; Realism; Surrealism; Symbolism.**

BIBLIOGRAPHY

Baker, Houston, Jr. *Modernism and the Harlem Renaissance.* Chicago: University of Chicago Press, 1987.

Berman, Marshall. *All That Is Solid Melts into Air: The Experience of Modernity.* New York: Simon and Schuster, 1982.

Bürger, Peter. *Theory of the Avant-Garde.* Translated by Michael Shaw. Minneapolis: University of Minnesota Press, 1984.

Butler, Christopher. *Early Modernism: Literature, Music and Painting in Europe 1900–1916.* Oxford: Clarendon, 1994.

Calinescu, Matei. *Five Faces of Modernity: Modernism, Avant-garde, Decadence, Kitsch, Postmodernism.* Durham: Duke University Press, 1987.

Eliot, T. S. "'Ulysses,' Order and Myth." In *Selected Prose,* edited by Frank Kermode. New York: Harcourt Brace Jovanovich; Farrar, Straus and Giroux, 1975.

Felski, Rita. *The Gender of Modernity.* Cambridge, Mass.: Harvard University Press, 1995.

Flaubert, Gustave. *The Selected Letters of Gustave Flaubert.* Edited and translated by Francis Steegmuller. New York: Farrar, Straus and Young, 1953,

Gikandi, Simon. *Reading the African Novel.* London: James Currey, 1987.

———. *Writing in Limbo: Modernism and Caribbean Literature.* Ithaca, N.Y.: Cornell University Press, 1992.

Gilbert, Sandra M., and Susan Gubar. *No Man's Land: The Place of the Woman Writer in the Twentieth Century.* New Haven, Conn.: Yale University Press, 1988.

Kenner, Hugh. *The Pound Era.* Berkeley: University of California Press, 1971.

Levenson, Michael. *A Genealogy of Modernism: A Study of English Literary Doctrine, 1908–1922.* New York: Cambridge University Press, 1984.

Marinetti, Filippo Tommaso. *Selected Writings.* Edited by R. W. Flint. New York: Farrar, Straus and Giroux, 1972.

Moretti, Franco. *Signs Taken for Wonders: Essays in the Sociology of Literary Forms.* Translated by Susan Fischer, David Forgacs, and David Miller. London: New Left Books, 1983.

Perloff, Marjorie. *The Poetics of Indeterminacy: Rimbaud to Cage.* Princeton, N.J.: Princeton University Press, 1981.

Pound, Ezra. *ABC of Reading.* New Haven, Conn.: Yale University Press, 1934.

Sheppard, Richard. *Modernism-Dada-Postmodernism.* Evanston, Ill.: Northwestern University Press, 1999.

Rainey, Lawrence. *Institutions of Modernism: Literary Elites and Public Culture.* New Haven, Conn.: Yale University Press, 1998.

Symons, Arthur. *The Symbolist Movement in Literature.* New York: E. P. Dutton, 1919.

Michael Levenson

LATIN AMERICA

Modernism (sometimes referred to as *modern art* or, even less precisely, as *modernity* in the arts) is a term for various experimental languages in the arts with multiple meanings and conflicting aims, and was ascendant from the 1880s to the 1960s (although certain artistic techniques and tactics of early modernist art, such as collage and photomontage, have enjoyed a potent afterlife since the 1960s, especially in Latin America at moments of social insurgency).

According to one of the most famous versions of the history of modernism, associated especially with the writings of critic Clement Greenberg from the 1930s through the 1980s, modernism is an essentially Euro-American phenomenon; but this was never an accurate story about modernism and has been decisively overturned by the debate around postmodernism since the late 1980s. Greenberg has been a very prominent voice about modernism in the United States, with a certain following among Latin American critics like Marta Traba. In perhaps his most well-known definition, "Modernist Painting" (1965), he tried to limit modernism to little more than an engagement with the "essential" material properties of the medium by linking it to Western positivism. (Revealingly, positivism was the prerevolutionary ideology of the dictatorship of Portfirio Díaz in Mexico, even as this school of thought enjoyed considerable hegemony in the West long after the "postcolonial" Revolution of 1910.)

The unduly reductionist view of modernist painting championed by Greenberg was then qualified by a whole series of noteworthy scholars, including Dore Ashton, Thomas Crow, Rosalind Krauss, and Charles Harrison in the West. They respectively demonstrated how modernism from the beginning had carried on a dialogue at once both positive and negative with mass culture as well as popular culture, how modernism was less about a literal focus on the brute materials of a given medium and more about a self-critical look at the inherited languages with which modernist artists had to work, and, finally, that modernist art's activation of the spectator's faculties is meant "to confront the occasions of fantasy and distraction with the requirements of imagination and critical self-awareness" (Harrison, p. 154).

The historical coordinates for the advent of international modernism between 1880 and 1940 have been incisively plotted in a paper by Perry Anderson entitled "Modernity and Revolution." In it he noted that "modernism . . . flowered in the space between a still usable classical past [of official academicism], a still indeterminate technical present [when the 'machine age' was still replete with radical possibilities], and a still unpredictable political future [when the prospect of revolution was more proximate than it had ever been]" (p. 105). Indeed, this triangulated field of forces—a contested academic art representing the old regime; the possibility of technological innovation, not necessarily along capitalist lines; and an insurgent political movement that called for revolutionary change—is precisely what spawned the "epic modernism" of the Mexican Mural Movement from 1922 to 1940 and thus inaugurated modernism as a potent force in the visual arts throughout the Americas.

In contrast to Greenberg's assertion, modernism does not emerge in a linear artistic progression along national lines; instead there are several different multinational conceptions of modernism (and with them, divergent views of its relation to postmodernism) that have arisen within several geographic regions (including not only Latin America, but also Asia and Africa). Modernism's trajectory is more accurately described as a delta with numerous destinations around the globe, rather than as a one-lane highway with only one stop terminating in the West.

At once international in character and yet also unavoidably regional by nature, metropolitan modernism has been paradoxically linked through the arts either to cultural forms of marginalized groups in the West (such as those of Eastern European émigrés, Latinos, African-Americans, and Native Americans) or to so-called peripheral nations in the Third World, as in Latin America. For Raymond Williams in *The Politics of Modernism* (1989), it was in "a generation of 'provincial' immigrants to the great imperial capitals that avant-garde formations and their distanced, 'estranged' forms have their matrix" (p. 14).

An adequate description of Latin American modernism, then, must begin by considering the various definitions of modernism that have arisen within specific contexts, as well as by distinguishing modernism as a cluster of renovative and self-reflexive languages in the arts from modernity. The latter is instead a social experience that has been generated by modernization, which is a globalizing economic program centered in the West. All three of these historic phenomena have existed in complicated, asymmetrical relation to each other.

The Origin of "Modernism" in Latin America

Far from originating solely with intellectuals from metropolitan Western Europe, the term "modernism" first surfaced in print in the writings of a major author from a small "underdeveloped" country in Central America. It was in the late 1880s that the celebrated Nicaraguan poet Rubén Darío (1867–1916) first published the term *modernism* (or *modernismo* in Spanish). The earliest known appearance in print worldwide of this term was in 1888 in Darío's essay "La literatura en Centroámerica" (*Revista de arte y cultural*, Santiago, Chile), when he discussed how author Ricardo Contreas was then using "*el absoluto modernismo en la expresión . . . [de] su estilo compuesto*" ("absolute modernism in expression . . . through his synthetic style"). Subsequently, Darío published the word *modernismo* a second time in an article entitled "Ricardo Palma (Perú, 1833–1919)," which appeared twice in 1890: first, in the Peruvian journal *El Perú Ilustrado* (Lima), on 8 November 1890, and second, in the Guatemalan publication *Diario de Centro-América* (Guatemala City). Thus, by 1899, the *Real Academia Española* had incorporated the word *modernismo* into the latest edition of the *Diccionario de la Lengua* (Madrid, 1899)—although the proliferation of meanings triggered by Darío's usage of the term defied any lexicographical effort at a fixed definition.

This beginning was a prophetic one, for modernism in the arts, both here and elsewhere, has generally occurred at the historic intersection between competing cultures uneasily linked by colonial lineaments, yet starkly divided by the uneven nature of capitalist modernization. Often modernism has thus responded "nationally" to a set of unsettled transnational relationships, but it has generally done so in a cosmopolitan spirit of internationalism that moves beyond national boundaries. Such was the case not only in Nicaragua during the time of Rubén Darío, but also in India during "the age" of Rabindranath Tagore and Mahatma Gandhi or Nigeria in the period of painter Aina Onabolu (1882–1962). It was also true in turn-of-the century Paris, during *la belle époque*, that obviously existed in tense relation to France's contemporary colonial empire in Central Africa.

Although it hardly enjoyed common usage in either the English- or French- or German-speaking artworlds before the mid-1950s (when a group of critics, including Clement Greenberg, began defining it in English), the term *modernism* was invoked, defined, and debated in the Spanish-speaking world beginning in the 1890s on both sides of the Atlantic. In many countries, though, whether in the Americas or in Europe, the most common term for modernism in the teens or twenties was simply *the new art* (*el arte nuevo,* or *die neue Kunst*), while in the 1930s and 1940s, the most common designation of modernist art was "modern art" (*arte moderno, l'art moderne,* and *moderne Kunst*). In Spanish discourses, the term *modernismo* was, quite confusingly, used both to refer the Modernist movement and as the generic name for various modernist movements. This explains the recourse to *modernidad*—which in English would literally be translated as "modernity," although

in fact *modernidad* would be better translated more broadly in English as "modernism." An early example of the latter usage would be in a well-known 1926 essay by muralist Diego Rivera about the photographs of Edward Weston and Tina Modotti, which artistically demonstrated the "*modernidad extrema de la plástica [del arte],*" that is, an "extreme modernism"—not "extreme modernity" in the arts—in English.

A similar imprecision in terminology occurred in routine usage from the late nineteenth century until the 1960s, both in the Americas and in Europe, of the term *avant-garde* or *arte de la vanguardia*—which was then assumed to be a mere synonym for those attributes of painting and the other visual arts articulating *modernism* (or *modernidad*). This was clearly the case in the very first modernist manifesto by the Mexican muralists, when David Alfaro Siqueiros in May 1921 made "*3 llamamientos de orientación actual a los pintores y escultores de la nueva generación americana*" ("Three appeals for orientation right now among the painters and sculptors of the new American generation") in the journal *Vida-Americana: Revista Norte, Centro y Sud-Americana de Vanguardia*. In the public appeal, Siqueiros wrote of how: "*VIVAMOS NUESTRA MARAVILLOSA EPOCA DINAMICA! amemos la mecanica moderna que nos pone en contacto de emociones plasticas inesperadas . . . Abandondemos los motives literarios. HAGAMOS PLASTICA PURA*" ("We are living in our marvelously dynamic epoch! We love the modern technology that we are placing in contact with unexpected artistic emotions . . . . We are abandoning literary motives. Let us make pure visual art"). Revealingly, this two-page manifesto that equated "pure painting"—that is, painting freed of literary references and based on an evocation of "*la vie moderne*" in the machine age—with the "*arte del futuro*" of "*la vanguardia*" was accompanied by a frontispiece that featured a cubist painting from 1914 by Diego Rivera, the first major, internationally recognized modernist painter produced by Latin America.

Thus Siquieros clearly assumes that these formalist concerns of the modernist movements featuring post-literary painting are entirely synonymous with avant-garde art. In three much later essays by the art critic Clement Greenberg, comparable assumptions prevail, yet to more conservative political ends, and far more restrictive aesthetic aims: "Avant-garde and Kitsch" (1939), "Towards a Newer Laocoon" (1940), and the aforementioned "Modernist Painting" (1965).

As Latin America's earliest avant-garde movement, *modernismo* was first limited largely to literature: essays, poetry, and short stories. Such was the case with Rubén Darío's now legendary *Azul . . .* (1888; Azure . . .), which conjoined the innovative self-critical splintering of poetic language (based on enjambment and mid-line caesura) with broader critical reflections on the process of modernization. At issue was a heterogeneous new cultural force that linked self-consciously French-influenced vanguard language with period tropes from an agrarian-based Central America and unlikely recollections of little-known pre-Columbian cultural traditions. This tightly intertwined dynamic of formal disjunction and thematic displacement was summed up by Darío in *Prosas Profanas* (1896; Lay hymns). In this controversial text, he both called for an inward-looking revivification of poetic language in the most modern terms and insisted on an outward-looking reengagement with the precolonial past, since "If there is a [new] poetry in nuestra America, it is to be found in the old things."

Following the lead of Cuban author José Martí (1852–1895), another modernist poet (who also led the movement for national liberation in Cuba against Western colonialism), Darío interwove modernist texts with thematic references to anti-imperialism and to a racial harmony only possible in a postcolonial future. An exemplary and still well-known poem in that vein is found in Darío's *Cantos de vida y esperanza* (1905), in a piece entitled "To Roosevelt." In it, he challenged the United States, as "*el futuro invasor de la América ingénua que tiene sangre indígena*" ("the future invader of the ingenuous America that has indigenous blood"). As such, the colossus of the North, with its cynical fusion of the cult of Hercules and the worship of money, was critically contrasted with the other Americas, "*la América nuestra, que teniá poetas / desde l os viejos tiempos de Netzahualcoyotol.*" In this text, the modernism of Darío, and others, responded to the critique of Euro-American-centrism first voiced in the celebrated anti-positivist *Kulturkritik* by Uruguayan author José Enrique Rodó (1872–1917), namely, *Ariel* (1900).

Only after the word *modernism* crossed the Atlantic from Latin America to discover Europe, first Barcelona, then Paris, did it start designating certain formal strategies and thematic concerns in the visual arts that were linked to the literary project of Rubén Darío. The term *modernismo* (*modernisme* in French) or *arte modernista* (*l'art moderniste*) was used in the beginning to refer to such famous architectural projects by Antoni Gaudí as *Parque Guell* (1900–1914) and *Sagrada Familia* (1883–1926), in the fin-de-siècle city where both Pablo Picasso and Diego Rivera would work in the early twentieth century. It was this cosmopolitan city in Spain, as much as Paris proper, that would help to spawn such early modernist masterworks as Picasso's 1907 *Demoiselles d'Avignon* (named for a street in Barcelona) and Rivera's distinctive corpus from 1913 to 1917 of "Anáhuac Cubism," as Justino Fernández would so aptly call it in reference to the indigenous Mexican content of Rivera's work. In the case of Gaudí, for example, the term *modernismo* constituted both a distinct tendency within modernism proper and a point of departure for advancing other types of modernism as well, such as cubism. Indeed, almost all of the key formal tactics for every other variety of modernism were deployed in Gaudí's singular modernist artworks, like Parque Guell and Sagrada Familia: (1) a collage aesthetic featuring a mosaic of ruins or shards; (2) a multilateral sense of history based upon uneven development; (3) a multicultural *mestizaje* (hybridity) ranging from African components to pan-European elements; (4) a critique of capitalist modernization; and (5) an anti-imperialist aspiration (in this instance, one interlinked with the Catalan autonomy movement).

As for the ideologically charged use of the fragment to explain the historical import of modernism in the visual arts, we need only recall how Mexican painter Diego Rivera defined the unsettling language of cubism as "a revolutionary movement . . . [that] broke down forms as they had been seen for centuries, and was creating out of the fragments new forms, new objects, new

The Towers of Satellite City (constructed 1957), designed by Mexican architect Luis Barragan (1902–1988). Resembling abstract skyscrapers, the cement towers of this public artwork ascend over the Queretaro highway in Mexico City as a startling example of Latin American modernism. © RENE BURRI/MAGNUM PHOTOS

patterns, and—ultimately—new worlds" (trans. by March). Later, art critics would illuminate how *arte modernista*, like that of the cubist "collages" by Rivera, with their distinctive uses of modernist space, constituted a critique of the actual mechanics for pictorial logic in Western art. As Rosalind Krauss would point out in the 1980s, two of the key artistic strategies to develop out of collage space were figure/ground reversals and the restless transposition of negative space into positive form, so that no visual sign would exist without the attendant eclipse or negation of its natural referent. In this manner modernism, particularly as manifested in cubism, ended up critically exploring through a critique of artistic languages the preconditions of mainstream Western—that is, colonial—modes of representation.

As such, the modernist contestation by Latin American artists of Euro-American cultural hegemony is what permitted Diego Rivera to recruit cubism and several other artistic traditions, both modern and premodern, on behalf of the Mexican Revolution, when he (along with José Clemente Orozco, David Alfaro Siqueiros, Fernando Leal, and others) created an "epic modernism" during the Mexican mural renaissance from 1922 to 1940. Signs of this emergent "revolutionary modernism" (Rivera called it *"la revolución de arte moderno"*) already surfaced in such cubist period paintings in 1915 as *Paisaje Zapatista: El Guerrillero and Retrato de Martín Luis Guzmán* (a Mexican novelist who served with Pancho Villa). In that sense, one could justifiably recall the observation of Mexican writer Antonio Caso that Diego Rivera was to the modernist visual art of Latin America what Rubén Darío had been to modernist poetry from Latin America.

Modernism and Postmodernism

It is worth noting that, as was true of the term *modernism,* there was a south-to-north movement for circulating the word *postmodernism* (or *postmodernismo*). The latter first emerged in the Hispanophone literary world, in 1934, when it was coined by author Federico de Onis. He did so in *Antología de la Poesía Española e Hispanoamericana (1882–1933),* where he identified modernism as a worldwide movement in response to the "crisis of Western Civilization." De Onis contrasted a conservative artistic tendency within modernism, which he christened "postmodernism," in contradistinction to an *"ultra-modernismo."* The latter, linked to writers like Jorge Luis Borges from Argentina, was then reintensifying the most radical features of modernism, in a second wave of the original movement. Revealingly, it was only in the 1950s that the centrist Spanish term *postmodernism* would resurface in the English-speaking world—after which it then was redefined as a "radical development" and became a generalized cultural phenomenon in the arts "around the world" over the next three decades.

The art critic Hal Foster pointed out in a now-famous anthology entitled *The Anti-Aesthetic: Essays on Postmodern Culture* (1983) that postmodernism emerged not just as a "new set of styles" that chronologically superceded those of modernism. Rather, some tendencies of postmodernism have often been another way of reengaging critically with the competing legacies of international modernism, thus being yet another subaltern or dissenting phase of modernism proper in the form of "resistant post-modernism." Hence, in the period since 1900, there has been a concerted move by advanced critical theorists both to redefine modernism along postcolonial lines and to resituate the historical trajectory of modernism worldwide in response to the "new world order" (without, in either case, denying the ongoing neocolonization now being sanctioned by Western imperialism). Two noteworthy reconsiderations of modernism from "outside the West" encapsulate this hotly contested historiography of modernism and postmodernism: *La Modernidad después de la postmodernidad* (1990; Modernity after postmodernity) by the Argentine author Nestor García Canclini and "Postmodernity as Modernity's Myth" (2001) by the Slovenian philosopher Slavoj Žižek.

Conclusions

In Latin America and elsewhere in the "postcolonial world," the confining, Eurocentric position of Greenberg was then more broadly reworked through critiques by such notable thinkers as Juan Acha of Peru, Gerardo Mosquera of Cuba, Partha Mitter of India, Rasheed Araen of Pakistan, Olu Oguibe of Nigeria, and Kobena Mercer of the United Kingdom. In all of these cases, and others, they reminded us that a "postcolonial" redefinition of modernism (along with modernity and modernization), one that is adequate to the demands of the historical present, has only now begun to be written.

See also **Aesthetics: Europe and the Americas; Arts: Overview; Modernity: Overview; Postmodernism.**

BIBLIOGRAPHY

Anderson, Perry. "Modernity and Revolution." *New Left Review* (March/April 1984): 96–113.

Ashton, Dore. *A Fable of Modern Art.* New York and London: Thames and Hudson, 1980.

Berman, Marshall. *All That Is Solid Melts Into Air: The Experience of Modernity.* New York: Simon and Schuster, 1982.

Buchloh, B. H. D., Serge Guilbaut, and David H. Solkin, ed. *Modernism and Modernity.* Halifax: Nova Scotia College of Art and Design, 1982.

Bürger, Peter. *The Decline of Modernism.* University Park: Pennsylvania State University Press, 1992.

Clark, T. J. *Farewell to an Idea: Episodes from a History of Modernism.* New Haven, Conn.: Yale University Press, 1999.

Craven, David. *Diego Rivera as Epic Modernist.* New York: G. K. Hall, 1997.

———. "The Latin American Origin of 'Alternative Modernism.'" In *The Third Text Reader,* edited by Rasheed Araeen, Sean Cubitt, and Ziauddin Sarder, 24–35. London and New York: Continuum, 2002.

Crow, Thomas. "Modernism and Mass Culture."1980. In his *Modern Art in the Common Culture.* New Haven, Conn.: Yale University Press, 1996.

Darío, Rubén. *Prosas profanas.* Madrid: Mundial, 1896.

Eder, Rita. "El muralismo mexicano: Modernismo y modernidad." In *Modernidad y modernización en el arte Mexicano,* edited by O. Debroise, 67–81. Mexico City: Museo Nacional de Arte, 1991.

Fernández, Justino. *Arte Moderno y Contemporareo de México.* 1952. Mexico City: Universidad Nacional Autónoma de México, 1994.

Foster, Hal, introduction. *The Anti-Aesthetic: Essays on Postmodern Culture.* Port Townsend, Wash.: Bay Press, 1983.

Frascina, Francis, ed. *Pollock and After: The Critical Debate.* 2nd ed. London: Routledge, 2000. Includes the essays "Avantgarde and Kitsch" and "Towards a Newer Laocoon" by Clement Greenberg.

García Canclini, Néstor. *Modernidad después de Postmodernidad.* Mexico City: Siglo XXI, 1990.

Greenberg, Clement. "Modernist Painting." 1965. Reprinted in *Modern Art and Modernism: A Critical Anthology,* edited by Francis Frascina and Charles Harrison, 5–10. New York: Harper and Row, 1982.

Harrison, Charles. "Modernism." In *Critical Terms in Art History,* edited by R. S. Nelson and R. Shiff, 142–155. Chicago: University of Chicago, 1996.

Henríque Ureña, Max. *Breve historia del modernismo.* Mexico City: Fondo de Cultural Económica, 1954.

Manrique, Jorge Alberto. "La vanguardia de Diego Rivera." *Diego Rivera Hoy,* 25–32. Mexico City: Palacio Nacional de Bellas Artes, 1986.

Mitter, Partha. "Modernism in India." In his *Indian Art,* 189–200. Oxford: Oxford University Press, 2001.

Morgan, Robert C. "The Delta of Modernism." In his *The End of the Art World*. New York: Allworth Press, 1998.

Poggioli, Renato. "Modernity and Modernism." In his *Teoria dell'arte d'avanguardia*, 216–220. 1962. Translated as *The Theory of the Avant-Garde* by Gerald Fitzgerald. Cambridge, Mass.: Harvard University, 1968. 216–220.

Rivera, Diego. *My Art, My Life*. Translated by Gladys March. New York: Dover Press, 1991.

———. *Textos de Arte*. Mexico City: Universidad Nacional Autónoma de México, 1996.

Siqueiros, David Alfaro. "3 llamamientos . . ." *Vida-Americana: Revista Norte, Centro y Sud-Americana de Vanguardia* 1, no. 1 (May 1921): 2–3.

Williams, Raymond. *The Politics of Modernism: Against the New Conformists*. London and New York: Verso, 1989.

Žižek, Slavoj. "Postmodernity as Modernity's Myth." *Polygraph* no. 13 (2001): 39–58.

David Craven

MODERNITY.

This entry includes three subentries:

Overview
Africa
East Asia

OVERVIEW

Modernity is best understood as a condition, rather than as the designation for some particular period of time. Aspects of the modern condition can arise at any time and place, but they are most generally associated with historical trends arising out of Cartesian philosophy, industrial capitalism, revolutionary politics, and the cultural changes of the turn of the nineteenth century. The main lesson to be learned from the postmodernism of the late twentieth century is that the tensions of modernity are still with us.

Of course, the term *modern* has narrower uses in particular fields of human endeavor, including especially art and architecture. The use of the term in the sense discussed here, as a syndrome of conditions associated with the modern mode of human life, is relatively recent. The French revolutionaries, for example, did not think of themselves as modern. When characterizing the more forward-thinking aspects of his time, the philosopher Immanuel Kant (1724–1804) did not call them modern or even enlightened, but described the late eighteenth century as undergoing a process of enlightenment. Classically, the term *modern* contrasts the present day as opposed to some time in the past, or more specifically, it contrasts ancient times with the modern times subsequent to them, as in Bernard of Chartres's famous twelfth-century description of moderns as dwarves sitting on the shoulders of giants. *Modern* may also apply as an adjective denoting novelty, as in the phrase "modern conveniences."

From a general point of view, however, modernity should be understood as a condition, mentality, or syndrome presenting characteristic dilemmas to human beings that remain both defining and unresolvable. Elements of the modern condition include rejection of traditional authority, a progressive rather than cyclical notion of time, individual and collective emancipation, a broadly empiricist orientation toward understanding the world, and what John Dryzek has called a Promethean outlook that regards all difficulties as technical problems to be mastered through human endeavor. As a heuristic, contrasts with unmodern conditions may be useful, as in Jürgen Habermas's point that "before the French Revolution, before the workers' movements in Europe, before the spread of formal secondary education, before the feminist movement . . . the life of an individual woman or man had less worth—not regarded from our own point of view, of course, but from the contemporary perspective" (p. 106). The modern horrors of the twentieth century, however, should cause one to be careful to apply these distinctions to elements of human practice, rather than to specific individuals or groups. The impulse to define some people along a premodern/modern axis, itself an outgrowth of characteristically modern impulses toward rational social management, should be resisted, whether the people are described as characteristically modern, as Richard Wagner said of the Jews, or as characteristically premodern, as European colonists considered aboriginal residents of the New World. The tension in this very practice of defining modernity in people and practices, with its disparate results ranging from attempted extermination to processes of emancipation, respectively, reveals the inescapably dialectical nature of the modern condition.

Indeed, an accelerated and socially powerful process of conceptual change constitutes a key element of the modern condition. Reinhart Koselleck has argued that in modernity, "political and social concepts become the navigational instruments of the changing movement of history. They do not only indicate or record given facts. They themselves become factors in the formation of consciousness and the control of behavior" (p. 129). Koselleck illustrates this process with the quintessentially modern concept of emancipation: once the reflexive verb, to emancipate oneself, gained currency beyond its origins among philosophers and literati and began to be used widely among participants in the revolutionary politics of late-eighteenth-century France, it became linguistically impossible, as it were, to defend the institutions of the Old Regime. The linguistic turn in philosophy and social theory attests to the modern role of language as constituting experience itself. Martin Heidegger (1889–1976) argued that language illuminates specific, comprehensive modes of being in the world; Hans-Georg Gadamer (1900–2002) later refined this idea with the idea that human beings move within "horizons" of linguistic prejudgments. Philosophers as different as Habermas, Ludwig Wittgenstein, and Hannah Arendt have explored the potential for commonalities in language usage to overcome seemingly fundamental barriers among human beings.

Modern theorists do not agree about the role played by historical subjects in effecting the conceptual changes that seem to drive a constantly evolving public sphere. Whereas Georg Wilhelm Friedrich Hegel (1770–1831) spoke abstractly of the progress of *Geist* (mind, consciousness, spirit) and Michel Foucault (1926–1984) revealed the socially constructed nature of the concepts and practices that constrain human beings, Karl Marx (1818–1883) and his followers argued that false consciousness could be overcome, while Sigmund Freud

(1856–1939) and his successors sought to overcome the damage done to individual mental health by modern social pressures through psychoanalysis. Some lines of modern argument are characterized by progressive optimism regarding the power of enlightened human reason, once freed from the shackles of tradition, to remake society according to rational principles. Jeremy Bentham (1748–1832) and his fellow utilitarians, for example, supported a slate of social reform programs, including birth control and humane treatment of prisoners, based on their application of the principle of the greatest happiness for the greatest number to society at large. In another indication of the dialectical tensions inherent in modernity, Bentham's rationalist vision of prison reform, originally intended to redeem the inherent worth and social value of every individual, even those abandoned to the horrors of the premodern prisonhouse, has evolved, as Foucault has demonstrated, into a near-totalitarian vision of social control over the resisting individual. Bentham's modern design for a prison, the "panopticon," has become the blueprint for the present-day "supermax" vision not of rehabilitation, but of central control.

Alexis de Tocqueville's (1805–1859) seminal thinking about this dynamic between modern egalitarian democracy and quasi-despotic central control happened to begin with a study of the early-nineteenth-century American prison system, which in Pennsylvania and New York exemplified Benthamite reformist principles. In *Democracy in America,* Tocqueville warned his fellow Europeans that democratic equality was not a passing fad, that although it broadened opportunities for the masses, it threatened national and individual greatness, and that without a strong network of intermediate institutions, democracy was likely to resolve into centralized administrative despotism. Tocqueville's dystopian vision contrasts with Bentham's progressivist faith in reason's beneficence: modern individuals in American democracy may be free of the old tyrannies of class and king, but they are subject to new forms of despotism rooted in their very freedoms. Like John Stuart Mill (1806–1873), Tocqueville argued that modern social mobility requires individuals to devote most of their energy to economic well-being, to the exclusion of more noble pursuits. Worse, without the traditional intermediaries of the estates checking the central power of the state, democracies will tend toward ever more powerful government. As modern individuals torn by accelerating social pressures become alienated from their premodern social support systems, they are vulnerable to domination by "an immense tutelary power . . . which alone takes charge of assuring their enjoyments and watching over their fate. It is absolute, detailed, regular, far-seeing, and mild. It would resemble paternal power if, like that, it had for its object to prepare men for manhood, but on the contrary, it seeks only to keep them fixed irrevocably in childhood . . . can it not take away from them entirely the trouble of thinking and the pain of living?" (p. 693).

What Habermas calls the "enlightenment project" thus doubles back on itself. Whereas for Kant, republican government (that is, government responsible to the people) forms an essential part of the emancipation of human beings to autonomy, for Tocqueville this same institution could lead to autonomy's opposite, to the infantilization of the population under a paternal power far worse than any premodern royalist

opposed by the likes of John Locke and Thomas Jefferson. Jean-Jacques Rousseau (1712–1778) had identified this irony of modernity already in the eighteenth century. In his first *Discourse* he outlines the many sacrifices human beings have had to make to become modern, including even the possibility of authentic relations with each other. However, for Rousseau there is no going back: modern consciousness, once achieved, cannot be forgotten but must enable modern human beings to devise new institutions for achieving a modern kind of authenticity. Similarly, the English poet William Wordsworth (1770–1850) complained in an 1807 sonnet of the loss of authentic relations among newly rational modern human beings:

> The world is too much with us; late and soon,
> Getting and spending, we lay waste our powers:
> Little we see in Nature that is ours;
> We have given our hearts away, a sordid boon!
> The Sea that bares her bosom to the moon;
> The winds that will be howling at all hours,
> And are up-gathered now like sleeping flowers;
> For this, for everything, we are out of tune;
> It moves us not. —Great God! I'd rather be
> A Pagan suckled in a creed outworn;
> So might I, standing on this pleasant lea,
> Have glimpses that would make me less forlorn;
> Have sight of Proteus rising from the sea;
> Or hear old Triton blow his wreathèd horn.
> (Sonnet No. 18).

The loss of the old gods, of traditional ways and of the comforts of an unquestionable worldview worried Wordsworth, the German poet Friedrich Hölderlin (1770–1843), and many others, but presented an opportunity to those modern thinkers seeking to replace the Old Regime with rational modes of human being. Chief among these were Marx and Engels, who noted with pleasure that in modern life "all fixed, fast-frozen relations, with their train of ancient and venerable prejudices and opinions, are swept away, all new-formed ones become antiquated before they can ossify. All that is solid melts into air, all that is holy is profaned, and man is at last compelled to face with sober senses, his real conditions of life, and his relations with his kind" (p. 68). Marx's optimism was undergirded by his faith in the power of reason; he expects human "sober senses" to point out the direction to progress. Nietzsche has a similar diagnosis of the origins of contemporary institutions in the interests of the few, but no accompanying expectation that the application of modern human reason can end this dynamic:

> With the aid of such images and procedures [as flaying and quartering criminals], man was eventually able to retain five or six "I-don't-want-to's" in his memory, in connection with which a *promise* had been made, in order to enjoy the advantages of society—and there you are! With the aid of this sort of memory, people finally came to "reason"! —Ah, reason, solemnity, mastering of emotions, this really dismal thing called reflection, all these privileges and splendors man has: what a price had to be paid for them! how much blood and horror lies at the basis of all "good things"! (p. 42)

Faced with the failure of received ideas, and without the optimistic view that modern reason could replace previous illegitimate modes of life with authentic modes, Nietzsche calls on (at least some) modern human beings to embrace the disorientation that comes with recognition of the modern condition, and to create their own sets of values.

Such a solution has obvious shortcomings when it comes to social coordination. Most observers of the collapse of traditional values felt less exhilarated than paralyzed, waiting for the inevitable new mode of collective human being. The Irish poet Yeats, in his 1921 work "The Second Coming," an exquisitely modern poem, both formally and in its content, worries thus:

> Turning and turning in the widening gyre
> The falcon cannot hear the falconer;
> Things fall apart; the centre cannot hold;
> Mere anarchy is loosed upon the world,
> The blood-dimmed tide is loosed, and everywhere
> The ceremony of innocence is drowned;
> The best lack all conviction, while the worst
> Are full of passionate intensity.
>
> Surely some revelation is at hand;
> Surely the Second Coming is at hand.
> The Second Coming! Hardly are those words out
> When a vast image out of *Spiritus Mundi*
> Troubles my sight: somewhere in sands of the desert
> A shape with lion body and the head of a man,
> A gaze blank and pitiless as the sun,
> Is moving its slow thighs, while all about it
> Reel shadows of the indignant desert birds.
> The darkness drops again; but now I know
> That twenty centuries of stony sleep
> Were vexed to nightmare by a rocking cradle,
> And what rough beast, its hour come round at last,
> Slouches towards Bethlehem to be born?

The quintessentially modern poem depends on a fundamentally premodern concept of time: for Yeats, time is not progressive, but cyclical. Modernity as a human condition is characterized by such ironies: as democratic politics empowers the subject, social scientific research demonstrates the subject's disempowerment; as modern political thought looks to abstraction to resolve premodern injustices, that most particular institution of the national state is the main agent against them; as modern science enables increasing technical mastery of nature, it simultaneously demonstrates nature's mastery over individuals.

Small wonder, then, that antimodern movements of nearly infinite variety have sprung up around the globe in recent years. Responding to the arguments of Max Horkheimer, Theodor Adorno, and many others sympathetic to the critique of modernity, Habermas has argued that

> only further enlightenment . . . has grown from the devastation of enlightenment. . . . it is only through reason

that we can determine the limits of our rationality. *This* is the fundamental figure of Kantian thought that was definitive for modernity. And modernity can't just be peeled off like a dirty shirt. It's in our skin. We find ourselves in a condition of modern life: we didn't freely choose it; it is existentially unavoidable. But for the opened eyes of modernity, this condition also implies a challenge, and not just a disaster. (p. 94)

See also **Democracy; Enlightenment; Modernism; Public Sphere; Utilitarianism.**

BIBLIOGRAPHY

Benjamin, Walter. *Illuminations: Essays and Reflections.* Edited and with an introduction by Hannah Arendt. New York: Schocken Books, 1969.

Berman, Marshall. *All That Is Solid Melts into Air: The Experience of Modernity.* New York: Simon and Schuster, 1982.

Foucault, Michel. *Discipline and Punish: The Birth of the Prison.* Translated by Alan Sheridan. New York: Vintage, 1979.

Freud, Sigmund. *Civilization and Its Discontents.* Translated and edited by James Strachey. New York: Norton, 1989.

Habermas, Jürgen. *The Past as Future.* Translated and edited by Max Pensky. Lincoln and London: University of Nebraska Press, 1994.

Horkheimer, Max, and Theodor Adorno. *Dialectic of Enlightenment.* Translated by John Cumming. New York: Continuum, 1989.

Kant, Immanuel. "An Answer to the Question: What Is Enlightenment?" In *Practical Philosophy,* edited by Mary Gregor. New York: Cambridge University Press, 1996.

Koselleck, Reinhart. *The Practice of Conceptual History: Timing History, Spacing Concepts.* Translated by Todd Samuel Presner and others. Stanford, Calif.: Stanford University Press, 2002.

Marx, Karl, and Friedrich Engels. *The Communist Manifesto.* Edited by John E. Toews. Boston: Bedford/St. Martins, 1999.

Nietzsche, Friedrich. *On the Genealogy of Morality.* Edited by Keith Ansell-Pearson. Translated by Carol Diethe. New York: Cambridge University Press, 1994.

Tocqueville, Alexis de. *Democracy in America.* Translated by Harvey C. Mansfield and Delba Winthrop. Chicago: University of Chicago Press, 2000.

Wordsworth, William. *The Complete Poetical Works.* London: Macmillan, 1888.

Elisabeth Ellis

AFRICA

The debates and controversies over modernity, from its origins in sixteenth- and seventeenth-century western Europe to the various sites of its deployment following the formation of colonial empires, have given rise to an abundance of literature. Non-Western societies, by and large, in the formation of their cultural, political, economic, and social identities and their reactions to it, have appropriated or not, accommodated or not, resisted or not, in many different ways, what is usually referred to as the project of modernity (or modernization). Associated at first with colonization, and then with independence, modernity involves an understanding of several issues connected with modes of thought, action, and belief, the legitimacy and effectiveness of which are fed by absolute faith in human progress, thanks to the power of science and technology. This creative tension between a way of being (the philosophical dimension of modernity) and of acting (modernization, which involves concrete advances in the realms of social and economic, political and legal, military and health policy, with the aim of transforming agrarian peoples and non-Western communities into urban, industrial societies) is at the heart of the dispute between the partisans and opponents of an understanding of modernity as the exclusive sign of civilization, established and defined by Europe.

The philosopher Jürgen Habermas, supported by the arguments of Max Weber, established a strong internal link between modernity and Western rationalism. This led to the erosion of religious concepts and the emergence in Europe of a secular culture via both laicization and modernization. Habermas suggests that the concept of modernization proposed in the 1950s comprises a set of cumulative procedures that reinforce one another, such as the capitalization and mobilization of resources, the development of the forces of production, increasing productivity of workers, establishment of political power and formation of national identities, dissemination of the notion of the right to political participation, the growth of forms of urban life, public education, and the secularization of values and norms.

However, in the historical, anthropological, and sociological literature, the terms *modernity, modernization,* and, occasionally, *liberalism* are often interchangeable. Opposing the idea of modernity as a strictly European development set forth by Habermas is the approach of numerous authors who are non-European or who work on the periphery of non-European societies. They emphasize its pluralistic character and its responsiveness to local environments. Benjamin Schwartz, a scholar examining Chinese history, stresses two revealing signs of the ambiguous nature of modernity: first, the crises, shocks, and convulsions that have destabilized Western societies and have strongly influenced and redefined Western modernity, both in terms of its basic content and its having been put to the test nationally during and after World War I; and the multiple versions of modernity, in particular the Soviet Marxist version. Two other fundamental issues should be considered: Modernity is a preoccupation of intellectuals, centered on questions of tradition and development, with a focus on the description and understanding of certain practical procedures and ways of thinking and feeling; when modernity leaves the realm of the intellectuals and takes on the aspect of modernization, it involves practical problems of economic development. Modernity thus became a word connoting order and mobilization, a goal to work toward. Schwartz invites us to proceed by a double movement: first, accepting that modernity does not refer to a simple entity or to a homogeneous admixture of manifestations, practices, or modes of thought, neither in its place of origin nor in non-European cultures. And similarly, it is not any kind of complete or synthetic whole; rather, it is crossed with horizontal tensions and conflicts "among the various currents and countercurrents of the modern world" (Schwartz, p. 54). It is therefore necessary to pay close attention to the lively debates among the

intellectuals in their specific historical context. In fact, for intellectuals in developing nations, in China at the beginning of the twentieth century, or in areas under colonial domination in Asia and Africa, the essential concern is to find the resources indispensable to the preservation of a community identity in their complex relationships to the past, in their traditions, and in the "European canon." In the case of Africa, novelists have tried to present these clashing trajectories, as exemplified by Cheikh Hamidou Kane in *L'aventure ambiguë* (English trans., *Ambiguous Adventure*) and Laye Camara in *L'enfant noir* (1954; English trans., *The Dark Child*).

Signs of Modernity

The signs of modernity are considered here together, from the historical circumstances of European nations' global colonial expansion, and from the indigenous reading of the signs of this economic, political, and cultural hegemony that are expressed by the project of the civilizing mission. The civilizing mission rests on the promise of universal reason and emancipation that, prompted by the philosophers of the Enlightenment, is associated with modernity, progress, and the powerful capacity for destruction possessed by irrational and unreasonable practices, in the struggle between science and rationality on the one hand, and faith and religion on the other. According to P. Selinow, there are three pillars supporting this modernity: capitalism, analyzed by Karl Marx; bureaucracy, analyzed by Max Weber; and the norms, forms, and procedural regulations of modern society studied by Michel Foucault. In addition to this definition of modernity as a unique moment in the history of Western civilization, of which the principal signs are the scientific and technological progress of the industrial revolution and the economic and social transformations of capitalism, there is an approach that envisages modernity as an aesthetic concept. Though limited, this approach may help us trace the many changing ways in which non-Western societies have tried to understand, appropriate, resist, or define the efforts at modernization as they have been presented or understood. This is the case, for example, of Chinese literature, which was dominated in the first half of the twentieth century by an obsession with the notion that China was afflicted with a spiritual malady that created a break between tradition and modernity. Tradition was regarded as the source of the Chinese malady, and modernity was seen by intellectuals as a revolt against tradition and as a possible source of new solutions.

To this dichotomy of tradition/modernity one can add others, such as agrarian/industrial, authority/liberty, and prescientific thought/scientific thought. The case of China, as with Bengali intellectuals confronted with colonial domination by the British, illustrates the adoption and utilization of the language and categories available in (or proposed by) the "European canon" in order to assimilate, evaluate, select, and/or reject the new ideas from the West—that is, in establishing a correlation between the material gains and progress associated with the European presence and the moral decadence of indigenous sociability, civility, and religiosity.

Whereas Europeans view the history of modernity as a progressive triumph of Enlightenment ideas, in non-Western societies it is seen as beginning with colonial conquest, which is now regarded as being part of the same movement in enlightened places and in regions of total darkness.

Colonial Modernities

There are two important issues in the development of colonial modernities: the interpretation of manifestations of modernity in the process of imperial expansion, on the one hand, and the place assigned to indigenous people in the colonial enterprise, on the other. Regarding the former, authors such as C. L. R. James focus on the modernity of slavery in the Atlantic economies at the beginning of the modern period; similarly, others suggest that the Indian peasant is not an anachronism in a modernized colonial world but a veritable contemporary of colonialism, an indispensable member of modernity. The complicity between colonial history and modernity is precisely the cause of the circumstances underlying the statement, "The same historical process that has taught us the value of modernity has also made us the victims of modernity" (Chatterjee, pp. 8–9). This strong correlation has its origin in numerous attempts to reinterpret the manifestations of modernity from indigenous impressions of it, by trying to jettison certain of these signs while recognizing the revisionist efforts to which it is heavily subjected in non-Western societies. Such a perspective is notably more apparent in studies on India and China than in those on Africa. One observes in the former an abundance of qualifications that result from opposing the idea of modernity as a strictly European development and affirming it as a multivalent phenomenon. Partha Chatterjee provides the best insight on this point in his definition of an Indian (or rather, Bengali) modernity as "our modernity."

The many authors who have joined this debate after Chatterjee emphasize the ways in which non-Western societies remake modernity in their own images, revising rationality and capitalism by transforming general formulas and formulations in terms of their own interests, ideals, and enterprises—political, economic, and social. It is essential to recognize that in the case of Africa, the debate is less intense today than it has been. It does not necessarily take the same theoretical and epistemological approaches that color the writings in the social sciences on India and China, to give just two examples. It has always been presented as a double figure, each of which takes various forms, the pair tradition/modernity and the demands, expectations, and aspirations of development through the economic and social compensation by modern, industrial Europe. This figure, which does not always reflect democratic structures, secularism, or equality between the sexes, among other things, is part of a series of attempts to transform African societies by "modernizing bureaucrats" in the final phase of colonial domination. In Africa and among blacks in general, as has already been mentioned, writers and cultural critics—more than historians and social scientists—have drawn connections between Africa and Europe, whether in terms of conflict (Aimé Césaire, Camara Laye, and Cheikh Hamidou Kane) or a fruitful dialogue (Léopold Sédar Senghor and Ousmane Socé Diop). Only one author, Cheikh Anta Diop, a Senegalese philosopher, taking a brutal, ironic approach, reverses this problematic double. He has made a name for himself as a radical dissident and

has struggled to rethink and revise the genealogy of modernity to counter the notion of it as a strictly European development. On the contrary, he asserts, Europe has evolved under the aegis of Africa; it became rational by following the example and teachings of Africa, the mother of civilizations and the originator of modernity, which emerged along the banks of the Nile during the time of the Egyptian pharaohs.

This revision of the history of human rationality erases the boundary between traditional African societies and modern European societies. At the least, the idea of extreme difference between the two is interpreted as an ideological strategy for establishing the mission of civilizing native populations and the enterprises of colonization. By reintroducing Africa as a participant in the development of rationality and modernity, Cheikh Anta Diop reconfirms Africa as producer and consumer of modernity. Not many other African authors share his view, although it has been embraced by partisans of Afrocentrism, especially in the United States. On the contrary, at the heart of the debates, which intensified during the years of nationalism—after World War II to the 1970s—in the era of globalization, the crucial question is how to interpret the complex and paradoxical relationship between culture and modernization. At issue are the conflict-ridden associations between modernity and colonial cultures and violence, and the cultural and psychological renaissance that accompanied the founding of postcolonial nations and states. Two historians, J. F. A. Ajayi and Jacqueline Ki-Zerbo, have responded to this in the same way. Ajayi suggests that the colonial enterprise failed in its desire to erase the African past, having never succeeded in changing the path of African history or the strength and prevalence of African initiative. Ki-Zerbo warns against the assimilation and appropriation of the history and culture of others, which cannot provide any guarantee of success in terms of development and modernization. Among the novelists, Kane emphasizes the ambiguity of the venture. The Grande Royale, who argues for the education of the young people of the kingdom of Diallobés against his brother, the king and religious leader of the community, gives two reasons: to understand why the colonizers, even though they were in the wrong, were able to defeat them; and to enable his people to gain technological expertise. His reading considers that neither morals nor the values of authenticity can save one from domination. The experience at school and university of Samba Diallo, the book's main character, and his delving into the Koran and texts by the philosophers of the Enlightenment do not open any doors to him other than those of solitude and death, which sanctions failure, and of assimilation and hybridization. Kane is even more explicit in his theoretical texts.

In contrast, Socé Diop, in his novel *Karim* (1935), relates with gusto the metamorphoses of the main character, Karim, who assumes multiple identities, including an accountant trained at a French school, a Senegalese Muslim from Saint-Louis (the oldest French colonial settlement in Africa) educated in the traditions of Islam and the values of the Wolof aristocracy, a dancer and charmer cognizant of urban opportunities and colonial chances. For each identity, Diop gives Karim a corresponding clothing style, dance steps, a manner of being and acting that are superimposed with close attention to French,

African, and Islamic teachings and practices on issues of aesthetics and rhythm, dress, love, and sex. Karim represents the celebration of a hybrid form of being, rejecting the draconian choice that would have lethal consequences for the "ambiguous adventure." The approach taken by Socé Diop is shared by "the translators of colonial modernity" analyzed by Simon Gikandi.

Gikandi describes superbly the dilemma of constructing an indigenous culture that embraces the colonial political economy both internally and externally, and examines the production of colonial modernity through a never-ending negotiation between the desire to maintain the integrity and autonomy of colonized societies and the willingness to face up to the European presence and its political economy (pp. 23–41). Taking as an example the kingdom of Buganda (today the nation of Uganda), he shows how the elite adopts Christianity as a key element in developing a certain modernity, regarded as one way of participating in the colonial culture. Similar characteristics detected and analyzed by Gikandi, beginning with the account of the voyage of Ham Mukasa (*Uganda's Katikiro in England*) are found in the ethnographic and religious writings of David Boilat and in the militant intervention of Augustin Diamacoune Senghor, leader of Senegal's Casamance independence movement, who used the colonial culture to "develop"—in the photographic sense—indigenous moral values and religious beliefs. Through these different figures, people involved in such causes became interested in reorienting the ways of expressing and of satisfying the desires generated by colonial modernity toward indigenous ends. They tried in various ways to alter the very nature of the "colonial canon" by infusing it with their voices, passions, and anxieties, so that it would present them not as objects of European intervention but as the subjects of their own cultural destiny (Gikandi, in Mukasa's *Uganda's Katikiro*, p. 21).

This way of thinking led to the perception of the dual nature of tradition and the realities it conceals, involving both a constant reinvention of the colonial canon and an ever-shifting horizon due to the ceaseless work of translation, appropriation, and selection. By means of this work, the colonial experience is turned into an indigenous opportunity. The only question that troubles the carriers or translators of modernity is that of defining the colonial culture of modernity (including Christianity) in isolation from the "enlightenment" of the Christian message and colonial modernity, from the repressive, controlling mechanism of political power, and from its very authoritarian economic and cultural manifestations.

To understand the African debate on modernity is, in large measure, to identify the different ways in which the "package" (the concept and the different constructions that it has given rise to) and the numerous realities that it conceals have circulated in Africa, in various historical circumstances. The latter have been shaped by methods of appropriation, forms of opposition, and resistance, but perhaps still more fundamentally by demands and expectations regarding what is understood or proposed by the term. It still has to be made clear, as James Ferguson has suggested, that this modernity has a concrete meaning, reflecting subdivisions, pensions, and family allowances. The African modernity that he analyzes was a preoccupation for

certain groups in colonial and postcolonial African societies: political leaders, union leaders, students, specialists as well as workers in economic development. Modernity thus became synonymous with development and material progress.

This reading of the term *modernity* subscribes to the colonial objective of impeding Africa's modernity; especially after World War I, restrictions imposed by colonial authorities led to the politics of retribalization, assimilation, and the containment of the "carriers of modernity." The colonialists tried to hold them back by claiming all the fruits—material, cultural, spiritual, economic, and political. On this question, the case of the Tsawana people, studied by Jean and John Comaroff, demonstrates the perpetual production of a modernity that is a constant source of tensions between, on the one hand, the adoption of the material elements of colonial culture (clothing, architectural styles, sanitation) and, on the other hand, their consequences under the appearance of new forms of individuation that progressively threaten the customs of the community, especially spiritual and therapeutic traditions. According to the Comaroffs, it is precisely the shock between missionary will and the processes of resistance, selection, and alteration that the Tsawana people go through, successively or simultaneously, that has created modernity. It derives in some way from what the West and the colonial enterprise call *modern*, the first manifestation of which was the mission to civilize the native peoples, and the last of which was modernization. These have linked the colonial enterprise and the nationalist struggle and its pursuit of development and achieving parity with Western economies. The emblems of the colonial enterprise are roads, commerce, and sanitation; the nationalist emblems are schools, community clinics, and electricity.

Among the best available analyses of colonial modernity are the groundbreaking studies by two experts on the French colonial empire, Louis-Hubert Lyautey (1854–1934) and Joseph-Simon Gallieni (1849–1916), the former on Morocco and Indochina, the latter on the Sudan and Madagascar. According to Paul Rabinow, the oscillation between the extremes of colonial modernization and continuing poverty within a framework of authenticity is not an exclusive characteristic of the autochthonous elite of African colonial societies. Gallieni, for example, established a definitive correspondence between pacification and modernity. In contrast to Lyautey's cultural relativism, he was a universalist. He did not by any means imagine that one might regard the lack of sanitation and the nondistinction among domestic space, work space, and livestock pen as anything other than signs of a lack of civilization. For him, "the sign of civilization was a busy road; the sign of modernity was hygiene" (Rabinow, pp. 149–150). Here, the meaning of modernity is, by colonial logic, constructed around elements such as security, communications lines, agriculture, commerce, and population growth.

It is difficult to determine where this chaotic journey will end. The paths and detours that it has taken reflect the great difficulty involved in making sense of a concept that is so prevalent in everyday conversations and in philosophical, political, moral, aesthetic, and cultural analyses, and increasingly in the economic realm as well. The questions regarding the genealogy of the concept of modernity and its different forms, from its initial appearance to its commonplace deployment and the subsequent debates about it, have provoked numerous examinations of its heuristic value, its effects in terms of status in the narrative and scientific fields, its limits, possibility of application, and the different manipulations that it offers to those who lay claim to it, adapt it, or reject it. As much as the imaginations it recaptures, the historical traces it carries, the uses and abuses it has undergone, the possible or probable futures that one accords it partake of different modes of reference. And it is precisely for that reason that no one challenges it for having lost, during this journey, its capacities for setting in order or disorder realities, as much descriptive as figurative. For others, despite its epistemological and narrative weaknesses, reflecting a quasi-impossibility of relating other histories and conveying other circumstances, modernity is simultaneously a horizon line, a point of anchorage, a mode of being, and a means of constructing a geography of people, of cultures, of aesthetic forms. It is probably this plasticity that makes it what it is, always different, always debated, as expected, plural and unstable, between, on the one hand, European modernity and its desire to remake the world in its image or according to its dictates, and, on the other hand, the never-ending processes of rewriting, reinterpreting, and/or retreating from other societies.

See also **Colonialism; Modernity: Overview; Nationalism; Postcolonial Studies.**

BIBLIOGRAPHY
Ajayi, J. F. A. "Colonialism: An Episode in African History." In *Colonialism in Africa*, edited by L. H. Gann and Peter Duignan. 5 vols. Cambridge, U.K.: Cambridge University Press, 1969–1975.
Appadurai, Arjun. *Modernity at Large: Cultural Dimensions of Globalization.* Minneapolis: University of Minnesota Press, 1996.
Boilat, David. *Esquisses Sénégalaises.* 1853. Reprint, Paris: Karthala, 1984.
Calinescu, Matei. *Faces of Modernity: Avant-garde, Decadence, Kitsch.* Bloomington: Indiana University Press, 1977.
Camara, Laye. *The Dark Child.* Translated by James Kirkup and Ernest Jones. New York: Farrar, Straus, and Giroux, 1969.
Chakrabarty, Dipesh. *Habitations of Modernity. Essays in the Wake of Subaltern Studies.* Chicago: University of Chicago Press, 2002.
Chatterjee, Partha. *Our Modernity.* Dakar: Codesria, 1997.
Comaroff, Jean, and John L. Comaroff. *Of Revelation and Revolution.* Vol. 2: *The Dialectics of Modernity on a South African Frontier.* Chicago: University of Chicago Press, 1997.
———, eds. *Modernity and Its Malcontents. Ritual and Power in Postcolonial Africa.* Chicago: University of Chicago Press, 1993
Diop, Cheikh Anta. *Nations nègres et culture: De l'antiquité nègre égyptienne aux problèmes culturels de l'Afrique noire d'aujourd'hui.* Paris: Présence Africaine, 1955.
Diouf, Mamadou. *Histoire du Sénégal: Le modèle islamo-wolof et ses périphéries..* Paris: Maisonneuve and Larose, 2001.
Ferguson, James. *Expectations of Modernity: Myths and Meanings of Urban Life on The Zambian Copperbelt.* Berkeley: University of California Press, 1999.
Giddens, Anthony. *The Consequences of Modernity.* Stanford, Calif.: Stanford University Press, 1990.
Gikandi, Simon. *Maps of Englishness: Writing Identity in the Culture of Colonialism.* New York: Columbia University Press, 1996.
Habermas, Jürgen. *Le Discours Philosophique de la Modernité.* Paris: Gallimard, 1988.
Hall, Stuart. "A Conversation with Stuart Hall." *Journal of the International Institute* (fall 1999): 15.
Kane, Cheikh Hamidou. *Ambiguous Adventure.* Translated by Katherine Woods. London: Heinemann, 1972.
Kelly, J. "Alternative Modernities to 'Modernity': Getting Out of the Sublime Modernist." In *Critically Modern: Alternatives, Alterities, Anthropologies,* edited by Bruce M. Hauft. Bloomington: Indiana University Press, 2002.
Lee, Leo Ou-fan. "The Quest for Modernity, 1895–1927." In *An Intellectual History of China,* edited by Merle Goldman and Lee Ou-fan Lee. Cambridge, U.K.: Cambridge University Press, 2002.
Mitchell, Timothy, ed.. *Questions of Modernity.* Minneapolis: University of Minnesota Press, 2000.
Mukasa, Ham. *Uganda's Katikiro in England.* With notes and an introduction by Simon Gikandi. Manchester, U.K.: Manchester University Press, 1998.
Ong, A. "Anthropology, China and Modernities: The Geopolitics of Cultural Knowledge."In *The Future of Anthropological Knowledge,* edited by Henrietta L. Moore. London and New York: Routledge, 1996.
Rabinow, Paul. *French Modern. Norms and Forms of the Social Environment.* Reprint, Chicago, University of Chicago Press, 1995.
Schwartz, Benjamin I. *China and Other Matters.* Cambridge, Mass.: Harvard University Press, 1996.

Mamadou Diouf

EAST ASIA

Modernity (*kindaisei* in Japanese, and *xiandaixing* in Chinese) is a relatively recent term in the intellectual vocabulary of East Asia, becoming current only after World War II. Differing conceptions of "the modern" start much earlier, when terms long available in both languages acquired new connotations, as the region felt the impact of the West. The classical Chinese *jin* (close, nearby) provided the root for the Japanese *kinsei,* or "recent epoch," popularized in the sense of "modern period" by translations of European works in Meiji time. It was soon replaced by *kindai* to free Buddhist implications in *sei.* These came to China as loanwords *jinshi* and *jindai,* but gave way to *xiandai* in the early 1920s, indicating not "recent" but "present" age. Although intellectual exchange between the two countries was intense after the Opium War (1840–1842), ideas relating to the "modern" in fact developed along distinctive trajectories.

At the same time, certain shared features have been unmistakable. The notion of the modern, coming to the region accompanied by the military violence of Western imperialism, acquired a strongly spatial, not just temporal, force. It meant learning from the West in both enlightenment and material advance, and struggling for equal position with the West in national, cultural, and intellectual terms. This implied an inevitable element of borrowing or imitation, bringing with it anxieties of collective identity. Moreover, the very process of modernization brought unintended—or even uncontrollable—changes to social life, turning "modernity" into part of an unprecedented daily experience that demanded articulation. Consequently, hard claimed universal ideas have been constantly challenged by local experience, and the relation between universal aspiration and particular attributes is never stable. These were issues that have preoccupied thinkers in the region down to the present.

Civilization and Enlightenment: Meiji Japan (1868–1912)

The Meiji Restoration set the stage for the first major bid of modernization. The driving force behind the program was the determination to secure *fukoky kyōhei*—rich country, strong army. But Meiji culture contained other aspirations as well. The most popular catchwords of the early Meiji years—*bunmei kaika*, "civilization and enlightenment"—were significantly different. The most forceful crusader for them was the prolific writer Fukuzawa Yukichi (1835–1901), who coined the term *bunmei* itself. His books *Seiyō Jijō* (1866–1870; Conditions in the West, 3 vols.) and *Bunmeiron no gairyaku* (1876; Outline of a theory of civilization) sold numerous copies. According to Fukuzawa, "civilization can be defined as that which advances man's knowledge and virtue" with an open future; presently, Japan was only "semideveloped" (*hankai*), compared to Europe and the United States, a condition that defined the task in hand. Contrasting East and West, he wrote that "there must be some fundamental difference in the education of the Western and Eastern peoples. In the education of the East, so often saturated with Confucian teaching, I find two points lacking: that is to say, the lack of studies in 'number and reason' [science] in material culture, and the lack of the idea of independence in the spiritual culture" (*The Autobiography of Fukuzawa Yukichi*).

Fukuzawa's original teaching, influenced by John Stuart Mill (1806–1873), emphasized the values of personal independence and a disciplined but free individuality as bases for a modern society, and the need for public diversity of viewpoints. However his commitment to enlighten the "uncivilized" led him to embrace policies of Japanese imperial expansion that followed European and American examples. Coining the term *datsua nyūō* (de-Asianization and joining Europe), he said that "our country cannot afford to wait for the enlightenment of our neighbors and to co-operate in building Asia up. Rather, we should leave their ranks to join the camp of the civilized countries of the West" ("Datsua ron," 1885, On de-Asianization). By the end of his life, Fukuzawa had abandoned his earlier support for "people's rights" and expressed boundless enthusiasm at Japan's military victory over China.

In 1886, the twenty-three-year-old Tokutomi Soho (1863–1957) published his hugely successful *Shōrai no Nihon* (The future Japan). Announcing that "the democratic trend is the world trend," the book conveyed a new and more intense sense of the pace of modernity and the ceaseless transformations it would require of his countrymen. "The future of reform is reform, but what sort of reform will it be? What sort of reform should it be? After the deluge comes the deluge. But what sort of deluge will it be? What sort of deluge should it be? Time

flies faster than electricity." Looking forward to a more industrial and mercantile version of modernity, inspired by John Bright (1811–1889) and Herbert Spencer (1820–1903), he argued that Japan's vocation was to emerge from "a natural commercial nation" to become "an industrial country; and as a natural consequence . . . a democratic country."

Tokutomi had few doubts of the ability of his cohort to make the necessary changes, claiming confidently in his journal *Kokumin no tomo* (Friends of the nation) the next year: "The old men of the past are gradually making way for the young men of the New Japan. Oriental phenomena are on their way out; Occidental phenomena are beginning. The period of destruction is at an end and the age of building is soon to start." This was the age of the utopian political novels, too, with plots set in future times as in *Shin Nippon* (1886; New Japan, by Ozaki Yukio, 1859–1954) and *Setchūbai* (1886; Plum blossoms in snow, by Suchiro Tetchō, 1849–1896) finding an enthusiastic reception. Such enthusiasm easily turned to nationalism, as it did in Tokutomi's case, once the Sino-Japanese war started in 1894. Thereafter, he remained an ardent supporter of the ultranationalist cause.

By the end of the Meiji period, to the cancellation of liberal political stirrings, on one side, as reforming intellectuals were absorbed into the ideology of a militarized state, corresponded on the other side the distress of lonely individuals, unanchored in the new society, as a central experience in the arts. The foremost novelist of the period, Natsume Sōseki (1867–1916), gave striking expression to this theme in his fiction, rejecting naturalist conventions. Sōseki had little confidence in the results of Japanese modernization. Scornful of both Western imitation and nationalist swagger, he told himself in 1902: "People say that Japan was awakened thirty years ago, but it was awakened by a fire bell and jumped out of bed. It was not a genuine awakening but a totally confused one. Japan has tried to absorb Western culture in a hurry and as a result has not had time to digest it" (Sōseki's diary, 16 March 1902). He feared the worst from this force-fed diet. In his essay *Gendai Nihon no kaika* (1912; The enlightenment of modern Japan), Sōseki predicted:

> If by dint of physical and mental exertions, and ignoring all the difficulties and sufferings of our precipitous advance, we succeed in covering in half the time it took the more prosperous Westerners to arrive at the same stage of specialization, the consequences will indeed be serious. We will be able to boast of a fantastic acquisition of knowledge, and will inevitably suffer a nervous collapse from which there will be no recovery.

Belated Enlightenment: China (1880s–1920s)

On the East Asia mainland, ideas of modernity developed later. In Korea, most enlightenment thinkers were trained in Japan, and these became the leading spokespersons for modernizing reforms in the late nineteenth century, and, when Korea eventually fell to Japanese colonialism in 1910, for a cultural nationalism and political independence. Chinese thinking about modernity, by contrast, was shaped by a tenacious Confucian view of the world, intertwined with erratic strands of

Buddhism and Western learning, and was marked by the persistent failure of efforts to reform the late Qing state for most of the nineteenth century. The result was a development in which enlightenment discourse was overshadowed by utopian constructions.

The leading reformer of the period, Kang Youwei (1858–1927), was a generation younger than Fukuzawa, but his ideas were notably less Westernized. In the early 1880s, Kang envisaged the emergence in another hundred years of equal rights for all human beings, phasing out the Confucian hierarchy between emperor and ministers, between gentry and commoners, and between men and women. But by the 1890s, the vague notion of a "public agreement" that would "lead every living being into the paradise of supreme happiness" (*Kangzi nei wai pian*, 1884, Kangzi: Inter and outer chapters) had given way to an accommodating monarchism that promised to give present society a stage of "well being" (*shengping, xiaokang*), en route to a "grand peace" (*taiping*) of the whole world of "great harmony" (*datong*). The vision of progress in it offered utopian constructions dressed in Confucian discourse as a remedy to China's modern crisis.

The thinker-translator Yan Fu (1853–1921) was responsible for introducing Social Darwinism into China with a translation of T. H. Huxley's *Evolution and Ethics,* significantly rendered as *Tianyan lun* (1895; On Heavenly evolution). Convinced of the need for the Chinese to understand the implications of "the survival of the fittest," Yan warned his countrymen: "The weak invariably become the prey to the strong, the stupid invariably become subservient to the clever" ("*Yuanqiang,*" 1895, On strength). In an essay entitled "*Lun shi bian zhi ji*" (1895, On the urgency of change in the world), he noted that "[t]he greatest difference in the principles of West and East, that which is most irreconcilable, is that the Chinese love the ancient and ignore the present, whereas Westerners strive for present to overcome the past." Here what is modern in his evolutionary horizon was still more a matter of geographical contrast than of temporal advance. As time moved on, through the chaos of the early Republic, Yan became disillusioned with the idea of evolution itself.

The first to tackle problems of modernity more directly was Kang's disciple, Liang Qichao (1873–1929), who fled to Japan after the failed attempt at state reform in the summer of 1898. With far more access to works by Meiji thinkers and Japanese translations of Western literature, he wrote that the effect of reading them was as if "suddenly seeing the sun in a dark room and drinking on an empty stomach" ("Lun xue riben wen shi yi," 1899, On the benefit of learning Japanese). Here were the models for the modernization of China. Reconfiguring the crisis of the time, Liang effectively replaced "Western" with "new" as a defining adjective for the tasks of the time. In his article "Shanonian Zhongguo shuo" (1900, On young China), he wrote: "What has made China today a senile giant is the evil deeds of dying old men." The task of creating a new China fell to the young, and he enumerated all the fields—from morality and laws to institutions and conventions—that required recasting by them in "an independent spirit" (*Xinmin shuo*, 1902–1906, Discourse on the new citizen). He also called for a "new history" and "new novel," publishing a utopian fiction of his own, *Xin Zhongguo*

weilai ji (The future of new China) in 1902, while advocating a monarchical constitution under the Manchu rule.

Liang's call for a new historiography was challenged by the classical scholar Zhang Binglin (1868–1936), who argued that Confucius should be seen as the first great Chinese historian, founding a tradition of historical studies that retained its validity to the present. "Instead of persuading people to worship Confucianism as a religion, we should encourage them to treasure the history of the Han nation" (1906). Politically a resolute revolutionary committed to the overthrow of the Manchu court, Zhang sought intellectually to tie the nationalist movement to pre-Qing traditions: "Historical events and relics can move patriotic feelings." The ensuing debate between the two showed the persistent classical sense of the past that had to be overcome before "modern times" could be successfully conceptualized in China.

It was not until the following decade that these parameters changed to that similar to, but almost half a century later than, Fukuzawa's *bunmei kaika,* in both essence and scale. The two leading intellectuals of the period, Chen Duxiu (1879–1942) and Hu Shi (1891–1962), launched a sweeping campaign against Chinese traditions in the name of democracy and science in 1917, in a movement that culminated in the May Fourth Incident against the post–World War I Versailles Peace Conference in 1919. Hu Shi insisted on a "critical attitude" and the need to "revalue all values" (*Xin sichao de yiyi*, 1919, The significance of the new thought) in the light of modern reason. Chen Duxiu declared:

In support of Mr. Democracy, we must oppose Confucian teaching and rites, the value of chastity, old ethics and old politics. In support of Mr. Science, we must oppose old arts and old religions. In support of both Mr D and Mr S, we must oppose the "national essence" and old literature. . . . How many upheavals occurred and how much blood was shed in the West in support of Mr D and Mr S, before these two gentlemen gradually led Westerners out of darkness into the bright world. We firmly believe that only they can resuscitate China and bring it out of all the present darkness of its politics, morality, scholarship and thought. (*Xin qinqnian zui-an zhi dabian,* 1919, In defence of the *New Youth* against accusations)

It was in the urgency of this perspective that the semantic shift of the term for "modern" from *jindai* to the more sharply present-focused *xiandai* occurred.

It was left to China's greatest writer of the period, Lu Xun (1881–1936), to consciously hold skepticism while fighting under the banner of Mr. D and Mr. S against conformist tendency. One of the first in China to introduce literary works from weak and colonized countries in Europe and Asia, he most valued the patriotic affection and fighting spirit expressed by the people. Similarly, he quoted Byron and Neitzsche repeatedly as the model for noncompromised struggle. He attacked those who "dream not about the future, only in the present," and warned those optimistic about modernity that "the most painful experience in life is to wake up from a dream and find no road to follow" ("Nala zouhou zenyang," 1923, Now Nora is after leaving [the Doll's House]). With a clear understanding that no ready model for imitation was available, Lu Xun envisaged life in constant struggle of paving new roads: "What is a road? It is what comes out from tramping over where there was no road, paved out from where there were brambles only." It was also to rejuvenate "human being's potential in longing for perfection" ("Gusiang," 1921, Hometown) to march forward regardless of how difficult, how seemingly hopeless the future ahead might be.

Urban Cosmopolitan Modernity (1920s–1930s)

In interwar Japan a new kind of consciousness of modernity crystallized, around the scenes, rhythms, and sensations of big-city life, which spread to China some ten years later. This was the modern not of institutions or technologies but of the experience of life Charles Baudelaire (1821–1867) and Arthur Rimbaud (1854–1891) had celebrated in Europe. The 1920s saw a wave of translations of modernist literature from the West, and formal experiments by Japanese writers. Successive literary schools contended against each other, virtually all of them taking individualism as a given, with aesthetics of existential fragmentation and a mixture of fascination and repulsion for the transient surfaces of metropolitan life. The one ingredient, important in the West, that was missing from this modernism—it would be true of the Chinese variant as well—was the European anguish at loss of religious faith. The solitude of humankind in a world without God was never a major theme of East Asian modernism.

The most influential of its currents in Japan was the New Sensationalism—associated with Yokomitsu Riichi (1898–1947) and early Kawabata Yasunari (1899–1972)—which Kawabata defined as "Expressionism in epistemology and Dadaism in formal expression" ("Shinshin sakka no shin keikō kaisetsu," 1924, An explanation on the new tendency among young writers). The New Sensationalism came to Shanghai in the late twenties and early thirties. Yokomitsu entitled his first full-length novel *Shanghai*. It was in these years that the term *xiandai* became ubiquitous in fashion magazines and avant-garde journals alike, and that—as in Japan—the idea of a specifically aesthetic modernism arrived, associated with the breaking of formal conventions and social taboos, erotic or otherwise.

In both cases, cosmopolitan influences were celebrated and even worshiped, but in general without the revolt against "philistinism" or the spirit of rebellion against the established order that marked much of Western modernism. Yokomitsu's sense of universal cosmopolitanism ended with his "melancholy journey" to Europe in 1936, where a pilgrimage turned into disillusion, and he subsequently "returned" to the nationalist course, reaching the same end, via a different path, as Fukuzawa decades earlier. But something of the same feel for the urban landscape was also shown by the Chinese leftist writer Mao Dun (1896–1981) in his novel *Ziye* (1933; Midnight), which covered a wide range of lurid scenes in Shanghai in a style not dissimilar to that of the New Sensationalists. Despite China's national crisis by the late thirties, the younger generation's fascination with modernism continued into the war years, especially in poetry, before fading away in the 1950s.

"Overcoming Modernity" (1940s–1950s)

Intellectual reactions against modernity started early in East Asia, and were not confined to traditionalists. Alarm at the "madness" or "lost soul" of modern industrialism and militarism was soon expressed by enlightenment intellectuals in both China and Japan. Touring Europe after World War I, Liang Qichao (1873–1929) was shocked by what he found:

Countless total strangers live together, sharing the same market or factory, with absolutely no links of affection to each other, merely relations of material interest. Most people own no property, depend on wages only, and lack any roots for survival, like a withering lotus. Social complexity exceeds anyone's capacity for orderly responses to it, over-stimulating and exhausting the nervous system. After work, there is need for play, but abruptly it is time to work again; day and night there is no rest. Desires multiply constantly, the price of goods rises uninterruptedly, life becomes harder and harder, competition fiercer and fiercer. (*Ou you xin ying lu,*1920, Impressions from my European journey)

Yet he believed China, as a latecomer to modernity, still had a chance to draw its own critical lessons from European development; he had converted to the May Fourth conviction of science and democracy as the prerequisite of entry into the modern world.

At virtually the same time, the philosopher and reformer Liang Shuming (1893–1988) set out a severe critique of contemporary Western societies in his book *Dongxi wenhua jiqi zhexue* (1921; The cultures of East and West and their philosophies), attacking their separation of man and nature, individual and society. After the catastrophe of World War I, the world had arrived at a point where it had to alter direction. In Liang Shuming's view, this meant shifting from the agonistic reason, guided by intuition, of the "cultural will" of the West, to the intuition guided by reason of the Chinese cultural will—this was where the world was now heading—and eventually to the valuation of faith and devaluation of desire that was Indian cultural will. The modern society that had emerged in the West was a necessary step in this long-run development, and the spirit of democracy and science it had brought was precious. But a better civilization was possible beyond it.

The challenge to uncritical images of modernity issued by the two Liangs led to a series of controversies in China in the 1920s, in which the resources of traditional Chinese learning in a time dominated by Western configurations of human knowledge and the potential for an alternative path of modern development for China were hotly debated. Although Liang Shuming was subsequently considered a precursor of neo-Confucianism in late-twentieth-century China, at the time he was true to the May Fourth generation, becoming an active proponent and organizer of agrarian cooperatives, and like Liang Qichao in the same period advocating a variant of socialism as a remedy for China's ills.

Japan. In Japan, probing of the dilemmas and paradoxes of modernity began already in the Meiji period, and has lasted to this day. In the 1890s, the Christian thinker Uchimura Kanzō (1861–1930) questioned the purpose of his country's headlong drive to join the ranks of the West:

> Can present-day civilization compensate for the loss of the independence of our souls through modernization? Are the steam engine, radio, champagne, torpedoes, and guns better than peace? Does civilization mean spending six billion dollars to maintain standing armies of two and a half million soldiers in Europe, producing anarchists and increasing nervous disorder? ("Kyūanroku," 1893, A record of search for peace)

But by Taishō times, Uchimura's dissent was directed more at his fellow intellectuals than at the government:

> I rejoice at the news that the government has a plan to restore Chinese studies in school. It is not the time to argue over the difference between the ideas of the West and the East. What we should do now is to destroy modern man [*kindai-jin*] and modern ideas [*kindai-shiso*]. ("Hibi no shōgai,"1924, Daily life)

There was an echo here, however distorted, of Liang Shuming's desire to counter temporal divisions with a call for spatial unity.

Stark counterpositions of West and East nonetheless persisted—even for those who despised *kindai jin* and *kindai-shiso* no less than Uchimura—throughout the interwar and war years. For in this period the Meiji aspiration of climbing up the rungs of a hierarchical world order of "civilization" was replaced, on the one hand, by spatially stressed notions of a plurality of cultures and ethnicities, under the catchphrase of a "return to Japan." On the other hand, Fukuzawa's vision of enlightened individuals acting with a spirit of independence gave way to fear of the modern decadence of an ill-informed individualism that was the captive of a debased mass culture. At the same time, images of socioeconomic modernity itself became much more divided. In the 1870s it was taken for granted that there was just one basic model of civilization, even though the Meiji oligarchs had borrowed selectively from the West. By the 1930s this was no longer possible. Russian Communism, Italian Fascism, American capitalism, and German Nazism offered a range of completely different models of state and society.

Against this background, a symposium that would have enormous resonance was held in Kyoto in the summer of 1942, shortly after the outbreak of the Pacific War. Modeled on League of Nations symposia chaired by Paul Valéry in the 1930s, notably on "The Future of the European Spirit," this Japanese forum brought together philosophers from the Zen-and-new-Kantian influenced Kyoto School founded by Nishida Kitarō (1870–1945), writers from the Japan Romantic School Society, to discuss the problem of "Overcoming Modernity" (*kindai no chôkoku*). The political context of the symposium—Japanese fascism—featured prominently in the discussions, but these did not adhere to any rigid ideological agenda, ranging over many aesthetic, philosophical, cultural, and social issues. Modernity had to be overcome, some argued, because the failures of capitalism, democracy, and liberalism had led inevitably to the war. But was modernity simply a European or American phenomenon? Others doubted it, pointing to a Japanese modernity compounded of indigenous and foreign elements alike. By the end, the chairman of the symposium concluded it had failed in its task.

Yet, after World War II, the symposium became a landmark for intellectual inquiry into Japan's modern history and its future. This outcome was primarily due to the work of Takeuchi Yoshimi (1910–1977) in the early 1950s, who extracted its quest from the compromised setting of wartime Japan, and "refunctioned" it for an anti-imperialist politics in postwar Japan. Significantly, Takeuchi was the major Japanese editor and translator of Lu Xun. Writing after the Communist victory in China, he contrasted the trajectory of the Chinese Revolution with the Japanese experience of a military-fascist regime followed by American occupation. Yet, throughout East Asia modernity had been the result of imperial violence by the West that forced it upon the East, in a continuous process in which until 1949 the West had always claimed victory. Truly to overcome that modernity in Japan required a "double resistance"—resisting both the external imposed reason and the internal denial of the defeat of which it was the outcome. Such resistance was the task of the citizens of a politically responsible nation (*minzoku*), to exercise their independent subjectivity (*shutaisei*). It was not antimodern. "If I were asked what is resistance," he wrote, "the only answer I have is, 'It is what you find in Lu Xun'" ("Chūku kindai to Nihon no kindai," 1948, China's modern and Japan's modern; in later collections the title changes to "Kindai towa nanika," What is modernity).

In postwar Japan, subjectivity had become one of the central terms of political debates over the recent past, as intellectuals sought to understand the human agents of social change in the processes of modernization and Japan's war experience. Maruyama Masao (1914–1996), a leading thinker of the Occupation period, rejected the existential interpretation of subjectivity of the Kyoto School, which continued as a major influence in the 1950s. During the war, Maruyama had invoked Fukuzawa as a thinker who "could never conceive of national independence in the absence of individual autonomy" ("Fukuzawa ni okeru chitsujo to ningen,"1943, The order and humane in Fukuzawa); and in his path-breaking essay *Chôkokkashugi no ronri to shinri* (1946; "The logic and psychology of ultranationalism") he attributed the disastrous course of Showa politics to the "collective irresponsibility" of an elite drifting to war in the name of a mystified imperial rule transcending temporal or spatial boundaries, and commanding the passive obedience of its subject-citizens (*kokumin*).

A true democratic revolution in postwar Japan, Maruyama contended, required the "establishment of a modern personality," capable of responsible decision making. His ideal here was Max Weber's (1864–1920) ethic of responsibility, as set out in *Politics as a Vocation* (1918). This was an admiration shared by his contemporary Otsuka Hisao (1907–1996), an economic historian who energetically appropriated Weber's theory of the Protestant ethic as a model for the kind of self-discipline needed to build a robust civil society in Japan. In their different ways, Maruyama's championship of the "modern personality" and Takeuchi's call for resistance by the *minzoku* opened a new page of critical thinking in Japan. The themes of modernity or its overcoming were taken up by many others in subsequent decades and have lingered in various contexts as a persistent theme in Japanese thinking to this day.

The issue of a politically responsible citizenry, resonant in Maruyama and Takeuchi, reappeared in Korean intellectual life during the 1970s. Paik Nak-chung (b. 1938), a leading literary critic, advocated a "national literature" (*minjok munhak*), the modernity of which is defined by its opposition to Korea's North-South division, and its openness to the world at large from a Third World position. Paik has since actively promoted an independent, creative national subjectivity, in a series of debates on modernism, postmodernity, and globalization.

Modernization and Postmodernity: Ongoing Debates

If *modernity* and *modernization* were characteristically Weberian concerns, they had little place in Marxist thinking, since their generality blurs the distinction between capitalism and socialism as forms of postfeudal society that is central to Marx's theory of history. Thus the major historical controversy within the communist movement in the two countries developed quite independently of debates over modernity, and without reference to them. The Chinese Revolution might be objectively responsible for a vast modernization of the country, but for a quarter of a century the notion itself was essentially foreign to its vocabulary.

With the strong reaction against the Cultural Revolution (1966–1976) that came in the early seventies, this changed. The government adopted the slogan of the "Four Modernizations": industrial, agricultural, techno-scientific, and defense. In time the function of this semantic shift became increasingly clear—to cancel the long-held distinction between socialism and capitalism, as Mao had feared. But in doing so, it reopened the classic "wound" in the concept itself, which was first painfully exposed in Meiji times. Was modernity just a "rich country and a strong army," as the quartet of official goals implied? Dissidents did not think so. In 1978, Wei Jingsheng (b. 1950) called for a "fifth modernization"—the institution of political democracy—and was punished with a long prison sentence. Rapid economic growth and political repression have continued to date.

By the 1990s, debates on postmodernity had reached China, but in the early 2000s the principal stake in discussion remained the concept of modernity itself. The historian of theology Liu Xiaofeng (b. 1956) in his work *Xiandaixing shehui lilun xulun* (1996; A preface to social theory of modernity) believes that modernity manifests itself in the form of a social structure, whose inherent contradictions can never be put to rest by actions of "overcoming," but will regenerate themselves endlessly, and which is European in origin only through a series of historical accidents. Other countries then initiated modern processes of social change under external pressure, albeit with their own varied historical legacies. Since the late Qing period most Chinese intellectuals, Liu argues, failed to grasp the logic of modernity because they tended to accord priority to the nation instead. In his view, the moralistic party-state that came into being after 1949 is now decaying, and to fill the vacuum it has left, a religious community needs to be rebuilt through religion at the local level, both in order to protect individual freedoms and to ensure an ethical basis for people to cope with an ever-changing society. The modern human without God must find salvation in religion again.

Approaching the issue from another perspective, the intellectual historian Wang Hui (b. 1959) worked for more than a decade on his study *Xiandai Zhongguo sixiang de xingqi* (2003; The rise of modern Chinese thought). In this work he traces the origins of ideas of modernity in China back to the eleventh century, with the aim of showing that capitalism can hardly lay claim to everything that is today associated with the modern. Himself the author of a work on Lu Xun, he champions a spirit of resistance, similar to that in Takenuch, though without emphasizing the "double," to mystifying discourses of global modernization, and the historical teleology that he argues they always entail, with an obligatory class structure and empty representative institutions at the end of the road. Alternative modernities remain necessary and possible, even if these will now require a different international order, sustaining national innovations, rather than crushing them in a neoliberal straitjacket.

In Japan, on the other hand, the success of postwar capitalist development did not put an end to questioning of modernity. Among significant debates, one centered on literature. Karatani Kōn (b. 1941), in his study *Nihon kindai bungaku no kigen* (1980; *Origins of Modern Japanese Literature*) emphasized the "nearness" of the "origins" of Japanese modernity, instead of tracing it to a genealogically distant past. Pointing to a global simultaneity of multinational modern experience, he sought to unravel the historical specificity of the Japanese case. Karatani almost immediately drew sharp disagreement from a number of Japanese scholars, including Kamei Hideo (b. 1937), who charged him with disregarding the continuities in the Japanese experience of modernity. For Kamei, exclusive attention to a uniformly identified "modernity" has suppressed the multiple possibilities latent in the flourishing creativities of Meiji Japan, which developed out of Edo culture and still require an intellectual effort to recover. The national component of modernity, projected by Takeuchi, acquired a new level of depth for inquiry.

With the consumer boom of the eighties, many intellectuals began to wonder whether Japan was not witnessing a new way of "overcoming the modern"—entrance into postmodernity. In a famous intervention, Asada Akira (b. 1957) has given the interlinked problems of subjectivity and historicity a critical postmodern twist. Drawing playful inspiration from Nishida Kitarō, he has contrasted a senile capitalism in Europe, under the sway of transcendental traditions, and an adult capitalism in America, marked by an inner-directed sense of individual responsibility, with an infantile capitalism in Japan, displaying the "nearly purely relative competition exhibited by other-directed children." Asada has described the postindustrial psyche of

Japanese society in the following way: "Children are running around, each as fast as possible, at the front lines of the history of capitalism as infantilization proceeds. They are enveloped by a 'place' whose age is hardly known—the 'place' that is transhistorical in the sense Nishida demonstrated" (1989). Debates on modernity in East Asia have plainly not yet run their course.

See also **Empire and Imperialism; Modernism; Nationalism.**

BIBLIOGRAPHY

Alitto, Guy. *The Last Confucian: Liang Shu-ming and the Chinese Dilemma of Modernity.* Berkeley: University of California Press, 1979.

Arima Tatsuo. *The Failure of Freedom: A Portrait of Modern Japanese Intellectuals.* Cambridge, Mass.: Harvard University Press, 1969.

Asada, Akira. "Infantile Capitalism and Japan's Postmodernism: A Fairy Tale." In *Postmodernism and Japan,* edited by Masao Miyoshi and H. D. Harootunian. Durham, N.C.: Duke University Press, 1989.

Denton, Kirk A., ed. *Modern Chinese Literary Thought: Writings on Literature, 1893–1945.* Stanford, Calif.: Stanford University Press, 1996.

Doak, Kevin Michael. *Dreams of Difference: The Japan Romantic School and the Crisis of Modernity.* Berkeley: University of California Press, 1994.

Fukuzawa Yukichi. *Outline of a Theory of Civilization.* Translated by David A. Dilworth and G. Cameron Hurst. Tokyo: Sophia University, 1973.

Harootunian, Harry. *Overcome by Modernity: History, Culture, and Community in Interwar Japan.* Princeton, N.J.: Princeton University Press, 2000.

Hu, Shih. *The Chinese Renaissance: The Haskell Lectures, 1933.* Chicago: University of Chicago Press, 1934.

Jansen, Marius B. *The Making of Modern Japan.* Cambridge, Mass.: Belknap, 2000.

Kamei, Hideo. *Transformations of Sensibility: The Phenomenology of Meiji Literature.* Translated, edited, and with an introduction by Michael Bourdaghs. Ann Arbor: Center for Japanese Studies, University of Michigan, 2002.

Karatani Kōjin. *Origins of Modern Japanese Literature.* Translation edited by Brett de Bary. Durham, N.C.: Duke University Press, 1993.

Keene, Donald. *Dawn to the West: Japanese Literature of the Modern Era, Fiction.* New York: Holt, Rinehart, and Winston, 1984.

Koschmann, J. Victor. *Revolution and Subjectivity in Postwar Japan.* Chicago: University of Chicago Press, 1996.

Lee, Leo Ou-fan. *Shanghai Modern: The Flowering of a New Urban Culture in China, 1930–1945.* Cambridge, Mass.: Harvard University Press, 1999.

Maruyama, Masao. *Thought and Behavior in Modern Japanese Politics.* London and New York: Oxford University Press, 1969.

Sakai Naoki. *Translation and Subjectivity: On Japan and Cultural Nationalism.* Minneapolis: University of Minnesota Press, 1997.

Schwarcz, Vera. *The Chinese Enlightenment: Intellectuals and the Legacy of the May Fourth Movement of 1919.* Berkeley: University of California Press, 1986.

Seymour, James D., ed. *The Fifth Modernization: China's Human Rights Movement, 1978–1979.* Stanfordville, New York: Human Rights Publishing Group, 1980.

Shi, Shu-mei. *The Lure of the Modern: Writing Modernism in Semicolonial China, 1917–1937.* Berkeley: University of California Press, 2001.

Spence, Jonathan D. *The Search for Modern China.* New York: Norton, 1990.

Tokutomi, Sohō. *The Future Japan.* Translated and edited by Vinh Sinh, with Matsuzawa Hiroaki and Nicholas Wickenden. Edmonton, Canada: University of Alberta Press, 1989.

Wang, Hui. *China's New Order: Society, Politics, and Economy in Transition.* Edited by Theodore Huters. Cambridge, Mass.: Harvard University Press, 2003.

Chaohua Wang

MODERNIZATION. The term *modernization* conjures images of social change in the direction of general improvement over the past. In contemporary social sciences, the notion has been the basis of a theoretical orientation—variously referred to as modernization theory, approach, paradigm, or framework—to the study of the development of Third World or underdeveloped societies. The conception of development as a process of modernization gained prominence in the period after World War II, but its popularity ebbed in the 1960s. There were rival definitions of modernization in the social sciences; this entry, however, will be concerned mainly with the use of the term for a general theoretical orientation—a set of linked assumptions framing analysis of and debates about the nature and challenges of development. In this regard modernization was a historically unique type of social change, which was inexorable, transformational in its effects, and progressive in its consequences. The main institutional pillars for modern society were industrialism and the nation-state.

A product primarily of American social science, the modernization approach was inspired by two important and concurrent developments of the postwar era, the disintegration of European colonial empires and the Cold War. The emergence of many new nations out of the ashes of European colonial empires generated unprecedented intellectual and policy interest in their economic, political, social, and cultural makeup and development. With the United States and the Soviet Union as the two superpowers and respective leaders of the Western and Eastern blocs, the Cold War was, among other things, a competition between two ideologies—liberal capitalism versus socialism—each claiming to be the superior path to modernity. This ideological contest framed the superpowers' rivalry for the allegiances of developing countries. Modernization theory, directly or indirectly, was concerned with resolving the problems of underdevelopment by promoting market-based economies and pluralistic political systems. The approach thus appeared to be scholarship guided by and in support of specific Western policy objectives. The intellectual roots of modernization theory lie in pre-Socratic Western thinking about social change, and more immediately in the European Enlightenment of the seventeenth and eighteenth centuries, which gave birth to modern social sciences. The Enlightenment embodied a critique of the "Old Order," when European societies were at the threshold of industrialization and exposed to social dislocations that would only intensify. Convinced of the inevitable demise of the old feudal order and of absolutism, Enlightenment intellectuals propounded the "Idea of Progress," a dogma about the immanence and desirability of change. In opposition to defenders of the Old Order, of social arrangements governed by and political authority legitimated by religion and tradition, they argued that rational knowledge of society, based on scientific investigation and freed from religious dogma and superstition, was possible and represented a superior form of knowledge. Once validated and acted on, such knowledge would advance the material and cultural emancipation of society. The founders of modern social sciences, prominent among them Karl Marx, Émile Durkheim, and Max Weber, were products of the Enlightenment and enamored of the idea of progress as a universal historical process leading to a single modernity. In Marx's famous theory of history, for example, societies progressed through modes of production—primitive communism, slavery, feudalism, capitalism, and communism—and their corresponding political structures. In general, nineteenth-century evolutionary theories of social change were equally all-embracing, relied on dichotomous conceptions in which societies were characterized as composed of traditional and modern attributes, and saw social change as a process of structural changes resulting in the preeminence of the attributes of modernity. However conceived, emergent industrial societies and modern nation-states of the West represented the most advanced stage of societal transformation. They predicted the future of underdeveloped societies, the majority of which at the close of the nineteenth century had effectively been colonized by European states.

Modernization theory adopted the narrative of progress of nineteenth-century evolutionary theories of social change. It dispensed with the racist overtones of many, which tended to separate societies into "civilized" and "savage" and doubted the possibility of development of the latter. Adopting the nation-state as its main unit of analysis, the theory defined development as an endogenously driven process and maintained that modernization was a goal attainable by all societies. Retaining but elaborating the dichotomous conceptions of earlier evolutionary theories, the modernization approach conceived of underdeveloped societies as comprising traditional and modern sectors. The traditional sector was rural and agrarian, its sociopolitical organization defined by religion, superstition, primordial loyalties, and similar forces. In contrast, the modern sector was urban, its economy dominated by industry; social standing was determined by economic position (social class) and hence the result of personal achievement, and secularism defined the organization of social relations and public life. In effect, this equated development with the increasing Westernization of underdeveloped societies through elaboration of market-based economies and liberal, pluralistic political systems. One of the most famous articulations of the approach, W. W. Rostow's *The Stages of Growth: A Non-Communist Manifesto*, made this explicit. Modeling his analysis on Marx's theory of history, but blunt about his intention to present liberal capitalism as the superior path to modernity, Rostow argued that economies progressed through five historical phases: traditional, preconditions for takeoff, takeoff, drive to maturity, and the age of high mass consumption. Contrary to Marx, who saw capitalism as a way station to the ultimate modern society—stateless communism—Rostow argued that high–mass-consumption society, of which

the United States was the most fully realized incarnation, was the end of the modernization process.

In general, the two key conditions for successful modernization were economic growth through industrialization and modernizing elites with the "psychocultural attributes" to guide their societies through the process. Modernization of underdeveloped societies could be realized in a shorter period than had been the case for Western societies. In bequeathing ex-colonies with modern economic enclaves and Westernized elites, colonial rule had laid the foundations for accelerating the process. Interestingly, the narrative of progress that undergirded the approach resonated with the nationalist aspirations of Third World elites. The promise of development of their societies served as a ubiquitous trope for the legitimization of their power. Although they adopted different ideological positions, modernization for them was fundamentally about the elaboration of the two projects of economic development through industrialization and nation-state building.

The modernization approach was subjected, as the 1960s unfolded, to increasingly blistering criticism, brought on by the realities of Third World societies, which mocked its excessive optimism. The record of economic growth in developing societies was at best mixed, and what growth occurred appeared to be accompanied by increases in mass poverty and economic inequality. Whereas modernization theory presumed economic growth that expanded social groups and engendered behavioral changes that favored the emergence of pluralistic political systems, instability and authoritarian rule appeared to be the norm. Against this backdrop, criticisms centered on the theory's ideological character, its limitations as a conceptual framework, and its contributions to the foreign policy objectives of—especially—the American government. The ethnocentrism of the approach, with its dichotomous constructs like "tradition" and "modern"—transparently, abstractions from vague and generalized images of the nature of changes in Western societies attending the rise of industrialism and the modern nation-state—drew fire. Based on such ideal types, the approach imagined the historically contingent experiences of Western societies as relevant to all societies. Moreover, in implying that "modern" and "traditional" were self-contained, it lacked definitional specificity and was of dubious analytical value, for social structures and relations in all societies were complex, shaped by the interpenetration of traditional and modern attributes, however defined. This was obviously the case in developing societies that had felt the impact of European colonization.

For conservative critics, such as the political scientist Samuel Huntington, the ethnocentrism and teleology of modernization theory made it a poor guide to public policy. The conjecture of an unproblematic causal link between economic development and the advance of pluralistic political systems encouraged a moralistic approach to policy toward the developing world, which promoted democracy even if it was not necessarily in the best interest of the United States. The social dislocations caused by economic development fed political instability; therefore, the creation of political order—the institutionalization of political authority—was a precondition for economic development and democracy. According to this argument, the main objective of American policy toward the developing world ought to be support of regimes that are capable of maintaining order and amicably disposed toward America's economic and strategic interests.

Radical critics, on the other hand, such as dependency and world system theorists, dismissed modernization theory as well as its conservative critics as engaged in providing intellectual justification for American imperial designs. In adopting the nation-state as the primary unit of analysis and positing modernization as a primarily endogenously driven process, they were both guilty of misleading representation of underdevelopment as an "original condition." Capitalism was a hierarchically organized global system, with nations or regions belonging to the core, semicore, or periphery of the system. The pace and pattern of development of "national" economies were contingent on the manner of incorporation and position of countries or regions within the world capitalist system and its corresponding hierarchy of nation-states. The underdevelopment of peripheral Third World societies followed from their incorporation, through colonialism, as subservient members in the world capitalist system and the shaping of their economies to serve the interests of dominant core states. Their governing elites were not altruistic agents of progressive social change but groups primarily interested in advancing their class interests. This they did in part by the use of state power to create and manage beneficial alliances between themselves and foreign capitalists. For radical critics, then, modernization theory and its conservative critics were both advocating an approach to development that favored the expansion of the world capitalist system.

In the 1980s, modernization theory and its radical alternatives were queried by many influenced by the postmodernist turn in cultural and social analysis. For this new group of critics, variously labeled postmodernist, poststructuralist, or post-development theorists, modernization theorists and their radical critics had more in common than they dared to admit, for their understanding of development was rooted in the dogma of linear progress. Consequently, they were equally guilty of advocating, in the name of development, policies that fostered the repression and disempowerment of marginalized groups in Third World societies, whose right to determine their own futures they denied. The combined weight of criticisms leveled against it robbed modernization theory of its allure. But despite the changing conceptual and normative vocabularies at the twentieth century's end, modernization theory's goal of a world of receding mass poverty and disease and of social and political interactions marked by civility instead of incessant conflict remains a pivotal concern in development analysis.

See also **Dependency; Modernization Theory; Progress, Idea of; World Systems Theory, Latin America.**

BIBLIOGRAPHY
Engerman, David C. et al., eds. *Staging Growth: Modernization, Development, and the Global Cold War.* Amherst: University of Massachusetts Press, 2003.
Frank, Andre. "The Sociology of Development and the Underdevelopment of Sociology." 1967. In *Dependence and Underdevelopment,* edited by James Cockcroft et al. Garden City, N.Y.: Anchor, 1972.
Huntington, Samuel. "The Change to Change: Modernization, Development, and Politics." In *Comparative Modernization: A Reader,* edited by Cyril Black. New York: Free Press, 1976.
Janos, Andrew C. *Politics and Paradigms: Changing Theories of Change in Social Science.* Stanford, Calif.: Stanford University Press, 1986.
Lee, Raymond. "Modernization, Postmodernism, and Development." *Current Sociology* 42, no. 2 (1994).
Rostow, Walt W. *The Stages of Economic Growth: A Non-Communist Manifesto.* Cambridge, U. K., and New York: Cambridge University Press, 1960.
Tipps, Dean. "Modernization Theory and the Comparative Study of Society: A Critical Perspective." *Comparative Studies in Society and History* 15, no. 2 (1973): 199–226.

Dickson Eyoh

MODERNIZATION THEORY. For roughly one decade until the second half of the 1960s, modernization theory was in vogue in the social sciences, especially in the United States. The word *modernization* appeared widely in titles, the concept was commonly invoked in efforts to explain long-term change, and it figured in critiques of Marxist theory and discussions of Cold War differences over how newly independent countries should develop. If much of social science analysis at the time was seen as narrow, studies dressed in the mantel of modernization theory attracted attention as meeting an academic quest for cross-disciplinary breadth and a political imperative for lessons to disseminate around the world. Over the following two decades, an entirely different atmosphere arose; modernization theory became a target of far-flung criticism. It was attacked as an ahistorical effort to impose a U.S. or Western model, disregarding obstacles resulting from the actual world order. Many rejected any theory for postmodernist reasons, while others preferred neo-Marxist or world systems theories that put the blame for underdevelopment on the United States. It became popular to dismiss modernization studies as antithetical to solid social science analysis without bothering to mention any serious efforts to apply it systematically or the fact that, even under attack, many took for granted the lingering value of the theory as a framework for understanding modern development.

As the Cold War ended, the debate over modernization theory was rejoined, only to fade gradually in the face of rising disagreements over globalization. Some argued that the fall of communism at last supported the predictions about the danger of deviating sharply from requirements specified in the theory, while others replied that the failure of "shock therapy" and other abrupt changes in Russia and beyond proved once again that the theory was incorrect. Was failure of the socialist model at last proving that the modernization theorists were correct, or was failure of economic advice a sign that a Western model could not be transferred? Later, debates about globalization revisited many of the same themes as modernization theory. A half century after the theory burst into the academic limelight, social scientists are again weighing the pros and cons of opening to the outside world, political reform in order to improve state capacity and responsiveness, economic integration into a global division of labor, a breakdown of social barriers, and a knowledge orientation that maximizes absorption of information. At the same time, opinion is split on whether what is demanded includes a full-scale embrace of Western notions of individualism, democratic politics, and limited state management, or whether these features are not inherent in the model.

Defining Modernization Theory

Disagreements about what modernization theory is and what has been learned from comparisons bedevil discussions between users and critics. Those who applied the theory often failed to be specific or to supply supporting explanations to establish it as a powerful set of generalizations in the forefront of cross-disciplinary social science analysis, while critics usually neglected to define the theory precisely or to make an effort to balance its merits against alleged shortcomings. Although the theory exerted a huge impact on the disciplines of history, political science, and sociology, and on thinking about capitalism versus socialism, East Asia versus Western advanced capitalist countries, and more versus less developed countries, to many its legacy remains confusing, as does its connection to recent globalization theory. Even at the beginning of the twenty-first century, there is little agreement on what modernization theory is and how it has advanced social science analysis.

The theory of modernization normally consists of three parts: (1) identification of types of societies, and explanation of how those designated as modernized or relatively modernized differ from others; (2) specification of how societies become modernized, comparing factors that are more or less conducive to transformation; and (3) generalizations about how the parts of a modernized society fit together, involving comparisons of stages of modernization and types of modernized societies with clarity about prospects for further modernization. Actually, reasoning about all of these issues predated postwar theory. From the Industrial Revolution, there were recurrent arguments that a different type of society had been created, that other societies were either to be left permanently behind or to find a way to achieve a similar transformation, and that not all modernizing societies had equal success in sustaining the process due to differences in economic, political, and other institutions. In the middle of the 1950s, these themes acquired new social science and political casting with the claim of increased rigor in analysis.

In the early post–World War II era, approximately twenty societies were regarded as highly modernized and roughly another ten to twenty were depicted as having passed a threshold on the path to modernization. Definitions of *modernized* varied. Some noted structural features, such as levels of education, urbanization, use of inanimate sources of energy, and fertility. Others pointed to attitudes, such as secularization, achievement orientation, functional specificity in formal organizations, and acceptance of equality in relationships. Conscious of the ethnocentric nature of many earlier explanations for growth in national power and income, social scientists in the 1950s and 1960s generally omitted cultural traits associated closely with Western history from definitions of modernity. Yet, given the rhetoric of the Cold War and a preoccupation with democracy in U.S. national identity, political institutions became a central factor in many definitions.

Applying Modernization Theory

It is useful to distinguish two approaches to modernization in the heyday of the theory: applications of already identified steps along a unilinear path; and comparisons of variations along a path becoming more diverse geographically, even if long-term convergence was expected in social indicators. The former approach in its extreme form assumes that the histories of latecomers to modernization (after the first-comers had all been steeped in Western culture) are irrelevant, that they can best achieve economic growth and accompanying modernization by rapid democratization and copying of Western institutions, and that notions of the self and social relationships are destined to become much as they are idealized in the United States. Even if few writers explicitly made these arguments, critics insisted that this approach was the essence of modernization theory. In contrast, the latter approach looks for diversity in societies along the path of modernization, argues that historical legacies shape divergent paths to political and other institutions, and suggests that social relations can be expected to differ as well, even as some convergence occurs.

Clashing views of the Soviet Union may have underscored the two approaches to modernization at a time when Cold War divisions were uppermost in many minds. On the one side were those who expected the Soviet system to collapse. High rates of industrial growth and the ability to project national power presumably would amount to little when the people aspiring for freedom and the economy riddled with inefficiencies reached an impasse. From this perspective on modernization there was only one model, and any seeming alternatives did not merit comparative study. The universal model assumed a high degree of individualism, an intense quest for democracy, and an economy that allowed for little state intervention. If, for a time, a mobilizing state could produce rapid economic growth, this did not signify modernization and could not be sustained.

On the other side were those who recognized efforts to reform the Soviet system as well as the rise of East Asian societies that did not fit the supposedly universal model. They argued that levels of individualism vary, states differ in their involvement in society, and social relations historically have reflected different regional traditions. While modernization in some respects is a "universal social solvent," there is notable variation even among societies labeled the "West." The Soviet Union had the potential to concentrate on science and technology in education and the workplace in order to advance a new elite, while providing social welfare benefits to motivate a broader mass of the population. If totalitarianism only produces temporary results, then a technocracy based on rising interest groups could lead to more balanced modernization and eventual convergence with Western societies, where social welfare benefits and central coordination were gaining ground. A comparative approach to modernization theory began with studies of socialist countries, and, after Soviet reforms stagnated under Leonid Brezhnev (1906–1982; in power 1964–1982), shifted to East Asian countries and especially Japan.

In the 1970s and 1980s, the two orientations in comparative modernization studies contended with theories on the left and the right. The comparative study of East Asia, highlighting first Japan's model of modernization and then the Confucian development model, faced the dependency school and related arguments centered on Latin American cases. In contrast to the insistence of the Latin Americanists that societies integrated into the global system of capitalism were doomed to remain in the periphery, locked into an unfavorable division of labor that perpetuates backwardness, the East Asianists affirmed the opportunities within the world system for an industrious population led by farsighted state policies. Studies of Japanese modernization pointed to benefits from the family system that supported educational achievement, workplace dedication, and long-range planning; the school and examination system that encouraged intense learning and competition as well as loyalty in the classroom, which could be transferred to the enterprise; and the workplace system that favored lifetime employment for a large segment of the workforce, seniority wages, enterprise unions, and competition among firms under administrative guidance from state ministries. While debates proceeded over how much these unusual aspects of modernization would withstand forces of convergence as Japan reached a higher stage of modernization and openness to foreign competition, the comparisons stressed that significant differences could shape development even in countries whose per capita income ranked at the top of the world.

The dependency theorists were guilty of ahistorical analysis, arguing that the Confucian cultures in East Asia that had produced extraordinary premodern levels of literacy, urbanization, meritocratic governance, and commercial development did not matter. Yet politicians and vested interests in some East Asian countries who lauded Asian values and resisted reforms that would broaden democracy and openness to outside influences were guilty, too, of slanted analysis, ignoring the argument of modernization theory that convergence continues, and more complex societies at higher stages of modernization, with greater openness to foreign competition and influences, must give voice to younger generations espousing new values. Critics of modernization theory on the left insisted that struggle against an oppressive world system (not domestic consolidation around shared values) would be necessary, dismissing comparisons that alleged different pathways to success.

The collapse of the traditional socialist model and then the Soviet Union brought to the fore the other struggle between comparative modernization studies and established social science schools, this time of a more conservative character. The comparativists had long argued that the unbalanced nature of socialist modernization would lead to far-reaching reforms. As China experienced economic success through its reforms, these comparativists pointed to policies that work and lessons that the Chinese had drawn from their emphasis on learning from modernization theory, beginning in the late 1970s under the slogan "the four modernizations." Analysts attributed transformation under the Soviet leader Mikhail Gorbachev (b. 1931;

in power 1985–1991) less to pressure from the United States than to a domestic search to rekindle economic growth by activating Soviet society and joining the world economy. When early reforms failed and the emphasis shifted to democratization and more radical measures, social scientists diverged in their response. Many economists and political scientists who considered the Soviet system a failure prescribed universal solutions with little regard for the legacies of Russian society and the Soviet social contract. This was quite different from the thrust of comparative modernization studies that considered the Soviet record of unbalanced development and the high level of dependency on the state of various groups, suggesting reforms that built on this existing foundation. "Shock therapy" became the symbol of imposing an external model without regard for comparative study that points to different pathways based on historical circumstances.

Globalization Theory

Globalization theory is essentially modernization theory bolstered by greater emphasis on international integration and the power of external forces to induce rapid change. Again, one finds generalizations about individual modernization, adoption of attitudes in favor of personal choice for marriage, divorce, choice of work, migration, and views of authority. One also may observe organizational adaptation, with formal organizations transforming their roles in a market environment where a civil society is gaining ground and individuals are free to enter and leave. Likewise, state authority becomes subject to checks and balances, limited in creating monopolies and denying access to the outside world. If modernization theory emphasized competition among nations that would oblige, sooner or later, domestic adjustments, globalization theory stresses the powerful effects of the flow of resources, information, and people across national boundaries. The urgency of meeting the competition is accelerating, but the fundamental changes identified by modernization theory continue to occur.

Critics of globalization theory, both from the left and the right, repeat the accusations raised against modernization theory. Many on the left see it as justification for neo-imperialism or U.S. hegemonism, leading to unfair results, including one-sided gains and negative consequences for cultural diversity and the environment. On the right, there is continued fear that compromises will have to be made with others who follow different models, watering down national distinctiveness or sovereignty. Instead of comparing different approaches to globalization and accepting the need for all sides to adjust as competition proceeds in unpredictable ways, many prefer either to reject the process as inherently flawed or to insist that control by only one party must be ensured. As seen in a half century of modernization theory, politicized approaches to far-reaching questions of social change as well as narrow rejection of generalized social science analysis leave many critics unprepared to keep the focus on how to draw on empirical evidence and comparisons to keep improving existing theory. The theory of modernization may not have remained popular, but its message endures: states reorganize in an increasingly competitive environment; the quest for international power and economic growth leads to substantial changes in domestic policies; societies continuously adjust to economic growth and global integration; and the result is growing convergence, but there may be multiple models and sharp backlashes from those fearful or unsuccessful in the process.

Contemporary Theories

As in the Cold War era, there are three prevailing theories of global evolution at the beginning of the twenty-first century. The Marxist school that equated modernization reforms with promotion of imperialism and social class exploitation has transformed into a broader left-leaning agenda, appealing to conflict against the United States and its elitist allies as a mechanism for more just economic distribution and more checks in global political development. The target of globalization more clearly pinpoints the problem of an imposed foreign model reducing cultural diversity and autonomy, raising the profile of nationalism over the old theme of class struggle.

The hegemonic globalization school may be less vocal, but it is not hard to comprehend the meaning of its warnings of threats that can only be addressed in a world mobilized under clear leadership and newly attuned to containing political development that allows security dangers to emerge. Its neoconservative message calls for imposing a single model, more than comparing alternative approaches of nations and regions while accepting the virtues of diversity.

As developed in comparative studies and by the multilateral globalization school, modernization theory accepts that convergence is a long-term process that must remain incomplete as societies seek solace in what makes them distinctive. The quickening pace of technological change will fuel accelerated integration, and there will be dangers of increased interdependence and vulnerability that will demand more security cooperation. Yet the driving forces of the global system will remain states competing to gain an advantage in boosting their economies and national power. In the context of growing world integration, states will still be in competition to capitalize on modernization and shape the global system.

See also **Globalization; International Order; Modernization.**

BIBLIOGRAPHY

Black, Cecil Edwin. *The Dynamics of Modernization: A Study in Comparative History.* New York: Harper and Row, 1966.

Black, Cecil Edwin, et al. *The Modernization of Japan and Russia: A Comparative Study.* New York: Free Press, 1975.

Ingelhart, Ronald. *Modernization and Postmodernization: Cultural, Economic, and Political Change in 43 Societies.* Princeton, N.J.: Princeton University Press, 1997.

Inkeles, Alex, and David H. Smith. *Becoming Modern: Individual Change in Six Developing Countries.* Cambridge, Mass.: Harvard University Press, 1974.

Jansen, Marius B., ed. *Changing Japanese Attitudes toward Modernization.* Princeton, N.J.: Princeton University Press, 1965.

Levy, Marion J., Jr. *Modernization and the Structure of Societies: A Setting for International Affairs.* Princeton, N.J.: Princeton University Press, 1966.

Roberts, Timmons, and Amy Hite, eds. *From Modernization to Globalization: Perspectives on Development and Social Change.* Oxford: Blackwell, 2000.

Rozman, Gilbert, ed. *The Modernization of China.* New York: Free Press, 1981.

Wu, Eric, and Yun-han Chu, eds. *The Predicament of Modernization in East Asia.* Taipei: National Cultural Association, 1995.

Gilbert Rozman

MOHISM.

MOHISM. Mohism is a school of thought named after its founder, Mozi (or Mo Di; c. 460–390 B.C.E.). Mozi was the first known thinker to challenge systematically the ideas of Confucius (Kong Fuzi; 551–479 B.C.E.) and his followers and to provide an alternative vision of the ideal society and state. One of the most prominent intellectual currents of the Zhanguo (Warring States; 453–221 B.C.E.) period, Mohism declined rapidly soon after the imperial unification of 221 B.C.E., to be rediscovered by modern scholars in the first decades of the twentieth century.

Sources

The Mohists' ideas are presented in a book that bears the name of the school's founder. The so-called core chapters (8–37) may have been produced during Mozi's lifetime or immediately thereafter, and are believed to reproduce his original thought. These chapters present ten major Mohist doctrines, each of which is discussed in three versions; the subdivisions are believed to reflect different traditions within the Mohist movement. Later portions of the *Mozi* deal with epistemological questions (chapters 40–45) and military theory (52–71) and tell anecdotes about Mozi and his disciples (46–51). These chapters were produced between the fourth and the second centuries B.C.E. by the later Mohists, reflecting major developments within the Mohist school.

The *Mozi* suffered considerably in the process of its transmission: no less than eighteen chapters were lost, others were significantly damaged, and almost ten chapters (1–7, and probably 38–39) are considered to be forged by later transmitters. The book was restored due to the meticulous efforts of scholars from the eighteenth century on, although proper arrangement of many portions is still subject to heated scholarly debate. Several Mohist treatises are included in the Warring States' collectanea, such as the *Lüshi chunqiu* (c. 240 B.C.E.); valuable information about Mohist thought is also present in the writings of the Mohists' opponents, such as Zhuangzi (fl. late fourth century B.C.E.), Xunzi (c. 298–c. 230 B.C.E.), and Han Feizi (c. 280–233 B.C.E.), as well as in the Han period texts (206 B.C.E.–220 C.E.).

Mozi

Few reliable details are known of the life of Mozi. Most scholars agree that he was a person of relatively humble origin from one of the eastern Chinese states (either Song, Qi, or Lu). Like Confucius, he traveled through neighboring states in search of better appointments, but apparently to no avail. Even more than Confucius, he succeeded as an educator and organizer, turning his followers into a tight ideological group that remained active throughout the Chinese world for almost two centuries.

Mozi's sociopolitical views are a curious blend of utopian idealism and sober pragmatism. On the utopian side Mozi promulgated the egalitarian principle of "universal love" (or "concern for everyone," *jian'ai*) as a remedy to social and political fragmentation. He rejected the attachment to an individual's state and lineage, as well as to the self, suggesting instead an ideal society where all the people under Heaven would share extra labor, extra products, and proper teachings. This society would be maintained by a highly centralized state, which would implement universal surveillance to disclose deviant subjects and rectify them. The state would be ruled by a morally perfect individual, who would select his officials on the basis of their morality and then impose universal standards of benevolence (*ren*) and righteousness (*yi*) down to the lowest social levels. The unity, therefore, would be ideological and not only political.

On the more practical level, Mozi suggested a series of measures to improve the functioning of the state and the life of its populace in the immediate future. First, he proclaimed strong opposition to offensive wars, which he rejected both on moral grounds and as an inexcusable waste of public resources. The opposition was not only theoretical, as Mohists reportedly organized a kind of universal intervention force that promised military support to the weak states against their powerful and aggressive neighbors; this may explain the great interest displayed by later Mohists in questions of defensive warfare. Second, Mozi argued that improved livelihood would be attained only through reduction of needless expenses, such as those associated with lavish burials and extravagant ritual music. This rejection of mortuary rites and ritual music—the hallmark of the centuries-old aristocratic culture—reflects Mozi's staunch opposition to the pedigree-based social order. This opposition is prominent in the third of his major recommendations, namely the establishment of meritocratic instead of the aristocratic rule. A person's social rank and emoluments should be determined exclusively by his intellectual abilities and moral outlook: "If there is an able person even among peasants, artisans or merchants, he must be promoted, granted high rank, rich emoluments and an appointment . . . hence officials will not be forever noble; the people will not be forever base." "Promoting the worthy" (*Shang xian*) became the hallmark of Mozi's political recommendations.

Mozi proposed triple justification for his radical departures from the established sociopolitical patterns. First, he argued that his recommendations would benefit everyone, and hence should be adopted due to purely utilitarian considerations. Second, Mozi made painstaking efforts to prove that his views reflect the true legacy of the ancient sage kings. Third, in sharp distinction to most other thinkers from the Warring States period, Mozi sought supernatural support for his claims. He argued that the moral order he advocated is in perfect accord with the intent of the supreme deity, Heaven, which "wants justice and detests injustice." Heaven is assisted in upholding universal morality by multiple deities that act as minor guardians of Heaven's intent and also constantly intervene in human affairs to punish the vicious and reward the righteous.

Scholars in China and abroad continue to disagree over whether Mozi was a true believer or a mere manipulator of the others' religious beliefs. Aside from emphatic statements in favor of Heaven's just intent, Mozi displays a more sober approach when he rejects the possibility of blind fate and calls upon humans to rely on themselves, disregarding possible extrahuman intervention in their lives. Moreover, Mozi's explicitly instrumental approach toward Heaven's intent, which he defines as a tool to judge world rulers, raises further doubts as to his piety.

Later Mohists

For several generations after Mozi's death his disciples maintained their effective organization and remained intellectually active. The focus of their interest, however, gradually shifted from sociopolitical issues to epistemological questions. Mozi was the first to display interest in modes of argumentation, proposing three criteria for the validity of his doctrines: their origins in the legacy of the ancient sage kings, their corroboration by people's everyday experience, and their usefulness in everyday affairs. Later Mohists further developed the art of argumentation, which led them to focus on many previously unexplored issues, such as logic, the relation of names to reality, the validation of knowledge in face of changing circumstances, and so on. Six chapters of the *Mozi* (40–45) summarize their views, remaining the richest source for the largely extinct logical approaches in ancient Chinese thought. The sophistication of Mohists' argumentation had, however, a negative impact on their school. First, the increasingly active search for abstract truth fueled ideological confrontations among the Mohists, which resulted in inevitable splits. Second, preoccupied with epistemological issues, the Mohists turned their backs on political issues, becoming partly irrelevant in contemporaneous intellectual life. As a result, although at the end of the Warring States period Mohism was still defined as "bright learning," its appeal was shrinking. From the second century B.C.E. Mohists largely disappeared from the intellectual scene, although some of their ideas, such as reducing conspicuous consumption and advancing those worthy to the top of political apparatus, had a lasting impact on Chinese thought and Chinese political culture in general.

See also **Chinese Thought; Confucianism; Legalism, Ancient China.**

BIBLIOGRAPHY

Graham, A. C. *Divisions in Early Mohism Reflected in the Core Chapters of Mo-tzu.* Singapore: Institute of East Asian Philosophies, 1985.

———. *Later Mohist Logic, Ethics, and Science.* Hong Kong: Chinese University Press, 1978.

Maeder, Erik W. "Some Observances on the Composition of the 'Core Chapters' of the *Mozi.*" *Early China* 17 (1992): 27–82.

Mo tzu. *Basic Writings.* Translated by Burton Watson. New York: Columbia University Press, 1963.

Mozi jiao zhu. Compiled by Wu Yujiang. Beijing: Zhonghua shu ju, 1993. Collated glosses on the *Mozi.*

Yuri Pines

MOLECULAR BIOLOGY. *See* **Genetics.**

MONARCHY.

This entry includes two subentries:

Overview
Islamic Monarchy

OVERVIEW

Monarchy derives from a Greek term that refers literally to rule by one person (as distinct from oligarchy, rule by the few, or democracy, rule by the people). Among political systems of a post-tribal nature, monarchy is certainly the most common form of human governance globally throughout human history. While the modern Western world tends to venerate non-monarchic constitutions of the past—such as the city empires of Athens and early Rome, and, to a lesser extent, Babylonia—this elides the near-ubiquity of one-man rule. And while modern authoritarian or despotic regimes are not usually considered to be monarchies, they nevertheless contain elements associated with monarchic rule. The persisting appeal of monarchic governments may stem largely from the perception that, in contrast to populist and self-governing systems, they are more stable and more successful at maintaining peace and order. (This is perhaps encapsulated in Benito Mussolini's [1883–1945] famous declaration that in fascist Italy, under his quasi-monarchic leadership, the trains run on time.) Regardless of whether such a position is empirically true, it has been central to the ideology of monarchy.

The nearly universal acceptance of monarchic rule, at least until recent times, obscures important differences in the ways in which such regimes have been classified and legitimated. Monarchies are by no means of a piece in either their theory or their practice. Important questions remain open to dispute, including: whether the king should be dynastic or elected, and if the latter, by whom; whether in dynastic systems, women should be admitted to succession or men only, or indeed whether succession may even pass through a female line; and whether (and under what circumstances) a king may be removed from power, and if so, in what way. When viewed from this perspective, monarchy ought hardly to be treated as a singular phenomenon at all. Rather, examination of the diverging conceptions of the foundation and source of monarchic power yields recognition of the highly diverse principles upon which ideas about the nature of monarchy have rested over time and across cultural and geographical divides.

Religion

Assessed from a global perspective, perhaps the most common justification given for the rule of a single person is religious. Even in this category, however, many different approaches are available. The ancient Egyptians regarded their kings to be deities, albeit lesser gods in the pantheon. By virtue of his divinity, the Egyptian monarch was qualitatively superior to and at a remove from those over whom he reigned, and his powers were "absolutely absolute," to use Samuel Finer's phrase. Consequently, the king of Egypt was the undisputed owner of all the territories under his control and the master of his subjects, who were all equally inferior to him. The surviving cultural artifacts from three millennia of Egyptian monarchy, such

as architecture, paintings, and written treatises, all reinforce this absolutistic image of royal divinity.

The Romans also deified their emperors in the later stages of their empire, proclaiming them to be *dominus et deus* ("lord and god"). This has sometimes been considered to be a result of the influence of so-called oriental or Eastern monarchic ideas. But it is difficult to gauge how seriously this deification (and attendant absolutist language) ought to be taken, given the persistence of earlier Roman ideas of citizenship and legality. The ideological structure supporting the Chinese dynasties of antiquity, by contrast, approached the Egyptian model more closely. Confucius (c. 551–479? B.C.E.) lent philosophical credence to the long-standing doctrine that while emperors were not themselves deities, they enjoyed the "Mandate of Heaven" in their occupation of the imperial throne. Of course, this mandate did not ensure that the emperors would not be overthrown in a palace coup (any more than the divinity of Egyptian kings protected them against dynastic replacement). Rather, the mandate was an ever-shifting imprimatur that depended upon the emperor's conformity with the fundamental dictates of virtue and equity, in particular the practice of benevolence, according to Confucius.

The monotheistic Abrahamic religions all subscribed to the notion of the divine ordination of kings to some extent. Although the earliest government of the Israelites was a sort of proto-republican federated constitution, the shift to a monarchic regime described in Jewish scripture arose from God's assent to a popular plea for a king so that Israel might resemble the other nations of the region. Israelite monarchy thus emerged as a divine appointment, and kings remained subject to the judgment of God. Once Christianity reached an accommodation with the Roman Empire in the early fourth century, the emperor came to be viewed as a divine agent—free to sin, of course, but a servant of the Heavenly Lord even when he went astray. Christian authors often deployed a microcosmic argument to bolster monarchy: just as God was the king of His creation, so the monarch resembled the supreme master of the universe. Islam also involved religion in the defense of monarchy. In the early history of Islam, the caliph was held to be the agent of God insofar as his conquests facilitated the spread of the Muslim religion and he enforced adherence to the rites of the faith. During a later era, the caliphate was charged in theory, if not in practice, with the imposition of the punishments for violations of *shari'a* (the vast body of Islamic law).

Naturalism

More mundane explanations of a monarch's authority emerge out of images and analogies drawn from nature. In many cultural traditions, the ruling position of the head (or sometimes the heart) in the human body is regarded as an analogue of the monarch. Royal dominion is thus licensed by or in accordance with the observable natural world. One finds this position evinced in East and South Asian writings, such as the *Arthashastra* of Kautilya (fl. late 300s B.C.E.), as well as in Western thought from antiquity through modern times. Alternatively, the supposed dominance of a single leader in the nonhuman organic world (such as among bees or other social creatures) has often been taken as a sign of a natural order subordinate to monarchy. Even the arrangement of the cosmos and the movements of the stars and planets are found to support the monarchic principle.

Perhaps the most widespread naturalistic justification for monarchy, however, is its supposed imitation of the organization of the family. Monarchic government is directly authorized by the presence in the typical family of a father or other male head whose responsibility is to care and provide for all the other members of the household. The rest of the family is expected in turn to submit without question to the superior authority of the father. Confucius insisted that filial piety constituted the quintessential basis of all forms of social relationships, extending as far as the people's obedience to the king. This view enjoyed considerable currency through East Asia well into modern times. Likewise, European authors such as Jean Bodin (1530?–1596) and Sir Robert Filmer (d. 1653) advanced one or another form of the patriarchal thesis.

Modes of Virtue

An alternative to a naturalistic justification of royal rule derives from the view that the monarch should be obeyed on account of the personal qualities that inhere in him, whether these characteristics are physical or psychological or both. Hence many cultures accepted the principle that, in effect, might makes right, in the sense that the warrior who demonstrates the greatest prowess and courage in battle deserves to be revered and obeyed in matters of government. The Greek concept of *aretē* ("excellence" or "virtue"), as espoused in the Homeric epics, epitomized this martial conception of rulership; those who fought gloriously were accorded the greatest deference concerning all political decisions. Similar views can be found in many societies with strong chivalric traditions, such as Japan during the era of the Shogunate or feudal Western Europe during the Middle Ages.

Monarchy might also be justified by the intellectual or moral qualities acquired and refined by a leader. The *Republic* of Plato (427?–347 B.C.E.) speaks of a "philosopher-king" whose competence to govern a city (and even over other philosophers) stems from his preeminence in the exercise of his speculative reason as well as the fully just ordering of his soul. Likewise, Aristotle (384–322 B.C.E.) believed that kingship, as that species of monarchy in which a superlatively virtuous man rules, constituted the ideally best political system, even if he was skeptical that it could be attained in practice. The Roman Marcus Tullius Cicero (106–43 B.C.E.) also believed that among "simple" constitutions, kingship was optimal, as long as the occupant of the royal office remained morally upstanding. Cicero also identified kingship as the chronologically earliest form of human government, since it involves power without a formalized system of laws. But Cicero believed (as did Aristotle) that kingship could readily degenerate into a form of arbitrary rule in the interest of the incumbent, and so he preferred a law-based republican regime.

Niccolò Machiavelli (1469–1527) combined the martial and the psychological elements of monarchy in his *Prince* (written c. 1513–1514 but not published until 1532). Machiavelli stated explicitly that he was addressing a particular sort of monarch: one who came to power not as the result of heredity or divinity but solely on the basis of his own ability (which Machiavelli called, somewhat perversely, *virtù*). On the one hand Machiavelli claimed that military prowess constituted the salient quality of an effective prince; good "arms" must precede good laws. Yet Machiavelli also held that *virtù* had a psychological dimension, insofar as the prince who succeeds in gaining and retaining his state must shun conventional personal morality and adjust to the circumstances of his position in whatever way is required. Hence, while the "self-made" monarch should try to adhere to the precepts of everyday virtue when he can, he must be prepared to contradict the moral teachings of religion and philosophy at those times when following them would lead to political ruin.

Limited Monarchy?

Most ideas of monarchy assumed or even pronounced the absolute power of the ruler, so that despotism was readily licensed. Yet some attempts were made, especially in Western thought, to constrain the reach of royal office. Religion provided one source of limitation. A monarch who engaged in tyrannical actions could be threatened with divine judgment unless he mended his ways. In its most extreme form, as in the *Polycraticus* (completed 1159) by John of Salisbury (c. 1115/20–1180), God's hand might even reach out to an earthly source (human or otherwise) to punish the evil ruler, permitting tyrannicide as a remedy. Alternatively, thinkers looked to election or other mechanisms of consent to hold the monarch in check. During the Latin Middle Ages, scholastic authors widely debated whether monarchy should be elective or inherited, and in a later era, liberals such as John Locke (1632–1704) sought to confine the authority of monarchs by basing their powers on a preexisting social contract.

The attempt to balance constitutional and absolutist dimensions of monarchy produced some interesting, if not always entirely convincing, theories. In his *Six Books of the Commonwealth* (1576), Bodin insisted upon the unfettered power of the monarch but also claimed that the ruler was strictly limited by natural law in the extent to which he could exercise his royal office. G. W. F. Hegel (1770–1831), in the *Philosophy of Right* (1821), posited a system of constitutional government in which the king possessed a single yet still indispensable function: placing the final stamp of his unique, indivisible will on all legislation and thus rendering a bill into statutory force. Hegel believed that short of such an ultimate declaration of will, members of civil society and their legislative representatives would continue to debate the validity of laws and thus undermine the respect due to legal structures.

One might imagine that monarchy is an outmoded idea in the modern world, given the widespread ideology of democracy. In fact, however, numerous countries are still ruled by monarchic regimes, even in Europe. Allegiance to a monarch in countries such as the members of the Commonwealth, comprising former colonies of the British Empire, remains popular. In the same vein, the public and ongoing expression of grief following the death of Princess Diana of the United Kingdom suggests that royal identity, even if only by marriage, remains a very compelling reason for public attention. It seems unlikely that the monarchic principle is likely to disappear entirely any time soon.

See also **Democracy; Republicanism: Republic; State, The.**

BIBLIOGRAPHY

Boesche, Roger. *Theories of Tyranny, from Plato to Arendt.* University Park: Pennsylvania State University Press, 1996.

Brock, Roger, and Stephen Hodkinson, eds. *Alternatives to Athens: Varieties of Political Organization and Community in Ancient Greece.* Oxford and New York: Oxford University Press, 2000.

Currid, John D. *Ancient Egypt and the Old Testament.* Foreword by Kenneth A. Kitchen. Grand Rapids, Mich.: Baker Books, 1997.

Eisenstadt, S. N. *The Political Systems of Empires.* New York: Free Press, 1963.

Finer, S. E. *The History of Government from the Earliest Times.* 3 vols. Oxford and New York: Oxford University Press, 1997.

Loewe, Michael. *Divination, Mythology and Monarchy in Han China.* Cambridge, U.K., and New York: Cambridge University Press, 1994.

Mastnak, Tomaz. *Crusading Peace: Christendom, the Muslim World, and Western Political Order.* Berkeley: University of California Press, 2002.

Cary J. Nederman

ISLAMIC MONARCHY

The question of leadership in the Islamic world is a complicated one. Although until recently monarchies were the most common form of government, Muslim understandings of a ruler's role, qualifications, and relationship to religious and worldly authority have been the focus of intense discussion and have shifted radically since a very early period. Literally hours after the death of Muhammad in 632 C.E., disagreements arose about the identity, qualities, and selection of the caliph, or successor to the Prophet (Ar., *khalifah*). Although it was clear that the caliph should function as the political, military, and religious leader of the community, the method of choosing a caliph was ill-defined at first. Many felt that the caliph should possess special religious qualities, whether noteworthy piety, early conversion to Islam, or blood relation to Muhammad. But the first four caliphs—Abu Bakr (r. 632–634), 'Umar ibn al-Khattab (r. 634–644), 'Uthman ibn 'Affan (r. 644–656) and 'Ali ibn Abi Talib (r. 656–661)—all had varied reputations for piety and differing relations to Muhammad, and were chosen in four unrelated fashions.

It was only in 661 at the accession of Mu'awiya that the Umayyad caliphate (661–750) became the first Islamic dynastic and caliphal monarchy. Knowledge of the Umayyad family is difficult to extract from the generally negative portrayal of them in later historical sources, but one criticism of them did highlight the fact that they were considered by some to be temporal kings (Ar., *muluk*), not religious authorities. Although this charge is difficult to evaluate, it may be said that the Umayyads managed to restrict the caliphate to their own family, forming a dynasty of kings whose political and military authority was evident but whose religious authority may well have been in question.

Abbasids

Ultimately resistance to Umayyad rule led to the Abbasid revolution of 749–750. The Abbasid caliphs (750–1258) traced their descent from Muhammad's uncle 'Abbas, and therefore their claims to legitimacy were considered to be stronger than those of their predecessors, since they were seen as members of the Prophet's house. The Abbasids formed a dynasty in which religious and political power were mingled. According to Muslim thinkers such as Abu Yusuf (d. 798) and al-Mawardi (d. 1058), the Abbasid caliphs needed to possess justice and comprehensive religious knowledge, with which they were to uphold Islamic law and maintain Islamic society.

Caliphs were chosen through a variety of methods, including designation by a ruling caliph, election by a selected body of religious scholars, primogeniture, or any combination of these factors. A caliph had not only to be a member of the Abbasid house but also male, sane, and free of physical restrictions—such as blindness—that might hinder the fulfilment of his duties. While the Abbasids were in power, pre-Islamic Persian ideas about a remote and awe-inspiring monarch were adopted into the Islamic tradition. Eventually the caliph was transformed from the head of the community to the Shadow of God on Earth, elevated far above ordinary people, and supported by an elaborate state bureaucracy and a complicated court protocol.

Military Rulers

The ninth and tenth centuries witnessed the Abbasids' gradual loss of control to military strongmen (emirs, sultans) who were fast becoming the de facto rulers in the Islamic world. This period also saw the rise of anti-caliphs, whether the Sunni Umayyads in Iberia (756–1031) or the Ismaili Shiite Fatimids (909–1171) in North Africa. Both developments led to important changes in Islamic theories about rule, for Muslim thinkers were forced to reconcile the new reality of military rule with the purely theoretical superiority of the caliph.

This was accomplished by thinkers such as the celebrated bureaucrat Nizam al-Mulk (d. 1092) and his equally famous contemporary al-Ghazali (d. 1111). Such theorists penned elaborate manuals on the proper behavior of military rulers, who had no claims to religious authority. These works drew on pre-Islamic Persian ideas about the interdependence of kingship and religion, in which neither could exist without the other because religion furnished a base for kingship and kingship protected religion. Combined with this concept was the equally ancient notion of the Circle of Justice, which espoused a belief in the importance of balance within society among four elements: the king, the army, the subjects, and justice. According to this theory, there could be no king without an army, no army without the wealth obtained from subjects, no subjects without justice in the realm, and no justice without a king to uphold it. The military rule of a sultan fit easily into the models provided by the Circle of Justice and the notion of cooperation between religion and kingship; indeed, eventually the earlier designation of the caliph as the Shadow of God on Earth was transferred to the sultan. This model also allowed scholars and statesmen to function as interpreters of Islamic norms. In this way, rule became dominated by military monarchies and regulated by religious scholars, while the caliph became a figurehead who periodically bestowed recognition on the rulers. Pre-Islamic Persian cultural and literary traditions also contributed the notion of a king of kings (Pers., *shahanshah*), which was easily worked into Islamic ideology.

Turko-Mongol Ideals

These developments were also shaped by Turko-Mongol ideas of kingship, which arrived with nomadic tribes from the central and east Asian steppe in the eleventh century. For Turkic and Mongol nomads, a ruler (Turk., *bey, beg;* Turk. and Mongolian, *khan*) was a charismatic military leader who exercised a highly personal style of rule. Often merely a first among equals, he was directly responsible to his own followers and was expected to settle their disputes, lead them militarily, and reward them for their loyalty through the distribution of spoils and wealth. Although nomadic khans were often members of noble families, their positions depended not only on their lineage but also on their own merits.

The more successful khans believed that their charisma had a divine origin, which was often identified with the spirit or spirits of the Enduring Sky, or God (Mongolian, *Tenggeri;* Turk., *Tanrı*). Such divine favor was expressed through a special good fortune (Mongolian, *su;* Turk., *kut;* Pers., *bakht* or *farr*), which was bestowed on particular rulers by Divine Will and which was demonstrated through military victories. Divinely favored rulers were thought to possess special religious or shamanistic powers. An emphasis on nomadic law (Turk., *töre, türe;* Mongolian, *yasagh* (*yasa*); Ar. to Ottoman Turk., *kanun*) also formed part of nomadic ideals of rulership, since a nomadic khan was expected to uphold the law. These ideas first entered the Islamic world when the Sunni Muslim confederation of Seljuk Turks conquered Khorasan and the Iranian plateau under the charismatic military leader Tughril Beg (d. 1063), who reached Baghdad in 1055 and established the Great Seljuk dynasty (1055–1157) under the benevolent eye of a powerless Abbasid caliph. (Nizam al-Mulk and al-Ghazali both wrote under Seljuk rule.)

Genghis (Chinggis) Khan

The most nomadic famous recipient of divine favor was the Mongol Temüchin, or Genghis (Chinggis) Khan (d. 1227). Genghis Khan rose from a noble but impoverished background to absolute rule and was thought to possess the power bestowed by God in the form of a divine mandate, which later passed to his descendants. According to the divine mandate, God had granted universal rule to the Chinggisids, who were charged with implementing that rule on earth through territorial conquest. The divine mandate passed to all Chinggisids, male and female, although only men reigned openly; women ruled primarily as regents for their sons. The position of Great Khan was usually limited to the sons of a chief wife, but within this restriction such factors as primogeniture, ultimogeniture, the preference of the current ruler, and the approval of the Genghisid family and the Mongol nobility all could play a role. As a result of this new and powerful model of kingship, the death of the Abbasid caliph al-Musta'sim at Mongol hands in Baghdad in 1258 therefore spelled for many a sea-change in understandings of rule. Despite the hasty revival of an Abbasid caliphate in Cairo (1261–1517), not all Muslims recognized it as legitimate. At first, Muslim kings and their advisors

focused on the military defense of the Islamic world against the pagan Mongol invaders. When the religious scholar Ibn Jama'ah (d. 1333) wrote an advice work in the early thirteenth century, he elaborated in great detail on the king's responsibility for defending the community.

But soon Mongol sovereigns themselves began to convert to Islam and employ Islamic models of kingship. Among these new Muslims were the khans of the Golden Horde in southern Russia and central Asia (1241–1480) and their Ilkhanid cousins in Iran (1258–1335). Their conversions led to important changes in the development of Islamic monarchies, since Muslim Mongols ruled both as divinely chosen descendants of Genghis Khan and as Muslim sovereigns, advised by Islamic scholars. Theories of rule in this era drew not only on the well-established Persian Islamic models but also on Greek philosophical thought, which was embodied by the work of authors such as al-Razi (d. 1256), al-Tusi (d. 1274), and Kashifi (fl. 1494–1495). These ideas envisioned a society divided into four distinct classes: men of the sword, men of the pen, merchants, and cultivators. In this model the ruler functioned as an enlightened philosopher king, whose task was to maintain each class in its proper place through the just application of Islamic law.

Post-Mongol Period

After the political disintegration of Mongol rule in the fourteenth century, new Muslim Turkic monarchies arose and modeled themselves on the Muslim Mongol example. At first they struggled with the dominant Mongol ideology and styled themselves guardians of the Chinggisid heritage by marrying Chinggisid princesses, using Chinggisid puppets, and upholding Mongol law. Later, Turkic dynasties began to replace Genghis Khan with their own noble ancestors and promoted both their own tribal law codes and their own versions of Mongol-style divine favor. Simultaneously they ruled as Muslim military leaders and made use of the well-established themes of justice and order. Among these was the warlord Timur (Tamerlane, d. 1405), who began as a Genghis Khan imitator but also relied on Islamic models of kingship. Timur's own dynasty ultimately grew to rival that of Genghis Khan and reached a conclusion in the career of Babur (d. 1530), founder of the Mughal Empire in northern India (1526–1858). Babur epitomized the Muslim sovereign but also prided himself on his impeccable lineage: his paternal descent was from Timur, and his maternal descent from Genghis Khan.

A long-term problem for Muslim monarchs of nomadic origin was their tribal laws, which posed a potential challenge to Islamic law (Ar., *shari'a*). Under the longest-lived Islamic dynasty, the Ottomans (1281–1923), tribal laws coexisted uneasily with Islamic law until Muslim thinkers under Sultan Kanuni Süleyman (Süleyman "the Lawgiver," r. 1520–1566) reconciled the two into a single coherent legal system (Ar. to Ottoman Turk., *kanun*), which became identified with the Ottoman state in general and the person of Süleyman in particular. Under the Ottomans the Persian and Greek concepts of the ruler as the upholder of justice and order were also linked both to the nomadic idea of the ruler as a lawgiver and to Islamic law itself.

Safavids and Successors

In a more radical development of Turko-Mongol norms, especially the notion of divine favor, the Safavid monarchy in Iran (1501–1736) assumed that the ruler possessed a direct personal connection to God, which allowed him to implement God's will in his kingdom through law. Although the Safavids were eventually succeeded by the tribal dynasties of the Afsharids (1736–1796) under Nadir Shah (d. 1746) in the east, and the Zands (1751–1794) in the west, these successors were seen by some as monarchies of warlords, lacking legitimate claims to rule and devoid of the religious aura that had surrounded the Safavids. Indeed, Zand rulers were never addressed as *king* (Pers., *shah*), and maintained a Safavid puppet until 1773. Subsequently the Turkic tribal Qajar monarchy (1795–1925) eliminated both the Zands and the Afsharids and went on to control Iran as independent kings. Although perfunctorily religious, the Qajars lacked the religious charisma of the Safavids and ruled by drawing on their heroic Turkic history, their former support of the Safavid state, and the Iranian cultural tradition of the king of kings.

Modern Monarchies

In the nineteenth century the Ottoman sultans began to investigate European-style parliamentary monarchies, but this model was not fully established until the abolishment of the Ottoman Empire in 1923 and the creation of the modern republic of Turkey, which replaced the monarch with an elected president and a parliament. Similar in focus were the khedival dynasty of Egypt (1805–1952) and the Hashimite dynasty of Iraq (1921–1958), which also developed into parliamentary monarchies and which were likewise replaced by republican governments.

One particular challenge for twentieth-century monarchies was the concept of secularism, which in some cases removed the religious ideology used by earlier kings to legitimate their rule but left nothing in its place. A noted secular monarchy was the Pahlavi dynasty in Iran (1925–1979), which succeeded the Qajars. The Pahlavis downplayed Islamic ideas in favor of their own pre-Islamic Persian heritage, which combined with their oppressive rule to provoke their overthrow in favor of an Islamic Republic in 1978–1979.

In the early twenty-first century, monarchies in majority countries with an Islamic majority tend to rely on some evocation of religious legitimacy. The al-Saud family of Saudi Arabia and the Hashimite monarchy of Jordan, for example, practice official state versions of Islam and rule with either secular or Islamic law. However, some modern monarchies have been challenged by Islamist resistance groups, which have proposed alternate visions of society in which sovereignty belongs to God alone.

See also **Empire and Imperialism: Middle East; Law, Islamic; Monarchy: Overview.**

BIBLIOGRAPHY

PRIMARY SOURCES

Abū Yūsuf Ya'qūb. *Abū Yūsuf's Kitāb al-Kharāj.* Translated by A. Ben Shemesh. Leiden, Netherlands: E. J. Brill; London: Luzac, 1969.

Ghazali. *Ghazālī's Book of Counsel for Kings (Nas'īat al-mulūk).* Translated by F. R. C. Bagley. London and New York: Oxford University Press, 1964.

Ibn Jamā'ah, Badr al-Dīn Muhammad. *Tahrīr al-Ahkām fī tadbīr ahl al-islam.* Edited by Fu'ād 'Abd al-Mun'im Ahmad Al-Daha. Qatar: Dār al-Thaqāfah, 1988. In Arabic.

Kashifi, Husayn Va'iz. *Akhlaq-i Muhsini; or, The Morals of the Beneficent.* Translated by H. G. Keene. Hertford, U.K.: Austin, 1850.

Mas'udi. *The Meadows of Gold.* Translated and edited by Paul Lunde and Caroline Stone. London and New York: Kegan Paul International, 1989.

Mawardī, 'Alī b. Muhammad. *The Laws of Islamic Governance.* Translated by Asadullah Yate. London: Ta-Ha Publishers, 1996.

———. *The Ordinances of Government.* Translated by Wafaa H. Wahbah. Reading, U.K.: Garnet, 1996.

Najm al-Dīn Razi. *The Path of God's Bondsmen from Origin to Return: A Sufi Compendium.* Translated by Hamid Algar. Delmar, N.Y.: Caravan Books, 1982.

Nizām al-Mulk. *The Book of Government; or, Rules for Kings: The Siyar al-Muluk or Siyasat-Namah of Nizam al-Mulk.* 2nd ed. Translated by Hubert Darke. London and Boston: Routledge & Kegan Paul, 1978.

Tusi, Nasir al-Dīn Muhammad. *Akhlaq-i Nasiri.* Edited by Mujtaba Minuvi and Aliriza Haydari. Tehran: Khvarizmi Publishers, 1977. Translated into English as *The Nasirean Ethics, by Nasir al-Din Tusir.* Translated by G. M. Wickens. London: Allen and Unwin, 1964.

SECONDARY SOURCES

Allsen, Thomas T. "Changing Forms of Legitimation in Mongol Iran." In vol. 2, *Rulers from the Steppe: State Formation on the Eurasian Periphery,* edited by Gary Seaman and Daniel Marks. Los Angeles: Ethnographics Press, 1991.

The Cambridge History of Iran. 7 vols. Cambridge, U.K.: Cambridge University Press, 1968–1991.

Cobb, Paul M. *White Banners: Contention in 'Abbāsid Syria, 750–880.* Albany: State University of New York Press, 2001.

Fleischer, Cornell H. *Bureaucrat and Intellectual in the Ottoman Empire: The Historian Mustafa Āli (1541–1600).* Princeton, N.J.: Princeton University Press, 1986.

Golden, Peter B. "Imperial Ideology and the Sources of Political Unity Among the Pre-Činggisid Nomads of Western Eurasia." *Archivum Eurasiae Medii Aevi* 2 (1982): 37–76.

Hawting, G. R. *The First Dynasty of Islam: The Umayyad Caliphate AD 661–750.* 2nd ed. London and New York: Routledge, 2000.

Inalcik, Halil. "The Ottoman Succession and Its Relationship to the Turkish Concept of Sovereignty." In *The Middle East and the Balkans under the Ottoman Empire: Essays on Economy and Society.* Bloomington: Indiana University Turkish Studies, 1993.

Kostiner, Joseph, ed. *Middle East Monarchies: The Challenge of Modernity.* Boulder, Colo., and London: Lynne Rienner, 2000.

Lambton, A. K. S. "Justice in the Medieval Persian Theory of Kingship." *Theory and Practice in Medieval Persian Government.* London: Variorum Reprints, 1980.

Shaban, M. A. *The 'Abbasid Revolution.* Cambridge, U.K.: Cambridge University Press, 1970.

Woods, John E. "Timur's Genealogy." In *Intellectual Studies on Islam: Essays Written in Honor of Martin B. Dickson.* Salt Lake City: University of Utah Press, 1990.

Anne F. Broadbridge

MONASTICISM.

The "idea of monasticism" invites a misconception, because monasticism is not an idea but a practice. It is a discipline of life, encapsulated in a vow to obey a rule. Monasticism is not a theory about the good life, and still less an escape from practicality, but rather a commitment to live according to a rule handed down from a founder. In its classical Western form deriving from St. Benedict (c. 480–547), a rule directs a monastic to spend a lifetime in one cloister under one abbot following one routine. This secluded way of life begets institutions, some of them highly complex, and these in turn nurture the kind of inner life that in the early twenty-first century is called "spirituality." Monastic *orthopraxy* regulates behavior through conformity to a rule, and contrasts with doctrinal *orthodoxy* that regulates belief through a magisterium or teaching office. Implausible though it may seem, a rule shields monastics from obsession with theorizing. Day in and day out, monastics live an ethos that others may merely preach. To this extent Christian monasticism resembles Rabbinic Judaism. Both pivot on obeying rules, and both tend to disregard niceties of belief. A crucial difference pertains, however. Whereas Jews affirm that the mandates of Torah come from God, Christians acknowledge that any rule comes from a human lawgiver.

History

As a mode of life that vows obedience to a rule, monasticism originated not in the Near East but in India with Siddhartha Gautama the Buddha (c. 563–c. 483 B.C.E.). His rule or *vinaya* governed conduct of life initially for the Buddha's community or *sangha* of immediate followers. Nine months of the year they wandered, but during the three months of the monsoon they settled in a *vihara* or monastery. Eventually the Buddha delivered a separate rule for women. Parallel phenomena coexisted within Jainism and Hinduism. Christian monasticism emerged six or seven centuries later in the deserts of the Eastern Mediterranean. Although Rabbinic Judaism (together with Islam) repudiates asceticism, Jewish precedents for Christian extremism emerged in a wanderer such as John the Baptist (c. 7 B.C.E.–c. 27 C.E.) or in the Qumran community. Christian ascetics of whom little is known roved the deserts of Syria and Egypt. The lifestyle of these spiritual "athletes" crystallized in figures such as Anthony of Egypt (c. 251–356) and Pachomius (c.290–346). Experience as a soldier equipped Pachomius to write a rule for, as it were, an army-camp of ascetics. By mid-fourth century in Egypt, hermits living alone or in loose groups practiced *eremitical* monasticism, while desert fathers and mothers living in community practiced *cenobitical* monasticism. The head of a consecrated community was called an *abba* (father) or *amma* (mother). From the start monks were copying manuscripts, as they would continue to do for the next twelve centuries. Eastern desert monasticism passed to France through fourth-century intermediaries such as Martin of Tours (c. 316–400), Hilary of Poitiers (401–449), and above all John Cassian of Marseilles (360–435). Epitomized in the disputed figure of St. Patrick (c. 385–461), an Englishman who may have dwelt at Cassian's houses near Marseilles, Irish monasticism emerged in the mid-fifth century through contact with France. In sixth- and seventh-century Ireland, an island that had never known Roman cities, an abbot ruled as a kind of tribal chieftain who outranked bishops. No amount of asceticism could, however, prevent Celtic monasticism from collapsing in the Viking raids of the ninth century.

By 450, Eastern Christian monasticism was coalescing not just in the desert but also in cities such as Alexandria, Antioch, and Constantinople, while its Western counterpart kept spreading in self-sufficient rural communities. Monastics lived in an enclosure or cloister that fenced a church, a refectory, a library, dormitories, and subsistence farming. Monasticism produced vastly more varieties in Western Europe than anywhere else. Proliferation of types—notably during two periods, one from 1100 to 1250 and the other from 1520 to 1700—complicates the task of classifying Western monasticism. Fundamental differences separate cloistered orders who, at least until the thirteenth century, preferred to dwell in the country and Mendicant friars who, in the wake of St. Francis of Assisi (1182–1226), frequented cities and towns preaching and begging for alms. Stemming from the Black Monks, who only in the seventeenth century acquired the name of Benedictines, other rural orders were the Carthusians (founded 1084) and the Cistercians (founded 1098). Following the example of the Franciscan friars (organized 1209), thirteenth-century Mendicants came to include three other orders: the Dominicans (organized 1215), who preached against heresy; the Carmelites (organized by the pope in 1247) who originated as hermits on Mount Carmel in Palestine; and the Augustinian Friars (organized by the pope in 1256), whose most famous member was Martin Luther (1483–1546). Whereas the pre-1200 Benedictines had cultivated son-to-father obedience to an abbot, Mendicants cultivated sibling-to-sibling relations to one another. Excelling all these in martial vigor were the warrior monks of Crusader Palestine, including the Knights Templar (who emerged c. 1119 and were dissolved in 1312) and the Knights Hospitaller (who emerged c. 1080 and in 1530 took the name Knights of Malta).

A second crucial distinction differentiates *contemplative* orders founded before 1215 from post-Reformation *active* orders and congregations such as the Jesuits (founded 1540) or Oratorians (founded 1575). The latter comprise not monastics but clerks regular: priests who follow a rule while ministering in the world. Having no lay brothers, the Jesuits and Oratorians are not monastics, and neither are the numerous post-1520 female teaching or nursing congregations such as the Ursulines (founded 1535) or Sisters of Charity (founded 1633). Nevertheless, from 1298 until the early 1970s, canon law obliged women's congregations in solemn vows to stay cloistered.

A third distinction pertains to Eastern and Western Christianity. In contrast to Western organizational fecundity, Eastern Christian monasticism functions under just one rule: that ascribed to St. Basil the Great (329–379). As a result, Eastern Christian monasticism has upheld one model through sixteen centuries, while Western monasticism has initiated reforms in nearly every generation. To be sure, monastic reform means not launching a fresh departure but rather attempting to install a better version of the past. In Western Christianity the

Monastery on Mount Athos, Greece. The monastic community on Mount Athos is located at the tip of the Chalcidice Peninsula in north-eastern Greece. The first monasteries were built on Mount Athos during the ninth century. © YANN ARTHUS-BERTRAND/CORBIS

idea of monasticism implies constant renewal in quest of a founder's vision or "source experience."

Buddhist monasticism differs structurally from Christian or Hindu forms. When the Buddha founded his religion, he conceived it solely as a monasticism. Lay Buddhism emerged after his lifetime and in Asia still presupposes proximity to a *sangha*. In Christianity and Hinduism, by way of contrast, monasticism competes with many other embodiments of the religion. This means that at least until the late twentieth century, classification of types of Buddhist monasticism amounts to classification of the religion as a whole, whereas classification of Christian monasticism does not. Three major types of Buddhism stand out: (1) In Sri Lanka, Thailand, Burma, Laos, and Cambodia, Theravada or the "Way of the Elders" claims to descend directly from the historical Buddha. It offers to individual monastics rules for working out during this or later lifetimes gradual passage to enlightenment. (2) In India and then in China, Korea, Japan, and Vietnam, Mahayana emerged at least six to eight centuries after the historical Buddha, and the first three of those countries generated numerous schools of thought and practice, each with its own ritual, texts, and lineage of masters. Some schools promised enlightenment to laypeople and not just to monastics, while innovative "pure land" leaders in Japan such as Shinran (1173–1262) discarded monasticism. (3) Starting in the eighth century, Indo-Tibetan Buddhism or Vajrayana fostered many sects or schools in Northern India, Tibet, Nepal, and Mongolia. Under the leadership of the present Dalai Lama (1935–), leader of the Gelukpa school, Tibetan Buddhism has spread throughout the world. Many non-Buddhists in the early twenty-first century mistakenly regard Tibetan forms as synonymous with Buddhism

per se. This misperception overlooks the dozens of schools of Theravada, Mahayana, and Vajrayana that thrive throughout Asia and increasingly in the West.

Twentieth-Century Changes

Asian Buddhism enforces the *vinaya* strictly, not least because that is what the historical Buddha did. In order to promote meditation, traditional Asian Buddhism imposes a life of renunciation—including dietary restrictions, memorization of texts, and attendance at ceremonies—with a stringency that Western adepts often evade. In consequence monastic rigor is diminishing among new Buddhists in North America, Europe, and Australia. Many so-called Western Buddhists appear intent to de-monasticize their religion. As a countertrend, since the 1960s Buddhist and Christian monastics have delighted in comparing their ways of life. The Trappist monk Thomas Merton (1915–1968) and the Dalai Lama helped to initiate joint scholarly meetings and other intermonastic encounters.

In Eastern Christianity, monastics retain authority not least because most bishops come from their ranks. Moreover, liturgies remain quintessentially monastic through use of chant, an unhurried pace, and lay adherence to monastic rules for fasting. Characteristically, Eastern Christianity boasts a "monastic republic" of male monasteries on the Holy Mountain of Athos—the easternmost arm of the Chalcidice Peninsula in northeastern Greece. In order to uphold an autonomy that excludes women, the Holy Mountain enjoys exemption from laws of Greece and of the European Community. No Western monastic site—and least of all the rebuilt Monte Cassino south of Rome—so resoundingly epitomizes the idea of Western

Cloister inside monastery on Mount Athos. Mount Athos enjoys status as a separate political division from the rest of Greece, allowing its collection of monasteries to legally exclude women from the peninsula. No female has been allowed in the community since the eleventh century. © DAVE G. HOUSER/CORBIS

monasticism as Mount Athos does for the Eastern idea. As the English classicist Graham Speake explains, that idea entails a process of inner transformation known as *theosis,* whereby the image of God nurtured in each adept gradually transfigures, indeed divinizes him or her, in body, mind, and spirit.

The prestige of Western monasticism once stood equally high. The period of medieval history from 700 to 1050 is frequently labeled the "Monastic Era," and the reforms inaugurated by monastic popes such as Gregory VII (1020–1085; ruled as pope 1073–1085) can be viewed as having imposed on all priests the practice of celibacy previously reserved to monastics. Needless to say, Roman Catholic monastics no longer command such attention. To be sure, in Europe pilgrimages to monastic centers such as Santiago de Compostela in northwestern Spain or the shrine of the Black Madonna at Czestochowa in southern Poland draw hundreds of thousands, as do celebrations for youth sponsored by the ecumenical monastery of Taizé, founded in Burgundy during the 1940s. Nevertheless, apart from pilgrimages, the *institutions* of contemplative monasticism engage only a tiny minority of Western Christians, while the *spirituality* that developed there wins ever-greater admiration.

Meanwhile, gender studies has transformed the understanding of the idea of monasticism. This scholarly revolution

can make it embarrassing to read master historians such as the Benedictines' David Knowles (1896–1974) or Jean Leclercq (1911–1993), who too often wrote as though all monastics were male. Since the 1970s researchers have reclaimed phenomena as diverse as the Desert Mothers of fourth-century Egypt, double houses of male and female monastics in twelfth-century France and England, and the rather widespread acknowledgement before 1100 of the spiritual equality of women and men. The Benedictine Hildegard of Bingen (1098–1179) has come to be hailed widely as one of the most original Christian writers ever. Many have come to deplore the pronouncement of Pope Boniface VIII (c. 1235–1303; ruled as pope 1294–1303) in 1298 that placed under enclosure all women in solemn vows. The constraint remained in force until the early 1970s. As the American historian Jo Ann Kay McNamara and the English philosopher Grace Jantzen, among others, show, almost everywhere in the West women monastics have proven to be at least as creative as men. At first nearly every branch of Eastern Christianity fostered autonomous houses for women, but many of these communities withered under Islamic occupation. In Theravada Buddhism and in Tibetan Buddhism, by way of contrast, a millennium ago women lost permission to receive the highest ordination as nuns (*bhikkuni*), while in Mahayana countries such as China, Japan, and, above all, Korea nuns have held their own.

WHAT DO WE KNOW ABOUT ST. BENEDICT?

A scholarly controversy of utmost delicacy affects interpretation of the reputed founder of Western monasticism, the author of its major rule, St. Benedict of Nursia (c. 480–547). The words of his *Rule* have been pondered in thousands of monasteries, and episodes from his life have animated countless paintings and hagiographies. Regrettably, apart from his *Rule,* all record of St. Benedict and his life comes from a single source, Book II of the *Dialogues,* supposedly written in 593 by Pope Gregory I (c. 540–604; ruled as pope 590–604). That account interweaves miracle stories of a rural wonder-worker with tales of the saint's periods of residence at mountain locations in central Italy such as Nursia, Subiaco, and Monte Cassino. Since the sixteenth century, the authenticity of Gregory's authorship of the *Dialogues* has occasionally been questioned, but never so comprehensively as by Francis Clark in *The Pseudo-Gregorian Dialogues* (1987). Clark argues that Benedict's rule appeared only in 655 in Gaul and around 675 in Britain, being acclaimed only after 717 when Monte Cassino began to be built; and that a clerk in the papal archives ("the Dialogist") compiled the *Dialogues* (first reported to exist in the 680s) and ascribed the document falsely to Gregory I. The Dialogist's "literary patchwork" intersperses miracle legends (some originating after Gregory's death) with eighty genuine Gregorian passages presumably culled from archives in the Lateran Palace. These genuine passages comprise 25 percent of the whole, half of them in Book IV. The Dialogist recounts prodigies of recluses in a legalistic style quite different from Gregory's own. In themes, allusions, and word frequencies, the *Dialogues* differ from every known work by Gregory. Moreover, the tales glorify many persons, including St. Benedict's sister Scholastica, whom no other text from before 690 so much as mentions. Thus Clark's argument revises the entire account of "Benedictine" monasticism down to the 730s. In his view its true creators were not, as previously believed, monastics at Monte Cassino in the 540s or at the Gregorian papal court of the 590s, but rather Italian and French monastics of the 720s who drew inspiration from the newly available *Dialogues.* As yet only a few Benedictines have accepted this revision, not least because it demolishes their order's foundational narrative. Cognitive dissonance between the 1300-year-old account and Clark's revision remains too acute, but as Clark's sequel *The "Gregorian" Dialogues and the Origins of Benedictine Monasticism* (2003) shows, the tide is beginning to turn. One can no longer affirm the traditional account of how Benedictine monasticism began. All that is known is that a rule ascribed to a certain Benedict had surfaced by the 650s and had begun to establish its preeminence by 720. The idea of Western monasticism no longer enjoys an agreed-upon foundational story. Seldom has a legend accepted for so long dissolved so abruptly. A gigantic task of rethinking looms.

Monasticism as the Institutional Matrix of Spirituality
During the last decades of the twentieth century, postmodernists began to conflate the idea of monasticism with that of *spirituality.* The latter word means a process of inner transformation in the presence of God such as Christian monastics pioneered from the fourth century onward. In the twelfth century the Latin word *spiritualitas* came into use among Cistercians to denote the presence of the Holy Spirit within a monastic. Both the adjective *spiritual* and the noun *mysticism* sprouted in seventeenth-century France to describe inner religious experience of monastics and laity alike. But only in the 1920s did Roman Catholic theologians of asceticism adopt the noun *spiritualité* to denote anyone's experience of the divine within. Although many Eastern Christian monastics hesitate to apply this Latin-derived word to the process of inner reconditioning that they call *theosis* (i.e., divinization), no one doubts that it was monastics in East and West who propounded what has come to be called "spirituality." The years of postmodernity of the late twentieth and early twenty-first centuries in the West saw treasures from seventeen centuries of monastic interiority exit the cloister and invade the mainstream of religious publishing—for example, in the series *The Classics of Western Spirituality* published since the 1970s by the Paulist Press.

The Dutch literary scholar M. B. Pranger calls into question postmodern infatuation with spirituality by contrasting its eclecticism with the monotony of textual memory within pre-1200 monasteries. The practice of *lectio divina* invited a monastic to nestle inside a text as if it were a cloister, where the mind encountered memories of other scriptural passages. Across a lifetime of rereading the same texts, a monastic recalled previous acts of remembering, as each act of memory condensed previous ones into an eternal moment. Thus *lectio divina* called into being a community of monastic reciters of the same texts, above all of the psalms, the Gospels, and the Rule of St. Benedict. Naturally, no medieval author could have imagined the popularity that monastic writings rooted in centuries of *lectio divina* would attract at the turn of the twenty-first century. Mass marketing undermines the idea of monasticism as a life spent in a reciting community ruminating on a few texts.

Postmodernity has enlarged the community of readers of monastic texts to include nearly everyone who pursues a spiritual quest. Just as Western Buddhists are de-monasticizing the practice of Buddhism, so the "Spirituality Revolution" among Christians in Europe, North America, and Australia is de-monasticizing the legacy of Christian interiority. The very idea of monasticism as lifelong commitment to a rule is being diluted. At a time when texts of monastic origin are read more widely than ever before, consumers of these distillations of the cloistered life probably understand less of the idea of monasticism (i.e., of religious orthopraxy) than ever before. In response to the postmonastic ethos of the early twenty-first century, the idea of spirituality is being de-institutionalized, while texts by monastics are being spiritualized. Scholars such as M.B. Pranger, Marilyn Dunn, Frank Senn, and Kees Waaijman are laboring to re-insert the study of Christian spirituality into a monastic context, where obedience to a rule governs all.

See also **Orthodoxy; Orthopraxy; Practices; Sacred Places.**

BIBLIOGRAPHY
Clark, Francis. *The "Gregorian" Dialogues and the Origins of Benedictine Monasticism.* Leiden, Netherlands: E. J. Brill, 2003. Updates the controversy and refutes attempted rebuttals of the 1987 work.
———. *The Pseudo-Gregorian Dialogues.* 2 vols. Leiden, Netherlands: E. J. Brill, 1987. Summarized 1:10-30, the argument challenges the authorship of the *Dialogues* traditionally ascribed to Gregory I. See sidebar.
Dunn, Marilyn. *The Emergence of Monasticism: From the Desert Fathers to the Early Middle Ages.* Oxford: Blackwell, 2000. Covers East and West to c. 650.
Jantzen, Grace. *Power, Gender, and Christian Mysticism.* Cambridge, U.K.: Cambridge University Press, 1995. Reconceptualizes methodologies for interpreting male and female monastic mystics.
Johnston, William M., ed. *Encyclopedia of Monasticism.* Chicago and London: Fitzroy Dearborn, 2000. More than 500 articles on Buddhist and Christian monasticism of all periods and places with bibliographies. Whalen Lai's twelve articles abound in comparisons.
Kardong, Terrence, OSB. "Who Wrote the *Dialogues of Saint Gregory?* A Report on a Controversy." *Cistercian Studies Quarterly* 39:1 (2004): 31–39. Endorses Francis Clark's conclusions and acknowledges the Rule as our sole source of knowledge about Benedict.
McNamara, Jo Ann Kay. *Sisters in Arms: Catholic Nuns through Two Millennia.* Cambridge, Mass.: Harvard University Press, 1996. Compares male and female Christian monastics in depth with massive bibliography.
Mitchell, Donald W., and James A. Wiseman, OSB, eds. *The Gethsemani Encounter: A Dialogue on the Spiritual Life by Buddhist and Christian Monastics.* New York: Continuum, 1998. Judicious essays by twenty-four authors on a wide range of issues.
Pranger, M.B. *The Artificiality of Christianity: Essays on the Poetics of Monasticism.* Stanford, Calif.: Stanford University Press, 2003. Exhilarating reassessment of modes of reading and remembering among Western Christian monastics to 1700.
Senn, Frank C. *Christian Liturgy: Catholic and Evangelical.* Minneapolis: Fortress, 1997. Delineates Western monastic liturgies in chapters 4–7, 16–18.
Speake, Graham. *Mount Athos: Renewal in Paradise.* New Haven: Yale University Press, 2002. Superbly illustrated volume evokes Orthodox monasticism's archetypal site.
Waaijman, Kees. *Spirituality: Forms, Foundations, Methods.* Translated by John Vriend. Leuven, Belgium: Peeters, 2002. Reconfigures methodology in light of dozens of case studies of Christian monastics.

William M. Johnston

MONISM. Monism is the doctrine that there is only one principle in terms of which all reality is to be explained. Doctrines differ as to the nature and activity of this principle and its relations to the appearance and experience of multiplicity. Monists explain multiplicity or plurality in the world either as derivative from the one principle or as an illusion. Monism is found in philosophical, religious, and cosmological doctrines. The concept itself is ancient, though the first appearance of the term *monism* in Western philosophy is in Christian von Wolff's *Logic* (1728).

Religious Systems

Religious monism has two forms: atheism and pantheism. Both deny that there is a transcendent deity. Pantheism posits a deity that is immanent to the world and on which the world completely depends. Atheism states that there is no deity at all. Critics of pantheism sometimes conflate it with atheism, on the grounds that a true God must be transcendent.

Brahmanism. Among the most ancient forms of pantheism is Brahmanism. Many of its main tenets were expressed in the Upanishads and systematized by the Vedanta-sutras. Its beginning is traced to the seventh-century thinker Gaudapada, who denied individuation and plurality. Appearances, as well as individual minds, are only temporary manifestations of the all-soul. Master Sankara (c. 700–750, India), author of commentaries on the Brahma-sutra, on parts of the Upanishads, and on the *Mandukya-karika,* studied with a pupil of Gaudapada. For Sankara, only the Brahman is real, and plurality and difference are an illusion.

Gnosticism. Gnosticism is the name given to various doctrines of salvation through knowledge. The first gnostic sects were pre-Christian. Scholars argue about Persian Mazdeism, Greek mysteries, Egyptian doctrines, or Babylonian astrology and religions as possible roots of Gnostic thought. Gnosticism came into contact with Judaism and early Christianity, borrowing some names and concepts, though refusing the main tenets. Ancient Gnosticism held that everything flows from one purely spiritual principle. The origins of matter were explained as a flaw in a long line of successive emanations from the one principle. While matter is impure, its existence is temporary: Gnostic eschatology states that ultimately the original unity and purity will be restored. Gnostic sects include the Syrian school and the Alexandrian school (early second century).

Sufism. Only rarely do Judeo-Christian forms of mysticism accept monism. John Scotus Erigena (c. 810–c. 877) in Ireland, Johannes Eckehart (Meister Eckehart; c. 1260–?1327) in Germany, and Nicholas of Cusa (1401–1464) endorsed forms of pantheism. The same is true for Islamic Sufism, which appeared as a reaction to the overly worldly tendencies of Islam in the late seventh century C.E. While most Sufi authors stressed personal discipline, asceticism, and purity as necessary elements to prepare the soul to know and unite with a transcendent God (which hardly qualify them as monist), it is interesting to mention figures that stressed a metaphysical unity of all beings in God. In the thirteenth century, the Spanish-born Ibn al-'Arabi (1165–1240) created a theory of the "Unity of Being." According to this theory, all existence is one, a manifestation of the underlying divine reality. Sufi currents that stressed the unity of all reality were present also in Indian Muslim communities in the late sixteenth and early seventeenth centuries. Mainstream Sufi authors reacted against monistic trends, stressing that a unity of vision (the mystical experience) did not correspond to a unity of reality.

Philosophical Systems

In philosophical systems, three forms of metaphysical monism can be identified: materialism, idealism, and neutral monism (in which the first principle is neither matter nor mind).

Neutral monists. Parmenides (b. c. 515 B.C.E.) juxtaposes *doxa* (mere belief or nonbeing) and *aletheia* (truth or being). Being is one, unchangeable, and atemporal, and the experience of change and plurality is illusion. Parmenides's student, Zeno of Elea (c. 495–c. 430 B.C.E.), argued against the reality of plurality and motion. Plotinus (205–270 B.C.E.), the most famous and influential of the Neoplatonists, held that everything is an emanation from the One, flowing to lower and lower degrees of reality until matter is formed.

Another famous monist was Baruch Spinoza (1632–1677). In his *Ethics* (1677), Spinoza argues that there is at most and at least only one substance, God. His study of René Descartes (1596–1650) and the new science resulted in a metaphysical system where everything is a necessary manifestation (mode) of this single substance, which is conceived under the attributes of extension and thought.

Materialism. Materialists deny the existence of any nonmaterial substance. Materialists are often, but not necessarily, atheists: some, such as the Stoics, or Thomas Hobbes

(1588–1679), held that God is corporeal. Among the earliest forms of materialism was atomism. Leucippus (5th century B.C.E.) and Democritus (c. 460–c. 370 B.C.E.) believed in an infinite number of indivisible bodies (atoms) moving in a void (nonbeing). Their movements, aggregations, and interactions explain every aspect of experience, including mental life. Epicurus (Greece, 341–270 B.C.E.) developed an atomistic ethics, claiming that the pleasures of the mind and the deliverance from passions constitute human happiness. Lucretius's (c. 100 to 90–c. 55 to 53 B.C.E.) poem *De rerum natura* (On the nature of things) had the most developed exposition of ancient atomism. Other atomist-like schools include the Indian school of Vaisesika, founded presumably by Kasyapa (c. 2nd–3rd century C.E.), which posited an infinity of atoms, of which nine kinds are identified, which constitutes all reality. The Medieval Islamic group of Asharites known as the *mutakallimun* (8th–12th century) held that God was the direct and continuous cause of all created beings (composed of atoms) and of the maintenance of each atom, from instant to instant. This doctrine of atomic time presaged Descartes and the Occasionalists, though without the commitment to a transcendent God.

Seventeenth- and eighteenth-century materialism arose with the scientific revolution's mechanical philosophy. Most natural philosophers were not materialist monists (because they believed in a transcendent God and in incorporeal souls), yet there are exceptions. Giordano Bruno (1548–1600), who was burned as a heretic, presented a pantheistic system in which the world and its soul are one. Thomas Hobbes in *Leviathan* (1651) developed a geometrical account of natural, human, and political science, where he argued that reality is only bodies in motion and these explain perception, our human ideas and volitions, and the body politic.

During the Enlightenment materialists like Julien Offroy de La Mettrie (1709–1751) and Baron Paul-Henri-Dietrich d'Holbach (1723–1789) wrote about the material and "mechanical" nature of man and rejected any immaterial God. Some Enlightenment philosophers (Denis Diderot, Holbach) were atheists, others opted for deism, or the belief that God acted exclusively through natural laws. The borders between deism, pantheism, or downright atheism were often quite blurred (as in Anthony Ashley Cooper, third earl of Shaftesbury, or Jean Le Rond d'Alembert).

The first half of the nineteenth century saw a strong idealistic and romantic reaction to materialism, yet materialism returned with a vengeance in the second half with the successes of the theory of evolution by natural selection and of Marxism. Karl Marx (1818–1883) focused on economics, yet, in reacting against Hegelian idealism, endorsed a metaphysical materialism and atheism. In Marx, ideas (intellectual contents) are determined and explained through the material, economic processes of production and ownership, upon which rise social and political superstructures.

On the Origin of Species by Means of Natural Selection: Or, The Preservation of Favoured Races in the Struggle for Life (1859) by Charles Darwin (1809–1882) made it possible, in

Richard Dawkins's words in *The Blind Watchmaker,* "to be an intellectually fulfilled atheist." Darwin was held by many to have produced a fully naturalistic and scientifically robust explanation of the nature of life. Darwinian evolution and natural selection were taken to be a serious challenge to explanations of the creation and development of life by a designing God. While many aspects of Darwin's own theory underwent major revisions with the discoveries of molecular biology and genetics, natural selection has lost nothing of its power as an explanatory tool in contemporary evolutionary biology and is used in many fields to explain structures and functions that are seemingly designed.

Idealism. Idealism is metaphysical monism that rejects the existence of matter and founds the experience of matter on the mental. Ancient forms of idealism can be found in Buddhist schools.

The Yogacara (or Vijnanavada) school started around the fifth century C.E. in India. Its central doctrine is that only consciousness (*vijnanamatra*) is real, that thought or mind is the ultimate reality. External things do not exist; nothing exists outside the mind. Ultimately, the purified, undifferentiated state of the mind without objects or thought processes is what constitutes "Buddhahood." Among the principal figures were the brothers Asanga and Vasubandhu.

The Zen, or Chan school was founded by the Indian monk Bodhidharma, who traveled to China around 520 C.E. (according to the tradition). Zen stresses the use of meditation to experience the unity and indistinctness of reality, which cannot be understood otherwise (any form of verbalization or conceptualization falls into the trap of dualism).

In the Western tradition, idealism was reprised by George Berkeley (1685–1753), bishop of Cloyne, who held that all we can know are the ideas in our minds. All objects of perception, including matter, are only ideas produced by God. German idealism started later with Johann Gottlieb Fichte's (1762–1814) transcendental idealism, which he saw as a development of Immanuel Kant's (1724–1804) ideas. For Fichte, God is the All, and particular objects result from reflection or self-consciousness through which the infinite unity is broken up. Friedrich Wilhelm Joseph von Schelling (1775–1854) held that there is a unity between ideal and real. Absolute idealism explains the process of division of consciousness and nature, and their return to unity.

The culmination of German idealism came with Georg Wilhelm Friedrich Hegel (1770–1831), who believed that understanding *Geist* (Absolute Spirit) would overcome all (Kant's) contradictions in the realms of reason and science. *Geist* is *the* principle of reality that makes the universe intelligible as an eternal cyclical process whereby *Geist* comes to know itself, first through its own thinking, then through nature, and finally through finite spirits and their self-expression in history and their self-discovery in art, in religion, and in philosophy. Later in the century, Hegel's doctrines were developed by a group of English idealists, most notably Francis Bradley and John McTaggart Ellis.

In contemporary philosophy, monism is mostly materialism or physicalism. In psychology and philosophy of mind, it is held by many that the mental is reducible to the physical and may be explained in terms of physical laws. Eliminative materialism (Patricia and Paul Churchland) denies that the mental exists and claims that all "mental" talk will be ultimately eliminated as science progresses. Functionalism is a noneliminativist form of materialism claiming that descriptions of mental events and their intentional natures may be explained by systemic relations among the parts of the material brain (Hilary Putnam and William Lycan).

Anomalous monism (Donald Davidson and John Searle) holds that mental events are ultimately identical to brain states, but that there are no laws (hence *anomalous*) that connect brain states to mental states.

See also **Atheism; Deism; Gnosticism; Historical and Dialectical Materialism; Idealism; Materialism in Eighteenth-Century European Thought; Zen.**

BIBLIOGRAPHY
Bakar, Osman. *The History and Philosophy of Islamic Science.* Cambridge, U.K.: Islamic Texts Society, 1999.
Block, Ned, Güven Güzeldere, and Owen Flanagan, eds. *The Nature of Consciousness: Philosophical Debates.* Cambridge, Mass.: MIT Press, 1997.
Chittick, William C. *The Self-Disclosure of God: Principles of Ibn al-'Arabi's Cosmology.* Albany: State University of New York Press, 1998.
Churchland, Paul M. *The Engine of Reason, the Seat of the Soul: A Philosophical Journey into the Brain.* Cambridge, Mass.: MIT Press, 1996.
Dawkins, Richard. *The Blind Watchmaker.* New York: W.W. Norton, 1986.
Dennett, Daniel C. *Darwin's Dangerous Idea: Evolution and the Meanings of Life.* New York: Simon and Schuster, 1995.
Filoramo, Giovanni. *A History of Gnosticism.* Oxford: Blackwell, 1990.
Lloyd, A. C. *The Anatomy of Neoplatonism.* Oxford: Clarendon, 1990.
Lusthaus, Dan. *Buddhist Phenomenology: A Philosophical Investigation of Yogacara Buddhism and the Ch'eng Wei-shih Lun.* London: Routledge Curzon, 2002.
Lycan, William, ed. *Mind and Cognition: An Anthology.* Malden, Mass.: Blackwell, 1999.
Moran, Dermot. *The Philosophy of John Scottus Eriugena: A Study of Idealism in the Middle Ages.* Cambridge, U.K.: Cambridge University Press, 1989.
Phillips, Stephen H. *Classical Indian Metaphysics: Refutations of Realism and the Emergence of "New Logic."* La Salle, Ill.: Open Court, 1995.
Ruse, Michael. *The Darwinian Revolution: Science Red in Tooth and Claw.* 2nd ed. Chicago: University of Chicago Press. 1999.
Searle, John. *Minds, Brains, and Science.* Cambridge, Mass.: Harvard University Press, 1984.
Stern, Robert. *Hegel, Kant, and the Structure of the Object.* London: Routledge, 1990.
Wallis, Richard T., ed., and Jay Bregman, assoc. ed. *Neoplatonism and Gnosticism.* Albany: State University of New York, 1992.

Westphal, Kenneth R. *Hegel's Epistemological Realism: A Study of the Aim and Method of Hegel's "Phenomenology of Spirit."* Dordrecht: Kluwer, 1989.

Peter Machamer
Francesca di Poppa

MORAL SENSE.   Sentimentalism, of which moral sense theory was a part, initially had a short run. Until the end of the twentieth century, all the major versions of the theory were produced within a sixty-year period in eighteenth-century Britain. Anthony Ashley Cooper, third earl of Shaftesbury (1671–1713), initiated the sentimentalist line of thought with his theory that morality is grounded in the reflexive sentiments of the mind, but the idea that human beings possess a specific moral sense, in addition to their external senses, is due to Francis Hutcheson (1694–1746). David Hume (1711–1776) explains the moral sense in terms of more fundamental psychological principles of the mind, especially sympathy. Adam Smith (1723–1790) follows Hume in tracing the moral sentiments to sympathy while dispensing with the idea of a moral sense altogether. Joseph Butler (1692–1752) advocated a compromise between sentimentalism and rationalism, describing the deliverances of conscience as a "sentiment of the understanding."

The sentimentalists think morality is rooted in human nature in two ways. First, what has moral value are first-order sentiments, the passions and affections that motivate people to act, and actions expressive of these sentiments. Second, what gives these motives their value is our reflective, second-order sentiments; sentiments we have about our own or other people's sentiments. We feel approval or disapproval toward ourselves or others for having and acting on certain first-order sentiments and affections. The eighteenth-century sentimentalists compare moral qualities to secondary qualities such as color that result from our visual apparatus. Because we have a propensity to project color onto objects, we come to think of color as a property of objects themselves. Similarly, we project our approval onto people's motives, which explains why we think virtue is a property of actions themselves and approval is a response to that property. For the sentimentalists, however, an action is virtuous only because we approve of it.

Both sentimentalism and its rival, rationalism, initially developed in reaction to Thomas Hobbes's (1588–1679) moral theory. The rationalists objected to Hobbes's claims that there is no right or wrong in the state of nature, that rightness or wrongness is determined by the sovereign's will, and that morality requires sanctions if it is to motivate us. The sentimentalists took a different tack, opposing what they took to be Hobbes's "selfish" conceptions of human nature and morality. They argued that we are by nature social creatures. Other-regarding affections such as benevolence, gratitude, and compassion are an original and real part of human nature. Butler's criticisms of Hobbes's selfish conception of human nature are held in high repute to this day. The sentimentalists also tried to show that morality has nothing to do with self-interest. Self-interest neither provides the motive to act morally nor explains why we morally approve or disapprove.

By the middle of the century, rationalists and sentimentalists began to argue with each other. The rationalist Samuel Clarke (1675–1729) claimed that our moral ideas spring from reason and that the rational awareness that actions are fit or unfit has the power both to obligate and to motivate us. The sentimentalists objected to both claims. One surprising advantage that the sentimentalists had over the rationalists is that they had a more fully worked-out view of what reason is and does, and they interpreted the rationalists in terms of that theory. On that view, reason is inert in two ways. First, reason's operations are limited to the examination and comparison of ideas, that is, to ascertain facts and to determine a priori relationships. Rationalists and sentimentalists agree that basic moral ideas are simple. On the sentimentalist view, however, reason alone never gives rise to simple ideas, so reason alone cannot be the source of moral ideas. Reason is inert in another way: it cannot by itself give rise to a new motive. All reason does is notice the relations between ideas; noticing a relation cannot move us. Hume infamously added that there are no normative rational standards at all that apply to action. We are no more required by reason to act prudently than we are required to act morally.

Shaftesbury characterizes the reflective moral sense as a tendency to admire and approve what is beautiful in people's motives and characters. Butler agrees that the principle of reflection—or conscience—is an essential part of human nature but argues that Shaftesbury overlooked its most important feature. Conscience, he insists, has authority—a right to rule us—that is independent of its strength or power to move us. Both Shaftesbury and Butler conceive of human nature teleologically, as a system structured to promote good ends—one's own good and the good of other human beings. The constitution that is morally approved of is one appropriately balanced between other-regarding and self-regarding affections. Moral evil results not from evil affections, but from our affections being out of balance. As these philosophers see it, human nature is on the whole good.

Starting with Hutcheson, later sentimentalists began to move toward a more modern scientific conception of human nature as morally indifferent. They thus reject the teleological picture of human nature Shaftesbury and Butler endorsed. They continue, however, to think of our nature as benign. Hutcheson, for example, denies that human beings have such evil affections as disinterested malice.

Hutcheson is famous for two claims. First, taking over Shaftesbury's idea of a reflective sense and embedding it in the empiricist view that simple ideas must come from the senses, he claims that human beings possess a unique moral sense that disposes us to immediately and noninferentially approve and disapprove of people's characters and their actions. He also argues that the only character trait of which the moral sense approves is benevolence. The four cardinal virtues—temperance, courage, prudence, and justice—are virtues, he insists, only when motivated by benevolence. Hutcheson distinguishes three types of benevolence. The morally best kind is calm universal benevolence, which aims at the good of all sentient creatures. The moral sense also approves of benevolence directed toward smaller groups, such as love of family or country, as well as particular benevolent impulses, such as pity and gratitude, but only if they do not counteract universal benevolence. When Hutcheson turns from a discussion of why we approve or disapprove of certain actions to a discussion of what actions we should choose, he says we should always choose the action that "produces the greatest happiness for the greatest number." He is the first to enunciate the utility principle.

Even more than Hutcheson, Hume and Smith explicitly aimed at providing a naturalistic explanation of morality, one wholly consistent with the scientific picture of the world. They criticized Hutcheson not only for positing an extra sense but also for failing to explain its origins and workings. The moral project, as they see it, is to discover the fundamental principles of the mind that account for the origin of moral concepts. Both trace the moral sentiments to the operation of sympathy, although they conceive of sympathy differently. For Hume, sympathy is a propensity to feel what other people are feeling, even those wholly unrelated to and removed from us. For Smith, sympathy is the ability to put yourself imaginatively in another's situation and to feel what you would feel in that person's place.

Hume's explanation of moral approval and disapproval begins with our more ordinary loves and hatreds that are violent and vary from person to person. He then describes the process whereby we transform these feelings into a kind of calm, uniform moral love and hatred. On his view of sympathy, we sympathize more easily with people who resemble or are contiguous to us. Although our ability to enter into the feelings of others varies, Hume believes, like most other moral philosophers of this period, that our moral approvals do not. Accordingly, moral approval springs from sympathy but only when we take up a "general" or "common" point of view. There are two regulating features to the general point of view. The first is that we survey a character from the perspective of the person and his or her usual associates. We sympathize then with the person and the people with whom that person regularly interacts, and we judge character traits in terms of whether they are good or bad for these people. The second is that we regulate sympathy by relying on general rules that specify the general effects of character traits. We do sympathize not with the actual effects of a person's character traits but with their usual tendencies for a person's regular associates.

Hume offers as an empirical hypothesis the claim that the moral sense approves of motives that are pleasant and useful to agents themselves or to others. Smith criticizes Hume for ignoring another important way in which we judge people's sentiments. We judge the propriety of people's reactions—whether they are excessive or weak in relation to their object. When we blame someone for excessive anger we do so not only because of its bad effects on that person or others, but also because it is out of proportion to its object or occasion. Smith explains judgments of propriety in terms of his own distinctive conception of sympathy. We judge the propriety of someone's reaction by seeing whether his reaction is the same as our vicarious reaction. We imaginatively put ourselves in the other's shoes and feel what he should feel, given his situation. We then compare his reaction with our vicarious one.

If his actual feeling is excessive compared with the vicarious one we are feeling, we disapprove; if the feeling is similar, we approve. Smith's account of judgments of propriety is one of his most distinctive contributions to sentimentalism.

Subsequent sentimentalists objected to Hutcheson's reduction of virtue to benevolence, claiming that we approve of a wide variety of character traits and motives. Butler argued against Hutcheson that utility cannot be the basis of our approval of justice, since we disapprove of such injustices as theft and treachery even in those cases in which they are useful. Hume grants that acts of justice, taken singly, do not always promote the public good, but he argues that what is useful is the system of justice with rules and procedures that everyone is to follow. Hume also accommodated the rationalist idea that the good person does the right thing because she sees it as right. He argues that in the case of justice this is the morally best motive as well as our usual motive.

Although all the sentimentalists believe that we have the capacity to judge ourselves, Smith tries to explain how we acquire this capacity and in so doing become reflective agents. According to him, conscience, or the "man within," comes from our social nature. We first learn to internalize the judgments others have about ourselves, viewing ourselves through their eyes. But others may misinterpret or misunderstand our motives, praising or blaming us when we do not deserve it. Smith thinks we learn to distinguish the actual praise of others from judgments about whether we are worthy of praise. The sense of moral obligation arises when we internalize the gaze of the ideal spectator—the man within—and try to meet the standards of praiseworthiness he sets for us.

Sentimentalism is enjoying a revival. New versions of the theory have been produced at the end of the twentieth century and the start of the twenty-first, the most prominent of which are the neosentimentalist theories of Simon Blackburn and Annette Baier. Both are followers of Hume, although Blackburn incorporates important elements from Smith. Their main target is Kant, whom they misread as a traditional moral rationalist along the lines of Hume's main opponent, Samuel Clarke. Traditional moral rationalists were realists: they believed that moral truths are part of the framework of the universe. So for Blackburn the foundational issue of whether morality should be located in sentiment or reason is one that asks whether morality is grounded in the framework of the universe or in that of human nature.

Like Hume and Smith, Blackburn wants to provide a naturalistic theory that is consistent with the scientific worldview. According to his theory, to value something is to have a stable disposition in favor of that thing, a disposition we approve of having and are concerned to preserve. Blackburn believes human beings tend to share the same settled dispositions because we need to coordinate our actions with those of others and because we want to be loveable in their eyes.

Blackburn conceives of morality as a product of human nature, springing from second-order sentiments we have about our first-order sentiments. He explains this characteristically sentimentalist idea in terms of a "staircase of emotional ascent."

At the bottom are preferences, simple likes and dislikes. The next step up are our primitive aversions to some kind of action or character. Following Smith and going up another step, Blackburn argues that if you are angry and I come to share your anger, we come to see the matter as a moral one. The sympathetic identification causes us to see the sentiment as legitimate. We take the final step when we are moved to urge others to share the sentiment, effectively treating it as required.

Moral obligation and motivation result from a four-step process. Following Hume, Blackburn thinks the process begins with the natural emotion of love we feel toward certain character traits. We turn that love into moral esteem by taking up what Hume calls the common point of view. We then notice whether we have the character trait or not. Blackburn relies on Smith's theory that we become agents by internalizing the moral gaze of others and on his explanation of how we come to desire not just praise but praiseworthiness. For Blackburn, the latter is the desire to do what is right, so we are motivated to act morally.

Like the earlier sentimentalists, who compare moral properties with secondary qualities, Blackburn gives a projectivist explanation of why morality appears to us as a feature of reality. We tend to project our approval onto people's motives and see it as a property of the motives themselves. This "quasi-realism," as Blackburn calls it, is the aspect of his theory for which he is best known.

Blackburn provides a naturalistic explanation of what we are doing when we use normative concepts. According to him, we are expressing or voicing our values rather than describing something. He thus defends a form of noncognitivism, the view that ethical judgments cannot be true or false, since they do not describe facts. Borrowing the term from Allan Gibbard, he calls this type of noncognitivism "expressivism." The twentieth-century noncognitivists are often thought to be following in the footsteps of the classical sentimentalists. But the eighteenth-century sentimentalists were concerned with the question of where our moral concepts come from rather than with the analysis of moral language. They did not deny that sentences in which moral concepts appear could be true or false.

Blackburn adopts the Humean view that the role of reason is limited to informing us of the facts of the case, including the likely effects of proposed actions. Awareness of these facts will move us, but only if they are tied to some desire or contingent concern of ours. Like Hume, Blackburn denies that there are rational standards governing action. Nevertheless, he argues that there is a perfectly respectable sense in which people may be said to reason about their ends or are criticized for being unreasonable. Reasonableness stands for freedom from certain traits—ignorance, lack of foresight, lack of concern for the common point of view. Those of us who value these traits may condemn someone who lacks these traits as unreasonable.

Baier provides perhaps the most sympathetic and systematic reading of Hume's *A Treatise of Human Nature* in *A Progress of Sentiments*. The progress is a turn from a reliance on pure Cartesian intellect to an attempt to employ philosophically all the capacities of the mind: memory, passion, sentiment, and "chastened intellect." On her reading, Hume's "carefree" or liberated philosophy is an investigation of the whole mind by the whole mind, in contrast to the Kantian investigation of reason by itself.

Baier sees Hume's moral theory as friendly to women's moral experiences and the inspiration for a new approach to feminist ethics. She thinks Hume anticipated many important elements of feminist ethics. Agreeing with the classical sentimentalists that we are essentially social creatures, she believes, as she thinks Hume did, that relationships are at the heart of morality. She applauds Hume for realizing that the system of justice with its rules and rights is an offspring of family cooperativeness and love. She sees him as one of the first philosophers to emphasize intimate and involuntary relationships and relationships between unequals such as parents and children.

Baier advocates a feminist ethics in which trust underwrites both love and obligation. Her deepest debt to Hume comes from his insight into how trust can come to be progressively enlarged, a view she reconstructs from Hume's account of the artificial virtues and the conventions in which they are embedded. Unless people trust each other, they will have trouble loving each other. To recognize a set of obligations is to trust that those who have the power to impose sanctions will enforce sanctions if obligations are not met. It is to trust a group of people with coercive power. Important questions include whom we should trust as well as distrust. Baier looks at obligation from the point of view of the powerless, not the powerful.

Despite Hume's commitment to naturalism, Baier, along with the neo-Kantian Christine Korsgaard, claim to have found in Hume a general test of normativity that applies to the understanding and the moral sense. Both agree that for Hume the normative problem is not whether our beliefs and values are true in the sense that they correspond to some independent reality. The problem is whether our more unreflective beliefs and values and the faculties that give rise to them can withstand their own reflection without incoherence or self-condemnation. Both argue that, on Hume's view, when the moral sense turns on itself and its operations it survives its own survey; therefore its judgments are authoritative.

See also **Natural Law; Philosophy, Moral; Rational Choice; Utilitarianism; Virtue Ethics.**

BIBLIOGRAPHY

PRIMARY SOURCES

Butler, Joseph. *The Analogy of Religion.* London, 1736. Includes *Dissertation of the Nature of Virtue.*

———. *Fifteen Sermons Preached at the Rolls Chapel.* London, 1726. Reprint, *Five Sermons Preached at the Rolls Chapel and A Dissertation Upon the Nature of Virtue,* edited by Stephen L. Darwall. Indianapolis: Hackett, 1983. Contains the five most important of the original fifteen Sermons.

Hume, David. *Enquiry Concerning the Principles of Morals.* London, 1751. Reprint, edited by L. A. Selby-Bigge and P. H. Nidditch. Oxford: Clarendon, 1975.

———. *A Treatise of Human Nature.* 3 vols. London, 1739–1740. Reprint, edited by L. A. Selby-Bigge and P. H. Nidditch. Oxford: Clarendon, 1985.

Hutcheson, Francis. *An Essay on the Nature and Conduct of Passions and Affections with Illustrations Upon the Moral Sense.* London, 1728. Reprint, edited by Aaron Garrett. Indianapolis: Liberty Fund, 2002.

———. *An Inquiry into the Original of Our Ideas of Beauty and Virtue.* London, 1725. Reprint, edited by Wolfgang Leidhold. Indianapolis: Liberty Fund, 2004.

Raphael, D. D., ed. *British Moralists, 1650–1800.* Vols. 1 and 2. Indianapolis: Hackett, 1991. Contains important selections from the sentimentalists as well as their opponents.

Shaftesbury, Anthony Ashley Cooper, Third Earl of. *Characteristics of Men, Manners, Opinions, Times.* London, 1711. Reprint, edited by Lawrence E. Klein. Cambridge, U.K.: Cambridge University Press, 1999.

Smith, Adam. *The Theory of Moral Sentiments.* London and Edinburgh, 1759. Reprint, edited by D. D. Raphael and A. L. Macfie. Indianapolis: Liberty Classics, 1982.

SECONDARY SOURCES

Baier, Annette. *A Progress of Sentiments.* Cambridge, Mass.: Harvard University Press, 1991.

———. *Moral Prejudices.* Cambridge, Mass.: Harvard University Press, 1994.

Blackburn, Simon. *Ruling Passion: A Theory of Practical Reasoning.* New York: Oxford University Press, 1998.

Darwall, Stephen. *The British Moralists and the Internal "Ought": 1640–1740.* New York: Cambridge University Press, 1995.

Gibbard, Allan. *Wise Choices, Apt Feelings: A Theory of Normative Judgment.* Cambridge, Mass.: Harvard University Press, 1990.

Korsgaard, Christine. *The Sources of Normativity.* New York: Cambridge University Press, 1996.

Schneewind, J. B. *The Invention of Autonomy.* New York: Cambridge University Press, 1998.

Schneewind, J. B., ed. *Moral Philosophy from Montaigne to Kant.* Cambridge, U.K.: Cambridge University Press, 2003. Contains selections from moral philosophers from Britain as well as the Continent.

Charlotte R. Brown

MOTHERHOOD AND MATERNITY.

Motherhood the world over is commonly understood in terms of a generic terminology. Regardless of country, clime, or class, age-old mythologies in all cultures eulogize motherhood and impart to it an importance that goes well beyond the physical act of birthing. At the level of twenty-first-century popular culture, however, motherhood and maternity have been appropriated by modern-day consumerism, particularly in Western cultures where specialized stores like Mothercare sell fashionable maternity apparel, and Internet sites like The Mothersbliss Shopping Experience offer both goods and advice on mothering. While religious symbolism stresses motherhood as *creation*, modern-day marketing targets the "mother-consumer" to sell fashionable maternity clothing, lingerie, and accessories as a form of "Pregnancy Chic!"

Given all the numerous contextual underpinnings, the concept of motherhood lends itself to a variety of interpretations across culture and historical time. It therefore needs to be analyzed in terms of history, culture, myth, art, and more lately in terms of the scientific discourses that shape new reproductive technologies and population control policies, all of which focus on women's bodies and their biological ability to become mothers. This article touches upon all these contexts, drawing illustrations from diverse cultural, social, and geographical locations to point out that motherhood is valorized in all cultures, yet the notions, symbols, and cultural practices that constitute motherhood and maternity are neither homogenous globally nor stable chronologically.

History, Religion, and Myth

Motherhood is wrapped in many cultural meanings. Birthing and nurturing new life physically has led to a conflation of "feminine," "maternal," and "feminine spirituality" in many cultures and religious traditions. Motherhood has been painted as a sacred and powerful spiritual path. In literature and in nationalist discourses alike, motherhood is a recurrent theme across cultures.

Religious scriptures and myths place motherhood in an exalted realm. Christian, Judaic, and Hindu religious imagery sentimentalizes and idealizes motherhood. While Madonna images are characteristic to Christianity, conceptualizations of the Devi-Ma (Goddess-Mother) in Hindu tradition are reinforced by the many goddesses in the Hindu pantheon, each epitomizing an attribute (Durga/Kali: strength; Lakshmi: prosperity/abundance; Saraswati: knowledge; etc.). In West African, Afro-Caribbean, and Afro-Brazilian traditions, Yemaya (or Yemalla) is a creation goddess. Often depicted as a mermaid or a beautiful woman, and associated with the moon and ocean, Yemaya governs the household and rules over conception, birth, and ensures the safety of children. Local mythologies suggest that the fourteen Yoruba goddesses and gods spilled forth from Yemaya's womb, and the breaking of her uterine waters caused a great flood that created the oceans. From her body were born the first human woman and man, who became the parents of all mortal beings on earth.

Although Buddhism does not give motherhood such overwhelming spiritual status and significance, maternal imagery and symbolism are present in the concept of the archetypal female Bodhisattvas, seen as supreme mothers. Tara is compared to a mother with compassion and forbearance; Prajnaparamita is seen as the mother of all Buddhas. Interestingly, the Bodhisattvas (transcendental ideal mothers) are also essentially androgynous—thus distinguishing the Buddhist spiritual tradition from the Christian and the Hindu.

Influenced by religious mythologies and local lore, classical literature from Europe, Africa, and Asia is filled with examples of self-sacrifice in the name of motherhood. While mothers are revered as creators, nurturers, and goddesses, they also inspire awe because they are believed to both protect and destroy. At the heart of the sprawling metropolis Mexico City stands the Monumento a la Madre, a monument commemorating motherhood. Its location and the Spanish inscription on it, "Porque su maternidad fue voluntaria" (because their maternity was voluntary), emphasize the centrality of motherhood in Mexican society. In fact, two of Mexico's most important mythical figures are mothers, contrasting figures with origins in Mexican history and mythology. La Malinche (also known as Malintzin), a Mexican Indian princess born around 1500, was given as a slave to Hernán Cortés, the leader of the conquistadors in Mexico. She later bore him a child. Because of this sexual transgression and for her role as mediator between the Spanish and the native Indians, popular mythologies view her as a traitor and a bad mother responsible for the quick defeat of the indigenous peoples and the downfall of the entire Aztec Empire. In contrast, the Virgin of Guadalupe, a Madonna with indigenous features, is seen as incarnating all the values associated with the good Mexican mother: meek, kind, self-sacrificing.

Indeed, in modern societies the concept of mother has commanded popular appeal as a symbol of the nation-state. Nationalist discourses in diverse global contexts deploy the nation-as-mother symbolism to mobilize patriotic sentiments. Love of mother and love of nation have been conflated. The symbolism of the enslaved mother was at the heart of the anticolonial nationalist struggles, both in India to free Bharat-Mata (Mother India) in the 1940s and in South Africa in the 1980s and 1990s. While patriotic songs and monuments in many countries celebrate the nation-as-mother, there are exceptions. In Russia, for instance, patriotic songs often invoke sentiments of loyalty toward the land of birth (*rodina*), referring to it as *otechestvo* (fatherland).

Although maternal ideals are espoused and valorized in all cultures, in patriarchal societies that uphold a woman's central purpose to be her reproductive function, motherhood and mothering become intertwined with issues of a woman's identity. Essentializing theories that define women in terms of fertility are reinforced socially through many female archetypes (such as the Virgin, Venus, and Mother Earth) that remain bound to women's reproductive functions. Such cultural myths, perpetuated throughout the centuries, enforce the belief that motherhood is an essential part of being a woman. The Mexican writer Rosario Castellanos (1925–1974) pointed out that a Mexican woman does not consider herself to be a real woman unless she has proved herself to be fertile and the "halo of maternity" shines over her. This holds true for most women not only in Mexico but also in Iran, India, China, Korea, and many Latin American societies, where the index of motherhood is used to define "real" women. Given that motherhood becomes a prerequisite for social acceptance in such societies, many non-mothering women experience feelings of rejection and low self-esteem. In cultural practice, this means that patriarchies can deploy notions of motherhood to foster conservative traditions, through which motherhood becomes a means of female control.

Although in many cultures expectations of mothering roles are buttressed by intense social pressure to conform to them, this seems to be driven less by levels of modernity or urbanization than by the status accorded to norms of familial and community cohesiveness in a society. For instance, Japan's highly urbanized, industrialized society continues to perpetuate highly prescriptive notions of motherhood, just as in Egypt, Iran, India, or Afghanistan. Despite differences in economic status and levels of development, all these societies share widely held beliefs about the importance of family and community linkages. Regardless of whether a particular African society displays a patrilineal or matrilineal kinship system, mothers are the essential building block of social relationships and identities in most African cultures. Because mothers symbolize familial ties and unconditional loyalty, motherhood is invoked even in extrafamilial situations that call upon these values. Women-as-mothers, then, become key players in the maintenance of linkages and acquire important community responsibilities.

Birthing. Given such assumptions about motherhood, the act of birthing is both anxiety-producing and a dramatic moment in what is perceived as the cycle of creation. In many Islamic and Hindu communities, birthing is also associated with rituals of purity and pollution: While these traditions exempt the mother from household chores and burdensome tasks, they also regard her as unclean and force her to live somewhat segregated from community spaces for several days post-childbirth. In many societies in Africa and Asia, among Muslim, Hindu, and Christian families (both urban and rural), daughters still return to their natal family homes late in pregnancy, to be properly cared for and pampered during and after birthing. Given the high maternal and infant mortality rates in most developing countries, birthing is understandably regarded as a dangerous and life-threatening process, the successful completion of which calls for prayer and celebration.

African societies also widely posit birthing with great significance. Feminists in Africa, while conceding that this may at times operate in an oppressive manner, have attempted to recuperate other conceptualizations of motherhood that are empowering for women. Within such conceptualizations, birthing bestows a certain status on women—even mystical powers. Yoruba traditions are a case in point. Among the Yoruba, motherhood confers privileges that hark back to the very foundations of society and women's presumed roles in it. Women symbolize fertility, fecundity, fruitfulness. The Yoruba say, "Iya ni wura, baba ni jigi" (Mother is gold, father is a mirror). Mother is gold: strong, valuable, true, central to a child's existence, wise, also self-denying. The Yoruba also believe that *ikunle abiyamo*—the kneeling position that is assumed at the moment of birth—confers spiritual privileges on a mother. Thus there are powers, privileges, and entitlements that come with motherhood—even in the act of birthing.

Stereotypes of "ideal" mothers. Even in Western societies, at least until the postwar years, women were encouraged to produce large families, to find satisfaction and pride in motherhood. However, the nobility and respect assigned to full-time motherhood was still regarded as inferior to male pursuits. Thus, motherhood was simultaneously idealized and denigrated.

The importance of these cultural and religious symbols of motherhood is borne out by the fact that they are repeatedly invoked in art and literature and form part of ongoing mythologies that create icons and idealized stereotypes pervasive in communities. Literary and artistic works through the ages valorize those attributes of motherhood associated with Virgin-identified self-sacrifice, offset by myths of the bad mother, which are just as prevalent. Depictions of self-sacrificing mothers as creators who must bear pain with patience and nurture selflessly leave no space for mothers as women who feel pain, anger, frustration, or are simply drained by the responsibilities that accompany their mothering roles. Thus good mother stereotypes assist in sustaining a bad mother/good mother dichotomy within which patriarchy condemns the negative maternal feminine image.

Statistics, of course, prove that the universality of motherhood is a myth. Women across the globe are individual, multidimensional personalities who defy this super-construct. Their roles and self-perceptions as mothers are mediated by the complicated tapestry of culture, clime, and class that shape them. Feminists in the second half of the twentieth century have aimed to debunk these cultural myths.

Feminist Critiques

Debates over motherhood have been fundamental to feminist movements, whether in the United Kingdom, the United States, Japan, India, or China. In this context, the issues for feminism are numerous. Some of these are analyzed in a historical context below, with references to how literary representations use tropes of motherhood that reinforce patriarchies of race and gender. Finally, contemporary debates on issues such as abortion, the use of reproductive technologies, surrogate motherhood, and single mothers are examined.

Broadly speaking, critiques of motherhood argue that femininity is widely defined in essentialist terms that assume that women have instincts that make them selfless nurturers. Such assumptions, in turn, shape social practices that make women automatically responsible as caregivers. Feminist theorists argue that such myths, constructed by the patriarchy, undergird social practices that eventually restrict women. Although contemporary feminisms have widely vocalized these issues, it is important to recognize that the first formulations on this issue predate twenty-first-century feminism.

The French writer Simone de Beauvoir (1908–1986) argued that women are repeatedly told from infancy that they are "made" for childbearing. While the "splendors of maternity" are forever being sung to her, the drawbacks of her situation—menstruation, illnesses, and even the boredom of household drudgery—are all justified by this "marvelous privilege" she has of bringing children into the world. Beauvoir pointed out that such pervasive socialization shapes women's desire to "choose" motherhood.

The second-wave feminist movement in the United States (after the 1960s) brought these interrogations to center stage. Feminists argued that throughout human history, maternal experience has been defined and written by patriarchal culture. Religion, art, medicine, psychoanalysis, and other bastions of male power have objectified motherhood, have disregarded female subjectivity, and have silenced the voice of the mother. Feminist activists insisted on middle-class women's right to work and participate in public life beyond the family (working class and poor women had been working all along, while also raising their families), and, along with this, that mothering was not essential to women's fulfillment or necessary to every woman's life.

Feminists in the United Kingdom, North America, and Europe began to challenge the overemphasis on fertility, insisting that the link between childbearing and childrearing is socially manipulative and serves to exclude women from other productive roles. Feminist theorists debunked the social pressures of a mothering role that seeks to control women's bodies and energy. They argued that such notions limit women's possibilities to the domestic sphere and restrict their entry into the public domain, thus vitally feeding into patriarchal agendas.

Although the second-wave feminists vocalized the issue of fertility more aggressively than before, it is important to remember that the earliest efforts in this direction were made in the 1920s through activism of the suffragists and women like Margaret Sanger (1879–1966), who founded the American Birth Control League in 1921. Sanger's movement made an impact in North America, Britain, and India, and forcefully argued for "planned parenthood" as essential to ensure women's participation in the public domain. Since the work of the second-wave feminists, fertility has remained a crucial part of the feminist agenda.

Literary criticism. Since the 1970s, feminist critics have generated a prolific body of literary criticism that demands an inquiry into the nature of the maternal instinct and the psychology of the mother-child relationship. This task is common to feminism in the West and the widely different cultures of Japan and India. In the 1970s, Japanese feminist critiques began to assert that *bosei* (innate maternal instinct) was a social construct. They sought to demonstrate that modern Japanese conceptions of womanhood as motherhood, of motherhood as something natural and instinctive to women, were artifacts of contemporary society whose construction could be historically interrogated. Contemporary Japanese fiction such as *Child of Fortune* by Yuko Tsushima (1983), about a woman struggling between the reality of motherhood and the expectations of society influenced by an idealized good mother paradigm, presents a stinging critique of rigid and constraining constructions of motherhood.

Along a related trajectory, the work of Marianne Hirsch from the late 1980s captures the spirit of Western feminists' preoccupation with the literature of matrilineage in conjunction with an ongoing feminist pursuit of retrieving maternal subjectivity. The literary representations of mother-daughter voices in contemporary matrilineal narratives open up a new chapter in the feminist project of repositioning mothers as individuals and as subjects. This repositioning sheds new light in the study of relationality in the field of feminist maternal scholarship.

Feminist scholarship from Latin America has critiqued the implications of local mythologies and motherhood discourses for Latina women. A feminist analysis of the La Malinche/ Virgin of Guadalupe dichotomy reveals that the Virgin (symbolizing passivity, tenderness, and self-sacrifice) is central to the construction of femininity in Latin American cultures because she embodies virtues convenient for the patriarchal order. La Malinche—the sexualized, headstrong woman who freely chose her destiny—is dangerous to the patriarchal order and is presented as hateful. Women thus feel compelled to emulate the Virgin, a less threatening figure. In effect, the Virgin image serves to suppress the threatening or deviant femininity embodied La Malinche—regarded as the Mexican Eve. The Virgin becomes the embodiment of Mexican motherhood, while La Malinche's depraved sexuality becomes a reason to justify the oppression of women.

Motherhood and race. Feminism and the self-reflexive questionings within the women's movement in North America also drew attention to the fact that notions of motherhood are racially specific and conditioned by prevailing social hierarchies. For instance, in North America from the Reconstruction through the Progressive Era, African-American and white women were encouraged to view motherhood as a national racial imperative. The mother-nation symbolism was anchored in a patriotic discourse. Literary representations depict a conflated mother-nation as a protector who also needs protection by her children/citizens, who must ensure the mother-nation's perpetuation by reproducing her progeny. Novels of sexual awakening by Kate Chopin (1851–1904) and Edith Wharton (1862–1937) depict motherhood as personally limiting but racially necessary. Women writers and activists responded to this imperative by using diverse strategies that reflected the broader public debates about race, reproduction, and female agency.

In the American context, it has also been argued that early-twentieth-century depictions of motherhood for African-American women sought to depict mothers as active agents rather than passive instruments of reproduction. However, the narratives also revealed that women's agency as mothers comes at a price and was continually constrained by fixed gender roles and social expectations. The brutalizing effects of slavery marred the joys of black motherhood, as did complications of biracial identity (Berg). Such fictional and nonliterary texts also reflected the early twentieth-century debates over birth control, feminism, and eugenics in the United States, using motherhood and race as key tropes for discussions of social progress and decline. These texts also established that even notions of universal motherhood that fostered cross-racial conversations reinforced social and racial hierarchies.

Feminist critiques from South Africa point out how nationalist and patriarchal causes have appropriated the African-woman-as-mother. This figure has been used to extol the ostensibly unique qualities of nurturance, protectiveness, and altruism of African women, qualities that are often believed to make them morally and culturally superior to Western women. Celebrated in much of the nationalist poetry and prose during the 1950s and 1960s, the African mother recurs in a range of present-day discourses in public and domestic life.

From another context, ethnographic research from Asia and the Pacific shows that maternal experiences vary greatly depending upon historical time and local discourses. For instance, motherhood as embodied experience for women in colonized societies was shaped by colonial policies, missionary influence, and conflicts between Western medicine and biomedical birthing methods. All these shaped the experience of modern mothering in many colonial societies (Ram).

Feminist theorists and writers challenge valorizations of motherhood fostered by conservative patriarchies. However, it is important to emphasize that feminists do not reject maternity or devalue the woman-centered experience of birthing and mothering. Their project is to interrogate the myths and assumptions that impose oppressive role expectations and erase the reality of maternal experience. Feminist voices seek to liberate motherhood from the institution and the myth that confine it to the narrow playing field of the conventional family, leaving no space for women to choose alternative identities.

Motherhood and Development Discourses

Some of the public debates, campaigning, and policy-making that surround women's relationships to their bodies at the turn of the twenty-first century make evident the extent to which affirmations of motherhood constrain discursive frameworks of justice for women. The American feminist Patricia McFadden identifies this in relation to dominant trends within research, public debate, and policy-making around HIV/AIDS, while Jessica Horn discusses how the patriarchal emphasis on reproductive health anchors perceptions of women's sexual health firmly in stereotypical gender roles and identities (Narayan).

Along another axis, projects like the Population Council's "Save the Mothers Initiative" places attention on motherhood in development discourses. The Safe Motherhood Conference (Nairobi, 1987) of the International Federation of Gynecology and Obstetrics (FIGO) noted with alarm that almost half a million women die each year because of complications related to pregnancy and childbirth. FIGO sought global support, stressing that because 99 percent of maternal deaths occur in the developing countries and among women in the most deprived sections of the population, it was a socially unjustifiable phenomenon.

At the beginning of the twenty-first century, United Nations agencies and the World Bank supported several country projects in Asia, Africa, and Latin America to evolve cost-effective and sustainable ways to reduce maternal mortality and morbidity. Institutions like the London School of Hygiene and Tropical Medicine have maternal programs for conducting research and disseminating information on policy issues related to maternal and child health.

Critics of such population policies, however, argue that mass distribution of hormonal medicines used for population control in developing countries has serious implications for the health of millions of women who are unaware of the long-term impact of these drugs. Feminists also point out that notions of "reproduction" and "reproductive rights" have many possible interpretations, with varying degrees of social impact on gender and family. In the 1960s, the core issues around reproductive rights involved the access to family planning and to information on birth control; in the abortion debates, the right to privacy seems to encompass the right to decide whether to conceive and to carry a fetus to term. Since the 1990s and the struggle against AIDS, reproductive health has won new relevance.

Contentious Debates

In the light of the revolutionary changes that have come about since 1978—when the first test-tube baby, Louise Brown, was born—it is important to touch upon abortion, surrogacy, and new reproductive technologies (NRTs). Such contemporary issues relating to motherhood have provoked controversies that reflect diverse social and cultural perceptions of motherhood.

Abortion. The conscious decision to medically terminate pregnancy is controversial in religious and political terms in many countries, regardless of levels of modernity. Pro-life groups in the United States and Europe staunchly campaign for the closure of abortion clinics, while for women in contemporary China or India abortion is easy and inexpensive, given the population control policies in these two countries.

Buddhism, Hinduism, Christianity, perhaps all religious and secular philosophies, focus on two central questions relating to abortion: (1) When does the embryo/fetus acquire the property that makes the termination of pregnancy "killing"? and (2) Is abortion, before or after this point, ever justifiable? Orthodox strains in Christianity, Buddhism, and classical Hindu embryology (which maintain that the transmigration of consciousness occurs at conception) believe that all abortion is sin and incurs the karmic burden of killing (in Buddhist and Hindu terms). Before modern embryology, however, in both Buddhist countries and the West, ideas about conception were scientifically inaccurate. Although the findings of modern neuro-embryology provided scientific support for subsequent arguments developed by most Western ethicists to defend abortion, such legacies continue to impede pro-choice campaigns in asserting that any society that values liberty should not control a woman's reproductive rights by law (Luker).

Whether abortion is ever "justified" relates to whether religious ethics about motherhood are absolutist, utilitarian, or "virtuist" (i.e., seeing the good in the development of personal qualities). The absolutist would regard abortion akin to murder, whatever the justification. The utilitarian would justify it on compassionate grounds (based on the mother's health or the population crisis or parental inability to raise a child).

Traditional Jewish law (halakah) takes a positive stand on procreation and is comparatively lenient regarding the NRTs. In densely populated countries like China, India, or Bangladesh, state-sponsored family planning policies have enhanced the social acceptability of abortion. Japanese society combines both utilitarian and virtue approaches. Widely accepted as a "sorrowful necessity," abortion is openly ritualized in Buddhist temples selling rituals and statues intended to represent parents' apologies to the aborted. Some Buddhists have adopted a moderate position: abortion is akin to killing, but women should have that choice. Since most Buddhists support laws that discourage or punish murder, implicitly this position seems to suggest that abortion is either justifiable (when it conflicts with bodily autonomy) or that fetuses are closer in status to animals.

Such reproductive accommodations, while they reduce the impact of oppressive regimes on women's reproductive autonomy, do not necessarily emerge from debates that incorporate women's voices. Feminists also point out that pro-life activists (women and men) are not necessarily opposed to capital punishment or killings in war, implying thereby that anti-abortion positions are motivated by considerations of power and control over women rather than morality. Thus, feminist activists the world over stress that abortion should be viewed as an issue of autonomy, constitutionality, and economic status, rather than simply of ethics.

Surrogate motherhood. Like abortion, surrogate motherhood—which allows for a woman to carry and bear a child for childless couples, mostly as a commercial transaction—is a highly problematic issue. In pitting claims of mothering-as-biological birthing against those of mothering-as-nurturing, it poses ethical, legal, and, some would argue, moral issues. Although new reproductive technologies that enable childless women to raise genetically related offspring increase women's motherhood options, they are pitted against religious beliefs and conservative ethical systems. By creating alternative forms of parenthood and supplanting sexual intercourse as a means of reproduction, this branch of biomedicine has also unwittingly created challenges to kinship and family law. Ethicists generally view surrogate mothering arrangements in terms of stark moral choices: between the tragedy of infertility on the one hand, and the potential for exploitation of the host mother on the other. Among the many compelling objections, the likely economic exploitation of poor, working-class women by affluent childless couples remains a key concern. There are also concerns that widespread surrogacy would lead to a commodification of infants, while reducing motherhood to paid labor and the woman's body to an incubator that can be hired through a contract.

New reproductive technologies. Feminist theorists of different persuasions have been critical of the effects of NRTs as "potentially insidious forms of social control" over women's bodies. Radical feminists believe that by using NRTs, and participating in these technological processes that invade the autonomy of their bodies, women unwittingly aid patriarchy in gaining more control over their bodies. Feminist theorists Jana Sawicki and Donna Haraway, however, advocate a more complex reading of these technologies. For Sawicki, radical feminists ignore the resistance already emerging within this area. Haraway suggests that rather than view this simplistically, one should complicate our theories of experience. Haraway calls for a shift away from dualistic, oppositional thinking that posits technology as solely destructive and fragmentary. In short, Haraway proposes that while is it true that technology can and has been used as a negative force against women, to write it off as unredeemably patriarchal limits feminist thinking when more nuanced perspectives are needed.

Contemporary Redefinitions: Single and Lesbian Mothers

It is evident that notions of motherhood are culturally varied and shift over time. In Japan and in South Asian societies, for instance, where traditional abortion is readily available and relatively free of social stigma, single motherhood is highly stigmatized. In fact, given rising divorce rates in Japan, the institution of single motherhood has become a particularly salient issue for contemporary Japanese feminism. Single motherhood in Japan almost inevitably involves financial and physical hardship, perhaps more consistently than in the West, given that there is little provision for child support and that even a divorced father usually does not continue to pay child support to the mother when she has custody of the children. Only 10 to 20 percent of divorced Japanese mothers receive regular child support payments. In addition, given the mythologies surrounding the mother's role in childrearing, there tends to be social stigmatization of working mothers in Japanese society, which has historically restricted and problematized conditions of access to daycare and other facilities. Thus, in the Japanese context, there are issues of institutionalized discrimination against single mothers that are intertwined with social perceptions of what constitutes a family.

Other redefinitions of mothering and motherhood have emerged with the turn of the twenty-first century. These new definitions interrogate gender stereotypes and question social constructs of "family." Nontraditional models of mothering by lesbian mothers in North America and Europe have further destabilized received notions of motherhood. Research scholars such as Ellen Lewin have analyzed models of the lesbian mother and lesbian and gay commitment ceremonies in the United States.

Definitions of motherhood and assumptions about its intersection with womanhood have been central to feminist theory in anthropology. Often these ideas draw directly on notions of nature and culture, conflating particular components of motherhood with virtue and authenticity. Insofar as some theorists have presented motherhood as a set of practices, it might be argued that men who undertake basic childrearing and caretaking activities are in some ways "mothers" rather than "fathers." What are the implications of these social realities for enacting cultural notions of motherhood and fatherhood? If men can be mothers, then can the conventional, biologically drawn boundaries of the basic gender categories—female and male—be defended? These questions remain complex and unresolved.

Motherhood in Academia and National Policy

Although millions of women in the world become mothers, motherhood generally is not regarded in academia as a core issue relating to society and the nation-state. Some universities, such as York University in Ontario, Canada, are beginning to study motherhood as an academic discipline, yet much of the research looks at the psychological and sociological aspects. Feminists argue that if motherhood is viewed as a historical experience, it will be evident that it is shaped not just by personal experiences and desires but also by public policy in which the nation-state plays a significant role.

From the discussion above, which draws upon the heritage, traditions, literature, and art from various cultures, it may not be far-fetched to suggest that the failure of institutionalized religions to give women a visible and valid role has traditionally led many women to seek dignity and self-respect, salvation and status, in society through birthing and motherhood, a role and path unique to them. In the new millennium, however, the emerging reality, especially in the industrialized countries, is of a falling birth rate. As millions of women join the global workforce, as more and more women gain control over their lives and bodies, and as motherhood becomes one of many acceptable identities and choices, it would seem that fewer women become mothers (and those that do raise fewer children). The birth rate in Japan has been falling steadily since the 1970s. On average, the first postwar generation had four children, and the second, two. Trends in Europe are also alarming. Such statistical projections are causing concern to government planners and national policy-makers in many countries. If women increasingly begin to feel that the challenges outweigh the "joys of motherhood," demographers may well predict for the rapidly industrializing world a future of restructured family norms, labor shortages, fewer taxpayers to support a rapidly aging society, and fewer caregivers for the elderly.

See also **Childhood and Child Rearing; Gender; Men and Masculinity; Women and Femininity in U.S. Popular Culture.**

BIBLIOGRAPHY

Badinter, Elisabeth. *The Myth of Motherhood.* Translated by Roger Degaris. London: Souvenir Press, 1981.

Baruch, Elaine Hoffmann, Amadeo F. D'Adamo, Jr., and Joni Seager, eds. *Embryos, Ethics, and Women's Rights: Exploring the New Reproductive Technologies.* New York: Haworth Press, 1988.

Beauvoir, Simone de. *The Second Sex.* Translated by H. M. Parshley. New York: Knopf, 1952.

Berg, Allison. *Mothering the Race: Women's Narratives of Reproduction, 1890–1930.* Urbana: University of Illinois Press, 2002.

Copeland, Rebecca. "Motherhood as Institution." *Japan Quarterly* 39, no. 1 (1992): 101–110.

Chodorow, Nancy. *The Reproduction of Mothering: Psychoanalysis and the Sociology of Gender.* Berkeley: University of California Press, 1978.

Doer, Edd, and James Prescott, eds. *Abortion Rights and Fetal Personhood.* Long Beach, Calif.: Centerline Press, 1989.

Hirsch, Marianne. *The Mother-Daughter Plot: Narrative, Psychoanalysis, Feminism.* Bloomington: Indiana University Press, 1989.

Lewin, Ellen. *Lesbian Mothers: Accounts of Gender in American Culture.* Ithaca, N.Y.: Cornell University Press, 1993.

Luker, Kristin. *Abortion and the Politics of Motherhood.* Berkeley: University of California Press, 1984.

McMahon, Martha. *Engendering Motherhood: Identity and Self-Transformation in Women's Lives.* New York: Guilford Press, 1995.

Narayan, Uma. *Dislocating Cultures: Identities, Traditions, and Third-World Feminism.* New York: Routledge, 1997.

Oyewumi, Oyeronke, ed. *African Women and Feminism: Reflecting on the Politics of Sisterhood.* Trenton, N.J.: Africa World Press, 2003.

Parker, Rozsika. *Mother Love/Mother Hate: The Power of Maternal Ambivalence.* New York: Basic Books, 1995.

Ram, Kalpana, and Margaret Jolly, eds. *Maternities and Modernities: Colonial and Postcolonial Experiences in Asia and the Pacific.* Cambridge, U.K.: Cambridge University Press, 1998.

Rich, Adrienne. *Of Woman Born: Motherhood as Experience and Institution.* New York: Norton, 1976.

Sanger, Margaret. *Woman and the New Race.* New York: Brentano's, 1920.

Sawicki, Jana. *Disciplining Foucault: Feminism, Power, and the Body.* New York: Routledge, 1991.

Smart, Carol, ed. *Regulating Womanhood: Historical Essays on Marriage, Motherhood, and Sexuality.* London: Routledge, 1992.

Trebilcot, Joyce, ed. *Mothering: Essays in Feminist Theory.* Totowa, N.J.: Rowman and Allanheld, 1984.

Maina Chawla Singh

MOTIF.

This entry includes two subentries:

Motif in Literature
Motif in Music

MOTIF IN LITERATURE

George Steiner has described culture as a matrix of recurrent and interrelated elements, a motor fueled by revolving constants. Broadly speaking, cultural literacy relies on our ability to recognize these constants—in literature, music, painting, or any other form of cultural production—and to work out relationships between them, to translate and recycle the meaning we inherit from them. Thus, the single word *Roncevaux*, voiced offhandedly by one man to another in Ernest Hemingway's *The Sun Also Rises,* can echo for the reader with large themes of betrayal, ambush, rivalry, and national loss—but only if the word is recognized as an allusion to the death trap set treacherously for Charlemagne's twelve peers in the early-twelfth-century *Chanson de Roland.* The tone of Steiner's short reflection on cultural literacy is dire, his main point being that "elementary" allusions and "implicit motifs"—such as Roncevaux—go unrecognized even by today's most "privileged students and readers." A small literary element like Roncevaux, reused over time in various languages and genres, provides a useful example of a cultural "constant," and recognizing the rich depth afforded by such recycled bits of meaning is in fact a method of comparative literary analysis. *Motif* is one word that can be used to delimit and distinguish an element like Roncevaux. But our options are many, and terms prove in practice frequently interchangeable. Steiner writes generally of *topologies,* a term that lumps together and encompasses such overlapping concepts as *topos, archetype, motif,* and *genre.* Our focus here is on the motif and limits the cultural field to literature. And yet Steiner's more expansive notion of culture as a network of recurring, interrelated constants provides one of the more helpful and lucid introductions to the movement and persistence associated with literary motif, an otherwise ambiguous element in comparative analysis.

Ambiguity

Let us start with the ambiguity that has characterized *motif* since the term first appeared—used in reference to a musical rather than a literary work—in Denis Diderot's *Encyclopédie* of 1765. Even now, defining exactly what constitutes a single motif or a motif sequence in literature continues to be a thorny task for students and scholars alike, in large part because published definitions as well as general use in literary criticism offer very little agreement as to its nature (excepting a general agreement that there is no common agreement). Dictionaries, encyclopedias, and handbooks have defined *motif* variously as myth, theme, subject, central recurring idea, image, characteristic, symbol, archetype, leitmotiv, or outstanding trait. Adding to the confusion, *theme* and *motif*—potentially incompatible terms to Horst Daemmrich—tend to be used interchangeably, strings of motifs often made synonymous with legend and myth. The recurring narrative constant of the insatiable artist, for instance, analyzed as integral to and mutually dependent on the literary tradition of Faust, has been described by Stuart Atkins, without clear distinction of terms, as "motif," "theme," and "myth." General character types (holy hermit, evil dwarf, seer-hag, calumniated wife, warrior king, "flower" or "candle" of knighthood), objects (hero's sword, poet's pen, lover's ring, the Holy Grail), settings (paradise, hell, deserted wasteland, the otherworld, the city), situations (spilled wine, physical blow, quest, game or test, war, marriage), psychological states (madness, hysteria, paranoia), and general attributes (red hair, black eyes, hairy mole, hunchback) can all be traced over time and across genre and discussed as recurring literary motifs. Such lists are potentially endless and not necessarily new (see the Medieval Welsh Triads as well as Stith Thompson's motif-index and Daemmrich's handbook). We might even speak of instructional, didactic, or homiletic motifs, as has David F. Johnson; in a study that seeks ultimately to identify the origin of a narrative tradition, Johnson has culled medieval British manuscripts for references to the rewards and punishments of the afterlife, concluding that both the Seven Joys of Heaven motif and its reverse, the Five Horrors of Hell, are Irish (rather than English) homilies. Theorists and scholars have used *motif* to identify narrative elements such as detail, metaphor, image, symbol, idea, and subject matter. The term need not refer exclusively to content elements but can apply to formal elements as well, and motif sequences have been identified as structuring devices, integral to a text's configuration. Helen Vendler's study of "key words" in Shakespeare's sonnets, for instance, demonstrates how motifs provide structural coherence by "firmly connecting" the four units of a sonnet (three quatrains and a couplet); in Vindler's analysis, motifs prove equally essential to the form of a sonnet as to its meaning. (The semiotician A. J. Greimas, as well as two of the most significant modern indexers of literary motifs, Stith Thompson and Elisabeth Frenzel, restrict motifs to content units; Wolpers, Daemmrich, and others extend the term's scope into form and structure.) A literary motif, in other words, can be—and has been—defined with great fluidity: as an element of both narrative content and structural form, as a general literary theme, or as a question of the discrete units that make up that theme.

Size

And yet, however frequently equated with larger terms, motifs are invariably "small," autonomous units of meaning. With Werner Sollors, we might consider *theme* to be a text's "aboutness" and motifs the discrete elements that make up its "treatment." Motifs are the "basic components" of literary texts, "small substantial content units," or the "details out of which full-fledged narratives are composed." *Theme* is a structured group of motifs, and "wider thematic potential" is the result of recurring motifs. Thus, the two broken, failed

---

STITH THOMPSON'S *MOTIF-INDEX OF FOLK-LITERATURE*

The "alphabetical" organization of Thompson's six-volume motif-index may at first seem counterintuitive. Thompson arranges material into twenty-three index categories—A to Z (excluding I, O, and Y)—but the category headings themselves are not arranged alphabetically. There is no correspondence, in other words, between a category's letter and its topic—category A collects Mythological Motifs; category B, Animal Motifs; category C, Motifs of Tabu; D, Magic; E, the Dead; F, Marvels; G, Ogres; H, Tests; J, the Wise and the Foolish; K, Deceptions; L, Reversals of Fortune; M, Ordaining the Future; N, Chance and Fate; P, Society; Q, Rewards and Punishments; R, Captives and Fugitives; S, Unnatural Cruelty; T, Sex; U, the Nature of Life; V, Religion; W, Traits of Character; X, Humor; and Z, Miscellaneous Groups of Motifs. Each index category is subdivided, some much more so than others. For a detailed list of the categories and their divisions, see the beginning of volume one: "General Synopsis of the Index," 29–35.

---

swords of *Beowulf* can be said to add essential, thematic force to the sense of loss that pervades the poem: Hrunting and Naegling are not in and of themselves what *Beowulf* is about, but as object motifs, in failing the hero in a time of need, they function as distinct elements in the poet's elaboration of cyclical violence and social disintegration. Likewise, character and setting motifs reverberate throughout the poetry of Charles Baudelaire in ways that build an overall sense of anxiety about mechanized modernity: the idle dawdler (*flâneur*), for one, and the contrasting "traumatophile type"—a man propelled both by irrational fear and by sudden, nervous tics of the body—are both lost in the faceless, phantom masses of Baudelaire's big-city crowd. While not interchangeable, then, (small) motif and (larger) theme are nonetheless "mutually dependent" aspects of all literature—both integral "constants" that contribute to the intertextual matrix of literary culture.

Etymology: Dynamism

The fluidity of the term *motif,* and its conflation with other concepts, help emphasize the movement, mutability, and persistence that return us both to Steiner's cultural "motor" and to the root of the word itself. Derived from the Latin verb *movere,* "to move," and the Medieval Latin noun *motivum,* "cause" or "incitement," *motif* implies movement, stimulus, and dynamism; a recurring pattern or rhythm of motifs in effect propels narrative action. Motifs move in different ways: they are "mobile sequences" that conduct narrative action within individual texts, and they are also "translingual," "intertextual migrations" that move between texts and genres through time. Motifs moreover persist—constantly migrating and recycling, but surviving. Thus, George Steiner traces the combined motifs of poet's death, springtime, and resurrection from Horace, via the early modern poets William Dunbar, Thomas Carew, and John Milton, to Percy Bysshe Shelley and W. H. Auden—

tracking how diverse writers inherited and adapted meaning from classical antiquity into the twentieth century.

King Motifs in the Medieval Arthurian Tradition

Kingship, along with issues of power—who wields it, and how—can be said to obsess literature in general and medieval literature in particular. Take the weak king of Arthurian tradition—discussed by Edward Peters as an example of *rex inutilis* (the useless king) and frequently defined as exemplary of the *roi fainéant* (idle king) of medieval romance. Together with his Knights of the Round Table, he is already lost in decline, sliding toward the betrayal and civil war that will annihilate the Arthurian world. The Arthur of late medieval literature is himself largely absent from narrative action and almost always silent—his court a place of contention; his knights cowardly and his champions far away; his queen physically threatened, kidnapped, and ultimately unfaithful; his servants and realm vulnerable to violence and attack (as, for instance, in the works of Chrétien de Troyes [fl. c. 1170]). Exemplifying the character motif of weak, ineffectual king, this Arthur has persisted in literature, a king who is familiar today through Alfred, Lord Tennyson (*Idylls of the King*), T. H. White (*The Once and Future King*), and John Steinbeck (*The Acts of King Arthur and his Noble Knights*), or via the cinematic creations of Robert Bresson (*Lancelot du Lac,* 1974), John Boorman (*Excalibur,* 1981), or Jerry Zucker (*First Knight,* 1995).

And yet, far from first appearing on the literary scene as weak, Arthur is initially an impressive heir to the warrior kings of early medieval epic. The earliest and most complete literary version of King Arthur, that of Geoffrey of Monmouth, proves to be almost indistinguishable from the likes of *Beowulf*'s Shield Sheafson, a king whose name defines his role as defensive armament to his people, and whose violent leadership is praised in such terms as (in Seamus Heaney's translation) "scourge of many tribes," "wrecker of mean-benches," and "terror of the hall-troops." As encapsulated by the *Beowulf* poet, Shield Sheafson "was one good king." Arthur, too, conquers, and with similar abandon: in the early years of his reign, the fifteen-year-old king defeats all of Britain—exterminating (in Lewis Thorpe's translation) "without mercy" and with "unparalleled severity" the Saxons, Scots, Picts, and Irish—before expanding his realm with the subjection of Iceland, Gotland, the Orkneys, Norway, Denmark, and Gaul. Moreover, this Arthur delights in close combat and general slaughter. "White hot in the fierceness of his rage," he laughs as he singlehandedly slays the monster of Mont-Saint-Michel, "driving the whole length of the blade into his head just where his brain was protected by his skull." Though not explicitly named his nation's armament, as is Shield Sheafson, Geoffrey's Arthur is nonetheless memorable both for his sword, Caliburn (the Excalibur of later tradition), and for his shield, on which "was painted a likeness of the Blessed Mary, Mother of God, which forced [Arthur] to be thinking perpetually of her." When Arthur invokes the Virgin's name as his battle cry, her apparent blessing enables "unheard of slaughter." Thus, the savage violence of *Beowulf*'s kingship gains in Geoffrey's *History* divine sanction and favor.

Interestingly, the sword and shield of Arthur—in Geoffrey's *History* such forceful sources of the king's warrior might—are parceled out to knights in later tradition: in Chrétien de Troyes's *Story of the Grail*, Excalibur is wielded by Gawain rather than by Arthur, and by the end of the fourteenth century it is Gawain rather than Arthur who carries the Virgin Mary emblazoned on his shield. The literary Arthur and the objects that help define his kingship demonstrate how motifs can transform even while persisting; such character and object motifs contribute to and elaborate a changing thematic of kingship, one that moves from praise of the warrior king to general neglect, to a new emphasis on knights and their quests.

What is the point of tracking literary change in a character motif, or of conducting motif-based analysis in the first place? Motifs in and of themselves, after all, are not what literature is about; if we recall Sollor's distinction made above, they are merely the small elements that treat what literature is about. What exactly gives motif-based analysis methodological force? Even our brief consideration of the figure of King Arthur, of his transformation from inimitable warrior king to weak and inactive ruler in need of knights, allows us to raise much larger thematic questions about the nature of royal power. We can begin, for instance, to chart a literary trend away from the king as heroic conqueror toward a focus on the exploits of champion knights—toward a kind of redistribution and redefinition of power that in fact coincides with actual, historical change. Such wider thematic potential is arguably what makes motif so integral to literary criticism—and so useful to readers, students, and scholars.

Conclusion

It is precisely the persistence through tradition of motif that made motif-based classification such a fundamental aspect of the structural criticism of the mid-twentieth century: dis-

crete, shared units of literature were collected, alphabetized, numbered, and indexed, and relationships between literary genres and periods catalogued by type. A cursory glance at Stith Thompson's six-volume *Motif-Index of Folk-Literature*, in which Western literature is reduced to twenty-three motif categories organized alphabetically from A ("Mythological Motifs") to Z ("Miscellaneous Groups of Motifs"), may strike any reader as a vestige of the classification impulse that marked literary methodology of the past. And yet a quick keyword search on WorldCat will yield nearly one hundred "motif-indexes" of literature, very many of them published in the 1990s. Current trends in literary criticism and analysis, even if no longer explicitly indebted to formalist or structuralist vocabulary—and even if the term *motif* is not used—continue to illuminate connections and relationships between texts in ways identifiable as motif-based. Consider Werner Sollors's discussion of recent "thematic" studies as well as the great number of "treatment of" titles published annually in the bibliography of the Modern Language Association, or the ongoing series issued by the publisher Peter Lang, titled *Studies in Themes and Motifs in Literature*. Although it was in 1993 that Sollors called attention to "the return of thematic criticism," motif-based analysis, inherently intertextual, interdisciplinary, and comparative, has arguably never gone out of style.

See also **Structuralism and Poststructuralism.**

BIBLIOGRAPHY

PRIMARY SOURCES

Chrétien de Troyes. *The Complete Romances of Chrétien de Troyes.* Translated by David Staines. Bloomington and Indianapolis: Indiana University Press, 1990.
Geoffrey of Monmouth. *The History of the Kings of Britain.* Translated by Lewis Thorpe. Harmondsworth, U.K.: Penguin, 1966.
Heaney, Seamus. *Beowulf: A New Verse Translation.* New York: Farrar, Strauss and Giroux, 2000.
Sir Gawain and the Green Knight. Translated by Brian Stone. 2nd ed. Harmondsworth, U.K.: Penguin, 1974.
Trioedd Ynys Prydein, the Welsh Triads. Edited by Rachel Bromwich. 2nd ed. Cardiff: University of Wales Press, 1978.

SECONDARY SOURCES

Atkins, Stuart. "Motif in Literature: The Faust Theme." In *Dictionary of the History of Ideas: Studies of Selected Pivotal Ideas,* edited by Philip P. Wiener. New York: Scribners, 1973.
Benjamin, Walter. "On Some Motifs in Baudelaire." In *Illuminations: Essays and Reflections,* edited by Hannah Arendt. Translated by Harry Zohn. New York: Schocken, 1985.
Daemmrich, Horst S., and Ingrid G. Daemmrich. *Themes and Motifs in Western Literature: A Handbook.* Tübingen: Francke, 1987.
Frenzel, Elisabeth. *Motive der Weltliteratur.* 3rd ed. Stuttgart: Kröner, 1988.
———. *Stoffe der Weltliteratur.* 7th ed. Stuttgart: Kröner, 1988.
Johnson, David F. "The Five Horrors of Hell: An Insular Homiletic Motif." *English Studies* 5 (1993): 414–431.
Peters, Edward. *The Shadow King: Rex Inutilis in Medieval Law and Literature, 751–1327.* New Haven, Conn., and London: Yale University Press, 1970.

Steiner, George. "Roncevaux." In *The Return of Thematic Criticism,* edited by Werner Sollors. Cambridge, Mass.: Harvard University Press, 1993.

Thompson, Stith. *Motif-Index of Folk-Literature: A Classification of Narrative Elements in Folktales, Ballads, Myths, Fables, Mediaeval Romances, Exempla, Fabliaux, Jest-Books, and Local Legends.* Rev. ed. 6 vols. Bloomington: Indiana University Press, 1955–1958.

Vendler, Helen. *The Art of Shakespeare's Sonnets.* Cambridge, Mass.: Harvard University Press, 1997.

Kristen Lee Over

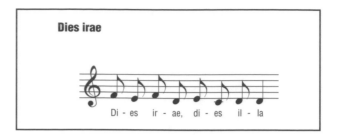

MOTIF IN MUSIC

A motif is a small but recognizable musical unit. The motif might consist merely of a series of pitches or a distinctive rhythm, or it might be harmonically conceived; quite often, pitch and rhythm are combined in a motif to create a discrete melodic fragment. No matter what its constituent elements, the motif needs to be repeated before it can be recognized as a unit. The repetition may be nearly continuous, as in the case of an ostinato—a short motif constantly repeated throughout a section of a composition—or the recurrence may be reserved for significant points in the structure of a work. (A form thus linked is often described as cyclical.) A motif needs to have clear boundaries, which might be established by immediately repeating the motif (as in the "Hallelujah" chorus in George Frideric Handel's *Messiah,* 1741), by placing a rest or pause after the motif (as in the beginning of Ludwig van Beethoven's Fifth Symphony, 1807), or by following the motif with contrasting material before repeating it. Although motifs vary in length, they are customarily only a portion of a complete melody.

Many motifs recur in note-for-note repetition, but a motif may be recognized even when modified. The modifications may involve rhythmic alterations (such as augmentation and diminution) and various sorts of melodic changes (including altered intervals or additional ornamentation) as well as retrograde (reversed) presentations or inversions, in which ascending pitches are substituted for descending pitches or vice versa. Sequential treatment, in which the motif is repeated at successively higher or lower pitch levels, is very common during transitional passages within large-scale structures, especially while the tonal focus is changing rapidly.

There is little consistency in terminology when discussing motifs. Some prefer the Anglicized *motive,* which, like *motif,* is derived from the Latin *motus,* the past participle of *movere* (to move). Other analysts use words such as *figure, subject, clause, pattern,* and *segment.* Both Western and non-Western cultures have terms for specialized motifs, such as leitmotifs, mottoes, head motifs, and the like.

Early History of the Motif

It is apparent in the earliest surviving music that composers were aware of the cohesive power of the motif. For example, the medieval sequence *Dies irae* (Day of wrath), a chant later incorporated into the Catholic requiem mass, opens with a descending eight-note melodic motif that unifies the entire chant by reappearing repeatedly through the course of the eighteen verses. The somber associations of its intervallic patterns, coupled with an ominous text concerning the biblical Judgment Day, have ensured the chant's opening motif a lasting place in music that strives to evoke the supernatural, ranging from Hector Berlioz's *Symphonie fantastique* (1830) to Stanley Kubrick's horror film *The Shining* (1980).

An early assessment of musical motifs appeared in Denis Diderot's monumental *Encyclopédie* in 1765. The *motivo* (as it is called there) is described as the principal thought or idea of an aria and thus constitutes "musical genius most particularly" (Grimm, p. 766a). Similar and expanded descriptions continued to appear on into the twentieth century. In 1906 the music theorist Heinrich Schenker argued that the "fundamental purpose" of a cyclical form is "to represent the destiny, the real personal fate, of a motif or of several motifs simultaneously" (p. 12). He added, "At one time, [the motif's] melodic character is tested; at another time, a harmonic peculiarity must prove its valor in unaccustomed surroundings; a third time, again, the motif is subjected to rhythmic change: in other words, the motif lives through its fate, like a personage in a drama" (p. 13).

Structural Uses of a Motif

Even among those uncomfortable with such anthropomorphic analysis, there is widespread recognition of the motif's role in creating unity within large or disparate pieces. Navajo traditions include an enormous body of Yeibichai songs, representing sacred ancestral spirits. Every one of the songs includes the call of the ancestors, a motif sung to the syllables "Hi ye, hi ye, ho-ho ho ho!" The Quechan tribe, in contrast, sings songs about natural history and lore, grouped into large cycles or series. In their Bird Series, all the songs are related by ending with the same "ha ha ha haaa" motif.

Melodic motifs. Melodic motifs have functioned structurally in many genres of music. The chief architectonic technique used by Renaissance composers of multivoice masses and motets was imitative counterpoint, in which subsequent voices repeated or echoed the opening motif presented by the initial singer. Similarly, in a Baroque fugue, the work begins with a subject that is reiterated in different registers, and the same motif reenters at later points in the work to start new series of imitative entrances.

Opera composers of the seventeenth and eighteenth centuries wrote arias with "motto openings," in which the first phrase of the song was performed by the singer, followed by a contrasting instrumental passage; the vocalist repeated the same opening phrase but then continued on with the remainder of the aria. In contrast, a single motif may serve as an introductory flourish for an entire set of pieces, such as the multiple movements of some Renaissance masses written in cyclical form, by having each movement begin with the same "head motif" or "motto."

Another common use of mottoes, especially in instrumental music, is the repetition of a clear-cut opening motif to signal important structural points within a movement. The slow, solemn fanfare that begins the first movement of Beethoven's "Pathétique" Sonata, Op. 13, is followed by the fast main section—the exposition—but it returns twice to underscore the start of the movement's development (tonally unstable) and coda (concluding) sections.

Harmonic motifs. Many cultures use certain harmonic motifs to provide a sense of completion or finality. In Western art music, these motifs are often described as cadence "formulas"; one of the most familiar of these is the Plagal (or "Amen") cadence that concludes hymns and other church music. Because cadence formulas are so ubiquitous, composers frequently embellish and prolong them in elaborate ways.

Harmonic motifs also occur in many styles of jazz music. Jazz performers often take the sequence of harmonies (or chord changes) underpinning a tune and use those borrowed chords as the basis for new melodic improvisations. The chords of George Gershwin's Broadway show tune "I Got Rhythm" (1930) are an especially popular source; numerous jazz hits have been based on these particular chord changes.

Rhythmic motifs. The organization of rhythm into recognizable groupings is a widespread motivic device. Many music analysts borrow from the vocabulary of poetic meter to describe short patterns of strong and weak pulses in music; thus a short note followed by a longer one would be called an iamb, while a longer note preceding a shorter note is a trochee. It has been traditional in Western literature and music to regard these different rhythms as possessing different emotional qualities.

Cultural customs lead to longer rhythmic patterns in varying contexts. Dances all over the world depend on set rhythmic motifs; a minuet has a different rhythmic pattern than a gavotte or a mazurka. In classical music of India, clap-patterns can be incorporated into a performance in accordance with one of the ancient rhythmic patterns, known as a tala. The complicated layering of much African drumming consists of the simultaneous presentation of diverse rhythmic motifs by various players, often repeated in ostinato fashion.

Representational motifs. In numerous cultures, a motif may carry symbolic meaning. Much of India's classical music, for example, is based on rāgas. Each rāga combines aspects of a mode—a certain set of pitches—with particular melodic motifs. Rāgas carry extramusical associations, sometimes linked to emotions, divinities, and even particular seasons of the year or times of day. Similarly the leitmotifs (leading motives) that Richard Wagner used in the four music dramas of his opera cycle *Der Ring des Nibelungen* (The ring of the Nibelungs;

1848–1874) are linked with a person, an object, or even an idea, and were repeated at different points in the work to bring that association back to our minds. For instance, in *Die Walküre* (the second music drama in the cycle), when Wotan refers to a "hero to come," the orchestra sounds the motif linked with Siegfried (even though at that point Siegfried has not yet been born).

Motifs can also portray more than just characters and objects in a story; at times, motifs have represented composers themselves. Since, in German musical nomenclature, the note B-flat is transcribed as a "B" and B-natural is transcribed as an "H," Johann Sebastian Bach was able to use a motif based on the letters of his last name as a subject for a fugue. Many other composers have embedded motivic messages into their works through this type of cryptography.

Despite its often tiny size, the motif's diversity makes it one of the most powerful tools at the disposal of composers and performers. It is one of the few musical characteristics that can be found in virtually all world cultures as well as throughout recorded history. Perhaps most important for listeners, a motif is a device by which music gains cohesion and, often, comprehensibility.

See also **Composition, Musical; Harmony; Motif; Motif in Literature.**

BIBLIOGRAPHY
Allanbrook, Wye Jamison. *Rhythmic Gesture in Mozart: Le nozze di Figaro and Don Giovanni.* Chicago and London: University of Chicago Press, 1983.
Grey, Thomas S. " . . . wie ein rother Faden: On the Origins of r'leitmotif as Critical Construct and Musical Practice." In *Music Theory in the Age of Romanticism,* edited by Ian Bent. Cambridge, U.K., and New York: Cambridge University Press, 1996.
Grimm, M. "Motif." In *Encyclopédie ou Dictionnaire raissoné des sciences, des arts et des métiers,* edited by Denis Diderot and Jean Le Rond d'Alembert. Vol. 10. Neuchâtel, Switzerland: S. Faulche, 1765.
Houle, George. *Meter in Music, 1600–1800: Performance, Perception, and Notation.* Bloomington and Indianapolis: Indiana University Press, 1987.
Koch, Heinrich Christoph. *Introductory Essay on Composition: The Mechanical Rules of Melody (Sections 3 and 4).* Leipzig, Germany, 1787. Translated, with an introduction, by Nancy Kovaleff Baker. New Haven, Conn., and London: Yale University Press, 1983.
Schenker, Heinrich. *Harmony.* Edited and annotated by Oswald Jonas, translated by Elisabeth Mann Borgese. Chicago and London: University of Chicago Press, 1954.

New Dictionary of the History of Ideas

Yeston, Maury. *The Stratification of Musical Rhythm.* New Haven, Conn., and London: Yale University Press, 1976.

Alyson McLamore

MULTICULTURALISM, AFRICA. Multiculturalism means different things to different people. For some it is directly linked to the politics of recognition and of difference (Taylor). In this regard, it concerns an appreciation of the necessity to deal with diversity in ways that affirm the value of different cultures and to respect the various claims made by minority groups. For others, multiculturalism concerns an explicit policy of protecting particularistic local cultures in the face of hegemonic and global cultures (both Australia and Canada have such self-conscious policies) or it can refer to a loose form of cultural pluralism (Kuper). Since multiculturalism is not a homogeneous concept or practice, it is important to differentiate between multiculturalism as a practical response to diversity and as an aspect of social philosophy advocating particular values with respect to cultural differences. There is no unifying theory of multiculturalism, and its respect for difference finds expression in a variety of political, social, and cultural approaches to problems of diversity.

The concept of multiculturalism does not enjoy widespread currency in African social thought. It is certainly not a topic of debate in early-twenty-first-century intellectual discourse on the continent. There are many reasons for this neglect, but it is undoubtedly connected to the fact that African societies are intrinsically multiethnic and multicultural. Diversity is not a new thing in Africa. Multiculturalism is premised on challenges to hegemonic cultures occasioned by the large-scale migrations of people who may experience alienation, marginalization, and exclusion in the host country. Sweden, for example, was remarkably homogeneous in a cultural sense prior to the influx of migrant laborers in the 1960s. African countries, in contrast, have entirely different histories. By and large, African states were formed by colonialism, usually to serve the interests of the colonists and, therefore, with little attention paid to the precolonial ethnic allegiances and other forms of belonging. These different histories play a critical role in the extent to which the concept of multiculturalism may be relevant in the African context.

Multicultural Problems in Africa

While the concept of multiculturalism has not enjoyed a great deal of scholarly attention in Africa, there are several practices that may fall neatly under its rubric. First, in the process of nation-building following independence, there was a concerted attempt to de-ethnicize the population and to construct a unitary conception of the nation. Second, multiculturalism is used in dealing with minorities, especially indigenous minorities in Africa. Third, it may be relevant in the various efforts at coping with and managing diversity in the workplace. Finally, multiculturalism plays a major role in education.

Even though ethnicity had a profound influence in African politics, the official rhetoric was dedicated to nation-building. Due to the generalized economic and political failures of the postcolonial state in Africa, these efforts have been thoroughly discredited. In the aftermath of massive resource limitations, the way has been opened up for a more explicit assertion of ethnic differences as a basis for economic and political claims. Since these perceived differences may form the basis of violent, sometimes genocidal, clashes between people, the topic of ethnic conflict has received considerable research attention from social scientists. The main area of debate is how to make citizens of everyone under conditions of such diversity and with so many subnational forms of belonging. This relates directly to the necessity of building legitimate polities in Africa in which all people have a sense of inclusion and national loyalties do not contradict cultural pluralism.

Dealing with minorities has become a major preoccupation of the Commission on Human Rights of the United Nations (CHR), which was established by the UN Economic and Social Council soon after the United Nations was formed in 1946. After years of dormancy and lack of effective functioning, in response to demands from below the CHR started to mobilize. A series of workshops, "Multiculturalism in Africa: Peaceful and Constructive Group Accommodation in Situations Involving Minorities and Indigenous Peoples," has been held across Africa over the last three years in Tanzania, Mali, and Botswana. These have served as starting points to provide both a voice for the articulation of people's concerns and a platform for cooperation among them on the basis of their common experiences of exclusion, marginalization, and displacement. It is of concern that, while the last meeting of this group was held in Botswana, the Basarwa/San were being forcibly removed from their ancestral land in the Kalahari.

Managing workplace diversity was at the center of the oppressive methods developed in the mining compounds in South Africa. Since many migrants came from all over southern Africa to work in the mines, the companies devised brutal divide-and-rule methods in an attempt to forestall the development of a common working-class consciousness by insisting on separate ethnic allegiances. In many ways, the apartheid experiment was an example of imposed cultural packaging of people and, in a perverse sense, it could fall under the rubric of multiculturalism in its imposition of cultural difference. The overwhelming emphasis in early-twenty-first-century South Africa, as in most postcolonial African states, is undoubtedly on de-ethnicizing the population in favor of a unitary national concept. However, parallel to this emphasis runs the idea of the promotion, and even celebration, of a rainbow nation, encapsulated constitutionally in the establishment of the Commission for the Protection and Promotion of the Rights of Cultural, Linguistic, and Religious Communities. Whether this represents a retreat into relativism and whether it will have a major impact on South African politics remain to be seen.

Multiculturalism has a profound influence on education in Africa. There are as many different positions on the virtues and vices of multicultural education as there are on multiculturalism itself. There is an abiding ambiguity here. Multiculturalism is supposed to promote diversity and contradictory perspectives, yet the goals attendant to these different positions differ sharply from those who are merely concerned with promoting tolerance to those who actively seek social change in the name of equal opportunities for all to learn. The question of language is, of course, of vital importance since it is established beyond all doubt that children perform much better when they are taught in their native language. Whether some people should be accorded special treatment in education because of historical disadvantage and whether, indeed, they should be given special curricula to cope with educational demands remain unresolved issues.

The cultural diversity of Africa has long been recognized. Audrey Richards, for example, provided a detailed account of the linguistic, religious, and cultural differentiation of communities in East Africa in a book presciently entitled *The Multicultural States of East Africa.* One of the contested concepts in multiculturalism is assimilation. An example from Ethiopia provides a unique insight into this policy. Bahru Zewde considers the situation of the Oromo in East Africa in the following manner: "[T]he Ethiopian emperor has three options with regard to the Oromo: enslavement and expropriation, assimilation, and indirect rule." While the first and the last mentioned are rejected for various reasons, "assimilation therefore remains the only credible and sensible option." In short, the Oromo should become Amhara since, "two peoples who are allowed to evolve separately will end up forming two different, and perhaps antagonistic, nations" (pp. 132–133). Assimilation thus implies the eradication of difference in favor of the dominant culture. It is essentially a homogenizing project that imposes itself on others on the basis of assumed cultural superiority. It is precisely this kind of cultural chauvinism that multiculturalism seeks to oppose, usually for the sake of the oppressed.

Multiculturalism and Culture

Any discussion of multiculturalism must include a definition of *culture* since multiculturalism literally refers to a plurality or a multiplicity of cultures. In this regard, *culture* refers to the collective material and nonmaterial accomplishments of particular groups, their ways of doing things, and the manner in which these patterns of behavior are transmitted from one generation to the next. A basic truism about culture is that it is never static. In this respect, multiculturalism has to accommodate changes if it is to remain relevant. This is very difficult though because multiculturalism tends to reify culture and freeze people into cultural particularisms on the assumption that certain people need to be treated differently because of their separate cultures. This is problematic because *culture* is then defined as an immutable entity based on primordial origins, and becomes a biological given rather than learned forms of behavior and creativity. Exemplifying this conflation of race and culture, Paul Kelly insists that the movement of "white European immigrants . . . and . . . the movement of non-white [sic] populations" (p. 2) lie at the heart of the reality of pluralism. Put bluntly, it is extremely difficult to emphasize cultural difference without also essentializing culture and ethnic identities, sometimes even understood in racial terms. Once group identities are politicized it

is virtually impossible to avoid packaging people in different categories and ensuring that they remain in their designated spaces. K. Anthony Appiah and Amy Gutman distinguish between cultures and identities but lament that "ethnic identities characteristically have cultural distinctions as one of their primary marks" and "in the United States, not only ethnic but also racial boundaries are culturally marked" (p. 89).

There are many other philosophical and political criticisms of multiculturalism, both as a concept and as a practice. In the first instance, the tendency to categorize people in this manner may lead to greater stereotyping, particularly if special treatment (for example, affirmative action in employment appointments) is expected. While multiculturalism pays a great deal of attention to recognition, it does not accord the problems of redistribution equal weight. In this sense, it does not deal adequately with the ways in which class intersects with other forms of differentiation. Since differences in people almost always imply differences in power and wealth, there is a great challenge for multiculturalism to recognize these inequalities in ways that do not entrench or solidify them, but simultaneously to appreciate that these inequalities are real in their consequences for many people. In this regard, there is a powerful argument that multiculturalists have retreated from economic struggles in favor of cultural struggles for recognition (Fraser).

Probably the greatest challenge for multiculturalism is how it can encourage cultural difference without promoting cultural chauvinism and its counterpart, xenophobia. Its insistence on cultural difference and separation makes the quest for equality elusive because of the reality of cultural hierarchies. The celebration of difference that it advocates rests awkwardly next to the reality of persecution, exclusion, and stereotyping. Thus, when people are recognized, it is their individual identities that should be recognized and not some preconceived caricature of who they should be or how they should behave because of their membership in a particular group. According to Brian Barry, for example, multiculturalism tends to conflate descriptions about the reality of cultural diversity with prescriptions of commitment to the program of normative multiculturalism (p. 22). Finally, there is the problem of how individual human rights can be protected in the context of such a pervasive emphasis on group rights, which raises the fundamental questions of identity and of choice. If cultural difference is so rigorously imposed, then it leaves little room for individual choice. Thus, one of the major issues around the concept of multiculturalism is how it meshes with individual rights because it so clearly emphasizes the recognition and rights of a collectivity. If identity is socially derived from particularistic cultural experiences, then it amounts to an ascribed status that allows for growth and development within the limited purview of the community.

Insofar as *multiculturalism* refers to the value of cultural tolerance and to the celebration of diversity, it has made a positive contribution in broadening narrow horizons and exposing people to the wide range of cultural heritages. However, multiculturalism in the sense of politicized group identities is problematic from the point of view of individual human rights in democracies because treating groups equally is much more difficult than treating individuals equally.

See also **Africa, Idea of; Assimilation; Black Consciousness; Communitarianism in African Thought; Ethnicity and Race: Africa; Identity, Multiple; Internal Colonialism; Migration: Africa; Nationalism: Africa; Pan-Africanism; Postcolonial Studies; Prejudice.**

BIBLIOGRAPHY

Alexander, Neville. *An Ordinary Country: Issues in the Transition from Apartheid to Democracy in South Africa.* Pietermaritzburg, South Africa: Natal University Press, 2002.

Appiah, K. Anthony, and Amy Gutmann. *Color Conscious: The Political Morality of Race.* Princeton, N.J.: Princeton University Press, 1996.

Barry, Brian. *Culture and Equality: An Egalitarian Critique of Multiculturalism.* Cambridge, U.K.: Polity Press, 2001.

Breytenbach, W. J. "The Protection of Minority Rights in Africa." In *Intergroup Accommodation in Plural Societies: A Selection of Conference Papers with Special Reference to South Africa,* edited by N. Rhoodie and Winifred C. Ewing, London: Macmillan, 1979.

Fraser, Nancy. "From Redistribution to Recognition: Dilemmas of Justice in a 'Post-Socialist' Age." In *Theorizing Multiculturalism: A Guide to the Current Debate,* edited by Cynthia Willet, 68–93. Oxford: Blackwell, 1997.

Kelly, Paul. "Introduction: Between Culture and Equality." In *Multiculturalism Reconsidered,* edited by Paul Kelly, 1–20. Cambridge, U.K.: Polity Press, 2002.

Kuper, Adam. *Culture: The Anthropologists' Account.* Cambridge, Mass.: Harvard University Press, 1999.

Richards, Audrey I. *The Multicultural States of East Africa.* Montreal: McGill-Queen's University Press, 1969.

Taylor, Charles. *Multiculturalism and the Politics of Recognition.* Princeton, N.J.: Princeton University Press, 1992.

Zewde, Bahru. *Pioneers of Change in Ethiopia: The Reformist Intellectuals of the Early Twentieth Century.* Addis Ababa, Ethiopia: Addis Ababa University Press, 2002.

Fred Hendricks

MUSEUMS. It is often assumed that museums have been a permanent feature of society, simply because they contain some of the oldest things in the world. In fact, in their current form, museums are surprisingly recent in origin, almost entirely Western in conception, internally confused about their identity, and unsure of their future role.

Museums in the early twenty-first century claim descent from the Museum in Alexandria established in the third century B.C.E., but this is only partly true. That museum—a Latin word derived from the Greek *mouseion,* meaning seat of the muses—was an attempt to bring all the fields of human knowledge together into one place. Its library was its most famous feature, complemented with a collection of artifacts. Contemporary accounts describe a huge complex of buildings, including seminar rooms and banqueting halls. It was more like a prototype university than a museum.

The British Museum, effectively the mother of all modern museums, was established in 1753 as a direct emulation of the museum in Alexandria, but this time as a public service, not as an educational institution open only to scholars. Its ambition also was to bring all human knowledge together into one place. Its library, again, was by far its most important feature. The idea that artifacts could be separated from books in the learning process did not emerge until well more than a century later, and then largely for reasons of administrative convenience. It was not until 1998 that the British Library was separated physically from the British Museum, which in the early 2000s is a totally different institution from the one that opened its doors 250 years ago, and yet it still proudly claims that its collection has remained "inviolable" since then. It is in this way that museums create myths about their permanence, though their role has in fact changed out of all recognition over the centuries.

Origins

Museums owe their origins to three traits in human nature: the desire to understand the universe, the wish to appreciate the artifacts museums contain, and the impetus to educate others. Each of these motivations has its own history, but none, by itself, necessitates the creation of a museum. One might, for example, have no more need for the objects used in one's research when what was being sought was found. Many archaeological remains are now replaced in the ground whence they came. If one wants to appreciate something, one will tend to look after it, but that does not mean that one will necessarily want to share it with anyone else, apart from a chosen few. This appears to have been the ethos behind the earliest art gallery in the world, the Pinakotheke, established on the Acropolis in Athens in the fifth century

Egyptian exhibit in the British Museum. Founded in 1753, the world-renowned British Museum houses a collection that spans two million years of history. The original incarnation of the museum also boasted an extensive library; the two were divided physically in the late twentieth century. PETER APRAHAMIAN/CORBIS

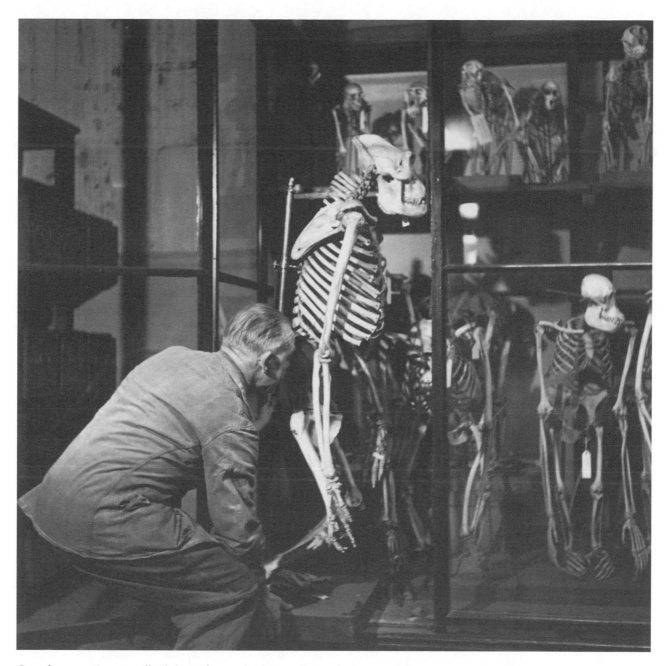

Caretaker removing a gorilla skeleton from a display case in London's Natural History Museum, 1953. The Natural History Museum began in the eighteenth century as a collection of exhibits in the British Museum. As the collection grew, Superintendent Richard Owen instigated a push for a separate natural history museum, and the new building was completed in 1880. © HULTON-DEUTSCH COLLECTION/CORBIS

B.C.E. As far can be determined from cursory contemporary accounts (nothing physical remains), the museum had a religious purpose and showed paintings for the initiates—and the gods themselves—to view. Though it might have been open to the general public, it would be two millennia before galleries were specially created with that purpose in mind. It was not until there was a commitment to universal education that the modern concept of the museum took root and flourished.

Museums did not emerge at all in societies where the scientific study of the material world was not valued, for example, in ancient China and India, nor in countries dominated by religions that focused people's attention on the spiritual rather than the material world, such as Christianity during certain periods of its history and, more generally, Islam. Museums sprang from the approach to learning advocated by Aristotle: that people can only learn by studying the world around them and trusting the evidence of their own eyes, not by listening to others or reading what they have written.

Early Development

Museums only started to develop in the form in which they are currently know them at the beginning of the Age of Enlightenment in Europe, when amateur scientists began to collect the material evidence of what was still widely assumed to be God's creation. By the sixteenth century many European noblemen had "cabinets of curiosities" containing the unaccountable wonders of nature, such as fossil teeth (thought to be satanic) and flint tools (thought to be thunderbolts) and, increasingly, natural and cultural artifacts gleaned from the newly discovered far-flung corners of the world. By the seventeenth century some of these collections had begun to be systematically studied and categorized. Ole Worm (1588–1654), a Danish doctor, used his vast collection to prove that so-called unicorn horns actually came from a species of Arctic whale—much to the chagrin of Scandinavian fishermen, who plied a lucrative trade in supplying such wonders.

The approach of these early scientific collectors was, as it had been in ancient Greece, encyclopedic. The mere activity of collecting similar objects together and placing them in some sort of order—the standard way of working in museums even in the twenty-first century—was then an extremely exciting activity. Barriers of accepted thought were being broken on every front. Geological specimens proved that the earth was far older than anyone had imagined, fossils demonstrated the fact of extinction (thought, by most, to be an impossibility within divine creation), and coins revealed the existence of cultures and dynasties previously unknown to history. Without his vast collection of natural history specimens, Charles Darwin (1809–1882) might never have formulated his theory of evolution. Working in the Museum of Northern Antiquities in Copenhagen, Christian Jurgensen Thomsen (1788–1865) developed the system of classifying prehistory according to the material evidence of the ages of stone, bronze, and iron, the names by which they are still known. It is significant that the formation of the British Museum (and library) was exactly contemporaneous with the publication of Denis Diderot's great *Encyclopédie* in France.

During the eighteenth and early nineteenth centuries public museums burgeoned throughout Europe and America, and soon in other societies influenced by them, such as South America, Australia, India, and South Africa. This was in response to two considerable and growing pressures: the new urge to collect and codify all material things, and the public's desire to see all these wonders. In those days the interests of the scholar and the general public were consanguineous. Crowds gathered to see the first stuffed kangaroo or dinosaur bone or the latest archaeological discovery from Peru. The field of enquiry that was opening was so vast that collectors—and therefore museums—soon began to specialize, dividing into subject areas such as natural history and geology, archaeology, and ethnology, which continue to define their form to this day.

Growth

The main impetus behind the extraordinary growth in museums during the last two centuries—few cities around the world are now without several—has been the growing awareness of the importance of public education. The roots of this egalitarian ideal also can be traced back to the Enlightenment, when people such as Diderot believed that knowledge would enable humankind to make the world a better place. His ideas for a national museum were put into practice by the leaders of the French Revolution: in 1792, just nine days after the Bourbon monarchy collapsed, the Louvre, at that time a royal palace, was transformed into a museum with the aim of embracing "knowledge in all its manifold beauty" so that it would, "by embodying these good ideas, worthy of a free people . . . become among the most powerful illustrations of the French Republic." Napoléon Bonaparte was following a time-honored tradition when his armies plundered masterpieces of art from the territories they conquered, particularly in Egypt and Italy, and sent them to the Louvre. (Napoléon was, in this case—at least ostensibly—acting solely in the interests of the people. The Italian treasures were returned after his fall from power.)

Individuals and institutions have, since the earliest times and in almost all cultures, collected rare and precious objects as manifestations of their status. There is archaeological evidence of royal and religious treasuries from ancient civilizations as widespread as Peru, Assyria, Greece, and China. What was new, however, during the Enlightenment, was the idea that these should become public treasuries. The members of the aristocracy of Europe were beginning to allow the general public to visit their collections in the eighteenth century; revolutions merely speeded up the process. The English Civil War, however, had come a century before such ideas had taken hold, and Charles I's extraordinary art collection was simply sold—Britain had to create its own National Gallery, from scratch, in 1824. The Hermitage, though still a royal palace, was first opened to the public in 1852, many decades before the Russian Revolution; its collections had been formed as part of Catherine II the Great's (ruled 1762–1796) strategy to bring education to Russia. The Bolsheviks boosted public collections by giving them religious treasures after religious worship had been outlawed. Many icons are now being returned as the churches reopen following the collapse of the communist regime.

Increasing access to culture dovetailed neatly with the Enlightenment's drive for knowledge. This was the great age of the formation of museums. Its high point, arguably, came in 1846 when James Smithson, a self-effacing English businessman, gave the American government the then celestial sum of half a million dollars to found a museum for "the increase and diffusion of knowledge among men." The Smithsonian Institution is now the greatest museum organization in the world, with its many galleries, most of which are ranged along the Mall in Washington, D.C., devoted to interests ranging from art to aerospace and from natural history to ethnography.

During the nineteenth and early twentieth centuries, the establishment of a museum became not just a response to educational need, but a matter of civic pride. This heady mix of political objectives accounts for the worldwide proliferation of museums at that time, from the Australian Museum in Sydney (opened 1828) to the Egyptian Museum in Cairo (1858) to the Museum of the History of China in Beijing (1915), and hundreds of thousands of smaller museums in towns and villages in between.

Museums had another advantage: they attracted tourists. Just as the churches of medieval Europe had competed with each other for relics, so museums sought out the best collections—for tourists, like pilgrims, bring income. Many museums in the late twentieth century were established as part of an economic strategy. Glasgow in Scotland was the first postindustrial city to rebuild itself on the back of an art gallery, the Burrell Collection, which opened in 1983. Gradually museum buildings, such as cathedrals, became beacons of attraction in themselves, which led to the extraordinary flowering of museum architecture in the late twentieth century. The Guggenheim Museum in Bilbao, Spain, designed by Frank O. Gehry and opened in 1997, is world-famous for its titanium-clad curves, though few could describe its collection—but then it is not really a museum so much as a temporary exhibition hall, exhibiting works on loan from its parent museum in New York.

Agencies of Influence

It wasn't long before people began to realize that museums could be used to influence people. The South Kensington Museum in London was created in 1857 specifically to encourage better industrial design in Britain. It was radical in that it combined engineering with art, and valued objects from the past purely for their capacity to inspire the present. It is difficult to quantify how effective it was—William Morris's famous wallpaper designs were directly influenced by its collections—but the museum gradually lost its motivation and in 1893 was split into the Science Museum and the Victoria and Albert Museum, thus creating new categories of museums for science and engineering and the decorative arts.

However, the proactive educational spirit sown by the South Kensington Museum became hugely influential. The push-button displays in the Science Museum were the direct inspiration for the Exploratorium in San Francisco, established in 1969 by Frank Oppenheimer, to help people understand new developments in science. The Exploratorium is not really a museum at all—it doesn't have collections—yet its approach has spawned science centers in almost every major conurbation.

The most radical recent developments in museums have sprung from the desire to educate, rather than to collect. Michael Spock put the old toys in the Boston Children's Museum into storage because he realized his young visitors weren't interested in them. He created a new type of museum in which children could explore the adult world through interactive displays. His methods, particularly his audience participatory programs, have been hugely influential on museums, and new-style children's museums have become almost as widespread as science centers.

Interior of the United States Holocaust Memorial Museum, c. 2001. This museum, located in Washington, D.C., is one of twelve in the U.S. alone dedicated to remembrance of the Holocaust. Chartered in 1980, the institution offers extensive programs, exhibitions, and publications. © PICTURENET/ CORBIS

Since the 1960s museums have been transformed by the introduction of modern media such as video and film, audio guides, and computers. It is now possible for museums to catch the imagination of a very wide public, but only a few, as yet, have begun to put their visitors first in this way. Most stick to their old, categorical presentations and assume that their visitors will want to learn about microliths, monstrances, and moths, without asking why they might be interested in such things, let alone if they would prefer to find out about something else. When he was commissioned to create what was to become the Museum of the Jewish Diaspora in Tel Aviv in 1968, Jeshajahu Weinberg, a former theater director, realized that it would not be possible to tell this story using original artifacts, because virtually none existed. He therefore created a display that used no original material at all, only reproductions. But, since it has no collections, it cannot really be categorized as a museum at all.

Weinberg's greatest museum, the United States Holocaust Memorial Museum in Washington, D.C. (opened 1993), uses all the storytelling techniques he developed in Israel together with real exhibits to mesmerizing effect, and attracts two million visitors per year. One reason for the recent proliferation of Holocaust museums (there are twelve in the United States alone in the early 2000s) is that its last living witnesses are being lost. One of the most important roles of museums in the future may be to preserve the evidence of past events, such as the Holocaust, of which it is imperative that they are not forgotten.

Future Challenges

A central issue facing museums in the early twenty-first century is to find ways to use their collections as a means of entertaining and educating a wide public, while developing their role as a resource for research. The felicitous atmosphere of the Enlightenment, when research and public interest coincided, has passed. Museum collections no longer represent, as they did then, the horizon of human understanding. The frontiers of science extend beyond the visible world collectable by museums, and it adds little to the sum of knowledge for museums to go on building up their collections, as most continue to do, according to categories laid down two centuries ago. But objects will still need to be preserved for future study and to make past experiences vividly meaningful to subsequent generations. Museums tend to go on doing what they have always done—adding another Carracci, crustacean, or car—and yet there is no museum about the history of communism (apart from a few remaining Soviet propaganda museums, which only tell one side of the story), or of marketing. Both are manifestations of ideas and practices that have vastly shaped the lives of people living in the early 2000s, and both have vivid material pasts, ideal for museum display. The challenge for museums is to decide what is important for them to collect in the present—because it is on these collections that their future will be built.

See also Arts; City, The: The City as a Cultural Center; Cultural History; Encyclopedism; Enlightenment; Visual Order to Organizing Collections.

BIBLIOGRAPHY

Asma, Stephen T. *Stuffed Animals and Pickled Heads: The Culture and Evolution of Natural History Museums.* Oxford and New York: Oxford University Press, 2001.

Coombes, Annie E. *Reinventing Africa: Museums, Material Culture, and Popular Imagination in Late Victorian and Edwardian England.* New Haven, Conn., and London: Yale University Press, 1994.

Dubin, Steven C. *Displays of Power: Controversy in the American Museum from the Enola Gay to Sensation!* New York: New York University Press, 2000.

Glaser, Jane R., and Artemis A. Zenetou, eds. *Gender Perspectives: Essays on Women in Museums.* Washington, D.C.: Smithsonian Institution Press, 1994.

Holo, Selma. *Beyond the Prado: Museums and Identity in Democratic Spain.* Washington, D.C.: Smithsonian Institution Press, 1999.

Holst, Niels von. *Creators, Collectors, and Connoisseurs: The Anatomy of Public Taste from Antiquity to the Present Day.* London: Thames and Hudson, 1967. Deals only with art collections.

Hudson, Kenneth. *Museums of Influence.* Cambridge, U.K.: Cambridge University Press, 1987.

Malraux, André. *Musée imaginaire.* Paris: Gallimard, 1965. Translated as *Museum Without Walls* by Stuart Gilbert and Francis Price. London: Secker and Warburg, 1967.

McClellan, Andrew. *Inventing the Louvre: Art, Politics, and the Origin of the Modern Museum in Eighteenth-Century Paris.* Cambridge, U.K.: Cambridge University Press, 1994.

McLoughlin, Moira. *Museums and the Interpretation of Native Canadians: Negotiating the Borders of Culture.* New York: Garland, 1999.

Norman, Geraldine. *The Hermitage: The Biography of a Great Museum.* London: Pimlico, 1999.

Schneider, Andrea Kupfer. *Creating the Musée d'Orsay: The Politics of Culture in France.* University Park: Pennsylvania State University Press, 1998.

Spalding, Julian. *The Poetic Museum: Reviving Historic Collections.* Munich: Prestel, 2002.

Staniszewski, Mary Anne. *The Power of Display: A History of Exhibition Installation at the Museum of Modern Art.* Cambridge, Mass.: MIT Press, 1998.

Weil, Stephen E. *A Cabinet of Curiosities: Inquiries into Museums and their Prospects.* Washington, D.C.: Smithsonian Institution Press, 1995.

Wilson, David M. *The British Museum: A History.* London: British Museum Press, 2002.

Julian Spalding

MUSIC, ANTHROPOLOGY OF. The phrase *anthropology of music* is most closely associated with Alan P. Merriam's 1964 landmark book bearing this title. In this prescriptive text, influential through the 1980s, Merriam defines ethnomusicology as the study of music in culture in relation to the mutual interactions of sound, behavior, and concepts. In consonance with many ethnomusicologists to this day, Mieczyslaw Kolinski (1967) responded that anthropological considerations should not dwarf an emphasis on the study of musical sound, per se, and he took Merriam to task for being too dogmatically anthropological. Kolinski argued that ethnomusicology is, in fact, a field at the juncture of two distinct disciplines: comparative musicology, which is the study of musical styles and systems from different societies, an integral part of general musicology; and musical anthropology, the study of the role music plays in human societies, an integral part of general anthropology. In 1987 Anthony Seeger described his book *Why Suyá Sing* as "a kind of musical anthropology as distinct from an anthropology of music—a study of society from the perspective of musical performance, rather than simply the application of anthropological methods and concerns to music" (p. xiii).

From these statements three general orientations emerge: (a) an emphasis on musical sound, styles, and performance in non-Western societies described in their cultural context; (b) an emphasis on analyzing musical sound and style in dialectic with social processes through the application of anthropological methods and concerns; and (c) an emphasis on social life and processes as studied through musical styles and performance ("musical anthropology"). Ethnomusicology emerged as an independent discipline in the 1950s, and the first two orientations characterize the majority of ethnomusicological work. The third orientation, that which uses musical data to understand social processes, might be identified with the disciplines of ethnomusicology and/or anthropology, often depending on the disciplinary identity of the scholar.

Anthropologists who focus on music represent a small minority within the discipline and, Bruno Nettl writes, "the practitioners of the types of study labeled as the 'anthropology of music' . . . have accounted, I reckon, for less than one-fifth of all ethnomusicologists, but among them have been many of the field's great leaders" (p. 62). Since the 1980s, the anthropology of music approach probably represents a larger portion of ethnomusicological work, and anthropological methods and theories have provided an important basis for the discipline as a whole throughout its development.

Musical Anthropology

Ethnomusicologists have documented the fact that many societies in the world do not have a single word or concept akin to the English term *music*. Nonetheless, scholars engaged with musical anthropology and the anthropology of music typically use the Western concept to define the boundaries of their study. Anthropologists have approached music in two basic ways: first, as a type of data to further general social theories or models, and second as a basic component of social life that deserves ethnographic description along with other cultural domains. An example of the first type is the Kulturkreis, or German diffusionist school in the decades around the turn of the twentieth century. Musical instruments and measurable musical traits, especially pitch organization, proved attractive data for determining the historical development of cultures and hypothetical contact between distant regions through mapping the distribution of cultural trait and artifact clusters. Anthropologists sought out help from their musicological colleagues such as Curt Sachs in this endeavor. Melville Herskovits used musical data prominently in his work on "Africanisms" in the Americas and in his theories about cultural continuity and acculturation. His study of musical styles and linguistic patterns led him to hypothesize that cultural practices that remain low in focal awareness tend to be more stable in situations of contact.

The defensive tone at the beginning of Robert Plant Armstrong's *The Affecting Presence: An Essay in Humanistic Anthropology* (1971) suggests that aesthetic systems and emotional experience were not well-accepted concerns in anthropology before this time, but an interest in such topics as *The Anthropology of Experience* (Victor Turner and Edward M. Bruner, eds., 1986), *The Anthropology of the Body* (John Blacking, 1977), and the anthropology of emotion has grown. These topics provide a natural point of intersection for anthropology and music scholarship. David P. McAllester, anthropologist and a founding father of American ethnomusicology, conducted groundbreaking research on Navajo social and aesthetic values through a study of music associated with the Enemy Way ceremony. Steven Feld's *Sound and Sentiment* (1982), a study of Kaluli myth, song performance, and emotional experience (a classic in the ethnomusicological literature), was widely read by anthropologists and has been particularly influential.

Recently, in relation to globalization, musical data has again appeared as significant to anthropologists for addressing broader theoretical issues. In discussing the cultural homogeneity-heterogeneity dialectic within late-twentieth-century processes of globalization, Arjun Appadurai, for example, writes:

We have a growing series of studies of cultural production worldwide, especially in the areas of music, film, and advertising, which let us look into the sites and institutions through which global commodities are locally interpreted by producers as well as consumers. The study of "world music" by ethnomusicologists is perhaps the best developed of these subfields. In general, these studies have produced a broad consensus that cultural differentiation tends to outpace homogenization, even in this most interactive of economic epochs. (p. 6,269)

The second type of anthropological engagement with music saw music simply as one component of culture that deserved ethnographic description along with other aspects. Merriam notes that "While anthropologists in the earlier history of the discipline almost always included music in their ethnographies, the tradition has become steadily less practiced, particularly over the past decade or two" (p. 18). Bruno Nettl likewise sees a decline in the description of music in anthropology textbooks and monographs generally after the mid-twentieth century. It may be that anthropologists who did not feel technically competent to deal with music simply decided to leave the topic to their ethnomusicological colleagues once this became a viable option. The perceived decline may also be partially a matter of disciplinary definition in that, increasingly after ethnomusicology became established in the late 1950s, anthropologists and specific works that predominantly focused on music simply came to be considered ethnomusicological.

It remains unclear, however, if the generalization about a former prominence and later decline in descriptive musical anthropology really holds. Franz Boas and his followers took a holistic view of culture and often discussed or at least mentioned music, as did Bronislaw Malinowski. George Herzog was an anthropologist so deeply concerned with music that he comfortably fits within comparative musicology. Nettl also cites Melville Herskovits, Robert Lowie on the Crow (1935), and Clark Wissler on the Blackfoot, among others, for including music in their ethnographies. He specifically highlights Margaret Mead's *Coming of Age in Samoa* (1928) as including a "short but insightful ethnography of music" (p. 63). The level of detail about music in this work, however, is easily matched and exceeded by anthropologists who published studies during the suggested period of decline—including Norman Whitten's work on *currulao* (an African-derived music-dance tradition from the Pacific coast of Colombia and Ecuador) in *Black Frontiersmen* (1974), Hans Buechler's study of Aymara panpipe performance in Bolivia as a window to social organization, William Mangin's work on migrant regional associations in Lima, Bruce Mannheim's work on Quechua songs, Jose María Arguedas's work on mestizo-indigenous relations in Peru, Ellen Basso's study of Kalapalo performance, Richard Price and Sally Price's work in Suriname, Fremont E. Besmer's study of the Hausa Bori cult, Colin Turnbull's discussion of Molimo music among the Mbuti, and Peter Fry's study of nationalism and spirit mediums in Zimbabwe, just to name a few examples. Morton H. Fried's general *Readings in Anthropology,* vol. 2, *Cultural Anthropology* (1968), includes two chapters on music and ethnomusicology—generous if one considers the number of facets of social life that needed to be covered. Conversely, founding father Edward Burnett Tylor's *Religion in Primitive Culture* ([1871] 1958), which considers a realm of life saturated with musical performance, barely mentions music at all. From the Boas camp, Ruth Benedict's *Patterns of Culture* (1934) does not mention music.

Comparative Musicology and Ethnomusicology

The emergence of contemporary ethnomusicology is typically traced to the 1880s. Thomas Edison invented the phonograph in 1887—ethnologist Jesse Walter Fewkes was the first to use the cylinder machine in his fieldwork (with Native Americans in 1890 and 1891). During the 1880s, British physicist and phonetician Alexander J. Ellis developed the cents system that divided the octave into 1,200 equal units and allowed for the measurement and comparison of scales from different societies. Ellis concluded that musical scales were not grounded on natural laws but "capriciously" differed from one society to the next. Thus he introduced the need for a culturally relativistic approach to musical analysis and understanding that became a fundamental cornerstone of ethnomusicological thinking, and that predated Boas's first direct statement about cultural relativism.

In 1885, Guido Adler published an article outlining the field of musicology. Adler divided the study of music into two subfields, historical and systematic musicology, and part of the latter was *Musikologie*—"comparative study [of non-Western music] for ethnographic purposes" (quoted in Nettl, p. 20)— a field that became known as comparative musicology, that grew into contemporary ethnomusicology, and that, along with historical musicology, has become one of the two main branches of musicology. As it has developed, historical musicology is devoted to the study of European and European-derived elite music repertories and composers with an emphasis on style development as well as studies that describe European elite music in its cultural context. By default, the remainder of the world's musics, including European and American "vernacular" musics, became the defining subject of comparative musicology and later ethnomusicology (e.g., see Kunst, p. 9).

Comparative musicology is most strongly associated with the "Berlin School" (originally based at the Psychological Institute of Berlin), and Carl Stumpf, Erich M. von Hornbostel, and Otto Abraham, and their students and associates including Curt Sachs, Kolinski, George Herzog, and Klaus Wachsmann. In his synthetic discussion, "The Problems of Comparative Musicology" (1905 [1975]), Hornbostel emphasizes the need to compare scales, intervals, and rhythmic organization of the world's peoples; his primary emphasis is on issues of musical sound, with theorizing about psychological and anthropological issues being secondary—a position maintained by Kolinski and many others.

Drawn generally from anthropological tradition, by the 1950s fieldwork became a basic prerequisite for professional standing in ethnomusicology. The early comparative musicologists, however, had little fieldwork experience and often based their research on recordings made by others—a style of work that became known as *armchair ethnomusicology.* The lack of in-depth fieldwork precluded the type of detailed social-musical analytical integration that began to emerge in the 1970s under the banner *the anthropology of music.*

The Anthropology of Music

Many musicologists maintain a Western aesthetic ideology of autonomous art. Against this backdrop, scholars with an anthropology of music orientation were faced with the challenge of finding theoretical approaches that would help them explain, or at least link, musical style with broader patterns of cultural and social processes. Ethnomusicologists frequently turned to the prominent anthropological theories and problems of any given period for this purpose. Social evolutionism, diffusionism, mapping culture areas, functionalism, problems of acculturation and culture change, structuralism, semiotics, "ethnoscience," feminist theory, theories of social power, practice theory, and problems of nationalism and globalization, prominently form the historical strata of ideas guiding work in the anthropology of music. Some scholars explicitly combined a variety of theoretical approaches in single publications. While it sometimes appears as if the newest problem or body of theory negates earlier approaches as faulty or outmoded, it is more accurate to view each as a theoretical layer that continues to inform later thinking.

Hornbostel, Curt Sachs, and the widely dispersed scholars influenced by this group (e.g., Carlos Vega in Argentina), are often associated with a social-evolutionist anthropological orientation. This is an oversimplification in that Hornbostel and Sachs, to cite but two examples, contributed to a variety of theoretical discussions and problems, for example, cultural diffusion, music perception, approaches to musical analysis, and the classification of musical instruments, among others. It is probably fairer to say that evolutionist ideas were part of common sense for this generation of scholars. Thus as a reason to study "foreign [contemporary] music" Hornbostel states that "we would like to uncover the remotest, darkest past and unveil, in the wealth of the present, the ageless universal in music; in other words: we want to understand the evolution and common aesthetic foundation of the art of music" (p. 269). In *The Wellsprings of Music,* Sachs views contemporary tribal peoples as "archaic" and as "the surviving tribes of palaeolithic culture" that provide a window to "early music," yet he also questions evolutionist ideas: "People do not stick to shallow secondal patterns because they stand on the lowest rung of the cultural ladder. . . . Often a person's sex appears to be the shaping power; women seem to prefer a smaller step [melodic interval], just as they do in dancing, while men proceed in larger strides and leaps" (p. 62). While social-evolutionism and such broad generalizing became largely discredited after the first part of the twentieth century, it might be argued that the evolutionist "primitive–civilized" contrast served as the paradigmatic background for the "traditional–modern" dichotomy that remains in currency, with many of the same problems.

Several ethnomusicologists followed the American anthropological trend of grouping different societies into culture areas. Bruno Nettl created a map of Native North American musical styles following the cultural mapping of anthropologists such as A. L. Kroeber; and Alan P. Merriam created a map of African musical culture areas following Herskovits. Later Alan Lomax attempted to map the world's musical areas. The musical areas that form the basis of Lomax's cantometrics project, especially, have been questioned for creating an overly homogenized view of constituent musical cultures based on rather thin data. Nonetheless, in practice the culture area idea, writ large, forms a fundamental basis for organizing courses in ethnomusicology, for defining scholars' specializations, and in the writing of textbooks and reference works—all typically organized according to geographical units.

During the 1950s and 1960s, practitioners of the anthropology of music embraced functionalism as a way to link music-making to social life. More akin to Malinowski's approach than A. R. Radcliffe-Brown's "structural-functionalism," ethnomusicologists began to emphasize what certain types of music contributed to certain realms of activity—healing, labor, political structure, family life, social cohesion. In *The Anthropology of Music,* Merriam states, "The uses and functions of music represent one of the most important problems in ethnomusicology" (p. 209). In contrast to Kantian ideas that the "aesthetic" and "functional" realms preclude each other, McAllester's Enemy Way study demonstrated that for many Navajo, the musically "good" or "beautiful" was defined according to its effectiveness for healing, that is, a performance was judged importantly in terms of how well it fulfilled its function. Although few ethnomusicologists after the 1960s would consider themselves functionalists, describing the deeper purposes that music serves remains a basic part of music ethnographies.

During this same time period and through the late twentieth century, an interest in musical change and acculturation echoed anthropological interests. One of the most widely accepted theories of musical acculturation, advocated by Merriam, Richard Waterman, and derived directly from Herskovits, held that musical cultures were more likely to blend together or influence each other if they shared a number of similar traits. Nettl and Margaret J. Kartomi created typologies for the different effects of culture contact. John Blacking published an influential article advocating the search for a unified theory of musical change emphasizing a distinction between change within a musical system and change of the system. Robert Kauffman argued that culture change or acculturation could not be read off surface forms, such as the adaptation of a foreign musical instrument, but rather, that modes of musical practice, organization, and aesthetics were the key variables for assessing culture change.

Practitioners of the anthropology of music loosely adapted Lévi-Straussian structuralism as a key approach in the 1970s and 1980s. Typically, ethnomusicologists were not concerned with Claude Lévi-Strauss's starting point, the common structure of the human mind. Rather, working on a culture-specific basis, they assumed that there would be deep structural patterns that would shape (surface) cultural practices and forms, creating homologies across different domains of social life. Thus, Charles Keil identified patterns involving circles and angles, in roof designs, visual arts, and in music, and Adrienne Kaeppler found homologies across different realms of Tongan art and society. Combining the earlier interest in homologies with the Peircian concept of iconicity, Judith Becker and Anton Becker found similar structures in Indonesian calendrical concepts and gamelan music; Steven Feld documented the iconicity of aesthetics, practices, and style across a number of domains of Kaluli social life; and Thomas Turino observed a series of symmetrical structures organized around a centerline in Aymara panpipe and flute ensembles, in Andean weaving, in the conceptualization of agricultural niches, and in the organization of space during festival celebrations.

During the same period, some ethnomusicologists took an interest in the premises and methods of structural linguistics for musical analysis; this represents a different trajectory than Lévi-Straussian structuralism, and the scholars involved tended to hail from the musicological rather than the anthropological side of the discipline. Other ethnomusicological approaches related (sometimes through opposition) to structuralism and linguistics involved "the ethnography of performance," following sociolinguistics and the "ethnography of speaking," and the "ethnoscience" approach.

Frequently, the early discussions of "culture contact" and acculturation did not take power relations between the groups into account as a primary variable. Beginning in the 1980s, younger scholars influenced by Marxian ideas, and especially the work of Antonio Gramsci, began to study the effects of asymmetrical power relations and identity politics on musical values and practices. During the 1990s, the study of music in relation to identity politics became a central topic in the anthropology of music. Since social identities are fundamental to political life, and public expressive cultural practices such as music and dance are key to formulating and representing social identities, ethnomusicologists have made major contributions to understanding the dynamics involved—often from a valuable grassroots perspective.

Jane Sugarman's work documents the fundamental ways musical performance functions in processes of socialization shaping conceptions of gendered identities and roles, and Christopher Ballantine provides an insightful essay on gendered power dynamics in South African popular music. Many others have studied the intersection of ethnicity, race, and class in relation to popular music practices and aesthetics. State intervention in indigenous and popular music has received significant attention. Another prominent ethnomusicological topic has been the effects of political nationalism on music. Finally, the study of transnational or "global" economic processes in relation to the production and reception of music—especially popular musics and styles within the "world music" rubric—has become a central focus in the anthropology of music.

Whereas European classical music was once deemed the primary type worthy of study, over the last three decades of the twentieth century "world music" classes and textbooks proliferated in response to several intersecting trends. The discourse of multiculturalism has certainly supported the growth of the interest in "non-Western" music. Multiculturalism itself may be seen as a liberal trend that is partially the result of anthropologists and ethnomusicologists advocating cultural relativism for over a century. It is also partially the result of the women's and civil rights movements' demand that artistic canons be expanded to include a variety of groups. Simultaneously, multiculturalism also functions as a new type of state strategy (e.g., in contrast to the "melting pot") to incorporate the variety of immigrant groups into nation-states and to mitigate challenges to the image of national unity.

Commercial music trends have intersected with the work of ethnomusicologists to expand the interest in, and familiarity with, a variety of musics from around the world. A fascination with the "exotic" has long been part of American and cosmopolitan popular culture—examples include nineteenth-century minstrelsy, "Latin" dance crazes and stars like Carmen Miranda throughout the twentieth century, and hippie (and the Beatles') interest in "Eastern" religion and sitar music. Following the international commercial success of Bob Marley and reggae, new marketing rubrics—"world beat" and "world music"—were adopted in the 1980s to sell a variety of musics from around the world. The more enterprising "world music" fans have turned to the work of ethnomusicologists to expand their knowledge of different styles, and ethnomusicologists have sometimes collaborated in commercial "world music" projects.

Finally, the contemporary discourse of globalism—which might be interpreted as ideologically supporting the expansion and control of trans-state capitalist interests and institutions in the post-Soviet era—has brought new recognition to the work of ethnomusicologists. The discipline has had a global perspective since its inception, but ethnomusicologists' detailed studies of the wealth of human creativity as well as the profound musical and aesthetic differences among social groups do not support views of an emerging "global culture," or its likelihood in the near future.

See also **Anthropology; Musicology.**

BIBLIOGRAPHY
Adler, Guido. "Umfang, Methode und Ziel der Musikwissenschaft." *Vierteljahrschrift für Musikwissenschaft* 1 (1885): 5–20.
Appadurai, Arjun. "Anthropology of Globalization." In *International Encyclopedia of the Social and Behavioral Sciences,* vol. 9, edited by Neil J. Smelser and Paul Baltes. Oxford: Elsevier Science, 2001.
Arguedas, Jose María. *Formación de una cultura nacional indoamericana.* Mexico: Siglo Veintiuno Editores S.A., 1977.
Armstrong, Robert Plant. *The Affecting Presence: An Essay in Humanistic Anthropology.* Urbana: University of Illinois Press, 1971.
Ballantine, Christopher. "Gender, Migrancy, and South African Popular Music in the Late 1940s and the 1950s." *Ethnomusicology* 44 (2000): 376–407.
Basso, Ellen. *A Musical View of the Universe.* Philadelphia: University of Pennsylvania Press, 1985.
Becker, Judith and Anton. "A Musical Icon: Power and Meaning in Javanese Gamelan Music." In *The Sign in Music and Literature,* edited by Wendy Steiner. Austin: University of Texas Press, 1981.
Béhague, Gerard, ed. *Performance Practice: Ethnomusicological Perspectives.* Westport, Conn.: Greenwood, 1984.
Benedict, Ruth. *Patterns of Culture.* New York: Penguin Books, 1934.
Besmer, Fremont E. *Horses, Musicians, and Gods: The Hausa Cult of Possession-Trance.* Zaria, Nigeria: Ahmadu Bello University Press, 1983.
Blacking, John. *The Anthropology of the Body.* London: Academic Press, 1977.
———. "Some Problems of Theory and Method in the Study of Musical Change." *Yearbook of the International Folk Music Council* 9 (1978): 1–26.
———. *Venda Children's Songs: A Study in Ethnomusicological Analysis.* Johannesburg: Witwatersrand University Press, 1967.
Boas, Franz. *The Central Eskimo.* Washington: Bureau of American Ethnology, 1888.
———. "The Limitations of the Comparative Method of Anthropology." *Science* 4, no. 103 (December 18, 1896).
Buechler, Hans C. *The Masked Media: Aymara Fiestas and Social Interaction in the Bolivian Highlands.* The Hague: Mouton, 1980.
Burnett, Robert. *The Global Jukebox: The International Music Industry.* London: Routledge, 1996.
Christensen, Dieter. "Erich M. von Hornbostel, Carl Stumpf, and the Institutionalization of Comparative Musicology." In *Comparative Musicology and Anthropology of Music: Essays on the History of Ethnomusicology,* edited by Bruno Nettl and Philip V. Bohlman. Chicago: University of Chicago Press, 1991.
Ellis, Alexander J. "On the Musicial Scales of Various Nations." *Journal of the Society of Arts,* xxxiii (1885), 3/27: 485-527; 10/30: 1102–1111.
Erlmann, Veit. *Music, Modernity, and the Global Imagination: South Africa and the West.* New York: Oxford University Press, 1999.
———. "The Politics and Aesthetics of Transnational Musics." *The World of Music* 35, no. 2 (1993): 3–15.
Feld, Steven. "Linguistic Models in Ethnomusicology." *Ethnomusicology* 15 (1974): 353–362.
———. *Sound and Sentiment.* Philadelphia: University of Pennsylvania Press, 1982.
———. "Aesthetics as Iconicity of Style, or 'Lit-Up-Over Sounding': Getting into the Kaluli Groove." *Yearbook for Traditional Music* 20 (1988): 74–114.
Fried, Morton H., ed. *Readings in Anthropology,* Vol. 2 of *Cultural Anthropology.* New York: Thomas Y. Crowell Company, 1968.
Frith, Simon. *World Music, Politics, and Social Change.* Manchester, U.K.: Manchester University Press, 1989.

Fry, Peter. *Spirits of Protest: Spirit Mediums and the Articulation of Consensus among the Zezuru of Southern Rhodesia (Zimbabwe).* Cambridge, U.K.: Cambridge University Press, 1976.

Herskovits, Melville J. "The Culture Areas of Africa." *Africa* 3 (1930): 59–76.

———. "Problem, Method and Theory in AfroAmerican Studies." *Afroamericana* 1 (1945): 5–24.

Herzog, George. "A Comparison of Pueblo and Pima Musical Styles." *Journal of American Folk-lore* 49, no. 194 (1936): 284–417.

Hornbostel, Erich M. von. "The Problems of Comparative Musicology." In *Opera Omnia I,* edited by Klaus P. Wachsmann, Dieter Christensen, and Hans-Peter Reinecke. The Hague: Nijhoff, 1905 [1975].

Kaeppler, Adrienne L. "Melody, Drone and Decoration: Underlying Structures and Surface Manifestations in Tongan Art and Society." In *Art in Society: Studies in Style, Culture and Aesthetics,* edited by Michael Greenhalgh and Vincent Megaw. London: Gerald Duckworth, 1978.

Kartomi, Margaret J. "The Processes and Results of Musical Culture Contact: A Discussion of Terminology and Concepts." *Ethnomusicology* 25 (1981): 227–250.

Kauffman, Robert. "Shona Urban Music: A Process which Maintains Traditional Values." In *Urban Man in Southern Africa,* edited by Clive Kileff and Wade C. Pendleton. Gweru: Mambo Press, 1975.

Keil, Charles. *Tiv Song.* Chicago: University of Chicago Press, 1979.

Kolinski, Mieczyslaw. "Recent Trends in Ethnomusicology." *Ethnomusicology* 11 (1967): 1–24.

Koskoff, Ellen, ed. *Women and Music in Cross-Cultural Perspective.* New York: Greenwood, 1987.

Kroeber, A. L. *Cultural and Natural Areas of Native North America.* Berkeley: University of California Press, 1947.

Kunst, Jaap. *Ethno-musicology: A Study of its Nature, its Problems, Methods and Representative Personalities to which Is Added a Bibliography.* The Hague: Martinus Nijhoff, 1955.

Lomax, Alan. *Folk Song Style and Culture.* Washington, D.C.: American Association for the Advancement of Science, 1968.

Lowie, Robert H. *The Crow Indians.* New York: Rinehart, 1935.

Malinowski, Bronislaw. *The Sexual Life of Savages.* London: Routledge, 1929.

Mangin, William. "The Role of Regional Associations in the Adaptation of Rural Populations in Peru." *Sociologus* 9 (1959): 23–35.

Mannheim, Bruce. "Popular Song and Popular Grammar: Poetry and Metalanguage." *Word* 37 (1986): 45–75.

McAllester, David P. *Enemy Way Music: A Study of Social and Esthetic Values as Seen in Navaho Music.* Cambridge, Mass.: Peabody Museum, 1954.

McLeod, Norma, and Marcia Herndon. *The Ethnography of Musical Performance.* Norwood, Pa.: Norwood, 1980.

Mead, Margaret. *Coming of Age in Samoa.* New York: Mentor Books, 1928 [1949].

Merriam, Alan P. *The Anthropology of Music.* Evanston, Ill.: Northwestern University Press, 1964.

———. "Definitions of 'Comparative Musicology' and 'Ethnomusicology': An Historical-Theoretical Perspective." *Ethnomusicology* 21 (1977): 189–204.

———. "The Use of Music in the Study of a Problem of Acculturation." *American Anthropologist* 57 (1955): 28–34.

Moore, Robin. *Nationalizing Blackness: Afrocubanismo and Artistic Revolution in Havana, 1920–1940.* Pittsburgh: University of Pittsburgh Press, 1997.

Myers, Helen. *Ethnomusicology: An Introduction.* New York: Norton, 1992.

Nettl, Bruno. *Encounters in Ethnomusicology.* Warren, Mich.: Harmonie Park, 2002.

———. *North American Indian Musical Styles.* Philadelphia: American Folklore Society, 1954.

Nettl, Bruno, and Philip V. Bohlman, eds. *Comparative Musicology and Anthropology of Music: Essays on the History of Ethnomusicology.* Chicago: University of Chicago Press, 1991.

Noll, William. "Music Institutions and National Consciousness among Polish and Ukrainian Peasants." In *Ethnomusicology and Modern Music History,* edited by Stephen Blum, Philip V. Bohlman, and Daniel M. Neuman. Urbana: University of Illinois Press, 1991.

Peña, Manuel. "From Ranchero to Jaitón: Ethnicity and Class in Texas-Mexican Music (Two Styles in the Form of a Pair)." *Ethnomusicology* 29 (1985): 29–55.

Perrone, Charles A., and Christopher Dunn, eds. *Brazilian Popular Music and Globalization.* Gainesville: University Press of Florida, 2001.

Powers, Harold S. "Language Models and Musical Analysis." *Ethnomusicology* 24 (1980): 1–60.

Radano, Ronald, and Philip V. Bohlman, eds. *Music and the Racial Imagination.* Chicago: University of Chicago Press, 2000.

Sachs, Curt. *The Wellsprings of Music.* Edited by Jaap Kunst. The Hague: Nijhoff, 1962.

Seeger, Anthony. *Why Suyá Sing: A Musical Anthropology of an Amazonian People.* Cambridge, U.K.: Cambridge University Press, 1987.

Stempfle, Stephen. *The Steelband Movement: The Forging of a National Art in Trinidad and Tobago.* Philadelphia: University of Pennsylvania Press, 1995.

Stokes, Martin, ed. *Ethnicity, Identity, and Music: The Musical Construction of Place.* Oxford: Berg, 1994.

Sugarman, Jane. *Engendering Song: Singing and Subjectivity at Prespa Albanian Weddings.* Chicago: University of Chicago Press, 1997.

Turnbull, Colin M. *The Forest People.* New York: Simon and Schuster, 1961.

Turner, Victor, and Edward M. Bruner, eds. *The Anthropology of Experience.* Urbana: University of Illinois Press, 1986.

Turino, Thomas. *Nationalists, Cosmopolitans, and Popular Music in Zimbabwe.* Chicago: University of Chicago Press, 2000.

———. "The State and Andean Musical Production in Peru." In *Nation-State and Indian in Latin America,* edited by Joel Sherzer and Greg Urban. Austin: University of Texas Press, 1990.

Tylor, Edward Burnett. *Religion in Primitive Culture,* Part II of *Primitive Culture.* New York: Harper and Brothers, 1871 [1958].

Wade, Peter. *Music, Race, and Nation: Musica Tropical in Colombia.* Chicago: University of Chicago Press, 2000.

Waterman, Richard. "African Influence on the Music of the Americas." In *Acculturation in the Americas,* edited by Sol Tax. Chicago: University of Chicago Press, 1952.

Waxer, Lise A. *The City of Musical Memory: Salsa, Record Grooves, and Popular Culture in Cali, Colombia.* Middletown, Conn.: Wesleyan University Press, 2002.

Whitten, Norman. *Black Frontiersmen: A South American Case.* 2nd ed. Prospect Heights, Ill.: Waveland Press, 1974 [1986].

Zemp, Hugo. "'Are'are Classification of Musical Types and Instruments." *Ethnomusicology* (1978) 22: 37–67.

———. "Aspects of 'Are'are Musical Theory." *Ethnomusicology* 23 (1979): 5–48.

Thomas Turino

MUSICAL PERFORMANCE AND AUDIENCES. Musical performance is an organized presentation of musical sounds (and, arguably, controlled silences), usually for the entertainment, edification, or enrichment of listeners. The parameters of a performance are often determined by culturally understood boundaries—symphony audiences disregard the warming up and tuning of orchestral musicians, whereas listeners to Indian classical music understand the *ālāpa* (a slow, improvisatory exploration of a rāga, or traditional melodic pattern) to be an intrinsic part of the performance, if not comprising the entire performance itself. Audiences must be conditioned, therefore, to understand the norms of performance and their own roles as listeners. An Indian audience might quietly snap along with a tala (a traditional rhythmic pattern), whereas the symphony audience is expected to maintain a strict silence until the final section of a multimovement work has concluded. A jazz audience, on the other hand, might chatter and drink beverages during a jazz combo's club performance, but would also respond to individual artistry during the course of a piece by applauding after each improvised solo (as seen in figure 1); an otherwise quiet opera audience would cheer a well-performed aria, and might even, in exceptional cases, demand an encore.

Despite the recognition that there are expected behaviors for performers and audiences, defining "musical performance" is as difficult as the attempt to pinpoint the nature of music itself. The immense diversity of human musical activity has led to a host of attitudes regarding the nature and purpose of musical events. The lines of demarcation between composer and composition, composition and performer, and performer and audience are sometimes almost impossibly blurred. Moreover, no universal standard exists by which to measure "good" performance; this assessment, too, is dependent on variable cultural and aesthetic expectations. However, the ongoing attempts of historians, ethnomusicologists, and philosophers (as well as composers and performers) to articulate and isolate var-

Figure 1. Jazz singer Ella Fitzgerald performs for an audience that includes bandleader Duke Ellington. Photographed in 1948 by Herman Leonard. HULTON ARCHIVE/GETTY IMAGES

Figure 2. Young Greek woman playing an aulos. © BETTMANN/ CORBIS

Figure 3. A man dressed as a *komuso* (beggar priest) plays a flute-like *shakuhachi*. Photograph c. 1901–1920. © UNDERWOOD & UNDERWOOD/CORBIS

ious parameters of musical activity help us to understand both the diversity and the similarities within musical performances.

Origins and Types of Performance

Without a doubt, performance is the oldest form of musical activity, but its origins are difficult to pinpoint. Steven J. Mithen posits a series of cultural "sparks" during the middle-upper Paleolithic transition, culminating in the first appearances of art objects in Europe some forty thousand years ago. Basing his theories on the work of cognitive scientists, Mithen argues that these sparks resulted from the coalescing of several human intelligences—technical, natural history, social, and linguistic—which in turn opened the door to the development of artistic and religious practices. Although archaeologists have discovered instruments made from mammoth bones in 18,000 B.C.E., the oldest known forms of written music survive on Mesopotamian clay tablets dating from at least 3,000 to 2,000 years B.C.E. Other tablets of the same era make reference to instrumentalists and singers. Ancient Egyptian hieroglyphics, c. 2400 B.C.E., comprise the earliest surviving representations of performing musicians. The ancient Greeks also depicted music-making (and listening); figure 2 portrays a young woman playing the aulos for a reclining male guest. Besides illustrating music as entertainment, Greek iconography also depicts other broad categories of musical performances, such as music for dance and music in support of religious beliefs.

Performance as background activity. The convention of an audience gathering specifically to listen to a scheduled musical event is a relatively modern phenomenon. Historically, much musical entertainment was presented at the convenience of its patrons, while many other forms of music-making were (and still are) almost entirely subordinate to some other fore-

ground purpose, such as worship, dancing, military maneuvers, and other activities.

Music in religious observance. Cultures all over the world incorporate music into their sacred and ceremonial activities. Jews and early Christians both made use of chant in their devotions, regarding this as a means of uplifting the mind as well as a method of worship. In the Fuke sect of Japanese Buddhism, *komuso* (beggar priests) play the flute-like *shakuhachi* (figure 3), not as an instrument per se, but rather as a spiritual tool that assists its player in reaching enlightenment. In contrast, the West African Ewe people believe they are guided through life by ancestral spirits, so a musician often regards music-making as his destiny, thanks to the inherited spirit of an ancestor who has determined the course of his life. An Ewe funeral is a celebratory affair because its ritual drumming, singing, and dancing enable the soul to become an ancestral spirit. According to Charlotte J. Frisbee, the Navajo Indians make a semantic distinction between "performing," which is the music-making during ceremonies, and "playing," which describes all other forms of musical activity. Music is even more deeply imbedded in the intertribal Native American Church; its adherents view music itself as prayer. Music as a function

Figure 4. A field show presented by the marching band of the University of California, Los Angeles. ALYSON MCLAMORE

of religious observance is by no means universal; for instance, music is forbidden in the Algerian Mozabite Muslim sect.

Music and dance. Music is also almost always an essential component of dance (and, indeed, dance and religion go hand in hand in many cultures). Customarily, music is subsidiary to the movements of the dancers, even though it controls (or reflects) their actions to varying degrees. In its simplest form, music for dance maintains the beat and tempo; various other aspects of the musical performance might guide more nuanced gestures. By actions such as foot stamping, whistling, clapping, or singing, the dancers themselves might produce the accompanimental music. Filipino Bontok musicians of Sadanga, Luzon, when playing *gangsa* (flat gongs) sound the gongs with sticks and dance in circles and spirals. More commonly, dancers move while stationary musicians perform, as in a processional Renaissance dance performed at a fifteenth-century Burgundian wedding. The shawm and sackbut players stand in an elevated side gallery apart from the dancers, and their status as "background" performers is reinforced visually by their plain, matching tunics.

Music in the military. Since antiquity, as armies grew too large for vocal commands to be heard, a system of musical signals was adopted by various military groups. Some of these "calls" regulated the soldiers' daily activities, ranging from the early-morning reveille to the bedtime tattoo; other forms of music passed along orders during battle. Military musical ensembles also supported morale among the troops, and although live musicians have seldom been used during actual warfare since the early twentieth century, many military units still use bands as a public-relations bridge feature, thereby moving their musical performances to the "foreground." In North America, in particular, the military bands influenced the development of various school ensembles; these ensembles consist of not only stationary "concert" bands of wind players and percussionists, but also marching bands. The mobile marching ensembles perform in two main contexts: street parades, in which they perform music while passing in front of viewers (who therefore hear only a portion of a work before the band passes

out of hearing range), and field shows (see figure 4), in which the band members create elaborate designs and patterns with their bodies while playing.

Music in other contexts. Musical performance has functioned as a backdrop to many other forms of human activity, ranging from lullabies sung to infants to children's games to banquet music to the elaborate vocal and orchestral performances that entertained strolling patrons in eighteenth-century Georgian pleasure gardens (see figure 5). The French composer Erik Satie was fascinated by the possibilities of what he called *musique d'ameublement* (furniture music), which was intended to be ignored, but found in 1920 that it was difficult to keep audiences talking and moving about while musicians were performing at a drawing exhibition. Nevertheless, modern-day shoppers seem to have little difficulty in ignoring live pianists playing in department stores, undoubtedly conditioned to this lack of response by the prevalence of recorded Muzak and other forms of "canned" environmental music.

Performance as foreground focus. Many cultures that use music for background purposes also host activities in which artistic music-making is the primary focus of the enterprise. Since the music itself commands attention, these endeavors might collectively be labeled "art music," although the term "classical music" is often used interchangeably. ("Popular music," in contrast, usually puts less emphasis on artistry and more focus on commercial qualities; in individual cases, of course, the level of artistic achievement in popular music may be extremely high.) In many instances, specialized venues (music rooms, concert halls, theaters) have been built to accommodate performances of art music (in figure 6, see Thomas Mace's 1676 plans for a dedicated "Musick-Roome"). Nevertheless, within art music's concert and theatrical presentations, the type of musical activity can vary widely; musicians might improvise freely or provide their own interpretations of traditional repertory, or, at the opposite extreme, they may be endeavoring to recreate a preexisting musical artwork as exactly as possible. Correspondingly, performers are viewed varyingly as free agents, composers' interpreters or "ambassadors," and even automatons.

Improvisation as performance. Various music education methodologies, such as Émile Jaques-Dalcroze's eurythmics or the Orff-Schulwerk pioneered by Carl Orff, allow children to improvise freely on instruments or vocally, which appears to be a natural tendency of childhood exploratory development. In most cultures, however, audiences expect improvisers to be highly trained experts in their media, and thus the improvised portions of performances carry great prestige; the cadenzas in concertos, the "solos" in jazz works, and the *taqsīm* in Arabic and Turkish music are all highlights for listeners. In both Western and non-Western traditions, some performers may study with masters for many years before embarking on their first public improvisations. Performers in other cultures may adopt entirely different attitudes toward improvisation, however; through fasting and self-torture, North American Plains Indians seek visions in which new songs might appear to them, whereas Pima Indians regard improvisation as a process of "un-

Figure 5. *Concert at Vauxhall Gardens* (1784) by Thomas Rowlandson. V & A IMAGES / VICTORIA AND ALBERT MUSEUM

raveling" the songs already present in the supernatural world. Of course, due to its spontaneous and unnotated nature, improvisation is one of the most difficult aspects of music to study historically.

Re-creative performance. In contrast to improvisation—or, sometimes, in partnership with it—much musical performance is the (re-)enactment of a piece according to predetermined specifications. In some traditions, the musical works are conveyed via oral transmission and rote mimicry, while other cultures have developed various forms of musical notation to guide performances (see figure 7 for a manuscript excerpt from a chorus of Thomas Linley's 1777 oratorio *The Song of Moses*). For performers, however, any score—the handwritten or printed record of a composer's intentions—is incapable of telling the "whole story." Just as in the case of skilled improvisers, musicians performing from scores usually need substantial prior training to understand the conventions of a particular style of music before they are considered ready for public performance.

Performance Considerations

There is no universal agreement as to what constitutes a musical performance, for the nature of music-making and listening varies greatly from culture to culture. Similarly, the parameters of *good* performance are equally hard to measure.

Many philosophers, historians, and performers have turned their attention to this problem, exploring varied issues of musical aesthetics and historical performance practice.

The quest for perfection No matter what impetus—improvisation or score transmission—has produced a performance of art music, audiences attending these presentations carry with them a set of aesthetic criteria, ranging from specific personal preferences to broad awareness of cultural norms. Listeners evaluate a performance on the basis of their blended personal and collective attitudes, which allows for enormous variety in the perception of a single performance as good or bad. It is impossible for a performer to anticipate and respond to all the individual standards by which his performance might be judged; as Jerrold Levinson quipped, "For a listener who wears earplugs, a very loud performance is the best" (p. 382). Nevertheless, in most instances in which performers bring "to sound" a notated score, their faithfulness to that score is often a leading measure of their success.

Philosophers and critics disagree as to how to measure that faithfulness. The relative imprecision of much early Western notation forces performers to make many basic choices: if a surviving work contains only vocal parts, but iconography from the same time period shows instruments playing alongside singers, should a contemporary conductor choose to double

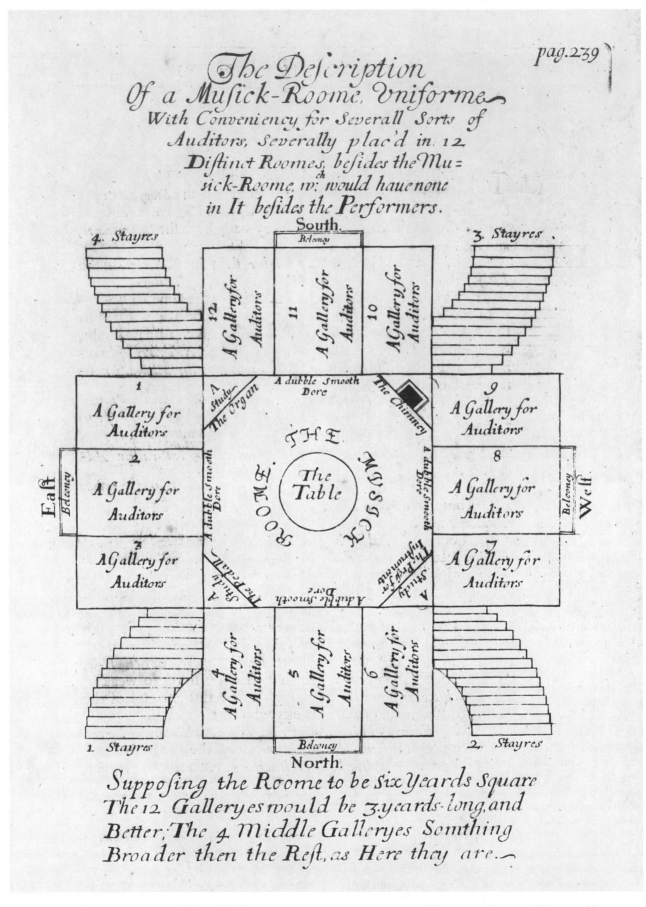

Figure 6. Plans for a "Musick-Roome" (1676) by Thomas Mace. BY PERMISSION OF THE HOUGHTON LIBRARY, HARVARD UNIVERSITY

New Dictionary of the History of Ideas

Figure 8. Vladimir Horowitz at the piano, 1986. CLIVE BARDA / ARENAPAL

Figure 7. Manuscript excerpt from the oratorio *The Song of Moses* (1777) by Thomas Linley. BY PERMISSION OF THE BRITISH LIBRARY, RM.21.H.9, FOL. 106V

the voices with instruments, despite no written indication to do so? Is this a better—or worse—performance than a presentation limited to voices alone? There has been a growing tendency in recent years to treat the score as sacrosanct, especially in repertories in which notation is increasingly exact. Many feel that when a musician exercises too much performance freedom, the original work's integrity is at risk of being lost. The philosopher Nelson Goodman takes this attitude to an extreme when he argues, "Since complete compliance with the score is the only requirement for a genuine instance of a work, the most miserable performance without actual mistakes does count as such an instance, while the most brilliant performance with a single wrong note does not" (p. 186). Although most listeners would disagree with Goodman's position, his view is in some ways at the heart of another controversial aspect of music: the goals of performance (or performing) practice.

Performance practice. The last half of the twentieth century witnessed an increasing desire among many musicians to reenact performances of historical works as closely as possible to the way (we think) they were first presented. No one objects to the notion that it is often pleasurable to hear Johann Sebastian Bach's preludes and fugues performed on a harpsi-

chord; the disagreements begin when we ask if it is still pleasurable (or desirable) to perform the same Bach works on a modern piano (see figure 8)—and if we should be allowed to use the pedal while doing so. Designating the attempts at exact reenactments of the past as "authentic" or "historically informed" (or "historically aware") has added heat to the debate. The problem, as Richard Taruskin and others have pointed out, is the invidious implication that a performer who does choose to play Bach on the piano is uninformed and that his performance is inauthentic or, worse, unaware. Moreover, as Paul Henry Lang recognizes, even the most exacting and thorough historical research will leave gaps that must be filled with "our own artistic beliefs and instincts"; he adds, "Unconditional conformity to authenticity in the interpretation of old music, in depending on archival fidelity, may fail in fidelity to the composer's artistic intentions" (p. 179). The conductor James DePreist argues that even living composers who are able to supervise rehearsals are inevitably surprised by the sound of their works in actual performance—"surprised," DePreist maintains, "because the gap between the musical blueprint, that is, the score, and the interpreted sound is a universe of options and potentialities" (p. 11). Looking at the issue of authenticity from another perspective, Peter Kivy discusses the challenge of creating historically aware listeners.

"Liveness" in performance. In the past, there has been an inherent two-fold assumption among Westerners that a performance entails live presentation of music before live listeners. The second component of this view is not universal, as J. H. Kwabena Nketia explains in his study of African music: "A physically present audience . . . is not always necessary . . . since a performance may well be for the benefit of someone who may not actually be present, or simply for the enjoyment of the performers" (p. 33). With the advent of recorded and electronic sound, however, the traditional expectation of "liveness" in the actual presentation of music has also been challenged. Recordings usher in a new host of metaphysical questions: in the case of a multilayered, overdubbed sound creation generated privately in a studio, is there no actual "performance" at all? Or is the artist performing during the process of adding each layer and effect? Or does a performance occur when the final product is transmitted to a listener? Simon Frith argues for the latter condition when he says, "I listen to records in the full knowledge that what I hear is something that never existed, that never could exist, as a 'performance,' something happening in a single time and space; nevertheless, it *is now* happening, in a single time and space: it is thus a performance and I hear it as one" (p. 211).

As Philip Auslander notes, a parallel "authenticity" problem exists when a presentation purports to be a live performance, yet in actuality the performers are miming their actions to a prerecorded soundtrack. In the Milli Vanilli scandal of early 1990, the pop singing-dancing duo had won a "Best New Artist" Grammy award, yet it was eventually revealed that not only did they use prerecorded vocals in their concert appearances but they had not been the actual singers on their prize-winning recording. This discovery led not only to the rescinding of their Grammy Award but to widespread American legislation that requires performers who plan to lip-synch during concerts to indicate this fact on advertising posters and on concert tickets. For some listeners, however, this caveat begs the question whether such a performance is "genuine," and if it is truly as good as a completely live presentation. It is frequently the case that touring productions of Broadway shows use "canned" (prerecorded) orchestral music, rather than sustaining the expense of traveling with a pit orchestra. Not only does such economy make union orchestral musicians unhappy, but it destroys the potential for flexibility during individual performances of the vocal numbers; singers must "keep up" with the recording, and so cannot indulge in nuanced interpretative variations from show to show. Perversely, however, it is precisely to enjoy those idiosyncratic moments that many listeners continue to attend and support live performance. At the same time, in some forms of art music, such as Milton Babbitt's *Philomel* (1964), composers have created electro-acoustic works in which live musicians perform in coordination with a prerecorded tape or electronic soundtrack. Is a performance "better" when the tape and live music are combined by artistic choice rather than economic motivations? This dilemma is yet another of the many puzzles confronting the assessment of good performance.

Jonathan Dunsby offers the provocative suggestion that the same technological innovations that are complicating our current valuations of performance may also be the impetus for an enormous change in human aesthetic judgment, since they will allow us to overcome the transient nature of our short lifespans. "The past," he observes, "is *silent*," but "it is interest-

ing to ask whether technology, in its sound recording, then vision and sound, holography, virtual reality, and who knows what may come next, is generating a fundamental shift in this situation." He adds,

> We may be witnesses, the only direct witnesses there will ever be, to the beginning of the music of the future. Is it not easy to imagine that two thousand years or five thousand years from now people will say that Western music really only got going properly during the twentieth century from which distant time there date the earliest proper sonic and visual records, following that strange 'mute' early period of music history that spanned the Greeks . . . to, say, Mahler . . . ? (pp. 15–16)

Dunsby's notion is a stimulating one, and its implications for performance have not yet been fully addressed. Certainly the ability of mass communication to shrink the globe and to link people (and their musics) has long been recognized; we are entering an age that enables us to join performances of the past to the music of the future. Any contemporary performer who has been influenced by the ideas, techniques, and artistry of long-dead twentieth-century musicians is already aware of the tremendous power of recordings; our aesthetic views now need to catch up. Mankind is not immortal, but through recorded performance we may now be able to live long beyond our time.

See also **Music, Anthropology of; Theater and Performance.**

BIBLIOGRAPHY

Auslander, Philip. *Liveness: Performance in a Mediatized Culture.* London and New York: Routledge, 1999.

Béhague, Gerard, ed. *Performance Practice: Ethnomusicological Perspectives.* Westport, Conn.: Greenwood, 1984.

Berleant, Arnold. *The Aesthetic Field.* Springfield, Ill.: Thomas, 1970.

Cone, Edward T. "The Pianist As Critic." In *The Practice of Performance: Studies in Musical Interpretation,* edited by John Rink. Cambridge, U.K.: Cambridge University Press, 1995.

Davies, Stephen. *Musical Works and Performances: A Philosophical Exploration.* Oxford: Clarendon, 2001.

DePreist, James. *Art for the Sake of Art: Musical Metamorphoses.* San Diego, Calif.: San Diego State University, 1999.

Dunsby, Jonathan. *Performing Music: Shared Concerns.* Oxford: Clarendon, 1995.

Frisbee, Charlotte J. "An Approach to the Ethnography of Navajo Ceremonial Performance." In *The Ethnography of Musical Performance,* edited by Norma McLeod and Marcia Herndon. Norwood, Pa.: Norwood, 1980.

Frith, Simon. *Performing Rites: On the Value of Popular Music.* Cambridge, Mass.: Harvard University Press, 1996.

Goodman, Nelson. *Languages of Art: An Approach to a Theory of Symbols.* 2nd ed. Indianapolis: Hackett, 1976.

Gracyk, Theodore. *Rhythm and Noise: An Aesthetic of Rock.* Durham, N.C., and London: Duke University Press, 1996.

Kivy, Peter. *Authenticities: Philosophical Reflections on Musical Performance.* Ithaca, N.Y., and London: Cornell University Press, 1995.

Lang, Paul Henry. *Musicology and Performance.* Edited by Alfred Mann and George J. Buelow. New Haven, Conn., and London: Yale University Press, 1997.

Levinson, Jerrold. *Music, Art, and Metaphysics: Essays in Philosophical Aesthetics.* Ithaca, N.Y., and London: Cornell University Press, 1990.

Mithen, Steven J. *The Prehistory of the Mind: The Cognitive Origins of Art, Religion, and Science.* London: Thames and Hudson, 1996.

Nettl, Bruno, with Melinda Russell, eds. *In the Course of Performance: Studies in the World of Musical Improvisation.* Chicago and London: University of Chicago Press, 1998.

Nketia, J. H. Kwabena. *The Music of Africa.* New York and London: Norton, 1974.

O'Dea, Jane. *Virtue or Virtuosity?: Explorations in the Ethics of Musical Performance.* Westport, Conn.: Greenwood, 2000.

Taruskin, Richard. "The Pastness of the Present and the Presence of the Past." In *Authenticity and Early Music: A Symposium,* edited by Nicholas Kenyon. Oxford and New York: Oxford University Press, 1988.

Alyson McLamore

MUSICOLOGY. Musicology is the scholarly study of music, where music can be considered either as a fixed object of investigation or as a process whose participants are the composer, the performer, and the listener. As a field of knowledge, it encompasses every aspect of the aesthetic, physical, psychological, and cultural dimensions of the musical art. In practice, consequently, the discipline includes not just music itself—considered either as a fixed object of study or as a process—but also anything that relates to music in any way. Thus, for example, the history of music patronage during the Renaissance is considered to be a musicological topic, as is the history of the development of printing presses able to reproduce music notation. The potentially unlimited scope of the discipline has led one contemporary musicologist to define musicology as "whatever musicologists do as musicologists" (Leech-Wilkinson, p. 216).

Historically, in the Western tradition, musicology has to a great extent been identified with the study of classical music ("art music"), as opposed to popular music. Neither of the terms "classical music" or "art music" is entirely satisfactory. The former is somewhat ambiguous, as it also refers less generally to music written in the Classical style of the late eighteenth and early nineteenth centuries by composers such as Franz Joseph Haydn (1732–1809) and Wolfgang Amadeus Mozart (1756–1791). And the term "art music," although it is widely in use, carries with it an undesirable and inaccurate connotation of elitism. Throughout this article, the phrase "classical music" is used, somewhat as the lesser of two evils, to refer generally to the notation-based music of the Western high-culture tradition.

Musicology has traditionally been differentiated from ethnomusicology, which in the most general terms is the comparative study of non-Western musics, as well as the study of popular and folk music from both Western and non-Western cultures and subcultures. However, recent developments within musicology (principally, the advent of what is referred to as the "new musicology" and the paradigm shift in musicological methodology described below under "The Critical Method")

have tended to diminish greatly previously significant differences between the two disciplines. (For an example of traditional ethnomusicological methodology applied to the study of Gregorian chant, see Jeffery, *Re-Envisioning Past Musical Cultures.*)

Subdisciplines of Musicology

The principal subdisciplines of musicology are as follows, briefly defined in the most general terms:

Music history: the careful construction of the historical record on the basis of available data from the past and the subsequent application of a historiographical methodology to that record. Traditionally, scientific historicism, which involves the postulation of historiographical categories such as causal relationships, periodization, and musical styles, has been the preferred methodology of music historians, whose field of investigation has generally been confined to the study of Western classical music (as noted above).

Performance practice and historically informed performance: the investigation of modes of musical performance that are particular to a specific time or place within music history, including methods of interpretation, tuning of instruments, types of musical ornamentation and improvisation, instrumental techniques, and performance conventions. An important late-twentieth-century development within this subdiscipline has been the increased interest, within the Western classical music tradition, in the historically informed performance of early music—that is, music for which an appropriate style of performance must be reconstructed on the basis of historical evidence.

Textual scholarship: generally, the systematic study and description of manuscripts and printed books, and the construction of scholarly editions that, assuming the existence of a most correct or "best" text, list and reconcile variant readings between two or more versions of the text in question. The study of manuscripts involves paleography, the science or art of deciphering and dating handwritten texts; within musicology, this frequently includes the study and transcription of early music notations.

Archival research: the study, for music-historical purposes, of documents issued by governments, churches, or any administrative authority in order to establish an important part of the historical record.

History and theory of music notation: the analysis of the process of translating the acoustical phenomenon of musical sound to the written page, employing both comparative and historical methodologies. (See the sidebar on "Music Notation.")

Music theory and analysis: the historical study of generalized descriptions of the structure of music and musical sound, both within and outside the Western classical-music tradition. Analysis, which is the detailed examination of individual pieces of music for the purpose of validating existing theoretical constructs or developing new ones, differs from music theory in that its object of investigation is music that has already been composed or performed, rather than the properties of the elements of musical sound or abstract musical principles.

Aesthetics of music: the study of issues of a primarily philosophical character connected to the art of music. Of principal concern is the question of whether or not music has either affective or semantic content. At issue also, given the ephemerality of music, is the ontological status of the musical work of art: does it exist as an ideal object, perhaps the faithful realization in performance of a musical score, or is it better conceived of as a sort of process, without any assumptions of an ideal existence?

Sociology of music: the systematic investigation of the interaction of music and society. This includes not only the ways in which music functions within a particular social context, but also the influence of that social context on characteristics of the musical work (such as genre, structure, form, and harmonic organization) or of the musical process (such as modes of performance and musical values).

Psychology of music: the scientific investigation, using psychological tools, of human musical behavior and cognition, with emphasis on the perception of various properties of musical sound, musical memory, performing and creating, learning and teaching, and the affective processes stimulated by aspects of musical sound. The three principal research orientations are psychophysics, cognitive psychology, and neuropsychology.

Criticism: the evaluation, description, and interpretation of an individual work of music, or of the musical process, according to a wide range of criteria drawn principally from the study of the aesthetics, psychology, and sociology of music. Criticism differs from analysis in its emphasis on music as it is actually heard, rather than on properties of music that can be ascertained in a written score, for example, but not necessarily easily perceived by an audience during the course of a performance.

Acoustics (the physics of musical sound): the science of sound and of the phenomenon of hearing applied to the description of the physical basis of music and to the determination of the nature of musical sound.

Organology: the scientific study of the history of the design and construction of musical instruments. This subdiscipline also addresses the extramusical functions of instruments in historical contexts, technology, and general culture.

Iconography: the study of the visual representation of musical subjects—such as musical instruments and

musicians—in texts, works of art, coins, and other media as a source of historical information about musical instruments, performance practices, biography, and the social and cultural roles of music.

Principal Methodologies for Musicological Research

In the face of a disciplinary definition of virtually unlimited scope and a diverse array of related subjects, the actual practice of musicology is probably best understood in terms of the principal methodologies or investigative paradigms that have been and are currently the bases for the scholarly study of music as it is carried out within each of the major subdisciplines: the scientific historical method, the analytical method, and the critical or interpretive method.

The scientific historical method. "Scientific" historicism—rather than just "historicism," to distinguish it from what is now commonly known as "new" historicism (see Treitler, "The Historiography of Music," p. 362)—is the traditional historiographical methodology of music history, taken (as indicated above) to mean the history of Western classical music. It is scientific in the sense that it seeks first to establish an accurate historical record and then, on the basis of that record, to identify patterns of influence and causal relationships that form the basis of the periodization of music historical time and the construction of a diachronic narrative.

Scientific music historiography has as its object of study "the history of music" in its most common sense—that is, the events of the past that can be related in some way to music. Because the investigation begins with whatever historical data are available, the subdisciplines of textual scholarship, archival research, history of music notation, organology, and iconography (as described above) are extremely important to the accurate and efficient construction of the facts and texts (for example, transcriptions or facsimiles of archival documents, biographical information, and scholarly editions) that will comprise the historical record and will serve as the bases of subsequent causal hypotheses. This first, empirical stage of investigation is frequently referred to as "historical positivism."

In general, once the historical record has been established, the scientific historiographer attempts to establish order among the various facts and texts by constructing plausible causal relationships and historical periodizations. In the case of music historiography, however, there exists at this point a tension between generalizations based on the entire historical record and those based on a consideration of specific pieces of music, objectified as works of musical art and considered to be semi-autonomous in the sense of existing within a continuum of musical works of art that are largely defined by their own internal processes of influence and causality, apart from those of history in general. In simplest terms, it is a question of what music history is about, traditionally a choice between two alternatives: either defining periods of musical history based on the guideposts provided by the lives of great composers (placed within their cultural context) and the schools of composition formed around them, or extrapolating periods defined by musical style from the patterns of influence, types of compositions (genres), and prevalent characteristics observed through the careful formal analysis of the properties of individual works of musical art. In either case, the result remains within the historicist paradigm; and in practice, twentieth-century music historiographers have tended to base their diachronic narratives principally on musical style, a process that permits the inclusion of historical and biographical facts but encourages the conviction that music history is really about the objectified musical work—and is therefore different in essence from other types of historical narratives. An instructive case in point is the extremely popular *History of Western Music* by Donald J. Grout and Claude V. Palisca, now in its sixth edition. A sampling from the table of contents shows a pragmatic mixture of chapters defined, respectively, by stylistic period, composer, genre, and historical grab bag: "Music of the Early Baroque Period," "Sonata, Symphony, and Opera in the Early Classic Period," "Ludwig van Beethoven," "The American Twentieth Century."

One result of nineteenth-century scientific historicism was the consolidation of what is known as the "musical canon," a collection of works that are generally regarded as having extraordinary aesthetic value and therefore able to serve as the building blocks of an historical narrative whose subject is the musical work. During the twentieth century, the wide popularity of historical accounts based on style, dealing almost exclusively with the composers and works of the musical canon, resulted in the nearly complete exclusion of minor composers and women and in an increasing emphasis on formal analysis. This emphasis led to, and was in turn nourished by, intense positivist activity in the production of new and more accurate editions of the composers and works of the canon, and answered many open questions about chronology, authenticity, and the process of composition. Thus, it encouraged an even greater focus on the inner workings of individual pieces of music and an increasing absence of any consideration of those pieces of music as historical documents produced within a specific social and political context. By the late 1970s, in fact, German musicologist Carl Dahlhaus, in the Introduction to his study of nineteenth-century music, lamented the decline of history and reasserted the task of a music historiographer as the establishment of "a relation between the aesthetic and the historical substance of works of music" (Dahlhaus, *Nineteenth-Century Music,* p. 1; see also Dahlhaus, *Foundations of Music History*). Similar ideas were expressed at about the same time by the American musicologist Leo Treitler: "Music history is possible only insofar as the historian is able to show the place of individual works in history by revealing the history contained within the works themselves, that is, by reading the historical nature of works from their internal constitution" (Treitler, *Music and the Historical Imagination,* p. 173).

Contemporaneous with these somewhat premature announcements of the triumph of formal analysis over music history was the rise of a flourishing practical application of various positivist historical projects: a branch of performance practice known variously as "the early music movement," "authentic performance," "period performance," and "historically informed performance." Beginning around 1970, performers of music written during the seventeenth and eighteenth centuries began to use the data of the historical record—editions, information about period instruments, knowledge of the composer's intentions, original performance conditions, and so on—to produce performances that were intended to be as historically appropriate as possible. Nourished by a thriving recording industry, the movement soon included music from every period and style, even that of the twentieth century. The movement has been widely criticized on the basis of its claims to authenticity and for what is described as its "essential modernism" (see Kivy, *Authenticities,* and Taruskin, *Text and Act,* respectively). However, it cannot be denied that the historically informed performance movement, which continues to be both vigorous and vital, has generated interest in a wide variety of repertories and introduced a broad spectrum of possibilities for both performance and hearing. (See Butt, *Playing with History,* for a thorough discussion of issues surrounding historically informed performance.)

The analytical method. The analytical method in musicology begins with a consideration of the music itself—either in written form in a notated musical score or in sounded form in performance—and attempts to identify the structural characteristics of that piece of music in terms of broadly definable elements such as form (including motivic and harmonic analysis), musical detail (such as dynamics and tone quality), and the music's relationship to a text. In the most straightforward sense, the musical analyst attempts to uncover what it is that makes a piece of music "work" as music. Musicological analysis differs from ethnomusicological analysis in that the latter necessarily places the investigation squarely within a particular cultural context, whereas musicologists may consider the musical work, either in score or in performance, completely removed from its context. As indicated above, musical analysis is related to music theory in that analysis provides the data that can be used to validate existing theories or to construct new ones; it is, as Nicholas Cook observed, "the practical application of theory" (*Music,* p. 93). It is also at least implicitly involved in critical musicology (see "The Critical Method," below), since the very act of careful analysis of a work of music indicates a prior judgment as to the worth of that music.

Musical analysis, though synchronic rather than diachronic in nature, provides the data that allow the scientific historian to assess the possibility of a causal relationship between the works of two composers, given the existence of stylistic similarities: Did the two composers know each other's work? Did they come into direct contact? Were they both influenced by a third composer rather than directly by each other? And the historian may be able to determine a chronology of composition of works of one or more composers on the basis of the stylistic information provided by analysis. Likewise, historical information can be of great use to the analyst, who must on occasion step outside of the work itself in order to decide which of several hypothetical structures best fits the music in question.

Whether the music is in musical score or in performance, the question of what is actually being analyzed, the "subject" of analysis, is difficult to answer. Music is by nature ephemeral, not subject to scientific observation and measurement. Should one concentrate on the musical sound that the composer may have had in mind as he composed the work, or on the sound of a particular performance, or on the work as it is represented in a notated score? In the Western classical-music tradition, the notated score—the written image of a work—is generally used as the starting point for analysis, which may then go on to consider various possibilities of how it might sound. Here again, the analyst often uses the output of the scientific historian, specifically the editions of works and composers produced by textual scholarship and the study and interpretation of music notations (see the sidebar on "Music Notation").

As mentioned above (in the discussion of scientific historicism), in recent years the popularity of historical accounts based on musical style and the accompanying emphasis on the formal analysis of the inner workings of individual pieces of music gave rise to a feeling among many historical musicologists that the analytical method had to a great extent succeeded in removing the historical component from works of music that were in fact historical documents and should not be considered entirely out of context. In short, the concern was that the two methodologies, rather than existing in peaceful symbiosis, were in danger of becoming a single approach based on formal analysis. Perhaps the most virulent denunciation of this tendency came from the musicologist Joseph Kerman, who objected strongly to the formalist preoccupation of music analysts with the internal structure of the individual work of art, considered as an autonomous entity. "The potential of analysis is formidable," he wrote, "if it can only be taken out of the hothouse of theory and brought out into the real world" (Kerman, *Contemplating Music*, p. 18). In fact, many of Kerman's points were well taken, although unquestionably overstated. Much of the structural analysis during the early years of the twentieth century tended to accept uncritically the works of the Western musical canon and to seek analytical methods to explain the "greatness" of these works; in other words, the truly critical dimension was missing. And in the years following World War II, music analysis became increasingly formalist, abstract, and even arcane in nature, using scientific language and symbolism, as well as drawing directly on areas of theoretical mathematics such as set theory.

In the years since 1985, the analytical method has continued in the old directions (which are ably defended in Pieter Van den Toorn, *Music, Politics, and the Academy*), while also—somewhat in response to Kerman's charge of excessive formalism—moving in new ones that attempt to strike a balance between the consideration of the musical work out of context and an investigation of the historical and social forces evident in that music. Among these new approaches are semiotic analysis; surface rather than structural analysis; a more vigorous investigation into the history of the reception of musical works; and attempts at experimental verification, based on perception, of the importance to the listener of various abstract analytical properties. (See, in this context, the collection of essays included in Cook and Everist, *Rethinking Music*.)

The critical method. The critical method in musicology undertakes the comprehensive interpretation and evaluation of what a musical work means within all of its contexts—historical, political, sociological, and economic, as well as aesthetic. In this, it differs from the analytical method, which generally considers the work of music to have a partially, if not completely, autonomous status with respect to any of its possible contexts. Scholarly music criticism has a long tradition, but the critical method in musicology has taken on much of its importance as a reaction and a response to Kerman's previously mentioned attack, in the mid-1980s, on excessive analytical formalism (see "The Analytical Method," above) and unrealistic historical positivism. With respect to the latter, Kerman and others questioned the assumption by scientific historians of the existence of a unique "best text" (ur-text) that can be reproduced in a scholarly edition, noting that for much early music the concept is anachronistic, and that even nineteenth-century composers such as Beethoven and Chopin were continually making changes to their compositions.

Deploring what he perceived as a substantial gap between academic musicology and the human experience of music, Kerman called for a methodology that would draw upon "all modes of knowledge, including the theoretical and the analytical, the historical and the intuitive, to help achieve a critical response to a piece of music" (Kerman, *Contemplating Music*, p. 154). And indeed, whether in response to Kerman specifically or simply as part of the "postmodernist" climate of the late 1980s and 1990s, the critical method in musicology has come to encompass a variety of historiographies and research methodologies, showing the influence of the literary critical theory of the 1990s as well as recent developments in disciplines such as anthropology and philosophy. This new wave of critical thinking is often included under the omnibus term "new musicology." Among the most productive and promising are the following, not necessarily mutually exclusive, directions:

Hermeneutic historiography. In answer to criticism of the claims of "certain" knowledge put forth by scientific historians, proponents of a hermeneutic historiography in musicology advocate a synchronic rather than a diachronic historiographical model: that is, narratives based on causal relationships constructed according to the scientific historical method should be replaced by thorough contextual descriptions of a musical work of art, a goal much influenced by the work of the anthropologist Clifford Geertz. The aim of such an investigation, given the wide range of contextual information, is the well-informed interpretation, or exegesis, of all aspects of the creation in a particular time and place of a musical work or of a musical process, involving details and conditions of performance and reception. (See, for example, Small, *Musicking*, especially his Geertzian "thick analysis" of a symphonic concert of classical music.) The issue of the status of the work of music is generally unresolved. Some musicologists argue that contextual interpretation is not enough, that the musical work of art must also be considered with respect to the aesthetic experience that it produces. It must therefore retain some degree of autonomy within its historical context and should be analyzed accordingly. (See, for example, Treitler, "Historiography of Music.") Others reject entirely the idea of a "close reading"

MUSIC NOTATION

The fundamental aim of music notation is to make a lasting visible indication of musical sound, which is invisible and ephemeral. In this respect, it is intimately related to writing in general; and, in fact, music notation is a technology found in societies that have already developed a script for language. Frequently the elements of that script are used in the music notation. And indeed, wherever they have been developed, systems of music notation fulfill two of the functions of script: conservation and communication. Moreover, just like writing in general, systems of music notation are selective in what they specify, ignoring certain aspects of performance judged to be less significant. For example, just as the written record of a speech provides little information about modes of delivery, music notations generally specify pitch or duration—which can be seen as the analogues of letters and words—but leave unfixed many elements of performance. Western notations are of two major types: instrumental tablature and phonetic or pitch notations. A tablature provides specific instructions for playing a piece of music on a stringed instrument, including proper placement of fingers and performance technique, and sometimes rhythm and the relative duration of notes. Pitch notation is a collection of signs (frequently letters of the alphabet), each representing a specific pitch, and possibly other information such as rhythm and duration.

The earliest surving notation is from Mesopotamia; and the musical cultures of India, China, Korea, and Japan, as well as the Arabic-speaking cultures, have made extensive use of music notation of various types, principally pitch notation, tablature, and solmization (the system of using syllables to denote the pitches of a musical scale). (See the articles on notation in the *New Grove Dictionary of Music* for a discussion of Western and non-Western music notations.) Western classical music, however, has relied more on notation than any other, because notation is fundamental to the conception of Western classical music as a collection of enduring works of art, objects that can be replicated in performance but that have a separate fixed existence independent of any specific sonic realization. This is not the case in other musical cultures, or even in non-classical Western musics, which place a higher value on performance and improvisation—on the act of making music—than on a written set of musical instructions.

The metaphor of the musical "object" came into use at some point during the nineteenth century (see Goehr, *The Imaginary Museum of Musical Works*). Prior to that time, imprecision was a generally accepted aspect of music notation, and a piece of music was generally thought of as something that existed only in specific performances made possible by the skill of performers in using a notational "sketch" to produce musical sound. But during the nineteenth century, composers increasingly sought to control performances of their works by means of more specific notation. This led to a view that performers were not "making music" but were "producing" musical works. According to this interpretation, the canon of Western music is a collection of imaginary musical objects (which are given a sense of reality by the fact that they are notated) and temporal experiences (the performances of these musical objects, made possible by the fact that they are notated). In this scenario, the responsibility of performers is to be true to the work (in German, *werktreu*)—that is, true to the intentions of the composer, true to scholarly edition, true to the authentic conditions of performance. These ideas have been challenged on many grounds, as discussed above. Most notably, the actual circumstances of composition indicate that often there is no single "correct" version of a musical work. And the degree of "authenticity" of a performance is difficult if not impossible to assess. These objections notwithstanding, Western classical music is largely conceived not in terms of performance but as a collection of notated musical objects.

of musical text, preferring to base their analysis entirely on a theoretically dialogic (two-way) conversation with the producer through the cooperation of archeological investigation and sympathetic hermeneutics. (See, for example, Tomlinson, *Music in Renaissance Magic.*) The most extreme advocates of this position interpret all musical detail—tonality, form, and so on—culturally.

Studies in gender and sexuality.

Beginning in the 1970s, some music historians began to take an interest in writing the history of women in music, a subject that until then had been almost entirely ignored; the resulting studies concentrated largely on the location of sources and the recovery of biographical information. These efforts were followed in the late 1980s and 1990s by the development of serious musicological criticism based on gender. In addition to identifying gender representations in various types of music, writers have used the results of formal analysis to argue that the music itself can produce these representations. Often this type of research has resulted in the destabilization of conventional assumptions about the events of Western music history. For example, Susan McClary, in *Feminine Endings,* has examined music spanning the period from the sixteenth century to the present and has identified the ways in which historically constituted ideas of gender, sexuality, and the body have informed musical procedures. (See Solie, *Musicology and Difference,* for a diverse and fascinating collection of critical writings on gender and sexuality in music.) The emergence of gender criticism in musicology during the 1990s was accompanied by scholarship based on gay and lesbian issues, demonstrating the relevance of issues of sexuality to musical criticism. (See, for example, Brett, *Queering the Pitch.*)

Sociohistoriography.

Since the late 1980s, musicologists and other scholars have increasingly studied Western classical music as a type of cultural practice. This rich methodological development includes work such as that of economist Jacques Attali, who, in a study of the political economy of music, argues that music can in fact challenge normative social orders and thus presage social development (Attali, *Noise;* see also Walser, *Running with the Devil*).

Rhetorical historiography.

Recently, the very ways in which musicologists present the results of their research, rather than the research methodologies themselves, have come under critical examination. Notably, Daniel Leech-Wilkinson, employing ideas drawn from Pierre Bourdieu (especially *Homo academicus*) and others, argues that the nature of the academic workplace guarantees that the presentation of new research is necessarily influenced by the shared ideology of the group of scholars for whom that research is largely intended (see, *The Modern Invention of Medieval Music,* especially chapter 4, "Evidence, Interpretation, Power, and Persuasion"). Furthermore, paradigm shifts in musicology, like that accompanying the "new" musicology of the late 1980s and 1990s, are more a result of the importance of creativity and novelty to academic promotion than of a successively closer approximation to the "truth" that is the purported goal of musicological research. Rather than viewing this as a drawback, Leech-Wilkinson concludes that rhetorical excellence of the sort that generates interest and creativity among the scholarly community should be the admitted goal of musicological research.

"Decentered" historiography.

Since the late 1980s, many musicologists have questioned the concentration by music historians on the group of works known as the canon of Western classical music (see "The scientific historical method," above), a concentration that has tended to marginalize or to ignore completely types of music that have in fact been extremely influential in the West and throughout the world. Advocates of the decentralization of music history argue that the very procedures by which scientific historians construct linear chains of causal relationships and ultimately propose periodizations based on elements of musical style are flawed; these historical analyses are diachronic and too narrowly focused, and the tidy narratives that they construct are misleading and should be corrected by a more synchronic and open-minded historiography. Susan McClary, for example, has written, "My history of Western music contains Bach, Mozart, and Beethoven, but it also includes Stradella and the Swan Silvertones, Bessie Smith and Eric Clapton, k. d. lang, Philip Glass, and Public Enemy" (*Conventional Wisdom,* p. 30). A fine example of decentered historiography is Robert Walser's detailed study of the heavy metal genre of rock music (*Running with the Devil*). Walser approaches his subject in various ways, integrating methods of musical analysis and cultural criticism; in particular he devotes a chapter to what he calls the "intersection" of heavy metal and Western classical music, comparing the techniques of heavy metal musicians to those of classical musicians (chap. 3).

See also **Absolute Music; Arts; Composition, Musical; Cultural History; Cultural Studies; Harmony; Music, Anthropology of; Musical Performance and Audiences.**

BIBLIOGRAPHY

Attali, Jacques. *Noise: The Political Economy of Music.* Translated by Brian Massumi. Foreword by Frederic Jameson. Afterword by Susan McClary. Minneapolis and London: University of Minnesota Press, 1996.

Bourdieu, Pierre. *Homo academicus.* Translated by Peter Collier. Cambridge, U.K.: Polity Press; Stanford, Calif.: Stanford University Press, 1988.

Brett, Philip, Elizabeth Wood, and Gary C. Thomas, eds. *Queering the Pitch: The New Gay and Lesbian Musicology.* New York: Routledge, 1994.

Butt, John. *Playing with History: The Historical Approach to Musical Performance.* Cambridge, U.K., and New York: Cambridge University Press, 2002.

Cook, Nicholas. *Music: A Very Short Introduction.* Oxford and New York: Oxford University Press, 1998.

Cook, Nicholas, and Mark Everist, eds. *Rethinking Music.* Oxford and New York: Oxford University Press, 1999. Reprint with corrections, 2001.

Dahlhaus, Carl. *Foundations of Music History.* Translated by J. B. Robinson. Cambridge, U.K., and New York: Cambridge University Press, 1983.

———. *Nineteenth-Century Music.* Translated by J. Bradford Robinson. Berkeley and Los Angeles: University of California Press, 1989.

Goehr, Lydia. *The Imaginary Museum of Musical Works: An Essay in the Philosophy of Music.* Oxford: Clarendon; New York: Oxford University Press, 1992.

Grout, Donald J., and Claude V. Palisca, eds. *A History of Western Music.* 6th ed. New York: Norton, 2000.

Jeffery, Peter. *Re-Envisioning Past Musical Cultures: Ethnomusicology in the Study of Gregorian Chant.* Chicago and London: University of Chicago Press, 1992.

Kerman, Joseph. *Contemplating Music: Challenges to Musicology.* Cambridge, Mass.: Harvard University Press, 1985.

Kivy, Peter. *Authenticities: Philosophical Reflections on Musical Performance.* Ithaca, N.Y.: Cornell University Press, 1995.

Leech-Wilkinson, Daniel. *The Modern Invention of Medieval Music: Scholarship, Ideology, Performance.* Cambridge, U.K.: Cambridge University Press, 2002.

McClary, Susan. *Conventional Wisdom: The Content of Musical Form.* Berkeley, Los Angeles, and London: University of California Press, 2000.

———. *Feminine Endings: Music, Gender, and Sexuality.* Minneapolis: University of Minnesota Press, 1991.

Pendle, Karin, ed. *Women and Music: A History.* 2nd ed. Bloomington: Indiana University Press, 2001.

Small, Christopher. *Musicking: The Meanings of Performing and Listening.* Middletown, Conn.: Wesleyan University Press; Hanover, N.H.: University Press of New England, 1998.

Solie, Ruth A. *Musicology and Difference: Gender and Sexuality in Music Scholarship.* Berkeley, Los Angeles, and London: University of California Press, 1993.

Taruskin, Richard. *Text and Act: Essays on Music and Performance.* Oxford: Oxford University Press, 1995.

Tomlinson, Gary. *Music in Renaissance Magic: Toward a Historiography of Others.* Chicago and London: University of Chicago Press, 1993.

Treitler, Leo. "The Historiography of Music: Issues of Past and Present." In *Rethinking Music,* edited by Nicholas Cook and Mark Everist. Oxford: Oxford University Press, 1999. Reprint with corrections, 2001.

———. *Music and the Historical Imagination.* Cambridge, Mass., and London: Harvard University Press, 1989.

Van den Toorn, Pieter C. *Music, Politics, and the Academy.* Berkeley, Los Angeles, and London: University of California Press, 1995.

Walser, Robert. *Running with the Devil: Power, Gender, and Madness in Heavy Metal Music.* Middletown, Conn.: Wesleyan University Press; Hanover, N.H.: University Press of New England, 1993.

Blair Sullivan

MYSTICISM.

This entry includes six subentries:

Chinese Mysticism
Christian Mysticism
Islamic Mysticism
Islamic Mysticism in Asia
Kabbalah
Mysticism in African Thought

CHINESE MYSTICISM

The term *mysticism* represents a modern approach to a cultural path rooted in antiquity, and given anthropological considerations it is timeless. Mysticism usually concerns any work, study, or praxis that aims at transcendence (the experiencing "self" moving beyond normal limits) or union with the divine. It was (is) often private or even secret, perhaps involving special teachers. To reflect on the experience requires placing it into everyday language and expression.

Mysticism in Chinese thought and society should neither be reified nor reduced to one cultural path or genre of thought. It resonates with some, if not all, ancient Mediterranean practices to which the Greek word *mustikos* (from the word *muo,* to be secret) was applied, as well as with mysticism found among thinkers from Jewish, Christian, and Muslim communities. Chinese society produced its own textual adepts and adherents, both within and outside of religious structures. And there are examples of guarded (in some sense hermetic) pursuits and transmittals of curricula and skills.

Three important aims of Chinese mysticism have been: (1) mantic knowledge and divination; (2) individual enlightenment and/or transcendence; and (3) union and cooperation with divinities. Social contexts range widely: individuals, village groups, and royal courts. A village scholar might employ an artisan-practitioner for mantic insight into his place in the cosmos, and priests might pursue hermetic texts and praxis of a rarefied nature.

China's "Mantic Way": Knowledge through Insight and Technics

The oldest, deepest element within Chinese mysticism is the society's diffuse mantic approach to both special knowledge and everyday life; one may call it the mantic way—enduring to the present. Archaeological work on ancient China has inspired deductions about the impact that mantic pursuits had upon politics, natural philosophy, religions, and technics. David Keightley has argued, via late-Shang royal divination records (around 1200 B.C.E.), that court decisions often were mantically "charged" in order to both detect and induce the influence of ancestors; thus, specialists, operating with divination materials, manipulated the rituals and linguistic processing of the charges not just to show how to act, but to verify that a ruler had acted correctly or had effective ancestral connections.

The mantic way infused all social levels and mundane contexts (court rites, tomb appurtenances and texts, household almanacs, manuals, and situational fortune-telling) and was a basic context for Chinese sciences. In this last regard, a trend developed from about 500 B.C.E. to 200 C.E. toward precision in the mantic arts (for example, numero-astral and calendric devices, and *Yi jing* numerate and correlative theoretics). Courts desired the best-trained and most effective practitioners with their impressive techniques. By Tang and Song times the arts were practiced widely, in urban areas and the countryside, and also became fairly regularized in state offices. Practitioners usually transmitted skills only within their own families. This alloy of intuitive, artisanal knowledge, precision

---

ANCIENT MYSTICISM EMERGES LATER IN DAOIST TEXTS

"[T]he five tones originate in the breath blown in and out from the mouth. . . . Spread out energy forms the six roots of the senses." Mystical practice as described in fifth-century Daoist text "Xisheng jing." Note the reference to ritual music, similar to the deep context of the earlier, non-religious "Wenyan" commentary to *Yi jing*.

SOURCE: *Taoist Mystical Philosophy: The Scripture of Western Ascension,* translated by Livia Kohn. Albany: State University of New York Press, 1991, p. 237.

---

technics, and protectiveness has cast an aura of "mystery" over arts that Westerners have found attractive, such as *fengshui,* medicine, and astrology. But it is more important to understand how arts and systems were both connected to and made sophisticated outside of the diffuse mantic way.

Self-Cultivation as a Secular Pursuit: c. 400 B.C.E.–1600 C.E.

"Self-cultivation" shows how a certain praxis grew out of the substrate to become an important cultural artifact. At an early point it became entangled in the catch-all (and confusing) category "Daoism." By the late 1700s European sinologists began to examine texts haphazardly denominated "Daoist." For example, the roughly third century B.C.E. commentary to *Yi jing* (The book of changes) titled "Wenyan," in a passage that discusses "aesthetic grace" (*mei*), reads at one point: "A man of quality: [attuned to basal] yellow [at the] center; transmitting a system-pattern. He uprightly sets [his] position; makes an abode [within his] outline-shape. With [aesthetic] grace on his inside, [he can be] at ease in [his] four limbs." Interpreters conflated ideas like this with what little they knew of "philosophic Daoism," which often was seen as a crypto-Legalist Confucianism. In the 1920s Richard Wilhelm translated the foregoing, in part, as "The superior man is yellow and moderate . . . makes his influence felt . . . through reason. . . . His beauty is within" (*The Yi jing,* p. 395), the assumption being that "yellow" referred to moderation and a yielding nature. This relates to late-imperial Confucian ethics and eremitism, but misses important links to an ancient context.

Scholars are now able to apply finer nuances. Since about 1975, archaeology has brought to light manuals, implements, and texts from pre- and early-Han tombs (roughly 400 to 100 B.C.E.) that evidence practices of divination, siting, sexual hygiene, demon-quelling, longevity arts, and mind-evacuation. Examples are "Recipes for Nurturing Life" and "Ten Questions," texts from the Mawangdui cache. Donald Harper carefully explains that these may have been the practical bases from which later self-cultivation pursuits developed. Such tombs were constructed in an era when imperial courts devoted money and energy to complicated rites programs, which in turn found parallels in local culture. Thus the commentary passage, above, apropos of the *Yi jing* phrase "yellow lower garment," actually carries a *mustikos*—objects in closed-off tombs and the secretive, frequently agonistic, court struggles over systems of music and dress. In fact, "Yellow Bell" was the name of an elusive, theoretical pitch regulation for establishing tuning "systems." Harmonics in turn were seen as "transmitting" cosmic beauty, which emanated from the "man of quality" at the "center"—that is, local royalty or, later, the emperor. The "Wenyan" passage thus glides on the edges of several readings: an indirect, mostly metaphorical exhortation on centering; a paean to court music and the computations of its harmonics experts; an alchemy of nurturing the homunculus emperor (or sage) within oneself; and reconciling inner and outer commitments in one's public life. Later in the Han period, and with important revivals during Tang and Song (see below), other texts carried self-cultivation forward, with instructions in mystical practice that became more specific.

If the above interpretation of a passage of commentary to *Yi jing* is controversial, nevertheless, self-cultivation is read quite confidently from passages of famous works such as Laozi, Huainanzi, Guanzi, and Zhuangzi that discuss breathing, sitting still, and removal of all perception and emotion. Such readings are seen by Harold Roth to reflect a historical development whose very earliest period emphasized "cosmology and the inner transformation of the individual leading to the attainment of 'mystical gnosis'" (Roth, pp. 6–9). Through the textual work of Roth, Livia Kohn, and others it is better understood that early China contained a whole culture of self-cultivation, with fairly common terminologies, texts, and aims.

Beginning around 100 C.E., scholar-officials restored and reinterpreted ancient texts. The *Yi jing,* especially its anonymous commentaries (as above), was researched anew, as was the relativistic and transcendent logic of Laozi and Zhuangzi. The second to fourth century scholar-Daoists, often referred to as "neo-Daoists" or "Mystery Adepts," brought relativist logic and psychological inquiry into public discourse, and many practiced eremitic stances and withdrawals. Most did not identify the ancient traces of mystical praxis per se in their classics, but

---

FROM MEDIEVAL TANTRA TO MODERN TIMES

The following snippet of recitation (from a 600-year-old text) was performed in the 1990s in Fukien, China, for local Daoist rites: ". . . with complete obedience [to] . . . Perfected Lord Wu/ . . . Wrote talismans, let fall seal-scripts . . . that his Sacred Spell would have awesome power. . . ."

SOURCE: *Taoist Ritual,* translated by Kenneth Dean, p. 93.

---

their metaphysics and ontology spurred mystical speculation later on among monk-scholars and Daoist revelators.

In this same period, anonymous writings known as "weft-texts" (*wei*) and numero-calendric "charts" (*tu*) were thought to augment hermetically the "warp" of the Confucian classics. Essentially, they were revelatory texts that claimed sage-authorial voice for their political predictions and comments on sociocosmic timing and justice. Beginning about 350 C.E., revealed texts of various types influenced southern Daoist scholars and scriptural communities; and they remain in use in Daoist communities of the early twenty-first century.

Around 1000 C.E. neo-Confucian discussions reclaimed ancient approaches to self-cultivation, this time fully conscious of the mystical program, unlike earlier reclaimers. Many judged Daoist practices as undesirable and the cosmologies and belief-systems of Mahayana Buddhism as anathema; but the influential Shao Yong (1011–1077), for example, borrowed from both, sparking interest among scholar-intellectuals in psychocosmic resonance and correlation, as well as in self-cultivation. In fact, self-cultivation became prominent in the aspirations and writings of Wang Yangming (1472–1529), his disciple Wang Ji (1498–1583), and follower Li Zhi (1527–1602), to name a few. Their mysticism centered around the notion (even praxis) of "innate knowledge"—promoting instinctual mental (and moral) response over the machinations of academic learning. In fact, Wang Yangming wrote of practicing a Zen-like contemplation and the subsequent redirecting of it into political action. His ideas made a deep impact on elite-scholar life for over two hundred years.

The Buddho-Daoist Melange: Tantra, Zen, and Mediums, 400 C.E.–Present

By about 300 C.E., northern Chinese polity had collapsed under pressure from proto-Turkic invaders. Many northern social and political elite had reestablished themselves in the south, a general area long known for expressions of ecstatic vision and song and escapist literature. When Daoism and Buddhism, as organized monastic-lay communities, flourished in the south, detailed instructions in mystical practice became more frequent, while at the same time the themes and types of practice changed. When the nation was unified under the Tang dynasty in 618, the two religions achieved widespread official sanction.

Buddhism's Hinayana roots in China (from about 100–300 C.E.) had emphasized mind-body exercises (breathing, counting, and recitation). Mahayana Buddhism, a bit later, shared with Daoist scriptures the desire to impart protection for individuals and communities against demons and apocalyptic chaos. The resulting Buddho-Daoist melange reflected the entrance (and frequently the forging) of Indic Tantrist technics and scriptures from Tibet and Central Asia. The Buddhist scripture titled *Book of Consecration* (c. 450s) is a collection of various spells, oracles, talismans, and even instructions for rebirth into a heaven of medicinal herbs. It is a total package of Chinese mysticism. Seemingly Indic and Tantric, it is nonetheless solidly Chinese, presenting practices in the mantic way, in self-cultivation and transcendence, and finally tutelary divinities who defend against demonic forces.

The *Book of Consecration* provides the first example of physical implements and practices as tools for transitory union with divinities. This was a new twist, since previously divinities were mainly powerful, official-like beings to whom one petitioned. "Officials to be petitioned" and "gods with whom to gain union" continue in modern Daoist communities throughout the Chinese world. Rites and festivals require chanting for divine intercession, writing of magical calligraphic documents, and direct transmission of divine will through medium-shamans.

In Tang times, "Double Mystery" (chengxuan) Daoist priests such as Liu Jinxi (d. c. 640), who resided at a Daoist monastery in Changan and defended Daoism at court debates in the 620s, exhibited Buddho-Daoist blending. Liu's *Benji jing* uses a Buddhist debate style as well as notions of the Dao as cosmic deity. Tang Daoists developed the older strains of "self-cultivation" more systematically. Instructions were set out to effect the discarding of all desires, then even the discarding of the state of no-desires, a logical ploy borrowed from Mahayana Buddhism. Chan (Zen) Buddhism matured as a sect from the 700s to 900s, transmitting texts, oral teaching, and even implements in guarded fashion, through disciple-master lineages. Chan rules for meditation were codified, for example, the "Regulations of the Chan School" (1004), and Zongze's "Principles of Seated Meditation" (1103), which prescribe how to enter the practice room, how to sit, the placing

New Dictionary of the History of Ideas

of the limbs, and the positioning of tongue and mouth for breathing practice.

Conclusion

Chinese mysticism was, and is, a vibrant phenomenon with ancient, secular roots that over time, and via religious enterprises, developed new forms. Not only did Chinese mysticism mix the secular and religious, but also the social range was total. To see this better, one must not think of Chinese mystical practice as simply its tools, for example, alchemically larded manuals of healing and longevity, or *fengshui* (mantic siting). Such arts often draw on China's mantic way by employing instinctive—nontextual, nonmechanistic—skills. The artisan becomes a psychopomp, a shaman leading a client to special knowledge, clarity, or health. And arts were guarded within family groups, which made them in some sense *mustikos*. But they could also be entirely mechanical. One cannot describe as mystical the act of looking up an interpretive symbol inscribed on a calibrated siting compass. Chinese mysticism is best seen in the long arc of textual guides to, and metaphysical supports for, self-cultivation. All three paths interlaced, eventually in the practices of cult communities, and eventually as techniques for establishing relations with divinities.

See also **Buddhism; Confucianism; Daoism; Religion: East and Southeast Asia; Zen.**

BIBLIOGRAPHY

Chang, K. C. *Art, Myth, and Ritual: The Path to Political Authority in Ancient China.* Cambridge, Mass.: Harvard University Press, 1983. An eloquent exploration of the role of ancient shaman-priests in asserting text and symbol as political tools.

Csikszentmihàlyi, Mark. "Traditional Taxonomies and Revealed Texts in the Han." In *Daoist Identity: History, Lineage, and Ritual,* edited by Livia Kohn and Harold D. Roth, 81–101. Honolulu: University of Hawai'i Press, 2002.

Dean, Kenneth. *Taoist Ritual and Popular Cults of Southeastern China.* Princeton, N.J.: Princeton University Press 1993.

DeWoskin, Kenneth J. *Doctors, Diviners, and Magicians in Ancient China: Biographies of Fang-shih.* New York: Columbia University Press, 1983.

Harper, Donald. "Warring States Natural Philosophy and Occult Thought." Chapter 12 in *The Cambridge History of Ancient China: From the Origins of Civilization to 221 B.C,* edited by Michael Loewe and Edward L. Shaughnessy. Cambridge, U.K., and New York: Cambridge University Press, 1999.

Harper, Donald. "Warring States, Qin, and Han Manuscripts Related to Natural Philosophy and the Occult." In *New Sources of Early Chinese History: An Introduction to the Reading of Inscriptions and Manuscripts,* edited by Edward L. Shaughnessy, 223–252. Berkeley: The Society for the Study of Early China and The Institute of East Asian Studies, University of California, 1997.

Keightley, David N. "Shang Divination and Metaphysics." *Philosophy East & West* 38, no. 4 (1988): 367–395.

Kohn, Livia. *Early Chinese Mysticism: Philosophy and Soteriology in the Taoist Tradition.* Princeton, N.J.: Princeton University Press, 1992. The first chapter gives a useful anthropological summary of recent discussions on the nature of mysticism.

Roth, Harold. *Original Tao: Inward Training and the Foundations of Taoist Mysticism.* New York: Columbia University Press, 1999.

———. "Psychology and Self-Cultivation in Early Taoistic Thought." *Harvard Journal of Asiatic Studies* 51 (1991): 599–650.

Sivin, Nathan. "State, Cosmos, and Body in the Last Three Centuries B.C." *Harvard Journal of Asiatic Studies* 55, no. 1 (1995): 5–37.

Strickmann, Michel. *Mantras et mandarins: Le bouddhisme tantrique en Chine.* Paris: Gallimard, 1996. Groundbreaking insights into the way Tantric-seeming tools of individual transcendence, demonifugic protection, and salvation wove through Daoism and Buddhism.

———. "The Mao Shan Revelations: Taoism and the Aristocracy." *T'oung Pao* 63 (1978): 1–64.

Wilhelm, Richard. *The I Ching, or Book of Changes.* 3rd ed. Translated by Cary F. Baynes. Princeton, N.J.: Princeton University Press, 1967.

Howard L. Goodman

CHRISTIAN MYSTICISM

Since the Baroque age, the concept of mysticism (first in French, *la mystique*) has been used to describe religious phenomena that can hardly be restricted to a certain geographical space or a certain epoch. These phenomena are primarily symbolic expressions (in act, speech, literature, art, music, etc.), of persons trying to communicate knowledge that has been gained through mystical experiences.

A commonly accepted definition of "mystical experience" does not exist. St. Thomas Aquinas (1225–1274) says that beyond speculation, there is an experimental cognition (*cognitio experimentalis*) of the divine, "thereby a man experiences in himself the taste of God's sweetness, and complacency in God's will" (*Summa theologiae* II/II q.97, a.2, re2). In order to include forms of mysticism that reject the notion of a personal god, one could more generally speak of immediate experiences of divine presence. For an additional clarification of the concept it is still useful to consider the four characteristics of the "mystical state of consciousness" as provided by William James (pp. 294–296):

1. Ineffability: The paramount experiences exceed the intellect, defy verbal expression, and can therefore not be imparted or transferred to others.

2. Noetic quality: Mystical experiences are not mere feelings but also insights and participations in a nonintellectual and nondiscursive knowledge.

3. Passivity: Although the mystic may actively prepare body and mind, the actual experience is rather one of being grasped and held by a superior power.

4. Transiency: Mystical experiences are limited in time and can only imperfectly be reproduced by memory. This last characteristic, however, has been questioned by more recent scholarship, since there are sources that speak of permanent mystical states.

The symbolic expressions as well as the modes of mystical experience are, to a certain degree, predetermined by their social, religious, and intellectual environment. This observation, however, does not contradict the assumption that there is a "numinous" dimension of reality from which all mystical experiences originate. Accounts of mystical states of consciousness occur in every religion, philosophy, and doctrine of wisdom, involving a dimension of divine eternity, which on the one hand transcends the sphere of temporal beings and sense perceptions and, on the other hand, is the ground and source of all being. Besides this ontological presupposition an anthropological one is required. Mystics claim that a feature of human nature—most often identified as the "soul" or its highest parts—is divine or can assume a divine form. Therefore, it can free itself from the bodily and temporal sphere of existence in order to enter the transcendent realm of the divine.

Basic Problems of Christian Mysticism

Christian mysticism inherited most of its ontological and anthropological foundations from the Hellenistic environment from which it emerged. But it also derived a great deal of its imagery and inspiration from the Old Testament, first of all from the Song of Songs. Nevertheless, the original contributions of Christianity must be related to the revelations of the New Testament. The history of Christian mysticism begins with the oldest documents of Christianity, the letters of Paul. The Apostle writes:

> I know a man in Christ who fourteen years ago was caught up to the third heaven. . . . And I know that this man . . . was caught up into Paradise and he heard things that cannot be told, which man may not utter. (2 Cor. 12:2–4)

This quotation shows the problems that scholarship on Christian mysticism confronts. Paul's memory of his mystical ascent seems to lie at the periphery of his religious consciousness. It is his experience as a "man in Christ" and can only be understood as one of the consequences of the Damascus experience, his vision of the Resurrected. The paramount experiences that lie at the foundations of the Christian symbolic universe are not understood as the results of individualistic efforts by religious virtuosos but as the self-revelation of a merciful god. At least in Western Christianity, the paradigm of the saint is not the ascetical hero, who attained mystical states, but the converted sinner, who did not deserve the grace of his calling. The notion of a God who not only created the world but also mediates himself through sending his Son and the Holy Spirit, in other words a God who acts toward man, seems to contradict the mystical notion of an ever-transcendent God that must be approached by meditative ascent.

Moreover, if the climax of God's self-revelation is the incarnation of his word (logos), how can there be a higher knowledge, gained in an experimental realm beyond language? The union of the soul with the ground of being, which can be regarded as the climax of mystical experiences, seems to undermine the orthodox understanding of divine union, that is

the sacramental union with the body of Christ, provided by the institution of the church. It is therefore no wonder that Christian mystics often fell under the suspicion of heresy and that even modern theologians regard the concept of Christian mysticism as a contradiction in terms. Of course, a closer look at their writings would show that almost all Christian mystics did not doubt that membership in the church, faith in Christ, and the dispensation of divine grace is the presupposition of their ascent. Nevertheless, the tension remains.

History of Christian Mysticism

The tension first became manifest in the mysticism of the Egyptian hermits who, influenced by the Platonic theology of Origen (185?–254? C.E.), felt dissatisfied with the community life of the church and were searching for a more immediate experience of God in the isolation of the desert. In their view, the *parousia,* the presence of Christ, was no longer a historical event but rather a personal encounter and a result of ascetical purification. Until the High Middle Ages, occidental mysticism was limited by the authority of St. Augustine of Hippo (354–430). Other than in his early work, which drew heavily on the mystical Neoplatonism of Plotinus and Porphyry, the church father more and more opposed the self-confident individualism of the ascetics. Rather, he insisted on the general sinfulness of man and God's autonomous dispensation of grace. But the manifold richness of his experiential world would not allow him to completely abandon the Neoplatonic idea of mystical ascent. Augustine shows the orthodox Western attitude that mystical experience does not necessarily lead to a mystical theology. Rather the awareness of divine presence confirms earlier theological assertions and removes doubts. An account in the *Confessions* (c. 400) betrays its Neoplatonic background as it sketches the parallel ascent through the hierarchies of the ontological order of beings and the anthropological order of human capacities.

> And so step by step I ascended from bodies to the soul which perceives through the body, and from there to its inward force, to which the bodily senses report external sensations, . . . From there again I ascended to the power of reasoning to which is to be attributed the power of judging the deliverances of the bodily senses. This power, which in myself I found to be mutable, raised itself to the level of its own intelligence, and led my thinking out of the ruts of habit. It withdrew itself from the contradictory swarms of imaginative fantasies, so as to discover the light by which it was flooded. . . . So in the flash of a trembling glance it attained to that which is. At that moment I saw your "invisible nature understood through the things which are made." (*Confessions* VII, 17, 23)

Augustine's "moderate mysticism," which laid greater emphasis on the mutability and misery of all earthly existence and the limitedness of human knowledge, has been challenged throughout the history of Western Christianity. Influences from Eastern Christianity always provided alternative approaches to mysticism. The most important of these sources were the writings of an unknown (probably Syrian) author, published around the year 500 under the name of Dionysius the Areopagite (cf. Acts 17, 34). Unlike Augustine, Pseudo-Dionysius provides a mystical theology in the strict sense. His negative (*apophatikē*) theology teaches the contemplative ascent through the realm of language by the successive reduction of words and negation of all positive propositions about God. Its purpose is a translinguistical meditation on and union with the superessential (*hyperousion*) "It."

> . . . ascending, we say, that It is neither soul, nor mind, nor has imagination, or opinion, or reason, or conception; . . . neither is standing, nor moving; nor at rest; neither has power, nor is power, nor light; neither lives, nor is life; neither is essence nor eternity, nor time; . . . neither one, nor oneness; neither Deity, nor Goodness; nor is It Spirit according to our understanding; nor Sonship, nor Paternity; nor any other thing of those known to us, or to any other existing being. . . . (*Mystical Theology* V)

The inherent tension of Christian mysticism becomes again manifest because the mystical insights transcend everything that Christian theology teaches about God. The "It" lies in the "overbright darkness" (*hyperphōtos gnophos*) beyond the essence of the triune God.

St. Bernard of Clairvaux (1090–1153) became the most influential representative of a genuine Christian version of mysticism, the mysticism of love. In his *Sermons on the Song of Songs,* he provides a sophisticated doctrine of four types of love. The highest one is the paradoxical "self-love for God's sake," an ecstatic state in which the self is almost completely annihilated through the union with the divine. On the one hand, Bernard could more easily reconcile his mysticism with the doctrine of grace, since he could understand the mystical ascent as the loving answer of the human soul to the loving call of God. On the other hand, his doctrine implied the degradation of other forms of Christian love. According to Bernard, the love of neighbor belongs to the lowest type of love.

This view was rejected by one of the most singular personalities of medieval Christian thought, Johannes Eckehart, called Meister Eckhart (c. 1260–?1327), a German Dominican. His philosophy was a turn back to the heritage of Neoplatonism and faced vehement opposition by the church. Mystical ascent is not a movement through ever-higher stages of love but an intellectual endeavor. Its end is the contemplation of the "divinity" (*Gottheit*), a higher preexistent unity that precedes and transcends the ontological difference between God and man. Eckehart also insisted on the priority of the active life.

Nevertheless, the mysticism of love dominated female mysticism, which first began to flower in the middle of the twelfth century. Thousands of mostly wealthy married women, who were dissatisfied with their subordinate status in society and the ecclesiastical order of charismas, joined the Cistercians in order to change their "carnal marriage" into a "spiritual marriage" with Christ. In the thirteenth century, the more freely organized but orthodox movement of the Beguines began to attract many women from all social ranks, primarily in the new urban centers of western Europe. Contemplation of and union with Christ is the typical form of female love mysticism, which ranges from loving compassion with Christ's suffering to explicit accounts of erotic encounters with the Savior. Female mysticism reached an intellectual climax in the writings of the Spanish nun St. Teresa of Ávila (1515–1582). Her symbol of the "interior castle" and its various rooms signifies the different stages of perfection the soul must pass to achieve final perfection and the union with God in the "innermost chamber." Although the exclusion of women from scholastic education was one of its motivations, female mysticism may not be regarded as a feminist protest movement. The more significant currents remained orthodox and did not oppose church authority. Moreover, many of its spiritual leaders were male. Female mysticism, however, shows that contemplative life does not necessarily lead to the renunciation of the active life. Many female mystics were extraordinarily active in charity and politics. One of the best examples is St. Catherine of Siena (1347–1380), who was sent on diplomatic missions and played a mediating role in the Great Schism.

Some other important representatives of Christian Mysticism have not been mentioned so far: St. Gregory of Nyssa (c. 335–c. 394) was one of the most brilliant and influential church fathers of the East and described mystical experience as the "fruition of God." The Flemish mystic Jan van Ruysbroeck (1293–1381), known as the "Ecstatic Teacher" and the "New Dionysius," developed a "spiritual ladder of Christian attainment," consisting of the three steps of active life, inward life, and contemplative life. St. Gregory Palamas (1296–1359) was an important theorist of the Eastern mystical movement of the "hesychasts" and taught the fusion of the soul with divine energies. Johannes Tauler (c. 1300–1361), a German mystic and Dominican monk, emphasized ethical perfection as the presupposition of mystical union. The English female mystic Julian of Norwich (1342–after 1416), insisted on the love and benevolence of God. The unknown English author of *The Cloud of Unknowing* (written around 1375) continued the negative theology of the Areopagite. St. John of the Cross (1542–1591) was the most brilliant of all mystical poets. Edith Stein (1891–1942), a student of phenomenologist Edmund Husserl (1859–1938), developed the inward mysticism of Teresa of Ávila and John of the Cross.

See also **Christianity; Mysticism: Kabbalah; Sacred Texts.**

BIBLIOGRAPHY

PRIMARY SOURCES

Augustine of Hippo. *Confessions.* Translated with an introduction and notes by Henry Chadwick. Oxford and New York: Oxford University Press, 1991.

Bernard of Clairvaux. *Selected Works.* Translated with a foreword by G. R. Evans. New York: Paulist, 1987.

Dupré, Louis, and James A. Wiseman, eds. *Light from Light: An Anthology of Christian Mysticism.* 2nd ed. New York: Paulist, 2001.

Meister Eckhart. *The Essential Sermons, Commentaries, Treatises, and Defense.* Translated with an introduction by Edmund Colledge and Bernard McGinn. New York: Paulist, 1981.

Pseudo-Dionysius, the Areopagite. *The Divine Names; and, Mystical Theology.* Translated with an introductory study by John D. Jones. Milwaukee, Wis.: Marquette University Press, 1980.

Teresa of Ávila. *The Interior Castle.* London: Fount, 1995.

SECONDARY SOURCES

Beierwaltes, Werner, Hans Urs von Balthasar, and Alois M. Haas. *Grundfragen der Mystik.* Einsiedeln, Germany: Johannes, 1974.

James, William. *Varieties of Religious Experience: A Study in Human Nature.* Centenary edition. London and New York: Routledge, 2002.

Lossky, Vladimir. *Mystical Theology of the Eastern Church.* London: Clarke, 1991.

McGinn, Bernard. *The Presence of God: A History of Western Christian Mysticism.* New York: Crossroad, 1991–.

Otto, Rudolf. *The Idea of the Holy: An Inquiry into the Non-rational Factor in the Idea of the Divine and Its Relation to the Rational.* 2nd ed. London and New York: Oxford University Press, 1970.

Ruh, Kurt. *Geschichte der abendländischen Mystik.* 4 vols. Munich: Beck, 1990–1999.

Matthias Riedl

ISLAMIC MYSTICISM

The mystical dimension of the Islamic religious tradition has roots in the divinely revealed text of the Koran. One passage often pointed to in this regard is the "Light Verse" (24:35), in which God is described as the Light of a blessed lamp, lit by a burning oil "neither of the East nor the West." One episode from the Koran, involving the prophet Moses, provided key evidence for the mystics' claim that an unseen world runs parallel to our own. The story describes Moses' meeting and deferring to one whom God had taught knowledge from His "own presence" (18:65). The understanding is that the prophets have their exoteric missions and knowledge, but that esoteric knowledge has a parallel, if not superior, position.

The earliest mystical practices seem to have been ascetic, probably based on earlier Syrian and Iraqi Christian models. The term *Sufism*, for example, probably derives from the early mystics' practice of wearing wool (*suf*). A lost collection of biographies of ascetic women from the eighth and ninth centuries has been recovered. This work, by al-Sulami (d. 1021), presents themes such as scrupulous attention to God's law; excessive crying and fainting in response to one's guilt or to God's love; sincerity and control of the material appetites. These and the many other collections of ascetic exemplars that followed could evoke the prophet Muhammad's own spiritual retreats and supererogatory praying, as preserved in the Koran and the Tradition as precedents.

The concern with the self in this ascetic environment gave rise to theories of spiritual exercise that the aspirant would pursue in order to progress along the path to wisdom, purity, or even the presence of God. Among the most influential teachers and writers of the early period were Hasan al-Basri (d. 728), al-Muhasibi (d. 857), and the poet al-Bistami (d. 875). The tenth and eleventh centuries saw efforts at systematizing these paths, with the composition of a series of manuals describing and explaining such experiences as "extinction of the self in God," "trust in God," "certainty," "sincerity," and "repentance." These manuals (by al-Makki, d. 996; al-Hujwiri, d. 1071; al-Qushayri, d. 1074; and others) also present the mystical teachings of prominent Sufi masters.

Mystical thinking among the Shi'a also begins early. The sixth imam of the Twelver tradition, Ja'far al-Sadiq (d. 765) is taken by the Shi'a (and certain Sunni Sufis) to have been a master of esoteric teaching. The very concept of Shi'a leadership, or *imama*, included esoteric or mystical elements. The vibrant mystical tradition among the Twelver Shi'a, which came to be recognized as one of the religious sciences, would be known as *'irfan* (literally, "knowledge").

The twelfth and thirteenth centuries saw the rise of the Sufi brotherhoods, or *turuq* (singular, *tariqa*). The most prominent are probably the Qadiriyya, the Shadhiliyya, the Rifa'iyya, the Naqshbandiyya, and the Chistiyya. As an institution based on the teachings and model of a saintly founder, each *tariqa* would give rise to its own devotional practices, mystical doctrines, and literature. Central among these practices are the *dhikr*, or remembrance of God—a ritual group recitation of the name(s) of God. Along with *dhikr* goes the stylized recitation of long prayers, usually passed down from the founder of the order. Mystical doctrines vary widely. One issue that has been debated recently among scholars is that of "neo-Sufism." This is the term given to the perceived shift in Sufi practice, from about the middle eighteenth century, which inflated the role of the prophet Muhammad as a figure of devotion. This shift also challenged the traditional structures of the established Sufi brotherhoods and saw itself as reformist.

The heyday of Islamic mystical thought, however, took place outside the brotherhood organizations. Independent thinkers such as Ruzbehan Baqli (d. 1209), Najm al-Din Kubra (d. 1221), Ibn 'Arabi (d. 1240), Ibn al-Farid (d. 1235), and Jalal al-Din Rumi (d. 1273), provided dynamic mystical perspectives on God, creation, and existence itself. Also, the Koran could be illuminated by mystical exegesis. Ruzbehan Baqli's writings describe dramatic visions of the divine and the intense experiences these provoke. He also defended the phenomenon of ecstatic utterances (*shatahat*), for which the early Sufi al-Hallaj (d. 922) in particular had been known. Much of this defense rests on the notion that mystical language must be recognized as a reflection of the essentially nonverbal reality that is mystical experience. Kubra's innovative interpretation of the soul's mystical ascent associated certain colors with the levels of experience leading to sanctity.

Ibn 'Arabi's thought introduces a hermeneutic based on the assumption that an interpretation based on mystical insight is as true as that from any other human perspective. His elaboration of a qualified "oneness of being," that is, the recognition that only God's existence stands, has had an immense influence on the mystical tradition. The concept of sanctity (*walaya*) was to undergo dramatic elaboration in his writings. Ibn al-Farid, poet and mystic, composed some of the most sophisticated verses ever in the Arabic language. His great poem, the *Ta'iyya*, reframes classical images such as love and drunkenness to point to the mystic's experience of and devotion to the divine. The Persian poet Rumi made an even larger impact with his epic the *Mathnawi*. This collection of fables and wisdom tales presents a sophisticated and humane perspective, which although mystical in approach has a universal appeal.

These thinkers introduced and elaborated a set of concepts that constitute the touchstones of Islamic mysticism. One of these is an extension of the idea of the Light of the prophet Muhammad. This is the Muhammadan Reality, which gave the Prophet a cosmic and existential role to play—quite a leap from the earliest understanding of the man in Islamic tradition. The Muhammadan Reality stands between God and creation, an intermediary similar to the Universal Intellect of the Neoplatonists. The "oneness of being" concept has remained debated, but a fruitful subject for speculation up to the present. The concept of sanctity, and in particular the theory of the identity and nature of the "seal of saints" has provoked much thought among later mystics.

See also **Islam; Miracles; Sacred Texts.**

BIBLIOGRAPHY

Knysh, Alexander. *Islamic Mysticism: A Short History.* Leiden, Netherlands and Boston: Brill, 2000.

Schimmel, Annemarie. *Mystical Dimensions of Islam.* Chapel Hill: University of North Carolina Press, 1975.

Sells, M. *Early Islamic Mysticism: Sufi, Qur'an, Miraj, Poetic and Theological Writings.* Edited and translated by Michael A. Sells. New York: Paulist Press, 1996.

Trimingham, J. Spencer. *The Sufi Orders in Islam.* New York: Oxford University Press, 1998.

Richard McGregor

ISLAMIC MYSTICISM IN ASIA

There are a number of mystical movements within Islam, but by far the dominant tradition is that of Sufism, one of the most dynamic and interesting dimensions of Islamic religious and cultural expression. *Sufism* is an umbrella term for a variety of philosophical, social, and literary phenomena occurring within the Islamic world. In its narrowest sense, the term refers to a number of schools of Islamic mystical philosophy and theology, to the phenomenon of religious orders and guilds (*tariqat*) that have exerted considerable influence over the development of Islamic politics and society, and to the varied expressions of popular piety and devotion to shrines found throughout the Islamic world. In a wider sense, Sufism is often seen as the spiritual muse behind much of premodern verse in the Islamic world, the idiom of much of popular Islamic piety, the primary social arena open to women's religious participation, and a major force in the conversion of people to Islam in Africa and Asia. The Sufi orders served as educational institutions that fostered not only the religious sciences but also music and decorative arts. Their leaders sometimes functioned as a challenge to the power of the juridic and theological establishment. In modern times (as at other periods in history), the Sufi orders have been praised for their capacity to serve as instruments of religious reform at the same time as they have been vilified for a lack of respect for Islamic law and

for fostering ignorance and superstition in order to maintain control over the community.

The term *Sufism*—or *tasawwuf*, as the tradition is called in Arabic—may derive from the practice of wearing wool (*suf* in Arabic), or possibly from the Arabic word for purity (*safa*). The earliest Sufis spent almost all their waking hours in prayer, and frequently engaged in acts of self-mortification, such as starving themselves or staying up the entire night, as a form of prayer exercise. They renounced their connections to the world and possessed little other than the clothes on their backs. A large percentage of these early Sufis were women, several of whom, such as Rabi'a al-Adawiyya (d. 801), are revered to this day.

History: Early Period

In Muslim understanding the origins of Islamic mysticism in the form of Sufism lie in the life of Muhammad. His earliest biographies emphasize his habit of meditating in a cave and living a life of material simplicity bordering on asceticism, both of which are seen as prototypes of mystical belief and practice in Islam. As an organized movement, Sufism too owes its official origins to Muhammad and his cousin and son-in-law, 'Ali, who is viewed by the majority of Sufis as the first of their kind. Ali was the first male convert to Islam and the man closest to Muhammad in his private life. As such, he is said to have received levels of spiritual guidance from Muhammad that were not available to anyone else. Part of this was a body of mystical knowledge that was passed down through Ali to future generations. The concept of esoteric or mystical knowledge (*'ilm al-batin, al-'ilm al-batini,* or simply *al-batin*) became central to the theology of Shiism, one of the two main sectarian divisions in Islam. It also remains at the center of Sufi understanding.

The historically traceable origins of Sufism begin approximately a century after Ali's death. Very little biographical information is available on some of the earliest Muslim ascetic and mystical figures, but they are important for their impact on the development of Sufism. By the late eighth century, members of the school of a famous mystical ascetic named Hasan al-Basri (d. 728) had established a convent (*ribat*) at Abadan, and others had composed important treatises on Sufi etiquette. Important mystical figures of this period include Dhu'l-Nun Misri (d. c. 859), an Egyptian figure who is of importance to the development of Sufism in western Asia because later Sufis quote him frequently, seeing him as a Muslim exponent of the Hellenistic tradition. An Iranian Sufi named Bayazid Bistami (d. 874) became famous for ecstatic utterances (*shathiyat*), which he was the first to use consistently as an expression of Sufi mystical experience. These somewhat scandalous declarations were dramatic statements made to demonstrate the merging of Bistami's individuality with the divine identity. This sense of union with God was the result of a life-long process of self-purification at both a physical and a spiritual level. In his practice of prayer and meditation Bayazid showed strong ascetic tendencies while at the same time ridiculing traditional asceticism because he felt that trying to renounce the physical world was to afford the physical realm an existence that it did not actually possess. The theme of asceticism appears frequently in Iranian Sufism in the ninth century even though many Sufis, like Bistami, rejected the outward trappings of an ascetic life.

The end of the tenth century marks a transition in the development of Sufism from the early formative period that was characterized by a high degree of individualism in practice and a central focus on asceticism to a classical age wherein there is greater emphasis on organization and systematization. This is also a time when Sufism in western Asia appears somewhat divided between two schools, the first being the Iraqi one (which was transplanted to Nishapur in Iran) and the second being the Khurasani one, centered in northeastern Iran and Afghanistan. The differences between these two schools are not altogether clear and at times appear to have more to do with the theological and legal affiliations of Khurasani Sufis than with any major differences over mystical theory and practice.

The transitional phase of the tenth and eleventh century also witnessed an increased emphasis on the formalization of Sufi doctrine, the canonization of earlier Sufi figures, and an apologetic attempt to show potential Sufis and the society at large that Sufism was in complete harmony with orthodox Islam. Two of the most important figures in this regard are Abu Bakr Kalabadhi (d. between 990 and 995) and Abu 'Abd al-Rahman Sulami (d. 1021).

Kalabadhi is most famous as the author of the *Kitab al-ta'arruf li-madhab ahl al-tasawwuf,* a widely circulated book that attempts to explain Sufi terminology and beliefs and to show the essential orthodoxy of Sufism. Among Sulami's many works his *Tabaqat al-sufiyya* served as a model for many later Sufi biographical works. He also wrote treaties on Sufi ethics, particularly on the concept of Sufi chivalry (*futuwwa*) and on antinomian trends in Islamic mysticism.

Two of the most important mystical figures of the formative period of Sufism in Asia are Khwaja 'Abd Allah Ansari (d. 1089) and Abu Sa'id ibn Abu al-Khayr (d. 1049). They are both central to the development of organized Sufism but represent two distinct models of leadership. Abu Sa'id is perhaps the most colorful of the famous Iranian Sufis of this period. He studied law, theology, and other religious sciences before adopting a contemplative life, which he pursued under the guidance of a master for fifteen years. Following his teacher's death, Abu Sa'id entered into a flamboyant, public phase of his life during which he ran two Sufi centers, one in his home town of Mehana and the other in Nishapur, the biggest city in Iran at the time. Abu Sa'id was accused by his critics of accepting too much money from devotees, living too luxurious a lifestyle, and having attractive young men dance and sing in public. Abu Sa'id is one of the key figures in the earliest evolution of successful Sufi orders and centers.

Khwaja 'Abd Allah Ansari is a Sufi of a very different kind, though comparable in importance to Abu Sa'id. Ansari was a committed polemicist belonging to an important school of Sunni Muslim legal thought. His personal and professional fortunes changed as the religious pendulum swung in different directions. It was toward the end of his life, after he had gone blind and at the urging of his disciples, that Ansari dictated his main works, including the very popular *Kitab manazil al-sa'irin,* a brief didactic text providing an itinerary for the soul's journey to God. His other important works include a mystical treatise emphasizing the importance of love in the journey toward God.

The period immediately before and after the Mongol invasion of Iran in the early thirteenth century was perhaps the single most vibrant phase in the history of Iranian Sufism. The social and political instability of the era combined with a high degree of intellectual vitality to produce major thinkers and teachers. Undoubtedly the most famous of these is the Andalusian emigré Muhyi al-din Ibn al-'Arabi (d. 1240). Ibn al-'Arabi's mystical and philosophical ideas reshaped much of Sufi thought and, to a large extent, fashioned the language if not always the content of Sufi discussions since his time. His central philosophical idea was that the universe is the physical manifestation of God; as such, it is not entirely distinct from him but represents one of his aspects, the other being his uniqueness. This doctrine came to be known as "Oneness of Being" (*wahdat al-wujud*). The doctrine that God is utterly separate from creation is a central belief of many Muslims for whom Ibn al-'Arabi's teachings represent an unorthodox position. Over the two centuries after his death a modified version of the theory of "Oneness of Being" emerged; named "Oneness of Witnessing," it attempted to reconcile the philosophical aspects of Ibn al-'Arabi's philosophy with common Muslim theological beliefs.

It was in the fourteenth and fifteenth centuries that Islamic mystical ideas and institutions consolidated their positions in South and Central Asia, although mystical thought and Sufi individuals had been common in these regions since the eleventh century. The Naqshbandi Sufi order started in present-day Uzbekistan. Its eponymous founder, Baha' al-din Naqshband (d. 1389), had a tremendous impact on the development of Islam all across Central and inner Asia, as well as in South Asia and the Ottoman Empire. It remains one of the most influential Sufi orders in modern times and is involved in global Muslim debates over the place of religion in modern society.

Of similar importance is the Chishti order, which derives from Mu'in al-din Sijzi (d. 1235), a Sufi master from Afghanistan who settled in the Indian town of Ajmer. The Chishti order had tremendous importance in popularizing Islam among non-Muslim or nominally Muslim Indians, at the same time as Chishti Sufi masters maintained closed relationships with the ruling elite of South Asia. To this day the Chishti order remains notable for its openness to outsiders, in terms of both its warm welcome into its gatherings and its widespread use of music.

Doctrine and Practices

Sufis are motivated by the desire to have a direct, personal experience of God while they are still alive, rather than waiting until after resurrection when, according to Muslim belief, all human beings will share this experience. The direct experience of God is considered so overwhelming as to be indescribable and can only be spoken about in metaphors, the most commonly used ones being those of falling in love and of being intoxicated with wine. These images are frequently encountered in Sufi literature, particularly in poetry, which tries to express the indescribable joy that Sufis experience through their relationship with God, combined with the heartache of being separated from Him.

The Sufi concept of union with God is expressed in many different ways. The main problem in Sufi philosophical circles is how a mortal human being can unite with the omnipotent, omniscient deity who is unlike us in every way. The union with God is normally called *fana'*, which literally means "destruction" or "annihilation." Sufis believe that in the final stage of an individual's spiritual development, she loses any consciousness of her individual identity and is only aware of the identity of God. In effect, God's identity then replaces the identity of the Sufi.

There is disagreement among Sufis over whether the final spiritual goal of Sufism is to lose one's identity completely in the identity of God or to reach a stage where one's own concerns no longer prevent us from seeing the world in its true nature. A common metaphor for the first approach is to describe the Sufi's individuality as a drop that vanishes into the ocean. It ceases to exist as an identifiable entity but does not actually cease to exist, since it is now part of the vastness of the sea. The latter view, that one sees things more clearly, depicts the human heart (which was the seat of the intellect in medieval Islamic thought) as a mirror that is normally dirty, tarnished by our everyday concerns and petty desires. Through engaging in mystical exercises we effectively polish the mirrors of our hearts and cleanse them to the point that they can accurately reflect the light of God.

The Sufi Path

Sufis believe that average human beings are unable to understand the true nature of spirituality because of their petty concerns. The quest for spiritual understanding in Sufism is seen as a path that each Sufi must travel under the guidance of a teacher or master. This path has many stages, the number and names of which vary according to the school of Sufi thought.

The Sufi path relies on the use of meditation to accomplish its goals. The various Sufi forms of mediation are called *zikr* (or *dhikr*). *Zikr* literally means "repetition," "remembrance," "utterance," or "mentioning" and is a term that appears several times in the Koran. At its most basic level, Sufi *zikr* consists of repeating one of God's names over and over. In Islam, God is believed to have many names that describe some aspect of his nature. Of these, ninety-nine are considered special and are called the "Most Beautiful Names." The purpose of reciting these names is to concentrate wholly on what one is to lose all self-awareness by repeating the *zikr* formula enough times that it permeates one's entire being so that even if the person ceases to actively engage in *zikr*, it continues to be repeated in his heart.

Impact on Literature and the Arts

Islamic mysticism has had a tremendous impact on shaping literature and the arts in Islamic society. This impact has been felt particularly in poetry and music. Mystical poetry has been composed in all languages spoken by Muslims. In Persian in particular, as well as Turkish, Urdu, and other languages that borrow much of their poetics from Persian, mystical poetry has traditionally represented one of the most important literary genres. Its influence has been so pervasive that almost all premodern love poetry in these languages borrows mystical metaphors, with the result that romantic poetry is ambiguous as to whether it refers to God or an earthly beloved. Complementing mystical poetry is a large literature of allegorical romances.

Among the many excellent mystical poets, the most famous is Mawlana Jalal al-din Rumi (d. 1273), whose three-volume didactic poem *The Masnavi* has been translated into all major Western languages. The Mevlevi Sufi order, which derives from him, is distinctive for the importance it gives to music and dance in its *zikr* practices. The Chishti order also makes extensive use of music in its religious exercises. Called *qawwali*, they involve a group of musicians singing religious songs in Persian or one of the languages of South Asia set to a very rhythmic beat. *Qawwali* music has attained global popularity over the past three decades.

See also **Islam; Mysticism: Islamic Mysticism; Sacred Texts: Koran; Sufism.**

BIBLIOGRAPHY

Arberry, A. J. *The Doctrine of the Sufis: Translated from the Arabic of Abu Bakr al-Kalabadhi.* New York: Cambridge University Press, 1935. Reprint, 1979.

Chittick, W. C. *The Sufi Path of Knowledge: Ibn al-'Arabi's Metaphysics of Imagination.* Albany: State University of New York Press, 1989.

Ernst, C. *The Shambala Guide to Sufism.* Boston: Shambala, 1997.

Ghazali, Abu Hamid M. al-. *The Alchemy of Happiness.* Translated by C. Field and E. Daniel. London: Octagon Press, 1980.

Ibn al-Munawwar, M. *The Secrets of God's Mystical Oneness, or, The Spiritual Stations of Shaikh Abu Sa'id.* Translated by John O'Kane. Costa Mesa, Calif.: Mazda, 1992.

Khan, H. Inayat. *The Mysticism of Sound and Music.* Boston: Shambala, 1991.

Lewis, F. D. *Rumi Past and Present, East and West: The Life, Teachings and Poetry of Jalal-Din Rumi.* Boston: Oneworld, 2000.

Lewisohn, L., ed. *The Legacy of Mediaeval Persian Sufism.* London: Khaniqahi Nimatullahi Publications, 1992.

Massignon, L. *The Passion of al-Hallaj.* 4 vols. Translated by Herbert Mason. Princeton, N.J.: Princeton University Press, 1982.

Nizami. *The Story of Layla and Majnun.* Translated by R. Gelpke et al. New Lebanon, N.Y.: Omega Publications, 1997.

Radtke, B., and J. O'Kane. *The Concept of Sainthood in Early Islamic Mysticism.* Richmond, U.K.: Curzon Press, 1996.

Schimmel, A. *Mystical Dimensions of Islam.* Chapel Hill: University of North Carolina Press, 1975.

Jamal J. Elias

KABBALAH

Kabbalah is a Hebrew term that has many meanings. Its basic meaning is derived from the root *QBL*, which means to receive, and thus the term means "reception." In rabbinic literature it stands mainly for a tradition that is received orally. However, beginning in the tenth century, testimonies appeared for a more specific form of Kabbalah: an esoteric tradition deal-ing basically with details related to divine names. In the be-ginning of the thirteenth century this esoteric tradition became more common in written sources, and ultimately imposed it-self as the main meaning of the noun. This widespread use of the term *Kabbalah* as secret knowledge reflects the emergence of a huge, primarily Hebrew literature that claimed to reflect the secret meanings of Judaism. Numerous authors were des-ignated as *Mequbbalim,* kabbalists, and in their books they re-sorted to the term *Kabbalah,* which became a technical term.

During the thirteenth century, kabbalistic writings were composed primarily in Southern France, Spain, and Italy. However, kabbalistic thought radiated immediately to North Africa, Germany, and the land of Israel. In the late decades of the thirteenth century and the early decades of the fourteenth century the classic of kabbalistic literature, the book of the *Zo-har,* was composed in Castile. It is only after the end of the fifteenth century, with the expulsion of the Jews from the Iber-ian Peninsula, that full-fledged centers of Kabbalah were es-tablished also in North Africa, Poland, Iraq, and especially the land of Israel. In the Galilean town of Safed, kabbalistic liter-ature was represented by the different systems of Moses ben Jacob Cordovero (1522–1570) and Isaac ben Solomon Luria (1534–1572) and their followers. A second peak of kabbalis-tic creativity developed in the mid-sixteenth century.

Kabbalistic ideas were connected with messianic aspirations from the very beginning, especially in Abraham ben Samuel Abulafia's (c. 1240–after 1291) ecstatic Kabbalah and in some parts of the *Zohar,* as well as in Safedian Kabbalah. In the sec-ond half of the seventeenth century these ideas produced cer-tain expectations in some Jewish elite figures, which led to a widespread messianic mass-movement around the figure of Shabbetai Tzevi (Sabbatai Zebi; 1626–1676). Drawing antin-omian conclusions from some earlier sources, Tzevi and his prophets and theologians Nathan of Gaza and Abraham Michael Cardozo resorted to a variety of kabbalistic themes in order to foster their messianic beliefs, creating a moment of exhilaration at the beginning of the movement. An ensuing disappointment followed Tzevi's forced conversion to Islam.

Though understood to be an esoteric tradition of Judaism that should not be disclosed to an ordinary Jew and even less to a gentile, at the end of the fifteenth century a gradually ex-panding Christian Kabbalah became visible. It started in Florence with the succinct theses of Giovanni Pico della Mirandola (1463–1494), and then in the more systematic writ-ings of Johannes Reuchlin (1455–1522) and Heinrich Cor-nelius Agrippa of Nettesheim (1486–1535), based on various elements from kabbalistic texts, often read in Latin translations made by converts to Christianity. Characteristic of Christian Kabbalah is the integration of the kabbalistic elements—mostly the theosophical, the hermeneutical, and the magical ones, which were separated from their ritualistic background—within structures of thought found in translations of Greek and Hellenistic material prepared and printed during the Re-naissance, especially by Marsilio Ficino (1433–1499).

European occultism, like various forms of European theos-ophy and Freemasonry, had been substantially influenced by kabbalistic thought, as seems to be the case in early Mor-monism. The most viable mystical mass-movement created by the popularization of Kabbalah is late Polish Hasidism. This eastern European mystical phenomenon remained the most lasting form of the penetration of Kabbalah in the lives of many nonelitist Jews. Under the combined influence of Kabbalah and Hasidism, concepts like *dibbuk* (possession) and *golem,* or *qelippah* (demonic shell), became part of the beliefs of larger segments of Jewish population in the late eighteenth century.

Types of Kabbalah

The vast literature assumed to belong to Kabbalah, composed in many countries and continents over the span of more than eight centuries, is hardly a unified literary corpus. Many capital divergences may be discerned in the thousands of texts and manuscripts, and it is difficult to offer a definition to cover those corpora. Differing speculative models informed the thought, the praxis, and subsequently also the writings of kabbalists and Ha-sidic masters. Far from representing a unified or monochromatic line of thought that allegedly has changed throughout history, the diverse kabbalistic literature focused around at least three ma-jor models: the theosophical-theurgical, the ecstatic, and the mag-ical-talismanic model. The interplay and interactions between these three models characterize many important aspects of kab-balists' concerns and of kabbalistic creativity.

The three models of kabbalistic thought interpreted the ear-lier Jewish corpora, the Bible and rabbinic literatures, in novel ways. However, these new interpretations were only rarely totally new impositions of medieval intellectual constructs on older ma-terial. The kabbalists claimed that their writings constituted the ancient, hidden Jewish tradition, which contains the essence of Judaism. This contention notwithstanding, the conceptual di-vergences between the various kabbalistic schools render such an assertion difficult to support. The impact of ancient and me-dieval material from non-Jewish sources—for example, Hel-lenistic sources of Neoplatonic, hermetical, and Neopythagorean extraction—is significant and discernible in all the brands of Kabbalah. Most of those sources had been mediated, changed, and sometimes enriched by Muslim authors. In addition to the contribution of those speculative types of materials, medieval kabbalists also developed some modes of thought found in ear-lier kinds of Jewish written literature, like the rabbinical and the magical ones, and had access to some forms of earlier mytho-logical themes, which have parallels in ancient times and which might have reached them orally.

Theosophical-theurgical model. The most widespread among the kabbalistic models is the theosophical-theurgical. It deals with the different and complex maps of the divine realm—this area of speculation is described by scholars as theosophy—and with the manner in which human religious deeds impact on it—what may be called theurgy. The belief in the impact of the performance of the commandments, or of transgressions, on supernal realms is crucial for the under-standing of theosophical-theurgical Kabbalah.

Cardinal for this kabbalistic model is the widespread vision of the realm of the divine as constituted of a series of ten divine powers, designated as *sefirot*, originally a term standing for mystical numbers, and sometimes of a higher power, designated as infinity, *'Ein Sof.* This is a dynamic system, in which processes of interaction between those powers and themselves, and between human religious activities and some of those divine powers are quintessential for both the divine and human realms.

'Ein Sof—Infinity

Keter—Crown

Binah—Understanding

Hokhmah—Wisdom

Gevurah—Judgment

Gedulah—Mercy

Tiferet—Splendor

Hod—Majesty

Netzah—Eternity

Yesod—Foundation

Malkhut—Kingship

Some kabbalists assume that the ten *sefirot* constitute the divine essence and that the divine realm is a complex system, while other kabbalists assume that those powers are instruments of the divine activity—creation, revelation, and providence—or vessels mediating the presence of the divine in the extra-divine realms. Fewer kabbalists assume that those *sefirot* constitute the divine presence in the world, while some others assume the presence of those powers within the human soul. The emergence of the system of ten *sefirot* from the higher realm is described in terms of emanation, in Hebrew *'Atzilut,* or expansion, *hitpashetut,* processes that create some form of chain, *shalshelet,* between the highest divine realm and the lower worlds that are produced by the *sefirot.* In the sixteenth-century Lurianic Kabbalah the divine configurations have even more pronounced anthropomorphic natures, called five *partzufim,* which constitute the main structure of the divine realm.

There are three main ways to explain this affinity between the higher and the lower realms: the isomorphic model, the augmentation model, and the ritualistic reconstitution of the shattered divine world—*tiqqun.* The isomorphic model assumes a structural similarity between the lower and the higher realms, as evident in many texts, and a sympathetic affinity between them, which allows the impact of the lower structure on the higher one. The Torah as a symbol is conceived of as a faithful representation of the divine form. By knowing the correspondences between the two structures, the Kabbalist is able to activate the supernal realm by performing religious rites.

The theosophical-theurgical model informed many of the discussions in Spanish Kabbalah and flourished afterward in an even more vigorous manner in sixteenth-century Safed. This model assumes that language reflects the inner structure of the divine realm, the *sefirotic* system of divine powers. Language was conceived also as influencing this structure, by means of theurgical activities that aim to restore the harmony within the divine realm. Either in its cognitive-symbolic role or in its theurgical-operational function, language has been conceived by this type of Kabbalah as hypersemantic. This means that not only is the ordinary sense of language maintained by the kabbalists, but its basic function as part of the kabbalistic enterprise is due to a surplus of meaning, which adds semantic fields to that or those designated by the ordinary meaning. The two aspects, the symbolic, or referential, and the theurgical, or performative, should not be conceived as totally independent: the symbolic role of language, namely the concept that it reflects the structure of the divine powers, is often only one face of the coin, whose other face is the use of the symbolic knowledge in order to amend processes taking place within the divine realm.

The scroll of the Torah is conceived of as a graphic symbol of the divine form, and this is the reason why the Kabbalist assumes that it is not only the semantic message involved in it that is religiously important but also the very contemplation of the manner in which the text has been written. This comprehensive symbol constitutes a faithful representation of the entire divine realm within the lower reality—a sort of icon of God, which incorporates all the details of the divine form.

Another widespread symbol is Jerusalem. This city was conceived of in both Biblical and rabbinic sources as the unifying place between the mundane and the divine realms, an omphalic locus. However, because of its geographical distance from most early kabbalists, Jerusalem was the starting point for the transition to guessing the higher divine reality. Still, even in such a case—when the symbolizing reality existed but was distant and essentially unapproachable—the function of the symbol was essentially the same. Jerusalem was still a functioning city during most of the Middle Ages, but was practically unknown, at least in a direct manner, by those Spanish kabbalists who viewed it primarily as a symbol. Jerusalem as a symbol functions on two levels: as a present, available literary symbol it works because of the special nature of the biblical text understood by the kabbalists as reflecting the divine sphere of existence; and on an ontological level, as a *symbolum in factis,* the temporally absent and geographically remote city represents a spiritual and thus cognitively remote divine power. These two separated symbolic channels were supposed to lead to one and the same divine entity, in most of the cases the last *sefirah, Malkhut.*

However, in order to understand how two so different entities—a name (a linguistic unit), and a city designated by the name—may help someone to reach the invisible divine power, the Kabbalist would assume that there is a profound affinity between a name and the entity it designates, a phenomenon that can be described as a linguistic immanence. Jerusalem is not merely a conventional name for the city—it summarizes by the structure of the word the very essence of the earthly city and at the same time, points to her supernal, divine counterpart. The triad of a name, a geographical entity, and a superessential, divine attribute that governs both the name and the geographical entity, is therefore a rather com-

Dov-Der Haskelevich, a Jewish rabbi who makes predictions based on the Kabbalah, New York City, 2000. Prophecies and other paranormal experiences are characteristic of the ecstatic model of kabbalah, which began to appear in the writings of some authors as early as the late thirteenth century. © COONEY REBECCA/CORBIS SYGMA

mon triad that informs many symbolical processes in Kabbalah. However, given the fact that the starting point of the vast majority of kabbalistic symbols is the biblical texts and their intricacies, whose counterparts on the historical or geographical realms were either no longer existent or geographically very remote and beyond the scope of the more ordinary medieval Kabbalist living in Europe, kabbalistic symbolism should be defined as predominantly inspired by authoritative texts and their religious values and as functioning by means of the linguistic units that constitute these texts. Kabbalistic symbolism is fundamentally a code to interpret the canonical texts, while ignoring forms of realia that are divorced from the contents of the sacred scriptures. Rhetoric about the absorbing nature of the Torah is found in the theosophical Kabbalah, and it provides the nexus between claims of symbolizing everything via the absorbing characteristic of the Torah.

The ecstatic model. Ecstasy is a constant of human religious experience, as the wide dissemination of this type of experience in so many cultures demonstrates. Ecstatic experiences became more and more evident in the written documents of Jewish mysticism in the mid-thirteenth century. It seems that a process of adoption and accommodation of paranormal experiences was characteristic of medieval and early modern

Jewish thought, which addressed with a growing seriousness paranormal experiences as legitimate events. The concomitant spread of the Maggidic experiences in the late fifteenth and sixteenth centuries—particularly in the diary of Joseph ben Ephraim Karo (1488–1575), Isaac Luria's claims of paranormal revelations, and the discussions of cases of possession in the sixteenth century—may bear testimony to the legitimation of their discussion in public rather than to the emergence of new forms of experiences. No movement in Judaism emphasized the importance of the pneumatic experiences, in their most intensive and extreme forms, as did Polish Hasidism.

The ecstatic model is concerned with inner processes taking place between the powers of imagination, the human intellect and the cosmic one, called the agent intellect. This sort of Kabbalah gravitates around the ideal of *devequt,* understood as pointing to moderate or extreme types of union with the Godhead. The other vital parts of this model are devices, or techniques, to ensure the attainment of this ideal. *Hitbodedut,* both as solitude and as mental concentration, *hishtawwut* or equanimity, and linguistic techniques of combining Hebrew letters or contemplating divine names are integral constituents. Paranormal experiences, like revelations and prophecies are congenital to this type of mystical model, and more consonant with it than to the theosophical-theurgical Kabbalah. The coherence between these concepts and practices rests in an organic continuum between strong mystical techniques and extreme mystical experiences, which include experiences of self-transformation.

The ecstatic model was visible at the end of the thirteenth century and the beginning of the fourteenth century in the writings of some kabbalists, like Isaac ben Shemuel of Acre, Nathan ben Sa'adyah, the author of *Sha'arei Tzedeq, Ner 'Elohim,* and *Sefer ha-Tzeruf,* and in the sixteenth century in the writings of Yehudah Albotini, Moshe Cordovero (1522–1570), and Hayyim ben Joseph Vital (1542 or 1543–1620). Many of the concepts were disseminated by means of the widespread writings of Cordovero's disciples, though some folios of Abraham Abulafia's Kabbalah were in print as early as 1556. Some of Abulafia's manuscripts were known in the eighteenth century in eastern Europe by both Hasidim and Mitnaggedim.

This model, though formulated in a systematic way by a Spanish Kabbalist, was not accepted by the Spanish kabbalists in the Iberian Peninsula. In Safed, however, Cordovero and his students were positively predisposed toward this type of mysticism. He described the major revelation concerning the messianic mission of Tzevi as the result of a path reminiscent of ecstatic Kabbalah. Abulafia's influence may also be discerned in Hasidism.

The ecstatic approach assumes that the Kabbalist can use language and the canonical texts in order to induce a mystical experience by means of manipulations of elements of language together with other components of the various mystical techniques. This approach is much less concerned with divine inner structures, focusing as it does on the restructuring of the human psyche in order to prepare it for the encounter with the divine. The ecstatic theory of language is less mimetic, and thus less symbolic and theurgic, than the view espoused by the theosophical Kabbalah. While the theosophical-theurgical approach to language assumes the paramount importance of information that is either absorbed by the human mind or transmitted by the soul to the divine, in many cases the ecstatic view of language encourages the effacement of knowledge as part of the opening toward the divine. According to ecstatic Kabbalah, language helps cleanse someone's consciousness by breaking, using a mystical technique, the words of the sacred scripture into nonsemantic units. While the theosophical Kabbalah emphasizes the given, structured aspects of language as manifested in the canonical writings, in ecstatic Kabbalah the deconstruction of the canonical texts, and of ordinary language as well, is an important mystical tool for restructuring the human psyche.

Significant for this model is the antinomian feature of the techniques, which means that according to the various descriptions of his paths the rabbinic rites are not essential for achieving the supreme religious experience. Prophecy is the main purpose of Abulafia's entire kabbalistic project, and he conceived himself to be a prophet. The recurrence, at least in principle, of this topic is visible in a Kabbalist who was also well acquainted with the theosophical-theurgical Kabbalah. Isaac Luria, like his teacher Rabbi Nathan, did not have

prophetic claims; his vision of prophecy is quite similar to Abulafia's. The linguistic components of these techniques are of paramount importance. Also conspicuous are the strong individualistic proclivities of this kind of mysticism and the deep influence of philosophy, especially Aristotelianism in the case of Abulafia, and Neoplatonism in the case of his followers. The existence of various elements of the ecstatic model is easily detectable in Neoplatonic philosophy and in Spanish Kabbalah.

The magical-talismanic model. While the two models of Kabbalah surveyed above are represented in distinct kabbalistic literatures, the magical-talismanic model is found in a variety of writings belonging to those models, and only rarely constitutes a literature of its own. Jewish magic is an old lore, having a variety of forms already in late antiquity. Some parts of it survived in Hebrew and Aramaic texts, some had an impact on Hellenistic magic. No doubt early kabbalists were acquainted with Jewish magical texts and appropriated some of its elements, while others criticized them. From the beginning of the fourteenth century, a distinction between two types of Kabbalah gradually came to the fore: Speculative Kabbalah (*Qabbalah 'Iyyunit*) and Practical Kabbalah (*Qabbalah Ma'asit*). In the fifteenth century this distinction appeared several times and in the sixteenth century it became a standard tool for differentiating various types of Kabbalah. The emergence of this distinction may have something to do with the distinction between speculative and practical philosophy, as formulated by Moses ben Maimon (1135–1204).

The greater interest in magical Kabbalah became evident toward the end of the fifteenth century in the writings of both the Spanish and the Italian kabbalists. The extent of the magical influence on Jewish mysticism is an issue that still waits for detailed treatment. There can be no doubt as to the importance of various forms of magic within some of the important forms of Jewish mysticism, starting with the *Heikhalot* literature. The magical view of the Hebrew language is crucial for most of the forms of magic in Judaism and remained influential in numerous texts, especially in Kabbalah. In the Middle Ages under the influence of philosophical views found among the Arabs, an additional explanation appeared, contending that by cleaving to the spiritual celestial source that rules this world—the universal soul—the mystic, or the philosopher, is able to channel the events in the sublunar world. The operation is a spiritual one and takes place in the supernal world. This understanding of magic uses Neoplatonic elements.

In ancient Hellenistic magic, and in Arabic and Jewish medieval magic, the dominant view asserted is that it is possible to attract downward the spiritual forces of the celestial bodies. These spiritual forces—named *pneumata* in Greek, *Ruhaniyyat* in Arabic, and *Ruhaniyyut* in Hebrew—were conceived as being able to be attracted and captured by special types of objects and rituals, whose natures are consonant to features of corresponding celestial bodies.

In fifteenth-century Kabbalah the use of the Hebrew language as a technique to draw down the spiritual force became explicit, and it was increasingly assumed that each and every *sefirah* had a spiritual force of its own. Thus, the astrological structure of this model was projected onto the "higher" theosophical structure, thereby diminishing the potential critiques that a strong astrological stand could provoke. While not totally obliterating the astral meaning of the term *ruhaniyyut*, kabbalists attributed to the *sefirotic* realm a structure, which they adopted from astrological thought: on high, a distinction should be made between the more material and the spiritual aspects of reality. It is possible to detect some translations of features of the astral bodies to the corresponding divine powers, the *sefirot*.

While the Arab astrologists differentiated between *haikhalat* and *ruhaniyyat*, the kabbalists introduced this distinction in the realm of the intradivine: the *sefirot* have an external aspect, the vessels named *kelim* and the more inner component, the spirituality of each *sefirah*. Though this division also served other theological goals, the terms used by Yohanan Alemanno (1433–c. 1504) and Moses Cordovero in this context betray their sources. Especially important is the emergence of the term *ruhaniyyot ha-Sefirot*, the spiritual forces of the *sefirot*. This phrase still maintains the concept of a multiplicity in the spiritual world: each *sefirah* possesses a distinct inner power that reflects the specific quality of the respective divine power. This "elevation" of the term *ruhaniyyutm* to the rank of divine realm did not supercede the magical use of the term in the writings of those kabbalists who adopted this projection.

While accepted by some kabbalists, the magical-talismanic model was changed in two major points: the theological, actually the theosophical plane, supplanted the celestial-astrological one, whereas the magical practices were substituted, to a great degree, by the Jewish rites and especially by the ritualistic use of the Hebrew language in prayer and in study. This pivotal change took place in a conspicuous way in the writings of Alemanno, S. Alqabetz, and Cordovero. It was part of an attempt to offer an explanation of the efficacy of the commandments in addition to, or different from, the more common theurgical rationales recurrent in the kabbalistic literature.

In adopting the Jewish ritual for the sake of magical attainments, or by interpreting these rites as magically effective, the more difficult philosophical aspects of magic, as an operation performed by acts that are not part of regular behavior, were attenuated to a great extent. The material and spiritual attainments are drawn down by fulfilling the divine will, and not by an attempt to short-circuit the order of nature, or by forcing the divine will. In many cases the term *ruhaniyyut* preserves overtones from its magical sources, while in many other instances, both in Cordoverian Kabbalah and Hasidism, this term designates the ideal, spiritual realm, without maintaining any of the astral-magical meanings.

The essence of Kabbalah involves both the theosophical core, the nature of the *sefirot* and their luminous manifestations (the theoretical Kabbalah), and the experimental factor, the visualization of the colors, which is the essential component of the mystical intention during prayer. As in descriptions stemming from Nahmanides's (1194–c. 1270) school,

where the supernal realm and the commandments are mentioned altogether, Kabbalah is presented as a synthesis between theosophical and theurgical elements. The culmination of the kabbalistic lore and practice, as envisioned in one of the most influential treatises in its history, assumes that a mystical element is essential, in addition to the knowledge of the map of the divine world.

The magical brand of Kabbalah remained part and parcel of this lore. Nevertheless there are important cases in which kabbalists rejected, or minimized, the importance of the magical aspects of their lore. Astral magic is paramount in the writings of Alemanno and of Cordovero. The astral spiritualities were projected in the intradivine realm and were presented using magical categories. The basic technique in this type of magic is the drawing down of divine powers, or the overflow of the *sefirot*, in accordance with the needs of the magician.

Cordovero was aware of the affinity of his conception to that of astral magic and considered the knowledge of the preparation of amulets or talismans as a revealed gnosis, which serves as an introduction to the knowledge of the Kabbalah. His reluctance to acknowledge the conspicuous affinity of his Kabbalah with a certain type of magic is understandable but it does not detract from the profound similarity and the historical filiation of his Kabbalah to magic. Like Alemanno, Cordovero did not intend to disrupt the natural order by appealing to demonic forces, which could destroy the natural order. Instead he proposed a type of activity that complemented natural activity by adding a dimension of praxis based on laws already in existence but hidden from the eyes of the uninformed. The kabbalistic activity was supernatural not because it intruded into the regular course of events but because its orderliness was superior.

According to other texts, inducing the supernal influx upon the righteous by the combination of letters of the divine names is similar to causing the descent of the overflow of the *sefirot* by employing the color technique. Whereas the names can be conceived as static talismans, there are instances in which there is a dynamic process that induces the spiritual force from above, and it is a dynamic descent that is incited by a combination of letters. The talismanic implications of Abulafia's techniques were enhanced by some of his disciples, who vigorously introduced the talismanic view of language. Thereby, the human body was conceived as the locus where the divine influx is received and becomes a vessel of the descending influx. It is the mystical-magical technique that may induce an experience of the divine, present in and working through the human body.

A certain shift from the theurgical ideal toward a more magical view, represented by the ideal of drawing upon someone the divine efflux, is evident. As in the case of the acculturation of the hermetic type of magic into the Jewish ritual, the Kabbalist performing the practice of concentration and pronunciation of the combinations of letters is presented as a righteous—that is, as an ideal—religious type. Though not part of the regular ritual, the above technique is nevertheless considered to be a licit practice as it is attributed to an ancient source, and the practitioner is described as a righteous man.

An important development taking place in Cordovero's thought that had deep repercussions later is the vision of the human righteous, the *Tzaddiq,* as functioning in a manner reminiscent of the ninth *sefirah, Yessod,* transmitting the influx it receives from the higher to the lower parts of the *sefirotic* realms. The influx is received from the *sefirotic* realm, to which the righteous cleaves, and is transmitted then to others.

In the magical model the world depends upon the higher powers, the spiritual force attracted on the low by the very body of the *Tzaddiqim* and their religious acts as well as the secrets of the Torah. It is a magical universe that is described by Cordovero: the *Tzaddiq* is not only able to change the earthly realm but is also conceived as governing the celestial world. By the dint of the divine soul that dwells in man, the righteous rules over the world because of his cleaving to the world of emanation. This expansion of divine influx depends on the religious behavior, which is instrumental in attracting the "light of the world of emanation" onto all the worlds. Cordovero distinguishes between this type of influence on the world—for him a type of natural magic similar to the view of his Renaissance contemporaries in Italy—which is drastically different from a more radical form of Jewish magic that operates by the virtue of the divine names, and which should be avoided as much as possible.

The drawing down consists of two stages: the intradivine, from the peak to the last *sefirah, Malkhut,* a stage that can be designated as a theurgical act, and drawing the influx from the last *sefirah* toward the lower entities, which can be called magic. What is significant is the fact that a ritualistic term and its performance as a ritual act are involved in the process of attracting spirituality downward. The use of the term *hamshakhah* reflects a magical aspect, which may be a return to a more ancient layer of thought. Cordovero inherited a tradition from a long series of kabbalists who connected two topics: the concept and practice of blessing, *berakhah,* and the drawing down, *hamshakhah.*

Differences and Overlaps

The three models differ insofar as their objectives: the ecstatic one is concerned with the changes a certain mystical technique may induce in humans; the talismanic model emphasizes the effects someone's ritualistic linguistic acts may have on the external world, while the theosophical-theurgical model is concerned with inducing harmony within the divine realm. These models have been only rarely exposed as completely separate approaches. The ecstatic model was sometimes combined with the talismanic. The theurgical operation, which ensures the continuing pulsation of energy within the divine realm, has sometimes been combined with the magical or talismanic approaches, and drawing the emanation from the higher *sefirot* to the lower ones was followed by causing the descent of this emanation into the extra-divine world. A strongly anthropocentric attitude, the talismanic model envisages the enhancing of the spiritual and material well-being of an individual, and often of the whole religious group, as an important core of religion.

The theosophical-theurgical and the talismanic models assume that, in addition to the semantic aspect of the sacred text, and of Hebrew language in general, there is an energetic aspect that is also effective, either by affecting the supernal world or, respectively, by attracting it downward. In ecstatic Kabbalah these two aspects are sometimes present but play a relatively marginal role. It recognizes the magical powers of language, though it conceives them as exercising an influence on a lower, inferior level of existence, when compared to the cathartic role language plays in purifying the soul, or the intellect, in order to prepare them for the reception of the supernal effluvia. The talismanic model as exemplified by linguistic magic is a synthesis between the particularistic tendency, characteristic of the theurgical model and the more universalistic tendency of the hermetic sources. Focused on Hebrew words as major tools, the linguistic talismanics and sometimes the ecstatic kabbalists assume that not only Hebrew words, but also Hebrew letters, and especially, what can be called according to them "Hebrew" sounds or phonemes, may serve as talismans. The three models had an impact on the particular understanding of many central issues like the nature of the Messiah, metempsychosis, and cosmic cycles, which have been reinterpreted in accordance to each of these models' logic.

Impact of Kabbalah

Due to the dissemination of Christian Kabbalah, and the impact of modern scholarship of Kabbalah represented in the seminal studies of Gershom Scholem (1897–1982), elements of kabbalistic thought have been integrated in a variety of modern intellectual and literary realms. Well-known figures in European thought had been attracted to Kabbalah, like the seventeenth-century Cambridge Neoplatonists, Gottfried Wilhelm Leibniz (1646–1716), Emanuel Swedenborg (1688–1772), Friedrich Wilhelm Joseph von Schelling (1775–1854), and Salomon Maimon (1753–1800).

In literature Kabbalah influenced writers like William Blake (1757–1827), Franz Kafka (1883–1924), Ivan Gol, Paul Celan (Paul Antschel; 1920–1991), Jorge Luis Borges (1899–1986), Isaac Bashevis Singer (1904–1991), Umberto Eco (b. 1932), and, on the Israeli scene, Shmuel Yosef Agnon (1888–1970), David Shahar (1926–1997), and Uri Tzvi Greenberg, as well as some literary criticism and philosophy of text by Maurice Blanchot (1907–2003), Harold Bloom (b. 1930), Jacques Derrida (b. 1930), George Steiner (b. 1929), and Eco. In modern philosophy kabbalistic elements are conspicuous in the speculative systems of Franz Rosenzweig (1886–1929), Abraham Isaac Kook (1865–1935), Joseph Baer Soloveitchik, Abraham Joshua Heschel (1907–1972), and Emmanuel Levinas (1906–1995).

A revival of interest in Kabbalah was visible at the turn of the twenty-first century in a return of role of kabbalists in some segments of Israeli society, and the resort to kabbalistic ways of thought used by some New Age thinkers in the United States, like Rabbi Zalman Schechter. Even orthodox kabbalists, active basically only in Israel, are inclined now to allow a previously unthinkable large-scale dissemination of this lore in large audiences, by a new politics of printing and teaching.

See also **Christianity; Judaism; Magic; Religion.**

BIBLIOGRAPHY

Dan, Joseph. *Jewish Mysticism.* Northvale, N.J.: Aronson, 1998–1999.

Giller, Pinchas. *Reading the Zohar.* New York: Oxford University Press, 2001.

Ginsburg, Elliot. *The Sabbath in the Classical Kabbalah.* Albany: State University of New York Press, 1989.

Green, Arthur, ed. *Jewish Spirituality.* New York: Crossroad, 1986–1987.

Halamish, Mosheh. *An Introduction to the Kabbalah.* Translated by Ruth Bar-Ilan and Ora Wiskind-Elper. Albany: State University of New York Press, 1999.

Idel, Moshe. *Absorbing Perfections: Kabbalah and Interpretation.* New Haven, Conn.: Yale University Press, 2002.

———. *Hasidism: Between Ecstasy and Magic.* Albany: State University of New York Press, 1995.

———. *Kabbalah: New Perspectives.* New Haven, Conn.: Yale University Press, 1988.

———. *Messianic Mystics.* New Haven, Conn.: Yale University Press, 1998.

———. *The Mystical Experience in Abraham Abulafia.* Albany: State University of New York Press, 1988.

Liebes, Yehuda. *Studies in Jewish Myth and Jewish Messianism.* Translated by Batya Stein. Albany: State University of New York Press, 1993.

———. *Studies in the Zohar.* Translated by Arnold Schwartz. Albany: State University of New York Press, 1993.

Ruderman, David. *Kabbalah, Magic, and Science: The Cultural Universe of a Sixteenth-Century Jewish Physician.* Cambridge, Mass., and London: Harvard University Press, 1988.

Scholem, Gershom. *Kabbalah.* New York: Quadrangle, 1974.

———. *Major Trends in Jewish Mysticism.* New York: Schocken, 1961.

———. *On the Kabbalah and Its Symbolism.* Translated by Ralph Manheim. New York: Schocken, 1965.

———. *On the Mystical Shape of the Godhead.* Translated by Joachim Neugroschel. New York: Schocken, 1991.

———. *Origins of the Kabbalah.* Translated by Allan Arkush. Princeton, N.J.: Princeton University Press, 1987.

———. *Sabbatai Sevi: The Mystical Messiah, 1626–1676.* Princeton, N.J.: Princeton University Press, 1973.

Tishby, Isaiah, and Fischel Lachower. *The Wisdom of the Zohar.* 3 vols. Translated by David Goldstein. Oxford and New York: Oxford University Press, 1989. An anthology of texts arranged and rendered into Hebrew by Lachower and Tishby, with introductions and explanations by Tishby.

Wolfson, Elliot R. *Abraham Abulafia—Kabbalist and Prophet: Hermeneutics, Theosophy, and Theurgy.* Los Angeles: Cherub, 2000.

———. *Along the Path.* Albany: State University of New York Press, 1995.

———. *Circle in the Square.* Albany: State University of New York Press, 1995.

———. *Through a Speculum That Shines.* Princeton, N.J.: Princeton University Press, 1994.

Moshe Idel

MYSTICISM IN AFRICAN THOUGHT

The term *mysticism* typically denotes a complex of beliefs and practices related to the personal experience of the di-

---

> Mysticism in indigenous African thought is:
>
> distinct from conceptions of mysticism in Judaism, Christianity, and Islam;
>
> characterized by a social, worldly orientation;
>
> united with indigenous religious practices;
>
> primarily focused on interaction with spirits, rather than the supreme God;
>
> preserved in and transmitted through oral traditions; and
>
> not aimed at unification with the divine through eradication of or purification of the self.

---

vine. Much, although not all, mystical thought and practice derives from or draws upon formal religious doctrines, emphasizing reflective, introspective, and meditative practices as the keys to cultivating perception and awareness that will ultimately lead to knowledge of and communion with the divine.

When one turns to mysticism in African thought, and specifically to the mystical tenets extant in indigenous religious beliefs and practices, the common Western definition is necessarily altered. *Mysticism* continues to describe the realm of interaction between humanity and the divine or supernatural, but owing to the prevailing nature of indigenous African belief systems, the orientation and manifestations of mystical practices are of a different character. The orientation is social and utilitarian, and the manifestations occur within the structure of indigenous rites; mystical practices aim to fulfill needs in society, and they do not exist as a separate body of practices. This reflects the general African cosmology and understanding of arenas of interaction between humanity and the divine or supernatural.

Cosmology and Interaction

African cosmology, in general, posits three categories of agents: God, spirits, and man. A supreme God, who is the creator of the universe and all that is in it, is acknowledged and revered in indigenous practices, through libations, praises, and proverbs. Although knowledge of his existence is present, the majority of indigenous beliefs and rites do not focus on God, nor do they aim to bring the individual closer to him. God is an acknowledged reality, but a distant, somewhat nebulous one.

In addition to God, there exist other agents, typically referred to as spirits. These spirits are part of the creation, as are humans, but they possess certain powers and abilities. They interact with human beings and have agency in the world.

Man, the third category, is created by God and coexists with the spirits in the world. Human orientation in the world is social, and action to uphold social ties and foster social cohesion is held in high regard and even seen as the primary goal of life. Humans can, through reciprocal affiliation with and worship of spirits, gain access to their power and channel that power for positive or negative ends.

Man does not, in mystical and spiritual endeavors, aim solely to gain knowledge of the supreme creator God through contemplation and negation of worldly existence and self; rather, being socially oriented, a person seeks to obtain utilitarian agency that will foster change in the world. Mystical and spiritual practices in indigenous African traditions do not, therefore, center on the individual in isolation; they maintain social orientation and purpose. The goal of the mystical endeavor is not to obliterate individual consciousness or physicality; it is rather to garner knowledge and power that can be used in the human world.

Individuals and spirits interact with each other. Laypeople may have encounters with spirits, and they may also seek guidance and physical assistance from them. Individuals who are initiated in specific indigenous traditions may mediate the latter form of interaction; individuals can experience the divine or supernatural to only a certain extent without an intermediary. Furthermore, the role of the intermediary is of central importance because that experience alone is not the end; the goal is to acquire and use knowledge to bring about change in human society. In many cases, these practitioners, commonly referred to as priests, are "chosen" by the spirits, as evidenced in physical or spiritual crises. Such crises are seen as signs that the individual should be initiated into the service of a particular spirit. Initiation is characterized by intensive ritualistic, spiritual, physical, and intellectual training, which is carried out in seclusion, under the supervision of an elder priest. Mystical traditions and knowledge, preserved and transmitted orally, are passed from the priest to the initiate and onward.

Once initiated, priests and other practitioners interact with and seek assistance from the spirits for themselves and others. One common method is the possession trance, typically induced through music and dance or consumption of herbs or intoxicants, in which the spirit enters the priest's body and communicates information to those present. Another common form of interaction is divination, the best-known example being the complex Ifa system among the Yoruba of Nigeria.

Indigenous Religions Compared with Christianity and Islam

The impact of Christianity and Islam on the African continent has been and continues to be profound. In most places, indigenous religious and practices coexist with, and may form new syncretic traditions with, Christianity and Islam. This results, increasingly, in the overlap and combination of mystical practices and trends. Many of these manifestations, readily observable today, take on a form that departs from the "pure" manifestation of African mysticism and is more in line with

the common understanding of mysticism. Nevertheless, in trying to isolate mysticism in indigenous African thought, it becomes apparent that African mysticism is of a different variety than mysticism in Christianity and Islam. To begin with, whereas mysticism in Christianity and Islam primarily focuses on knowledge and communion with the divine, African mysticism focuses on interaction with spirits. Mysticism in Christianity and Islam involves practices such as meditation and asceticism that require the individual to withdraw from the physical world in order to undergo a subjective experience of the divine and the resultant transformation. African mysticism retains a social, worldly focus, deriving its purpose and value from its functionality in effecting change in the society, rather than in the individual only. Christianity and Islam are based on prophetic traditions and written texts. Their respective mystical practices and beliefs have evolved as specific "paths" within the larger traditions, sometimes differing drastically from mainstream practice. These paths have been documented in written form and have developed into types of theology. Indigenous African mysticism is derived from oral traditions that have been evolving over many millennia. In most cases, these traditions are not contained in formal texts and are not associated with prophetic traditions. Mystical practices and beliefs are integrated into the larger, dynamic belief structure, which has no prophetic ideal.

See also **Personhood in African Thought; Religion: Africa; Religion: African Diaspora.**

BIBLIOGRAPHY

Gray, John. *Ashe, Traditional Religion and Healing in Sub-Saharan Africa and the Diaspora: A Classified International Bibliography.* New York: Greenwood, 1989.

Idowu, E. Bolaji. *African Traditional Religion: A Definition.* London: S. C. M. Press, 1973.

Mbiti, John. S. *African Religions and Philosophy.* Oxford and Portsmouth, N. H.: Heinemann, 1988.

———. *Introduction to African Religion.* Oxford and Portsmouth, N. H.: Heinemann, 1991.

Ray, Benjamin C. *African Religions: Symbol, Ritual, and Community.* Englewood Cliffs, N. J.: Prentice Hall, 1976.

Jerusha T. Lamptey

MYTH. The study of myth across the disciplines is united by the questions asked. The main questions are those of origin, function, and subject matter. *Origin* in this context means why and how myth arises; *function,* why and how myth persists. The answer to the why of origin and function is usually a need, which myth arises to fulfill and persists by continuing to fulfill. What that need is varies from theory to theory. *Subject matter* here means the referent of myth. Some theories read myth literally, so that the referent is the apparent one, such as gods. Other theories read myth symbolically, and the symbolized referent can be anything.

For example, a myth told by the Trobriand Islanders of Melanesia, as described by Polish-born anthropologist Bronislaw Malinowski (1884–1942) in *Myth in Primitive Society* (1926), says that the world "was originally peopled from underground. Humanity had there led an existence similar in all respects to the present life on earth. Underground, men were organized in villages, clans, districts; they had distinctions of rank, they knew privileges and had claims, they owned property, and were versed in magic lore. One day humans came to the surface and established themselves, bringing with them all their culture to continue it upon this earth."

According to Malinowski, whose theory will be considered in detail below, this myth was devised to secure support for the social divisions, ranks, and rights that were still to be found among the Trobrianders. Because no people will readily tolerate impositions, this myth was intended to provide a limited kind of justification. It does not assert that the impositions are deserved, but rather that they are traditional and go back even to the time before the proto-Trobrianders emerged from underground. The need being fulfilled is on the part of society itself, not on the part of individuals. Malinowski reads the myth literally: the subject matter is the social life of the Trobriand Islanders, both while underground and once above ground.

It is commonly said that theories of the nineteenth century focused on the question of origin and that theories of the twentieth century have focused on the questions of function and subject matter. But this characterization confuses historical origin with recurrent origin. Theories that profess to provide the origin of myth claim to know not where and when myth first arose but why and how myth arises wherever and whenever it does. The issue of recurrent origin was as popular with twentieth-century theorists as with nineteenth-century ones, and interest in function and subject matter was as common to nineteenth-century theorists as to twentieth-century ones.

Disciplines differ in their definitions of myth. Not all even assume that myth is a story. For political scientists, for example, myth can be a credo or an ideology, which may be illustrated by stories but is not rooted in them. Even when myth is assumed to be a story, disciplines differ over the contents. For folklorists, myth is about the creation of the world. In the Bible, only the two creation stories (Genesis 1 and 2), the Garden of Eden story (Genesis 3), and the Noah story (Genesis 6–9) would thereby qualify as myths. All other stories would instead constitute either legends or folktales. For theories drawn from religious studies, the main characters in myth must be gods or near-gods, such as heroes. Theories from anthropology, psychology, and sociology tend to allow for secular as well as religious myths.

Myth and Science

In the West, the ancient challenge to myth was on ethical grounds: Plato (c. 428–348 or 347 B.C.E.) bemoaned Homeric myths for presenting the gods as practitioners of immoral behavior. The chief modern challenge to myth has come from science.

One form of the modern challenge to myth has been to the scientific credibility of myth. Did creation really occur in a mere six days, as the first of two creation stories in Genesis (1:1–2:4a) claims? Was there really a worldwide flood? The most unrepentant defense against this challenge has been to claim that the biblical account is correct, for, after all, the Pentateuch was revealed to Moses by God. This position, known as *creationism*, assumes varying forms, ranging, for example, from taking the days of creation to mean exactly six days to taking them to mean "ages." At the same time, creationists of all stripes tout their views as scientific *as well as* religious, and they enlist scientific evidence to refute "pseudoscientific" rivals such as evolution.

A much tamer defense against the challenge of modern science has been to reconcile myth with that science. Here elements at odds with modern science are either removed or, more cleverly, reinterpreted as in fact scientific. There might not have been a Noah who was single-handedly able to gather up all living species and to keep them alive in a wooden boat sturdy enough to withstand the strongest seas that ever arose, but a worldwide flood did occur. What thus remains in myth is true because it is scientific—modern scientific.

By far the most common response to the challenge of science has been to abandon myth for science. Here myth is taken as an explanation of its own kind, not a scientific explanation in mythic guise. The issue is therefore not the scientific credibility of myth but the compatibility of myth with science. Myth, here a part of religion, is considered to be the "primitive" counterpart to science, which is assumed to be exclusively modern. Because moderns by definition accept science, they cannot also have myth, and the phrase *modern myth* is self-contradictory. Myth is a victim of the process of secularization that constitutes modernity.

The pioneering English anthropologist E. B. Tylor (1832–1917) remains the classic exponent of the view that myth and science are at odds. Tylor subsumes myth under religion and in turn subsumes both religion and science under philosophy. Primitive philosophy is identical with primitive religion. There is no primitive science. Modern philosophy, by contrast, is divided into religion and science. Primitive religion is the primitive counterpart to science because both are explanations of the physical world. The religious explanation is personalistic, the scientific one impersonal. The explanations are incompatible because both are *direct* explanations of the *same* events. Gods operate not behind or through impersonal forces but in place of them. One cannot, then, stack the religious account atop the scientific account.

Modern religion has surrendered the explanation of the world to science and has instead become a combination of metaphysics and ethics, neither of which is present in primitive religion. One now reads the Bible for not for the story of creation but for the Ten Commandments, just as for Plato a bowdlerized Homer (fl. 9th or 8th century B.C.E.) would enable one to do. This irenic position is like that of the American evolutionary biologist Stephen Jay Gould (1941–2002). Yet for Tylor, myths are too closely tied to gods as agents in the world to permit any transformation like that of the rest of religion. Where, then, there is "modern religion," albeit religion shorn of its prime role as explanation, there are no modern myths.

In pitting myth against science, as in pitting religion qua explanation against science, Tylor epitomizes the nineteenth-century view of myth. In the twentieth century, the trend was to reconcile myth as well as religion with science, so that moderns can retain myth as well as religion.

Closest to Tylor stands J. G. Frazer (1854–1941), the Scottish classicist and fellow pioneering anthropologist. For Frazer, as for Tylor, myth is part of primitive religion; primitive religion is part of philosophy, itself universal; and primitive religion is the counterpart to natural science, itself entirely modern. Primitive religion and science are, as for Tylor, mutually exclusive. But where for Tylor primitive religion, including myth, functions as the counterpart to scientific *theory*, for Frazer it functions even more as the counterpart to *applied* science, or technology. Where for Tylor primitive religion, including myth, serves to *explain* events in the physical world, for Frazer it serves even more to *effect* events, above all the growth of crops. Where Tylor treats myth as an autonomous text, Frazer ties myth to ritual, which enacts it.

The biggest difficulty for Tylor's and Frazer's view of myth as the primitive counterpart to science is that it conspicuously fails to account for the retention of myth in the wake of science. If myth functions to do no more than science, why is it still around?

Reacting against the views of Tylor and Frazer and other members of what he imprecisely calls "the English school of anthropology," the French philosopher and armchair anthropologist Lucien Lévy-Bruhl (1857–1939) insisted on a much wider divide between myth and science. Where for Tylor and Frazer "primitives" think like moderns, just less rigorously, for Lévy-Bruhl primitives think differently from moderns. Where for Tylor and Frazer primitive thinking is logical, just erroneous, for Lévy-Bruhl primitive thinking is plainly nonlogical.

According to Lévy-Bruhl, primitives believe that all phenomena are part of a sacred, or "mystic," realm pervading the natural one. Phenomena become one another yet remain what they are. The Bororo of Brazil deem themselves red araras, or parakeets, yet still human beings. Lévy-Bruhl calls this belief "prelogical" because it violates the law of noncontradiction: the notion that something can simultaneously be both itself and something else.

For Lévy-Bruhl, as for Tylor and Frazer, myth is part of religion, religion is primitive, and moderns have science rather than religion. But where Tylor and Frazer subsume both religion and science under philosophy, Lévy-Bruhl associates philosophy with thinking *freed* from mystical identification with the world. Primitive thinking is nonphilosophical because it is not detached from the world. Primitives have a whole mentality of their own, one evinced in their myths.

One reaction to Lévy-Bruhl was to accept his separation of myth from philosophy but not his characterization of myth as pre-philosophical or pre-scientific. The key figure here was Malinowski. Invoking Frazer, Malinowski argues that primitives are too busy scurrying to survive in the world to have the luxury of reflecting on it. Where for Frazer primitives use myth *in place of*

science, for Malinowski primitives use myth as a *fallback* to science. Primitives possess not just the counterpart to science but science itself. Where science stops, they turn to magic. Where magic stops, they turn to myth—not to secure further control over the world, as Frazer would assume, but to reconcile themselves to aspects of the world that cannot be controlled, such as natural catastrophes, illness, aging, and death. Myth explains how, say, illness arose—a god or a human brought it about—but primitive science and magic try to do something about it. By contrast, myth says that nothing can be done about it.

Reacting both against Malinowski's view of primitives as practical rather than intellectual and against Lévy-Bruhl's view of primitives as mystical rather than intellectual, the French anthropologist Claude Lévi-Strauss (b. 1908) has boldly sought to revive an intellectualist view of primitives and of myth. At first glance, Lévi-Strauss seems a sheer throwback to Tylor. Yet in fact Lévi-Strauss is severely critical of Tylor, for whom primitives concoct myth rather than science because they think less critically than moderns. For Lévi-Strauss, primitives create myth because they think differently from moderns—but, contrary to Lévy-Bruhl, still think and still think rigorously. For both, myth is the epitome of primitive thinking.

Where for Tylor primitive thinking is personalistic and modern thinking impersonal, for Lévi-Strauss primitive thinking is concrete and modern thinking abstract. Primitive thinking focuses on the observable, sensible aspects of phenomena rather than, like modern thinking, on the unobservable, insensible ones. Yet antithetically to Tylor, Lévi-Strauss considers myth no less scientific than modern science. Where for Tylor myth is the primitive counterpart to science per se, for Lévi-Strauss myth is the primitive counterpart to *modern* science. Myth *is* primitive science, but not thereby inferior science.

If myth is an instance of primitive thinking because it deals with concrete, tangible phenomena, it is an instance of thinking itself because it classifies phenomena. Lévi-Strauss maintains that all humans think in the form of classifications, specifically pairs of oppositions, and project them onto the world. Many cultural phenomena express these oppositions. Myth is distinctive in resolving or, more accurately, tempering the oppositions it expresses. Those contradictions are to be found not in the plot but in what Lévi-Strauss famously calls the "structure."

Karl Popper (1902–1994), the Viennese-born philosopher of science who eventually settled in England, breaks radically with Tylor. Where for Tylor science simply replaces it, for Popper science emerges *out of* myth—not, however, out of the *acceptance* of myth but out of the *criticism* of it. By "criticism" Popper means not rejection but assessment, which becomes scientific when it takes the form of attempts to falsify the truth claims made.

Myth and Philosophy

The relationship between myth and science overlaps with that between myth and philosophy. Yet there is an even greater array of positions held on the relationship between myth and philosophy: that myth is part of philosophy, that myth *is* philosophy, that philosophy is myth, that myth grows out of philosophy, that philosophy grows out of myth, that myth and philosophy are independent of each other but serve the same function, and that myth and philosophy are independent of each other and serve different functions.

The most abrupt reaction to Lévy-Bruhl's opposing of myth to both science and philosophy came from the Polish-born anthropologist Paul Radin (1883–1959), who was brought to the United States as an infant. Radin grants that *most* primitives are far from philosophical but observes that so are most persons in any culture. Both the average "man of action" and the exceptional "thinker" types of temperament are to be found in all cultures, and in the same proportion. If Lévy-Bruhl is therefore wrong to deny that any primitives are reflective, Tylor is equally wrong to assume that all are. But those primitives who are get credited by Radin with a philosophical prowess keener than that granted even myth makers by Tylor. Contrary to Tylor, primitives, furthermore, are capable of rigorous criticism. Likely for Radin, as definitely for Popper, the capacity for criticism is the hallmark of thinking.

A far less dismissive reaction to Lévy-Bruhl came from the German-born philosopher Ernst Cassirer (1874–1945). For Cassirer, wholly following Lévy-Bruhl, mythic, or "mythopoeic," thinking is primitive, is part of religion, and is the projection of mystical oneness onto the world. But Cassirer claims to be breaking sharply with Lévy-Bruhl in asserting that mythic thinking has its own brand of logic. In actuality, Lévy-Bruhl says the same and invents the term *prelogical* exactly to avoid labeling mythic thinking "illogical" or "nonlogical." Cassirer also claims to be breaking with Lévy-Bruhl in stressing the autonomy of myth as a form of knowledge—language, art, and science being the other main forms. Yet Cassirer simultaneously maintains, no differently from Lévy-Bruhl, that myth is incompatible with science and that science succeeds it. For both Cassirer and Lévy-Bruhl, myth is exclusively primitive and science exclusively modern. Still, Cassirer's characterization of myth as a form of *knowledge* puts myth in the same genus as science—not quite where Lévy-Bruhl puts it.

As philosophical as Cassirer's approach to myth is, he never contends that myth *is* philosophy. The theorists who do so are the German theologian Rudolf Bultmann (1884–1976) and the German-born philosopher Hans Jonas (1903–1993), who eventually settled in the United States. They apply to their specialties, Christianity and Gnosticism, a theory from the early, existentialist work of Martin Heidegger (1889–1976).

Myth and Religion
Myth approached from the field of religious studies naturally subsumes myth under religion and thereby directly exposes myth to the challenge to religion from science. Twentieth-century theories from religious studies sought to reconcile myth with science by reconciling religion with science.

There have been two main strategies for doing so. One tactic has been the recharacterization of the subject matter of religion and therefore of myth. Here religion is not about the physical world, in which case it is safe from any encroachment by science. The myths considered under this approach to religion are traditional myths such as biblical and classical ones, but they are now read symbolically rather than literally. Myth, it is claimed, has been taken to be at odds with science because it has been misread—by those who, like Tylor, read myth literally.

The other tactic for retaining myth in the wake of science has been the elevation of seemingly secular phenomena to religious ones. Here myth is no longer confined to explicitly religious ancient tales. There are now overtly secular modern myths as well. For example, stories about heroes are at face value about mere human beings, but the humans are raised so high above ordinary mortals as to become virtual gods. This approach retains a literal reading of myth but recategorizes the literal status of the agents in myth.

The grandest exponents of a symbolic rendition of traditional religious myths were Bultmann and Jonas. Taken literally, myth for Bultmann is exactly what it is for Tylor and should be rejected as uncompromisingly as Tylor rejects it. But unlike Tylor, Bultmann reads myth symbolically. In his celebrated, if excruciatingly confusing, phrase, he "demythologizes" myth, which means not eliminating, or "demythicizing," the mythology but instead extricating its true, symbolic meaning. To seek evidence of an actual worldwide flood, while dismissing the miraculous notion of an ark containing all species, would be to *demythicize* the Noah myth. To interpret the flood as a symbolic statement about the precariousness of human life would be to *demythologize* the myth.

Demythologized, myth ceases to be about the world and turns out to be about the human *experience* of the world. Demythologized, myth ceases to be an explanation at all and becomes an expression, an expression of what it feels like to live in the world. The New Testament, when demythologized, contrasts the alienation from the world felt by those who have not yet found God to the at-home-ness in the world felt by those who have found God. Myth ceases to be merely primitive and becomes universal. It ceases to be false and becomes true. It depicts the human condition.

Taken literally, myth, as a personalistic explanation of the physical world, is incompatible with science and is therefore unacceptable to moderns. Once demythologized, however, myth is compatible with science because it now refers at once to the transcendent, nonphysical world and, even more, to humans' experience of the physical one. But to say that myth is acceptable to scientifically minded moderns is not to say why it should be accepted. In providing a modern *subject matter* of myth, Bultmann provides no modern *function*.

Jonas argues that ancient Gnosticism presents the same fundamental view of the human condition as modern existentialism—but of atheistic rather than, as for Bultmann, of religious existentialism. Both Gnosticism and existentialism stress the radical alienation of human beings from the world. Unlike Bultmann, who strives to bridge the gap between Christianity and modernity, Jonas acknowledges the divide between Gnosticism and modernity. Yet for Jonas, Gnostic mythology can still speak to moderns, and not to modern believers, as for

Bultmann, but to modern skeptics. Like Bultmann, Jonas seeks to reconcile myth with science by recharacterizing the subject matter of myth. Yet no more than Bultmann does he offer any function of myth for moderns.

Hagiographical biographies of celebrated figures transform them into near-gods and their sagas into myths. For example, immediately after the First Gulf War, biographies of the American commander-in-chief, "Stormin' Norman" Schwarzkopf (b. 1934), touted him as the smartest and bravest soldier in the world—so much smarter and braver than anyone else as to make him almost more than human.

The chief theorist here is the Romanian-born historian of religions Mircea Eliade (1907–1986), who spent the last three decades of his life in the United States. Unlike Bultmann and Jonas, Eliade does not seek to reconcile myth with science by interpreting myth symbolically. He reads myth as literally as Tylor does. Unlike Bultmann and Jonas, Eliade does not try to update traditional myths. But rather than, like Tylor, sticking to traditional, explicitly religious myths, he turns to modern, seemingly nonreligious ones. Yet instead of trying to reconcile those myths with science, as Bultmann and Jonas would, he appeals to the sheer presence of them to argue for their compatibility with science: if moderns, who for Eliade no less than for the others have science, also have myth, then myth simply must be compatible with science. Where Bultmann and Jonas argue meekly that moderns *can* have myth, Eliade argues boldly that they *do*. Where Tylor and Frazer assume that myth is the victim of the process of secularization, Eliade argues that only a superficial secularization has occurred.

Myth and Ritual

Myth is commonly taken to be words, often in the form of a story. A myth is read or heard. It says something. Yet there is an approach to myth that finds this view of myth artificial. According to the myth and ritual, or myth-ritualist, theory, myth does not stand by itself but is tied to ritual. Myth is not just a statement but also an action.

The myth-ritualist theory was pioneered by the Scottish biblicist and Arabist William Robertson Smith (1846–1894). Smith argues that belief is central to *modern* religion but not to *ancient* religion, where instead ritual was central. He grants that ancients doubtless performed rituals only for some reason. But the reason was secondary and could even fluctuate. The reason was a story, or a *myth,* which simply described the origin of the ritual. In claiming that myth is an explanation of ritual, Smith was denying Tylor's conception of myth as an explanation of the world.

Yet Smith is like Tylor in one key respect. For both, myth is wholly ancient. Modern religion is without myth—and without ritual as well. Myth and ritual are not merely ancient but "primitive." In fact, for both Tylor and Smith, ancient religion is but a case of primitive religion, which is the fundamental foil to modern religion.

J. G. Frazer developed the myth-ritualist theory far beyond Smith. Frazer, rarely consistent, actually presents two distinct versions of myth-ritualism. In the first version myth describes the life of the god of vegetation, and ritual enacts the myth describing his death and rebirth. The ritual operates on the basis of the voodoo-like Law of Similarity, according to which the imitation of an action causes it to happen. The ritual directly manipulates the god of vegetation, but as the god goes, so automatically goes vegetation. The ritual is performed when one wants winter to end, presumably when stored-up provisions are running low. A human being, often the king, plays the role of the god and acts out what he magically induces the god to do.

In Frazer's second version of myth-ritualism, the king is central. Here the king does not merely act the part of the god but is himself divine, by which Frazer means that the god resides in him. Just as the health of vegetation depends on the health of its god, so now the health of the god depends on the health of the king: as the king goes, so goes the god of vegetation, and so in turn goes vegetation itself. To ensure a steady supply of food, the community kills its king while he is still in his prime and thereby safely transfers the soul of the god to his successor. As in the first version, the aim is to end winter, which now is attributed to the weakening of the king.

While this second version of myth-ritualism has proved the more influential by far, it actually provides only a tenuous link between myth and ritual. Instead of enacting the myth of the god of vegetation, the ritual simply changes the residence of the god. The king dies not in imitation of the death of the god but as a sacrifice to preserve the health of the god. What part myth plays here, it is not easy to see. Instead of reviving the god by magical imitation, the ritual revives the god by a transplant.

Outside of religion, the most notable application of the myth-ritualist theory has been to literature. The English classicist Jane Harrison (1850–1928) daringly derived all art, not just literature, from ritual. Using Frazer's first version of myth-ritualism, she speculates that gradually people ceased believing that the imitation of an action caused that action to occur. Yet rather than abandoning ritual, they now practiced it as an end in itself. Ritual for its own sake became art, her clearest example of which is drama. More modestly than she, fellow classicists Gilbert Murray (1866–1957) and Francis Macdonald Cornford (1874–1943) rooted specifically Greek epic, tragedy, and comedy in myth-ritualism. Murray then extended the theory to the works of William Shakespeare (1564–1616).

Other standard-bearers of the theory have included Jessie Weston on the Grail legend, E. M. Butler on the Faust legend, C. L. Barber on Shakespearean comedy, Herbert Weisinger on Shakespearean tragedy and on tragedy per se, Francis Fergusson on tragedy, Lord Raglan on hero myths and on literature as a whole, and Northrop Frye and Stanley Edgar Hyman on literature generally. As literary critics, these myth-ritualists have understandably been concerned less with myth itself than with the mythic origin of literature. Works of literature are interpreted as the outgrowth of myths once tied to rituals. For those literary critics indebted to Frazer, as the majority are, literature harks back to Frazer's second myth-ritualist scenario. "The king must die" becomes the familiar summary line.

For literary myth-ritualists, myth becomes literature when myth is severed from ritual. Myth tied to ritual is religious literature; myth cut off from ritual is secular literature, or plain literature. Bereft of ritual, myth can no longer change the world and is demoted to mere commentary.

Perhaps the first to temper the dogma that myths and rituals are inseparable was the American anthropologist Clyde Kluckhohn (1905–1960). The German classicist Walter Burkert (b. 1931) has gone well beyond Kluckhohn in not merely permitting but assuming the original independence of myth and ritual. He maintains that when the two do come together, they do not just serve a common function, as Kluckhohn assumes, but reinforce each other. Myth bolsters ritual by giving mere human behavior a real, not to mention divine, origin: do this because the gods did or do it. Conversely, ritual bolsters myth by turning a mere story into prescribed behavior of the most dutiful kind: do this on pain of anxiety, if not punishment. Where for Smith myth serves ritual, for Burkert ritual equally serves myth.

Ritual for Burkert is "as if" behavior. The "ritual" is not the customs and formalities involved in actual hunting but dramatized hunting. The function is no longer that of securing food, as for Frazer, for the ritual proper arises only after farming has supplanted hunting as the prime source of food. The communal nature of actual hunting, and of ritualized hunting thereafter, functioned to assuage anxiety over one's own aggression and one's own mortality, and at the same time functioned to cement a bond among participants. This shift of focus from the physical world to the human world typifies the shift of focus from nineteenth-century theories of myth to twentieth-century ones.

Myth and Psychology

In the field of psychology, the theories of the Viennese physician Sigmund Freud (1856–1939) and of the Swiss psychiatrist Carl Gustav Jung (1875–1961) have almost monopolized the study of myth. Freud's key discussion of his key myth, that of Oedipus, fittingly occurs in *The Interpretation of Dreams* (1913), for he, and Jung as well, compare myths with dreams.

On the surface, or manifest, level, the story of Oedipus describes that figure's vain effort to elude the fate that has been imposed on him. Latently, however, Oedipus most wants to do what manifestly he least wants to do. He wants to act out his "Oedipus complex." The manifest, or literal, level of the myth hides the latent, symbolic meaning. On the manifest level Oedipus is the innocent victim of Fate. On the latent level he is the culprit. Rightly understood, the myth depicts not Oedipus's failure to circumvent his ineluctable destiny but his success in fulfilling his fondest desires.

Yet the latent meaning scarcely stops here. For the myth is not ultimately about Oedipus at all. Just as the manifest level, on which Oedipus is the victim, masks a latent one, on which Oedipus is the victimizer, so that level in turn masks an even more latent one, on which the ultimate victimizer is the myth maker and any reader of the myth smitten with it. Either is a neurotic adult male stuck, or fixated, at his Oedipal stage of development. He identifies himself with Oedipus and through

him fulfills his own Oedipus complex. At heart, the myth is not biography but autobiography.

The Austrian psychoanalyst Otto Rank (1884–1939), who was Freud's protégé at the time but who later broke irrevocably with the master, works out a common plot, or pattern, for one key category of myths: those of male heroes. The heart of the pattern is the decision by the parents to kill their son at birth to avert the prophecy that the son, if born, will one day kill his father. Unbeknownst to the parents, the infant is rescued and raised by others, grows up to discover who he is, returns home to kill his father, and succeeds him as king or noble. Interpreted psychologically, the pattern is the enactment of the Oedipus complex: the son kills his father to gain sexual access to his mother.

Mainstream psychoanalysis has changed mightily since Freud's day. Contemporary psychoanalysts like the American Jacob Arlow (1912–2004) see myth as contributing to normal development rather than to the perpetuation of neurosis. Myth abets adjustment to the social and the physical worlds rather than childish flight from them. Furthermore, myth now serves everyone, not merely neurotics.

The classical Freudian goal is the establishment of oneself in the external world, largely free of domination by parents and instincts. Success is expressed concretely in the form of a job and a mate. Jungians accept that goal, but as that of only the "first half" of life, or from infancy to young adulthood. The goal of the uniquely Jungian second half of life—of adulthood—is consciousness—not, however, of the external world, as summed up by the Freudian term *reality principle,* but of the distinctively Jungian, or collective, unconscious. One must return to that unconscious, from which one has unavoidably become severed in the first half of life, but not to sever one's ties to the external world. On the contrary, the aim is return in turn to the external world. The ideal is a balance between consciousness of the external world and consciousness of the unconscious. The aim of the second half of life is to supplement, not abandon, the achievements of the first half.

The American mythologist Joseph Campbell (1904–1987) provides the classical Jungian counterpart to Rank on hero myths. Where Rank's pattern, limited to males, centers on the hero's toppling of his father, Campbell's centers on a journey, undertaken by an adult female or a male hero, from the known, human world to the heretofore unknown world of gods. Interpreted psychologically, that journey is an inner, not outer, trek from the known portion of the mind—ordinary, or ego, consciousness, the object of which is the external world—to the unknown portion of the mind—the Jungian unconscious. The successful hero must not only reach the strange, new world but also return. In psychological terms, success means the completion of the goal of the second half of life.

The most influential Jungian theorists of myth after Jung himself have been Erich Neumann (1905–1960) and James Hillman (b. 1926). Neumann systematizes the developmental, or evolutionary, aspect of Jungian theory. Jung himself certainly correlates myths with stages of psychological development, but Neumann works out the stages, beginning with the "uroboric" stage of sheer unconsciousness and proceeding to the incipient emergence of the ego out of the unconscious, the development of an independent ego consciousness, and the eventual return of the ego to the unconscious to create the self. Neumann's emphasis on heroism in the first half of life complements Campbell's devotion to heroism in the second half.

By far the most radical development in the Jungian theory of myth has been the emergence of archetypal psychology, which in fact considers itself post-Jungian. The chief figure in this movement is Hillman. Another important figure is David Miller. Archetypal psychology faults classical Jungian psychology on multiple grounds. By emphasizing the compensatory, therapeutic message of mythology, classical Jungian psychology purportedly reduces mythology to psychology and gods to concepts. In espousing a unified self (or "Self") as the ideal psychological authority, Jungian psychology supposedly projects onto psychology a Western, specifically monotheistic, more specifically Christian, even more specifically Protestant outlook. The Western emphasis on progress is purportedly reflected in the primacy Jungian psychology accords hero myths and the primacy it accords the ego, even in the ego's encounter with the unconscious: the encounter is intended to abet development. Finally, Jungian psychology is berated for placing archetypes in an unknowable realm distinct from the known realm of symbols.

As a corrective, Hillman and his followers advocate that psychology be viewed as irreducibly mythological. Myth is still to be interpreted psychologically, but psychology is itself to be interpreted mythologically. One grasps the psychological meaning of the myth of Saturn by imagining oneself to be the figure Saturn, not by translating Saturn's plight into clinical terms like depression. Moreover, the depressed Saturn represents a legitimate aspect of one's personality. Each god deserves its due. The psychological ideal should be pluralistic rather than monolithic—in mythological terms, polytheistic rather than monotheistic, or Greek rather than biblical. Insisting that archetypes are to be found *in* symbols rather than outside them, Hillman espouses a relation to the gods in themselves and not to something beyond them. The ego becomes but one more archetype with its attendant kind of god, and it is the soul rather than the ego that experiences the archetypes through myths. Myth serves to open one up to the soul's own depths.

Myth and Structure

Lévi-Strauss calls his approach to myth "structuralist" to distinguish it from "narrative" interpretations, or those that adhere to the plot of myth. Nonstructuralists deem myth a story, progressing from beginning to end, be the story interpreted literally or symbolically. Where the plot of a myth is that, say, event A leads to event B, which leads to event C, which leads to event D, the structure, which is identical with the expression and resolution of contradictions, is either that events A and B constitute an opposition mediated by event C or, as in the Oedipus myth, that events A and B, which constitute the same opposition, are to each other as events C and D, an analogous opposition, are to each other. Apparently, all oppositions for Lévi-Strauss symbolize the tension between humans as part of nature and humans as part of culture.

Lévi-Strauss is not the only or even the earliest theorist of myth labeled a structuralist. Notably, the Russian folklorist Vladimir Propp (1895–1970) and the French Indo-Europeanist Georges Dumézil (1898–1986) wrote both before Lévi-Strauss and independently of him. The French literary critic Roland Barthes (1915–1980) was a contemporary of Lévi-Strauss but was his own person.

The common plot that Propp deciphers in Russian fairy tales is his structure, which thus remains on the narrative level and is no different from the kind of structure found by Rank and Campbell. By contrast, the structure that Dumézil unravels lies as much beneath the surface level as Lévi-Strauss's. But it reflects the order of society rather than, as for Lévi-Strauss, that of the mind, and is three-part rather than two-part.

Barthes is concerned with myth as ideology. In Lévi-Straussian terms, he writes to expose the way that French bourgeois culture creates myths to make itself seem natural—a fusion of culture with nature rather than the mere alleviation of the opposition between them. For Barthes, the function of myth is social rather than, as for Lévi-Strauss, intellectual. For Barthes, the structure of myth is its cultural context. By "myths" he means artifacts and activities more than stories. His clearest example is of professional wrestling, which, much more than a sport, is an attempt to alleviate lingering misgivings over the behavior of some French citizens during the Occupation by presenting clear-cut Good (the wrestler) as triumphing over clear-cut Evil (his opponent).

A group of French classicists headed by Jean-Pierre Vernant (b. 1914) have proved the most faithful followers of Lévi-Strauss's brand of structuralism, though even they have adapted it. Lévi-Strauss has regularly been lambasted for isolating myth from its various contexts—social, cultural, political, economic, even sexual. In his essay on the American Indian myth of Asdiwal, he does provide a detailed ethnographic analysis of a myth. But he does so almost nowhere else. Vernant and his fellow classicists—notably, Marcel Detienne, Pierre Vidal-Naquet, and Nicole Loraux—have taken the analysis of Asdiwal as their model. As the heirs of Lévi-Strauss, these classicists have sought to decipher underlying, often latent patterns in myths, but they have then sought to link those patterns to ones in the culture at large.

Myth and Society

Where for Tylor and Frazer myth deals exclusively, or nearly exclusively, with physical phenomena—flooding, disease, death—for Malinowski myth deals even more with social phenomena—classes, taxes, rituals. Myth still serves to reconcile humans to the unpleasantries of life, but now to unpleasantries that, far from unalterable, *can* be cast off. Here, too, myths spur resigned acceptance by tracing these unpleasantries, or at least impositions, back to a hoary past, thereby conferring on them the clout of tradition. Myth persuades denizens to defer to, say, ranks in society by pronouncing those ranks long-standing and in that sense deserved. Here the beneficiary of myth is society, not the individual. The modern counterpart to myths of social phenomena—if for Malinowski moderns lack myths—would be ideology.

As the Frazerian counterpart to Rank and Campbell, Lord Raglan extends Frazer's second myth-ritualist scenario by turning the king who dies for the community into a hero. The function of myth is now as much social as agricultural: inspiring present kings to sacrifice themselves so that their communities will not starve. The French-born, American-resident literary critic René Girard (b. 1923) offers an ironic twist to Raglan. Where Raglan's hero is willing to die for the community, Girard's hero is killed or exiled by the community for having caused the present woes of the community. Indeed, the "hero" is initially considered a criminal who deserves to die. Only subsequently is the villain turned into a hero, who, as for Raglan, dies selflessly for the community. Both Raglan and Girard cite Oedipus as their fullest example, though both scorn Freud. For Girard, the transformation of Oedipus from reviled exile in Sophocles' *Oedipus the King* to revered benefactor in Sophocles' *Oedipus at Colonus* typifies the transformation from criminal to hero.

Yet this change is for Girard only the second half of the process. The first half is the change from innocent victim to criminal. Originally, the community selects an innocent member to blame for the violence that has erupted. This scapegoat, who can be of any rank, is usually killed, though, as with Oedipus, sometimes exiled. The killing is the ritualistic sacrifice. Rather than directing the ritual, as for Frazer, myth for Girard is created *after* the killing to *hide* it. Myth comes from ritual, as for Smith, but it comes to mask rather than, as for Smith, to explain the ritual. Myth turns the scapegoat into a criminal who deserved to die and then turns the criminal into a hero, who has died voluntarily for the good of the community.

Like Burkert, Girard roots myth in sacrifice and roots sacrifice in aggression. Yet like Burkert, myth functions to secure peace and not, as for Frazer, food. Myth deals with the human world; science, with the physical world. This shift of focus again typifies the shift from nineteenth-century of theories of myth to twentieth-century ones.

See also **Fundamentalism; Literature: Overview; Psychoanalysis; Psychology and Psychiatry; Religion; Ritual: Religion; Science: Overview; Structuralism and Poststructuralism: Overview.**

BIBLIOGRAPHY

Arlow, Jacob A. "Ego Psychology and the Study of Mythology." *Journal of the American Psychoanalytic Association* 9 (1961): 371–393.

Barthes, Roland. *Mythologies.* Translated by Annette Lavers. New York: Hill and Wang, 1972.

Bultmann, Rudolf. "New Testament and Mythology." In *Kerygma and Myth,* edited by Hans-Werner Bartsch. Translated by Reginald H. Fuller. London: SPCK, 1953.

Burkert, Walter. *Creation of the Sacred: Tracks of Biology in Early Religions.* Cambridge, Mass.: Harvard University Press, 1996.

Campbell, Joseph. *The Hero with a Thousand Faces.* New York: Pantheon, 1949.

Cassirer, Ernst. *The Philosophy of Symbolic Forms.* Vol. 2: *Mythical Thought.* Translated by Ralph Manheim. New Haven, Conn.: Yale University Press, 1955.

Dumézil, Georges. *Archaic Roman Religion.* 2 vols. Translated by Philip Krapp. Chicago: University of Chicago Press, 1970.

Eliade, Mircea. *The Sacred and the Profane: The Nature of Religion.* Translated by Willard R. Trask. New York: Harcourt, Brace, 1959.

Frazer, J. G. *The Golden Bough: A Study in Magic and Religion.* 3rd ed. 12 vols. London: Macmillan, 1911–1915.

Freud, Sigmund. *The Interpretation of Dreams.* In *Standard Edition of the Complete Psychological Works of Sigmund Freud.* 24 vols. Edited and translated by James Strachey et al. London: Hogarth Press, 1953–1974.

Girard, René. *Violence and the Sacred.* Translated by Patrick Gregory. Baltimore: Johns Hopkins University Press, 1977.

Harrison, Jane Ellen. *Ancient Art and Ritual.* London: Williams and Norgate, 1913.

Hillman, James. *Re-Visioning Psychology.* New York: Harper and Row, 1975.

Jonas, Hans. *The Gnostic Religion: The Message of the Alien God and the Beginnings of Christianity.* 2nd ed. Boston: Beacon Press, 1963.

Jung, Carl Gustav. *The Archetypes and the Collective Unconscious.* 2nd ed. Translated by R. F. C. Hull. Princeton, N.J.: Princeton University Press, 1968.

Lévi-Strauss, Claude. "The Structural Study of Myth." In *Myth,* edited by Thomas A. Sebeok. Bloomington: Indiana University Press.

Lévy-Bruhl, Lucien. *How Natives Think.* Translated by Lilian A. Clare. London: Allen and Unwin, 1926. Reprint, Princeton, N.J.: Princeton University Press, 1985.

Malinowski, Bronislaw. *Myth in Primitive Psychology.* New York: Norton, 1926.

Popper, Karl. *Conjectures and Refutations.* 5th ed. London: Routledge and Kegan Paul, 1974.

Propp, Vladimir I.A. *Morphology of the Folktale.* 2nd ed. Translated by Laurence Scott. Austin: University of Texas Press, 1968.

Radin, Paul. *Primitive Man as Philosopher.* 2nd ed. New York: Dover, 1957.

Raglan, Lord. *The Hero.* London: Methuen, 1936. Reprinted in *In Quest of the Hero,* edited by Otto Rank, et al. Princeton, N.J.: Princeton University Press, 1990.

Rank, Otto. *The Myth of the Birth of the Hero.* 1st ed. Translated by F. Robbins and Smith Ely Jelliffe. New York: Journal of Nervous and Mental Disease Publishing, 1914. Reprinted in *In Quest of the Hero,* edited by Otto Rank, et al. Princeton, N.J.: Princeton University Press, 1990.

Segal, Robert A. *Myth: A Very Short Introduction.* Oxford: Oxford University Press, 2004.

———. *Theorizing about Myth.* Amherst: University of Massachusetts Press, 1999.

Smith, William Robertson. *Lectures on the Religion of the Semites.* Edinburgh: A. and C. Black, 1889.

Tylor, E. B. *Primitive Culture.* 2 vols. London: Murray, 1871.

Vernant, Jean-Pierre. *Myth and Thought Among the Greeks.* London: Routledge and Kegan Paul, 1983.

Robert A. Segal

N

NARRATIVE. Although the study of narrative goes back as far as Aristotle's *Poetics,* narrative theory emerged as a distinct field of inquiry only in the second half of the twentieth century. At that point, work on the theory of the novel intersected with structuralism's project of writing the grammar of stories and storytelling. This intersection in turn opened out to other streams of traffic in narrative studies, including the analysis of oral narrative by sociolinguists; reflections on historical narrative by historiographers; and the varied investigations of film scholars, among others. In the early twenty-first century many other disciplines—medicine, law, business, and psychoanalysis, prominent among them—both draw upon and contribute to narrative theory (see sidebar). In this respect, contemporary interdisciplinary thought has undergone a "narrative turn."

From Novel to Narrative

The most influential figures in the early theorizing of the novel were novelists themselves, particularly Henry James (1843–1916) and E. M. Forster (1879–1970). In "The Art of Fiction" (1888) and in the Prefaces to the New York Edition of his novels (1909–1910), James describes and defends his own novelistic practice. He argues that the artistry of the novel depends on its representation of "felt life," and, in the Prefaces, he describes, often with rich, extended metaphors, how he came to view the "treatment" (the technique) of his novels as even more important than their "subject" (their characters and situations). More specifically, James explains why he came to prefer the technique of narrating from the consciousness of his central character(s): such treatment highlights the impression of felt life even as it allows him to offer fresh ways of exploring his subjects. James's distinction between treatment and subject is a distinction between the how and the what of the novel that reappears in some form in every major theoretical approach to narrative. James's specific preferences soon became codified by his followers into a set of rules for good novelistic practice: use scenes rather than narrative summaries because they are more impersonal and objective; narrate from the perspective of a central consciousness rather than from the perspective of an external narrator because that treatment involves less rhetoric and more artistry. In short: show, don't tell.

If James is the theorist of treatment (the how), Forster is the theorist of character (one element of the what). In *Aspects of the Novel* (1927), he introduces a distinction between "round" and "flat" characters that is still frequently cited in the early 2000s: Round characters are capable of surprising in a convincing way, while flat characters can be summed up in a single sentence. Forster also distinguishes between story and plot (see sidebar), viewing the first as a kind of necessary evil ("yes, oh dear, yes,

the novel tells a story"), and the second with its inclusion of causality as what makes the recounting of events worthwhile. But he regards character as the most important element of the novel. In fact, he sees plot and character as often in conflict—one requires closure, the other does not—and he laments those novels in which he thinks character is sacrificed for plot.

Contemporaneous with Forster's theorizing, the Russian Formalists, a group including Victor Shklovsky, Boris Eichenbaum, and Yuri Tynanov, develop ideas about the novel that provide an especially interesting comparison with James's. They introduce a more formal and ultimately more influential distinction between the what and the how, identifying the *fabula* as the abstract chronological sequence of events independent of their expression in the *sjuzhet,* the actual presentation of those events in the novel's text. This distinction explains one's intuition that there can be different versions of the same narrative: different *sjuzhets* do not constitute different narratives unless they also are based on different *fabulas.* The Formalists also go James one better by arguing that the purpose of literature in general and the novel in particular is not the representation of felt life but defamiliarization or estrangement: the purpose of literature is to renew or revise our perceptions—in Shklovsky's famous phrase, to make the stone stony. This view leads the Formalists to an account of literary change built on the formal necessity of innovation, especially in the how of the novel: novelistic forms that once provided estrangement gradually lose that effect as they themselves became familiar, and so the inventive novelist discovers new devices of estrangement.

The next significant literary critical approach to form, that of the Anglo-American New Critics, emphasizes the distinctiveness of literary language itself, and so focuses on the image patterns of novels (the how) as containing the key to their thematic concerns (the what) and, thus, their formal artistry. The rivals of the New Critics, the Chicago School neo-Aristotelians, though generally unsuccessful in their effort to unseat New Criticism as the orthodoxy of the critical mainstream, turn out to be more influential than the New Critics in the evolution of narrative theory. R. S. Crane, working without knowledge of the Russian Formalists, develops a concept of plot that distinguishes between its "material action" (the what, roughly equivalently to the *fabula*) and the "plot proper" (the synthesis of what and how in the service of a given purpose and set of effects—roughly equivalent to *sjuzhet*). Crane's student Wayne C. Booth reexamines, from the neo-Aristotelian perspective, the Jamesian rules for novelistic success and repudiates them with a method that transforms Crane's neo-Aristotelian poetics into a rhetoric. In *The Rhetoric of Fiction* (1961), Booth argues that techniques of showing are as rhetorical as techniques of telling; the choice is not between impersonal art and inartistic rhetoric but rather between different ways of trying to influence the audience—in short, different kinds of rhetorical appeals. More generally, Booth's insight that the novel is rhetorical from top to bottom paves one road for the entry of ethical and ideological approaches to narrative.

Another Russian scholar of the 1920s, Vladimir Propp, provides a model for a different approach to narrative in *The Morphology of the Folktale* (1929). Propp identifies thirty-one functions that occur in invariable order (for example, hero perceives a lack; hero meets a magical agent) in every Russian folktale. But more important than his specific account of the folktale itself is Propp's insight that underlying the surface variety of the folktale is a single deep structure (an Ur-*fabula,* if the reader will). The structuralist narratologists of the 1960s and 1970s, such as Tzvetan Todorov, Claude Bremond, and, in one phase of his work, Roland Barthes, look back to Propp and to Ferdinand de Saussure in their effort to uncover the underlying structures of narrative. Saussure's distinction between *langue,* the abstract system of language that underlies any utterance and makes it intelligible, and *parole,* actual utterances, provides an analogy for the structuralist project of describing the grammar of narrative that makes any given narrative intelligible.

Strikingly the results of these efforts are not a comprehensive grammar but a number of conceptual tools that remain both useful and influential to this day. Chief among these tools are the *story/discourse* distinction, a new version of the what/how distinction, and Gérard Genette's analyses of discourse. Story encompasses the characters, events, and settings (or states, events, and existents) of narrative, and discourse encompasses all the devices for rendering the story in one way rather than another. Genette groups these devices into three main kinds: (1) those of temporality, which include order, duration (the relation between story time and its expression in discourse time, for instance, twenty years may be summarized in a single sentence, just as one minute may be treated in several pages), and frequency (the relation between the number of times an event happens in story and the number of times it is reported in discourse); (2) voice, the answer to the question "who speaks?"; and (3) vision, the answer to the question "who perceives?" Even more significantly, as the link between Propp and the structuralist project suggests, the emergence of narratology makes possible the shift from novel to narrative—that is, storytelling of all kinds—as the central object of study, even if literary fiction narrative retains a special status within the project. Genette, for example, develops his conceptual toolbox from his analysis of Marcel Proust's *A la recherche du temps perdu* (1913–1927; Remembrance of things past). Consequently, in the 1980s the field of narrative theory emerged with a recognizable identity.

Contemporary Narrative Theory: Contextual and Interdisciplinary Models

Even as the field was emerging, it was being affected by the larger "theory revolution" of the last quarter of the twentieth century in two main ways: (1) the field's focus on narrative form expands and becomes complicated through attention to the relations between form and ideology; and (2) as already noted,

the field becomes increasingly interdisciplinary. The discovery and dissemination in the West of the work of Mikhail Bakhtin, another Russian scholar of the 1920s and 1930s, is especially significant in the complication of formal approaches. Bakhtin, in one sense, is as concerned with the form of the novel as Shklovsky or any other Russian Formalist; indeed one of his goals was to earn for the novel as a genre the kind of respect and status accorded to poetry in 1920s Russia. But Bakhtin conceives of the novel's form as inseparable from its ideological component, because he conceives of language as always already ideological. He views any national language (English, French, Russian) not as a unified system but rather as a collection of sociolects or minilanguages, such as the language of the working class, the language of the law, or the language of the academy, each of which carries the values of its group. Bakhtin argues that the novel necessarily draws upon multiple minilanguages and puts them into dialogic relationships with each other; this dialogue among languages is also a dialogue among ideologies.

Feminist narratologists such as Robyn Warhol and Susan Lanser participate in the spirit of Bakhtin's work by linking technique to ideology, though they are most concerned with ideologies of gender and their interests extend beyond novelistic language to other features of narrative discourse, especially the devices and techniques of woman writers and female narrators. Although other ideologically based theoretical approaches such as Marxist theory and postcolonial theory have not yet spawned their own branches of narratology, these theories also contribute to a general understanding of the inseparable connection between form and ideology: Each shows how an author's choice of particular narrative techniques and structures occurs within both a formal and a political context and therefore has both formal and ideological consequences.

Another significant complication of the formal model has been the rise of narrative ethics, itself a subfield of the burgeoning area of ethical criticism. Martha Nussbaum argues that narrative, due to its concrete particularity and its capacity to draw on the cognitive power of the emotions, is, in the hands of a novelist such as Henry James, a site for ethical exploration that rivals the explorations of philosophical ethics. Booth extends the rhetorical approach of *The Rhetoric of Fiction* to the ethical realm by focusing on the quality of one's life in the hours spent reading narrative. More specifically, Booth proposes the metaphor of "books as friends" and suggests the reader can judge the quality of such friendships by attending to the trajectory of desires they invite the reader to follow. Adam Zachary Newton and others develop approaches to narrative ethics through attention to the relation between the specifics of story and discourse, on one hand, and ethical categories derived from philosophers such as Emmanuel Levinas, on the other. James Phelan seeks to extend the work of both Booth and Newton by exploring the ethics of technique as much as the ethical dimension of characters' situations.

Contemporary narrative theory is interdisciplinary in two related ways. As the example of narrative ethics shows, it either brings the insights of other disciplines to the study of narrative or it brings the conclusions of narrative theory to the concerns of other disciplines. In each case, the interdisciplinarity is a two-way street: Not only does philosophical ethics illuminate narrative's

---

E. M. FORSTER'S KING AND QUEEN AND NARRATIVE ACROSS THE DISCIPLINES

"The king died and then the queen" is a story. "The king died and then the queen died of grief" is a plot. Thus spake E. M. Forster, who also points out that the difference between the two is causality. Theorists have debated the validity of the distinction since Forster proposed it in the 1927, arguing, for example, that the very temporality of "and then" entails causality (or at least invites the reader to supply it) so that the only difference between the two versions is the *explicit* naming of the cause in the second. The debate also includes objections to defining plot solely in terms of causality, since many narrative artists build plots on other principles. Nevertheless the debate itself shows that Forster identified four elements of narrative—character (or agent), event, temporality, and causality—that are essential to the contemporary interest in "narrative across the disciplines." Because narrative spells out the specific relations among agents, events, time, and causality, it is capable of explaining phenomena that escape more abstract analyses such as those based on science-oriented ideas of general laws. In twenty-first-century culture, with its widespread abandonment of a belief in eternal verities, this capability is of great importance for many disciplines.

Many legal cases, for example, involve disputes about the relation among the agents involved, the temporal order of events, and the causes of those events; judges and juries often render their verdicts according to which side constructs the most convincing narrative about that relation. In medicine, the narrative of an onset of an illness with its particular relation of what the patient did when and for what reason can provide clues to both to the nature of the illness and the appropriate treatment. Furthermore many patients find the opportunity of relating their "illness narrative" to a sympathetic medical professional to be salutary in itself. The talking cure of psychoanalysis is a narrative cure: an analysand comes to recognize how the relation among agents, including herself, events of her past, and their causality are still affecting her and, thus, how she can break the grip of that narrative and write another one for her life. More generally, narrative's interest in character, event, temporality, and causality provides the basis for claims that people's identities are constituted by the narratives they tell about their lives. The queen died, in other words, because the event of the king's death made her own passing the inevitable next event in her narrative of her life.

---

representations of ethical situations, but those representations have implications for philosophy's investigations into ethics. Similarly not only does, say, medicine benefit from drawing on narrative theory, but medicine's use of it has consequences for the field's ongoing efforts. Among other things, this aspect of interdisciplinarity corrects literary study's attraction to the experimental or innovative case and helps keep the focus on what seems to be the fundamental elements of narrative's power (see sidebar).

One of the most promising current interdisciplinary developments is the cognitive approach to narrative taken by such scholars as David Herman. In a sense, this movement is an extension of classical narratology because it also has the goal of giving a comprehensive view of narrative, its elements, and their combinations. But rather than fashioning that comprehensive view by analogy with Saussure's theory of language, the cognitivists start with the idea that narrative is a way of organizing experience, one that involves, in both its production and consumption, the development of a mental model of that organization. This starting point means that the cognitivists draw upon both the findings of narrative theory broadly conceived—including, for example, classical narratology, rhetorical theory,

and sociolinguistics—and the findings of cognitive science about how the human mind processes information, forms patterns from diverse data, and so on. Whether the cognitive approach succeeds in establishing a new dominant paradigm for understanding narrative or becomes, like classical narratology, a movement that is more significant for its local successes than the achievement of its ultimate goal remains to be seen. But the cognitive project is a telling example of the interdisciplinary nature of contemporary narrative studies and strong evidence, along with the undeniable ubiquity and amazing variety of narrative itself, that the future of narrative theory is very bright.

See also **Formalism; Literary Criticism; New Criticism.**

BIBLIOGRAPHY

Bakhtin, Mikhail. "Discourse in the Novel." In his *The Dialogic Imagination.* Translated by Caryl Emerson and Michael Holquist. Austin: University of Texas Press, 1981.

Barthes, Roland. "An Introduction to the Structural Analysis of Narrative." Translated by Lionel Duisit. *New Literary History* 6 (1975): 237–272.

Booth, Wayne C. *The Company We Keep: An Ethics of Fiction.* Berkeley: University of California Press, 1988.

———. *The Rhetoric of Fiction.* Chicago: University of Chicago Press, 1961. Reprint, Chicago: University of Chicago Press, 1983.

Forster, E. M. *Aspects of the Novel.* New York: Harcourt, Brace, 1927.

Genette, Gérard. *Narrative Discourse: An Essay in Method.* Translated by Jane Lewin. Ithaca, N.Y.: Cornell University Press, 1980.

Herman, David. *Story Logic: Problems and Possibilities of Narrative.* Lincoln: University of Nebraska Press, 2002.

James, Henry. *The Art of Criticism: Henry James on the Theory and Practice of Fiction.* Edited by William Veeder, and Susan M. Griffin. Chicago: University of Chicago Press, 1986.

Lanser, Susan. *Fictions of Authority: Women Writers and Narrative Voice.* Ithaca, N.Y.: Cornell University Press, 1992.

Newton, Adam Zachary. *Narrative Ethics.* Cambridge, Mass.: Harvard University Press, 1995.

Nussbaum, Martha. *Love's Knowledge: Essays on Philosophy and Literature.* New York: Oxford University Press, 1990.

Phelan, James. *Living to Tell about It: A Rhetoric and Ethics of Character Narration.* Ithaca, N.Y.: Cornell University Press, 2004.

Propp, Vladimir. *Morphology of the Folktale.* 2nd ed., rev. Translated by Laurence Scott. Austin: University of Texas Press, 1968. Originally published in 1929.

Saussure, Ferdinand de. *Course in General Linguistics,* edited by Charles Bally and Albert Sechehaye in collaboration with Albert Reidlinger and translated by Wade Baskin. New York: Philosophical Library, 1959.

Shklovsky, Victor. *Theory of Prose.* Translated by Benjamin Sher. Elmwood Park, Ill.: Dalkey Archive Press, 1990.

Warhol, Robyn. *Gendered Interventions: Narrative Discourse in the Victorian Novel.* New Brunswick, N.J.: Rutgers University Press, 1989.

James Phelan

NATION.

Natio derives from the Latin verb to be born (*nasci*) and refers to societies constituted by (assumed) common birth or descent, a meaning akin to the English word *race*.

Prepolitical Usages

In late Roman and early medieval texts, *natio* was less frequently used than *gens,* which also meant groups of common descent, though emphasizing kinship and family rather than race. Another group noun, *populus,* referred to the assembled citizens of a city-state. (*Plebs* referred to people in the negative sense of the masses.) This meaning translated from Greek city-states to the Roman Republic and then to the Roman Empire. Romans used *gens* and *natio* to describe *other* peoples perceived as extended kinship groups or subjects of quasi-religious dynasts.

Such groups were given specific names. Tacitus (c. 55– c. 117) in *Germania* (98 C.E.) named the people (*gens*) of "Germania," differentiating distinct nations and subnations. However, there was no consistency in relating general labels to specific names. This ethnography was taken over by the late Roman Latin-writing intellectual elite and continued by their successors, the Roman Catholic clergy. The names given to certain territories (England, France, Germany) derive from Latin labels.

The Nation and Political Authority, 1000–1500

The Venerable Bede (673?–735), in the *Ecclesiastical History of the English Nation* chose the name *Anglii* or *gens Anglorum* for the subjects of Christian kings. As Roman Christianity expanded and the number of kingdoms contracted, clerics following Bede fixed the name to one kingdom and its people. Something similar happened with Franks, France, and the French. Why names like French and English survived, others disappeared (Goth, Lombard, Norman), and others attached themselves to the same group (German, Deutsch) is unclear.

Name that prevailed were detached from original connotations of race and kinship. Even before the Norman conquest in 1066, "English" rulers and elites were drawn, and were conscious of being drawn, from beyond the ranks of the Anglo-Saxons. The conquest of 1066 introduced a new ruling class with a clear sense of ethnic identity. Yet the names England and English quickly reasserted themselves. Possible explanations include the facts that Anglo-Saxon institutions were taken over by the new rulers; they married English-speaking women; later rulers identified with the land of their conquest rather than with Normandy.

The political concept of nation referred to monarchy and the ruling class. When the eastern Frankish empire took the name "The Holy Roman Empire of the German Nation," nation meant the princes and high nobility of the empire. The nation, in becoming political, divested itself of populist elements associated with language and customs. Insofar as descent was claimed, this was dynastic and aristocratic.

Nation was used inconsistently and descriptively in political discourse. Sustained arguments about legitimate rule were couched in terms of religion, dynasty, and privilege. The king of "England" could claim the "French" crown; indeed such a claim by Henry V was recognized in a treaty even though his premature death prevented the agreement coming into effect. Rulers invoked the nation when rejecting jurisdictional claims by the papacy or other princes but dropped it when making such claims themselves. Occasionally they drew upon older ethnographic meanings to appeal to their subjects, though we have no idea how this was received. The word also figured in conflicts between princes and elite subjects, especially when nobles defended privileges as properties of the nation.

Natio was used in many other ways. Delegations to the Council of Constance (1414–1418) and bodies of students at the University of Paris were called nations and given specific names. The word broadly referred to specific groups of foreigners but lacked stable meaning, suggesting it was not disciplined by constant deployment in political arguments. So long as arguments about legitimate political authority excluded notions of equal citizenship and popular participation, the nation remained a marginal concept. Only when *natio* took on attributes of *populus* did it become politically significant.

Making Politics National, 1500–1800

There were two principal ways in which the political concept of nation developed. The first was during the Reformation. Protestants invoked the biblical idea of God's chosen people, or elect nation, associating this with sacred territory and promised land. It is difficult to gauge the long-term significance of this.

Protestant resistance to authority took mainly sectarian and international forms; salvation was for individuals or small groups. Radical Protestantism was crushed by Catholic and mainstream Protestant regimes before the later emergence of popular national movements. However, by then it was commonplace to combine state, confession, and nation in political arguments.

Second, the growth of state power meant that ever-larger groups were brought into contact with the central government. If government was "national," then groups deployed that term in political conflict. A significant example is eighteenth-century France. As the crown attacked privileged groups, its publicists portrayed these as factional interests undermining national interests. Those opponents in turn conflated nation with privileged institutions, insisting they were defending "national liberty." These ideas of national interest and liberty could be combined and extended. Revolutionaries generalized the concept of the nation to *all* subjects of the crown.

New Ways of Thinking about the Nation

The Enlightenment view that human beings choose and construct their institutions, that society and state are contractual associations, and that all human beings are equal, endowed with reason and rights, entailed profound consequences for the concept of nation. It took on qualities of *populus*, extended to the populations of territorial states.

In February 1789 in France, the abbé Emmanuel Joseph Sieyès (1748–1836) published a pamphlet entitled *What Is the Third Estate?* His answer was that it was not one estate among others in a society of privileges, but was *everything*. The actual representatives of the Third Estate, meeting in the Estates-General summoned in 1789, acted out this answer by transforming themselves into the National Assembly and inviting members of the other Estates to join them. The Assembly issued a Declaration of Rights: "The Nation is essentially the source of all sovereignty; nor can any individual or any body of men, be entitled to any authority which is not expressly derived from it" (Article III). The French Revolution abolished privileges and devised political arrangements to realize national sovereignty. Despite the failure of these experiments the notion became entrenched as a basic tenet of modern democracy.

Apart from practical problems of implementing national sovereignty, there was a conceptual difficulty: Who belonged to the nation? If the nation was defined in relation to the state over which it claimed sovereignty, then it should consist of the subjects of that state, with all their accidental differences of customs, beliefs, and conditions. Even this required one to define state boundaries precisely, itself a novel practice. Then one had to devise rules for turning subjects into citizens. Citizens and inhabitants were two different notions. Children and women as well as foreigners were excluded from citizenship. Above all, there was the problem of reconciling nation as the sum of individual citizens with nation as a group bound by ties of culture and values. The Jacobins tried expanding the idea of politics so that these ties flowed from, rather than toward the state, but they failed. It seemed necessary to look beyond politics to find the nation.

This was already happening during the Revolution. Radicals in Paris suggested that Bretons, Basques, and other reactionaries were infected by cultures and languages that made them incapable of appreciating new truths. Conservatives in and beyond France, notably Edmund Burke (1729–1797), argued that revolution was destructive because it ignored the importance of the traditions and customs that made each society (nation) distinct; revolutionaries mistakenly imagined that human reason could design an ideal society and state.

The German thinker Johann Gottfried von Herder (1744–1803) moved from the idea of variety to that of uniqueness. Different languages were not variants on a universal language; human beings had not rationally constructed languages. Each language expressed and transmitted across individuals and generations unique values that embodied the national spirit. The argument could be extended to music, architecture, customs, laws, indeed, to every aspect of society. The Romantic movement promoted the view that societies were organisms; art, the expression of uniqueness; and human beings, bound together by feelings and emotions not by reason and interest.

Two kinds of nation? These two ways of thinking about the nation appear diametrically opposed. One stresses politics, reason, and choice; the other, culture, emotions, and belonging. This distinction has been linked to two kinds of nationalism variously called "western" and "eastern," "civic" and "ethnic," "political" and "cultural." The distinctions differ in important ways but all relate to these opposed ways of thinking. We need to see how such ideas were combined or opposed as the nation became the justification for statehood.

Nation and State in Europe after 1800

The opposed elements combined in many ways. In the first half of the nineteenth century, nationality as citizenship was linked to "high" culture. Basques and Catalans, Welsh and Scots, Bretons and Provencals must become Spanish, British, and French, respectively, to belong to the nation. Educational and other policies were pursued to this end. Such policies were explicitly assimilationist.

The situation was more difficult when one could not link the state to a dominant culture. Habsburg, Romanov, and Ottoman rulers were reluctant to do this. In some regions they confronted subjects with their own elites and high culture, such as the Poles and Magyars. There were also large and culturally subordinate groups, especially Slav speakers. These ranged from peoples with indigenous elites, a literary language, autonomous institutions, and national consciousness to peasant communities with distinct ethnic qualities but without national consciousness. Other areas were splintered into small states with one dominant nationality, above all the German lands and Italian peninsula.

As the nation as the bearer of popular sovereignty became a central political concept, these nonnational states were confronted with difficult questions. The "answer" in the German lands and the Italian peninsula was "unification," although these unifications included people who did not share in the national culture and excluded people who did.

In multinational empires no single national culture could assimilate others. The Russification project in the Russian Empire failed. The Habsburgs in the western half of the Austro–Hungarian Empire recognized distinct German and Czech nationalities. The Magyars practiced harsh assimilationist policies that alienated subordinate groups. The Ottomans conceded autonomy to Christian subjects but by the late nineteenth century had been expelled from areas claimed for "nations" using names such as Serbian, Greek, Bulgarian, Rumanian. Apologists for these "nations" legitimized political claims in cultural terms: creating a national literature, constructing a confessional identity, elaborating national customs, ceremonies, and histories. Ethnic-cultural ideas figured more centrally than they had in the national movements of dominant cultural groups in western European territorial monarchies.

Linking ethnicity and nationality was one response to problems in multinational empires. Ethnic censuses asked people whether they were Germans or Czech (one could not answer "both" or "neither"). The Austrian socialists Otto Bauer (1882–1938) and Karl Renner (1870–1950) elaborated arguments separating political citizenship from national identity, anticipating contemporary debates on multiculturalism. However, with the collapse of multinational empires at the end of World War I, the stage was set for the ethnic nation-state.

National cultures did not neatly distribute themselves as territorial blocks. Nationalities were brought together, as in Czechoslovakia and Yugoslavia (meaning "south Slav," a name designed to bridge differences between Croatians, Serbs, and Slovenes). National minorities were created. One attempt to address resultant problems was by entrenching minority rights, to be monitored and enforced by the new League of Nations. This failed. Without strong and united support from the major Western powers, the League could not enforce rules. The doctrine of national sovereignty was understood to mean majority rule in a state that recognized no higher authority. The notion of citizenship as a property of *individuals* made it difficult to frame limitations on state power with respect to *groups*.

The Soviet Union had a national policy. Vladimir Ilyich Lenin (1870–1924) recognized the need to gain support from non-Russians. The state was a *union* of republics named by their dominant or "titular" nationality. The state recognized "personal" nationality, embodying this in passports and educational claims. The destruction of all political autonomy under Joseph Stalin (1879–1953) included the autonomy conceded to nationality. Nevertheless, cultivation of national identity and a system of national republics shaped the way the Soviet Union collapsed.

The breakdown of political order in central Europe saw ethnonationalism taken to extremes. Nationalist and racist movements aimed to destroy "inferior" nations or races by expulsion, exploitation, and murder. Arguably, racist justifications for race empire and genocide go beyond the idea of the nation that, if only implicitly, recognizes plurality and difference. However, fascism and Nazism drew upon arguments about the nation.

These extreme forms of ethnonationalism were defeated by 1945, but not before they had altered the map and mentality of Europe. The national states created after 1945 were ethnically more homogenous than those formed in 1919. Ethnic cleansing continued with the expulsion of Germans from other states. Yet the doctrine of national sovereignty was qualified by the formation of supranational blocs centered on the Soviet Union and the United States, as well as the formation of the United Nations. The title of this organization, as that of its predecessor the League of Nations, equates nation with state.

The Concept of Nation beyond Europe

The United Nations, an association of formally sovereign states, excluded colonies. Colonial nationalists argued for independence in political terms. Imperial powers could not reject democratic arguments, as these legitimized their own states. Racism, even if endemic in Europe and the United States, had been discredited. Imperialists could only argue that circumstances were unpropitious, divisions too acute, indigenous resources for self-rule inadequate.

There were other reasons for making the nation purely political. Boundaries of colonial states were arbitrary, dividing close-knit groups. The small-scale nature of many indigenous groups made it difficult, if not impossible, to identify a dominant culture. Nationalists confined themselves to challenging imperial rule within given boundaries. Hardly any postcolonial state has seen its boundaries change. The most important such case, Bangladesh, took the form of a separation within otherwise unchanged boundaries. Yet tension between nation as culture and as citizenship presented itself in the first important act of postwar decolonization, when Muslim movements achieved the separation of the state of Pakistan from India. The justification was that Muslims constituted a separate nationality.

Internal conflicts within postcolonial states have been explained in terms of cultural difference, variously described as ethnic, tribal, or national. Sometimes federal arrangements have been implemented to try to reduce these conflicts; sometimes there have been civil wars, expulsions, and genocides. However, in other cases a conception of nationality as citizenship has brought unity at the state level, even if multiple ethnic differences remain important.

Contemporary Problems with the Nation

There is tension between nation as citizenship and as culture, but such tension is frequently manageable. In specific cases it is difficult to imagine how, in the foreseeable future, Israelis and Palestinians or Croats and Serbs, for example, could live peaceably together in one state. Equally, it is difficult to see how the world could be stably organized on a thoroughgoing ethnonational basis.

First, there are problems of creating many small states and coping with the geographical intermixing of different nationalities. Second, there is the theoretical problem of what constitutes a nation. Making the nation-state the political norm encourages minorities to formulate demands in the name of the nation. When does a distinct cultural feature qualify for recognition as a separate nation? For some theorists the answer lies not in ethnonational states but in enabling nationalities to live together in one state. One approach seeks to divide political authority between nationalities geographically through federalism or explicit division of powers at the state level. Another approach is to entrench nationality rights on issues such as language, education, and worship. An alternative to these public recognitions of multiple nationalities is to make a firm public-private distinction, regarding nationality as a private cultural preference and the state as a secular and public authority above such preferences. All these policies confront severe problems and are matters of fierce political and intellectual debate.

For some the nation is banal, equated with existing state, society, and everyday life. For others it is under threat. For a few it is a prison they wish to leave. All these experiences are modern. The premodern political lineage of *natio* relates to *populus;* its premodern cultural lineage to *gens.* The rise of the sovereign, territorial, public, and participatory state made the question "Who are the people/nation?" acute. Once the argument that the nation was the sum of the citizens of the existing state proved inadequate, the search moved on to consider the claims of culture. Nation as a significant political concept represents a series of attempts to answer that modern question.

See also **Citizenship; Ethnicity and Race; Feudalism, European; Sovereignty; State, The.**

BIBLIOGRAPHY

Cobban, Alfred. *The Nation-State and National Self-Determination.* Rev. ed. London: Collins, 1969.

Forde, Simon, Lesley Johnson, and Alan V. Murray, eds. *Concepts of National Identity in the Middle Ages.* Leeds, U.K.: School of English, University of Leeds, 1995.

Greenfeld, Liah. *Nationalism: Five Roads to Modernity.* Cambridge, Mass.: Harvard University Press, 1992.

Hutchinson, John, and Anthony D. Smith, eds. *Nationalism.* Oxford and New York: Oxford University Press, 1994.

Kemilainen, Aira. *Nationalism: Problems concerning the Word, the Concept and Classification.* Jyväskylä, Finland: Jyväskylän Kasvatusopillinen Korkeakoulu, 1964.

Koselleck, Reinhart, et al. "Volk, Nation, Nationalismus, Masse." In *Geschichtliche Grundbegriffe: Historisches Lexikon zur politisch-sozialen Sprache in Deutschland,* edited by Otto Brunner, Werner Conze and Reinhart Koselleck, 141–431. Vol. 7. Stuttgart, Germany: E. Klett, 1978.

Miller, David. *On Nationality.* Oxford and New York: Oxford University Press, 1995.

Motyl, Alexander, ed. *Encyclopaedia of Nationalism.* 2 vols. Vol. 1: *Fundamental Concepts.* San Diego, Calif., and London: Academic Press, 2001.

Reynolds, Susan. *Kingdoms and Communities in Western Europe, 900–1300.* New York: Oxford University Press, 1997.

Scales, Len, and Oliver Zimmer, eds. *Power and the Nation in European History.* London: Palgrave, 2005.

Smith, Anthony D. *Nationalism and Modernism: A Critical Survey of Recent Theories of Nations and Nationalism.* London and New York: Routledge, 1998.

John Breuilly

NATIONAL HISTORY. The professionalization of history in nineteenth- and twentieth-century European universities was so closely related to the construction of the nation-state that national histories came to be seen as the only objective form of historical writing—indeed, criticism of national histories was seen not only as unpatriotic, but as a threat to the integrity of the historical profession and its claim to objectivity.

National histories regard the nation-state as the primary unit of historical analysis, and social, economic, intellectual, and other processes are contained within it. The nation is the subject of history, and the object of historical development is the realization of the nation-state. The nation is said to have long existed in a latent state, and its members are regarded as having an unchanging character. In Hegelian fashion, the nation becomes conscious of itself by overcoming obstacles such as linguistic diversity, fragmented trade patterns, and foreign occupation. National histories are morally judgmental and teleological. Specific periods of history are judged—in all senses of the term—according to the degree to which they advanced or retarded the national cause. "Great men" figure prominently in national histories: they act creatively because they understand the movement of history. National histories are also populated with villains—representatives of foreign powers and traitors to the national cause. While noxious in the short term, their efforts are doomed historically.

Nation Building and Professionalization

National histories were written before history was professionalized. Whig historians like Thomas Babington Macauley (1800–1859) located the English national genius in the development of parliamentary liberty. The Whigs' French counterparts held that history provided the unifying force that prevented individualism from undermining the social body, and that the Orleanist regime (1830–1848) represented the culmination of French history because it reconciled individual liberty with the national good. Some amateur national historians, influenced by positivism, felt that the triumph of the nation was scientifically inevitable. National histories represented one element in disparate amateur historical writing, which also included social, economic, religious, revolutionary, and women's history, and which were united by special pleading—often explicit. They were written as much to inspire as to inform.

The professionalization of history in the nineteenth century was predicated, as Lord Acton (1834–1902) put it, upon the removal of the poet and patriot from history. Acton's hero, Leopold von Ranke (1795–1886), rejected Hegelian teleologies on the grounds that individual periods should be understood in their own terms. The uniqueness of a set of events would be grasped by careful criticism of primary sources and their arrangement into an interpretation. Historians would constitute a profession, endowed with a special ability to understand the past objectively through the mastery of special skills.

In practice, it might be argued, professional historians merely provided scientific authority for existing ideas about the nation-state. Modern universities were created in periods of nation building, for which governments expected historians to provide historical legitimacy. In Prussia the universities expanded after defeat in the Napoleonic wars, in France after defeat at the hands of Prussia in 1870, and in Britain during a period when global preeminence seemed to be threatened by the rise of Germany and America.

It was not inevitable that nationalism should have acquired a historical dimension. The French revolutionaries (at least in theory) had preached a territorial nationalism, dependent upon the democratic choice of a people to live under a particular government. It was widely believed, however, that abstract rights had led to the dissolution of the social body and to the Jacobin Terror. Even democratic nationalists feared that abstract rights nationalism might permit the overthrow of any government at the behest of the people. A historically rooted nationalism limited a people's freedom to choose and provided a defense against unrestrained individualism, anarchy, and the recourse to despotism.

Moreover, nationalists and national historians were impressed by the pseudo-scientific pretensions of theories of race, Social Darwinism, and group psychology that depicted individuals as products of national and racial origin. But the extent to which individuals were prisoners of their nationality varied. Women, "inferior" races, workers, and peasants were seen as passive embodiments of the nation, who grasped the national idea "instinctively," or through the "fetishization" of national symbols and great men. The active carriers of the national idea were bourgeois men, who alone possessed the ability to understand the national idea rationally. To govern effectively, this elite needed to take account of national character and provide a people with a system of government in keeping with their characteristics. National history became an essential part of training for government, and in societies where gendered separate spheres were an integral part of bourgeois culture, it became an essential attribute of manliness too.

There were also intellectual reasons for privileging the nation-state. Ranke followed Johann Gottfried von Herder (1744–1803) in seeing peoples as "thoughts of God." Through a process of intuition, combined with careful documentary research, the historian could grasp the nation's unique spirit. While the historian could not discern the end of history, God was present in history, and the objective historian could glimpse something of God's divine plan.

Varieties of National History

Historians varied in the extent to which they were willing to endorse the particular version of nationalism espoused by their governments. In Germany professors were appointed by authoritarian conservative governments that monopolized power until 1918, and they shared the ruling nationalist ethos. In Britain political pluralism and the greater autonomy of the universities ensured a more diverse profession, but most historians wrote national histories of one sort or another.

The structures of national histories were flexible enough to encompass many different types of national history, including left and right wing, state and opposition nationalism. For some national historians the core of the nation is parliament, for some the state; for others it is the people defined in linguistic, historical, cultural, ethnic, or other terms. Contest over the meaning of national history was all the greater because professionals have never monopolized the writing of history.

Germany

Ranke's nationalism was relatively benign. He saw all nations as equal before God and urged historians to understand rather than judge. He was also conservative in an age when nationalism was a movement of the revolutionary and democratic left. His *History of Prussia* (1847) depicted Prussia as a territorial state rather than as the precursor of German unity. Nevertheless, Ranke held in *The Great Powers* that "the greatest possible unfolding of the rule of the spirit reveals itself among the most resolute" and believed that history should serve the state. The latter ideas were taken up by the neo-Rankeans of the 1890s. Max Lenz (1850–1932) saw the state as the expression of a people, engaged with other states in a struggle to preserve its uniqueness. He justified the expansionism of the German Reich while claiming to be wholly objective. Lenz's nationalism was not, however, aggressive enough for some extreme nationalists, who attacked both the "caution" and the "narrow specialization" of university historians. Amateur writers like Julius Langbehn (1851–1907) rewrote the history of Germany with a racially defined *Volk*, rather than the monarchical state, as its subject, and developed ambitious schemes for expansion in eastern Europe. Conservative nationalists survived the challenge of the extreme right, just as they did the German Revolution of 1918. Like *Völkisch* historians, the Nazis were critical of the "bloodless objectivism" of the historical establishment, but they too failed to breach the hegemony of the professoriat. While professional historians largely rejected the extreme racism of the Nazis, early medievalists in particular made concessions to the notion that the *Volk* was the agent of history, thus providing historiographical legitimation for Germany's mission in the east. From 1936 the prestigious *Historische Zeitschrift* published a rubric on the history of the "Jewish Question." After 1945 most historians continued to write traditional national history, denying German guilt for the outbreak of the Great War and reducing the Third Reich to a diversion from the normal path in German history. The German destiny was updated to lie in the Western alliance.

This picture was upset only in 1961, when Fritz Fischer published his *Griff nach der Weltmacht: Die Kriegszielpolitik des kaiserlichen Deutschlands 1914/18* (1961; English trans. *Germany's Aims in the First World War,* 1967). Whereas German historians had traditionally regarded all powers as equally responsible for the outbreak of war in 1914, Fischer claimed that German politicians had consciously risked world war. Furthermore, in a reversal of the usual assumption that foreign policy determined the character of a nation, he argued that both the Great War and the accession to power of Nazism were the result of the attempts of the Prussian aristocracy to preserve a social position threatened by modernization. Neither Fischer nor his many heirs broke with the national framework, however. Borrowing from Max Weber (1864–1920), they assumed a normal pattern of national "modernization" (an updated version of the idea of "progress") and attributed the disasters of German history to the attempts of her leaders to work against the grain of history—they did not act as "great men."

Britain

British historians embraced national histories as enthusiastically as their German counterparts. They assumed an unchanging national character and rooted the English constitution in the forests of Germany, but they disagreed on whether state or parliament was the vehicle of the national idea. Some historians had much in common with German partisans of power politics. The conservative J. R. Seeley saw Britain's racial destiny in imperial conquest and wrote his *Life and Times of Stein* in 1878. Geoffrey Elton did not speculate on the racial origins of English virtue but felt nevertheless that the English had discovered the perfect blend of order and liberty. In his *Tudor Revolution in Government* (1953), he claimed that the foundations of a unitary modern state had been laid in the 1530s by Thomas Cromwell, chiefly through the removal of the influence of the Catholic Church from government. He added that English rule over the "disordered" and "wild" Irish and Welsh was both beneficial and necessary. Interestingly, Elton, although a vociferous defender of value-free empirical history, argued for the theoretical primacy of political history. It concerned, he said, the ways in which people used their reason to organize society into a "properly constructed, continuously living body"—note again the Hegelian notion that through the development of the state a society becomes conscious of itself. Like Fischer, Elton assumed a necessary process of modernization, and the greatness of Cromwell lay in his ability to realize the meaning of history.

The liberal E. H. Freeman (1823–1892) developed the idea of an innate English love of liberty into a vast Aryan project, and his history of the Norman Conquest took the side of the Anglo-Saxons against despotic French invaders. In the interwar period, in the face of the Nazi threat, George Macauley Trevelyan wrote a history of England as the home of liberty yet repeated conventional prejudices about the Irish. Postwar left-wing historians abandoned racism but retained the notion of an English predisposition to liberty. For A. J. P. Taylor, German authoritarianism represented the antithesis of Englishness. The crux of his *Origins of the Second World War* (1961) was that Hitler's foreign policy represented a continuation of traditional German national aims. Taylor was a member of the Campaign for Nuclear Disarmament and believed that the peace-loving British were ideally placed to find a middle way between the two superpowers. The Marxist historian E. P. Thompson was also a leading campaigner against nuclear weapons. In "The Peculiarities of the English," Thompson described himself as a "socialist internationalist speaking in an English tongue" (p. 37). In his classic *Making of the English Working Class* (1963), he argued that the English bourgeoisie, frightened by the French Revolution, had betrayed the cause of liberty and failed to carry out a bourgeois revolution. The working class became the bearers of the tradition of the free-born Englishman.

The adaptability of the structures of national historical writing is illustrated by the historical works of opposition nationalists. John Davies's *History of Wales* (1993) is based on the assumption that although Welshness might be expressed in many ways (the author is especially concerned to reconcile industrial English-speaking Wales with rural Welsh-speaking Wales), there is a core national identity. He traces the resistance of "Wales and its attributes" to predictions of imminent oblivion that go back to Tacitus in 100 C.E. "This book," he concludes, "was written in the faith and confidence that the nation in its fullness is yet to be." The nation constitutes the subject of the historical process, and its realization in the nation-state represents the end of history.

John Davies's book is one of the major sources for Norman Davies's *The Isles: A History* (1999), which attacks the Anglo-centric Whig view of history and predicts the break-up of the British state. The book was welcomed by the Left and condemned by the Right. Yet its structure is typical of national histories, and in its emphasis on the reconciliation of Celt and Anglo-Saxon, and in the author's interest in J. R. R. Tolkien's dream of harmony between races, the book owes something to the new right's vision of a Europe made up of unique peoples. For Norman Davies, Britain has since the fourteenth century consisted of four distinct nations, all integrated into a European culture. The long separation of Britain from Europe, beginning with the Reformation, is an "aberration" in the history of the Isles. Britain returns to its true vocation with membership of the European Union.

Nation and History Today

Challenged by social, demographic, women's, and gender history, national histories no longer occupy the monopolist position they once did. In *The Practice of History* (1967) Geoffrey Elton reacted to the rise of explicitly theoretical social history with a vigorous defense of the objectivity of political history. In fact, the national framework has remained essential to historical writing. The social and women's history of the 1970s and 1980s continued to be written within the confines of nation-states, and much of it, as in Thompson's *Making of the English Working Class,* dealt with the question of national specificities. The impact of poststructuralism upon historical writing has not substantially altered the situation. Poststructuralism has led to suspicion of essentialist definitions of nation, class, and gender but has caused historians to focus upon the historical, and mutual, construction of identities, including national identities. As yet few historians have taken up the critique of national histories advanced by cultural transfer theorists.

The international political climate also sustains interest in national histories. In the Balkans, contemporary diplomats are as ready as their counterparts at Versailles in 1919 to use historical arguments to justify territorial claims. In eastern Europe postcommunist states are engaged in reassessing their pasts—often presenting the communist period as an aberration in the normal path of national development, just as German, Italian, and French historians explained away Nazism, Fascism, and collaboration. The European Union is also tempted by the use of history for purposes of historical legitimation. The Maastricht Treaty (1992) called upon the commission to "bring the common cultural heritage to the fore."

See also **Historiography; Nationalism.**

BIBLIOGRAPHY

Berger, Stefan. *The Search for Normality: National Identity and Historical Consciousness in Germany since 1800.* New York: Berghahn Books, 2003.

Berger, Stefan, Mark Donovan, and Kevin Passmore, eds. *Writing National Histories: Western Europe since 1800.* London and New York: Routledge, 1999.

Boer, Pim de. *History as a Profession: The Study of History in France, 1818–1914.* Translated by Arnold J. Pomercans. Princeton, N.J.: Princeton University Press, 1998.

Bosworth, R. J. B. *Explaining Auschwitz and Hiroshima: History Writing and the Second World War, 1945–1990.* London and New York: Routledge, 1993.

Breuilly, John. "Historians and the Nation." In *History and Historians in the Twentieth Century,* edited by Peter Burke. Oxford and New York: Oxford University Press, 2002.

Burleigh, Michael. *Germany Turns Eastwards: A Study of* Ostforschung *in the Third Reich.* Cambridge, U.K., and New York: Cambridge University Press, 1988.

Espagne, Michel, and Michael Werner, eds. *Transferts. Les relations interculturelles dans l'espace Franco-Allemand.* Paris: Éditions Recherche sur les civilisations, 1988.

Kenyon, John. *The History Men: The Historical Profession in England since the Renaissance.* London: Weidenfeld and Nicolson, 1983.

Slavin, Arthur J., "Telling the Story: G. R. Elton and the Tudor Age." *Sixteenth Century Journal* 21 (1990): 151–169.

Smith, Bonnie G. *The Gender of History: Men, Women and Historical Practice.* Cambridge, Mass., and London: Harvard University Press, 1998.

Stuchtey, Benedikt, and Peter Wende. *British and German Historiography, 1750–1950: Traditions, Perceptions, and Transfers.* Oxford and New York: Oxford University Press, 2000.

Thompson, E. P. "The Peculiarities of the English." In his *The Poverty of Theory.* London: Merlin Press, 1979.

Kevin Passmore

NATIONALISM.

This entry includes five subentries:

OVERVIEW

Nationalism is one of the most significant political ideas of the nineteenth and twentieth centuries, at the heart of worldwide and local conflicts penetrating every region of the globe. It can be defined simply as a political ideology that aims to bring about or to increase the political representation or power of "the nation" and has appeared in many forms in a wide variety of circumstances. It is first and foremost a theory of political legitimacy, which arose and developed in opposition to various theories that derived political legitimacy from other principles. Firstly, nationalism contested the absolutist claim to the divine right of kings that had supported the monarchies of the European ancien régime, claiming that "the nation" was a more legitimate source of power than a monarch. Secondly, nationalism can be seen in opposition to the Marxist theories that aristocratic or bourgeois supremacy should or will be replaced by the unification of the proletarian lower classes around the world, where class is held to be legitimate, rather than a nation. Marxist theories give economics precedence over

culture and integrate the ideology of nationalism into a class-based understanding of the world by labeling it as a "bourgeois" theory of legitimacy. Thus nationalism in the nineteenth and twentieth centuries can be thought of as one theory of political legitimacy competing with others for acceptance.

In different historical contexts, nationalism has been compatible with a wide variety of other political positions, from nineteenth-century economic liberalism, to fascism in the early twentieth century, and indeed forms of Marxism in the post-colonial debate. It can be argued that much of its power as a mover of people comes from its flexibility and adaptability, which in turn can be attributed to the vagueness of the concept of the "nation" that underlies it. A nation is a group of people identified as sharing any number of real or perceived characteristics, such as common ancestry, language, religion, culture, specific institutions, historic traditions, or shared territory. The members of such a group can identify themselves and the others as belonging to the group, and who have the will or desire to remain as a group, united through some form of organization, most often political. Since no two nations need to be defined in the same way, many different combinations of characteristics may be used as the basis for a national identity at the foundation of a nationalist movement. Nationalism thus exists in a variety of forms, the common feature being the use of a culturally defined national identity in a quest for political representation, legitimacy, or power.

In order to understand the ideology of nationalism, it is helpful to examine several of the historical contexts in which nationalism has played a significant part, and then to turn to several theoretical approaches that have been used to classify and interpret nationalism, including areas of debate.

Historical Manifestations

Nationalism first came to prominence in the Western world during the late eighteenth and early nineteenth centuries. With roots in the Enlightenment, nationalism was proliferated during the French Revolution of 1789 and elsewhere by those who opposed absolutism, seeking the replacement of kings by nations as the source of all legal and political authority. The revolutionaries sought, for example, to bring about a constitutional, legal regime with a national assembly dedicated to representing the citizens of the nation, thereby overthrowing absolutism and the idea of a hierarchical society of privileges based upon birth.

The idea of the legitimacy of the nation was spread around Europe via the Revolutionary and Napoleonic French armies, who both took their ideology with them, as well as provoking "nationalist" reactions to the French conquests. Although following Napoléon's defeat in 1815 the absolute monarchies were restored around Europe, republican nationalism had already penetrated much of the Continent, and for the next half century there were repeated outbreaks of violence in support of popular nationalism. At this stage, many of the nationalists thought of each other as allies, that the fight against absolutism was one that needed to be fought by the many nations and peoples together. Secret societies of democratic, nationalist opposition, such as Young Italy, Young Germany, and Young Ireland, were affiliated with one another in the quest to overthrow absolutism. Wars and revolutions were fought both to

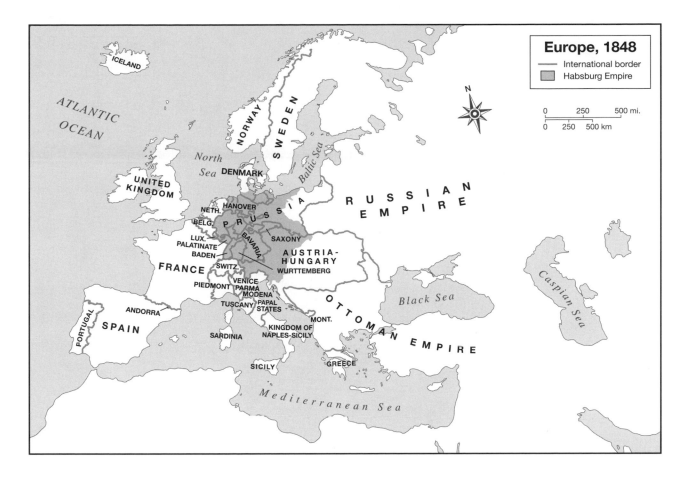

Europe, 1848

— International border

▓ Habsburg Empire

0 — 250 — 500 mi.

0 — 250 — 500 km

ICELAND

ATLANTIC OCEAN

NORWAY

SWEDEN

North Sea

DENMARK

Baltic Sea

UNITED KINGDOM

NETH.

HANOVER

BELG.

PRUSSIA

LUX.

PALATINATE

BADEN

BAVARIA

SAXONY

SWITZ.

FRANCE

AUSTRIA-HUNGARY

WURTTEMBERG

PIEDMONT

VENICE

PARMA

MODENA

TUSCANY

PAPAL STATES

ANDORRA

PORTUGAL

SPAIN

SARDINIA

KINGDOM OF NAPLES-SICILY

MONT.

SICILY

GREECE

RUSSIAN EMPIRE

OTTOMAN EMPIRE

Black Sea

Caspian Sea

Mediterranean Sea

overthrow an absolutist order and to bring about some kind of representative liberal assembly, and at the same time to create individual nation-states, either through the unification of numerous smaller states (such as Italy and Germany) or via the breakup of larger empires (such as Austria-Hungary). During the first half of the nineteenth century, nationalism was primarily supported by the educated middle classes and associated with the economic doctrines of liberalism.

The reaction to invasion during the Napoleonic period sowed the seeds for the type of nationalism that would become more common later in the nineteenth century, when constitutional monarchies and republics had replaced absolute monarchies in most of the European nations. Once absolutism ceased to be the enemy, the common cause of the nationalists disappeared and nation-states found their principal rivals in one another. National leaders concentrated on solidifying their position both with respect to their own populations and with other nations through the championship of their own nation's virtues, often relative to those of other nations.

In each nation-state, national identities were encouraged and developed by national school systems and the proliferation of the symbolism of each nation through flags, anthems, or monuments. Historians such as Jules Michelet (1798–1874) in France, musicians such as Frédéric Chopin (1810–1849) or Giuseppe Verdi (1813–1901), and poets and writers from all over Europe, convinced of their political mission, encouraged

national awareness and gave the weight of their popularity and of their academically recognized publications to their nation's glory. Wars involving the conscription of the common citizens used nationalist rhetoric to motivate their soldiers to fight, and many wars were fought in the name of the defense of nations and of national honor and glory, culminating in Europe in World Wars I and II.

At this stage, nationalism became associated with more right-wing, populist parties who sought to promote their own national cultural values and to increase the power and glory of their nation, often at the expense of other nations or of immigrants, at least rhetorically. This kind of populist nationalism can be understood as more than just patriotism, which is a sentiment of loyalty to the nation to which one belongs, because it includes the beliefs that one's own nation has a higher calling and greater value than other nations.

Nationalism was also a key motivating factor in European imperialist expansion throughout the nineteenth century. However, this very imperialist expansion provoked a nationalist reaction throughout much of the rest of the world. Nationalist ideas of independence were brought by the colonizers, and the occupation and rule by the imperial powers led to the anti-imperial national independence movements. From the principle of self-determination found in Woodrow Wilson's Fourteen Points and used as a basis for the post–World War I international settlement came the theory to support the numerous twentieth-century

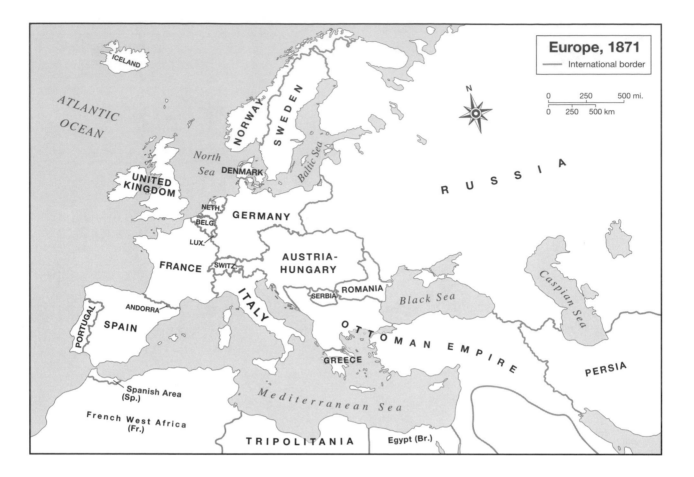

Europe, 1871
International border

wars of national liberation both from colonial powers and from larger states composed of more than one "nation."

The twentieth century saw innumerable conflicts in which nationalism was a motivating factor, and at the same time it saw the solidification of the system of nation-states as the primary form of social organization throughout the world. The United Nations became the primary international body, and nationhood became the goal of any group seeking to increase its political power.

Theories of Nationalism

In the same way that different nations may be defined according to quite different combinations of cultural characteristics, nationalism has not appeared in a single form, nor has it always conformed to the rough chronology outlined above. Sometimes nationalism emerges as a democratic antiauthoritarian movement, and at other times as a means to promote wars between nations, or obtain the unification or subdivision of territory, or as a force seeking the liberation of a territory from "foreign" domination. Nationalism's diversity has made it extremely difficult to develop an all-inclusive theory that can explain every historical apparition. Distinctions can be made between reformist, unificatory, and secessionist types, between revolutionary and counterrevolutionary forms, between successive liberal and conservative variants, and between European and colonial manifestations of nationalism. Many of these

systems of classification have as their base a fundamental distinction between two types of nation: civic and ethnic.

Civic and Ethnic Nations

According to this model, civic nations are characterized by the early development of a unified state, a long and shared political history and an emphasis on citizenship, whereas ethnic nations are characterized by threatened elites, early democratization or late modernization, the consolidation of a national culture, xenophobia, and the repressive presence of polyglot empires. The model tends to categorize northern and western European nations such as Britain, France, or the Netherlands as civic, with Germany, Italy, Russia, and nations of the Austro-Hungarian and Ottoman Empires as ethnic. Held occasionally to be "good" and "bad" types of nationalism, the model aimed in part to explain the phenomenon of violent, expansionist, or anti-Semitic nationalism without qualifying all nationalism as negative. Recent work has demonstrated the limitations of this model, as all nationalisms exhibited both civic and ethnic characteristics, and a simple classification is not always helpful.

The Perennialists

The question of how certain cultural characteristics come to be identified as those defining a nation, as well as how they come to exist in the first place, has inspired two scholarly

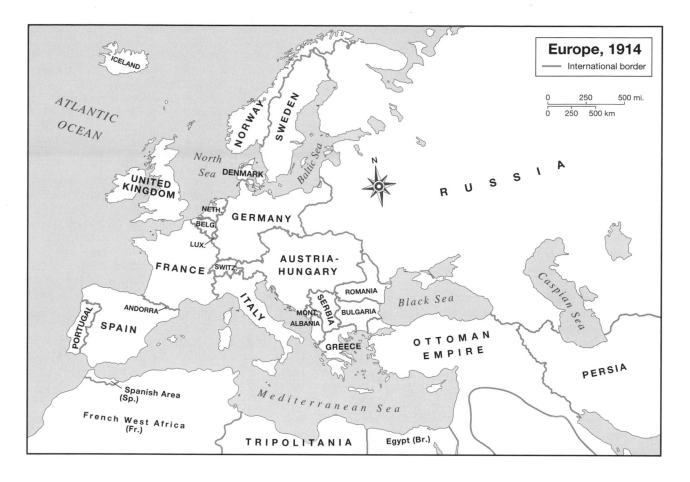

Europe, 1914
International border

0 250 500 mi.
0 250 500 km

debates: first the question of invention or preexistence of nations, and second whether nations and nationalism are linked with modernity. The first position with regard to the origins of the common cultural base is that national cultural characteristics exist and are a natural result of humans living in society. This is the position of the "perennialists," who argue that nations, whether natural or not, have existed as long as humans have lived in "society," as well as of many nationalists who seek to claim that their nations are "natural," having existed for many centuries. According to this position, the history of nations and nationalism can be found by tracing the evolution of the cultural characteristics that define each nation and their inscription on the human landscape over time. Even where the characteristics are considered to be symbolic or mythical, they are held to preexist consciousness of them by the members of the nation.

This debate is linked to, but not completely identical with, the question of the existence of nations in the premodern period. Historians such as Adrian Hastings argue that even if they have not "always" existed, nations have existed in Europe for several centuries, and their development is not directly linked to the arrival of modernity. Their arguments are based upon the certain existence and consciousness of large ethnic groupings, as well as the use of the word *nation* by these groups to describe themselves during the Middle Ages.

The Modernists

The opposite position to those who describe nation as perennial is that nations as they are understood now have developed within a particularly modern context and are invented or imagined rather than naturally existing. This is the position of Benedict Anderson, who defines nations as "imagined political communities." This imagination does not imply "falsity" but only that the reality of national cultural characteristics lies in the perception of them by both the members and those outside of the nation, rather than in an underlying "fact" of their existence independent of any consciousness of them. Further to this idea is the notion that much of the culture defined as national is made up of what Eric Hobsbawm and Terence Ranger have described as "invented" traditions: rituals or symbols that imply continuity with the past and seek, through repetition, to encourage certain patterns of behavior or thinking. According to this position, when examining questions about the nation it is more profitable to begin with nationalism and the nation than with the reality they represent. It is the differing concepts of the nation that eventually, through time, inscribe themselves into the very society that they claim to portray. Ernest Gellner writes that the high culture which characterizes nations is not something that is natural but that must be learned, and nationalism's roots must be found in the pervading social order rather than in human nature, instinct, or the human psyche. The defined national culture gradually infuses the rest of the population with the image(s) it has formed of itself.

According to this theory, the modern state is central in this endeavor as a framework within which nationalist movements can operate. It is also necessary as a mechanism to encourage the people's identification with national history and other images, as well as the extension of the national high culture that is at the center of the nation's identity. John Breuilly stresses this role of the modern state and its institutions in the growth of nationalism and argues indeed that the modern state is the most important feature of the political context in which a nationalist movement can arise. This does not imply that nationalism is a direct product of the modern state, only that within the context of such a state nationalism has much greater potential as a political force. Nationalism, seen as a form of political opposition to absolutism within the newly emerging type of state, leads directly to a conflict over organization and sovereignty. The increasing significance of the state, its institutions and administrative structure, as well as its ability to control and manipulate images in the modern period also contribute to the extension of both national ideologies or traditions and the literate culture to the masses once one group of nationalists has gained control.

The development of technology that enables mass communication, rapid travel, and sophisticated record keeping provided nation-states with enhanced resources to preserve the loyalty of populations and also to encourage what Michael Billig has termed *Banal Nationalism* (not "banal" in the sense of unimportant). He refers to the phenomenon of the reinforcement of national identity through numerous unconscious reminders of the nation in all of the small habits of social life, via expanding material culture and through the media. From "national" forms such as income tax or social security to the shape and color of mailboxes, lettering on license plates, vocabulary developed to describe diplomas, jobs, laws or customs, and national weather and news reports, everywhere there are subtle and subconscious reminders of the nation, in such a way as to make that which is national seem natural and given.

Permeating societies at a variety of conscious and subconscious levels, capable of application to any number of combinations of group characteristics, and compatible with a wide range of other political ideologies, nationalism is not yet a political idea that has inspired consensus among those analyzing it. Nevertheless, over two hundred years after its emergence as a political theory, it is still one of the most powerful political forces in the world.

See also Historiography; Nation; National History; Political Science.

BIBLIOGRAPHY

Anderson, Benedict. *Imagined Communities: Reflections on the Origin and Spread of Nationalism*. 2nd ed. London and New York: Verso, 1991.

Baycroft, Timothy. *Nationalism in Europe, 1789–1945*. Cambridge, U.K., and New York: Cambridge University Press, 1998.

Berger, Stefan, Mark Donovan, and Kevin Passmore, eds. *Writing National Histories: Western Europe since 1800*. London and New York: Routledge, 1999.

Billig, Michael. *Banal Nationalism*. London and Thousand Oaks, Calif.: Sage, 1995.

Breuilly, John. *Nationalism and the State*. 2nd ed. Manchester, U.K.: Manchester University Press, 1993.

Gellner, Ernest. *Nations and Nationalism*. Oxford: Blackwell, 1983.

Greenfeld, Liah. *Nationalism: Five Roads to Modernity*. Cambridge, Mass.: Harvard University Press, 1992.

Guibernau, Montserrat. *Nationalisms: The Nation-State and Nationalism in the Twentieth Century*. Cambridge, U.K.: Polity Press, 1996.

Hastings, Adrian. *The Construction of Nationhood: Ethnicity, Religion and Nationalism*. Cambridge, U.K., and New York: Cambridge University Press, 1997.

Hobsbawm, E. J. *Nations and Nationalism since 1780: Programme, Myth, Reality*. Cambridge, U.K., and New York: Cambridge University Press, 1990.

Hobsbawm, Eric, and Terence Ranger, eds. *The Invention of Tradition*. Cambridge, U.K., and New York: Cambridge University Press, 1983.

Smith, Anthony D. *Nationalism and Modernism: A Critical Curvey of Recent Theories of Nations and Nationalism*. London and New York: Routledge, 1998.

Woolf, Stuart, ed. *Nationalism in Europe, 1815 to the Present: A Reader*. London and New York: Routledge, 1996. Collection of important primary texts.

Timothy Baycroft

AFRICA

The topic of African nationalism has been repeatedly contested and redefined over the past century. At the end of the nineteenth century, the European powers divided the continent and ruled virtually all of Africa, and African nations lost their sovereignty. During the 1950s and 1960s, when Africans began to seriously resist colonial rule, Africa underwent a major transformation and each colony eventually gained its freedom. Africans, in general, united in hopes of regaining their sovereignty. *Nationalism* originally referred to the process of uniting and regaining freedom from European rule, but it was also defined by pioneer African leaders to mean the creation of new nations as well as their economic and political transformation.

Development of African Nationalism
While a country such as Britain or Germany is viewed as one nation, in reality each contains a variety of nations or peoples. Uniting these various groups through common interests creates a nation. These nations are, as Benedict Anderson writes, "imagined" rather than "real." Anderson explains:

> [A nation] is an imagined political community. . . . It is *imagined* because the members of even the smallest nation will never know most of their fellow-members, meet them, or even hear of them, yet in the mind of each lives the image of their communion. (p. 6)

A nation is a created community that believes that, though the community is diverse, as a whole it has a common interest that trumps all other interests; nationalism is the formation of this national identity.

African nationalism attempted to transform the identity of Africans. Rather than seeing themselves as Igbo or Hausa,

Kikuyu or Masai, nationalist leaders wanted Africans to view themselves as Kenyan, Nigerian, and so forth. While the idea appears simple in theory, it proved far more difficult in practice. The colonial powers never considered that the colonies would eventually form sovereign nations, and ethnic groups were treated as separate "tribal" or religious groups so that colonial officials could play them against each other, thereby keeping a colony's populace divided, and, thus, less likely to work together to overthrow European rule. Various groups continued such practices even after independence, and the African continent in general suffered from religious and ethnic strife during the latter half of the twentieth century.

To compound matters further, the modern boundaries of African nations are not age-old ones recognized for centuries but arbitrary lines decided by European rulers in Germany at the Congress of Berlin in 1885. The events following that Congress are known as the "Scramble for Africa." Whereas many European nations have one ethnic group, this was not the case for African nations, colonial boundaries throughout Africa were not in alignment with precolonial ones. Colonial borders often split ethnic groups, spreading them into various countries rather than uniting them into single nations. The Somali, for instance, were split up among four colonies. Therefore, when examining African nationalism, one must consider that borders are not "natural" or old, and that every African colony has many different factions.

A major dilemma that confronted early African nationalists was how to retain an African identity while appropriating the positive attributes of Western development. Whether to completely adopt English or French ways, to reject them completely, or find some sort of compromise were questions that Africans had to confront. Some, who realized the strengths of their missionary education and Christianity and were content to perpetuate colonial norms, felt that Africans should strive to mirror European culture and life.

Initially, African nationalist movements were led by middle-class intellectuals. These elites usually had a missionary education and viewed themselves as brokers between colonial officials and the African people. As Basil Davidson observes: "These were minority movements, restricted mostly to the 'lawyer-merchant class,' timid in their protests, opposed to any call for mass support" (p. 74). In other words, these early nationalist movements were inherently elitist, not true mass movements, and, thus, were not representative of "the people." These elites were much wealthier and better educated than their peers, grateful for the advantages bestowed on them by their missionary education, and loyal to the colonial powers. Instead of transferring governing power to the African people, many of these early leaders felt that the colonial state should simply hand over power to them.

Others envisioned an "Africa for Africans" and sought to reclaim Africa for the native peoples. They refused to adopt European values and many aspects of Europe's cultures, and thought it fruitless to do so. Edward Wilmot Blyden (1832–1912), widely regarded as "the Father of Cultural Nationalism," felt that Africans must revive their cultures and relearn their traditions from those least influenced by colonial rule. Throughout the period of colonial rule, Africans were repeatedly told that their cultures were uncivilized, primitive, evil, and barbaric, and that their history began with the arrival of Europeans. Therefore, nationalist leaders had to "decolonize" the African mindset as well as overthrow colonial rule. African nationalists sought to "reeducate" their followers, and began to promote black pride. African foods, music, dress, architecture, and religion were celebrated and promoted as equal to, if not better than, their European counterparts. While these steps may seem minor, nationalists believed that, without such a cultural revival, Africans would forever perceive themselves as inferior to Europeans if they failed to regain the pride and self-worth that colonization had taken away from them.

This return to "tradition," however, was also problematic because African traditional rituals, leaders, governments, and policies were exploited or manipulated by colonial governments, often unintentionally. As Hobsbawm and Ranger explain:

> British administrators set about inventing African traditions for Africans. Their own respect for "tradition" disposed them to look with favour upon what they took to be traditional in Africa. They set about to codify and promulgate these traditions, thereby transforming flexible custom into hard prescription. (p. 212)

Pan-Africanism

A major advance in African nationalist movements came with the Pan-Africanist movement. Though its roots were in early abolitionist movements, Pan-Africanism, which sought to unite Africans and overcome ethnicity by stressing the similarities and connections among all Africans, blossomed in the early twentieth century. Originally led by blacks in America, Britain, and the Caribbean, the movement did not initially fully represent the needs of Africans, but blacks throughout the world came to view themselves in a position similar to those of others of African descent in Britain, the United States, and throughout Latin America.

The two most notable leaders of early Pan-Africanism were Marcus Garvey (1887–1940) and W. E. B. DuBois (1868–1963). Garvey, whose outspoken nature attracted many followers, believed that blacks would never be treated as the equals of whites in America and must return "home" to Africa if they were to be free. DuBois, who had earned a doctorate in history from Harvard in 1896, may be the greatest Pan-Africanist intellectual ever. He argued that Africa had a glorious past and that Africans had deeply influenced Western civilization. He believed that Africa had to be freed from colonial rule if African Americans were to be liberated, and his work sought to end the caricatures of blacks as the "clown of history, football of anthropology, and the slave of industry" (p. ix).

The Great Depression hurt Africa greatly. Employment, especially in rural areas, was scarce. Many migrated from the countryside to urban areas, and the populations of cities swelled. These areas became overcrowded and poverty was rampant. The European powers were ill-equipped to combat these developments because resources and attention were focused on World War II. This furthered discontent and Africans became more disorderly. Bolstered by the influx of returning soldiers, nationalist movements throughout Africa were energized. By the 1940s, nationalist movements were becoming more radical, and Africans everywhere began to protest colonial rule as they increasingly realized how wrong and oppressive it was.

As the century progressed, the nationalist movements began to attract more people and to wield more influence. Leaders who could relate to and represent more than one group or class became household names and heroes. These leaders mobilized "the people" rather than a select few or one ethnic group. Obafemi Awolowo (1909–1987; Nigeria), Kwame Nkrumah (1909–1972; Ghana), Jomo Kenyatta (1889–1978; Kenya), Julius Nyerere (1922–1999; Tanzania), and Nelson Mandela (b. 1918; South Africa) belong to this new generation of leaders who successfully reached out and enlisted the support of their countries' population.

The Italian invasion of Ethiopia in 1935 marked a turning point in African history. Ethiopia was Africa's only truly independent nation. The invasion radicalized African nationalist movements and caused Africans to see themselves as peers and comrades in similar struggles. In general, they felt that Ethiopia symbolized a free, proud, civil, and successful Africa. As long as Ethiopia remained free of colonial domination, many believed that their dream of freedom and independence remained alive and achievable. If Ethiopia fell, however, then the hope for an independent Africa would die with it. Africans across the continent rallied to support Ethiopia, and blacks around the world attempted to supply both military and financial support for the Ethiopian cause.

African Nationalism after World War II

The next significant event in the development of African nationalism was World War II. Nearly two million Africans were recruited as soldiers, porters, and scouts for the Allies during the war. When these soldiers returned home, they returned to colonial states that still considered them inferior. Many veterans had expected that their dedication to colonial governments would be recognized and they would be rewarded accordingly. This was not to be, and these soldiers returned home to conditions worsened by a weak global economy. Because they had fought to protect the interests of the colonial powers only to return to the exploitation and indignities of colonial rule, these men became bitter and discontented.

In 1945, the Pan-African Manchester Congress in England marked a turning point because it attempted to address the needs of all blacks. Pan-Africanism began to stress common experiences of blackness and sought the liberation of all black people around the world. African leaders became more influential in the movement as they used it to attack colonial rule, and the movement would become more African-based after 1945.

Pan-Africanism proved very popular among nationalist African leaders because it offered a way for them to overcome both regionalism and ethnic divides by stressing commonalities and a common oppression. By the 1950s, Pan-Africanism had profoundly influenced almost every African nationalist leader: Kwame Nkrumah, Kenyatta, Nyerere, Kenneth Kaunda (1964–1991; Zambia), Haile Selassie (1892–1975; Ethiopia), Albert Luthuli (c. 1898–1967; South Africa), and Nnamdi

Azikiwe (1904–1996; Nigeria), all were deeply affected by the movement.

Kwame Nkrumah is regarded as the father of "Africanized" Pan-Africanism. Nkrumah detested colonial rule. Schooled in the United States, he was deeply influenced by the African American civil rights struggle, and began to emphasize the similarities between those struggles and those of African peoples. He argued that African workers and peasants needed to reclaim their independence, and advocated the use of force if necessary. For this to happen, Africans had to shed their strong ethnic or religious identities and see themselves simply as black or African rather than Yoruba or Fante. Nkrumah's intense disdain for colonial rule, zealous enthusiasm for independence, and the ideal of a United States of Africa made him popular among Africans throughout the continent. Nkrumah argued that they could not look to any outside power for support, and believed that foreign economic and political forces eroded African values. He also disagreed with the idea of returning to "African tradition." Instead, he argued that a new African identity must be created out of Islam, Christian, and traditional cultures.

Nnamdi Azikiwe was a prominent Pan-Africanist and an important thinker. Unlike most Pan-Africanists, Azikiwe rejected various aspects of Africa's past such as chieftaincy and informal education. He also rejected Nkrumah's united Africa, and advocated the use of colonial boundaries to define nations. For him, a united Africa meant cooperation, but not an actual unification of the continent. As Nigeria achieved independence and rapidly moved toward regionalism, Azikiwe abandoned his Pan-Africanist ideals for regional politics.

Pan-Africanism reinforced notions of black pride, and African history was used to foster a national identity. Many nationalist leaders stressed past empires (for example, the Mali and Asante), achievements (such as those of great Zimbabwe and ancient Egypt), and leaders (Shaka Zulu [c. 1787–1828] and Emperor Menelik of Ethiopia [1844–1913] among them) as a means to instill pride among African peoples. By stressing the continent's successes throughout its history, African leaders sought to convince their followers of their own worth and that Europeans were not superior to them. Again, the aim was to restore pride in Africa and create a sense of unity that nations could use to foster nationalism.

African women were major contributors to resistance to colonial rule and the promotion of nationalism. Many argue that women fared the worst under colonial rule. Governments such as those in Rhodesia, Kenya, and South Africa sought to restrict women's movement and even banned them from urban areas. In rural areas, they were often expected to maintain food production and raise children while their husbands rotted in jails, migrated to other areas in search of wage labor, or fought in wars (both in World War II and various liberation struggles). These women did not idly sit back and allow colonial governments to impinge on their rights, and, in response to their harsh situation under colonial rule, they organized protests, boycotts, workers' strikes, and demonstrations. In Kenya, Zimbabwe, Algeria, and other areas that attempted armed struggle, women as well as men carried messages, spied, and prepared meals. Overall, their impact on the anticolonial and nationalist movements throughout Africa was profound.

While Africans were widely successful in fostering nationalism in order to overthrow colonial oppressors, maintaining this unity after independence proved far more difficult. African nationalism was overtly anticolonial. For these nationalist movements, energy was concentrated on gaining freedom rather than planning how to run a country once freedom was achieved. Overthrowing colonial regimes was quite difficult, so these leaders could not afford to spend manpower, funds, and effort planning how to govern their new nations if they were successful.

Postcolonial Nationalism in Africa

Each African nation took a unique path toward independence. Some, such as Algeria, Mozambique, and Zimbabwe, took extreme measures like waging a guerilla war on the colonial state; most countries pursued nonviolent means and achieved a peaceful transfer of power. But there were varying degrees of success. Some countries, such as Ghana, became completely independent while others, such as Congo, continued to depend on Europe, and their independence was superficial rather than absolute.

As the age of independence dawned, African leaders faced the daunting tasks of developing their vastly underdeveloped economies and reversing the economic ills of imperialism. Largely, African nations leaned toward leftist ideologies (such as Marxism and socialism) or capitalism. Because the Soviet Union possessed no African colonies, it was perceived as an ally of anticolonial movements. Nyerere, Nkrumah, Ahmed Sékou Touré (1922–1984), and Muammar Gadhafi (b. 1942; Libya) attempted to "indigenize" leftist doctrines and became the continent's leading leftist thinkers. They blamed Western capitalists' imperialism for Africa's ills, and believed the overthrow of capitalism and imperialism was the only way to truly liberate Africa. Precolonial African societies were based on communalism, and many viewed socialist and Marxist ideologies as a way for African nations to return to their precolonial ways of living because they promised economic equality and a classless society. Others felt that nations on the left, such as Cuba, the USSR, and China, should be looked to as allies and for aid; the leftist powers proved incapable of providing enough aid and support, however, and both socialism and Marxism have been abandoned throughout Africa. Nations that chose capitalism proved equally unsuccessful because African economies were not diverse enough to sustain development. World Bank and structural adjustment programs proposed by the West only worsened Africa's underdevelopment. The debt of these nations increased exponentially and their economies weakened considerably.

Consequently, African nationalistic ideals of the 1950s and 1960s have waned. African nations have not succeeded in convincing their countries' populations to put national interests ahead of regional, ethnic, or religious ones. In various parts of Africa, politics has progressed so that leaders must rely on the backing of their own ethnic group, and, if one branches out too far, he or she will be replaced by someone who will better represent interests of the specific ethnic group. In other words, being loyal to one ethnic group, religious faith, or

geographical region can offer protection, but it also creates great divides in society. Ethnic divisions have hurt both nationalism and development in Africa. Countries such as Nigeria, Burundi, Rwanda, Uganda, and Zimbabwe have had their share of ethnic rivalries, civil wars, and genocide. In order to avoid ethnic clashes, some leaders advocated socialism, military rule, or one-party states, but these ideas have failed and such maneuvers have served only to widen ethnic divisions.

Many African nations have failed to maintain a strong sense of nationalism or national identity. Ethnic rivalries, diseases, unemployment, globalization, corruption, greed, and natural disasters have all played major roles in the dire reality that is post-independence Africa. African nationalism of the 1950s and 1960s was overtly anticolonial or anti-European. Once the colonial powers formally pulled out, Africans looked inward to consolidate power and rid themselves of political rivals. Military coups, one-party political systems, widespread corruption, and tyrannical autocrats became the norm.

As a result, numerous scholars have provided many valid criticisms of nationalist movements. Initially, scholars harshly criticized African ruling parties and political systems as they tended to promote corruption, violence, and tribalism as well as sponsoring useless plans for development. Most experts of the 1960s believed that independence would bring about progress and development. By the late 1970s, such optimism had been eradicated, most scholars became pessimistic about Africa's future, and "Afropessimism" became an ideology of its own. Civil wars, depleted economies, increasing debt, skyrocketing unemployment, and despotic leaders led many to become disheartened and to give up hope.

More recent critiques have been twofold. One type offers deeper analyses of how these negative systems operate and goes beyond identifying the problems in order to fully understand how coups and tyrants can be eliminated. Leroy Vail's work is an example of this approach. His *The Creation of Tribalism in Southern Africa,* an edited collection of essays, aims to explore why and how tribalism has been employed throughout both the colonial and postcolonial eras. Instead of accepting tribalism as inevitable, Vail discusses how ethnic identities have been manipulated and strengthened over the past century, while demonstrating how the educated elites and the continent-wide movement toward one-party rule promoted tribalism: it was a way for leaders to secure support even when their policies failed. As he puts it, "They concentrate upon its heroes, its historical successes, and its unsullied cultural purity, and are decked out with the mythic 'rediscovered' social values of the past" (p. 14). In other words, tribalism and ethnic affiliations became easy ways to achieve or consolidate power when development failed. They have allowed regional nationalism to blossom while weakening national identities as a whole.

The second type of critique emphasizes areas where Africans themselves have succeeded despite such difficult surroundings. Richard Werbner and Terence Ranger document how Africans, in general, react and cope with despotic leaders and harsh political realities. Werbner and Ranger aim "to show how and why the present reconstructions of personal and collective identity, of social subjectivity, and of moral agency draw on the culturally nuanced resources of social memory for negation, for affirmation, and for playful fun" (p. 4). Their work recognizes agency on the part of the African masses, instead of assuming them to be helpless pawns in the hands of tyrants. While these achievements are not monolithic, acknowledging them does serve to diminish the pessimistic view that Africa is doomed to remain lawless and antidemocracy.

While Africa has failed to develop along the lines of nations such as Japan or the United States, nationalism has not been completely erased. Manifestations of nationalism and national unity are most apparent during times of natural disaster, sporting events, and international crises. For Africa to compete in the twenty-first-century's global economy, African nations must foster stronger national identities that can be sustained for an extended period. The unity has to be permanent and not as easily dissipated as the attempts of the 1960s. It must also be strong enough to overcome ethnic divisions and rivalries that have plagued the continent since independence. Poverty, AIDS, starvation, globalization, and negative interference by the West may be common problems that will finally unite Africans and foster such nationalism.

See also **Africa, Idea of; Afropessimism; Anticolonialism: Africa; Black Atlantic; Black Consciousness; Capitalism: Africa; Colonialism: Africa; Development; Empire and Imperialism; Ethnicity and Race: Africa; Globalization: Africa; Neocolonialism; Pan-Africanism; State, The: The Postcolonial State; Westernization: Africa.**

BIBLIOGRAPHY
Anderson, Benedict R. *Imagined Communities: Reflections on the Origin and Spread of Nationalism.* New York: Verso, 2002.
Bayart, Jean Francois, Stephen Ellis, and Beatrice Hibou. *The Criminalization of the State in Africa.* Oxford: The African Institute, 1999.
Boahen, A. Adu. *African Perspectives on Colonialism.* Baltimore: John Hopkins Press, 1987.
Davidson, Basil. *Modern Africa: A Social and Political History.* New York: Longman, 1994.
DuBois, W. E. B. *The Autobiography of W. E. B. DuBois.* New York: International, 1968.
Esedebe, P. Olisanwuche. *Pan-Africanism: The Idea and Movement, 1776–1963.* Washington, D.C.: Howard University Press, 1982.
Falola, Toyin, ed. *Africa,* Vol. 4: *The End of Colonial Rule, Nationalism, and Decolonization.* Durham, N.C.: Carolina Academic Press, 2002.
———. *Nationalism and African Intellectuals.* Rochester, N.Y.: University of Rochester Press, 2001.
———. *The Power of African Cultures.* Rochester, N.Y.: University of Rochester Press, 2003.
Hobsbawm, Eric, and Terence Ranger, eds. *The Invention of Tradition.* New York: Cambridge University Press, 2002.
Hodgkin, Thomas. *Nationalism in Colonial Africa.* New York: New York University Press, 1957.
Joseph, Richard, ed. *State, Conflict, and Democracy in Africa.* Boulder, Colo.: Lynne Rienner, 1999.
Mazrui, Ali A., and Michael Tidy. *Nationalism and New States in Africa: From About 1935 to the Present.* Nairobi, Kenya: Heinemann, 1984.
Nkrumah, Kwame. *Neo-Colonialism: The Last Stage of Imperialism.* New York: International, 1965.
Vail, Leroy, ed. *The Creation of Tribalism in Southern Africa.* London: James Currey, 1989.
Webner, Richard, and Terence Ranger. *Postcolonial Identities in Africa.* London: Zed Books, 1996.
Zachernuk, Philip S. *Colonial Subjects: An African Intelligentsia and Atlantic Ideas.* Charlottesville: University Press of Virginia, 2000.

Toyin Falola
Tyler Fleming

CULTURAL NATIONALISM

Literary critics and historians use *cultural nationalism* to refer to collective practices that form modern political communities within, unsanctioned by, or even undercutting state authority. Such collective practices include the "high" culture disseminated via public media, established in publicly funded institutions such as universities and museums; as well as the "low" culture of popular performance and markets. Cultural nationalism, then, is distinct from patriotism, national literatures, or similar state-referenced collective identities. At present, cultural nationalism figures in discussions of why English literature should be taught in universities, as well as those concerning the content and selection criteria for what is taught as comparative literature. Even though Britain plays a minor role in international trade and politics, Britain's works of literature continue to serve as the standard of taste and literary value. Bill Ashcroft, Gareth Griffiths, and Helen Tiffin (1989) note that, even when postcolonial societies achieve political independence, the issue of colonialism remains relevant. Early-twenty-first-century historians also use cultural nationalism to discuss affinities, experiences, or practices that serve as the basis for common political views; what unites individuals (who may even carry different passports) could be common language and ethnic identity—even literary and musical tastes, dramatic films, cuisine, and sports spectatorship.

Two references to the definition of culture can serve as starting points for a discussion of cultural nationalism in literature. The first is from Raymond Williams's *Culture and Society* (1958). His four-part definition considers culture from both humanistic and anthropological perspectives, granting the same importance to those who define cultural practices for the global North's institutions of higher education, as to those who live culture every day. Williams liberates nationalism from the state and its patriotisms. Those who were denied privileged access to the state and public institutions—women, economic under classes, and others—participated in forming the nation even though Empire was a fundamental and constitutive part of Europe's social fabric, intellectual discourse, and the imaginary lives of its citizenry. Politically committed British academics led by Stuart Hall (*Popular Arts* [1965] and *The Young Englanders* [1967]) insisted that ongoing economic and political relations with the postcolonial United States formed "universal" traditions increasingly identified with European-American modernity.

Culture and Nationalism: Separate Ideas
The term *cultural nationalism* has gained increasing acceptance since the late twentieth century. Previously, however, the ideas of culture and nationalism were treated separately.

Jean-Jacques Rousseau (1712–1778) was identified as the father of modern political nationalism, a role he shared with Johann Gottfried von Herder (1744–1803). Culture, that is, as defined before the idea of cultural nationalism was embraced, was closely tuned to Europe's classical and modern history and philosophies: Etymologies and definitions for culture and civilization could be traced from the classical Mediterranean, including those provided by Giambattista Vico (1668–1744), von Herder, and Immanuel Kant (1724–1804).

Focus on the separate ideas of culture and nationalism continued among certain communities in the late twentieth century. In addition to accepting von Herder on culture, Ernst Gellner (1983) returned to Kant's ideas regarding Europe's "modern" ways of thought. Gellner relied on both von Herder and Kant to describe how education imposed "high culture" on industrial societies. National identities were not Europe's primordial heritage; rather, for Gellner, nationalism was awakened or invented to accomplish the kind of cultural homogeneity industrial society considered necessary: "nations, like states, are a contingency, and not a universal necessity" (p. 6). Elie Kedourie gives von Herder his due with the assertion that nationalism was invented in Europe in the early nineteenth century. For Kedourie, nationalism seemed alien to the non-European world, the residents of which are denied authentic recourse to the claims of the nation: expression of unique character, self-determination, or contribution from their natural genius to humanity's common fund.

From Europe to a Worldview

In the mid-1970s, observations concerning modern Europe and its ability to represent a universal ideal became increasingly contentious. Thus the discussion in this article turns from Europe's culture to a worldwide perspective, following a brief detour from structuralist to poststructuralist philosophy, since that transition influenced studies by historians and literary critics of the world outside Europe.

Structural philosophy and linguistics used such binary oppositions as true/false, civilized/savage, culture/nature, modern/primitive, and public/private to decide what was worthy of study, and what was not. These opposing terms were indebted to the same forms of authority that created modern nation-states in Europe, and therefore owe some part of their power to states' monopoly over coercive force. Jacques Derrida and other poststructuralist philosophers recognize that such binary terms are not equally valued since the term in the structurally dominant position assumes the power to define its opposite. Such hierarchical oppositions grant mind power over nature, cognition privilege over feeling, and reason over desire, as discussed in Derrida's article, "La Différance" (1972). Feminists adopted similar strategies to conceptualize masculinist authority. For others, the West enjoyed a cultural nationalism not merely over "The Rest," but at its expense.

Scholars employed in English and comparative literature departments around the world may describe their work as Third World literature, or literature of resistance. Discussions of cultural nationalism cluster around language, genre, and analogy. While postcolonial intellectuals recognize neocolonial economic and political relations, many write in European languages. Drama and poetry in local languages were central to postcolonial politics of global literature; among prose genres, fiction and travelogue, which are closely tied to European forms, are used for critiques of nineteenth-century modernities. And by means of analogy, the feminine is marked as differentiated from European modernities.

Franz Fanon's work—in particular, an address to the second Congress of Black Writers and Artists, which met in Rome in 1959, published as a chapter in *Wretched of the Earth* (1963)—asserts that the demand for a national culture and the affirmation of such culture's existence represents a special battlefield. Reference to the dignity, glory, and solemnity of a past culture rehabilitates the nation when addressing colonialism's distortion, disfiguration, and destruction of precolonial histories. Yet in discussing Arab cultural nationalism and negritude, Fanon notes the fatally ambiguous position of the native intellectual as it develops through three phases: unqualified assimilation, poetic exoticism, and finally the literature of national struggle. It is the "progress of national consciousness among the people" that "modifies and gives precision to the literary utterances of the native intellectual" (p. 239).

Ngugi wa Thiong'o noted that colonialism entailed a double procedure. Colonialism meant the deliberate discounting or even destruction of the colonized culture, whether its art, dance, religion, history, geography, education, or oratory, as well as the conscious elevation of the colonizers' language (1986, p. 16). Beginning with the founding authors of liberalism (David Hume, Thomas Jefferson, and Georg Wilhelm Friedrich Hegel), nineteenth-century modernity denigrated the colonized. This system of domination's final triumph was symbolized by the dominated singing the system's virtues; the literature Africans penned in European languages was identified as African literature, as if there had never been a literature in the languages of Africa. But writing in African languages will only bring about an African cultural renaissance if these texts convey a struggle to create postcolonial political and economic community.

Michel Foucault's philosophical/historical work, *Discipline and Punish* (1977), provided flexibility to those working in cultural nationalism outside Europe. Prison authorities, he notes, maintain discipline among the incarcerated through surveillance, normalization, and examination; the written language was essential to the influence of these techniques. The power of writing, Foucault explains, is that description and classification function not as procedures for creating heroes, but for transforming humans into objects and subjects. Taking direction from Foucault, Edward Said found coercive force exercised through those texts describing the predominately Islamic world. The radical otherness of the Islamic world need neither be praised nor condemned; once differentiation has been accomplished, an exemption has been made for universal humanism. Said's *Orientalism* (1979) was widely read for its ability to forge a link between the literature that described the Orient, and Europe's exercise of coercive force on overseas territories.

Barbara Harlow queried whether poststructural literary criticisms could be useful outside the cultural traditions that produced them: does "deconstruction" facilitate "decolonization"? Armed struggles for national liberation were and are no more or less crucial than the struggle for cultural productivity and historical record. In describing the literature of Africa, the Middle East, and Latin America as resistance literature, Harlow notes that such works bear the mark of national liberation movements, that the commitment to political struggle prohibits "academic objectivity" or "scientific dispassion." Postcolonial literature is always public, never private: "Resistance literature calls attention to itself, and to literature in general, as a political and politicized activity. The literature of resistance sees itself furthermore as immediately and directly involved in a struggle against ascendant or dominant forms of ideological and cultural production" (pp. 28–29).

Frederic Jameson (1987) argues that Third World literatures are distinguished by their use of allegory; in such texts, ostensibly personal issues such as libidinal investment are understood to bear public significance. However Jameson notes the incompleteness of African states' independence, in that new state structures were not matched with the reconfigured social relationships and consciousnesses formed in revolutionary struggle. Indeed reference to cultural nationalism remains indebted to the new social movements: conscious public activism against militarization and environmental abuse, against class, race, gender, and sexual oppression. As Ella Shohat notes, due to "the collapse of the Soviet communist model, the crisis of existing socialisms, the frustration of the hoped for tri-continental revolution (with Ho Chi Minh, Frantz Fanon, and Che Guevara as talismanic figures) the realization that the wretched of the earth are not unanimously revolutionary (nor necessarily allies to one another), and the recognition that international geo-politics and the global economic system have obliged even socialist regimes to make some kind of peace with transnational capitalism" (p. 100).

Benedict Anderson built on the work of Gellner, Eric Hobsbawm, and Terence Ranger. Hobsbawm most usefully noted that those practices that seek to inculcate norms through reputation, and automatically imply continuity with the past, may be of quite recent origin or even invented. Ranger noted that European militaries and administrations in Africa relied on the practice of disseminating invented traditions. While for Gellner, the word invent meant fabricate or falsify; for Anderson, nations were "created," "thought out," or even "imagined" communities. Anderson identifies the nexus of market capitalism and the print industry as the institutional space for development of modern, national languages.

In responding to Anderson, Partha Chatterjee notes that Europe's history was not that of the rest of the world: historically specific correspondences between economic change and epistemic privilege were unique to European society. Chatterjee identifies three "moments" for nationalist thought, as expressed in literature and political polemic. The first, the moment of departure, is predicated on essential differences between the West and the Rest, noting that while those not living in Europe or North America are deficient in European modernities, that lack is compensated for with spiritual gifts. The second, the moment of maneuver, described as the embrace of modernities antitheses as the national culture, may lie closest to Fanon's ideals for postcolonial intellectuals. In the third, the moment of arrival, nationalist thought is phrased in its own vocabulary of modernist order. In another work,

Chatterjee notes the rhetorical significance of women's issues to national movements. The discovery of tradition by nationalist movements relegates "the women's question" to inner domains. Given the power of European modernist claims in the material sphere, colonial rule threatened the very institutions of home and family. The nationalist project justified selective appropriation of Western modernity along the lines of public/private life, specifying that women's bodies and the domestic circle would occupy a central position in cultural nationalism.

Gayatri Spivak sharpened poststructuralist thought's importance for worldwide cultural nationalism. She noted the exclusivity of Immanuel Kant's metaphor "the turning of the mind to the feeling of the sublime" in *Critique of Judgment* (1790). Where other poststructuralists note the presence of unbalanced power, Spivak argues that universal observations exclude entire categories. The West's knowledge hegemonies work at two levels enabling cultural imperialism to crush cultural nationalism. At one level, they define the system of concepts by which social and political reality is lived. These concepts need not be consensual or universal in order to be effective. At another level, hegemonies fragment the social order, so that divisions—along boundaries of class, race, and gender—proliferate.

One of the new locations for studies of cultural nationalism was the United States. While the United States witnessed a civil rights movement and university-based protests throughout the 1960s, such disturbances were only indirectly responsible for politicizing the movement for new forms of knowledge in academia. Rather, increasing university enrollment following general prosperity throughout the country meant that history and literature departments continued to hire scholars. The academic profession became more inclusive as international scholars and scholar-activists became tenured. While class-aware, subaltern, and feminist approaches may remain marginalized in Europe (whether shunted to Britain's new universities or parked in France's provincial institutions), they are surprisingly well represented in the most richly endowed institutions of the United States.

While discussions of cultural nationalism remain active in scholarly monographs in the early twenty-first century, interest in the subject is also widening in academic publishing. During the 1970s, editors at journals such as *Comparative Studies in Society and History,* the *Journal of African History,* the *Journal of Modern African Studies,* and the *Journal of the History of Ideas* entertained discussions of cultural nationalism. By the 1980s, literary journals such as *Callaloo,* MELUS, *Social Text,* the *New German Critique, Public Culture,* and *Yale French Studies* printed articles that mingled culture with nationalism; for example, a 1995 issue of *Boundary 2* was titled "Beyond National Cultures."

See also **Anticolonialism; Colonialism; Orientalism; Other, The, European Views of; Postcolonial Theory and Literature.**

BIBLIOGRAPHY

Anderson, Benedict. *Imagined Communities: Reflections on the Origin and Spread of Nationalism.* London: Verso, 1983.

Ashcroft, Bill, Gareth Griffiths, and Helen Tiffin. *The Empire Writes Back: Theory and Practice in Post-Colonial Literatures.* New York: Routledge, 1989.

Chatterjee, Partha. *The Nation and its Fragments: Colonial and Postcolonial Histories.* Princeton, N.J.: Princeton University Press, 1993.

———. *Nationalist Thought and the Colonial World: A Derivative Discourse?* London: Zed Books, 1986.

Fanon, Frantz. *The Wretched of the Earth.* Translated by Constance Farrington, with a preface by Jean-Paul Sartre. New York: Grove Press, 1963.

Foucault, Michel. *Discipline and Punish: The Birth of the Prison.* Translated by Alan Sheridan. New York: Pantheon Books, 1977.

Gellner, Ernest. *Nations and Nationalism.* Ithaca, N.Y.: Cornell University Press, 1983.

Harlow, Barbara. *Resistance Literature.* New York: Methuen, 1987.

Hobsbawm, Eric, and Terence Ranger, eds. *The Invention of Tradition.* New York: Cambridge University Press, 1983.

Jameson, Frederic. "World Literature in an Age of Multinational Capitalism." In *The Current in Criticism: Essays on the Present and Future in Literary Theory,* edited by Clayton Koelb and Virgil Lokke, 139–158. West Lafayette, Ind.: Purdue University Press, 1987.

Ngugi wa Thiong'o. *Decolonising the Mind: The Politics of Language in African Literature.* Portsmouth, N.H.: Heinemann, 1986.

Rich, Adrienne. *Dream of a Common Language: Poems 1974–1977.* New York: Norton, 1978.

Said, Edward. *Orientalism.* New York: Vintage Books, 1979.

Shohat, Ella. "Notes on the Post Colonial." *Social Text* 31/32 (1992): 99–113.

Spivak, Gayatri. *A Critique of Postcolonial Reason: Toward a History of the Vanishing Present.* Cambridge, Mass.: Harvard University Press, 1999.

Elizabeth Bishop

MIDDLE EAST

Nationalism is generally regarded as a recent development in the Middle East, a contingent phenomenon produced by the unique conditions of the modern era. Prior to the nineteenth century, concepts of collective identity and allegiance appear to have been defined primarily on the basis of lineage, locale, or religion—communities of sentiment and solidarity either smaller or larger than the nationalisms that subsequently emerged. For the region's agricultural and pastoralist majority, living in largely self-contained village or nomadic communities, one's clan, tribe, or village are presumed to have been the primary objects of self-identification and affiliation. For the area's literate minority, usually urban residents and immersed in a milieu dominated by religion, collective identity was defined by a combination of locale (loyalty to one's city), polity (being a member of the ruling elite), and most vitally religion (self-definition as Muslim, Christian, or Jew). Ethnic or linguistic concepts of identity, on the other hand, were conspicuous by their absence. Terminology illustrates the point. Prior to the twentieth century the word *Turk* denoted a rural resident of Anatolia, not a member of the educated multiethnic elite of the Ottoman Empire. In Arab usage the term *Arab* referred to the wild Bedouin of the desert, not the area's sophisticated urban population.

The Emergence of Modern Nationalisms

The nineteenth century was the seedtime of nationalism in the Middle East. The region's geographic, linguistic, and religious heterogeneity has provided the basis for numerous and competing nationalist movements.

Fueled by their religious distinctiveness and their contacts with the European milieu where nationalism was becoming the hegemonic referent for collective identity, some of the region's Christian minorities developed nationalist movements prior to the region's Muslim majority. Most prominent in this regard were the Maronites of Mount Lebanon and the Armenians of eastern Anatolia, among whom constructs emphasizing their historical separateness and right to political autonomy took hold in the nineteenth century. Thanks to European assistance, Lebanon gained autonomous status within the Ottoman Empire by the 1860s. Such was not the case in historic Armenia, where an active nationalist movement came into conflict with the Ottoman state as well as with the area's Turkish and Kurdish population in the later nineteenth century, and where fear of nationalism led to the mass expulsion and massacre of Armenians by the Ottoman government in the early twentieth.

In both Egypt and Iran, distinct geographical areas existing as autonomous polities with their own ruling structure (Iran since the sixteenth century, Egypt since the early nineteenth) led Westernized Egyptian and Iranian intellectuals to assert the existence of historically unique Egyptian and Iranian "nations" by the later decades of the century. Egyptian nationalism took political form by the later 1870s, when indigenous Egyptian elites sought greater control over an originally Ottoman ruling family and the European financial domination that dynastic extravagance was producing; their movement's slogan "Egypt for the Egyptians" succinctly expresses its overall thrust. Active nationalist activity in Iran dates from the 1890s and was produced by much the same combination of dynastic incompetence and foreign economic penetration; in the Iranian case it generated a formally successful Iranian constitutional movement in the early years of the twentieth century.

For the Turks of Anatolia and the Arabs of the Fertile Crescent, both living under Ottoman rule through the long nineteenth century, the causes producing nationalism were parallel. A precondition for modern Turkish and Arab nationalism was the development of a firm sense of ethnic identity. This was stimulated in the Turkish case by the discoveries of European Turkology, the uncovering of the pre-Islamic history of the Turkic-speaking peoples in Central Asia and beyond that fostered identification with a historic ethnie distinct from both the Muslim community and the multiethnic Ottoman Empire, in the Arab case by the process known as the "Arab Awakening," the blossoming of Arabic literature and history that occurred in the middle decades of the nineteenth century. As elsewhere in the Middle East, increasing elite contact with Europe and a growing awareness of European ideas also played a role. Nationalism is a modular concept, "available for pirating" (to pirate Benedict Anderson's phrase) by all those impressed by Europe and the world supremacy its nations were able to achieve in the modern era.

The catalyst turning a heightened sense of ethnic identity into visible Turkish and Arab nationalist movements was the trajectory taken by the Ottoman Empire over the course of the nineteenth century. On the one hand, the empire's territorial crumbling as European powers established their control over its African dominions and the peoples of the Balkans gained independence raised the possibility of a similar dismemberment of its Asian heartlands, thereby generating a search for an alternative base for viable community. On the other hand, the Ottoman government itself assumed a more reactionary character by the later decades of the nineteenth century. For educated Turks and Arabs, who were absorbing the values of individual liberty and participatory politics from their European mentors, the Ottoman Empire increasingly came to be seen as an undesirable framework for modern life.

Turkish and Arab ethnic nationalism became active movements only in the early twentieth century, specifically in the "Young Turk" era (1908–1918). Among Turks new organizations with an explicitly Turkish emphasis (the Turkish Society, formed 1908; the Turkish Hearth Clubs, formed 1912) emerged; in the press, extravagant ideas of uniting all Turkic-speaking peoples in a ethnically based "Turanian" state were voiced; on the governmental level efforts at increased centralization emphasized the primacy of the Turkish language within the state and sometimes gave precedence to ethnic Turks (although not to the degree once assumed). Similar organizational and intellectual trends occurred in the Arabic-speaking provinces of the Fertile Crescent: new Arab societies with a political agenda (the Ottoman Administrative Decentralization Society, 1912) emerged; demands for Arab autonomy were expressed in the press; and an Arab Congress was held in Paris in 1913 to promote Ottoman decentralization. The continued drive for centralization being undertaken by the Young Turk regime ran counter to what was originally an Arab demand for provincial decentralization. By the eve of World War I, a new trend was developing in the Arab provinces as prominent individuals and secret societies began to think of Arab independence as the only way to avoid subjugation within what politicized Arabs were coming to see as an oppressive "Turkish" state.

Modern Jewish nationalism (Zionism) did not require a similar process of the rediscovery of national distinctiveness. A sense of collective uniqueness and solidarity existed among Jews well before the nineteenth century. This sense was solidified by Judaism's liturgical language (Hebrew), the rich tapestry of distinctive customs, and the shared isolation of and discrimination against Jews living in European countries. An active Jewish nationalist movement based on this sense of distinctiveness was produced on the one hand by the gradual process of emancipation and assimilation experienced by Jews in parts of Europe during the nineteenth century, a process of historical change that also involved the acceptance of modern nationalist concepts, and on the other by growing European anti-Semitism, a phenomenon that led Jews to question their future in national states where powerful movements were now defining Jews as an alien element. In direct response to rising anti-Semitism in the Russian Empire, in the 1880s Zionist societies emerged in eastern Europe and began to organize Jewish immigration to Ottoman Palestine. By the late 1890s an international organization of Jews, the World Zionist Organization (WZO; established 1897), had been founded "to create for the Jewish people a homeland in Palestine secured by public law" (its founding declaration), and in the years prior to World War I the WZO worked to encourage Jewish migration and the initial development of distinctive Jewish national institutions in Palestine itself.

World War I and Its Settlement

World War I and its settlement had a crucial impact on nationalism in the Middle East. Ottoman entry into the war on the side of the Central Powers led to Ottoman military defeat. At war's end, the victorious allies began the process of partitioning the Ottoman Empire in accord with secret wartime arrangements. The postwar attempt at Allied domination was unsuccessful in the primarily Turkish-speaking Anatolian portion of the empire, where a vigorous Turkish nationalist movement led by the charismatic General Mustafa Kemal (later Atatürk) successfully resisted European domination and in the process abolished the Ottoman Empire and replaced it with the new state of Turkey (1923). Quite a different course of events were obtained in the Fertile Crescent, which Great Britain and France divided between themselves. France received a League of Nations mandate for "Syria" (initially including Lebanon, defined as a separate state in 1920), Great Britain mandates for the territories of "Iraq" and "Palestine" (the latter comprising today's Israel and Jordan). In the process of imperial partition, a nascent Arab nationalist movement that had emerged during the war and established an Arab government in Damascus was crushed by French military action. In Palestine, where the terms of the mandate allowed for large-scale Jewish immigration in order to facilitate the emergence of the Jewish "national home," the postwar settlement also laid the basis for the subsequent emergence of the state of Israel.

The contrast between the course of events in Turkish-speaking Anatolia and in the Arabic-speaking Fertile Crescent deserves emphasis. Turkish nationalism emerged successful out of the turmoil of World War I and its settlement, realizing its goal of the creation of a Turkish national state predicated on the existence of a linguistically based Turkish ethnic community. Nothing succeeds like success; Turkey has remained the object of national self-definition and allegiance for its Turkish-speaking majority ever since its creation in the early 1920s. In the Arab case a nationalist movement similar in genesis and aspiration, but geographically more vulnerable, was eliminated by European force of arms. In its stead the Fertile Crescent was divided into several artificial political units according to imperial fiat. None possessed deep roots; the reality and viability of all were to be deeply contested in the years to come.

Differential Nationalist Trajectories

The several nationalisms considered above have taken very different paths since World War I and its settlement. In Iran the territorially based nationalism that emerged in the nineteenth century remained dominant under the Pahlavi dynasty (1921–1979). It was never fully accepted, however, by more religious Iranians, particularly by the country's powerful Shiite religious hierarchy. In the late 1970s the religious class played a leading role in overthrowing the secular nationalist government of the shahs. In the 1980s the promotion of worldwide Islamic solidarity and international Islamic revolution became the leitmotif of Iranian foreign policy. In the 1990s, as the Iranian revolution moderated, the concept of Iran as a distinct national community again received greater emphasis. The precise nature and implications of Iranian collective identity is a contested issue at the start of the twenty-first century, part and parcel of the struggle between more liberal and more conservative Iranians.

With the creation of a cohesive independent state in Anatolia, Turkish nationalism largely shed the grandiose visions of pan-Turkic unity that had been expressed by some of its early proponents. Reified and promoted by the government of the new Turkish state during the long ascendancy of Mustafa Kemal Atatürk in the 1920s and 1930s, belief in the construct of a Turkish nation centered in Anatolia gradually disseminated beyond the elite circles in which Turkish nationalism had been born. The post-Atatürk decades have seen intensive debate among Turks as to the orientation of the Turkish state, particularly over the question of the role of religion in public life; but the participants in these debates have by and large not challenged the existence of a Turkish nation. The one partial exception is Turkey's marginalized Kurdish-speaking population, among whom demands for cultural and political autonomy surfaced in the later decades of the twentieth century and generated a prolonged civil war in eastern Turkey in the 1980s and 1990s.

The Zionist movement realized its main goal with the creation of the Jewish state of Israel in 1948. Some religiously oriented groups have never accepted the legitimacy of a Jewish state created as a result of human rather than divine agency. Moreover, fierce debates over the internal character of the state (for example, the role of religion in public life and the relationship of the Palestinian Arab minority to state institutions), as well as over the territorial extent of the state (the fate of the Palestinian-inhabited territories of the West Bank and Gaza Strip occupied by Israel in 1967), have continued to perturb Israeli public discourse. However, these debates occur among a Jewish population the vast majority of whom have accepted Israel as their national community of destiny.

Egypt was granted formal independence by Great Britain in 1922 in response to a nationalist uprising after World War I, and territorially based nationalism remained the dominant political construct in Egypt for most of the three decades of the parliamentary monarchy (1922–1952). Its cutting edge was Pharaonicism, an intellectual movement that posited the existence of a distinctive national character deriving from the ancient Egyptians. From the later 1930s the primacy of this locally based nationalism was challenged by voices that insisted upon Egypt's Arab affiliations and that emphasized the common problem of imperialist domination facing all Arab regions. Thereafter, both Egyptian opinion and Egyptian state policy evolved in a more Arabist direction, especially after the Egyptian revolution of July 1952. Under the leadership of Gamal Abdel Nasser, by the late 1950s Egypt had become the champion of Pan-Arabism. In 1958 it joined with Syria in the major experiment in Arab unity of the twentieth century, the United Arab Republic (1958–1961). The collapse of the UAR when Syria seceded in 1961 in effect marked the turning point in Egypt's involvement in the Arab nationalist movement. A drift away from commitment to Arab nationalism set in Egypt from the 1960s onward. It accelerated under Nasser's successors Anwar al-Sadat and Husni Mubarak, both of whose policies have emphasized Egypt as a separate political entity with its own national interests.

The fate of nationalism in the Arabic-speaking lands of the Fertile Crescent since the post–World War I settlement has been complex. In the interwar era the new states created after the war gradually acquired a degree of reality in the minds of their inhabitants. The effectiveness of state consolidation varied from country to country. It was probably strongest in Lebanon, where spokesmen among the country's slight Christian majority expounded an exclusively Lebanese nationalist ideology focused on the country's long history since the era of the Phoenicians as a uniquely "Mediterranean" nation different from other Arabic-speaking lands. It was probably weakest in Syria, where much of the political elite clung to the vision of the united Arab state that had been destroyed by imperialist partition in 1920. Among Palestinian Arabs a distinctive local identity was on the one hand fostered by the conflict with Zionism, but on the other was undercut as Palestinians sought outside Arab solidarity and support in the same struggle.

The process of Arab state consolidation in the Fertile Crescent was uneven. Continuing foreign domination reinforced the perception that the new states created after World War I were artificial entities established to suit imperial interests. An aura of what-should-have-been hovered over Arab politics in the Fertile Crescent, a belief that Arabs had been swindled out of the unity that was their proper destiny. After World War II this disaffection with existing states and belief in the desirability of their replacement by a state uniting most Arabs blossomed into Pan-Arabism, the drive for integral Arab unity that was a central component of Arab politics through the 1950s and 1960s.

The process of territorial state consolidation was facilitated with the recession of Pan-Arabism from the later 1960s onward. Over the decades the expanding institutions of the territorial state (bureaucracy, schools, vested interests) and its new symbols (flags, monuments, national holidays) bound the population to the state and gave greater substance to what had been artificial entities. At the level of policy-making there has been a clear trend away from the pursuit of Arab unity toward the realization of state interests since the 1960s. Wider Arab nationalist sentiments—belief in the existential reality of an Arab nation transcending existing state borders—have not totally faded. There is also an impressive degree of inter-Arab economic and cultural cooperation that has developed over time under the auspices of the League of Arab States and similar agencies. Pan-Arab issues, especially Palestine, are capable of arousing deep emotions across the Arab world. But, in the shifting relationship between the alternative concepts of local/statal allegiance and a broader identification with an Arab nation based on the bonds of language and history, the former appears to be the more prominent tendency at the beginning of the twenty-first century.

After Nationalism?

A significant challenge to nationalism has emerged in the Islamist movements that have gained prominence in recent decades. At the abstract level, the primacy of the religious bond over loyalty to territory, polity, or *ethnie* is basic to Islamist ideology. The formulation of Sayyid Qutb, founding father of Sunni Arab Islamism, states the position starkly: "There is no country for a Muslim except that where the law of God is established. . . . There is no nationality for a Muslim except his belief, which makes him a member of the Islamic community" (*Milestones*, p. 103). In political terms, a considerable measure of sympathy, mutual aid, and collaborative action have marked the relations between Islamist activists and movements originating in different countries. From the galvanizing impact of the Iranian Revolution of 1979 on Islamist activism elsewhere, through international support for the mujahideen opposing Soviet occupation in Afghanistan in the 1980s, to the international makeup and operations of Al Qaeda in the 1990s and after, a revived emphasis on the Islamic *umma* (Arabic, "community" of believers) as the most meaningful community of solidarity and destiny for Muslims has reasserted itself in the contemporary era.

But this is not the whole story. Territorial and ethnic nationalism still have their advocates, ideologues, and public figures who question the political salience of the religious bond and who posit that political behavior should be based on nonreligious criteria. The current division of the Muslim world into numerous states inevitably influences the practical articulation of contemporary Islamism. Many Islamist activists accept the reality of existing territorially or ethnically based states and operate within the political field determined by state structures, directing their activism toward infusing existing states with a more Islamic content.

By reasserting the centrality of a previously recessive collective identity, the Islamic resurgence of the late twentieth and early twenty-first centuries has complicated but not totally transformed the nationalist landscape of the Middle East. Sentiments of religious solidarity coexist with territorial, local, and ethnic/linguistic nationalism. The result is a complex, crowded, and unstable universe of imagined communities in which individuals are faced with determining the relevance of alternative referents for self-definition, allegiance, and action.

See also **Pan-Arabism; Pan-Turkism; Zionism.**

BIBLIOGRAPHY

PRIMARY SOURCES

Antonius, George. *The Arab Awakening.* London: H. Hamilton, 1938. The classic account of the genesis of Arab nationalism.

Haim, Sylvia G., ed. *Arab Nationalism: An Anthology.* Berkeley: University of California Press, 1962. A lengthy introductory essay followed by excerpts to the 1960s.

Hertzberg, Arthur, ed. *The Zionist Idea: A Historical Analysis and Reader.* Garden City, N.Y.: Doubleday, 1959. A lengthy introductory essay and a wide range of excerpts from Zionist thinkers.

SECONDARY SOURCES

Avineri, Sholmo. *The Making of Modern Zionism: Intellectual Origins of the Jewish State.* New York: Basic Books, 1981. A probing intellectual history.

Dawisha, Adeed. *Arab Nationalism in the Twentieth Century: From Triumph to Despair.* Princeton, N.J.: Princeton University Press, 2003.

Gelvin, James L. *Divided Loyalties: Nationalism and Mass Politics in Syria at the Close of Empire.* Berkeley: University of California Press, 1998. A pioneering analysis of the relationship of elite and nonelite Arab nationalism.

Hanioğlu, M. Şükrü. *Preparations for a Revolution: The Young Turks, 1902–1908.* New York: Oxford University Press, 2001. The continuation of his 1995 work.

———. *The Young Turks in Opposition.* New York: Oxford University Press, 1995. A detailed account of the genesis of the main Turkish nationalist movement.

Jankowski, James, and Israel Gershoni, eds. *Rethinking Nationalism in the Arab Middle East.* New York: Columbia University Press, 1997. Essays suggesting new approaches to the study of nationalisms in the Arab world since World War I.

Khalidi, Rashid, et. al., eds. *The Origins of Arab Nationalism.* New York: Columbia University Press, 1991. Studies of the development of Arab nationalism up to World War I.

Khoury, Philip S. *Urban Notables and Arab Nationalism: The Politics of Damascus, 1860-1920.* Cambridge, U.K.: Cambridge University Press, 1983. A thoughtful exploration of the social basis of Arab nationalism.

Laqueur, Walter. *A History of Zionism.* New York: Holt, Rinehart and Winston, 1972. A comprehensive political and intellectual history of Zionism to 1948.

Lewis, Bernard. *The Emergence of Modern Turkey.* London: Oxford University Press, 1961. A classic exploration of Turkish political and intellectual history.

Mottahedeh, Roy. *The Mantle of the Prophet: Religion and Politics in Iran.* New York: Simon and Schuster, 1985. A masterful study of how religious and nationalist thought intertwine.

Qutb, Sayyid. *Milestones.* Indianapolis, Ind.: American Trust Publications, 1990.

Sternhell, Zeev. *The Founding Myths of Israel: Nationalism, Socialism, and the Making of the Jewish State.* Translated by David Maisel. Princeton, N.J.: Princeton University Press, 1998. A revisionist interpretation arguing for the nationalist over socialist ideas in Zionism.

James Jankowski

NATIONALISM IN MUSIC, EUROPE AND THE UNITED STATES

Nationalism in music has traditionally been described as a late-nineteenth-century phenomenon associated with countries or regions aspiring to nationhood whose composers strove to wed a national (most often folk-based) musical idiom to existing "mainstream" genres. Some of these accounts begin with Frédéric Chopin (1810–1849), but he is more often understood as "cosmopolitan" or "universal," a Romantic composer of Polish and French parentage whose work was often based on Polish dance forms but was too early to count as nationalist. Most accounts of musical nationalism start with Russians in the next generation, especially the *moguchaya kuchka*—the "mighty little heap," or the "mighty five," including Nikolay Rimsky-Korsakov (1844–1908),

Modest Musorgsky (1839–1881), and Aleksandr Borodin (1833–1887)—and continue with the Czechs Bedřich Smetana (1824–1884) and Antonín Dvořák (1841–1904), the Norwegian Edvard Grieg (1843–1907), and the Finnish Jean Sibelius (1865–1957). Within this narrative line, the rise of a musical form of Impressionism in France and the genesis of a distinctively American music may be seen as late developments, somewhat out of step with general trends.

Yet nationalism has provided the principal cultural and political framework for musical expression within European-based traditions for most of the nineteenth century and has continued to do so up to the present. This tendency has not been widely noted for two main reasons: First, it remained overlooked because of the entrenched habit of considering European music history apart from history more generally, as encouraged by the doctrine of absolute music; and second, the genesis and development of musicology—the discipline entrusted to tell the history of music—were both intimately connected to nationalist ideologies.

Musicology and Nationalism

Music history in the nineteenth century has generally been perceived in terms of "mainstream" traditions continuing from the late eighteenth century, the general rise of Romanticism across these mainstreams, and the splintering into a variety of "nationalist" musics in the later part of the century. But nationalism lay at the heart of all facets of this master narrative, from the maintenance of the "mainstreams" to Romanticism and, most especially, to the narrative perspective. The principal task of historical musicology, for much of the time since about 1850, has been the promotion and development of a historicist canon to support a particular nationalist ideology. Moreover, as European nationalism, especially in Germany and Italy, led to two world wars in the twentieth century, some of its victims who fled to the United States (especially in the 1930s) established the American scholarly tradition in musicology, teaching the same history they had been taught and thus perpetuating the view that the most important musical tradition was German, which was to be understood as the least nationalist and most universal (Bach, Beethoven, Brahms, etc.), trailed by Italian opera and older Italian traditions, a few isolated "cosmopolitan" geniuses such as Chopin, and various "national" schools at the margin of respectability, whose legitimacy was cast in doubt not least because their music was widely enjoyed.

Nationalism and Art

Nationalism holds that a "people," whether defined in terms of cultural or ethnic roots, constitutes the only legitimate basis for a political state. This belief took root in Europe around the beginning of the nineteenth century, as an outgrowth of German Romanticism, the French Revolution, the Napoleonic wars, and (according to some views) human inclinations. The merger of nationalist feeling and art was accomplished using the model proposed by German poet and philosopher Friedrich von Schiller (1759–1805) of how an artist might project—for those in the urbanized present who stand in imperfect relation to a more ideal past—either a fuller sense of that lost past (through idyll and elegy), a critical account of

the present (through satire), or a believable future restoration. Coupled with the idea of the *Volksgeist* (the spirit of a people) promulgated by fellow German Johann Gottfried von Herder (1744–1803), Schiller's structure became a recipe for the nationalist artist: the idealized past, for the nationalist, is the past of a "people" who survive into the present (i.e., in the *Volk* of the countryside), and the ideal future for which one strives is a "nation" in which they are restored to their earlier oneness with the land of their past. Images, narratives, and projections that instill belief in a people's valued past—that is, mythologies—thus quickly became a core ingredient in the artistic advancement of nationalism.

German Nationalism

The early stages of a specifically musical engagement with nationalism may be found in the late-eighteenth-century fascination with folk song, which fed the development of early nineteenth-century German lieder, folk-based chamber songs expressive of a yearning subjectivity. In his lieder, Franz Schubert (1797–1828) placed that subjectivity, often alienated, within a specific landscape, frequently carried within the piano's figuration. Such placement of people within a landscape became a core strategy of nationalist art, and was more elaborately accomplished in German Romantic Opera, beginning with *Der Freischütz* (1821) by Carl Maria von Weber (1786–1826) and continuing in the next generation with the operas and music dramas of Richard Wagner (1813–1883); particularly effective were Weber's evocations of the German woods, through horn choirs, and his (and Wagner's) frequent recourse to mythology. Beethoven's Ninth Symphony (1824) is implicitly nationalist, but in a forward-looking way, projecting a temporal and geographic fusion of classical Greek ideals (Elysium), "oriental" ("Turkish") tropes, and modern German Christianity. In the generation following his death, Beethoven became the cornerstone of Germany's nationalist claims to preeminence in music. By the middle of the nineteenth century, older German musical treasures from the past (especially those by J. S. Bach) were being systematically collected, establishing a milestone in the nascent field of musicology. After the Franco-Prussian War (1870–1871) and the unification of Germany that resulted from it, the Festspielhaus in Bayreuth—the opera house designed and built by Wagner—became an enduring monument to "Holy German Art."

During the same general period, Italy also became unified, led by a movement—the Risorgimento—whose slogan ("Vittorio Emanuele Re D'Italia," championing a leader of the movement) was based on the letters spelling the name of the foremost Italian composer, Giuseppe Verdi (1813–1901). After the Franco-Prussian war, French composers, who until then competed primarily with Italy, and mainly in the domain of opera, began to engage deliberately with Germany's proclaimed mastery of instrumental music, at which point various musical nationalisms began to proliferate according to the familiar narrative outlined above.

Features of Nationalist Music

While musical nationalism could adopt a variety of specific profiles according to the "nation" involved, these all had a number of features in common. Many nationalist musics relied on folk idioms that, however inaccurately, could be claimed as a national heritage. Opera and program music lent themselves easily to national themes; and opera also had recourse to rousing choruses, which could not only evoke the character and presence of a people—most notably "Va, pensiero" in Verdi's *Nabucco* (1842) and the coronation scene in Mussorgsky's *Boris Godunov* (1872)—but also cross over into popular currency. Ethnographic studies could either add legitimacy to native folk idioms or form the basis for a nationally conceived exotic "other" to be assimilated and synthesized in national terms. Thus, "Spanish" music provided both Russian and French composers an opportunity to indulge in coloristic orchestration that was itself a source of nationalist pride; such as in *Carmen* (1874) by Georges Bizet (1838-1875) and *Capriccio Espanole* (1887) by Rimsky-Korsakov. Similar use was made of Asian sources (e.g., in Rimsky-Korsakov's *Sheherezade*, 1888), analogous to the earlier tradition regarding the "Turkish" topic. Eventually, ethnographic research evolved from a kind of colonialist interest in the "other" into another vehicle for nationalist endeavor, with some ethnomusicologists holding that only "authentic" members of a group ought to conduct research into its musical traditions.

The Legacy of Nationalism and the Special Case of the United States

Nationalism must be at least partly blamed for the Holocaust and other instances of "ethnic cleansing" in the twentieth century, given that nationalism's intense focus on defining an authenticating group identity entailed a corollary focus on what that group was not. The most notorious early instance of this in musical discourse was Wagner's essay *Das Judentum in der Musik* (1850; rev. 1869), which helped give nationalism a racialized profile it has never lost.

Nationalism has often moved in quite another direction in the United States, which, according to the European model, would have had either to elevate the American Indian as the core part of its authenticating past or to foster an alternative mythology of a "virgin" land settled by Europeans, transformed by their new setting. A third alternative, which has helped absorb the contradictions between the first two, has been to claim some form of "melting pot" nationalist basis; such was Dvořák's approach in his "New World" Symphony, op. 95 (1893), blending "Negro" melodies (spirituals), Indianist idioms, and a European-based style, in a recipe later taken up by William Grant Still (1895–1978) in his blues-based *Afro-American Symphony* (1930), for example. More central exemplars of American nationalist music are the often nostalgic "New England" idiom of early modernist Charles Ives (1874–1954), the jazz-based concert idiom of George Gershwin (1898–1937), and the "wide-open spaces" idiom of Aaron Copland (1900–1990), which was often allied with an emergent American style of balletic dance. Departing from these "high art" traditions, many have chosen to locate America's most distinctive musical profile within popular music, either within jazz ("America's classical music") or song, which has, historically, absorbed a wide number of influences. In terms of musical nationalism, perhaps the most fully realized American tradition—based on popular song styles and a variety of mostly assimilationist plots—is that of the American musical, both for the stage and in films.

See also **Absolute Music; Musicology; Motif: Motif in Music.**

BIBLIOGRAPHY

Applegate, Celia. "How German Is It? Nationalism and the Idea of Serious Music in the Early Nineteenth Century." *Nineteenth-Century Music* 21, no. 3 (spring 1998): 274–296.

Beckerman, Michael. "In Search of Czechness in Music." *Nineteenth-Century Music* 10, no. 1 (summer 1986): 61–73.

Beller-McKenna, Daniel. "How Deutsch a Requiem? Absolute Music, Universality, and the Reception of Brahms's Ein deutsches Requiem, op. 45." *Nineteenth-Century Music* 22, no. 1 (summer 1998): 3–19.

Gellner, Ernest. *Nationalism*. New York: Weidenfeld and Nicolson, 1997.

Gossett, Philip. "Becoming a Citizen: The Chorus in Risorgimento Opera." *Cambridge Opera Journal* 2 (1990): 41–64.

Hamm, Charles. "Dvořák in America: Nationalism, Racism and National Race." In his *Putting Popular Music in Its Place*, 344–353. Cambridge, U.K., and New York: Cambridge University Press, 1995.

Kallberg, Jeffrey. "Hearing Poland: Chopin and Nationalism." In *Nineteenth-Century Piano Music*, edited by R. Larry Todd, 221–257. New York: Schirmer Books, 1990.

Kramer, Lawrence. "The Harem Threshold: Turkish Music and Greek Love in Beethoven's 'Ode to Joy.'" *Nineteenth-Century Music* 22, no. 1 (summer 1998): 78–90.

Pederson, Sanna. "A.B. Marx, Berlin Concert Life, and German National Identity." *Nineteenth-Century Music* 18, no. 2 (fall 1994): 87–107.

Rumph, Stephen. "A Kingdom Not of This World: The Political Context of E.T.A. Hoffmann's Beethoven Criticism." *Nineteenth-Century Music* 19, no. 1 (summer 1995): 50–67.

Steinberg, Michael P.. *The Meaning of the Salzburg Festival: Austria as Theater and Ideology, 1890–1938*. Ithaca, N.Y.: Cornell University Press, 1990.

Stokes, Martin, ed. *Ethnicity, Identity and Music: The Musical Construction of Place*. Oxford and Providence, R.I.: Berg, 1994.

Taruskin, Richard. *Defining Russia Musically: Historical and Hermeneutical Essays*. Princeton, N.J.: Princeton University Press, 1997.

———. "Nationalism." In *The New Grove Dictionary of Music and Musicians*, edited by Stanley Sadie and John Tyrrell, vol. 17, 689–706. London: Macmillan, 2001.

Tischler, Barbara. *An American Music: The Search for an American Musical Identity*. New York: Oxford University Press, 1986.

Weiner, Marc A. *Richard Wagner and the Anti-Semitic Imagination*. Lincoln: University of Nebraska Press, 1995.

Raymond Knapp

NATIVE POLICY. Before Europeans from a variety of countries began arriving on the shores of the two continents of the western hemisphere in the late fifteenth century, there were no "Indians." At that point in time, millions of human beings, members of hundreds of distinctive societies speaking mutually unintelligible languages, inhabited the lands between Alaska and Patagonia. The category of person called "Indian" resulted from the imposition of colonial rule by Spain, Portugal, France, England, and Holland upon the diverse societies the Europeans encountered on these two continents. Following European colonialism, the creation of independent republics in what came to be known, by another misnomer, as "the Americas" was also marked by dynamic relations between states controlled by elites of European descent and the peoples called Indians. First colonial regimes and then independent nation-states in Latin America and in North America have been concerned with the classification and regulation of who is Indian and what constitutes "Indianness." We can call the operationalization of these systems of classification "Indian policy."

Such a perspective, of course, is necessarily also a historical phenomenon itself. Historians and anthropologists have alternately ignored or obsessed over the indigenous peoples of the Americas that by convention are still called "Indians," and have gone from understanding Indianness as an identity entirely tangential to the histories of nation-states, to the contemporary approach described above, in which Indianness and state policy are intertwined. Thus, at the same time that we review contemporary anthropological approaches to understanding Indian policy, we must simultaneously reflect upon those perspectives as substantially different from pre-1970 anthropological understandings of Indianness. This entry will discuss how Indian policy has developed in colonial and post-colonial nation-states of Latin America, and compare the evolution of Indian policy in Latin America as a whole with its evolution in the United States, acknowledging that this comparison increasingly parallels the pan-hemispheric struggles of indigenous peoples who themselves are engaging in such comparisons. Finally, describing indigenous struggles within and against the nation-states of the Americas in the twentieth century prefigures where those controversies are headed in the twenty-first.

Anthropology's Changes

Up until the 1970s, most anthropologists approached Indian communities as discrete cultural units (a classic example would be Redfield and Villa Rojas), and were particularly fascinated by and drawn to those aspects of cultural practice and belief that appeared least influenced, distorted, or destroyed by European colonialism. Anthropologists were spellbound by the mystique of pristine, if not always primitive, Indian cultures—the more isolated and removed from the mainstream of nation-states, the better. Even attempts to move anthropology beyond an obsessive focus upon an "Other" that contrasted with "the West" did not necessarily conceptually reconnect Indians to the world system to which they had historically been joined since the fifteenth century. For example, Eric Wolf's early taxonomy of peasantries, and much subsequent ethnography of Indian communities as peasant communities, also characterized such communities as discrete and bounded units, albeit in a different analytic light.

A major breakthrough was achieved by June Nash in her study of Bolivian tin miners, who in her work appeared clearly as simultaneously members of the industrial working class and as Indians. Nash elaborated an analysis that did not downplay the distinctively Indian religious and cultural practices of the miners, their complex political ideological relationship with the Bolivian state, or their emplacement within the capitalist world system. After Nash, it became possible to study Indian communities not only as part of global economic and political systems, but also as part of Latin American nation-states. Describing the policies that such nation-states were developing in response to Indian communities was a logical next step in anthropological work.

Perspectives on Colonialism and Postindependence Latin America

In the 1980s and 1990s, historians and anthropologists alike elaborated new analyses of the colonial and early independence eras in Latin America. These analyses made clear that from the beginning of the Spanish colonial era, ruling elites legislated and implemented policies for governing Indians that consigned them to an exploited, subaltern class position, and distinguished Indians from the non-Indian population. Many scholars also emphasized that the peoples who became known as Indians were not simply passive recipients of the brutalities colonial conquest wreaked upon them. Such scholars portrayed Indian peoples as dynamically responsive to the national and global political and economic systems. This latter point is still controversial, and Orin Starn has shown that well into the 1990s many anthropologists working in the Andes remained wedded to views of Indians that emphasized their cultural discreteness and isolation from nationalist ideologies and identities.

While the conquest indeed precipitated a demographic collapse among all indigenous groups, caused by massacres, enslavement, and pernicious epidemics, many Indian peoples survived through their own efforts. Acknowledging Indians as active makers of their own destinies draws attention to the key differences in how different Indian peoples negotiated the policies imposed upon them by colonial authorities. In the urban centers of the old indigenous empires in Mesoamerica and the Andes, colonial authorities were eager to utilize the labor afforded by their domination of Indian societies, while using the markers of Indian identity to signify subaltern status. These regimes wanted to diminish distinctive Indian identities by converting Indian peoples to Christianity, eliminating their native languages, and controlling Indian lands and resources. Yet they also wanted to maintain a large mass of servile, exploitable laborers. The dual motivations behind colonial Indian policy likely made it possible for Indian communities and leaders to at least partly subvert the intentions of colonial regimes.

Roger Rasnake elaborates the creation of postcolonial Indian authorities and social systems in the regions that became Bolivia, showing that Indians were able to manipulate state policies to achieve forms of local political and cultural autonomy. In colonial Mexico, Claudio Lomnitz-Adler has shown that the semiautonomous communities referred to as the "Indian Republics" of the eighteenth century ultimately "meant that the Spanish system recognized the existence of two nations with political representation within the Spanish state" (p. 267). In the collection edited by Carol Smith, authors writing about colonial Guatemala agree to a certain extent, arguing that the segregationist policies of the Spanish colonial state helped to establish strong Indian communities. In another quite different region, Joanne Rappaport's work in the Cauca region of colonial Colombia shows that Indian communities subverted the Spanish *resguardo* institution, intended to concentrate and manage the supply of coerced Indian labor to the Spaniards' haciendas (plantations), resulting in the creation of regions of refuge for Indian communities.

Florencia Mallon, a historian, established similar dynamics in the early independence period in both Mexico and Peru, emphasizing the dynamic role of Indian and non-Indian peasants in the making of those two nation-states. By contrast, Smith argues that successive nineteenth-century state forms built the Guatemalan nation around Indian policies that decisively excluded Indians from national identity, even as Guatemala's economy was increasingly developed and incorporated into the global economy. In other countries, nineteenth-century Indian policy aimed to continue, in effect, the work of the conquest by ultimately eliminating Indian ethnic identities. This process of assimilating Indian peoples in Latin America through biological miscegenation and the suppression of sociocultural distinctiveness, which Les Field has elaborated in Nicaragua, has for centuries been called *mestizaje*.

Indian Policies of the Twentieth-Century Nation-States

Shifts in the ways that anthropologists have been analyzing contemporary state policies toward native peoples in Latin America are highlighted in two important anthologies published since the early 1990s. In Joel Sherzer and Greg Urban's collection *Nation-States and Indians in Latin America* (1991), contributors elaborated a galaxy of distinctive Indian identity formations, within the context of national identities. As in colonial times, these national identities have in the main excluded indigenous peoples from full citizenship as Indians, but instead utilized state policy to culturally assimilate Indian peoples to thereby gain full control over Indian lands and resources. In this collection, authors document how Indian identities have resisted state-sponsored assimilation, but also experienced marked transformations of the cultural traits, practices, languages, and symbols that demarcate Indianness.

Twelve years later, the publication of Kay Warren and Jean Jackson's *Indigenous Movements, Self-Representation, and the State in Latin America* (2002) crystallizes the changes among Indian peoples in the interim, as well as the new anthropological responses to current conditions. Contributors in this collection have documented the importance of indigenous political movements as they marshal Indian cultural identities toward the twin goals of auto-representation (for local, national, and global audiences) and reordering the place of Indians in nation-states. The second goal signifies no less than the wholesale reconceptualization of national identities in Latin America, at the formal level of constitutions, political parties, laws, and leadership, as well as at the popular level. This anthology demonstrates anthropologists' commitment to even closer analysis of state policies and their multifarious effects upon Indian peoples.

Two other ethnographies demonstrate the vast differences evolving in state policy toward Indians in Latin America. In Charles Hale's exploration of "contradictory consciousness"

among the Miskitu of the Nicaraguan Atlantic coast, an Indian identity coalesced around opposition to the integrationist policies of the revolutionary Sandinista state. Even though this opposition became the banner for a florescence of Miskitu language and culture, it was allied to the United States' war against the Sandinistas. By contrast, left-wing coalition politics in the Juchitán region of Oaxaca, Mexico, described by Howard Campbell, created the local political conditions for both opposition to the federal Mexican state and the opportunity for Zapotec cultural renaissance. In these ethnographies, it is clear that state policies are having unpredictable effects upon and interactions with Indian peoples and cultures.

Comparisons with Indian Policy in the United States

Comparing the history of Indian policy in Latin America versus that history in the United States is instructive, particularly with respect to the issue of cultural assimilation of Indian peoples through *mestizaje*. *Mestizaje* as an intrinsic part of Latin American state policy profoundly departs from Indian policies in the United States, as elucidated by Les Field and Circe Sturm. In North America, treaty-making between indigenous peoples that began with the British colonial regime and continued under successive U.S. administrations in the eighteenth and nineteenth centuries ultimately created a category of officially acknowledged Indian people, the "federally recognized Indian tribe."

While the federal government has since the 1880s on at least three occasions attempted to disengage from the premise of federal recognition, which more or less accepts the indefinite existence of Indian peoples, these attempts have so far failed to put an end to this officialized status. Federally recognized tribes hold onto a sharply circumscribed, but nevertheless always potentially valuable, set of properties, that is, Indian reservations; furthermore, recognized tribes are authorized to make claims upon various parts of the U.S. federal bureaucracy. Indians who do not live on reservations but are members of recognized tribes can return to their designated reservations and make claims to resources. Even in urban areas, Indians from federally recognized tribes still maintain access to certain federally funded services, such as health and education. These resources are substandard in the estimation of Indians and non-Indians alike, and in no way compensate for the loss of immense territories, not to mention economic and political liberty. For this reason, Indian identities in the United States are closely policed by both federal and tribal authorities; tribal membership is substantiated via genealogy, or blood quantum, and the policies of both the tribes (acting as semiautonomous internal state forms) and the federal bureaucracy are obsessed with counting Indians and allocating resources.

Compared with the United States, state policy in Latin America is much less concerned with policing Indian identities for three reasons. First, whatever rights accrue to being Indian in Latin America are minimal, and wherever such rights exist, they depend upon residence in demarcated Indian communities. Second, popular genealogical theories in Latin America, that is, theories of "blood," encourage *mestizaje* as a means toward social mobility, rather than serving as legitimation for Indian identities as in the United States. Finally, nationalist ideologies in Latin America profoundly stigmatize

THE ANTI-QUINCENTENNIAL

The year 1992 marked the 500th anniversary of Columbus's fateful voyage that initiated the destruction of indigenous civilizations and the rise of nation-states dominated by elites of European descent. Pan-hemispheric organizing among Indian peoples mixed resistance to the plans by many countries in both North and Latin America to treat the anniversary as a cause for celebration, as well as an opportunity to express demands for profound changes in the relationship between Indian and national identities. Ecuador's indigenous confederation, CONAIE, which brings together diverse peoples from the Pacific coastal region, the Andean region, and the Amazon, formulated its demands during a series of uprisings in 1990, 1992, and 1994 (for a full description of the formation and politics of CONAIE, see CONAIE). CONAIE leaders called for a new kind of nation-state—*el estado plurinacional*—in which Indian identities would become by definition central to the nation, and for state policies explicitly intended to build the economic infrastructure for technologically advanced and politically autonomous Indian communities.

Such demands are mirrored in the post-1992 pan-Mayan movement in Guatemala described by Kay Warren. Similarly, since the beginning of Mexico's Zapatista uprising in 1994, many anthropologists have been concerned to show this movement as both indigenous and national in scope. The economic and political goals enunciated by these indigenous movements in some ways resembled but in other ways markedly diverged from the objectives of the Latin American left in the 1990s. The differences manifested in anthropological analyses as well, with some anthropologists deciding to act as advocates for Indian movements, while others critiqued the Indian movements from Marxist or neo-Marxist perspectives (see, for example, the critical analysis in Alcida Rita Ramos's *Indigenism* [1998]). One area of future anthropological research will likely focus upon what happens when Indian movements in Ecuador, Mexico, Guatemala, and elsewhere achieve even some of their political and economic goals. Will finding a political and economic place in reconfigured Latin American nation-states exacerbate class differentiation and inequalities within and among Indian communities? How will new state policies affect such outcomes?

Indianness, associating it with poverty, ignorance, backwardness, and powerlessness. In the last regard, nationalism in the United States, and state policy over the last two centuries, do concur with state policies in Latin America. Yet without the history of treaties, reservations, and federal recognition that exists in the United States, which with all of its problems still provides a basis for both establishing and maintaining Indian identities, Latin American *mestizaje* has acted as a powerful ideological force aiding and abetting state policies aimed at disenfranchising and disarticulating Indian societies and cultures. Indeed, the struggles of indigenous movements to reconfigure nation-states in Latin America discussed above are aimed precisely at creating political and economic structures that will support the survival of Indian peoples into the future.

Indianness, National Policy, and Anthropology in the Twenty-First Century

Anthropologists sometimes exaggerate and sometimes underestimate the importance of their work and their ideas to "the real world"—the world of governments and families, health and disease, happiness and despair. But in the case of Indian policy, anthropological knowledge has buttressed and often been the accomplice to national "regimes of truth" about Indian peoples. In the United States, an "official anthropology" funded and sponsored by the federal government has been a historic partner to state Indian policy. In Latin America, such an official anthropology has generally not had the same effects historically, with the exception of Brazil and Mexico. However, the rise of indigenous movements demanding control over lands and resources will likely oblige Latin American governments to act as "gatekeepers" and to utilize anthropological knowledge much more in order to ascertain and legitimize Indian identities in the twenty-first century. Anthropological knowledge in this century will therefore be simultaneously yoked to forging new state–Indian relations and new kinds of Indian policies, while also being engaged in reflective and critical analysis of these new relationships. These often contradictory roles will unfold in both North and Latin America.

See also **Anthropology; Colonialism; Empire and Imperialism; Indigenismo; Mestizaje; World Systems Theory, Latin America.**

BIBLIOGRAPHY

Campbell, Howard. *Zapotec Renaissance: Ethnic Politics and Cultural Revivalism in Southern Mexico.* Albuquerque: University of New Mexico Press, 1994.

CONAIE (Confederación de Nacionalidades Indígenas del Ecuador). *Las nacionalidades indígenas en el Ecuador.* Quito: Ediciones Tincui-Abya-Yala, 1989.

Deloria, Vine, Jr., and Clifford M. Lytle. *The Nations Within: The Past and Future of American Indian Sovereignty.* Austin: University of Texas Press, 1998.

Dyck, Noel, and James B. Waldram, eds. *Anthropology, Public Policy, and Native Peoples in Canada.* Montreal and Buffalo, N.Y.: McGill-Queen's University Press, 1993.

Field, Les W. "Blood and Traits: Preliminary Observations on the Analysis of Mestizo and Indigenous Identities in Latin vs. North America." *Journal of Latin American Anthropology* 7, no. 1 (2002): 2–33.

———. *The Grimace of Macho Ratón: Artisans, Identity, and Nation in Late-Twentieth-Century Western Nicaragua.* Durham, N.C.: Duke University Press, 1999.

Hale, Charles R. *Resistance and Contradiction: Miskitu Indians and the Nicaraguan State, 1894–1987.* Palo Alto, Calif.: Stanford University Press, 1994.

Lomnitz-Adler, Claudio. *Exits from the Labyrinth: Culture and Ideology in the Mexican National Space.* Berkeley: University of California Press, 1992.

Mallon, Florencia E. *Peasant and Nation: The Making of Postcolonial Mexico and Peru.* Berkeley: University of California Press, 1995.

Nash, June. *We Eat the Mines and the Mines Eat Us: Dependency and Exploitation in Bolivian Tin Mines.* New York: Columbia University Press, 1979.

Ramos, Alcida Rita. *Indigenism: Ethnic Politics in Brazil.* Madison: University of Wisconsin Press, 1998.

Rappaport, Joanne. *The Politics of Memory: Native Historical Interpretation in the Colombian Andes.* Cambridge, U.K., and New York: Cambridge University Press, 1990.

Rasnake, Roger Neil. *Domination and Cultural Resistance: Authority and Power among an Andean People.* Durham, N.C.: Duke University Press, 1988.

Redfield, Robert, and Alfonso Villa Rojas. *Chan Kom: A Mayan Village.* Reprint. Chicago: University of Chicago Press, 1962. Originally published in 1934.

Sherzer, Joel, and Greg Urban. *Nation-States and Indians in Latin America.* Austin: University of Texas Press, 1991.

Smith, Carol A., ed. *Guatemalan Indians and the State, 1540 to 1988.* Austin: University of Texas Press, 1990.

Starn, Orin 1992. "Missing the Revolution: Anthropologists and the War in Peru." In *Rereading Cultural Anthropology,* edited by George Marcus, 152–179. Durham, N.C.: Duke University Press, 1992.

Sturm, Circe. *Blood Politics: Race, Culture, and Identity in the Cherokee Nation of Oklahoma.* Berkeley: University of California Press, 2002.

Warren, Kay B. *Indigenous Movements and their Critics: Pan-Maya Activism in Guatemala.* Princeton, N.J.: Princeton University Press, 1998.

Warren, Kay, and Jean Jackson, eds. *Indigenous Movements, Self-Representation, and the State in Latin America.* Austin: University of Texas Press, 2002.

Wolf, Eric R. *Peasants.* Englewood Cliffs, N.J.: Prentice-Hall, 1966.

Les W. Field

NATURAL HISTORY. Natural history, the study of natural objects, has been a feature of all literate civilizations. In the Western tradition, starting with Aristotle, natural history has engaged scholars and has been an important feature of Western literature. The perspective with which writers have approached natural objects, and the aspects of interest to them, have varied as much as their cultures. Natural history has been written about as a form of philosophy, as entertaining literature, and as a form of didactic lesson. Aristotle, Pliny, Albertus Magnus, and Ulisse Aldrovandi's "natural histories" in many ways have little in common other than the objects about which they wrote. In addition, non-Western civilizations have rich literatures that go back centuries, on plants, animals, and minerals. And, anthropologists make the claim that numerous nonliterate peoples have developed sophisticated conceptions of the natural world and its objects.

As a scientific discipline, however, natural history has a more restricted domain. When the term *natural history* is used today, it is most often in reference to the subject as it emerged in the mid-eighteenth century. In this modern form, natural history is the systematic study of natural objects (animals, plants, minerals)—that is, naming, describing, classifying, and searching for their overall order. As such, it has been at the heart of the life sciences. The modern scientific discipline of natural history that emerged in the middle of the eighteenth century was closely tied to the careers of two individuals: Carolus Linnaeus and Georges Louis Leclerc, comte de Buffon.

Naturalists, particularly those interested in plants, faced a serious problem at the time. An enormous quantity of material had come into Europe from areas recently explored by colonial powers. Naming and classifying the new plants presented a challenge because they did not fit easily into previously established systems. The Swedish naturalist Carlus Linnaeus (1707–1778) created a classification system for plants that placed them into twenty-four classes according to their number of stamens (male part) and their relative positions. The classes, in turn, were broken down into sixty-five orders primarily on the basis of the number and position of the pistils (female part). He used other characteristics to break the orders into genera and species. Overall, the system was simple, easy to remember, and easy to use.

Of equal importance, Linnaeus also provided a set of rules for naming plants. Before his reform of nomenclature, the scientific names of plants consisted of two parts, a word or set of words that identified a group of plants, and then a string of words that distinguished the characteristics of the plant from other plants. As a result, the scientific name was awkward, and because various writers had used different characteristics to distinguish different plants, considerable confusion existed. Linnaeus proposed a simple reform that made plant names like human names, a single name common to all the species in a genus, and a second specific name that distinguished the species from others in the genus. He used this binomial nomenclature in his *Species plantarum* (1753; The species of plants) and recorded all the known species of plants in it. Later he extended his approach to animals. His reform quickly caught on and is the basis for contemporary nomenclature.

Although Linnaeus's main goal was the naming and classifying of natural products, he described them as part of a divine order, a balanced and harmonious system. In his mind, every plant and animal filled a particular place in a balanced order and functioned to help maintain it. Carnivores, for example, daily destroyed animals that if not checked would reproduce at a rate that would outstrip their source of food in short order.

While Linnaeus labored in Sweden, to the south, Georges Louis Leclerc, comte de Buffon (1707–1788), worked on a more secular vision of nature, and in a somewhat different manner. Louis XV of France had appointed Buffon as director of his royal garden in Paris. The Jardin du Roi was an institution that provided public lectures in natural history, cultivated a large public garden, and housed the royal collection of natural history objects. Buffon had a brilliant career there: he expanded the physical space to double its former size, increased the collections, and helped make it into the foremost institution for the study of the living world. More important, Buffon set out to prepare a catalog of the royal natural history collection, a standard practice in most large collections. But instead of planning a mere annotated list of the curiosities and rare objects in the collection, Buffon envisioned a much grander project: a complete natural history of all living beings and minerals. Over a period of almost fifty years he published thirty-six quarto volumes containing a theory of the earth, and natural histories of human beings, minerals, quadrupeds, and birds. (The rest was completed by a team of specialists in the two decades after his death.)

Buffon's *Histoire naturelle, générale et particulière* (1749–1789; Natural history, general and particular) comprises an encyclopedia that reflects the goals of the French Enlightenment. In his introductory essays, he elaborated a general philosophy that stressed the importance of observation and claimed that through empirical investigation naturalists might uncover the order in nature. He had little use for the work of people like Linnaeus who devoted their attention to naming and arranging specimens. In contrast, Buffon envisioned natural history to be a general survey of the natural world and an attempt to summarize all available knowledge about it. Also unlike Linnaeus, Buffon did not conceive of natural history as a handmaiden to Christianity, but rather for him nature is a creative natural power responsible for the harmony, balance, and fullness of life. Natural history should be the portrait of nature. Like the physical world, so well described by the Newtonian physical scientists of his day, the living world follows natural laws that investigation would reveal. Buffon's secular vision provided an attractive alternative to Genesis and explains the importance of his reputation in the French Enlightenment.

1782 drawing of nutmeg by botanist Elizabeth Blackwell. In the eighteenth century, Swedish naturalist Carolus Linnaeus began classifying plants based on the number and positions of their stamens. He also pioneered the system of binomial nomenclature still used in the twenty-first century to identify individual plants. © STAPLETON COLLECTION/CORBIS

Collections and the Growth of Natural History

Buffon and Linnaeus, although different in perspective, each contributed to molding natural history and inspiring others. They had each relied primarily on natural history collections for their work, rather than going out into the field in search of information. The fourteen thousand species of plants and animals described by Linnaeus, and the extensive accounts of quadrupeds, birds, and minerals that comprise Buffon's thirty-six volumes, reflected the extensive empirical base of knowledge available in private and public collections in the later half of the eighteenth century. But as impressive as the collections were compared to those of the previous century, they were just the beginning. An enormous expansion of natural history collections took place in the early nineteenth century and completely transformed them as well as natural history. Explorers, colonial officials, traveling naturalists, and commercial natural history houses had supplied collectors in the eighteenth and early nineteenth centuries. With the conclusion of the Napoleonic Wars, however, a new wave of European colonial expansion began, one reflecting the vast industrial and commercial revolutions that had been taking place in western Europe. Merchants and governments increasingly sought international markets and commercial products, and with these new developments there came what must have seemed like limitless opportunities for the collection of plants, animals, and minerals. The resulting new collections were not only larger, but they were more scientifically valuable because trained collectors in the field were instructed in what was of scientific interest. They knew how to adequately preserve specimens and how to label them with appropriate information.

Combined, the new opportunities to collect on a global scale made a new sort of natural history collection possible. Until the end of the eighteenth century, most natural history collections had been primarily amateur ones whose owners were not scientists and who did not publish anything other than the occasional catalog. The reorganization during the French Revolution of the royal garden into a national museum of natural history provided a new model and led to the establishment of the leading natural history collection in the world for many decades. The new public and semi-public museums that were inspired by the Paris museum had professional curators who were active scientists.

Not only did the nature of the collections change in the early nineteenth century, but the number of individuals involved in the study of natural history increased dramatically. In large part, this reflected the many new opportunities that became available for those interested in the subject. Not only were more museums created, with curator positions, but also private companies supplied paid positions for those willing to travel to exotic places to collect specimens. The increase in literacy and the revolution in printing created new markets for those interested in writing for the general public. As a consequence, more people came to be engaged in the study of natural history, and the subject became, overall, more rigorous and more specialized.

Although the specialization in natural history created new specialized subdisciplines, such as ornithology and entomology, the legacy of Linnaeus and Buffon continued to guide research—that is, description, classification, and the search of a general order in nature. New empirical data raised interesting new questions. The carefully collected and labeled specimens that poured into European collections showed interesting patterns of distribution of animals and plants. Fossils from local and exotic quarries led researchers to ponder the relationship of extinct forms to contemporary ones. And the immense number of specimens showed that even within a species there was an astonishingly large amount of variation. What did it all mean?

Maturity of Natural History

The nineteenth century was rich in new theoretical approaches that attempted to explain the vast diversity in nature and the patterns that were emerging. On a more practical level, international commissions were established and worked to produce agreed-upon standards in nomenclature, bringing Linneus's goal of unity in naming closer. Museum curators developed taxidermic techniques that eliminated the threat of insect pests and pioneered new methods of display that would culminate in the wonderful dioramas of the American Museum of Natural History in New York, the Biological Museum in Stockholm, and in the hundreds of other large museums that were established. Natural history museums became standard

institutions in all major cities, and the new museums were large, well funded, and well attended. By 1900, there were 250 natural history museums in the United States, 300 in France, and 150 in Germany. Beyond the United States and Europe there were museums from Melbourne to Bombay, from Buenos Aires to Montreal. Along with the development of museums, there was a parallel development of zoological and botanical gardens that displayed and did research on living specimens. These were extraordinarily popular: In its first year, 1828, the Zoological Gardens in London's Regent Park had 130,000 visitors, and over the following decade that number swelled to a quarter of a million a year. By the 1880s, the garden attracted more than 600,000 people a year. With size and public support, the zoological and botanical gardens played new and important roles other than public entertainment and scholarly research. Kew Garden, outside London, functioned in an important manner in the global agricultural network that linked British interests to the transfer of important economic plants such as rubber plants and cinchona trees (important for quinine) throughout the empire. The New York Zoological Society Park pioneered the preservation of endangered species.

Important as these institutional and technical developments were, they have been somewhat overshadowed by the major intellectual synthesis provided by Charles Darwin (1809–1882). His theory of evolution by means of natural selection resolved the leading questions in natural history and also provided an intellectual structure that has proved to be the unifying theory of the life sciences. Like other naturalists of the nineteenth century, Darwin had been struck by the enormous diversity in nature and the interesting patterns of distribution that he and others observed. He was, similarly, curious about the relationship of fossils to living forms, and like many of his contemporaries who were trying to classify large groups, he attempted to sort out the differences between varieties and species. He approached the study of natural history with a secular perspective and sought natural explanations for the questions he asked. In an interesting sense, he combined and synthesized the traditions stemming from Linnaeus and Buffon. He sought the key to a classification and nomenclature system, and was searching for a secular vision of the order in nature. His *Origin of Species* (1859) has served as a model for how to envision and study nature.

Not that everyone agreed with his conclusions or his methods. For several decades scientists debated Darwin's theory. Some, like Louis Agassiz (1807–1873), did not want to break the tie between natural history and religion, while others were disturbed by numerous scientific problems: the age of the earth was not believed to be old enough for the process to have occurred, the theories of inheritance did not adequately explain how variation arose or how it could be transmitted in a way that supported the theory. Those in the medical sciences had been making great strides in investigations by using the experimental method and were elaborating a theory of the body based on an understanding of the cell. It was not clear how Darwin's science fit with that body of research. This latter issue was of special importance because many universities and other institutions were tending to see natural history as "old fashioned" by the end of the century and sought a new synthesis for the life sciences in the exciting research stemming from the experimental sciences that were elucidating how the body functions.

Modern Synthesis and Contemporary Natural History

Life scientists in the late nineteenth century were agreed that life had evolved over time, but there was considerable disagreement over how that evolution had taken place. Darwin's emphasis on natural selection was thought to be problematic, and a variety of alternatives were proposed. The research on genetics in the early decades of the twentieth century provided tools for a new examination of the subject. Starting with Theodosius Dobzhansky's (1900–1975) *Genetics and the Origin of Species* (1937), naturalists were able to bring together several different lines of research to construct a new theory of evolution, one based on natural selection and the genetics of population change. Like Darwin's earlier theory, the modern synthesis, as the new theory is called, proved widely synthetic. Dobzhansky once wrote that nothing made sense except in the light of evolution, and this very well sums up the tremendous generalizing power of the modern theory. It has brought an evolutionary perspective on traditional subjects like the study of fossils and distribution, or the foundations of classification and nomenclature, as well as subjects like animal behavior, ecology, and conservation biology. With techniques and information from molecular biology, the theory of evolution has been extended to an understanding of evolution on the molecular level.

With contemporary interest in molecular biology, and especially the potential medical applications that it promises, it is easy to lose sight of the importance of natural history today. The unifying theory of the life sciences is still the theory of evolution that emerged from the naturalist tradition and is deeply rooted there. Contemporary naturalists like Edward O. Wilson argue that natural history still provides the vantage point from which to stand back and conceptualize the general order in nature. By studying a particular group from its molecular aspects to its widest ecological dimension, Wilson contends, we can go beyond much of the narrow research and discover general features of life. On a more practical side, natural history provides the tools for examining environmental issues and has been central in the call for preserving the biodiversity of the planet.

Natural history has been at the heart of the life sciences for over two centuries and remains a powerful set of ideas about the study of nature and its order. It has given rise to the major unifying theory of the life sciences, and it remains the repository of what we know about natural objects on the earth.

See also **Biology; Ecology; Environment; Nature; Science.**

BIBLIOGRAPHY

Allen, David Elliston. *The Naturalist in Britain: A Social History.* Princeton, N.J.: Princeton University Press, 1994.

Allen, Garland E. *Life Science in the Twentieth Century.* New York: Wiley, 1975.

Barrow, Mark V., Jr. *A Passion for Birds: American Ornithology after Audubon.* Princeton, N.J.: Princeton University Press, 1998.

Blunt, Wilfrid. *The Compleat Naturalist: A Life of Linnaeus.* New York: Viking, 1971.

Browne, Janet, *Charles Darwin: Voyaging.* New York: Alfred A. Knopf, 1995.

Coleman, William. *Biology in the Nineteenth Century: Problems of Form, Function, and Transformation.* New York: Wiley, 1971.

Farber, Paul Lawrence. *Finding Order in Nature: The Naturalist Tradition from Linnaeus to E.O. Wilson.* Baltimore: Johns Hopkins University Press, 2000.

Gunther, Albert E. *A Century of Zoology at the British Museum through the Lives of Two Keepers, 1815–1914.* London: Dawsons, 1975.

Jardine, N., J. A. Secord, and E. C. Spary, eds. *Cultures of Natural History.* Cambridge, U.K., and New York: Cambridge University Press, 1996.

Mayr, Ernst, and William B. Provine, eds. *The Evolutionary Synthesis: Perspectives on the Unification of Biology.* Cambridge, Mass.: Harvard University Press, 1980.

Rothfels, Nigel. *Savages and Beasts: The Birth of the Modern Zoo.* Baltimore: Johns Hopkins University Press, 2003.

Shteir, Ann B. *Cultivating Women, Cultivating Science: Flora's Daughters and Botany in England, 1760–1860.* Baltimore: Johns Hopkins University Press, 1996.

Paul Farber

NATURALISM. Naturalism was one of a wave of "isms" that swept through the cultural world of the late nineteenth century. Its most vocal advocate was the French author Émile Zola (1840–1902), a prolific novelist, dramatist, essayist, and critic. Highly controversial in the period between the heyday of realism (1830–1860) and the emergence of early forms of modernism at the end of the century, naturalism in France was so closely identified with Zola's fiction that few claimed the label after his death. The widespread translation of his work, however, gave Zola a global influence that led to the emergence of naturalist schools around the world. The influence of Zola's naturalism was particularly prominent in Russia, which in the nineteenth century had very strong cultural ties to France; in western European nations; and in the United States. The naturalist charge in the United States was led by novelist and critic Frank Norris (1870–1902), dubbed "the boy Zola" by contemporary critics. Although Norris is now considered somewhat of a secondary figure in U.S. literature, the naturalist aesthetic he popularized influenced major twentieth-century writers such as Theodore Dreiser, Upton Sinclair, and John Steinbeck.

In popular use, the term *naturalism* is sometimes used to mean fiction that exaggerates the techniques of realism, sacrificing prose style and depth of characterization for an exhaustive description of the external, observable world. Literary critics often accept this view, but add to it a laundry list of features used to identify the naturalist novel:

- a deterministic plot of decline or degeneration, where characters are crushed by the forces of a universe they can neither understand nor control;

1868 Portrait of Émile Zola by Édouard Manet. Oil on canvas.
Zola's works turned an unflinching eye on the minutiae of human behavior, and he portrayed his characters with unstinting and often provocative detail. PORTRAIT OF EMILE ZOLA (1840–1902) 1868 (OIL ON CANVAS), MANET, EDOUARD (1832–83)/MUSEE D'ORSAY, PARIS, FRANCE, LAUROS/GIRAUDON/BRIDGEMAN ART LIBRARY/WWW.BRIDGEMAN.CO.UK

- attenuation of exceptional or heroic characters, so that each character is a balance of merits and flaws; the critic Philippe Hamon calls this an "aesthetic of normative neutralization" (p. 102);

- attention to lurid or squalid subject matter, particularly focused on the aspects of human experience conceived to be base or instinctual; main characters are often perverted by uncontrollable appetites, drives, or lusts;

- characters drawn from the working class—in U.S. naturalism particularly, perversion and degeneration are associated with working-class characters;

- a modern or contemporary setting, most often urban or industrial, rather than the geographically or temporally distant settings favored by adventure and romance fiction;

- sociological research by the author, including onsite investigation of a workplace, subculture, or location, expert advice, and incorporation of specialized vocabularies.

This list is derived in large part from Zola's most emblematic (and best-selling) novels, such as *L'assommoir* (1877), *Nana* (1880), *Germinal* (1885), and *La bête humaine* (1890), and closely matches other naturalist monuments, such as Frank Norris's *McTeague* (1899).

Origins of the Term

The precise meaning of the term *naturalism* varies across the disciplines: a literary critic, philosopher, theologian, and political scientist would each use the term in a slightly different way. In its broadest sense, naturalism is a doctrine holding that the physical world operates according to laws discernible through empirical science. The naturalist method, modeled after nineteenth-century innovations in the experimental sciences, involves informed, systematic observation of the material world. For the naturalist thinker, human beings are nothing more than a part of this world—like rocks, plants, and animals, they are subject to the laws of physics, chemistry, and biology, which govern human behavior as inexorably as they govern the natural world. Naturalism is thus materialist and anti-idealist in that is does not recognize the existence of nonmaterial or nonobservable phenomena (such as a spiritual realm or higher moral law); it is also antihumanist in that it grants no exceptional status to human beings. Every action taken by a human being, according to the strict naturalist view, has a cause in the physical plane; human behavior is thus entirely determined by the laws of cause and effect in the material world.

In applying this theory to literature, Zola drew on the work of an older contemporary, the French philosopher, historian, and literary critic Hippolyte Taine (1828–1893). Taine's monumental *Histoire de la littérature anglaise* (1863–1864; History of English literature)—a philosophical treatise disguised as literary criticism—sought to demonstrate that a nation's culture and character are products of material causes; as he put it in a famous quip, "vice and virtue are products, like vitriol and sugar" (p. 3). Taine argued that works of art are the products of three factors: *race, moment,* and *milieu.* Taine's English translator renders this phrase as "race, epoch, and surroundings" (p. 12), though the French term *race* is much closer to the English words *nation* or *people* than to *race.* In the analysis of literature, Taine claimed, "we have but a mechanical problem; the total effect is a result, depending entirely on the magnitude and direction of the preceding causes" (p. 13).

Zola's Understanding of Naturalism

While Taine sought to develop a scientific method for the analysis of literature, Zola's naturalism was a method for writing novels; where Taine sought to understand a nation through its literary output, Zola used naturalist philosophy as a basis for creating characters, and with them a portrait of French society in the second half of the nineteenth century. Combining Taine's theories with research developments in the biological and behavioral sciences, Zola conceived of the novel as a laboratory for the study of human behavior under the influence of heredity and environment. By his mid-twenties, having published several novels, he began to plot out his massive life's work, a twenty-novel series entitled *The Rougon-Macquart*—a work to rival the vast *Human Comedy* of Honoré de Balzac (1799–1850), to be based in science rather than intuition.

Zola tirelessly promoted his theories in columns that appeared in newspapers, magazines, and journals. Unfortunately, the most widely anthologized expression of this theory is also among the least thoughtful. This essay, "The Experimental Novel" (1880), is essentially an extended paraphrase of the physician Claude Bernard's influential 1865 work, *Introduction to the Study of Experimental Medicine.* The essay is now regarded as historically interesting if theoretically naïve, and contemporaries—including former disciples of Zola, such as the author Henry Céard (1851–1924)—ridiculed it as a misunderstanding of Bernard's work.

To take this essay as representative of Zola's thinking about naturalism would be a serious error. Naturalism in literature was as much a promotional concept as a literary-critical one, and the range, variety, and energy of Zola's writing about the term indicates he was perhaps less interested in providing a final definition than in keeping alive the heated debates about naturalism. As a literary critic, theater critic, and essayist, Zola was a provocateur: he was strident, often caustic, and prone to dramatic and sensationalist gestures. Early in his career, Zola came to understand and exploit the value of notoriety; his first volleys of criticism were collected in 1866 under the title *My Hatreds,* and his unrepentant slogan "I am here to live out loud" is still occasionally cited by artists and activists. "The Experimental Novel"—along with many of Zola's defenses of naturalism—is best understood from this perspective: to criticize the essay for its lack of theoretical rigor is to miss entirely its brilliance as a provocation and a promotion.

If Zola's criticism is more confrontational than systematic, a broader look at his writing on naturalism nonetheless reveals several consistent ideas. First, Zola often claimed that the lurid, pornographic subject matter of many his novels was incidental to naturalism; what counted was the method—which, as his former disciple Céard observed, could hardly be called "experimental," but that nonetheless shared the careful, systematic observational methods of the emerging social sciences of psychology, sociology, and anthropology. For audiences that consumed Zola's novels as quickly as he could write them and for critics and government censors who called naturalism "putrid literature," the graphic content of the novels was naturalism's most salient feature, and Zola and his publishers often faced obscenity charges in France and abroad (cheap pulp editions with racy covers appeared in the United States as late as the 1950s). For Zola, however, unflinching analysis was the substance of naturalism.

A second, often overlooked theme that runs throughout Zola's writing on naturalism is his repeated association of naturalism and democracy. Perplexed scholars have called this connection a double dysfunction, a strange marriage, a paradox: nineteenth-century theories of biological determinism seem hardly compatible with the Enlightenment ideals of citizenship and self-government. In the words of the critic Harold Kaplan, for naturalist literature in the United States, "democracy seemed to require strong idealizations to support free choice" (p. 37). But for Zola, naturalism in literature and democracy in politics were logical, even necessary evolutionary developments. Zola likened the outsized protagonists of Romanticism to kings and princes, out of place in the modern world. For him naturalism, like democracy, was a representation—faithful if at times unflattering—of the common people.

Critical Debates

Naturalism was politically controversial in its heyday—conservatives called Zola a "literary anarchist," while liberals saw his work as a "calumny of the people"—and its place in literary history has been hotly debated by scholars. By the mid–twentieth century, three major strands of thinking about naturalism's legacies had emerged in Europe. In the early part of the century, Zola was adopted by the French left and elevated to the status of one of France's great writers. Thanks in part to Zola's courageous role in the Dreyfus affair, a political scandal that rocked France in the 1890s, naturalism—once reviled for its unsympathetic portrayals of the working class—was reassessed as an eye-opening portrait of the exploitation of the weak. As a result Zola, spurned by the literary establishment and prosecuted by the French government during his lifetime, was eventually laid to rest in the Pantheon, France's secular cathedral to the "Great Men" of France.

Twentieth-century critics who favored the difficult modernist writing of James Joyce or Marcel Proust, however, were suspicious of this popularity. Naturalism's accessibility and faith in science were incompatible with the modernist turn toward self-consciousness, interiority, opacity, and style; from the modernist perspective, Zola's naturalism looked like a kind of dead end of realism, an overextension of realist strategies at a time when modernist artists were turning away from representational art forms. As the critic James McFarlane put it, naturalism "exhausted itself taking an inventory of the world while it was still relatively stable, [and as a result] could not possibly do justice to the phenomena of its disruption" (p. 80).

A third response to Zola and naturalism is best represented by the Hungarian philosopher Georg Lukács (1885–1971), a prominent figure in leftist aesthetic debates in Europe in the mid–twentieth century. Lukács affirmed the common antithesis between realism and modernism, but saw naturalism as a form of modernism, not an outgrowth of realism. The differences between naturalism and modernism were, for Lukács, merely superficial differences of style. On a more substantive level—for Lukács, the ideological level—naturalism is a form of modernism. As he put it, "There is a continuity from Naturalism to the Modernism of our day"—a continuity of "underlying ideological principles" (1963, p. 29). In contrast to "critical" realism's "dialectical unity," both naturalism and modernism, despite their widely divergent styles, deny the possibility of understanding and action, instead presenting the human condition as one of alienated subjectivity, isolation, and psychopathology. For Lukács, then—in spite of Zola's courageous politics (see his 1940 essay "The Zola Centenary")—naturalism was, like modernism, "not the enrichment, but the negation of art" (1963, p. 46).

Naturalism in the United States

Naturalism was a short-lived phenomenon in France, where it was closely associated with Zola himself. Of Zola's acolytes (known as the "Médan group, after the location of Zola's country estate), only one, Guy de Maupassant (1850–1893), has achieved a lasting reputation. Although short-lived, Zola's influence was global: his work was translated into nearly every language, and writers from Tokyo to Buenos Aires to Moscow saw in his work both a modern sensibility and a fierce critical edge. Scholars have long discussed naturalist literary movements in England, Russia, Germany, and Spain, but are still hard at work mapping naturalism's influence outside Europe: in the 1990s, two journals devoted to Zola and his legacy, *Excavatio: Nouvelle Revue Émile Zola et le naturalisme* and *Les Cahiers Naturalistes,* published a number of essays tracing naturalist movements, often short-lived, in eastern Europe, Asia, and South America.

The U.S. version of naturalism proved to be more enduring: the novelist Frank Norris succeeded in establishing naturalism as a permanent part of the lexicon of literary critics (in spite of his rather idiosyncratic view of naturalism as a magnification of Romanticism rather than a form of realism). Although naturalism was initially associated with Norris and his contemporaries Stephen Crane (1871–1900) and Jack London (1876–1916), a wide range of authors over the next seven decades have been shown to have been influenced by naturalism. As the U.S. scholar June Howard put it, "the name taken by a clearly defined, relatively short-lived movement in France [became] in America a broad term used by some writers and many critics to characterize a diverse group of works . . . over a long period of time" (p. 30). The critic Donald Pizer, in particular, has mapped naturalism's influence on twentieth-century U.S. literature.

Although Norris also wrote adventure novels, his *McTeague* (1899), *The Octopus* (1901), and the posthumously published *Vandover and the Brute* (1914) are the touchstones of U.S. naturalism and were strongly influenced by Zola; some critics accused Norris of lifting passages directly from the French novelist. Although Crane's novella *Maggie: A Girl of the Streets* (1893) is sometimes used to mark the beginning of naturalism in the United States, Norris's criticism established the term in an American context. Norris also used his influence as a reader at Doubleday to promote naturalism; his most notable success was Theodore Dreiser's masterpiece *Sister Carrie* (1900), which the publisher pursued on the strength of Norris's recommendation in spite of his own distaste for the book.

Beginning in the 1980s, U.S. naturalism saw a critical revival, as new theoretical developments led to a fresh perspective on the genre—and indeed, on the notion of genre itself. For traditional literary criticism, focused largely on concerns of aesthetic merit and often, if implicitly, moral value, naturalism had been somewhat of a problem: as a genre, U.S. naturalism privileges blunt artlessness and—like Zola—posits an essentially amoral universe. Critical works such as Walter Benn Michaels's *The Gold Standard and the Logic of Naturalism,* a tour de force of New Historicism, and June Howard's *Form and History in American Literary Naturalism,* broadly informed by the theoretical developments of structuralism and poststructuralism, examine naturalism as a complex meditation on cultural contradictions faced by U.S. culture at a pivotal

moment in its history. Michaels, for example, sees both literary naturalism and debates about the gold standard as part of an entire culture's struggle with the relationship between the material and the ideal—a struggle that, for Michaels, is constitutive of personhood itself. Howard, drawing on the French philosopher Louis Althusser's notion of ideology, argues that naturalism was one way for turn-of-the-twentieth-century U.S. culture to process threatening contradictions in the social order, such as contradictions between the egalitarian ideals of democracy and prominent social and political inequalities of the period. For Howard, the most notable of these are the dominance of industrial capitalism and the increasingly visible presence of groups—a largely immigrant urban working class, women, and African Americans—seeking to be included as agents in U.S. political life.

See also **Literature; Naturalism in Art and Literature; Realism.**

BIBLIOGRAPHY

Hamon, Philippe. *Texte et idéologie: Valeurs, hiérarchies et évaluations dans l'œuvre littéraire.* Paris: Presses Universitaires de France, 1984.

Howard, June. *Form and History in American Literary Naturalism.* Chapel Hill: University of North Carolina Press, 1985.

Kaplan, Harold. *Power and Order: Henry Adams and the Naturalist Tradition in American Fiction.* Chicago: University of Chicago Press, 1981.

Lukács, Georg. *The Meaning of Contemporary Realism.* Translated by John Mander and Necke Mander. London: Merlin Press, 1963.

———. "The Zola Centenary." 1940. In his *Studies in European Realism,* pp. 85–96. London: Merlin Press, 1972.

Masson, Pierre. *Le Disciple et l'insurgé: Roman et politique à la Belle Époque.* Lyon, France: Presses Universitaires de Lyon, 1987.

McFarlane, James. "The Mind of Modernism." In *Modernism: 1890–1930,* edited by Malcolm Bradbury and James McFarlane. New York: Penguin, 1976.

Michaels, Walter Benn. *The Gold Standard and the Logic of Naturalism: American Literature at the Turn of the Century.* Berkeley: University of California Press, 1987.

Mitterand, Henri. *Zola et le naturalisme.* Paris: Presses Universitaires de France, 1986.

Pizer, Donald. *The Theory and Practice of American Literary Naturalism: Selected Essays and Reviews.* Carbondale: Southern Illinois University Press, 1993.

Schor, Naomi. *Zola's Crowds.* Baltimore: Johns Hopkins University Press, 1978.

Taine, Hippolyte. *History of English Literature.* Translated by H. Van Laun. New York: Henry Holt, 1879.

Walcutt, Charles C. *American Literary Naturalism, a Divided Stream.* Minneapolis: University of Minnesota Press, 1956.

Jonathan P. Hunt

NATURALISM IN ART AND LITERATURE.

Naturalism, a term widely used in the nineteenth century, was employed by novelists, artists, and art critics as a synonym for *realism.* But, in fact, *naturalism* was a much more complex term. The term derived from the theory of positivism developed by the French philosopher Auguste Comte (1798–1857). The roots of scientific naturalism, emerging from the eighteenth century and coming to fruition in the nineteenth century, considered knowledge as a pure science that was to be reinforced by a clear understanding of the laws of nature and an objective observation of facts. In the last half of the nineteenth century writers, primarily novelists, subscribed to this innovative positivist view of the world around them.

In the course of the nineteenth century the philosopher Hippolyte Taine applied scientific methods to the study of art and literature. From 1864 to 1884, as a professor at the influential École des Beaux-Arts in Paris, Taine taught students that the character and development of visual culture were determined by two qualities: race and the environment in which art was created. Taine presented the foundation for an evolutionary approach toward human nature and the importance of family genes in determining the ways in which people reacted. Similarly, this author's advocacy of studying the locale or place in which an individual was brought up emphasized societal implications in shaping an individual. Taine's widely read book *The Philosophy of Art* conveyed his beliefs to a broad audience.

Taine's ideas also provided a scientific method for historians that allowed them to understand the past and even predict the future since it was based on immutable historic laws. His approach contributed a foundation upon which contemporary thinkers could build literary and artistic examples of works that were meant to reflect their own era through a factual reconstruction of the "spirit of the time." This need to be "of one's own time" affected writers and visual artists until the end of the nineteenth century and into the twentieth.

The Father of Naturalism

The best-known "proponent of naturalism" was the novelist and French art critic Émile Zola (1840–1902); he was one of the most passionate defenders of Taine's theories, putting them to use in his novels. Zola's foreword to his novel *Thérèse Raquin* (1867) became the fundamental manifesto of literary naturalism. He maintained and enlarged his ideas in his *Experimental Novel* (1880) and *The Naturalist Novelists* (1881), where he advocated that modern literature needed to be as accurate as possible in order to provide a record of "modern history." To Zola, literature could only be truly real if it examined life in a verifiable way, similar to a medical experiment or analysis, where humanity, as an organism, would be able to function only by following predetermined hereditary laws that were to be studied within a very precise social environment. As a careful note taker of the world in which he lived, Zola used the documents he compiled as necessary building blocks in the construction of his novels.

Zola's naturalism created no less a sensation than the earlier realism of Gustave Courbet when he showed his paintings at the Salon in Paris (1850–1851). Very quickly, and certainly by the early 1880s, if not before, literary (and eventually visual) naturalism became the most popular method of creativity

The Haymakers **(1877) by Jules Bastien-Lepage. Oil on canvas.** Bastien-Lepage (1848–1884) was considered by many to be the pioneer of the naturalist style in painting. Though he died quite young, his work inspired the art of numerous other adherents of naturalism. THE HAYMAKERS, 1877, BASTIEN-LEPAGE, JULES (1848–84)/MUSEE D'ORSAY, PARIS, FRANCE, CREDIT: PETER WILLI/WWW.BRIDGEMAN.CO.UK

throughout Europe. Much of this influence was due to the wide dissemination of literary texts through popular journals. The consistent discussion of Zola's theories by writers and painters in the public eye made it clear by the world's fairs of 1878 and 1889 that naturalism was everywhere; it had become an international phenomenon.

The Early Naturalist Painters

As an art critic, beginning in the 1860s, Zola was a very passionate and effective critic of contemporary art. He profoundly admired the work of the French painter Jules Bastien-Lepage (1848–1884), an artist who was seen at the time as one of the leading naturalist painters, if not the primary painter working in this vein. Many younger painters idolized Bastien-Lepage's work, especially after his early death from cancer. Zola, along with the art critic Albert Wolff, saw Bastien-Lepage as the inheritor of the tradition of Jean-François Millet (1814–1875) and Gustave Courbet (1819–1877). Zola, and to a slightly lesser degree Albert Wolff, affirmed Bastien-Lepage's superiority over the Impressionist painters active at the time, since Bastien-Lepage could, it was believed, factually recreate his impressions in a most organized way. Bastien-Lepage's canvases, such as his *Hay Gatherers* (Musée d'Orsay, Paris) and *Potato Harvesters* (National Gallery of Victoria, Melbourne), because of their sense of the momentary and their large-scale presence, created lively discussion. Critics, and other artists, believed the artist had originated a naturalist painting style that was photographic and environmentally specific. The painter used the landscapes of his native region, the Meuse, for his naturalist reconstructions of rural life.

Bastien-Lepage's work excited the imagination of painters beyond France; he was seen as a pivotal figure in the international naturalist movement. His death was viewed as cataclysmic for the visual arts, and he was assured a position of importance in the creation of a "new style." His canvases became models for emulation in Scandinavia, eastern Europe, England, and the United States, where his example demonstrated that naturalism was a viable and fertile mode of representation.

Using Bastien-Lepage as a touchstone, other painters, including P. A. J. Dagnan-Bouveret, created a heightened naturalism that relied extensively on the use of photography as a tool, an aide-mémoire, without revealing photography as a primary source. Photography became for visual artists what note taking was for the novelist; it allowed them to gather visual facts they could use later in their reconstructions of reality. A number of well-accepted painters created a compelling version of "virtual reality" that deeply engaged the general public, who saw, accurately recorded, elements from their environment and types from society that they knew well.

Another French painter, one linked briefly with the Impressionist movement, was Jean-François Raffaelli (1850–1924). In a series of mostly small compositions, he represented people from the lowest level of society in order to convey authenticity and ugliness. Raffaelli's ragpickers, wanderers, and social outcasts revealed that beauty and strength came from character, no matter where this was found. He helped shift the visual perspective from "ideal nudes" toward the examination of those whose life was unfortunate, similar to many of the types in Zola's novels. Raffaelli's vision of the world suggested that sadness and hopelessness were aspects of life experiences that a modern naturalist painter needed to understand. With Edgar Degas and Gustave Caillebotte, painters with a strong naturalist streak in many of their works, the Impressionist canon was expanded to include themes drawn from urban life, thereby helping to fulfill the call from many art critics of the era that themes from modern life could be found everywhere. In his series of articles on realism published in the review of the same name, Edmond Duranty (1833–1880) foreshadowed Zola's ideas about the position of the artist, writer, or painter vis-à-vis nature. For Duranty, as for Zola, artists should be concerned with the truth, with an exacting study of nature. He called for the artist to portray the practical conditions of human life, the milieu in which people lived, in order to represent the social side of man and the influences that affected him.

Spreading Naturalism

As Zola's novels gained an international following, a large number of imitators appeared who helped promote the naturalist aesthetic in popular literature that was available to the masses. Writers such as Guy de Maupassant (1850–1893) based their stories on Zola's methodology. At the same time, Zola's best-known novels were turned into plays: Nana was one character who dominated the French stage in productions of L'assommoir from the 1880s onward; Zola's mining novel, Germinal, provided additional evidence of his influence when performed in popular theaters. During the 1890s, a series of printmakers furthered the appearance of visual naturalism in posters and lithographs published by the ever increasing socialist press. Théophile Steinlen, an avowed radical, saw that such types as the print "The Barge Man" provided an opportunity to comment on the implied threat found in disgruntled wanderers; other images, for the periodical Gil Blas, stressed that those who were out of work and destitute could be found everywhere. The plight of the poor became a naturalist battle cry that many artists, in varied artistic media, answered. By using these themes, writers and visual artists enlarged the social dimension of the naturalist movement, which had first brought these types to the fore.

But it was the haunting impact of the environment and of the social milieu on life that remained one of the most trenchant aspects of the naturalist heritage after the turn of the century. In America, in the novels of Theodore Dreiser (1871–1945) or Frank Norris (1870–1902), the influence of Zola's brand of naturalism was paramount. In Vandover and the Brute or in the cataclysmic McTeague: A Story of San Francisco, Norris's characters were flawed, often overwrought, brutes whose nature was determined by genetic and environmental factors. Their pursuit of money underscored uncontrollable drives; naturalism was now focusing on obsessive traits. Significantly, Norris's novel McTeague led to another level of naturalist appeal: the influence on early cinema. When Erich von Stroheim completed his extremely long film Greed, based directly on McTeague, in 1924, he revealed that the naturalist aesthetic could be transferred to another medium, where it was used as a means of revealing fatal character traits that cast light on the lives of troubled people. In effect, Zola's idea of making art understandable for the masses by creating a detailed narrative had come full circle with the motion picture.

See also **Aesthetics: Europe and the Americas; Impressionism; Literary History; Realism; Symbolism.**

BIBLIOGRAPHY

Brown, Frederick. *Zola: A Life.* New York: Farrar Straus Giroux, 1995.

Egbert, Donald Drew. *Social Radicalism and the Arts, Western Europe: A Cultural History from the French Revolution to 1968.* New York: Knopf, 1970.

Furst, Lilian R. *Naturalism.* London: Methuen, 1971.

Gauss, Charles Edward. *The Aesthetic Theories of French Artists: 1855 to the Present.* Baltimore: Johns Hopkins University Press, 1949.

Guieu, Jean-Max, and Alison Hilton, eds. *Émile Zola and the Arts.* Washington, D.C.: Georgetown University Press, 1988.

Hauser, Arnold. *Naturalism, Impressionism, the Film Age.* Vol. 4 of *The Social History of Art.* 3rd ed. New York: Routledge, 1999.

Mitterand, Henri. *Émile Zola: Fiction and Modernity.* Edited and translated by Monica Lebron and David Baguley. London: Emile Zola Society, 2000.

Nochlin, Linda. *Realism.* Harmondsworth, U.K.: Penguin, 1971.

Nochlin, Linda, ed. *Realism and Tradition in Art, 1848–1900, Sources and Documents.* Englewood Cliffs, N.J.: Prentice-Hall, 1966.

Papke, Mary E., ed. *Twisted from the Ordinary: Essays on American Literary Naturalism.* Knoxville: University of Tennessee Press, 2003.

Sacquin, Michèle, ed. *Zola.* Paris: Bibliothèque Nationale de France/Fayard, 2002.

Stromberg, Roland N. *Realism, Naturalism, and Symbolism: Modes of Thought and Expression in Europe, 1848–1914.* New York: Walker, 1968.

Weisberg, Gabriel P. *Beyond Impressionism: The Naturalist Impulse.* New York: Abrams, 1992.

Weisberg, Gabriel P., ed. *The European Realist Tradition.* Bloomington: Indiana University Press, 1982.

Gabriel P. Weisberg

NATURAL LAW. Natural law theories have a venerable place in the history of philosophy, stretching back to the time of Plato (428–348 or 347 B.C.E.) and Aristotle (384–322 B.C.E.) when the relationship between law and nature first became a central dynamic of discussion in ethics. Since then such theories have provided staple ingredients within each major phase in Western philosophy down to the time of Immanuel Kant (1724–1804) and beyond into the contemporary era. While such accounts have often been short on detailed and practical guidance on right action, the outlook of natural jurisprudence has been highly influential in ensuring a continuous focus on the alleged rationality of the natural world and the constant and uniform accessibility to the human mind of such principles of observed regularity. However, there has always been a tension between the claim that these principles are eternal and unchanging, and the particular forms and uses assigned to natural law: in Ancient Greece the focus was more on the apparently unchanging character of nature and the distressing mutability of actual law; in the medieval age St. Thomas Aquinas (c. 1224–1274) above all emphasized the accessibility of regular patterns in nature to human nature; and in the early modern era natural law theories evolved as responses first to skepticism about the sources of knowledge, and secondly in reaction to the political turbulence that followed the Reformation, which seemed to shatter the easy symmetry between the uniformity of church and state both across Europe as a whole and also within its constituent political units. In each case the position of natural law was ambiguous, both very much of its time, and yet claiming its authenticity and authority from its position outside history.

Natural jurisprudential approaches to ethics have proved difficult to integrate into the historiography of philosophy because of just this same ambiguous relationship to history itself. On the one hand, natural law was viewed as a set of eternal verities presented by God to humanity in finished and perfect shape, and found embodied in the moral and civil order as evidence of its divine fashioning, albeit in a form diminished by the Fall of Man. But on the other hand, natural jurisprudence is a product of the interaction not just of different and succeeding schools of moral philosophy, but also of the interaction of the range of plausible accounts of divine instigation and human response within wider politics and society. So, for example, the neo-Thomist and Lutheran-Aristotelian systems of natural law that evolved in the sixteenth and seventeenth centuries in Spain and Germany were both a reaction to the

new ideological circumstances of the Reformation and Counter-Reformation eras as much as they were internal modifications and realignments within academic institutions of the legacy, above all, of Aquinas and Aristotle. The same epistemological ambiguity runs through the natural law systems of the early Enlightenment era and the interpretation that they laid upon the works of Hugo Grotius (1583–1645) and Thomas Hobbes (1588–1679), which were their foundation and self-conscious inspiration. The writings of Samuel Pufendorf (1632–1694), Gottfried Wilhelm von Leibniz (1646–1716), Christian Wolff (1679–1754), and Christian Thomasius (1655–1728) sought both to anchor themselves in a newly revealed metaphysics that stood outside time, and also to comment powerfully upon and if necessary direct the course of the world of contemporary practical politics.

Natural Law in the Ancient and Medieval World

At the heart of natural law is an attempt to extract general principles out of the confusing multiplicity of legal and social convention; in the Greek world, this was represented by the contrast and tension between those areas of human life governed by contingency and those controlled by the ineluctable force of nature. Given the variability of positive law both across cultures and within them, the question arose of how legal certainty could be identified and located; and immediately battle-lines were drawn between those who held that such a moral law could be found—usually as a divine creation—and those who remained skeptical of such normative claims, and either denied that there was any essential morality, or located it elsewhere. This pattern, which originated with the Sophists, was to be repeated throughout the history of natural law arguments.

Part of the explanation of why Aristotle's writings are regarded as the first important contribution to this discourse is that they adeptly try to reconcile the distinction between nature and convention. He achieves this by elevating human reason as humankind's dominant and defining characteristic, whose proper exercise mediates between what is permanent and what is ephemeral. This is taken up with greater vigor by the Stoics, and by Marcus Tullius Cicero (106–43 B.C.E.) in particular. He regarded human reason as the apex of a rational world order: human nature rather than an innate law outside human beings now provided the ground and basis for distinguishing between positive law and natural law. Moreover, all humans possessed the rational means, when properly exercised, to identify this law unaided by God, whose divine spark reason essentially is. The Stoics also initiated what was to become one of the most influential strands of natural law thinking—namely, the view that one of the core principles of natural law is a sense of broad sociability towards one's fellow humans, tempered though not obliterated by one's own personal priorities.

The rationalism of natural law still runs as a clear thread through the massive *Summa Theologiae* of Aquinas, despite its elaborate metaphysical architecture. Human nature and the rational conclusions that can be generated from it continue to be his point of departure. However, Aquinas is concerned to reinstate divine eternal law within his framework, and that does lead to some tension within his overall concept of natural law as a bridge between positive and divine law. He tries to overcome this by recourse to a categorical division of natural law into primary and secondary principles, thus making natural law both fixed and mutable simultaneously. This sophisticated synthesis of pre-existing views within a Christian framework proved highly influential, and was continually refined, most notably by the later Spanish Jesuit Francisco Suarez (1548–1617); but ultimately the pressures generated by the Reformation and Thirty Years' War on the one hand and Renaissance skepticism on the other required a reconfiguring of the relationship between divine and natural law, a renewed emphasis on the Stoic formulas, and a fresh initiative to link the core principles of natural law to the emergent law of nations.

Early Modern Germany

In the era that followed the conclusion of the Thirty Years' War in 1648, it was generally held that the combined effects of Renaissance skepticism and the fragmenting effect of endemic confessional strife had destroyed the coherence of pre-existing accounts of political sovereignty. The rights and duties of monarchy, most especially in respect to churches and the enforcement of doctrinal and liturgical uniformity, were left open to question and redefinition as Europe sought to come to terms with the permanence of confessional division and the necessity of its diplomatic recognition. How could sovereignty remain unified and cohesive when religious truth had become fissiparous? How could absolutism be redefined in a way that preserved unity of political decision-making while paying due pragmatic recognition to the complexities of the new European order?

Nowhere were these tensions more visible than in the Holy Roman Empire, the epicenter of the recent military conflict, and the most graphic illustration in its uneasy religious tessellation of the need to find a new legitimization for political sovereignty. It is therefore no accident that it was from this region that there emerged the most systematic attempts to re-unify politics with metaphysics and devise new explanations of the appropriate exercise of political and ecclesiological power by the ruler. The pathbreakers in this respect were Grotius and Hobbes, far more than René Descartes (1596–1650), whose relative silence on morals gave no clear assistance in this area. Grotius was admired and praised above all for showing first in a series of specific works on the legal implications and meaning of colonial acquisition, and second in his larger work of synthesis, *On the Law of War and Peace* (1625), that there were still general principles of natural law that could be discerned right across the spectrum of international customary law. These were accessible to all, and, crucially, would obtain even if God and God's revealed intentions for humankind were taken out of consideration. From Hobbes European readers drew the key arguments of what is generally known now as voluntarism: that laws of general validity arose from the imposition of a unified, sovereign, rational will rather than the progressive discovery of general principles benignly imprinted on humanity's consciousness in the form of innate ideas. It was in the combination of Grotius's arguments in favor of the possibility and content of universal natural law, and Hobbes's insight into

how those laws may be isolated and implemented in contemporary, fragmented practical politics that produced a truly modern theory of natural law, associated with Pufendorf and Thomasius. It evoked in turn a powerful hostile reaction in the work of Leibniz and Wolff, which tried to rework the views of Aquinas in a different idiom.

The contest (for that is what it effectively became) between the voluntarism of Pufendorf and the essentialism of Leibniz was mainly played out within a framework of university disputation, but also spilled over importantly into the public arena in debates over such issues as confessional reunion. At stake here in essence was the way in which the principles of moral knowledge were obtained, an apparently recondite area of learning, but nevertheless one with crucial implications for method in all areas of modern philosophy. In his major work *On the Law of Nature and Nations* (1672), Pufendorf argued that humans gain knowledge of morals in a way that parallels the manner in which they devise languages, that is, through the imposition of categories and meanings to create shared, mutually accessible structures. God may give humans revealed truths, but this forms but one part of human duties; the majority of these duties are devised through unaided reason, which God gave to humans to use in this free fashion. From this initial insight, explicitly grounded in Stoic thought, emerges a complex analytical structure that frames an elaborately contractarian politics weighted heavily through the prudential calculations of individuals in an absolutist direction. It also resulted in a clearly articulated Erastian church politics, vesting the civil power with final control and powers of resolution in religious disputes.

In contrast to this, Leibniz and Wolff regarded the work of Pufendorf and his followers as an attempt to provide practical resolutions of disputes from poorly argued philosophical premises that either guilefully or ineptly justified secular voluntarism. In its place, Leibnizian posited an elaborately conceived metaphysical approach that sought to explain natural law in terms of divine justice and the "charity of the wise," arguing in essence that all practical morality can be derived from the reservoir of truth located in the perfect wisdom of God. Less daring in the practical politics with which it eventuated, Leibnizian natural law nevertheless performed virtuosic surgery on the corpse of Protestant-Aristotelian natural law, ensuring that Wolff's textbooks enjoyed equal credibility and popularity in both Protestant and Catholic universities until the later eighteenth century. Leibniz also pointed out disquietingly secular overtones in the work of the followers of Pufendorf that inhibited their unequivocal acceptance of their work even within Protestant Germany.

Early Modern France

While the grandest systems of natural law emerged in Germany, there was also a sustained focus on ethical discourse of this type among the French Huguenots, exiled by Louis XIV (1638–1715) after the Revocation of the Edict of Nantes in 1685, and forced therefore to construct a new political identity for themselves within a cosmopolitan intellectual framework, rather than that of a state. Their most eloquent writers, such as Jean Barbeyrac (1674–1744) and Jean-Jacques

Burlamaqui (1694–1748), sought to defend a right to religious conscience while retaining a political order that was primarily absolutist in character. The particular circumstances of their ideological preferences therefore led them to develop a proto-liberal language of rights in association with religious toleration that was genuinely original and powerfully influential, not least on John Locke (1632–1704). But the Huguenots also had to confront more directly than any other group of writers the potentially illiberal and austerely utilitarian (using that term loosely) aspects of Pufendorfian absolutism, whose voluntarist assumptions sometimes appeared to produce results rather similar to the divine-right absolutism pursued for wholly different reasons by Louis XIV. This was a paradox not lost on Jean-Jacques Rousseau (1712–1778), who, with intimate knowledge of the local Swiss context of these writers, later castigated the Huguenots, and the natural law school as a whole, as a very clear case study in subservience to absolutism and a failure to follow through an analysis of the rights of conscience with sufficient rigor.

In four particular respects, the natural law disputes of the period between 1625 and 1760 left an important philosophical legacy. Firstly, the issues of how far religious toleration was to be permitted, what its political consequences should be, and what were the sources of its intellectual justification were played out within and refracted through the discourse of natural law above all others. Natural law theories therefore provided the framework for the discussion of the major question of the day on the interface between political theory and practical politics. Secondly, although this was not fully intended, the crucial separation of the fields of ethics and moral theology, argued for by Grotius, Pufendorf, and their followers, ultimately resulted in the final downgrading and devaluing of the formal divine content and origin of ethics and the promotion of individuals as separate self-sufficient moral persons capable of undertaking rational voluntary transactions. Thirdly, this Pufendorfian argument produced several very important discussions of the nature of contractarian government, of the right to own property and to pursue economic interactions untrammeled by the state, that powerfully anticipated some of the most radical and influential ideas of the philosophes and of the Scottish Enlightenment. Finally, the natural lawyers' preoccupation with securing links between the law of nature and the law of nations established the view that reason of state arguments were not sufficient in the world of public affairs, thus—ironically—reinstating a link between "eternal" principles of human ethics and the law of nations, just when the link between divine and natural law had been irretrievably severed.

Natural Law and Natural Rights

The disappearance of natural law arguments from mainstream philosophy was not nearly so abrupt in the nineteenth century as is often made out, as can be seen from the curricula and textbooks adopted at many universities. Nevertheless, the combined influence of Kantian idealism and utilitarianism did serve ultimately to undercut several of the key claims of the theorists of the preceding two centuries. In his *Foundations of the Metaphysics of Morals* (1785), Kant essentially generated a fresh account of moral obligation that was located not in the principles of human nature, but in an autonomous will freely exercising practical reason: Obligation lay not in the harmony of a principle with human nature, but in whether a law could be objectively generalized in relevantly comparable circumstances. Thus it appeared that natural law arguments only yielded empirical "counsels of prudence" about human behavior, not conceptually coherent moral yardsticks. A second blow was struck by Jeremy Bentham (1748–1832), who stressed that there was no "external consideration" that permitted natural jurisprudence to distinguish between one person's judgment of the law of nature and another's: natural law had to act as its own circular proof and guarantor, which was unacceptable. Attempts to distill a common set of principles from the infinite variety of the law of nations were bound to fail; he believed it to be far better to move outside the categories of reason and human nature altogether, accept the pluralist nature of human definitions of the good life, and reassert the supremacy of legal positivism, based on accommodating majority preferences. This point was particularly difficult for natural lawyers to answer, given that they had failed to observe how easily their view that knowledge of the law of nature was not reliant on God could slide into a statement that grounds for obeying natural law are not dependent on God either—a conclusion that left no clear criterion of obligation to fall back upon.

However, the eclipse of natural law arguments was by no means complete even at the beginning of the twenty-first century. While natural rights theories have pursued their own separate trajectory towards an assertion of the protection of individual rights as a good in itself, perhaps best embodied in the American philosopher Robert Nozick's *Anarchy, State and Utopia,* a number of Catholic theorists, most notably the Australian author John Finnis in *Natural Law and Natural Rights,* have reworked the idea of shared goods inherent in human nature, though the content of that list of shared goods and the relationship between them has proved to be controversial. As with the earlier versions of natural law theory that have taken their stand on human nature and its attributes, this version too stands or falls on the richness or poverty of its conception of that human nature, and on the clarity and self-awareness with which human nature is neutrally described or prescribed in relation to other norms at each step in the argument. All such theories explore very difficult philosophical territory because they seek to unify two essentially different projects: to provide specific prudential advice on how best to achieve one's objectives (implying a recognition that human nature and its needs change in line with historical circumstances in ways that reason alone does not always fully comprehend), together with a parallel recognition that for human insights to be generalized as valid law, they need to be assessed according to a sole and unvarying standard, usually identified as rational truth. Those thinkers who have best overcome these paradoxes, such as the Stoics, Grotius, and Pufendorf, lived in periods of significant social dislocation, but were stimulated to identify and narrow general principles attributable to reason that were also imaginatively rich enough to meet the shifting empirical shoals of their own political and existential crises. That is why they are still worth studying in the twenty-first century, for this juxtaposition of moral philosophy with moral exigencies is a task that is never completed, despite the shift in intellectual frameworks that makes the natural law era seem so distant and different from that of the present.

See also **Christianity; Human Rights; Scholasticism; Toleration.**

BIBLIOGRAPHY

PRIMARY SOURCES

Aristotle. *Nicomachean Ethics.* Edited by Roger Crisp. Cambridge, U.K.: Cambridge University Press, 2000.

Cicero, Marcus Tullius. *De Legibus and De Republica.* Edited by Niall Rudd and J. G. F. Powell as *The Republic and the Laws.* Oxford: Oxford University Press, 1998.

Finnis, John. *Natural Law and Natural Rights.* Oxford: Oxford University Press, 1980.

Grotius, Hugo. *De Jure Belli ac Pacis.* 3 vols. 1625. Edited by Francis W. Kelsey and published as *The Law of War and Peace: De Jure Belli ac Pacis.* Indianapolis: Bobbs-Merrill, 1962.

Nozick, Robert. *Anarchy, State and Utopia.* Oxford: Blackwell, 1974.

Pufendorf, Samuel. *De Jure Naturae et Gentium.* 1672. Translated by Basil Kennett as *Of the Law of Nature and Nations: Eight Books.* Clark, N.J.: Lawbook Exchange, 2003.

Thomas, Aquinas St. *Summa Theologiae.* 1265–1273. Reprint, n.p.: Blackfriars; New York: McGraw-Hill, 1964–1976.

SECONDARY SOURCES

Buckle, Stephen. *Natural Law and the Theory of Property: Grotius to Hume.* Oxford: Oxford University Press, 1991.

George, Robert P. *In Defense of Natural Law.* New York: Clarendon, 1999.

Haakonssen, Knud. *Natural Law and Moral Philosophy: From Grotius to the Scottish Enlightenment.* Cambridge, U.K.: Cambridge University Press, 1996.

Hunter, Ian, and David Saunders, eds. *Natural Law and Civil Sovereignty: Moral Right and State Authority in Early Modern Political Thought.* New York: Palgrave; Cambridge, U.K.: Cambridge University Press, 2002.

Tierney, Brian. *The Idea of Natural Rights: Studies on Natural Rights, Natural Law, and Church Law, 1150–1625.* Atlanta: Scholars Press, 1997.

Tuck, Richard. *Natural Rights Theories.* Cambridge, U.K.: University Press, 1979.

T. J. Hochstrasser

NATURAL RIGHTS. *See* **Human Rights; Natural Law.**

NATURAL THEOLOGY. The primary sense of the term *natural theology* rests on the contrast between natural and revealed knowledge. Natural theology concerns knowledge of the existence and attributes of God arrived at using only the natural faculties of sense and reason. Philosophical arguments for the existence, intelligence, power, and goodness of God based on the order and beauty of the world, or on purely intellectual considerations, are examples of natural theology. Knowledge of God that is based on divine revelation as set down in scripture is the subject of revealed theology.

A central metaphor for the distinction between natural theology and revealed theology is that of the "two books"—the book of God's word (scripture) and the book of God's works (nature). The mainstream theological position has always been that the primary source of truth was revelation and that natural reasoning—reading the book of God's works—can provide ancillary support for revealed truths. Reason can confirm what is already known by faith. Natural theology has, therefore, been a more or less important, and more or less welcome, secondary support for Christian doctrine over the centuries. A constant worry for theologians has been the possibility of relying too heavily on natural theology and thus giving too much away to rationalistic and secular ways of understanding the world and placing insufficient emphasis on the importance of scripture and revelation.

Although the primary sense of "natural" in the phrase "natural theology" is natural as opposed to revealed knowledge, there is a secondary sense that is also important. Works of natural theology produced from the seventeenth to the nineteenth centuries frequently focused on the wonders of the natural world and on developments in natural science. The phrase "natural theology" thus came to stand for a rather particular kind of natural theology—a celebration of the beauty of the natural world and the power, wisdom, and goodness of its Creator, as revealed by the scientific study of nature. This sort of natural theology might also be thought of as a kind of "theology of nature," to distinguish it from the broader intellectual enterprise of arguing about God independently of revelation.

Natural Theology and the Birth of Modern Science
Although it had roots both in ancient Greek philosophy and in medieval Christian theology (for instance, in Thomas Aquinas's famous "five ways" of demonstrating the existence of God), the heyday of natural theology was between the seventeenth and nineteenth centuries and was intertwined with the rise of modern science (see Brooke, 2003; Brooke and Cantor).

Nature was investigated and interpreted in new ways in sixteenth- and seventeenth-century Europe. These innovations (which have traditionally been summed up as the "scientific revolution") included the use of new scientific instruments (such as the telescope, the microscope, and the air pump), a new emphasis on experimentation, and the use of mechanical models to explain natural phenomena. The natural theological genre was one that both allowed practitioners of the new mechanical and experimental philosophy to justify their work to a sometimes skeptical religious establishment and also allowed religious apologists to enlist new knowledge in the service of Christian piety.

Many of the early members of the Royal Society in London (founded in 1660) saw a connection between their experimental investigations and their Christian faith. (Robert K. Merton famously argued that the Puritan religious beliefs of many of the founder members played a key role in shaping the activities of the Royal Society.) Robert Boyle (1627–1691), for instance, as well as conducting important experiments with his air pump to investigate the pressure of air and other gases, wrote on *The Excellency of Theology, Compared with Natural*

Philosophy (1674) and composed a work entitled *The Christian Virtuoso* (1690), subtitled, "shewing that by being addicted to experimental philosophy, a man is rather assisted than indisposed to be a good Christian." Another early Fellow of the Royal Society whose writings explored the way that the new experimental and mechanical philosophy could be used to support theology was John Ray (1627–1705), whose *The Wisdom of God Manifested in the Works of the Creation* (1691) was to become a classic of the natural theological genre. In this work, Ray argued that since the creativity of God was present throughout the natural world, no part of it was too low or insignificant to be a subject of natural-philosophical study.

The experimental investigation of nature in seventeenth-century England was, then, justified as being to the greater glory of God and for the good of man. The natural theology produced by men such as Boyle and Ray reflected the character of the new natural knowledge they were engaged in producing. Their God was an able mathematician, a geometer, a designer, a mechanic. If the experimental philosopher displayed his ingenuity by designing and constructing a telescope or a microscope, how much more ingenious must be the God who could design and construct the human eye? If the man of science gave evidence of his intelligence by discovering that natural phenomena were governed by elegant mathematical laws, how much more intelligent and powerful must be the God who drew up and laid down those laws?

In his will, Boyle left money to pay for a series of lectures to promote this natural theological vision, which he hoped would prove the truth of the Christian religion "against notorious infidels, viz. Atheists, Pagans, Jews, and Mahometans" (quoted in Brooke, 2003, p. 157). The result was a series of Boyle Lectures, which were delivered for around forty years, annually, starting in the year of Boyle's death, 1692, when the first Boyle lecturer was Isaac Newton's friend, the Reverend Richard Bentley (1662–1742). Another Newtonian and theologian, Samuel Clarke (1675–1729), was the Boyle lecturer in 1704–1705.

Natural Theology and Its Critics in the Eighteenth and Nineteenth Centuries

Lectures and treatises in this same natural theological tradition continued to be produced throughout the eighteenth century and into the first half of the nineteenth century, across Europe, but with a particular popularity in Britain. Natural theologians argued from the harmonious, law-governed, architecturally sophisticated, mathematically precise wonders of nature—animate and inanimate—to the existence and attributes of a good, powerful, and intelligent deity. Natural theological works frequently relied on arousing their readers' aesthetic feelings, but these could then be used in support of very different political programmes, from Joseph Priestley's and Thomas Paine's versions of radical republicanism to William Paley's and William Whewell's more conservative Anglicanism.

The most famous philosophical critique of natural theology, David Hume's (1711–1776) *Dialogues Concerning Natural Religion,* appeared, posthumously, in 1779. Although the use of the dialogue form meant that Hume did not claim any view directly as his own, some have thought that the arguments against natural religion voiced by the skeptical Philo are closest to Hume's own views. In addition to throwing doubt on the soundness of the analogy between the universe and human artifacts, Philo suggests that if the analogy is to be taken seriously, then the correct inference should be to a cause more closely resembling the cause of human artifacts—namely, a being (or, more likely, a collaborating group of beings) of limited skill and foresight, not a single being of unlimited power and intelligence. Pressing the point even further, Philo asks why the natural theologian, once embarked upon the project of comparing human and divine designers, should not become a perfect anthropomorphite. Why not assert that the deity or deities has eyes, a nose, mouth, ears and so on, he asks.

Although the attacks upon the argument from design put forward in Hume's *Dialogues* are often seen, in retrospect, as devastating to the natural theological enterprise, that was not how they were perceived at the time. The most famous treatise in the natural theology tradition postdated the *Dialogues* and did not consider the arguments put forward in them to be seriously troubling. This was William Paley's (1743–1805) *Natural Theology* (1802), which is still considered the classic expression of the argument from natural design to divine designer. The Paleyite version of natural theology, with its focus on adaptation and design, was taken up by the authors of the *Bridgewater Treatises.* It was also the version of natural theology to which the young Charles Darwin (1809–1882) was introduced as a Cambridge undergraduate with a passion for natural history, in the late 1820s.

As the nineteenth century unfolded, however, the natural theology of Paley and the *Bridgewater* authors came under attack from a variety of different directions. Discussions about the intellectual status of natural theology overlapped with debates about the political desirability of church-dominated education. In Britain, for instance, the second half of the nineteenth century saw the Anglican monopoly on the universities and education being gradually eroded. Anglican men of science and their natural theological arguments were gradually displaced by agnostics and secularizers, with their more materialistic interpretations of scientific results, as the leading scientific authorities in Victorian Britain.

There had been, for some time, a radical, anti-Christian strand of natural theology—a deistic sort of natural religion promoted most famously by Thomas Paine (1737–1809) in his *Age of Reason* (1794–1807). On this view natural theology was not a supplement to revealed theology but a self-sufficient alternative to it. Paine argued that the book of nature was the only book that was needed to understand God and his creation. All churches, scriptures, and doctrines were anathema to Paine. Christianity was pilloried as a corrupt and oppressive system, run by a self-serving and power-hungry priesthood. The true theology—as opposed to the immoral superstitions of the churches—was to be found in the results of science and philosophy. Writing in the same freethinking tradition as Paine, but replacing Paine's deism with outright atheism, the secularist campaigner George Jacob Holyoake

---

PALEY'S WATCHMAKER

William Paley (1743–1805) was an Anglican clergyman and successful writer whose *Principles of Moral Philosophy* (1785) and *Natural Theology* (1802) were widely read, especially by students, well into the nineteenth century. The central argument of *Natural Theology* was that living things are comparable to mechanical contrivances, such as watches; and just as from a mechanical contrivance we infer a human designer, so, by analogy, from natural contrivances we should infer a divine designer (see Addinall; Brooke, 2003; Nuovo). The opening paragraph of Paley's *Natural Theology*, quoted below, set the tone for the central analogy of the book. The title of Richard Dawkins's 1988 book, *The Blind Watchmaker*, alludes to this argument by suggesting that blind Darwinian processes of variation and natural selection have replaced Paley's divine watchmaker.

> In crossing a heath, suppose I pitched my foot against a *stone,* and were asked how the stone came to be there; I might possibly answer, that, for any thing I knew to the contrary, it had lain there for ever: nor would it perhaps be very easy to show the absurdity of this answer. But suppose I had found a *watch* upon the ground, and it should be inquired how the watch happened to be in that place; I should hardly think of the answer which I had before given, that, for any thing I knew, the watch might have always been there. Yet why should not this answer serve for the watch as well as for the stone? Why is it not as admissible in the second case, as in the first? For this reason, and for no other, viz. that, when we come to inspect the watch, we perceive (what we could not discover in the stone) that its several parts are framed and put together for a purpose, *e.g.* that they are so formed and adjusted as to produce motion, and that motion so regulated as to point out the hour of the day; that, if the different parts had been differently shaped from what they are, of a different size from what they are, or placed after any other manner, or in any other order, than that in which they are placed, either no motion at all would have been carried on in the machine, or none which would have answered the use that is now served by it. . . . This mechanism being observed (it requires indeed an examination of the instrument, and perhaps some previous knowledge of the subject, to perceive and understand it; but being once, as we have said, observed and understood), the inference, we think, is inevitable, that the watch must have had a maker: that there must have existed, at some time, and at some place or other, an artificer or artificers who formed it for the purpose which we find it actually to answer; who comprehended its construction, and designed its use.

(1817–1906), while serving a prison sentence for blasphemy, composed a pamphlet entitled *Paley Refuted in His Own Words* (1847). Holyoake pressed arguments similar to those put forward in Hume's *Dialogues* seventy years earlier. Holyoake's conclusion was that he had shown natural theology to be logically flawed, and thus also shown that revealed theology was groundless (since he held that revealed theology presupposed natural theology). He then went on to denounce Christian religion as a barrier to human progress and demand that it be replaced by a utilitarian and scientific secular morality.

Charles Darwin's explanation in *The Origin of Species* (1859) of how the processes of random variation and natural selection could combine to produce what appeared to be instances of "design" in the natural world is often described as the final nail in natural theology's coffin. If blind natural forces could create adaptation, then surely no role was left for Paley's God. It was not quite that simple, however. Historians of science have shown that Darwin took over much of the language of natural theology (the discourse of "adaptation" and "design") as well as some of its leading assumptions—such as the idea that every anatomical and behavioral trait should be assumed to have a function. Darwin was certainly no Holyoake. Whatever his own personal doubts about theology, he presented his ideas not as an argument for atheism but as an explanation of how the creator could make new species through the operation of laws rather than through miraculous interventions. Paley's watchmaker-God may have been banished in Darwin's new view of nature, but that had only ever been one of the

THE *BRIDGEWATER TREATISES*

In February 1829 the Reverend Francis Henry, earl of Bridgewater, died. His will made provision for £8000 sterling to be held at the disposal of the president of the Royal Society in London and used to finance the publication of one thousand copies of a work on the power, wisdom, and goodness of God as manifested in the creation. The result, eventually, was not one but eight such works. These works of natural theology were written by leading religious and scientific figures of the day and were published between 1833 and 1836 (see Addinall; Topham):

1. Thomas Chalmers (1780–1847), *On the Power, Wisdom and Goodness of God as Manifested in the Adaptation of External Nature to the Moral and Intellectual Constitution of Man* (1833).

2. John Kidd (1775–1851), *On the Adaptation of External Nature to the Physical Condition of Man: Principally with Reference to the Supply of His Wants and the Exercise of His Intellectual Faculties* (1833).

3. William Whewell (1794–1866), *Astronomy and General Physics Considered with Reference to Natural Theology* (1833).

4. Charles Bell (1774–1842), *The Hand: Its Mechanism and Vital Endowments in Evincing Design* (1833).

5. Peter Roget (1779–1869), *Animal and Vegetable Physiology: Considered with Reference to Natural Theology* (1834).

6. William Buckland (1784–1856), *Geology and Mineralogy Considered with Reference to Natural Theology* (1836).

7. William Kirby (1759–1850), *On the Power, Wisdom and Goodness of God as Manifested in the Creation of Animals and in Their History, Habits and Instincts* (1835).

8. William Prout (1785–1850), *Chemistry, Meteorology, and the Function of Digestion: Considered with Reference to Natural Theology* (1834).

In 1837 Charles Babbage (1791–1871), the creator of the famous "difference engine" (a calculating machine often cited as the earliest forerunner of the modern computer), wrote an unsolicited *Ninth Bridgewater Treatise*, which argued that a system operated entirely by mathematical laws could result in the appearance of unexpected novelties. Babbage's suggestion that divine intervention could thus be replaced by the operation of natural laws was explicitly taken up in the evolutionary work *Vestiges of the Natural History of Creation*, published anonymously in 1844 (the author was later revealed to have been the Edinburgh journalist and publisher Robert Chambers), and, more tacitly, in Darwin's *Origin of Species* (1859).

images of God with which natural theologians had been concerned.

The Twentieth Century

Twentieth-century developments add weight to the view that Darwin's writings, while requiring theologians to rethink natural theology, did not compel them to abandon it. One of the institutions through which natural theological endeavors were continued was the Gifford lectures. These lectures, set up to promote the study of natural theology, were instituted by the will of Adam Gifford, who died in 1887. Delivered in the Scottish universities of Edinburgh, Glasgow, St Andrews, and Aberdeen, by a range of distinguished philosophers, scientists, historians, and theologians since 1888, the Gifford lectures have resulted in a lively and ongoing series of natural theological reflections, conceived in the broadest sense. Gifford lecturers have included William James, Nils Bohr, Charles Raven, and Paul Tillich; and, more recently, the physicist and Anglican minister John Polkinghorne, historians of science John Hedley Brooke and Geoffrey Cantor, and the American theologian Stanley Hauerwas.

Discussions of natural theology have, ever since the mid-1930s, been carried out under the shadow of the figure of Karl Barth (1886–1968). In reaction to a 1934 treatise on *Nature and Grace* by Emil Brunner, Barth wrote a response titled simply *No!* In this and other works, Barth (and many others in twentieth-century academic theology who shared his dissatisfaction with nineteenth-century theological accommodations with scientific rationalism) emphasized the centrality of revelation and a religious relation to Christ. For the Barthian, rational argumentation undertaken on secular foundations could never produce distinctively Christian knowledge, and to suppose that it might was a theological mistake (regardless of whether it was also a philosophical and scientific one). Interestingly, both Barth and Brunner were subsequently Gifford lecturers; Stanley Hauerwas, in his recent Gifford lectures, argues in favor of a form of natural theology reconceived along Barthian lines.

Given the Humean, Darwinian, and Barthian objections to any form of natural theology grounded in the sciences, attempts to revive it in the later twentieth century certainly seemed to be doing so in the face of formidable opposition. Nonetheless, such attempts have been made. In the area of "science and religion," authors such as Ian Barbour, Arthur Peacocke, John Polkinghorne, Bob Russell, and Nancey Murphy have argued that divine purposes can still be discerned in the findings of modern science. There has been particular interest in the question of whether the "fine-tuning" of the fundamental physical constants of our universe might indicate that it was made by a deity with an interest in creating intelligent life. Another area of lively revived natural theological speculations has been quantum physics.

In the United States, the twentieth century saw the invention of another new variety of natural theology, namely "creation science" or "scientific creationism," whose advocates continue to resist mainstream neo-Darwinian orthodoxy and to call for "balanced treatment" of Darwinian science and "creation science" in the classroom. In this American controversy, not only the relationship between church and state but also the ancient question of the relationship between the book of nature and the book of scripture continues to be contested. Each group has its own view about this relationship. For creationists, revealed theology (specifically a literalist interpretation of the book of Genesis) and natural theology (specifically an antievolutionary interpretation of scientific evidence) concur in teaching that God created separate forms and that humans do not have a common ancestry with other animals. For other Christians, revelation and nature can be brought into harmony by reading Genesis less literally and accepting mainstream science. For others again—those who take a view like Thomas Paine's—churches and supposed revelations are all nothing more than human creations: the only real source of transcendent knowledge is the study of the natural world, and the most fruitful means of studying it are science and philosophy. It thus continues to hold true that debates about natural theology are closely connected with debates about the relationship between church and state, especially in the area of education.

See also **Creationism; Evolution; Mechanical Philosophy; Natural History; Nature; Religion and Science.**

BIBLIOGRAPHY

PRIMARY SOURCES

Aquinas, Thomas. *Summa Theologiae.* Translated by the Dominican Fathers. London: Blackfriars, 1964–1981.

Brunner, Emil, and Karl Barth. *Natural Theology.* Translated from the German by Peter Fraenkel, with an introduction by John

Baillie. London: Geoffrey Bles, 1946. Reprint, Eugene, Ore.: Wipf and Stock, 2002. Comprising *Nature and Grace* by Emil Brunner and the reply *No!* by Karl Barth.

Hume, David. *Dialogues Concerning Natural Religion.* Edited by J. C. A. Gaskin. Oxford: Oxford World's Classics, 1998. First published 1779.

Paley, William. *Natural Theology; or, Evidences of the Existence and Atributes of the Deity, Collected from the Appearances of Nature.* 1802. Reprint, Oxford: Oxford University Press World Classics Series, 2005.

SECONDARY SOURCES

Addinall, Peter. *Philosophy and Biblical Interpretation: A Study in Nineteenth-Century Conflict.* Cambridge, U.K., and New York: Cambridge University Press, 1991.

Barr, James. *Biblical Faith and Natural Theology.* Oxford: Clarendon, 1993.

Behe, Michael. *Darwin's Black Box: The Biochemical Challenge to Evolution.* New York and London: Free Press, 1996.

Brooke, John Hedley. "Darwin and Victorian Christianity." In *The Cambridge Companion to Darwin,* edited by Jonathan Hodge and Gregory Radick. Cambridge, U.K., and New York: Cambridge University Press, 2003.

———. *Science and Religion: Some Historical Perspectives.* Cambridge, U.K.: Cambridge University Press, 1991.

Brooke, John Hedley, and Geoffrey Cantor. *Reconstructing Nature: The Engagement of Science and Religion.* Edinburgh: T. and T. Clark, 1998. See especially section 3.

Buckley, Michael. *At the Origins of Modern Atheism.* New Haven, Conn.: Yale University Press, 1987.

Dawkins, Richard. *The Blind Watchmaker.* London: Penguin, 1988.

Dembski, William. *Intelligent Design: The Bridge between Science and Theology.* Downers Grove, Ill.: Intervarsity Press, 1999.

Desmond, Adrian, and James Moore. *Darwin.* London: Penguin, 1992.

Hauerwas, Stanley. *With the Grain of the Universe: The Church's Witness and Natural Theology.* Grand Rapids, Mich.: Brazos Press, 2001.

Jaki, Stanley L. *Lord Gifford and His Lectures: A Centenary Retrospect.* 2nd ed. Edinburgh: Scottish Academic Press, 1995.

Merton, Robert K. "Puritanism, Pietism, and Science." In *Science and Religious Belief: A Selection of Recent Historical Studies,* edited by C. A. Russell. London: University of London Press, 1973.

Numbers, Ronald L. *The Creationists.* New York: Knopf, 1992.

Nuovo, Victor. "William Paley." In *The Dictionary of Eighteenth-Century British Philosophers,* edited by John Yolton, John Valdimir, and John Stephens. Bristol, U.K., and Sterling, Va.: Thoemmes Press, 1999.

Olding, Alan. *Modern Biology and Natural Theology.* London: Routledge, 1990.

Ospovat, Dov. *The Development of Darwin's Theory: Natural History, Natural Theology, and Natural Selection, 1838–1850.* Cambridge, U.K., and New York: Cambridge University Press, 1981.

Polkinghorne, John. *Science and Christian Belief.* London: SPCK, 1994. Published in the United States as *The Faith of a Physicist: Reflections of a Bottom-up Thinker.* Princeton, N.J.: Princeton University Press, 1994.

Richards, Robert. *Darwin and the Emergence of Evolutionary Theories of Mind and Behavior.* Chicago: University of Chicago Press, 1987.

Ruse, Michael. *Darwin and Design: Does Evolution Have a Purpose?* Cambridge, Mass.: Harvard University Press, 2003.

Topham, Jonathan. "Beyond the 'Common Context': The Production and Reading of the *Bridgewater Treatises.*" *Isis* 89 (1998): 233–262.

Thomas Dixon

NATURE. No interpretation of the idea of nature is good for all people in all places at all times. The interpretive position here reflects pivotal conceptual developments of the nineteenth and twentieth centuries.

Charles Darwin's century brought home forcefully the reality of time, of evolutionary process that ultimately transforms all things. Darwin's contemporary T. H. Huxley believed that evolution forced the question of our place in nature upon us. Twentieth-century science posed a further interpretive challenge. We have reached the end of credible claims to certainty concerning nature. Given uncertainty, open-ended inquiry becomes the hallmark of rationality, and the idea of nature remains inevitably in flux. A third interpretive factor emerges at the intersection of the twentieth and twenty-first centuries. The present cultural trajectory is on a collision course with the evolved biophysical scheme. The interpretive challenge is to account for the predicament of a naturally evolved species whose cultural evolution has led to maladaptive ideas of nature that must be transformed in order to avert biophysical catastrophe.

Nature before Literacy

Arguably, the nineteenth-century discovery of the Paleolithic, the period of human development stretching from about two million to about ten thousand years ago, is exceeded in significance only by the discovery of biological evolution. Ensconced within cultural cocoons of literacy and technology, we believe that paleo-people were stupid savages since they were not literate and possessed only rudimentary technology. There are two rejoinders to such notions. First, the paleo-strata unequivocally confirm that the historical epoch of literacy is a mere moment in a human past stretching across several hundred thousand years. And second, the assumption that we monopolize intelligence and genius is untenable. Our paleo-ancestors were capable of imaginings that rival those of the greatest minds of history.

Nevertheless, any reconstruction of Paleolithic ideas of nature remains conjectural. Interpretation depends on reading "texts" that, rather than being alphabetic, are material artifacts—stone points and knives, cave paintings and megalithic constructions, and tens of thousands of other artifacts. Additional evidence comes from paleo-notions of nature that resonate in surviving aboriginal cultures. Collectively these materials support three conjectures. First, Paleolithic hunter-gatherers realized that there was an order to the world that they inhabited. While the pattern varied seasonally, there was regularity in the movement of animals, in the growth of plants, in the presence or absence of water. Second, paleo-people

believed the inherent order of nature was cyclical, since the world moved in repeating cycles. Third, paleo-people believed their role was to harmonize with rather than change the circumstances of existence.

These conjectures can be challenged across multiple fronts. For example, there is evidence of climatic upheavals that through natural selection eliminated all but the most behaviorally adaptable hominid bands. How, then, could paleo-people believe in a cyclical nature? And yet evidence from the Neolithic strata suggests that the myth of the eternal return and the belief in the Magna Mater (the Great Mother) were foreshadowed during the Paleolithic.

Nature in Antiquity

Antiquity is defined here as a zone of cultural transition at the boundary between the Old and the New Stone Age, the Paleolithic and the Neolithic. Climate change is increasingly accepted as the environmental driver that ended the era of the great hunt. Whereas utility vanished at the margin of portability for paleo-people, the Neolithic brought profound changes to material culture and thus to notions of nature. Sedentarism, the cultivation of cereal grasses, and the domestication of animals transformed human relations to nature. Forests were cleared for fields and building materials. Crops were planted and tended. Rivers were diverted into canals to support irrigated agriculture. Permanent habitation was constructed. Wild creatures, such as bears and wolves, formerly totems with which humans empathically identified, became predators.

Materials for the conceptual reconstruction of ancient ideas of nature can be found in texts marking the passage from orality into alphabetic literacy, such as the Sumerian-epoch *Gilgamesh* and the Old Testament, the latter a primary source for prevailing if conflicting Western notions of nature. The Old Testament manifests two antagonistic ideas of nature. One reflects agriculture, where humankind increasingly asserts its dominion over the earth while paying the price of great toil. The other is that of a world of milk and honey where humans wandered the earth freely, living in an Edenic condition. On either account a creator god is posited as the agency of creation. A cosmos is constructed and populated, culminating on the sixth day with the arrival of Adam and Eve. Life is good, until the original pair fall into temptation and sin. The consequence was expulsion from the Garden, arguably a remembrance of a deep past free of the woes of agricultural existence.

Pre-Socratic Ideas of Nature

Alphabetic literacy changed the way that humans thought of nature. It is the pre-Socratics, the Greeks, and to a lesser extent the Egyptians and Romans, who in their theorizing of nature appear as our kindred spirits, even if we believe their theories are mistaken, in their commitment to rational explanation. A clear line separates pre-alphabetic from post-alphabetic accounts of nature; the mythical accounts of antiquity become topics of derision. Nature increasingly becomes a conceptual entity known only through rational inquiry.

The pre-Socratic philosophers Heraclitus and Parmenides laid down two basic channels in which contemporary ideas still flow. According to Heraclitus (c. 540–c. 480 B.C.E.), reality is a moving river into which humans cannot step twice. And yet, since total chaos would defeat knowability, he posits the strife of opposites as a limit on chaos. Hot becomes cold, wet becomes dry, winter gives way to summer. The wise person behaves according to these basic insights into evanescence and its limits. Heraclitus's notions resonate with contemporary evolutionary thinkers, systems ecologists, and chaos theorists. Chaos theorists celebrate Heraclitus as the conceptual source of a second scientific revolution in the twentieth century. We can also recognize Paleolithic resonances in Heraclitus, including his notion of nature as a cyclical process with which humans should exist in harmony.

Heraclitus's conceptual antagonist was Parmenides (born c. 515 B.C.E.), who argued that reality does not move since "all is one." The apparent motion of nature was for him just that: appearance and not reality. His immediate followers, such as Zeno, devised the famous paradoxes of motion, such as the tortoise and the hare, that conceptually defeated all challenges until the twentieth century. If the tortoise, however slow, starts ahead of the hare, however fast, and if in any given unit of time the hare closes one-half of the distance to the tortoise, the hare can never pass the tortoise because there will always remain an unclosed interval between them. The appearance, then, that the hare catches and passes the tortoise is a deception—"the way of seeming," as Parmenides termed it, and not the "way of truth." The conceptual truths of nature deny perceptual appearances.

The best-known successors to Parmenides are the atomists, Leucippus and Democritus. Perhaps the first truly modern theorists, they corrected Parmenidean conceptual excess. The variety and phenomena of nature were constituted by the arrangement of many "ones"—that is, the atoms themselves. The perceptions of a changing world could now be admitted without undercutting nature's conceptual knowability. Atomic theory today traces its roots to Leucippus and Democritus.

Nature in Greek Rationalism

All these thinkers pale in comparison with Aristotle (384–322 B.C.E.), the greatest classical theorist. Aristotelian ideas of nature dominated Western civilization until the scientific revolution of the seventeenth and eighteenth centuries. So pervasive is his influence that some believe Western intellectual history is little more than footnotes to his work. Only a partial description showing Aristotle's continuing influence can be included here.

First, Aristotle introduced the category of cause as a key explanatory feature for theorizing nature. He understood the diverse phenomena and different kinds in nature in terms of four causes: the formal, material, efficient, and final. Aristotle's account of causation surpasses the theories of his predecessors. For example, his notion of material cause chimes with the atomism of Leucippus and Democritus, and yet the atoms themselves are neither a final cause, since they have been set into original motion, nor an efficient cause, since they can be rearranged by other factors, including human agency.

Second, Aristotle argued that all motion is a consequence of an original, unmoved mover. Without the unmoved mover

any causal sequence would entail an infinite regress. Aristotle's notion of an unmoved mover, while driven by his logical commitment to avoiding motion that cannot be explained, resonates not only with earlier Hebraic conceptions of a creator god but also with Parmenidean commitments to a final rational explanation for all that is, was, or ever will be. It also resonates with the Heraclitean stream of influence: natural processes and creatures move.

Third, Aristotle offered a theoretical account of living nature manifesting a sensitivity to the explanatory and descriptive requirements of the behavior of plants and animals. These motions could not be explained in the same way as those of inanimate objects. While not an evolutionary thinker in modern terms, he recognized the diversity of natural kinds with their characteristic patterns of reproduction and growth.

The theoretical legacy of the Greeks is highly significant. While it is an exaggeration to say that the period between the fall of Rome and the Middle Ages was a conceptual wasteland, and while descriptive accounts of nature flourished (in astronomy, for example), there were few developments beyond Aristotelian ideas. The Middle Ages brought some conceptual refinements, but no paradigmatic breakthroughs. For example, William of Ockham (c. 1285–1349?) deduced that a simpler explanation was to be preferred to a more complicated explanation when the explanatory power was equal—a logical principle of parsimony known as Ockham's razor. But it is the theorizing of classical Greek civilization that lives on, even if implicitly.

Nature during the Scientific Revolution

Facilitated in part by advances in instrumentation, such as the telescope and microscope, the scientific revolution brought paradigmatic change to the idea of nature. When Galileo Galilei (1564–1642) observed moons orbiting Jupiter on a predictable schedule, the consequences were enormous. Earth could no longer be conceived as the center of the cosmos, as the focal point of a godly creation. Bacteria were first observed by the Dutch naturalist Anton van Leeuwenhoek (1632–1723) in 1683 (although the science of bacteriology had not yet arrived). As with Galileo, so with Leeuwenhoek: the apparent reality of nature visible to the naked eye was not what it seemed.

Changes in instrumentation were accompanied by changes in the powers of mathematical analysis. Working independently, Gottfried Wilhelm von Leibniz (1646–1716) and Sir Isaac Newton (1642–1727) developed what is now called the calculus. The move into conceptual abstraction that began with the Greeks was radically transformed by such mathematics. The scientific idea of nature was more and more represented in terms of equations and laws, devoid of so-called secondary qualities such as color and sound. There was an increasing commitment to Parmenidean tendencies—that is, the reduction of nature to permanence through mathematically described mechanical relations. The hallmark of rationality thus continued in the tradition of Parmenidean One—nature as an unchanging and therefore totally knowable singularity—while admitting to diverse mathematical characterization of natural phenomena.

The scientific revolution is often thought of as culminating in the work of Newton and the view of nature according to what is now termed "classical physics." But Newton is best understood as both an original thinker and a synthesizer. The work of three other thinkers is indicative of his precursors.

The first of these thinkers was Francis Bacon (1561–1626), aptly characterized as the man who saw through time because he straddled the medieval and modern ages. A practicing scientist, his scientific discoveries are less significant than his radical new ideas concerning nature itself. Science, he realized, was power—power over the natural world. And that power could lead human beings to a second world fashioned according to their wants and desires. Much of the utopian character of our own time, the belief that through the advance of theoretical knowledge and its technological application all problems might be solved, was first articulated by Bacon. His arguments effectively became a legitimating rationale for societal support of the natural sciences. While our rationales are primarily economic, his were ethical. He addressed the ancient problem of the fall into sin, which effectively sundered godly relations between humankind and nature. Toil and suffering, the ruined earth, affliction with drought and storm, insects and disease, were the consequences of the Fall. On the Baconian view a New Jerusalem could be had through the power of science to set nature right again, returning humans to an Edenic condition. Contemporary studies, including those based in critical, feminist theory, argue that the Baconian view of nature reflected an intensely hierarchical and patriarchal society. "Man" (meaning, the male members of the human species) would wrest scientific knowledge from an unwilling and unruly natural world, and through such knowledge gain power over "her."

The second was Galileo, an Italian physicist and astronomer famous for his encounters with the Inquisition, whose work in physics fundamentally undercut Aristotelian physics. Building on the theoretical work of Nicolaus Copernicus (1473–1543), who overturned geocentrism, Johannes Kepler (1571–1630), who first theorized the laws of planetary motion and the sun's influence on planetary orbits, and Tycho Brahe (1546–1601), who had achieved unparalleled accuracy in measuring the motions of the heavens, Galileo brought a new mathematical precision to the description of planetary motion (ironically, believing wrongly that the motion was circular rather than elliptical) and to falling material objects. Through his many experiments and observations, Galileo realized that there was but one kind of motion in nature, whether celestial or terrestrial, not two as the Greeks had believed.

Third, the work of the Frenchman René Descartes (1596–1650) had a profoundly important influence on physics. Descartes invented analytical geometry, a technique that allowed the precise description of the trajectories of material bodies in motion—later refined by Newton. His further work on methodology (the method of analysis) was likewise crucial. He argued that the way to understand complex physical phenomena was to reduce them to simpler components until reaching the level of irreducibility. Finally, Descartes argued that the new science of physics, built on mathematical description and prediction, would make humankind the master and possessor of nature.

Isaac Newton's Nature

While the advances made by Galileo, Bacon, and Descartes were considerable, history's judgment is that Newton revolutionized Western thinking, dominating his age much as Aristotle did that of the Greeks. Many of his notions, such as the absolute nature of space and time, were repudiated in the twentieth century. And yet Newtonian ways of thinking rule today's culture, lying at the heart of our notion of human dignity as control over nature. We have institutionalized notions that nature is little more than atoms in mechanical and therefore predictable motion. So construed, nature becomes nothing but raw material awaiting technological conversion into goods of economic value.

Newton himself was not concerned with such derivations from his ideas, but with nature as matter in motion, especially the movements of the heavenly and terrestrial bodies. His invention of the reflecting telescope, the calculus (which he called his "fluxional method"), and the laws of motion coalesced in an ability to describe physical systems mathematically and thus to make accurate predictions. For Newton material atoms were the fundamental characteristic of nature, bound together by the force of gravity. Newton theorized the law of planetary attraction, which he argued varied inversely to the square of the distance from the sun. However, Edmond Halley (1656–1742) did more to popularize the Newtonian idea of nature than Newton himself. Using a Newtonian reflector and Newtonian physics, Halley calculated the orbit of what is now called Halley's Comet, accurately predicting its appearance in the night sky in the year 1758.

Classical science, as Newton's science is now called, and the scientific picture of the world and humankind's relation to it, became the way that Western civilization understood nature. But several problems with the classical view soon appeared. For one, nowhere in the cognizable world picture did human beings appear—as if nature was devoid of human presence. Further, the Newtonian notion of nature facilitated naive realism, the notion that nature was known without interpretation, as if Newton had given us a "God's eye" view of nature as the way it was and forever would be. These conundrums continued throughout the twentieth century and remain with us today.

Nature in Darwin's Century

Classical science assumed that objectivity depended upon the separation of the knowing observer from the world of nature. Charles Darwin's (1809–1882) theory of evolution upset that assumed separation forever, reinserting humankind into a cognizable view of nature. Darwin's penetrating insights into the nature of our own humanity—and the importance of language—are effectively a Copernican revolution in our self-understanding of the idea of nature itself. Humankind can no longer be thought of as separate from the cognizable world picture. The status of humankind as something apart from, rather than a part of, nature becomes, after Darwin, increasingly incomprehensible (consider, for example, Werner Heisenberg [1901–1976], who makes clear that not only are humans embedded within biophysical systems but that our observations themselves profoundly color what can be known).

As with Newton, so with Darwin's precursors, who framed the stage upon which he stood. First, the work of scientists in disparate disciplines, such as geology and paleontology, combined with Darwin's work in natural history, led to what can be termed the discovery of time in four crucial dimensions, beginning with geological time. Irish Archbishop James Ussher (1581–1656) had calculated the age of the Earth, based on biblical interpretation, as no more than 6,000 years. Charles Lyell (1797–1875) heralded the arrival of a scientifically informed grasp of the enormity of geological time. Lyell's theory of very slow but uniform change in the Earth upset the dominant theory of catastrophism—the notion of a ruined Earth as God's punishment for sin. Geological inquiry expanded the notion of time over almost unimaginably large temporal scales: Ussher's estimate was off by nearly six magnitudes.

Second, paleontology disclosed through the discovery of successive layers of the fossil record a continual transformation of the forms of life. The natural world could no longer be rationally understood as frozen into eternal forms, but only as a ceaseless flux. The work of Georges Cuvier (1769–1832) drew in part from the geological law of superposition. Fossilized life forms found in lower strata were necessarily older than those lying above. Cuvier also observed that the various strata themselves had characteristic life forms, suggesting a coming and going of great epochs of life.

Third, Darwin's own studies made clear that the process of natural selection had not only shaped but continued to shape the flora and fauna. His five-year voyage on the HMS Beagle provided the data that were soon interpreted as evidence for natural selection over biological time. The adaptive radiation manifest in his famous finches, whose beaks illustrated the evolutionary diversification of forms through adaptation, became an exemplary case study. While Darwin lacked any knowledge of the genetic basis for inheritance of advantageous characteristics, discovered by Gregor Mendel (1822–1882), he clearly understood that natural selection was governed by the principle of survival of the fittest—an idea that the economist Thomas Malthus (1766–1834) had developed in relation to human populations.

Finally, near the end of the century, archeologists discovered the Paleolithic strata, a clear record of cultural transformation as successive generations of humans adapted their lives to the natural world. However dimly, these discoveries coalesced in a dawning awareness that humankind is a naturally evolved species that has moved into culture—a symbolically mediated space from where nature is increasingly and continuously theorized. The ongoing inquiries of prehistoric archeology and paleoanthropology have fundamentally changed both the ways we think of ourselves and our ideas of nature.

Nature in the Twentieth Century

Reflecting the dominant notion of nature as nothing more than atoms–in motion subject to mechanical laws, an unparalleled fusion of science, technology, and market capitalism colored the twentieth century. During the eighteenth century the Newtonian worldview was translated into an economic theory of marketplace capitalism by Adam Smith (1723–1790). Market societies of the twentieth century believed they possessed the power to bend nature to any and all human purposes. The rational exploitation of nature for human benefit was publicly and privately institutionalized. Wild rivers were tamed, deserts made to bloom, old-growth forests harvested. The apparent mastery of the atom heralded an era of nuclear energy in which power would be too cheap to meter. Modern chemistry promised better living. The "green revolution" offered agricultural plenty to the hungry masses. There would be no Malthusian limits to the growth of human population nor to its steady economic advance. Mirroring the dreams of Bacon's New Jerusalem, cultural progress seemed to be virtually a law of nature.

But perhaps the greatest changes were in the life sciences, especially biology and ecology. Both were profoundly affected by the molecular revolution and the Cartesian belief that complexity must be reduced to analytical simplicity. James D. Watson's and Francis Crick's discovery of the double helix as the structure of DNA in 1953 promised mastery over life itself. Molecular biology, supported by advances in scientific instrumentation, combined with market capitalism to offer the promise of organisms better than those produced by nature. Genetically modified organisms (GMOs) became the rage in the late twentieth century. Biotechnology reinvigorated the Baconian dream of a second world. And yet, as the twentieth century wound down, scientific and other critics raised fundamental questions about the sustainability of a cultural trajectory built around the ideas of the scientific revolution. Classical physics, while theoretically useful, was neither the one, true view of nature nor the final word.

Twentieth-Century Ideas

There is no definitive twentieth-century idea of nature. The turn of the century marked the beginning of a virtual revolution in the work that collectively constitutes the new physics. Albert Einstein's (1879–1955) theory of special relativity challenged the Newtonian notion of absolute space and time. And yet Einstein's theories did not support conceptual relativism. He was a Parmenidean in modern guise. God, in his account, did not play dice with the universe. Einstein dedicated the last half of his life to discovery of what came to be known as God's equation—a mathematical expression of the fundamental reality that explains all that there is, was, or will be.

The middle of the twentieth century might be represented through the work of Werner Heisenberg (1901–1976). If Einstein is a Parmenidean, then Heisenberg's principle of indeterminacy and quantum theory manifest a Heraclitean vision. In his account, the very activity of the observation of nature made a profound difference in what was observed. Physical sciences could achieve relative precision in one measurement only by sacrificing certainty in another. Heisenberg's insights into the atom were equally brilliant. The particles within atoms did not, Heisenberg demonstrated, behave according to Newtonian mechanics. While the picture of nature offered by classical physics remains useful in certain domains—for example, calculating the trajectories of flying objects or predicting the motions of planets and stars—the Newtonian view has lost intellectual hegemony.

The latter decades of the twentieth century can be represented by work of another Nobel laureate, Ilya Prigogine (1917–2003). Prigogine and many others constitute a rapidly growing epistemic community studying the phenomena of nature that are in disequilibrium—including life itself. After embracing chaos theory, the possibility of definitive description disappears, as does the notion that complex phenomena can be disassembled into constituent parts and then reassembled. Biological and ecological scientists in particular have challenged reductionistic mechanism. The principle of superposition, which underlies the description and explanation of linear phenomena, has been repudiated by the life sciences, where nonlinearity rules.

The implications of such accounts for our idea of nature, as well as the conceptualization of our place in nature, are enormous. The belief that humankind has sure and certain knowledge of nature is untenable. While remaining useful assumptions at some scales of inquiry, atomism, reductionism, and mechanism are not absolutes. Laplacian determinism, the notion that, given sufficient knowledge of nature, sure and certain prediction of the future is possible, has been discredited. Radically new perspectives on the nature of nature and the cosmos itself have started to emerge. Time itself has clearly been recognized as a fourth and absolutely essential dimension of any comprehensive idea of nature.

The notion that humankind has dominion over the evolved world has also been discredited. Our knowledge of nature is limited, more contingency and probability than necessity and certainty. Increasingly the lack of equilibrium in the natural world gives evidence that our present interactions with it are unsustainable over biologically and ecologically meaningful scales of time. Political and economic temporal scales are known to be discordant with nature's temporal horizons. The fragility of humankind's dominion is clearly manifest in multiple dysfunctional relations between cultural and natural systems. Despite the received idea of nature, nature profoundly acts on culture. The idea of nature as a passive material world over which humankind has dominion has failed, gravely intensifying the question of humankind's place in nature. Conceptual developments in areas such as cosmology also lead to a chastened view of our place in nature. The visible material cosmos is a very small portion of reality. Dark matter, as it turns out, while unseen, is as consequential in understanding the cosmos as visible matter.

As the twentieth century ended, the notion of a discord between the culturally dominant idea of nature and nature itself gained credence. The cultural system, which had given birth to and nurtured the idea of nature as passive matter in motion, subject to reductionistic explanation and technological control, began to experience pervasive environmental dysfunctions. The anthropogenic depletion of stratospheric ozone, collapse of oceanic fisheries, deforestation of Amazonia, disruption of global weather patterns, and extinction of biodiversity posed ominous warnings as well as major conceptual challenges that can only be met by articulating alternative ideas of nature and humankind's place therein.

Nature in the Third Millennium

Clearly, the idea of nature is semantically and conceptually conflicted. If we think of nature as meaningful across multiple temporal and spatial scales, from the cosmic to the subatomic, then we can also understand that our dysfunctional relations are due in part to our lack of either the ability or the commitment to integrate knowledge of nature across scales. Contemporary thinkers argue that the hold of ancient dreams, especially the return to the Garden, must be put behind. And the failed idea of nature inherited from classical science must be replaced by alternative ways of conceptualizing nature and our place therein.

Some of these emerging ideas were first broached in the late nineteenth and early twentieth centuries by alternative voices such Henry David Thoreau and Aldo Leopold, and then more vigorously in the latter part of the twentieth century by Ilya Prigogine and Edward O. Wilson. Thoreau argued that the best humankind could hope for was a sympathy with the intelligence of nature rather than sure and certain knowledge. Leopold, observing the destruction of nature at an unprecedented scale, argued that humans should think of themselves as citizens of the land community rather than as the conquerors of nature. Near the end of the century Prigogine argued that humankind must, for the first time in its history, engage the evolved complexity of the natural world in dialogue, as a conversational partner. And Wilson made clear that humankind's actions over the first few decades of the new millennium would have profound consequences for the future of life.

As a linguistically reflexive, naturally evolved yet culturally self-conscious species, we might yet find our way into more tenable and less destructive notions of nature. But the challenge is enormous. How might we break free of the notion that we are the dominators of a brute, blind, material world of nature into an idea that leads us to restore some sense of ourselves as natural creatures, living in harmony with nature, while also retaining our distinctive cultural identity? There is no ready answer. Perhaps we will come to know the idea of nature more fully when we have come more fully to realize the enormity of time and our own historicity. There are reasons to think, as we enter the twenty-first century, that humankind might come to embrace an idea of nature that includes ourselves as cognizing subjects within it while not reducing ourselves to it.

See also **Aristotelianism; Biology; Development; Ecology; Evolution; Life; Life Cycle; Natural History; Naturphilosophie; Newtonianism; Organicism; Physics; Science, History of; Scientific Revolution; State of Nature.**

BIBLIOGRAPHY

Aczel, Amir D. *God's Equation: Einstein, Relativity, and the Expanding Universe.* New York: Four Walls Eight Windows, 1999.

Bernstein, Richard J. *Beyond Objectivism and Relativism: Science, Hermeneutics, and Praxis.* Philadelphia: University of Pennsylvania Press, 1983.

Cohen, I. Bernard. *Revolution in Science.* Cambridge, Mass.: Harvard University Press, 1985.

Collingwood, R. G. *The Idea of Nature.* Oxford: Clarendon, 1939.

Darwin, Charles. *The Descent of Man, and Selection in Relation to Sex.* London: John Murray, 1871.

Einstein, Albert. *Ideas and Opinions.* Translated by Sonja Bargmann. Rev. ed. New York: Modern Library, 1994.

Evernden, Neil. *The Social Creation of Nature.* Baltimore: Johns Hopkins University Press, 1992.

Firor, John. *The Changing Atmosphere: A Global Challenge.* New Haven, Conn.: Yale University Press, 1990.

Glacken, Clarence J. *Traces on the Rhodian Shore: Nature and Culture in Western Thought from Ancient Times to the End of the Eighteenth Century.* Berkeley: University of California Press, 1967.

Kirk, G. S., J. E. Raven, and M. Schofield. *The Presocratic Philosophers: A Critical History with a Selection of Texts.* 2nd ed. Cambridge, U.K.: Cambridge University Press, 1983.

Kuhn, Thomas S. *The Structure of Scientific Revolutions.* 2nd ed. Chicago: University of Chicago, 1996.

Lederman, Leon M. *The God Particle: If the Universe is the Answer, What is the Question?* New York: Dell, 1993.

Leopold, Aldo. *A Sand County Almanac: With Essays on Conservation from Round River.* San Francisco: Sierra Club Books, 1970.

Levin, Simon A. *Fragile Dominion: Complexity and the Commons.* Reading, Mass.: Perseus, 1999.

Mayr, Ernst. *The Growth of Biological Thought: Diversity, Evolution, and Inheritance.* Cambridge, Mass.: Harvard University Press, 1982.

Merchant, Carolyn. *The Death of Nature: Women, Ecology, and the Scientific Revolution.* New York: Harper and Row, 1980.

———. *Earthcare: Women and the Environment.* New York: Routledge, 1990.

Oelschlaeger, Max. *The Idea of Wilderness: From Prehistory to the Age of Ecology.* New Haven, Conn., and London: Yale University Press, 1991.

Prigogine, Ilya. *From Being to Becoming: Time and Complexity in the Physical Sciences.* San Francisco: W. H. Freeman, 1980.

Prigogine, Ilya, and Isabelle Stengers. *Order Out of Chaos: Man's New Dialogue with Nature.* New York: Bantam, 1984.

Rees, Martin J. *Our Final Hour: A Scientist's Warning: How Terror, Error, and Environmental Disaster Threaten Humankind's Future in This Century—On Earth and Beyond.* New York: Basic Books, 2003.

Williams, Raymond. *Keywords: A Vocabulary of Culture and Society.* Rev. ed. New York: Oxford University Press, 1983.

Wilson, Edward O. *The Diversity of Life.* Cambridge, Mass.: Harvard University Press, 1992.

———. *The Future of Life.* New York: Knopf, 2002.

Max Oelschlaeger

NATURPHILOSOPHIE. *Naturphilosophie* refers both to the specific philosophical program Friedrich Wilhelm Joseph von Schelling (1775–1854) initiated with his *Ideen zu einer Philosophie der Natur* (1797; Ideas for a philosophy of nature) and to the movement during the German Romantic period that Schelling's work is said to have spawned. The context of both is the achievement of Immanuel Kant (1724–1804), whose philosophical system formed the background against which many of the themes of Romantic thought emerged. In this case, dissatisfaction with Kant's treatment of nature, in which there could be cognition only of the appearances of nature but not of nature-in-itself, provided the occasion for several individuals to attempt to complete what they thought Kant had only begun.

Schelling was by no means the first thinker who departed from Kant's understanding of the natural philosopher's role as a lawgiver to nature. Others from the 1790s who independently of Schelling addressed for various reasons what they saw as the inadequacy of Kant's system where nature was concerned included Franz Xaver von Baader (1765–1841); Carl Friedrich Kielmeyer (1765–1844); Karl August Eschenmayer (1768–1852); and in his dissertation of 1799, Hans Christian Ørsted (1777–1851).

The Work of Schelling

But it was Schelling who set out to locate the knowledge of nature within a larger system of philosophy. He came to this task as a participant in the general philosophical examination of Kant's system that was underway in the 1790s. In addition to those largely sympathetic to Kant, there were others, especially Johann Fichte (1762–1814), who questioned Kant's reliance on the existence of things-in-themselves. Since we cannot have knowledge of things-in-themselves, how could Kant insist that they were the source of the sense data that reason utilized to create knowledge of the world? Schelling's initial sympathy for this critique made it appear that he agreed with Fichte's claim that even the manifold of sense had been produced by us out of our own creative faculty. But in spite of his agreement with Fichte that the possibility of our knowledge of nature did not depend on the existence of Kant's things-in-themselves, it was Schelling's ultimate disagreement with Fichte's reliance on the absolute ego that led to his wish to construct a system of philosophy in which nature retained its own integrity.

At first, in the *Ideen,* Schelling insists merely that our belief in a reality outside ourselves grew up at the same time that our belief in our own existence appeared, that one was as necessary as the other. But this first book is best seen as a preliminary attempt, a beginning to the new enterprise. In it Schelling does not yet himself realize the basic foundation of his later *Naturphilosophie.* The *Ideen* contains, like Baader's work before it, an attack on atomism as an outlook sufficient to capture the depth of nature's reality. In place of atomism Schelling proposed a dynamic conception of underlying polar forces he believed were more up to the task. With these he felt that he could show how what we experience of nature derives from the same source that gives rise to our belief in a nature outside ourselves.

So far he has not gotten outside the mind, since he is here speaking about instances of our belief. But with the rapid appearance of a series of works between 1798 and 1801, in which the work of Benedict de Spinoza (1632–1677) was influential, he would make clean the break from Fichte and insist that the realm of the real has equal status to that of the ideal. It was these works that inspired many to abandon the viewpoint of Kant in favor of what they saw as the more realistic understanding that Schelling's approach provided.

It was likely while he was writing the *Ideen* that Schelling came to the realization that the realm of the organic, which had been dealt with only cursorily in his first work, altered fundamentally the direction in which he had been going. In the next book, *Von der Weltseele* (1798; On the world soul), the new emphasis became clear in the subtitle: *An Hypothesis of Higher Physics to Explain General Organism.* By recognizing that the metaphor for reality was not mechanism but organism, Schelling found a means by which he could overcome Kant's fracturing of human experience into two separate realms. If nature was an organism, then knowledge of organism would include knowledge of nature as a living whole. And that whole would include the life of the mind and soul as well as that of the body. There would not be, as Kant taught, two separate realms, only one of which was accessible to knowledge. For Schelling there was only one realm.

This perspective resonated with many in the early years of the nineteenth century. As a prolific author in Jena, Schelling had become an important member of the famous Romantic circle that had assembled there. He also got to know Johann Wolfgang von Goethe (1749–1832), who spent many hours together with Schelling reading the latter's work. Because of his youth—he was twenty-three when he received the call to Jena—Schelling established a reputation as a successful young genius.

Supporters and Detractors

Physicians were especially drawn to Schelling's focus on nature as an organic whole. Many of them found his emphasis on the organic especially appealing because they felt that healing was impossible without seeing the body in intimate connection to the soul that inhabited it. Of forty readily identifiable sympathizers of Schelling's system, for example, more than 70 percent held medical degrees. Given the development of what has been called an ideology of *Wissenschaft* that accompanied the upsurge of German culture during the latter half of the eighteenth century, scholars have also pointed to the promise some physicians felt that organic *Naturphilosophie* held for medicine. Because in these years medicine suffered from criticism that it lacked the systematic structure enjoyed by other *Wissenschaften,* physicians hoped that the rigorously reasoned program Schelling had outlined in his many works would supply the kind of intellectual foundation medicine needed.

Other natural philosophers were also attracted to Schelling's attempt, as he once said, to give wings to physics, that is, to give the natural philosopher the responsibility to move from particular empirical results to the larger meaning of the entire enterprise of natural science. Regarding nature as a living whole, for example, entailed the assumption that all of nature's forces were interrelated. A number of experimenters from the physical sciences persisted in exploiting this assumption, including Hans Christian Ørsted, whose commitment to the philosophical unity of nature's forces played a direct role in his discovery of electromagnetism in 1820.

While Schelling himself always retained great appreciation of and respect for empirical research, eventually the charge arose, in some cases justifiably, that his followers dealt primarily with the play of speculative ideas and had little interest in the empirical side of natural science. In addition, those still devoted to a Kantian position on nature and natural science, like the philosopher-physicist Jakob Fries (1773–1843), composed informed critiques of Schelling's work.

After the first decade of the century, Schelling turned in his writing to other matters, and his influence as the founder of *Naturphilosophie* waned. By the 1820s there were only a few who were willing to identify themselves as *Naturphilosophen.* Among those who were, however, was Lorenz Oken (1779–1851), who was the motive force behind the emergence of a German scientific community in the modern sense of the term. His founding of the journal *Isis* and his leading role in establishing the Society of German Natural Investigators and Physicians in 1822 were accomplished in spite of his reputation as an unrepentant *Naturphilosoph.*

See also **Biology; Kantianism; Life; Medicine: Europe and the United States; Organicism; Philosophy; Physics; Religion and Science; Romanticism in Literature and Politics; Science.**

BIBLIOGRAPHY

Beiser, Frederick. *The Fate of Reason: German Philosophy from Kant to Fichte.* Cambridge, Mass.: Harvard University Press, 1987.

Bonsiepen, Wolfgang. *Die Begründung einer Naturphilosophie bei Kant, Schelling, Fries und Hegel: Mathematische versus spekulative Naturphilosophie.* Frankfurt am Main: Klostermann, 1997.

Broman, Thomas. *The Transformation of German Academic Medicine, 1750–1820.* Cambridge, U.K.: Cambridge University Press, 1996.

Gregory, Frederick. "Kant, Schelling, and the Administration of Science in the German Romantic Era." *Osiris* 5 (1989): 17–35.

———. "Die Kritik von J. F. Fries an Schellings Naturphilosophie." *Sudhoffs Archiv* 67 (1983): 145–157.

Richards, Robert. *The Romantic Conception of Life: Science and Philosophy in the Age of Goethe.* Chicago: University of Chicago Press, 2002.

Frederick Gregory

NEGRITUDE. An aesthetic and literary movement inaugurated in the 1930s that centers on the creative potential of black consciousness, negritude was one of the premier cultural phenomena of the twentieth century. Curiously, negritude has no originating text as such; it took root and flourished in Paris in the mid-1930s, fed by the writings of two black scholars from the French colonies, Aimé Césaire (b. 1913) of Martinique and Léopold Sédar Senghor (1906–2001) of Senegal. Both of these figures would go on to become major writers, and each would play a leading role in the political life of his respective country of origin. Senghor became the first president of an independent Senegal, and Césaire served simultaneously as mayor of the Martinican capital, Fort-de-France, and as Martinique's representative to the French National Assembly for more than forty-five years.

Influences

Negritude became internationally recognized with the publication of Césaire's book-length poem, *Cahier d'un retour au pays natal* (Return to my native land) in 1939. The Césaire-Senghor collaboration that led up to this moment was indeed serendipitous. They met as colonial scholarship students in Paris. Each had been strongly influenced by the scope for rehabilitating black history and culture evinced by such recent movements as the Harlem Renaissance, and admired greatly the work of such poets as James Weldon Johnson, Jean Toomer, and Claude McKay. René Menil, a constituent member of the Parisian group that published the radical manifesto *Légitime défense* (Legitimate defense) in 1932, was also a major influence on Césaire, and joined him later in launching the Martinique-based periodical *Tropiques*. The *Revue du monde noir* (Review of the black world), published 1931–1932, introduced them to the work of such writers and educators as Langston Hughes and Alain Locke; they were also influenced by the presence in Paris of the French Guyanese author René Maran, the author of *Batouala,* which had won the French Prix Goncourt in 1921 and was subsequently banned in French African colonies. Together with a group of fellow students, they launched a literary magazine, *L'Etudiant noir* (The black student), which took a militant stand against black cultural assimilation by actively seeking to explore and valorize the singularity of the black cultural experience. The publication inaugurated the use of the word *negritude,* and appeared roughly half a dozen times before closing in 1936. During this period Césaire and Senghor, along with their friend and collaborator, the French Guyanese poet Léon Dumas, culled from these influences a framework for rehabilitating and resituating the articulation of black consciousness and its attendant cultural expression, even within an ongoing context of colonialism and racism.

Philosophy and Practice: Césaire

Drawing on a binary structure that, as we shall see, would ultimately lead to its undoing, negritude sought to ground and, indeed, to legitimize the difference of the black aesthetic in a set of biological concepts meant to firmly separate the black experience from the white experience. Initially, however, from an artistic perspective, its founders drew heavily on French surrealism. This radical mode of poetic expression, which first made its appearance in postwar France, afforded a means of discursive liberation from French rationalism through the abandonment of traditional aesthetic and expressive constraints. To this expressive vein must be added the work of Leo Frobenius, whose groundbreaking *Histoire de la civilisation africaine* (1936; History of African civilization) exploded the myth of Negro barbarity as a European invention and was of cardinal importance in allowing the founders of negritude scope for a needed valorization of Africa-based civilizations and cultures. This concatenation of beliefs and arguments allowed them to posit that what was unique to the black experience—what separated it from Western subjectivity and provided the basis for the new aesthetic—was a predetermined predilection

for art, emotion, intuition, and rhythm, which were opposed to supposedly Western characteristics of order, reason, and logic. These, then, were the enabling categories of expression that mediated the appearance and argumentation of negritude.

In literary terms, and especially in the *Cahier,* which is typically seen as its foundational text, negritude functions as an illumination and affirmation of pride in black subjectivity. The sentiments voiced in the poem derive their importance equally from their form and their content as the poet joins lyricism to self-revelation in a rediscovered empathy with his African ancestry. This black subject revels in the rebirth of a black identity that is both historically and culturally grounded; negritude becomes a framework for creative cultural expression that valorizes black civilizations past and present and thus, at least in the *Cahier,* goes beyond a reductive essentialism based on biology. Ultimately, what is emphasized is the process of self-discovery and self-actualization, an ongoing voyage into blackness that replaces the static acceptance of colonial inferiority with the active uncovering of viable alternative identities.

Philosophy and Practice: Senghor

Senghor differed from Césaire in both his vision and his practice of negritude; for him, opposing the values of Europe to those of the African world led him to valorize life forces as the essential framework grounding his poetic portraits of African civilization. Arriving in Paris in 1928 on a partial scholarship in literary studies, he studied at the Lycée Louis-le-Grand and the Sorbonne. It was during this period that he began to be influenced by his discussions with Césaire, Maran, McKay, and the Haitian author and intellectual Dr. Jean Price-Mars. It was around this time that Senghor formed the belief that blacks could benefit by assimilating European culture without severing themselves from their own cultural origins. He promulgated a return to historical and cultural sources through the cultivation of indigenous languages and traditions, and sought to instantiate this value system through the vocabulary, themes, and symbolism of his published poetry. His *Hosties noires* (Black offerings) and the collection *Anthologie de la nouvelle poésie nègre et malgache de langue française* (Anthology of new black and Malagasy poetry in French) appeared to mark the centennial of the French abolition of slavery in 1948, joining the already-published collections by Césaire in rehabilitating the perceived "primitive" character of black colonial civilizations.

Senghor's primary themes are alienation and exile, along with a recognition of the central role played by the culture and tradition of his African homeland. The importance of the cultural heritage that he was thus able to describe and define for his fellow blacks cannot be overemphasized. This valorization of a cultural patrimony became a catalyst for black self-realization, demonstrating negritude's capacity to engender pride in authenticity and racial difference. Much more so than did Césaire's, Senghor's writing stressed claims for a particular black emotional and psychological experience, an affective rapport that draws on a specifically African relationship to the forces of the universe that are separate and apart from those of the West. Where the black African perceives and internalizes in a subjective way (the argument goes), relating to external stimuli in primarily emotional terms, the Westerner, in his turn, relates to the world through analysis and reason. This is not to claim a monopoly on either category for either group, in his view. While not denying the rational power of blacks or the emotive capacities of whites, Senghor does see very real differences in temperament and worldview that determine the ways in which certain cultures view and relate to the world. As limited and reductionist as this argument might seem today, it extended an elaborate and perhaps necessary ontology to the concept of negritude, providing an enabling framework for literally hundreds of African and Caribbean writers to express their vision of their own cultural and historical experience well into the 1960s.

Negritude, then, was in a certain sense a product of its time; despite its own claims to the contrary, its primary shortcoming was perhaps that it drew unconsciously on the binaries of the colonial era. It opened the way for a flood of creative black expression, but it would in time be superseded by alternative approaches to, and theories of, black identity. Critiques that would be leveled at negritude by Frantz Fanon, the Martinican intellectual, and Wole Soyinka, the Nigerian novelist and Nobel laureate, among others, would center on the concept's racial grounding and its implicit essentialisms, contradictions, and limitations. Given the widely varying social and historical situations involved in the development of black culture, any theory that sought to contextualize and mediate this development needed to be deracialized. By moving away from a race-based analysis of culture to one that reflects the range of influences inflecting black historical reality, the differing cultural expressions of black people could be taken into account, catalyzed, and valorized. The theories of Césaire and Senghor would in time give way to those of Glissant and Bernabé, Chamoiseau, and Confiant, among others, acknowledging the opening up of the categories of race and culture whose binary, colonially driven structures established the boundaries of blackness even as they sought to endow them with value and meaning.

See also **Africa, Idea of; African-American Ideas; Afrocentricity; Authenticity, Africa; Black Atlantic; Black Consciousness; Colonialism: Africa; Communication of Ideas: Africa and Its Influence; Diasporas: African Diaspora; Humanity: African Thought; Race and Racism.**

BIBLIOGRAPHY

Arnold, A. James. *Modernism and Negritude: The Poetry and Poetics of Aimé Césaire.* Cambridge, Mass.: Harvard University Press, 1981.

Bâ, Sylvia Washington. *The Concept of Negritude in the Poetry of Léopold Sédar Senghor.* Princeton, N.J.: Princeton University Press, 1973.

Cailler, Bernadette. *Proposition poétique: une lecture de l'oeuvre d'Aimé Césaire.* Sherbrooke, Que.: Naaman, 1976.

Confiant, Raphaël. *Aimé Césaire: une traversée paradoxale du siècle.* Paris: Stock, 1993.

Davis, Gregson. *Aimé Césaire.* Cambridge, U.K.: Cambridge University Press, 1997.

Eshleman, Clayton, and Annette Smith, trans. *Aimé Césaire: The Collected Poetry.* Berkeley: University of California Press, 1983.

Popeau, Jean Baptiste. *Dialogues of Negritude: An Analysis of the Cultural Context of Black Writing.* Durham: Carolina Academic Press, 2003.

Richardson, Michael. *Refusal of the Shadow: Surrealism and the Caribbean.* Translated by Krzysztof Fijalkowski and Michael Richardson. London: Verso, 1996.

Sartre, Jean-Paul. "Orphée noir." In *Anthologie de la nouvelle poésie nègre et malgache de langue française.* Edited by Léopold Sédar Senghor. Paris: Presses universitaires de France, 1948.

Scharfman, Ronnie. *Engagement and the Language of the Subject in the Poetry of Aimé Césaire.* Gainesville: University Press of Florida, 1987.

Senghor, Léopold Sédar. *Négritude et humanisme.* Paris: Seuil, 1964.

Taylor, Patrick. *The Narrative of Liberation: Perspectives on Afro-Caribbean Literature, Popular Culture, and Politics.* Ithaca, N.Y.: Cornell University Press, 1989.

H. Adlai Murdoch

NEOCOLONIALISM. Neocolonialism can be defined as the continuation of the economic model of colonialism after a colonized territory has achieved formal political independence. This concept was applied most commonly to Africa in the latter half of the twentieth century. European countries had colonized most of the continent in the late nineteenth century, instituting a system of economic exploitation in which African raw materials, particularly cash crops and minerals, were expropriated and exported to the sole benefit of the colonizing power. The idea of neocolonialism, however, suggests that when European powers granted nominal political independence to colonies in the decades after World War II, they continued to control the economies of the new African countries.

The concept of neocolonialism has several theoretical influences. First and foremost, it owes much to Marxist thinking. Writing in the late nineteenth century, Karl Marx argued that capitalism represented a stage in the socioeconomic development of humanity. He believed that, ultimately and inevitably, the capitalist system in industrially developed countries would be overthrown by a revolution of the working class; this would result in the establishment of socialist utopias. In 1916, Vladimir Lenin modified this thesis, claiming that the rapid expansion of European imperialism around the world in the last decade of the nineteenth century had marked the highest stage of capitalism. Presumably, then, the end of imperialism (which Lenin believed would be the result of World War I) would mark the beginning of the end of capitalism. However, neither imperialism nor capitalism came to an end after the war or in future years. European empires persisted well into the 1960s.

With the granting of independence to colonies, a theory of modernization took hold. This suggested that independent countries would begin to develop very rapidly, politically and economically, and would resemble "modern" Western countries. It soon became clear, however, that this was not happening. Postcolonial theorists now sought answers for the continued underdevelopment of African countries and found a second influence in dependency theory.

Dependency theory first gained prominence as a way to explain the underdevelopment of Latin American economies in the 1960s. It proclaims that underdevelopment persisted because highly developed countries dominated underdeveloped economies by paying low prices for agricultural products and flooding those economies with cheap manufactured goods. This resulted in a perpetually negative balance of payments that prevented underdeveloped countries from ever becoming competitive in the global marketplace. Economic theorists of postcolonial Africa, such as Walter Rodney and Samir Amin, combined the Marxist-Leninist concept of colonialism as a stage of capitalism with the concept of underdevelopment to create the concept of neocolonialism, which Kwame Nkrumah called "the last stage of imperialism."

According to Rodney and Amin, European countries, and increasingly the United States, dominated the economies of African countries through neocolonialism in several ways. After independence, the main revenue base for African countries continued to be the export of raw materials; this resulted in the underdevelopment of African economies, while Western industries thrived. A good example of this process is the West African cocoa industry in the 1960s: during this time, production increased rapidly in many African countries; overproduction, however, led to a reduction in the selling price of cocoa worldwide. Neocolonial theorists therefore proclaimed that economies based on the production of cash crops such as cocoa could not hope to develop, because the world system imposes a veritable ceiling on the revenue that can be accrued from their production. Likewise, the extraction and export of minerals could not serve to develop an African economy, because minerals taken from African soil by Western-owned corporations were shipped to Europe or America, where they were turned into manufactured goods, which were then resold to African consumers at value-added prices.

A second method of neocolonialism, according to the theory's adherents, was foreign aid. The inability of their economies to develop after independence soon led many African countries to enlist this aid. Believers in the effects of neocolonialism feel that accepting loans from Europe or America proved the link between independent African governments and the exploitative forces of former colonizers. They note as evidence that most foreign aid has been given in the form of loans, bearing high rates of interest; repayment of these loans contributed to the underdevelopment of African economies because the collection of interest ultimately impoverished African peoples.

The forces of neocolonialism did not comprise former colonial powers alone, however. Theorists also saw the United States as an increasingly dominant purveyor of neocolonialism in Africa. As the Cold War reached its highest tensions at roughly the same time that most African countries achieved independence, many theorists believed that the increasing levels of American aid and intervention in the affairs of independent African states were designed to keep African countries within the capitalist camp and prevent them from aligning with the Soviet Union.

If the forces of neocolonialism were so obvious to many theorists at the time, why then could independent African countries not simply recognize them and steer toward economic models that would allow them to be more competitive in the world market? Most students of neocolonialism had theories about the continuing drain of African resources. Perhaps the two most prolific were Kwame Nkrumah and Frantz Fanon. Many theorists and politicians came to espouse the ideas of these two men; a general understanding of the causal theories of neocolonialism may therefore be gained through a brief summary of their writings.

Kwame Nkrumah was a major figure in African politics for more than four decades. Born in Gold Coast (later Ghana) in 1909 and educated in Philadelphia and London, Nkrumah became a powerful leader in the movements for African independence and pan-African unity in the 1930s and 1940s. He became the first president of independent Ghana in 1957 and ruled until 1966, when his regime was overthrown by a military coup. Aside from his political activity, Nkrumah also wrote several books dealing with issues facing contemporary Africa. Of particular importance was his 1965 *Neo-Colonialism: The Last Stage of Imperialism* in which he sought to prove the existence of neocolonial forces in Africa and explain the impediments to overcoming them.

According to Nkrumah, the most important factor allowing for the perpetuation of neocolonialism in Africa was the "balkanization" of the continent that had occurred as a result of European colonialism. Colonizers had broken Africa into dozens of administrative units in order to govern it more effectively, and the colonial boundaries had become the lines within which African countries had been given independence. Nkrumah believed that the interests of Africa were being damaged by the need of each new country to fend for itself. For instance, the fact that each produced and exported its cocoa crop independently was what resulted in lower prices. Nkrumah believed that through African unity and cooperation, the continent could best combat neocolonialism. This required a policy of nonalignment in the Cold War. Believing that Africa had all the resources necessary to achieve true economic independence, Nkrumah promoted inter-African trade, so that the continent could wean itself from Western imports. He also believed that African unity would help to strengthen African countries' bargaining power on the world market, as well as in international politics. If Africans aligned with each other, rather than with the various Western countries that wished to exploit them, the future could be safeguarded. Nkrumah also believed that concerted efforts toward industrialization should complement agricultural and mineral exports in order that African countries become able to produce their own finished goods and reduce their reliance on European and American manufactured products. By enacting such policies, the spell of neocolonialism could be broken, ushering in an era of distinctly African "socialism." Many African leaders of the day, including Sékou Touré of Senegal and Julius Nyerere of Tanzania, held similar beliefs. Although these men fought diligently for African unity and economic development, their goals were mostly not achieved.

Frantz Fanon offered a different perspective on the dilemma facing independent African countries. Fanon was born in

Martinique, in the West Indies, in 1925. Educated in France, he moved to Algeria in 1953 to practice psychiatry, and soon became embroiled in that nation's violent struggle to gain independence from France. As the Algerian war of independence was nearing its end, Fanon wrote his most celebrated book, *The Wretched of the Earth* (*Les damnés de la terre*), in which he discussed, among other things, the causes of neocolonialism in Africa, and the solution he foresaw.

Fanon took much of the basis for neocolonialism for granted, seeing the exploitative tendencies of Western countries as inherent to their capitalist nature. He saw no place for Africa in this system. The African petty bourgeoisie, which had received power from the exiting colonial government, was the primary cause of neocolonialism in Africa. Fanon believed that the Africans who took power at the time of independence had been favored by European powers because they were willing to effect a smooth transition from colonialism to neocolonialism. Since they were generally of the Western-educated middle class who had in many ways benefited from the colonial system, they had the most to gain from a continuation of colonial economic policies. Fanon accused them of collaborating with the colonial power to ensure that the interests of both would continue to be met after the declaration of formal political independence; this class of Africans had betrayed the masses on whose backs the various nationalist movements had been borne. In order to achieve complete and final independence for African countries, "a rapid step must be taken from national consciousness to political and social consciousness" by the masses in order to check the power of the governing class, which had merely replaced the colonial administration as the most direct exploiters of African people. Violent revolution was the only means to drive oppressive neocolonial forces from the world. Fanon's ideology was supported by several political actors in Africa, including Amilcar Cabral of Guinea-Bissau, who warred against a deeply entrenched Portuguese colonial regime until his assassination in 1974.

Of course, neocolonial theory has its detractors as well. Opponents argue that the concept is merely an attempt to continue to blame colonialism for Africa's problems rather than confront the major issues hampering independent African governments, such as corruption, inefficiency, and protectionism. They argue that these problems, more than any systematic process of external exploitation, have been responsible for the poor performance of African economies since independence. Others continue to argue that neocolonialism persists, if in slightly different form. Transnational corporations, such as petroleum and mining companies, and international organizations such as the International Monetary Fund, World Bank, and World Trade Organization are responsible for much of the neocolonial influence in African countries in the early twenty-first century. The activities of these corporations and organizations transcend the boundaries and powers of the traditional nation-state, making it difficult to talk about interregional relationships except in terms of such paradigms as united North (Europe, Canada, and the United States) and underdeveloped and desperate South (Africa, Asia, and Latin America). As the understanding of international and intercontinental relations becomes more and more refined, the idea

of neocolonialism will continue to be revisited. It is for this reason that *neocolonialism* has entered the vocabulary of all students of Third World affairs and is an important concept in the history of ideas.

See also **Anticolonialism; Colonialism; Dependency; Internal Colonialism; Modernization; Modernization Theory; Third World.**

BIBLIOGRAPHY

Amin, Samir. *Neo-Colonialism in West Africa.* Translated from the French by Francis McDonagh. Harmondsworth, U.K.: Penguin, 1973.

Falola, Toyin, ed. *Africa* (Volume 5, *Contemporary Africa*). Durham, N. C.: Carolina Academic Press, 2003.

Fanon, Frantz. *The Wretched of the Earth.* Translated by Constance Farrington. New York: Grove Press, 1963. Originally published in French, 1961.

Museveni, Yoweri K. *What Is Africa's Problem?* Minneapolis: University of Minnesota Press, 2000. Originally published in 1992.

Nkrumah, Kwame. *Neo-Colonialism, The Last Stage of Imperialism.* New York: International, 1966.

Rodney, Walter. *How Europe Underdeveloped Africa.* Rev. ed. Washington, D.C.: Howard University Press, 1981. Originally published in 1972.

Woddis, Jack. *Introduction to Neo-Colonialism.* London: Lawrence and Wishart, 1967.

Toyin Falola
Matthew Heaton

NEOLIBERALISM. The concept of neoliberalism is an interesting one in that, first, it is a label commonly used by its opponents rather than by its adherents. As with all such labels, the tendency for caricature may at times overtake the need for faithful rendition of the underlying idea. As the term implies, neoliberalism refers to what some view as a new form of liberalism, and what others view as a mere reassertion and ascendancy, in intellectual and policy circles, of classical liberalism. Neoliberalism has its roots in classical liberalism, which on the one hand criticized the constraints inherent in the old and dying feudal and mercantilist orders, and on the other hand advocated for political and economic freedom underpinned by a market economy based on private property rights in the form of the newly emerging capitalist mode of production.

History and Meaning

The terms *neoliberal* and *neoliberalism* have been variously used to refer to leading political exponents of the ideology, such as former U.S. president Ronald Reagan (yielding the label "Reaganomics") and former prime minister of the United Kingdom Margaret Thatcher ("Thatcherism"); particular intellectual trends, such as supply-side economics and monetarism, associated with academics such as Milton Friedman (b. 1912); intellectual traditions associated with particular institutions, such as the Chicago School (after the University of Chicago, where most of the leading proponents originated);

the policy stance of particular institutions that have been crucial in promoting its policy implications, such as the Bretton Woods Institutions (the World Bank and the International Monetary Fund, yielding the "Washington Consensus"); or more forthrightly "market fundamentalism" and "neoclassical orthodoxy." In the developing world, neoliberalism emerged in the form of stabilization and structural adjustment programs (SAPs) that entailed a standard package of the above policy measures regardless of the situation in a given country.

Neoliberalism arose as a major paradigm shift facilitated by the conjuncture of a number of eventualities: persistent and intractable recessions beginning in the 1970s for which standard economic policy tools, primarily based on Keynesianism, appeared ineffectual; the impasse in economic policy at national and global levels; and the unsustainability of some welfare regimes, including those of social democracy, in the developed world in the face of recessionary trends and fiscal constraints. In the context of these developments, proponents of neoliberalism saw the state as the major constraint on the efficient operation of the market and the resuscitation of growth at both national and global levels. Accordingly, neoliberalism directed its criticism against what was seen as an overextended role of the state in the economy consequent upon Keynesianism, socialism, and social democracy. Thus the main thrust of neoliberalism entails the need to roll back the state by restricting its role to the provision of pure public goods and the need to ensure that the state provides the appropriate environment for the market to operate by protecting property rights and associated contractual obligations, facilitating the free mobility of resources within and across nations, and ensuring safety and security.

As the term is applied in the early 2000s, *neoliberalism* refers to an all-embracing economic and political ideology that advocates the supremacy of the market over any alternative social arrangements, viewed from both a comparative and historical perspective, in ensuring the efficient allocation and utilization of scarce resources for the maximum satisfaction of relatively unlimited human wants. The market, based on freedom of choice and respect for private property and individual rights, and underpinned by competition among producers and consumers alike, is seen as the ideal and optimal vehicle for the realization of human ends. Thus neoliberalism leads to the conclusion that individuals, rather than collectives, are the best basis for decision making and that the role of the state (or any similar collective agencies) should be limited to creating and ensuring an environment conducive to individuals freely and competitively making decisions and choosing between alternatives, thereby facilitating and consolidating the expansion of the market and protecting private property rights, and to the provision of pure public goods, which, by definition, cannot be provided for efficiently by the market. This recalls the "invisible hand" notion of the market in enhancing economic welfare articulated by Adam Smith in the eighteenth century in his *The Wealth of Nations* (1776).

Policy Implications of Neoliberalism

The foregoing tenets of neoliberalism are based on certain assumptions. A philosophical assumption is made that human beings are driven by self-interest (as contended by Adam Smith) and that society is best advised to accommodate this drive since the welfare of society as a whole is best maximized by ensuring that individual self-interest is promoted and satisfied. Politically, neoliberalism accepts that individuals are formally equal and that they possess civil liberties that should be respected and protected, but it insists on the recognition that individuals have different capacities and potentialities which should be allowed to flourish, even if the result is income and wealth. Indeed, inequalities are seen as a major impetus to maximizing individual self-interest because inequalities require greater exertion and effort to acquire the most from the market. The philosophical assumptions about self-interest and freely arrived-at choices under conditions of competition have been relied upon to develop mathematically rigorous economic theories aimed at demonstrating the superiority of the unfettered market as a form of economic organization. In addition, neoliberalism has extended its terrain to the analysis of political and social behavior and arrangements to justify the superiority of the market as the major guarantor of both economic and social welfare, with minimum government involvement.

Some of the key economic policy implications of neoliberalism are found in the following prescriptions, which are rigorously and uncompromisingly promoted by its proponents:

Sound macroeconomic policy: The need for what are referred to as "sound macroeconomic fundamentals" by ensuring stable and predictable prices and positive real interest rates. This requires tight fiscal and monetary policy by ensuring that budget deficits and money supply are assiduously controlled to minimally acceptable minimum levels in relation to gross domestic product. The aim here is to stabilize key indicators of the market such as overall price levels, interest rates, and the exchange rate in the belief that the ensuing stability and predictability of the indicators provide a basis for rational economic behavior and decision making for all economic agents, thereby enhancing overall efficiency.

Trade liberalization: The need for trade liberalization by reducing tariffs and non-tariff barriers and freeing the exchange rate in order to enhance competition internationally.

Labor market flexibility: The call for flexible labor markets, in particular the freedom of entrepreneurs to hire and fire workers at will and to reorganize work as needed; and, for some, the need for the free mobility of labor within and across countries.

Privatization: The need for the state to exit from productive activities that can be undertaken by the private sector by transferring ownership or management functions from the state to the private sector. Over time, neoliberals have been able to drastically circumscribe areas that are seen to be legitimate government activities, thereby expanding those areas that need to be privatized. Thus, for instance, areas such as health, education, provision of water and sanitation, security, and certain routine administrative functions such as the issuing of licenses, collection of fees and rates, issuing of fines, and so forth, have increasingly been identified as areas that need privatization.

Deregulation: The need to remove any regulations that may act as barriers or constraints to the mobility of goods and services, capital, and labor or that may interfere with the optimal functioning of firms. By the same token, it is demanded of the state that it provide an appropriate regulatory environment for the functioning of the market and the protection of property rights and contracts.

Export-oriented sectoral policies: A policy environment that is neutral in relation to export promotion or import substitution, or preferably biased through the use of narrowly targeted supply-side incentives, in favor of export promotion and integration into the global economy based on open trade and free movement of capital across nations.

The foregoing policies are also seen by neoliberals to be compatible with the increased globalization of economic activities, so that support for neoliberalism and support for increased globalization have become conjoined and indistinguishable.

Effects of Neoliberal Policies

Neoliberalism has also fostered a value chain that begins with theoretical activity in academia and various research institutions and feeds into various institutional vehicles that uphold and promote particular aspects of the neoliberal paradigm, right up to the production and reproduction of policy advisors and implementers who attempt to sustain and implement the policy implications of the paradigm at national and international levels. Neoliberalism has benefited from the support of key national and global-level corporations whose influence is exerted through their ability to shift funds instantaneously across the globe in response to changing environmental conditions, through financing various activities in the value chain and influencing policy in the government of developed countries, and through key multilateral and bilateral financial, trade, and development agencies.

The neoliberal agenda has had a tendency to effectively close out any competing ways of looking at economics and economic policy. At the political level, the promotion of neoliberalism approached tyrannical levels with some governments, such as the United States and the United Kingdom, seeing any challenge to neoliberalism as a challenge to a national way of life—and, indeed, to the protection of this way of life. This has been used as a justification to initiate campaigns for regime change in some countries. More generally, fairly effective sanctions and incentives are deployed throughout the value chain to ensure compliance with, or promotion of, the neoliberal agenda. However, neoliberalism has negatively affected large numbers of people though retrenchments, degradation of work, misuse of the environment, increased poverty, and marginalization of nationalities and households, particularly those in the non-formal sectors of the developing world, while the net social gains have been spurious and remain quite open to debate. It is clear, however, that some financiers and corporations (and some countries in the developed world) have benefited immensely.

Nevertheless, it appears that neoliberalism has peaked as its presumed benefits have become more questionable and as the ideology is challenged from a number of quarters. The empirical evidence supporting neoliberalism is mixed in the developed world and is particularly dismal in the developing world. In the developed countries, the social implications of neoliberal policies have undermined social safety nets with no viable substitutes emanating from the market. In developing economies, particularly those in Africa, the pursuit of structural adjustment and stabilization programs has not yielded the desired benefits in either inclusive or equitable growth, which should be the aim of development. In these countries neoliberalism has had the consequence of jettisoning any semblance of development or strategic planning that those countries had attempted prior to the adoption of the recent economic reforms, so that the economies are currently in disarray. The early-twenty-first-century consensus on the creative manner in which the East Asian Tigers (Taiwan, South Korean, Singapore, and Hong Kong) combined the roles of the market and a proactive state have also done much to deflate the dogmatic opposition to the state advocated by neoliberals. At the theoretical level, the contributions arising from the new institutional economics, the economics of information, and the economics of risk and uncertainty are beginning to question neoliberal assumptions and prescriptions regarding the role of the state. And at the social and political level, global movements have arisen to challenge neoliberal policies.

In the wake of these challenges, shifts have begun to occur in the neoliberal camp in the early twenty-first century, and new syntheses of approaches have been proposed. The neoliberal agenda has begun to include welfare issues by supporting the promotion of sustainable livelihoods, social safety nets, and poverty reduction. In addition, given that neoliberal policies have tended to be unilaterally imposed, particularly in developing economies, there has been a shift to accommodating popular participation and good governance, as in the development of Poverty Reduction Strategy Papers (PRSP) associated with the Highly Indebted Poor Countries (HIPC) debt initiative of the Bretton Woods Institutions. More generally, there is less of a dogmatic stance on the nature and content of policy packages comprising economic reform initiatives, yielding what has been labeled the "post-Washington Consensus." At another level, some have worked toward synthesizing lessons from neoliberalism with those from social democracy, resulting in the proposal for a "third way." Finally, from a philosophical point of view, the assumptions underlying the neoliberal model have also been challenged, particularly as to whether methodological individualism assumed in the model, to the exclusion of other plausible assumptions that could be made, is necessarily the most appropriate or adequate assumption to guide formulation of social theories; and, if it can be contended that a particular proclivity of human beings is natural and inevitable, such a proclivity must necessarily be pandered to as a normative ideal. Thus, while as deductive theory and approach neoliberalism may appear unchallengeable and highly persuasive, its benefits are increasingly viewed as unsustainable on intellectual, philosophical, social, and political grounds.

See also **Conservatism; Economics; Globalization; Liberalism.**

BIBLIOGRAPHY

Bond, Patrick, and George Dor. "Neo-Liberalism and Poverty Reduction Strategies in Africa." Discussion paper, Regional Network for Equity in Health in Southern Africa (EQUINET), 2003.

Chomsky, Noam. *Profit over People: Neoliberalism and Global Order*. New York: Seven Stories Press, 1999.

Giddens, Anthony. *The Third Way: The Renewal of Social Democracy*. Cambridge, Mass.: Polity, 1998.

Stiglitz, Joseph. *Globalization and Its Discontents*. London: Allen Lane, 2002.

Guy C. Z. Mhone

NEOPLATONISM. Neoplatonism is a modern term that refers to the philosophical movement that dominated the intellectual life of the Roman Empire from the third to the sixth centuries C.E.; its most prominent representatives were the pagan philosophers Plotinus, Porphyry, Iamblichus, and Proclus. These thinkers strove to elucidate ambiguities in Plato's philosophy with insights drawn from Neopythagoreanism, Aristotelianism, and Stoicism in order to establish a thorough summation of ancient learning. As such, Neoplatonism was the last flowering of pagan philosophy, which flourished until it was supplanted and to a certain degree absorbed by Christian theology. Christian thinkers who were deeply influenced by pagan Neoplatonism are often regarded as Neoplatonists as well, most significantly Augustine of Hippo, the Greek Fathers known as the Cappadocians, Boethius, and the author called Pseudo-Dionysius the Areopagite. The term is often applied to movements during the Middle Ages and Renaissance that were informed by Neoplatonic doctrines. All Neoplatonists, regardless of religious orientation, shared a belief in the superior quality of immaterial reality and regarded Plato as the greatest of ancient philosophers.

Terminology

Neoplatonism initially had a negative connotation. Enlightenment historians developed the term to dissociate the Platonists of the late Roman Empire from Plato, believing that they had distorted his philosophy beyond all recognition by their eclecticism. Jacob Brucker (*Historia critica philosophiae,* 1742–1744) branded them "the Eclectic Sect" before A. F. Büsching (*Grundriß einer Geschichte der Philosophie,* 1772–1774) dismissively suggested the appellation "new Platonists" (*neue Platoniker*). Edward Gibbon similarly disparaged the philosophy of the "new Platonicians" (*History of the Decline and Fall of the Roman Empire,* 1776). The prefix *neo* did not appear in English until the 1830s. Yet the idea of Neoplatonism is, in certain ways, unsatisfactory. It implies a sharp break with the thought of preceding generations, whereas considerable continuity is evident; moreover, the Neoplatonists did not regard themselves as innovators but as elucidators of the true philosophy established by Plato. The word is now simply a term of convenience denoting a late phase in the reception of Plato's philosophy.

Before Neoplatonism

The Academy founded by Plato went through two major phases. The Old Academy (387–c. 250 B.C.E.) emphasized metaphysics, whereas the New Academy (c. 150–c. 110 B.C.E.) took a skeptical turn and focused on epistemology. The fall of Athens in 86 B.C.E. apparently ended the school, and circa 80 B.C.E. a former member, Antiochus of Ascalon, took the opportunity to found his own "Academy," which revived a dogmatic approach. This development marked the beginning of a phase known as Middle Platonism (c. 80 B.C.E.–c. 250 C.E.), which reaffirmed the centrality of metaphysics and coincided with a turn toward mysticism. In attempting to clarify Plato, the Middle Platonists did not hesitate to borrow ideas from rival schools of philosophy. Although this approach has traditionally been described as "eclectic," John Dillon recommends avoiding the term, since it implies an arbitrary recombination of ideas based on personal preference rather than a thoughtful reformulation made in light of ongoing philosophical discussion, which was surely the motivation behind both Middle Platonic and Neoplatonic adaptations.

Middle Platonists divided reality into three parts: God, the Ideas, and matter. God was subdivided into three hierarchical levels—the Primal God, Mind, and Soul—as outlined in a second-century Platonic handbook by Alcinous. The Ideas, or Platonic Forms, were identified as the thoughts of God. This metaphysical framework was further developed in Neoplatonism.

Plotinus

Plotinus (205–270) is commonly regarded as the founder of Neoplatonism. He studied in Alexandria before founding his own school circa 244 in Rome, where he devised a comprehensive philosophy that has been preserved in the *Enneads*. For Plotinus, philosophy was not exclusively an effort of reasoned argument, since he equated the love of wisdom with assimilation to God, which is possible only through mystical ecstasy—a state Plotinus himself experienced. Discursive reasoning merely assists in attaining this higher end by clarifying what constitutes reality.

Plotinus's ontology reflects his mystical vision. Adapting the Middle Platonists' threefold division of God, Plotinus called the highest level of divinity, or first hypostasis, "the One"—a perfect unity, infinite and unknowable. Its superabundant goodness impels it to emanate existence in a cascading chain of being. As the source of all existence, the One itself actually transcends being. Hence the highest being is the divine Mind, which is emanated directly by the One. This second hypostasis, in which the Ideas are located, further emanates a third hypostasis, which is called Soul as it contemplates the intelligible realm and Nature as it previews what it will produce. Time and the physical world thus emanate from Soul/Nature. The process of emanation ends when being is so attenuated that a limit is finally reached. This lowest stage of emanation is matter, which exists only potentially. Inasmuch as being is linked with goodness, matter's virtual absence of being is seen as the source of evil. Although matter is not *substantially* evil, since it ultimately emanates from the One, nevertheless evil resides in its state of privation.

Human souls, like the third hypostasis, are divided into a higher part that perceives the intelligible world and a lower part that cares for a material body. The individual soul falls into degradation when it is excessively concerned with material things and forgets its true identity. Philosophy reminds the wayward soul that it is an immaterial substance and thus opens the way for salvation, whereby the enlightened soul chooses to return to the intelligible world, from which it can ascend to the bliss of union with the One.

Later Neoplatonists

Plotinus's legacy was preserved by his pupil, Porphyry of Tyre (c. 232–c. 304), who wrote a biography of the master and published his tractates under the title *Enneads.* Porphyry's own writings include a manual of Plotinian metaphysics (*Sentences*) and commentaries on various texts, including Homer's *Odyssey* (*On the Cave of the Nymphs*) and Aristotle's *Categories* (*Isagoge*). Porphyry took a religious view of the philosophical enterprise and, while denouncing Christianity as an irrational cult, introduced into the Neoplatonic canon the second-century *Chaldean Oracles,* Platonic texts that he regarded as true revelation.

These writings also inspired the Neoplatonist Iamblichus (d. c. 330), who founded what is sometimes called the Syrian school. Iamblichus did not share the optimistic Plotinian view about the ease of salvation; he supplemented philosophy with theurgy—rituals invoking the divine powers for aid. His innovations were adopted by the schools in Alexandria and Athens, the other major centers of Neoplatonism. The inclusion of traditional pagan elements in Iamblichus's system made it attractive to Emperor Julian (331?–363), who promoted Syrian Neoplatonism in his attempt to revive paganism.

The foremost representative of the Athenian school was Proclus (410?–485), who wrote two influential works of systematic metaphysics, the *Elements of Theology* and *Platonic Theology.* He was head of a revived academy, which remained a bastion of paganism, and attacked the Christian doctrine of creation. The Alexandrian school, however, was diverse; it included some Christians, one of whom, John Philoponos (c. 490–570), wrote a rebuttal to Proclus's attack. The Alexandrian school displayed a keen interest in Aristotle, and Philoponos is often regarded as an Aristotelian rather than a Neoplatonist, although his independence of mind makes either characterization questionable. Other noteworthy Neoplatonists were the Athenians Plutarch (d. c. 432), Syrianus (d. c. 437), Damascius (d. after 538), and Simplicius (d. 560) and the Alexandrians Hypatia (d. 415), Hierocles (fifth century), Ammonius (d. after 517), and Olympiodorus (d. after 565).

Ancient Christian Neoplatonism

Since Neoplatonists and Christians shared many common beliefs, the latter sometimes borrowed insights from the former,

in spite of the polemic between them. Among the Latin Fathers, Augustine of Hippo (354–430) remarked in his book *On True Religion* (chap. 7) that one need only change a few words to make Christians of the Platonists. The Greek Fathers, especially the fourth-century Cappadocians (Basil the Great, Gregory of Nazianzus, and Gregory of Nyssa), were similarly responsive to Neoplatonism, since men such as Origen (185?–254?) had already brought Middle Platonism into the Greek theological tradition. Neoplatonism waned, however, as the Roman Empire disintegrated. The emperors after Julian firmly championed the Christian religion, and in 529 Justinian closed the doors of the Academy. Neoplatonism's continuing influence would depend on the tolerance of religious thinkers.

Medieval Neoplatonism

The reception of Neoplatonism during the thousand years of the Middle Ages is an immensely intricate subject, complicated by the mediated nature of the transmission (largely through theological assimilations) and by the division of the Mediterranean world into rival cultural spheres. Hence Neoplatonic adaptation developed differently among Greek and Latin Christians, Muslims, and Jews.

In each culture, enthusiasts tried to reconcile Neoplatonism with their religion. Most extraordinary was the Christianization of Proclus's philosophy circa 500 by a Byzantine using the pen name of Dionysius the Areopagite, the first-century convert of St. Paul (Acts 17:34). This assumed name lent his writings an air of authority that was undeserved yet guaranteed their dissemination. The texts provided instruction in the "affirmative" and "negative" theologies—methodologies for achieving mystical union with God through the use and suppression of symbolic language. The affirmative theology describes what God is by way of analogy, but since God is ultimately unlike anything that exists (for God is beyond being), the alternative theology is required to transcend the limitations of language by negating the analogy. This contemplative process of description and denial prepares the soul for ecstatic union by correcting its misapprehensions about God. The Pseudo-Dionysian texts were translated into Latin and studied in western Europe, where they inspired the ninth-century Neoplatonic system of John Scotus Eriugena (c. 800–c. 877).

Greek Christians were the only group able to read the Neoplatonic texts in the original language, yet this direct access actually increased the difficulty of using the old pagan philosophy in the theologically charged atmosphere of the Byzantine Empire. Philosophers who attempted to further the patristic effort at assimilation sometimes endured accusations of heterodoxy—as did Michael Psellos (1018?–1096?) and John Italos (c. 1023–1085). Arabic culture was at times more tolerant. Muslim thinkers were impressed with Greek philosophy and tended to equate it with its final, Neoplatonic form. Even Aristotle seemed a Neoplatonist, perhaps due to Neoplatonic commentaries that minimized his differences with Plato but also due to the misattribution of certain Neoplatonic texts, such as the *Theology of Aristotle* (extracts from Plotinus) and the *Book of Causes* (extracts from Proclus). The most prominent Muslim Neoplatonist was Ibn Sina (Avicenna, 980–1037), whose works were favorably received before Al-Ghazali (1058–1111) wrote a critique that prompted a phase of intolerance. Jewish thinkers were also impressed with the Greek heritage, most notably Ibn Gabirol (Avicebron, c. 1021–c. 1058), whose *Fountain of Life* featured Neoplatonic doctrines. Neoplatonism was the main philosophical influence on the Kabbalah of thirteenth-century Provence.

Neoplatonism in the Latin West

Compared with the other three traditions, Latin Christianity was slower in absorbing Neoplatonism, largely due to a paucity of sources, yet it became the most vibrant by the end of the Middle Ages. After Augustine, the principal Neoplatonic thinker was the Roman philosopher Boethius (c. 475–525), who brought Porphyry's *Isagoge* to a Latin audience and presented many Neoplatonic ideas in his own *Consolation of Philosophy*, which became a standard schoolbook. Two commentaries were also significant in the medieval schools: one on Plato's *Timaeus* by Calcidius (third or fourth century, considered by some a Middle Platonist rather than a Neoplatonist), another on the *Dream of Scipio* (an excerpt from Cicero's *Republic*) by the fifth-century Macrobius. The latter provided a concise summary of Plotinian metaphysics, which occasioned a controversy in the eleventh century, featured in Manegold of Lautenbach's *Book against Wolfhelm*.

A cultural revival during the twelfth century led to renewed interest in old texts and an influx of new translations. After thinkers such as Peter Abelard, William of Conches, Thierry of Chartres, and Bernardus Silvestris fruitfully reexamined the Calcidian *Timaeus,* their successors discovered that the newly arriving translations of Aristotle's treatises had more to offer the scholastic enterprise of systematic theology than did the less direct dialogues of Plato, of which only the *Meno* and *Phaedo* were added to the Latin corpus. However, since Aristotle came to the West via the Arabs, he was initially read as a Neoplatonist. Thomas Aquinas (1225–1274) was instrumental in correcting this error when he identified Proclus as the source for the Pseudo-Aristotelian *Book of Causes* after reading a Latin version of the *Elements of Theology* translated in 1268.

Although Aquinas was principally Aristotelian in outlook, his teacher, Albertus Magnus (c. 1200–1280), was partial to Neoplatonism and inspired a Neoplatonic approach in three other Dominican friars: Dietrich of Freiberg (c. 1250–c. 1310), whose interest in the Neoplatonic metaphysics of light inspired him to study optics; Meister Eckhart (c. 1260–c. 1328), the controversial mystic; and Berthold of Moosburg (c. 1300–after 1361), who wrote an extensive commentary on Proclus's *Elements*. Nicholas of Cusa (1401–1464) later drew upon these thinkers, as well as the twelfth-century Platonists and earlier sources, in constructing his own Neoplatonic worldview outlined in *Learned Ignorance* (1440), a reaction against the Aristotelianism dominant in the universities. Petrarch (1304–1374) had already urged a return to Plato, and this tendency within Italian Renaissance humanism culminated in the work of the Florentine philosopher Marsilio Ficino (1433–1499), whose translations and studies of the complete Plato, Plotinus, and other Platonic authors were influential throughout Europe for centuries.

See also **Christianity; Microcosm and Macrocosm; Platonism; Scholasticism.**

BIBLIOGRAPHY

Armstrong, A. H., ed. *The Cambridge History of Later Greek and Early Medieval Philosophy.* London: Cambridge University Press, 1967.

Carabine, Deirdre. *The Unknown God: Negative Theology in the Platonic Tradition, Plato to Eriugena.* Louvain, Belgium: Peeters, W. B. Eerdmans, 1995.

Dillon, John. *The Middle Platonists, 80 B.C. to A.D. 220.* Rev. ed. Ithaca, N.Y.: Cornell University Press, 1996.

Gersh, Stephen. *Middle Platonism and Neoplatonism: The Latin Tradition.* 2 vols. Notre Dame, Ind.: University of Notre Dame Press, 1986.

Gersh, Stephen, and Maarten J. F. M. Hoenen, eds. *The Platonic Tradition in the Middle Ages: A Doxographic Approach.* Berlin and New York: Walter de Gruyter, 2002.

Goodman, Lenn E., ed. *Neoplatonism and Jewish Thought.* Albany: State University of New York Press, 1992.

Gregory, John. *The Neoplatonists: A Reader.* 2nd ed. London and New York: Routledge, 1999.

Morewedge, Parviz, ed. *Neoplatonism and Islamic Thought.* Albany: State University of New York Press, 1992.

O'Meara, Dominic J., ed. *Neoplatonism and Christian Thought.* Albany: State University of New York Press, 1981.

Tatakis, Basil. *Byzantine Philosophy.* Translated by Nicholas J. Moutafakis. Indianapolis: Hackett, 2003.

Wallis, R. T. *Neoplatonism.* 2nd ed. London: Duckworth; Indianapolis: Hackett, 1995.

Robert Ziomkowski

NEW CRITICISM. The New Criticism is the name given to the work of a school of formalist-oriented Anglo-American literary critics whose writings appeared in the years following World War I and came to prominence in the 1940s and 1950s. John Crowe Ransom (1888–1974) coined the moniker itself in his 1941 study *The New Criticism,* in which he provided an overview of the work of key "New" Critics, including I. A. Richards (1893–1979), T. S. Eliot (1888–1965), William Empson (1906–1984), and Yvor Winters (1900–1968). Other important critics associated with this school included F. R. Leavis (1895–1978), Kenneth Burke (1897–1993), Allen Tate (1899–1979), Cleanth Brooks (1906–1994), Robert Penn Warren (1905–1989), and René Wellek (1903–1995), to name a few. Arising, in part, as a response to earlier approaches such as comparative philology and biographical and impressionistic criticism, the New Criticism focused on the individual work of literature, usually the poem, as the sole object of study. These critics placed special emphasis on the formalistic aspects of the literary work, highlighting connotative and associative usage of words and the many figurative devices of language that functioned within the poem.

Beginnings in England

The poet and critic T. S. Eliot gave shape to many of the concerns that would eventually coalesce as New Criticism. Eliot articulated a sense of literary tradition that wrenched criticism away from historical and biographical assessment. In essays such as "Tradition and the Individual Talent," rather than emphasizing the greatness of the individual poet, Eliot stressed the importance of directing criticism upon the poem itself. In turn, the tradition of poetry became the collective vessel through which cultural greatness was transmitted. By distinguishing levels of poetic appreciation, he stressed the benefit of technical appreciation as opposed to the more popular (and coarse) emotional. The aim of the critic was to mine "*significant* emotion, emotion which has its life in the poem and not in the history of the poet" (Eliot, p. 11). Eliot, then, was establishing a way of reading poetry that acknowledged Western tradition as a continuum dating back to Greek antiquity, in which "art never improves, but that material of art is never quite the same" (p. 6). In doing so, he sought a rigorous, formalist appreciation of art as a corrective to more popular modes of modern culture. Eliot, like later New Critics, hoped to cultivate an understanding of great literature as a countervailing force to the vulgar and degradative thrust of modern mass society.

The emphasis on rigorous technical understanding of the literary work would become the hallmark of New Criticism. Most practitioners generally eschewed explicit formulation of theoretical orientation but, rather, focused on the practical application of certain, specific ways of reading. This orientation was captured in the title of I. A. Richards's 1929 work *Practical Criticism,* in which the notion of criticism was allied with careful or "close" readings of poetic works. Richards used his Cambridge Honors students' responses to poetry to reveal the reading deficiencies of ostensibly well-trained readers. These misreadings allowed him to distinguish four distinct meanings that the critic needed to draw out in order to understand a poem: Sense, Feelings, Tone, and Intention. Such an emphasis on reading as a practice, whose focus was to be directed solely upon formal aspects of the literary object, would become a key trait of New Critical thought.

Indeed, the status of the literary object, isolated from historical and cultural context, would gain strength over the next two decades. The poem was the literary object par excellence, its condensed and intense use of language particularly conducive to close reading. For most of the New Critics poetry *was* literature, and they eschewed more lengthy and convoluted genres such as fiction and drama. In the 1920s, Richards had defined the poem as an autonomous and organic being whose unity as an aesthetic object was essential to its study. In the 1930s and 1940s, critics based in the American South would develop this idea further.

American New Criticism

In the United States, several poets and critics based in the South would pick up on Richards's work. This group, associated with the Agrarian Revival, would elaborate upon close reading and the autonomy of the poem, eventually developing these principles into a full-fledged critical ethos. In the 1930s, John Crowe Ransom's writing on poetry positioned literature against the rapacious force of dehumanizing scientific logic. Considering the Revivalists' opposition to Southern industrialization, the turn to poetry as a means to maintain

contact with a humanistic, organic, and agrarian tradition made sense. Most of the Agrarians shared a sense of distrust in technology and were religious and conservative in their social views. Ransom, Allen Tate, and others saw poetic knowledge as a remedy to an oppressive scientific modernity. For them, poetry offered access to means of human expression and communication that were not available in other, modern discourses.

Organic unity and the heresy of the paraphrase. In the journal *Southern Review,* the editors Cleanth Brooks (1906–1994) and Robert Penn Warren (1905–1989) provided an influential platform for New Criticism. From 1935 to 1942, Brooks and Warren, in addition to raising the profile of Southern writers, also established New Critical principles of criticism as central to American literary studies. In his 1947 work *The Well Wrought Urn,* Brooks brought together many of his previous essays into a key text for the movement. Not only articulating its principles, Brooks also provided exemplary New Critical readings of poetry. In positioning poetic against scientific knowledge, he argued that paradox was characteristic of the unique knowledge of the poem. Unlike science, which sought to eliminate paradox, the poetic work achieved its ontological status through contradictions, oppositions, and ambiguity. Brooks also described the "Heresy of the Paraphrase" in order to highlight the importance of the poetic object as a complete and unified whole. No part of the poem could be read outside of the whole, and the whole was constituted by each individual part. Thus, any summarization or paraphrase of a poem was grossly inadequate, as the internal multiplicities of the poem could not be reduced in such a way. Brooks would, in later work, elaborate upon William K. Wimsatt (1907–1975) and Monroe Beardsley's (1915–1985) concepts of the intentional fallacy and the affective fallacy to reaffirm the organic unity and autonomy of the poem. Aimed at biographical and impressionistic criticism, the former dismissed attempts to gauge the poet's intentions through examination of historical context, whereas the latter argued that the poem is not to be judged based upon its emotional impact on the reader.

Decline of the New Criticism and Continuing Influence

In the years following World War II, New Criticism became a force in Anglo-American literary studies. Its rise was attributed not only to the focus it placed on literature as a discipline unto itself but also to its ease of pedagogical transmission. In an era when universities were flooded with returning soldiers, the New Criticism offered a clear and direct approach to the analysis and appreciation of literature as a rigorous, objective form of study. Several prominent literary critics challenged New Critical methods during its heyday. Alfred Kazin (1915–1998), in the early 1940s, charged that it fetishized formalism. In the latter part of the same decade, R. S. Crane (1886–1967) attacked Brooks and others for their "critical monism," which was exemplified by their slavish adherence to poetry, and primarily lyrical poetry at that. While Brooks responded to this charge by setting his sights on fiction, he was forced to concede that historical context was an important component in the structure of the novel. But it was in the 1960s, with increasing social flux, when New Criticism began to see its influence diminish. Its ahistorical approach to the study of literature was faulted for depoliticizing literature and, thereby, upholding a political status quo. With increased interest paid to Marxist, hermeneutic, structuralist, and feminist criticism in the 1960s, New Criticism ceded ground to a variety of theoretical and historicist concerns. While in the early twenty-first century the New Criticism is faulted for its limitation of focus and methodological austerity, the impact it has had on the rise of a discipline of literary studies in the United States and that discipline's underlying reliance upon various methods of "close" reading are lasting achievements.

See also **Literary Criticism; Literary History; Literature.**

BIBLIOGRAPHY
Brooks, Cleanth. *The Well Wrought Urn.* Norfolk, Conn.: New Directions, 1941.
Eliot, T. S. *Selected Essays.* New York: Harcourt, Brace and World, 1964.
Ransom, John Crowe. *The New Criticism.* New York: Harcourt, Brace and Company, 1947.
Richards, I. A. *Practical Criticism.* 1929. Reprint, London: Routledge and Kegan Paul, 1964.
Wimsatt, W. K., Jr., and Monroe C. Beardsley. "The Intentional Fallacy." In *The Verbal Icon.* Lexington: University of Kentucky Press, 1954.

Amit Ray

NEW HISTORICISM. *See* **Literary Criticism; Literary History.**

NEWTONIANISM. A standard definition of *Newtonianism* or *Newtonian philosophy* found in early eighteenth-century dictionaries such as John Harris's *Lexicon Technicum* (5th ed., 1736) is: "The doctrine of the universe, and particularly of the heavenly bodies; their laws, affections, etc., as delivered by Sir Isaac Newton." An almost identical definition appears around thirty years later in the *Encyclopédie* of Denis Diderot and Jean le Rond d'Alembert: "Newtonianisme ou philosophie Newtonienne: c'est la théorie du méchanisme de l'univers, & particulierement du mouvement des corps célestes, de leur lois, de leur propriétés, telle qu'elle a été enseignée par M. Newton" (Newtonianism or Newtonian philosophy: the theory of the mechanism of the universe, and particularly of the motion of the heavenly bodies, of their laws, their properties, as delivered by Mr. Newton).

The authority of Newtonian philosophy was established through the publication of the two major works of Sir Isaac Newton (1642–1727) in natural philosophy, *The Principia* (*Philosophiae Naturalis Principia Mathematica,* 1687) and the *Opticks* (*Opticks; or, A Treatise of the Reflections, Refractions, Inflections & Colours of Light,* 1704). The former was a work in rational mechanics where Newton aimed to study "the motion that results from any force whatever and of the forces that are required for any motion whatever." His major stake was

to overcome the model of impact that dominated the mechanical philosophy of his time and to introduce the notion of attractive force as a proper dynamic factor of motion. Accordingly, he aimed to explain Kepler's laws through the use of universal attraction and to discard the Cartesian theory of vortices. The latter work was a study in the spirit of mechanical philosophy, where Newton investigated the phenomena of light. He introduced his experimental method and he elaborated the atomistic model of matter. In the successive editions of the work he enriched it with a number of "queries" where he developed his theoretical and metaphysical contemplations about the nature of matter, the various instances of attractive and repulsive force, and the theoretical grounding of experimental induction.

The publication of the *Principia* clearly marked the establishment of a new spirit in European natural philosophy. It is equally clear, though, that Newton's contemporaries differed significantly in the appreciation of his magnum opus. Followers like Edmond Halley (1656–1742) and Voltaire (1694–1778) were so excited by Newton's achievements that they placed him in the highest position of the philosophical firmament of the time. At the same time, however, Christiaan Huygens (1629–1695) was astonished by the fact that such an elaborate synthesis in mechanics was founded upon the notorious notion of universal attraction. Along a similar line, Gottfried Wilhelm Leibniz (1646–1716) accused Newton of turning the entire operation of Nature into a perpetual miracle. Having been nourished by the Cartesian rationalistic tradition, Huygens and Leibniz found that the adoption of attraction by natural philosophers would bring about a reversion to the "occult qualities" of Scholasticism.

Historians assume that the *Principia* is one of the least read documents in the history of ideas. Even in the early eighteenth century influential philosophers like John Locke (1632–1704) and Voltaire adopted its message without having read or understood its technical part. The reputation of the *Principia* was based primarily on the authority of very few competent readers. At the same time, quite a few nonmathematical philosophers made a systematic attempt to bring Newton's message to the general reader. To this purpose, they proceeded with the compilation of comprehensive treatises where they presented an outline of Newtonian mechanics and experimental philosophy.

The *Opticks* was a far more widely read work. A reason for this was its deceptive accessibility. The *Opticks* was not a revolutionary work in the sense the *Principia* was. It was rather a brilliant display of the art of experimentation, and it was often cited as a model of how to approach a difficult problem by experiment and how to conduct precise quantitative experiments. What was important in the *Opticks* from the point of view of the Newtonian synthesis was that Newton elaborated there the most comprehensive public statement he ever made of his experimental method:

As in Mathematics, so in Natural Philosophy, the Investigation of difficult Things by the Method of Analysis, ought ever to precede the Method of Composition [or Synthesis]. This Analysis consists in making Experiments and Observations, and in drawing general Conclusions from them by Induction, and admitting of no Objections against the conclusions, but such as are taken from Experiments, or other certain Truths. For Hypotheses are not to be regarded in experimental philosophy. . . . By this way of Analysis we may proceed from Compounds to Ingredients, and from Motions to the Forces producing them; and in general from Effects to their Causes, and from Particular Causes to more general ones, till the Argument end in the most general. (*Optics,* 1979, p. 404)

Newtonianism, however, is much more than the direct impact of Newton's two major works on European intellectual life. First of all, Newtonian philosophy was neither a given system nor a definitive synthesis in natural philosophy. It was rather a multifaceted current shaped by the interpretations of Newton's works and, to a significant degree, by the adaptations of these works to various intellectual environments all over the European continent. Moreover, throughout the eighteenth century "Newtonianism" meant much more than a physical theory. It was an amalgam of scientific, political, and religious ideas, which only partially went back to Newton's original works. It was quite common for people who endorsed Newtonian philosophy to have only a vague idea of his mathematical and experimental investigations. Nevertheless, Newton became something of an authority people drew upon in order to resolve matters concerning not only nature's interpretation but also the conduct of man, the function of the state, and the doctrines of religion. Thus, in what follows we will briefly examine the many aspects of Newtonianism in a variety of intellectual contexts that assigned an accordingly variable meaning to the term.

The author of the aforementioned article in the *Encyclopédie* was Jean Le Rond d'Alembert. Being one of the protagonists in the developments that took place in the field of Newtonian natural philosophy in the mid-eighteenth century, he was well aware of the inadequacy of a general definition of Newtonianism. Hence, after the short descriptive definition he gave in the opening of the article, he immediately proceeded with the delineation of a broad spectrum of notions and practices that contributed to the formation of this intellectual current. Some authors, he notes, perceive Newtonian philosophy as a version of "corpuscular philosophy," enriched and corrected by the discoveries of Newton. In this sense, Newtonian philosophy is nothing else than a new philosophy, distinct from the Cartesian, the peripatetic, and the other ancient philosophies of the body. Others perceive Newtonian philosophy as the method Newton employs in his philosophy. This method consists in deriving conclusions directly from the phenomena, without feigning hypotheses, in starting from simple principles, in deducing the primary laws of nature from a small number of selected phenomena, and in using these laws in order to explain all the other natural effects. In this sense, Newtonian philosophy is nothing else than "experimental physics," opposing to the ancient philosophy of the body. Others perceive Newtonian philosophy as the branch of philosophy that examines natural bodies mathematically and applies geometry

and mechanics in the resolution of the respective problems. In this sense, Newtonian philosophy is nothing else than "mechanical and mathematical philosophy." It is clear, thus, that for d'Alembert and his contemporaries, even in the narrow field of natural philosophy Newtonianism means at least three different things: a new philosophy of body, experimental philosophy, and rational mechanics. In fact, all these philosophical and mathematical traditions have a bearing on Newton's own work and mark the distinctive research and philosophical directions that stem from the various pieces of the Newtonian synthesis.

The Philosophy of Body

The "philosophy of body" was deemed a crucial branch of philosophy in the eighteenth century dealing with the nature of matter. According to the traditional Cartesian view, the only essential property of a material body was extension. Figure, position, and motion were only "modes of existence" of an extended being. As a result, all natural effects should be processed on the basis of changes that occur in the shape, the relative positioning, and the motion of the bodies or of their parts. A significant advantage of this approach, according to the proponents of Cartesian philosophy, was that it made clear the distinction between the material agent of natural phenomena and the external cum immaterial causes of motion. This way it was made possible to disengage material bodies from the notorious "occult qualities" they inherited from Renaissance and some aspects of ancient philosophy.

Newtonianism brought about two important transformations to this view: Firstly, it maintained the implicitly theological idea that it is in principle impossible for people to grasp all the qualities of natural bodies. Thus, not only is extension not a unique essential quality of material bodies, but also the few other qualities we are able to know are but a subtotal of the qualities God may have provided the bodies with. Almost all the followers of Newtonian philosophy subscribed to this voluntaristic view of the divine design. Voltaire, Willem Jacob 'sGravesande (1688–1742), and Petrus van Musschenbroek (1692–1761)—to mention only the most active of them—insisted on the constitutional inability of human beings to penetrate God's will so as to acquire a definitive knowledge of the nature of material bodies.

The second transformation has to do with a new addition to the list of attributes of natural body, namely the force of attraction. According to the definition of Musschenbroek,

those things which we find to be in all bodies, we call their attributes. . . . Among these attributes there are some, which can never be intended or remitted, and others, which are capable of intension and remission. The former are extension, solidity, inactivity, mobility, a capacity of being at rest or having a figure. The latter are gravity and the power of attraction. (Musschenbroek, p. 10)

It is true that in the course of time, this addition gave much trouble to the proponents of Newtonian philosophy. Even in the early eighteenth century, it was not clear whether attraction was an inherent active principle of the matter, or a force transmitted through an ethereal substance filling the whole universe. As a result, the supporters of this view were accused of reverting to the "occult qualities," which had been banished from philosophy thanks to Cartesian philosophy. Concerning this issue, the Newtonians attempted to articulate a moderate philosophical thesis maintaining that attraction was simply a force of unknown origin that dominated the interactions between material bodies:

> And lest any one should think, because we do not assign the Cause of the abovemention'd attracting and repelling Forces, that they too are to be reckon'd among the Occult Qualities: We shall say, with the great Newton, we do not consider those Principles, as Occult Qualities, which are imagin'd to arise from the specifick Forms of Things; but as the universal Laws of Nature, by which Things themselves are form'd; for the Phaenomena of Nature shew us, that such Principles do really exist, tho' no one hath explain'd yet what are the Causes of them. ('sGravesande, p. 24)

Concerning the idea that attraction might be an inherent quality of matter, however, things were more troublesome. Such an interpretation of Newtonian dynamics by some supporters of Spinozistic philosophy, like John Toland (1670–1722), favored materialism, which was much repudiated by the "orthodox" Newtonians, as we shall see below.

Experimental Philosophy

The second field where the contribution of Newtonian philosophy was considered decisive was "experimental philosophy." Newton applied two new principles in this field. Both of them were an outcome of the aforementioned methodological approach he developed in the *Opticks* and the accompanying "queries."

The first principle was that the only safe way to derive natural laws from the phenomena is to proceed inductively. Hypotheses have no place in this process. Moreover, sticking to this methodological commitment is the only way to protect ourselves from producing natural interpretations built upon "chimerical" suppositions, as was actually the case with Cartesian natural philosophy. "Analysis" (or resolution), as opposed to "Synthesis" (or composition), comprised the core of this method. According to extreme advocates of analytical method, like Abbé Étienne Bonnot de Condillac (1714–1780), analysis was the only correct method of reasoning, because it was taught to humans by nature herself. As a result, even composition would lose its significance: The demonstration of every proposition ought to go over the path of discovery; and the only due method to do so was analysis, not synthesis. It is true that the pronouncement of analytical method has been the source of much confusion, since it has been read by many Newtonians and, evidently, by Newton himself, as if it applies equally to mathematics and to experimental philosophy. On the other hand, however, this same aspect of Newtonian philosophy epitomized the anti-Cartesian stance of many

eighteenth-century scholars and became a cornerstone of the natural theology of the time.

The second element Newton introduced to his contemporary experimental philosophy was the quantitative principle. Some fifty years after the first edition of the *Opticks,* d'Alembert described experiments as processes that aim at intentionally producing new phenomena in order to force nature to disclose her hidden principles. The man who had brought experimental philosophy to its current state was Newton. He had done so by introducing geometry into physics and by unifying experimental practice with mathematical techniques. Thus, he achieved an exact, scrupulous, and innovative science. The object of this science was the study of the general qualities of bodies; observation might help us perceive these properties superficially, but only experiment could bring them forth in a precise and measurable manner. The outcome of this process was the formulation of general quantitative laws, especially for those natural phenomena that were perpetually repeated without making evident their causes or the principles that governed their succession. This same perception, however, was also the limit of Newtonian experimental philosophy: Although Newtonian method was considered the key to unlocking the secrets of nature, from the moment the fundamental laws had become known—as most philosophers believed, in the mid-eighteenth century—the usefulness of experimental physics was rendered limited. Any further investigation of natural effects should come under the field of "mathematical sciences," that is, rational mechanics.

Rational Mechanics

Rational mechanics was, indeed, the third field where the Newtonian legacy was of major importance. In the seventeenth century, the term *mechanics* had a double meaning. In his preface to the *Principia,* Newton made a clear-cut dichotomy between "practical mechanics" and "rational mechanics." The former referred to all manual arts people used to practice in varying degrees of exactness. Practical mechanics was closely related to geometry, for geometry "is nothing other than that part of universal mechanics which reduces the art of measuring to exact propositions and demonstrations." However, this was not the kind of mechanics Newton wanted to deal with. "Since the manual arts are applied especially to making bodies move, geometry is commonly used in reference to magnitude, and mechanics in reference to motion. In this sense, rational mechanics will be the science, expressed in exact propositions and demonstrations, of the motions that result from any forces whatever and of the forces that are required for any motions whatever" (Cohen and Whitman, p. 382). Half a century after the publication of the *Principia,* rational mechanics was a well-established branch of Newtonian physics, clearly distinguished from other aspects of natural investigation. A standard definition of the term implied three significant features:

- Rational mechanics was the mathematical study of motions generated from specific forces as distinguished from statics, which examined the forces of a system being in equilibrium.

- The mathematical analysis employed in rational mechanics should be able to represent the generation of the trajectories of moving bodies as distinguished from geometry, which sufficed only for the description of static curves.

- The current formulation of rational mechanics was based on the *Principia,* as opposed to practical mechanics, which originated in classical and Hellenistic antiquity.

The major contribution of Newton to the establishment of modern rational mechanics was threefold. First, he introduced the notion of attractive force as a dynamic factor of motion. He did so by mathematically constructing the modus operandi of a centripetal force acting as the inverse square of distance; subsequently, he assigned it a natural status by unifying terrestrial and celestial physics on the basis of attraction. His second contribution was that he clearly showed the limits of Euclidean geometry as far as the problems of motion were concerned. Although he himself did not totally reject Euclidean geometry when he composed the *Principia,* the modification of traditional geometry he suggested there, as well as his mathematical studies on "fluxions" and "fluents," indicated that the only proper mathematical way to treat the problems of motion was infinitesimal calculus. His third contribution was the comprehensive study of celestial mechanics and the explanation of a wide range of celestial phenomena on the basis of universal attraction.

Although the last contribution established Newton as a heroic figure throughout the eighteenth century, the two former did not have an equally straightforward effect on his philosophical profile. There is no doubt that Newtonian mechanics bridged the gap between astronomy and cosmology by presenting a concise physico-mathematical model for the operation of the Keplerian laws. However, the mathematical and ontological foundations of Newton's synthesis became the object of much discussion on the part of his successors. It is somewhat ironic that the transcription of Newtonian mechanics in the language of infinitesimal calculus was carried out on the basis of the mathematical notation suggested by Leibnitz, his major philosophical opponent. In fact, it was characteristic of Newtonian mechanics throughout the eighteenth century that many of the people who undertook the further advancement of Newtonian achievements combined the legacy of the *Principia* with the philosophical and mathematical ideas of Leibniz. The incorporation of the vis viva, or living force, theory in many Newtonian treatises that circulated widely on the Continent, along with various attempts aiming to render the laws of motion compatible with the metaphysical principles of Leibniz, were two other instances of this characteristic.

The thorn of Newtonianism, however, was the ontological status of attractive force. Thus, by the mid-eighteenth century quite a few significant mathematicians, like d'Alembert and Lazare Carnot (1753–1823), insisted that the notion of force should be expelled from mechanics. Others, like Johann Bernoulli (1667–1748) and Leonard Euler (1707–1783), suggested that a dynamic factor was, indeed, necessary in mechanics, but they also tried to keep a distance from the metaphysical consequences of such an assumption. In any case,

the major pursuit of the time was the transformation of the Newtonian mechanics so that it might work exclusively on the basis of kinetic laws. This process culminated with the publication in 1788 of *Méchanique analytique.* Joseph Louis Lagrange's (1736–1813) work was entirely analytical in contrast to the method employed by Newton in the *Principia,* which was entirely geometrical. Lagrange was an admirer of Newton but he was also a disciple of d'Alembert. Thus, he shared with the latter the desire to develop a new science of mechanics that would not need the metaphysically laden concept of force. As a result, his *Méchanique analytique* drew upon d'Alembert's principle, the conservation of vis viva, and the principle of least action, none of which had a counterpart in Newton's work. Additionally, he applied his method to constrained systems of masses, rigid bodies, and continuous media, which was again a substantial departure from Newton's preoccupation with the legitimization of centripetal force acting at a distance.

Religion and Politics

Newton was not only a natural philosopher and Newtonianism was not only a scientific theory. Newton was also a pious Christian and an active theologian. Newtonianism, on the other hand, besides its scientific content or because of it, was gradually identified with the rise of a Whig oligarchy and with the new balance of power that resulted from the Revolution of 1687–1689 in England. Thus, soon after the publication of Newton's two major works, Newtonianism became the cornerstone of a new intellectual program that affected significantly the political and theological trends of the time. The people who set out this program in England were Newton's friends and supporters, including Richard Bentley, Samuel Clarke, William Whiston, John Harris, William Derham, and Jean Desaguliers. They actively propagandized the idea that Newton's intellectual achievements provided a perfect model for social order, political harmony, and liberal but orthodox Christianity. Although the promotion of this aspect of Newtonianism employed the technical achievements of Newtonian natural philosophy, the discourse built on this basis was not technical in itself. It was primarily through the Boyle lectures (a series of lectures established in Robert Boyle's will to defend Christian orthodoxy against the various forms of atheism) that Newton's followers unfolded the ideological implications of Newtonian science and turned it into a component of moderate Enlightenment.

One major problem with Newtonian philosophy was that it was used by both freethinkers and its religious-minded supporters. The former adopted the mathematical and experimental method as a clue that provided a liberal spirit in the investigation of the natural world; the latter, in addition to this, championed the moral and metaphysical implications of Newton's thought to wage war against pure rationalists and the various representatives of "irreligious pluralism." The other major problem, however, was that in the course of this confrontation, the Newtonian philosophy gave rise to a "heretic" approach to Christian theology, which was much denounced by the official Anglican Church.

Freethinkers and materialists of the time picked up those elements of Newtonian philosophy that fitted their perception of nature. The doctrine of universal gravity was of prominent importance to this process of adaptation. People with a preference for Spinozistic philosophy, like John Toland, gladly adopted this principle, but they suggested that one should perceive gravity as inherent to matter. Thus, in the hands of freethinkers, the power of gravity provided another evidence that matter is inherently active and offered further support to a purely naturalistic explanation of the universe, devoid of supernatural agencies and occult qualities.

In this atmosphere, even Newton himself was credited with potential atheism. Quite a few Christian thinkers held him responsible for the "misinterpretations" of his theories that resulted in the rejection of divine providence. They cautioned that despite the obvious usefulness of modern science, one should not confuse human knowledge with absolute truth, since the latter becomes known only through revelation. Other thinkers, however, believed not only that Newton's achievements were in accordance to Christian faith, but also that if the new theories were seen in their proper perspective, they would enhance the belief in a universe created and governed by God. Thus, Samuel Clarke (1675–1729), in order to fight Toland's views on the inherently active character of matter, drew upon Newton's argument about the reality of empty space. In his Boyle lectures of 1704 he argued that according to Newton's own demonstration, the existence of a void space is a necessary consequence of the existence of gravitation. And this void space is, of course, the most clear demonstration that the existence of matter is not necessary.

Clarke's belief in the existence of an empty space turned out to be decisive to his metaphysical investigations. This belief was firmly based on the notions of absolute space and time introduced by Newton in the scholium to Definition VIII of the *Principia*. Newton had stressed that only absolute space and time are real and Clarke extended this thought by stating that they are "affections which belong, and in the order of our Thoughts are antecedently necessary, to the Existence of all Things." Space was not a substance in its own right, but from the fact that it is necessarily existent, Clarke inferred that it must be a property of God. This conclusion provided a decisive argument for the necessity of a universal self-existent Being whose attributes are eternity, infinity, and unity. Clarke was well aware, however, that at the theological level there was a potential conflict between the doctrine of Trinity and the view of God's unity that ensued from the notion of absolute space. Although his initial intention was to fight Toland's idea that both God and matter could be considered self-existent principles, in the course of the debate he came to entertain serious doubts about the validity of the doctrine of Trinity. Thus, what initially was an argument against materialism led him to a radical reinterpretation of the Bible in favor of Divine unity. By 1711, in the third edition of his Boyle lectures, Clarke had made this interpretation quite explicit, and one year later he culminated his scriptural investigations with the publication of the *Scripture-Doctrine of the Trinity*. The outcome of his analysis confirmed the distinction between the attributes of God and those of the Son; the former belonged to the eternal being and thus were absolute, whereas the latter belonged to a product of the divine will, and therefore were relative.

Newtonian philosophy found itself in the basis of the heterodox theology suggested by Clarke. It is now well-known that Newton himself was also an anti-Trinitarian. William Whiston, another disciple of Newton, publicly supported the same belief at the expense of his academic career. In the uncertain atmosphere of postrevolutionary England, all these manifestations of heterodoxy could not escape the attention of those who defended religious "orthodoxy" and a certain aspect of social order. As a result, Newtonianism was engaged in the political debate of the time. The degree to which the basic concepts of the Newtonian natural philosophy became acceptable by various groups of English society depended on the political and religious affiliations of these groups. The fact that Newtonianism might be viewed as a faction in philosophy caused a major discomfort to those who held "Tory sensibilities." Political factionalism of the seventeenth century was deemed one of the factors that subverted the political basis of the Stuart monarchy. In this sense, the Newtonian philosophy represented much more than a new trend in the investigation of nature: for a significant part of the English society it symbolized potential social disorder, and Newton was largely held responsible for this. Therefore, words like *attraction* and *inertia*, as well as methodological commitments like experimentalism and the mathematical representation of nature, became part of a polemic.

This was not the case with another aspect of Newtonianism that prevailed on the Continent during the eighteenth century, namely Voltaire's Newtonianism. It took nearly fifty years for the Newtonian worldview to find its first devoted advocates in France. Pierre Louis Moreau de Maupertuis (1698–1759) was the first who pleaded with his countrymen not to dismiss unwisely the exegetical power of attraction. Subsequently, Voltaire, convinced by Maupertuis's assurance about the worth of Newton's synthesis, launched a systematic attempt to familiarize the French educated public with the new natural philosophy. Inevitably, the propaganda for the Newtonian system had to go hand in hand with the undermining of the Cartesian tradition. The French public recognized numerous defects in Descartes's natural philosophy but they believed that an advancement in philosophy would correct these errors and restore the primacy of Cartesian tradition; under no circumstances were they willing to cure Descartes's deficiencies by replacing his philosophy with the Newtonian synthesis. Voltaire dated the beginnings of the decline of the "chimerical philosophy" of Descartes in France to 1730. The main objective of his own attack was to secure Newton's primacy on the basis of the superiority of his analytical method: Newton was superior to Descartes because his discoveries were a product of a systematic inductive investigation of nature confirmed by geometry. Newton never mistook conjectures for truth as was, in fact, the case with Descartes.

An equally important aspect of Voltaire's undertaking was related to the theological dimension of Newtonian philosophy. Quite unexpectedly, Voltaire proclaimed the superiority of Newtonian theology over the Cartesian conception of God, whose "rational" character might seem, at first glance, more appropriate to the atmosphere of the rational Enlightenment. What basically annoyed Voltaire was the inclination of many followers of the Cartesian tradition to adopt a quasi atheist stance, in the context of which the universe was the poor product of matter and motion. In Leibnizian philosophy, the counterpart of this stance was a kind of "rational" atheism, since the principle of sufficient reason held good even for God. Newton's voluntarism was a decisive answer to these stances. The will of God was absolutely impenetrable by human intellect. The universe was not a product of natural or logical necessity but the outcome of God's unrestrained will. Fallen man had access only to the results of His choices as they were revealed by the order of universe and the laws that govern the natural phenomena.

Voltaire's interpretation of the Newtonian philosophy became popular in a great part of the European continent. The favorable attitude toward Christian faith and the countering of the Aristotelian and Cartesian dogmatism that ensued from this interpretation was an invaluable tool for those who promoted religious tolerance and moderate political reform. John Locke's survey of the limits of human knowledge served as the counterpart of this aspect of Newtonianism and comprised the basis of an intellectual current that defended freedom of thought in a variety of sociopolitical environments. As a result, experimental philosophy came to represent far more than a scientific method. It epitomized the ability of citizens to overcome the restrictions of the established authorities without disturbing the social order, to participate in the acquisition of knowledge by their own means, and to establish paradigmatic procedures of social consent that would guarantee human progress and happiness.

See also **Cartesianism; Mathematics; Mechanical Philosophy; Physics; Philosophy.**

BIBLIOGRAPHY

PRIMARY SOURCES

Algarotti, Francesco. *Sir Isaac Newton's Philosophy Explain'd for the Use of the Ladies: In Six Dialogues on Light and Colours.* Translated by Elizabeth Carter. 2 vols. in 1. London: Printed for E. Cave, 1739. First Italian edition published 1737.

Châtelet, Gabrielle-Émilie le Tonnelier de Breteuil, marquise du. *Institutions Physiques adressées à Mr. son Fils.* Amsterdam, 1742. Reprint, Hildesheim, Germany, and New York: Georg Olms Verlag, 1988. First edition published 1740.

Clarke, Samuel. *The Scripture-Doctrine of the Trinity. In three parts: Wherein all the texts in the New Testament relating to that doctrine, and the principal passages in the liturgy of the Church of England, are collected, compared, and explained.* London: Printed for James Knapton, 1712.

Cohen, I. Bernard, and Anne Whitman. *Isaac Newton, The Principia. Mathematical Principles of Natural Philosophy. A New Translation.* Berkeley and London: University of California Press, 1999. First Latin edition published 1687.

Desaguliers J. T. *The Newtonian System of the World, the Best Model of Government: An Allegorical Poem. With a Plain and Intelligible Account of the System of the World, by Way of Annotations . . . To Which is added, Cambria's Complaint Against the Intercalary Day in the Leap-Year.* Westminster: Printed by A. Campbell for J. Roberts, 1717.

Gravesande, Willem Jacob 's. *Mathematical Elements of Natural Philosophy confirm'd by experiments; or, an Introduction to Sir Isaac Newton's Philosophy.* Translated by J. T. Desaguliers. 2 vols. London: Printed for J. Senex and W. Taylor, 1720–1721. The Latin original and another English translation made by J. Keill were published in 1720.

Maclaurin, Colin. *An Account of Sir Isaac Newton's Philosophical Discoveries.* London: Printed for the author's children and sold by A. Millar and J. Nourse, 1748. Reprint, New York and London: Johnson Reprint Corporations, 1968.

Martin, B. *A panegyrick on the Newtonian philosophy: shewing the nature and dignity of the science, and its absolute necessity to the perfection of human nature; the improvement of arts and sciences, the promotion of true religion, the increase of wealth and honour, and the completion of human felicity.* London: Printed for J. Owen, J. Leake, and J. Frederick, 1749.

Musschenbroek, Petrus van. *The Elements of Natural Philosophy. Chiefly intended for the Use of Students in Universities, by Peter van Musschenbroek, M.D., Professor of Mathematicks and Philosophy in the University of Leyden. Translated from the Latin by John Colson, M.A. and F.R.S., Lucasian Professor of Mathematicks in the University of Cambridge.* 2 vols. London: Printed for J. Nourse, 1744. First Latin edition published 1734.

Newton, Isaac. *Opticks; or, A Treatise of the Reflections, Refractions, Inflections and Colours of Light.* 4th ed. London: Printed for W. Innys, 1730. Reprint, New York: Dover, 1979. First edition published 1704.

Pemberton, Henry. *A View of Sir Isaac Newton's Philosophy.* London: Printed by S. Palmer, 1728.

Toland, John. *Letters to Serena.* London: Printed by B. Lintot, 1704. Reprint, New York: Garland Publications, 1976.

Voltaire, *The Elements of Sir Isaac Newton's Philosophy. Translated from the French, revised and corrected by John Hanna, teacher of Mathematics.* London, 1738. Reprint, London: Frank Cass, 1967. First French edition published 1738.

SECONDARY SOURCES

Cohen, I. Bernard. *Franklin and Newton: An Inquiry into Speculative Newtonian Experimental Science and Franklin's Work in Electricity as an Example Thereof.* Philadelphia: The American Philosophical Society, 1956.

Dobbs, Betty Jo Teeter, and Margaret C. Jacob. *Newton and the Culture of Newtonianism.* Atlantic Highlands, N.J.: Humanities Press, 1995.

Ferrone, Vincenzo. *The Intellectual Roots of the Italian Enlightenment: Newtonian Science, Religion, and Politics in the Early Eighteenth Century.* Translated by Sue Brotherton. Atlantic Highlands, N.J.: Humanities Press, 1995. First Italian edition published 1982.

Force, James E., and Richard H. Popkin, eds. *Newton and Religion: Context, Nature, and Influence.* Dordrecht and Boston: Kluwer Academic, 1999.

Gascoigne, John. "From Bentley to the Victorians: The Rise and Fall of British Newtonian Natural Theology." *Science in Context* 2 (1988): 219–256.

Guerlac, Henry. *Newton on the Continent.* Ithaca, N.Y.: Cornell University Press, 1981.

Hankins, Thomas L. *Jean d'Alembert: Science and the Enlightenment.* Oxford: Clarendon, 1970.

Jacob, Margaret C. *The Newtonians and the English Revolution, 1689–1720.* Ithaca, N.Y.: Cornell University Press, 1976.

Rattansi, P. M. "Voltaire and the Enlightenment Image of Newton." In *History and Imagination: Essays in Honour of*

H. R. Trevor-Roper. Edited by Hugh Lloyd-Jones, Valerie Pearl, and Blaire Worden. New York: Holmes and Meier, 1982.

Rousseau G. S., and Roy Porter. *The Ferment of Knowledge: Studies in the Historiography of Eighteenth-Century Science.* Cambridge, U.K., and New York: Cambridge University Press, 1980.

Stewart, Larry. *The Rise of Public Science: Rhetoric, Technology, and Natural Philosophy in Newtonian Britain, 1660–1750.* Cambridge, U.K., and New York: Cambridge University Press, 1992.

Theerman, Paul, and Adele F. Seeff. *Action and Reaction: Proceedings of a Symposium to Commemorate the Tercentenary of Newton's* Principia. Newark: University of Delaware Press; London: Associated University Presses, 1993.

Truesdell, Clifford. "A Program toward Rediscovering the Rational Mechanics of the Age of Reason." *Archives for the History of Exact Ideas* 1 (1960): 1–36.

Manolis Patiniotis

NIHILISM.

In a history that spans more than two and a half centuries, the term *nihilism* has been employed to denote a wide range of phenomena. It has been variously used to express contempt or horror on the one side, approval and admiration on the other. In the twentieth and twenty-first centuries, it has almost always been an emotional and axiological term, frequently employed to cut off debate on a moral issue by representing a particular position as absolute, totalizing, and extreme.

Early History of the Term

The word *nihilism* is constructed from the Latin *nihil,* "nothing," and the Greek suffix *ism.* In the compendious *Historisches Wörterbuch der Philosophie* (Historical dictionary of philosophy), Wolfgang Müller-Lauter gives 1733 as the earliest known date for the occurrence of the German *Nihilismus* and notes the rise of the word *nihilisme* in France at the end of the eighteenth century.

From the late eighteenth century through the first half of the nineteenth century, nihilism followed a course that scholars have already traced in considerable detail. Enemies of German idealism threw the term at Immanuel Kant and Johann Gottlieb Fichte, for example, protesting against the emptiness of a philosophy that denies the possibility of any reliable contact with the world of things in themselves. As European thought increasingly moved toward dispassionate, secular explanations of religious belief (holding, for example, that such belief is a natural and predictable product of human consciousness or that it reflects a natural, human tendency to generate myths), those seeking to defend traditional faith increasingly leveled the charge of nihilism against secularizing thinkers. David Friedrich Strauss (1808–1874), the famed and much reviled author of *Das Leben Jesu: kritisch bearbeitet* (1835–1836; The life of Jesus: critically examined), one of the nineteenth century's many biographies of Jesus, and Ludwig Feuerbach (1804–1872), the equally noted author of the skeptical *Das Wesen des Christentums* (1845; The essence of Christianity), were both accused of propagating nihilism. Max

Stirner (pseudonym of Johann Caspar Schmidt; 1806–1856), author of the primary gospel of egoism, *Der Einzige und sein Eigentum* (1845; The ego and his own), and pre-Nietzschean messenger of the death of God, has been described as an early nihilist. All such thinkers, it was felt, had reduced to nothing (*nihil*) both faith and its transcendent object.

Nihilism in Russia and As a Russian Export

The term *nihilism* (*nigilizm* in Russian) had been used in Russia early in the nineteenth century, but it burst on the scene with particular force and with an entirely new meaning in January 1862, when Ivan Turgenev (1818–1883) published *Fathers and Sons.* Turgenev's hero, Evgeny Vasil'evich Bazarov, is a man of science, a member of the new generation who has decided that, at least in theory, nothing in the universe lies beyond the explanatory power of the empirical method. He is, in a word, a nihilist. As his callow young friend puts it to members of the older generation (the "fathers"), a nihilist is a man "who approaches everything from a critical point of view . . . who does not bow down before any authorities, who does not accept a single principle on faith, no matter how much respect might surround that principle." Bazarov dissects frogs (the better to understand human beings), denies the value of artistic expression, and is predictably flummoxed when he finds himself hopelessly in love, that is, in a condition that completely defies the very foundation of his materialist worldview.

If nihilism, as Turgenev's hero understood it, comprised both a thoroughgoing materialism and a thoroughgoing anti-aestheticism, it was already possible to find both in the apostle of the new progressive generation, Nikolai Gavrilovich Chernyshevsky (1828–1889), who would gain notoriety in 1863 as the author of the didactic novel *What Is to Be Done?* In his master's thesis, *The Aesthetic Relation of Art to Reality* (1855), Chernyshevsky had denied the existence of beauty as an autonomous quality in art, saying that beauty can be nothing more than life itself. And in *The Anthropological Principle in Philosophy* (1860), he had reduced human freedom and, for that matter, human distinctiveness, to nothing, arguing that individual freedom is an illusion as much in humanity as in the lower forms of animal life. Chernyshevsky would add a third feature to the definition of nihilism in *What Is to Be Done?* The idealized characters in his novel behave in accordance with an odd amalgam of utilitarianism and enlightened egoism, thus reducing traditional ethical values to nothing.

After the publication of *What Is to Be Done?* nihilism as a term or attitude took three principal directions in Russia. First, in literary life, it nurtured the trend toward realism. Dmitry Pisarev (1840–1868), the young critic who in a favorable review of *Fathers and Sons* helped disseminate a positive image of Turgenev's hero, took Chernyshevsky's anti-aestheticism one step farther in the 1860s, devoting a series of essays to the "destruction of aesthetics" and to the promotion of a rigidly realist style in literature. Second, in political life, the term *nihilism* came to be used, often with hostile intent, to describe a group within the revolutionary movement characterized by its unscrupulous methods and its unprincipled aims. Fyodor Dostoyevsky helped popularize this sense of *nihilism* by offering up the savage caricatures of left-wing political operatives that we see, above all, in *The Devils* (also called *The Possessed*; 1871). The chief "devil" in this book, Peter Verkhovensky, is a self-described nihilist notable for his desire to bring about terrible destruction and for his utter lack of concern about what might follow that destruction. As Peter Verkhovensky's real-life prototype, the notorious anarchist Sergei Nechaev (1847–1882), had written in the *Catechism of a Revolutionary* (1869), "The revolutionary disdains all doctrinairism and has repudiated all peaceful science. . . . He knows one science only: the science of destruction." Third, the term *nihilism* came to be used, again in political life, in a sympathetic sense to denote the Russian revolutionary movement broadly speaking. The Russian revolutionary Sergei Mikhailovich Kravchinsky (1851–1895; better known by the pseudonym Sergius Stepniak), after fleeing Russia in 1878, spent much of his life publishing—in English and Italian—apologias for the Russian liberation movement that he broadly termed *nihilism*. And the anarchists Emma Goldman (1869–1940) and Alexander Berkman (1870–1936), both Russian immigrants to the United States, used the term *nihilist* in their memoirs to refer to the heroes of the Russian revolutionary movement, heroes that had inspired them to embark on their own revolutionary careers.

Nietzsche and Nihilism

Had it not been for Friedrich Nietzsche (1844–1900), nihilism—the word and what it came to designate—would no doubt have been very different from what it in fact became. We find an enigmatic reference to "nihilism according to the Petersburg model" (an apparent reference to Turgenev) in part 5 (1887) of *The Gay Science,* but the term occurs in his published writings mostly in connection with philosophies that Nietzsche views as world- or life-denying. In *The Genealogy of Morality* (1887), for example, he offers the term *nihilism* as a synonym for *Buddhism,* meaning a renunciation of the affairs of the world. In *The Anti-Christ* (1888), nihilism is essentially synonymous with "denial of life," and Nietzsche defines pity, the root sentiment of Christianity, as "the praxis of nihilism."

The bulk of Nietzsche's comments on nihilism, however, appear in unpublished writings (the *Nachlass,* or "literary legacy") from the 1880s. It is here that Nietzsche describes nihilism as a condition in which "the highest values devaluate themselves" and in which the answer to the question "Why?" is missing. There are two possible responses to this condition, Nietzsche explains in a notebook he kept in 1887. We may rise up in strength and recognize that existing goals are no longer adequate, establishing new values in place of the older ones, or we may resign in weakness ("Buddhism," as Nietzsche puts it), thus failing to generate new values. The first response is called "active nihilism," the second "passive nihilism."

There has been some debate over the years about whether Nietzsche himself was a nihilist. The debate is misguided. A cursory reading of what Nietzsche says on the subject shows that for him nihilism is alternately a lamentable and a potentially fruitful condition, but in either case a temporary one. Anyone inclined to construe the proclamation that God is dead as an expression of nihilism should remember that Nietzsche declared the religion whose God was allegedly dead to be itself a form of nihilism. Nietzsche's true legacy was the association

Conspiracy in Russia: A Nihilist Meeting Surprised. **Illustration, 1880.** In late nineteenth-century Russia, *nihilism* was often used as a pejorative term meant to characterize certain left-wing radicals as dangerous and amoral, but supporters appropriated the same term to refer to the Russian revolutionary movement in a positive fashion. © BETTMANN/CORBIS

of nihilism with values (their absence, their rejection, their synthesis). Future social commentators who invoke the term *nihilism* to mourn the loss of traditional morality may blame or not blame Nietzsche; what they wittingly or unwittingly owe him is a definition that is at least implicit in what they say.

Nihilism and the Twentieth Century's Ills

From 1936 to 1946, Martin Heidegger (1889–1976) wrote the component parts of what became a two-volume study of Nietzsche. A simple glance at the chapter and subchapter headings will show to what extent nihilism, in Heidegger's eyes, was fundamental to Nietzsche's thinking. World War II and the period immediately preceding it were an appropriate backdrop for Heidegger's sense that we must view Nietzsche's nihilism in the broader context of what he calls "the end of metaphysics" in Europe. He defines this end as "the beginning of a taking-seriously of that 'event,' 'God is dead.'" As Heidegger sees it, nihilism is one of five "principal headings" (*Haupttitel*) in Nietzsche's thought, the other four (with which it is inseparably connected) being the revaluation of all prior values, the will to power, the eternal recurrence of the same, and the superman. If Heidegger's comments on Nietzsche's nihilism are partly a comment on the contemporary European

> Listening to my teacher revived the ghastly sight: the bleeding body, the piercing shrieks, the distorted faces of the *gendarmes,* the knouts whistling in the air and coming down with a sharp hissing upon the half-naked man. Whatever doubts about the Nihilists I had left from my childhood impressions now disappeared. They became to me heroes and martyrs, henceforth my guiding stars.
>
> SOURCE: Emma Goldman, in *Living My Life* (1931), on learning of the flogging of peasants in Russia.

situation, they are also partly a comment on his own earlier work. In his chapter on the five principal headings, for example, Heidegger defines what he calls Nietzsche's "classical nihilism" as "that bringing-to-completion of nihilism in which nihilism considers itself to be released from the necessity of thinking precisely that which its essence constitutes: nihil, nothing—as the veil of the truth of the Being of that-which-is [*des Seins des Seienden*]." A passage like this is probably helpful more to the student of Heidegger's *Being and Time* (1926) than to the student of nihilism.

World War II and the entire history of totalitarianism in the first half of the twentieth century provoked one of the most forceful uses of *nihilism* as a moral and political term. In 1951, Albert Camus (1913–1960) published *L'homme révolté* (Man in revolt; translated into English as *The Rebel*). As Camus put it in the first few pages of his book, "If our age easily allows that murder can have its justifications, it is because of that indifference to life that is the mark of nihilism." The central question becomes whether it is possible to offer a rational justification for murder, as is done in this "age of ideologies." Nihilism has to do with values, as it did for Nietzsche. When Camus comes to show the inner contradiction in "the absurd" (his term for the attitude born of nihilism or "absolute negation"), he has this to say: The absurd is a contradiction "because it excludes value judgments while still wishing to preserve life, whereas to live is itself a value judgment. To breathe is to judge." One might argue that this position represents a petitio principii (begging the question), but even so, it is obvious that, to Camus, it serves as a palliative in a world still reeling from the Stalinist purges and the horrors of the Holocaust.

Outside Russian revolutionary circles, *nihilism* has been a term whose alleged exponents rarely embrace it, particularly because it is seldom used favorably. Some scholars have attempted to classify it into several subtypes. Donald A. Crosby, in *The Specter of the Absurd,* sees five types of nihilism: political (essentially the Russian revolutionary sort), moral (in which all moral judgments are rejected as individual or arbitrary), epistemological (in which all truth claims are seen as purely relative), cosmic (in which the cosmos is seen as meaningless), and existential (in which human existence is seen as pointless). Karen L. Carr, in *The Banalization of Nihilism,* proposes a similar taxonomy. In her view, there are five types of nihilism: epistemological ("the denial of the possibility of knowledge"), alethiological ("the denial of the reality of truth"), metaphysical ("the denial of an independently existing world"), ethical ("the denial of the reality of moral or ethical values"), and existential or axiological ("the feeling of emptiness and pointlessness that follows from the judgment, 'Life has no meaning'").

With categories as broad as these, nihilism can be applied to a host of phenomena associated generally with a loss of values or centeredness. One might even say that nihilism as a label became so popular in the second half of the twentieth century that it was often left unspoken. A famous issue of *Time* magazine in 1966 posed the question "Is God Dead?" in stark red letters against a black background on its cover. In the article, whose immediate inspiration was the rise of the "death-of-God theology" practiced by a particular group of American theologians, John T. Elson reflected on his age as "a time of no religion," cited Søren Kierkegaard (1813–1855) and Nietzsche as prophets of modern godlessness, and offered this comment on modern art: "From the scrofulous hobos of Samuel Beckett to Antonioni's tired-blooded aristocrats, the anti-heroes of modern art endlessly suggest that waiting for God is futile, since life is without meaning."

Many, however, have not hesitated to name the illness. In 1987, for example, Allan Bloom (1930–1992) published his assault on American higher education, *The Closing of the American Mind.* He titled Part 2 of that book "Nihilism, American Style," taking aim at a pathological condition he saw in America both inside and outside the academy: "value relativism." The ultimate culprit is none other than Nietzsche. As Bloom saw it, Nietzsche's target was not only God but modern democracy. Displaying Nietzsche's own fondness for unsubstantiated, sweeping claims, Bloom declares, "Nobody really believes in anything

> Although nihilism and its accompanying existential despair are hardly anything but a pose for Americans, as the language derived from nihilism has become a part of their educations and insinuated itself into their daily lives, they pursue happiness in ways determined by that language. There is a whole arsenal of terms for talking about nothing—caring, self-fulfillment, expanding consciousness, and so on, almost indefinitely.
>
> SOURCE: Allan Bloom, *The Closing of the American Mind* (1987).

anymore, and everyone spends his life in frenzied work and frenzied play so as not to face the fact, not to look into the abyss."

The Future of Nihilism

If the word *nihilism* during the twentieth century was frequently used to denote the condition—and the accompanying feeling of despair—that arises when established and fixed moral values are missing, it is not surprising that it gained currency at a time when much of the world was dominated by ideologies that rejected such values or openly embraced destruction. At the turn of the century, a major political source of obsessive fear in Western Europe and the United States was anarchism. For much of the remainder of the century, it was fascism and communism. At the beginning of the twenty-first century, it appeared to be Islamic fundamentalism. Whatever the phrase "Islamic fundamentalism" might be construed to mean, it is safe to say that, if it indeed represents a threat to the West, it is because of values that are perceived as alien, not because of the loss of all values. At this stage, *nihilism* as a term has perhaps become a mere relic.

See also **Anarchism; Atheism; Existentialism.**

BIBLIOGRAPHY

Bloom, Allan. *The Closing of the American Mind: How Higher Education Has Failed Democracy and Impoverished the Souls of Today's Students.* New York: Simon and Schuster, 1987.

Camus, Albert. *The Rebel.* Translated by Anthony Bower. London: H. Hamilton, 1953.

Chernyshevsky, Nikolai. *What Is to Be Done?* Translated by Michael R. Katz. Ithaca, N.Y.: Cornell University Press, 1989.

Crosby, Donald A. "Nihilism." In *Routledge Encyclopedia of Philosophy,* edited by Edward Craig. Vol. 7. London and New York: Routledge, 1998.

———. *The Specter of the Absurd: Sources and Criticisms of Modern Nihilism.* Albany: State University of New York Press, 1988.

Elson, John T. "Is God Dead?" *Time* 87, no. 14 (April 1966): 82–87.

Goerdt, W. "Nihilismus." In *Historisches Wörterbuch der Philosophie,* edited by Joachim Ritter and Karlfried Gründer. Vol. 6. Basel and Stuttgart: Schwabe, 1984.

Goldman, Emma. *Living My Life.* 2 vols. New York: Knopf, 1931.

Goudsblom, Johan. *Nihilism and Culture.* Oxford: Blackwell, 1980.

Heidegger, Martin. *Nietzsche.* Pfullingen, Germany: Neske, 1961.

Nechayev, Sergei. "The Catechism of the Revolution." In *Apostles of Revolution,* by Max Nomad. Rev. ed. New York: Collier, 1961.

Nietzsche, Friedrich. *The Anti-Christ.* In *Twilight of the Idols and The Anti-Christ.* Translated by R. J. Hollingdale. New York: Penguin, 1990.

———. *The Gay Science.* Translated by Walter Kaufmann. New York: Random House, 1974.

———. *On the Genealogy of Morality.* Translated by Maudmarie Clark and Alan J. Swensen. Indianapolis, Ind.: Hackett, 1998.

Rosen, Stanley. *Nihilism: A Philosophical Essay.* New Haven, Conn., and London: Yale University Press, 1969.

Turgenev, Ivan. *Fathers and Sons.* Edited and translated by Ralph E. Matlaw. New York: Norton, 1966.

Steven Cassedy

NOMADISM.

While numerous types of migrating peoples can be referred to as *nomads,* this entry focuses on *pastoral nomadism,* defined as human cultures that depend solely or primarily on herds of domesticated animals. People in these cultures as a result are required to relocate their homes to new pastures on a regular basis in order to sustain these herds— what anthropologists call *transhumance.* Such nomads are historically represented in three significant regions, all of which are characterized by sufficient grass for animals but insufficient rain and soil quality for sustained agriculture. These regions are Sudanic and East Africa, where herds consisted primarily of cattle and camels; Arabia, southwest Asia, and the Iranian plateau, with herds of camels, sheep, and goats; and the vast steppe region of Central Eurasia, famous for herds of horses.

Nomadic Society and Culture

The necessity of regular migration shapes almost all aspects of nomadic society and culture. While often seen by outsiders as "wandering," the seasonal migrations of nomadic herdsmen are generally over fixed routes traveling between established pastures and water resources. These migrations begin in spring, as adequate rainfall or snowmelt (or both) open up additional pasturelands. In Central Eurasia, the general pattern was for nomads to move their herds northward as much as 500 miles as the weather warmed, and then to reverse course and work their way south as temperatures cooled. In other areas, nomads covered shorter distances, often following circular routes, or shifting from lower altitudes to higher pastures in mountainous regions. During these migrations the nomad's animals were vulnerable to dramatic shifts in climate, including droughts and harsh winter freezes, as well as disease. Since they depended on their herds for survival, any significant loss of animals could spell disaster for the nomads themselves.

Socially and politically, most nomadic peoples have been organized according to kinship structures, which generally include legends of origin tracing all members of a particular group to a common ancestor. However, as more recent scholarship has demonstrated, historically these kinship ties have incorporated an element of flexibility, with individuals and even larger groups changing clans due to conflicts and other crisis events. Still, the dominant pattern has been to maintain tight bonds of family loyalty, tested and reaffirmed during economic crisis or during feuds with outsiders. Thus the famous cliché of both scholars and tribesmen themselves: "Me against my brothers; my brothers and me against our cousins; my brothers, cousins, and me against the world." It is this aspect of nomadic life that was emphasized by the great Muslim social historian Ibn Khaldun (1332–1406) in his discussion of *'asabiyya* or "group feeling," which he saw as key to the Bedouins' success in warfare against outsiders.

Pastoral societies were frequently resistant to large-scale political organization, at least under a single leader, due to the availability of flight as an option when faced with authoritarian claims to power. In fact, many scholars argue that leadership among nomads was often the creation of sedentary powers who sought someone to deal with in their contacts with nomadic peoples. While the general pattern of disunity limited the political power of nomadic peoples, it also served as an

Afghan nomads near Kabul, 1997. Afghanistan is one of several countries that still maintains a substantial nomadic population in the twenty-first century. During the summer, the Afghan nomads graze their herds in the highlands, but as winter approaches they drive the livestock to the lowlands to ride out the inclement weather. AP/WIDE WORLD PHOTOS

effective political adaptation to outside threats, making it much more difficult to conquer nomadic peoples who, lacking a centralized leadership, simply broke up into ever smaller autonomous units rather than concede defeat.

Among the many distinctive features of nomadic culture, military prowess has no doubt historically attracted the most attention. While many have sought to locate the martial skills of nomads within some cultural essentialism or even genetic predisposition, it is hard to sustain the notion that nomads are more war-like than anyone else. Rather, the military advantages of nomadic populations, as shown, for example, by the horse nomads of Inner Asia, derived primarily from a nomadic lifestyle that was in many ways "paramilitary" in its orientation, including the harshness of life on the move, and constant practice in horsemanship and archery while defending one's herds. This, combined with greater mobility and speed of movement to, within, and (if necessary) away from the battlefield, gave nomadic peoples an advantage over their sedentary opponents.

Relations with Sedentarists

Much has been made historically of the so-called clash between the "desert" and the "sown," the "barbarians" versus the "civilized," exemplified even by the ancient Hebrew story of the first murder, when Cain the farmer killed Abel the herdsmen. In fact, one must beware false oppositions and note that the relations between pastoral nomads and sedentary societies have, for the most part, been peaceful, symbiotic, and mutually beneficial. Indeed, as Anatoly Khazanov argues, nomadic cultures can be seen as to some extent dependent on sedentary cultures, at least economically, especially as the former became more specialized. Throughout recorded history nomads have provided sedentary populations with items such as horses, furs, meat, and wool, in exchange for grains, luxuries, and other manufactured goods. These trade relationships have impacted the course of human history in many ways, not the least of which was the role of nomads in supporting and maintaining the so-called silk roads across Eurasia, which served as the conduit of long-distance interactions between sedentary civilizations for centuries.

Still, it is undeniable that the written historical record is dominated by numerous accounts of hostilities between nomadic and sedentary communities. This is due in part to the fact that these records generally emanate from sedentary writers seeking to portray nomads as "the other," enemies in every sense to sedentary society. At the same time, hostilities were a significant part of the relationship, often initiated by nomads for various reasons. For example, nomads sometimes struck at sedentary regions in an effort to compel the latter to engage in trade. This was particularly true along the border with China, where officials would seek to dominate their nomadic neighbors by denying them access to Chinese markets. In other instances, climatic changes in nomadic regions could lead to overpopulation or, conversely, to loss of herds, driving nomads to invade sedentary areas to fend off starvation. And finally, it is certainly the case that nomads often attacked sedentary communities to obtain loot, especially when the nomads enjoyed clear military superiority.

State and Empire Building

The most significant and lasting influence of nomadic peoples historically has come as a result of supratribal cooperation that led to the conquest of and rule over sedentary states. The two great examples of this are the Arabs from the seventh century and the Inner Asian Turco-Mongolian tribes from the tenth century. In the famous analysis of Ibn Khaldun, the Arabs were able to put aside their differences and unite due to the influence of the non-tribal principle of Islam. Once accomplished, this unified Arab force successfully spread its power from Spain to the Indus.

For the Turco-Mongolian tribes of Inner Asia, who more readily accepted the notion of hierarchical distinctions in their societies, leadership arose from charismatic tribal chiefs and their families, who were then able to form tribal confederations, sometimes numbering in the millions, and spread their power over vast regions. The quintessential example of this type of leadership was the thirteenth century Mongol chieftain Genghis (Chinggis) Khan (who ruled from 1206–1227), under whose leadership the Mongols and their Turkish confederates established the largest land empire the world has ever seen.

For both nomadic Arabs and Mongols, the irony of their success in conquering sedentary regions is that, once they began to rule, the nomads invariably became sedentary themselves, thus leading to the weakening of the state's initial military power base. Thus began the frequently discussed cycle of powerful nomadic conquerors, growing weaker in successive generations, until finally overthrown by more nomadic elements of their own people or by newly arrived nomads from outside.

Nomadism as a way of life has survived into the twenty-first century, though in much limited scope, due to the fact that nomads are still able to utilize parts of the earth's environment that are of no use to anyone else. Still, with the vastly improved technology of sedentary cultures, nomads are not likely to ever again play the central role in history that they once did.

See also **Borders, Borderlands, and Frontiers, Global; Migration; Tribalism, Middle East.**

BIBLIOGRAPHY
Barfield, Thomas J. *The Nomadic Alternative*. Englewood Cliffs, N.J.: Prentice Hall, 1993.
Khaldun, Ibn. *The Muqaddimah: An Introduction to History*. Translated by Franz Rosenthal, edited and abridged by N. J. Dawood. Princeton, N.J.: Princeton University Press, 1967.
Khazanov, Anatoly M. *Nomads and the Outside World*. 2nd ed. Madison: University of Wisconsin Press, 1994. Very rich bibliography.
Lindner, Rudi Paul. *Nomads and Ottomans in Medieval Anatolia*. Bloomington: Research Institute for Inner Asian Studies, Indiana University, 1983.

William A. Wood

NONVIOLENCE. Gandhian nonviolence (*ahimsa*) is an active civic virtue that habitually disposes individuals, social groups, and political authorities to resist violence through nonviolent means and to resolve conflicts using peaceful methods. It recognizes violence as a fact and nonviolence as a norm of social life. Its normative character arises from the assumed natural sociability of human beings. Its focal point is the good of society, which includes the good of the individual as well. It is an active virtue, inasmuch as it imposes a twofold obligation on its adherents to resist violence in all its forms and to seek effective nonviolent means to resolve conflicts. To be nonviolent in the Gandhian sense, it is not enough to refrain from committing acts of violence; it is equally necessary to take positive steps to remove the causes of violence wherever they are found, whether in the political, social, economic, or religious arena.

In the Indian context, the organized practice of this virtue is called *satyagraha*. Coined by Mohandas Karamchand Gandhi (1869–1948), this Gujarati term means "firmness in adhering to truth"—practical truth. The discovery of the truth underlying a conflict situation by the parties to the conflict is a distinguishing feature of satyagraha. The parties to a conflict are considered not so much adversaries as partners in search of a common end. There is no question of one party losing and the other party gaining. On the contrary, the goal is for both parties to make some moral advance for having engaged in a conflict.

Nonviolence may be practiced by individuals or by groups. In either case, it requires careful moral training and the use of appropriate techniques. Its practice may take several forms: noncooperation (if the offending party is the state), boycott (if the offending party is a business or corporation), strikes (in labor disputes), or protest marches, and so forth. Joan Bondurant's *Conquest of Violence* (1965) and Mark Juergensmeyer's *Gandhi's Way* (2002) give excellent accounts of the techniques that Gandhi used in the organized exercise of this virtue.

Distinctions

Gandhi makes a number of distinctions that clarify the meanings of nonviolence: active nonviolence distinguished from passive nonviolence, nonviolence as creed distinguished from nonviolence as policy, and the nonviolence of the brave distinguished from that of the morally weak.

Active nonviolence is the disposition to use not only existing nonviolent means in settling disputes, but also to invent new means if the existing ones prove to be ineffective. Its active character makes it a creative and dynamic force in the culture of a given society. Passive nonviolence, by contrast, is a private, monastic virtue whose goal is the spiritual perfection of the individual. In and of itself, it is indifferent to, if not blind to, the violence that exists in society.

Nonviolence as creed prohibits, always and everywhere, the use of violent means to resist violence. Nonviolence of the brave raises the practice of this virtue to a heroic level, making personal suffering, even death, an acceptable consequence of practicing it. Gandhi saw these two forms of nonviolence as options open only to exceptional individuals; he did not make them mandatory for those who practice nonviolence as a civic virtue.

Nonviolence as policy is preeminently a civic virtue. It too is based on a strong moral conviction against the use of violence to resolve conflicts. At the same time, it permits the lawful use of violence in certain circumstances, as, for instance, in the maintenance of public order or public welfare. Also, wars of legitimate self-defense, conducted under strict rules of natural justice and international law, do not violate the norms of nonviolence as policy. Its object is not the total elimination of violence from society—which is taken as being existentially impossible—but the gradual reduction of its frequency and intensity. It stands for a realist, not pacifist, vision of society and polity. However, its practitioners too are obliged to seek, wherever possible, nonviolent ways of resolving conflicts. Finally, the nonviolence of the morally weak is hardly a virtue, since it is practiced for reasons of expediency, not moral conviction.

The Historical Context

The origin and development of Gandhian nonviolence were owed to four forms of violence that Gandhi had to face throughout his career. They were, first, colonialism as practiced in South Africa and India at the turn of the twentieth century; second, the rise of Indian nationalism aligned to terrorism; third, the violent treatment of the untouchables by upper-class Indians; and fourth, the rise of religious extremism in India.

Gandhi viewed colonialism as a product of modern Western civilization (the other product being Marxism). By definition, colonialism legitimized aggressive wars of conquest and condoned the treatment of the colonized as "lesser breeds" without rights. Its twin maxims, he claimed, were "might is right" and the "survival of the fittest." The immediate context of the birth of satyagraha (1906) was Gandhi's confrontation with what was perhaps the most violent form of colonialism—that practiced in South Africa.

Although in its early years Indian nationalism adhered to liberal values, by the turn of the twentieth century an extremist faction was turning to terrorist violence as a means of ending colonialism. Terrorist secret societies, such as the Abhinav Bharat (1904) and the Anusilan Samiti (1905), had gained ground in several regions of India. Gandhi was keenly aware of the dangers that political terrorism posed for Indian society.

Although racism was part of the colonial ideology, Gandhi was appalled more by the quasi-racist treatment of India's so-called untouchables by the Indians themselves than he was by the racism of the whites against nonwhites. The eradication of this form of violence from India was one of the major objects of his nonviolent campaigns. The Vykom Satyagraha (1924–1925) was directed specifically against untouchability.

What troubled Gandhi most, however, was the rise of religious extremism in India in the first quarter of the twentieth century. Vinayak Damodar Savarkar's (1883–1966) *Hindutva*, the basic text of Hindu extremism, was published in 1923, and Abul Ala Mawdudi's (1903–1979) *Jihad*, a basic text of modern Muslim fundamentalism, was published in 1927. Both rejected Gandhi's nonviolent vision of society and polity. Gandhi's position was that religious fundamentalism was corrupting both Hinduism and Indian Islam. His philosophy of nonviolence appealed to both moderate Hindus and moderate Muslims, but failed to prevent the partition of India along religious lines.

The Intellectual Context

The ideas that shaped Gandhian nonviolence were drawn both from Western and Indian sources. The trial of Socrates as described in Plato's *Apology* had a profound impact on Gandhi. In 1908 he published a paraphrase of this work in English and Gujarati under the title *The Story of a Soldier of Truth*. Socrates was a model for all those who would resist nonviolently the violence of the state. The ethics of the Sermon on the Mount, as interpreted in Leo Tolstoy's *The Kingdom of God Is within You* (1893), had a lifelong influence on him. Another of Tolstoy's writings, *Letter to a Hindu* (1908), made Gandhi rethink the role of violence in Indian society. Tolstoy had argued that the British were able to hold India by violence because Indians themselves believed in violence as the basis of society. That is why they submitted themselves to their rajas and maharajas, and treated the untouchables with extreme cruelty. Under these circumstances, the complaints of Indians against colonial violence seemed to him to resemble the complaints of alcoholics against wine merchants. The removal of colonial violence would not solve India's problems with violence. They would be solved only if Indians made nonviolence the basis of a new India. Gandhi was so persuaded by the *Letter* that he translated and published it in both English and Gujarati.

Gandhi's study of Western jurisprudence made him a lifelong defender of the idea of the rule of law and the legitimacy of the limited, constitutional state. The fight against violence needed such a state as its ally. Here Gandhi departed from Tolstoy's radical pacifism that rejected the state as such.

John Ruskin's *Unto This Last* (1860) opened Gandhi's eyes to the hidden structures of violence in industrial capitalism. This work, too, Gandhi paraphrased and published in English and Gujarati (1908) under the title *Sarvodaya* (The welfare of all), a title that he later gave to his own economic philosophy.

Finally, there was the question of nationalism and how to free it from ethnic or religious or terrorist violence. Here he found help in the liberal nationalism of Giuseppe Mazzini, whose *An Essay on the Duties of Man*, published in 1892, became one of the recommended readings for all those who wanted to understand Gandhi's own fundamental work, *Hind Swaraj* (1909).

However, it was Indian philosophical thought that helped Gandhi to integrate the ideas he had absorbed from the West. Here three philosophical traditions were significant. The first was the pacifist tradition of Jainism, as interpreted by Rajchand—businessman, poet and mystic, and a personal friend. His advice was that a nonviolent way of life was possible only if one withdrew from politics and concentrated all one's energies on achieving inner harmony. Gandhi accepted the point about inner harmony but rejected the idea of withdrawing from politics. On the contrary, he sought to link the quest for inner harmony with that for outer harmony in society and polity.

The philosophy of yoga as expounded in the classic text, the *Yogasutra* of Patanjali, had also impressed Gandhi greatly. Like Jainism, it too believed in the incompatibility between maintaining inner harmony and engaging in active politics. However, it had recommended five moral virtues as being necessary for inner harmony. Nonviolence was one of them; the other four were truthfulness, abstention from theft, celibacy, and moderation in the use of material possessions. Gandhi gladly incorporated nonviolence into his ethical system—with one modification. He modified it from being a moral virtue into a civic virtue, thereby making it appropriate for political action.

But the philosophy that influenced him most was that of the *Bhagavad Gita*. He interpreted it as teaching the negative lesson of the futility of war. On the positive side, he interpreted it as teaching that the good life called for the disinterested service of one's fellow human beings, sustained by a deep love of God. Obstacles to the good life came from violence and the undisciplined state of the passions, notably anger, hatred, greed, and lust. Self-discipline therefore was the psychological key to nonviolence.

The philosophical anthropology underlying Gandhi's theory of nonviolence is adapted from that underlying the *Bhagavad Gita*. Humans are composites of body and soul (atman). As such, body force and soul force were both seen as active in human affairs—the first as a fact and the second as a norm. The body was the source of violence and the passions; the soul was the source of sociability and of the knowledge of good and evil. It was because the spiritual soul was a constitutive element of human beings that nonviolence remained the norm of their behavior. A materialistic view of human life, in Gandhi's view, could not justify, much less sustain, a nonviolent way of life.

The philosophical anthropology of the *Bhagavad Gita* also gave Gandhi's nonviolence its ethical realism. Because humans are composite beings, perfect nonviolence was possible only in the atman's disembodied state, not in its embodied state. In its embodied state, the will to live always brought with it the will to use force in legitimate self-defense. In the embodied state, one must always abstain from culpable violence—that is, offensive violence used for illegitimate gains. Defensive violence used in legitimate self-defense is not judged culpable.

Fields of Nonviolence

Although nonviolence is a universal norm, Gandhi was insightful enough to recognize that its application depended on the nature of the society (or "field," to use his terminology) in which it was to be applied. He distinguished four such fields—the family, the state, the religious community, and the community of sovereign states.

The family, or family-like communities such as the ashram, were best suited to learn the basics of nonviolence. How to treat one another with love and forbearance and how to settle disputes amicably were first learned in the family.

Historically, nonviolence had notable success in liberal states, or colonial states functioning under the supervision of a metropolitan liberal state. Also, it operated well within religions that displayed a capacity for internal self-criticism. That was why it was able to rid Hinduism of untouchability. However, it was less successful in preventing the revival of jihad in South Asia.

In the international field, Gandhian nonviolence operated *suo modo*. Gandhi's philosophy permitted sovereign states the right to use military force in legitimate self-defense. However, a commitment to nonviolence also required them to strive for progressive disarmament and to increase the effectiveness of international organizations. Never a radical pacifist, Gandhi urged sovereign states to experiment with nonmilitary ways of securing national defense such as using "armies without lethal weapons." He did not envision a warless world, but at the same time he held out the possibility of wars becoming less frequent and less destructive.

The "Vast Majority" Principle

Gandhi's thoughts on the future of nonviolence led him to realize that unless the "vast majority" of the people in a state were nonviolent, that state could not be governed nonviolently. The vast majority principle distributed the responsibility for nonviolence equally on the shoulders of the leaders and ordinary citizens; political leaders could promote nonviolence only to the extent that their own people became nonviolent. And their own people could become nonviolent if they—the people—could dismantle, through non-governmental organizations, existing structures of internal violence.

The sociological insight contained in the vast majority principle led Gandhi to write his last major thesis on nonviolence, *Constructive Programme* (1941). In it he analyzed, among other things, the structures of violence active in Indian society, and concluded that unless Hindus and Muslims in India learned to live in harmony, unless caste violence was set aside, and unless mass poverty was eliminated, there was no chance of India's becoming a nonviolent country.

A corollary of the vast majority principle is that unless a circle of sovereign states became nonviolent in the manner described above, there was no chance of their relations becoming peaceful. Gandhi's vast majority principle is reminiscent of Immanuel Kant's "republican principle," enunciated in his *Perpetual Peace* (1795).

The Impact of Nonviolence

Gandhian nonviolence has affected global culture in four ways. First, it changed for the better aspects of the political culture of particular countries. In India, for example, it influenced the manner in which colonialism was brought to an end and a new political philosophy introduced. In the United States, it had an impact on the civil rights movement led by Martin Luther King Jr.

Second, it inspired many individuals across the world to adopt active nonviolence as their own public philosophy. Those so inspired include the Dalai Lama, Lech Walesa of Poland, Lanza del Vasto of France, Aung San Suu Kyi of Myanmar (Burma), Anglican Archbishop Desmond Tutu of South Africa, Cesar Chavez of the United States, and Thomas Merton, the American Trappist monk.

Third, it contributed to the emergence of several nongovernmental organizations worldwide, among them those devoted to disarmament, economic development from below, the green movement, and the dialogue between religions.

Finally, it gave further impetus for nonviolence to become a subject of serious academic study and research in institutions of higher learning throughout the world, notably in the fields of history, sociology, religious studies, theology, and comparative political philosophy.

See also **Colonialism; Hinduism; Jainism; Peace; Resistance and Accommodation.**

BIBLIOGRAPHY

Bondurant, Joan V. *Conquest of Violence: The Gandhian Philosophy of Conflict.* Rev. ed. Berkeley: University of California Press, 1965.

Brown, Judith M. *Gandhi: Prisoner of Hope.* New Haven, Conn.: Yale University Press, 1989.

Dalton, Dennis. *Mahatma Gandhi: Nonviolent Power in Action.* New York: Columbia University Press, 1993.

Gandhi, Mohandas K. *Gandhi, an Autobiography: The Story of My Experiments with Truth.* Boston: Beacon, 1993.

———. *Hind Swaraj and Other Writings.* Edited by Anthony J. Parel. Cambridge, U.K.: Cambridge University Press, 1997. Contains the text of Gandhi's *Constructive Programme.*

———. *Satyagraha in South Africa.* Stanford, Calif.: Academic Reprints, 1954.

Juergensmeyer, Mark. *Gandhi's Way: A Handbook of Conflict Resolution.* Berkeley: University of California Press, 2002.

Merton, Thomas, ed. *Gandhi on Non-violence.* New York: New Directions, 1965.

Parekh, Bhikhu. *Gandhi.* Oxford: Oxford University Press, 1997. Past Masters series.

Terchek, Ronald J. *Gandhi: Struggling for Autonomy.* Lanham, Md.: Rowman and Littlefield, 1998.

Wolpert, Stanley. *Gandhi's Passion: The Life and Legacy of Mahatma Gandhi.* New York: Oxford University Press, 2001.

Anthony Parel

NUCLEAR AGE.

The nuclear age began in mid-July 1945 when an 18.6-kiloton nuclear bomb was detonated at the Trinity test site near Alamogordo, New Mexico. Three weeks later, on 6 August 1945, the world became aware of the existence of nuclear weapons when a U.S. B-29 bomber known as *Enola Gay* dropped a nuclear bomb on the Japanese city of Hiroshima. That was followed three days later by the dropping of another bomb on Nagasaki. The term *nuclear age* was coined almost immediately after the two bombs were used. Within days of the Nagasaki bombing, the publisher Pocket Books put out a special primer titled *The Atomic Age Opens,* edited by Gerald Wendt. The phrase *atomic age* remained more common than *nuclear age* through the mid-1950s, but *nuclear age* already enjoyed wide use in 1945. By the end of the year, it had even been inserted into the title of the second edition of a physics textbook by Harvey Brace Lemon. The title of the original edition, published in 1934, was *From Galileo to Cosmic Rays,* whereas the second edition, published in early 1946, was retitled *From Galileo to the Nuclear Age.*

Since those early days, the term *nuclear age* has been incorporated into almost every language as a designation for the international security system that has existed since 1945. Implicit in the term is the notion that the advent of nuclear weapons marked a far-reaching change from the system that existed until 1945. Although scholars have differed in their estimations of the extent to which the system has genuinely changed, few would deny that nuclear weapons have been one of the major elements in international politics since the mid-1940s.

Contending Ideas about Nuclear Weapons

The publication of a volume edited by Bernard Brodie, *The Absolute Weapon: Atomic Power and World Order,* in 1946 marked the first systematic attempt by specialists in international relations to think through the political and strategic implications of the nuclear age. Brodie and his colleagues—F. S. Dunn, P. E. Corbett, Arnold Wolfers, and W. T. R. Fox—sought to determine how warfare and international politics would be altered by nuclear weapons. Their findings prefigured many of the themes that came up over the next several decades in scholarly and official analyses of nuclear arms. Brodie argued that nuclear weapons had made total war obsolete and that U.S. military strategy from then on would have to emphasize deterrence: "Thus far the chief purpose of our military establishment has been to win wars. From now on its

chief purpose must be to avert them. It can have almost no other useful purpose" (p. 5). This view, which adumbrated the U.S. shift to a declaratory policy of "massive retaliation" in the 1950s, was broadly accepted by the other contributors. Brodie and his colleagues left no doubt that, in their view, nuclear weapons had fundamentally changed the nature of world politics and military strategy.

The Soviet Union's acquisition of nuclear weapons in 1949, and the subsequent emergence of a U.S.-Soviet nuclear standoff, seemed to strengthen Brodie's basic point. Nonetheless, from an early stage, his thesis had many detractors. Some analysts argued that Brodie failed to take account of the importance of limited wars, such as those fought in Korea and Vietnam. In two highly acclaimed books, *The Strategy of Conflict* (1960) and *Arms and Influence* (1966), Thomas Schelling elaborated the theory of what he called "compellence," that is, the use of nuclear threats (and threats of the massive use of conventional weaponry) to coerce the adversary into taking a particular course of action. Schelling contended that nuclear deterrence did not eliminate the need for U.S. policymakers to deal with contingencies short of nuclear war and to think about how to use nuclear weapons to influence political and strategic outcomes.

Schelling also argued that even in relations between the two superpowers, strategy was not obsolete in the nuclear age. One of the other purposes of his books was to develop a better strategy for great-power competition within the context of deterrence. Schelling argued that deterrence of Soviet aggression in Europe or East Asia was crucially dependent on credibility. Unless the threat of retaliation was credible, Soviet leaders would have little reason to yield during a crisis. To cope with this problem, U.S. leaders, Schelling maintained, would have to demonstrate that they were prepared to act in ways that ordinarily would seem irrational. Schelling stressed that by actively preparing to carry out "threats that leave something to chance" (the title of a chapter in *The Strategy of Conflict*), U.S. policymakers would bolster their own credibility and thereby reduce the chance that they would ever be forced to make good on those threats.

Other analysts went a good deal further than Schelling in contesting Brodie's views about nuclear weapons. Strategic analysts such as Herman Kahn in the 1960s and Colin Gray in the 1970s and 1980s rejected the whole notion of an "absolute weapon." Kahn and Gray contended that even large-scale nuclear warfare between the two superpowers was not "unthinkable." They acknowledged that nuclear weapons might induce greater caution on the part of policymakers, but they stressed that this did not mean that the chance of war was zero. On the contrary, Kahn and Gray argued, there was a possibility that nuclear war would break out, and therefore they believed that U.S. policymakers must be prepared to fight such a war and to win it. Gray summed up this view in an article he coauthored in 1980 with Keith Payne. The article stressed that "the United States must possess the ability to wage nuclear war rationally" and must develop "a plausible theory of how to win a war or at least insure an acceptable end to a war." Gray and Payne urged the U.S. government to "plan

Mushroom cloud caused by atomic bomb, Bikini Atoll, 1946. In the 1940s, scientists began experimenting with atomic devices—the first nuclear weapons—and the first controlled explosion took place in August, 1945, in Alamogordo, New Mexico. © CORBIS

seriously for the actual conduct of nuclear war" and to develop a strategy "to defeat the Soviet Union and do so at a cost that would not prohibit U.S. recovery." As they saw it, a combination of robust strategic anti-missile and air defenses, a comprehensive civil defense program, and a large and diverse arsenal of nuclear missiles and bombers would ensure victory.

Not surprisingly, the views expressed by Kahn and Gray proved controversial. Stanley Kubrick satirized the nuclear war-fighting school in his 1964 film *Dr. Strangelove.* (Many viewers guessed that the title character was based on Kahn, but Kubrick never confirmed this.) More seriously, critics argued that theories of victory in a large-scale nuclear war rested on untenable assumptions about nuclear weapons and strategic defense technology. In a widely cited article published in early 1982, Wolfgang Panofsky and Spurgeon Keeny maintained that a "effective protection of the population against large-scale nuclear attack is not possible" and that an exchange involving only a few thousand of the more than fifty thousand nuclear weapons deployed by the United States and the Soviet Union "could destroy most of the urban population and destroy most of the industry of both sides." Even much smaller nuclear exchanges, they added, would have "very severe consequences." Nuclear war-winning strategies, in their view, were based on "wishful thinking."

Mutual Assured Destruction

Much of the intellectual debate about the U.S.-Soviet nuclear relationship was encapsulated in the perennial controversy about what became known as Mutual Assured Destruction (MAD). The concept of MAD was first enunciated in the early 1960s when both the United States and the Soviet Union

began deploying large numbers of intercontinental-range ballistic missiles (ICBMs) armed with nuclear warheads. Defense Secretary Robert McNamara and other U.S. officials at the time argued that, in a situation of MAD, any large-scale use of nuclear weapons by either side would provoke retaliation in kind by the other side, resulting in the effective destruction of both. Under this logic, no rational leader on either side could hope to gain a meaningful advantage by starting a nuclear war, and therefore mutual deterrence would prevail. Many observers construed these statements as an accurate reflection of U.S. nuclear doctrine.

The intellectual debate about MAD often was reflected in concerns raised in public discussions and policy circles. The notion that, as Winston Churchill put it, the "safety" of each side rested on the prospect of "mutual annihilation" was a discomfiting one for many Americans. The vulnerability inherent in MAD was in contrast to the relative invulnerability that the United States had always enjoyed by virtue of its geography. The desire to move beyond MAD and restore a sense of invulnerability lay behind periodic attempts to build defenses against ICBMs and submarine-launched ballistic missiles (SLBMs) and to develop more credible nuclear warfighting strategies. The Strategic Defense Initiative (SDI) of President Ronald Reagan's administration, announced in 1983 as a program to develop a comprehensive system of protection against ICBMs and SLBMs, was explicitly justified on the ground that indefinite reliance on MAD was too perilous an option.

Critics of these attempts to move beyond MAD, including Keeny and Panofsky, focused on two basic points. First, they argued that MAD was not a mutable doctrine but was instead a codification of the underlying strategic and technical realities.

New Dictionary of the History of Ideas

In their view, MAD followed from the technical nature of nuclear missiles and the inherent vulnerability of urban populations to nuclear destruction. No plausible doctrinal or technological innovations could alter this reality. Second, they maintained that attempts to move beyond MAD were dangerous because they would create the illusion that MAD was a doctrine and could be changed. This misperception, they contended, would increase the risk of nuclear war. Keeny and Panofsky argued that if policymakers erroneously believed it was possible to fight and win a nuclear war without suffering "unacceptable damage," they might be more willing to risk the use of nuclear weapons.

Unease about MAD also led in a very different direction. From the start of the nuclear age, a relatively small but vocal group of critics insisted that the only acceptable course of action was to ban all nuclear weapons. This school of thought was especially prevalent among scientists and intellectuals associated with the *Bulletin of the Atomic Scientists,* a specialized monthly publication that became famous for its doomsday clock on the cover. In later decades, many intellectuals supporting complete nuclear disarmament became active in ban-the-bomb campaigns and the nuclear freeze movement. Jonathan Schell's best-selling *The Fate of the Earth* (1982), published at the height of the nuclear freeze movement in the early 1980s, laid out the case for the elimination of nuclear weapons. The book came under harsh criticism from many specialists on nuclear strategy and arms control, but it struck a chord with the U.S. "peace" movement and with a considerable number of ordinary Americans who were concerned about the sharp increase in U.S.-Soviet tensions in the early 1980s. Not until the Cold War drew to an end in the late 1980s and early 1990s—and Washington and Moscow agreed to much sharper reductions in their strategic nuclear arsenals—did the antinuclear weapons movement wane in influence.

Nuclear Thinking in the Post–Cold War World

After the Soviet Union disintegrated at the end of 1991, the formerly antagonistic relationship between Moscow and Washington ceased to exist. The U.S.-Soviet nuclear standoff, which had dominated strategic thinking in the nuclear age, was no longer relevant. Instead, thinking about the nuclear age shifted mainly to issues of nuclear proliferation and efforts to prevent (or dissuade) non-nuclear weapons states from acquiring nuclear arms. Although the United States and post-Soviet Russia continued to possess large numbers of nuclear-armed ICBMs that were maintained at full alert, fears of a large-scale nuclear war all but disappeared. Instead, strategic analysts worried about the possibility of nuclear terrorism and nuclear weapons programs under way in so-called rogue states like North Korea, Libya, Iran, and Iraq under Saddam Hussein.

Some analysts, such as Kenneth Waltz and Shai Feldman, had long argued that nuclear proliferation should be welcomed rather than discouraged. Waltz maintained that nuclear weapons would enable relatively weak states to deter stronger and more aggressive neighbors from attacking them, in much the same way that the United States and the Soviet Union had relied on mutual deterrence to ensure peace between them.

The "optimists" about nuclear proliferation (a label that was later attached to Waltz and others who shared his views) were never particularly numerous, however. In the post–Cold War world, the "pessimists" like Scott Sagan were far more common. In an illuminating exchange with Waltz, Sagan pointed to a number of dangers regarding potential accidents and unauthorized uses of nuclear weapons that would make nuclear war more likely, not less likely, in a proliferated world. Sagan and others also contended that nuclear proliferation would increase the risk that weapons might be diverted to terrorists.

Analysts who wanted to prevent nuclear proliferation differed in their views of how to achieve that goal. Some argued that unless the security concerns of proliferating states were allayed (or at least greatly mitigated), those states would be unlikely to forswear nuclear weapons. They cited the case of India and Pakistan, both of which openly acquired nuclear weapons in 1998 (though India had tested a nuclear bomb as far back as 1974), as an example of the pressures on states to build nuclear weapons in order to deter hostile neighbors. Analysts who subscribed to this view maintained that the best way to prevent nuclear proliferation was to address the underlying security concerns of potentially vulnerable states through international mediation. Other analysts wanted a more active policy to discourage nuclear proliferation. They advocated a "counterproliferation" strategy that would deal with regional security concerns but would also include a variety of sanctions against states that continued to pursue nuclear weapons programs. These sanctions would range from diplomatic pressure to condemnations by the UN Security Council to economic penalties and ultimately to military action. Scholars who believed that military action might, in the end, be desirable argued that Israel's successful raid in 1981 against Iraq's Osiraq nuclear plant underscored the importance of not ruling out the military option. Had Israeli jets not bombed the facility, Iraq most likely would have been able to build a nuclear weapon by the late 1980s, well before its program came under aggressive international scrutiny.

The prospect of nuclear terrorism was the other major issue of concern to specialists on nuclear weapons in the post–Cold War world. Contrary to popular wisdom, the threat of nuclear terrorism was not at all new. Concerns about the possibility that a nuclear bomb would be smuggled into a U.S. port had arisen as far back as the mid-1950s. Analysts such as Schelling, Brian Jenkins, and Paul Leventhal had written books and articles about the risk and implications of nuclear terrorism in the 1970s and 1980s. For the most part, however, the question of nuclear terrorism during the Cold War was generally overshadowed by the U.S.-Soviet nuclear standoff. Only in the post–Cold War world, when the U.S.-Soviet confrontation no longer dominated strategic thinking, did analysts devote much greater attention to the terrorist threat. This focus intensified, for understandable reasons, after the large-scale terrorist attacks on the United States on September 11, 2001.

Although experts on nuclear proliferation generally agreed that few if any terrorist groups had the wherewithal to build a nuclear weapon on their own, they warned that a weapon (or at least crucial components, including fissile material) might be furtively supplied to a terrorist group by a state like North Korea or by a group of rogue scientists. The nuclear-supply trail involving the nuclear weapons programs of both Pakistan and North Korea that came to light in 2004 reinforced these concerns. Most analysts believed that such channels could be closed through concerted international action, but they held out little hope that the risk could ever be fully eliminated. Thus, even after the Cold War ended, the perils of nuclear weapons continued to dominate thinking about the nuclear age.

See also **Peace; Technology; War.**

BIBLIOGRAPHY

Brodie, Bernard, ed., *The Absolute Weapon: Atomic Power and World Order.* New York: Harcourt Brace, 1946.

Freedman, Lawrence. *The Evolution of Nuclear Strategy.* 3rd ed. New York: Palgrave Macmillan, 2003.

Gray, Colin S. *The MX ICBM and National Security.* New York: Praeger, 1981.

Gray, Colin S., and Keith B. Payne. "Victory Is Possible." *Foreign Policy* 39 (summer 1980): 14–27.

Herring, Eric, ed. *Preventing the Use of Weapons of Mass Destruction.* London and Portland, Ore.: Frank Cass, 2000.

Jenkins, Brian M. *Will Terrorists Go Nuclear?* Discussion Paper No. 64. Santa Monica, Calif.: California Seminar on Arms Control and Foreign Policy/RAND Corporation, 1975.

Kahn, Herman. *Thinking about the Unthinkable.* New York: Horizon Press, 1962.

———. *On Thermonuclear War.* Princeton, N.J.: Princeton University Press, 1960.

Kaplan, Fred M. *The Wizards of Armageddon.* New York: Simon and Schuster, 1983.

Keeny, Spurgeon M., Jr., and Wolfgang K. H. Panofsky. "MAD versus NUTS: Can Doctrine or Weaponry Remedy the Mutual Hostage Relationship of the Two Superpowers?" *Foreign Affairs* 60, no. 2 (winter 1981–1982): 287–304.

Sagan, Scott D., and Kenneth N. Waltz. *The Spread of Nuclear Weapons: A Debate.* New York: Norton, 1995.

Schelling, Thomas C. *Arms and Influence.* New Haven, Conn.: Yale University Press, 1966.

———. *The Strategy of Conflict.* Cambridge, Mass.: Harvard University Press, 1960.

Waltz, Kenneth N. *The Spread of Nuclear Weapons: More May Be Better.* London: International Institute for Strategic Studies, 1981.

Mark Kramer

NUDE, THE.   Although the English word *nude* is derived from the Latin *nudus* meaning "naked," "bare," it connotes, especially in such phrases as "in the nude" or "The Nude," more than a state of undress; rather it indicates a work of art, a cultural convention, and a socioreligious attitude. The term *The Nude* signifies a Western cultural ideology while nudity is a universal human condition.

The British painter Walter Sickert (1860–1942) is credited with the first art critical discussion of "The Nude" as a formal convention of academic art (1910). Formal academic analyses were initiated with Kenneth Clark's 1953 Mellon Lectures in the Fine Arts on the meaning and motif of "The Nude" in Western art that he subtitled "a study in ideal form." Clark described the distinction between "The Nude" and "the naked" as a cultural attitude predicated on political, religious, and societal perceptions of the body and human sexuality. The classical Greek was nude while the medieval Christian was naked. The former recognized the body as an embodiment of sacred energy and form interdependent with philosophic and cultural attitudes toward the individual person, human dignity, and creativity. The latter was premised upon the recognition of human finitude and the sinful state in which Christians lived, and thereby affected Christian perceptions of the individual person, human dignity, and creativity.

As a state of both physical nakedness and spiritual power, the nude figure is an elemental component of the cultural legacy of human civilization. The vast differences in the spirit and the reception of both the human body and the meaning of nudity from the prehistoric to modern, from East to West, deepens the layers of cultural accumulations. Nude figures are found in gendered formations of both male and female in the guises of divinities, heroes, warriors, or mythological beings. This iconology is bequeathed visually from Egyptian monuments, Khajuraho reliefs, Cypriote statues, Indian and Persian miniatures, and classical sculptures.

"The Nude" as defined by Clark is not a proper iconographic category, although it appears in Western art both in religious iconography and in a variety of artistic topoi ranging from historical, mythological, biblical, allegorical, narrative, and pornographic themes to genre scenes. "The Nude," however, is a Western type relating concepts of the body, philosophy, religions, and aesthetics that begin with the recognition of "The Nude" as an aesthetic object and as "high art" first in classical Greece and then in the Renaissance.

Portrayals of the human figure as incarnation or manifestation of the deity is a fundamental connector through the arts and religious values of East and West. The Western disposition is premised upon the classical Greek tenet that the idealized perfection of the physical denotes the model of divine beauty. The Eastern classification proceeds from the Indian principle that the creation of supernatural beauty is through abstractions of the physical body. Nonetheless, there are regional interpretations on the meaning of nudity throughout Eastern and Western cultures. In India, nudity suggests simultaneously the sensuality of fertility spirits (female nudity) and supreme yogic control (male nudity); whereas the human body is a didactic illustration of moral and ethical teachings in the Far East, especially with the advent of Confucian ethics.

The decision to depict nudity whether for a male or a female figure is as much a decision of aesthetic and artistic appropriateness as it is a moral issue. For example, many world religions identify those believers who celebrate religious rituals and ceremonies "sky clad," that is, naked. Among Tantrics, the state of being "sky clad" signifies the state of being without rank, caste, or socioeconomic class. For Jains, because the Jain path to enlightenment is through extreme asceticism, there was a conflict between nudity as a state of purity and the impurity of women. Nudity represented the highest ideal of nonattachment; however, the question was whether women could attain enlightenment and salvation. By 80 C.E., Jainism was divided into two factions over the relationship between nudity, salvation, and women. Digambara advocated the necessity of nudity and extreme asceticism as the path to salvation; and that, because female nudity was unacceptable, there was no salvation for women. Shvetambara recognized that ascetic nudity was not the only salvific path, thereby affirming the possibility of female enlightenment.

Other religious traditions, whether premised on mythology, revelation, or scriptures, identified female nudity as a positive value. For example, "the goddess" was identified as dwelling in her flesh, not in her garments. Her sacred power, as with that of mortal women, was released by a state of nudity, whereas the magic power of gods and men required the condition of being fully clothed as self-definition was concretized in uniforms, badges, and decorations of rank. Body types, attitudes toward the body, and the artistic renderings of the human form reflected religious and societal values as much

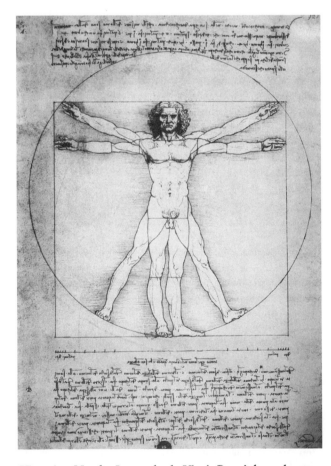

***Vitruvian Man* by Leonardo da Vinci. Pen, ink, and watercolor.** The classical perspective on the nude, said to be represented by da Vinci's 1492 sketch, held that man symbolized the harmony of God's universe and a kind of divine beauty and integrity. © CORBIS

as the decision to depict an individual as an identifiable person or as simply a male or female type.

There are four principal philosophic perspectives on "The Nude" in Western culture. The classical perspective is established from the Platonic mathematical foundation of all forms in combination with the Neoplatonic conviction that the human was a symbol of the harmonious arrangement of the universe as a reflection of God. Christianity reversed this view in response to the theological attitudes toward human fallibility, finitude, and original sin as pronounced by Augustine of Hippo (354–430) and Jerome (c. 347–?420). Renaissance philosophers retrieved and reframed the classical definition as epitomized by Leonardo da Vinci (1452–1519), who identified "Man as the measure of the Universe" and envisioned "The Nude" in his *Vitruvian Man* (1492; Gallerie dell' Accademia, Venice). The modern position is predicated on the liberation of "The Nude" from the boundaries of mythology and religion during the Enlightenment, and finds its fullest expression in Gustave Courbet's *The Origin of the World* (1866; Musée D'Orsay, Paris).

Survey in Western Culture

Western art and culture have premised "The Nude" upon the classical Greek legacy and Christian transformations until the mid-nineteenth century when the philosophy and political revolution of the Enlightenment bore fruit in realism and the secularization of twentieth-century art movements. The Greek "cult of the nude" was imbued with cultural, philosophic, and religious meaning. Beyond the ideal of divine beauty was the Greek philosophy of freedom and dignity of the individual—nudity was synonymous with integrity. Legendary heroes, ideal figures, mythological personalities, and triumphant warriors were characterized as being "in the nude." As the first flowering of "The Nude," Greek art praised what it knew in daily life: the handsome beauty of the male form. Public nudity was a normative condition for men who participated in athletic competitions, exercised at the gymnasium, and partook of the public baths. The Greek ideal of a sound mind and a healthy body was attained in the gymnasium, which was simultaneously a center for education and athletics; all the academies of philosophy had their centers in a gymnasium. Clothes were removed in order to exercise and to be able to think without restraints. The Greek root of gymnasium is *gumnos,* "to be naked, nude, or bare." Nudity was a condition of physical and mental freedom.

With the advent of Christianity, "The Nude" and the idea of nudity were transformed into reminders of human finitude and guilt, and of the sinful state, especially for women. Augustine of Hippo and Jerome, among other early Church fathers, decried the classical glorification of the human body and denounced the connection between "The Nude" and human sexuality, thereby transmogrifying nudity from a condition of innocence, idealism, and integrity into one of guilt, materialism, and vice.

Descriptions and depictions of "The Nude" in Christian iconography were restricted to scriptural narratives. The biblical narratives recount varied episodes in which nudity is

Giorgione's *The Sleeping Venus* (c. 1510). Oil on canvas. During the Renaissance, artistic works featuring the nude female figure became popular, although Church authorities disapproved of such frank and revealing treatment of the human body. © ERICH LESS-ING/ART RESOURCE, NY

appropriate for the story, as in a bathing sequence, and for either men or women. For example, Adam, Eve, Susannah, David, Bathsheba, Salome, and Jesus of Nazareth are depicted in states of total or partial undress. However in Christian iconography nudity embodied more often than not the condition of shame, especially with regard to women as the "daughters of Eve." The artistic and literary tradition of Western culture, especially Christianity, may be characterized as influenced by the legacy of Eve, and in particular, established the motif of the *femme fatale,* or fatal woman, from the characterization of women as seducers of men as prefigured in the scriptural stories of Eve, Delilah, Bathsheba, Salome, and eventually, even, the Jewish heroine Judith.

The Renaissance recovery of classical philosophy, art, and literature promoted a revival of interest in "The Nude" beyond the confines of scriptural narratives and Christian morality lessons. However, the Renaissance was distanced by centuries of political, social, and economic meliorations from classical Greece and Rome, and even further distanced from the classical philosophy and culture that were the foundation for the classical nude. Although premised upon classical models, Renaissance nudes differed in constructions of musculature and gender. The female nude, with the familiar exception of the *Venus pudica,* was absent from the mainstream of the classical arts. She became a popular motif in the Renaissance arts even up to Giorgione's (1477–1510) creation of the reclining female nude found in his *Sleeping Venus* (1508–1510;

Gemaldegalerie, Dresden). This Renaissance flowering of interest in "The Nude" extended into northern Europe where Albrecht Dürer (1471–1528) fashioned his famous study of the principles of perspective and anatomy in *Artist Drawing a Reclining Nude* (c. 1527: Metropolitan Museum of Art, New York), which affirmed the dichotomy of female passivity and male activity.

The popularity of "The Nude," whether male or female, among both Renaissance artists and their patrons garnered the attention of ecclesiastical leaders. This impropriety was dramatically decried by the Dominican monk Girolamo Savonarola (1452–1498), whose preaching influenced significant Renaissance artists including Michelangelo (1475–1564) and Botticelli (1445–1510), and ultimately led to the infamous "Bonfire of the Vanities" in the public square in Florence. However, official Church condemnation of "The Nude" was not pronounced until the Council of Trent (1545), and then, only tangentially. From the Tridentine decree forward, artworks intended for the Church were to be inspected and approved by the bishop of each diocese; appropriate local or regional decrees were promulgated clarifying or expanding upon the phrase "all lasciviousness avoided."

The modern conception of "The Nude" is premised upon the multiple political, social, and cultural revolutions of the late eighteenth and the mid-nineteenth centuries. It found expression in the arts of the realists, such as Gustave Courbet

(1819–1877), and the Orientalists, beginning with Eugène Delacroix (1798–1863) in *Death of Sardanapalus* (1827; Musée du Louvre, Paris), who present the plausibility and eroticism of "The Nude," especially of the female nude. Freed from confinement of mythology, history, or narrative, the female nude flowered in the arts of the Impressionists, who reinterpreted the classical motif of the bathing Venus into secularized female bathers and who were influenced by Japonisme. (For example, Torei Kayonaga's depictions of restrained geishas were translated into Édouard Manet's [1832–1883] defiant prostitutes.) Furthermore, in the nineteenth century, the introduction of female students into art academies and ultimately into life drawing classes began a transformation of the "male gaze" into the "female gaze" whether the subject was a female or male model. Commensurately, the central position of the male nude was diminished, so that from the perspective of late twentieth-century art criticism and feminism to speak of "The Nude" is to speak of the female nude.

The female nude extends beyond the boundaries of allegory and metaphor to become an expression of sexual provocativeness, eroticism, sexual appeal, and potentially, voyeurism throughout twentieth-century art beginning with Pablo Picasso's (1881–1973) famed *Les Demoiselles d'Avignon* (1907; Museum of Modern Art, New York). "The Nude," which had been a motif of spiritual and moral uplift for the classical world, was transformed not simply into an image of Christian shame and embarrassment but into a modern object of profane physicality.

The relationship of "The Nude" as both an object and a subject of high art to voyeurism and pornography has been raised since the mid-nineteenth century. As Clark so perceptively noted, there is no innocent depiction of a naked body. Each of us sees through a distinctive but personalized lens, so one person's aesthetic encounter with "The Nude" is another person's moment of voyeurism. Further, definitions of pornography shift with cultural attitudes as witnessed in the commentaries by the American writer Mark Twain or Supreme Court rulings.

Eastern and Western Attitudes toward "Nudity"

Eastern and Western attitudes toward nudity can best be compared through discussions of both the male and the female nude. The former signify the ideal of moral perfection and the latter the vitality of the life principle.

The Greek image of Apollo is that of a standing, aloof, proud, and nude male figure. He is the ultimate ideal athlete. He was anthropomorphized into the *kouros* who is distinguished by his rigid frontal pose accented by arms pressed closely down his sides. This stasis is relieved by the placement of one foot, thereby also the leg, forward from the other to signify human dynamism. The visual combination of ideal male beauty through an identifiable muscular structure and movement provides the viewer with the sensation of a vital man. The Greek ideal of the athlete is the conjunction of physicality and spirituality through the vehicle of "The Nude."

The Jain image of the ascetic, or *tirthankara*, is that of a superhuman and heroic figure whose broad shoulders and narrowed waist were similar to that of Apollo or the *kouros*. This figuration of a frontal pose with firmly indented arms is balanced by his straight legs. The portrayal of suspended animation fulfills the requirements of the spiritual tenet of *kayotsarga*, or the dismissal of the body, as this yogic trance permits complete withdrawal from all earthly distractions. The Jain image of nudity is a signifier of asceticism and of the spiritual ideal. The identifiable, and thereby natural, muscular structure and intimated movement of the *kouros* promoted divine-human association, while the suppression, thereby abstractions, of muscular structure and motion of the *tirthankara* emphasized his symbolic value.

In both East and West, the female nude is predicated on a cult image that is provocative and sensuous in appeal. The Greek goddess, Aphrodite, was simultaneously the personification of love and beauty and the achievement of the idealized female body. The captivating undulations of the feminine form combined with softness and delicacy of skin and muscle denoted the sensuality necessary for procreation. Greek representations of the topography of the female nude vacillated between depictions of innocence, as in the motif of *The Birth of Aphrodite* (470-460 B.C.E.; Museo Nazionale Romano delle Terme, Rome), and of flirtation, as in the topos of the *Venus pudica* found in the *Medici Venus* (first century B.C.E.; Galleria degli Uffizi, Florence). The body proportions, like those of the Apollo and the *kouros*, were based upon mathematical formulations.

The Indian *yakshi*, the oldest indigenous nature goddess or fertility spirit, signifies fecundity through the abstractions of her nude body. Her spherical breasts, like her ample hips and conspicuous pudenda, are enlarged in mathematical relation to the female frame and head to emphasize feminine sensuality and maternal potential. *Yakshi* are situated in exaggerated

---

The English language, with its elaborate generosity, distinguishes between the naked and the nude. To be naked is to be deprived of our clothes, and the word implies some of the embarrassment most of us feel in that condition. The word 'nude,' on the other hand, carries, in educated usage, no uncomfortable overtone. The vague image it projects into the mind is not of a huddled and defenseless body, but of a balanced, prosperous, and confident body: the body re-formed.

SOURCE: Kenneth Clark, *The Nude: A Study in Ideal Form* (Mellon Lectures, 1953), p. 3.

And they were both naked: to wit, Adam and his wife: and were not ashamed. (Genesis 2:25)

And the woman saw that the tree was good to eat, and fair to the eyes, and delightful to behold: and she took of the fruit thereof, and did eat, and gave it to her husband, who did eat.

And the eyes of them both were opened: and when they perceived themselves to be naked, they sewed together fig leaves, and made themselves aprons.

And when they heard the voice of the Lord God walking in paradise at the afternoon air, Adam and his wife hid themselves from the face of the Lord God, amidst the trees of paradise.

And the Lord God called Adam, and said to him: Where art thou?

And he said: I heard thy voice in paradise; and I was afraid, because I was naked, and I hid myself.

And he said to him: And who hath told thee that thou wast naked, but that thou hast eaten of the tree whereof I commanded thee that thou shouldst not eat? (Genesis 3:6-11)

SOURCE: Douay-Rheims Bible.

postures and positions to denote the erotic abstractions of the female body. The naturalistic harmony of the human standards of feminine beauty found in Aphrodite made both the divine and the human female approachable and tangible, whereas the symbolic abstractions of the nude *yakshi* tempered physicality with yogic restraint.

The Conundrum of Non-Western Culture and the Idea of "The Nude"

Discussions and scholarship on "The Nude" are decidedly Western in form and focus. Ostensibly, this is not a result of Western imperialism but more likely than not the influence of the Western monotheistic traditions with their distinctive morality and defense of the integrity of the one God. For example, Islamic art is normatively interpreted as aniconic, or nonfigural, in its emphasis on geometric abstractions. Although there is no Koranic prohibition against figural art or art, there is clear prohibition of images of either of idols or of God. For some commentators, the absence of the figure, especially the nude figure, is interpreted as a visual sign distinguishing Islam and Islamic art from Christianity and Christian art, which is fundamentally obsessed with Eve's nakedness and her role in the Fall. By contrast, Eve when she is depicted in Islamic art is the joyous companion of Adam. Commensurately, when those exceptionally rare nude figures are painted, whether male or female, they appear only in commissioned works of what might be best termed "secular Islamic art."

However in the non-Western world, attitudes toward nudity and the nude figure are characterized by their naturalness and ease and not categorized as a special art category or motif, except when the arts of Africa, Oceania, or Meso-America are examined with Western criteria. The first reality of nudity as a state of undress, whether ritually required or common to daily life experience, is a universal condition. The second reality of nudity is that neither the art nor religion of these indigenous cultures is monolithic as Western art and monotheism is perceived to be. Rather, for example, African figural art is naturalistic among the Ife and Benin of Nigeria but other African peoples image themselves with simplified and/ or exaggerated anatomical features. A third reality of nudity is that differing climates and their resident cultures require a variety of dress in both fabric and style to accommodate native meteorological conditions. So thinner materials and lighter colors are more appropriate to warmer climates while heavier fabrics and darker colors conform to the needs of cooler climates. From the Western perspective, especially that of the nineteenth-century missionaries, the exposed breasts and bare feet of Polynesian or African women were considered a social affront. Simultaneously for some nineteenth-century European colonialists, the shock of this tribal or societal nudity was the foundation for the myth of "The Noble Savage" as the concept of the *le primitif* was for their twentieth-century counterparts. This Western myth of idyllic innocence and primal energy coincided with a belief that primitive peoples were free of moral constraints and middle-class concerns. However defined, the arts of these varied primitive cultures were highly influential on twentieth-century art from Picasso and Henri Matisse (1869–1954) to the Abstract Expressionists.

Scholarship of "The Nude"

Kenneth Clark, who distinguished between naked and nude with relation to cultural, philosophic, and religious attitudes in the classic and Western Christian worlds, initiated the formal study of "The Nude." His masterful analysis of the postures, gestures, poses, and body formations of the undressed human figure defined the parameters of analyses on this topic. Whether consciously or not, all following studies on "The Nude," whether differentiating between the male and the female nude, or looking at both gendered figurations, are dependent upon Clark's fundamental definition either as a point of departure or argument. John Berger's investigation of the relationship between the spectator and "The Nude," particularly the female nude, and that between fine art and modern advertising, was a significant development in the study of "The Nude."

Since the late 1960s, the establishment of the new scholarship of "the marginalized," with its origins in the questions of race, gender, class, or ethnicity (Melody Davis, Julia Kristeva, Edward Lucie-Smith, Lynda Nead) has expanded the boundaries of examination. Feminist scholarship, for example,

---

The painting described is the motif of the reclining Venus:

> You enter [the Uffizi] and proceed to that most-visited little gallery that exists in the world—the Tribune—and there, against the wall, without obstructing rag or leaf, you may look your fill upon the foulest, the vilest, the obscenest picture the world possesses—Titian's Venus. . . . There are pictures of nude women which suggest no impure thought—I am well aware of that. I am not railing at such. What I am trying to emphasize is the fact that Titian's Venus is very far from being one of that sort. (Mark Twain, *A Tramp Abroad* [1880], 578.)

---

disproved the cultural concept of a "hermeneutics of aesthetic innocence" and thereby of "The Nude" as neutral. Feminists then proceeded to examine the political and societal minefield of domination and submission when "The Nude" was created by a male artist for a male patron. Further, the critique of *le regard* as the (male) gaze was crucial for feminist and gender scholars who advocated the existence of a female gaze in which women artists painted either male or female nudes to be admired and to stimulate the female viewer. The presumption here is that men and women see, and experience art regardless of the subject matter, the same way; however, the primary question of whether seeing is engendered remains a lacuna. Early-twenty-first-century categories of scholarly conversation, including the issues of the body, the reclining (female) nude, body language, and gesture (Kristeva, Peter Brown, Camille Paglia, Marcia Pointon, Alison Smith), are reframing the central questions of "*who* is 'The Nude?'" and "*what* is the character of nudity?"

See also **Body, The; Gender in Art; Humanity in the Arts.**

BIBLIOGRAPHY

Adler, Kathleen, and Marcia Pointon, eds. *The Body Imaged: The Human Form and Visual Culture Since the Renaissance.* New York: Cambridge University Press, 1993.

Beckwith, Sarah. *Christ's Body: Identity, Culture and Society in Late Medieval Writings.* London and New York: Routledge, 1993.

Belting, Hans. *Likeness and Presence: A History of the Image before the Era of Art.* Chicago: University of Chicago Press, 1994.

Berger, John, et al. *Ways of Seeing.* Harmondsworth, U.K.: Penguin Books, 1972.

Bowie, Theodore, and Cornelia V. Christenson, eds. *Studies in Erotic Art.* New York: Basic Books, 1970.

Brown, Peter. *The Body and Society: Men, Women, and Sexual Renunciation in Early Christianity.* New York: Columbia University Press, 1988.

Clark, Kenneth. *The Nude: A Study in Ideal Form.* Princeton, N.J.: Princeton University Press, 1972. First published in 1956.

Cormack, Malcolm. *The Nude in Western Art.* Oxford: Phaidon, 1976.

Davis, Melody D. *The Male Nude in Contemporary Photography.* Philadelphia: Temple University Press, 1991.

Goldstein, Laurence, ed. *The Male Body: Features, Destinies, Exposures.* Ann Arbor: University of Michigan Press, 1994.

Lucie-Smith, Edward. *Race, Sex, and Gender in Contemporary Art.* New York: Abrams, 1994.

———. *Sexuality in Western Art.* New York: Thames and Hudson, 1991.

Miles, Margaret R. *Carnal Knowing: Female Nakedness and Religious Meaning in the Christian West.* Boston: Beacon Press, 1989.

Mullins, Edwin. *The Painted Witch: How Western Artists Have Viewed the Sexuality of Women.* New York: Carroll and Graf, 1985.

Mulvey, Laura. *Visual and Other Pleasures.* Bloomington: Indiana University Press, 1989.

Nead, Lynda. *The Female Nude: Art, Obscenity, and Sexuality.* London and New York: Routledge, 1992.

We can now begin to see the difference between nakedness and nudity in the European tradition. In his book on *The Nude* Kenneth Clark maintains that to be naked is simply to be without clothes, whereas the nude is a form of art. According to him, a nude is not the starting point of a painting, but a way of seeing which the painting achieves.

To be naked is to be oneself.

To be nude is to be seen naked by others and yet not recognized for oneself. A naked body has to be seen as an object in order to become a nude. (The sight of it as an object stimulates the use of it as an object.) Nakedness reveals itself. Nudity is placed on display.

To be naked is to be without disguise.

SOURCE: John Berger, *Ways of Seeing* (1972), pp.53, 4.

Perchuk, Andrew and Helaine Posner, eds. *The Masculine Masquerade: Masculinity and Representation.* Cambridge, Mass.: MIT Press, 1995.

Pointon, Marcia R. *Naked Authority: The Body in Western Painting, 1830–1908.* Cambridge, U.K.: Cambridge University Press, 1990.

Pollock, Griselda and Roszika Parker. *Old Mistresses: Women, Art, and Ideology.* New York: Pantheon Books, 1981.

Rudofsky, Bernard. *The Unfashionable Human Body.* Garden City, N.J.: Doubleday, 1971.

Saunders, Gill. *The Nude: A New Perspective.* New York: Harper and Row, 1989.

Smith, Alison. *The Victorian Nude: Sexuality, Morality, and Art.* Manchester, U.K.: Manchester University Press, 1997.

———, ed. *Exposed: The Victorian Nude.* London: Tate Publications, 2001. Exhibition catalogue.

Steinberg, Leo. *The Sexuality of Christ in Renaissance Art and in Modern Oblivion.* New York: Pantheon, 1983.

Suleiman, Susan Rubin, ed. *The Female Body in Western Culture: Contemporary Perspectives.* Cambridge, Mass.: Harvard University Press, 1986.

Üster, Celâl, ed. *Nude in Art.* Special issue of *P Art and Culture Magazine* 9 (spring 2003): 1–132.

Walters, Margaret. *The Nude Male.* Harmondsworth, U.K.: Penguin Books, 1979.

Diane Apostolos-Cappadona

O

OBJECTIVITY. Objectivity is the idea that the truth can be known independently of viewpoint, perspective, or bias. For example, "Gustav Mahler completed nine symphonies," is an objectively true statement, independent of the person who utters it. "Gustav Mahler was the greatest composer in history" is not an objective truth—some people would agree, others would disagree, depending on their subjective aesthetic values. Objectivity has often been presented as diametrically opposed to subjectivity, the idea that people's beliefs and value judgments reflect their individual situation and interests; historicism, the consideration of people's opinions as reflections of the historical era in which they live; and relativism, which considers all points of view to be equally correct and inevitable.

History of the Term

The terms *subjective* and *objective* were introduced in European medieval philosophy. Their meanings then were nearly the reverse of their current use: *subject* meant that which exists, whereas *object* referred to what is perceived in consciousness. These uses of the terms persisted at least until George Berkeley in the eighteenth century. Lorraine Daston suggests that the current use of the terms was introduced in 1856 by Thomas De Quincey, although the concept of objectivity as knowledge based on fact had already been made in the seventeenth century. Previously, the Aristotelean tradition considered factual knowledge, historical knowledge of specific events, or knowledge of anomalies and novelties inferior to knowledge of "essences" and generalities. Daston attributes to Francis Bacon the novel promotion of facts to a level worthy of natural philosophy. These facts are the precursors of objective knowledge.

Immanuel Kant in his *Critique of Pure Reason* (1781, 1787) is probably responsible more than any other single thinker for spurring a debate about objectivity by "splitting" the world into "things for us" and "the thing in itself" (*Ding an Sich*). Kant analyzed human cognition and concluded that for anything to appear in our consciousness, it must fit into certain innate internal categories such as temporality and causation. It is impossible for us to perceive any phenomenon but within the matrix of these categories. For example, all phenomena must appear in time and be caused by other phenomena. Kant concluded that it is impossible to have knowledge of the world as it is, independent of human observers, beyond our categories, or to use later terminology, objectively.

Much of subsequent philosophy attempted to rise to the Kantian challenge. Phenomenology has attempted to reunite the world by eliminating the distinction between subject and object. Georg Wilhelm Friedrich Hegel (1770–1831) sought

to unite them as aspects of an ideal world spirit that we can know by an act of self-consciousness, because we are parts of this world rather than distinct from it. Edmund Husserl (1859–1938) designed his phenomenology to study pure consciousness through the method of epoche, the suspension of belief in subject-object distinction. Husserl claimed that prior to cognitive processes, such as scientific abstraction, that distinguish the objective from the subjective, we live in an immediate asubjective "life-world." Husserl and his immediate and remote intellectual progeny (Hannah Arendt, Jürgen Habermas) attempted to recapture this lost preobjective life-world. However, their analysis resulted in a new chasm between what they considered to be universal immediate human consciousness and the objective scientific world view.

Conversely, the nineteenth-century school of positivism (Auguste Comte, John Stuart Mill) and the twentieth-century school of logical-empiricism (Ernst Mach, the early Ludwig Wittgenstein, Rudolph Carnap) claimed that the scientific method offers objective knowledge of the world, and therefore philosophy should explicate this method, and other disciplines would do well to use this philosophic blueprint to reform themselves. The logical empiricists shared an analysis of language as composed of distinct units that correspond with distinct chunks of reality. The objective meaning of words or propositions is then their empirical truth condition, a state of affairs in the world. For example "the cat is on the mat" is objectively true if and only if indeed the cat is on the mat.

The objectivity of our beliefs has been criticized by traditions that descend from Karl Marx (1818–1883)and Friedrich Nietzsche (1844–1900). Marx thought that the material conditions of production are the objective aspect of society. Systems of belief merely reflect economic interests. Nietzsche tended to reduce beliefs to power relations. Karl Mannheim (1893–1947), the founder of sociology of knowledge, and Max Horkheimer (1895–1973), one of the founders of the Frankfurt School, concentrated on economic or political influences over apprehensions of reality. Horkheimer argued that it is impossible to produce a metatheory to transcend the limits of a temporal worldview. Later, Michel Foucault (1926–1984) and Bruno Latour showed the dependence of research on social power relations, on what Foucault called discourses.

Contemporary Debates

Since the 1960s the debate about the objectivity of knowledge in English-speaking countries concentrated on explaining the history of science. Thomas Kuhn (1922–1996) and others demonstrated that there are no simple objective scientific facts because scientific concepts are always embedded in conceptual frameworks, and so are confirmed holistically. After Kuhn, those who believe that science offers objective knowledge attempt to explain scientific change by referring to internal scientific reasons, the interaction between theory and reality. Those who claim that science is at least in some cases not objective, including sociologists of knowledge of "the strong program" (which is based on a critique of traditional philosophy of science), feminists (such as Helen Longino, Miriam Solomon, and Kathleen Okruhlik), and postcolonial thinkers explain scientific change by external social factors. They may be divided into moderates who argue that in many cases science did not adhere to its objective criteria, and radicals who claim that the very ideas of objectivity and rationality reflect the biases of male, heterosexual, and white European scientists.

These debates led contemporary philosophers like Nicholas Rescher to attempt to understand objectivity without referring to the world or truth conditions, to reduce objectivity to universal impersonal reason that should lead to the same cognitive output given the same informational or evidential input. Objectivity then is a general human point of view, avoiding the idiosyncratic.

One of the most influential twentieth-century discussions of objectivity was introduced by Thomas Nagel. He considered objective–subjective propositions to have different degrees of reliance on an individual's makeup and position in the world. Since there is no "view from nowhere," a point of view is inevitable. The subjectivity of consciousness is irreducible to its physical properties (the brain). In ethics, moral subjectivism considers moral principles personal; moral objectivism argues that moral judgments are defensible rationally and moral values exist objectively. Nagel considered the good to be subjective and irreducible, since we cannot act impersonally. According to Nagel the problem facing contemporary philosophy is the integration of our subjective-personal and objective-impersonal views of ourselves in the same worldview.

See also **Idealism; Paradigm; Phenomenology; Positivism; Relativism; Science, History of.**

BIBLIOGRAPHY

Megill, Allan, ed. *Rethinking Objectivity*. Durham, N.C.: Duke University Press, 1994.

Nagel, Thomas. *The View from Nowhere*. New York: Oxford University Press, 1986.

Natter, Wolfgang, Theodore Schatzki, and John Paul Jones, eds. *Objectivity and Its Other*. New York: Guilford, 1995.

Rescher, Nicholas. *Objectivity: The Obligations of Impersonal Reason*. Notre Dame, Ind.: Notre Dame University Press, 1997.

Aviezer Tucker

OBLIGATION. Since Plato wrote of political obligation in his dialogue *Crito*, obligation in general has been of ongoing interest to philosophers. In that dialogue, Socrates argues that he was under an obligation to obey the laws of Athens and comply with a sentence of death. During the course of the argument, he raises and offers solutions to many of the central issues about obligation that philosophers still puzzle over. For instance, how can obligations have the grip on us that they do—in some cases, so that we are willing to die rather than not fulfill them? What is the nature and justification of moral and legal obligations? Do we have an obligation to obey the state, and if so, why?

The range of issues and positions relating to obligation is vast, given that there are few areas of moral and political philosophy in which obligation does not play a role. In what follows, four topics that have been of particular interest to contemporary philosophers are discussed: (1) the analysis and justification of obligations; (2) legal and moral obligations; (3) obligations, roles, and identities; and (4) agent-relative obligations.

The Analysis and Justification of Obligations

Obligation is normative, concerned with how things should be (not necessarily with how they are). In particular, it is a deontically normative—concerned with duty, or what is permissible, forbidden, and the like—as opposed to axiologically normative, concerned with what is good, bad, better, or worse. A given deontic normative perspective classifies actions, laws, institutions, or whatever as permissible (acceptable) or impermissible (unacceptable, wrong, forbidden). The classifications are interdefinable. For instance, an option is permissible when it is not impermissible, obligatory when permissible and every alternative option is impermissible.

Obligation is a relation with as many as three places: the person or entity who *has* an obligation (call this the *agent*), what that agent is obligated to do (the *performance*), and the person or entity to whom the agent owes the performance (the *object*). Because the object of an obligation is owed the performance, that person or entity has a *right* to it, and when an obligation has an object, obligations and rights are reciprocal: if someone has a right to your ϕing, then you have an obligation to ϕ; and if you have an obligation to someone to ϕ, then that someone has a right to your ϕing. Philosophers differ over whether all or just some obligations have objects, and so whether all or just some obligations come with reciprocal rights. For instance, some hold that a person is morally obligated to help others, but this obligation does not give anyone a right to be helped. Often, obligations that do not generate reciprocal rights for their objects are called *imperfect* obligations, while those that do generate reciprocal rights are called *perfect* obligations.

Some obligations are *agent-relative* (or *agent-centered*) and others are *agent-neutral*. Agent-relative obligations are those whose performance contains within its scope an essential reference back to the agent and to the agent carrying out that performance (McNaughton and Rawling, 1991). Hence, such obligations state that the agent is obligated himself to perform some action. An agent-neutral obligation, by contrast, states only that the agent ought to ensure the performance of the action, whether by himself or someone else. For instance, my obligation to help a stranger is really just the obligation that I make sure the stranger is helped—whether by me or by someone nearby does not matter. By contrast, my obligation to go to my son's birthday party is an obligation that *I* go to his party. I do not discharge that obligation by sending someone else. Likewise, if I promise that *I* will baby-sit your children, the obligation I have undertaken is that *I* baby-sit, not that a baby-sitter of some sort is provided. To the degree that obligations and rights are reciprocal, this distinction in agent-relative and agent-neutral obligations brings with it a distinction in agent-relative and agent-neutral rights. For instance, you have an agent-relative right that I baby-sit if I have promised as much.

What is obligatory is what one *must* do. A citizen has an obligation to obey the law, and so *must* obey the law; it is obligatory for a Boy Scout to keep himself physically strong, thus he *must* do so; parents are under an obligation and so *must* care for their children. Because of this, deontic classifications have been treated as modal notions—as what it is normatively *necessary, possible,* or *impossible* to do. Moreover, these modalities are often characterized much like causation and other kinds of necessity, as relations grounded in the governance of laws. Heat must boil water because there is a natural law governing these events; likewise, a Boy Scout must keep himself physically strong because there is a Scouting law governing his actions. Thus, an action is obligatory when a normative law or rule makes it normatively necessary, permissible when a normative law makes it normatively possible, and so on. The differences between moral, legal, etiquette, and club obligations can thus be made out as differences in the sets of normative rules or laws grounding the modal categorization. For instance, a club obligation is an action made necessary by the rules of the club.

An obligation is thus typically held to be an action that is normatively necessary according to some normative rule or law. A normative law, however, does not necessitate one's action, in the way that the law of gravitation makes a person stay on or near the surface of the earth. The laws of a state, club, or morality necessitate one's action not as nature or logic makes things necessary, because it is logically and naturally possible for a person not to act as these laws direct. What is normatively necessary is both logically and naturally not necessary, even if both logically and naturally possible.

For any deontic realm, there will be obligations *within* or defined by that realm, and there may also be obligations not defined by that realm, but whose performance is *regarding* the obligations within that realm—separate obligations to fulfill the obligations laid down by that deontic realm (Green, 1988). For instance, legal systems define certain legal obligations, such as the obligation not to exceed a certain speed on a given road. These are obligations *within* the law. Yet a club, such as the Boy Scouts, may define certain obligations regarding those obligations created within the law. Hence, one obligation of the Boy Scouts is never to fail in one's legal or moral obligations. This is an obligation within one deontic realm, the Boy Scouts, regarding the obligations within a distinct deontic realm, the law. In general, if there is an obligation regarding a given deontic realm (i.e., an obligation to fulfill the obligations laid down by a club, a state, or etiquette), then there must be some second deontic realm independent of it within

which the obligation regarding that realm exists. One of the most important kinds of obligation regarding a deontic realm is the moral obligation to conform to legal obligations, often termed *political obligation.*

Normative laws can make one's actions necessary in a variety of ways. One way in which they might do this is if the laws are created as means to ends that one has. In order to vote, one must register; in order to get badges in the Boy Scouts, one must keep oneself physically strong; and so on. This can be called *instrumental necessity.* Many have thought that the necessity of any obligation must be instrumental. The laws of a state, for instance, would generate obligations for a given person when and only when those laws necessary are necessary for her security and the avoidance of sanctions for disobedience.

Most philosophers, however, have thought instrumental necessity is neither necessary nor sufficient for deontic necessity. It is not sufficient because a law backed up by sanctions alone seems not to be an obligation but rather extortion. The law must at least be in some sense a legitimate law of that deontic realm. Following the legal philosopher John Austin, a mechanism to establish the legitimacy of a normative law or rule can be called a *pedigree.* Systems of normative rules or laws require a pedigree that establishes the legitimacy of those laws or rules in creating a genuine obligation.

Instrumental necessity is not necessary for deontic necessity either. For instance, according to the rules of chess, it is necessary that the bishop stay on his color; this is a normative necessity arising from a rule of chess. But that rule is not backed up by some clause such as "in order to avoid such and such penalty." The rules of chess are in this sense "categorically" necessary. What is required for deontic necessity are laws that are nonoptional rules of behavior, and that at a minimum have a pedigree that makes them legitimate rules of the system.

Different deontic realms can have different pedigrees, and philosophers have offered different pedigrees for some deontic realms. For instance, philosophers such as St. Thomas Aquinas tied the legitimacy of a state's laws to divine pedigree. Genuine obligations, both within and to the law, arise only from demands conforming to laws God laid down for our nature when he created us. Hence, genuine legal obligations arise only from laws that comport with this natural law. And the moral obligation to obey the law is grounded in our obligation to obey God. The view that the legitimacy of law arises from acts of will, or "voluntarism," underwent a transformation as the vision of the universe grounded in God's will receded (for recent accounts of the history of modern thought about obligation, see Darwell, 1995, and Schneewind, 1998). Human acts of will—acts of choice, consent, agreement, promise—came to take the place of God's will as a source of authority. Thomas Hobbes and John Locke, for instance, rejected Thomas's view that each person's good naturally comports with the good of others. Although we are naturally entitled to seek our own good, each person's good is at odds with that of others. This conflict inevitably leads to a devastating loss for all as everyone tries to secure their own good at the cost of others. It is only by leaving this natural state that all can secure their good. Each person's natural authority over himself is transferred to the sovereign or the community, which then comes to possess an authority to enact and enforce laws obligating them. And our obligation to obey those laws is based on something like a promise we have made.

Some version of the law-based source of obligation and some version of voluntarism as a source of the legitimacy of those laws and the obligation to obey has held a dominant position among philosophers since the modern era began. Nevertheless, many have defended nonvoluntarist positions and/or have rejected the model of obligations as actions made necessary by a law. Some, for instance, hold that obligations are a special kind of reason that make actions necessary. Hence, the obligation to obey the law, for instance, is a reason that necessitates obeying it. Among voluntarism's important detractors was David Hume, who had misgivings both about the law-based analysis of obligation and about voluntarism as the required pedigree. Hume argued that consent "has very seldom had place in any degree, and never almost in its full extent" (II.XII. 20). We are born into or find ourselves with obligations. Obligations that we have because of our consent, such as promises, are few and far between. Hume's own view of obligation was complex and hard to deem entirely consistent. Nevertheless, the gist of his view was that deontic necessity should be explained in subjective terms: When I judge that someone has an obligation to perform some action, I judge that there is a admirable motive impelling her to do it. The motive might be unreflective and natural, as is the love of children. Or it may arise from reflection on the advantages of various institutions, such as property or promising. Such a motive gains legitimacy through my approval of it from an impartial point of view.

John Stuart Mill followed the spirit of this pattern of analysis, but focused on external actions rather than internal motives. His still influential account holds that an action is obligatory just in case failure to perform it justifies internal or external sanctions, "if not by law, by the opinion of his fellow creatures; if not by opinion, by the reproaches of his own conscience" (pp. 48–49). The pedigree granting authority to such internal or external punishments in the case of moral and legal obligations is general happiness. As David Lyons (1977) has argued, however, Mill's analysis in terms of justifiably sanctionable behavior is itself quite separate from his view of what justifies such sanctions, namely, the general happiness. Indeed, anarchists argue for a given analysis of political obligation but then deny that any such thing exists on the grounds that no legitimacy can be given for it (see, e.g., Simmons, 1979; Wolff, 1998).

Most philosophical positions separate the legitimacy or authority of a law laying down obligations (moral or legal) from the reason to comply. Whether a rule or law in some deontic realm is valid is one thing; whether a person has reason to comply with its obligations is quite another. The most famous attempt to unify the legitimacy and reason to comply with moral obligations was that of Immanuel Kant. Kant's insight was to view moral obligations as stemming from laws that each person imposes on himself rather than from laws whose origin is external to the agent. In particular, moral laws are requirements stemming from deep inside—from a person's very capacity to act and choose on the basis of reason itself. If the source of a law was the moral agent himself, that is, if it were created and enacted by the agent's own rational will, then its authority would come from the agent himself, namely, the authority of his own rational will over his actions. Kant referred to this as the "autonomy" of a rational will. Moral obligations, in his view, stem from the demands of our own reason, and it is in virtue of this source that we have reason to comply.

Legal and Moral Obligations

The two most salient deontic realms are law and morality. But how are legal and moral obligations related?

Positivism is the doctrine that our legal and moral obligations are quite distinct, that what the law *is* is a separate issue from what it ought to be. In the form originally propounded by Jeremy Bentham and Austin, legal obligations are generated by commands of the sovereign, or that entity whom society is in the habit of obeying, who is not in the habit of obeying anyone else, and who has the power to sanction noncompliance. H. L. A. Hart showed that this form of positivism is subject to fatal objections. It can account for neither the continuity of legal authority across sovereigns nor the persistence of legal obligation after a given sovereign is gone. Moreover, he noted that it assumes that normative necessity must be instrumental necessity, which, as discussed above, is a mistake. What is needed are nonoptional *rules,* and sanctions are neither necessary nor sufficient for these (such as in the chess example). Part of the problem, Hart thought, was that Austin used *criminal law,* in which the law is a *barrier* to doing certain things, as his model for the whole of the law. *Civil law* (such as the law of contracts), in which law is a solution for various problems that would otherwise exist, is a much better model.

The law, Hart argued, is "a union of primary and secondary rules" (1994, p. 107). Primary rules direct each how to act ("don't eat shellfish," "no one may sit higher than the king," and so on). These rules impose genuine obligations, but not in the way that Austin thought. For Austin, rules are little more than means by which one can predict when the state will harm you. To see a rule in this way is to take an "external" view of it: conforming to the rules has no part in defining one's membership in the society. The first step in having a legal system is to have a system of rules that most take an internal view of, or see as standards of criticism and justification of one's behavior.

Hart argued that problems will inevitably arise in a system composed only of primary rules. First, in such a system, there will be *uncertainty* about whether a rule exists covering many situations and what to do when rules conflict. Second, the system will be too *rigid* to deal with changing circumstances. How will new rules come into and go out of existence? Third, the system will be *inefficient* in enforcing the rules and determining whether they apply in any case. What is required is a system of *secondary rules,* or rules concerning how to determine, introduce, abolish, change, and apply *primary* rules. Most importantly, what is required are *rules of recognition* that identify those features in virtue of which a rule is a rule of the group, to be supported by social pressures of various sorts. Rules of recognition are the sorts of rules that define lawmaking in U.S. state and federal legislatures. Thus, a rule exists as a rule in some system if its pedigree can be traced to rules of recognition defining legality for that system. Notice that, in contrast to Austin's view, rules can exist even if nobody ever obeys them. As long as a rule is enacted in the right rule-defining and -creating way, it exists. Hart insisted, however, that the rule of recognition itself need not be backed in any sense by any standard of authority, legal or moral. A rule of recognition exists in the sense of an "external statement of fact," that is, if it is generally not disregarded in defining and creating law.

Positivism's stark separation of legal and moral obligation has been challenged most forcefully by Lon L. Fuller and Ronald Dworkin. Fuller argued that if a given system of directives is immoral in a formal sense, then it will fail to be a legal system because it will fail to be a genuine system of rules. A system of directives is arbitrary if it does not conform to principles such as treating like cases alike, making its directives public, or not introducing directives after the fact. And an arbitrary system is not a system of rules. Moreover, a system possessing precisely these nonarbitrary features is also considered to be formally just. Thus, a system of directives that is not formally just is not a system of rules. If legal systems are systems of rules, then it follows that a formally unjust system of directives is not a legal system at all and does not generate legal obligations.

Dworkin's view challenges Hart's positivism by arguing that the law requires more than merely formally moral features. He argues that the actual practice of judges shows that legal systems contain elements from the moral traditions within which they arise and to which a judge's decisions must appeal to be valid. In cases that are not clearly covered by an existing law, judges in his view actually legislate, reaching outside of the law to make laws on the basis of good social policy. Dworkin argued that this does not match either actual or good judicial practice. Legal systems are composed of more than rules. They include principles invoking moral rights and obligations that judges are bound by in deciding cases. Indeed, what litigants are typically claiming is that some principle protecting a right is on their side. For Dworkin, there is always a determinate answer to the question of who has a right. Thus, there is always a determinate solution to legal conflicts to which litigants have a right and the judge is bound to find and deliver. Dworkin's own account of the pedigree of law therefore requires invoking moral principles and so implies that judges do not have discretion to create legal obligations as required by Hart's account. They must find the answer to which litigant's rights to protect, and not by intuition, but by articulating and defending a view of rights. Thus, for Dworkin, there is no sharp separation of legal and moral obligations.

Obligations, Roles, and Identities

The problem of political obligation is the problem of establishing an obligation within the moral deontic realm regarding the legal deontic realm—a moral obligation to obey the law, for instance. Many offer the voluntarist account, that the moral obligation is based on what is in effect a promise. Others think that moral obligations, and *a fortiori* political obligation, are all tied to promoting the overall good. Still others follow Socrates in thinking we owe an obligation of gratitude to the state for preventing harms and facilitating our good.

Some have argued, however, that the whole issue is illusory because "it is part of the concept, the meaning of 'law,' that those to whom it is applicable are obligated to obey it" (Pitkin, p. 214). "U.S. citizen" *means* "person obligated to comply with U.S. laws." Obligations are in effect parts of our ordinary concepts defining our positions and roles. The seemingly deep question of whether a U.S. citizen is "really" obligated to follow U.S. laws either betrays a confusion about what "U.S. citizen" means or takes the language "on holiday"—that is, uses terms such as *obligation* and *law* outside of the contexts in which they have a meaning.

In the early twenty-first century, this conceptual argument has few adherents on the grounds that it does not dissolve the problem so much as relocate it (see, e.g., Pateman, 1979; Simmons, 1996). Suppose "citizen" *does* just mean "someone with a genuine obligation to conform to the law." Then we may legitimately ask, is anyone genuinely a citizen in this sense? Clearly, the selfsame problem has returned dressed in new clothing. Many, however, agree with the view that obligations come with one's social roles and positions. So although the connection between role and obligation is not *analytic,* it is still true in a deeper substantive sense that to occupy many roles means having certain obligations. The origins of the position are in Georg Wilhelm Friedrich Hegel, and a version of it was defended in F. H. Bradley's famous essay, "My Station and Its Duties." It can be found most prominently in "communitarian" views of such late twentieth-century figures as John Charvet, Margaret Gilbert, Michael Hardimon, and John Horton.

The basic outline of the idea is as follows: the conception of the bare presocial individual who voluntarily takes on various obligations and agreements is illusory, an abstraction. A person *just is* a collection of social roles, a nexus of connections to other roles in a social fabric, very few of which are voluntarily assumed, and none are in any deep sense voluntary. When you tell someone who you are, you tell them about the collection of positions you occupy in a variety of social structures and institutions—a parent, an American, a teacher, a lawyer, an Oregonian, a writer. Your social identity may include your gender, race, and sexual preference. If each person is made up to a significant degree or other by these roles, then we are deeply identified with them, in the sense that we are attached to these positions as "who we are." Each of these roles comes with a set of obligations: To be a parent is to be someone genuinely obligated to care for her child, to be a teacher is to be someone genuinely obligated to instruct students, and so on. The view is thus not that the meaning of the word *teacher* is "someone obligated to instruct," but that what it is to actually occupy this position is to have such a genuine obligation.

This viewpoint has come to enjoy wide acceptance. It faces serious difficulties, however, not the least of which is an analog of the question facing the conceptual argument. For even if to have a certain obligation just is to occupy a certain role, there seems to be a meaningful question about the normative status of that role and the practices that create it—a question of whether one *ought* to occupy that role, and moreover whether its obligations are genuinely binding. A defender of such obligations has to deny that there is any question of what one is genuinely obligated to do *beyond* what is laid down by one's social positions. The question "Ought I occupy this role and take on these requirements?" can be understood only from the perspective of some *other* role and its requirements. It asks only which social position or role should win out when there is a conflict. No single distinctive question about what one ought or ought not to do can be asked of social positions and their directives in general, because there is no single distinctive position or role that every person has in common with every other person.

In her 1996 book, *The Sources of Normativity*, Christine M. Korsgaard applied a similar strategy to the problem of moral obligation. In her view, this is a requirement stemming from one's "practical identity"—an identity that is constituted by ongoing commitments to act in various ways in various circumstances. Her insight is that the power and legitimacy of obligations are tied to a sense of one's own identities. As mentioned earlier, most of us think that there are some actions about which we say "I would rather die than do that"—that the necessity of some moral obligations is sufficient to put the acceptance of death on the table as an option. Korsgaard takes this talk seriously. If death is the loss of identity, the necessity of obligation comes from the threat of this loss. There are actions one would rather die than perform, or at least things the doing of which would be as good as dying. But combining the idea that death is a loss of identity with the idea that everyone has a multiplicity of identities tied to various positions and roles yields the idea that we might die *as an F*, where *F* names some role or position we occupy. Thus, to be a parent *requires one* to pursue the care of one's child. To stop this pursuit *just is* to give up that practical identity (insofar as this is a "person who cares for her child"), and hence to *die* as a parent. The necessity of parental obligation is thus tied to the persistence of one's identity as a parent. Where Korsgaard differs from the neo-Hegelian turn discussed above is that she holds that some identities are not merely social roles. In particular, our deepest identity—an identity it is impossible for us rationally to lose or throw off—is our identity as a reflective rational agent. This identity, she argues, is constituted by a requirement to respect this reflective agency in oneself and others. Failures of respect are in this way moral deaths, ways of giving up one's identity as a rational agent. This, she contends, explains the special grip or authority of moral obligation.

Agent-Relative Obligations

Much debate in late twentieth-century moral philosophy has been over how deep the distinction between agent-relative and agent-neutral obligations goes and whether the existence of agent-relative obligations is compatible with utilitarian moral theories. Recall that agent-relative obligations seem to have a special attachment to the person whom they bind. This is particularly the case regarding moral obligations: I see children who need caring for and can with no cost to myself care for one but not all. I have a moral obligation to care for one, then, but it does not seem to matter which. Indeed, everything else being equal, any other person in my place would have this obligation too. By contrast, suppose one of the children is my own son. It seems that I ought to care for my son over the other children, that it now matters morally which one I care for and that I do the caring. This is an

agent-relative obligation: I have an obligation that *I* care for *my* son. The puzzle is that every child is equally valuable in objective terms; my son's care has no more and no less intrinsic value than the care of anyone else's child. Of course, he is more valuable *to me,* but that is not an objective measure of his value. Further, it would be abominable for me to care for my own child, but justify it by saying "I can't care for all children, so I flipped a coin and my son won." I seem to have an obligation *to him,* and he has a claim on my care that no other person has. How is that possible if there is no more objective value in my son's care than in the care of any other child?

To take another example, we are morally obligated not to torture. But suppose you could reduce the number of torturings in the world by a few by torturing some one innocent person. It is very tempting to think that you still have an obligation not to torture that person, even if by doing so you could bring about the reduction in torturings. You seem to have here an agent-relative obligation that *you* should not torture, rather than simply an agent-neutral obligation to prevent torturings. How is this possible? Surely if one torturing is evil, two are more evil, three even more so, and so on. Surely you should bring about as little evil as possible in the world. Moreover, if we increase the number of torturings you could prevent, there will be some number at which everyone will relent and say you ought to torture to prevent other torturings. So how could it be wrong to prevent more of the very same ills that one thinks one should bring about oneself, and only in some cases but not others? Much late twentieth-century work on obligation has focused on just this question.

Utilitarianism has been most often associated with the view that there are no genuinely agent-relative obligations, that all of our obligations are agent-neutral. Our fundamental obligation is always to bring about the better state of affairs. This is indeed a very intuitive position: How could it ever be impermissible to bring about the most good? Shouldn't one always do this? Some, such as Samuel Scheffler (1994), have argued that agent-relative *permissions* can be defended, but not agent-relative *obligations*. That is, we can be permitted, but not obligated, to tell the truth even when our lying would bring about more truth-telling. What justifies a permission here for Scheffler is the agent's need to preserve his integrity (or, for Thomas Nagel, his autonomy) as a moral agent. Others have taken a stronger position that there are genuine agent-relative obligations. For example, you have an obligation not to torture even if by torturing you would bring about fewer torturings overall. Nagel argues that such an obligation is justified on the grounds that one must never be led by evil. Whether these or related arguments will ultimately prove successful is an ongoing concern of moral philosophers.

See also **Altruism; Law; Philosophy, Moral; Virtue Ethics.**

BIBLIOGRAPHY

Austin, John. *The Province of Jurisprudence Determined.* 1832. Reprint, edited by Wilfrid E. Rumble. Cambridge, U.K.: Cambridge University Press, 1995.

Bentham, Jeremy. *Of Laws in General.* Edited by H. L. A. Hart. London: University of London, Athlone Press, 1970.

Bradley, F. H. "My Station and Its Duties." In his *Ethical Studies*. 2nd ed. 1876. Reprint, with an introduction by Richard Wollheim. Oxford: Oxford University Press, 1988.

Darwall, Stephen. *The British Moralists and the Internal "Ought," 1640–1740*. Cambridge, U.K.: Cambridge University Press, 1995.

Dworkin, Ronald. *Taking Rights Seriously*. Cambridge, Mass.: Harvard University Press, 1977.

Flathman, Richard E. *Political Obligation*. New York: Atheneum, 1972.

Fuller, Lon L. "Positivism and Fidelity to Law: A Reply to Professor Hart." *Harvard Law Review* 71, no. 4 (1958): 630–672. Reprinted in *Philosophy of Law*, 7th ed., edited by Joel Feinberg and Jules Coleman, 67–81. Belmont, Calif.: Thomson/ Wadsworth, 2004.

Gilbert, Margaret. "Group Membership and Political Obligation." *Monist* 76, no. 1 (1993): 119–131.

Green, Leslie. *The Authority of the State*. Oxford: Clarendon, 1988.

Hardimon, Michael. "Role Obligations." *Journal of Philosophy* 91, no. 7 (1994): 333–363.

Hart, H. L. A. *The Concept of Law*. 2nd ed. Edited by Penelope A. Bulloch and Joseph Raz. Oxford: Clarendon, 1994.

Hume, David. "Of the Original Contract." Part II, Essay XII in *Essays Moral, Political and Literary*, ed. E. Miller. Indianapolis: Liberty Fund, 1987.

Korsgaard, Christine M. *The Sources of Normativity*. Cambridge, U.K.: Cambridge University Press, 1996.

Lyons, David. "Mill's Theory of Morality." *Noûs* 10 (1977): 101–120.

McNaughton, David, and Piers Rawling. "Agent-Relativity and the Doing–Happening Distinction." *Philosophical Studies* 63 (1991): 167–185.

Mill, John Stuart. *Utilitarianism*. 2nd ed. Reprint, edited, with an introduction, by George Sher. Indianapolis: Hackett, 2001.

Nagel, Thomas. *The View from Nowhere*. New York: Oxford University Press, 1986.

Pateman, Carole. *The Problem of Political Obligation*. Chichester, U.K.: Wiley, 1979.

Pitkin, Hanna. "Obligation and Consent—II." Reprinted in *Concepts in Social and Political Philosophy*, edited by Richard E. Flathman, 201–219. New York: Macmillan, 1973.

Scheffler, Samuel. *The Rejection of Consequentialism*. Rev. ed. Oxford: Clarendon, 1994.

Schneewind, J. B. *The Invention of Autonomy*. Cambridge, U.K.: Cambridge University Press, 1998.

Simmons, A. John. "Associative Political Obligations." *Ethics* 106, no. 2 (1996): 247–273.

———. *Moral Principles and Political Obligations*. Princeton, N.J.: Princeton University Press, 1979.

Wolff, Robert Paul. *In Defense of Anarchism*. Berkeley and Los Angeles: University of California Press, 1998.

Robert N. Johnson

OCCIDENTALISM. The term *Occidentalism* refers primarily to the many ways in which non-Western intellectuals, artists, and the general public perceive and present the West. Though it seems to be an inversion of Orientalism, it has acquired some unique aspects defying a simple definition. In fact, the practices and discourses of Occidentalism vary a great deal, from time to time and region to region. If we can arbitrarily divide certain parts of the world into West and East, then the people of the East, like their counterparts in the West, had approached an understanding and knowledge of the West long before such terms as Occidentalism and Orientalism were coined. However, it was largely due to the seminal influence of Edward Said's *Orientalism* that the discussion and use of the term *Occidentalism* gradually, from the 1990s on, gained currency in academic circles. Also, the two discourses not only juxtapose but also overlap with one another, in that the non-Western people do not perceive the West solely on their own cultural terms; rather, given the presence of Western discursive hegemony, they present the West either as a contrast, or an exemplar, reminding one of the principal practices of Orientalism among the Westerners. Different from the Orientalist discourse, which is mostly made by and for the Westerners, however, the Occidentalist discourse is made by non-Westerners for both Westerners and themselves. In the early twentieth century, for example, when a group of Japanese Buddhists attended the World's Parliament of Religion, they exercised, to borrow James Ketelaar's terminology, a "strategic Occidentalism" in promoting Buddhism both at home and to the world. They appropriated elements from Christianity, and Western culture in general, and constructed an image of the West as the contrasting Other. In so doing, they threw into relief the value of Buddhism as a more integral part in Japanese culture. They also emphasized the potentials of Buddhism for complementing Christianity and redressing its shortcomings.

East-West Dialogue and the Other

While the discussion of Occidentalism is often in juxtaposition with that of Orientalism, it can also amount to a criticism of the latter. Edward Said's critique of Orientalist writings and studies raised important questions about the Western hegemonic power in shaping the imagery of the "Orient." But like the Orientalists, as Mohamad Tavakoli-Targhi charges, Said, in presenting his thesis on the Western discursive hegemony, underestimates and overlooks the intellectual power and contribution of the people in the Orient. In his study of the Persianate writings in history and travelogue by Iranians and Indians during the seventeenth and nineteenth centuries, Tavakoli-Targhi notes that prior to the spread of European power, the Asians not only traveled to and wrote about Europe, contributing to Persianate Europology, but they also helped the early European Orientalists to acquire a knowledge of the Orient. In other words, in the exchanges between East and West, the East was not a passive, silent Other, as portrayed by the Orientalists (and also, ironically, as endorsed by Edward Said). Rather, argues Tavakoli-Targhi, the Persianate writers displayed equivalent intellectual capability to engage in cross-cultural communications with their Western counterparts. That the Orientals contributed to the gestation of Orientalism has also been noticed by Arif Dirlik in his study of South and East Asian history, although he casts this contribution in a more critical light.

Moreover, Occidentalism can be used, as Couze Venn has attempted, to describe the rise of Europe in modern times. In this usage, the term no longer refers to the construction of the image of the West only by the non-Western peoples. It now

Still from Zhang Yimou's 1995 film *Shanghai Triad.* In the late twentieth century, Chinese filmmakers like Yimou found critical success outside of their home country for works that depicted a China customized to Western tastes and expectations. ALPHA FILMS/THE KOBAL COLLECTION

also includes attempts by Europeans to turn their historical experience into a universal, hegemonic model. "Occidentalism," states Venn, "thus directs attention to the becoming-modern of the world and the becoming-West of Europe such that Western modernity gradually became established as the privileged, if not hegemonic, form of sociality, tied to a universalizing and totalizing ambition" (p. 19). Engaging in this study of how Europe rose to become the West entails careful examination of the development of capitalism and spread of colonialism, not only during the seventeenth and nineteenth centuries, but also, as Venn suggests, in today's world. The legacy of both are well reflected in such global forms of regulations and organizations as the World Bank, the International Monetary Fund (IMF), and the United Nations. All of them have accompanied the Western hegemony in academic discourses. While different from Edward Said's theory of Orientalism, Couze Venn's study of Occidentalism defined as such suggests a similar interest in revealing the repressive side of modernity. In this regard, Occidentalism extends, as does Said's work, the project of postcolonial critique of the modern world.

If the definition of Occidentalism is complex, this is because the interaction and dialogue between East and West have been a diverse experience, shaped by different forces under different circumstances. Even if we confine our discussion to the non-Western construction of the Western imagery, it still defies the simple understanding of it as a form of internalized Orientalism, in which the West is perceived as the exemplary Other, or of it as a defensive reaction against the West, in which the West is seen as a devilish Other. In addition to the various attempts to portray the West, Occidentalism has another dimension, or "double reflection" in Meltem Ahiska's analysis, that the non-Western also seeks to imagine how its image is perceived by the West. This is because the Occidentalist discourses often emerged as a result of the Western expansion to the world, which made it urgent and necessary not only for the non-Western to form its national and cultural identity, but also to do so by emulating and extending the Western model. It demands that the non-West seek identification of the West on the one hand in forming its modernity and, on the other hand, draw a line of demarcation between Self and Other in order to bolster its own contradistinctive identity.

China and Occidentalism

In the discussion on Occidentalism, scholars in the China field, including native Chinese scholars living in China and overseas, are quite active. This is perhaps because compared to its neighbors in Asia, China boasts a long historical and cultural entity and, since the mid-nineteenth century when its conflict with the West commenced, has remained quite resilient in resisting the Western influence and maintaining its cultural heritage. This marks a stark contrast to Meiji Japan in which a wholesale Westernization was set in motion almost as soon as the country was opened by and to the West. In China's cultural terrain until today, the China–West dichotomy appears quite salient, which suggests that the Chinese by and large have maintained, despite the ups and downs of their history, a clear self-awareness while constructing their relation with and perception of the West. In the New Culture movement of the early twentieth century, which was often perceived as a radical rupture of the Chinese cultural tradition, this self-awareness remained quite visible. In seeking a national identity, which was a main goal of the movement, the participants not only drew inspiration from the West, but also considered the Soviet experience. Moreover, despite its iconoclastic appearance, the movement did not entirely discard tradition. Instead, it gave rise to the National Studies project, in which the enthusiasm for modern science was translated into an endeavor at identifying similar, indigenous elements in the past.

This keen and persistent self-awareness bore upon the ways in which the modern Chinese imagined and construed the West. In her *Occidentalism: A Theory of Counter-Discourse in Post-Mao China,* Xiaomei Chen has identified two tracks of Occidentalist discourses in modern China. One is called Maoist, or official Occidentalism, in which the West is portrayed as the demon. The other is anti-official Occidentalism, advanced by various groups of the intelligentsia, in which the West becomes a useful metaphor for their critique of domestic oppression. Though the origin of Maoist Occidentalism can be traced back to the second half of the nineteenth century, marked by China's defeats in confronting the Western intrusion, it culminated in the 1940s and the 1950s as the Communists rose to power and founded the People's Republic of China (PRC). By depicting the West as the imperialist aggressor, it incited nationalist sentiment among the Chinese and instigated their animosity toward the West. In so doing, it enabled the PRC government, in Chen's words, to use this essentialized West "as a means for supporting a nationalism that effects the internal suppression of its own people. In this process, the Western Other is construed by a Chinese imagination, not for the purpose of dominating the West, but in order to discipline, and ultimately to dominate, the Chinese self at home" (p. 5). While Chen's work mainly describes this type of Occidentalism in 1980s China, judging from China's situation today, its practice seems to have not only persisted but also intensified as the country often sees surges of ultranationalistic behavior in its (young) populace. This ultranationalistic, anti-West sentiment is not entirely spontaneous, but has a good deal to do with the PRC government's decades-long nationalist propaganda, which often taps into the historical pride of the people.

Like its counterpart, anti-official Occidentalism also has a history that predated the founding of the PRC. It originated in the New Culture movement of the 1920s, if not earlier, in which the Western idea of democracy was invoked as a means to shore up the fledgling Republic in the face of warlordism and factionalism. In the post-Mao years when the PRC intellectuals reflected critically upon the tragic legacy of the Cultural Revolution (1966–1976), they sought to revisit and revive certain themes of the New Culture movement. This revivalist endeavor gave rise to "a powerful anti-official discourse using the Western Other as a metaphor for a political liberation against ideological oppression within a totalitarian society" (Chen, p. 8). Central to this anti-official Occidentalist discourse was the production of *Heshang* (River elegy), a TV documentary mini-series that aired nationally in China in 1988. It became a cause célèbre in the history of the PRC's TV industry, for while it attracted hundreds and thousands of viewers across social strata, it was also criticized by professional historians and later banned by the government. The criticisms centered on *Heshang*'s presentation of Chinese cultural tradition vis-à-vis modern Western culture, or Orient versus Occident, because the producers and writers, elevating the iconoclasm of the New Culture movement to a new level, vilified the Chinese cultural heritage and denied its relevance to modern life. Meanwhile, it glorified Western civilization, praising its openness, adventurousness, and youthfulness, to which the advance of capitalism and technology of the modern world were attributed. This China–West dichotomy was rendered vividly in *Heshang*'s cinematic presentation, in which the Yellow River and yellow earth, symbols of Chinese civilization, conveyed a deeply sorrowful feeling of death and stagnation, whereas the West was symbolized by the azure blue ocean, emanating energy and liveliness. These contrasting images appealed to the Chinese audience who, in the aftermath of the Cultural Revolution, were still haunted by the terrible memories of the country's recent past and frustrated by the setbacks in the century-long search for wealth and power. While seemingly a cultural critique, marking a climax of the "Culture Fever" (*wenhua re*) movement prevalent at the time, *Heshang*'s Occidentalism was, argues Xiaomei Chen, a counterdiscourse to official Occidentalism, because it indirectly and

effectively translated this public frustration into a veiled criticism of the palpable failure of the Communist government.

The divergent ways in constructing the Western imagery in contemporary China underscore that it is important for us to consider the context in which various forms of Occidentalist discourse have occurred. The attention paid to this context question can also help highlight the essential difference in the constructions of Orientalism and Occidentalism. Different from Edward Said's critique of Orientalism, in which he presents the East-West dichotomy in an invariable manner in order to stress the Western dominance of power, the presentation of the Occidentalist discourse has shown that such relationships can be quite flexible, depending on the specific sociocultural context. This is because when the Orientals perceive the West, their perception is shaped not only by the international and global climate of the modern world, but also by the domestic context in which such perception is called for. This consideration, too, should be applied to the Orientals' construction of the Self, because such an image is also often constructed and presented under and for the Western gaze. This practice of presenting Self for the Western Other has been given various terms, such as "Orientals' Orientalism," "self-imposed Orientalism," and "cooperative Orientalism." But to the extent that it is predicated on a projection by non-Westerners onto the West on which they set out to present their own cultures, it also amounts to a form of Occidentalism. The Japanese Buddhists' endeavor at promoting their persuasion to the Western world is a good example of this.

A more current example is shown in the success of the "fifth-generation" Chinese movie directors, led by Zhang Yimou, in winning numerous awards for their productions at movie festivals in the West from the 1990s on. What made their success particularly salient as a form of Occidentalism is that while Zhang and others produced works about China and Chinese culture, their productions were often not shown within China. This was sometimes the result of government bans, but a more important reason seemed to be that these movies were originally tailored to the taste of the Western audience. While the moviemakers visualize and represent China, what they actually accomplish is rather an imaginary West based on their own projections. Judging from their successes at Western movie festivals, their understanding of the West and, moreover, their imagination of how China would likely be perceived by the West, are quite correspondent with the reality. However, their presentations of China, ironically, were often not approved by their compatriots back home.

If this exercise of Occidentalism acts on an anticipation of how the Western Other is to gaze at the Self, there seems another way in which the Western Other is shown more accessible and cooperative for the Self. After China opened its doors to the world in the early 1980s, there appeared a series of novels (some of them also made into TV shows) depicting the experiences of Chinese students and immigrants living in the West, such as Zhou Li's *Manhadun de Zhongguo nuren* (1993; A Chinese woman in Manhattan), Yu Heizi's *Bolin de tiaozao* (1993; Fleas in Berlin), and Cao Guilin's *Beijingren zai niuyue* (1994; A native of Beijing in New York). A recurrent theme in these novels is that in order for a Chinese to succeed in the West, he or she must first know how to approach a thorough understanding of Western lifestyle and culture and adjust his or her life accordingly. But the Other never dominates the Self completely. Rather, it works with the Self in effecting the latter's ultimate success, an end that most of the protagonists managed to achieve. In this presentation, the East and West/Self and Other divide central to Said's critique of Orientalism becomes increasingly blurred. It thus calls for considerations of various contexts in which such conceptions are imagined and construed. This call for historical specificity perhaps marks the most notable contribution that the discourses of Occidentalism have made to our understanding of the world.

See also **Orientalism; Other, The, European Views of.**

BIBLIOGRAPHY

Ahiska, Meltem. "Occidentalism: The Historical Fantasy of the Modern." *The South Atlantic Quarterly* 102, nos. 2/3 (2003): 351–379.

Chen, Xiaomei. *Occidentalism: A Theory of Counter-Discourse in Post-Mao China.* 2nd ed. Lanham, Md.: Rowman and Littlefield, 2002.

Dirlik, Arif. "Chinese History and the Question of Orientalism." *History and Theory* 35, no. 4 (1996): 96–118.

Ketelaar, James. "Strategic Occidentalism: Meiji Buddhists at the World's Parliament of Religions." *Buddhist-Christian Studies* 11 (1991): 37–56.

Snodgrass, Judith. *Presenting Japanese Buddhism to the West: Orientalism, Occidentalism, and the Columbian Exposition.* Chapel Hill and London: University of North Carolina Press, 2003.

Tavakoli-Targhi, Mohamad. *Refashioning Iran: Orientalism, Occidentalism, and Historiography.* Basingstoke, U.K.: Palgrave, 2001.

Venn, Couze. *Occidentalism: Modernity and Subjectivity.* London and Thousand Oaks, Calif.: Sage, 2000.

Q. Edward Wang

ONTOGENY. *See* **Development.**

ORAL TRADITIONS.

This entry includes two subentries:

Overview
Telling, Sharing

OVERVIEW

The challenge of reconstructing the history of nonliterate or preliterate societies makes necessary the study and interpretation of oral traditions. Many such societies have gone to great extents to preserve and transmit the knowledge of their past in oral forms. The phrase *oral traditions* refers to folklore, legends, tales, taboos, and stories through which knowledge of the past is preserved and transmitted from one generation to

another. Oral traditions must be differentiated from *oral evidences,* which are experiential. Such traditions record the origins, movements, and settlements of peoples; the genealogy and chronology of royalty, priests, and citizens; and the important landmarks in history. Besides, much oral tradition can be gleaned from surviving cultural practices such as burials, rituals, games, and language.

Virtually all societies, including literate ones, have depended on oral traditions for the reconstruction of their histories at one point or other. "Once upon a time" or "long, long ago" are the usual introductions to the oral narratives that European and Native American children heard throughout their childhood and early adolescence. The knowledge of preliterate historical periods is derived in some form from oral accounts. As writing and documentation developed and literacy became widespread, however, this genre of historical recollection became less important in the literate societies. This is because of the presumed unreliability of oral traditions as compared with documents. Indeed, by the nineteenth century, a form of historiographical tradition had become established in Europe that held that only written sources could produce historical reliability. This was not unconnected to the development of archives and the documentary traditions of the medieval European courts. Europe-based historians of the nineteenth century tended to consider that nonliterate societies had no history.

Oral Tradition and the Search for the African Past

Thus, although oral traditions are not peculiar to black Africa; their use as a source for the construction of African history has attracted the most attention. Not many of the continent's peoples developed any extensive form of writing. Thus, the earliest written sources on African peoples were the accounts of European and Arab traders, travelers, and explorers who wrote about their experiences primarily for home audiences, or as personal memoirs. For this reason, many of the historical studies on Africa were considered not history but anthropology. Archaeological findings of early African civilizations were attributed to foreign influences. It is in this context that the British historian Hugh Trevor-Roper contended that Africa had no history apart from the activities there of Europeans and Arabs. This contention drew sharp responses from the intelligentsia on both sides of the Atlantic—including representatives of the evolving colonial African historical consciousness. There is also a sense in which the denigration of the African past was a replication of the European racial and colonial enterprise, referred to by Edward Said as a "race construct" of "otherness," that is, the creation of a negation of the European ideal in conquered and dominated peoples. The challenge for colonial African and indeed intellectual responses to the question of African history was to prove its existence through the only source that seemed available at the time: oral traditions.

Oral Traditions as a Source and as a Method of Historical Construction

African and Africanist historians have professed the value and reliability of oral traditions for the reconstruction of the history of African peoples. Their weaknesses as a source of historical reconstruction have been argued as no worse than those of other sources of history, including written records. Various processes have been developed for the mitigation of these weaknesses by the methodical gathering and treatment of oral traditions. This has also involved the conceptualization of oral tradition and the classification of the genres that make up oral traditions. Each of these typologies has peculiar treatment types.

Oral traditions, among many African peoples, are more complex, better-organized forms of recording history than the stories and legends of some other preliterate societies. Traditional controls in the form of training and taboos have served to guarantee the reliability of historical accounts. "Palace historians" and griots often occupy hereditary positions, and the training of custodians of a society's history usually begins at an early age. Special occasions such as coronations, burials, births, and other rituals present opportunities to perfect their arts. Stringent sanctions are attached to any distortion of historical accounts. The fact that in such societies crimes and punishments are communal and that physical and spiritual influences guide social compliance provides added checks against manipulation of accounts. Oral traditions have thus been successfully employed to reconstruct the history of many societies in Africa. In Nigeria, the pioneering works of Kenneth Dike—*Trade and Politics in the Niger Delta* (1956)—and Saburi Biobaku—*The Egba and Their Neighbours* (1957, based on a 1951 thesis) relied mainly on gathered oral traditions and have survived much historiographical scrutiny to remain national historical classics. Substantial works on East African history have also depended on the collection and use of oral traditions following the pioneering works of B. A. Ogot. Jan Vansina's seminal theoretical work, *Oral Tradition: A Study in Historical Methodology*, articulated the major theoretical advances for the defense of the use of oral traditions in historical reconstruction. The case for oral tradition was further taken up in his more recent study, *Oral Tradition as History*. Vansina, however, not only makes a case for the validity of oral tradition in historical reconstruction but has produced historical works that fully utilize the method. These include *The Tio Kingdom of the Middle Kongo 1880–1892* (1973) and *The Children of Wool: A History of the Kuba People* (1978). Vansina's influence as the foremost theoretician of oral tradition historiography is not in doubt.

The Use of Oral Traditions and Its Critics

There are obvious problems with the use of oral traditions. Critics easily point out that they lack absolute chronology, are extremely selective in their content, and are compromised by possible human errors. William G. Clarence-Smith argued that the value of using oral traditions has been not for their intrinsic worth but sentimental, as they offer African historians the opportunity to present an independent history, "uncontaminated by colonialism." Many of the theoretical advances in oral tradition have focused on how to lessen the impact of these weaknesses. The use of oral traditions demands a distinct professionalism that is not altogether dissimilar to that employed by historians who rely on other, "conventional" sources. Historians employing oral traditions, though, need to acquire additional qualities, including, as Phillips Stevens has com-

mented, intuition, which is not usually required by conventional historians.

Oral traditions have had much wider influence on global historiography that its critics would concede. The emphasis on written sources as the only reliable source of historical reconstruction has mellowed with the acknowledged contributions of other sources of history including archaeology, paleography, and linguistics, as well as oral traditions. An interdisciplinary approach to historical reconstruction has gained much currency among historians. Besides, the debate over oral traditions has also shed some critical light on written documents as sources of history, with a view to strengthening their reliability. It has become realized, for instance, that many written documents are in reality processed oral traditions. The study of oral traditions has developed as a recognized discipline and various projects in the collection and processing of these traditions are being undertaken in research institutions across the world.

See also **Historiography; History, Idea of; Memory; Oral Traditions: Telling, Sharing.**

BIBLIOGRAPHY

Afigbo, A. E. "Oral Tradition and the History of Segmentary Societies." In *Perspectives and Methods of Studying African History,* edited by Erim O. Erim and Okon E. Uya. Enugu, Nigeria: Fourth Dimension Publishers, 1984.

Clarence-Smith, William G., and Fernand Braudel. "A Note on the 'École Des Annales' and the Historiography of Africa." *History in Africa: A Journal of Method* 4 (1977): 275–281.

Curtin, Phillip D. "Oral Traditions and African History." *Journal of the African Folklore Institute* vi, nos. 2/3 (1969): 137–155.

Oosten, Jarich G., ed. *Text and Tales: Studies in Oral Tradition.* Leiden: Research School CNWS, 1994.

Stevens, Phillips, Jr. "The Uses of Oral Traditions in the Writing of African History." *Tarikh* 6, no 1 (1978): 21–30.

Vansina, Jan. "Oral Tradition and Its Methodology." In *UNESCO General History of Africa* I: Methodology and African Prehistory. Edited by Joseph Ki-Zerbo. Paris: UNESCO; London: Heinemann; and Berkeley: University of California Press, 1981.

———. *Oral Tradition as History.* Madison: University of Wisconsin Press, 1985.

———. *Oral Tradition: A Study in Historical Methodology.* Translated by H. M. Wright. Chicago: Aldine, 1965. Originally published in 1961.

Sola Akinrinade

TELLING, SHARING

For the vast majority of human history, the only way people could transmit information has been by speaking, listening, and remembering. Indeed, the capacity for speech and the connected capacities for learning and remembering might be thought of as the defining elements of human consciousness, shared perhaps with other, now extinct, members of the hominid lineage but not shared with any other existing species. Through speech, humans did more than coordinate cooperation necessary for individual and group survival; they transmitted knowledge. They taught new generations techniques and ideas. They developed the ability to use abstract and theoretical thinking that allowed them to adapt to new circumstances. They created moral codes that regulated behavior between genders, between generations, between ranks, and between communities, and devised elaborate justifications for these codes. They speculated about the sublime question of the reason for the existence of it all and made up great cosmological explanations that usually placed humanity at the center of some sort of creation. For the vast majority of the at least 100,000 years that *Homo sapiens* has walked the earth (and perhaps longer if earlier hominid species had the power of speech), humans transmitted all of this orally. It would seem then that speaking and listening are the "natural" way humans learn.

Humans used several techniques to help them remember what they had learned. They created objects that served to remind them of the spirits that watched over them and needed succor. They made images of those that had gone before. They portrayed their fears on available rock surfaces. Perhaps most importantly, and in some ways seemingly universally, they used meter and rhyme in language, pitch and syncopation in sound, noises created by the ingenious noisemakers they devised, and the movement of bodies in time to music to remind them of what was important to know.

What they needed to know and to remember, though, changed over time. Humans learned to forget that which seemed no longer important. Knowledge flowed seamlessly from past to present, from the ancestors to the living, from God or the gods to the mortal. What was told always sought relevance with what the hearers of the words lived.

Sometime about five thousand years ago, in Mesopotamia and Egypt, some human societies began to use symbols etched in clay tablets, painted on papyrus scrolls, or carved into stone to record at first basic data. Eventually people developed the ability to use writing to capture the most complex of abstractions and the most beautiful of poetic expressions. Gradually literacy developed in other places and spread to still others. Almost everywhere it was associated with power. Those in power wielded the written word as one of the tools of domination. They determined what was truth, what was history, what God wanted people to do or be. While the struggles among the literate over these issues are the stuff of literate history, for most people knowledge continued to be transmitted orally. Even with the development of printing, the rise of mass literacy, and the spread of "universal" education, many elements of culture and community remain expressed primarily if not wholly in oral form. Especially among communities in some way or another disempowered by the apparatus of literate knowledge, oral tradition remains an important means of transmitting knowledge and maintaining social solidarity.

Oral Tradition

The introduction above sketches an expansive definition of oral tradition, using the term to refer to any form of knowledge transmitted in a regular way between generations verbally. This definition, while broad, does distinguish between oral tradition and oral history. Researchers (who need not be professional historians or scholars) elicit oral history by interviewing informants. Oral history is information about the past that is spoken only in the context of personal memory. Generally, it includes life histories and personal recollections. It can include information told to an informant by others, such as parents. In the context of collecting oral histories, though, the research may also collect oral traditions.

While the expansive definition also allows for the existence of oral tradition in societies with literacy, oral traditions are usually associated with "preliterate" societies. In such societies, information can be passed on only through oral means. All known societies have oral texts that validate a moral order. Many have texts that depict the proper relationships between groups within a community and often with those outside a community. To the extent that social divisions exist, component groups often have their own form of traditions. In particular, women quite often have a distinctive body of oral texts circulated only among themselves. In addition to traditions that bind a community together, some types of traditions celebrate hierarchy and power. In particular, praise songs—panegyrics—not only signify power and prestige during the honoree's lifetime but often become eulogies remembered long afterward. Finally, great narratives, epics, and sagas served to tell the story of heroes and founders, of creators and minions.

Even when literacy emerged and spread, knowledge often continued to be transmitted and developed orally. Only elites often had extensive literacy in large parts of the world for long periods of time. While they might codify the epics into scripture and history, oral traditions often remained alive as folk wisdom and oral literature. Sometimes, oral traditions served as ideological justifications for counterhegemonic movements among subject classes or communities. Often, a complex interplay developed between oral and literate traditions. Even after the rise and spread of mass literacy, oral tradition has continued to play an important role in helping create popular, folk, and subaltern identities; however, the interaction between oral and literate in those cases often becomes more intimate and immediate.

The broad definition of oral tradition used here does not deny that there are sharp differences between situations where the only means of transmission of information is through oral communication and those where oral transmission serves as a refuge for a group in some way marked different from the rest of society. This definition, though, sees the differences more in terms of genre and function, than in terms of oral and literate societies or oral and literate people.

Genres in Oral Literature

Scholars working with orally transmitted information have identified a number of broad genres. Scholars define the genres by both function and form. Not every society has each of the genres. Scholars often approach these genres as different types of oral literature (a seeming oxymoron that acknowledges the creative energy involved in the preparation of oral texts), so different are they in form and function. Genres of oral literature include epics and sagas, panegyrics, prose stories, lyric poems, ritual songs, and genealogies. While all transmit knowledge, the genres do have different but sometimes overlapping functions.

Epics and sagas. More narrow definitions of oral tradition often limit it to epics and sagas. Epics, defined by the use of poetics, and sagas, prose, serve as foundational texts for societies. They tell the stories of the culture heroes who create society, of the origins of civilized behavior, of the creation of heaven and earth and the people who populate it. Epics (used hereafter for convenience) sometimes tell history. Other times they reveal God's or the gods' design to humans.

Perhaps the epics best known to Western readers are the *Iliad* and the *Odyssey,* which date in their recorded form to about the eighth century B.C.E. Classical Greek authorities named a bard called Homer as their author. They exhibit, however, characteristics that define them as oral literature. They are recorded as verse with many elements of repetition. While they are historical, as opposed to sacral, they serve as foundation texts for ancient Greek ideas of civilization and culture. They focus on the deeds of "great men" and the ways the gods intervene in the affairs of people. The structure of the *Odyssey*—the plight of a "wanderer" and his spouse who must wait for him—follows a structure found in many other epics in other cultures and times. The question for these epics comes from their transcription. Were they the production of one or two authors who worked with oral literature but made the finished products their own (given, of course, the possibility of changes to the texts in later copies)? Or are the epics in their present form truly composite examples of oral literature in which no guiding author can be seen in form as well as narrative? Such debates have also animated scholars when they consider sacred texts such as parts of both the Old and New Testaments as well as texts from India and China. Clearly, many of these texts, for example the Torah or first five books of the Bible, began as oral literature, functioning as creation myths that define the proper relationship between God and humanity.

Understanding the nature of the question of authorship requires understanding oral traditions, and especially epics, not just as texts but as performances. Over the centuries since Homer and the codification of the Torah, records have come down on the transcription of oral performances and the preparation for them by performers. Each time the song is sung, the tale told, the epic performed, it changes. Bards often served as more than just entertainers. Telling the tale, singing the song involved making a link with the audience, and giving the audience what it came to hear or admonishing the audience for what it has failed to do.

Tellers and performers usually plan such variations in advance to make their point or curry favor with their audience. Jan Jansen tells of witnessing the preparations for the performance—which happens once every seven years—of the Sundiata epic of the Mande people at the shrine of Kamabolon at Kangaba in the Republic of Mali. The epic tells of the founding of the Malian empire in the fourteenth century. The Diabate griots, or bards, members of the clan that supplied Sundiata with his griot, perform the full epic in the sanctuary as it has a new roof placed on it by a newly initiated age group. The only others present in the sanctuary are members of the Kieta, or royal, clan of the old empire. Outsiders may not see or record the actual ceremony. Griots tell the epic itself throughout the region, but the people hold the version told at Kangaba as the orthodox version, filled with secrets. Jansen, an outsider, attended the many practice sessions for the performance, as did almost anyone who wanted to. He reports that the griots debated quite intensely the wording and arrangement of the performance and the significance of its message. At the performance itself, Jansen noted that the griots cut it somewhat short. The performance, for a collection of royal clan members who had all heard it before, lacked the immediacy of the rehearsals, which featured the necessity both of working out the correct version of the epic among the professionals and of getting it right for the visitors who had come out of interest.

Even in cases where the performer is clearly subordinate to the intended audience, the performance of oral tradition creates a social persona for the performer. In most cases the performance creates society and social norms through linking people, communities, and institutions together. Whether the recitation of the Mansa Jigin, the Mande "gathering of kings," that confirms the centrality of the empire of Mali for the far-flung Mande peoples in diaspora all across West Africa (and in the early twenty-first century, New York and Paris), or the recital of a clan history at a funeral in central Tanzania by the heir to the deceased that recreates the ties of kinship and marriage linking people together across the region, oral traditions as performed generate community.

While epics and sagas are foundational documents akin to scripture in preliterate societies (and indeed scribes have sometimes converted them into scripture), they have component parts that bards stitch together (a direct translation from the ancient Greek of the bard's art). These components comprise some of the other genres of oral tradition. Bards can often recombine or condense or elaborate using these elements in the telling, combining them in different ways to fit audience and occasion. Taken as a whole, an epic is often no more than the most expansive collection of such components held together by the unity of theme and sometimes character.

Panegyrics. One of the most interesting and historic of these genres is the praise poem. This type of poetry, the panegyric, is found in a wide variety of societies. These poems are often composed for specific occasions, as happens among the Xhosa people of southern Africa. However, while the metaphors and similes used in them may sometimes be tropes of deep cultural significance, in particular cases praise poems become linked to particular historic figures, and hence become an important part of a culture's historic memory. The following quote comes from the praise poem of Shaka, the founder of the Zulu kingdom in South Africa in the early nineteenth century:

> Shaka went and erected temporary huts
> Between the Nsuze and the Thukela,
> In the country of Nyanya son of Manzawane;
> He ate up Mantondo son of Tazi,
> He felt him tasteless and spat him out,
> He devoured Sihayo.
> He who came dancing on the hillside of the Phuthiles,
> And he overcame Msikazi among the Ndimoshes.
> He met a long line of hah-de-dahs [ibis birds]

When he was going to destroy the foolish Pondos;
Shaka did not raid herds of cattle,
He raided herds of buck. (Owomoyela, p. 15)

These lines tell of several of the peoples and rulers Shaka conquered. Praise poems can then become one of the building blocks of epics, but in many cases they themselves become the most important form of historic memory. Cases where the elements of oral tradition do not coalesce into epics are more common than those where they do.

Stories. Stories, whether called folktales, fables, or even oral history, often serve the function of oral tradition. People use them to impart moral lessons and to promote a feeling of group solidarity through a sense of common history. They can be told in formal situations, such as initiation rituals or informally, such as around the hearth. Stories often tell moral tales, and sometimes they use structures, plots, and motifs spread quite widely across different cultures. However, with the addition of appropriate cultural detail, they also can refer to very specific episodes in local historical memory. As tellers tell and retell the story, it changes to provide a community with an agreed-upon explanation for the topic of the story. For example, in central Tanzania among the Gogo people, elders tell a story of something they say happened during the most serious famine in their history during World War I. A group of people fled hunger in their village to seek food from the newly established British administration in the wake of the East African campaign. They received no food at the administrative headquarters nor from the merchants in the small town along the rail line. They decided to camp for the night in a dry gully under the railroad tracks before trying to find food again the next day. That night a rainstorm filled the gully, and they all drowned. This author collected twenty-five versions of this story from throughout the region in Tanzania. While some details varied, all but one agreed that it occurred sometime between 1917 and 1919. The one outlier came from an elder who had been a colonial-era chief. He said he had known the people to which this tragedy had occurred and that it had happened not during World War I but during a famine several years later. As he was adamant, knowledgeable, and could name names, this author believes the former chief's oral history is "true." But the oral tradition created by the people out of this event encapsulates a complete explanation of colonial rule in the region. The people were conquered and ruled by Europeans who fought among themselves during World War I and killed many. They were exploited by an ever expanding market economy. Given these disruptions to the social order, they were abandoned by the forces of nature that first brought drought and then killed them with too much rain. Hence, the story became part of an agreed-upon explanation for colonial rule, and in memory they moved it back in time to the worst famine of their history.

As with panegyrics, some societies stitch such stories together to form epics. Stories such as this, though, often stand alone; and many societies never develop full-blown epics. Groups within societies often have their own sets of stories that emphasize their own particular place within society and relationship to other groups in it. Often, for example, women tell stories markedly different from those told by men, and they often tell them in contexts reserved for women alone. These stories, which may emphasize gender solidarity or debunk the claims made for well-known characters in other stories, are often labeled by men or other dominant groups as fables or as untrue. Just as much as stories told by men or dominant groups, though, they represent an agreed-upon explanation for why the world is the way that it is.

Ritual songs and lyric poetry. Songs and lyric poetry function much like stories in that they focus on particular events or situations. Like stories, they are sometimes historic but often fabulist. They change as bards and singers change them to fit audiences and circumstances. While they are often individual performances, groups can also perform them. The demands of meter and music impose a certain stability on them, especially those performed by groups. Work songs and ritual songs fall into this category. Work songs can consist sometimes of little more than a few lines repeated rhythmically for as long as the task lasts, but they can also impart moral or historic lessons. They can recall individuals or events associated with particular activities.

Ritual songs likewise can impart both historic and moral lessons. Songs performed at sacrifices, at celebrations of life passages, at healing rituals, at divining sessions all can serve the function of oral tradition. Songs or chants used in rituals can call upon historically important people or groups as intercessors with the divine. People often use music and dance to compliment the words of the songs. Dance in particular can act out, as well as act as a mnemonic device for, the story.

Genealogy. Genealogy is the final genre of oral tradition considered here. Genealogies quite literally link the past with the present by charting the ancestors to those still living. Genealogies usually contain more than mere lists of names. Tellers usually include both stories and praise poems for the ancestors as well as often detailed descriptions of relationships between different kin groups. Genealogies, like other forms of oral tradition, change as conditions change. In the long run, genealogies telescope with generations and relatives lost over time. Often, founders remain in the story, but the number of generations between the founder and the present may remain constant. Sometimes genealogies expand, as with king lists that proclaim consistently long reigns. Genealogies also often regularize relationships between generations, especially for holders of positions of authority. Usurpers become legitimate heirs. Inheritance through the female line gets changed to the male line in patrilineal societies and visa versa in matrilineal societies. Finally, genealogies in performance change to fit the circumstances. Social networks become embedded in genealogies as fictive kin relations. Such is the case in central Tanzania, where the principal heir recites the clan genealogy at a funeral. As with other genres, genealogies often make up an important part of epics, with bards stitching them into the narrative to highlight the proper relationship between groups.

The Modern Study of Oral Traditions

Over the course of the last two centuries, scholars have developed three distinct approaches to the study of oral traditions.

One, the oldest, sees oral traditions as "oral literature" or "folklore" and promotes analysis on literary and humanistic elements, often focusing on comparative analysis. The second sees oral traditions as expressions of cultural values and norms. Anthropologists, especially ethnographers, analyze such traditions as functional promoters of group solidarity or structuralist explanations for the workings of society. Scholars working in both of these approaches focus little on the historical veracity of traditions and sometimes argue they contain no historically valid information. Historians, particularly of preliterate societies, on the other hand, attempt to derive from oral traditions historically valid evidence. All three approaches complement one another. Understanding the cultural and historical context of an epic enriches the appreciation of it as literature. Ethnographic analysis requires historical grounding and an understanding of the importance of performance. Historical analysis must take into account both the performative aspects of oral tradition and the cultural structuring that occurs in it.

Two issues, however, often divide students of oral traditions. One is the perceived difference between oral and literate societies. Some scholars argue that literate societies promote entirely different ways of comprehending the world than do those without or with only limited literacy. Oral traditions transmit knowledge in metaphor and ahistorical essences. Critics of this approach maintain that it minimizes the creativity and logical ability of people in preliterate societies. The second main issue dividing scholars is the historical validity of oral traditions. Many suggest they have none, that oral traditions are so attuned to the present that all information about the past is structured beyond relevance. Other scholars argue that properly understood oral traditions do transmit historically valid evidence.

The first field that developed around what is now called oral traditions was that of folklore. Folklorists sought to collect oral texts both from societies perceived as nonliterate as well as from among marginalized groups in literate societies. In the nineteenth century the field became tied with the Romantic project of recovering the "true" culture of the nations of Europe. In its less politicized form, folklore turned to the comparative method, seeking to show relationships between epics and tales found in different parts of the world. Early folklorists tended to work in Western societies, although by the middle of the twentieth century many had begun to work with non-Western oral literatures, bringing their emphasis on textual analysis to oral literatures hitherto the domain of ethnographers.

Folklore studies became the study of oral literature as the works of Milman Parry and his student Alfred Lord dramatically transformed the field in the first half of the twentieth century. Parry and Lord collected epics and songs among the Muslims of Bosnia. Their work, most famously elaborated in Lord's *Singer of Tales,* generally saw epics as literature composed in performance but based on a formula that used meter to string together episodes and clichés from a common fund of such tales. Each performance, then, is different, and performers do introduce innovation, often to fit a particular audience. Epics, however, retain a broad stability over long periods of time. Lord, in particular, used the *Iliad* and the *Odyssey* as models for epics, and the great questions they sought

to answer concerned the actual "authorship" of such epics. Later scholars, such as Walter Ong and Werner Kelber, brought this approach to biblical studies.

Later scholars have criticized this oral literature approach for emphasizing textual analysis over context. The explicitly comparative approach minimizes the cultural and historically specific circumstances that have called forth the production of oral literature. They have charged that the importance placed on the difference between orality and literacy in the remembrance and performance of oral literature reduces it to a "formula" that denies the creativity of performers and the ways in which oral historians generate their histories.

Anthropologists, especially those engaged in ethnography, have also long used oral traditions as sources for their analyses of cultures and societies. Like folklore, anthropology originated as the study of a phenomenon outside the perceived mainstream of "Western civilization" in the nineteenth century. It began as the study of "primitive" societies. During the twentieth century, it quickly evolved into the study of culture broadly defined. As such, ethnographies have continued to draw heavily on a variety of genres of oral traditions in their efforts to portray culture.

Like folklorists, anthropologists have deemphasized the historicity of oral traditions. They have seen them functionally as means of promoting group solidarity and defining social norms. As such, they have seen them as entirely flexible, altered to suit changing circumstances. By the 1960s, the work of Claude Lévi-Strauss came to dominate such views. His argument that much of culture itself, as well as the expressions that defined and underpinned it, was structurally determined led to such important studies as Luc de Heusch's *The Drunken King.*

Starting in the late 1950s, the rise of new fields of historical studies led to a movement among historians to reevaluate oral sources for history. In particular, historians engaged in trying to recover a usable past for African societies, as nations on the continent began to emerge from colonialism, turned to oral traditions to recover a precolonial past often derided by colonial sources. Jan Vansina pioneered the collection of oral traditions, by which he meant mostly epics. In addition, the widespread epic tale of the founder of the kingdom of Mali, Sundiata, also attracted scholarly attention. The epic, performed by casted bards, *griots* in French or *jeli* in Mande, among many of the Mande-speaking peoples, tells of the founding of the empire in the thirteenth century and yet continues to be performed as a living oral tradition in the early twenty-first century.

Over the 1960s and 1970s, historians scoured Africa for oral traditions and produced works of incredible subtlety and incredible naïveté. While very few historians argued for the literalness of oral traditions as history, some took a more critical look at the context of the production of oral tradition than others. Ruth Finnegan, a leading folklorist, felt compelled to take historians to task for such naïveté. By the 1980s, historians had refined their approach to oral traditions. Some, such as David William Cohen, had moved close to a structuralist position. Vansina himself reworked his position on the collection of traditions, and many of his students showcased their work in *The African Past Speaks,* edited by Joseph Miller. Many scholars focused on the range of ways that historical information passed from generation to generation and the uses to which it was put. Since many African societies lack epic traditions, scholars have learned to use historical anecdotes, songs, stories, and life histories in innovative ways to answer questions about the past. These innovations have gone on to inform oral historical approaches in other areas and general historical debates about popular memory and history.

Oral Traditions and the Modern World

In a narrow sense, the rise of mass literacy and its spread (although still incomplete) across the globe has transformed the role of oral traditions in society. Just as happened in ancient Greece around 800 B.C.E., so it has happened repeatedly that when an epic is reduced to writing, it ceases to change. Written versions, with their stability, become orthodox, canonical versions. Yet, to see the gradual decline in importance of oral epics as the end of oral tradition takes much too narrow a view of the importance of the field. In some places, epics retain important functions and continue to be performed. The descendants of the royal griots of Mali who perform the full epic of Sundiata in a ritual reroofing of his shrine every seven years remain adamant that only they know the full version and that the transcriptions made over the years by many writers and scholars are pale glosses on the fullness of the epic.

More to the point, oral traditions in many parts of the world, including many communities in Western, wealthy, and industrialized nations, remain vibrant ways of expressing group solidarity. Oral traditions in the form of stories and songs continue to circulate widely in many communities as alternative takes on the world and its workings. They often express counterhegemonic tendencies and sometimes focus on communalism. They exist in situations where literate and especially formal discourse is dominated by state power.

Oral traditions have served to place humanity in the universe and to explain the workings of the world to humanity. The narrative mode of explanation embodied in the epic is a big part of what makes us human. But also the other genres of oral literature—the song, the riddle, the praise poem, the proverb, the genealogy—help delineate social relationships that define human society. Oral tradition remains the most immediate, the most "natural" way for humans to bring past and present together.

See also **Genre; Language, Linguistics, and Literacy; Reading.**

BIBLIOGRAPHY
Cohen, David William. "The Undefining of Oral Tradition." *Ethnohistory* 36, no. 1 (1989): 9–18.
Finnegan, Ruth H. *Oral Literature in Africa.* London: Clarendon, 1970.
Heusch, Luc de. *The Drunken King; Or, The Origin of the State.* Translated by Roy Willis. Bloomington: Indiana University Press, 1982.
Jansen, Jan. "Hot Issues: The 1997 Kamabolon Ceremony in Kangaba (Mali)." *African Studies Review* 31, no. 2 (1997): 253–278.
Kelber, Werner H. *The Oral and the Written Gospel: The Hermeneutics of Speaking and Writing in the Synoptic Tradition, Mark, Paul, and Q.* Philadelphia: Fortress, 1983.
Lord, Albert. *The Singer of Tales.* 2nd ed. Cambridge, Mass.: Harvard University Press, 2000.
Miller, Joseph, ed. *The African Past Speaks: Essays on Oral Tradition and History.* Hamden, Conn.: Archon, 1980.
Owomoyela, Oyekan. *African Literatures: An Introduction.* Waltham, Mass.: Crossroads Press, 1979.
Scheub, Harold. "A Review of African Oral Traditions and Literature." *African Studies Review* 28, no. 2/3 (1985): 1–72.
Tonkin, Elizabeth. *Narrating Our Pasts: The Social Construction of Oral History.* Cambridge, U.K.: Cambridge University Press, 1992.
Vail, Leroy, and Landeg White. *Power and the Praise Poem: Southern African Voices in History.* Charlottesville: University Press of Virginia, 1991.
Vansina, Jan. *Oral Tradition: A Study in Historical Methodology.* Translated by H. M. Wright. Chicago: Aldine, 1965.
———. *Oral Tradition as History.* Madison: University of Wisconsin Press, 1985.

Gregory H. Maddox

ORGANICISM. Organicism refers to the idea that some object or entity shares an important property or quality in common with a living or animate being. It is related to, although remains distinct from, holism, in the sense that organicist doctrines tend to uphold the view that the living creature is an integrated whole containing precisely the range and number of parts necessary for the maintenance of its existence and for its flourishing. Hence, organicism is closely aligned with the concept of "organic unity." Organicism enjoys a long intellectual history in a number of fields of endeavor, including metaphysics and logic, aesthetics, theology, and social and political thought. While perhaps most fully articulated by Western thinkers, organic ideas seem to have a global purchase.

Logic and Metaphysics

Plato's (c. 428–348 or 347 B.C.E.) metaphysical theories constitute an important starting place for organicism in the West. In the *Philebus,* he examined the problem of "how the one can be many, and the many one," that is, the ways in which diversity comports with unity. The Platonic doctrine of the Forms, as presented in the *Republic,* constituted one such solution. Even when Plato later criticized the failings of his own metaphysical teachings, as in the *Theatetus,* he remained committed to the principle that the totality is greater than the sum of its parts.

Aristotle (384–322 B.C.E.), in turn, rendered organicist doctrine a precept of logic by asserting that the whole is prior to its parts because it is only possible to conceive of the parts qua parts once one has grasped the whole. Hence, Aristotle maintained that the analysis of any organic unity requires a "decompositional" method that commences with the whole and then dissolves it into its constituent parts precisely in order to discover the contribution that each element makes to the totality. One finds applications of this logical method throughout the Aristotelian corpus, including his metaphysics, aesthetics, politics, and natural philosophy.

Organicist metaphysics thus stands in stark contrast to metaphysical atomism. The organicist believes that some inhering force—the Good, *telos*—unites beings into a single Being and therefore that apparent clashes or disparities between opposites are entirely illusory. The neo-Platonic doctrine of a concordance or coincidence of opposites follows an organicist track, as does Hegelian dialectical logic.

Aesthetics

While the idea that a work of art was an organic unity whose very "beauty" was constituted by its totality can be traced back to the ancient Greeks (for example, Aristotle's *Poetics*), this idea enjoyed its culmination in the modern world, especially among the Romantics. Johann Gottfried von Herder (1744–1803) emphasized the idea of an "inner form" that animated a poetic work, a precept that he applied, for instance, to Shakespearean drama. Herder's disciple, Johann Wolfgang von Goethe (1749–1832), soon adapted his insight. The *Critique of Judgment* (1790) by Immanuel Kant (1724–1804) developed more broadly and explicitly the analogy between a work of art and a living creature, which was developed by German Romantics such as Friedrich Wilhelm Joseph von Schelling (1775–1854) and Friedrich von Schlegel (1772–1829). Georg Wilhelm Friedrich Hegel (1770–1831) declared in his *Lectures on Aesthetics* (posthumously published in 1835) that genuine art required "self-enclosed completion" to be judged beautiful.

The most influential English critics expounded similar doctrines. Samuel Taylor Coleridge (1772–1834) proclaimed that the principle of "unity in multiplicity" constituted the essential feature in human imagination. That is, the genius of imagination was to draw together disparate and even contrary elements into a single, unified, seamless whole. William Blake (1757–1827) seconded this organicist aesthetics, and it was restated regularly by the English as well as Italian schools of neo-Hegelian philosophy of the late nineteenth and early twentieth centuries, represented by figures such as Bernard Bosanquet (1848–1923) and Benedetto Croce (1866–1952).

Theology and Cosmology

Many of the world's religions and philosophies have regarded the universe as possessing an organic unity as a macrocosm of a living body. For example, Hinduism, Sufism, the Russian philosophy of All-Unity, and numerous strains of Christianity (especially those of a mystical or neo-Platonic bent) display organicist tendencies by viewing the world as a collection of diverse beings that nevertheless possesses an integral unity. In this way, human beings may connect with God by submitting to the purposes found in the larger order of the cosmos; divinity is found in all things and orders diversity.

Perhaps the most controversial example of organic unity within the frame of religion is the Christian doctrine of the Trinity, that is, the idea that God is Three-in-One. Debates about the trinitarian character of divinity have long raged among theologians, who have been repeatedly challenged to explain how God can be composed of a single substance if He

is also three different and distinct beings. (Adherents to more strictly monotheistic doctrines, including Jews and Muslims as well as unitarian Christians, have found this teaching absurd or even polytheistic.) Some version of organicism has afforded trinitarian theologians a way to explain the three-fold yet single nature of God.

Social and Political Thought

Perhaps the most common expression of organicism on a global scale is the analogy between the living body (human or animal) and human community. The so-called metaphor of the body politic may be found in a number of ancient sources, including Asian works such as the *Analects* of Confucius (551–479 B.C.E.) and the *Arthashastra* of Kautilya (fl. 300 B.C.E.). In all cases, the aim of authors in deploying the analogy is to move beyond a strict hierarchical system of subordination and rule in social relations and to proclaim a principle of "reciprocity." A reciprocal relation connotes a natural self-regulating harmony or balance between the parts of the organism that aims at a higher goal such as justice within, or the material welfare of, the whole. Thus, the common tendency to equate organic theories of society with hierarchy per se is misinformed, although some conceptions of the body politic are stridently hierarchical.

In Western thought, the origins of the body politic can again be traced back to Greece and Rome in the writings of Plato, Aristotle, Cicero, and others. It was during the Latin Middle Ages, however, that the organic metaphor for society became commonplace. In its earliest expression, and perhaps under the influence of Plato's *Timaeus,* medieval society was divided into a three-fold yet unified functional order of those who fight, those who work, and those who pray. This was later replaced by a more self-consciously organic doctrine, the most influential exponent of which was John of Salisbury (1115 or 1120–1180). His *Policraticus* (completed 1159) contained an extensive account of how each of the organs and limbs of the human body—from the head to the toes—had a direct counterpart in society, from the king all the way down to the peasants and artisans. John's depiction of the organic community was widely disseminated and repeated by philosophers and political commentators, although many different implications (including surprisingly egalitarian ones) were drawn from it. In 1406, Christine de Pisan (1364–c. 1430) became the earliest author to construct an entire political treatise, *Le Livre du corps de policie (The Book of the Body Politic),* around the analogy. Christine made a special point of including advice even to the humblest of subjects—artisans and peasants—that explicitly demonstrated her respect for their contributions to the social whole.

Decline of Organicism

The rise of modern scientific thought and of moral and political individualism profoundly challenged and damaged the organicist outlook. The tendency to consider nature in mechanistic and evolutionary terms devalues the distinctively organic and purposive character of biological creatures, as does the emphasis on the individual as the building block of social institutions. Organicism has been conflated with methodological holism in logic and metaphysics or, worse still, with collectivism and authoritarianism in politics. Likewise, poststructuralism and other twentieth-century movements in criticism disputed the very uniqueness of the work of art as a cultural form distinct from its surroundings. Still, the popular invocation of phrases such as "body politic" suggests that the inclination to conceive of diversified unities in organicist terms has not completely disappeared from the intellectual stage.

See also **Logic; Metaphysics; Philosophy; Society.**

BIBLIOGRAPHY

Abrams, M. H. *The Mirror and the Lamp: Romantic Theory and the Critical Tradition.* New York: Oxford University Press, 1953.

Constable, Giles. *Three Studies in Medieval Religious and Social Thought.* Cambridge, U.K.: Cambridge University Press, 1995.

Feher, Michael, with Ramona Naddaff and Nadia Tazi, eds. *Fragments for a History of the Human Body.* 3 vols. New York: Zone, 1989.

Struve, Tilman. *Die Entwicklung der organologischen Staatsauffassung im Mittelalter.* Stuttgart, Germany: Hiersemann, 1978.

Cary J. Nederman

ORIENTALISM.

This entry includes two subentries:

Overview
African and Black Orientalism

OVERVIEW

The Arab-American political activist and professor of European literature Edward Said (1935–2003) durably redefined the term *Orientalism* with the publication in 1978 of his book by the same name. Before Said's book, Orientalism had two distinct meanings. Both were politically neutral and marginal to the central concerns of the humanities and social sciences. After Said's *Orientalism,* these two meanings have been collapsed into one that is highly charged politically and central to contemporary debates in the humanities and social sciences, while at the same time covering a smaller historical span than either of the two earlier meanings of the term.

One of the older meanings was the presence of motifs, themes, subjects, or allusions in the music, art, or literature of the Western world that were borrowed from, or meant to evoke or represent, the Orient. For the purpose of these artistic trends, the Orient meant, effectively, the lands immediately to the East and South of Europe: the Ottoman Empire (which included much of Southeast Europe), North Africa, the Arab lands, Iran, and Islamic Central Asia. While these lands have been in recent centuries the core of the Islamic world, Orientalist artists and writers did not separate the Islamic from the earlier ancient Orient in their imaginative constructions. And their interests could run from the current affairs of their own times to far earlier periods. Hence, Gustave Flaubert (1821–1880) wrote of nineteenth-century Egypt in his travel literature, but set his novel *Salammbô* in ancient Carthage. Similarly, the painter Eugene Delacroix (1798–1863) could exploit the same imagery to portray current events such as the Greek revolt (like most Romantics, he took the Greek, anti-Turkish, side) or the death of the ancient Assyrian ruler, Sardanapalus.

Oriental elements played several important roles in European creative arts. Musicians from Ludwig van Beethoven (1770–1827) and Charles Camille Saint-Saëns (1835–1921) to Nikolai Andreevich Rimsky-Korsakov (1844–1908) and Mikhail Mikhaylovich Ipolatov-Ivanov (1859–1935) borrowed instrumentation or characteristic modes. Writers introduced Oriental tales and settings to create exoticism and/or to gain critical distance from European mores and institutions (for example, the work of Voltaire [1694–1778] and Montesquieu [1689–1755]). Painters sought dramatic exotic subjects, different light, and often also the titillation of harem scenes. But such erotic exploitations were also made of classical antiquity.

The second meaning of Orientalism was the scholarly study, in the West, of the Orient. Scholarly Orientalism was based upon the study of ancient languages, other than Greek and Latin and their modern descendents. This meant Hebrew and the other Semitic languages, including Arabic, as well as Ancient Egyptian and Coptic (along with Assyriology) and eventually Persian and Turkish in their various historical manifestations. Methodologically, such Oriental studies were the extension of Classical studies. Philology was the queen of the sciences and the critical edition carried pride of place among scholarly achievements.

As a scholarly endeavor, Orientalism was pursued in a variety of European countries, as well as the United States. While scholars in some countries were naturally drawn to areas of local interest (for example, Spaniards in the Muslim domination of the Iberian peninsula, Italians in the Muslim occupation of Sicily), the most important sources of Orientalist scholarship were Britain, France, and Germany (with an important U.S. role beginning after World War II). Of these countries, Germany was for many years the most important (and of the three, the most influential in the development of American Orientalism), in line with the general leadership role of German scholarship in the West in the nineteenth and early twentieth centuries.

For most of the years preceding Said, the Middle Eastern response to scholarly Orientalism was mixed, but low-key. Archaeologists were considered in most quarters to be treasure hunters, especially as markets in antiquities (black and otherwise) continued to parallel archeological activities. There was also a widespread suspicion, not always misplaced, that Western scholars in the region were spies for their governments. Yet, despite this, Orientalists were always well down on the list of suspicious foreigners, preceded, for example, by missionaries, Zionists, and the more formal actors of military, political, and economic imperialism. There have always been many in the region who have openly collaborated in the Western scholarly enterprise. Middle Eastern scholars even attended European Oriental congresses at the turn of the twentieth century. Some among Middle Eastern educated elites were flattered by Western attention to their culture, some bemused, and most indifferent.

The attitudes of Western scholars to the imperialism that characterized so much of the nineteenth and twentieth centuries were also mixed. A few supported it, but many opposed it, taking the sides of the peoples they studied. Among cultural Orientalists, many Romantics (and some socialists such as the followers of Comte de Saint-Simon [1760–1825]) sought a strong East whose powerful spirituality could balance what they saw as the overly materialistic West.

Said conflated the two earlier meanings of Orientalism while associating the new amalgam with Western imperialism in the lands of Islam. For Said, both the cultural Orientalism of artists and writers and the scholarly study of the Middle East were separate facets of the same phenomenon: a hegemonic Western vision of the Islamic world. This vision was not a reflection, however distorted, of a Middle Eastern reality. Instead, it was an entirely Western construct reflecting Western fears and appetites in association with Western imperialism, which it both aided and benefited from. The usefulness of Orientalist knowledge to imperialism was based in its essentials not on the accuracy of practical information but on the notion of Western strength, activity, and superiority contrasted with Oriental weakness and passivity.

The thesis of Orientalism as the handmaiden of imperialism (or the other way around) was reinforced by Said's decision to ignore German scholarship and concentrate instead on British and French and, later, American production. If such a choice does not fit the history of scholarly Orientalism, it fits well the cultural marks that European imperialism left on the Arab world. A knowledge of English or French (and sometimes both) is common among the more Westernized members of the Arab intelligentsia. Many are those (such as Said himself) who received their instruction in French- or English-language schools in the region. German is rarely found outside of Turkey.

The same can be said of Said's choice of epochs. For scholarly Orientalism, the connection with the Ancient Near East was crucial. Arabic and Hebrew were studied together under the intellectual canopy of Comparative Semitics. Not only philologists but also anthropologists thought that studying the Arabs could help them understand the Hebrews of the Bible. In *Orientalism* as well as subsequent writings, Said concentrated on Western attitudes to the region in its Arab and Islamic periods. This, too, reflects cultural politics on the ground. Popular attitudes as well as the dominant political movements have almost always based their sense of identity on the region as it was remade by the great Arab Islamic military (and only later cultural) expansion of the seventh century. This is as true of the Arab nationalism whose influence is waning at the turn of the twenty-first century as it is of the Islamic revivalism simultaneously in the ascendant.

Interest in the pre-Islamic world has virtually no popular existence and is confined to relatively marginal branches of the Westernized intelligentsia and occasional clumsy manipulation by authoritarian governments. It should be noted that during the heyday of imperialism, local participation in the study of the pre-Islamic East was not always encouraged, although since independence in the mid-twentieth century the situation has been completely reversed.

Focusing on the Arab-Islamic periods and especially on the period of Western imperialism supports the political claims of both Arab nationalists and Islamic revivalists. Attention to the period before the rise of Islam has the opposite effect, and instead could carry grist to the mill of Zionists, since it is on ancient history that the latter base their historical claims.

Said's insistence on the hegemonic implications of intellectual and cultural discourses harks back to Antonio Gramsci (1891–1937). But both the Arab-American professor's focus on discursive practices and their association with power, and his identification of a virtual episteme whose essence remains unchanging while its forms vary superficially, show the influence of Michel Foucault (1926–1984). One difference is that Foucault wrote of the invention of the human sciences while Said treated only a specific application, that of one civilization's vision of another. A second difference would be that in several of his most famous works, Foucault specifically linked intellectual discourses with institutional practices (for example, in medicine and penology). Said, by contrast, leaves the relationship between cultural discourses and specific imperialist practices unarticulated.

As cultural politics, Said's *Orientalism* brought together Zhdanovism, *tiers-mondisme,* and American multiculturalism. Zhdanovism, or intellectual Stalinism, is the extreme version of intellectual engagement. It argues that knowledge must be judged according to whether or not it serves the political interests of the forces of historical progress. In the original version, this meant the interests of the proletariat as confounded with those of the Communist movement and the Soviet Union. Said makes no such bald claim, but his assumption that Orientalist knowledge is vitiated by its association with imperialism, along with his complaint that such scholarship did not represent the historical aspirations of the peoples of the Middle East, leads to Zhdanovist conclusions. And this is certainly how his followers have applied Said's work. *Tiers-mondisme,* as associated for example with the work of Frantz Fanon (1925–1961), substituted the third world for the proletariat of advanced industrial societies as the carrier of historical progress, turning Western imperialism and resistance to it from relatively marginal events to the center of the story of the emancipation of humanity. As an academic practice, American multiculturalism redefines scholarly domains by the ethnic or other identity groups considered the subject of study. At the same time, academic multiculturalism stresses the distinct experiential knowledge of members of the group, implying that they should have a dominant, for some even exclusive, role in the study and teaching of these newly defined subjects. Multiculturalism then intersects with social policy as it blurs the distinction between diversity in the faculty and diversity in the curriculum.

Most reviewers of *Orientalism* found the work to be seriously damaged by errors that showed its general ignorance of the Middle East and scholarship on it. This was even true of reviewers who sympathized with Said's political positions on the Middle East. Many also called attention to his tendentious arguments and highly debatable interpretive leaps. Yet despite these reviews, Said's extraordinarily dense prose, and his thinly stretched reasonings, *Orientalism* was an international best-seller. It has been translated into numerous languages and made of Said the best-known professor of English in the United States and one of the most influential academics on the world scene. In the field of Middle East studies, his impact was dramatic. Never, it would appear, has a long-established episteme been so swiftly overthrown, or at least never have so many run away from it so quickly. Orientalism became a dirty word. The international Orientalist congress even changed its name.

When Said's book appeared in 1978, Middle East studies in the United States, and to a lesser degree in Europe, was already at a turning point. The old philologically based Orientalism was ceding leadership to the new area studies paradigm supported by massive U.S. government post-Sputnik Cold War expenditures. If the old Orientalism favored ancient and medieval civilizations with their classical languages, the new area studies favored the imperial and post-imperial world while deemphasizing language knowledge. Institutionally, the rivalry was reflected in competition between the American Oriental Society, for the old school, and the Middle East Studies Association, for the new. In this environment, it was relatively easy for the area studies specialists to claim distinction from the Orientalists. And this despite the fact that Said was careful to include the new area studies in his condemnation.

The triumph of anti-Orientalist sentiment operated dialectically with other trends. The European-trained immigrants who founded American Orientalism after World War II largely failed to reproduce themselves. Some circles in the old Orientalism discouraged the participation of natives of the region. New waves of professors came less and less from the old classical languages mode. Increasingly, they were immigrants from the Middle East, aided by the contemporary cult of native-speaker language teachers. Or these professors were Peace Corps veterans who had fallen in love with their country of assignment (especially with Iran), and often with one of its citizens. Such experts were naturally more sympathetic to the political interests of the region they studied. In this, they reflected most area studies in which, with the pointed exception of Communist Eastern Europe, practitioners identified with the causes of chosen regions and were often sharply critical of U.S. government policy. Just as French *tiers-mondisme* was in many ways a reflection of the brutal and divisive Algerian War, American anti-Orientalism was nourished by the sequels of the Vietnam trauma. American elites after the civil rights movement were justifiably sensitive to any charge of racism, and anti-racism became a leading value in American academic circles. This is one of the reasons why anti-Orientalism has had a deeper impact on American scholarly production than that in Europe, despite the latter continent's history of direct imperial administration of the Middle East.

Said's public, and courageous, political assumption of his Palestinian identity and his outspoken defense of the Palestinian cause also strengthened the reception of his ideas. Few knew in those early years that Said grew up in comfortable circumstances in Alexandria, Egypt, studied in English language schools such as the prestigious Victoria College, and was not at home in the language of his ancestors. The 1980s and 1990s also saw intellectual and academic sentiment in the United States, originally sympathetic to Israel, become increasingly critical of the Jewish state and concerned with the plight of the Palestinians.

Said's intellectual influence was apparent among graduate students in the early 1980s. Those who taught in those years remember the earnest objections to any comments or materials that seemed to cast the Middle East or its peoples in an unflattering light. A number of ideas, based upon Said, became common currency among students who later became professors. Generalizations about the region were vulnerable to opposite critiques. Applying a Western model to the Middle East was Europocentric. Creating a distinct model for the region was censured as the fabrication of an Oriental essence. Critics who were ignorant of the history of their field of study, or who doubted the cultural and economic reality of the Islamic Middle East, argued that Orientalism (or Middle East studies) was the only field that had created its own object of research before describing it. Charges of reification and reductionism fell like rain.

The intellectual fracas around Orientalism played to predilections in the American academic market, especially the national reluctance to learn foreign languages. A movement dedicated to fighting Western arrogance has had the paradoxical effect of restricting knowledge. The Orientalists were language buffs and commonly worked in more than one Near Eastern language and half a dozen European ones. Their successors do not often have a command of more than one Near Eastern language, and regular use of more than one European language (other than English) is rare. At the same time, the scholarly study of the Western image of the Orient has blossomed from a minor subfield of English or French literary studies into a central area of inquiry, even among scholars of Middle East studies for whom such topics are politically safer and linguistically easier. The unflattering examination of images of the Arabs and the Middle East in American popular culture also flourished. Paradoxically, the Orientalism controversy has shifted relative attention from the region and back to an American society obsessed with identity politics.

But the impact of Professor Said and the *Orientalism* paradigm has gone far beyond Middle Eastern or other Oriental studies. Among scholars of English—and to a lesser degree of other European—literatures, Said was a major if not the most important force behind a shift in emphasis in literary studies. To his supporters, this was a salutary move from formal literary-textual properties to historical situations of creation and reception, from aesthetic interests to political ones. To its critics, this trend represents a license for writing on history and politics by scholars who have neither the background, training, nor methodological awareness provided by the disciplines of history and political science.

Knocking Orientalism off its academic pedestal also led to the creation of a self-consciously new academic subfield: postcolonial studies. Though some historians and anthropologists have adopted this model, its major intellectual home remains departments of English and, to a lesser extent, those newly created departments and programs of Cultural Studies. The area treated by postcolonial studies is for the most part coterminous with the domain previously assigned to Third-World Studies. The greatest novelty of postcolonial studies is a relative shift of emphasis. On the one hand, by constantly referring to the post-colony, this approach deemphasizes both the earlier precolonial history of the societies in question and the differences in the nature of the imperial impact on different cultures. Postcolonialism emphasizes relations between the colony and the metropole, making imperialism the most important factor in the history of non-Western peoples, just as the term colony expresses the greatest degree of imperial subjugation. At the same time, postcolonial studies have highlighted the increasing interpenetration of Third World and First World societies associated with globalization. Said is generally credited as the godfather of postcolonial studies.

Events of September 2001 inaugurated a new phase in the evolution of Middle Eastern studies in the United States and at the same time in the debate over Orientalism. These 2001 phenomena have done so by accelerating trends already present. The better-known event was the terrorist attacks on New York and Washington, D.C. on September 11, 2001, carried out in the name of Islam. But only a few days before, an international conference against racism that took place in Durban, South Africa, inaugurated a new member into the club of social evils: Islamophobia. As an irrational fear of Islam, or even just a fear of Islam, Islamophobia is the progeny of Said's *Orientalism.*

But the attacks of September 11 were also the most violent expression of larger trends in the Middle East. The popularity of Said and of his works among the relatively secularized branches of the Middle East intelligentsia has masked the fact that the positions championed by Said—cultural openness and progressive politics combined with vigorous anti-imperialism and anti-Zionism—have lost ground to a frequently reactionary Islamic revival in religion and politics. Middle East experts did pay some attention to this trend, but they tended to underestimate its importance, its reactionary nature, and its capacity for violence. Ironically, this underestimation was at least partly caused by the effects of the Orientalism controversy. On the one hand, scholars were reluctant to broadcast bad news from the region. On the other hand, the attack on the Orientalists discredited, by association, everything they stood for. This included knowledge of the more classical forms of Arabic. Said's work accelerated the trend, already present in area studies, to shift Arabic instruction in American and European universities from the more classical to the more modern versions of the language, sometimes going so far as to seek to replace the modern literary idiom (which is universal for the region) with instruction in the local spoken dialects.

And yet the classical form of Arabic has been the preferred medium, in some ways the cultural signature, of the Islamic revival. The twenty-first century's Islamists and Jihadists use classical formulations and quote medieval sources and examples with great frequency. This goes well beyond the citation of the Koran and hadiths (the sayings and actions of the

Prophet Muhammad) to include medieval theologians, commentators, and historians. Academic Middle Eastern studies in the West was moving away from the classical idiom at the precise moment when the Arabs were returning to it.

The September 11 attacks reversed this trend by creating a new model for Middle Eastern studies, the institute or department of Islamic Studies. Increased public demand for knowledge on this now apparently important subject has been met with increased supply as both Muslim governments and Islamic groups in the United States have combined to support new university positions. This trend, when added to the slightly earlier expansion of Jewish studies, has further strengthened the identity-based nature of American university scholarship on the Middle East.

In the wake of September 11, American media, both popular and elite, are engaged in a debate about the nature of Islam and its role in the modern world. Is Islam a religion of peace? Or one that advocates holy war? Did the terrorists hijack a religion or merely express one of its options? Are those who criticize Islamic movements, institutions, or leadership echoing a long-held Western prejudice based on ignorance? Are fears of Muslims as potential terrorists in the United States prudence or prejudice? Would airport profiling or selective immigration rules be part of American racism? Are Arabs in America subject to discrimination as people of color? All these debates come back to the fundamental issue of Orientalism, as redefined by Said—a deeply held Western prejudice against the East, serving imperialist causes. In this way, the controversy over Orientalism continues, though the word itself has almost disappeared, victim of the political success of its critics.

See also **Ethnocentrism; Eurocentrism; Occidentalism; Orientalism: African and Black Orientalism; Other, The, European Views of.**

BIBLIOGRAPHY

"After the Last Sky: The Humanism of Edward Said." *Intersections: The Near Eastern Center Newsletter of The G.E. Von Grunebaum Center for Near Eastern Studies, University of California, Los Angeles* XXIV, no. 2 (2004).

Charnay, J. P. *Les Contre-Orients, ou, Comment penser l'Autre selon soi.* Paris: Sindbad, 1980.

Fanon, Frantz. *Les damnés de la terre.* Paris: François Maspéro, 1961. Translated into English as *The Wretched of the Earth.*

Foucault, Michel. *Les mots et les choses, une archéologie des sciences humaines.* Paris: Gallimard, 1966.

———. *Surveiller et punir: Naissance de la prison.* Paris: Gallimard, 1975.

Lewis, Bernard, Edmund Leites, and Margaret Case, eds. *As Others See Us: Mutual Perceptions, East and West.* New York: International Society for the Comparative Study of Civilizations, 1985.

"L'Orientalisme, Interrogations." Special issue. *Peuples Méditeranéens/Mediterranean Peoples* 50 (1990): entire issue.

Malti-Douglas, Fedwa. "Dangerous Crossings: Gender and Criticism in Arabic Literary Studies." In *Borderwork: Feminist Engagements with Comparative Literature,* edited by Margaret R. Higonnet. Ithaca, N.Y.: Cornell University Press, 1994.

———. "Re-orienting Orientalism." *Virginia Quarterly Review* 55, no. 4 (1979): 724–733.

Rodinson, Maxime. *La fascination de l'Islam.* Paris: F. Maspéro, 1980.

Said, Edward W. *Covering Islam: How the Media and the Experts Determine How We See the Rest of the World.* New York: Pantheon, 1981.

———. *Orientalism.* New York: Pantheon, 1978.

Shaheen, Jack G. *The TV Arab.* Bowling Green, Ohio: Bowling Green State University Popular Press, 1984.

Tidrick, Kathryn. *Heart-Beguiling Araby.* Cambridge, U.K.: Cambridge University Press, 1981.

Allen Douglas
Fedwa Malti-Douglas

AFRICAN AND BLACK ORIENTALISM

Edward Said's 1978 book, *Orientalism,* is the harshest critique to date of Western scholarship on the Muslim orient. However, its focus is almost exclusively on the Near and Middle East. The policy statements of William Ponty, the French governor-general in Senegal (1907–1915), quoted below suggest a link between Orientalism, as understood by Edward Said, and colonial scholarship on Muslim societies in sub-Saharan Africa.

It is our duty to study the Muslim society of our colonies in the minutest details. . . . It presupposes special studies of Islam which the great Orientalists of France and of Europe have now virtually succeeded in establishing. . . . [The study] will seem very attractive to many because of the scientific interest attached to it. But above all it is interesting for political and administrative reasons. It is almost impossible to administer an Islamic people wisely, if one does not understand its religious faith, its judicial system and its social organization, which are all intimately connected and are strongly influenced by the Coran [*sic*] and the prophetic tradition. It is this understanding of native society which, alone, will enable a peaceful and profound action on the minds of the people. It is, therefore, in this study . . . that we will find the surest bases and the most suitable directions for our Muslim policy. (Harrison, p. 107)

Writings such as these have prompted scholars to explore the links between Orientalism and European-language scholarship on Africa, produced notably during the colonial period.

Africa and European Colonial Scholarship

European governments commissioned much of Western scholarship on African Muslim societies produced in the colonial period. The most influential writers on African Islam were scholar-administrators, or at least closely linked with colonial administrations. Britain, Germany, Holland, and France commissioned the most respected specialists on Islam to study the Muslim societies that were coming under their rule. The scholarship therefore studied Islam as a focus of resistance to colonial rule. Sometimes the scholars sought to justify the colonial undertaking.

For example, the writer of the apology of British occupation of Northern Nigeria, *A Tropical Dependency* (1905), was Flora Shaw, the colonial correspondent for the London *Times,* who eventually married Lord Luggard, the first high commissioner of the British protectorate of Nigeria. Lady Luggard argued that African Islam had lost its initial grandeur and had betrayed its own ideals. Britain could, therefore, no longer ignore her historic responsibility to take over.

An anthology of works on African Islam by colonial-administrators would be encyclopedic. François Clozel, Maurice Delafosse, Jules Brévié and Paul Marty, Lady Luggard, Christiaan Snouck Hurgronje, and C.-H. Becker, to name a few, all adapted their writings for use by the colonial establishments that they served. Other scholars, such as Edward Wilmot Blyden, were missionaries, who by and large saw Islam either as an obstacle in their bid to Christianize Africa or else as a temporary and intermediary stage in the black African's journey from "paganism" to Christianity.

The image of African Islam that emerges from these writings is not consistent. Islam is revolutionary; it is fatalistic. It is misogynist; it elevates the status of the African woman. It is egalitarian; it allows a small clique of religious men (*marabouts*) to live at the expense of their gullible followers. All these perceptions and more had a lot to do with the concrete experiences of the scholars, the diversity of the societies studied, and the changing priorities and political landscapes of the colonizing countries. In consonance with the essentialism that Edward Said decries, writers tended to explain the behaviors of individuals and communities by evoking the single, universal, and unchanging reality of their being Islamic.

Not all of the images about African Muslim societies in colonial scholarship are, therefore, negative. Moreover, one has to acknowledge the great contributions made by some of the Orientalists to our knowledge of the societies they studied. For example, it was Octave Houdas, a French Orientalist, who studied and translated into French, over a hundred years ago, two of the most significant histories of West Africa, the *Tarikh el-Fettach* and the *Tarikh es-Soudan.* He was aided in this by Maurice Delafosse, a French linguist and ethnologist, who also a French colonial administrator. It is the view of some modern commentators that many of the Orientalist approaches to African Islam have been carried over into contemporary scholarship on Africa and African literature.

Orientalism, African Literature, and Criticism

George Lang is likely one of the first scholars to draw attention to Orientalist features in European-language African writing. Lang explores the effects of the reductions of Islam's complexity upon Africanist writing. The denial of the complexity of Islam impedes the understanding not just of Islam but of Africa. In the area of literary criticism, very frequently one or other dimension of Islam is either missed by Western critics or cast out of context. This also leads to significant misinterpretations of African novels of Islamic inspiration. Similar arguments are developed in Ahmed Bangura's book *Islam and the West African Novel: The Politics of Representation* (2000).

Edris Makward acknowledges a new shift in the African novel from a linguistic (English-French) to a religious polarity based on writers' attitudes to Islam. The thought was impressed upon him by an address given in 1979 by Wole Soyinka in which Soyinka praises Sembène Ousmane, a Senegalese writer, for being critical of Islam in his work while denying Cheikh Hamidou Kane, another Senegalese writer, the merit of authenticity for depicting Islam as part of Senegal's heritage rather than as an alien religion that was imposed through violence and other coercive means.

Similarly, in the early 1990s Ali Mazrui and Wole Soyinka were locked in a debate pertaining partly to the question of African authenticity and the Islamic factor. Ali Mazrui wrote the article "Wole Soyinka as a Television Critic: A Parable of Deception" in response to Soyinka's negative critique in *Index to Censorship* of Ali Mazrui's television series, *The Africans: A Triple Heritage*. In his article, Soyinka accuses Mazrui of denigrating indigenous African culture in the series. Perhaps more significantly, he alludes to the fact that Mazrui is not only culturally Arabized, he is also by both blood and vocal identification part Arab. In both the address alluded to by Edris Makward and the debate between Soyinka and Mazrui, Soyinka repeats some of the negative opinions about Islam that one finds in colonial writings: Islam is a seductive superstition that was imposed on the Africans through the sword. Perhaps more significantly, Soyinka is ready to discredit an African scholar's interpretation of African history on the bases that the scholar is a Muslim and has allegedly Arab-Islamic sympathies.

Wole Soyinka's critique of Islam is part of an intellectual current that some commentators would consider to be Orientalist. It is related to the issue of Islam and African or black identity. Some African and black scholars assert that black Americans and black Africans who profess or advocate Islam are committing a form of cultural apostasy. They are critical of all "alien" ideologies such as Islam, which have allegedly brought havoc to Africa and the Black Diaspora.

Black America and Black Orientalism

Ali Mazrui was probably the first person to use the term *Black Orientalism* in his critique of the PBS documentary *Wonders of the African World*, produced by Henry Gates, an African-American professor. According to Mazrui, Gates is a Black Orientalist because he made condescending, paternalistic, ideologically selective, superficial, and uninformed depictions of Africa. He also suggests that Gate's emphasis on black Africans' participation in the Atlantic slave trade ends up exonerating the West. Just as Western Orientalist scholarship was used to justify and promote colonialism, Gate's work is an apology for European colonization and domination of the African continent.

Mazrui's use of Orientalism is very unconventional. He does not focus on Gate's attitudes toward Arabs, Muslims, and Islam, although Gate's documentary made what could be construed as negative and problematic portrayals of Arabs in the segments on Egypt and East Africa. Moreover, it is not clear why Mazrui calls Gate's alleged Orientalism "Black" and not African-American or just American.

Black Orientalism and "Immigrant" Islam

Sherman Jackson's article on "Black Orientalism" helps one to see Orientalism in the context of the African-American experience. Jackson detected a major shift in black American responses to Islam and the immigrant Muslim community in America. Prior to the wave of Muslim immigration to America in the 1970s, Islam was by and large perceived in the black community as an authentic expression of African-American spirituality and identity. The gains of Islam that resulted from this perception constituted a loss to other African-American religious denominations and movements.

Then the new immigrants came with historical Islam from the Middle East and other parts of the Muslim world. The center of Islamic religious authority started shifting away from its erstwhile black core to new forms of orthodoxy that did not always manifest an understanding of African-American religious and ideological aspirations. "Real Islam" came to be perceived in segments of the African-American community as the religion of Arabs and foreigners, and black Americans who professed Islam increasingly faced the criticism of being cultural heretics, "self-hating 'wannabees' who had simply moved from the back of the bus to the back of the camel" (Jackson, p. 22).

Jackson makes a distinction between a critique of Islam, Arabs, and Muslim societies based on experience and sound knowledge and criticism based on imagination, ideology, and projection. It is the latter that can be called Orientalist. Black Orientalism seeks to undermine the popularity of Islam among African-Americans by highlighting the alleged race prejudice of the Muslim world. Jackson singles out for particular criticism the Afrocentric movement as it is best articulated in the writings of Professor Molefi Kete Asante, notably in *Afrocentricity* and *The Afrocentric Idea*. While Jackson reveals the problems in Black Orientalism, he also cautions immigrant Muslims to be sensitive to African-American Muslims' historical experience and to be active in building bridges with indigenous American Muslim communities. A failure to do so will alienate African-American Muslims and provide evidence to Black Orientalists, who are all too eager to portray Islam as a foreign and racist religion.

Jackson's study indicates that Black Orientalists are critical of Islam mainly on racial grounds. It would have been more helpful had it addressed the interlocking issue of Islam and the black American Muslim woman's experience. After all, Islam is more commonly perceived as holding women in subordination. This perception is, however, at odds with the enduring attractiveness of Islam to many accomplished black American women. The illustrious life of the late Betty Shabazz is worth citing, and so are the endeavors of other African-American Muslim women such as the professors Aminah McCloud and Carolyn Moxley Rouse, as well as many others, who are making their mark in different spheres of life.

Incidentally, Rouse's book *Engaged Surrender: African American Women and Islam* (2004) seeks precisely to clarify what Islam may mean to some black American women who have accepted it as their faith.

Conclusion

Based on the foregoing analysis, one can see that Orientalism, as it applies to Blacks and Africa, describes realities that are not necessarily in consonance with Edward Said's original use of the term. In Said's usage, Orientalism is place-bound. It refers to scholarship on the Muslim orient. George Lang, Sherman Jackson, and other scholars have focused on the central targets of Orientalist discourse—Arabs, Islam, and Muslims—regardless of the geographical location.

See also *Ethnocentrism; Eurocentrism; Orientalism: Overview; Other, The, European Views of.*

BIBLIOGRAPHY

Bangura, Ahmed. *Islam and the West African Novel: The Politics of Representation.* Boulder, Colo.: Lynne Rienner, 2000.

Harrison, Christopher. *France and Islam in West Africa, 1860–1960.* Cambridge, U.K.: Cambridge University Press, 1988.

Jackson, Sherman. "Black Orientalism: Its Genesis, Aims and Significance for American Islam." In *Muslims in the United States,* edited by Philippa Strum and Danielle Tarantolo. Washington, D.C.: Woodrow Wilson Center for Scholars, 2003.

Lang, George. "Through a Prism Darkly: 'Orientalism' in European-Language African Writing." In *Faces of Islam in African Literature,* edited by Kenneth Harrow, 299–311. London and Portsmouth, N.H.: Heinemann, 1991.

Makward, Edris. "Women, Tradition and Religion in Sembène Ousmane's Work." In *Faces of Islam in African Literature,* edited by Kenneth Harrow. London and Portsmouth, N.H.: Heinemann, 1991.

Mazrui, Alie. "Black Orientalism." *West African Review* 1, no. 2 (2000).

———. "The Dual Memory: Genetic and Factual." *Transition* 57 (1992): 134–146.

———. "Wole Soyinka as a Television Critic: A Parable of Deception." *Transition* 54 (1991): 165–177.

Rouse, Carolyn. *Engaged Surrender: African American Women and Islam.* Berkeley: University of California Press, 2004.

Soyinka, Wole. "Footnote to a Satanic Trilogy." *Transition* 57 (1992): 148–149.

———. "Religion and Human Rights." *Index on Censorship* 17, no. 5 (1988): 82–85.

———. "Triple Tropes of Trickery." *Transition* 54 (1991): 178–183.

Ahmed S. Bangura

ORTHODOXY. The very suggestion of a unified tradition implicit in the idea of the word *orthodox* renders its meaning problematic for the simple reason that conceptions of any religion's traditions are notoriously pluralist. Moreover, the term is hardly universal, since it is seldom applied to indigenous traditions around the world, even though there are some beliefs and practices within each aboriginal group that might be regarded as orthodox to some practitioners—for example, the Plains peoples in North America regard the Sundance as an "orthodox" rite. Generally the articulation of a theological system is one requirement of an orthodox tradition, and indigenous traditions rarely have such a publicly acknowledged construction. Despite its problems, though, major religions continue to use the term, and believers, external observers, and sometimes scholars find it useful. In the contemporary period, it embraces notions of the traditional, conservative, basic, and customary, all of which point to a normative idea about a religion's self-understanding. Because history, rituals, institutions, and doctrines all combine in manifold ways in each religion, orthodoxy really has to be understood from within each religion. Key notions will be drawn from diverse religious traditions.

Christianity
Christianity, for example, has a major group of churches whose links to each other in a single communion constitutes the Orthodox Church. Adherents look back to the great ecumenical councils and even to Jesus's apostles as the root of their identity, but the groups that make up national churches known as autocephalous (meaning that they are in full communion with each other, but independent of external, patriarchal authority) also acknowledge autonomous churches—that is, those that are not in full communion with them (usually because of some jurisdiction issue). Other issues related to identity also play a role; Orthodox Christianity makes much of its connection to the Greek fathers, has adopted the Julian calendar, affirms the validity of married parish priests, and gives an important place to monasticism, especially that of Mount Athos, from which the episcopacy is drawn.

Orthodox Christianity's central doctrinal difference with Western Christianity concerns the Trinity as developed by St. Augustine; Orthodoxy rejects the *filioque* affirmed by the Latin Church; the Latin idea was that the Holy Spirit proceeded from both the Father *and* the Son. Orthodoxy made the rejection of this doctrine a central fixture of its beliefs. Perhaps as a result, a different spirit is to be found in Orthodox liturgy, where the worshipper is encouraged to experience the presence of God in the sacraments, the icons, and the beauty of the rituals. This emphasis implies an engagement with God's mystical presence in many forms, whereas the Western Church emphasizes the person of Jesus Christ as the principal focus of that engagement.

Beyond this reference to particular institutional churches, however, one must acknowledge that Christianity in general holds certain notions to be orthodox: the idea of a sacred writing called the Scriptures, the role of the community of believers, the church, the central place of Jesus Christ in the understanding of revelation, and a firm commitment to the concept of God. While each of these doctrines is configured according to each group's theological instincts, all Christian groups insist on these conceptions as normative, and in some sense they all see them as existing from the beginning of the tradition. Feminist theologians have raised questions about the representativeness of such "orthodoxies," since, they hold, the orthodox theologians ignore the patriarchal substratum within which conventional theology was framed. The feminist claim is to a more authentic equality and inclusionary model before the official orthodoxy shaped the accepted discourse. Despite these claims, one point seems convincing: included in the term *orthodoxy* is the idea that it reflects a loyalty to the original or authentic content and expression of the religion.

Judaism
Religious orthodoxies are not necessarily historically ancient. Judaism's distinctive Orthodox tradition is fairly recent: 1791.

In this year, France recognized Judaism as a separate religion. This was partly in response to Moses Mendelssohn's influence, but also to Hasidism (established by Shem Tov [1700–1765]), which became an international movement emphasizing the return to the fundamentals of the tradition. By the beginning of the nineteenth century it had become clear to practicing Jews that the Orthodox way of life could be demarcated from those who affirmed a reforming vision of the tradition. Those who believed that the law, whether oral or written, was divine came to be known as Orthodox; for them, Torah could not be subject to modernization or cultural alteration, as the Reform Tradition insisted should be done.

For the Orthodox believers, however, the central ideas of their faith had nothing to do with Reform doctrine. Rather, Orthodoxy was based on limitations on the kinds of food that could be eaten under the laws of *kashrut,* proper observance of the Sabbath (i.e., restraint on activities on the day of rest), and a vigorous commitment to family purity. In effect, Orthodoxy was (and is) home-centered in ways other Judaic traditions were not, for the purity of the family arose out of relations between husband and wife and could not be observed by outsiders, while the laws of *kashrut* were principally practiced in the home. A life of training at home coupled with school-supported teachings and solid synagogue attendance constituted the main parameters of the Orthodox way of life; a corollary of this approach was (and is) a certain reluctance toward participation in modern life and even a trend towards isolation, especially in the face of contemporary secularism.

These beliefs have institutional impact; a central perception is that both non-Orthodox rabbis and converts to Judaism are beyond Orthodoxy and hence outside the community of those who practice the true Torah life. Consequently, community membership is hence strongly defined. In North America, Orthodox communities have steadily maintained their presence through an emphasis on the Hebrew language, *yeshivot* (day schools), and a trained rabbinate through Yeshiva University. Such an emphasis on a "true" Torah education also sets the Orthodox tradition apart from believers in the Conservative, Reform, and Reconstructionist branches of modern Judaism. The experience of the Orthodox in Judaism highlights the fact that orthodoxy is not always rooted in religion's antiquity.

Islam

Islam also reflects how difficult it is to define the term *orthodoxy,* even for a tradition that holds that the *umma* (the Islamic community) is theoretically united as one because God is one and He has given one divine Scripture, the Koran. There is, for example, no word in the Koran that is equivalent to the English word *orthodox.* Western writers often regard Sunnism, the tradition to whom the majority of Muslims belong, as orthodox, and many introductory texts define orthodoxy that way. But such a view is not valid, because Shiism, the other important group in Islam, does not regard Sunnism as defining Muslim orthodoxy for a variety of reasons, and even Sunnis would be reluctant to regard their beliefs as "normative," implying that others are not, because the Koran insists that one's true religion is to be judged by God, not by humans.

JEWISH ORTHODOXY

Of all the things you can teach, Gemara (explanations of the Mishna) is more important than anything else. Gemara is everything. It is *Torah sheh ba'al peh'* (the Oral Law). It's the real stuff. Everything else will follow. In this world it is *Torah sheh ba'al peh',* which is the harder way, not the sweet way; it's demanding . . . . But we also give them what the guys call "bags of candy." We always laugh about it. They themselves call other studies bags of candy after a while. The rabbi calls it that, too. He says, "Okay. Give out bags of candy."

SOURCE: Murray Danzger, *Returning to Tradition: The Contemporary Revival of Orthodox Judaism.* (New Haven: Yale University Press, 1989), p. 118.

Moreover, contemporary Islam has been challenged by Islamism, or fundamentalism, which cuts across traditional distinctions between Sunni and Shii and embraces a neoconservative ideology that its practitioners regard as orthodox. Part of the doctrine of that stance involves an antipathy to all non-Muslim ideas and cultural expressions. Currently the West, in all its cultural diversity, is the object of that negative reading. This perception of Islamic orthodoxy is rejected by both mainstream Sunnis and Shiis.

Some scholars prefer to regard Sunnism as an orthopraxy, meaning that the way of life developed by most Muslims around the world reflects important common elements of belief and practice. The formation of a normative path for the believer to walk, particularly by means of the *shari'a* (Islamic law), became the preferred idea. Insisting on such a view accords with Sunni notions of their own tradition, because at a critical time in its development (c. 900 C.E.), Islamic doctrine moved away from Greek intellectual categories and the use of the mind to construct theologies. Such a movement reduced the input of the mind in constructing the true understanding of Islam. Still, even Shiis would accept that restriction with some modifications.

Despite these important qualifiers, orthodoxy does have a place in Islamic self-expression. For example, the Koran itself implores, "guide us in the *mustaqiam* [straight] path" (1:6), thereby implying that there is a singular way of being Muslim that all should follow. Moreover, Muslims have always valued the noun *salaam,* a word whose meanings include soundness of being, an attribute of God, as well as peace; in its verbal form it means "surrender" or "submit," and in another form it gives the name of the religion, Islam. Furthermore, submitting to God is held to bring a special perfection to the human

---

> The method of final salvation that I have propounded is neither a sort of meditation, such has been practiced by many scholars in China or Japan, nor is it a repetition of the Buddha's name by those who have studied and understood the deep meaning of it. It is nothing but the mere repetition of the "Namu Amida Butsu," without a doubt of his mercy, whereby one may be born into the Land of Perfect Bliss. The mere repetition with firm faith includes all the practical details, such as the three-fold preparation of mind and the four primordial truths. If I as an individual had any doctrine more profound than this, I should . . . be left out of the Vow of the Amida Buddha.
>
> SOURCE: Honen's *Pure Land Buddhism*. In Ryūsaku Tsunoda, Wm. Theodore de Bary, and Donald Keene, compilers, *Sources of Japanese Tradition*. (New York: Columbia University Press, 1958), p. 208.

being, a perfection called *salaam*. Finally, from the Koran, the verbal form *waqaa*, which means to protect, defend, or preserve, has a noun form *taqwa*, god-fearing or righteousness. This word takes on special meanings in pious circles, for it suggests someone who lives according to normative Islam.

Some contemporary Muslim women have argued that too much of traditional scholarship, and indeed, most of the tradition since the Prophet, has been crafted without proper regard to the principles of equality. They therefore maintain that the true orthodox position of Islam was essentially gender-neutral; male scholarship subsequently skewed the true orthodox position away from women's equal rights (see Ahmed). They contend that Islam must return to the true orthodox position on gender relations. All these interpretations delineate the idea of ethical and religious exemplariness involved in any definition of orthodoxy.

Hinduism

Hindu tradition has always privileged diversity, and at first blush, discovering any form of orthodoxy in Hinduism may seem to be impossible. Indeed, there is no institutional form that the majority of Hindus would consider the orthodox group. Nevertheless, there are ideas within Hinduism that fulfill the notion of orthodoxy, such as those designated by the word *astika*, or assenting to the authority of the Vedas. Almost all Hindus would acknowledge the singular importance and basic religious authority of the collection of texts known as the four Vedas. Moreover, the ordinary believer would probably insist that the most important marker of orthodoxy is the religious activity and interpretation approved by the local Brahman; he defines normativeness for the common folk.

Scholars acknowledge that some rituals are not propounded in the Vedas—rituals such as cremation, for example. Yet cremation acts are certainly *smriti* ("that which is remembered"); they are required acts that go beyond the Vedic record but are held to be essential for an acceptable Hindu life. Such requirements may be found in writings such as the *Laws of Manu,* a work that provides evidence that local custom can also be a

source of the true *dharma* (duty). Yet once again such teachings are likely to be defined for the faithful by the most respected local authority. Those of a more philosophical bent might insist that the system of belief known as Vedanta is likely the most orthodox "theology," even where some of the notions of the philosophical system pose serious problems.

Finally, in Hinduism, even if orthodoxy is not enshrined in any one particular sect or group, it does take a social form. An orthodox Hindu social form is represented most plainly by the caste system. Following one's designated caste in everything, from how and with whom one associates, to the minutia of life (i.e., what caste the person is who prepares lunch) indicates a marker of special gravity in Hindu tradition. Hindu women are deeply affected by the traditional stance of the dharma on caste, for it has defined women's roles almost completely within the role of marriage. The subordination of women to their husbands is most graphically expressed in the rite of suttee (from the Sanskrit *sati,* "faithful wife"), in which the widow immolated herself on her husband's funeral pyre. Modern Hindu women struggle with the implication of an identity tied to husbands and not to their own dharma. Still, for many Hindus, whether male or female, proper caste interaction is a true measure of one's orthodoxy.

Buddhism

The issue of orthodoxy in Buddhism has been a matter of no little disputation; the earliest form of the teachings of the Enlightened One (the Buddha) held sway for several centuries before the variety of Buddhist converts pushed the tradition to embrace doctrinal diversity. The "original" dharma, meaning the teachings or truth taught by the Buddha, was embodied in a *sangha,* or religious order, which encompassed both lay and ordained disciples. These "three jewels"—the Buddha, dharma, and sangha—constitute the fundamental building blocks upon which the worldwide Buddhist community rests. Yet the tradition became so diversified and those who pursued enlightenment so far removed from the milieu of ancient India, where the Buddha flourished, that three distinctive ways or "vehicles" developed: the Theravada, the Mahayana, and the Vajrayana.

The Theravadans hold that they are loyal to the original Buddhist tradition, insisting, then, that they are orthodox in their teachings. They are often dubbed Hinayana ("Little Vehicle") by rival Buddhists, implying that they have restricted the means of enlightenment to a single kind of experience. Both the other vehicles, however, hold that they are just as orthodox. They maintain that they accept other cultural frameworks for configuring the dharma and they notably give great significance to the Bodhisattva in the practice of Buddhism. For the ordinary believer, weighed down by the chores of life, the assistance of one who has completed the way is a magnificent boon: the Bodhisattva puts off entering into nirvana in order to assist those who are less endowed with good karma by transferring some of the merit obtained in the process of enlightenment to the less advanced searcher for enlightenment.

Debates about orthodoxy arose largely because of Buddhism's swift successes across manifold cultural frontiers, and these debates pitted those committed to the earliest texts and most common social forms associated with earliest Indian Buddhism (termed the Way of the Elders) against more manifold expressions. Buddhist orthodoxy, then, rests upon claims of authentic connection to the ideas, doctrines, and social forms deemed consistent with those of this early period. Those committed to the Theravadan tradition believe that theirs most closely follows these normative dimensions of that early Buddhism. Others insist that their enlightenment truth is the same (i.e., is orthodox) but that the formulas for expressing it in human language must be diversified in order to appeal to humans in their rich cultural environment. Initially such groups designated themselves as Mahayanist or "Big Vehicle."

In addition, Mahayanist tradition developed several philosophical schools as ways to comprehend the true impact of the Buddha's teachings for all kinds of minds. One of the most important of these was begun by a Brahman convert called Nagarjuna. His position is referred to as the "Middle Way," or *Madhyamika*. It is sometimes regarded as the most orthodox of the many schools in Mahayana Buddhism. Nagarjuna declined to debate whether or not one could talk about what is absolutely real. He insisted, rather, that anything that could be claimed to be real had to be "empty" of self-essence or absolute truth claims. This was because all the evidence around us in the world of phenomena points to the fact that nothing is permanent. Nagarjuna noted that everything appears to have an essence that abides forever, but in truth it does not. Thus what is true must be empty of such claims—it is truly "nothing" in its most authentic expression.

His orthodoxy of thought is often contrasted to orthodoxy of practice, such as that expressed in the great Yogacara school of meditation practice developed by a *bhiksu,* or monk, named Maitreya (270–350 C.E.), who insisted on the momentariness of all conscious awareness. Once one had meditated to the point where the false nature of substance became apparent, one could then proceed to the point where consciousness itself would merge into ultimate reality. His sketch of the processes of meditation provided the foundation for subsequent meditational developments and hence took on a kind of conservative orthodoxy. The citation of these schools as orthodox shows that the term relates to fundamental stances toward what is real or what exists.

Buddhist women in particular have no problem with the traditional religious understandings of the way, whichever of the three vehicles they belong to, but more and more they are objecting to the social restrictions imposed by the patriarchal structures of the Buddhist societies in which they live. Traditionally, monks were regarded as superior to nuns, and seldom were female practitioners of any Buddhism school accorded a leadership role. Monastic codes almost always insisted that females adopt a male stance in order to progress along the path. Currently women are insisting on the equality expressed by the Buddha's original teachings, a notion of orthodoxy that differs considerably from the norm. In the final analysis, the case of Buddhist orthodoxy raises the issue of whether orthodoxy's meaning can be limited to a single linguistic or cultural expression. Rather, it might well rest upon a core intuition which is then embodied in many cultural forms and languages, all of them ultimately unreal but all provisionally necessary for human knowledge.

This survey does not exhaust the religious environments in which the ideas of orthodoxy flourish, but what has been noted here should throw into relief some of the key ideas and affirm the multidimensionality of the term. Since the very use of the word implies exclusion, it runs counter to the more positive instincts of inclusion important today, especially in the West. Still, orthodoxy reminds us again of the immense power that religious affirmation and division have encapsulated in the human family.

See also **Buddhism; Christianity; Hinduism; Islam; Judaism; Orthopraxy; Religion.**

BIBLIOGRAPHY
Ahmed, Leila. *Women and Gender in Islam: Historical Roots of a Modern Debate.* New Haven, Conn.: Yale University Press, 1992.
Allen, Michael, and S. N. Mukherjee, eds. *Women in India and Nepal.* Canberra: Australian National University, 1982.
Basham, A. L. *The Wonder that Was India: A Survey of the Culture of the Indian Sub-Continent before the Coming of the Muslims.* New York: Grove Press, 1959.
Carmody, Denise Lardner. *Women and World Religions.* 2nd ed. Englewood Cliffs, N.J.: Prentice Hall, 1989.
Carmody, Denise Lardner, and John Tully Carmody. *Roman Catholicism: An Introduction.* New York: Macmillan, 1990.
Danzger, Murray Herbert. *Returning to Tradition: The Contemporary Revival of Orthodox Judaism.* New Haven, Conn.: Yale University Press, 1989.
Esposito, John J. *Islam: The Straight Path.* New York: Oxford University Press, 1988.
Gross, Rita M. *Buddhism after Patriarchy: A Feminist History, Analysis, and Reconstruction of Buddhism.* Albany: State University of New York Press, 1993.
Klostermaier, Klaus K. *A Survey of Hinduism.* Albany: State University of New York Press, 1989.
Meyendorff, John. *The Orthodox Church: Its Past and Its Role in the World Today.* Translated by John Chapin. New York: Pantheon, 1962.

Robinson, Richard H., and Willard L. Johnson, assisted by Kathryn Tsai and Shinzen Young. *The Buddhist Religion: A Historical Introduction.* 3rd ed. Belmont, Calif.: Wadsworth, 1982.

Ruether, Rosemary Radford, ed. *Religion and Sexism: Images of Women in the Jewish and Christian Tradition.* New York: Simon and Schuster, 1974.

Sharma, Arvind, ed. *Today's Woman in World Religions.* Introduction by Katherine K. Young. Albany: State University of New York Press, 1994.

Tsunoda, Ryūsaku, Wm. Theodore de Bary, and Donald Keene, compilers. *Sources of Japanese Tradition.* New York: Columbia University Press, 1958.

Williams, Paul. *Mahāyāna Buddhism: The Doctrinal Foundations.* London and New York: Routledge, 1989.

Ware, Timothy. *The Orthodox Church.* Baltimore, Md.: Penguin, 1964.

Earle H. Waugh

ORTHOPRAXY.

This entry includes two subentries:

Asia
Western Orthopraxy

ASIA

The term *orthopraxy* means "right practice," and stands as a contrast term for *orthodoxy* "right belief." It is often said of Asian traditions generally that—in contrast to most Western traditions—right practice is of more importance that right belief, and to a certain extent this is true. For instance, Confucianism is primarily concerned with the rituals and practices that constitute a properly ordered society, while Buddhism is ultimately concerned with the practices that bring about enlightenment. This emphasis should not be overstated, however, as particular beliefs often undergird the practices of Asian traditions (as in Confucian beliefs about the nature of cosmic order) and the practices themselves sometimes vary so widely as to call into question the very notion of right practice (as in Buddhism). As the following accounts will indicate, orthopraxy plays an important role in Asian traditions, but the definition of this role is always strewn with the challenges of diversity, consistency, and regulation within each of these traditions.

Hinduism

Orthopraxy is difficult to define for Hinduism, not because there is no mention of what constitutes right action, but rather because there is such diversity within Hinduism that it becomes difficult—if not impossible—to say anything definitive about the tradition as a whole. For any practice that might be considered "right practice" within Hinduism, there are usually a few traditions for which it is either irrelevant or even "wrong practice" (*heteropraxy*). Yet whatever diversity there is pertaining to practice, there is still more diversity pertaining to belief. For example, some Hindus believe in one god, others believe in many gods, and still others believe in no gods at all;

yet, within Hinduism, none of these beliefs necessarily renders a person unorthodox. Indeed, Hindus have at times demonstrated a remarkable pluralism with respect to belief (although variations in belief have often been seen as inferior alternatives), but have tended to identify themselves and their tradition with the rites and practices that underlie Hindu society.

Perhaps the most consistent trait of Hindus is that some relation to the Vedic texts plays an important role in their religious and cultural lives. Hindus tend to distinguish between two broad groups: the *astika* (those who accept the authority of the Vedas) and *nastika* (those who do not accept the authority of the Vedas). It should be noted that such acceptance says nothing about what beliefs a person or group holds, but rather whether they are participating in the preservation and enrichment of Hindu society as inaugurated in the Vedas. Thus, "orthoprax" Hindus are considered *astika,* while Buddhists, Jainas, and Carvakas (those who reject the tradition stemming out of the Vedas) are considered *nastika.* The Vedic tradition is ultimately a belief in the dharma revealed by the Vedas—the cosmic order of reality that, when embodied in the structure of Hindu society, leads to social and cosmic harmony.

The most basic exemplification of the dharma is proper observation of caste distinctions (although there are additional distinctions made according to age, social position, etc.). Within Hindu thought, caste distinctions are not artificial constructs, but natural designations: one is born into a particular caste because of karmic residue from past lives. Moreover, society functions well only when these distinctions are respected, because each caste was created with particular capacities that correspond to particular needs within society. Traditionally, *Brahmans*—typically seen as the highest caste—are priests and scholars, *kshatriyas* are warriors and rulers, *vaishyas* are merchants and artisans, and *shudras* are farmers and laborers (the so-called untouchables typically fall outside of the caste system, and are seen as even lower than the *shudras*). Right practice for a Hindu is thus a matter of living according to one's caste and performing the duties and obligations of that caste (that is, living according to the dharma); however, because those duties and obligations are often different for each caste, what constitutes right practice for any Hindu is typically dependent on their caste (as well as a number of other related social considerations). Needless to say, caste intermarriage and attempts at social mobility have traditionally been censured within Hinduism.

Just as there are exceptions to the aforementioned adherence to the tradition stemming out of the Vedas, so there are other, less central practices that are widespread among Hindus (for example, reverence for the cow, refraining from harming other creatures, etc.). Furthermore, there are a number of *dharmashastras* (texts of religious laws) and other post-Vedic literature that further specify right action with respect to rituals, caste relations, and personal discipline (e.g., the *Manava Dharmashastra* or *Manusmrti, Laws of Manu*). What all of these manifold specifications of practice have in common, however, is that they all exemplify the attempt to act in accordance with the dharma for one's position in life and to do so while accruing as little negative karma as possible. Thus, while the

Vedas may not be in the forefront of every Hindu's understanding of "right action," they ultimately inform the traditions that make such action properly Hindu.

With the *Brahman* class at the head of the Hindu caste system, one would expect authority to reside with them for interpreting orthopraxy with respect to the dharma. Historically, *Brahman* scholars have in fact seen themselves as the protectors of the dharma and have argued in the courts of their rulers (typically *kshatriya*) for the preservation and enforcement of a social structure based on the Vedic rules and ritual practices. However, because there has traditionally been no prevailing institutional authority for Hinduism, such preservation and enforcement has typically been possible only at the level of broad social pressure. Moreover, any authority the *Brahmans* have for interpreting the dharma has been at least matched by the authority afforded to extraordinary devotees and saints of any caste for reinterpreting it. Perhaps the most prominent recent example of this is found in Mahatma Gandhi (1869–1948), who proposed a radical shift in the structure of Hindu society by renaming—and thus repositioning—the so-called untouchables (those who reside in India but fall outside of the caste system); he renamed them *harijan,* or "God's people," and gave them equal status among other Hindus in temples. As Gandhi's case illustrates, the authority for reinterpreting the dharma does not necessarily reside with social position (Gandhi was a member of the *vaishya* caste), but rather with the moral authority—usually understood in terms of devotion and service—to speak on behalf of the dharma.

In the end, orthopraxy is crucial to the understanding of Hinduism not because Hinduism entails no particular beliefs or because it makes no claims for orthodoxy; different traditions do espouse particular beliefs, and many will not hesitate to claim orthodoxy for those beliefs. Rather, orthopraxy is important for Hinduism because the commonality of practices among Hindus far exceeds the commonality of beliefs. Indeed, it is not merely religious scholars but also Hindus themselves who define Hindu identity in terms of practices more than beliefs. This emphasis on practice rather than belief runs counter to the typical Western model of religions, but it is an emphasis that proves characteristic not only of Hinduism but also of Asian religious and social traditions generally.

Buddhism

Strictly speaking, Buddhism is not interested in right action, as action itself is tied up in the ignorance and desire that Buddhism is intended to overcome. At least with respect to its ultimate aims, Buddhism is primarily interested in realizing the emptiness (*shunyata*) of action (as well as all other things, especially the self), and thus achieving enlightenment (nirvana). As Buddhists find themselves faced with a world that demands decisions in the midst of this quest for enlightenment, however, they have found it useful and appropriate to comment on what would constitute right practice in such a context. The most prominent example of this is found in the Eightfold Path for achieving enlightenment, as laid out in Gautama Buddha's (c. 563–c. 483 B.C.E.) first sermon. This path consists of right views, right intention, right speech, right action, right livelihood, right effort, right mindfulness, and right concentration

(*Samyutta-nikaya,* 420). From this account, at least two things become clear: The first is that Buddhism is not entirely antinomian—it is quite possible to follow the wrong path; the second is that, while right beliefs play an important role in Buddhist practice, greater emphasis is placed on right practice. At least at the origins of Buddhism, enlightenment was possible only when one's practices were consistent with the Eightfold Path.

Following the death of Gautama Buddha, however, Buddhism ceased to have any centralized religious authority and thus found it difficult to maintain any consistency with respect to its interpretation of the Buddha's message. It is notable that the early Buddhists held councils to determine right belief and practice, but—as evidenced by the various accounts of different schools—they proved less than effective at achieving any substantive degree of consistency. Rather, as Buddhism was interpreted by different persons in increasingly different contexts (in Tibet, China, and Japan), this diversity only compounded. Indeed, such diversity of practice is often considered a virtue: according to the doctrine of *upaya-kaushalya* (skillful means), the Buddhist message is not seen as something static but rather something to be altered in such a way as to be effectively communicated to its intended audience. Thus, at least in theory, the diversity of forms that Buddhist practices can take is potentially limitless. These differences should not be overstated, because there is still an underlying consistency to Buddhism that affirms prevalence of illusion and the need for enlightenment; however, the practices that are pursued as a means to that end vary remarkably among the various schools of Buddhism.

Aside from the Eightfold Path, Buddhist orthopraxy is also exemplified in rituals and monastic orders. Rituals of one form or another are practiced by all Buddhists—monks and nuns, as well as laypersons—and pertain to actions whose merit can be applied toward achieving nirvana or a better position in the next reincarnation. This includes not only engaging in virtuous behavior and avoiding vicious behavior, but also participating in ceremonies, acts of devotion, and other symbolic acts. Significantly, whereas ritual is seen as secondary to meditation in most Buddhist traditions, it is given equal status and prominence in Tibetan Buddhism for the attainment of enlightenment. Monastic orders, in turn, offer a more disciplined approach, including an increased enforcement of orthopraxy in order to assist in aligning one's actions with the path to enlightenment (as the path is understood by that particular monastery). These practices differ from monastery to monastery, but they generally follow from the doctrinal commitments of each monastery. Like their monastic practices, Buddhist practices in general also vary markedly from context to context; what holds true in Buddhism across the board, however, is that these practices—whatever they are—are always designed to bring local Buddhists ever closer to nirvana.

Chinese Religion

From its very beginnings, Chinese society has placed a particular emphasis on the right performance of rituals. In the Shang dynasty (c. 1554–1045/1040 B.C.E.), this had to do primarily with performing rituals to appease the High God (Shangdi), one's ancestors, and other spiritual powers. It should be noted that the larger part of ritual activity was applied to the

> Consider this doctrine as utilized some centuries later by Zhu Xi's (1130–1200) to (somewhat one-sidedly) compare Confucians and Buddhists on the question of ritual propriety.
>
> > [A student] asked how to tell the difference between Confucianism and Buddhism. The teacher said: just take the teaching 'what heaven has endowed is called the nature.' The Buddhists simply do not understand this and dogmatically say that the nature is empty consciousness. What we Confucians talk about is solid principles, and from our point of view they are wrong. . . .
> >
> > Take the human mind-and-heart, for example. In it there must be the five moral relations between parent and child, ruler and minister, elder and younger, husband and wife, and friends. When the Buddhists are consistent in action, they show no affection in these relationships, whereas when we Confucians are consistent in action, there is affection between parent and child, rightness between ruler and minister, order between elder and younger, attention to their separate functions between husband and wife, and trust between friends." *Zhuzi quanshu* (*The Complete Works of Zhu Xi*) 60:14a. Translated by Wm. Theodore de Bary. In de Bary, p. 713.

veneration of ancestors, as it was generally felt that their approval was easier to attain than the more powerful but less reliable Shangdi. In all of this, the king bore a particular responsibility in performing the right rituals, since the success or failure of the state was seen to be a direct result of such performance. Indeed, proper performance of these rituals was seen to influence everything from harvests and weather patterns to illnesses and military campaigns. It should be noted, however, that this performance of ritual also served to legitimize the king's position, as it afforded him a special position as a mediator between spiritual forces and the welfare of the state.

In the Zhou dynasty (1045/1040–256 B.C.E.), this relationship became more formalized, largely in the attempt to legitimize the Zhou overthrow of the Shang. As recorded in the *Shujing* (Classic of documents), Shang rulers had once been virtuous and mindful of their ancestral obligations; toward the end of the dynasty, however, they became cruel and negligent. As a result, Heaven allowed the Zhou to rise up and overthrow the Shang, and thus to become the rightful rulers of China. As this account illustrates, the Zhou began to see the highest spiritual power as the impersonal Heaven (*tian*) rather than as the personal God, Shangdi; likewise, they saw the survival of the state as dependent on observance of a moral principle—the Mandate of Heaven (*tianming*)—rather than the allegiance of spiritual powers. Of course, this does not do away with the veneration of ancestors— a hallmark of Chinese practice—but begins to reinterpret it in terms of ritual responsibility rather than appeasement.

By the time of Confucius (Kong fuzi; 551–479 B.C.E.), the Zhou was in serious decline, such that there was military upheaval, social unrest, and general devastation throughout the empire. Confucius's message, as found in the *Analects,* was that this devastation was the result of the fact that the order of Earth no longer reflected the order of Heaven and the order of Heaven could only be exemplified by reviving the classic virtues (most significantly, *ren,* or humaneness). These virtues, in turn, could only be realized by a revival of the rituals (*li*) that guide human relations. Confucianism brought ritual propriety to the fore by taking a term that had indicated guidelines for deference among the nobility and imbuing it with ethical implications for all people. In short, for Confucius, right practice is not a matter of mere politeness but is rather the very heart of a stable and prosperous society.

A good example of ritual propriety is found in the *Zhongyong* (*Doctrine of the Mean*), one of the central texts of the Confucian tradition. Among other things, it emphasizes acting in accordance with one's position: effectively, a person of lower position acts with deference without resentment, while a person of higher position acts with graciousness without disdain. Such ritual propriety applies on a diminishing scale as family relations become more distant and official positions less distinguished. Most importantly, the *Zhongyong* gives expression to the five relations taken to be the most important foci of right relation: "The five are those governing the relationship between ruler and minister, between father and son, between husband and wife, between elder and younger brothers, and those in the intercourse between friends. These five are universal paths in the world" (*The Doctrine of the Mean,* quoted in Chan, p. 105). It should be noted that, while Confucianism is often associated with patriarchy, not all of the relations listed above are hierarchical. Thus, while many of its relations have historically been patriarchal, there is reason to believe that there is room in Confucian orthopraxy for more equitable relations.

While Confucianism is rightly seen as the dominant tradition informing social practices, it was only one of many approaches introduced during this tumultuous period; Mozi (fifth century B.C.E.), for example, argued for the eradication of all ritual (in that all people were equal before Heaven), while the so-called legalists argued for the strict enforcement of certain practices within the context of a system based on punishment and reward. Perhaps the most persistent counterpoint to the Confucian emphasis on ritual, however, was the Daoist tradition. Where the Confucians praised structured interactions, the Daoists prized spontaneity. To Daoists, the social constructs of the Confucians were unnatural at best, if not outright destructive. The opposition of these two schools of thought, however, should not be overstated, as each balanced the other and even borrowed from the other in its own development. Stated simply, even Daoists had their rituals, though they were less centralized than those of their Confucian counterparts (see, for example, Daoist liturgies, ordination rites).

Historically, however, it is the Confucians who have enjoyed the most government sponsorship, and have thus had the greatest influence on the nature and breadth of ritual practice in China. Consistent with the Confucian account, therefore, right practice was not enforced on any official level (as evidenced by its Daoist and Buddhist detractors), but it was upheld on an unofficial basis as a standard of social morality and decorum. Indeed, the prominence that ritual propriety still enjoys in Chinese society can be attributed in large part to the longstanding influence of the Confucian tradition on its history. Although the Confucian tradition is no longer officially sanctioned by the government in the early twenty-first century, the importance of ritual propriety continues to be very evident in Chinese social practices, and arguably will remain so for many generations to come.

See also **Buddhism; Confucianism; Daoism; Hinduism.**

BIBLIOGRAPHY

Chan, Wing-tsit. *A Source Book in Chinese Philosophy.* Princeton, N.J.: Princeton University Press, 1963.

De Bary, Wm. Theodore, and Irene Bloom, and comps. *Sources of Chinese Tradition: From Earliest Times to 1600.* 2nd ed. Introduction to Asian Civilizations Series. New York: Columbia University Press, 1999.

Eno, Robert. *The Confucian Creation of Heaven: Philosophy and the Defense of Ritual Mastery.* Albany: State University of New York Press, 1990.

Flood, Gavin D. *An Introduction to Hinduism.* New York: Cambridge University Press, 1996.

Flood, Gavin D., ed. *The Blackwell Companion to Hinduism.* Malden, Mass.: Blackwell, 2003.

Fowler, Merv. *Buddhism: Beliefs and Practices.* Portland, Ore.: Sussex Academic Press, 1999.

Kinsley, David R. *Hinduism: A Cultural Perspective.* 2nd ed. Englewood Cliffs, N.J.: Prentice Hall, 1993.

Klostermaier, Klaus K. *A Survey of Hinduism.* 2nd ed. Albany: State University of New York Press, 1994.

Lagerwey, John. *Taoist Ritual in Chinese Society and History.* New York: Macmillan, 1987.

Lopez, Donald S., Jr. *The Story of Buddhism: A Concise Guide to its History and Teachings.* San Francisco: HarperSanFrancisco, 2001.

———, ed. *Religions of China in Practice.* Princeton, N.J.: Princeton University Press, 1966.

Michaels, Axel. *Hinduism: Past and Present.* Translated by Barbara Harshav. Princeton, N.J.: Princeton University Press, 2004.

Miller, Jeanine. *The Vision of Cosmic Order in the Vedas.* Foreword by Raimunda Panikkar. London and Boston: Routledge and Kegan Paul, 1985.

Radhakrishnan, S., and Charles Alexander Moore. *A Source Book in Indian Philosophy.* Princeton, N.J.: Princeton University Press, 1957.

Reynolds, Frank E., and Jason A. Carbine, eds. *The Life of Buddhism.* Berkeley: University of California Press, 2000.

Sharma, Arvind. *Classical Hindu Thought: An Introduction.* New York: Oxford University Press, 2000.

Tu Wei-Ming. *Centrality and Commonality: An Essay on Confucian Religiousness.* Revised and enlarged edition of *Centrality and Commonality: An Essay on Chung-Yung.* Albany: State University of New York Press, 1989

———. "Probing the 'Three Bonds' and 'Five Relationships' in Confucian Humanism." In *Confucianism and the Family,* edited by Wlater H Slote and George A. De Vos, 121–136. Albany: State University of New York Press, 1998.

Walpola, Rāhula. *What the Buddha Taught,* rev. ed. New York: Grove Press, distributed by Random House, 1974.

Robert Smid

WESTERN ORTHOPRAXY

Orthopraxy or *orthopraxis* (from Greek *orthos,* "correct," and *praxis,* "action") denotes proper action, particularly in a religious context. It is contrasted with *orthodoxy* (*orthos* and *doxa,* "opinion"), which denotes proper belief. The word *orthopraxy* is of relatively recent invention and has been used above all in connection with Latin American "liberation theology." It does not otherwise have a significant history of its own in the West. Because of its pairing with *orthodoxy,* however, it is useful for a discussion of the conflict between action and belief, works and faith, obedience to law, and commitment to creed.

There has been some limited use of the term *orthopraxy* in connection with Islam. Malise Ruthven, for example, in his *Islam: A Very Short Introduction* (1997), speaks of Muslim fundamentalists (a term he disapproves of), commenting that for Muslims opposed to modern secularism, the emphasis is on action rather than belief. "Throughout history," he writes, "Islamic rectitude has tended to be defined in relation to practice rather than doctrine. Muslims who dissented from the majority on issues of leadership or theology were usually tolerated provided their social behaviour conformed to generally accepted standards. It is in enforcing behavioural conformity (ortho*praxy*) rather than doctrinal conformity (ortho*doxy*) that Muslim radicals or activists look to a 'restoration' of Islamic law backed by the power of the state."

But in the West, the dominant debates on orthopraxy and orthodoxy (whether or not these terms are used) take place in connection with Judaism and Christianity. This article will examine the conflict in those two religions.

Judaism

The Hebrew Bible is filled with statements that emphasize the importance of obedience to God's commandments. After his forty days and nights on Mount Sinai, Moses proclaims to his people, "So now, O Israel, what does the Lord your God require of you? Only to fear the Lord your God, to walk in all his ways, to love him, to serve the Lord your God with all your heart and with all your soul, and to keep the commandments of the Lord your God and his decrees that I am commanding you today, for your own well-being" (Deuteronomy 10:12–13). Elsewhere God directs Moses to say this to his people: "My ordinances you shall observe and my statutes you shall keep, following them: I am the Lord your God. You shall keep my statutes and my ordinances; by doing so one shall live: I am the Lord" (Leviticus 18:4–5).

In the twelfth century, Moses ben Maimon (Maimonides; 1135–1204) published his *Mishneh torah* (Repetition of the Torah, c. 1178), in which he gave definitive form to the list of 613 commandments (*mitsvot*) that pious Jews accept as binding on their daily conduct. Another milestone in the codification of Jewish practice is the *Shulchan'arukh* (literally, "the set table"), written by the Spanish-born Joseph Karo (1488–1575) in the mid–sixteenth century. This work presents a legal code that many observant Jews continue to the present day to regard as definitive in the settlement of religious disputes. The emphasis that these works and Jewish tradition have placed on obedience has led many modern commentators, both Jewish and non-Jewish, to conclude that Judaism is a religion characterized primarily by its insistence on proper practice and obedience to God's law or, to put it in terms of this entry, a religion characterized by its insistence on orthopraxy over orthodoxy.

At the end of the eighteenth century, Immanuel Kant (1724–1804) declared Judaism to be a religion of "purely statutory laws" and therefore no religion at all. Georg Wilhelm Friedrich Hegel (1770–1831), in his early days, had followed Kant and (in "The Positivity of the Christian Religion") described Jews as struggling "under a burden of statutory commandments . . . that pedantically prescribe a rule for every casual action of everyday life." In their view of Judaism as a primarily legalistic religion, both men were following the German-Jewish philosopher Moses Mendelssohn (1729–1786), father of the modernizing Jewish *Haskalah* ("Enlightenment"). In *Jerusalem; or, On Religious Power and Judaism* (1783), Mendelssohn had stressed "divine legislation" (*göttliche Gesetzgebung*)—by contrast with "revealed religion" (*geoffenbarte Religion*) in the Christian sense—as an essential fact of Judaism.

A number of modern Jewish commentators agree that Judaism is a religion whose essence lies not in theory or belief but in practice. Samuel Belkin (1911–1976), president of Yeshiva University in New York and a respected Jewish leader, wrote, "Many attempts have been made to formulate a coherent and systematic approach to Jewish theology. All such attempts,

however, have proved unsuccessful, for Judaism was never overly concerned with logical doctrines. It desired rather to evolve a corpus of practices, a code of religious acts, which would establish a mode of religious living. . . . In Judaism, articles of faith and religious theories cannot be divorced from particular practices . . . the theology of Judaism is contained largely in the Halakha [Jewish law]—in the Jewish judicial system—which concerns itself not with theory but primarily with practice."

The issue arises with particular force in connection with the modern Orthodox movement. That movement arose in late-eighteenth- and early-nineteenth-century Germany, in response to various attempts to modernize Judaism, including the *Haskalah* and Reform Judaism. Orthodoxy's principal proponent, German rabbi Samson Raphael Hirsch (1808–1888), saw his movement as a means of accommodating traditional Judaism to the conditions of modern life. Still, Hirsch favored a strict interpretation of the practical duties of the Orthodox Jew. In his eyes, the fact of the revelation to the entire Jewish people at Mount Sinai obviated the need for faith or belief. The revelation is an established historical fact, and Judaism is thus a religion of law, not of belief. "Statutes of faith?" he asks in the fifteenth Letter. "Judaism knows 613 duties, but no commandments of faith." In light of such remarks, Jacob Katz, an historian of the movement, declared that *orthopraxy* would have been a more accurate term for the new movement than *orthodoxy*.

But Hirsch and modern commentators like Samuel Belkin by no means have the last word on this issue. There is a lively debate within rabbinic Judaism on the issue of whether belief should be considered a component of the religion alongside practice. After all, though Moses ben Maimon codified Jewish practice in his list of the *mitsvot* ("commandments"), he was also the author of the Thirteen Principles (*shloshah asar yesodot*) published in his commentary on Tractate *Sanhedrin* of the *Mishnah* (the codified oral law that forms the core of the Talmud). The Principles cover such matters as the existence (*metsi'ut*), unity (*yichud*), and incorporeality (*shlilat hagashmut*) of God, the divine revelation of Torah (*heyot hatorah min hashamayim*), and the resurrection of the dead (*techiyat hametim*). But the focus of the Principles is belief, so, for example, when Moses ben Maimon speaks of the existence of God, rather than simply declare it a fact, he tells us that we must believe (*leha'amin*) it. In the *Mishneh Torah,* he emphasizes the importance of *kavanah,* or intention, in prayer. *Kavanah* (from the verbal root *kun,* meaning "to be established" or "to be steadfast") had already appeared in the Talmud in roughly this sense, but Moses ben Maimon gives the word what is quite possibly its *locus classicus,* when he declares, "Any prayer that is not [said] with *kavanah* is not a prayer."

The history of Judaism is filled with challenges to what is perceived to be a rigid adherence to the letter of the law. Kabbalah (Hebrew *qabalah,* "tradition"), with its mystical emphasis on direct communication with the divinity, has roots that go back almost two thousand years. Some might regard this movement as representing a departure from legalism. The eighteenth century in eastern Europe brought a significant reaction to the aridity of Talmudic scholasticism, as practiced by then-powerful rabbis in Lithuania. The leader of the opposition was Israel Ben Eliezer (c. 1700–1760), known popularly as the Ba'al Shem Tov ("master of the good name"), and his movement came to be known as Hassidism (from Hebrew *chasid,* "pious," "righteous"). The Ba'al Shem Tov emphasized a nonintellectual, spiritual communion with God (though he certainly did not advocate a rejection of Jewish law). The Paris Sanhedrin, the group of Jewish notables that Napoleon convened in 1806 to determine the legal position of Jews in France, helped establish as a principle in French law that Jews would be regarded as one religion among others, in other words, that, because religious duties must fall in place behind loyalty to the nation, Jewishness in France would henceforth be determined by one's faith, not by one's birth or one's actions. The Reform Movement started out in Germany with a quasi-Hegelian notion of the progressive, historically unfolding spirit of Judaism, something very different from traditional "orthopraxy." In the United States, the movement marked out its turf by expressly rejecting what it regarded as the religion's anachronistic legalism. The Pittsburgh Platform of 1885, which established the guiding principles of the American Reform Movement, contained this bold statement: "We hold that all such Mosaic and rabbinical laws as regulate diet, priestly purity and dress originated in ages and under the influence of ideas altogether foreign to our present mental and spiritual state." The contemporary world, especially in the United States, offers the Jew a varied menu of choices, from the strictly regulated life of the "ultra-Orthodox," to the secular humanism of Reconstructionism, to the mysticism of the modern Kabbalah movement.

While it might be tempting to claim that Judaism has traveled the path from orthopraxy to various forms of spirituality, one must not forget that many branches of Judaism in the modern world have emphasized praxis, but in the social and political rather than the personal, religious sphere. The Pittsburgh Platform, having affirmed the immortality of the human soul, concludes with this principle: "In full accordance with the spirit of Mosaic legislation, which strives to regulate the relation between the rich and poor, we deem it our duty to participate in the great task of modern times, to solve, on the basis of justice and righteousness, the problems presented by the contrasts and evils of the present organization of society." The Reform Movement is not the only branch of Judaism to have dedicated itself to this cause.

Christianity

The debate about proper belief and proper practice began almost at the moment Christians became conscious of themselves as members of a new religion distinct from Judaism. The debate was framed as faith (Greek *pistis,* Latin *fides*) versus works (Greek *erga, praxeis,* Latin *opera, facta*), and it attracted virtually every prominent figure in the history of Catholic theology, as well as the founding fathers of Protestantism.

The apostle Paul set the terms of the debate. In the decades following the death of Jesus, Paul's mission was to consolidate and universalize the new Christian church, to establish the principle that Gentiles need not pass through a conversion to Judaism in order to join the church, and finally to formulate an explanation of the position that Judaism and its laws were

to occupy in the church. The doctrine of justification by faith was perfect for Paul's purposes. It demonstrated that all were eligible to join the fledgling church since faith alone—not works or Pharisaic obedience to Jewish law—was necessary, and it assured new converts that obedience to the law and loyalty to the legacy of Abraham would follow naturally from a profession of faith in Christ. We find this doctrine in the Epistle to the Galatians (probably one of Paul's earlier letters, written between 52 and 55 C.E.). "We ourselves are Jews by birth and not Gentile sinners," he wrote, "yet we know that a person is justified not by the works of the law but through faith in Jesus Christ. And we have come to believe in Christ Jesus, so that we might be justified by faith in Christ, and not by doing the works of the law, because no one will be justified by the works of the law" (Galatians 2:15–16). Under this principle, the church becomes universal, as former distinctions among people disappear. At the same time, members of the church are implicitly incorporated into the traditions of Judaism: "There is no longer Jew or Greek, there is no longer slave or free, there is no longer male and female; for all of you are one in Christ Jesus. And if you belong to Christ, then you are Abraham's offspring, heirs according to the promise" (Galatians 3:28–29).

In his Epistle to the Romans, Paul reintroduces justification and once again links it with the principle of universality: "For we hold that a person is justified by faith apart from works prescribed by the law. Or is God the God of Jews only? Is he not the God of Gentiles also? Yes, of Gentiles also, since God is one; and he will justify the circumcised on the ground of faith and the uncircumcised through that same faith. Do we then overthrow the law by this faith? By no means! On the contrary, we uphold the law" (Romans 3:28–31). He also introduces two related principles that will guide discussions of faith and works for centuries to come: predestination (from Greek *proorizō,* "predetermine," Latin *praedestino*) and election by grace (Greek *eklogē kharitos,* Latin *electio gratiae*). "For those whom he foreknew he also predestined to be conformed to the image of his Son, in order that he might be the firstborn within a large family. And those whom he predestined he also called; and those whom he called he also justified; and those whom he justified he also glorified" (Romans 8:29–30). "So too at the present time there is a remnant [of the Jews], chosen by grace. But if it is by grace, it is no longer on the basis of works, otherwise grace would no longer be grace. What then? Israel failed to obtain what it was seeking. The elect obtained it, but the rest were hardened" (Romans 11:5–7).

What might well have begun as an effort to distinguish a new religious sect from Judaism quickly and lastingly came to be incorporated into the very core of Christian theology. The ultimate victory of Saint Augustine of Hippo (354–430 C.E.) in his long polemic with Pelagius, a theologian of the same era who had insisted that volition and action proceed from men themselves and not from Christ or God, established by the early fifth century C.E. the position that the Catholic Church would retain permanently: faith is a gift from God; our freedom of will both to believe and to act proceeds from God's grace; God predestines some, but not all, to faith; and the reasons for which some are elected while others are not is "inscrutable" (*On the*

Predestination of Saints, 428 or 429 C.E.). "Predestination is a preparation for grace; grace itself, however, is a gift [*donatio*]." When it comes to faith and works, Augustine is unequivocal: "faith is given first." Faith takes precedence and is the sign of the new covenant: "As the law of works [*lex factorum*] is written on tablets of stone," he says, "so the law of faith is written in hearts." The rewards of the former are associated with the Old Testament, those of the latter with the New Testament (*On the Spirit and the Letter,* 412 C.E.).

In the writings of Saint Thomas Aquinas (c. 1225–1274), we find a shift in emphasis to the inwardness of the human will and the dominance of reason. But Thomas is careful to safeguard the divine origin of the human faculties that he exalted: "The movement of the will is from within, just like natural movement. . . . The cause of the will, however, can be nothing other than God, and for two reasons: first because the will is a power of the rational soul, which is caused by God through creation . . . and second because the will tends toward the universal good, from which it follows that nothing can be the cause of the will except God himself, who is the universal good" (*Summa Theologica,* 1265/1266–1273). To be sure, Thomas attributes to man a greater degree of autonomy than we find in Augustine and many other Christian theologians. For example, he distinguishes between two types of grace, under one of which, "operating grace" (*gratia per operantem*), God is our sole mover and under the other of which, "cooperating grace" (*gratia per cooperantem*), our actions stem from both God and our minds. But when it comes to judging actions, Thomas is quite clear: "our actions are meritorious in so far as they proceed from free choice, *moved by God through grace*" (emphasis added).

With the new emphasis on individual, subjective freedom that we find in Luther and the Protestant Reformation, we might expect to see man newly invested with the dignity of free choice in his actions. But for Martin Luther (1483–1546), John Calvin (1509–1564), and others, freedom meant freedom from the tyranny of the Catholic Church, not freedom in the sense of an autonomous volition that is the source of our actions. In Luther's view, faith and grace once again precede actions, and righteous actions by themselves do nothing to render righteous the individual who commits those actions: "Not he who works much [*multum operatur*] is just but rather he who without works [*sine opere*] believes much in Christ" (*Heidelberg Disputation,* 1518). Luther wrote *The Bondage of the Will* (1525) expressly to refute the existence of free will, on the strength of the argument that original sin deprives us of the freedom to choose. "God foreknows and foreordains [*praescit et praeordinat*] all things," he writes, thus only what God wills can take place, and "there can be no such thing as free choice [*liberum arbitrium*] in man or angel or any creature." "The Gospel," he writes in the preface to his German translation of the New Testament, "does not demand works of us, so that we might become devout and blessed [*frum und selig*] thereby; in fact, it condemns such works but demands only faith in Christ" (*Preface to the New Testament,* 1522).

By the end of Luther's life, John Calvin had completed his *Institutes of the Christian Religion* (1536). To the modern reader, Calvin's theology appears, as regards the issue of faith and works, to differ very little from that of Augustine. But for a sixteenth-century reformer extending the work of Luther, the doctrine of justification by faith served as a repudiation of the temporal authority of the pope and thus had a resonance different from what it had had for the bishop of Hippo. Faith for Calvin is a gift of God, as it was for Augustine, Thomas Aquinas, and Luther, and righteousness arises not from works but from faith. Works are not the cause of holiness but are, rather, gifts of God (*Dei dona*), signs of his calling (*vocationis signa; Institutes of the Christian Religion,* 1536–1559). If Calvin's thought represents a departure from that of his predecessors, it is largely owing to his attitude toward life. Contempt for our present life (*praesentis vitae contemptus*) and the practice of abstinence, sobriety, frugality, and modesty in that life are the guides to proper conduct.

With the age of Enlightenment and its increasing tendency to ground moral issues in nature and humankind, we see the emphasis in Christianity shift increasingly from faith to the human arena. The nineteenth century produced a spate of books, in a variety of European languages, under the title *The Life of Jesus,* most prominently *Das Leben Jesu* (1835–1836), by David Friedrich Strauss (1808–1874) and *La vie de Jésus* (1863), by Ernest Renan (1823–1892). The kenotic tradition in nineteenth-century German Protestant theology emphasized the human dimension of Jesus ("kenotic" refers to the process, described in Philippians 2:7, by which Christ "emptied himself" [*ekenosen*] and became a man). French socialist theory in the first half of the nineteenth century modeled its conceptions of social justice on a vision of the early Christian church and the teachings of Jesus. In *Le nouveau christianisme* (1825; English trans. *The New Christianity,*" 1834) by Henri de Saint-Simon (1760–1825), the "new Christian" expresses what he sees as the "divine part" of Christianity: "men must conduct themselves as brothers with respect to one another. . . .They must make it their aim to ameliorate as promptly and as completely as possible the moral and physical existence of the most numerous class."

The late nineteenth and early twentieth centuries produced a spate of socially conscious Christian thinkers and activists, especially in the United States. The Social Gospel movement, from roughly 1870 to 1920, encouraged followers to devote themselves to social justice, in imitation of Christ. Walter Rauschenbusch (1861–1918), one of its leaders, went so far as to embrace communism as a Christian principle in his *Christianity and the Social Crisis* (1907). Reinhold Niebuhr (1892–1971) helped define theological liberalism in the United States in the first half of the twentieth century.

In the second half of the twentieth century, two developments steered the Catholic Church (or some of its members) increasingly in the direction of praxis. In 1965, Pope Paul VI issued, as one of the sixteen decrees of Vatican II, *Gaudium et spes* (Joy and hope; titled in English "Pastoral Constitution On the Church in the Modern World"), which affirmed the church's commitment to service in the human world: "What does the Church think of man? What needs to be recommended for the upbuilding of contemporary society? What is the ultimate significance of human activity throughout the world? People are waiting for an answer to these questions.

From the answers it will be increasingly clear that the People of God and the human race in whose midst it lives render service to each other. Thus the mission of the Church will show its religious, and by that very fact, its supremely human character." The Society of Jesus (the Jesuit order) today has an Office of Social and International Ministries, whose purpose is to serve the "Social Apostolate (ministries addressing domestic and international social problems)." One Jesuit priest, Philip J. Rosato, has suggested that Karl Barth (1886–1968), the great twentieth-century Protestant theologian who became increasingly committed to social justice during his long career, helped, through dialogue with Catholics, to steer the post–Vatican II church toward orthopraxy in social affairs.

In 1968, a Peruvian priest named Gustavo Gutiérrez published *Teología de la liberación* (English trans. *A Theology of Liberation,* 1973), which served as the central text for the Catholic "liberation theology" movement in Latin America. Gutiérrez is explicit about the orthopraxy/orthodoxy relationship. Human history, says Gutiérrez, is an "opening to the future" (*abertura al futuro*), and this means an emphasis on action, or "doing the truth" (*hacer la verdad*). "Only by doing this truth will our faith *veri-fy* itself, speaking literally," he says. "Hence the recent use of the term *orthopraxis,* which might shock certain sensibilities. Nor should this be understood as denying the meaning of *orthodoxy,* understood as a proclamation and reflection of affirmations considered to be true." Liberation theology represents an odd amalgamation of Marxist theory (the last of Marx's "Theses on Feuerbach," 1845, reads, "The philosophers have merely *interpreted* the world in various ways; the point is to *change* it.") and Christian theology.

It would probably be safe to say that many branches of Christianity in the twentieth century have placed an increasing emphasis on orthopraxy at least in addition to, if not to the detriment of, orthodoxy. The praxis that has come to be favored is of the sort that takes place in the social and political world and not just of the sort that is directly connected with the rituals of a particular institution. Waging a struggle against poverty and waging a struggle against abortion rights can both be expressions of religious principle, but they are different in kind from practices like taking communion and confessing.

See also **Christianity; Islam; Judaism; Orthodoxy; Religion.**

BIBLIOGRAPHY

Augustine, Saint. *De praedestinatione sanctorum, De spiritu et litera.* In Vol. 43: *Patrologiae cursus completus, series latina,* edited by Jacques-Paul Migne. Paris: Migne, 1844–1891.

———. *Saint Augustin: Anti-Pelagian Writings.* In Vol. 5: *Select Writings of Nicene and Post-Nicene Fathers of the Christian Church,* edited by Philip Schaff. Peabody, Mass.: Hendricks, 1994.

Belkin, Samuel. *In His Image: The Jewish Philosophy of Man as Expressed in Rabbinic Tradition.* New York: Abelard-Schuman, 1960.

Calvin, John. *Institutes of the Christian Religion.* 1568. Modern edition, edited by John T. McNeill. Translated by Ford Lewis Battles. Philadelphia: Westminster, 1960.

Gutiérrez, Gustavo. *A Theology of Liberation: History, Politics, and Salvation.* Translated and edited by Sister Caridad Inda and John Eagleson. Maryknoll, N.Y.: Orbis, 1988. First Spanish edition, 1968.

Hegel, Georg Wilhelm Friedrich. "The Positivity of the Christian Religion." In *Early Theological Writings,* edited and translated by T. M. Knox. Chicago: University of Chicago Press, 1948.

Hirsch, Samson Raphael. *The Nineteen Letters.* 1836. Translated by Karin Paritzky. Jerusalem and New York: Feldheim, 1995.

Kant, Immanuel. *Religion within the Boundaries of Mere Reason and Other Writings.* Translated and edited by Allen Wood and George Di Giovanni. Cambridge, U.K., and New York: Cambridge University Press, 1998.

Katz, Jacob. "Orthodoxy in Historical Perspective." In *Studies in Contemporary Jewry.* Vol. 2. Bloomington: Indiana University Press, 1986

Luther, Martin. *Martin Luther's Basic Theological Writings,* edited by Timothy F. Lull. Minneapolis: Fortress Press, 1989.

Maimon, Moses ben. Commentary on Tractate *Sanhedrin* of the *Mishnah,* chap. 10.

———. "Helek: Sanhedrin, Chapter Ten." In *A Maimonides Reader,* edited by Isadore Twersky. New York: Behrman House, 1972.

———. *Mishneh torah.* Hilkot tefilah, IV, 15.

Mendelssohn, Moses. *Jerusalem; or, On Religious Power and Judaism.* Translated by Allan Arkush. Hanover, N.H.: University Press of New England, 1983.

Montefiore, C. G., and H. Loewe, eds. "The Importance of Motive or Intention. *Kawwanah,* and *Lishmah.* The Love, the Fear, and the Praise of God." In *A Rabbinic Anthology.* New York: Schocken, 1974.

Nessan, Craig L. *Orthopraxis or Heresy: The North American Theological Response to Latin American Liberation Theology.* Atlanta: Scholars Press, 1989.

Paul VI, Pope. "Pastoral Constitution on the Church in the Modern World: *Gaudium et Spes.*" Available at http://www.vatican.va/archive/hist_councils/ii_vatican_council/documents/vat-ii_cons_19651207_gaudium-et-spes_en.html.

Privat, Edouard ed. *Le Grand Sanhédrin de Napoléon.* Toulouse: Edouard Privat, 1979.

Rauschenbusch, Walter. *Christianity and the Social Crisis.* New York: Macmillan, 1907.

Rosato, Philip J., S. J. "The Influence of Karl Barth on Catholic Theology." In *Gregorianum* 67 (1986): 659–678.

Ruthven, Malise. *Islam: A Very Short Introduction.* New York and Oxford: Oxford University Press, 1997.

Saint-Simon, Henri, comte de. *New Christianity.* Translated by J. E. Smith. London: B.D. Cousins, 1834.

Senn, Frank C. "Orthodoxia, Orthopraxis, and Seekers." In *The Strange New Word of the Gospel: Re-Evangelizing in the Postmodern World,* edited by Carl E. Braaten and Robert W. Jenson. Grand Rapids, Mich.: William B. Eerdmans, 2002.

Thomas Aquinas, Saint. *Basic Writings of Saint Thomas Aquinas.* Vol. 2. Edited by Anton C. Pegis. New York: Random House, 1945.

Steven Cassedy

OTHER, THE, EUROPEAN VIEWS OF.

All epistemological and hermeneutical investigations are predicated on the observation that the human self, like all objects around a person, gains an understanding of its identity through the binary opposition of self and other. No value can be established for any element in the material and abstract world without the differentiation from "the Other." The famous linguist Ferdinand de Saussure described all essential components of language in terms of value units that develop their identity by being separate from all other elements surrounding them both in the syntagmatic and associative context. The same applies to the historical subject, man (here understood not in gender-specific terms), who discovers himself only when he realizes that he is different from all people around him. When a small child begins to recognize its environment, it also observes its own self. Hans-Georg Gadamer defines the phenomenon of selfhood versus otherness in the following way: "Whatever is being distinguished must be distinguished from something which, in turn, must be distinguished from it. Thus all distinguishing also makes visible that from which something is distinguished" (p. 272). All individuality is intimately connected with the recognition of the Other as a phenomenological entity outside of the self, and all cultures, religions, and peoples have relied on this fundamental truth in order to establish their own selfhood, legitimacy, culture, religion, and nationhood. The "I" discovers itself, as Martin Buber pointed out, through the separation from the "You," which, in its ultimate manifestation, proves to be God. Once the individual realizes that there is the Other, expressed by the pronoun you, the process of speaking, dialogue, discourse, and epistemology, both in the mundane and spiritual dimensions, begins.

The phenomenon of "otherness," as a subject of philosophical discourse led, in the 1980s, to the development of a new academic discipline, xenology, or the study of "alterity." Xenology focuses on the Other as a critical component of cultural anthropology, and as a key issue in the history of mentality, of the Church, and also of everyday life (Sundermeier, Wierlacher, Hallson). Study of the Other cannot be limited to the history of the Western world—the same phenomena also determine cultures in all other parts of the world to a lesser or greater degree—but for pragmatic purposes this article concentrates on the Judeo-Christian tradition. Most military conflicts throughout time can be explained either by religious disputes or material greed, or the two combined. These sentiments, however, result from hostility against or disregard of the Other whose own identity is not acknowledged but instead is treated as a dangerous challenge, if not an actual threat, to the existence and social construct of the dominant culture.

Considering military conflicts since the mid-twentieth century, including the Kosovo War in 1999, the terrorist attack on the World Trade Center on September 11, 2001, and the Iraq War in 2003, hostility against the Other and xenophobia in global terms continues and represents a major source of discord in increasingly multicultural societies and among nations (Gioseffi).

Since the end of World War II, the number of legal and illegal immigrants to Western nations has grown steadily. Once these asylum seekers or economic refugees settle in the new home country, they often face prejudice, rejection, hatred, and physical violence. In fact the early-twenty-first-century world is undergoing a major paradigm shift because the ethnic composition of Western societies is experiencing a transformation, bringing representatives of different religious, ethnic, and cultural groups into close proximity. The degree to which foreigners are integrated into a particular society undoubtedly represents a benchmark of its developmental stage as an enlightened, tolerant, and humanistic community. Earlier societies had to cope with similar phenomena, but throughout history the fundamental conflict between self and other has shaped most cultural, religious, military, and political developments. As Irvin Cemil Schick observed, identity is the result of a construction process, not simply a given, "and narrative is the medium through which that construction is realized" (Schick, p. 21).

Perspectives in the Ancient World

In ancient Greece, peoples of other ethnic backgrounds were identified as *barbarophonoi* (Homer, in the *Iliad* [c. 800 B.C.E.]), or as those who spoke nonunderstandable languages. However since the Greek world did not have the concept of a larger national unit, everyone outside the family or urban community was perceived as foreign, as other (*allos, allodapos,* and *xenos*). Significantly the Greeks did not necessarily differentiate between members of a foreign polis (city-state) and non-Greeks. Nevertheless the Greeks espoused the ideal of hospitality, which extended especially to foreigners; in later centuries many cities appointed a *proxenos* whose task it was to serve as a host for foreigners, perhaps comparable to the modern diplomatic institutions. At the turn of the sixth century B.C.E., a more xenophobic concept of the barbarian developed in Greece, triggered by a feeling of cultural superiority and also by fear of the growing Persian threat. Both Euripides and Aristotle, for instance, identified the barbarian with subhuman creatures and argued that their sole function was to serve as slaves—an attitude that slowly changed only after Alexander the Great's conquest of the Persian Empire (Stutzinger). Whereas the early Roman republic was built on a fairly strict division between Roman citizens and foreigners, during the time of the Roman Empire the Roman *civitas* was extended to additional population groups. The *Constitutio Antoniniana* (212 C.E.) awarded Roman citizenship to all free people living within the borders of the state. Nevertheless the entire ancient world accepted the idea of slavery and treated all defeated foreigners as objects that could be sold or killed at will. During the age of migration, Germanic tribes attacked the Roman Empire strengthening the notion of the barbaric others, especially since Romans regarded their nomadic opponents—in close parallel to the ideology espoused by modern colonialists, especially in the Americas and Africa—as primitive, lacking in culture and civilization.

During late antiquity the concept of monsters—teratology—living at the outskirts of the Roman world became popular; these monsters have populated literary and artistic imagination ever since. Pliny the Elder collected some of the most influential accounts about these monsters in his *Naturalis historia* (before 79 C.E.), followed by Caius Julius Solinus's *Collectanea rerum memorabilium* (c. 250 C.E.), which medieval and early modern encyclopedists and naturalists eagerly copied. Solinus's works became the source for scores of artists and writers who blithely integrated this "information" about strange beings on the periphery of human civilization into their texts and images (Williams).

Medieval Perspectives

The ancient world primarily projected images of the Other as a matter of curiosity, with the specific purpose of populating worlds far from the eastern Mediterranean to satisfy general scientific interest. But in the early Middle Ages the contrast between self and other gained in intensity because of the sharp conflict between the Christian Church and pagan cultures, the constant threat of famine due to undeveloped agriculture and farming, and constant military threats from other places (Huns, Saracens [Arabs], Vikings, and later the Magyars). A remarkable expression of the fear of the Other can be found in the myriad monster images depicted in churches, on government buildings, on the facades of houses, in wall paintings, in sculptures, and in numerous manuscript illuminations (Benton, Camille). Some of the best medieval art focuses on these monstrous figures and elaborates on their fearful, hideous features, reflecting a highly ambivalent and contradictory attitude toward the Other. Whereas Christian theologians established rigid criteria to determine good versus evil, or self versus other, in accordance with biblical teaching, popular culture continued to be dominated by strong undercurrents of paganism that derived strength from its fascination with and abhorrence of the Other (Milis). In the Old English heroic epic *Beowulf* (early eighth century), for example, the protagonist's struggles, first against the monster Grendel, then against its mother, and finally against a dragon, represent the individual stages of interaction with a foreign world and establishment of an identity for a particular social group. Many other heroic epics in Old Norse and Old and middle-High German literature can be explained in terms of their treatment of the Other and their interest in offering a medium of self-identification for the reader/listener (Lionarons).

Religious Perspectives

All early-twenty-first-century world religions, especially Judaism, Christianity, and Islam, are predicated on the exclusivity and absoluteness of their own religion and the truth of their faith, since the monotheistic concept negatively determines the relationship with all other religions, rejecting them as other and hence as false. By contrast, people in ancient Greece and Rome recognized many different gods and easily tolerated representatives of other religions as long as they demonstrated loyalty to the secular authorities and obeyed the rules of public mores (Assmann).

Since the early Middle Ages, factions of all three major religions have demanded absolute adherence to their own faith and have not hesitated to persecute and execute members of the other religions, unless the latter voluntarily submitted to the dominant religion. The history of the Western world is deeply influenced by constant, bitter struggles among these three religions, whether in the form of Arab conquests in the seventh and eighth centuries, or Christian crusades between 1096 and 1291. In antiquity and the Middle Ages, these conflicts and tensions were often addressed with violence (crusades, pogroms, expulsions, imperialistic warfare, and hostile

persecutions), victimizing the Jewish population above all. There were a number of attempts by Christian philosophers and theologians from the thirteenth to the fifteenth centuries to enter into critical discourse with Jews (Paris Disputation [1240], Barcelona Disputation [1263], Tortosa Disputation [1413–1414]; Maccoby), but these were intellectual experiments and ultimately yielded no positive changes in the relationship between the religions; the situation for Jews became increasingly worse (expulsion from Spain in 1492). Although Augustine (354–430) had firmly argued for a tolerant attitude toward Jews, insisting that they were "living testimony to the antiquity of the Christian promise" (Cohen, p. 33), and although Bernard of Clairvaux (1090–1153) had emphasized that Jews were the "living letters of the law" (Cohen, p. 388), anti-Semitic attitudes grew in intensity throughout the late Middle Ages and were promulgated even by prominent theologians and philosophers including Thomas Aquinas (1225–1274), who argued that Jews willfully rejected the true faith and could be compared to recalcitrant heretics. In the early sixteenth century, the Christian convert Johannes Pfefferkorn, who had been a Jew, became one of the most vicious enemies of Jews and made highly controversial allegations against them, allegations that even some Christian thinkers, such as the Hebrew scholar Johannes Reuchlin (1455–1522), severely criticized (Kirn).

Legal Perspectives

The modern, post-Reformation world witnessed at least some attempts to establish principles of coexistence, toleration, and, especially, since the age of Enlightenment, tolerance. Nevertheless intolerance, xenophobia, religious tensions, and subsequent military conflicts have continued to torture humankind, and the contentious relationship between self and other, both in its philosophical and political contexts, remains highly fragile and subject to manipulation and distortion. Racism, sexual intolerance, marginalization of minority groups, misogyny, and numerous forms of violence against weaker members of society are results of this binary opposition in which the self sometimes desperately struggles against the Other in order to establish its identity.

The First Amendment to the U.S. Constitution, ratified in 1791, clearly specifies a modern, tolerant attitude toward the Other: "Congress shall make no law respecting an establishment of religion, or prohibiting the free exercise thereof; or abridging the freedom of speech, or of the press; or the right of the people peaceably to assemble, and to petition the government for a redress of grievances." Athough the meaning of this statement and its practical application have remained contested, the amendment continues to serve as the basis for intensive discussions about the relationship between the individual citizen and the state for the United States and many other Western societies in the early twenty-first century (Mittal and Rosset, Amar).

One of the most far-reaching and pragmatic expressions of the ideals of the Enlightenment was the legal code established under Napoléon, the *Code Napoléon* (1804), that stipulated the following: (a) equality of all in the eyes of the law; (b) no recognition of privileges due to the happenstance of birth; (c) freedom of religion; (d) separation of church and state; and

(e) freedom to work in an occupation of one's own choosing (Martin). Many of the principles in the *Code* decisively influenced legal systems developed in other countries in the Western world and continue to be cornerstones of modern societies.

Religious differences, even in the early-twenty-first-century West, are a major source of conflict and may always exist, as documented by numerous expressions of anti-Semitism, manifested most virulently in the Holocaust committed by the German Nazis. Each generation struggles with problems of cultural identity and differentiation from the Other, which is the basis for the exploration of the self. However when weakness on one's own part or ideological manipulation by authority figures are involved in the epistemological process, the Other can easily be abused for a wide range of political purposes. People are vulnerable to brainwashing, which relies on an underdeveloped sense of individuality and a high degree of insecurity in the face of ethnic, cultural, religious, linguistic, and political otherness. Fear, intolerance, and dogmatic thinking have always acted to strengthen the group identity and denounce the Others. This is evident in the centuries-old rejection of Sinti and Roma (formerly known as Gypsies), the persecution of Jews since late antiquity, the expulsion of the French Huguenots and the Amish and Mennonites in the sixteenth and seventeenth centuries, the abuse of blacks by colonialists and slaveholders worldwide, the genocide of North and South American Indians, the massive purge of alleged enemies of the Russian, Chinese, and Cambodian communist regimes, and the genocides in Armenia, Burundi, Kosovo, and elsewhere in the twentieth and early twenty-first centuries.

Mysticism, Demons, and the Other

Since the Middle Ages, belief in ghosts, demons, spirits, and other elements have represented a challenge to the Church, and philosophers and authorities stuggle in vain against various forms of superstition and fear (Delumeau, Dinzelbacher). During the high Middle Ages, supernatural phenomena were often associated with the divine, or regarded as emanations of the Godhead, leading to a widespread mysticism movement. Bernard of Clairvaux exerted great influence on his contemporaries and posterity not only due to his learnedness, but also because of his intensive examinations of mystical phenomena. His *super Cantica Canticorum* particularly developed a highly affective interpretation of the Song of Songs and its imagery of the Godhead as bridegroom and the soul as bride. Contemplation was the first stage in the quest for the religious other, followed by mediation, prayer, fasting, sleep deprivation, and grace, which ultimately allowed the mystic to experience revelations. Hildegard of Bingen (1098–1179), leader of a Benedictine convent, gained fame for her mystical visions, which were accepted as authentic by Church fathers (especially Bernard of Clairvaux and Pope Eugene III), who authorized her to go on preaching tours throughout Germany. Other famous mystics were Mechthild of Magdeburg (1208–1282), Mechthild of Hackeborn (1241–1299), Gertrud the Great (1256–c. 1301), Bonaventura (1217–1274), Henry Suso (1295–1366), Meister Eckhart (c. 1260–1327), Bridget of Sweden (1302–1373), and Catherine of Siena (1347–1380) (Szarmach). Although each mystic experienced individualized

visions, all mysticism commonly dealt with the ineffable quality of the Godhead and the absolute realization of the Other in the religious context (Classen, 2002a). Since there are no adequate words to explain the phenomenon of the soul's encounter with the divine, mystics commonly resorted to an apophatic discourse, or, as in the case of Meister Eckhart, to negative theology, which contended that man cannot really talk about God, the absolute Other, and emphasized the need to subjugate the self in the presence of the divine (Milem).

In the late Middle Ages and particularly from the sixteenth century, the Church intensified its control over individualized forms of religious experience and rejected those who claimed to have had visions or been privy to divine revelation (Caciola). As a consequence, women with prophetic abilities, visionaries, and ecstatics were increasingly regarded with suspicion and became victims of the Holy Inquisition.

Although attempts were made to reject magic and to oust different types of seers and sorcerers, such as *harioli, auspices, sortilegi,* and *incantatores,* these practioners preserved their secret influence far into the modern age (Flint, 1991). Throughout Europe, both the rural population and intellectuals, even as late as the eighteenth and nineteenth centuries, subscribed to various forms of superstitions, including witchcraft, fear of the devil, and evil spirits (Ginzburg), not to mention a belief in astrology.

Surveying the eighteenth century, Theodor Adorno and Max Horckheimer identified the phenomena as the "dialectics of enlightenment." But such beliefs continue in early-twenty-first-century society as well, allowing technocrats and bureaucrats to manipulate the Other for their own purposes without regard for the latter's nature, interests, and needs: "Enlightenment behaves toward things as a dictator toward men. He knows them in so far as he can manipulate them" (Adorno and Horckheimer, p. 9).

Even as rationality offers logical explanations of the world around us, people fall back to superstitions and irrational thinking, which permits ideologues to stereotype groups and blame them for a wide range of general ills. In the Middle Ages, the preferred object of this manipulative strategy was the Jews. In early modern Europe, women were accused of witchcraft and burned at the stake, serving as scapegoats for a heightened sense of religious insecurity, fear of the scientific paradigm shift occurring at the time, the growing pressure of the centralized power of the state, and a brewing conflict between popular culture and beliefs and intellectualism (Levack, Scholz Williams).

Ancient and medieval authors, chroniclers, and writers of travelogues projected images of a fabulous East, which was paradise-like in its luxuries and sophistication, but sometimes also populated by monsters. By contrast, early twenty-first-century authors, filmmakers, and artists have resorted to technological utopias, relying on a stereotypical fear of and fascination with extraterrestrial beings, but in anthropological and epistemological terms the differences are minimal. From the late Middle Ages, people imagined the East, especially India, as a sensuous paradise, just waiting for European colonization. This form of Orientalism, which Edward Said discussed in his famous study (1978), continues to be a pervasive and manipulative concept of the Other both in its epistemological and social-literary dimensions in the early twenty-first century. Overcoming the monster, defeating extraterrestrial creatures, or colonizing their exotic worlds represent the triumph of the self over the Other and offer the chance to establish the self's identity. This phenomenon seems to have characterized all developmental stages of the Western world. Medieval monster lore was deeply influenced by ancient concepts developed by Herodotus (c. 484–between 430 and 420 B.C.E.), Ctesias (c. 400 B.C.E.), Pliny the Elder (23–79 C.E.), and Solinus (third century C.E.). Though Augustine, in his *City of God Against the Pagans* (BK. XVI, ch. 8) expressed doubts, he accepted the possibility that monsters might exist. He suggested that if these monstrous races were real, they should be treated as God's creatures: "He Himself knows where and when anything should be, or should have been, created; and He knows how to weave the beauty of the whole out of the similarity and diversity of its parts" (Augustine, p. 708). Decidedly excluding the idea that God might have erred when he created monsters, Augustine concludes that "just as some monsters occur within the various races of mankind, so there should be certain monstrous races within the human race as a whole" (Augustine, p. 710). One of the earliest examples of monster imagery in the Middle Ages can be found in the Anglo-Saxon *Wonders of the East* (c. 970–1150).

Throughout the Middle Ages, theologians and artists, writers and philosophers were deeply divided over the correct explanation of monsters, the absolute Other within human epistemology (Cohen, J. J., 1999). Jacques de Vitry (1160–1240) attempted to describe the European perspective of monsters: "And just as we consider Pygmies to be dwarfs, so they consider us giants. . . . We consider the black Ethiopians of bad character; among them, however, the one who is blackest is judged most beautiful" (Friedman, p. 164). The fascination that monsters exerted throughout the centuries was undeniable, as documented by numerous manuscript illustrations, sculptures, chronicle accounts, travelogues, textile images, and ivory, stone, and wood carvings (Bovey). Many bestiaries depict not only a wide variety of animals, but also a broad spectrum of monsters whose grotesque features were interpreted as signaling moral decrepitude or who were seen as symbols of imminent apocalypse. Often the treatment of monsters reflected a profoundly Manichean worldview that divided everything into good and evil. Late-medieval poets took a more diversified approach and developed accounts of basically good monsters, such as Melusine, half human and half snake (Classen, 1995, p. 141–162), who was eventually expelled from human society because of her human husband's failure to keep her true nature a secret (see the text versions by Walter Map, Gervasius of Tilbury, Jean d'Arras, Couldrette, and Thüring von Ringoltingen). Many medieval manuscripts, especially Psalters, contained images of hybrid creatures, grotesque beings, and monsters, which could have hardly served as deterrence from sinfulness; instead they represented a growing fascination with the Other and an emerging playfulness in the visual depiction of the world (Camille, Yamamoto). The encyclopedist Thomas of Cantimpré (1201–1272), relying on Augustine's ruminations, urged his readers to "consider the

forms of creatures and delight in the artificer who made them" (Friedman, p. 123). When explorers reached the shores of the New World in 1492, they used monster images to describe and depict the indigenous population, thereby casting them as other from the start (Flint, 1992, p. 53–54, 61, et seq.).

Tolerance and Toleration

The term "tolerance," reflecting a unique approach to the Other, requires a detailed explanation as to its meaning and manifestations during different cultural periods. While classical Greece and Rome generally tolerated people of different beliefs, it would be more correct to identify the openness toward Others as toleration. The persecutions of Jews, and later of Christians, was not the result of religious doctrines, but rather the consequence of claims by Jews and Christians as to the absolute truth of their respective beliefs. Augustine was the first to formulate a preliminary concept of tolerance toward those who embraced different religions (Jews) or were sinners in the eye of the Church, such as prostitutes (*Epistola ad Vincentium V* [1649]), as long as such open-mindedness contributed to the cohesiveness and stability of the Christian community. However, Augustine vehemently attacked those Christians who followed deviant teachings (Donatists), and approved of their persecution. In the Middle Ages, scholastic writers pursued the idea of tolerance in the light of sinful behavior that could be accepted as long as it did not affect the principles of Christian belief. Thomas specifically differentiated among heathens, Jews, and heretics, and argued for the toleration of various religious practices among Christians as long as they supported the truth of the New Testament. Moreover Thomas rejected forced conversion and baptism since such acts constituted a violation of natural law (Bejczy, p. 370).

A number of medieval writers explicitly advocated tentative models of tolerance. In his middle High German epic *Willhelam* (c. 1218), Wolfram von Eschenbach's female protagonist Gyburc pleads for humane treatment of the heathens, her own relatives who she had left behind when she fled to the Christian world with her lover and future husband Willhelam. In the pan-European love story *Floire et Blanchefleur* (Old French version, c. 1160), just as in *Aucassin et Nicolette* (Old French, early thirteenth century), the difference in religion of the young couple has no significance, whereas love is described as the dominant force that overcomes all social, ethnical, military, and political conflicts (Shutters, 2004). In the anonymous middle High German verse romance *Reinfried von Braunschweig* (c. 1280), the protagonist at first intends to force his opponent, the Prince of Persia, to convert to Christianity. But, upon the latter's plea, Reinfried allows the Persian to maintain his religion because he realizes that a forced conversion would never make the Prince into a true Christian. In fact the protagonist abandons all his religious goals and becomes a secular tourist who simply admires the wonders of the East. The Catalan mystic and poet Ramon Llull (c. 1232–1316) strongly advocated openness toward the Other in his *Book of the Gentile and the Three Wise Men* (c. 1275–1290). Similar to Peter Abelard's *Dialogue between a Philosopher, a Jew, and a Christian* (c. 1136–1139), Llull's treatise is built upon dialogues among representatives of the three world religions about their specific form of belief. Although Llull, like Abelard, explicitly advocated Christianity, he accepted other religions as valid belief systems that he could not and did not want to condemn absolutely. On the contrary, both Abelard and Llull suggested that conversion to Christianity must be based on true conviction, which in turn was based on an intellectual, rational discourse in which the opponent was convinced of the falsity of his or her original belief and convinced by logical arguments and a newfound faith to accept Christianity (Nederman, Muldoon). Although in reality openness toward other religions was hardly ever practiced—as evidenced by the many persecutions and expulsions of and pogroms against Jews—many medieval and early modern philosophers can be credited with bold, farsighted exploration of the possibilities for various religions to exist side by side. Nicolaus of Cusa (1401–1464), in *De pace fidei* (1453), proposed embracing the concept of *concordia* (concordance) of the *religio una in ritum varietate* (one religion in a variety of rituals). Some humanists such as Thomas More (1485–1535) and Erasmus of Rotterdam (c. 1466–1536) advocated acceptance of religion as an individual worldview that should not be imposed on other people. Heretics should be persecuted, but only by the state and only when they represented a danger to the entire community (*De amabili ecclesiae concordia liber* [1533]). Conversely Martin Luther (1483–1546), although he had broken with the Catholic Church, strongly defended the persecution of Jews and members of various Protestant sects, and approved of the death penalty. John Calvin (1509–1564) defined tolerance as friendliness of the spirit (*mansuetudo animi*), but he did not raise any objections to imposing the death penalty on heretics, such as the Spanish theologian Miguel Serveto (c. 1511–1553).

On the opposite side of the debate was the French philosopher Jean Bodin (1530–1596) who defended the freedom of individual consciousness and tolerance (*Six Livres de la République* [1576]). In the tradition of Abelard and Llull, Bodin composed a dialogue text in which representatives of various religions discuss their theological differences (*Colloquium heptaplomeres* [c. 1593]).

Religious tolerance was an important issue in the wake of religious wars on the European continent and in England up to the end of the Thirty Years' War because the dominant religions persecuted minorities, which in turn led to military conflicts. Thomas Hobbes (1588–1679) was the first to define religious convictions as "private opinions" (*Leviathan* [1651]), which paved the way for John Locke's famous "Letter Concerning Toleration" (1689): "For no man can, if he would, conform his faith to the dictates of another" (Locke, see Zagorin). Nevertheless even Locke refused to accept atheists and charged them with refusing to abide by the basic rules of human society, which were predicated on the concepts of covenants, promises, and oaths.

Traditional scholarship argues that Locke's "Letter Concerning Toleration" represents the first attempt in the history of the Western world to establish philosophical principles of tolerance, followed by comparable statements by Wilhelm von Humboldt (1767–1835), Benjamin Constant (1767–1830), and John Stuart Mill (1806–1873). But even though the term

tolerance might not be fully applicable in other contexts, as early as late antiquity and the Middle Ages writers and philosophers embraced certain types of tolerance, or at least toleration, for example Augustine, John of Salisbury (c. 1115–1180), Marsiglio of Padua (1275–1342), Nicholas of Cusa (1401–1464), and Bartolomé De Las Casas (1484–1566) (Nederman, 2000). Francisco de Vitoria (1483–1546), insisting upon the inalienable rights of all peoples, formulated such astonishingly open-minded views regarding the North and South American Indians and their inhumane treatment at the hands of the Spanish conquistadors that his works were almost put on the papal index of forbidden books (Schmidinger, pp. 194–202). In particular, de Vitoria argued that conversion to Christianity can only be possible if the prospective convert has been convinced rationally. Infidels can never be forced to convert, since faith is also a matter of reason. This attitude resonated profoundly in John Locke's "Essay Concerning Human Understanding" (1690): "Such is the nature of the understanding that it cannot be compelled to the belief of any thing by outward force. Confiscation of estate, imprisonment, torments, nothing of that nature can have any such efficacy as to make men change the inward judgment that they have framed of things. . . . It is only light and evidence that can work a change in men's opinions; and that light can in no manner proceed from corporal sufferings, or any other outward penalties" (Vernon, p. 17). In other words, tolerance, or acceptance of the Other, in his inalienable character and nature, has been explored by philosophers throughout history, but has remained a fleeting concept regularly undermined and challenged by social, economic, political, and military realities.

Major breakthroughs in the history of modern tolerance did not occur until the late eighteenth century. Emperor Joseph II of Austria issued a law of tolerance for the various religious (Christian) communities in his inherited lands, giving members of non-Catholic communities recognition, as long as the dominance of the Catholic Church was not compromised. In letters that he exchanged with his mother Maria Theresa, he said that he remained an ardent defender of Catholicism, but wanted to give Protestants equal rights, at least in terms of their status as citizens, and to grant them the right to practice their religion. The Constitution of the United States was based on the principle of tolerance, best reflected in the Bill of Rights, as formulated by Thomas Jefferson (1743–1826), and Thomas Paine (1737–1809) in his enormously popular *Rights of Man* (1791).

The most influential and far-reaching public defense of tolerance, however, might well be that of the German Enlightenment writer Gotthold Ephraim Lessing (1729–1781) in *Nathan the Wise* (1779). Based on an episode from Boccaccio's *Decameron* (c. 1348–1350), the key component of the story is a parable that the Jew Nathan tells the Sultan Saladin. The Sultan, short of money, encourages Nathan to identify which of the three world religions is the only true one, hoping to extort money from Nathan who is sure to reveal his preference of Judaism. Nathan, however, does not provide a straightforward answer, and instead relates the parable of a man who owned a valuable ring that had the power to make its bearer loved by all people. The ring's owner leaves the ring to the son who is dearest to him. The pattern of that legacy is continued for many generations, until one day a father has three sons whom he loves equally. When death approaches, the father has two perfect copies of the ring made and secretly gives one to each of his three sons, pretending that it is the only and true ring. After his death the sons go to a judge to determine who owns the authentic ring and hence who is heir to the father's estate. The judge refuses to decide and advises the three brothers to "Let each of you demonstrate his belief in the power of his ring by conducting his life in such a manner that he fully merits—as anciently promised—the love of God and man." The brothers are told to return to the ultimate judge, God, within a thousand years and to confirm before Him who had been the most loved because of his kindness and piety. Saladin understands Nathan's message and discharges him, accepting him as a friend. Saladin has learned that all three religions are equal in their basic essence and that believers of all faiths should tolerate each other, competing only in an attempt to be most worthy of the love of families and neighbors.

Assessment

Despite numerous efforts by lawmakers, philosophers, theologians, and poets, the deep gulf between self and the Other has continued to plague the modern world. Although Jews gained more freedoms after the early nineteenth century and were increasingly integrated into Christian society, by the 1890s anti-Semitism had reached new levels of intensity, making possible the atrocities committed by the Nazis during the Holocaust, and subsequent pogroms in Poland and Russia following World War II and continuing into the early twenty-first century. The world continues to struggle with the dialectics of self and other, in intellectual and popular culture, in economic and military terms, and in issues regarding the legal rights of immigrants, refugees, prisoners of war, criminals, and others who society at large does not accept or tolerate (Levinas, pp. 145–149. Ancient man regarded barbarians or even members of neighboring city-states as other. Medieval people used images of monsters to characterize believers of other religions as dangerous infidels or heretics. These as well as homosexuals, apostates, the possessed, and even women were considered to be the Other, both threatening and dangerous (Goodich). In the early twenty-first century, dominant societies have created a variety of new images of the Other, such as illegal immigrants, asylum seekers, political refugees, Muslim terrorists, and imagined creatures from outer space (Schreiner).

The content of the theoretical template of the Other has changed over the centuries but its fundamental binary opposition that the self always establishes barriers to the Other in order to create an identity—a process that is possible only through deliberate differentiations—remains. While not inherently hostile or dangerous, in most cases, throughout history people have tended to cast the Other in the worst possible light because the self usually chooses a path toward itself by rejecting the Other and establishing a close-knit community (family, village, church group, country, and people). Since the Middle Ages individual writers, poets, philosophers, and theologians have argued in defense of the Other and have made

serious attempts at breaking down the rigid barriers between it and the self, demonstrating that open-mindedness and tolerance are values that have long been important in human society. In other words, arguments for the humane, integrative treatment of the Other have been proposed throughout history, with the idea of tolerance arising in different contexts in different cultures and historical periods. Since the creation of the U.S. Constitution and the *Code Napoléon,* however, Western societies, particularly, have struggled, more or less successfully, to establish institutional frameworks and legal, social, economic, and religious conditions through which the constructive interaction between self and other have become increasingly possible (Wierlacher, 1993).

See also **Anti-Semitism; Demonology; Enlightenment; Heresy and Apostasy; Humanity; Mysticism; Occidentalism; Orientalism; Toleration.**

BIBLIOGRAPHY

Adorno, Theodor W., and Max Horckheimer. *The Dialectics of Enlightenment.* Translated by John Cumming. New York: Continuum, 1972. Originally published in 1944.

Bejczy, István. "Tolerantia: A Medieval Concept." *Journal of the History of Ideas* 58, no. 3 (1997): 365–384.

Amar, Akhil Reed. *The Bill of Rights: Creation and Reconstruction.* New Haven, Conn.: Yale University Press, 1998.

Assmann, Jan. "Praktiken des Übersetzens und Konzepte von Toleranz im Alten Orient und in der hellenistisch-römischen Antike." In *Kulturthema Toleranz: Zur Grundlegung einer interdisziplinären und interkulturellen Toleranzforschung,* edited by Alois Wierlacher, 283–306. Munich: Iudicium, 1996.

Augustine. *The City of God against the Pagans.* Edited and translated by R. W. Dyson. Cambridge Texts in the History of Political Thought. Cambridge, U.K.: Cambridge University Press, 1998.

Benton, Janetta Rebold. *Holy Terrors: Gargoyles on Medieval Buildings.* New York: Abbeville Press, 1997.

Bovey, Alixe. *Monsters and Grotesques in Medieval Manuscripts.* Toronto: University of Toronto Press, 2002.

Caciola, Nancy. *Discerning Spirits: Divine and Demonic Possession in the Middle Ages.* Ithaca, N.Y.: Cornell University Press, 2003.

Camille, Michael. *Image on the Edge: the Margins of Medieval Art.* Cambridge, Mass.: Harvard University Press, 1992.

Classen, Albrecht, ed. *The German Volksbuch: A Critical History of a Late-Medieval Genre.* Lewiston, N.Y.: Edwin Mellen Press, 1995.

———. *Meeting the Foreign in the Middle Ages.* New York: Routledge, 2002.

———. "*Die Suche nach dem Ich in der Gottheit. Mystische Literatur als epistemologisches Phänomen im Spätmittelalter: Zu Hildegard von Bingen, Mechthild von Magdeburg und Agnes Blannbekin.*" *Etudes Médiévales* 4 (2002): 21–34.

Cohen, Jeffrey Jerome. *Of Giants: Sex, Monsters, and the Middle Ages.* Minneapolis: University of Minnesota Press, 1999.

Cohen, Jeremy. *Living Letters of the Law: Ideas of the Jew in Medieval Christianity.* Berkeley: University of California Press, 1999.

Delumeau, Jean. *Sin and Fear: the Emergence of a Western Guilt Culture: 13th–18th Centuries.* Translated by Eric Nicholson. New York: St. Martin's Press, 1990.

Dinzelbacher, Peter. *Angst im Mittelalter: Teufels-, Todes- und Gotteserfahrung: Mentalitätsgeschichte und Ikonographie.* Paderborn, Germany: Schöningh, 1996.

Flint, Valerie I. J. *The Imaginative Landscape of Christopher Columbus.* Princeton, N.J.: Princeton University Press, 1992.

———. *The Rise of Magic in Early Medieval Europe.* Princeton, N.J.: Princeton University Press, 1991.

Friedman, John Block. *The Monstrous Races in Medieval Art and Thought.* Cambridge, Mass.: Harvard University Press, 1981.

Gadamer, Hans-Georg. *The Hermeneutic Reader: Texts of the German Tradition from the Enlightenment to the Present.* Edited by Kurt Mueller-Vollmer. New York: Continuum, 1985.

Ginzburg, Carlo. *The Night Battles: Witchcraft and Agrarian Cults in the Sixteenth and Seventeenth Centuries.* Translated by John Tedeschi and Anne Tedeschi. Baltimore: Johns Hopkins University Press, 1992.

Gioseffi, Daniela. *On Prejudice: A Global Perspective.* New York: Anchor Books, 1993.

Goodich, Michael, ed. *Other Middle Ages: Witnesses at the Margins of Medieval Society.* Philadelphia: University of Pennsylvania Press, 1998.

Hallson, Fridrik. *Xenologie: Eine Begriffserläuterung.* Bielefeld, Germany: Universität Bielefeld, 1994.

Kirn, Hans-Martin. *Das Bild vom Juden im Deutschland des frühen 16: Jahrhunderts.* Tübingen, Germany: Mohr, 1989.

Levack, Brian P. *The Witch-Hunt in Early Modern Europe.* 2nd ed. London and New York: Longman, 1995.

Levinas, Emmanuel. *Alterity and Transcendence.* Translated by Michael B. Smith. New York: Columbia University Press, 1999.

Lionarons, Joyce Tally. "The Otherworld and its Inhabitants." In *A Companion to the Nibelungenlied,* edited by Winder McConnell, 153–171. Columbia, S.C.: Camden House, 1998,.

Locke, John. "A Letter Concerning Toleration." In *Two Treatises of Government and a Letter Concerning Toleration,* edited by Ian Shapiro. New Haven, Conn., and London: Yale University Press, 2003.

Maccoby, Hyam, ed. and trans. *Judaism on Trial: Jewish-Christian Disputations in the Middle Ages.* London: Associated University Press, 1982.

Martin, Xavier. *Nature humaine et révolution française: Du siècle des lumières au Code Napoléon.* Bouère, France: D. M. Morin, 1994.

Milem, Bruce. *The Unspoken Word: Negative Theology in Meister Eckhart's German Sermons.* Washington, D.C.: Catholic University of America Press, 2002.

Milis, Ludovicus, ed. *The Pagan Middle Ages.* Translated by Tanis Guest. Woodbridge, Suffolk, U.K., and Rochester, N.Y.: Boydell Press, 1998.

Mittal, Anuradha, and Peter Rosset, eds. *America Needs Human Rights.* Oakland, Calif.: Food First Books, 1999.

Muldoon, James, ed. *Varieties of Religious Conversion in the Middle Ages.* Gainesville: University Press of Florida, 1997.

Nederman, Cary J. *Worlds of Difference: European Discourses of Toleration c. 1100–1550.* University Park: Pennsylvania State University Press, 2000.

Said, Edward W. *Orientalism.* New York: Pantheon Books, 1978.

Saussure, Ferdinand de. *Saussure's Third Course of Lectures on General Linguistics (1910–1911).* Translated by Roy Harris. New York: Pergamon Press, 1993. Translation of *Troisième cours de linguistique générale (1910–1911).* French text edited by Eisuke Komatsu.

Schick, Irvin Cemil. *The Erotic Margin: Sexuality and Spatiality in Alteritist Discourse.* London, New York: Verso, 1999.

Schmidinger, Heinrich, ed. *Wege zur Toleranz: Geschichte einer europäischen Idee in Quellen.* Darmstadt, Germany: Wissenschaftliche Buchgesellschaft, 2002.

Scholz Williams, Gerhild. *Defining Dominion: The Discourses of Magic and Witchcraft in Early Modern France and Germany.* Ann Arbor: University of Michigan Press, 1995.

Schreiner, Klaus. "Toleranz." In Vol. 6 of *Geschichtliche Grundbegriffe: Historisches Lexikon zur politisch-sozialen Sprache in Deutschland,* edited by Otto Brunner, Werner Conze, and Reinhart Koselleck, 445–605. Stuttgart, Germany: Klett-Cotta, 1990.

Shutters, Lynn. "Christian Love or Pagan Transgression?: Marriage and Conversion in *Floire et Blancheflor.*" In *Discourses on Love, Marriage, and Transgression in Medieval and Early Modern Literature,* edited by Albrecht Classen. Tempe, Ariz.: MRTS, 2004.

Stutzinger, Dagmar. "Das Fremde und das Eigene: Antike." In *Europäische Mentalitätsgeschichte: Hauptthemen in Einzeldarstellungen,* edited by Peter Dinzelbacher, 400–415. Stuttgart, Germany: Kröner, 1993.

Sundermeier, Theo. *Den Fremden wahrnehmen: Bausteine für eine Xenologie.* Gütersloh, Germany: G. Mohn, 1992.

Szarmach, Paul E, ed. *An Introduction to the Medieval Mystics of Europe.* Albany: State University of New York Press, 1984.

Vernon, Richard. *The Career of Toleration: John Locke, Jonas Proast, and After.* Montreal: McGill-Queen's University Press, 1997.

Wierlacher, Alois, ed. *Kulturthema Fremdheit: Leitbegriffe und Problemfelder kulturwissenschaftlicher Fremdheitsforschung.* Munich: Iudicium, 1993.

Williams, David. *Deformed Discourse: The Function of the Monster in Medieval Thought and Literature.* Montreal: McGill-Queen's University Press, 1996.

Yamamoto, Dorothy. *The Boundaries of the Human in Medieval English Literature.* Oxford: Oxford University Press, 2000.

Zagorin, Perez. *How the Idea of Religious Toleration Came to the West.* Princeton, N.J.: Princeton University Press, 2003.

Albrecht Classen

P

PACIFISM. The issues summoned up by the term *pacifism* are complex and varied because different concepts, traditions, and definitions exist throughout the world, often creating misunderstanding and confusion—sometimes intentionally so. For example, the term may be used pejoratively in political debates by individuals seeking to portray opponents who refuse to support a specific military action, or by those who prefer nonviolent approaches to a problem or conflict while not being principled pacifists. The term underwent a bifurcation, redefinition, and narrower specification with the watershed years of the so-called Great War of 1914. The distinction between absolute pacifism and "pacific-ism"—the latter a term coined by the modern historian A. J. P. Taylor and used by his successors—or other less ethically rigid "pacifist" positions emerged then. Before 1915 the term *pacifist* was employed as a more general term to describe one who opposed war as an institution, rejecting violence in favor of turning "swords into plowshares." But the earlier definition of *pacifist* did not necessarily exclude violence—still less all force—as a means to an end, for example, in opposing slavery.

This more general understanding of pacifism did not necessarily imply a refusal to support, or indeed fight in, a war once it broke out. The more rigid position became defined as "absolute" or "pure" pacifism, identifying those whose stance in 1914 or from 1915 to 1916 was based on consistent principles. The terms *pure* or *absolute* have been dropped from the political debate since then, and the term *pacifist* now tends to mean rejection of all and any war—especially since the 1960s, when some "pacifists" remained equivocal on violence in Indochina.

The Religious Concept of Pacifism

The individual moral concept of "turning the other cheek" is one that belongs to a number of religious traditions, though the position has perhaps arguably been most fully developed as an ethical position in Judaism and then Christianity and as a spiritual position in Buddhism—and, mainly through Mahatma Gandhi (1869–1948), as a revision of Hindu thought. The major religious tradition with the least apparent pacifist dimension seems to be Islam. Secular ethical pacifism emerged in the nineteenth century alongside other "isms" based on humanist and universalist ethics and overlaps with several ideological strands from liberalism to anarchism and, since the 1970s, feminism.

Pacifism and Resistance to War

The biblical commandment "thou shall not kill" does not specifically refer to organized war and can thus be taken as a prohibition of individual murder, perhaps not the "legitimate" killing by soldiers in war—an ethical sleight of hand that has been convenient to states and rulers and allows the concept of just war, elaborated by the Christian Church when it became institutionalized in the West in the fifth century and continuing for a millennium. The injunction to turn the other cheek in the face of violent provocation has been seen not as a theory of nonviolence but as one of passivity, suffering, and stoicism. Pacifist idealism and ethics have evolved toward a more formal position of war refusal or war resistance. More generally, pacifism worldwide has evolved from an ethic of suffering and detachment to active engagement through nonviolence as an alternative to war. The invention of Gandhian nonviolence thus represented a critical moment in the evolution of pacifist ethics—though Gandhi was not an absolute pacifist in the strictest sense.

Conscientious Objection Based on Pacifist Principles

Since laws of universal military service—conscription or the draft—and claims of conscientious objection spread gradually during the nineteenth century, the issue of refusal to fight in war did not appear to be a universal issue of conscience. It had been possible to avoid the choice if faced with it. Pacifism as opposition to war as an institution did not mean refusal to participate in it until the drafts of 1914–1918, when those who accepted the call of country (so-called pacificists) divided themselves from the minority absolute pacifists who remained antiwar in practice as well as theory.

War Resistance versus Pacifism

Similar ethical divisions over war in general and specific (just) wars have continued. War resistance (often to specific wars) and pacifism are not the same; some have refused to participate in specific "unjust" wars or opposed an arms race or particular (for example, nuclear) weapons without being pacifists in regard to all war. For example, the peace movement was often partisan regarding whose weapons and wars it most actively opposed—divided over emancipatory or "progressive" war or violence (such as the defense of the Spanish Republic against fascism after 1936). Other ethical issues for pacifism have arisen over the moral duty to counsel others to refuse military service (under some laws "incitement to disaffection")—or to take nonviolent action, even sabotage, to obstruct war or destroy weapons.

Further examples of this dilemma abound. Should continued religious teaching against war or military combat be interpreted as treasonable or subversive of a state in time of war? Certainly not all those who refuse to be involved in war on ethical grounds are advocates of nonviolence or turning the other cheek in other situations. Equally those who accept a nonviolent discipline in domestic politics (such as Gandhi's) do not necessarily condemn all war. The grounds for opposing war and conscription are often not strictly ethical; they may be political or personal—ethics of justice, liberation, equality or "national liberation" may be more important than nonviolence in antiwar protests.

The Personal versus the Political in Pacifism

The term pacifism is usually used of an ideological position that is more than purely personal—the U.S. anarchist Paul Goodman (1911–1972) called himself a "fist-fighting pacifist." For others personal nonviolence in life, or a meditative path, is more important than whether one dons a uniform or picks up a weapon or takes a position against a war or revolution. It is essentially retreatist. There are many variants of these positions.

The millennia of otherworldly retreat—monastic or utopian—from a world that appears lost repeats itself as communitarian pacifism and recurrently inherits recruits from failed or dissipated antiwar movements. There is an emphasis on child development, peace education, and the construction of a more peaceful culture, which has had an impact on modern pedagogy.

Mahatma Gandhi (1869–1948). Gandhi's policy of passive resistance—or, as he preferred to call it, *satyagraha* (truth and firmness)—was first manifested during his sojourn in South Africa in the late nineteenth century and continued upon his return to his homeland of India. AP/WIDE WORLD PHOTOS

Gandhi's own ambivalence on these dilemmas, expressed in his retreat after the mass 1920s campaigns became violent—again is symptomatic of this ambiguity in pacifist idealism; yet by the 1930s and 1940s he once again advocated mass nonviolent resistance to British colonial rule in India, even during wartime, while also urging such resistance to Hitlerism from the 1930s on—for those brave enough to do so. Violence in this view was the inferior weapon of the weak, preferable to cowardice, but a lesser evil at best. Gandhi's model was reproduced in Ghana to some extent, but more violent methods adopted by leftist or nationalist revolutionaries tended to dominate such struggles thereafter.

Gandhi was also a political pacifist, however, in seeking programs of social and institutional change, not merely personal transformation. He saw them as being linked—following the teachings of Leo Tolstoy—but went further than the Russian Christian anarchists in creating a political ethic of nonviolent collective action (drawing also from Thoreau's principles of civil disobedience). These ideas in turn inspired Dr. Martin Luther King Jr. (1929–1968) and other human rights leaders. In the early New Left of the 1960s and the women's movements of the 1970s and 1980s and since, the personal and the political came together again in a fusion of pacifism and antipatriarchal women's peace activisms that sought to "take the toys from the boys" not least the Cruise missiles deployed in the United Kingdom by U.S. President Ronald Reagan in the 1980s. The Greenham Common Women's Peace Camp at the Greenham missile base in the United Kingdom was symptomatic of hundreds of such projects, militantly antimilitarist but linked to feminist and pacifist ideologies and predominantly nonviolent in methodology.

Twentieth-Century Developments

In the twentieth century new forms of pacifism emerged that were linked to political traditions: anarchist or socialist pacifism, nationalist pacifism (for example, in Wales), nuclear pacifism or the refusal to support or tolerate the stockpiling manufacture, use, or threatened deployment of weapons of mass destruction. Many pure pacifists were ambivalent about such a movement against only one form of war, while others took leadership roles in movements opposing the atomic bomb, in turning the movement to the use of Gandhian nonviolence. Feminism took an interest in pacifism from the first women's movements, burgeoning in the antinuclear women's peace movements of the 1980s and reflected in writers such as Barbara Deming.

Since 1918 the link between individual pacifist ethics and political pacifism has been shown to be most obvious; the sum of individual conscientious stances can create a social force based on ethics that can have an impact on policy. While more noticeable in liberal democratic contexts, even in authoritarian and repressive situations, such movements have had enormous effectiveness. Acting against the military draft, opposing the threat to engage in war, or the planned deployment of a new weapon (for example, to target civilians), or the invasion of another country—such movements have suffered many short-term setbacks but some long-term successes. Yet often pacifist and pacifist groups have remained marginal in their attempt to bring ethical stances into political life; the peace churches and "prophetic minorities" have kept ethics alive and provided leadership but are at best pressure groups or lobbies for change, as was the attempt to stop the strategic bombing of cities in World War II (1943–1945). In retrospect this was, even from the mainstream, not considered treasonable behavior but a legitimate ethical position. At the time it was seen as disloyal and questionable and was therefore marginalized by the allied military-political elites.

The war in Vietnam is another instance where, in hindsight, the pacifist positions that were marginalized in 1965 seemed justifiable only a decade later. The draft resistance movement led by pacifist groups has gained a respectable if not heroic image. However, this opportunistic application of just war or pacifist theories is anathema to absolute pacifists for whom even World War II, the "good war," remains ultimately an injustice—to the victims and those forced to fight in it.

Ethical pacifists who have emerged in the twentieth century with leading roles in social movements—Dr. Martin Luther King, Jr., Mahatma Gandhi, and many others—have, like some of the great pacifist religious prophets of the distant past, had an impact on social consciousness and cultural history far beyond their immediate actions. Yet pacifist ethics are in tension not only with the institution of war but even with the violent origins, foundations, and operations of the state and its penal and security systems. Despite the Gandhian model, pacifism often finds itself in tension with nationalist aspirations, or the urge toward armed emancipation from oppression. The "Balkan Gandhi," Ibrahim Rugova (b. 1945), witnessed two decades of nonviolent struggle for the autonomy of Kosovo, but also saw his nonviolent movement overtaken by a violent reaction to Serb oppression in 1998–1999 and ultimately by military intervention by NATO.

The episode in Kosovo, like the Spanish Civil War of 1936, underlines the dilemmas of pacifist ethics in a highly militarized world, socialized toward violent solutions to conflict. Such events do not prove pacifism right or wrong; they do raise issues of immediate effectiveness in the last resort (especially where peoples are under threat, or as in Spain where the long-term consequences of inaction may be disastrous), as against aspirations for long-term cultural and political change, and the failure to break the cycle or self-sustaining character of violent action. The great social structural insight of pacifism (as opposed to its ethical probity) is that violent conflict and change begets violent institutions, authoritarianism, and further violence. Whether nonviolence as a method can slowly replace that structural dynamic remains open to question, yet it is surely one of the prime issues of all human politics.

See also **Nonviolence; Peace; Resistance and Accommodation; War.**

BIBLIOGRAPHY

Bondurant, Joan V. *The Conquest of Violence: The Gandhian Philosophy of Conflict.* Princeton: Princeton University Press, 1958. Still the classic academic work of political theory on the ideas and practice of nonviolence by political scientist.

Brock, Peter. *Pacifism in the United States: From the Colonial Era to the First World War.* Princeton: Princeton University Press, 1968. The foremost historian of pacifism.

——. *Pacifism since 1914 An Annotated Reading List.* 3rd ed. Toronto: P. Brock, 2000. Best bibliography on Modern pacifism

——. *Varieties of Pacifism: A Survey from Antiquity to the Outset of the Twentieth Century.* 4th ed. Syracuse, N.Y.: Syracuse University Press, 2000. Short essays.

Brock, Peter, and Nigel Young. *Pacifism in the Twentieth Century.* Syracuse, N.Y.: Syracuse University Press, 1999. Strongest on religious debates and useful as a comprehensive reference work.

Carter, April. *Peace Movements: International Protest and World Politics Since 1945.* London and New York: Longman, 1990. Sympathetic critical account of pacifist and nonpacifist movements by an academic once active in the movements.

Ceadel, Martin. *Pacifism in Britain 1914–1945: The Defining of a Faith.* Oxford: Clarendon, 1980. Written by a nonpacifist who has written several other works critically examining pacifism.

Cooney Robert, and Helen Michalowski. *The Power of the People: Nonviolent Action in the United States.* Philadelphia: New Society Press, 1988. Accessible, well-illustrated general accounts of pacifist campaigns mostly twentieth century.

Gandhi, Mahatma. *The Moral and Political Writings of Mahatma Gandhi.* Edited by Raghavan Iyer. 3 vols. Oxford and New York: Oxford University Press, 1986–1987. Contains "My Experiments with Truth" (Gandhi's autobiography).

Nuttall, Geoffrey. *Christian Pacifism in History.* Oxford and New York: Blackwell, 1958. A summary of the religious standpoint.

Young, Nigel. "War Resistance and the Nation State." Ph.D. diss., University of California, Berkeley, 1976. An academic political sociology of pacifist action written by an academic peace researcher, observer, and participant, who has written extensively on war resistance, peace, and radical movements.

——. "War Resistance in Britain." In chap. 1, *Campaigns for Peace,* edited by Richard Taylor and Nigel Young. Manchester, U.K.: Manchester University Press, 1987. This collection contains several other useful and pertinent essays including on the women's peace movement; the introduction has a useful tabulation of peace traditions following R. Overy and others.

Nigel Young

PAN-AFRICANISM.

Because it refers neither to a single political ideology nor a clearly discernible philosophical tradition, *Pan-Africanism* is difficult to define. Many scholars avoid defining it, noting that black internationalism has varied drastically according to time and place. Indeed, various conceptions of Pan-Africanism have been aligned with disparate political and theoretical positions, from largely religious to communist to even, Paul Gilroy suggests, fascist forms. Yet, the concept can be said to signify a set of shared assumptions. Pan-Africanist intellectual, cultural, and political movements tend to view all Africans and descendants of Africans as belonging to a single "race" and sharing cultural unity. Pan-Africanism posits a sense of a shared historical fate for Africans in the Americas, West Indies, and, on the continent itself, has centered on the Atlantic trade in slaves, African slavery, and European imperialism.

Cultural and intellectual manifestations of Pan-Africanism have been devoted to recovering or preserving African "traditions" and emphasizing the contributions of Africans and those in the diaspora to the modern world. Pan-Africanists have invariably fought against racial discrimination and for the political rights of Africans and descendants of Africans, have tended to be anti-imperialist, and often espoused a metaphorical or symbolic (if not literal) "return" to Africa.

Origins and Development of Pan-Africanism

The modern conception of *Pan-Africanism*, if not the term itself, dates from at least the mid-nineteenth-century. The slogan, "Africa for the Africans," popularized by Marcus Garvey's (1887–1940) Declaration of Negro Rights in 1920, may have originated in West Africa, probably Sierra Leone, around this time. The African-American Martin Delany (1812–1885), who developed his own re-emigration scheme, reported in 1861 the slogan after an expedition to Nigeria during 1859–1860 and Edward Wilmot Blyden (1832–1912) adopted it when he arrived in West Africa in 1850. Blyden, originally from St. Thomas, played a significant role in the emergence of Pan-Africanist ideas around the Atlantic through his public speeches and writings in Africa, Britain, and the United States, and proposed the existence of an "African personality" resembling contemporary European cultural nationalisms. Blyden's ideas informed the notion of race consciousness developed by W. E. B. DuBois (1868–1963) at the end of the nineteenth century.

The growth of Pan-African sentiments in the late nineteenth century can be seen as both a continuation of ethnic, or "pan-nationalist," thinking and a reaction to the limits of emancipation for former slaves in the diaspora and European colonial expansion in Africa. There are a number of reasons why black internationalism had particular resonance during this period. African contact with Europeans, the slave trade from Africa, and the widespread use of African slaves in the New World colonies were the most salient factors, leading first those in dispersion and then many in Africa to envision the unity of the "race." At the same time, as abolition spread gradually around the Atlantic during the nineteenth century, Europeans increasingly viewed race as a biological and, thus, inherent difference rather than a cultural one.

Back-to-Africa movements—particularly the establishment of Sierra Leone by the British in 1787 and Liberia by the American Colonization Society in 1816—also contributed to the emergence of Pan-Africanism, and were probably the original source of the phrase, "Africa for the Africans." From 1808, English Evangelicals at the CMS Grammar School in Freetown taught their "liberated" students that there were other Africans around the globe, which instilled a sense of a common destiny. Many mission-educated Sierra Leoneans like Samuel Crowther (c. 1807–1891) and James Johnson (1836–1917) moved or, in some cases, moved back to Nigeria, primarily Lagos, beginning in the mid-nineteenth century, where they were joined by returning freed people from Brazil and the Caribbean. These groups quickly coalesced into the Christian, African upper class that produced the leaders of early Nigerian nationalism and Pan-Africanism. Pan-Africanism was the product of extraordinary, European-educated Africans and African-Americans, in other words, those most exposed to metropolitan culture and the influences of the modern world.

Ethiopianism. Apart from the contributions of West Africans and African descendants in the New World, South Africa developed a distinctive form of race consciousness in the form of Ethiopianism. Up to the contemporary Rastafarian movement in Jamaica, the word *Ethiopian* has enjoyed a privileged position in the Pan-Africanist vocabulary as a term for all Africans and as one referring only to the inhabitants of a specific state (Abyssinia). The movement denoted by the term *Ethiopianism* draws on the former denotation and takes its name from the "Ethiopian Church" founded in 1892 by Mangena M. Mokone (1851–1931) who separated from the African Methodist Episcopal mission over discrimination in the church.

Ethiopianism emerged in response to European colonial settlement, the institutionalization of white supremacy, and rapid industrialization, particularly in mining areas like the Rand region near Johannesburg. Its leaders were largely graduates of missionary schools, but most in their audiences were illiterate. Thus, Ethiopianism became a significant means of spreading proto-nationalist ideas and a sense of Pan-African unity in southeastern and South Africa. Following the last Zulu uprising in 1906, white South Africans and the British associated the movement with the insurrection and became hypersensitive to any potential expressions of the "peril." The notion of Ethiopianism, however, had spread to West Africa, notably the Gold Coast and Nigeria, by the end of the nineteenth century, where it blended with other Pan-Africanist currents.

Transnational Pan-Africanism

Although the exact origins are disputed, the term *Pan-African* first appeared in the 1890s. P. O. Esedebe maintains that the Chicago Congress on Africa held in 1893 marks both the transition of Pan-Africanism from an idea to a recognizable movement and the first usage of the word itself. In their collection on Pan-African history, however, Adi and Sherwood point to the creation of the African Association in 1898 and the convening of the first Pan-African conference in 1900 in London, both organized by the Trinidadian lawyer Henry Sylvester Williams (1869–1911), with the objective of "bringing into closer touch with each other the Peoples of African descent throughout the world," as the beginning of the "organised Pan-African movement." Despite these differences, scholars agree on the important role that the African American intellectual W. E. B. DuBois played in developing the idea of Pan-Africanism and marshalling a transnational political movement around it. Indeed, DuBois contributed significant speeches to the proceedings of the Chicago Congress and the Pan-African 1900 conference. In his "Address to the Nations of the World" at the latter, DuBois declared:

> the problem of the twentieth century is the problem of the colour line, the question as to how far differences of race . . . are going to be made, hereafter, the basis of denying to over half the world the right of sharing to their utmost ability the opportunities and privileges of modern civilization. (1995, p. 11)

Although Williams was unable to bring plans for a second conference to fruition, DuBois soon initiated his own movement, resulting in five Pan-African Congresses during the first half of the twentieth century (1919, Paris; 1921, London, Brussels, Paris; 1923, London and Lisbon; 1927, New York; 1945, Manchester, England). During this period the nature and tenor of Pan-Africanist cultural and political activities changed drastically.

Pan-Africanism in the Early Twentieth Century

World War I brought thousands of African-Americans, Afro-Caribbeans, and Africans into contact with one another. The exigencies of war also led the imperial powers of Europe—Britain, France, and Germany—to train and employ colonial subjects in crucial industries while, as colonial combatants, many others saw firsthand the depravity that a supposedly superior European civilization had produced. Colonial soldiers also pointed to the racism implicit in being asked to fight to "make the world safe for democracy" when this world would not include them, a suspicion confirmed for many when the Allies refused to include a guarantee against racial discrimination in the League of Nations charter following the war. As a result, the interwar years witnessed an unprecedented growth in a sense of racial unity and the popularity of black internationalism.

Marcus Garvey. The most famous Pan-Africanist movement of the period was Garveyism. After struggling for some time to attract an audience in his native Jamaica, Marcus Garvey emigrated to Harlem in 1916, where he and a young, educated Jamaican woman, Amy Ashwood (who later married Garvey), relocated the Universal Negro Improvement Association (U.N.I.A.; founded 1914) on firmer footing. The U.N.I.A. quickly became the largest African-American organization in history due, in large part, to the diligent work of black women in the movement, especially West Indian emigrants like Ashwood and Marcus Garvey's secretary and second wife, Amy Jacques (1896–1973).

The apogee of the U.N.I.A.'s success was probably its international convention in 1920, at which Garvey presented the Declaration of the Rights of the Negro Peoples of the World, demanding "self-determination for all peoples" and "the inherent right of the Negro to possess himself of Africa." Garvey's hubris—in declaring himself "the provisional president of Africa," for instance—and autocratic leadership, however, cost him important friends and supporters, and his flair for ostentatious public spectacles and inflated expectations led many leading African-American writers and scholars, for example, Alain Locke (1885–1954) and DuBois, to decry him as a liability to the race. With most of his commercial enterprises like the Black Star shipping line failing or already bankrupt, in 1922 the U.S. government arrested and jailed Garvey for five years before deporting him in 1927, effectively ending the organizational life of the U.N.I.A. in the United States. Nevertheless, Garvey's life and work left a powerful legacy around the African diaspora, and his ideas have reappeared in many guises, from the violent labor clashes in the Caribbean during the 1920s and 1930s to the more millenarian form of Garveyism that developed in South Africa.

Pan-Africanist literary and cultural movements. The interwar period also witnessed the flowering of a number of Pan-Africanist literary and cultural movements, especially in New York, London, and Paris, and the emergence of a trans-Atlantic periodical culture. In the United States, the New Negro movement of the 1920s, better known as the Harlem Renaissance, not only drew attention to the work of African American artists but also displayed distinct Pan-Africanist sensibilities. Writers like James Weldon Johnson (1871–1938) inspired others around the Atlantic, for example, the Nardal sisters from Martinique (Paulette, Jane, and Andrée, who ran a salon out of which came *La Revue de Monde Noir* [The Journal of the Black World] edited by Paulette Nardal and Léo Sajous) and Una Marson from Jamaica (1905–1965; the first major woman poet of the Caribbean and a playwright), to assert positive images of blackness while experimenting with stylistic innovations, often informed by black musical forms like the blues. Yet, the New Negro movement was not solely a literary or artistic movement: Pan-Africanist political organizations, including the explicitly communist African Blood Brotherhood, can also be seen as manifestations of it.

Pan-Africanists and communism. However, it was across the Atlantic in Britain—where by the mid-1930s a key group of West Indian and African radicals had assembled—that communism and, particularly, the recent of success of the Bolshevik Revolution (1917) had its greatest impact on Pan-Africanist activists and intellectuals. The Trinidadians George Padmore (1902–1959) and C. R. L. James (1901–1989) were most significant in this regard. Padmore served as head of the International Trade Union Committee of Negro Workers and editor of its monthly newspaper, the *Negro Worker,* and James was an internationally known Trotskyite.

Growing awareness of Stalin's abuses in the Soviet Union and, more importantly, the apathy with which the governments of Europe and the League of Nations greeted Mussolini's invasion of Abyssinia (Ethiopia) and Haile Selassie's pleas for intervention ultimately led them both to split from the Communist Party and foreground Pan-Africanism in their political and intellectual work. In 1938, James published two important books of Pan-African history, the *Black Jacobins* and *A History of Negro Revolt.* Both situated contemporary anti-imperialist struggles in Africa within a larger tradition of resistance stretching back to slave uprisings in the New World. As James explains in a revealing footnote that he later added to the *Black Jacobins,* "such observations, written in 1938, were intended to use the San Domingo revolution as a forecast of the future of colonial Africa."

James formed the International African Friends of Abyssinia in 1935 along with Padmore, Amy Ashwood Garvey, the Trinidadian musician and journalist Sam Manning, Ras Makonnen (1892–1975) from British Guiana, the Sierra Leonean trade unionist I. T. A. Wallace-Johnson (1895–1965), and the future president of postcolonial Kenya, Jomo Kenyatta (1889–1978). The group soon became the International African Service Bureau and published a series of short-lived but important journals: *Africa and the World* (July–September 1937), *African Sentinel* (October 1937–April 1938), and *International African Opinion* (July 1938–March 1939).

Sojourners from Africa and the Caribbean created a number of other organizations in interwar Britain, most notably the West African Student Union (WASU) and the League of Coloured Peoples (LCP). Harold Moody (1882–1947), a West Indian doctor who was outspokenly anticommunist, founded the latter as an interracial association with the intention of fostering greater understanding and cooperation across racial boundaries. A small group of law students from West Africa, led by Ladipo Solanke (1884–1958), established the WASU to challenge racial discrimination and racist representations in Britain. However, they were also encouraged by the example of the National Congress of British West Africa under the leadership of J. E. Casely Hayford (1866–1930), which envisioned the creation of an independent "United States of West Africa." The LCP and the WASU also published two significant mainstays of the black British press during the period, *The Keys* and *Wãsù* (Preach), respectively. Though initially neither was radical politically, by World War II both organizations had begun to call for an end to British colonial rule in Africa and the Caribbean, and the WASU's local hostel in particular had become an important clearinghouse for Pan-Africanist ideas. In fact, several members of WASU went on to become prominent politicians in postcolonial Africa.

Pan-Africanism in France.   Though they have received far less attention in the extant literature, students, writers, and activists from the Francophone Antilles and French West Africa also developed a distinct form of Pan-Africanism, or *internationalisme noir* (black internationalism), in Paris between the wars. After serving in World War I, the ambitious lawyer and philosopher Prince Kojo Tovalou-Houenou (1887–1925) from Dahomey founded the *Ligue Universelle pour la Défense de la Race Noire* (International League for the Defense of the Black Race), which published the first black newspaper in France, *Les Continents,* during the second half of 1924. The Martinican novelist René Maran (1887–1960) also played a major role in the paper as both an editor and writer.

However, the most well-known expression of black internationalism in interwar France was the literary and philosophical movement known as Negritude. The Martinican poet Aimé Césaire coined the term during 1936–1937. In addition to Césaire, the work of Léon-Gontran Damas (1912–1978) and Léopold Sedar Senghor (1906–2001) are usually credited with establishing and defining the movement. Yet, Negritude emerged within a broader spectrum of Pan-Africanist activities, from the Senegalese communist Lamine Senghor's (1889–1927) Comité de Défense de la Race Nègre (Committee for the Defense of the Black Race), which was founded in 1926 and published the short-lived journal *La voix des nègres.*

Women's contributions to Pan-Africanism.   The essential contributions of women to the development of both Anglophone and Francophone forms of black internationalism were overshadowed by their male contemporaries and have fared little better in scholarship on Pan-Africanism. Recently, however, the feminist-inflected Pan-Africanism of Jamaican women—Amy Ashwood Garvey, Una Marson, and Claudia Jones (1915–1964)—and West African women such as Constance Cummings-John (1918–2000) and Stella Thomas

has received more attention. Likewise, the crucial role of the Martinican Nardal sisters in initiating and articulating *internationalisme noir* in Paris—as illustrated, for example, by *La revue du monde noir*—is only beginning to be acknowledged. Moreover, as Brent Hayes Edwards points out, historians have failed to recognize the ways in which various formulations of Pan-Africanism and, more specifically, the Negritude movement were implicitly gendered.

Pan-Africanism after World War II and Postcolonialism

Coming as it did immediately after the upheavals of World War II, the 1945 Pan-African Congress in Manchester marked a watershed in black internationalist activities around the Atlantic. Though ostensibly under DuBois's guidance, it was organized primarily by socialist Pan-Africanists in Britain, especially George Padmore, and was the first Congress to include a significant number of Africans like Jomo Kenyatta and Kwame Nkrumah (1909–1972), who served as assistant secretary and joint secretary, respectively.

Following the Manchester Congress, the site of Pan-Africanist activities shifted from the United States and Europe to the colonies in the Caribbean and, particularly, Africa. In fact, many of the key figures in the movement—DuBois, Padmore, and Alphaeus Hunton—relocated to Africa during this period. In 1956, Padmore's classic *Pan-Africanism or Communism?* appeared, and in 1958 Nkrumah hosted the first All-Africa People's Conference at Accra in the wake of independence from British colonial rule in 1957 and the creation of an independent Ghana.

In the postcolonial era, the nature of Pan-Africanism and the problems facing Pan-Africanist projects changed dramatically. For the first time, Pan-Africanism became a broad-based mass movement in Africa and enjoyed its greatest successes as an international liberation movement in the first two decades after the war. Through his rhetoric and, most importantly, his example as president of independent Ghana, Nkrumah dominated this period in the history of Pan-Africanism. The context of the Cold War profoundly shaped the struggle for independence in Africa, as it did global politics in general, but in spite of his commitment to Marxism, Nkrumah avoided taking sides in the East-West Cold War and, instead, emphasized African unity. As some historians have noted, the All-Africa People's Conference at Accra in 1957, attended by some 250 delegates, established the basic tenets of Pan-Africanism for decades to come: the attainment of political independence, assistance to national liberation movements, diplomatic unity between independent African states at the United Nations, and nonalignment. As Nkrumah asserts in *I Speak of Freedom,* "a Union of African states will project more effectively the African personality."

In 1963, due primarily to the efforts of Nkrumah, President Sékou Touré (1922–1984) of Guinea, President Modibo Keita (1915–1977) of the Republic of Mali, and Haile Selassie, the emperor of Ethiopia, the Organization of African Unity (OAU) was founded in the midst of decolonization and the euphoria of independence in West Africa. However, economic neocolonialism and the limits of political independence quickly extinguished the optimism of the immediate postcolonial period, leading Pan-Africanist scholars like the Trinidadian historian Walter Rodney (1942–1980) to reevaluate the long-term repercussions of the Atlantic slave trade and European imperialism for Africa. The 1960s also witnessed a number of intra-African disputes between newly independent states, many of which were precipitated by border issues inherited from colonialism.

Pan-Arabism and Pan-Africanism. Another significant feature of the postwar period was the convergence of Pan-Africanism and Pan-Arabism, which had hitherto remained distinct movements in North Africa. Traditionally, Pan-Arabism focused on North Africa's historical links to the east, to the Arabian Peninsula and the Fertile Crescent, while sub-Saharan Pan-Africanism looks across the Atlantic to African descendants in the Americas. Moreover, religion (Islam) enjoys pride of place in Pan-Arabism as the basis of the perceived unity of the Arab world, but loosely defined cultural similarities and "racial" solidarity or, in Nkrumah's words, a distinctive "African personality" underlie Pan-Africanism.

The flowering of anti-imperialist, nationalist movements in North African after World War II, and especially the Egyptian revolution of 1952, however, signaled the emergence of a fusion of the two movements. Initially, this resulted principally from the political vision of Gamal Abdel Nasser (1918–1970), who succeeded Muhammad Naguib (1901–1984) as Egypt's leader. He maintained that his country had historically occupied the center of three concentric circles—the Arab world, the Muslim world, and Africa—and argued on this basis that Egypt should not remain indifferent to liberation struggles in sub-Saharan Africa. Despite his exaggeration of the importance of Egypt to Africa's future, the appearance in 1959 of his book, *The Philosophy of Revolution,* marked an important moment in the intersection of the Pan-Arab and Pan-African movements.

The triumphant resolution of the Suez Crisis in 1956 also enhanced Nasser's international standing, making him a source of inspiration and a symbol of the larger struggle to free Africa and the Arab world from European hegemony. The pioneering works of the Senegalese historian and politician Cheikh Anta Diop (1923–1986), such as *The Cultural Unity of Black Africa* (1963) and *The African Origin of Civilization: Myth or Reality* (1974), which resituated Egyptian history within its larger African context, represent another important intellectual manifestation of this moment in the history of Pan-Africanism.

The final, bloody years of the Algerian war of independence (1954–1962) also strengthened ties between Pan-Arabism and Pan-Africanism. The anticolonial war in Algeria had originally split intellectuals and politicians in Francophone Africa, due largely to the special status accorded the territory as a legal part of France. This began to change, however, after Ghana's independence in 1957 when Nkrumah, an outspoken proponent of the Algerian cause, became the new state's first president. In addition to Nkrumah's Ghana, Guinea and Mali joined the predominately Arab, pro-Algerian Casablanca Group, and Nkrumah became the first sub-Saharan African leader to support Arab nations in denouncing Israel as a "tool of

neocolonialism" in Palestine when he endorsed the Casablanca declaration.

After Algeria gained its independence in 1962, the Organization of African Unity (OAU) emerged as the primary agent of Arab-African cooperation after 1963. Many then interpreted the June War of 1967 between Arabs and Israel as an attack on a member of the OAU and an occupation of African territory by Israeli forces, which only served to strengthen the importance of anti-Israeli sentiment as a basis for Arab-African solidarity. By the time of the October War of 1973 between Arab nations and Israel, politics in the Middle East and Africa were more intertwined than ever due to the nearly unanimous severing of African states' diplomatic ties to Israel.

Pan-Africanism in the Late Twentieth Century
The mid-1970s saw the elaboration of a new philosophy and a new outline for long-term economic, technical, and financial cooperation between Africa and the Arab world. In some respects, oil and, particularly, the creation of the Organization of Petroleum Exporting Countries (OPEC) were important in this regard and transformed Nigeria into a crucial state in Arab-African relations. Oil profits and the institutional framework of OPEC enabled significant capital transfers from Arab to African states between 1973 and 1980. Yet, those funds fell well short of Africa's real needs for development capital, and these factors often proved to divide rather than promote unity. Ultimately, the dramatic downturn in oil prices beginning in the early 1980s not only hurt oil-producing countries but drastically reduced Arab aid to Africa.

At the end of the twentieth century, debates surrounding "globalization" and renewed interest in transnational communities and cultural networks sparked a number of attempts to "reconsider" the history of Pan-Africanism, particularly among scholars associated with the nascent fields of African diaspora studies and Atlantic history. The delegates at the Sixth and Seventh Pan-African Congresses—held in Dar es Salaam, Tanzania, and Kampala, Uganda, in 1974 and 1994, respectively—also revisited this history. They did so, however, in an attempt to emphasize the need for unity in confronting contemporary economic exploitation in Latin America and Africa as well as the revolutionary potential of Pan-Africanism for the future. Likewise, following the end of both the Cold War and apartheid in South Africa, the new African Union, founded at Sirte, Libya, in March 2001 to replace the OAU, was called on to address problems as diverse as the marginalization of Africa in international affairs, the global economy, and the AIDS pandemic on the continent.

The Future of Pan-Africanism
The career and rise to international prominence of Thabo Mbeki (b. 1942) as South Africa's second freely elected president exemplify the mixture of promise and immense difficulties facing Pan-Africanist projects and Africa in general in the twenty-first century. Like Nelson Mandela (b. 1918), Mbeki devoted his life to the fight against apartheid in South Africa, but, whereas Mandela was imprisoned for much of his adult life, Mbeki spent years in forced exile in Britain after 1962, earning a Master's degree in economics from Sussex

University in 1968 and working with Oliver Tambo (1967–1991), the effective leader of the African National Congress (ANC) in Mandela's absence.

In 1969, like most ANC leaders, many of whom were also long-time members of the South African Communist Party (SACP), Mbeki went to the Lenin International School in Moscow for a year to receive military training. After serving as political secretary for Tambo, the ANC president in the late 1970s, he became the ANC's chief diplomatic liaison, which increased the antiapartheid movement's profile abroad as well as his own, and rose to the SACP's central committee in the late 1980s. However, following F. W. de Klerk's (b. 1936) lifting of the ban on dissident organizations like the ANC, SACP, and the Pan-Africanist Congress on February 2, 1990, Mbeki gradually distanced himself from the SACP, allowing his membership to lapse at the same time as he spearheaded attempts to transform the ANC from a prohibited liberation movement into a legal political party. Then, having served as Mandela's deputy president from 1994 to 1999, Mbeki was inaugurated as his successor in June 1999.

Mbeki's presidency became mired in a series of controversies, most famously concerning his flirtation with "dissident" views on the nature and treatment of HIV/AIDS, but his espousal of an "African Renaissance" made possible discussions over the relevance and potential of Pan-Africanism in the twenty-first century and, more specifically, the role of a free South Africa on the African continent. Mbeki's notion of an "African Renaissance," though deliberately vague, has a number of ideological roots. For one, it is situated within the long tradition of South African leaders who, regardless of their ideological or physical hue, have asserted the country as the driving force behind development on the continent in general. This is a position that, it is said, South Africa must reclaim and would otherwise already occupy had it not been for the artificial privileges accorded by race under apartheid.

The international stature of Nelson Mandela reaffirmed this assumption of the naturalness of South African leadership in both internal diplomatic relations in Africa and projecting Africa's interests into the global market and international political organizations like the United Nations. Yet, as Peter Vale and Sipho Maseko observe, it was largely "the appeal of Mbeki's lyrical imagery that turned the obvious . . . into a tryst with destiny." It is clear that Mbeki's thought rests on a social-contractual reading of the African Renaissance. It represents essentially a double-edged agreement that not only commits the South African state to a democratic concord with the people of South Africa but also to the cause of peace and democracy across the continent.

Unfortunately, the emancipatory potential of Mbeki's message remained unrealized and, by and large, more promise than policy, limited changes like South Africa's assumption of a peacekeeping role in Africa notwithstanding. Moreover, some have criticized the limitations of Mbeki's approach: buoyed by the same modernization theory that inspired economic ambitions under apartheid, though directing attention backward to Africa's past, it fetishizes new technologies, endowing the latter with the power to trigger profound social changes almost single-handedly. Nevertheless, the ambiguity and potential weaknesses of Mbeki's rhetoric have created a political space in which a multiplicity of competing interpretations of Africa's future can be debated.

Vale and Maseko identified two distinct approaches to the idea of an "African Renaissance," one "globalist," the other "Africanist." Based firmly in the modernist tradition, the former seems to assume that what is good for South Africa is also good for the rest of Africa, views the continent as principally an expanding market, and sees free markets, privatization, and cuts in public expenditure as prerequisites to curtailing the power of authoritarian governments. The latter, however, envisions an African Renaissance to promote a series of complex social constructions that turn on issues of identity and call for a reinterpretation of African history and culture outside of the analytical frameworks and narratives of European imperialism. Thus, representatives of the Africanist approach eschew the modernizing tendency toward Africa's encounter with Europe, or "chasing of scientific glory and money," and maintain that the globalist perspective will merely result in an externally driven consumerist movement in Africa. According to this view, Africans will continue to be valued solely for their capacity to absorb foreign goods if development on the continent continues to follow the globalist path. Despite advancing a powerful critique of globalist/modernist assumptions and encouraging alternative visions of Africa's future, Africanist arguments rarely appear in mainstream political discussions of interstate relations in Africa. This is due in large measure to prevailing socioeconomic conditions on the continent in which states, suffocating under the burden of international debt, increasingly fail to provide their constituencies with basic amenities like water, electricity, and adequate housing.

One final development in black internationalism—the emergence of the concept of the "Black Atlantic"—figures in the future of Pan-Africanism. The idea was originally introduced by black British scholars, most famously Paul Gilroy, who emerged from the Cultural Studies group under the leadership of Stuart Hall at Birmingham University and whose work focuses heavily on African American and black British literature and popular culture. The notion of the Black Atlantic injected new life into attempts to examine the historical formations outside of the analytic framework of the nation-state by highlighting the singular importance of the legacy of the Middle Passage and African slavery around the Atlantic. In *Black Atlantic* (1993), Gilroy offered a compelling critique of the increasingly unproductive impasse between "essentialist" and "anti-essentialist" positions on racial and ethnic difference and what became known in the late twentieth century as "identity politics." Many of the insights—as well as the potential pitfalls—of this approach have been picked up by academics in the Americas, and especially the United States. For example, Brent Hayes Edwards expands on this scholarship while also exposing the tendency of much work on the African diaspora to overemphasize similarities and obscure differences rather than recognizing the management of difference (cultural, economic, linguistic, etc.) as an inescapable and, indeed, constitutive aspect of the elaboration of any particular vision of diaspora.

See also **Africa, Idea of; Black Atlantic; Black Consciousness; Diasporas: African Diaspora; Nationalism: Africa; Nationalism: Cultural Nationalism; Negritude.**

BIBLIOGRAPHY

PRIMARY SOURCES

Bowen, J. W. E., ed. *Africa and the American Negro: Addresses and Proceedings of the Congress on Africa 1895.* Atlanta, Ga.: Gammon Theological Seminary, 1896.

Campbell, Horace. *Pan-Africanism: The Struggle against Imperialism and Neocolonialism, Documents of the Sixth Pan-African Congress.* Toronto: Afro Carib Publications, 1975.

Cunard, Nancy, ed. *Negro: An Anthology.* 1934. Reprint, New York: F. Ungar, 1970.

DuBois, W. E .B. *W. E. B. DuBois: A Reader.* Edited by David Leavering Lewis. New York: Owl Books, 1995.

James, C. L. R. *The Black Jacobins: Toussaint L'Ouverture and the San Domingo Revolution.* 1938. Reprint, New York: Vintage, 1963.

———. *A History of Pan-African Revolt.* Introduction by Robin D. G. Kelley. Chicago: C. H. Kerr, 1995. Originally published in 1938 as *A History of Negro Revolt.*

Makonnen, Ras T. *Pan-Africanism from Within.* Recorded and edited by Kenneth King. London: Oxford University Press, 1973.

Nasser, Gamal Abdel. *The Philosophy of the Revolution.* Buffalo, N.Y.: Smith, Keynes, and Marshall, 1959.

Nkrumah, Kwame. *I Speak of Freedom: A Statement of African Ideology.* London: Heinemann, 1961.

Padmore, George, ed. *History of the Pan-African Congress.* London: Hammersmith, 1947.

———. *Pan-Africanism or Communism? The Coming Struggle for Africa.* London: D. Dobson, 1956.

Report of the Pan-African Conference held at the 23rd, 24th and 25th July, 1900 at Westminster S.W., London. London: n.p., 1900.

Rodney, Walter. *How Europe Underdeveloped Africa.* London: Bogle L'Ouverture, 1972.

SECONDARY SOURCES

Adi, Hakim. "Bandele Omoniyi—A Neglected Nigerian Nationalist." *African Affairs* 90 (1991): 581–605.

Adi, Hakim, and Marika Sherwood. *Pan-African History: Political Figures from Africa and the Diaspora since 1787.* London: Routledge, 2003.

Appiah, Kwame Anthony. *In My Father's House: Africa in the Philosophy of Culture.* New York: Oxford University Press, 1992.

Cooper, Frederick. *Africa since 1940: The Past of the Present.* New York: Cambridge University Press, 2002.

Decraene, Philippe. *Le Panafricanisme.* Paris: Presse universitaire de France, 1959.

Edwards, Brent Hayes. *The Practice of Diaspora: Literature, Translation, and the Rise of Black Internationalism.* Cambridge, Mass.: Harvard University Press, 2003.

Egonu, Iheanachor. "*Les Continents* and the Francophone Pan-Negro Movement." *Phylon* 42 (September 1981): 245–254.

Esedebe, P. Olisanwuche. *Pan-Africanism: The Idea and Movement, 1776–1963.* Washington, D.C.: Howard University Press, 1994.

Geiss, Imanuel. *The Pan-African Movement: A History of Pan-Africanism in America, Europe, and Africa.* Translated by Ann Keep. New York: Africana, 1974.

Gilroy, Paul. *Between Camps: Nations, Cultures, and the Allure of Race.* London: Penguin, 2000.

———. *The Black Atlantic: Modernity and Double Consciousness.* Cambridge, Mass.: Harvard University Press, 1993.

Hooker, James. *Black Revolutionary: George Padmore's Path from Communism to Pan-Africanism.* New York: Praeger, 1967.

Jacobs, Sean, and Richard Callard, eds. *Thabo Mbeki's World: The Politics and Ideology of the South African President.* London: Zed, and Pietermaritzburg, South Africa: University of Natal Press, 2002.

James, Winston. *Holding Aloft the Banner of Ethiopia: Caribbean Radicalism in Early Twentieth-Century America.* London: Verso, 1998.

Jarrett-Macauley, Delia. *The Life of Una Marson, 1905–65.* Manchester, U.K.: Manchester University Press, 1998.

Kodjo, Edem, and David Chanaiwa. "Pan-Africanism and Liberation." In *History of Africa.* Vol. 8: *Africa since 1935,* edited by Ali A. Mazrui. Oxford: Heinemann, Berkeley: University of California Press, and Paris: UNESCO, 1993.

Langley, J. Ayodele. *Pan-Africanism and Nationalism in West Africa, 1900–1945: A Study in Ideology and Social Classes.* Oxford: Clarendon, 1973.

Lemelle, Sidney J., and Robin D. G. Kelley, eds. *Imagining Home: Class, Culture, and Nationalism in the African Diaspora.* London: Verso, 1994.

Sharpley-Whiting, T. Denean. *Negritude Women.* Minneapolis: University of Minnesota Press, 2002.

Shepperson, George. "Pan-Africanism and 'Pan-Africanism': Some Historical Notes." *Phylon* 23 (1962): 346–358.

Sherwood, Marika. *Kwame Nkrumah: The Years Abroad, 1935–1947.* Legon, Ghana: Freedom Publications, 1996.

Vale, Peter, and Sipho Maseko. "South Africa and the African Renaissance." *International Affairs* (April 1998): 271–288.

Zachernuk, Philip. *Colonial Subjects: An African Intelligentsia and Atlantic Ideas.* Charlottesville: University of Virginia Press, 2000.

Marc Matera

PAN-ARABISM.

Pan-Arabism is the concept that all Arabs form one nation and should be politically united in one Arab state. The intellectual foundations of pan-Arabism were laid down in the early decades of the twentieth century, in the context first of Arab alienation from Ottoman rule and later in response to the imperialist partition of the Arab provinces of the Ottoman Empire after World War I. The doctrine became politically significant in the post–World War II era, when it produced the drive for integral Arab unity that culminated in the union of Egypt and Syria in the United Arab Republic (1958–1961). Since the 1960s pan-Arabism has receded as a meaningful political aspiration, giving way to the acceptance of the reality of the existing Arab state structure overlaid by a continuing sense of Arab cultural unity and political solidarity.

Both as theory and practice, pan-Arabism was a child of its times. Its roots lay in the linguistic unity of elite culture across the Arabic-speaking world, where classical Arabic provided a common means of communication transcending geographical barriers, and in Arab awareness of their historical importance as the people responsible for the spread of Islam. This latent Arab consciousness was politicized in the early twentieth century, when educated Arabs in the Fertile Crescent provinces of the Ottoman Empire began to chafe at growing Ottoman centralization as well as at their partial exclusion from participation in Ottoman rule due to the growth of Turkish nationalism. With parallel aspirations for autonomy developing in the several Arabic-speaking provinces of the empire by the pre–World War I years, these first nationalist stirrings in the Fertile Crescent had an implicitly pan-Arab character. The proximate referent for an explicit pan-Arabist ideology was the Arab-run state that emerged in greater Syria by the close of World War I as a result of the wartime Arab Revolt. Although crushed by the French in 1920, Emir/King Faisal's short-lived Arab Kingdom was thereafter a constant reminder of the united Arab polity that might have been were it not for the machinations of imperialism.

An explicit ideology positing the existence of one Arab nation and calling for the unity of all Arabs emerged in the interwar years. Articulated particularly by ideologues from the new mini-states of Iraq, Syria, and Palestine, it was in large part a reaction to the externally imposed division of the Arab East. Its key spokesman was the Iraqi educator Sati' al-Husri (1880–1968), whose numerous essays hammered home the message that language and history were the main determinants of nationhood and consequently that the Arabs, united as they were by one language and a shared history, deserved a parallel political unity. Husri's message was reinforced and deepened by Arab pedagogues of the interwar era, whose histories of the Arab nation expounded on the concepts of linguistic unity and a glorious Arab history reaching into antiquity. By the 1940s the doctrine of the existential reality of the Arab nation had been internalized by much of the younger generation, generating new political movements dedicated to working for Arab political unification. The most important of these was the Ba'th or Renaissance Party formed in Syria in the 1940s, an organization that rapidly found adherents in other eastern Arab lands. Its slogan—"one Arab nation with an eternal mission"—encapsulated the pan-Arabist vision; its 1947 program—that "[t]his nation has the natural right to live in a single state and to be free to direct its own destiny"—set the pan-Arabist agenda.

Pan-Arabism became a major political force in the decades after World War II. The circumstances of the postwar era—the entry into political life of a younger generation imbued with pan-Arabist ideas; individual Arab countries obtaining a greater measure of independence from foreign domination, and with it a greater ability to pursue pan-Arabist goals; the existence of the common problems of Western imperialism and the new state of Israel, both of which were perceived as necessitating Arab cooperation to be successfully addressed—provided a receptive medium for the flourishing of political pan-Arabism. The new League of Arab States (formed 1945), although strictly a confederative arrangement in which the separate Arab states retained freedom of action, nonetheless indicated the new postwar mood envisaging greater inter-Arab cooperation in the future. The Ba'th and other pan-Arabist political parties grew in size and influence in states such as Syria, Iraq, and Jordan from the 1940s onward, occasionally succeeding in stimulating a measure of inter-Arab political cooperation and at least lip-service to the goal of Arab unity

from their governments. Most meaningful politically was the emergence of a new champion for pan-Arabism in the 1950s, in the person of Jamal 'Abd al-Nasir (Nasser) of Egypt. Although his own nationalist outlook was at base primarily Egyptian nationalist, Nasser nonetheless perceived the desirability of greater inter-Arab cooperation in order to attain the goal of complete independence for the Arab world. Nasser's successes in opposing Western imperialism in the mid-1950s made Nasser and Egypt the natural focus of pan-Arabist hopes.

The high point of pan-Arabism as a political movement came in 1958, when pan-Arabist activists in Syria approached Nasser to request the integral unity of Egypt and Syria. Not without reservations, but also snared by his own previous advocacy of Arab nationalism as a mobilizing slogan, Nasser assented. The result was the United Arab Republic (UAR), a new state uniting Egypt and Syria under Nasser's leadership. The creation of the UAR set off considerable agitation for unity with the UAR by pan-Arabist enthusiasts in other eastern Arab states such as Lebanon, Jordan, and Iraq, agitation resisted only with difficulty by more localist leaders and forces concerned about their own prospects in any unified Arab state.

In the end Nasser's reservations about the UAR were borne out. Frustrated by their marginalization within the counsels of the regime, and opposed to the socialist measures being introduced by the early 1960s, in September 1961 elements of the Syrian military revolted, expelled their Egyptian overlords, and effectively terminated the reality of the UAR (although Egypt retained the name until 1971). The breakup of the UAR was a crucial setback for the pan-Arabist goal of integral Arab unity. To be sure, the dream did not die; when Ba'thists seized power in Syria and (more briefly) in Iraq in 1963, both governments immediately entered into "unity talks" with Nasser. These collapsed (as did the subsequent but less substantial initiatives aimed at negotiating Arab federation initiated by Mu'ammar Gadhafi of Libya in the early 1970s) on the rock of political power-sharing. A further and greater setback for pan-Arabism came in June 1967 with the stunning military defeat of Egypt, Jordan, and Syria by Israel, an Arab catastrophe in which the leading exponents of pan-Arabism, Nasser and the Syrian Ba'th, were indelibly discredited as potential leaders of the drive for Arab political unity.

As a political movement, pan-Arabism has receded since the 1960s. Just as the context of the post–World War II decades provided the necessary medium for its earlier flourishing, so changed conditions since the 1960s have contributed to pan-Arabism's fading. The gradual consolidation of the power and legitimacy of what were initially artificial Arab states; the end of overt imperialist domination, thereby undercutting much of the reason for inter-Arab solidarity; the growing acceptance of the reality of Israel; the increased clout of the Arab oil monarchies, regimes apprehensive about what Arab unity might mean for them; not least the growth of the rival transnational ideology of Islamism, many of whose spokesmen view Arab nationalism as an alien, Western-inspired concept designed to subvert Muslim unity: all these developments of the 1970s, 1980s, and 1990s have worked against significant movement toward Arab political unity.

Politically, pan-Arabism has stalled since the 1960s. Other than the union of Yemen and North Yemen in 1990, a local development with no broader nationalist implications, there have been no further mergers of separate Arab states since the formation of the UAR in 1958 (the forced "merger" of Kuwait with Iraq in 1990 was quickly reversed by international opposition, including that of most other Arab states). The post-1970 leaders of those states that had led the pan-Arabist movement in the 1950s and 1960s—Anwar al-Sadat and Husni Mubarak of Egypt; Hafiz al-Asad of Syria; intermittently Saddam Husayn of Iraq—all concentrated on promoting the interests of their respective states, rather than on pursuing integral Arab unity, during their long tenures in power. There have been various regional organizations of Arab states created since the 1970s, the Gulf Cooperation Council formed in 1981 by the six Arab monarchies bordering the Persian Gulf being the most durable and meaningful; but these have been confederative arrangements that guarantee the territorial integrity of their members.

If political pan-Arabism is in eclipse, what remains? The League of Arab States continues to exist, and through its various subsidiary organizations has fostered an impressive level of interstate Arab cooperation in the economic, social, and cultural fields. Inter-Arab migration for occupational or educational reasons boomed in the 1970s and 1980s, driven particularly by the demand for Arab labor in the Arab oil states. Literally millions of Arabs lived, worked, or studied in Arab countries other than their homelands in the 1970s and 1980s; this inter-Arab migration decreased from the mid-1980s onward. Perhaps most important in perpetuating and deepening a shared Arab consciousness in recent decades has been the mass media. First radio, then television, more recently the Internet and the emergence of Arab media outlets capable of reaching Arabs everywhere have spread a common Arab culture and kept "Arab" issues, Palestine being the most vital, at the forefront of Arab awareness. Political pan-Arabism may be stalled; but an abiding sense of the Arabs as one people with a common culture, similar problems, and shared aspirations has increased and penetrated more deeply into the fabric of Arab society.

The temporal trajectory of political pan-Arabism was thus significantly different from that of the cultural Arabism on which it was in part based. Whereas the former emerged, flourished, and then declined over the course of the twentieth century, the latter has steadily increased and disseminated more widely. Arabism is by no means an exclusive identity; it exists in tandem with affinal ties, a longstanding self-definition as part of the Muslim community (for most Arabs), and a more recent loyalty to the state in which Arabs live. But it remains part of the blend of referents that define collective identity, shape popular sentiment, and inspire political action.

See also **Anticolonialism: Middle East; Nationalism: Middle East; Pan-Islamism; Pan-Turkism.**

BIBLIOGRAPHY

Cleveland, William L. *The Making of an Arab Nationalist: Ottomanism and Arabism in the Life and Thought of Sati 'al-Husri.* Princeton, N.J.: Princeton University Press, 1971. A careful biography of the seminal pan-Arabist ideologue.

Dawisha, Adeed. *Arab Nationalism in the Twentieth Century: From Triumph to Despair.* Princeton, N.J.: Princeton University Press, 2003. A recent comprehensive survey.

Dawn, C. Ernest. "The Formation of Pan-Arab Ideology in the Interwar Years." *International Journal of Middle East Studies* 20 (1988): 67–91. Focuses on pan-Arabist histories.

Devlin, John. *The Ba'th Party: A History from Its Origins to 1966.* Stanford, Calif.: Hoover Institution Press, 1976. An account of the main pan-Arabist political party.

Haim, Sylvia G., ed. *Arab Nationalism: An Anthology.* Berkeley: University of California Press, 1962. A useful anthology with an extended introductory essay.

Hourani, Albert. *Arabic Thought in the Liberal Age, 1798–1939.* London: Oxford University Press, 1961. A magisterial survey of modern Arab thought including nationalism.

Jankowski, James. *Nasser's Egypt, Arab Nationalism, and the United Arab Republic.* Boulder, Colo.: Lynne Rienner Publishers, 2002. A study of Nasser's and Egypt's pan-Arabist involvement.

Jankowski, James, and Israel Gershoni, eds. *Rethinking Nationalism in the Arab Middle East.* New York: Columbia University Press, 1997. A collection of essays suggesting new perspectives on Arab nationalism.

Nuseibeh, Hazem Zaki. *The Ideas of Arab Nationalism.* Ithaca, N.Y.: Cornell University Press, 1956. An articulation of the premises of Arab nationalism written at the height of the movement.

James Jankowski

PAN-ASIANISM.

Pan-Asianism as a general term refers to a wide range of ideas and movements that called for the solidarity of Asian peoples to counter Western influences in the late nineteenth and early twentieth centuries. In Japan, where Pan-Asianism had a decisive influence on the course of its modern history and served as an ideological justification for its military expansionism through 1945, it is referred to as "Asianism" or "Greater Asianism."

Origins and Development in Japan

In the late nineteenth century, when the leaders of the Meiji government pursued Western-style modernization, Pan-Asianists emphasized Japan's affinity with Asia. They felt that Japan's progress could not be secured without the liberation of Asian neighbors from poverty and backwardness and that the Japanese had a mission to lead Asians out of stagnation. Many of the early Pan-Asianists began their political activities in the Freedom and People's Rights movement, demanding democratic participation in the national government. Miyazaki Tōten (pen name of Miyazaki Torazō; 1871–1922) came from a family of rural samurai well known in their area for their devotion to the People's Rights movement. He was an outstanding example of romantic Pan-Asianism who devoted some thirty years of his life to the cause of Sun Yat-sen's republican revolution in China.

Anxiety over national security was at the root of Pan-Asianism. Tarui Tōkichi (1850–1922), who explored the coast of Korea in the early 1880s, wrote *Daitō gappōron* (Federated states of great East), a proposal for a federation of Japan and Korea. His idea, that the only hope for survival for the small Asian nations was in joining forces, reflected a perception among the contemporary Japanese that the "white race" was superior in physical, intellectual, and financial power to the "yellow race."

Defense of indigenous tradition was another issue at this time of rapid modernization. Miyake Setsurei (Yūjirō; 1860–1945) and other cultural nationalists formed in 1888 a political association, Seikyōsha, for the purpose of raising national pride in *kokusui* (cultural essence of the nation), and published a series of popular periodicals, *Nihonjin* (the Japanese), *Ajia* (Asia), and *Nihon oyobi Nihonjin* (Japan and the Japanese). Naitō Konan (Torajirō; 1866–1934), a prominent Sinologist, associated with this group in his early career as a journalist. He held China's culture in high esteem but maintained that China had lost its vigor and needed Japan's guidance for reform. Okakura Tenshin (Kakuzō; 1862–1913), a gifted art historian who studied with Ernest Fenollosa at Tokyo University, called for the resurgence of the East. He underscored the creative vitality of Chinese and Indian civilizations that had adapted to changing historical circumstances over millennia and attained high levels of maturity. "Asia is one," stated at the opening of Okakura's *Ideals of the East,* was frequently quoted and had enormous influence.

Pan-Asianist Organizations in Japan

To promote good will among Asian neighbors, the Japanese government encouraged Pan-Asianist organizations. Kōakai (Raise Asia society) was the earliest among them, organized in 1880 by Japanese literati and members of the Chinese legation. In 1898 Prince Konoe Atsumaro (1863–1904), the chairman of the House of Peers, formed the Tōa dōbunkai (East Asia common culture society). It played a major role in enhancing Japan's cultural policies in China through 1945. Tōyama Mitsuru (1855–1944), of Fukuoka, the most influential Pan-Asianist outside the government, founded Gen'yōsha (Black ocean society), an expansionist association, in 1881 and named it after Genkainada, the sea between Fukuoka and Korea. Uchida Ryōhei (1874–1937), one of Tōyama's followers, headed Kokuryūkai (Amur River [black dragon] society), organized in 1901. They cooperated with government authorities as unofficial handlers of visitors from Asia. Numerous Pan-Asianist groups were organized under their influence. Their followers served as freelance agents for the Japanese government, military, and commercial establishments in China.

Development in Twentieth-Century Japan

After Japan joined the ranks of colonial powers following its victories over China in 1895 and Russia in 1905, the Japanese government adopted a policy of cooperation with the Western powers. At the same time it asserted Japan's special interest in China. Around World War I phrases like "Asia for Asians," "Asian Monroe Doctrine," and "White Peril" appeared in newspapers and popular periodicals. The earlier emphasis on solidarity with Asian neighbors was replaced by emphasis on Japan's leadership and supremacy in Asia. The opinions of Tokutomi Sohō (Iichirō; 1863–1957), the long-lived influential publicist, reflected the changing mood in Japan. Kita Ikki (1884–1937),

who once joined the revolutionary activities in China, urged Japan's aggressive expansion in Asia and called for a radical reform in Japan to establish a kind of state socialism under the emperor. Ōkawa Shūmei (1886–1957) believed that Japan had a mission to replace white men's imperialism with a federation of all nations and to create a new world blending the civilizations of the East and the West. Ōyawa had close ties with ultranationalist army officers, including Ishiwara Kanji (1889–1949), the mastermind of Japan's conquest of Manchuria in 1931. During the 1930s and early 1940s, when the Japanese government openly adopted military expansionism, Pan-Asianist ideas were expressed in official declarations proclaiming a "New Order in East Asia" and the "Greater East Asia Co-Prosperity Sphere."

Asians and Pan-Asianism

Japan's 1905 victory over Russia, a European power, was received as an exhilarating event throughout Asia. During the following decade, a large number of students and revolutionaries from China, Korea, Philippines, India, and other areas of Asia came to Japan hoping to find encouragement for their nationalistic causes. Sojourners in Tokyo developed a sense of community as Asians. In 1907 Zhang Binglin, Zhang Ji, Liu Shipei, and other revolutionaries from China organized a Yazhou heqin hui (Asiatic humanitarian brotherhood) with revolutionaries from India, Vietnam, Burma, Philippines, and Korea, as well as Japanese socialists, to help each other's anti-imperialist activities. Among its members and their associates were Phan Boi Chau of Vietnam and Mariano Ponce of Philippines. This organization and other similar associations did not last long because Tokyo became a less hospitable place for expatriate revolutionaries. Other Asians increasingly criticized Japanese Pan-Asianism as mere rhetoric for Japanese imperialism. In 1919 Li Dazhao wrote that weak nations in Asia must unite themselves to form a "new Greater Asianism" to defeat Japan's "Greater Asianism." Sun Yat-sen gave a lecture on Pan-Asianism in Kobe in 1924 and tried to persuade the Japanese to join a truly pan-Asian movement instead of becoming a watchdog for Western imperialists. To the 1926 Japanese call for a Pan-Asian conference in Nagasaki, Chinese and Korean newspapers responded with strong protest against Japan's "Twenty-one Demands" on China and imperialist oppression of Koreans.

In India, in the early decades of the twentieth century, Bengali intellectuals had lively debates on the civilizations of the East and the West. Rabindranath Tagore (1861–1941) eloquently advocated the revival of Asian culture and the unity of Asia, but was against political nationalism. Jawaharlal Nheru followed Tagore in spirit in promoting the ideal of united Asia giving peace to a troubled world.

See also **Colonialism: Southeast Asia; Empire and Imperialism: Asia; Pan-Africanism; Pan-Arabism; Pan-Islamism; Pan-Turkism.**

BIBLIOGRAPHY

Hay, Stephen N. *Asian Ideas of East and West: Tagore and His Critics in Japan, China, and India.* Cambridge, Mass.: Harvard University Press, 1970.

Jansen, Marius B. *The Japanese and Sun Yat-sen.* Cambridge, Mass.: Harvard University Press, 1954.

Kuzuu, Yoshihisa. *Tōa senkaku shishi kiden.* 3 vols. Tokyo: Kokuryūyai, 1933–1936.

Miyazaki, Tōten. *My Thirty-three Years' Dream: The Autobiography of Miyazaki Tōten.* Translated by Etō Shinkichi and Marius B. Jansen. Princeton, N.J.: Princeton University Press, 1982.

Okakura, Kakuzō. *The Ideals of the East, with Special Reference to the Art of Japan.* 2nd ed. New York: Dutton, 1905.

Tarui, Tōkichi. *Daitō gappōron.* In *Nihon shisōshi shiryō sōkan,* vol. 1. Tokyo: Chōryō Shorin, 1975.

Yamamuro, Shin'ichi. *Shisō kadai to shite no Ajia.* Tokyo: Iwanami Shoten, 2001.

Noriko Kamachi

PAN-ISLAMISM.

A term of European origin, *pan-Islamism* denotes the intellectual and institutional trends toward Islamic unity that emerged among Muslim peoples, starting in the mid–nineteenth century and continuing throughout the twentieth century. The need for a unified Islamic identity was a product of the challenges posed by Western intervention in and domination of Muslim societies during the colonialist period. Leaders throughout the Muslim world appealed to the Islamic tradition to solidify public opposition to foreign occupation and thereby gain political independence. Like its European namesakes pan-Hellenism and pan-Slavism, pan-Islamism used cultural ideas to achieve nationalist political ends. Unlike the ethnic identities emphasized in European nationalisms, however, pan-Islamism emphasized the religious heritage and symbols that both united all Muslims and set them apart from their Western Christian colonialist occupiers. The nationalist purposes to which pan-Islamism was primarily directed may seem at odds with the universal principles on which it rests, but this tension was largely resolved in the practical drive for political, economic, and social progress that enveloped Muslim societies. Nowhere is this resolution more clearly defined than in the life and work of Jamal al-Din al-Afghani (1839–1897), a Muslim reformer and key advocate of pan-Islamism.

Jamal al-Din al-Afghani

Born in Persia, not Afghanistan as his name suggests, al-Afghani led the life of an itinerant scholar and activist. After his initial education in Persia, he studied in India and then worked in Afghanistan, Istanbul, Egypt, and Paris. Al-Afghani's travels provided him with a unique insight into the modern condition affecting all Muslim peoples, a condition he believed was characterized by political weakness, social instability, and cultural ignorance. Contact with the West did not cause this condition, according to al-Afghani, but it did bring it into high relief; it also alerted Muslims to an essential but long-dormant element of their own tradition: rational thought. For al-Afghani, the power and success of the modern West rested on its rejection of the stultifying restrictions of Christianity and its turn toward reason; since Islam, by contrast, was rooted in rationalism, Muslims need only return to the essence of their faith to overcome the developmental asymmetry that had come to differentiate Western and Muslim societies.

Arguing for the rational nature of Islam was a common strategy among Muslim reformers, who wanted to facilitate change while maintaining cultural identity. It was a strategy that recognized the Western orientation of modern development and the threat this orientation posed to cultural authenticity in the Muslim world. Indeed al-Afghani believed that social and political change could only be brought about if Muslims had a firm sense of the civilization to which Islam had given birth. By *civilization,* al-Afghani meant the intellectual and moral achievements that contributed to the unity and greatness of a people—a notion he borrowed from the French statesman-historian François Guizot (1787–1874) and employed to foster a usable Islamic past. This past did not lead inexorably to the unification of the entire Muslim community (the *umma*) under a single Islamic state. Instead, al-Afghani viewed Islamic civilization, the foundation of pan-Islamism, as a common cultural stream that fed the national political aspirations of such distinct countries as India, Persia, and Egypt. Here the logical appeal of Islam as universal glue for all Muslim peoples was subordinated to the practical realities of a world where nation-states had become the political norm. Pan-Islamism, however, had served a very different political purpose under the Ottomans.

Late Ottoman Politics

If al-Afghani was the father of pan-Islamist thought, Ottoman sultans were the first to implement pan-Islamism as official state policy, a policy with imperialist, not nationalist, goals. As early as the 1860s, the then-sultan, Abdul Aziz (r. 1861–1876), tried to extend his political authority beyond the Ottoman Empire by casting himself as the caliph, the designated ruler of all Muslims and the defender of the faith. His successor, Abdul Hamid II (r. 1876–1909), adopted the same mantle of authority. This pan-Islamic appeal was tied to the growing Western influence in the Muslim world that the Ottomans themselves had facilitated through their efforts to reform. The need to reform had become apparent as European peoples began to win back territory in the seventeenth and eighteenth centuries that had been lost to the Ottoman expansion into Europe during the fifteenth and sixteenth centuries. The same rising tide of technological advancement that had allowed European nations to defeat the Ottomans in Europe also permitted them to project their power abroad. This new political reality was made clear to the Ottomans when, in 1798, one of their autonomous possessions, Egypt, was invaded and occupied by the French under Napoléon Bonaparte.

Conscious of their declining power, the Ottomans embarked on a series of military, educational, social, and governmental reforms throughout the first half of the nineteenth century, and they sought technical assistance and advice from the very European nations that threatened the empire's territorial sovereignty. While dramatic and far-reaching, the reforms came too late to prevent the Ottomans from becoming known as the Sick Man of Europe, an inefficient and weakened empire whose lands in the Middle East and Central Asia looked ripe for the picking. The competition to take control of Ottoman possessions was widespread in Europe in the late nineteenth century and early twentieth century, but it was played out on a grand scale—referred to as the Great Game—by two imperialist powers bent on world domination, Great Britain and Russia. For the Ottomans, pan-Islamic propaganda seemed a viable means of reasserting its sway over Muslim subjects whose loyalty was being tested by new ideas like nationalism and undermining the progress of European influence among Muslim peoples in places such as India. Ultimately unsuccessful as an imperialist ideology, pan-Islamism did serve the nationalist desires of Muslim peoples trying to break free from both Ottoman and European rule. It failed, however, to take hold in modern Turkey, the nation that arose out of the heartland of the defeated and dismembered Ottoman Empire.

The Khilafat Movement

The first popular pan-Islamist political movement, the Khilafat movement (1919–1924), emerged in India after World War I, though support for the caliphate locally among Indian Muslims had been gaining momentum throughout the second half of the nineteenth century. Chafing under British occupation and mindful of the glory days of Mogul rule, Indian Muslims directed their spiritual and later political longings toward the remaining seat of independent Muslim rule: the Ottoman caliphate. With the Ottoman Empire in ruins after World War I and the office of the caliph, the caliphate, under threat of extinction, Indian Muslims organized to preserve what many viewed as the last vestige of Islamic unity and power. In 1919 activist groups like the Association of Servants of the Ka'ba and the Council of the All-India Muslim League convened a Khilafat Conference, during which the movement took official form as the All-India Central Khilafat Committee.

The politics of the Khilafat movement were clearly anti-imperialist and pro-independence, which accounts for the popular support it received across Muslim sectarian lines in India and across the Muslim world. Activists within the movement spread their message through publications at home and abroad. Delegations were sent to England, France, and Switzerland to shape public attitudes and government policy regarding the caliphate and the future of Muslim societies. In the end, however, it was not European leaders but the new leaders of Turkey who decided the fate of the movement by adopting a secular path for the nation based on a narrowly conceived ethnic identity—a path that mirrored European strains of nationalism—and then abolishing the office of the sultan in 1922 and that of the caliph in 1924. The Khilafat movement protested Turkey's actions, but with no power to impose its will and with its reason for existence eliminated, the movement had gradually faded from public view by the late 1920s. Pan-Islamism in India, however, continued to play a part in Muslim cultural and political life, especially the communal debates that resulted in the formation of Pakistan in 1947.

A World of Nation-States

The division of the Muslim world into nation-states has given rise to new strands of pan-Islamism. First, transnational organizations like the Organization of Islamic States (OIC) have been formed to express the collective sentiments and concerns of Muslim peoples. It remains to be seen whether the OIC or similar organizations can be effective in a world of nation-states, a

question made more serious in light of the events following September 11, 2001. Like the United Nations, the OIC depends on its integrity and moral authority to effect change unless it has the backing of a strong state. Second, Islamism, or Muslim fundamentalism, has laid claim to the pan-Islamic heritage in order to remake, if not undermine, the modern system of nation-states that divides Muslim societies. While pan-Islamism advocates Muslim unity and strength, it is not conducive to the totalizing agenda espoused by Islamists who wish to (re-)Islamize every aspect of society. Lastly, pan-Islamism remains a current of feeling and thought—typically associated with calls for justice and hope—that runs throughout Muslim societies and also minority Muslim communities in the West. Like religion itself, there is a certain ambiguity and ambivalence about the purposes to which it is put and the events that evoke it. The only certainty surrounding pan-Islamism is its perennial nature.

See also **Cultural Revivals; Empire and Imperialism: Middle East; Ethnicity and Race: Islamic Views; Fundamentalism; Islam; Nationalism: Middle East; Pan-Africanism; Pan-Arabism; Pan-Asianism; Pan-Turkism; Westernization: Middle East.**

BIBLIOGRAPHY

Choudury, M. A. *Reforming the Muslim World.* London and New York: Kegan Paul, 1998.

Eickelman, Dale F., and James Piscatori. *Muslim Politics.* Princeton, N.J.: Princeton University Press, 1996.

Hourani, Albert. *Arabic Thought in the Liberal Age, 1798–1939.* Cambridge, U.K.: Cambridge University Press, 1983.

Keddie, Nikki R. *An Islamic Response to Imperialism: Political and Religious Writings of Sayyid Jamāl ad-Dīn "al-Afghāni."* Berkeley: University of California Press, 1968.

Kramer, Martin S. *Islam Assembled: The Advent of the Muslim Congresses.* New York: Columbia University Press, 1986.

Landau, Jacob M. *The Politics of Pan-Islam: Ideology and Organization.* Oxford: Clarendon, 1994.

Lewis, Bernard. *The Emergence of Modern Turkey.* 2nd ed. London: Oxford University Press, 1968.

Mandaville, Peter. *Transnational Muslim Politics: Reimagining the Umma.* London: Routledge, 2001.

Piscatori, James P. *Islam in a World of Nation-States.* Cambridge, U.K.: Cambridge University Press, 1986.

Sheikh, Naveed S. *The New Politics of Islam: Pan-Islamic Foreign Policy in a World of States.* London: RoutledgeCurzon, 2003.

Jeffrey T. Kenney

PAN-TURKISM. The term *Pan-Turkism* refers to an intellectual and political movement advocating the union of all Turkic peoples. Although some promoters of this ideology went as far as calling for a political union including all Turkic groups, many others envisioned only a cultural unity.

Intellectual Origins and the Impact of European Works

European works such as Joseph de Guignes's *Histoire générale des Huns, des Turcs, des Mogols, et des autres Tartares occidentaux,*

&c. avant et depuis Jésus-Christ jusqu'à present (Paris, 1756–1758) and Arthur Lumley David's *A Grammar of the Turkish Language with a Preliminary Discourse on the Language and Literature of the Turkish Nations* (London, 1832) paved the way for a debate on Turkish peoples living under different administrations and their common ethnic bonds. David rejected the lumping together of all Turkic tribes under the rubric of Tatars, and proposed the generic name Turk for all these peoples; this made many intellectuals in the Ottoman Empire and other Turkic states reevaluate their approach to their peoples' ethnic origins. A French translation of the work was submitted to the Ottoman Sultan Mahmud II in 1833, and was widely read by Ottoman intellectuals and linguists. A Polish convert, Mustafa Celâleddin Pasha (Constantine Borzecki), who had fled to the Ottoman Empire after the unsuccessful 1848 revolution, liberally used de Guignes's work in preparing his own study, *Les turcs anciens et modernes* (Constantinople, 1869). Mustafa Celâleddin Pasha maintained that Turks and Europeans were from the same "Touro-Aryan" race. Works of Arminus Vámbéry, who traveled widely in Central Asia and underscored the common racial "Turanian" characteristics of the Turkic peoples, and Léon Cahun's *Introduction á l'histoire de l'Asie* (Paris, 1896) presented the "Turanian" race as one that brought civilization to Europe; this strongly influenced many Turkish intellectuals. Vámbéry should be credited as the first non-Turkish savant who, in 1865, entertained the idea of a Turkic "empire extending from the shore of the Adriatic far into China." Many Ottoman intellectuals paid close attention to these new ideas. It is interesting to note that in the prefatory article of the Young Ottoman journal *Hürriyet* (established 1868), the Turks were portrayed as "a nation in whose medreses Farabis, Ibn Sinas, Ghazzalis, Zamakhsharis propagated knowledge." Another leading Young Ottoman, Ali Suavi, underscored the common ethnic origins of the Turkic groups in his journal *Mukhbir* (1878). In an essay on Khiva he criticized the Ottoman policy toward this Central Asian khanate and described its people as "Muslim Turks who belong to our religion, nation, and ethnic family." In 1876 Süleyman Pasha prepared the first volume of his "World History" to be used as a textbook at the Royal Military Academy; in it he underscored the common bond uniting the Turkic peoples by drawing heavily on de Guignes's work. Beginning in 1877 history textbooks referred to the Turkish ancestry of the Ottomans, and the Ottoman press developed a keen interest in Turks living in Central Asia and the Caucasus, publishing many articles on them.

First Pan-Turkist Ideas

Despite the emergence of a national consciousness among the Turks living in the Ottoman Empire and the Turkic peoples of the Caucasus, Central Asia, and Iran, and a strong focus on their common origins, no intellectual or politician openly promoted unification of the Turkic groups until 1904. In an essay published in 1881 Gaspıralı İsmail (Isma'il Bey Gasprinskii) debated the reasons for the decadence of the great "Turco-Tatar nation scattered in Asia and parts of Europe." He argued that "Turks, Turcomans, Mongols, Tatars, Uzbeks, and Yakuts [were] all from the same family." He advocated similar theses in his journal *Tercüman,* published in Bakhchesaray in the Crimea. The importation of this influential newspaper was occasionally banned by the Ottoman authorities. Nevertheless, it was widely read by Ottoman intellectuals and strongly influenced them.

In 1903 a Young Turk journal called *Türk* started publication in Cairo. This journal promoted a more developed Turkish nationalism and devoted its efforts toward "the moral and material progress of the Turkish world." In it Yusuf Akçura, a Young Turk intellectual and a former military officer of Tatar origin, published an essay entitled "Üç Tarz-ı Siyaset" (Three kinds of policy). He asserted that there were three alternatives before the Ottoman administration—Pan-Ottomanism, Pan-Islamism, and Pan-Turkism—and that the best choice would be "to pursue a Turkish nationalism based on race." This essay, which first appeared in 1904, might be considered the first clear-cut intellectual formulation of the Pan-Turkist idea. Following the Russian Revolution of 1905, Gaspıralı started using the motto "Unity in Language, Thought, and Work" under the masthead of his journal *Tercüman.* He presented his aim as an attempt to create a united front of Turks living under tsarist rule. He maintained that such unity would enable the Turks to defend their rights better. There is no doubt, however, that in reality he intended more than uniting Turks living in Russia. The Russian Revolution of 1905 and the increased cultural activities of the Turkic peoples under tsarist rule made the Ottoman press in the empire and in exile pay more attention to these groups and to relations between them and the Ottoman Empire. Many Turkic journals, mostly published by Azerbaijani and Tatar intellectuals, promoted closer cultural relations among Turkic peoples.

Another organization that developed an interest in such ideas was the Ottoman Committee of Union and Progress. Following its reorganization in 1905–1906, this committee established ties with Turkic intellectuals and provided finance to help some of them publish their journals. The committee supported the creation of a "Turkish Union in the regions from the Adriatic Sea to the Chinese Sea" and promised to extend a helping hand to these Turkic groups once it had toppled the regime of Sultan Abdülhamīd II. Strident letters sent from Azerbaijani and Tatar organizations to this committee reveal that such an idea was also popular among the intellectuals of these peoples.

Pan-Turkism, 1908–1922

The Young Turk Revolution of 1908 brought the Committee of Union and Progress to power in the Ottoman Empire. Many Turkic intellectuals participated in its policy-making bodies along with Turkist intellectuals. The committee supported the establishment of various organizations such as the Türk Ocağı (Turkish Hearth) (established in 1912), and it published journals such as *Türk Yurdu* (Turkish homeland) promoting cultural or political Pan-Turkism and Pan-Turanism. It should be remembered, however, that despite their Turkist and Pan-Turkist proclivities, the leadership of the Committee of Union and Progress viewed these ideologies as tools with which to save the Ottoman Empire and employed them alongside the rival ideologies of Ottomanism and Pan-Islamism. The Ottoman entry into World War I against Russia gave a considerable edge to Pan-Turkism and a free hand to the Committee of Union and Progress leaders in propagating it. The leading ideologues of Pan-Turkism and Pan-Turanism, such us Moiz Cohen (Tekin Alp), Ziya Gökalp, and Ömer Seyfeddin, further entertained the idea of a future Turanian state including all Turkic peoples. Ottoman war propaganda made much use of this idea. Despite this fact, the accomplishment of that goal had been envisioned by its major promoters as a gradual and long-drawn-out development. Even in 1918 Ziya Gökalp likened the accomplishment of this distant ideal to reaching a pure communist society. During the war, Ottoman agents worked in the Caucasus and Central Asia and were aided by the German government in their efforts to spread Pan-Turkist sentiments. In the final phases of the war, new governments promoting Pan-Turkism were set up in the Caucasus through Ottoman military incursions. Even after the war, the Young Turk leaders in exile made efforts aimed at arousing Pan-Turkish sentiment in an area stretching from the Caucasus to Central Asia and Afghanistan. During this period between 1918 and 1922, Pan-Turkish ideas were put to a test on the ground; however, the Soviet victories and the establishment of the Turkish Republic reduced Pan-Turkist activities to the publication of a few journals by various Turkic expatriate groups in France, Germany, Poland, and Romania.

Pan-Turkism from 1922 to the Present

Both the Soviets and the Turkish Republic, which was established in 1923, officially shunned Pan-Turkism and considered it a harmful form of adventurism. This view continued to be the official Soviet position on Pan-Turkism until the end of the Soviet Union. In Turkey, however, various Pan-Turkist groups were allowed to publish journals beginning in 1931. They were nevertheless closely scrutinized by the government. These groups were later backed by the Nazi government and tolerated by the Turkish administration, which wanted to avoid a confrontation with Germany; but with the waning of the German power in 1944, the leading Pan-Turkists were tried and sentenced to hard labor. The subsequent deterioration of Turco–Soviet relations, however, triggered a retrial in 1946 resulting in the dismissal of all charges against the leading Pan-Turkists. Later, Pan-Turkism was promoted by various cultural groups and political parties, the most important of which was the Nationalist Action Party under the leadership of Alparslan Türkeş.

The collapse of the Soviet Union and the emergence of new Turkic states gave fresh hope to many Pan-Turkists in Turkey, the Caucasus, and Central Asia. Developments to date, however, suggest that the most that they can hope for is a better cultural understanding between peoples living in nation-states with clearly molded identities and well-defined borders.

See also **Ethnicity and Race; Pan-Africanism; Pan-Arabism; Pan-Islamism.**

BIBLIOGRAPHY

Akçuraoğlu, Yusuf. *Türk Yılı, 1928.* Istanbul: Yeni Matbaa, 1928.

Ali Suavi. *Hive.* Paris: n.p., 1873.

Arai, Masami. *Turkish Nationalism in the Young Turk Era.* Leiden: Brill, 1992.

Cohen, M. *Türkismus und Panturkismus.* Weimar, Germany: G. Kiepenheuer, 1915.

Hanioğlu, M. Şükrü. *Preparation for a Revolution: The Young Turks, 1902–1908.* New York: Oxford University Press, 2001.

Ismail Bey. *Gaspirinski, Russkoe musul'manstvo: mysli, zametki i nabliudeniia musul'manina.* Simferopol', Russia: Tipografiia Spiro, 1881. Republished, Oxford: Oxford University Press, 1985.

Kushner, David. *The Rise of Turkish Nationalism, 1876–1908.* London: Frank Cass, 1977.

Landau, Jacob. *Pan-Turkism: From Irredentism to Cooperation.* Bloomington: Indiana University Press, 1992.

———. *Tekinalp, Turkish Patriot, 1883–1961.* Istanbul: Nederlands Historisch-Archaeologisch Instituut, 1984.

Ömer, Seyfeddin. *Yarınki Turan Devleti.* Istanbul: Kader Matbaası, 1914.

Ziya, Gök Alp. *Yeni Hayat.* Istanbul: Yeni Mecmua, 1918.

M. Şükrü Hanioğlu

PARADIGM.

Paradigm is the key term in Thomas Kuhn's (1922–1996) very influential book, *The Structure of Scientific Revolutions* (1962). As is frequently the case when new ideas are presented, Kuhn took an existing term and gave it a specialized meaning. The term *paradigm* now occurs frequently in every kind of discourse, usually to mean something like "way of thinking" or "approach to a problem." Kuhn has generally been given credit for introducing this usage, but the way that *paradigm* is popularly used misses a central aspect of his argument. Kuhn emphasizes that a paradigm cannot be reduced to a set of beliefs or to a list of rules and indeed that a paradigm cannot be put into words. Scientists have to learn by doing, both by thinking in terms of the concepts that are used in a particular science and by physically manipulating material to create phenomena.

Kuhn argues that the history of science is best understood as exhibiting stable periods, which he calls normal science, punctuated by revolutionary changes. *Paradigm* is the central concept that Kuhn uses to make his case, since a period of normal science is defined by its paradigm and a scientific revolution is, in Kuhn's terms, a change in paradigms. Typically a paradigm is first established by the publication of a groundbreaking book that sets out problems and solutions, then others adopt the aims and methods of the original, thus establishing a period of normal science. Contrary to the traditional view that science was founded in Renaissance Europe by "the scientific revolution," Kuhn sees multiple revolutions in the history of science, that is, multiple cases of the overthrow of one scientific paradigm by another.

Paradigm is defined in the *Oxford English Dictionary* as a pattern, exemplar, or example. Kuhn acknowledges this meaning by giving the conjugation of a regular Latin verb as an example of a paradigm. Furthermore, since he believes that a normal science is typically established by an important book and often by a series of experiments, it is clear that Kuhn has the idea of a paradigm as a pattern that will be followed very much in mind when he is explaining his view. A key aspect of paradigms is that they set out problems and also show how to solve them. Newton's laws of motion and the force of gravity combine to explain planetary motion, for example. There is more to a paradigm than a good model to follow, however. Kuhn also thinks that among scientists who are working under the same paradigm, the historian can find common methods, common standards, common aims, and fundamental agreement about the nature of the world and the nature of the processes in it. Periods of normal science are characterized by consensus, especially about fundamentals, and this agreement allows for specialization, or as Kuhn puts it, "professional and esoteric work" (1996, p. 23). The function of normal science is to extend the original work by applying its methods to new areas as well as to revisit old ground in order to refine the paradigm. Because normal science is based on agreement and has well-defined parameters, it can make progress and accumulate knowledge.

On Definition

Kuhn compresses his discussion of the centrality of the notion of paradigm into a single chapter entitled "The Priority of Paradigms." Paradigms have priority because there is nothing more basic by which "paradigm" could be defined. In logical terminology, the word *paradigm* functions as a primitive term. Properties of paradigms can be given and examples of paradigms can be enumerated, but the word cannot be defined, any more than *number* can be defined in arithmetic. Kuhn justifies his introduction of the term *paradigm* by arguing that, for the historian, it is a better organizational concept than any other. By looking for paradigms and changes in paradigms, the historian can classify scientists and historical periods in ways that lead to productive research and a better understanding of the history of science. Turning to philosophers to justify the undefinability of paradigms, Kuhn invokes Michael Polyani's (1891–1976) idea of tacit knowledge and Ludwig Wittgenstein's (1889–1951) idea that some human activities cannot be captured by a set of rules, arguing that while paradigms cannot be reduced to a set of methods and beliefs, they are recognizable to the historian as the organizing principle underlying a period of normal science.

The root definition of *paradigm* as both pattern and example exhibits both sides of a classical philosophical debate over the nature of definition. Plato (c. 428–348 or 347 B.C.E.) argued forcefully that providing examples is not adequate; the real definition of a term must specify what the examples have in common and thus explain why they all properly fall under the concept being defined. In the terminology of later philosophy, Plato argues that a definition must tell us the essence of a thing. For Plato, this is the *eidos*, the eternal form or idea to which all objects falling under a concept must conform. Kuhn sides with David Hume (1711–1776) and Wittgenstein in rejecting Plato's requirement that the essence be given in the proper definition of a concept. Like Hume, Kuhn argues that it is enough to say that the objects falling under a concept resemble one another in various aspects that can be specified and to take that resemblance as a starting point. Kuhn claims that paradigms do not have an essence, since there is always some disagreement and some difference in emphasis among scientists who are working under the same paradigm. In Wittgenstein's terminology, the historian can find a family resemblance among the views of these scientists rather than single common set of beliefs and methods.

Kuhn also defends his view that paradigms cannot be reduced to a set of beliefs and rules of method by pointing out that scientists learn by working through concrete examples of problems, not by learning rules. Thus learning a paradigm is more like learning a skill than like learning a body of knowledge, a point that Joseph Rouse has rightly emphasized. Kuhn is very close to using *paradigm* in its original meaning here, since the problems and solutions through which students learn are to be taken as patterns of scientific thought and work.

Criticism of Kuhn's Paradigms

Kuhn's use of the term *paradigm* was immediately criticized, especially by philosophers, for being too broad and vague. In the postscript to *Structure* (1962), Kuhn conceded that the term was perhaps too broad, saying that he would use *paradigm* to mean "exemplar," that is, the founding book or experiment of a particular science, and that the rest of the elements that make up normal science will be called the "disciplinary matrix." However, this change in terminology played no role in Kuhn's later work, so it provides little gain in understanding his viewpoint.

Kuhn was also accused of circularity, since it seems that in order to determine the nature of the paradigm behind a particular period of normal science, the historian must first determine which scientists belong to that group and then study their work to discover their aims, methods, and assumptions. However, since normal science is defined in terms of a paradigm, it seems that the historian must also recognize a paradigm first in order to know which scientists are working under it. Kuhn acknowledged that this was indeed a problem, suggesting that scientists should be categorized first on purely sociological grounds, such as who works with whom, and then the paradigm that underlies these connections be can determined.

Revolutions

Kuhn argued that his use of the term *revolution* to describe changes in science is appropriate because, like political revolutions, scientific revolutions overturn existing rules and institutions in order to establish new ones. By definition, there can be no legal way to have a political revolution, since any changes that follow the processes of the old regime would merely be reform, not revolution. For Kuhn the key point of the analogy between political and scientific revolutions is that in both cases there are no rules that could help adjudicate between the two systems. The supporters of the old and the new paradigms will each follow their own methods, emphasize their own aims, and accept their own solutions to problems, without necessarily accepting any of the methods, aims, or standards of supporters of the other paradigm. In an influential paper that helped redirect criticism of Kuhn's book, Gerald Doppelt emphasized the apparent relativism of Kuhn's view, given that there is no right or wrong answer to the question of when an old paradigm should be abandoned and a new paradigm adopted. Antoine-Laurent Lavoisier (1743–1794) and Joseph Priestley (1733–1804) independently discovered oxygen, but while Lavoisier used this discovery as a basis for a new chemistry, Priestley never accepted Lavoisier's revolution and maintained the old phlogiston paradigm instead. Kuhn argued that

Thomas S. Kuhn. The Harvard-educated Kuhn first proposed his personalized theory of paradigm in his 1962 *Structure of Scientific Revolutions.* Kuhn posited that paradigms were conceived through thought and physical experimentation, rather than by representing established sets of beliefs. PHOTOGRAPH BY STANLEY BROWN. REPRODUCED BY PERMISSION OF THE ESTATE OF THOMAS S. KUHN

both of these famous scientists were acting reasonably. Nothing can force a scientist to change paradigms, according to Kuhn, because a scientist can always find a way either to incorporate new data into the existing paradigm or to show why the new data can be dismissed as unimportant from the point of view of the existing paradigm. It is important to note, however, that Kuhn is not saying that anyone can believe anything. Paradigms must be well developed and cover a wide range of phenomena. It is not easy to develop a new science that will justify the overthrow of an established paradigm.

Rather than promoting general relativism, Kuhn saw himself as rejecting particular philosophical accounts of science. He criticizes the idea of confirming scientific theories and comparing how well they are confirmed, a view of science associated with Rudolf Carnap (1891–1970), and he criticizes the idea of testing scientific theories to show that one theory is false, a view of science associated with Karl Popper (1902–1994). Both of these views require that a body of neutral evidence be available to scientists, a position that Kuhn disputes because, he claims, all evidence is acquired on the basis of a paradigm and therefore an element of it. He also points out that Popper's view that theories should be rejected when negative evidence is found is unrealistic, since there are always anomalies—problems that the paradigm cannot solve.

Leaps of Faith

Given that no new evidence or argument could overthrow a paradigm, Kuhn needs to explain "What causes the group [of professional scientists] to abandon one tradition of normal research in favor of another" (1996, p. 144). After pointing out that it is possible for a revolution to take place over generations without requiring individual scientists to change from one paradigm to another, Kuhn sets out four reasons that scientists may have for deciding to change paradigms. Two of these reasons, aesthetic considerations (including simplicity, unity, and so forth) and personal or political beliefs, are clearly subjective. We can understand how Lavoisier could have reasons to revolutionize chemistry that Priestley did not share, if the reasons given are personal and subjective. We do not expect others to have the same personal or subjective views or tastes that we do. Kuhn also says that a scientist may change from one paradigm to another if the new paradigm solves problems that the old one could not. New paradigms are successfully introduced when there is a crisis, that is, when scientists feel that the old paradigm is not working. To revolutionary scientists, what had been anomalies are now seen as refutations of the old paradigm. Although this reason for changing paradigms sounds objective, Kuhn argues that there is no objective way to know how seriously anomalies should be taken. Some, like Lavoisier, will feel that there is a crisis and a need for revolutionary change, while others, like Priestley, can look at the same situation and feel no need for change. To add to the sense that these two positions are subjective, Kuhn famously describes the change from one paradigm to another as a Gestalt shift, in which a picture of an old woman suddenly looks like a young woman or a duck suddenly looks like a rabbit. When they are seen from the perspective of the new paradigm, what had been minor anomalous puzzles suddenly show that the old paradigm was terribly wrong. Finally, Kuhn points out that in a revolutionary period, scientists must decide which paradigm is more promising for future success. Such forward-looking predictions are bound to be based on partial information and require belief in the promise of the paradigm. Kuhn calls this a matter of faith and argues that it too is subjective, like all of the reasons that scientists may have to change paradigms.

Criticism of Kuhn's Relativism

Kuhn was rather surprised at the reaction of many philosophers and scientists to his work. He did not see himself as claiming that science is irrational or subjective but rather as developing a philosophy of science that was true to the actual history of science. While this may be true, it is also clear that Kuhn was quite capable of using inflammatory rhetoric that was bound to offend many supporters of science. For example, when explaining the analogy with political revolution, he says that the defender of a new viewpoint must resort to "techniques of mass persuasion, including force" when political recourse fails (1996, p. 93). In the mythology of modern science, the church represents the Dark Ages, superstition, and jargon-filled Scholastic rationalizations, whereas science represents reason, knowledge, and the objective quest for the truth. Yet Kuhn says that science textbooks are as dogmatic as orthodox theology, and, in arguing that there is no objective criterion

THOMAS KUHN

Thomas Samuel Kuhn was born on 18 July 1922 in Cincinnati, Ohio. He graduated summa cum laude from Harvard in 1943 with a bachelor's degree in physics, and after some work in the government Office of Scientific Research and Development during World War II, he returned to Harvard for his master's and doctoral degrees in physics in 1946 and 1949. He remained at Harvard until 1956 teaching in the Department of the History of Science that had just been created by his mentor James Conant, who aided his transition from theoretical physics to the history and philosophy of science. Kuhn next joined the faculty of the University of California at Berkeley, where he developed the idea for his most influential book. In 1964 he moved to Princeton, where he was the M. Taylor Pyne Professor of

Philosophy and History of Science. Kuhn returned to Boston to complete his career at the Massachusetts Institute of Technology as professor of philosophy and history of science from 1979 to 1983 and the Laurence S. Rockefeller Professor of Philosophy from 1983 until 1991. Kuhn was the author or coauthor of five books and scores of articles on the philosophy and history of science. He was a Guggenheim Fellow in 1954–1955, the winner of the George Sarton Medal in the History of Science in 1982, and the holder of honorary degrees from many institutions, among them the University of Notre Dame, Columbia University, the University of Chicago, the University of Padua, and the University of Athens. Kuhn suffered from cancer during the last years of his life and died in 1996.

for deciding between paradigms, he says changing from one paradigm to another is a "conversion experience" (1996, p. 151). Explaining how the existence of multiple revolutions has been covered up by traditional histories of science, Kuhn compares these histories to those given to the population in George Orwell's (Eric Arthur Blair; 1903–1950) *1984* (1949), which is about as far from objective truth as can be imagined. Kuhn also compares science textbooks to tourist brochures.

Incommensurable Worlds

In order to justify his claim that there is no neutral set of observations or experiments that could help scientists determine which paradigm is true, Kuhn argues that the Gestalt experiments show how it is possible to think of a scientist as seeing the world very differently after a change of paradigm. Examples of scientists s eeing different things after a change of paradigm include the following: The earth was seen as the center of the universe, then as a planet orbiting one of millions of stars. Light was seen first as a particle, then as a wave, and finally as a photon. Uranus was first seen as a star, then as a comet, then finally as a planet when William Herschel (1738–1822) "discovered" it. Dephlogisticated air was later seen as oxygen. Stones restrained from falling to their natural place were later seen as the repetitive motion of a pendulum. Kuhn argues that the revolutionary changes described in these examples are not simply changes in the name of something: Phlogiston is not anti-oxygen, the pendulum is not a falling stone, and so forth. Scientists working in different paradigms collect different data and work on different problems. Something that formerly needed to be explained may be seen as natural under a new paradigm, and what seemed natural before may now seem to need an explanation. Therefore "the historian of

science may be tempted to exclaim that when paradigms change, the world itself changes with them" (1996, p. 111).

Although he occasionally said contradictory things on this issue in *Structure,* Kuhn later insisted that the scientists working under different paradigms really do live in different worlds. Paradigms cannot be said to be different interpretations of a single objective world because "interpretation" only happens within a paradigm. We do not see the world as it really is but rather have to learn how to see, guided by the paradigm. Without a paradigm, there would be no science at all; rather there would only be confusion, a point that Kuhn makes with his reference to the experiments of Jerome S. Bruner and Leo Postman with anomalous playing cards and of George M. Stratton with inverted vision. Kuhn introduced the term *incommensurability* to describe the difficulty of comparing one paradigm to another. There is no way to test a paradigm as a whole or to compare the predictions that derive from paradigms against one another, as scientists do when they test theories. Kuhn argues that in cases where the same word is used in two different paradigms or when it seems that the same phenomenon can be described in both, the words in fact have different meanings in each paradigm and the phenomenon is not the same.

Revolutions have been covered up by textbooks, whose job it is to teach current science, not to teach history of science. Words are applied anachronistically, and the development of science is made to look linear and cumulative. As a historian, Kuhn discovered that there are radically different ways of doing science. He sought a way of expressing his discovery and of explaining the immersion into a historical text that is required for understanding. The concept of a paradigm is central to Kuhn's expression of his discovery and to his attempt to correct philosophical misrepresentations of science.

See also **Knowledge; Relativism; Science.**

BIBLIOGRAPHY

Barnes, Barry. *T. S. Kuhn and Social Science.* New York: Columbia University Press, 1983.

Bird, Alexander. *Thomas Kuhn.* Princeton, N.J.: Princeton University Press, 2000.

Doppelt, Gerald. "Kuhn's Epistemological Relativism: An Interpretation and Defense." *Inquiry* 21 (1978): 33–86.

Fuller, Steve. *Thomas Kuhn: A Philosophical History for Our Times.* Chicago: University of Chicago Press, 2000.

Gutting, Gary, ed. *Paradigms and Revolutions.* Notre Dame, Ind.: University of Notre Dame Press, 1985.

Hacking, Ian, ed. *Scientific Revolutions.* Oxford Readings in Philosophy. New York: Oxford University Press, 1981.

Horwich, Paul, ed. *World Changes: Thomas Kuhn and the Nature of Science.* Cambridge, Mass.: MIT Press, 1993.

Kuhn, Thomas S. *Black-Body Theory and the Quantum Discontinuity, 1894–1912.* Chicago: University of Chicago Press, 1987.

———. *The Copernican Revolution: Planetary Astronomy in the Development of Western Thought.* Cambridge, Mass.: Harvard University Press, 1957.

———. *The Essential Tension: Selected Studies in Scientific Tradition and Change.* Chicago: University of Chicago Press, 1977.

———. *The Road since Structure: Philosophical Essays, 1970–1993, with an Autobiographical Interview.* Edited by James Conant and John Haugeland. Chicago: University of Chicago Press, 2000.

———. *The Structure of Scientific Revolutions.* Chicago: University of Chicago Press, 1996.

Nickles, Thomas, ed. *Thomas Kuhn.* Cambridge, U.K., and New York: Cambridge University Press, 2003.

Nola, Robert. *Rescuing Reason: A Critique of Anti-Rationalist Views of Science and Knowledge.* Dordrecht, Netherlands: Kluwer Academic, 2003.

Nola, Robert, and Howard Sankey, eds. *After Popper, Kuhn, and Feyerabend: Recent Issues in Theories of Scientific Method.* Dordrecht, Netherlands: Kluwer Academic, 2002.

Rouse, Joseph. "Kuhn's Philosophy of Scientific Practice." In *Thomas Kuhn,* edited by Thomas Nickles. Cambridge, U.K., and New York: Cambridge University Press, 2003.

Sankey, Howard. *The Incommensurability Thesis.* Aldershot, U.K., and Brookfield, Vt.: Ashgate, 1994.

Sardar, Ziauddin. *Thomas Kuhn and the Science Wars.* London: Icon, 2000.

Von Dietze, Erich. *Paradigms Explained: Rethinking Thomas Kuhn's Philosophy of Science.* Westport, Conn.: Praeger, 2001.

David J. Stump

PARADISE ON EARTH. The word *paradise* develops in Western languages from the Greek word *paradeisos,* the old Persian word *pairidaeza,* and the modern Arabic and Persian *firdaus,* all of which originally denoted a walled garden. In the arid environment of the Near East, a garden must be carefully and laboriously constructed with watercourses for irrigation, and its precious flowers and fruits protected from theft by a surrounding wall. The conflation of this term for a type of garden built and cultivated in the Near East with religious imagery of heaven, especially in Judaism, Christianity, and Islam, has given the term a far more complex set of meanings, which have come to permeate the cultures of the Christian West and the Islamic world, creating a metaphoric bridge between divine paradise and paradise on earth.

In these cultures the concept of paradise developed in two related levels. The first was scriptural and thus a part of religious belief: paradise is either a place for life after death—often serving as a more tangible and concrete substitute for the vaguer term *heaven*—or the setting for a primal, idealized epoch in human history: the Garden of Eden. The second way in which the concept developed was through the actual physical depiction or recreation of the religious image of paradise on earth, either in the form of actual gardens or through the use of certain types of garden imagery—with or without religious connotations—in music, literature, and the visual arts.

Religious Conceptions of Paradise

In the Jewish Torah, paradise first appears as the Garden of Eden in Genesis. It also is regarded as the abode of God, to which the righteous are welcome (Psalm 73:24–25):

> Thou shalt guide me with thy counsel, and afterward receive me to glory. Whom have I in heaven but thee? And there is none upon earth that I desire besides thee.

In terms of concrete imagery, the most famous Old Testament vision of paradise is set forth in Psalm 23:2: "He maketh me to lie down in green pastures: he leadeth me beside the still waters." In Christianity paradise is the blessed afterlife promised by Christ in the Gospels—"And Jesus said unto him, Verily, I say unto thee, To-day shalt thou be with me in Paradise" (Luke 23:43)—or the more complex, mystical, and tangible paradise of the Book of Revelation (22:1–2):

> And he showed me a pure river of water of life, clear as crystal, proceeding out of the throne of God and of the Lamb. In the midst of the street of it, and on either side of the river, was there the tree of life, which bare twelve manner of fruits, and yielded her fruit every month; and the leaves of the tree were for the healing of the nations.

In Islamic scripture the image of paradise (Ar. *janna,* garden) is far more concrete and descriptive, a garden with flowering trees, running streams, silken cushions, and chaste companions promised in so many passages in the Koran:

> This is the picture of Paradise promised to those who fear God: it contains rivers of ever-fresh water, rivers of milk that never sours, rivers of wine that are a delight to those who drink, and rivers of pure honey; also for those who fear God are found every fruit, and their Lord's forgiveness. (47:15)

> They will be attended by youths perpetually young, carrying chalices and ewers and cups filled from a flowing spring, neither giving a headache nor intoxication, and

The Adoration of the Lamb (c. 1425–1429) by Jan and Hubert van Eyck, from ***The Ghent Altarpiece,*** open-center panel. Christian interpretations of paradise in art were often drawn from passages in the Bible and other religious works, a practice discouraged by other faiths. The van Eyck brothers drew partly upon the Book of Revelations to create *The Ghent Altarpiece.* © Archivo Iconografico, S.A./Corbis

such fruits as they wish, and the meat of birds as they wish. They will have as companions beautiful black-eyed maidens, pure as well-guarded pearls, a recompense for their righteousness. There will not be heard any vain or profane words, but only: "peace, peace, peace." (56:10–25)

Although the concept of paradise as a religious afterlife is primarily found in the three monotheistic religions originating in the Near East, the association of a garden with religious repose is also found in Buddhism, where it ultimately influenced secular garden culture in China and Japan. Of course for those of a secular bent, the metaphor of a heavenly garden may ultimately derive from the ancient use of a garden as a place of earthly pleasure, rest, or contemplation, but in the world of metaphor the heavenly garden precedes and influences its earthly counterpart.

In an intermediate step from scriptural sources toward earthly recreation in the arts, paradise forms a part of various liturgies, especially those involving funerals. Thus paradise is invoked in the Jewish prayer for the dead, the Islamic *mawlid,* and the Roman Catholic requiem mass, where paradise is also seen as the heavenly Jerusalem, what St. Augustine of Hippo termed the City of God: "May the Angels lead you into paradise; may the martyrs receive you and lead you into the holy city of Jerusalem."

Representations in Western Culture

From scriptures and liturgical texts the concept of paradise emerges as a dominant image in the religious art of Christianity and Islam over the centuries and eventually develops what we might term quasi-secular cognates as well, in which theological paradise in effect loans part of its meaning to secular palaces, poetry, and visual arts. In the Christian tradition, images of an essentially scriptural paradise figure prominently in literature of the West. These range from the Neoplatonic vision of a multi-tiered heaven in the early-sixth-century *Celestial Hierarchy* of Dionysius the Areopagite through the paradise described by the ninth-century Beatus of Liebana in his *Commentaries on the Apocalypse* to the lofty poetic visions of Dante's *Divine Comedy* in the early fourteenth century and Milton's *Paradise Lost* in the seventeenth, finding echoes in the earthy twentieth-century representations of Roark Bradford and Marc Connelly, epitomized in the latter's *The Green Pastures.*

These scriptural, liturgical, and literary images of paradise in turn had a profound influence on music and the visual arts, starting with illustrations to the texts in question. The medieval sculptural reliefs of the Last Judgment that so often grace the doorways of eleventh- and twelfth-century Romanesque churches traditionally depicted the rewards of paradise on the left (to the right of a central figure of Christ) and the torments of hell to the right or below, with details taken from Revelation and from the Beatus manuscripts. From Dante's late medieval exegesis and expansion of biblical texts came a view of paradise that was to influence later generations of visual artists. From Genesis combined with Milton's poetic text came Franz Joseph Haydn's musical depiction of paradise in *The Creation* as well as a number of depictions in painting.

Court of the Lions in Casa Real Palace, Alhambra, Granada, Spain. The concept of paradise on earth developed partly through physical representation in gardens, palace courtyards, or the cloisters of medieval monasteries. © PATRICK WARD/CORBIS

The image of paradise on Earth in the Western tradition is not exclusively Christian in inspiration. An idyllic earthly paradise is also evoked in the rich tradition of poetry and art inspired by the Greek myths of Arcadia and given defining shape in the poetry of Virgil. The classical Arcadia is a land of shepherds and idyllic peace that returns again and again in the poetry, prose, and painting of the West, given perhaps its most characteristic form in the paintings of Claude Lorrain and Nicolas Poussin in seventeenth-century France.

In Western art of the Christian tradition, where the illustration of religious texts is encouraged rather than actively discouraged as in Judaism and Islam, depictions of paradise are as likely to recall the primal innocence of Eden as they are the reward awaiting Christians in the afterlife. Seen from a strictly narrative perspective, the artistic potential of Christian hell is rich in pictorial possibilities, full of emotion and activity, while that of heaven or paradise is, comparatively speaking, both formulaic and limited, with the exception of the high drama of the expulsion of Adam and Eve from Eden. The Western art tradition does not, however, possess the embedded cultural tradition of the walled garden, and so, to paraphrase Freud, in Western art a flower is often simply a flower.

Among the many depictions of paradise in Western art, two may serve to illustrate the gamut of imagery. In the famous Ghent altarpiece painted by the Van Eyck brothers between 1425 and 1432, a literal depiction of paradise in the lower central panel of the open altarpiece shows a green meadow populated by crowds of angels, apostles, clerics, martyrs, and other saints, adoring the Holy Lamb on a stone altar, while an octagonal basin in the foreground, recalling the baptismal font with its water of salvation, contains a playing fountain of life. The inspiration for the imagery comes in part from Revelation and probably in part from the liturgy of All Saints, and the imagery itself is Roman Catholic in conception and detail. By contrast, the various depictions of the *Peaceable Kingdom* by the American naive painter Edward Hicks recall the Old Testament prophecy of Isaiah 11:6, the peaceable kingdom that will

arrive on earth with the coming of the Messiah: "The wolf also shall dwell with the lamb, and the leopard shall lie down with the kid; and the calf and the young lion and the fatling together; and a little child shall lead them."

Explicit physical recreations of paradise in Western landscape architecture are rare. The enclosed cloisters of medieval monasteries sometimes carried such an association, and the forecourts or enclosed gardenlike settings for some churches, referred to as *parvises,* carry the same connotation.

Islamic Art and Literature

In Islamic culture there is likewise a literary tradition of direct depiction of paradise, most typically represented by Mir Haydar's *Miraj-nama* (Book of the ascension), a fourteenth-century poetic description of the Prophet's mystical journey to heaven and hell, which takes much of its imagery of paradise directly from highly descriptive scriptural passages of the Koran. The most famous illustrated manuscript of the poem, created for the Timurid ruler Shah Rukh in Herat in about 1435, depicts a paradise with triple gates, four flowing rivers of water, milk, wine, and honey, and flowering trees, among which the houris engage in games and provide refreshments. In a *fal-nama* or "book of divination" manuscript created in Istanbul around 1600, a famous miniature depicts Adam and Eve expelled from paradise along with the serpent, as an astonished angel and a peacock look on.

In the complex metaphorical imagery of Persian poetry, the drinking of wine in the setting of a garden combines secular cultural praxis with the mystical notion of divine intoxication. For this reason, illustrations to the texts of poets such as Hafiz often show couples or individuals drinking wine in a garden, or even, in one famous example painted around 1529 by the Tabriz artist Sultan-Muhammad, a sort of half-earthly, half-heavenly saturnalia of elderly sheikhs and heaven-sent angels.

While paradisiacal imagery is found in many different Islamic arts, from ceramics and metalwork to miniature painting, some of the most memorable evocations of the heavenly garden are seen in textile arts. Many of the most famous Islamic carpets created under the Safavid dynasty in Iran in the sixteenth century are in the form of what one scholar has termed a "paradise park" format, in which an outer border symbolic of the surrounding wall encloses a lush vision of paradise that often includes depictions of the drinking of wine, the royal sport of hunting (itself often a metaphor of the soul's search for paradise), and lovers enjoying the floral ambience of the garden. The same motifs grace many of the famous figural Safavid velvets, in which the images of lovers in a garden are conflated with the idea of the soul's love of God. The two celebrated Ardebil carpets, probably woven in Kashan around 1537, depict the reflection of the sun's medallion—a metaphor for God as the giver of light—in a dark blue formal pool filled with countless floating lotus flowers on scrolling stems. Other Islamic carpet forms, such as the *sajjadah* or prayer rug, often depict a gateway to a tree- and flower-filled paradise, while one carpet form, the garden carpet, actually depicts a traditional Islamic garden with its cruciform axial watercourses (often filled with fish) and rectangular plantings, in a woven form that conveniently remains in bloom throughout the year.

Detail from Edward Hicks's *Peaceable Kingdom* (c. 1833; oil on canvas). Many of Hicks's paintings were illustrations of scenes in the Bible, such as his famous *Peaceable Kingdom,* which was based on a prophecy from the Book of Isaiah in the Old Testament. © BURSTEIN COLLECTION/CORBIS

In the Islamic world, the combination of a pre-Islamic form of walled garden from Iran known as a *char bagh*—literally a "fourfold garden"—and the imagery of the Koranic texts combined to foster a long tradition of princely garden building in which religious ideas formed a sort of symbolic overlay. The four long pools arranged in cruciform fashion that divide the garden into four represent the four heavenly rivers; a pavilion set in the middle of the garden might then take on equally heavenly symbolism, as in the Hasht Bihisht ("eight heavens") Safavid palace from seventeenth-century Isfahan. Among the countless Islamic attempts to create an earthly paradise, two gardens have achieved unusual historical prominence. The earlier of these, known today as the Court of the Lions, graces the fourteenth-century Nasrid Alhambra palace in Granada, Spain. Its four streams, fed by a central playing fountain in a basin borne on the backs of twelve sculpted lions, recall the heavenly rivers of the Koran, together with the fountain Salsabil that graces Islamic paradise (Koran 76:12). The other Islamic garden of special prominence is the great *char bagh* arrayed before the Mughal royal mausoleum known as the Taj Mahal, created in the mid-seventeenth century in Agra, India, by the Mughal emperor Shah Jahan. The inscriptions of the Taj Mahal itself stress the metaphor of an earthly depiction of heavenly paradise, in which the mausoleum itself is a symbol for the throne of God. The popularity of the *char bagh* in Islamic cultures from India to Iberia is a strong testament to its Islamic religious associations with paradise, as well as to the astonishing persistence of pre-Islamic forms in Islamic art.

East Asia

While the concept of an earthly paradise as a reflection of a heavenly paradise permeates much art in cultures under the influence of Christianity and Islam, a somewhat similar concept of a heavenly presence on earth—not specifically derived from the west Asian *firdaus*—can also be seen in other cultures, notably those influenced directly or indirectly by Buddhism. A final example of a constructed heaven on earth may

be seen in the succession of Chinese capital cities and royal palaces built in Beijing by the Jin, Yuan (Mongol), Ming, and Qing dynasties. The elevation of the emperor in China to semi-divine status encouraged the creation of a quasi-celestial abode for the emperor on earth. The hierarchical organization of the Forbidden City, with its succession of courts and gateways, each leading to a more rarified and exclusive precinct, also represents an attempt to create a heavenly city on earth, if not embodying direct metaphors for a scriptural paradise such as those found in the Christian and Islamic West. This in turn led to reflections of an earthly paradise in the palace architecture (and, in Japan especially, in the construction of palace gardens as places of aesthetic as well as religious contemplation) in other cultures of East Asia.

See also **Garden; Heaven and Hell; Landscape in the Arts; Utopia.**

BIBLIOGRAPHY

Blair, Sheila S., and Jonathan M. Bloom, eds. *Images of Paradise in Islamic Art.* Hanover, N.H.: Hood Museum of Art, 1991.

Gardet, L. "Djanna." In *Encyclopedia of Islam.* Vol. 2. Leiden: Brill, 1965.

Lehrmann, Jonas. *Earthly Paradise: Garden and Courtyard in Islam.* Berkeley: University of California Press, 1980.

Moynihan, Elisabeth B. *Paradise as a Garden in Persia and Mughal India.* New York: Braziller, 1979.

Psaki, Regina, and Charles Hindley, eds. *The Earthly Paradise: The Garden of Eden from Antiquity to Modernity.* Binghamton, N.Y.: Global Publications, Binghamton University, 2002.

Walter B. Denny

PARADOX. *See* **Logic.**

PATRIOTISM. Patriotism is one of a large class of words that are linked to the virtues of membership. To participate in relations of, for example, friendship, community, nationhood, citizenship, or marriage implies normative conventions. In other words, there are value expectations built into such membership. One important dimension of any membership relation is an expectation of loyalty. Fidelity or loyalty to a nation, community, friend, citizenship, marriage, or state is thus implied in the actual practice. To participate openly and self-consciously, therefore, in any of these membership practices involves adherence to loyalty-based virtue. In this context, the term *patriotism* usually denotes a specific loyalty virtue, consequent upon membership of a country or state. However, the term *loyalty* alone does not quite cover the range of values associated with patriotic membership. Patriotism also signifies a sense of personal identification with, and concern for, the well-being or welfare of that country or state. Further, it entails a readiness to make sacrifices for its defense or welfare. In addition, it provides (for some) the ground for all moral action—in the sense that morality, in itself, is seen to be, quite literally, premised on patriotic membership. Patriotism also indicates a special affection, feeling, or emotive response. This emotive response is commonly designated as a "love of country."

Origins

A distinction is often drawn between the terms *patriot* and *patriotism.* The former is seen as an older usage, traceable back to the ancient Roman republic, while the latter is viewed as an eighteenth-century neologism. Patriotism, as in most ideological "isms," is therefore often considered a more recent word. However, the older term *patriot* still covers many of the conceptual aspects of patriotism. The term *patriotism* figured in European and North American political discussion (and poetry) over the nineteenth and early twentieth centuries. However, during the larger bulk of the twentieth century its academic usage diminished. Certainly up to the 1990s it was considered, in academic debate, to be an antiquated term—particularly in liberal and Marxist political theory. However, there has been, over the last decade, a rediscovery of patriotism (among other membership-related concepts) within political theory and related disciplines. This rediscovery began in the 1980s with communitarianism and then developed into a renewed academic interest in nationalism, multiculturalism, citizenship, and the like. Patriotism is one of the latecomers to this process. It should be stressed, though, that this academic interest, or lack of interest, has little bearing on the ordinary political usage of these terms. Patriotism, regardless of academic concerns, persisted in lay political vocabularies throughout the twentieth century.

The deep roots of the word *patriot* lie in Roman antiquity, particularly in terms such as *patria* and *patrius,* which indicate fatherland, city, native, or familiar place. *Familiar* has links with the word *family* (*familia*). This also has ties with the term *father* or *paternal* (*pater, père, Vater, padre*), or what is implied by the "role of the father" within a family. In terms of the "role of father," *patria* and *patrius* have subtle connections with property, authority, and status. The word *patriarch* evolves from this dimension. The links between father, authority, family, property, and politics can be observed, for example, in the Roman patrician class, who possessed considerable wealth in land and were dominant in the older Roman political structure. Their property enabled wide-ranging political influence. This was also connected to the original use of the cognate terms *patron* and *patronage.* Early Roman political factions, as in later European monarchies, worked through powerful wealthy families. Loyalty to kin in politics was supremely important for survival and political success. Early Roman *pietas* was, therefore, originally loyalty to the family hearth. However, Roman republican writers, such as Cicero, also saw a wider patria in the res publica (the public thing). The later Roman legal *Digesta* and *Institutiones* referred to two patrias affecting citizens: the more local (*patria sua*) and the more abstract public Rome (*communis patria*). Under the later Roman Empire (and again under later European absolute monarchies), this second patria became increasingly more abstract and legalistic.

In effect, the highest patria (status and estate) became synonymous with the state. The state was, in a sense, paternal authority "writ large." This idea can still be seen in seventeenth-century doctrines of political rule, such as patriarchalism, where all authority is traced to the paternal role. The prince thus embodied the essence of the state. Traces of this can still be seen in eighteenth-century writings, such as Henry St. John, first viscount Bolingbroke's (1678–1751) *Idea of a Patriot King* (1749). The opposition to this reading of the state also employed the language of patriotism. Yet it wanted to colonize the state with a different set of values. Thus, liberty under the law became a motif for a divergent set of arguments. Consequently, if republicans, dissenters, and revolutionaries absorbed the language of patriotism, they could claim to be struggling for the "real" rights and freedoms of the people, and consequently for the soul of the state. At this point in the argument, in the early nineteenth century, the language of patriotism began slowly to mutate into nationalist language.

In summary, the qualities of "local familial or community loyalty" and an "impersonal abstract legal loyalty" have remained part of the vocabulary of patriotism to the present day. Local communal identification implies a more visceral loyalty, an attachment and love for the "familiar." This is why some contemporary commentators can still insist that patriotism is more of an emotion than an intelligible political idea. Yet at the same time, the loyalty to the remote authoritative legal abstraction of the state or city-state embodies another important formal aspect of the legacy of patriotism.

Objects of Patriotic Loyalty

First, in the medieval period, the patria could be identified with a locality, hamlet, clan, village, township, or city. The patriot was one who submitted to the village or city and was prepared to defend it. Second, in terms of the feudal structure, defending homelands could also entail defending the lands of a local lord or prince. In this sense, feudal and vassal relations became integral to patriotic argument. Third, in Augustinian Christian thought the significant patria was the "city of God," which transcended all cities and states. During the later medieval period, Roman imperial thought was utilized by secularizing territorial states (initially city-states) in Europe. However, "abstract legal Rome" (*communis patria*) was a movable feast. It could apply equally to Venice, Florence, Paris, or London. Princes became, in effect, supreme lawmakers (sovereigns) and emperors in their own realms. The objects of patriotism thus became the new territorial states with their fatherly princes.

From the twelfth century, the notion of patria often arose in the context of defense of a state territory. Defense of patria was a key ground for "just war." This identification with patria intensified with renewed study of writers such as Cicero (106–43 B.C.E.), and later, with the thirteenth-century rediscovery of Aristotle's political writings. Thomas Aquinas (1225–1274) also touched on the issue of the religious duty of citizens to render themselves vulnerable to death for their patria—*pro patria mori*. Religious language was immensely important here. Death for patria and death for the Christian faith became virtually coeval by the late medieval and early modern period. The emotive religious memorials and formal recognition we still give to patriotic war dead are a testimony to how deeply this idea has permeated state theory. It is crucial to the understanding of patriotism to the present day. Finally, it is important to underscore the point that patriotism is formally compatible with any political creed or "object of attachment." Family, locality, city, tradition, land, absolute monarch, total state, and republic have all been objects of patriotic loyalty.

Forms of Patriotism

In contemporary discussion there have been a number of renderings of patriotism. These can be distinguished between two forms—strong and moderate patriotisms. The stronger version argues that patriotic loyalty is the sole source of any meaningful moral claims. The content of patriotism is therefore always particular or local. In this context, the loyalties demanded from the patriot are simply to whatever values are regarded as dominant within a state or community. The key critical opposition to this perspective comes from universalist forms of argument, such as universal human rights claims. However, the larger bulk of recent writings on patriotism have appeared within the moderate category. The moderate category tries to mediate between universalism and localism.

Strong patriotism. The strong variant of patriotism does not have as many proponents as the moderate form. One key example of this is strong communitarian patriotism. In his 1984 essay, "Is Patriotism a Virtue?," Alasdair MacIntyre sees patriotism as one of a class of "loyalty-exhibiting virtues." These virtues exhibit "action-generating regard" for particular persons or groups, and they are embedded in highly particular relationships. Morality is thus rooted within communal relations. For MacIntyre, morality is always learned from within a particular way of life. Goods are always the particular goods of communities. The morality of patriotism is therefore seen as perfectly natural to us as communal beings. MacIntyre's citizen is basically a very mild-mannered political animal; however, it is important, nonetheless, to realize that the strong particularist arguments he deploys have been utilized by much more worrying forms of politics. Racial exclusivism or political authoritarianism could well be justified within this framework. The dangers implicit within this perspective are those of extreme exclusion and the lurking possibility of communal jingoism. In the twentieth century, strong variants of patriotism have been associated (rightly or wrongly) with the militaristic or bellicose stance of German national socialism and Italian fascism in the 1930s.

Moderate patriotism. The more recent moderate account of patriotism contains four subtle variants. First, for neoclassical republicans the distinctive character of patriotism is its focus on political liberty and civic virtue. Love of country is not love of a language or ethnicity, but rather of political liberty. This is not a love of a particular liberty, but a generic nonexclusive liberty as embedded in law. It is seen essentially as a universalizing force. A republic is seen to embody a powerful sense of local solidarity contained within a universal vessel of liberty under law. For its proponents, republican language is thus a viable alternative to current liberal foundationalism, ethnic nationalism, and strong patriotic arguments.

Second, for recent theorists such as Charles Taylor, moderate communitarian patriotism envisages a direct link between patriotism, republicanism (although some would categorize it

as civic humanism), and communitarian motifs. Communitarians are clearly not of one mind here. The distinction between strong and moderate patriotism has direct parallels with the distinction, made within communitarian theory, between strong and moderate senses of community. Whereas MacIntyre sees a direct synonymity between nationalism and patriotism and adopts a narrower, stronger, and more exclusive sense of community, Charles Taylor seeks some separation between patriotism and nationalism and adopts a more differentiated view of community (incorporating multicultural diversity). Further, whereas, for Taylor, moderate patriotism is a matter of self-conscious citizen identification with a polity, strong patriotism swims in murkier waters, usually envisaging patriotism as a prepolitical, nonintentional attachment. Moderate communitarian patriotism, for Taylor, has no "prepolitical" reference. It rather implies more intentional attachment to a country and its laws. Patriotism is therefore always "politically defined," as in the American and French Revolutions. However, most moderate communitarian patriots admit that in the nineteenth and twentieth centuries the vocabularies of nationalism and patriotism became confusingly intermeshed.

Third, Stephen Nathanson, in constructing his moderate liberal patriotism, has contrasted it with both the "extreme patriotism" of MacIntyre and communitarian arguments. Moderate liberal patriotism basically sees certain liberal universalist, essentially neo-Kantian, moral constraints acting upon patriotic goals. Too much patriotism, or too much liberal universalism, is to be avoided. Patriotism therefore requires a middle way. Thus, liberal universalism can and should legitimately restrain local solidarities and membership loyalties. Nathanson's position is at least a salutary reminder to republicans that liberal universalist language is not necessarily always antipatriotic.

The fourth, final strand is constitutional patriotism. This is associated with the writings of Jürgen Habermas on what he calls *Verfassungspatriotismus*. This is essentially, again, a neo-Kantian orientated loyalty to the universalistic principles of liberty and democracy embodied in a constitution. The emphasis is quite explicitly legalistic. Constitutional patriotism is an allegiance to a constitutional juristic tradition embodying certain fundamental rational values. The background to this is Habermas's own deep sensitivity to the events of World War II in Germany, particularly in relation to nationalism. In Habermas's case, constitutional patriotism is patriotic loyalty to the universalistic principles embodied in the German constitution. Citizens, in this scenario, are linked together by a formal common agreement on the shared values of the constitution. Habermas is insistent that constitutional patriotism has no connection with any prepolitical attachments, characteristic of nationalism or strong patriotism. This kind of general constitutional theme can be found, for some Habermasians, in the polity of the United States and, possibly, even the burgeoning European Union legal structures.

Nationalism and Patriotism

There are negative and positive arguments for both separating and fusing nationalism and patriotism. The positive statement for their fusion is contained in stronger views of communal identity. Both concepts embody powerful statements on the moral priority of the community. The positive view therefore involves the direct normative assimilation of nationalism and patriotism to communitarianism. This can be termed the "positive assimilation model." MacIntyre articulates this view, in which patriotism and nationalism become indistinguishable.

The negative reading of the "fusion" views patriotism and nationalism with equal contempt as blemishes on political and moral discourse. This can be termed the "mutually disagreeable model." There are a number of background points to this model. First, patriotism is seen as a verbal "sleight of hand" to avoid the pejorative connotations of nationalism; however, basically they are the same. The separate use of patriotism therefore has a face-saving character. Second, it might well be the case that patriotism did have an older individual meaning, but since the nineteenth century that older sense has been totally lost. Patriotism is exactly the same appalling entity as nationalism. Patriotism should therefore share all the opprobrium heaped upon nationalism. The "mutually disagreeable model" was well formulated by Leo Tolstoy at the beginning of the twentieth century. Tolstoy found both ideas repellent. Despite great efforts by states to foster patriotism, it is the same doctrine as nationalism. In the final analysis, both entail the renunciation of all human dignity, common sense, and moral conscience.

The opposite thesis to the above is the separation of nationalism from patriotism. This again has positive and negative dimensions. The positive reading of the separation is most forcibly rendered by recent republican writers. Thus, true patriotism must be kept completely distinct from nationalism. For such republicans (as Maurizio Viroli), the language of patriotism invokes a specific love of the political institutions and laws that embody a nondominatory concept of liberty. It is therefore about sustaining a particular way of life in a republic. Nationalism, on the other hand, is seen as a highly exclusive, prepolitical, culturally oriented attachment that is antagonistic to liberty. It is therefore deeply pernicious to confuse patriotism and nationalism, since patriotism is the theoretical and practical antidote to nationalism.

The negative reading of their separation suggests that patriotism and nationalism should be kept distinct on negative grounds. The concepts are historically different. Each has a distinct historical trajectory. Patriotism, for example, is an older terminology that has a much more intimate connection with both the state and religious language, whereas nationalism has closer connections to modernity and secularism. However, both terms are to be mistrusted for different reasons. Both are equally objectionable as narrow, exclusive, tribal, and deleterious to human dignity. In this context, the separation between patriotism and nationalism is valid, but this redeems neither doctrine.

See also **Nation; Nationalism; State, The; Romanticism in Literature and Politics.**

BIBLIOGRAPHY

Dietz, Mary. "Patriotism." In *Political Innovation and Conceptual Change,* edited by T. Ball, J. Farr, and R. L. Hanson. Cambridge, U.K.: Cambridge University Press, 1989.

Habermas, Jürgen. "Citizenship and National Identity: Some Reflections on the Future of Europe." *Praxis International* 12 (1992): 1–19.

Ingram, Attracta. "Constitutional Patriotism." *Philosophy and Social Criticism* 22 (1996): 1–18.

MacIntyre, Alasdair. *Is Patriotism a Virtue?* Lawrence: University of Kansas Press, 1984.

Nathanson, Stephen. *Patriotism, Morality, and Peace.* Lanham, Md.: Rowman and Littlefield, 1993.

Nussbaum, Martha Craven. *For Love of Country: Debating the Limits of Patriotism.* Edited by Joshua Cohen. Boston: Beacon, 1996.

Primoratz, Igor, ed. *Patriotism.* New York: Humanity Books, 2002.

Taylor, Charles. "Nationalism and Modernity." In *The Morality of Nationalism,* edited by Robert McKim and Jeff McMahan, 31–55. Oxford: Oxford University Press, 1997.

Tolstoy, L. N. "Christianity and Patriotism." In his *The Kingdom of God and Peace: Essays.* Translated by Aylmer Maude. London: Oxford University Press, 1935.

Vincent, Andrew. *Nationalism and Particularity.* Cambridge, U.K.: Cambridge University Press, 2002.

Viroli, Maurizio. *For Love of Country.* Oxford: Clarendon, 1995.

Andrew Vincent

PEACE. The peace concept has a long history both in the Western and Eastern intellectual traditions. While Greco-Roman and Judeo-Christian ideas regarding peace have expanded and changed over time, this is not so much the case in Muslim, Hindu, and Buddhist thought.

Ancient and Early Christian West

For the ancient Hebrews, *shalom* signified a state of prosperity and well-being as well as security. The Greek word, *eirēnē* from which we get the word *irenic,* also denotes the contentment and fruitfulness that comes from concord and harmony. Order (*tranquillitas ordinis*), quiet (*quies*), and repose (*otium*) inhere within the Latin word *pax,* which Romans sought and maintained as a higher good. Altars to peace were erected by both Greeks and Romans, and the Stoic view of the universe visualized an intrinsic natural harmony, which the virtuous endeavored to restore. In all of these ancient conceptualizations, there was a belief that an Eden-like time of peace had existed before war and disorder disrupted it. Peace, then, was understood mostly as a cessation of the chaos of the created disorder, including war. While it may have been the natural state of humankind at one time, in the early twenty-first century it is an idyll that can only be approximated by a good government that can ensure the security necessary for the achievement of concord and personal well-being.

The corresponding development of just-war ideas provided a program for realizing peace, or the restoration of order. Strict guidelines were erected in an attempt to prevent any behavior, especially by governments, that would be disruptive, unless it resulted in the ultimate acquisition of peace. While the earliest Christian writers eschewed war altogether, seeing it as contrary to the "way of love" taught by Christ, by the third century some Christians were fighting in Roman wars without compunction. Augustine of Hippo (354–430) did much to establish the components of the just war that would affect subsequent attitudes toward war in the West; but he also more fully defined what peace meant in a Christian context. For this early church father, peace was largely a spiritual concept. In his famous *City of God,* as well as in other works, Augustine incorporated the earlier Greek, Roman, and Jewish elements and contended that peace is essentially a right relationship with God that, through the indwelling of the Holy Spirit, will advance love and concord among human beings. The earthly city is a fallen one and original sin will prevent temporal peace from being established fully; thus, only when Christ returns to judge humanity will true, lasting peace be possible. By removing true temporal peace from the realm of possibility, Augustine bequeathed to the European Middle Ages a concept that was relatively idealistic and millennialistic, even as he sought to mitigate the horrors of warfare with a rigorous just-war doctrine.

Western Middle Ages

The medieval period produced elaborations of Augustine's idea of peace within the context of crusade and feudal politics. The fall of Rome in the late fifth century led to the foundation of numerous bellicose Germanic kingdoms, which struggled to create a new basis for social and political order while adopting gradually much of the culture of antiquity, especially as the Germanic peoples converted to Christianity. The Western Church in the early Middle Ages required exacting penances for the shedding of blood, which were enhanced in early Carolingian laws (eighth century). In this context it was often difficult to distinguish between war and peace, and peace came to be viewed mostly in practical terms as simply a respite from fighting, sometimes even being depicted as the goddess of victory. The Peace of God (*pax Dei*) movement around the turn of the first millennium attempted to regulate warfare through strict papal restrictions on times of fighting and types of weaponry used, violations of which could lead to excommunication or interdict. As feudal relationships came to provide a new negotiated basis for order and peace by the twelfth century, the emerging chivalric code incorporated just-war theory, and set as one of its objectives the perpetuation of order or peace. The inclusion of the Augustinian motivation of love as necessary in any just war helped to ensure that the Christian spiritual ideal regarding peace would remain the goal even if in practical terms it would always remain elusive. The Crusades became the ultimate expression of the just war in continental Europe, but the barbarous actions of the knights who journeyed to the Holy Land compromised the church's credibility in fostering peace, since plenary indulgences seemed to excuse all kinds of violence and manslaughter in this supposedly sacred cause. This situation also created the intellectual climate for the first real investigation of peace as an idea, coming as it did on the heels of charges of corruption against the clergy.

While there were new investigations of peace in continental Europe—such as Dante's (1265–1321) vision of a Christian emperor in *Monarchia* (c. 1315), who established a one-world government that would provide true peace and order—the concept of peace itself underwent little change. Only in England during the Hundred Years' War (1337–1453) is there found a protracted military enterprise provoking extensive criticism of warfare as an institution and, subsequently, suggesting a more complicated notion of what peace itself means. By the 1380s, writers such as John Gower (1330?–1408), Geoffrey Chaucer (c. 1342–1400), William Langland (c. 1330–c. 1400), Thomas Hoccleve (1368 or 1369–c. 1450), John Bromyard (d. c. 1390), John Lydgate (c. 1370–c. 1450), and John Wyclif (c. 1330–1384) all were attacking the justifications for wars, and the insincerity behind the putative goal of restoring order and peace. A new typology of peace emerged from this crucible of war and critique that would remain the basis for understanding peace right up until the modern period. First, the original Augustinian idea of personal, spiritual peace remained, along with its association with mercy, love, and patience. But for the critics of war, it was no longer enough to expect spiritual renewal to end the killing on a one-to-one basis. Relying on personal forbearance did not seem to reduce incidence of war at all. The other, older view of peace as order, including its affiliates—quiet, rest, concord, and law—now took on new resonance as writers excoriated the behavior of knights who supposedly followed a strict, peace-loving code of arms.

Two new elements of peace, however, which had been introduced by the early fifteenth century, proved to be more practical. First, Wyclif and the Lollards, who could easily be termed pacifists, emphasized the un-Christlikeness of war, and thus attempted to return to an early Christian ideal of peace as reflecting the image of Christ (*imago Christi*), demonstrated through acts of love. Unlike the Augustinian concept, here, to live like Christ is to work to stop war and to promote peace, not just in one's spiritual journey, but in society at large. The idea is that Christ believed that peace was possible, and in fact the Gospels say the angels proclaimed peace at his birth. Regardless of whether a cause seems just or not, war is always wrong and it must be a matter of conscience for all Christians to oppose it. By undercutting just-war arguments as inimical to God's way of peace, the concept for the first time emerged from the cloak of impossibility and became an obligatory pursuit. Issuing from this was the related idea that peace offered many practical benefits, thereby stressing its pragmatic nature. Lydgate, Hoccleve, and works such as *The Libelle of Englyshe Polycye* (c. 1436) equated temporal peace with economic well-being, personal security, and the growth of learning. From the late fifteenth century the value of peace was located increasingly in the language of political economy with its complex associations to the public good, which war was less likely now seen to promote.

Renaissance and Reformation

Renaissance humanists, especially those in northern Europe who had spent time in England, took the peace imperative and fashioned it into an ethic based on a dedication to the public good, or commonwealth. Desiderius Erasmus (1466?–1536), Thomas More (1478–1535), Juan Luis Vives (1492–1540), and John Colet (1466 or 1467–1519) all published works hostile to war, promoting all four meanings of peace elucidated above. Within the context of emerging nation-states in western Europe, Erasmus, in his *Complaint of Peace* (1517) and many other works, argued that spiritual peace, embodied in the virtuous Christian prince, would be the foundation of a true and lasting temporal peace. His somewhat Stoic view of the kinship of humanity emphasized the *concordia* aspect of *pax*, which would lead to a personal closeness to God, Christ-like behavior, an absence of strife, and the practical rewards of greater happiness such as the promotion of learning and economic prosperity. While events tended to make humanist pacifists appear idealistic in their own day, their endeavors enshrined peace as an uncontested value and its advancement a virtuous pursuit.

The Protestant reformers, many of whom were also humanists, came to stress the obligations to pursue peace as well through their literal interpretation of the Bible, although they were less optimistic concerning the depraved nature of humankind. One group, however, the Anabaptists, took Christ's words literally when he said "blessed are the peacemakers," and their devotion to all forms of peace became one of their most distinctive characteristics. Not since the time of the early church had a Christian position been so unilaterally in favor of peace; and later groups, such as the Quakers, also came to adopt this position. For these "separatists" peace continued to be understood as both a spiritual condition and a way of life, in all of its practical applications leading to a harmonious and godly society.

The Modern West

The peace concept in the Western tradition from this point onward changed very little in meaning. In the modern period, however, a humanitarian ethos largely replaced the once Christian foundations for valuing peace, but the growing interdependency of nations also produced new concerns about the survival of human existence. By the eighteenth century, many intellectuals opposed the unreasonableness and barbarism of war, and as a result, construed peace as a rational pursuit by enlightened peoples. The philosopher Immanuel Kant (1724–1804), in his *Perpetual Peace* (1795), argued that a world order built upon reason and prudence, which is basically enlightened self-interest, will produce a peaceful society, and bring with it all that is good. The nineteenth century witnessed few large-scale wars in Europe, leading some to believe that Kant's admonition had become a cultural reality. Attempts at balances of power up through the early twentieth century seemed to prove that the West had found the practical solution to the problem of war, and that temporal peace could be realized and perpetuated by sophisticated diplomacy and the careful and humane study of international politics. This rather hegemonic view of peace recalls the ideas of Aristotle and of later officials of the Roman Empire, both of whom believed that empire—that is, rule by a presumably superior civilization—was best positioned to ensure peace. Peace took on the additional nuance then of a planned arrangement for cooperation among nations, even as its moral and practical elements remained prominent.

World War I, the rise of fascism, and the development of nuclear and atomic weapons, all in the twentieth century, left the West once again arguing for peace more from an ethical stance. Since diplomacy and international institutions devoted to peace (such as the United Nations) often fail to prevent wars, the survival of humanity may depend more on people recognizing the moral necessity for keeping peace. This outlook tends to reduce the peace idea to its most basic meaning as the guarantor of continued human existence, a good for which there is universal agreement and support across cultures.

By the early twenty-first century, especially in Western societies, the concept of peace was most often linked to notions of justice and fairness. The modern ethical paradigm for peace espoused by most pacifists assumes that only when economic and political inequities are minimized or eliminated can we provide a basis for real and lasting peace and the consequent guarantee of prolonged human existence. Many contemporary intellectuals, such as Peter Brock, Peter Calvocoressi, Martin Ceadel, Michael Howard, and Charles Chatfield, have explored creatively the implications of this connection and have tried to offer specific and practical means for achieving true justice and, successively, peace.

Muslim, Hindu, and Buddhist Traditions

The Arabic word *salam,* a cognate of the Hebrew *shalom,* means "making peace." For Muslims, one comes to a purest state of peace by submitting to the will of Allah (*isalm*), and anyone who has accomplished this is a *muslim. Salam* is even one of the ninety-nine names of Allah in the Islamic religion. In the Koran, anyone doing the will of God and giving all to exalt his sacred name, including the making of holy war (*jihad*), will receive the divine blessing of peace and eventually live with God in that perfect state. Peace also can become an earthly state, in that good Muslims desire temporal peace, not war, realizing that only through an Islamic polity, serving Allah faithfully, can people prosper and live in harmony with one another. Thus, in Islam, ultimate peace, both spiritual and temporal, harmonizes within a submission to the divine will.

In eastern intellectual traditions the spiritual and practical elements of peace have cohered much more intricately and consistently than they have in the west. The Chinese word for peace, *heping,* is comprised of two characters meaning harmony and level (or flat), which suggests equalizing and balancing. (This type of peace may be inherent in the famous Taoist cosmic principles of *yin* and *yang,* which when symmetrical restore order and oneness to the universe.) The Japanese cognate *hewa* means much the same.

In classical Sanskrit *shanti* is the word closest in meaning to peace, usually denoting tranquility, calm, bliss, eternal rest, and happiness, but usually in connection to destruction or death. The term is often synonymous with *sandi* (association, combination) and the opposite of *vigraha* (separation, isolation, hostility). Peace here is contrary to the "absence of isolation" (*vigrahabhava*) or the "absence of strife or war" (*yuddhabhava*). From earliest Hindu thought it became the goal of the individual to escape from the necessity of being reborn, which was accomplished through deep meditation and the avoidance of bad *karma,* thus bringing ultimate peace. Another Indian concept, *ahimsa,* which is found first in the sacred *Upanishads* (c. eighth century B.C.E.), means nonviolence to animals and humans, and is based on the assumption that harm to living creatures produces bad *karma* by endangering or killing the soul of another. All life is one, and any animal could contain the soul of a relative who has been reincarnated, and so harming it is wrong. Mahatma Gandhi's (1869–1948) pacifism owed a great deal to this tradition of peace. By the time caste distinctions separated the ancient Indians, and led to warfare and strife, the famous meditation known as the *Bhagavad Gita* found in the epic classic Indian poem, the *Mahabharat* offered another means for achieving ultimate peace. *Krishna* tells the warrior Arjuna that in honoring the conditions of caste/race he brings honor to himself, and since souls return to new bodies after the old ones die, death does not matter. But one must reject all greed and anger, and therefore one can, even in the midst of battle, have peace within. Peace is ultimately an inner state that will beget positive ramifications as well for society as a whole.

Buddhist ideas of peace derived from these early Hindu notions that asserted self-denial was the key to contentment and ultimate peace with the universe of which we are all a part spiritually. Also centered in the idea of *ahimsa,* Buddhists have believed that true peace and happiness come from the eradication of all desire, including the desire for permanence that creates conflict and division. Through meditative practices, selfish desire can be gradually eliminated until absolute peace, in this case, *nirvana,* is reached when our state of being ends. Part of this process entails the gradual shutting down of all sensory awareness and feeling, in what is known as *sannavedayi-tanirodha.* Since one does not stay in this state of contemplation permanently, this does not provide a lasting peace. Buddha believed that peace (*shanti*), both internally and externally, can only be achieved truly when it becomes part of one's conception of the world and of those who live within it. Peace is conditional for Buddha as he taught that the insistence on any type of permanence led to inflexibility, and ultimately, to conflict. This recognition of "dependent arising" forms the path to enlightenment and brings freedom and peace within, but also peace without, since it allows for change and newness.

Conclusion

In summary, while the Eastern and Western intellectual traditions historically have construed peace differently, there are certain characteristics that appear to transcend culture and that are held in common, even if the emphasis varies. There persists a spiritual notion of peace that represents inner calm, wholeness, contentment, and selflessness. The internal condition tends to affect the external so that if individuals are not at peace with themselves, they are unlikely to engender temporal peace. On the contrary, they are more apt to participate in wars, since conflict among peoples usually comes from a dissatisfaction with the current state of being (or affairs) that needs redress, perhaps even violently. In most cultural traditions, peace is the natural state of the universe, and throughout history one of the most universal endeavors of humankind has been the quest to end strife and to restore a beneficial order and tranquility. In linking these various but complementary aspects of what it means to be at peace, peace scholar Gerald James Larson has concluded:

> To be at peace with oneself is to accept what or who one is and to have stopped warring with oneself. To be

at peace in community is to make an agreement to end hostility, to live together in harmony, accepting the presence of one another. To be at peace in the cosmos is to accept, largely on faith, that the universe is benign, a more or less fitting habitat for the sorts of beings and forces that dwell or operate within it. (Rouner, p. 138)

See also **Buddhism; Christianity; International Order; Islam; War; Yin and Yang.**

BIBLIOGRAPHY

Bainton, Roland H. *Christian Attitudes toward War and Peace: A Historical Survey and Critical Re-evaluation.* New York: Abingdon Press, 1960.

Dyck, Harvey L., ed. *The Pacifist Impulse in Historical Perspective.* Toronto: University of Toronto Press, 1996. Includes many good essays, including Roy C. Amore's "Peace and Non-violence in Buddhism," Klaus K. Klostermaier's "Himsā and Ahimsā Traditions in Hinduism," and Charles Chatfield's "Thinking about Peace in History."

Gallie, W. B. *Philosophers of Peace and War: Kant, Clausewitz, Marx, Engels, and Tolstoy.* Cambridge, U.K.: Cambridge University Press, 1978.

Johnson, James Turner. *The Quest for Peace: Three Moral Traditions in Western Cultural History.* Princeton, N.J.: Princeton University Press, 1987.

Kalupahana, David J. *The Buddha and the Concept of Peace.* Sri Lanka: Vishva Lekha Publishers, 1999.

Kelsay, John, and James Turner Johnson, eds. *Just War and Jihad: Historical and Theoretical Perspectives on War and Peace in Western and Islamic Traditions.* New York: Greenwood, 1991.

Lowe, Ben. *Imagining Peace: A History of Early English Pacifist Ideas, 1340–1560.* University Park: Pennsylvania State University Press, 1997.

Rouner, Leroy S., ed. *Celebrating Peace.* Notre Dame, Ind.: University of Notre Dame Press, 1990. A number of excellent essays, including Sissela Bok's "Early Advocates of Lasting World Peace: Utopians or Realists?," Gerald James Larson's "The Rope of Violence and the Snake of Peace: Conflict and Harmony in Classical India," and Bhikhu Parekh's "Gandhi's Quest for a Nonviolent Political Philosophy."

Zampaglione, Gerardo. *The Idea of Peace in Antiquity.* Translated by Richard Dunn. Notre Dame, Ind.: University of Notre Dame Press, 1973.

Ben Lowe

PEASANTS AND PEASANTRY. The words *peasants* and *peasantry* are generally associated with a way of life and mind-set that is the opposite of modernization. The terms referred, initially, to small-scale agricultural producers, also known as serfs, who comprised the majority of the populations of Western Europe from the fall of Rome in the fifth century C.E. and during the Middle Ages. Deriving their livelihood mainly, but not exclusively, from agriculture, medieval peasants depended heavily on landlords to whom they had sworn an oath of loyalty and on whose land they lived and farmed. They were expected to provide certain services and to meet specified obligations such as paying rent and taxes, in cash or in kind, and providing free labor as well giving tithes to the church. Lords, on their part, were obligated to protect the peasants under their care. While most peasants lived directly off the land, some earned their living from nonagricultural activities, namely as blacksmiths, tavern owners, or millers. Dependence on small-scale agriculture, lack of ownership of land, and subservience to a dominant class to which they gave their surplus were, thus, early characteristics of peasant societies and influenced the manner in which scholars conceived of them. Hence, Eric Wolf defined peasants as "rural cultivators whose surpluses are transferred to a dominant group of rulers" (1966, pp. 3–4). Similarly, Douglas Kincaid maintained that peasants were "rural cultivators from whom an economic surplus is extracted, in one form or another, freely or coercively, by non-producing classes" (p. 145).

Defining the Modern Peasantry

Currently concentrated in Africa, Asia, and Latin America, the peasantry has been defined differently by various scholars, depending on the degree of emphasis placed on any one of several characteristics. Definitions of the peasantry embrace some of the following characteristics: ownership and use of land, production methods, subordination to other social sectors, and the degree of integration into the market. For some scholars, therefore, peasants are agriculturalists who control most of the land they work, produce for the market, and who have obligations to other social classes, while for others, they are farmers who lack control over the land, labor, and capital they need to produce crops. For yet others, peasants are farmers who control the land they work as tenants or smallholders and who produce for the market and have obligations to other social classes.

Generally, however, with the exception of the more well-to-do peasant classes who own land and exploit the labor of poorer peasants, most peasants are associated with poverty; primitive production methods using little if any modern technology; small-scale production, mostly for subsistence purposes; and economic exploitation by and political and social subservience to a dominant elite class such as landlords or urban elites. They also lack capital and other production resources and, often, do not have control over the land on which they live and work. Where they do own the land, they tend to regard it as family property and not a commodity. In peasant societies, the family tends to be the central economic unit of production, consumption, reproduction, socialization, and welfare, while socially and culturally, peasant communities tend to be isolated from mainstream society and to have a distinctly local culture, as opposed to the dominant wider or higher national culture. They also have a conservative, inward-looking worldview revolving around the household and the kin group and are suspicious of outsiders and new ideas. Peasant communities are sometimes looked down upon by other social sectors who regard them as not only poor, ignorant, and subservient, but also backward, parochial, and closed.

Scholars, however, sometimes make a distinction between closed and open peasant communities; describing closed societies as being highly exclusive, suspicious of outsiders and new ideas, separated from wider society, and determined to protect their way of life by, among other things, discouraging the accumulation and display of wealth. Open societies, on the other hand, are characterized as being plugged into the modern capitalist economy and made up of individuals who own their own land, welcome change, and are largely integrated into the larger society. According to some scholars, therefore, open peasant societies are relatively independent actors who produce for the market and exercise considerable autonomy in deciding what to produce, depending on their analysis of inputs that have to be sourced outside the community and rent and tax requirements.

Clearly, while there are certain characteristics common to most peasant societies, there can be no simple all-embracing definition of peasants and peasantry, as scholars tend to highlight different aspects of what marks peasants as a class. Indeed, while the terms are widely used to describe rural communities all over the world, it is evident that they can no longer be regarded in their classical sense, since the groups that are now referred to as peasants in most countries no longer live exclusively by agriculture, as did most of the serfs in medieval times, but combine various survival strategies that often include wage labor, craft making, trading, and other off-farm activities. They can be part-time farmers, factory workers, small business people, traders, and workers on commercial agricultural establishments or seasonal workers in urban factories, all at the same time. Others maintain links with members of the family unit who are urban workers and who send money to supplement the rural family members' income. This leads to the conclusion that, although large populations who live in rural areas derive most of their livelihood from agriculture and regard themselves as peasants, it no longer really makes sense to identify rural society with the role of the peasant farmer.

Yet other scholars insist that the terms peasant and peasantry can only be appropriately applied to medieval or early modern Europe, as the African, Asian, and Latin American situations are so different as to make any comparisons meaningless. With respect to Africa, specifically, the question of whether small-scale agrarian communities on the continent can be regarded as peasants or not has been contentious, with some scholars arguing that Africa did not have distinct social classes, let alone a class that could be identified as peasants. Consequently, Africa only had primitive, rather than peasant, economies. According to this view, distinguishing features of peasant economies include production for the market by the majority of the people and access to resources such as land, labor, and tools, either for purchase or for rent. African rural dwellers, on the contrary, neither had access to nor produced for the market, being merely subsistence producers.

Thereafter, following a prolonged debate, the existence in Africa of a distinct class that could be called peasants was gradually and begrudgingly acknowledged, and discussion moved on to analyze the experiences and role of this class in recent history. By the 1980s, studies were recording peasants' lived experiences and analyzing peasant social structures, histories, inter- and intrapersonal relations, and relationships with the dominant social and economic structures and systems such as colonialism or the postcolonial state and elites. Peasants had, thus, become fully integrated into African studies.

Phases of Historical Study

Meanwhile, in world history in general, the peasantry long occupied the attention of economists, political scientists, sociologists, and anthropologists. The first phase of scholarly interest in the peasantry began with classical economists, such as Adam Smith (1723–1790), who recognized rural workers as a group, but one that was insignificant in the evolving division of labor that he was interested in. Later, Karl Marx also recognized the presence and importance of peasants, but he, too, dismissed them as an economically and politically backward and doomed class, destined to fall into one of the two antagonistic classes of capitalism, namely, the bourgeoisie or the proletariat. Where Smith and Marx had treated peasants as a homogenous mass, the Russian theorist and revolutionary Vladimir Lenin highlighted the existence of peasant class differentiation, identifying three layers, namely, rich, middle, and poor peasants, according to land area, capital accumulation, and wage or family labor and sought to analyze their role in the twin processes of industrialization and socialist revolution.

The second phase of scholarly attention to the peasantry began in the 1960s and 1970s, mainly due to peasant political activism and insurgence in Africa evident in the anticolonial struggles throughout the continent, and in Asia in the form of the Vietnam War and the Chinese Cultural Revolution following the Chinese Revolution of 1949. This second phase is characterized by revived and growing interest by Western anthropologists in the rituals, social structures, and belief systems of peasant societies and the place of poor agricultural areas at the periphery in the world capitalist system with its center in the developed countries. It was a time of peasant activism in the immediate aftermath of the Cuban Revolution in Latin America that led to agrarian reforms that undermined the latifundio agrarian structure in Chile, Peru, Ecuador, Colombia, and other countries. It was also the period characterized by scholarly debates on "articulation of modes of production," of development economists and donor agencies promoting the green revolution and encouraging peasants to participate fully in the world market in the belief that this would modernize "smallholder" agriculture and make rural producers full participants in the world economy.

Meanwhile, the development economists' optimism was countered by some scholars who pointed out that peasants would forever remain exploited because of the problems of declining terms of trade and "unequal exchange." Faced with the failure of the peasantry in the developing world to rise to expectations by raising their food productivity despite the efforts of development specialists to diffuse modern production values to them, Western governments began to blame this on developing country governments' flawed food pricing policies and inefficient marketing structures and to call for economic structural adjustment programs in order to correct these ills. These programs, sponsored by multilateral financial agencies, by ending government subsidies to the agricultural sector, worsened the plight of the peasantry at a time when the establishment of the World Trade Organization (WTO) had exposed peasants to the harsh environment of international market forces.

Historical Precedents

Although marginalized and oppressed by other social sectors, such as landlords and urbanites, and dismissed by Karl Marx and Friedrich Engels as lacking revolutionary consciousness, peasants have periodically asserted themselves politically throughout history either single-handedly as a class or in alliance with other deprived groups such as workers. Among some of the most known peasant political actions was the Peasants' Revolt of June 1381 in England when peasants from the English counties of Kent, East Anglia, Somerset, and Yorkshire rose up in protest at their oppression. They were particularly unhappy with the labor demands placed on them by the church and the poll tax that King Richard II had imposed in 1380. Under the leadership of John Ball and Wat Tyler, they destroyed tax records and registers, and burned down buildings housing government records before capturing the Tower of London and compelling King Richard to negotiate with them at Mile End. By late 1381, however, the movement had fizzled out after its leaders were hanged.

Another important peasant uprising in Europe was the Peasants' War in Germany from 1524, when the peasantry and the lower classes of the towns rose up against their feudal overlords protesting growing economic, religious, and judicial oppression under the nobles and clergy. The peasants' demands included the right to choose their own ministers, the abolition of serfdom, the right to fish and kill wild game, the abolition of many kinds of feudal dues, and the guarantee of fair treatment in courts presided over by the feudal nobles. Peasants also played an important role in the French Revolution and in the Russian Revolution in 1917. In Russia, although nominally emancipated by Tsar Alexander I through the Emancipation Manifesto of 1861, which decreed an end to serfdom and permitted former serfs to rent or buy land from the landlords, most Russian peasants, numbering some twenty-three million, were still landless by the turn of the twentieth century, as most land remained in the hands of the rich landlords. Among the grievances that the 1917 Russian revolutionaries were able to exploit, therefore, was the peasants' land hunger. The peasants' reluctance to fully embrace the socialist goals of the Bolshevik Party, particularly under Joseph Stalin, made them targets of Stalin's sustained campaign to destroy them during his collectivization drive of the 1930s, which resulted in the death and exile of thousands of peasants.

In Africa, peasants played a crucial role in resisting colonialism and its prescriptions, as evident in the 1905 Maji Maji uprising in Tanganyika (Tanzania), where German conquest and colonization between 1895 and 1900 provoked a massive uprising when African peasants objected to the taxes, forced labor, and harsh working conditions that came with German colonialism. Although it failed to dislodge German colonialism, the Maji Maji mass uprising forced the German colonial authorities to reform their administration and practices. Another example of armed peasant resistance is the 1896–1897 Chimurenga/Umvukela uprising in Zimbabwe (Southern Rhodesia) where, following British occupation in 1890, African peasants lost their land and cattle to colonial settlers and were subjected to forced labor and an array of taxes designed to force them into the labor market. Similarly, in

Namibia, German colonial rule also provoked armed resistance from the Herero and the Nama between 1904 and 1907. Here, too, colonialism brought with it massive land alienation, loss of sovereignty, loss of cattle to incoming German settlers, numerous taxes, openly racist policies and practices that marginalized Africans, corporal punishment, and other ills associated with European colonialism in Africa. In January 1904, the Herero rose up against German rule. In late 1904, the Nama began a three-year guerrilla campaign against German rule that was only crushed by German forces in 1907.

After the first wave of resistance, peasant protest continued throughout the interwar years and, thereafter, flowered into militant mass nationalism that finally led to the demise of colonialism. In Kenya, Zimbabwe, Angola, Mozambique, and Namibia, peasants participated in the armed struggle that brought about independence in those countries. Their contribution to the struggle for independence notwithstanding, most peasants benefited little from political independence, as postcolonial political and economic systems were dominated by the urban elite who promoted their interests at the expense of the peasant majority. Meanwhile, in Asia, peasants also participated in political movements, the most notable being the struggle of the Red Army organized by the Chinese Communist Party in the late 1920s, which ended with the setting up of the People's Republic of China in 1949.

In attempting to understand why peasants rebel, J. C. Scott contended that peasants tend to rebel when they perceive their traditional moral order or moral economy as being violated. The above examples seem to validate this claim, as they show that peasants have not been merely passive victims of other classes' machinations but have asserted and defended their rights and way of life when they felt that these were threatened.

See also **Anticolonialism; Capitalism; Colonialism; Feudalism, European; Poverty; Revolution; Work.**

BIBLIOGRAPHY

Bryceson, Deborah, Cristóbal Kay, and Jos Mooij, eds. *Disappearing Peasantries? Rural Labour in Africa, Asia, and Latin America.* London: Intermediate Technology Publications, 2000.

Bundy, Colin. *The Rise and Fall of the South African Peasantry.* London: Heinemann, 1979.

Dalton, George. "The Development of Subsistence and Peasant Economies in Africa." *International Social Science Journal* 16 (1964): 378–389.

———. "Economic Theory and Primitive Society." *American Anthropologist* 63 (1961): 1–25.

De Janvry, Alain. *The Agrarian Question and Reformism in Latin America.* Baltimore: Johns Hopkins University Press, 1981.

Emanuel, Arghiri. *Unequal Exchange: A Study of the Imperialism of Trade.* Translated by Brian Pearce. New York: Monthly Review Press, 1972.

Evans, David. "Unequal Exchange and Economic Policies: Some Implications of the New-Ricardian Critique of the Theory of Comparative Advantage." *IDS Bulletin* 6, no. 4 (1975).

Fallers, Lloyd. "Are African Cultivators To Be Called 'Peasants'?" *Current Anthropology* 2, no. 2 (1961): 108–110.

Frank, Andre Gunder. *Capitalism and Underdevelopment in Latin America: Historical Studies of Chile and Brazil.* Harmondsworth, U.K.: Penguin, 1969.

Isaacman, A. "Peasants and Rural Social Protest in Africa." *African Studies Review* 33 (1990): 1–120.

Kincaid, Douglas A. "Peasants into Rebels: Community and Class in Rural El Salvador." In *Constructing Culture and Power in Latin America,* edited by Daniel H. Levine. Ann Arbor: University of Michigan Press, 1993.

Klein, Martin, ed. *Peasants in Africa: Historical and Contemporary Perspectives.* Beverley Hills, Calif.: Sage, 1980.

Landsberger, Henry A. "The Role of Peasant Movements and Revolts in Development." In *Latin American Peasant Movements,* edited by H. A. Landsberger. Ithaca, N.Y.: Cornell University Press, 1969.

———. *Rural Protest: Peasant Movements and Social Change.* London and New York: Macmillan, 1974.

Mafeje, Archie. "Peasants in Sub-Saharan Africa." *African Development* 10, no. 3 (1977): 412–422.

Ranger, Terence. *Peasant Consciousness and Guerrilla War in Zimbabwe: A Comparative Study.* Berkeley: University of California Press, 1985.

Scott, James C. *The Moral Economy of the Peasant: Rebellion and Subsistence in Southeast Asia.* New Haven, Conn.: Yale University Press, 1976.

Shanin, Teodor, ed. *Peasants and Peasant Societies: Selected Readings.* 2nd ed. Oxford and New York: Blackwell, 1987.

Wolf, Eric R. *Peasants.* Englewood Cliffs, N.J.: Prentice-Hall, 1966.

———. *Peasant Wars of the Twentieth Century.* Reprint, Norman: University of Oklahoma, 1999.

Alois Mlambo

PERIODIZATION. Periodization, which became a branch of historical method and the philosophy of history in the twentieth century, has to do with the division of time's arrow—the theoretical timeline of the movement from past to present and future. In Western tradition this speculative aspect of history has its roots in myth and in the Bible—in Hesiod's succession of gold, silver, and bronze ages, for example, and in the periods and generations of the nation of Israel since Creation and the Fall, which long furnished the framework for the Judeo-Christian story of humanity, within which other cultural traditions were synchronized. To these, Christian theologians added ideas of particular ages (*aetates*), especially those before the law, under the law, and under grace, and later the ages of the Father, Son, and Holy Ghost, inspired by Joachim of Fiore (c. 1130 or 1135–1201 or 1202); and such messianic periodization passed also into eastern Europe, especially Poland. In ancient and medieval times, as in the work of St. Augustine of Hippo, Isidore of Seville, and the Venerable Bede, there was much speculation about the natural "ages of man"—three, four, six, or seven of them—which carried the analogy of the trajectory of human life (birth, youth, maturity, degeneration, and death) into the collective experience of nations or of humanity as a whole. Thus in the twentieth century Claude de Seyssel adapted Joachim's conceit of four ages to French history, marking infancy from the legendary Pharamond, youth to the end of the Merovingian dynasty, maturity under the Carolingians, and old age under the Capetian. On the political level the commonest way of describing the structure of history was through the biblically inspired conceit of the succession of four world monarchies—Medes, Persians, Greeks, and Romans, which included the Carolingian refoundation, the "Holy Roman Empire of the German Nation," down to its extinction by Napoleon in 1806. The notion of periods defined through political dominance was continued in the modern European tradition by recognition of Spain, France, England, Germany, and the United States (and the Soviet Union) as leading powers in their respective hours of glory.

For five or more centuries Western history has been dominated by the ancient-medieval-modern periodization, which arose from the conception of a "middle age" between ancient cultural splendor and its modern recovery by the humanists of the fourteenth and fifteenth centuries and by Protestant Reformers reacting to the intellectual "barbarism" of medieval scholasticism. As Petrarch (1304–1374) wrote in one of his sonnets (*Epistolae metricae* 3.33): "Long before my birth time smiled and may again, / for once there was, and yet will be, / more joyful days. / But in this middle age time's dregs / sweep around us. . . . " And "in order to forget my own time, I have constantly striven to place myself in spirit in other ages"— whence the conceit of a rebirth of antiquity and the aforementioned triad of periods. Similar to Petrarch's perspective was the view of Christian humanists and reformers like Martin Bucer (1491–1551), who wrote of "the various periods of the church," from the purity of the primitive church to the centuries of oppression under Antichrists to his own time of a return to the true gospel in the Kingdom of Christ. The seventeenth-century notion of "a middle time between ancient and modern," fixed in the textbook tradition by Conrad Cellarius (1574–1636), and continued into the later period, when the "renaissance of letters" was essentialized and publicized as simply "the Renaissance" by Jules Michelet, Jacob Burckhardt, and their epigones, later became the subject of debate by twentieth-century scholars. In the nineteenth century his convention of three ages was applied by European historians also to India, China, and America.

Periodization focused first on literary and artistic change, but from the eighteenth century it attended also to the material base and, in the work of Adam Smith, Anne Turgot, and Y.-A. Goguet, developed a stadial conception of human history. "The four stages of society," wrote Smith in 1762, "are hunting, pasturage, farming, and commerce." He explained these stages and the "origins of government" with the help of the ancient theory of three constitutional forms: "In the age of hunters there can be very little government of any sort, but what there is will be of the democratical kind. . . . The age of shepherds is that where government properly commences, followed by agriculture, property, and rule by a few rich men, and then by the emergence of chieftains, marking a monarchical government." Arts and manufactures are then cultivated, "as property arrangements and disputes are multiplied and civilized through writing" (pp. 201, 459). By the end of the century this thesis, promoted also by Lord Kames, James Dalrymple, John Millar, Lord James Barrett Monboddo, William Russell, Christoph Meiners, and others had become

commonplace in Britain as well as the continent, and it had a significant impact on the ideas of Karl Marx, Friedrich Engels, and later world historians and textbook writers.

This line of inquiry and interpretation were part of what Dugald Stewart called "conjectural history," and there were many examples of efforts at periodization in this connection, beginning with the old biblical narrative, which Bishop Bossuet (1627–1704) divided into twelve "epochs" from Adam and the Flood down to Charlemagne's empire. A more secular periodization was devised by Giambattista Vico, who posited a succession of three ages—poetic (barbaric), heroic (feudal), and human (civil). Perhaps the most famous system was that of Marie-Jean Caritat, Marquis. de Condorcet (1743–1794), who, like Bossuet a century earlier, divided universal history into "epochs," but ten instead of twelve and following not Biblical chronology but rather a "reasoned" sort of history, analogous to Lockean psychology but projected onto a collective tabula rasa. Condorcet followed the improvement of social skills, technology, and the advancement of learning— from tribal, pastoral, and agricultural society, through the ancient and medieval periods, down to the invention of printing, the rise of modern philosophy, the founding of the French Republic in the age of revolutions, and his own agenda—"reason, toleration, and humanity"—which he presented in the form of prophecy. So he made his transition from the ninth to the tenth epoch, which was devoted to "the future progress of the human mind" and which represented a secular version of the eschatological dimensions of Christian tradition. As humanity approaches perfection, so history becomes futurology, and this heritage was taken up by French Utopians, Socialists, Positivists, Marxists, and not a few historians in the next century, who offer a wide range of ideas of progress.

Marx continued the economic interpretation, making the primary mode of production and class conflict the criteria, and the result was the threefold division of history of (primitive) feudal, capitalist, and proletarian, which inspired research, speculation, and polemic for over a century. For Marx history begins in barbarism and its kinship relations and moves on to the higher form of feudalism, based on control of landed property and serfdom, and then, with the development of trade, commerce, and finance, to a capitalist mode of production and industrialization that, generating proletarian class consciousness, looks forward to a transition to communism. The materialist view of history, inherited by Marx from Enlightenment political economy, was taken up as well by prehistorians, who on the basis of archeological researches distinguished the ages of stone (old and new—paleolithic and neolithic), bronze, and iron, which replaced or gave solid reinforcement to the "four-stage" system of eighteenth-century conjectural history, by connecting it with more precise chronological—that is, stratigraphic— calibrations. In the twentieth century the *Annales* school shifted attention from events and periodization to structures of long duration, and historians of women have questioned the relevance of traditional periodization to the turning points in the history of women.

Systems of periodization continue to appear, but most are variations on these old themes, applying ideas of evolution and "modernization," if not decadence and decline. Of course there are lower levels of periodizing, that is designating periods, whether by centuries, decades, cultural styles (Romantic, Baroque, Gothic, fin de siècle), political domination (Elizabethan, Napoleonic, Victorian, Soviet, Nazi), or individual celebrities (the age of Shakespeare, Bach), and the like. As for the time line for the story of the human species the parallel columns started by Eusebius and filled in by later chroniclers has been vastly expanded by geographical, archaeological, and anthropological discoveries, and periodization in the old sense has been marginalized, although appending a "postmodern" age to a modern one suggests that the impulse still survives.

See also **Historiography; History, Idea of; Periodization of the Arts.**

BIBLIOGRAPHY

Burrow, J. A. *The Ages of Man: A Study in Medieval Writing and Thought.* Oxford: Clarendon, 1986.

Ferguson, Wallace K. *The Renaissance in Historical Thought: Five Centuries of Interpretation.* Boston: Houghton Mifflin, 1948

Koselleck, Reinhart. *Futures Past: On the Semantics of Historical Time.* Translated by Keith Tribe. Cambridge, Mass.: MIT Press, 1895

Meek, Ronald L. *Social Science and the Ignoble Savage.* Cambridge, U.K., and New York: Cambridge University Press, 1976

Smith, Adam. *Lectures on Jurisprudence,* edited by R. L. Meek, D. D. Raphael, and P. G. Stein. Oxford: Clarendon, 1978.

Van der Pot, J. H. J. *De Periodisiering der Geschiedenis.* The Hague: W. P. van Stockum, 1951.

Donald R. Kelley

PERIODIZATION OF THE ARTS.

Notions of boundaries, categories, and periods frame discussions of art and visual culture. The desire to organize visual information and material into clearly defined, manageable units has provided an irresistible impetus for periodization since the emergence of art historical and critical studies in the Renaissance. The application of periods to art and visual culture was extended in the nineteenth and twentieth centuries, when philosophers, historians, and critics of the arts searched for objective ways to explore their world. Their search for objectivity resulted in their conceptualization of periods as a metalanguage rooted in empiricism through which to communicate ideas. Centuries of scholarship have produced a multiplicity of periods underscoring diverse perspectives and serving diverse ends. For some observers, the study of periodization is an exercise in disillusionment. The absence of any single, consistent system of periodization is construed as a symptom of the failure of the intellectual disciplines surrounding the arts. For other observers, the study of periodization is an affirmative endeavor. The existence of alternative schemas for periodization indicates that intellectual discourse about the arts is open to debate, reconsideration, reorganization, and reinterpretation.

What Is a Period?

Art historians and aesthetic philosophers employ a number of ways to group world arts into systems of classification, known as *periods.* Periodization subdivides the continuous flow of artworks through time and space into groupings. Period groupings are defined by the perception that the artworks within them share a single quality or a set of qualities that are significant. Significant qualities can include the formal, stylistic, iconographic, thematic, or other aspects of art. Moreover, period groupings are further defined by the perception that the quality or qualities by which each grouping is defined is distinctive.

Rather than being neutral, periodization organizes art according to critical viewpoints and explanatory hypotheses. The definition of a period reflects judgments about the nature of meaningful connections between artworks and between art and its larger context. The divisions made between periods reveal judgments about the paths of artistic development or moments of artistic disjunction.

Periodization also influences the perception of the audience according to the quality or qualities that are used to group artworks. Qualities in individual artworks that are deemed significant to the period are more visible to viewers, while other qualities in the same artworks tend to be overlooked.

Is it necessary to periodize? Some theorists object to the concept of periods as a contradiction against the very nature of the art. According to this viewpoint, periodization merges the individuality of the artist and the uniqueness of artworks into homogeneity that is inherently the antithesis of creativity. Other theorists object to the utilization of periods as a distortion of the historical process. According to this viewpoint, periodization falsely divides the continuity of history. Critics of periodization argue that history should be written as a continuous chronicle of occurrences and their interrelations and that the principal purpose in writing art history should be to enhance our appreciation of the uniqueness of individual works of art.

One such critic was Roger Fry (1866–1934). While employing period names in his critical writings, Fry applied an overall approach that is essentially timeless. In his analysis of early-twentieth-century art, Fry denied that modern art was the next element in a cycle or sequence of periods. Artworks, in Fry's view, should be construed as the fruitions of independent creative acts, and hence as fundamentally unhistorical. Instead, Fry postulated a great tradition whose representatives can belong to any age.

Despite objections, most art historians and critics have utilized systems of periodization. Heinrich Wölfflin (1864–1945) both recognized that time can be convincingly presented as an uninterrupted flow and asserted that systems of periodization were crucial apparatuses to intellectual understanding. While acknowledging that, at some level, the concept of periods is invented, Wölfflin felt that periodization was necessary for the self-preservation of the scholar. He pragmatically observed that the infinity of images and events was overwhelming unless structured in some way.

The pragmatic justification for periodization offered by Wölfflin has been extended beyond its utility on the personal level. Periodization is defended as a necessity in educational enterprises, including community programs, college and university courses, and media programs. According to this viewpoint, periods offer institutions a useful way to package information into topics and courses; periods offer introductory students a reasonable way to absorb information; and periods offer professional teachers a commonly acknowledged way to define a special area of study by which to justify inclusion in the academy. When education is treated as a businesslike enterprise selling a commodity, the information must be packaged in a manner that meets the expectations of all its consumers to some extent.

There is a widespread consensus that periodization is a convenient and utilitarian schema. At the same time, debate persists over whether periodization is an arbitrary system that segments historical continuity or an embedded structure that reveals historical meaning. Proponents of the second viewpoint argue that, without periodization, observations about artworks would consist of little more than masses of unrelated visual observations and historical incidents. With periodization, it is suggested, not only is visual data collected and organized but relevant comparisons about artworks over time and space can be discerned; the past visual traditions can be described in a meaningful way; and the present imagery can be interpreted as a logical outcome of the past. Periodization is defended as being embedded in history because with it intentions, patterns, and purposes can be revealed, and without it some types of visual analysis and interpretation become impossible.

What types of periods are used? Both extrinsic and intrinsic periods are applied to the visual arts. Extrinsic models that are used to categorize and organize art rely on elements external to the artworks themselves, particularly chronological time and political history. Most extrinsic systems of classification are anchored by firm dates to mark beginning and end points. Therefore, extrinsic period names can be shared between various disciplines (the Neolithic period, for example).

Models of periodization that correspond to specific centuries and decades are among the most conventional and most deeply entrenched systems used to divide Western art into groups. These models result in familiar periods such as the medieval, Renaissance, and modern periods.

Additional factors extrinsic to the artworks themselves can also provide the frameworks through which periods may be defined. Some systems of periodization are determined by political figures and events. These models generate periods based on factors including the reign of particular rulers (as in the Georgian, Victorian, or Edwardian periods) or dynasties (Carolingian, Ottonian, Tudor), revolutions (such as the French and Bolshevik Revolutions), wars (such as World Wars I and II), and other public events. Still other extrinsic models of periodization are grounded in factors such as inventions (for example, the invention of writing as the endpoint of the "prehistoric period" or of metallurgy as the beginning of the "Bronze Age").

Extrinsic periods can become internal factors that influence artists and imbue artworks with particular qualities. Artists in the last decades of the nineteenth century were conscious of their art as fin de siècle, just as artists in the last years of the twentieth century were aware that they were producing art at the end of a millennium. But passages of chronological time and even events in political history are rarely determinants of aesthetic changes or stylistic choices. Since extrinsic periodizations are usually extraneous to the arts, many systems of periodization group artworks on the basis of factors intrinsic to art. Differences in the appearance of artworks, changes in the production of artworks, shifts in the purposes of artworks, and other factors particular to the history of art are frequently cited as more significant bases for the definition of periods. Therefore, some systems of periodization are considered to be intrinsic, rather than extrinsic, in nature. Intrinsic periods can be determined by either single or combined qualities, including skills (such as the discovery of foreshortening, perspective, light and shade in painting), materials (oil painting, ferroconcrete), content (dada, surrealism), and formal choices (abstract expressionism, cubism). Changes in these qualities are often explained as the result of changes in the ideals, interests, beliefs, and/or lifestyles of artists and audiences. Thus intrinsic periods are correlated with sets of values that are distinctive to themselves and assumedly or demonstrably different from sets of values prevailing in previous or successive periods. The most common paradigm used to explain changes in the values considered normative for a period is a gradual process during which ideas are first proposed, then fully realized, later regarded ambivalently, and eventually replaced by newly formulated ideas.

In contrast to extrinsic period names that can be extended to many disciplines, intrinsic period names are usually appropriate to only a few areas or to a single field (such as abstract expressionism or pop art). Although they arise directly from the study of the artworks, intrinsic periods in art history can become complex. The complexity of intrinsic period names is exemplified by the term *Baroque*. *Baroque* initially was a pejorative label for shapes and designs that were regarded as bizarre or extravagant. It was applied as a negative characterization for the art of the seventeenth and first half of the eighteenth centuries that followed after and differed from Renaissance art. It later became identified with a period style admired for distinct values of its own. As a period, the Baroque takes on a spatial character defined by the spread of those characteristics to different regions. This spread is recognized as occurring earlier in some countries and later in others, resulting in chronological dates of the Baroque period that vary according to region. Moreover, the Baroque period is also differently regarded in terms of a period sequence. Sometimes it is regarded as the last major subdivision of the Renaissance and sometimes as reaction against the "classicism" of Renaissance art. But the Baroque also appears in geographical regions in which Renaissance art is absent and therefore is sometimes independent of the paradigmatic style by which it is defined. Finally, the Baroque is sometimes regarded as a set of values that infuses morphological unity into all artworks of the period. This viewpoint stresses putative shared values underlying the artworks of contemporaneous painters such as Georges de La Tour, Nicolas Poussin, and Pietro da Cortona, artists who were born within three years of each other. In contrast, the

Notre Dame Cathedral, c. 1900. Notre Dame was built during the intrinsic High Gothic period in architecture, which art historians note was marked by high, vaulted ceilings, a sense of flowing, uninterrupted space, and an abundance of light. © BETTMANN/CORBIS

Baroque is alternatively regarded as what James Ackerman described as one of several "confluent, overlapping, and intersecting" stylistic trends. This viewpoint stresses the evident dissimilarities in the visual qualities of the same artworks by the same painters.

The complexity of intrinsic period terms is further illustrated by other uses of the term *Baroque. Baroque* is used as a period concept either to imply that a set of ideals or values pervaded an age or to suggest a set of visual elements that were predominant in a given spatiotemporal context. At the same time, *Baroque* is used as a style name that imputes a certain visual quality independent of time and space. Thus the term *Baroque* can be applied to one of the visual arts to designate formal elements that were widespread in the seventeenth century. But it can also be applied to other cultural phenomena, such as the "Baroque" organ, that share a common temporal context but none of the formal elements by which the Baroque was originally characterized. And it can be applied to visual designs produced in distant regions at unrelated dates, such as contemporary Latin American Baroque art.

The complexity of periodization is compounded by the convergence in the practical usage of extrinsic and intrinsic periods. Some extrinsic periods become identified with distinctive cultural and intellectual attitudes (such as "the Roman Empire"), others with a set of shared myths and memories (the 1960s, "the Reagan years"), or still others with a specific aesthetic outlook ("the Victorian era"). Because they can assume attributes of intrinsic periodizations, extrinsic period terms can mistakenly imply that each period automatically had a distinctive and unified visual character and necessarily differed from its predecessor or successor.

Periodization is complicated by at least one more issue, the issue of whether every period is unique or whether periods can be analogous. Meyer Schapiro (1904–1996) argued that periodization must recognize the fixed and unrepeatable order of events. However, intrinsic definitions of periods are based on qualities that are potentially applicable to more than a single period. One strategy that is frequently used in order to preserve the uniqueness of a period employs a dual method of description. A period description can be defined principally in

The Annunciation (c. 1432) **by Fra Angelico. Tempera on panel.** Critic Henrich Wölfflin (1864–1945) composed an analytical study of art that divided the discipline into three phases based on conflicting visual concepts. He applied his model to European art during the Renaissance. PHOTO CREDIT: ERICH LESSING/ART RESOURCE, NY

terms of intrinsic qualities but can also claim that those qualities are fully realized only in the extrinsic context of a specific time and place. As a consequence, for example, many periods might contain art with baroque qualities, but the claim is sometimes made that only one period can be Baroque.

How do periods change? Because periods, with their beginning and ending moments, purportedly chart shifts in visual expression, the use of periodization poses questions about the nature of artistic change over long durations of history. The nature of these changes has been addressed by many writers, among them Alois Riegl (1858–1905). According to Riegl, art always develops under universal laws, and these laws dictate that art always moves in a forward, unremitting progression. Riegl saw the final phase of a period as a necessary stage because it formed the foundation upon which the next phase would rest. Period endings and beginnings, therefore, blurred together almost seamlessly.

The use of periodization also poses questions about the nature of change within shorter spans of time. Periods are generally subdivided into shorter units of time that purport to track internal dynamics of stylistic development. Descriptions of the progression of art through sequential subperiods generally employ metaphors of either organic evolution or physical mechanics.

Metaphors of organic evolution describe change in terms of the biological processes of birth, florescence, decay, and death. An early, and highly influential, art critic who utilized such a metaphor was Giorgio Vasari (1511–1574). In his *Lives of the Artists* (1568), Vasari celebrated the accomplishments of fellow Renaissance artists in an anthology of biographies. While Vasari portrayed the lives of famous painters, sculptors, and architects in a roughly chronological order, he divided the corpus of biographies into three distinctive groups. In the prologues that introduce each section, Vasari reveals the purpose for his divisions.

According to Vasari, the quality of the artists' works paralleled the relative time period in which they worked. Vasari

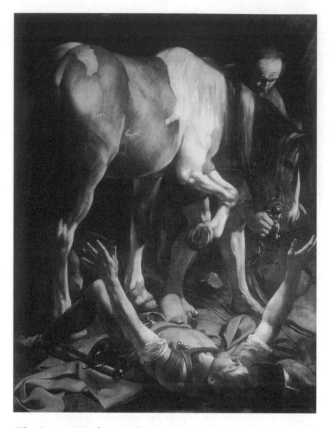

The Conversion of St. Paul (1600–1601) by **Michelangelo Merisi da Caravaggio. Oil on canvas.** During the Renaissance scholars and historians first began to divide works of art into specific units or periods. © ARALDO DE LUCA/CORBIS

placed the earliest Renaissance artists, such as Cimabue (Bencivieni di Pepo) and Giotto di Bondone, into his first group. The works of Piero della Francesca and Andrea Mantegna occupied the second category, while the third, and temporally latest, group included the works of Leonardo da Vinci, Raphael, and Michelangelo. Vasari's primary criterion for judging the quality of the artworks was based on the degree to which the art adhered to nature. Thus Vasari admired those artists, including Cimabue and Giotto, who initiated naturalistic styles of representation. He awarded high acclaim to Piero della Francesca and Mantegna for their increasing facility in accurately depicting nature, but Vasari bestowed the maximum degree of praise upon Leonardo, Michelangelo, and Raphael for not only masterfully portraying nature but also surpassing nature by perfecting its flaws.

Vasari's scheme established a biological model as a way both of dividing periods and of judging the quality of artworks. According to Vasari, internal cycles dictated the progression of art, and these perpetual cycles transcended any individual artist's talents. Vasari equated the artistic change to the human life cycle, a cycle governed by a clock beyond human control. To Vasari, art was born, grew to maturity, and eventually died. The artists who were described by Vasari as surpassing nature itself and as thereby attaining the highest level of artistic mastery were placed in the category of growth and florescence; they

represented the blossoming maturity that would eventually decline with subsequent artists of the seventeenth century.

The biological analogy utilized by Vasari has been adapted and applied to the arts for centuries. The twentieth-century literary critic Northrop Frye (1912–1991) also compared stylistic change to organic growth. Frye attributed the dynamics of change to the necessary process of technical mastery required of artists and craftsmen. He argued that, in any art form involving complex technical knowledge, each generation of practitioners must learn from its elders as it also struggles to introduce innovations. The phase of initial experimentation is followed by another of mature development and a final one of exhaustion and abandonment.

In counterpoint to metaphors of organic evolution, metaphors of physical mechanics have also been applied to periods. These metaphors describe change in terms such as cycles, oscillations, waves, and pendular swings. An influential critic who used a cyclical model was Heinrich Wölfflin. Wölfflin ushered in a phase of artistic inquiry in which formal qualities of art constituted primary data. Using this primary data, Wölfflin devised a new method of analysis that centered on comparing the observable formal qualities. According to Wölfflin, art follows cycles of three phases, early, classic, and baroque. In order to identify these phases, Wölfflin identified five pairs of opposed visual concepts by which art could be analyzed: linear versus painterly; plane versus recession; closed versus open; multiplicity versus unity; and absolute versus relative clarity. Wölfflin applied his comparative scheme of vision to European art of the fifteenth, sixteenth, and seventeenth centuries and associated the early Renaissance, or quattrocento, with the early phase of an artistic cycle, the High Renaissance, or cinquecento, with the classic phase of the cycle, and the Baroque with the late or baroque phase of the same cycle.

Some eighteenth-century aesthetic theorists, including Edmund Burke (1729–1797) and Johann Christoph Friedrich von Schiller (1759–1805), described period changes in terms of a series of pendular swings between polar opposites such as optic and haptic, additive and divisive. In the twentieth century, Martin Warnke (b. 1955) proposed a model of pulsation in which every age of classicism will be followed by an age of anticlassicism.

While pointing out the shortcomings in the pendular and pulsation metaphors, Ernst H. Gombrich (1909–2001) utilized the dialectic of the classical with the nonclassical. To Gombrich, every form of unity represented by classicism is followed by nonclassicism, that is, by disintegration. But Gombrich also consistently stressed the relevance of the changing functions of images in their social context and proposed an ecological metaphor for art. Similarly, Marxist and social historians of art have explained period dynamics in demographic and socioeconomic terms.

Critics have objected to analogies drawn from biology and physical mechanics. In the view of Horst W. Janson (1913–1982), such analogies result from the imposition of similar critical viewpoints rather than from an inherent organic unity.

According to Janson, these analogies amount to no more than pathetic fallacies in which living consciousness is attributed to historical accident. Other skeptics include James Ackerman (b. 1919) and George Kubler (1912–1996). Ackerman refuted the premise that change follows innate dynamics. He considered the process of change to be motivated by the constant incidence of probings into the unknown. Kubler cautioned that changes within a period often result from myriad randomly timed shifts rather than from a patterned progression.

Why should accepted periodizations be challenged? Periodization can be regarded as intellectually restrictive if it is accepted as the inevitable foundation of art history and theory rather than as a trigger for critical analysis and debate. Revisions to accepted periodizations often arise when researchers recover materials that have been ignored or dismissed. Reevaluations of the art corpus that are initiated to redress social injustices and to counter stereotypical imagery lead not only to the expansion of the visual record but also to the reconsideration of periodizations. Revisions to accepted periodizations also arise when new art theories are promulgated or when new visual styles are formulated. Challenges to existing periodizations can consist of modifications within an accepted structure or the proposal of an entirely different scheme. Rival periodizations do not necessarily diminish their utility or discredit the concept of periods. Instead, they may serve to underscore the dynamics of artistic complexity and to express the multiplicity of aesthetic creativeness.

Periodization and Globalization: Mesoamerica as a Case Study

When scholars encountered the artistic traditions outside of the Western world, they applied conventional systems of periodization that had initially been developed to organize the investigation of Western art. One non-Western region to which conventional, formalist periodization was applied was ancient Mesoamerica. Present-day Mexico, Guatemala, Belize, and Honduras constitute a region described as Mesoamerica, based on its position between North and South America and a number of cultural practices and characteristics shared among the many peoples who occupied this area between 1800 B.C.E. and the sixteenth century C.E. When the explorer Hernán Cortés arrived in the New World early in the sixteenth century, he immediately became interested in indigenous artworks fashioned of gold and precious stones. Cortés sent a sampling of Aztec-crafted gold objects back to Spain as evidence of the potential richness of the region, along with a few Aztec books and maps. Despite this early appreciation of indigenous artworks, within a few years of the Spanish arrival, Spanish governors and religious leaders ordered the mass burning of thousands of native books and the destruction of sculptures. Europeans entering the New World saw native artworks as dangerous purveyors of indigenous religious beliefs, as crafts, and as "idols," which were far inferior in quality to known Western art.

It was not until the nineteenth century that scholars took an interest in analyzing the aesthetic qualities of the arts of the ancient Americas. An early system of periodization was designed by Wendell Bennett and Junius Bird to classify the great

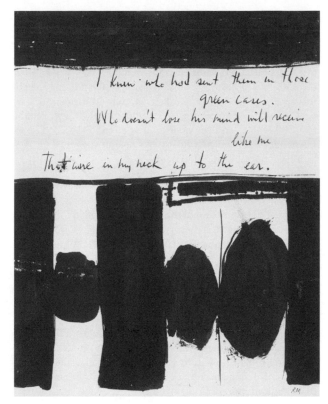

Elegy to the Spanish Republic No. 1 (1948) **by Robert Motherwell. India ink on paper.** Motherwell's Spanish Republic series comprises some one hundred images he painted between 1949 and 1976. The series can be considered representative of the intrinsic period of abstract expressionism. ROBERT MOTHERWELL, "ELEGY TO THE SPANISH REPUBLIC NO. 1," 1948, INDIA INK ON PAPER, DIGITAL IMAGE © THE MUSEUM OF MODERN ART/LICENSED BY SCALA/ART RESOURCE, NY; ART © DEDALUS FOUNDATION, INC./LICENSED BY VAGA, NEW YORK, NY

variety of artifacts from the central Andean region of South America. Bennett and Bird consciously addressed theoretical issues involved with the creation and application of periods in artistic traditions outside Western, literate society. They noted that the choice of features by which a culture was identified was in some respects an arbitrary outcome of historical preservation and archaeological recovery. They further recognized that the problem of determining general periods was compounded by the absence of absolute dates and by the use of differing relative systems of dating employed in local regions. These relative systems included dating by the use of stratigraphy, surface collections of ceramics, sampling pits, and trade pieces. In addition, Bennett and Bird realized that a single system of periodization risked obscuring regional cultural variation within the central andean region.

Nonetheless, Bennett and Bird argued for the definition of overall cultural horizons as a means to permit the central Andes to be treated as a single unit and to be compared in its cultural developments and achievements with other parts of the world. The system designed by Bennett and Bird simplified relative chronologies of different regions named after local sites into cultural horizons named by terms that cross-cut local terminology. Their system of periodization employed accessible period names, in part because period names were based on Western perceptions of indigenous economic and political organization. Those periods were termed Early Farmers (c. 2500–1200 B.C.E.) Cultist (c. 1200–400 B.C.E.), Experimenter (c. 400–1st C. B.C.E.), Master Craftsman (c. 1st c. C.E.–900), Expansionist (c. 900–1200), City Builder (c. 1200–1450), and Imperialist (after c. 1450–1532). The sequencing of periods in a linear progression suggested an evolutionary model of development.

The principles by which the Andean system of periodization was created were subsequently adapted for use in Mesoamerica. The occupation of the region was divided into Archaic (prior to 1500 B.C.E.), Formative (c. 1500 B.C.E.–250 C.E.), Classic (250–900), and Postclassic (after 900). While this periodization utilized less descriptive names, it was nonetheless based on the same Western perceptions of indigenous economic and political organization as the Andean scheme. Thus Archaic corresponded to Cultist, Formative to Experimenter, Classic to Master Craftsman, and Postclassic to Expansionist, City Builder, and Imperialist. Similarly to the Andean scheme, this periodization suggested an evolutionary model of developmental progression in its linear serialization while the subdivision of periods into phases echoed Vasari's organic model of biological cycles.

Still another Western model of periodization was also applied to Mesoamerica. The artworks created by the ancient Maya particularly interested Western scholars, and Maya artworks and style became a measuring stick against which all Mesoamerican artistic traditions were judged. The Maya occupied much of the eastern portions of Mesoamerica. Between 250 and 900 C.E. they constructed numerous large cities, with elaborate palace complexes, soaring temples, and vast plaza systems. They lavished their built environments with hieroglyphic inscriptions, paintings, and large-scale sculpture. The great architectural achievements evident in ancient Maya cities, combined with a style of sculpture that portrayed the human subject in an especially naturalistic manner, impressed Western viewers, who saw affinities between Classic Maya art and the celebrated Greek art of the Classic period (480–323 B.C.E.).

Like Greek sculpture during the Classic period, Maya art created between 250 and 900 seemed to exhibit the highest degree of naturalism and idealization, as though the indigenous artists looked to nature for their models and fused this observation with native ideals. Like the Classic period in Greece, the Classic period for the Maya was seen as the pinnacle of civilization—a time in which the Maya excelled in the realm of sciences, especially astronomy, and a time when Maya scribes recorded temporal and mythical histories using sophisticated calendrical systems. Western scholars also saw the Classic period as a moment in which theocratic rulers, guided by piety, religion, and logic, governed the activities of the Maya cities (an assumption that has subsequently been disproved in both the cases of Classic Greek and Classic Maya periods). With the term *classic* denoting a period of brilliance and the pinnacle of Greek cultural production, *classic* was similarly employed to describe the apparent florescence of the Maya world between the years 250 and 900 C.E.

The periodization of Maya art thereby grafted Western perceptions of qualities described as "classical" or "less than classical" into a system of periods originally based on Western principles of economic and political organization. The resultant schema resembles the pendular models of periodization based on physical mechanics and parallels Gombrich's theory of periodization and style. In the literature on Maya art, the time period that chronologically preceded the Classic period frequently was termed the Preclassic rather than the Formative. The choice of this term suggested that the period represented a stage of infancy that would eventually mature and blossom into the splendor of the Classic. In examining the artworks created after the Classic period, scholars observed that artists no longer lavished monuments with lengthy hieroglyphic texts; artists no longer focused their attention on building large-scale architecture; and sculptors no longer placed priority in inscribing each monument with the most sophisticated systems of calendrical notation. In addition, Maya artists no longer imbued the human subject with the elements of naturalism and idealism that they had in the past. Thus the period known as the Postclassic was seen as a period of decline and decay.

Far-reaching consequences emerged as a result of the assumptions intrinsic to the system used for periodizing Mesoamerican art. These assumptions implicate the scholarly, economic, and social spheres that surround the artworks themselves. For decades, Maya art created during the Classic period received the most acclaim. Acclaim translated into importance, and Classic period art drew greater numbers of scholars than Preclassic and Postclassic art.

The desire to celebrate aesthetic qualities deemed Classical has promulgated a skewed picture of Mesoamerican art. Far greater financial support is directed, especially by North American and European institutions, toward the preservation, restoration, and exhibition of Classic period Maya art than to any other Mesoamerican artistic tradition. By extension, a distorted concept of Mesoamerican culture has also resulted. Far more archaeological investigations are proposed and funded for the purpose of studying Classic period Maya sites than any other set of Mesoamerican sites. As a result, both art historical and archaeological scholarship presents a lopsided view of Mesoamerica in which the importance of the Classic Maya period is overestimated.

By the turn of the twenty-first century scholars attempted to eliminate the attendant value judgment from conventional models of periodization by replacing value-laden terms with more neutral terms. The period named "Formative," for example, gained popularity over the period name "Preclassic." In addition, scholars strove to present the names of periods simply as temporal boundaries without attached notions of quality or sophistication.

Technology and periods in Mesoamerica. Technologies that had been unavailable in the formulation of early models of periodization now allow for the discussion of artworks based solely on time. Radiocarbon dating, for example, provides a simple and reliable way to date ancient artifacts (if they contain organic matter), by measuring the residue of radiocarbon. Another useful dating method termed obsidian hydration is especially useful since Mesoamerican peoples frequently fashioned local obsidian into tools and artworks. Thermoluminescence, a more recently discovered dating technique, is employed to date rocks, minerals, and pottery. These recently developed methods allow investigators the option to remove artworks from previously codified systems of periodization, to reinterpret past models, and to define periods in new ways.

Western and indigenous traditions of time and periodization.

Western-imposed modes of periodization often clash with indigenous traditions of dividing time and indigenous approaches to conceptualizing their material past. Among the ancient Maya, time was seen not as a single linear progression but as a series of unremitting cycles. Divided into subcycles and almanacs, native concepts of temporality dictate that time itself possesses distinctive qualities and purposes. Unlike some Western theories of time, which operate outside the boundaries of intrinsic nature, the Maya situated time as an entity that acts upon and shapes the content that it frames.

Feminism and Periodization

Voiced principally by women, radically new questions about artists and artistic canons emerged during the late 1960s and early 1970s. Feminist artists and writers, particularly Linda Nochlin (b. 1931), vigorously probed the history of art in order to understand why female artists were not celebrated in Western history and in contemporary culture. Deep within the internal structures of the discipline itself, feminist writers located inherently exclusionary foundations. One exclusionary strategy has been identified as the construction of definitions of art. Women traditionally created artworks that were often made, used, and exhibited within their homes. Media conventionally seen as "crafts," such as embroidery, miniature painting, and ceramic production and decoration, constitute some examples of artistic production in which women historically participated. Conformist notions of "high art" and canons disregarded artworks created by women and subsequently excluded such art from the majority of periodization models (Alois Riegl is a notable exception who regarded crafts as equally important as figural arts). In the 1960s and 1970s women identified this exclusion and fought to unravel the system.

While designers of periodization paradigms ignored women, the trajectory of feminism itself gradually became divided into periods. Rather than hinging on factors external to feminism, feminist ideologies operated as the content around which periods were framed. Known as "waves," these periods became incorporated into discussions of the differing interests within feminism, which loosely correlate with periods of time. Writers now place some of the earliest feminists in the first wave of feminism, which began in the late nineteenth and early twentieth centuries, when women fought for legal rights, including suffrage. Influential women such as Simone de Beauvoir and Susan B. Anthony have been placed within the first period or wave.

During the 1960s and 1970s, women concentrated on reviving the efforts and trajectories of issues explored by feminists during feminism's first wave. This new movement, now known as second-wave feminism, strove to elevate the position of women, especially in professional contexts. Women of this period wanted to "have it all," including equal access to privileges and positions along with equal compensation. Other paramount concerns for second-wave feminists included rights and control over their bodies. Other trajectories of feminism within the second wave focused on the difference between male and female in terms of sex and different reactions to gender. Cultural feminism and radical feminism, for example, held opposing views about the goal of feminism. The radical view argued for the cultural reconstruction of gender, reducing gender differences of males and females. Cultural feminism, on the other hand, emphasized the need to liberate, valorize, and preserve female difference as an absolute category.

The second wave of feminism bears particular relevance to periodization of the arts because it is within this period that Nochlin and others began to deconstruct the cultural paradigms that omitted women artists from the canon of masters. Second-wave feminist artists include Judy Chicago, Audrey Flack, and Miriam Schapiro, all of whom subverted notions of artistic canons by creating artworks that foreground the feminine through subjects and techniques that reference the artistic traditions of women and femininity itself.

Beginning in the 1980s and 1990s a new wave of feminism took shape and aimed at probing and revising some of the aspects of second-wave feminism. The third wave of feminism recognized exclusionary tendencies that characterized the interests of second-wave agendas and doctrine. Blurring the loose boundaries that separate the second and third waves, some feminists from the second wave shifted their interest and entered the third. Third-wave feminists recognized that the second wave had advocated social change primarily directed to the rights of white, straight, middle-class women. Third-wave feminism deemphasized the role played by sexual difference and explored the social structures, material and economic, that oppressed both women and men. As a result gender was framed in more neutral terms and as a product of enculturation rather than an innate quality.

Third-wave feminism's multiplicity of foci and fluid boundaries oftentimes incite criticism. This strategy simultaneously generates power to sustain the movement. By their presence in popular media, participation in politics, and commitment to academic discourse and critique, proponents engage feminism with other discursive modes. Because they share the quality of persistent cultural subversiveness, second-wave artists such as Judy Chicago and Audrey Flack are embraced by new feminist artists. With its roots broadly anchored in cultural dialogues, third-wave feminism addresses immediate issues and influences that affect far-ranging audiences.

Conclusion

No single system of periodization has emerged. Some observers regard the existence of multiple systems based on varying criteria as a symptom of the arbitrariness and illogicality of period schemes, while others interpret the same multiplicity as a positive result of the study of history. In this view, each periodization offers a possible strategy for the study of art, which encompasses widely diverse activities, including writing surveys, artistic biographies, catalogues raisonnés, iconographic analyses, or cross-cultural overviews. If the definition of periods and their temporal limits can be regarded as provisional strategies rather than objective reality, then the choice of periodization schema can be determined by the problem at hand. Different systems of periodization can be regarded as beneficial rather than chaotic when they permit the same masses of data to be organized by different principles and to yield different insights. Thus the ongoing debate about periodization contributes to the continuing vitality of the disciplines related to the visual arts.

See also **Aesthetics; Classicism; Communication of Ideas; Historiography; Impressionism; Mechanical Philosophy; Modernism; Organicism; Renaissance.**

BIBLIOGRAPHY

Ackerman, James S. "Style." In *Problems in Aesthetics: An Introductory Book of Readings,* edited by Morris Weitz, 308–324. 2nd ed. New York: Macmillan, 1970.

Bennett, Wendell C., and Junius B. Bird. *Andean Culture History.* New York: Natural History Press, 1964.

Buszek, Maria Elena. "Waving not Drowning: Thinking about Third-Wave Feminism in the U.S." *Make: The Magazine of Women's Art,* no. 86 (December 1999–February 2000): 39–40.

Davis, Whitney. "Periodization." In *The Dictionary of Art,* edited by Jane Turner. Vol. 24. London and New York: Grove's Dictionaries, 1996.

Dolan, Jill. *The Feminist Spectator as Critic.* Ann Arbor: University of Michigan Press, 1988.

Fernie, Eric, ed. *Art History and Its Methods.* London: Phaidon, 1995.

Focillon, Henri. *The Life of Forms in Art.* Translated by George Kubler. New York: Zone Books, 1992.

Fogle, French Rowe. *A Critical Study of William Drummond of Hawthornden.* New York: King's Crown Press, 1952.

Fry, Roger. *Vision and Design.* London: Chatto and Windus, 1920. Reprint, London: Oxford University Press, 1947.

Frye, Northrop. *Anatomy of Criticism: Four Essays.* Princeton, N.J.: Princeton University Press, 1957.

Gallie, W. B. *Philosophy and the Historical Understanding.* 2nd ed. New York: Schocken, 1968.

Gombrich, E. H. *Norm and Form: Studies in the Art of the Renaissance.* 4th ed. Oxford: Phaidon, 1985.

———. "Style." In *International Encyclopedia of the Social Sciences,* edited by David L. Sills. Vol. 15. New York: Macmillan and Free Press, 1968

Hart, Joan Goldhammer. *Heinrich Wölfflin: An Intellectual Biography.* Ph.D. diss., University of California at Berkeley, 1981.

Kubler, George. *The Shape of Time: Remarks on the History of Things.* New Haven, Conn.: Yale University Press, 1962.

———. *Studies in Ancient American and European Art: The Collected Essays of George Kubler.* Edited by Thomas F. Reese. New Haven, Conn.: Yale University Press, 1985.

Miller, Mary Ellen. *The Art of Mesoamerica.* 3rd ed. London and New York: Thames and Hudson, 2001.

Minor, Vernon Hyde. *Art History's History.* 2nd ed. Upper Saddle River, N.J.: Prentice Hall, 2001.

Nochlin, Linda. *Women, Art, and Power: And Other Essays.* New York: Harper and Row, 1988.

Podro, Michael. *The Critical Historians of Art.* New Haven, Conn.: Yale University Press, 1982.

Riegl, Alois. *Late Roman Art Industry.* Translated and annotated by Rolf Winkes. Rome: Giorgio Bretschneider, 1985.

Schapiro, Meyer, H. W. Janson, and E. H. Gombrich. "Criteria of Periodization in the History of European Art." *New Literary History* 1, no. 2 (winter 1970): 113–125.

Sparshott, F. E. "Notes on the Articulation of Time." *New Literary History* 1, no. 2 (winter 1970): 311–334.

Vasari, Giorgio. *Lives of the Artists.* Translated by Julia Conaway Bondanella and Peter Bondanella. Oxford and New York: Oxford University Press, 1991.

Warnke, Martin. *Political Landscape: The Art History of Nature.* Cambridge, Mass.: Harvard University Press, 1995.

Wölfflin, Heinrich. *Principles of Art History: The Problem of the Development of Style in Later Art.* Translated by M. D. Hottinger. 7th ed. New York: Dover, 1940.

———. *Renaissance and Baroque.* Translated by Kathrin Simon. Ithaca, N.Y.: Cornell University Press, 1964.

Kaylee Spencer-Ahrens
Linnea Wren

PERSON, IDEA OF THE. Western European ideas about the person have long centered on the duality between body and soul (in religious discourse) or between body and mind (in the domains of philosophy and psychology). Consequently, early anthropological interest in non-European ideas of the person tended to mirror such deep-seated European conceptualizations, focusing on the origins of the concept of the soul.

The preoccupation of evolutionary Victorian anthropologists with religion focused on the question of its origins. By and large, these thinkers were apostles of secularism and science, committed to the notion that religion and its associated ideas (the soul included) were outdated, survivals from human prehistory. Religion was a repository of conceptions, which, while not entirely irrational in and of themselves, were fallacious or erroneous. In particular, Edward Tylor, in his book *Primitive Culture* (1871), saw in the idea of the soul the most ancient and fundamental of all religious beliefs, the key to understanding the subsequent development—but also the ultimate irrelevance—of religious ideas:

It seems as though thinking men, as yet at a low level of culture, were deeply impressed by two groups of biological problems. In the first place, what is it that makes the difference between a living body and a dead one; what causes waking, sleep, trance, disease, death: In the second place, what are those human shapes which appear in dreams and visions? Looking at these two groups of phenomena, the ancient savage philosophers probably made their first step by the obvious inference that every man has two things belonging to him, namely, a life and a phantom. These two are evidently in close connexion with the body, the life as enabling it to feel and think and act, the phantom as being its image or second self; both, also, are perceived to be things separable from the body, the live as able to go away and leave it insensible or dead, the phantom as appearing to people at a distance from it. The second step would seem also easy for savages to make, seeing how extremely difficult civilized men have found it to unmake. It is merely to combine the life and the phantom. As both belong to the body, why should they not also belong to one another, and be manifestations of one and the same soul? (pp. 12–13)

In Tylor's scheme, the idea of the soul constituted the core of the most primitive form of religion, Animism, both in the form of the worship of the souls of departed ancestors and in the idea that inanimate objects—trees, rocks, bodies of water—also possessed souls and could be worshiped in their own right.

Durkheim's Critique

Émile Durkheim's (1858–1917) monumental treatise of *The Elementary Form of Religious Life* (1912) begins with the bold assertion that "a human institution cannot rest upon error and falsehood . . . when I approach the study of primitive religions, it is with the certainty that they are grounded in and express the real" (p. 2). Durkheim definitely had Tylor in mind when he wrote these lines, and devoted an entire chapter of the book to a refutation of Tylor's theories. Specifically, he argued that Tylor's account of the generation of ideas of the double and the soul from primitive explanations of dreams was radically circular. Rather, such notions presupposed the very ideas whose origins they were supposed to explain. For Durkheim, ideas such as the soul, ancestor spirits, totems, or gods could not be derived from the experience, much less the speculations, of individuals. Rather, they were intrinsically social phenomena.

Nonetheless, Durkheim concurred with Tylor that the idea of the soul was fundamental to religion: "Just as there is no known society without religion, there is no religion, however crudely organized, in which we do not find a system of collective representations dealing with the soul—its origin and destiny" (p. 242). Unlike Tylor, who drew for examples for his theories from around the globe and throughout history, Durkheim's examination of primitive religion focused on ethnographic accounts from Australia, and his discussion of the idea of the soul was correspondingly centered on Australian examples. According to native Australians, there exists a limited stock of souls. Each individual is a reincarnation of an ancestor, and all people are ultimately reincarnations of the original totemic *alcheringa* ancestors, powerful beings who existed in dreamtime and whose natures were merged with those of totemic species. For Durkheim, these representations addressed the critical problem of the relationship of society to the individual. The ancestral souls embodied the fundamental reality of society of which the individual was a particular manifestation.

Within the context of his discussion of the soul, Durkheim quietly introduced the idea of the person. The person, Durkheim suggested, represents the conjunction of an impersonal and personal principle, the soul and the body. The first, impersonal, derives from "the spiritual principle that serves as the soul of the collectivity . . . the very substance of which

individual souls are made" (p. 273), whereas the body, by situating this impersonal principle in a specific location in space and time, serves as the differentiating element. Hence, "individuation is not the essential characteristic of the person. A person is not only a singular subject that is distinguished from all the others. It is, in addition and most of all, a being to which a relative autonomy is imputed in relation to the milieu with which it interacts most directly" (p. 274).

The idea of the person, for Durkheim, squarely embodied the relationship between the individual and society at the very core of his approach to sociological theory. While it still reflected European dualistic thinking about body and soul, reading his own society's dichotomies into the thought of native Australians, it opened the way to new, less ethnocentric ways of understanding non-European conceptions of the person.

Mauss: The Person as "A Category of the Human Mind"

In a seminal lecture, which he delivered (in French) to a British audience in 1938, Durkheim's nephew, Marcel Mauss (1872–1950), was the first to bring the ideal of the person to center stage. Like Durkheim, he saw in the religious categories of so-called primitive societies a key to the understanding of modern European ideas. Citing examples from Australian societies as well as from Native Americans—Zuñi, Kwakiutl, Winnebago—he stressed the importance of names for the establishment of personhood. Names as such were not necessarily the hallmark of the individual, but rather of a persona, a fixed role or position within a society. Thus, a clan or other similar group might possess a finite stock of names. The name typically represented, not only membership in a group but also a specific position within it, and so individuals might change names within the course of their lives. Such names, Mauss suggested, were akin to masks—another phenomenon he related to ideas of personhood. The theatrical metaphor was intrinsic to Mauss's argument. In relatively "primitive" societies, there were a relatively fixed number of "roles." Personhood in such instances reflected the individual's place within such a fixed scheme.

In his essay, Mauss contrasted this relatively fixed conception of personhood in non-European societies with a dynamic vision of the changing idea of personhood in Western Europe, through Greek philosophy, Roman law, Christian theology, and ultimately the Enlightenment. The end result of this evolution was a conception of personhood in terms of individual consciousness rather than as the embodiment of set social relationships. These ideas have been rejected by the overwhelming majority of anthropologists who reject any teleological dichotomy between European societies as essentially dynamic and non-European ones as static. However, if this part of Mauss's argument has fallen by the wayside, his insistence that conceptions of the person are culturally and historically constituted constantly subject to change provided the foundation for most subsequent anthropological writing on the subject.

The Anthropology of the Person since Mauss

While Mauss's essay provided inspiration to both French and British anthropologists, the implications of his work were developed in substantially different ways by anthropologists belonging to different national schools. At the same time, American anthropologists were to approach the problem from a very different starting point. In all three cases, concepts of the person were explored in the context of extensive fieldwork in specific cultures. Rather than generalizing from the vantage point of European categories, taken as the end point of a process of evolution, anthropologists grappled with non-European conceptualizations firsthand.

Griaule and the French school.
Marcel Griaule's work among the Dogon of modern Mali (then French Sudan) was to mark the French approach for at least a generation afterward. For Griaule, the complex esoteric cosmology of the Dogon, as revealed to him by his key informant, Ogotemmeli, constituted an intricate and sophisticated philosophical system, an alternative way of thought in no way inferior to European equivalents. Dogon ideas of the person are consequently one element of this entire system. Crucial to these ideas is the principle of the ideal duality of all creatures. In the original acts of creation, only the Creator's firstborn—the jackal—was created single, and it is for this reason that the jackal is the quintessential trickster and embodiment of disorder, but also the agent through whom truth is revealed to the diviner. After the jackal, a couple, the Nommo, were born: demiurges who represent the ideal dual order. Twins consequently represent the ideal birth, and human twins become the object of a cult as soon as they are born. Even ordinary humans have double souls—*kinndou-kinndou*—one for each gender. The female principle resides in the man's foreskin, the male in the woman's clitoris; rites of circumcision and excision are consequently required at adolescence to transform ambivalently gendered children into fully male or female adults. In short, for Griaule, the Dogon myth of creation contained the key to their conceptions of personhood and of the world in general.

British social anthropology.
The British school of social anthropology, also profoundly influenced by the work of Durkheim and Mauss, adopted a less abstract and more sociological approach to the study of ideas of the person. E. E. Evans-Pritchard's pioneering study of *Witchcraft, Oracles and Magic among the Azande* (1937), published a year before Mauss's lecture, did not explicitly mention the concept of the person, but his explanation of Azande notions of witchcraft nonetheless represented a landmark in the ethnographic exploration of personhood. Witchcraft is a common explanation of misfortune among the Azande, and is caused by a grudge or ill will on the part of a witch. However, not all people are witches. Witches are born with innate witchcraft substance, inherited by boys from their fathers and girls from their mothers. It operates through *mbisimu mangu,* the soul of witchcraft, which travels from the body of the witch to the body of the victim, although the witch himself may not be conscious of the harm he is perpetrating. However, Evans-Pritchard was not simply concerned with the ideology of witchcraft in itself, but in the way in which these ideas underpinned the everyday actions of Azande, so that they understood and reacted to the ordinary misfortunes of everyday life through consulting oracles, attempting to cool the anger of witches, and ultimately pursuing vengeance when witchcraft proved fatal.

In an essay titled "On the Concept of the Person among the Tallensi" (1973), Meyer Fortes explicitly developed Mauss's insights with specific reference to a particular West African culture:

> observance of prohibitions and injunctions relating to the killing and eating of animals, to distinctions of dress, to speech and etiquette, to a wide range of ritual norms, to the jural regulations concerning marriage, property, office, inheritance and succession, play a key part in the identification of persons. Persons are kept aware of who they are and where they fit into society by criteria of age, sex, and descent, and by other indices of status, through acting in accordance with these norms. By these actions and forms of conduct they, at the same time, show to others who they are and where they fit into society. (p. 282)

Seen in this light, an individual's birth is merely the first step in the process of turning him or her into a full person, a process which only ends with death, when, as an ancestor, one may eventually become a full person. Tallensi personhood is thus not a feature of the individual per se, but of the individual's interaction with society as a whole. For Fortes as for Evans-Pritchard, this process of interaction was played out in the miniature crises of everyday life.

American anthropology and the problem of personality.
During the first half of the twentieth century, anthropologists in the United States were far less influenced by the theories of Durkheim and Mauss than by the work of Sigmund Freud (1856–1939). Rather than evincing interest in "the person" as a category of thought, they focused on the formation of the individual personality in different cultures. Ruth Benedict's *Patterns of Culture* (1934) is the most famous example of this approach. For Benedict, each culture has its ethos, its style, which characterizes its art, its ritual, its ideology, the emotional tenor of social relationships, and so on. Individual children are raised in conformity with this ethos, internalizing patterns of feeling as well as of behaving. Those with little natural aptitude for the predominant ethos are deviants, though deviance in one culture can well be normality in another. Moreover, cultures may also have established deviant roles, such as the *berdache* in Native North America, a person who was born biologically male but who dressed as a woman, adopted women's occupations, and sometimes even married another man.

In the 1960s, Clifford Geertz attempted a synthesis between the American emphasis on personality and Mauss's conception of the person, most notably in his essay, "Person, Time, and Conduct in Bali" (1966). Geertz focused on those aspects of Balinese culture—names and titles—central to Mauss's formulation of the development of the idea of personhood. However, for Geertz, these component features of the Balinese conception of personhood were expressions of an overall Balinese ethos. Children are given a personal name, but this is generally a nonsense term and rarely used to address or refer to them. Children are more generally known by standard birth order names, and adults (except for childless adults, who in some sense remain socially children themselves) by tekonyms—"father (or mother) of so-and-so (their first child)." Balinese status titles as well as names serve

> to stress and strengthen the standardization, idealization, and generalization implicit in the relation between individuals whose main connection consists in the accident of their being alive at the same time and to mute or gloss over those implicit in the relation between consociates, men intimately involved in one another's biographies, or between predecessors and successors, men who stand to one another as blind testator and unwilling heir. (Geertz, pp. 389–390)

In short, the Balinese concept of the person, in keeping with the Balinese ethos, is depersonalizing, at least from a European point of view.

These different approaches to the study of the idea of the person, whether French, British, or American, have convincingly demonstrated that there is no single "primitive" conception of personhood, much less of "the soul." The different cultural constructions of "personhood" around the globe cannot be interpreted in terms of narratives of the progressive emergence, either of rationality or of individuality, in Europe as opposed to the rest of the world, as nineteenth and early twentieth century theorists attempted to argue.

See also **Identity: Identity of Persons; Identity: Personal and Social Identity; Personhood in African Thought; Religion; Sociability in African Thought; Society.**

BIBLIOGRAPHY
Benedict, Ruth. *Patterns of Culture.* Boston: Houghton Mifflin Company, 1934.
Carrithers, Michael, Steven Collins, and Steven Lukes, eds. *The Category of the Person: Anthropology, Philosophy, History.* Cambridge, U.K.: Cambridge University Press, 1985.
Durkheim, Emile. *The Elementary Forms of Religious Life,* Translated by Karen Fields. New York: The Free Press, 1995.
Evans-Pritchard, E. E. *Witchcraft, Oracles and Magic among the Azande.* London: Oxford University Press, 1937.
Fortes, Meyer. "On the Concept of the Person among the Tallensi." In *La Notion de Personne en Afrique Noire.* Paris: Colloques Internationaux du Centre National de la Recherche Scientifique, No. 544, 1973. Reprinted in his *Religion, Morality and the Person: Essays on Tallensi Religion,* edited with an introduction by Jack Goody, 247–286. Cambridge, U.K.: Cambridge University Press, 1987.
Geertz, Clifford. *Person, Time, and Conduct in Bali: An Essay in Cultural Analysis.* Yale Southeast Asia Program, Cultural Report Series 14, 1966. Reprinted in his *The Interpretation of Cultures,* 360–411. New York: Basic Books, 1973.
Griaule, Marcel. *Conversations with Ogotemelli: An Introduction to Dogon Religious Ideas.* London and New York: Oxford University Press for International African Institute, 1970.
Mauss, Marcel. "A Category of the Human Mind: The Notion of Person; the Notion of Self." Translated by W.D. Halls. In *The Category of the Person: Anthropology, Philosophy, History,* edited

by Michael Carrithers, Steven Collins, and Steven Lukes, 1–25. Cambridge, U.K.: Cambridge University Press, 1985.
Tylor, Sir Edward Burnett. *Primitive Culture,* London: John Murray, 1871. Reprinted in 2 vols. as *The Origins of Culture* and *Religion in Primitive Culture.* New York: Harper and Brothers, 1958.

Robert Launay

PERSONHOOD IN AFRICAN THOUGHT.

What is a person? Two basic types of considerations are apparent in African answers to this question. The first is ontological, the second ethical. Ontologically a person is a combination of a physical constituent, namely the body and a set of two or in some cases three constituents of a rarefied character requiring careful elucidation.

The nonbodily constituent on which all the accounts of personhood seem agreed is what might be called the life principle. This is thought of as an entity whose presence in the body means life and its absence death. The Akans call it *okra,* the Yoruba *emi,* and the Nuer, roughly, *yiegh.* By common agreement it derives directly from God himself. Indeed the Akans are explicit that it is a speck of the divine substance. As metaphorically and often literally understood, this entity or an ontologically analogous one goes before God to take leave of him before coming to the world to be born of man and woman. It is at this meeting that God apportions the prospective person's destiny.

The Yoruba account of this meeting is the most dramatic of all. For them, unlike the Akans, it is not the life-giving constituent, like the Akan *okra* or Yoruba *emi,* but another nonbodily entity called the *ori-inu* that receives the apportioned destiny. It stands before God and proposes a destiny, which God either confirms or refashions. Or it kneels before God and has a destiny affixed to it. Either way, the apportionment is ultimately God's own. Moreover the destiny, which is the outline of one's earthly career, is doubly sealed, for on its way down to the world the individual encounters God's gatekeeper, who typically asks, "Where are you going? . . . What are you going to do?" To which the individual replies with a recitation of the destiny just assigned. The gatekeeper then says *"To,"* which Bolaji Idowu translates as "It is sealed." Idowu comments, "And so the person passes into the world with his destiny doubly sealed" (p. 174).

This doctrine is widely received, though not universal, in Africa. Okot p'Bitek (chap. 9) argues that the Central Luo do not have a place in their worldview for a predetermined destiny. Wherever entertained, however, it is significant as indicating the moral uniqueness of every human individual, but it is also the source of some of the deepest problems at the intersection of morals and metaphysics. The African mind has been sorely challenged to fathom how an individual can be held responsible for his or her conduct if what he or she does is in fulfillment of a divine plan. Furthermore, even though it is generally supposed that the destiny assigned by God is unalterable, various African peoples are known to seek the help of "specialists" to rectify a dreary destiny.

Some writers on African thought, such as Idowu, content themselves with the observation that "the paradox involved in this two-sided conception is accepted by the Yoruba without question" (p. 183). Kofi Opoku writes similarly with regard to the Akans. It is, however, possible that the apparent inconsistency, euphemistically described by Idowu as a "two-sided conception," is due to the fact that what one is dealing with is the confluence of a variety of unnamed sources amalgamated into a strand of the oral tradition. Kwame Gyekye (1995) and Kwasi Wiredu (1996) offer further suggestions. But the priority here is to elucidate the ontological character of the nonbodily components of personhood. In addition to those already noted, the Akans, for example, speak of *sunsum,* which may be rendered as that which is responsible for an individual's personal presence. This seems to be thought of as a kind of entity. The *tali* of the Lugbara seems to be a similar conception.

In general the nonbodily constituents of personhood, as conceived by African peoples, number at least two. How do they compare, ontologically speaking, with the analysis of personhood best known in Western philosophy, namely that a person consists of body, mind, and soul, with the soul usually, as in René Descartes, identified with the mind? In both the African and the Western conceptions, all the items named are regarded as entities. But the similarity ends there. The elements of the African inventory of human personality are conceived as material, save only that they are supposed to be exempt from the ordinary laws of optics and dynamics. If such entities are, for convenience, called quasi-material, then the contrast might be expressed as follows. The nonbodily components are, as a rule, conceived as quasi-material in Africa, while among thinkers of a Cartesian predilection they are thought of as spiritual, in the sense of being immaterial, nonextended.

The quasi-material orientation of African thought is especially apparent in notions of the afterlife, which are often heavily laden with material imagery. On the present interpretation, this marks a fundamental difference between the many African and Western systems of ontology. Whereas the categories of material, quasi-material, and immaterial entities are widespread (though not universal) in Western ontologies, only the material and the quasi-material are admissible in the African counterparts (Wiredu, 1996, pp. 52, 55). This interpretation of African thought is not uncontested (see Gyekye, 1995, pp. 85, 89). Still it is interesting that, on the quasi-material interpretation of the nonbodily aspects of personhood, it is an ontological mistake to identify any of them with the Western concept of the soul.

According to the foregoing account, a person, in African thought, consists of a body combined with quasi-material entities that account for its animation and for its destiny and other marks of uniqueness. Nothing has been said of mind. But this is not a mindless omission. Africans do not appear to construe mind as a kind of entity. Certainly the Akans do not. For them, mind is the capacity to engage in various activities, such as perceiving, reasoning, feeling, talking, and dancing. (For more on this conception, see Wiredu, 1987; for a

contrary view, see Gyekye, 1995, chap. 6.) To the question as to what is the basis of this capacity, the answer is implicit but unmistakable. In Akan discourse it is the *amene* (the brain). The Yoruba too cite the *opolo* (the brain) as the seat of the human power of reasoning. They also, presumably metaphorically, invoke the *okan* (the heart) as the seat of will and emotion. In this, Bantu thought resembles closely that of the Yoruba. In his exhaustive study of the concept of personhood entertained by the Bantu peoples of Africa, Alexis Kagame, a Rwandan philosopher and linguist, found that the Bantu generally think of a human person as consisting of a body, an animating force (which he describes metaphorically as "shadow"), a principle of intelligence, and finally, the heart, which is not thought of as a pump. According to Kagame, the Bantu, exactly like the Yoruba, also speak of the heart as the seat of will and emotion.

In whatever way one looks at African conceptions of personhood then, mind, though not generally conceived as an entity, is accorded a high degree of importance. The topic of mind moreover brings up the second basic type of consideration discernible in African thought about personhood. Mind is crucial in a special way in the definition of personhood. In the normative part of the African conception, a person is not just an individual of human parentage. To ascend to the status of a person, an individual has to have attained a certain degree of moral maturity and social responsibility. This obviously is a matter of the quality of one's mind.

Probably every conception of a person has the notion of a certain degree of moral competence annexed to it. This is certainly the case in English language discourse. But among many African peoples, such as the Akans and the Yoruba, such a notion is not additional to the concept of a person; it is an integral part of it. The comparison may be illustrated with the following anecdote. At the conclusion of the peace conference between the freedom fighters and the white settlers of present-day Zimbabwe that led to independence in 1980, Kenneth Kaunda, then president of Zambia, wishing to pay the highest compliment to Margaret Thatcher, then prime minister of Great Britain, for her contributions to the success of the negotiations said to her that she was very much a person. Not wishing to be considered (presumably by the Western press) as the author of the greatest understatement of the century, he hastened to explain that in his language to be said to be a person was praise indeed. Without this clarification, Western observers, he must have thought, would have had to be excused immeasurable puzzlement. On the other hand, any Akan journalists present would have been pleasantly surprised to discover that the concept of a person in the president's language was, in this respect, exactly the same as their own.

But this linguistic clarification needs amplification. The word for a person in Akan, for example, is *onipa.* This carries an ambiguity. In one sense it means simply a human being; in another it refers to a human being of a certain moral and social status. Even the most elementary sense of context, however, suffices to disambiguate. An individual, for example, who is by reason of confirmed laziness or waywardness unable to hold down a job long enough to make worthwhile contributions to the welfare of the family and community would be said not to be an *onipa* (person). But if one kills such an individual, one has killed an *onipa* (a human being), and there will be severe consequences. Any human being, according to the traditional understanding, contains an element of divinity and is, on that ground alone, entitled to life, liberty, and an ample dispensation of natural rights (Wiredu, 1996, chap. 12).

A similar circumspection is necessary regarding the status of children. In the normative conception, a child is not yet a person, not having reached the time of the requisite maturity in moral thinking and social action. But there is not here the criticism that would normally be intended of, say, a constitutionally wayward adult. The adult has taken the test of personhood and failed; the child is not yet due for the test and deserves the kindest solicitude. Even in the case of the adult, criticism is reformative in intent and soon gives place to concerted efforts at helping the individual achieve or regain personhood.

The following propositions therefore should not seem paradoxical. Personhood, to the African, is not something one is born with. It is something one has to work for and something at which one can fail. Furthermore there are degrees of personhood, and its lower gradations can shade off into nonexistence in the life of a human individual. Life then, on the African conception, is a struggle for personhood.

One might now ask what accounts for this conception among Africans. The answer is quite simple. African societies are, famously, communalistic. The individual is brought up, from the beginning, with a sense of belonging and solidarity with an extensive circle of kith and kin. The basis of this solidarity is a system of reciprocity in which each individual has obligations to a large set of other individuals. These are matched by rights owed him or her by the same number of individuals. Living amid the reality of this reciprocity, one soon begins to see oneself as presupposing the group. This is the mainspring of the normative conception of a person.

In contemporary African philosophy the locus classicus of the normative conception of a person is Ifeani Menkiti's "Person and Community in African Traditional Thought" (1984). But the anthropologist Meyer Fortes had already in the 1940s noted the normative character of the concept of a person held, for example, by the Tallensi of northern Ghana. Wiredu's independent interpretation of the Akan concept of personhood as normative is in total agreement with Menkiti's main position on this matter. John S. Mbiti's now classic remark that the African individual "can only say 'I am, because we are'" may perhaps be called Africa's communalist answer to Descartes's *Cogito;* it is only one step away from the normative conception as outlined above. Gyekye's (1997) "moderate communitarianism" is, broadly speaking, an interpretation of normative personhood, and Gbadegesin is also sympathetic. These are some of the signs that the normative conception of a person, preached and practiced by the African ancestors, may perhaps become a source of insight and commitment for the larger community of contemporary African philosophers as well, possibly, as others.

See also **Communitarianism in African Thought; Person, Idea of the.**

BIBLIOGRAPHY

Evans-Pritchard, E. E. *Nuer Religion.* Oxford: Clarendon, 1956.

Fortes, Meyer. *Religion, Morality, and the Person: Essays on Tallensi Religion.* Edited with an introduction by Jack Goody. Cambridge, U.K., and New York: Cambridge University Press, 1987.

Gbadegesin, Segun. *African Philosophy: Traditional Yoruba Philosophy and Contemporary African Realities.* New York: Peter Lang, 1991.

Gyekye, Kwame. *An Essay on African Philosophical Thought: The Akan Conceptual Scheme.* Rev. ed. Philadelphia: Temple University Press, 1995.

——. *Tradition and Modernity: Philosophical Reflections on the African Experience.* New York: Oxford University Press, 1997.

Idowu, Bolaji E. *Olódùmarè: God in Yoruba Belief.* London: Longmans, 1962.

Kagame, Alexis. "The Problem of 'Man' in Bantu Philosophy." *African Mind: Journal of African Religion and Philosophy* 1, no. 1 (1989).

Kaphagawani, Didier Njirayamanda. "African Conceptions of a Person: A Critical Survey." In *A Companion to African Philosophy,* edited by Kwasi Wiredu. Malden, Mass.: Blackwell, 2004.

Little, Kenneth. "The Mende in Sierra Leone." In *African Worlds,* edited by Daryll Forde. New York and Oxford: Oxford University Press, 1954.

Mbiti, John S. *African Religions and Philosophy.* 2nd ed. Oxford and Portsmouth, N.H.: Heinemann, 1990.

Menkiti, Ifeanyi. "On the Normative Conception of a Person." In *A Companion to African Philosophy,* edited by Kwasi Wiredu. Malden, Mass.: Blackwell, 2004.

——. "Person and Community in African Traditional Thought." In *African Philosophy: An Introduction,* 3rd ed., edited by Richard A. Wright. Lanham, Md.: University Press of America, 1984.

Middleton, John. *Lugbara Religion.* Oxford: Oxford University Press, 1960.

Opoku, Kofi Asare. *West African Traditional Religion.* London: FEP International, 1978.

p'Bitek, Okot. *Religion of the Central Luo.* Nairobi, Kenya: East African Literature Bureau, 1971.

Wiredu, Kwasi. "The African Concept of Personhood." In *African-American Perspectives on Biomedical Ethics,* edited by Harley E. Flack and Edmund D. Pellegrino. Washington, D.C.: Georgetown University Press, 1992.

——. "The Concept of Mind with Particular Reference to the Language and Thought of the Akans." In *Contemporary Philosophy,* vol. 5: *African Philosophy,* edited by Guttorm Fløistad. Boston: Kluwer, 1987.

——. *Cultural Universals and Particulars: An African Perspective.* Bloomington: Indiana University Press, 1996.

——. "Death and the Afterlife in African Culture." In *Person and Community: Ghanaian Philosophical Studies I,* edited by Kwasi Wiredu and Kwame Gyekye. Washington, D.C.: Council for Research in Values and Philosophy, 1992.

——. "Determinism and Human Destiny in an African Philosophy." *Hamline Review* 25 (spring 2001).

Kwasi Wiredu

PERSPECTIVE.

In the visual arts, the English word *perspective* refers to the optical illusion whereby a picture on a flat, two-dimensional plane appears to be three-dimensional; as if the represented objects were actually in a deep space receding behind the picture surface (like looking at them through a window or in a mirror), and in some cases seeming even to project forward in front of the picture. The term itself derives from the Latin participle *perspectus* of the verb *perspicere,* meaning "to see through." While artists in nearly every world culture since the beginning of the human race have sought to create some kind of illusion of visual reality in their image-making, none were so preoccupied with perspective mathematics as the painters of the Italian (and then pan-European) Renaissance.

Renaissance-Style Linear Perspective

Alternative means of creating the illusion of visual reality in other times and cultures will be discussed later, but this entry will begin with a review of what is generally taken for granted in our Western culture as the one "legitimate" construction, the method invented during the early Italian Renaissance (or rediscovered, if one believes the ancient Greeks and Romans already had discerned the basic geometric principles). Sometime in the late thirteenth century in central Italy, artists hired to paint frescoes on the walls of the new churches began to conceive of their pictures not as flat patterns in the traditional Romanesque manner, but as if they thought of their painted spaces as framed theatrical *proscenia* behind which the sacred scenes of the life of Christ and his saints were being acted out. Indeed, these artists may well have been inspired by the plethora of miracle plays performed on street corners, town squares, and even in the portals of churches in cities all over Europe during those intense years of religious uncertainty after the Crusades failed and the papacy fell into schism. Italian painters from Rome (who still remembered ancient wall-painting techniques) and from Florence—including the brilliant Giotto di Bondone (c. 1266/67–1337)—all working in the new basilica dedicated to the recently canonized Saint Francis in the Umbrian town of Assisi (Fig. 1), inadvertently began a revolution that was to radically change the style, and ultimately the content of Western art for the next six hundred years. No longer would artists simply repeat traditional medieval formulas for representing the sacred narratives. No longer would viewers sense these images only as abstracted iconic symbols. Rather, they should now feel as if they could reach beyond the frames right into the picture space and actually touch the holy beings represented on the other side—"seeing and believing" in the manner of St. Thomas, who, according to Scripture, put his finger into the very wounds of Christ in order to prove his Savior had really come back from the dead.

While these early perspective paintings did not depend on the old two-dimensional symbolic manner of representation, they also did not employ any systematic geometry for creating their exciting new optical illusions. The Italian artists were simply intent on depicting religious scenes as if they were being acted out before their eyes *de naturale,* or according to nature. They even introduced cast shadows and modeling as if the subjects they painted were illuminated on one side and in shade on the other, giving an effect of sculpture in relief. This nascent perspective style is often called *empirical* to distinguish it from the more systematic mathematization of art that followed in the fifteenth century.

Art historians remain in some disagreement as to whether this early development of perspective from the thirteenth to the fifteenth century was an evolution within the painters' profession itself, that is, isolated from the ideology and politics of contemporaneous Christian Europe, or whether it was nudged, so to speak, by a remarkable science, ancient to the Greeks and Arabs, but quite new to the Latin West when manuscripts of it were first discovered in Moorish Spain and Sicily after the Christian reconquest in the twelfth century. This science was called, in Greek, *optika,* that is, *optics,* which translated into Latin as *perspectiva,* but having no association yet to the art of painting, later termed *perspectiva artificialis* to distinguish it from the original *perspectiva naturalis.* In fact, the original *perspectiva* had only to do with explaining the nature of light rays, how they always travel in straight lines, how they are reflected in mirrors, refracted when entering a denser medium, and, especially, how they affect the way the human eye sees.

Perspectiva naturalis was regarded as the special handmaiden of Euclidean geometry, the latter also just revealed in the West in the twelfth century. Since light rays were understood by the ancient Greeks as always radiating from their source in the shape of a pyramid (a three-dimensional triangle), Euclid reasoned that the images framed by them must conform to his fundamental law of similar triangles; for instance, in Fig. 2, if A be the point of light source, and BCD the surface illuminated, then a consistent proportion always exists between the distance of AC from BCD and the relative size of BCD; in other words, AC:BCD as AF:EFG as AI:HIJ, etc. Greek and Arab commentators on Euclid were quick to realize the significance of this in explaining how the images of very large objects can penetrate the tiny pupil of the eye. Let A in Fig. 2 now stand for the human eye, and HIJ the object being observed (Arab commentators liked to use the camel as their example). As the distance AI between these points diminishes to AF and then to AC and so on, the illuminated "camel" will grow ever smaller in proportion until it is finally able to enter the eye and be "seen."

Medieval Christian theologians were fascinated by these Greek and Arab revelations. The English bishop Robert Grosseteste (c. 1175–1253) noted that since God created light on the first day (Genesis), he intended to apply the absolute laws of geometry in the creation of the universe. Indeed, he must have formed its tiny shape a priori in his divine mind's eye and then projected it full-scale into the void, creating the world's three-dimensional space and volume according to the same Euclidean theorems. In other words, the science of optics seemed to be the very key to the mind of God.

Members of the young Franciscan order, headquartered in the Basilica of their founding saint in Assisi, were especially moved by these ideas, and none more so than his fellow Englishman, Roger Bacon (c. 1220–1292). Bacon's famous treatise, the *Opus majus* (Great work), is replete with calls upon Christian leaders to study both Euclidean geometry and *perspectiva naturalis* as weapons against the Moors. Bacon was particularly intrigued by the way concave mirrors can convert light to heat, and so considered how they might be made to

Figure 1. Mural by Giotto di Bondone; Bay B, right wall, upper church, Basilica of San Francesco, Assisi, Italy (late thirteenth century). SCALA/ART RESOURCE, NY

burn Moorish ships! Furthermore, he advised, geometry had application to the visual arts. If only religious pictures of, say, the Ark of Noah and other sacred objects mentioned in Scripture, were represented in the exact scale of their biblical description, Christians would be inspired as never before to renew the holy crusade and retake Jerusalem.

Speculum, Latin for mirror, became almost a synonym for divine revelation during the Middle Ages. Numbers of treatises with titles like *Speculum salvationis humanis* (Mirror of human salvation) were published everywhere in Christian Europe. Moreover, the technology of manufacturing mirrors was improving at this time, too, particularly in Venice where both flat and convex mirrors of glass began to be manufactured in convenient size, eventually becoming upper-class household items where their reflections might be compared, both actually and symbolically, with painted pictures.

According to medieval optical theory, the eye itself was nothing less than a mirror. The convex lens within the eye was understood (incorrectly, as we now know) to receive and display the minutely scaled image of whatever object is being seen,

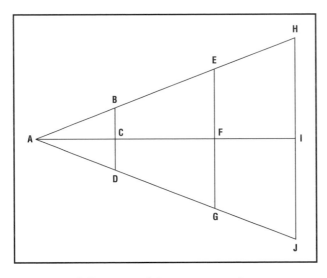

Figure 2. Euclid's concept of *Perspectiva naturalis.*

just as if reflected in a mirror; the image then passed to the optic nerve for cognition in the brain. It should come as no surprise that the next critical development in the history of Renaissance perspective involved comparison to a mirror reflection. It is now generally agreed that the great Florentine architect, engineer, and impresario Filippo Brunelleschi (1377–1446) created the first picture ever to be constructed by adapting the geometric laws of *perspectiva naturalis.* The fact is that the optical pyramid explains both how a large image can be reduced to scale, and also how a small image might be similarly increased in reverse, in much the way that a modern film projector magnifies a small transparency that becomes enlarged to the same scale when it reaches the screen. Indeed, by this means, God must have formed the universe: first, it was a tiny shape in His divine mind's eye, and then God projected it full-blown into the void. What Brunelleschi apparently realized is that the eye level of the person looking into a mirror sees not only his or her own eye reflected at that same level, but the edges of other reflected objects parallel to the ground on which the viewer stands, all appearing to converge to "vanishing points" on that same eye-level line. This is referred to as the "horizon" principle (Fig. 3).

In any event, sometime between 1413 and 1425, Brunelleschi did paint a small picture of the Baptistery of Florence as seen from the portal of the Duomo. Unfortunately, this historic painting is lost, but its composition was probably based on a geometric diagram combining mirror principles with certain other traditional measuring techniques employed by land surveyors, and possibly new projection methods inspired by cartography. We may presume the mirror connection because Brunelleschi's biographer distinctly recalled that his hero demonstrated the first perspective picture by having the viewer hold its back side against one eye, the front side of the picture facing away, then peep through a small hole bored through the back side and see the painted image of the Baptistery on the obverse side reflected in a flat mirror held in the viewer's other hand (Fig. 4). This was apparently the earliest acknowledgement of the true vanishing point in a perspective picture on line with the artist's eye from which the depicted scene was imagined, and at which all receding perpendicular edges of objects represented in the picture appear illusionistically to converge.

Figure 3. The horizon principle. COURTESY OF THE AUTHOR

Figure 4. A demonstration of Brunelleschi's exercise with a mirror to establish perspective. COURTESY OF THE AUTHOR

In 1435 and 1436, the humanist Leon Battista Alberti (1404–1472), having just returned to Florence after a lifelong exile from the home of his forefathers, was so impressed by the city's fecund artistic activities that he wrote a treatise, *Della pittura* (On painting), dedicated to Brunelleschi and other contemporary artists. At the beginning of his book, Alberti advocated that painters must learn geometry if they are to be successful; he even spelled out the basic Euclidean definitions of point, line, and plane, and then proposed a simple geometric optical formula for laying out a perspective picture, perhaps a simplified codification of Brunelleschi's method. (See the sidebar for Alberti's textual explanation with accompanying illustrations.) Rather than comparing his system to a mirror, he likened it to looking through a window fixed with a gridwork of strings (Fig. 6). "Alberti's window" has since become the metaphor of Western civilization's concept of linear perspective, that is, perspective determined only by drawn lines signifying edges of things seen that converge or recede toward a single horizon.

Why was linear perspective so unique to Western civilization? As argued above, the advent of artificial linear perspective in the West had much to do with an idealized geometry that seemed to reveal the workings of God's mind, and thus, when applied to the making of holy pictures, should reenergize Christian faith. Perhaps it was no coincidence that the very first monumental painting to be constructed according to Brunelleschi's perspective had as its subject the *Holy Trinity* (Fig. 5), a large fresco depicting near-life-size figures on the nave wall of the Church of Santa Maria Novella painted c. 1425 by his friend Masaccio (1401–1428). This picture was certainly an attempt

Figure 5. The fresco *Holy Trinity* (c. 1425) by Masaccio. Church of Santa Maria Novella, Florence, Italy. ERICH LESSING/ART RESOURCE, NY

to convince Christian viewers that the most metaphysical mystery in all Christian theology could actually be manifested in physical form before their very eyes.

Some present-day scholars, nonetheless, still maintain that Masaccio's *Trinity,* as well as Renaissance perspective from the very beginning, were secular reactions to medieval religiosity. Hubert Damisch, for example, thinks its advent is better explained ahistorically, by means of postmodern structuralism and Lacanian psychoanalysis (Damisch, 1994). In any case, by the sixteenth century, artists and their aristocratic patrons were showing less interest in applying perspective to uplifting religious pictures than to the revival of pagan antiquity. Indeed, instead of elevating human eyes to an intensified contemplation of the divine, Alberti's window had actually succeeded in

Figure 6. Leon Battista Alberti's method for laying out a perspective picture.

bringing heaven down to earth, revealing more materiality than spirituality in its ethereal essence. Even angels were henceforth transmogrified as secular solids, rigid Euclidean volumes that raised questions as to how they could convincingly appear to take flight. Galileo Galilei (1564–1642), beginning his career as a teacher of perspective at the Florentine Academy of Art, grew so expert that he built his own optical telescope in order to observe the moon. With an eye long nurtured by artificial perspective, especially from drawing shades and shadows of spherical solids, he was able to discern what no one in the world had ever understood before: that the lunar surface was covered not with mysterious supernatural blotches, but high mountains and low valleys catching sunlight and casting shadows—just like the Alpine region of northern Italy.

In the long run, linear perspective's most important contribution to Western art has been to its technology rather than its aesthetics. Even more importantly, it changed not just the way we draw pictures, but how we can actually see what we draw—but that's another story.

Other "Perspectives"

Although every human being (of whatever ethnicity) experiences the natural visual illusion of parallel edges—like

Figure 7. Drawing by five-year-old Anna Filipczak. Pen and crayon. COURTESY OF ANNA FILIPCZAK, WILLIAMSTOWN, MASS.

Figure 8. Leaf from a Khamsa of Nizami, Persia, Herat (c. 1491). *LEAF FROM THE KHAMSA OF NIZAMI,* PERSIAN, TIMURID, 15TH CENTURY. OBJECT PLACE: PERSIA. PAPER. 33.5 X 20.3 CM (13 3/16 X 8 IN.). MUSEUM OF FINE ARTS, BOSTON. GIFT OF JOHN GOELET, 60.176. PHOTOGRAPH © 2004 MUSEUM OF FINE ARTS, BOSTON

Anna, a five-year-old Ukrainian girl. Notice how she shows the trees and hammock in schematic side view but, because she wants to indicate her mother lying inside the hammock, depicts her posed as teetering on the edge; it is as if her mother is now imagined as being viewed from above. Until the infusion of Euclidean geometry and optics in the arts of western Europe during the early Renaissance, no artists anywhere had cultural need to have their pictures replicate the optics of single-viewpoint vision, and almost all the conventions they employed for signifying solid form and distant space—even in the most sophisticated art of the pre-Renaissance West and all other non-Western cultures—evolved from similar expressions found in the instinctive art of children.

This does not mean that non-perspectival pictures should be labeled "childlike" in the sense of being primitive (or inferior) to the Western style. Quite the contrary. Multiple viewpoints and other innate pictorial signifiers, such as placing nearby figures and objects at the bottom of the picture surface and those more distant at the top, have been refined into some of the most aesthetically beautiful and stylish painting in all art history. Manuscript illumination in medieval Persia is a fine example (Fig. 8). Interestingly, while medieval Islam possessed Greek optics, including Euclidean geometry, long before the West—with Muslim philosophers even adding their own commentary—Muslim painters never applied optics to art, and only used geometry for the creation of elaborate abstract designs in their magnificent architecture.

Artists in China and Japan, on the other hand, refined two perspective conventions that had naught to do with optical geometry. (Euclid was unknown in the Far East until the seventeenth century.) One method was a kind of axonometric projection whereby rectilinear objects were drawn as if their perpendicular sides were set at an angle, just as in Western perspective, but with their parallel edges remaining parallel and never converging (Fig. 9). The other convention, called aerial or atmospheric perspective, provided an effective illusion of distant landscape simply through the tonality of color. Far-off mountains, for instance, were painted in hazy gray or blue in contrast to the brighter colors of nearer foreground objects, thus creating an ideal complement to the Chinese predilection for philosophic contemplation. During the Renaissance, atmospheric perspective was also explored by Western artists, notably Leonardo da Vinci.

Another perspective convention, foreshortening, does not necessarily involve optical geometry and was also independently realized in other cultures. This is the pictorial illusion of an object appearing to extend forward or backward in space even though only one end of it can be observed, such as a body limb depicted as if thrust directly at the viewer. (Think of James Montgomery Flagg's famous "I Want You" World War I recruiting poster.) Ancient Mayan artists in Central America, for ideological reasons peculiar to their culture, applied a similar foreshortening convention when representing their rulers seated with one leg bent sharply sideways (Fig. 10): note the twisted right foot of the seated male. This pose had special meaning because it signified the auto-sacrificial ritual in which Maya

roadsides or railroad tracks—appearing to converge toward a point as they approach the horizon, it is not natural to reproduce this illusion in pictures. In other words, while everybody sees the same phenomenon in reality, no one, no matter how artistically talented, is innately predisposed to picture it (except, remarkably, certain autistic prodigies). Perspective is a technique that generally must be learned. Therefore there is no reason to believe that nature rather than nurture had anything to do with why artists in other ages and cultures did not pursue the "realism" preferred in the West.

Young children do instinctively make pictures from a number of viewpoints simultaneously, as in Fig. 7, a drawing by

New Dictionary of the History of Ideas

Figure 9. *The Literary Gathering at a Yangzhou Garden* (1743) by Fang Shishu and Yeh Fanglin. DETAIL, FANG SHISHU AND YEH FANGLIN, CHINESE, LATE 17TH–EARLY 18TH CENTURY, QING DYNASTY. *THE LITERARY GATHERING AT A YANGZHOU GARDEN*, 1743. HANDSCROLL, INK AND COLOR ON SILK, 31.7 X 201 CM. © THE CLEVELAND MUSEUM OF ART, 2004. THE SEVERANCE AND GRETA MILLINKIN PURCHASE FUND, 1979.72

Let me tell you what I do when I am painting. First of all, on the surface of which I am going to paint, I draw a rectangle of whatever size I want, which I regard as an open window through which the subject to be painted is seen; and I decide how large I wish the human figures in the painting to be. I divide the height of a man into three parts, which will be proportional to the measure commonly called a *braccio* [.5836 meters]; for, as may be seen from the relationship of his limbs, three *braccia* is just about the average height of a man's body. With this measure I divide the bottom line of my rectangle into as many parts as it will hold; and this bottom line of the rectangle is for me proportional to the next transverse equidistant quantity seen on the pavement [Illus. A]. Then I establish a point in the rectangle wherever I wish; and as it occupies the place where the centric ray [from the painter's eye] strikes, I shall call this the centric [vanishing] point [Illus. B]. The suitable position for this centric point is no higher from the base line than the height of the man to be represented in the painting, for in this way both the viewers and objects in the painting will seem to be on the same plane. Having placed the centric point, I draw straight lines from it to each of the divisions on the base line. These lines show me how successive transverse quantities visually change to an almost infinite distance [Illus. C]. . . .

I have [another] drawing surface on which I inscribe a straight line, and this I divide into parts

Illustration a. ILLUSTRATIONS A–G COURTESY OF THE AUTHOR

(continued on the next page)

(continued from previous page)

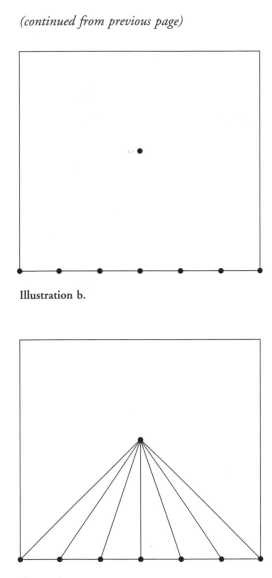

Illustration b.

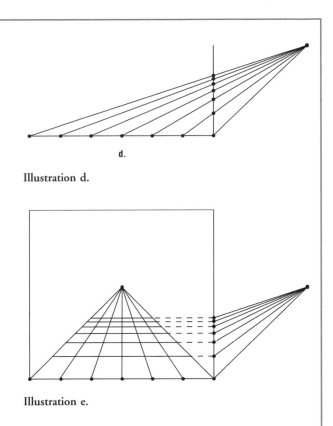

Illustration d.

Illustration e.

Illustration c.

like those into which the base line of the rectangle is divided. Then I place a point above this line, directly over one end of it, at the same height as the centric point is from the base line of the rectangle, and from this point I draw lines to each of the divisions of the line [Illus. D]. Then I determine the distance I want between the eye of the spectator and the painting, and, having established the position of the intersection at this distance, I effect the intersection with what mathematicians call a perpendicular. . . . This perpendicular will give me, at the places it cuts the other lines, the measure of what the distance

should be in each case between the transverse equidistant lines of the pavement. In this way I have all the parallels of the pavement drawn [Illus. E]. . . . A proof of whether they are correctly drawn will be if a single straight line forms a diameter of connected quadrangles in the pavement [Illus. F]. When I have carefully done these things, I draw a line across, equidistant from the other lines below, which cuts the two upright sides of the large rectangle and passes through the centric point [Illus. G]. This line is for me a limit or boundary, which no quantity exceeds that is not higher than the eye of the spectator. As it passes through the centric point, this line may be called the centric [horizon] line. This is why men depicted standing in the parallel furthest away are a great deal smaller than those in nearer ones, a phenomenon which is clearly demonstrated by nature herself, for in churches we see the heads of men walking about, moving at more or less the same height, while the feet of those further away may correspond to the knee-level of those in front.

(continued on the next page)

(continued from previous page)

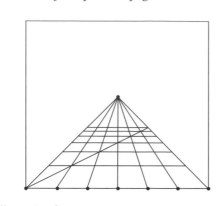

Illustration f.

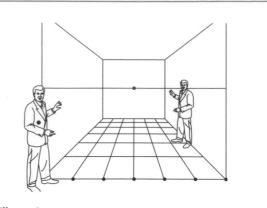

Illustration g.

SOURCE: Leon Battista Alberti, *On Painting* and *On Sculpture*. Translated by Cecil Grayson, 55–57. London: Phaidon, 1972.

Figure 10. King Bird Jaguar and his wife auto-sacrificing, Lintel 17 (c. 752) Yaxchilan, Mexico. "DRAWING OF YAXCHILAN LINTEL 17 FROM *CORPUS OF MAYA HIEROGLYPHIC INSCRIPTIONS*, VOL. 3, PART 1, *YAXCHILAN*, REPRODUCED COURTESY OF THE PRESIDENT AND FELLOWS OF HARVARD COLLEGE

kings spread their legs apart in order to draw blood from the penis and offer it to the gods.

See also **Arts; Geometry; Landscape in the Arts; Realism; Visual Culture.**

BIBLIOGRAPHY

Damisch, Hubert. *The Origin of Perspective.* Cambridge, Mass.: MIT Press, 1994.

Edgerton, Samuel Y. *The Renaissance Rediscovery of Linear Perspective.* New York: BasicBooks, 1975.

Kemp, Martin. *The Science of Art: Optical Themes in Western Art from Brunelleschi to Seurat.* New Haven: Yale University Press, 1990.

Summers, David. *Real Spaces.* New York, Phaidon, 2003.

White, John. *The Birth and Rebirth of Pictorial Space.* Cambridge, Mass.: Belknap, 1987.

Samuel Y. Edgerton

PHENOMENOLOGY. Phenomenology is the study of experience, how things appear to us. The word comes from the Greek but was elaborated in the early nineteenth century on the basis of Immanuel Kant's conception of the world as phenomenon, the world of our experience (as opposed to the world as noumenon, the world as it is "in itself"). Georg Wilhelm Friedrich Hegel famously employed the term in *Phänomenologie des Geistes* (1807; *The Phenomenology of Spirit*), suggesting that all knowledge was a matter of appearance with no world "in itself" other than the one we know. But phenomenology came of age with Edmund Husserl, who turned the Hegelian perspective into a rigorous philosophical method. Husserl in turn gave birth to a number of remarkable students, who together would set the tone for much of European philosophy in the twentieth century. Among them are Martin Heidegger, Max Scheler, Emmanuel Lévinas, Jean-Paul Sartre, and Maurice Merleau-Ponty.

Edmund Husserl

As a movement and a method, as a "first philosophy," phenomenology owes its life to Edmund Husserl (1859–1938), a

German-Czech (Moravian) philosopher who started out as a mathematician in the late nineteenth century and wrote a book on the philosophy of mathematics, *Philosophie der Arithmetik* (1891; *The Philosophy of Arithmetic*). His view was that there was a strict empiricism, but on being shown (by the great German logician Gottlob Frege) that such an analysis could not possibly succeed, Husserl shifted his ground and started to defend the idea that the truths of arithmetic had a kind of necessity that could not be accounted for by empiricism. Thus, one of the main themes of his next book, *Logische Untersuchungen* (1913, 1921; *The Logical Investigations*), was a protracted argument against "psychologism," the thesis that truth is dependent on the human mind. Rather, Husserl argues that necessary truths are not reducible to our psychology. Phenomenology was Husserl's continuing and continuously revised effort to develop a method for grounding necessary truth.

Given Husserl's beginnings in the rigorous field of mathematics, one must appreciate the temperament that he brought to his new discipline. By the end of the nineteenth century, a new perspectivism (or some would say a relativism) had come into philosophy. Friedrich Nietzsche, in particular, had argued that all knowledge is perspectival and that philosophy could not be reduced to a single perspective, that philosophy might be relative to a people, or to our particular species, or even to individual psychology. Husserl's contemporary Wilhelm Dilthey defended a milder but similar thesis, and the "sociology of knowledge" was just beginning its ascension. Against any such relativism, Husserl insisted on philosophy as a singular, rigorous science, and his phenomenology was to provide the key.

It is often debated whether phenomenology is a philosophy or a method, but it is both. As a "first philosophy," without presuppositions, it lays the basis for all further philosophical and scientific investigations. Husserl defines phenomenology as the scientific study of the essential structures of consciousness. By describing those structures, Husserl promises us, we can find certainty, which philosophy has always sought. To do that, Husserl describes a method—or rather, a series of continuously revised methods—for taking up a peculiarly phenomenological standpoint, "bracketing out" everything that is not essential, thereby understanding the basic rules or constitutive processes through which consciousness does its work of knowing the world.

The central doctrine of Husserl's phenomenology is the thesis that consciousness is intentional, a doctrine that is borrowed from Franz Brentano. That is, every act of consciousness is directed at some object or other, perhaps a material object, perhaps an "ideal" object—as in mathematics. Thus, the phenomenologist can distinguish and describe the nature of the intentional acts of consciousness and the intentional objects of consciousness, which are defined through the content of consciousness. It is important to note that one can describe the content of consciousness and, accordingly, the object of consciousness without any particular commitment to the actuality or existence of that object. Thus, one can describe the content of a dream in much the same terms that one describes the view from a window or a scene from a novel.

In *Ideas: A General Introduction to Pure Phenomenology* (1931), Husserl distinguishes between the natural standpoint and the phenomenological standpoint. The former is our ordinary everyday viewpoint and the ordinary stance of the natural sciences, describing things and states-of-affairs. The latter is the special viewpoint achieved by the phenomenologist as he or she focuses not on things but on our consciousness of things. (This is sometimes confused by the fact that Husserl insists that the phenomenologist pay attention to "the things themselves," by which he means the phenomena, or our conscious ideas of things, not natural objects.) One arrives at the phenomenological standpoint by way of a series of phenomenological "reductions," which eliminate certain aspects of our experience from consideration. Husserl formulates several of these, and their nature shifts throughout his career, but two of them deserve special mention. The first and best-known is the *epoché* or "suspension" that he describes in *Ideas*, in which the phenomenologist "brackets" all questions of truth or reality and simply describes the contents of consciousness. (The word is borrowed from both the early Skeptics and René Descartes.) The second reduction (or set of reductions) eliminates the merely empirical content of consciousness and focuses instead on the essential features, the meanings of consciousness. Thus Husserl (like Kant) defends a notion of "intuition" that differs from and is more specialized than the ordinary notion of "experience." We have intuitions that are eidetic, meaning that we recognize meanings and necessary truths in them, and not merely the contingent things of the natural world.

In his early work, including *Ideas*, Husserl defends a strong realist position—that is, the things that are perceived by consciousness are assumed to be not only objects of consciousness but also the things themselves. A decade or so later, Husserl made a shift in his emphasis from the intentionality of the objects to the nature of consciousness as such. His phenomenology became increasingly and self-consciously Cartesian, as his philosophy moved to the study of the ego and its essential structures. In 1931 Husserl was invited to lecture at the Sorbonne in Paris, and on the basis of those lectures published his *Cartesianische Meditationen* (1938; *Cartesian Meditations*, 1960). (The *Paris Lectures* were also published some years later.) He argues there that "the monadically concrete ego includes the whole of actual and potential conscious life" and "the phenomenology of this self-constitution coincides with phenomenology as a whole (including objects)" (*Cartesian Meditations*, 68, para. 33). These statements suggest the strong idealist tendency in his later philosophy.

As in the 1930s, Husserl again reinvented phenomenology, this time with a shift toward the practical, or what some might call the more "existential" dimension of human knowledge. Warning of a "crisis" in European civilization based on rampant relativism and irrationalism (an alarm that the logical positivists were raising about the same time in Vienna), Husserl published his *Krisis der Europäischen Wissenschaften* (1937; *Crisis of European Sciences and Transcendental Phenomenology*). In *Crisis*, the focus turned to the "lifeworld" and the nature of social existence, topics that played little role in his earlier investigations of the philosophy of arithmetic and the nature of individual consciousness but would come to play a much greater role in the "existential" phenomenology that would follow. But it is much to Husserl's credit that he continued to see the inadequacies of his own method and correct them, in ever-new efforts to get phenomenology right.

Martin Heidegger

Martin Heidegger (1889–1971) was a student of Husserl. Before that, he was a theology student, interested in much more concrete matters of human existence than his teacher, and his questions concerned how to live and how to live "authentically"—that is, with integrity, in a complex and confusing world. His use of phenomenology was subservient to this quest, although the quest itself soon transcended the phenomenological method. Heidegger's phenomenology is most evident in his first (and greatest) book, *Sein und Zeit* (1927; English trans. *Being and Time,* 1962). Like his teacher Husserl, Heidegger insists that philosophical investigation begin without presuppositions. But Husserl, he says, still embraced Descartes's basic picture of the world, assuming that consciousness, or "the mind," was the arena in which phenomenological investigation took place. Such a philosophy could not possibly be presuppositionless. So Heidegger abandons the language of mind, consciousness, experience, and the like, but nevertheless pursues phenomenology with a new openness, a new receptivity, and a sense of oneness with the world.

Heidegger's early work is defined by two themes: first, Heidegger displays a profound anti-Cartesianism, an uncompromising holism that rejects any dualism regarding mind and body, any distinction between subject and object, and the linguistic separation of "consciousness," "experience," and "mind." This also demands a reconsideration of the Cartesian thesis that our primary relationship to the world is one of knowledge. Second, Heidegger's early philosophy is largely a search for authenticity, or what might better be described as "own-ness" (*Eigentlichkeit*), which we can understand, with some qualification, as personal integrity. This search for authenticity will carry us into the now familiar but ever-renewed questions about the nature of the self and the meaning of human existence.

To ensure that we do not fall into Cartesian language, Heidegger suggests a new term (the first of many). *Dasein* (literally, "being-there") is the name of this being from whose perspective the world is being described. *Dasein* is not a consciousness or a mind, nor is it a person. It is not distinguished from the world of which it is aware. It is inseparable from that world. *Dasein* is, simply, "Being-in-the-World," which Heidegger insists is a "unitary phenomenon" (not being + the world). Thus, phenomenology becomes ontology (the nature of being) as well.

Being-in-the-World is not primarily a process of being conscious or knowing about the world. Science is not the primary concern of *Dasein. Dasein's* immediate relation to the world is better captured in the image of the craftsman, who "knows his stuff," to be sure, but might not be able to explain it to you nor even know how to show it to you. What he can do—what he does do—is engage in his craft. He shows you that he knows how to do this and that by simply doing it. This knowing *how* is prior, Heidegger tells us, to knowing *that.* In effect, our world is essentially one extended craft shop, a world of "equipment" in which we carry out various tasks and only sometimes—often when something goes wrong—stop to reflect on what we are doing and look at our tools as objects, as things. They are, first of all, just tools and material to be used, and in that sense we take them for granted, relying on them without noticing them. Our concept of "things" and our knowledge of them is secondary and derivative.

Thus the notion of *Dasein* does not allow for the dualism of mind and body or the distinction between subject and object. All such distinctions presuppose the language of "consciousness." But Heidegger defends an uncompromising holism in which the self cannot be, as it was for Descartes, "a thinking thing," distinct from any bodily existence. But, then, what is the self? It is, at first, merely the roles that other people cast for me, as their son, their daughter, their student, their sullen playmate, their clever friend. That self, the *Das Man* self, is a social construction. There is nothing authentic, nothing that is my own, about it. The authentic self, by contrast, is discovered in profound moments of unique self-recognition—notably, when one faces one's own death. And so Heidegger's phenomenology opens up the profoundly personal arena of existentialist phenomenology.

Max Scheler and Emmanuel Lévinas

Max Scheler (1874–1928) was also a student of Husserl, but he, too, took phenomenology in a different direction, toward ethics (which had been ignored by both Husserl and Heidegger). Scheler was an intense man whose considerable contribution to philosophy was the introduction of emotion into the overly formal Kantian conception of ethics that still ruled the Continent. In *Wesen und Formen der Sympathy (*1913; English trans. *The Nature of Sympathy,* 1954), he resurrected moral sentiment theory and gave a central place in ethics to such emotions as love and hate. He argued that emotions have been understood by philosophers as merely "subjective" and argued a "cognitive" view, such that emotions could be construed as a source of knowledge. There is even, he argued, an emotional a priori, a universal and necessary status to the emotions that philosophers had neglected.

Scheler summed up the theme of the unfolding century between the wars in his book, *Ressentiment* (1961), in which he develops Nietzsche's accusation that modern morality is a "slave morality," a morality of resentment. But where Nietzsche blames Christianity, Scheler (a Catholic) exonerates his religion and shifts the blame instead to the bourgeoisie. Scheler's phenomenology, unlike Husserl's, was primarily concerned with value and, in particular, the source of values in feelings. What was becoming evident in phenomenology—and in European philosophy more generally—was a loosening up, a rejection of formality, an acceptance and an attempt to understand the less rational aspects of human existence. Worth mentioning here as well is Emmanuel Lévinas (1906–1995), who also elaborated a phenomenological ethics based on our felt relations with other people. "The face" is the focus of Lévinas's phenomenology. It is an interpersonal phenomenology rather than an Ego- or

Dasein-based phenomenology, and interpersonal ethics, including love, plays a central role in it.

Jean-Paul Sartre

Jean-Paul Sartre (1905–1980) attended Husserl's lectures at the Sorbonne, and he became an enthusiast of phenomenology. He was first of all concerned with the nature of human freedom and the correlative sense of responsibility. Sartre's phenomenology is largely modeled on Heidegger's work, but in his *L'être et le néant* (1943; English trans. *Being and Nothingness,* 1956) he retreats from Heidegger's attack on the Cartesian view of consciousness, Sartre argues that consciousness (described as "being-for-itself") is such that it is an activity, not a thing or substance ("no-thing"), and it is always to be distinguished from the world it intends. Consciousness is free to choose and free to "negate" (or reject) the given features of the world. Thus, Heidegger's "being-in-the world" phenomenon gives way to a conflicted portrait of human consciousness resisting and challenging the world.

As in Husserl, consciousness is essentially intentionality, but for Sartre it is nothing but intentionality, an activity directed at the world. Consciousness is active, essentially critical, and consists not just of perception, thoughts, and ideas but as much of desires, wishes, emotions, moods, impulses, and imaginings, negating the world as it is. Sartre celebrates our remarkable freedom to imagine the world other than it is. Our perceptions of the world, he argues, are always permeated by imagination, so that we are always aware of options and alternatives. Furthermore, there is no self or ego behind consciousness, no agent behind the activity. Thus, Sartre distinguishes consciousness from the self, and self, he insists, is "in the world, like the self of another [person]." The self is an ongoing project in the world.

Sartre defines his ontology in terms of the opposition of "being-in-itself" and "being-for-itself," manifested in the tension between the fact that we always find ourselves in a particular situation defined by a body of facts that we may not have chosen—our "facticity"—and our ability to transcend that facticity, to imagine, and choose—our transcendence. He tells us that consciousness "is what it is not, and is not what it is"—a playful paradox that refers to the fact that we are always in the process of "transcending" ourselves. He also defines a third ontological category, "being-for-others," which makes our lives with other people an essential part of our existence.

Maurice Merleau-Ponty

After the war, Sartre's younger colleague Maurice Merleau-Ponty (1908–1961) convinced him that he should modify his "absolute" insistence on freedom in his later works, although his insistence on freedom and responsibility remains. Merleau-Ponty went on to develop his own radical revision of the phenomenology of freedom and the essentially embodied nature of human consciousness. Following Sartre, Merleau-Ponty expanded the role of the body in phenomenology. Accordingly, Husserl's intentionality becomes motility, and instead of disembodied perception we have the body's orientation to the world. It is a radical move, and phenomenology could not

quite keep up with it. So when phenomenology was replaced in French thinking, by the new wave of poststructuralism, the body retained its now privileged position but phenomenology moved to the margins. It is still practiced by diehard Husserlians and Sartreans, and it has become a valuable tool—one among many—for researchers on all sorts of psychological topics, but as an exclusive approach to philosophy, a "first philosophy," it is now for the most part simply a part of history.

See also **Continential Philosophy; Existentialism; Kantianism; Structuralism and Poststructuralism.**

BIBLIOGRAPHY

Brentano, Franz. *Psychology from an Empirical Standpoint.* Edited by Oskar Kraus and Linda L. McAlister. Translated by Antos C. Raucella et al. London: Routledge, Kegan and Paul, 1973.

Heidegger, Martin. *Being and Time.* Translated by John Macquarrie and Edward Robinson. New York: Harper, 1962.

Husserl, Edmund. *Cartesian Meditations.* Translated by Dorion Cairns. The Hague: Nijhoff, 1964.

———. *Ideas: General Introduction to Pure Phenomenology.* Translated by W. R. Boyce-Gibson. London: Macmillan, 1931.

Sartre, Jean-Paul. *Being and Nothingness.* Translated by Hazel E. Barnes. New York: Philosophical Library, 1956.

Scheler, Max. *Formalism in Ethics and Non-formal Ethics of Values.* 5th rev. ed. Translated by Manfred S. Frings and Roger L. Funk. Evanston, Ill.: Northwestern University Press, 1973.

———. *The Nature of Sympathy.* Translated by Peter Heath. New Haven, Conn.: Yale University Press, 1954.

Solomon, Robert C. *From Hegel to Existentialism.* New York: Oxford University Press, 1987.

———. *From Rationalism to Existentialism: The Existentialists and Their Nineteenth-Century Backgrounds.* New York: Harper and Row, 1972.

Robert C. Solomon

PHILANTHROPY. Active in English usage by the seventeenth century, *philanthropy* has been shown more recently to have a long, complex, and controversial history displaying multiple meanings of the term. Now *philanthropy* is normally construed as love of mankind, a voluntary, practical benevolence toward others, or an effort to promote the welfare of humanity by gifts without self-benefit. However, philanthropy over the long span of its use in Western civilization has gained and shed a more diverse array of meanings. Historically, the dynamic succession of human ambitions and virtues associated with the term implicate philanthropy in the creation of cosmic and social hierarchies, the politics of city life, the proliferation of faiths, the making of laws, and the governance of states. Philanthropic behavior also helped to form economic systems like capitalism and has accelerated both the pursuit of knowledge and the pace of artistic innovation. To comprehend the significations of philanthropy over time requires a multidimensional perspective attentive to its many spatial, material, cultural, psychological, and ethical impacts over time.

For much of recorded history, charity and philanthropy are indistinguishable and must be analyzed together to understand

New Dictionary of the History of Ideas

the evolution of the latter term. Historically, such giving has more often been construed as an imperative duty rather than as a choice of the fortunate toward the misfortunate. Only recently have forces of religious schism, liberalism, and individualism broken charity's traditional lien on property. Ancient service to the needy requires attention not only to the actual poor and their real needs, but also to the social imagination of the rich. Perceptions of dangerous want by the wealthy, accurate or not, more often determined the type and direction of their giving. The demand for and the supply of philanthropy rarely accord. Past disjunctures here, grown unbearable to new generations of aspiring benefactors, have caused epochal changes in the practice and meaning of philanthropy, religion, and politics.

Ancient Mediterranean Examples

The peoples of the ancient Mediterranean world made enduring contributions to the definitions and practices of philanthropy. In their law codes from the third millennium B.C.E., Babylonian kings decreed special punishments for the strong who abused the weak. These provisions made justice and clemency hallmarks of nobility. Babylonian epic poetry, exemplified by the *Gilgamesh* cycle (c. 2000 B.C.E.), reiterated this message. Verses retold the misfortunes of misanthropic kings while celebrating generosity and self-sacrifice as vital steps toward civilization. Contemporaneous Egyptian sacred writings such as *The Book of the Dead* make it clear that anyone's successful passage to the afterlife depended on a lifetime record of benevolent acts toward the suffering. Egyptian deities expected postulants for immortality to swear that they had never denied food to the starving, drink to the thirsty, and clothing to the ragged. Islam's many later commandments that the faithful must be charitable derive from philanthropy's sacred character among Semitic peoples in antiquity.

Judaism. Ancient Judaism went farther, postulating a single God as the epitome of generosity. All of creation belonged to Jehovah, but he gave the Israelites the promised land, sheltering them as refugees ("for the land is mine; for you are strangers and sojourners with me"; Lev. 25:23). Israel itself is defined in Jewish sacred writings as a foundling nation, rescued by the Lord. Repeated Mosaic descriptions of the deity as an avenger of the orphaned, the widowed, and the homeless compel Jews, in turn, to help the bereft ("Love the stranger therefore, for you were strangers in the land of Egypt"; Deut. 10:19). Here, misanthropy equals apostasy, and pious Jews are required to be givers. Charity becomes a mode of divine worship, and rituals of giving organize all Hebrew calendars. Days of celebration and atonement marking the lunar year must be accompanied by shared meals and presents. Seasonal harvests close with free gleanings in the fields accorded to the impoverished. Tithes to benefit the poor, priests, and slaves run at three-, seven-, and fifty-year cycles, perpetuating acts of charity among the tribes of Israel. Synagogues themselves embodied Judaism's charitable imperatives with spaces designed for the kindly deposit and distribution of alms. Donors left gifts secretly in one room of the temple. Beneficiaries collected the offerings in a second room unseen by contributors and thus immune to any shame in the transaction. Such philanthropic constructs prefigure the hierarchies of giving explained by

Jewish sages such as Moses ben Maimon (1135–1204 C.E.). Voluntary donors who act anonymously and who succeed in organizing others in durable networks of mutual aid get highest praise in this literature.

By the turn to the common era, gifts in Jewish communities had intensified as markers of social status and priestly privileges. More punctilious but also more debatable charitable acts invigorated Jewish sectarianism. Out of this controversy, disaffected Jews, like the Galilean, Jesus, sought for a more humble and true charity.

Greek models. Westerners owe the word *philanthropy* to the Greeks, who, since the fifth century B.C.E. ceaselessly elaborated on their idea of *philanthropia*. This concept they first embodied in the benevolent god Prometheus, who dared to share divine fire with mortals and suffered Zeus's wrath for his generosity. Greeks also revered their gods Hermes and Eros as especially philanthropic for the gifts of wisdom and desire they imparted to men. Greek fascination with knowledge as a gift freely communicated to mortals by other wise men registers in Plato's presentation of the philosopher Socrates stating the philanthropic nature of teaching (*Euthyphro,* c. 400 B.C.E.). The love of learning and discriminating art patronage employed by the Persian ruler Cyrus the Great induced his Greek biographer Xenophon to praise the monarch's supremely philanthropic soul (*Cyropaedia,* c. 380 B.C.E.). Here are the origins of the honorific by which Greek subjects addressed the emperors of Byzantium for centuries: "Your Philanthropy." This title was doubly appropriate since, by the sixth century C.E., a "philanthropy" in Greek also meant the tax exemption Byzantine emperors regularly gave to their favorite charities such as hospitals, orphanages, and schools. The tax-exempt condition of many modern philanthropies is ancient, and this type of privilege has long contributed to shaping various status hierarchies within Western societies.

In Greek cities, many forms of philanthropy combined to strengthen urban culture. Most important were the civic liturgies rich men assumed either voluntarily or under heavy peer pressure. These duties obligated wealthy citizens to subsidize personally the cost of temples, city walls, armories, granaries, and other municipal amenities promoting inhabitants' common identity and welfare. Prominent citizens vied with one another in the performance of these indiscriminate gifts to show the superiority of their own civic virtue. Personal vanity was a prime motive for donors, but rich citizens risked ostracism by peers and plebs if they failed to appreciate their wealth as a trust in which the community had a share. Greek philanthropists showed a genius for converting their gifts into potent symbols of communal strength and solidarity. Groups of wealthy men regularly paid for all the equipment necessary to stage the great Greek dramatic festivals. Such gifts of theaters, scripts commissioned from leading playwrights, costumes, and actors shaped the physical and cultural environments of Greek cities, gave audiences memorable lessons in civility, and enshrined drama as one of the greatest media of collective artistic expression in the West.

Roman philanthropia. As conquerors, heirs, and cautious emulators of the Greeks, the Romans assumed better regulation of what they called *philanthropia* to be among the greatest obligations of their civilization. Influential authors like Cicero and Seneca composed manuals on the arts of proper gift giving and receipt. Seneca, tutor to the emperor Nero, emphasized that elite giving must generate gratitude between the vertical ranks of Roman society and argued that philanthropy rightly done formed the "glue" that held the Roman people together (*On Benefits,* composed c. 60 C.E.). Thus benefactors had to select appreciative beneficiaries carefully and choose presents capable of eliciting maximum acknowledgment from recipients. Heads must rule hearts in discriminate Roman philanthropy. Roman rulers took this advice with emperors asserting exclusive right to make choice gifts of baths, gymnasia, fountains, and gladiatorial games to the Roman population. The elaboration of Roman law aided less exalted philanthropists by giving legal status to trusts, charitable endowments, and mutual-aid societies. But the propensity of many donors to use such legal instruments for self-glorification, personally advantageous politicking, and the conservation of family wealth did little to help larger numbers of the destitute in growing Roman imperial cities. To Latins, philanthropy also meant the proper conduct of diplomacy, special respect for foreign ambassadors, fidelity to sworn treaties, and generous terms of alliance offered to defeated enemies. The propagandists of empire cited these philanthropies as justifications of Roman imperialism and the superiority of Roman civilization.

Christian Regimes of Philanthropy

The radical, roving holy man Jesus of Nazareth rebelled against all existing regimes of self-serving philanthropy in the ancient world simply by proclaiming: "Blessed are the poor" (Luke 6:20). The master commanded early apostles to abandon without recompense all material possessions by almsgiving and to strive for ever deeper humility through personal alms seeking, courting rejection and abuse at every door. The earliest Christian writings, the letters of Paul—composed c. 54–58 C.E.—advocate in part this radical social ethic demanding that all believers become tireless benefactors. Those formerly accustomed to being mere protégés of greater patrons must now aspire themselves to become protectors of their neighbors no matter how humble they all may be. Paul raised up new communities of donors to be inspired by Jesus's manifest love and empowered spiritually and philanthropically through the church. New Testament evangelists amplified this charitable theme, emphasizing how Jesus immediately cared for the suffering even by doing good works on the Sabbath in contravention of Jewish worship protocols (Mark 3:4 and 6:2–5). Jesus personified as the Good Samaritan (Luke 10:29–37) emphasized that one's obligation to help the stricken must extend to all and transcend ethnocentric notions of racial superiority, caste privilege, and self-interest. Fundamental tenets of Christianity formed as its exponents did battle with more ancient regimes of philanthropy.

Early Christian bishops, locked in vicious power struggles with old pagan elites for control of crumbling Roman imperial cities, could not be so generous. Anxious to portray themselves as potent "lovers of the poor," they continually revised Christian doctrines on alms, riches, and the poor to gain disciplined blocks of loyal followers. Fidelity to Jesus's more selfless teachings was sacrificed as bishops toned down earlier rebukes of the wealthy, courted rich donors with preferred places in new congregations, and increasingly described almsgiving as a means by which the ordinary faithful could atone for their personal sins under reinforced church discipline. The crucial Christian linkage of philanthropy and penance enticed givers to look upon their alms as a form of spiritual capital accumulation and intensified self-centered motives for giving. Worldly charitable deposits would ultimately enable pious donors to boast in heaven about the purity of their own souls and to secure personal salvation.

Church efforts to monopolize regulation and distribution of alms, especially through fixed monastic offices, were continually challenged during the Middle Ages. Philanthropic insurrectionaries—like St. Francis of Assisi—embraced poverty in apostolic fashion and preferred direct care to the wretched within recovering European cities. Lay members of medieval civic confraternities, who pledged to help one another and to care for needy fellow citizens, thereby diminishing urban violence, also challenged ecclesiastical control of philanthropy. Voluntary brothers and sisters sought to convert their good works into better lives for fellow citizens, enhancing the social and spiritual capital of all.

Early Modern Refinements

Both the rise of the state and intensified religious conflict in early modern times contributed to critical redefinitions of philanthropy. This was especially true if kings meddled in religious affairs, as when King Henry VIII of England organized a new English Episcopal Church in the 1530s while systematically destroying Catholic institutions of worship and charity within his realm. These royal actions promoting the English Reformation first made it imperative for Tudor rulers to create a tax-supported poor-relief program to replace vanished Catholic charities. Then statesmen became determined to increase the efficiency of all remaining private philanthropic organizations so as to spare the state from unnecessary subventions of the needy. The result was the famous Elizabethan Statute of Charitable Uses (1601) that defined in passing legally acceptable charities. But this legislation far more amply encouraged private citizens and government officers to investigate and to sue surviving philanthropies and their private trustees for any suspected mismanagement of endowments now deemed vital to maintenance of public order.

The Reformations became a manifold gift crisis as Europeans questioned God's bounty to man, what humans could offer the divine, and what they owed to one another. With Protestants facing off against Catholics, the integrity of Christian charity collapsed as giving became more sectarian. Surviving benevolent organizations competed fiercely for the smaller pools of total gift capital rival faiths could muster. Charity officials turned to perpetual fundraising campaigns and creatively diversified their funding sources, enhancing tactics of resource management vital to capitalism's success. Churchmen on all sides complained that impetuous philanthropy would be not only wasteful, but also a boon to heresy if it wrongly benefited religious opponents. Agents of police, including clerics, denounced the poor as disruptively irreligious and denied them any legitimate right to aide from the rich.

These conditions sanctioned a reconceptualization of philanthropy as a riskier matter of choice and optional capital investment that should produce demonstrable returns in accord with the sacred and secular beliefs of donors. The current vogue for "entrepreneurial philanthropy" has ample precedents in early modern history.

Modern "Scientific" Philanthropy

Reformation-era debates over giving accelerated the secularization, rationalization, and nationalization of philanthropy. Disgusted with doctrinaire religious bickering and giving, statesmen-philosophers of the European Enlightenment sought to define and effect a "scientific philanthropy" that would efficiently benefit the truly needy and entire nations as well. Legislators in England, France, and central Europe simultaneously denounced private and religious endowed charitable foundations whose limited antique purposes or beneficiaries had been rendered obsolete by the passage of time. Parliamentarians enacted legislation to curb the creation of foundations via gifts of land to permanent endowments and they favored methods of ad hoc fundraising to meet any community's pressing needs. Utilitarians of the nineteenth century, like John Stuart Mill, advocated closer national supervision of all charities and politically mandated investment of their liquid assets in state bonds to enhance their public benefit and economic partnership with government. Britain's national Charity Commissioners, first deputized by Parliament in 1818 and made permanent in 1853, soon exercised authorization and annual inspection powers over all philanthropic organizations.

In America, colonial and then state constitutions differed widely in the encouragement and discouragement of private philanthropy leading to the failure of many interstate charitable bequests and organizations. This frustrating situation spurred many legal battles and multiple interventions by the U.S. Supreme Court, including the famous Dartmouth College case decision in 1819. Here, the justices quashed an attempt by the governor and state legislature of New Hampshire to take over Dartmouth College and change its curriculum to meet state needs. The court held that the state's plan violated the school's charter and grossly abused the law of contracts. That charter, obtained from the royal provincial governor by the college's founders in colonial times, was itself a contract between the government that issued it and the trustees of the college. By the U.S. Constitution, such agreements could be altered only if all parties to the original contract, or their successors, concurred. This point of law reinforced the separation of church and state while also promoting the freedom of conscience and speech for the agents of philanthropic corporations.

Early Americans fought hard in the courts to compile a body of law stipulating the rights of incorporated philanthropies and protecting them against government spoliation. Boosters of charity organization societies in England and America campaigned successfully for greater coordination and professionalization of philanthropic work, castigating "mere charity" as wasteful, sentimental, and incapable of solving the modern socioeconomic problems caused by urbanization and industrialization. The rise of "social work" as an accredited, data-driven service vocation in modern times exemplifies the triumph of a professionalized and scientific philanthropy. This trend strengthened when immensely wealthy and influential captains of U.S. industry, like Andrew Carnegie and John D. Rockefeller Sr., transferred their millions to personal philanthropic corporations organized and operated in accord with rigorous business principles. Foundation executives, confronted with the necessity of managing endowments now more often comprised of corporate stock, recruited highly skilled staffs to handle the accumulation and pay out of philanthropic capital.

Jewish benefactors contributed to these trends by subsidizing a wider array of causes and organizations, like loan funds, hospitals, and support networks for Eastern European immigrants, the aid being more practical and scientific than pious in nature. The advent of Zionism in the nineteenth century, the calamity of the Holocaust, and the creation of the state of Israel catalyzed modern Jewish philanthropy as a means of nation building and commemoration of historic events.

By contrast, ancient Islamic forms of philanthropy have remained very influential in Muslim communities throughout modern times, especially support of Koranic schools, mosques, public works, and poor relief. Vital here is the enduring medieval institution of the *waqf* (pl. *awqaf*), a transfer in perpetuity of real estate or productive property to support a religious or charitable institution forever. Islamic law stipulates the inviolability of such endowments, postulating Allah himself as their owner. This level of material security greatly appealed to elite Moslem property owners living under rapacious monarchs and without recourse to fixed laws of testation and property succession by heirs. They created many family *awqaf* with immediate kin and descendants richly rewarded as the direct beneficiaries or well-paid administrators of these endowments. Here, institutionalized philanthropy as protection of clan interests and as projection of political protest elicited the wrath of Muslim state rulers, ancient and modern. In the post-colonial Mid-East, secularizing Turkish and Arab nationalist governments (in Algeria, Egypt, Syria, and Tunisia) have resorted to confiscations of *waqf* properties, advancing state policies at the expense of traditional philanthropies and their prime beneficiaries, especially clerics. Such tactics underscore the fragility of civil society in the region and promote sectarian conflict.

In modern times, the rise of mass-circulation daily newspapers and muckraking exposés significantly reshaped Western philanthropy, as journalists produced stories decrying socioeconomic problems, the irrelevance of existing charities, and the need for better benevolent organizations. Learned societies and professional bodies—like bar associations, incorporated as nonprofit organizations, contributed their journals and specialized studies to a growing flood of information about the best means, measures, and objectives of effective philanthropy. Generalized contempt for charity's dead hand made constant self-scrutiny and a capacity for self-renewal to meet new social problems prized attributes of modern philanthropic organizations. Many newer charitable foundations are even primed to spend themselves out of existence and self-destruct after a set period of time so as to prevent their social obsolescence. These achievements have often brought greater coherence between the demand and supply of philanthropy. The remarkable dynamism of the nonprofit sector in the United States and abroad, signaled by the proliferation of private family foundations, grassroots community foundations, and donor-advised funds highly responsive to the fluid social awareness and giving interests of contributors, demonstrates broader public participation in historic debates over the real meaning of philanthropy. For the moment, this agitation confirms rather than subverts modern philanthropy's scientific pretensions.

See also **Christianity; Poverty; Property; Wealth.**

BIBLIOGRAPHY

Andrew, Donna. *Philanthropy and Police: London Charity in the Eighteenth Century.* Princeton, N.J.: Princeton University Press, 1989.

Brown, Peter. *Poverty and Leadership in the Later Roman Empire.* Hanover, N.H.: University Press of New England, 2002.

Cavallo, Sandra. *Charity and Power in Early Modern Italy: Benefactors and Their Motives in Turin, 1541–1789.* Cambridge, U.K.: Cambridge University Press, 1995.

Davis, Natalie. *The Gift in Sixteenth-Century France.* Madison: University of Wisconsin Press, 2000.

Himmelfarb, Gertrude. *Poverty and Compassion: The Moral Imagination of the Late Victorians.* New York: Knopf, 1991.

Jones, Gareth. *History of the Law of Charity, 1532–1827.* London: Cambridge University Press, 1969.

Loewenberg, Frank M. *From Charity to Social Justice: The Emergence of Communal Institutions for the Support of the Poor in Ancient Judaism.* New Brunswick, N.J.: Transaction, 2001.

McCarthy, Kathleen D. *American Creed: Philanthropy and the Rise of Civil Society, 1700–1865.* Chicago: University of Chicago Press, 2003.

Miller, Howard S. *The Legal Foundations of American Philanthropy, 1776–1844.* Madison: State Historical Society of Wisconsin, 1961.

Safely, Thomas M. *Charity and Economy in the Orphanages of Early Modern Augsburg.* Boston: Humanities Press, 1997.

Veyne, Paul. *Bread and Circuses: Historical Sociology and Political Pluralism.* London: Penguin, 1992.

Weissman, Ronald. *Ritual Brotherhood in Renaissance Florence.* New York: Academic Press, 1982.

Winter, Bruce W. *Seek the Welfare of the City: Christians as Benefactors and Citizens.* Grand Rapids, Mich.: Eerdmans, 1994.

Kevin C. Robbins

PHILOSOPHIES.

This entry includes four subentries:

African
American
Feminist, Twentieth-Century
Islamic

AFRICAN

Ancient Egypt has been offered as a point of origin of African metaphysical speculation. According to the work of Senegalese historian Cheikh Anta Diop, Egypt is to Africa what the Greco-Latin civilization is to the West, and texts such as *The Book of the Dead,* written more than 3,500 years ago, could play the role of a founding text for a tradition of philosophical thinking on the African continent. Most of Diop's work has been devoted to demonstrating that the history of ancient Egypt cannot be separated from the history of the rest of the continent. The cosmogony of the Dogon people, for example, described by the sage Ogotemmêli and recorded by French ethnologist Marcel Griaule, is a testimony to the cultural and metaphysical continuity existing between the ancient Egyptians and the people living in the region of the Niger River's loop. Thus, the philosophy behind the practice of male and female circumcision is similar to what is found in ancient Egypt: that is, human beings have inherited from their divine origin an androgynous nature; at puberty, therefore, the right ontological order of things commands that the sexes be radically separated through circumcision and excision. Another important element of continuity is to be found in African languages, which, Diop claims, need to be studied in relation to the Egyptian language. In support of this, he presents in much of his work Egyptian philosophical concepts that survived in his native Wolof. Subsequently, Diop's disciple Theophile Obenga has emphasized the continuous presence in African tongues and cultures of the notion of *maat,* which is central in Egyptian philosophy and means "reality," "truth," "justice," "righteousness," "evenness," or "perfection." In Coptic and in other African languages spoken in Ethiopia, Congo, Gabon, Cameroon, Sudan, or Nigeria, recognizable derivatives from *maat* are indications of the permanence of this philosophical concept in the peoples' worldview as the expression of an African ideal of harmony in society. African philosophy could be characterized as a philosophy of *maat.*

Diop's views have provoked heated ideological debate, Egyptology being premised on the notion that ancient Egypt belongs to Asia rather than to the African continent, where it is and was situated. The German philosopher Georg Wilhelm Friedrich Hegel (1770–1831), in particular, insisted that Egypt and North Africa be culturally detached from Africa, the purpose being to erase any indication that what he called "Africa proper" could produce civilization, let alone philosophy, which for him uniquely represented the spirit of Europe.

The Islamic Past
To detach North Africa from the rest of the continent also meant to take out of it the chapters in the history of philosophy written in cities such as Alexandria, Carthage, or Hippo, where St. Augustine, "the most celebrated African thinker in history" as D. A. Masolo presents him, was a bishop in 396. It also meant ignoring the intellectual consequences of the penetration of Islam into Africa, starting in the eighth century, when the graphic rationality of the Muslim religion became part of African life. It is true that, by the end of the thirteenth century, the period of development of philosophy (*falsafa* in Arabic), which started in the ninth century, was coming to an end in the Sunni world. Still, Aristotelian logic was studied and philosophical thinking remained part of religious disciplines such as theology (*kalam*), commentary (*tafsir*), and mysticism (Sufism). In many learned centers in the Islamized regions of Africa, scholars in these

disciplines have created and developed an African written intellectual tradition, partly concerned with philosophical speculation. The legendary city of Timbuktu is the most famous of such centers. Ahmad Baba, who lived at the end of the sixteenth and in the early seventeenth century, was the best representative of the scholarly elite of Timbuktu. For Muslim scholars, the Saharan desert was not the wall Hegel supposed; they traveled in the Islamic world, North Africa, Egypt, and Arabia for intellectual purposes, often taking the opportunity of the pilgrimage to Mecca to do so. There is in the early twenty-first century a need to assess the importance of a written tradition of African philosophy in Arabic and in *Ajami,* that is, in African languages using Arabic script. This tradition is still widely unknown because many manuscripts kept in private family libraries are yet to be exhumed, restored, cataloged, and eventually published.

The Beginning of a Discipline

While Egyptian and Islamic components of African philosophy are now being researched, showing the historical depth of the intellectual tradition of speculation on the continent and questioning the received view that African cultures are naturally and essentially oral, the beginning of African philosophy as a discipline and an aspect of contemporary scholarship on Africa came after World War II. The publication in 1945 of Placide Tempels's *Bantu Philosophy* (in Dutch; it was translated into French in 1949 and English in 1959) was a crucial moment in this process, and so was the publication in 1948 of Griaule's *Conversations with Ogotemmêli.*

Both works represented a break from the colonial negation of African cultures. Ethnologists such as Lucien Lévy-Bruhl had characterized the Africans' approach to reality as prelogical and magical, therefore foreign to any systematic view and organized philosophy; his concept of "primitive mentality" epitomized the face of anthropology as a science of the "other," which justified the "mission" of colonialism to bring civilization and rational thinking to people who were devoid of both. *Bantu Philosophy* showed a different face of anthropology as it affirmed, beyond the cultural traits, customs, and behaviors studied by ethnographers, the existence of a systematic "philosophy" that gives meaning and coherence to these cultural features. African philosophy as a discipline continuing, questioning, or criticizing the fundamental approach of *Bantu Philosophy* was born at that time, when Tempels's book was acclaimed by African and European scholars as doing justice to an African tradition of speculative thought.

Major Themes

The concept of *vital force* is considered characteristic of African philosophy. According to Tempels and to Alexis Kagame, it is a fundamental trait of African thought to hold that the force of life is the supreme value and to posit "being" and "force" as equivalent: such ontology is said to be dynamic. Although Tempels and Kagame limited their description of it to the Bantu peoples, this ontology has been considered valid for other African cultures and regions as well. It is central to the philosophy known as Negritude, defined by one of its heralds, Léopold S. Senghor, as the concept of a specific black identity founded on a core set of values shared throughout the black world.

African *religion* is an area in which the philosophy of vital force is visible. Contemporary African philosophers have established a general structure of religions other than Christianity and Islam and based on the following elements: a supreme being or force who created the world, which depends on him for its continuous existence; divinities or spirits or forces that are active in the world; ancestors who are the departed elders of the community and whose forces are still active (they have reached after their death the status of spirits, and the custom of pouring libation to them is still alive even in Christianized or Islamized groups); living creatures that are mineral, vegetal, animal, or human forces. All these beings or forces form together a field of interaction. This explains the conventional opinion that the Africans' worldview is essentially religious and indicates why this religiosity has been misunderstood as magical thinking (according to which a "force" can act on another "force" to increase or diminish it, apparently without an actual causal relationship).

African conceptions of *personhood and community* are to be understood within this cosmology. Many African philosophers hold that at the foundation of African socioethical thought is a communitarian philosophy. John Mbiti, in his *African Religions and Philosophy,* has thus summarized this notion of a priority of the community over the individual: "I am because we are; and since we are, therefore I am." *Nit, nitay garabam,* "the remedy for a human is another human," is a Wolof proverb that expresses this feature of African humanism and communalistic ethics. But a slightly different form of it—*nit niteey garabam*—is also often offered, meaning: "the remedy for a human is human behavior." This play on words is significant. The emphasis is now on the person and on the goal set for individuals to become what they have to be: accomplished humans. The community is ontologically rich in the individuals who compose it and who must realize through it their potential as accomplished persons. This dialectics of the community and the individual is considered by Kwame Gyekye as the basis for an African notion of human rights.

African cosmologies are also said to convey a specific African philosophical concept of *time.* One very controversial question is whether the future truly exists in African worldviews. After an examination of a few Bantu languages, John Mbiti has stated that, for African people, time is a composition of events and not a frame that remains when the events are taken out of it. The implication is that the past is the most important temporal dimension, while the future barely exists beyond the tiny span ahead, a mere continuation of today's events. Other African philosophers have brought forward counterexamples from other African cultures to argue that Mbiti's account was mistaken and tantamount to the prejudice against Africans as supposedly culturally unprepared to plan, manage time, or project themselves into the future.

African art is a major domain of investigation for African philosophy, as it is arguably in the arts that the greatest contributions of Africa to world culture in the twentieth century have been acknowledged. The use of stylization, the obvious symbolism of art objects that deliberately use disproportion, geometrical figures, and emphasis on certain parts of the body have exercised influence on contemporary art worldwide and are regarded as expressive of an African metaphysics. This is also said of African music and drumming. The metaphysical significance of African dance as a way of participating in the life of the universe is central to Senghor's philosophy of African arts.

The Controversy about the Meaning of Philosophy

The radical rejection of the approach inaugurated by *Bantu Philosophy* came in the early 1970s from some African philosophers who characterized it as "ethno-philosophy," that is, a systematization of ethnological traits presented as philosophy. Paulin Hountondji and Marcien Towa are famous critics of the idea of a philosophy defined as the worldview of an ethnic group or a whole continent, arguing that philosophy is not the expression of a culture but the very possibility of stepping out of that culture and the unexamined collective opinions it carries in order to develop individual and critical thinking: folk wisdom expressed through proverbs cannot be considered the equivalent of philosophical argumentation, and one cannot speak of African philosophy in the absence of a written tradition because in oral cultures the function of memorizing is so demanding that it makes critical distance impossible. Hountondji also made the point that equating philosophy and culture would mean that everybody shares the same view in a society where unanimity would be a value; consequently, the political danger of legitimizing authoritarianism in the name of philosophical consensus could hardly be avoided. Thus traditionalism could be valued even when oppressive—to women, for example, when it comes to practices such as female circumcision.

The criticism of "ethno-philosophy" has been denounced as accepting an exclusivist Western notion of philosophy that fails to comprehend the challenge African and other speculative traditions present to this view.

For Odera Oruka, beyond the controversy about philosophy lies the task of establishing a program of research in African sagacity. Individual sages—such as the Dogon Ogotemmêli—have always existed in the different African societies, and these sages can explain, question, and often criticize the elements of the culture, not simply regurgitate them. Such sages are also living today, and their thoughts must be acknowledged and recorded as part of the African philosophical library at large. Another way out of the debate about the meaning of philosophy is for contemporary African philosophers to call for a critical approach to African cultures, not to excavate their latent philosophical content but to illuminate the African context and experience and the task ahead: philosophizing in matters pertinent to the African peoples. Thus Kwasi Wiredu insists on an African orientation in philosophy that would mean conceptual decolonization. The simple test of using African languages to examine concepts such as reality, being, truth, justice, God, self, and reason would be a crucial step toward such a conceptual decolonization.

See also **Negritude; Personhood in African Thought; Realism, Africa; Sage Philosophy.**

BIBLIOGRAPHY

Diop, Cheikh Anta. *Civilization or Barbarism, an Authentic Anthropology.* New York: Lawrence Hill, 1991. Translated from the French, this work was first published by Présence Africaine, Paris, in 1981. It is the last book by C. A. Diop, who died in 1986.

Eze, Emmanuel. *African Philosophy: An Anthology.* Malden, Mass.: Blackwell, 1998.

Griaule, Marcel. *Conversations with Ogotemmêli: An Introduction to Dogon Religious Ideas.* London and New York: Oxford University Press, 1965.

Gyekye, Kwame, and Kwasi Wiredu eds. *Person and Community.* Ghanaian Philosophical Studies, I. Washington, D.C.: Council for Research in Values and Philosophy, 1992.

Hountondji, Paulin. *The Struggle for Meaning: Reflections on Philosophy, Culture and Democracy in Africa.* Athens: Ohio University Center for International Studies, 2002. In this recent book the author presents his intellectual itinerary and softens some of the criticisms he leveled against "ethno-philosophy" in *African Philosophy: Myth and Reality* (London: Hutchinson, 1983).

Kagame, Alexis. *La philosophie bantu-rwandaise de l'Être.* Brussels, Belgium: *Mémoires de l'Académie royale des Sciences coloniales.* Classe des sciences morales et politiques. Nouv. Série., t. 6, fasc. 1, 1956.

Mbiti, John S. *African Religions and Philosophy.* 2nd ed. London: Heinemann, 1990 (1st ed. 1969).

Mosley, Albert, ed. *African Philosophy: Selected Readings.* Englewood Cliffs, N. J.: Prentice-Hall, 1995. Contains Léopold S. Senghor's discussion of Negritude in an article titled "On Negrohood: Psychology of the African Negro."

Oruka, H. Odera. *Sage Philosophy: Indigenous Thinkers and Modern Debate on African Philosophy.* Leiden, Netherlands, and New York: Brill, 1990.

Tempels, Placide. *Bantu Philosophy,* 2nd edition. Paris: Présence africaine, 1969.

Wiredu, Kwasi, ed. *Companion to African Philosophy.* Malden, Mass.: Blackwell, 2003. Theophile Obenga, who has published extensively on the Egyptian origin of African philosophy, has contributed an article titled "Egypt: Ancient History of African Philosophy." In the same volume are also: Souleymane Bachir Diagne, "Precolonial African Philosophy in Arabic" and D. A. Masolo's "African Philosophers in the Greco-Roman Era."

Souleymane Bachir Diagne

AMERICAN

American philosophies are as varied and diverse as the many backgrounds and cultures that collaborate to form American life. Even so, there are some similar emphases that cross these differences. Often, philosophies in America valorize action and the practical aspects of thought; American philosophers are regularly concerned with problems of race, class, gender, and other ethical and political forces that shape and undergird more abstract thought; and even the more religious and spiritual elements of American philosophies are characteristically addressed to matters of community and personal growth.

Native American Philosophy

Well prior to the arrival of European colonists, the Iroquois had developed sophisticated political thought and a government with a clear division of powers; Mississippian peoples had constructed one of the largest cities in the Western hemisphere at Cahokia, spreading Mississippian religious and cultural influence throughout the region; and the Pueblo people had created intricate agricultural innovations, community structures, and economies. While it is impossible to tie together all the diverse traditions of thought and belief among the various cultures indigenous to the Americas, a few basic contrasts may be made between much of Native American thought and much of Western thought. There are clear differences in the treatment of individuality and community, in emphasis upon writing and oral communication, and in the separation, or lack thereof, between humanity and nature.

Such differences have, throughout the history of the Americas, led to misunderstandings between Native American peoples and European-Americans, as well as served as excuses to lie to, abuse, and kill indigenous people. Perhaps the most important of contemporary Native American thinkers, writers, historians, intellectuals, and activists is Vine Deloria, Jr. (1933–), whose works are extremely critical of much of U.S. culture and call for a reevaluation of the richness of Native American ways of life and thought. In 2003 the philosopher Anne Waters published an anthology, *American Indian Thought: Philosophical Essays,* a work key to understanding the breadth and depth of traditional and contemporary Native American thought.

Puritan Thought

Puritan philosophy arises out of sense of the separation and uniqueness that developed as the Puritans left England because of religious persecution and settled in the New World. The difficulty of such a journey and the problems of living in an unfamiliar land combined to add a kind of rigor and harshness to the Puritans' Christian theology and a strict ethical and social control over the members of their communities.

The first truly influential and famous of Puritan philosophers, Jonathan Edwards (1703–1758), came years after the Puritans settled in the New World, and is perhaps best known for his fiery sermons and his active role in the religious revivals of the Great Awakening. His endeavor to reconcile Calvinist theology and Congregationalist religious practices with Enlightenment philosophy and science put him squarely in the middle of the conflict between religious traditionalism and the increasing secularization of American society. Edwards's philosophy sought to discard neither religion nor science; rather, his systematic study of both brought him to espouse a naturalized religion in which religious affections and their effects on human conduct replace the supernatural as the primary objects of concern.

Transcendentalism

Transcendentalism, which blended philosophy, religious thought, social reform, and environmental concern, was most active during the first half of the nineteenth century, and most of its key figures lived in New England. These figures include Ralph Waldo Emerson (1803–1882), Henry David Thoreau (1817–1862), and Margaret Fuller (1810–1850). Through its major outlet for publications, the journal *The Dial,* transcendentalists focused on the individual as the source of moral authority and truth. Far from believing that this gave everyone the right to

do whatever he or she pleased, however, the transcendentalists described how, by looking within oneself, one can experience and reflect upon the universal that exists through all things. People all have a spark of the divine with them, according to the transcendentalists, and thus can transcend, or overcome, their limitations by turning toward the beauty and truth that lies within. Criticized for being overly optimistic about the nature of humanity and impractical for their eschewing of accepted social norms in their quest for more esoteric and ephemeral insights, nevertheless, the transcendentalists had a long-lasting and far-reaching influence on American philosophy, literature, and social thought.

Pragmatism

Pragmatism developed primarily out of the work of Charles Sanders Peirce (1839–1914), William James (1842–1910), and John Dewey (1859–1952). Peirce, a logician, semiotician, and philosopher, first developed the notion of pragmatism as a theory of meaning, a way of clarifying terms used in philosophic debate. Peirce claimed that when one understands "all the conceivable experimental phenomena which the affirmation or denial of a concept could imply," one understands the definition of that concept. Peirce was attempting to force otherwise unending metaphysical speculation to come to terms with the effects and consequences of philosophic debate—to arrive at agreement as to the meaning of concepts by bringing those concepts into the shared realm of common experience.

While Peirce is normally heralded as the father of pragmatism, William James and John Dewey are usually credited with the popularization and refinement of this distinctly American philosophy. James, a psychologist, physician, and philosopher, emphasized the personal elements of pragmatic thought—focusing on what the adoption of pragmatic belief might mean for individuals confronted with difficult personal and philosophical dilemmas. James believed that by looking to consequences, and thus getting one's bearings through a consideration of the practical elements of a situation, one could resolve for oneself answers to otherwise endless difficulties. Dewey, also a psychologist and philosopher, and a key figure in the development of American educational theory, emphasized the social, political, and educational aspects of pragmatic thought. By looking to public and shared experience as the means of resolving philosophical debate, rather than antecedent arguments and abstract truths, Dewey's version of pragmatism focused on experimental inquiry and the refinement of practical, philosophic instruments of ongoing communication.

African-American Philosophy

African-American philosophy has historically struggled against the efforts of many European-Americans to marginalize and denigrate the importance of African-American experiences and reflections upon the unique situations of black Americans. For many centuries punished if they learned to read or write, black Americans communicated largely through the development of rich oral and religious traditions that cultivated unique and diverse philosophies of justice, morality, and human nature. As public participation and formal education among

African-Americans increased following the Abolitionist Movement of the nineteenth century and the American Civil War, African-American scholars and activists such as W. E. B. Du Bois (1868–1963), Alain Locke (1886–1954), and Martin Luther King Jr. (1929–1968) contributed to national and international debates on human rights and the nature of justice.

W. E. B. Du Bois is most famous for his explanation of the phenomenon of "double-consciousness," by which he described the ambiguous ways in which African-Americans see themselves both from their own perspectives and from the perspectives of others. Du Bois, throughout his long career, argued that racism separates the human community, thus betraying its interdependent natures. From the founding of the National Association for the Advancement of Colored People (NAACP) early in his career to his later development as a communist, Du Bois worked continuously to embody and refine his social philosophy and reflections upon African-American experience.

Alain Locke, a Rhodes scholar and the first African-American to earn a doctorate from Harvard University, remains perhaps the most famous of African-American philosophers. During his time at Howard University, the school became the prime location for the education of African-American social thought and philosophy. Locke also published *The New Negro* in 1925, an anthology of work meant to encapsulate and present the Harlem Renaissance. According to Locke, this movement embodied and carried forward the notion of value pluralism, a rejection of absolutist philosophies and a positive construction of alternatives to the essentializing tendencies of Western philosophy.

From his inspirational sermons, to his elaboration of the philosophy of non-violence, to his leadership role in the American civil rights movement, the life and work of Martin Luther King Jr. is a testament to the American spirit of uniting philosophy with action, theory with practice. Steeped in both the tradition of the Southern black churches and the philosophy of personalism espoused by Borden Parker Bowne (1847–1910) and Edgar S. Brightman (1884–1953), King believed in a living, personal God whose struggle for justice is evidenced in the concrete actions of ethical human persons. King urged that people treat each other with respect for the presence of God in the growth of individuals and communities—that is, he urged that individuals treat each other as persons. King's personalism and his encounter with the work of the Indian religious leader Mohandas Gandhi (1869–1948) led him to preach a philosophy of non-violent resistance toward social injustices, thus providing the grounds for one of the more momentous public movements in American history.

Feminist Philosophy

Women in American society have also been marginalized and their unique perspectives have been often overlooked and many times simply discarded. Despite this forced invisibility, American women have contributed to worldwide feminist movements, often in uniquely American ways far different from their counterparts in other nations and cultures.

> Western civilization seems clear, orderly, obvious, and without possibility of reform primarily because it defines the world in certain rigid categories. The product of this clarity, however, is a certain kind of insanity that can survive only by renewed efforts to refine the definitions and that, ultimately, becomes totally self-destructive.
>
> SOURCE: Vine Deloria Jr., *Spirit and Reason,* p. 4.

From childhood, Jane Addams (1860–1935) was deeply troubled by the blight of economic and social inequality. As a philosopher, social activist, and founder of Hull House, a settlement house for immigrants and the working poor in Chicago, her work focused on rehabilitating communities in theory and in practice, and rectifying inequalities not by philanthropic charity work, but by cultivating sympathetic understanding and mutual concern. Addams offered her principle of *reciprocity* as an important tool with which to approach the building of communities. Addams insisted that the interaction of otherwise separate social groups be treated as reciprocal, that is, as offering mutual benefit. Viewed in this way, what might otherwise become an impersonal philanthropic enterprise that serves to make more explicit the line between giver and taker becomes instead an opportunity for mutual enrichment and the sympathetic understanding necessary to create a community.

In the late twentieth century, feminist Carol Gilligan (1936–) wrote *In a Different Voice: Psychological Theory and Women's Development* (1982), calling for recognizing the different and valuable ways that women think and evaluate moral situations. Having done extensive study on moral and psychological development, Gilligan found most research to be biased toward the male point of view. Focusing instead on care for others and responsibility toward relationships, feminine morality should be valued for its own merits and not treated as secondary to a more masculine emphasis on rules, rights, and laws, according to Gilligan.

Catharine MacKinnon (1946–), an attorney, social activist, and writer, successfully argued that sexual harassment is, legally, a form of sexual discrimination. Her books and other writings have had a powerful impact on American and international movements in the legal status of pornography, hate speech, and women's rights. Other key contemporary American feminists are Sandra Harding (1935–), Nancy Fraser, Donna Haraway (1944–), and Alison Jaggar.

Anglo-American Philosophy

Anglo-American philosophy, also known as analytic philosophy, is largely an import from European thinkers who immigrated to the United States during the first half of the twentieth century and their followers. Perhaps the most famous of these immigrants was Bertrand Russell (1872–1970), who was a serious academic philosopher and a great popularizer of both analytic philosophy and his own controversial ethical and political beliefs. Analytic philosophy focuses on rigorous argumentation, is typically quite amenable to scientific evidence and concerns, and tends to primarily address linguistic, logical, epistemological, and metaphysical issues. In some ways, analytic philosophy arose as a reaction to what was seen as a weakness in much of European philosophy—its increasing tendency toward vagueness, metaphor, and literary conceit. By the end of the twentieth century, Anglo-American philosophy and its methods had become the most influential force in most academic philosophy departments in the United States, as well as in the largest group of professional philosophers, the American Philosophical Association.

See also **Analytical Philosophy; Philosophies: Feminist, Twentieth-Century; Pragmatism.**

BIBLIOGRAPHY

Addams, Jane. *Democracy and Social Ethics.* New York: Macmillan, 1902.

Deloria, Vine, Jr. *Spirit and Reason: The Vine Deloria, Jr., Reader.* Golden, Colo.: Fulcrum, 1999.

Flower, Elizabeth, and Murray Murphey. *A History of Philosophy in America.* 2 vols. New York: Putnam, 1977.

Harris, Leonard, ed. *Philosophy Born of Struggle: Anthology of Afro-American Philosophy from 1917.* Dubuque, Iowa: Kendall/Hunt, 1983.

Martinich, A.P., and David Sosa, eds. *Analytic Philosophy: An Anthology.* Malden, Mass.: Blackwell, 2001.

Myerson, Joel, ed. *Transcendentalism: A Reader.* Oxford: Oxford University Press, 2000.

Schneider, Herbert W. *A History of American Philosophy.* New York: Columbia University Press, 1946.

Seigfried, Charlene Haddock. *Pragmatism and Feminism: Reweaving the Social Fabric.* Chicago: University of Chicago Press, 1996.

Smith, John E., Harry S. Stout, and Kenneth P. Minkema, eds. *A Jonathan Edwards Reader.* New Haven, Conn.: Yale University Press, 1995.

Stuhr, John J., ed. *Pragmatism and Classical American Philosophy: Essential Readings and Interpretive Essays.* Oxford: Oxford University Press, 1999.

Waters, Anne, ed. *American Indian Thought: Philosophical Essays.* Malden, Mass.: Blackwell, 2003.

Stephen Barnes

FEMINIST, TWENTIETH-CENTURY

The term *feminism* is used both in reference to social movements, such as the late-nineteenth century women's rights movement or the mid-twentieth century women's movement in Europe and the United States, and to theories that identify and critique injustices against women, such as *A Vindication of the Rights of Woman* by Mary Wollstonecraft (1759–1797) or *The Book of the City of Ladies* by Christine de Pisan (c. 1364–1430). Although there are various uses of the term, a core connotation of *feminism* is the commitment to revealing and eliminating sexist oppression.

If one searches the discipline of twentieth century philosophy for philosophers who were feminists, few if any names surface prior to mid-century. It was only beginning in the last half of the twentieth century that philosophers systematically turned their attention to the issues of feminism and embraced the label of "feminist philosophy" to signify a method or focus of attention for doing philosophy. Although it would be a mistake to conclude from this that earlier philosophers were not concerned with the identification and elimination of gender injustice, it does reflect the fact that this was not a central concern of academic philosophy.

It could be argued that feminist philosophy in the late nineteenth and early twentieth centuries began outside the academy, birthed through the writings and radical activities of such feminists as Charlotte Perkins Gilman (1860–1935), Ida B. Wells-Barnett (1862–1931), Emma Goldman (1869–1940), Jane Addams (1860–1935), and Anna Julia Cooper (1858–1964). Indeed, one important tenet of feminist history of philosophy is an awareness of the fact that due to the systemic exclusion of most women from the dominant sites of philosophy—the academy and the seminary—one must look to those locations where women are doing philosophy at different historical periods, such as the salon, the convent, and the women's movement.

Many scholars have marked the genesis of contemporary feminist philosophy with *The Second Sex* by Simone de Beauvoir (1908–1986), and there is good reason for doing so. *The Second Sex* provides one of the first sustained analyses of the lived experience of "becoming woman." Beauvoir examines the institutions and practices that lead to women internalizing a sense of inferiority to men, that is, woman as Other. Beauvoir's philosophical insights are contained in her now famous phrase, "One is not born a woman: one becomes one." In this she presages feminist distinctions between sex and gender, and the ways in which women are "produced" through complex disciplinary practices such as marriage, motherhood, and sexuality.

Beauvoir's philosophy not only provided an important source of modern feminist philosophy, the reception of her work illustrates the very types of exclusions feminists have critiqued. Her writings were, until recently, often relegated to asides or footnotes, and typically treated as derivative of the philosophy of Jean-Paul Sartre (1905–1980). The 1967 *The Encyclopedia of Philosophy,* to cite just one telling example, only refers to Beauvoir in two entries, one on Sartre where she is described as one of the founders of the review *Les Temps Modernes,* and another on existentialism that asserts that she employed some of Sartre's analyses in her writings. Contemporary feminist philosophical scholarship on Beauvoir has transformed her position in the philosophical canon by demonstrating the significant impact of Beauvoir's ideas on Sartre's philosophy and by locating her work within the phenomenological tradition.

Social and Political Theory

Feminist philosophical work that emerged after Beauvoir's *Second Sex* was influenced by the women's movement and had a strong focus on issues of justice and equality. Feminist philosophers began by paying attention to women, to their roles and locations. What are women doing? What social and political locations are they part of or excluded from? How do their activities compare to those of men? What do women's roles and locations allow or preclude? How have their roles been valued or devalued? Because of the centrality of questions such as these, feminist philosophers grappled with political theories that would be adequate to such concerns.

Alison Jaggar's 1983 *Feminist Politics and Human Nature* provided an influential discussion of the various political theories feminists employed in efforts to argue for women's liberation. Jaggar delineated four primary frameworks: liberal feminism, which focuses on rights and equal access, and argues that the primary cause of women's oppression is laws and rules that limit women's equal access to educational, economic, and political institutions; Marxist feminism, which argues that at the root of sexist oppression is class oppression; radical feminism, which identifies patriarchy and male control over women's bodies, including sexuality and reproduction, as the cause of sexual subordination; and socialist feminism, which views economic and social institutions as interdependent and thus attempts to incorporate the insights of the class analysis of Marxism with the radical feminist critique of patriarchical social organizations.

Ethics

Contemporary feminist philosophers have also enriched and arguably transformed the field of ethics. Through their attention to the concerns of women, feminist philosophers have introduced new issues to feminist ethics and social theory, such as affirmative action, sexual harassment, and comparable worth, and have brought new insights to more traditional issues, for example, discussions of abortion, and the institutions of marriage, sexuality, and love.

Some feminists who work in the field of ethics have argued that traditional ethical theories are inadequate in that they ignore the experiences and perspectives of women by overstressing rights or duties and neglecting issues of care and relationships. Virginia Held argues for an enriched moral theory that is based not on the ideal of the "autonomous man" but rather on the ideal of the "relational woman." Others, such as Sara Ruddick, have argued that traditional Western ethical theories have trivialized those virtues historically associated with women and in so doing have neglected the fact that the typical moral situation is not between two completely autonomous and equal individuals, but rather, more like the relationship between parent and child: that is, between individuals with different strengths and weaknesses. Ruddick claims that maternal practices, with their aims of preservation, growth, and acceptability of children, provide a particularly rich alternative to the "contract model" of liberal social theory.

Feminist philosophers have also argued that attention to gender cannot be done in isolation from other axes of oppression, such as sexuality, race, ability, or class. The work of feminist philosophers such as Linda Martín Alcoff, Claudia Card, Nancy Fraser, Marilyn Frye, Sarah Lucia Hoagland, Eva

Kittay, María Lugones, Anita Silvers, Elizabeth Spelman, Iris Marion Young, and Naomi Zack reveal the importance of analyses that identify the structure and consequences of the interaction between different forms of discrimination or subordination.

While ethics and political theory have been a focal point of contemporary feminist philosophers, feminist philosophical work has included all the core areas of philosophy and has made use of all the philosophical traditions. The "difference" of feminist philosophy does not have to do with philosophical traditions or themes—indeed, feminist philosophers work in all the traditions of philosophy including analytic, Continental, and classical American philosophy, and their thematic focus is often influenced by the topics and questions highlighted by these traditions.

History of Philosophy

Feminist work in the history of philosophy was initially concerned with analyzing canonical philosophers' accounts of women and their conceptions of femininity. Although there were exceptions, the philosophical canon is rife with conceptions of women as lesser or misbegotten men, a bias that has had a profound structuring impact on the history of philosophical and scientific conceptions of men as the true form and women as inferior. Luce Irigaray argues that woman has been defined not in terms of true difference from men, but in terms of lack according to an A (male) / −A (female) logic. Men are the true form; women the deviation. Men are rational animals; women less capable of reason.

But the "question of women" in feminist scholarship in the history of philosophy is far broader than canonical (male) philosophical views of women. Much feminist philosophical scholarship has been devoted to recovering the work of women philosophers who have been "forgotten" or, like Beauvoir, seen as too marginal to be included in the canon. Philosophers of history such as Mary Ellen Waite, Eileen O'Neill, Therese Dykeman, and John J. Conley, who have devoted their attention to recovering the work of women philosophers, argue that the lack of women philosophers in contemporary histories of philosophy is due neither to the absence of women philosophers nor to the significance and value of their work, but is the result of complex values that inform the narratives of philosophy and determine what questions and styles count as philosophical and whose voices are sufficiently influential to be chronicled.

Feminists working in the history of philosophy have further argued that gender leaves traces not only on canonization processes, but deeply inscribes the very concepts of philosophy. One common theme in feminist histories of philosophy is the contention that many of the central categories of philosophy are formed through the exclusion of the feminine. In a complex two-step process, concepts such as reason, morality, and agency are produced through the prioritizing of masculine characteristics and the forgetting of gender. The concepts so constructed are then posited as objective and universal rather than gendered and particular. As just one example, Genevieve Lloyd argues that "rationality has been conceived as the transcendence of the feminine; and the 'feminine' itself has been partly constituted by its occurrence within this structure" (p. 104).

To the extent that the central categories of philosophy have been inscribed in this way, not only is philosophy *not* the objective, universal practice many philosophers have believed it to be, it is also complicit in a social organization that impoverishes the lives of women as well as men. The question of the maleness of reason, for example, may be what is behind common judgments of women as less capable of rational thought, but the question itself is far more complex. To investigate the maleness of reason, one must consider the extent to which conceptions of rationality have privileged traits historically associated with masculinity. In other words, one must consider the extent to which the attainment of rationality has been perceived as involving the control or transcendence of attributes historically identified as female—the body, the emotions, the passions, the appetites, the erotic. If it is the case that what Michèle Le Dœuff has called the "philosophical imagery of gender" (1989) is inscribed onto a philosopher's conception of reason, then one can not simply ignore his (or her) sexism for it is at the core of the values from which this central category emerges.

Feminist philosophy's attendance to the denigration of the feminine in the history of philosophy presents an important step, but one that must be seen as a first step of a much larger inquiry. Feminists delineate such bias not to simply reject a philosopher, but rather to participate in new ways of reading historical texts that identify resources for engendering the central concepts of philosophy in ways not predicated on the forgetting of gender. These reading strategies are diverse and reflect the different positions and training of feminists themselves. Some, such as Le Dœuff, Penelope Deutscher, Sarah Kofman, and Irigaray, bring deconstructive methods to bear on canonical texts. Others, such as Annette Baier, Barbara Herman, and Martha Nussbaum, read through the lens of contemporary feminist revaluing of the emotions.

Epistemology and Philosophy of Science

Feminist philosophers have also made significant contributions to epistemology and the philosophy of science. Lloyd's insights about the gendering of reason led to substantive analysis of contemporary conceptions of rationality, the process of inquiry, and the knowing subject. Epistemologists and philosophers of science such as Lorraine Code, Sandra Harding, Helen Longino, Lynn Hankinson Nelson, Elizabeth Potter, and Naomi Scheman have critiqued traditional "S knows that P" models of knowledge. A common theme of feminist epistemology is that the traditional view of the knowing subject as distinct but not distinctive is inadequate in that it occludes the ways in which human knowledge practices emerge out of and are influenced by social structures, including those of gender. In other words, the goal of a generic knower is misguided in that subjectivity is always at least partially socially constituted. On this position, no one, regardless of gender, race, class, or ability, is a generic subject.

This conception of situated knowers is a key component of many feminist epistemologies and philosophies of science.

Harding develops a version of standpoint theory to account for the ways in which social location can impact knowledge practices, and argues that this theory supports a strengthened conception of objectivity, one that is less susceptible to the production of community-wide biases than research modeled on the "neutrality ideal." Longino and Nelson have also critiqued the individualism of "S knows that P" accounts, arguing in the case of Longino that knowledge is held by persons who are part of complex social communities where both the knower and what is known are marked by that relationship. Nelson, building on a naturalized epistemology inspired by W. V. O. Quine's emphasis on studying how humans in fact reason, argues that it is communities rather than individuals who know.

The commitment to situated knowers has led to an appreciation of the role of embodiment in knowledge practices (for example, in the work of Susan Bordo, Elizabeth Grosz, and Gail Weiss), as well as the role of emotion, imagination, empathy, and values (for example, in the work of Louise Antony, Susan Babbitt, Lorraine Code, Longino, and Alison Wylie).

Conclusion

Feminist philosophical work is making an impact in other areas of philosophy such as metaphysics (Charlotte Witt, Sally Haslanger, Marilyn Frye, Christine Battersby), aesthetics (Peg Brand, Cynthia Freeland), and the philosophy of religion (Pamela Sue Anderson, Ellen Armour, Gail Jantzen).

For those who would critique feminist philosophy as motivated by political concerns and thus not a pure philosophy, Alcoff providers a reminder that much work in the history of western philosophy emerged out of particular political motivations, including the work of René Descartes (1596–1650), Immanuel Kant (1724–1804), John Locke (1632–1704), and Bertrand Russell (1872–1970). As Alcoff explains, "like Kant, feminist philosophers are committed to using philosophical methods to clarify and disempower the current dogmatisms that inhibit political advance" (p. 55).

See also **Feminism; Gender; Gender Studies: Anthropology; Human Rights: Women's Rights; Sexual Harassment; Womanism.**

BIBLIOGRAPHY

Addams, Jane. *Democracy and Social Ethics.* New York: Macmillan, 1902.

Alcoff, Linda Martín. 2001. "On Judging Epistemic Credibility: Is Social Identity Relevant?" In *Engendering Rationalities,* edited by Nancy Tuana and Sandra Morgen. Albany: State University of New York Press, 2001.

Anderson, Pamela Sue. *A Feminist Philosophy of Religion: The Rationality and Myths of Religious Belief.* Oxford: Blackwell, 1998.

Antony, Louise M. "Quine as Feminist: The Radical Import of Naturalized Epistemology." In *A Mind of One's Own: Feminist Essays on Reason and Objectivity,* edited by Louise M. Antony and Charlotte Witt. Boulder, Colo.: Westview, 1993.

Armour, Ellen T. *Deconstruction, Feminist Theology and the Problem of Difference: Subverting the Race/Gender Divide.* Chicago: University of Chicago Press, 1999.

Babbitt, Susan E. *Impossible Dreams: Rationality, Integrity, and Moral Imagination.* Boulder, Colo.: Westview, 1996.

Baier, Annette. *A Progress of Sentiments: Reflections on Hume's Treatise.* Cambridge, Mass.: Harvard University Press, 1991.

Battersby, Christine. *The Phenomenal Woman: Feminist Metaphysics and the Patterns of Identity.* New York: Routledge, 1998.

Beauvoir, Simone de. *The Second Sex.* Translated and edited by H. M. Parshley. New York: Knopf, 1953.

Bordo, Susan. *Unbearable Weight: Feminism, Western Culture, and the Body.* Berkeley: University of California Press, 1993.

Brand, Peg, and Mary Devereaux, eds. "Women, Art, and Aesthetics." Special issue of *Hypatia: A Journal of Feminist Philosophy* 18, no. 4 (2003), entire issue.

Card, Claudia. *Lesbian Choices.* New York: Columbia University Press, 1995.

Code, Lorraine. *What Can She Know? Feminist Theory and the Construction of Knowledge.* Ithaca, N.Y.: Cornell University Press, 1991.

Cooper, Anna Julia. *A Voice from the South.* Xenia, Ohio: Aldine, 1892.

Conley, John J. *The Suspicion of Virtue: Women Philosophers in Neoclassical France.* Ithaca, N.Y.: Cornell University Press, 2002.

Deutscher, Penelope. *Yielding Gender: Feminism, Deconstructionism, and the History of Philosophy.* London: Routledge, 1997.

Dykeman, Therese Boos, ed. *The Neglected Canon: Nine Women Philosophers First to the Twentieth Century.* Dordrecht, Netherlands: Kluwer Academic, 1999.

Fraser, Nancy. *Unruly Practices: Power, Discourse, and Gender in Contemporary Social Theory.* Minneapolis: University of Minnesota Press, 1989.

Freeland, Cynthia. *But Is It Art?: An Introduction to Art Theory.* Oxford: Oxford University Press, 2001.

Frye, Marilyn. *The Politics of Reality: Essays in Feminist Theory.* Trumansburg, N.Y.: Crossing Press, 1983.

Gilman, Charlotte Perkins. *Women and Economics: A Study of the Economic Relation between Men and Women as a Factor in Social Evolution.* Boston: Small, Maynard, 1898.

Goldman, Emma. *The Traffic in Women and Other Essays in Feminism.* New York: Times Change Press, 1970.

Grosz, Elizabeth A. *Volatile Bodies: Toward a Corporeal Feminism.* St. Leonards, Australia: Allen and Unwin, 1994.

Harding, Sandra. *Whose Science? Whose Knowledge?: Thinking with Women's Lives.* Ithaca, N.Y.: Cornell University Press, 1991.

Haslanger, Sally. "Feminism and Metaphysics: Negotiating the Natural." In *Cambridge Companion to Feminism in Philosophy,* edited by Miranda Fricker and Jennifer Hornsby. Cambridge, U.K.: Cambridge University Press, 2000.

Held, Virginia. *Feminist Morality: Transforming Culture, Society, and Politics.* Chicago: University of Chicago Press, 1993.

Herman, Barbara. *The Practice of Moral Judgment.* Cambridge, Mass.: Harvard University Press, 1993.

Hoagland, Sarah Lucia. *Lesbian Ethics: Toward New Value.* Palo Alto, Calif.: Institute of Lesbian Studies, 1988.

Irigaray, Luce. *Speculum of the Other Woman.* Translated by Gillian C. Gill. Ithaca, N.Y.: Cornell University Press, 1985.

Jaggar, Alison. *Feminist Politics and Human Nature.* Totowa, N.J.: Rowman and Allanheld, 1983.

Jantzen, Gail. *Becoming Divine: Towards a Feminist Philosophy of Religion.* Manchester, U.K.: Manchester University Press, 1998.

Kittay, Eva. *Love's Labor: Essays on Women, Equality, and Dependency.* New York: Routledge, 1999.

Kofman, Sarah. *The Enigma of Woman: Women in Freud's Writings.* Translated by Catherine Porter. Ithaca, N.Y.: Cornell University Press, 1985.

———. *Socrates: Fictions of a Philosopher.* Translated by Catherine Porter. Ithaca, N.Y.: Cornell University Press, 1998.

Le Dœuff, Michèle. *The Philosophical Imaginary.* Translated by Colin Gordon. Stanford, Calif.: Stanford University Press, 1989.

Lloyd, Genevieve. *The Man of Reason: "Male" and "Female" in Western Philosophy.* Minneapolis: University of Minnesota Press, 1984.

Longino, Helen. *Science as Social Knowledge: Values and Objectivity in Scientific Inquiry.* Princeton, N.J.: Princeton University Press, 1990.

Lugones, María. *Pilgrimages = Peregrinajes: Theorizing Coalition Against Multiple Oppressions.* Lanham, Md.: Rowman and Littlefield, 2003.

Nelson, Lynn Hankinson. *Who Knows: From Quine to a Feminist Empiricism.* Philadelphia: Temple University Press, 1990.

Nussbaum, Martha C. *Sex and Social Justice.* New York: Oxford University Press, 1999.

O'Neill, Eileen. "Disappearing Ink: Early Modern Women Philosophers and Their Fate in History." In *Philosophy in a Feminist Voice: Critiques and Reconstructions,* edited by Janet A Kourany. Princeton, N.J.: Princeton University Press, 1998.

Pisan, Christine de. *The Book of the City of Ladies.* Translated by Rosalind Brown-Grant. London: Penguin, 1999.

Potter, Elizabeth. *Gender and Boyle's Law of Gases.* Bloomington: Indiana University Press, 2001.

Ruddick, Sara. *Maternal Thinking: Towards a Politics of Peace.* Boston: Beacon, 1989.

Scheman, Naomi. *Engenderings: Constructions of Knowledge, Authority, and Privilege.* New York: Routledge, 1993.

Silvers, Anita, David Wasserman, and Mary B. Mahowald, eds. *Disability, Difference, Discrimination: Perspectives on Justice in Bioethics and Public Policy.* Lanham, Md.: Rowman and Littlefield, 1998.

Spelman, Elizabeth. *Inessential Woman: Problems of Exclusion in Feminist Thought.* Boston: Beacon, 1988.

Tougas, Cecile T., and Sara Ebenrick, eds. *Presenting Women Philosophers.* Philadelphia: Temple University Press, 2000.

Tuana, Nancy. 1993. *The Less Noble Sex: Scientific, Religious, and Philosophical Conceptions of Woman's Nature.* Bloomington: Indiana University Press, 1993.

———. *Woman and the History of Philosophy.* New York: Paragon House, 1992.

Weiss, Gail. *Body Images: Embodiment as Intercorporeality.* New York: Routledge, 1999.

Wells-Barnett, Ida B. *On Lynchings.* Amherst, Mass.: Humanity Books, 2002.

Witt, Charlotte. "Feminist Metaphysics." In *A Mind Of One's Own,* edited by Louise Antony and Charlotte Witt. Boulder, Colo.: Westview, 1993.

Wollstonecraft, Mary. *A Vindication of the Rights of Women.* London: J. Johnson, 1792.

Wylie, Alison. *Thinking From Things: Essays in the Philosophy of Archaeology.* Berkeley: University of California Press, 2002.

Young, Iris Marion. *Justice and the Politics of Difference.* Princeton, N.J.: Princeton University Press, 1990.

Zack, Naomi. *Race and Mixed Race.* Philadelphia: Temple University Press, 1993.

Nancy Tuana

ISLAMIC

All Muslims hold the Koran as the very word of God, who provides guidance and understanding of creation and proper human conduct by divine wisdom (*hikma*). This wisdom is also reflected in the oral statements of the prophet Muhammad collected in the Traditions (hadith) and in the reports of the life and deeds (sunna) of the Prophet. The study of these in the traditional Islamic religious sciences of Koranic commentary (*tafsir*), Traditions, religious law (*al-fiqh*), Arabic grammar, and related religious studies is the human response to the command of the Koran to seek out knowledge and understanding (20:114; 39:9). That search for knowledge and understanding is not limited to studies strictly religious since the whole of creation manifests divine wisdom. Hence medicine, mathematics, and study of nature can be included in the divine command, though these are classified as foreign sciences and rational or intellectual sciences. Philosophy, which retains its reference to its non-Islamic origins in its transliterated form as *falsafah*, is located in this second group but nevertheless came to be identified by the philosophers of the Islamic milieu with the wisdom (*al-hikma*) mentioned in the Koran and Traditions of the Prophet. In the classical period (eighth to twelfth centuries) the major philosophers of the lands of Islam (*dar al-islam*) characterized philosophical understanding at the highest levels as concerned with principles ultimately founded in God and thereby claimed a rightful stake in knowledge of the divine and of God's creation for the rational sciences. The significance of this idea can hardly be overemphasized since this controversial assertion of the value of independent rationality was a hallmark of philosophy in the classical period and has had a deep and lasting influence not only among Muslim, Christian, and Jewish philosophical thinkers in Islamic lands but also in the medieval Latin West, where its effect was shocking and altogether new.

Philosophical Theology in Islam

Among the most important participants in *kalam* or Islamic theological dialectics were the Mu'tazilis whose name came from their reasoned disassociation from extremist views of moral purists (Kharijis), who would exclude sinners from the community and from those more accepting of transgressors (Murji'is). The name came to be associated with theologians asserting the value of human reason in the judging of religious issues, famously insisting on rational coherence in regard to divine attributes by denying scriptural literalism in favor of allegorical interpretation and the denial of attributes to divine unity, on the rational necessity of the restraint of divine justice by human freedom, and on the created nature of the Koran. Abu'l-Hasan al-Ash'ari (873–935), breaking away from his Mu'tazili teacher, al-Juba'i (d. 915), argued for the literal understanding of divine attributes recounted in God's revelation, for what is now characterized as divine command moral theory (that Justice is itself defined as whatever God decrees), and for the eternal speech of God and the uncreated Koran. This was so, he asserted, because on such matters the statements of the Koran must be accepted *bi-la kayf*, "without asking how." Insofar as all power belongs to God, all actions are dependent upon God and are merely "acquisitions" (*aksab*) by humans of states and actions created by God. This led to the

development of an occasionalist atomism in which transitory atoms having no persisting natures are renewed in existence only by divine power and apparent regularity of nature is fully dependent on divine will. The Ash'ari analysis receives its most powerful expression in the later thought of al-Ghazali, who attacked Aristotelian accounts of natural causality by famously arguing that there is no metaphysically necessary connection between what purport to be cause and effect.

Transmission and Development of Greek Science and Philosophy

The quantity of important works of science and philosophy translated into Arabic was unrivaled until modern times. Among the philosophical writings translated were the entire corpus of Aristotle's works (with the notable exception of his *Politics*), the dialogues of Plato as well as their *Summaries* by Galen, a vast array of medical works by Galen and others, substantial portions of the *Enneads* of Plotinus, the *Isagoge* and other works of Porphyry, and works by nearly all of the writers of the philosophical commentary tradition, such as Theophrastus, Alexander, Iamblichus, Themistius, Syrianus, Proclus, Ammonius, Simplicius, Philoponus, Olympiodorus, and others.

The extraordinary transference of philosophical and scientific knowledge from Greek into Arabic that took place during the long period of the Abbasid caliphate may be traced to a large array of factors: a desire to enhance Abbasid power by opening Islamic society to many different peoples; concerns of the ruling class for future success (thus the interest in Greek astrology) and for good health (thus the interest in Greek medical writings); the needs of a new, powerful, and growing empire for knowledge both practical and theoretical; and perhaps also a cultural ideology of valuing knowledge in all its forms as part of a Zoroastrian heritage. Whatever the precise reasons, it is clear that the translation, assimilation, and development of Greek thought was a broad cultural movement involving Christians, Muslims, and Jews working in concert both as translators and as philosophers teaching students and developing new approaches that, though founded on Greek thought, inevitably led to new doctrines argued not solely on the basis of tradition but on the basis of new scientific analyses and on the basis of reason itself.

Al-Kindi and the Assimilation of Greek Neoplatonic Metaphysics

Research on the thought of al-Kindi (d. c. 870) and an early phase of the translation movement at Baghdad has led to the conclusion that this Arab philosopher was part of a circle or group of thinkers with special interest in Greek metaphysical texts concerning God, the higher intellects moving the heavens, and the soul. Among the works translated wholly or partially and studied by this group were Aristotle's *Metaphysics* by Eustathius; selections from Plotinus's *Enneads*, books 4–5 (portions of which were revised, edited, prefaced by al-Kindi to be issued as the *Theology of Aristotle*); Plato's *Timaeus*; Aristotle's *On the Heavens, Meteorology, Prior Analytics*; works on animals by Yahya Ibn al-Bitriq; and selections or perhaps all of the *Elements of Theology* of Proclus as well as other selections by Proclus attributed to Alexander of Aphrodisias by unknown translators (Endress). This group produced a paraphrase of the *De Anima;* the widely read and influential *Theology of Aristotle;* and the *Discourse on the Pure Good,* a creationist treatise based on the *Elements of Theology* of Proclus and the *Theology of Aristotle.* The *Discourse* was read in Arabic by a number of philosophers but had its greatest influence in the Latin West as the *Liber de causis,* where its highly influential discussion of the First Cause as being alone, devoid of form, was read as the completion of Aristotle's discussion of God in the *Metaphysics* (D'Ancona and Taylor). That metaphysical doctrine was borrowed from the Arabic Plotinus, which had already probably been "adapted" by the Christian translator Ibn Na'ima al-Himsi to monotheism and to an Aristotelian conception of God as the First Being and cause of all other beings (Adamson). In the pseudo-Aristotelian *Theology of Aristotle,* metaphysics ("what is after the physical") is presented as identical with divine sovereignty (*rububiyya*) and divine things (*ilahiyyat*). Al-Kindi as editor and presumed author of the preface of this work set forth the view that the subject matter of metaphysics is the same as that of dialectical theology or *kalam.*

Arguing against those theologians of his day who would reject any role for the foreign science of philosophy, al-Kindi boldly asserted in what is extant from his *On First Philosophy* that the goal of the philosopher is the attainment of truth by causal knowledge of the True One, which is the cause of existence for all things. Identifying the religious study of divine unity (*tawhid*) as having the same end as the philosophical pursuit of the truth, al-Kindi not only argues for a major role for philosophy in defending against unbelievers of various sorts but also asserts that philosophical metaphysics has the God of revelation as its ultimate object of study. By an examination of the nature of unity or oneness (*wahda*), al-Kindi concludes that there is no true or essential unity in created things and that unity must be derived from the True One. Creation is also argued in another work to be the only True Agent insofar as it alone acts by a creative agency presupposing nothing, while all other agents are mere metaphorical agents insofar as their agency is not essentially their own but rather derived from their being and power, which are to be traced to God. These accounts of God as True Unity and as First and Primary Cause of all are also found in the *Discourse on the Pure Good* and contribute to the view that al-Kindi himself may have been the author or editor of that work as well as of the *Theology of Aristotle.* Al-Kindi's philosophical psychology is also based on a mixture of genuine Aristotelian teachings and adapted teachings of Plotinus, though other sources from the Greek tradition are detectable. His treatise *On the Intellect* with its assertion of intellect as of four kinds (intellect eternally in act, intellect as potency in the soul, intellect as an actualized disposition in the soul, and intellect as act in the soul) shows more immediate dependence on the school account of the Christian Alexandrian John Philoponus. He also employed the arguments of Philoponus to assert for philosophical reasons the temporal creation, a doctrine thought to be in accord with the apparent sense of Koranic revelation. And in his ethical treatise, *On the Art of Dispelling Sorrows,* he draws upon the Stoic argument for restraint regarding earthly desires and the cares they engender for the sake of a hoped-for lasting and permanent intellectual fulfillment of the higher realm not further elaborated.

In his teachings al-Kindi clearly showed a degree of affinity with the rationalist goals of the Mu'tazili theologians of his day as well as a desire for conciliation of philosophy and Islam, though his commitment to Greek philosophy was foundational. That his followers used his works and those of his group for the understanding of Islamic teachings is particularly evident in the work of al-'Amiri (d. 992) who wrote *On the Afterlife,* drawing on Aristotelian and Neoplatonic sources for arguments for personal immortality promised in the Koran. He made use of a large array of materials from al-Kindi's group and was quite familiar with the Arabic Plotinus texts as well as with the *Discourse on the Pure Good,* which he paraphrased in *Chapters on Metaphysical Topics* (Rowson). The tradition of al-Kindi, however, was soon eclipsed by the work of Avicenna, who drew upon the thought of al-Farabi, a thinker who was less sanguine on the harmony of philosophy with Islam.

Hunayn ibn Ishaq and Baghdad Aristotelianism

Contemporaneous with the circle of al-Kindi, the Christian Hunayn ibn Ishaq (d. 873) initiated a tradition of sophisticated translation of Greek philosophical, medical, and scientific works into Syriac and Arabic. In contrast to the al-Kindi group, Hunayn's group of translators and their successors made extensive efforts to track down works for translation, exercised greater care in selecting and collating manuscripts, translated by consideration of whole phrases or sentences rather than individual words, and standardized much vocabulary. Translation, particularly of works by Galen and other physicians, was a lucrative business, and some of its practitioners were paid well by wealthy families for quality translations and the revision or retranslation of earlier versions. The enormous wealth of translations of this period recorded in the *Fihrist* or book catalogs of Ibn al-Nadim bears witness to the fertile ground for the rise of a new Aristotelianism in Baghdad fostered by Christian translators and philosophers of Syriac background, such as Abu Bashr Matta, Ishaq ibn Hunayn, and many others who were able to consult Syriac as well as Arabic translations. F. W. Zimmermann notes that "in the contemporary milieu of Baghdad the predominant language of Christian scholarship still was Syriac. Syriac Christianity, owing to its roots in the Greek church and a considerable tradition of Hellenic learning in Syriac, had a virtual monopoly of access to the Greek legacy" (al-Farabi, 1981, lxxvii). The tradition this movement inherited was that of late Aristotelianism of the Alexandrian School. And while he apparently did not know Syriac and depended on his teachers and colleagues for philosophical sources, the representative of this tradition most well-known today is al-Farabi.

Abu Nasr al-Farabi

Abu Nasr al-Farabi (c. 870–950) likely worked for the greater part of his eighty-year lifespan in Baghdad, where he was a student of logic with the Christian Yuhanna ibn Haylan and taught the Christian Yahya ibn 'Adi, who came to be a leading philosophical figure in Baghdad. Al-Farabi was thoroughly engaged in the great project of the establishment of a new

New Dictionary of the History of Ideas

Alexandrian Aristotelianism in the Arabic philosophical context. His apparently enormous literary output, of which only a modest portion survives, includes sophisticated paraphrases and commentaries on Aristotle's logical works as well as lost commentaries on Aristotle's *On Generation and Corruption* and *Nicomachean Ethics,* innovative emanationist accounts of principles governing the universe and human societies (*The Principles of the Opinions of the People of the Virtuous City* and *The Political Regime or the Principles of Beings*), a set of works on Plato and Aristotle (*The Attainment of Happiness, The Philosophy of Plato, The Philosophy of Aristotle, The Harmony of Plato and Aristotle*), complex works on the nature of metaphysics, logic, and language (*On One and Unity, The Book of Letters,* and *The Purposes of Metaphysics*), and more.

Al-Farabi worked to build a coherent understanding of philosophy as a systematic discipline founded on Platonic insights and Aristotelian principles. At the foundation of this was his apparent correction of the view of al-Kindi and his group that the end of philosophy and religion is the same, namely the knowledge of divine unity and truth. In his *Intentions of Aristotle's Metaphysics,* al-Farabi argues for metaphysics to be understood not as a special science dealing primarily with God, as in al-Kindi, but as a general science dealing with the principles of being. On this understanding the study of God and higher causes (special metaphysics) is understood as encompassed within general metaphysics, which deals with all being and unity. Since metaphysics deals with the more universal causes of beings of the material world, al-Farabi does not neglect special metaphysics but rather sets out to explain that causality by way of an account of emanation following Ptolemaic astronomy in *The Principles of the Opinions of the People of the Virtuous City* and *The Political Regime or the Principles of Beings.* From the noetic activity of the First Cause, which in Aristotelian fashion is self-thinking thought, another emanates and from this there emanate both another intellect and the outermost celestial sphere, a process that continues giving rise to intellects and planetary spheres terminating with the final and lowest intellect, the agent intellect (*al-'aql al-fa"al*), which oversees the sublunar realm, the matter for which comes from the celestial spheres. This last intellect in the emanative hierarchy al-Farabi identifies with the agent intellect that Aristotle posited in *De Anima* 3.5 to account for the understanding of intelligible universals in contrast with sensation and imagination, which apprehend only particulars. In his *Treatise on the Intellect* based on his study of Alexander of Aphrodisias rather than the *De Anima* directly (Geoffroy 2002), he explains that human happiness lies in the transcendence of the body and some degree of immaterial noetic identity with the agent intellect. The separate agent intellect enables abstraction and brings the potential intellect to act with intelligibles in actuality existing in individual minds. When the acquired intellect has been perfected by the understanding of universal principles, the philosopher no longer requires the body and is able to associate with the separate agent intellect. Although this doctrine of intellectual perfection plays an important role in al-Farabi's teachings, Averroës, Ibn Bajjah, and others report that he abandoned this view that a generated human knower could become immortal and eternal in his lost *Commentary on the Nicomachean Ethics* as an old wives' tale.

Al-Farabi's account of intellect and the knowledge of universal principles provides the noetic account essential for his understanding of human beings and society. Just as with Plato, who singled out the philosopher-king to rule because of his highest, most perfect knowledge in the ideal city-state of the *Republic,* so too according to al-Farabi the rightful place of rule belongs to the philosopher-king, who has exact scientific knowledge through philosophical demonstration and proof, not the mere dialectical accounts of poetry and rhetoric. While these are understood to be included in the *Organon* with Aristotle's logical works, they aim only at persuasion by the prompting of images in the hearer and not at the rigorous truth of demonstration. Ideally the images of religion conveyed by a prophet and taught by an imam work to prompt those receiving them into action in accord with the end of human beings, which is happiness in perfection of intellect. Yet few are intellectually capable of this, so rhetoric, poetry, dialectic—all of which are contained in religion and revelation—provide a way for the truth (which is known to the philosopher directly but to the others in the emotive movement of the soul's imagination) to be shared with the community. This allows for the prophet-imam-philosopher to guide the community toward its perfection, which is the perfection of individual human beings to the point that they ascend to the level of the agent intellect. In accord with this, al-Farabi says at the beginning of his *Book of Religion,* "religion is opinions and actions, determined and restricted with stipulations and prescribed for a community by their first ruler, who seeks to obtain through their practicing it a specific purpose with respect to them or by means of them" (al-Farabi, 2001, p. 93). Thus rather than being one with philosophical metaphysics as al-Kindi had it, religion is concerned with particular human responses to the general end of human intellectual perfection. For al-Farabi, metaphysics and philosophical theology concern the intellectual study of the essential matters of being, unity, and its causes, while religion is concerned with particular and varying ways for the establishment of the conditions for highest human intellectual fulfillment on the part of select individuals.

This was a period of great intellectual diversity and creativity at Baghdad and elsewhere. The renowned physician Muhammad Ibn Zakariyya al-Razi (d. 925) wrote a wide range of works in philosophy, theology, cosmology, medicine, and more; he gave an account of creation as the fall of soul infused with knowledge by God and permitted to fulfill its yearning to be in matter, space, and time. It is likely that at about this time at Basra the Brethren of Purity (Ikhawan al-Safa) crafted and assembled much of their collection of treatises drawing upon Aristotle and the Arabic Plotinus to weave a view of philosophy as an essential part of the religious goal of the saving of the soul. But much of the work of this era was dwarfed and nearly forgotten in the shadow of Islam's most influential philosopher, Avicenna.

Avicenna (Ibn Sina)

The brilliant Persian philosopher, physician, and vizier Avicenna (Ibn Sina; 980–1037) was born in the village of Afshanah near Bukhara in present-day Uzbekistan. A diligent and exceptionally insightful student according to his own autobiographical account, Avicenna mastered medical, legal, scientific, and philosophical studies in short order and went on to develop his own philosophical teachings. The context in which he worked was that of the harmonization of the philosophies of Plato and Aristotle and the effort to bring about a complete and consistent teaching of the sort found in the late commentator Ammonius and pursued by al-Farabi, whose work guided Avicenna's understanding of Aristotle's *Metaphysics*. From this and his studies of Islamic theology, Avicenna crafted a new synthesis most evident in his broadly influential teachings on God as the Necessary Being and the human soul's separability from the body.

Avicenna's arguments for the Necessary Being appear in a number of important works. In the *Metaphysics* of his *Shifa'* (Healing), the argument that leads to the Necessary Being begins in book 1, chapter 5, which is on being (*mawjud*) and thing (*shay'*). There Avicenna writes that there are three first intentions that arise initially in the soul: being or existent, thing, and necessary. These are primary intentions that naturally arise as first principles grasped by the mind in the consideration of reality in any of its forms. But apprehended quiddity or essence has of its very nature an indeterminate openness to various sorts of existence determined by something outside the essence. The arguments for the existence of the Necessary Being then proceed by rejection of the impossibility that all beings are merely possible or contingent and the acceptance that there must be necessary being for the actual existence. Since there cannot be an infinite regress of beings necessary by another, Avicenna concludes that there must be a first, the unique Necessary Being that causes the existence of the dependent necessary and possible beings and is itself uncaused. This analysis leads to the Avicennian distinction of essence and existence so influential in Arabic philosophy and in the Latin West. The First is the True One that is existence alone, free of the limitation of form, while all other things are form and being received ultimately from God. Causality here is by way of emanation, as with al-Farabi, in a hierarchy of necessary beings, except that for Avicenna there is an emanation of an intellect, a celestial sphere, and a celestial soul associated with the celestial intellect as its mover. Holding firm to the principle "from one only one can arise," Avicenna asserted that there first was emanated an intellect and from that plurality arose. This emanation continues down to the level of the moon, at which point the agent intellect generated the world and all the forms in it.

This agent intellect is denominated the "giver of forms" because it gives forms both to human minds and to natural entities of the world. The human soul has a temporal origination and its individuation in being is the result of its association and joining with the body. But its nature as intellectual shows that it is not merely the form of a body. Rather, its nature as rational indicated to Avicenna that the soul is incorruptible and that it does not die with the death of the body. This is illustrated (not proved) by the famous "Flying Man" argument which holds that it can be imagined that even if a man is suspended in the air and in complete sensory deprivation as if bodiless, he would nonetheless affirm his existence as a rational soul. According to his *Letter to Kiya,* the key principle is found in Aristotle's discussion of the atomism of Democratus

in the *De Anima* and the notion that intelligibles can only exist in immaterial subjects. The common explanation that these intelligibles come to be in the soul by emanation when the soul is prepared for their reception and not by true abstraction has been challenged recently with texts suggesting a greater role for the activities of the soul itself. Still for Avicenna the soul of a prophet has special powers of imagination to receive intelligibles directly from the agent intellect and to communicate them to the people in religious discourse.

Avicenna's philosophy dominated the tradition that continued to develop after his death even after the harsh attacks of the Ash'ari theologian Abu Hamid Muhammad al-Ghazali (1058–1111). In the *Incoherence of the Philosophers,* al-Ghazali attacked the thought of the philosophers (al-Farabi and Avicenna) as insufficiently founded and also as contrary to Islam on the eternity of the world, God's knowledge of particulars, and the resurrection of the body. While the stated purpose of this work is to undermine the pronouncements and arguments of the philosophers, al-Ghazali's own Ash'ari occasionalism plays a role, for example, when he argues that there is no necessary connection but rather only habitual association between what are customarily called cause and effect. Such connections must be traced to divine will and power and are not found in the natures of things themselves.

Philosophy in Andalusia

While philosophical texts and ideas are present in the eclectic thinking of the Cordoba native and Sufi Ibn Masarrah (883–931), who drew upon Mu'tazili theology and Neoplatonic and pseudo-Empedoclean texts, the beginnings of rigorous philosophical study are with Ibn Bajjah (d. 1138). This philosopher from Saragossa is most famous for his challenge to the understanding of motion in the natural philosophy of Aristotle with a theory of impetus and momentum, for his theory of intentional forms and intellect and for his political philosophy of solitude. His theory of intellect is based on the consideration of spiritual forms or intentions that are apprehended in sensation and must be traced to higher realities. Using arguments from Neoplatonic sources against Aristotle's rejection of Plato's transcendent forms, Ibn Bajjah holds in his *Treatise on Conjunction with the Intellect* that intelligibles in act or universals cannot be founded on abstraction from particulars but rather can only be grounded in forms located in the unique agent intellect. True knowledge is not tied in any way to the transitory world but rather is the grasp of the eternal and unchanging forms causative of things of this world. These are apprehended by an intellectual "conjoining" with the agent intellect that is a uniting in oneness without the destruction of the individual. In this the end is the perfection and happiness that consist in conjoining and uniting with a separate agent intellect, and the means is intellectual understanding. Those who are intellectual in nature either are in a society in which they can lead as philosopher-king or they are rejected by the ignorant masses and must live a solitary life. Most often they find themselves in an unreceptive society, as in Andalusa and elsewhere, where they are like weeds. A similar theme is found in Ibn Tufayl's tale *Hayy ibn Yaqzan,* in which the protagonists find it impossible to lead the people by religion and take refuge in a solitary life apart from society.

Averroës (Ibn Rushd)

The Cordoban jurist, physician, and philosopher Averroës (Ibn Rushd; 1126–1198), more influential in the history of philosophy by his commentaries on Aristotle translated into Latin in the thirteenth century than for his work extant in Arabic, is famous for his commitment to the proper interpretation of Aristotle's philosophy and the rejection of the innovations of Avicenna, for his detailed response to the theologian al-Ghazali's attack on the philosophers in his *Incoherence of the Incoherence* and his rationalist critique of *kalam,* and for his own creative completion of Aristotle's doctrine of human intellect with the theory of a single shared receptive and incorporeal intellect (called "material intellect" following Alexander of Aphrodisias). While Averroës thought philosophy had attained its highest achievement in the thought of Aristotle ("I believe that this man was a model in nature and the exemplar which nature found for showing ultimate human perfection" [Averroës, 1953, p. 433]), his *Short, Middle* and detailed *Long Commentaries* expounded the difficult texts of Aristotle and completed unfinished philosophical accounts. Although he followed emanationist views in some early works, in his own mature account he argued that God is "creator" as the ultimate final cause drawing generated things from potency into act, continuing the heavens in eternal motion, sustaining the separate intellects (angels in religious language), and generally attracting all things toward the perfection of which he is the exemplar. He rejected Avicenna's distinction of essence and existence as philosophically unwarranted insofar as it is founded on *kalam* and also Avicenna's theory of the soul as an immortal substrate for the reception of intelligibles by emanation from the agent intellect. While in his early works on psychology Averroës held that each person possesses a distinct receptive material intellect, his final position was that both the material intellect and the agent intellect are distinct immaterial substances in which human knowers share. He was prompted to this position by the need for there to be one set of intelligibles for intersubjective discourse and understanding and by the realization that intelligibles in act received into a plurality of particular minds would become particulars, not the universals needed for knowledge. As a consequence he held the eternality of the material and agent intellects and also of the human species that provides images for abstraction by the agent intellect to impress upon the receptive material intellect. Contrary to Ibn Bajjah, Averroës viewed conjoining with separate intellect not as the end itself but as the means to human happiness in intellectual understanding. These mature positions were expounded only after he had written several works critical of *Kalam* advocating for a central role for philosophy in the attainment of truth concerning God and his creation. Most famous of these is the *Decisive Treatise,* in which this jurist who served as chief judge (*qadi*) of Cordoba mounted a vigorous defense of the pursuit of philosophy on the basis of Islamic religious law. He argued that philosophy is not only permitted but is the surest method of the attainment of truth and philosophical demonstration and so is endorsed by the Koran. Holding that there can be no conflict between the truths of demonstration and religion, he declared, "Truth does not contradict truth but rather is consistent with it and bears witness to it"—without mention of his source in Aristotle's *Prior Analytics*— thereby dispelling any concerns about the issue of a double truth, one for religion and one for philosophy. Where conflict between religion and reason arises, particularly concerning scriptural interpretation, reason's method of demonstration of truth is primary in determining the need for allegorical interpretation of otherwise conflicting explanations.

Condemned and exiled toward the end of his life, Averroës founded no school, and his influence in the subsequent development of philosophy in the Islamic milieu is hardly detectible until a revival of interest in the nineteenth century in the Arab world, where his thought was used to support various causes current then and later. His greatest influence was through Latin and Hebrew translations of his work that taught Latin and Jewish thinkers to read Aristotle and stirred great controversies among religious authorities wary of reason acting independently of the traditions of faith.

Before, during, and after the time of Averroës, Sufi mystical thought was a strong presence in Andalusia, and it is reported that the elderly Averroës met the very young Sufi Ibn al-'Arabi (1165–1240). Ibn al-'Arabi's notion of the unity of all being (*wahdat al-wujud*) and the perfect human being as the mirror of the divine brought to the fore the importance of imagination in apprehending the divine and contributed powerfully to the development of mystical philosophy in the East. Detailed work on the texts of philosophy is evidenced in the work of the pantheistic Sufi Ibn Sab'in (c. 1217–1270), whose broad knowledge of philosophy made him a suitable candidate for answering philosophical questions posed by the emperor Frederick II of Sicily. Ibn Khaldun (1332–1406) of Tunisia was an astute reader of philosophy, including the work of Averroës, and in his *Muqaddimah* he set forth a philosophy of history explaining political change in terms of social and structural changes.

In the East, philosophy continued to flourish with new developments in which the philosophy of Avicenna was the centerpiece, particularly his *Pointers and Reminders* (*al-Isharat wa'l-tanbihat*), the last section of which was read literally as mystical and religious. The Ash'ari theologian Fakhr al-Razi (d. 1209) attacked Avicenna, as later did the mystic illuminationist Suhrawardi (d. 1191), for whom Avicenna's Peripatetic epistemology was to be replaced by the necessity of Platonic Forms for true knowing in a doctrine of knowledge by presence in the intellectual ability to apprehend essences. The illuminationism of Suhrawardi had a lasting impact on philosophy in the East, as did the continuing legacy of Avicenna in figures such as Nasir al-Din al-Tusi (d. 1274), who expounded Avicennian metaphysics and authored the widely influential *Nasirian Ethics*. The development of *ishraqi* or illuminationist philosophy was continued by Qutb al-Din al-Shirazi (d.1311), who studied Avicenna and wrote a commentary on Suhrawardi's *Philosophy of Illumination*. By the time of the founding of the School of Isfahan by Mir Damad (d. 1631) and Sadr al-Din al-Shirazi or Mulla Sadra (d. 1641), the Safavid dynasty had long supported mystical thinking in Twelver Shiism. This new school systematically completed the synthesis of philosophical and Sufi mystical teachings from Ibn al-'Arabi and others in ways that continue to be reflected dominantly in Shiite thought. One notion of lasting philosophical interest is that of knowledge by presence with a focus on the "I" as knowing subject in lieu of a role for Avicenna's separate agent intellect. In the early twenty-first century the writings of Mulla Sadra and Suhrawardi play a powerful role in Iran, where philosophy is taught not only in religious schools but also in universities. Contemporary thinkers of the Shiite tradition of Iran, such as Mehdi Ha'iri Yazdi, who studied in the West and published *The Principles of Epistemology in Islamic Philosophy* in 1992, continue these traditions by placing the thought of Avicenna, Suhrawardi, and Mulla Sadra in dialogue with modern Western thought.

See also **Aristotelianism; Death and Afterlife, Islamic Understanding of; Islam; Philosophy and Religion in Western Thought; Sacred Texts: Koran.**

BIBLIOGRAPHY

Adamson, Peter. *The Arabic Plotinus: A Philosophical Study of the Theology of Aristotle.* London: Duckworth, 2002.

al-Farabi. *Alfarabi, the Political Writings: Selected Aphorisms and Other Texts.* Translated and annotated by Charles E. Butterworth. Ithaca, N.Y., and London: Cornell University Press, 2001.

———. *Al-Farabi's Commentary and Short Treatise on Aristotle's De Interpretatione.* Edited and translated by F. W. Zimmermann. Oxford: Oxford University Press, 1981.

Averroës (Ibn Rushd). *Averrois Cordubensis Commentarium Magnum in Aristotelis De Anima Libros.* Edited by F. Stuart Crawford. Cambridge, Mass.: Medieval Academy of America 1953.

———. *Averroës: On the Harmony of Religions and Philosophy.* Translated by George F. Hourani. London: Luzac, 1961.

———. *Averroës' Tahafut al-Tahafut (The Incoherence of the Incoherence).* Translated by Simon Van Den Bergh. London: Luzac, 1969.

Corbin, Henry. *En islam iranien, aspects spirituels et philosophiques.* 4 vols. Paris: Gallimard, 1971–1972.

D'Ancona, Cristina, and Richard C. Taylor. "Le Liber de causis." In *Dictionnaire de Philosophes Antiques. Supplément.* Edited by Richard Goulet et al. Paris: CNRS Edition, 2003.

Davidson, Herbert A. *Alfarabi, Avicenna, and Averroës on Intellect: Their Cosmologies, Theories of the Active Intellect, and Theories of Human Intellect.* Oxford: Oxford University Press, 1992.

Endress, Gerhard. "The Circle of Al-Kindi. Early Arabic Translations from the Greek and the Rise of Islamic Philosophy." In *The Ancient Tradition in Christian and Islamic Hellenism: Studies on the Transmission of Greek Philosophy and Sciences,* edited by Gerhard Endress and Remke Kruk. Leiden, Netherlands: Research School CNWS, 1997.

Fakhry, Majid. *Al-Farab, Founder of Islamic Neoplatonism: His Life, Works, and Influence.* Oxford: One World, 2002.

Geoffroy, Marc. "La tradition arabe du Peri; noù d'Alexandre d'Aphrodise et les origines de la theorie farabienne des quatre degres de l'intellect." In *Aristotele e Alessandro di Afrodisia nella Tradizione Araba,* edited by Cristina D'Ancona and Giuseppe Serra. Padua, Italy: Il Poligrafo, 2002.

Gohlman, William E. *The Life of Ibn Sina: A Critical Edition and Annotated Translation.* Albany: State University of New York Press, 1974.

Gutas, Dimitri. *Avicenna and the Aristotelian Tradition: Introduction to Reading Avicenna's Philosophical Works.* Leiden, Netherlands: Brill, 1988.

———. *Greek Thought, Arabic Culture: The Graeco-Arabic Translation Movement in Baghdad and Early Àbbâsid Society (2nd–4th/8th–10th centuries).* London and New York: Routledge, 1999.

Hasse, Dag Nikolaus. "Avicenna on Abstraction." In *Aspects of Avicenna,* edited by Robert Wisnovsky. Princeton, N.J.: Markus Wiener Publishers, 2001.

Ha'iri Yazdi, Mehdi. *The Principles of Epistemology in Islamic Philosophy: Knowledge by Presence.* Albany: State University of New York Press, 1992.

Harvey, Steven. "The Place of the Philosopher in the City according to Ibn Bâjjah." In *The Political Aspects of Islamic Philosophy: Essays in Honor of Muhsin S. Mahdi,* edited by Charles E. Butterworth. Cambridge, Mass.: Harvard University Press, 1992.

Hourani, George F. "Ibn Sina on Necessary and Possible Existence." *Philosophical Forum* 4 (1972): 74–86.

Ibn al-Nadim. *The Fihrist of al-Nadîm: A Tenth-Century Survey of Muslim culture.* Edited and translated by Bayard Dodge. New York and London: Columbia University Press, 1970.

Ibn Bajjah. *Treatise on Conjunction with the Intellect (Risâlat Ittisâl al-fiAql bi-l-Insân).* Edited with introduction and Spanish translation, "Tratado de Ibn Bajja sobre al Union del Intelecto con el Hombre," by Miguel Asin Palacios. *al-Andalus* 7 (1942): 1–47.

Marmura, Michael. "Avicenna's 'Flying Man' in Context." *Monist* 69 (1986): 383–395.

Rowson, Everett K. "An Unpublished Work by al-Âmirî and the Date of the Arabic De causis." *Journal of the American Oriental Society* 104 (1984): 193–199.

Taylor, Richard C. "'Truth Does Not Contradict Truth': Averroës and the Unity of Truth." *Topoi* 19 (2000): 3–16.

Von Kügelgen, Anke. *Averroës und die arabische Moderne: Ansätze zu einer Neubegründung des Rationalismus im Islam.* Leiden, Netherlands: Brill, 1994.

Wisnovsky, Robert. *Avicenna's Metaphysics in Context.* Ithaca, N.Y.: Cornell University Press, 2003.

Zimmermann, F. W. "The Origins of the So-Called *Theology of Aristotle.*" In *Pseudo-Aristotle in the Middle Ages,* edited by Jill Kraye, W. F. Ryan, and Charles B. Schmitt. London: Warburg Institute, University of London, 1986.

Richard C. Taylor

PHILOSOPHIES, EASTERN. *See* **Chinese Thought; Japanese Philosophy, Japanese Thought.**

PHILOSOPHY.

This entry includes two subentries:

Historical Overview and Recent Developments
Relations to Other Intellectual Realms

HISTORICAL OVERVIEW AND RECENT DEVELOPMENTS
Philosophy is the noble art of thinking carefully, persistently, even obsessively, about the Big Questions of life—the meaning of life and with it the business of living, that is living well.

It is also, as Aristotle (384–322 B.C.E.) famously said, looking with wonder at ourselves and the world around us, being intrigued by both nature and the way we look and talk about nature, and the ways in which we think and talk about ourselves. But philosophy—and even the word *philosophy*—is shot through with contentiousness and is subject to endless debate. This was true in the days of Socrates, Plato, Aristotle (teachers and students, respectively) and it is certainly true today. The word itself is a Greek coinage, supposedly by Pythagoras (c. 580–c. 500 B.C.E.), who when asked if he was wise gave the modest answer "no, but I am a lover of wisdom." Thus the words love (*philein*) and wisdom (*sophia*) were fused into "philosophy," the love of wisdom. But the true nature of philosophy is perhaps better captured by Socrates, who showed quite clearly that philosophy is essentially the love of argument. Or, as Bertrand Russell cynically noted, "philosophy is an unusually ingenious attempt to think fallaciously."

The prototype of philosophical disagreement was captured by Raphael Stanza in his well-known painting *The School of Athens,* where he depicts Plato (c. 428–348 or 347 B.C.E.) and Aristotle in animated conversation, elderly Plato pointing up to the heavens and a younger Aristotle, no longer just the pupil, making a down-to-earth gesture, palm toward the ground. Thus the history of Western philosophy displays profound disagreement between those philosophers who would appeal to the otherworldly and those who would remain unabashedly worldly. If the long history of medieval philosophy kept its eyes fixed on the heavens, the subsequent history of "modern" philosophy has tended to be resolutely worldly and secular, even when religion remained lurking in the background, in awe of science and often taking philosophy itself to be a science—or to be at least "scientific." Since René Descartes (1596–1650) followed Galileo Galilei (1564–1642) and embraced the scientific revolution in the fifteenth century, philosophy has been primarily concerned about the objectivity of knowledge. Since the eighteenth-century Enlightenment, in particular, the philosophy of religion has been a marginal specialty and not the whole or at any rate the heart of philosophy, as it was from St. Augustine of Hippo (354–430) to St. Thomas Aquinas (c. 1224–1274), almost a millennium. But before that, Plato, writing in playful, witty dialogues, and Aristotle, whom we know only through his matter-of-fact lectures, exemplified a dramatic difference in philosophical style, already raising the question whether philosophy is a science or an art, the literal pursuit of truth or the metaphorical expression of deep inner longings. From Plato and Aristotle, two opposed but complementary threads of the history of philosophy continue to interweave.

Dialectic in Philosophy

The dialectic between religious and secular philosophy and the split between those who think of philosophy as akin to poetry and those who insist that it be exact and rigorous are not the only oppositions that rend modern philosophy. There is also the perennial tug-of-war between those philosophers who stubbornly hold onto the ancient paradigm of philosophy as the more or less practical search for the good life and those who insist on philosophy being "heavenly" in a different sense,

namely that philosophy is hopelessly impractical and esoteric and has nothing to do with the problems of real life. It is this opposition, perhaps, that best allows us to understand the current situation in philosophy. A good deal of contemporary philosophy has become quite technical, almost like mathematics. Philosophers are entranced by problems mainly of their own making and enraptured by the difficulty of solving them, with very little concern for others outside their academic circle, who have no interest anyway. Others have turned directly to real-life problems, in business and in medicine, for example, and "applied" the skills of philosophy to questions about fairness in the marketplace and to life and death issues in health care. Then, too, others have turned these skills at argument to an enhanced appreciation of the arts and aesthetics, to the improvement of psychology and the other social sciences, even to physics and evolutionary biology. For several decades, now, feminist philosophers have challenged the male archetypes of philosophy and argued that philosophy is in fact gender-defined and have elaborated in many directions, especially concerns with motherhood and "sisterhood," just what this amounts to. Still other philosophers, steeped in cultures outside the West, have turned their eye to comparing ideas and cultures, drawing sometimes dramatic contrasts between both strains of philosophy since Plato and Aristotle in the West and dramatically different (but sometimes dramatically similar) traditions in other parts of the world.

If one were to paint a broad-brush history of Western philosophy from ancient times, it would begin with the origins of philosophy and science together in ancient ontology and cosmogony (the Pre-Socratic philosophers from Thales to Democritus, culminating in Aristotle) along with a heavy emphasis on the Good and living well (Socrates, Plato, and Aristotle through the Stoics and the Skeptics). After Aristotle, science is almost totally eclipsed as the philosophy of religion becomes virtually the whole of philosophy, culminating in the rich convergence of Judaic, Christian, and Muslim ideas and cultures in the thirteenth century. With the Renaissance, the classics come alive again, humanism becomes the reigning philosophy, science is again on the rise, Niccolò Machiavelli (1469–1527) and Thomas Hobbes (1588–1679) revolt against the supposedly gentlemanly art of politics of the ancients. Then comes Descartes and with him the pre-occupation with epistemology ("the theory of knowledge") and skepticism. But whereas ancient Skepticism was always concerned with the best way to live, modern skepticism became narrowly epistemological, "absurd" even to its most illustrious defender, the Scot David Hume (1711–1776). Thus by the end of the nineteenth century, the German philosopher Friedrich Nietzsche (1844–1900) would complain, "Philosophy reduced to theory of knowledge—that is philosophy in its last throes." Over the course of the nineteenth century, philosophers in both Europe and America tried to regain their cosmic reach, in the magnificent multiple *Critiques* of Immanuel Kant (1724–1804), by way of the cranky pessimism of Arthur Schopenhauer (1788–1860), through the all-bracing Spirit of Georg Wilhelm Friedrich Hegel's (1770–1831) phenomenology, and in the German-inspired American "Transcendentalism" of Ralph Waldo Emerson (1803–1882), Henry David Thoreau (1817–1862), Amos Bronson Alcott (1799–1888), and Margaret

Fuller (1810–1850). This brings us to the border of the twentieth century and then philosophy today.

Philosophy West and East

If there is a single word that best captures the spirit of twentieth-century philosophy, it would be *relativism*. Nietzsche prefigured the new century in the 1880s with his doctrine of "perspectivism," the idea that there is no singular truth and no "God's eye" view of the world. Albert Einstein (1879–1955) defended relativity in physics at the same time that Pablo Picasso (1881–1973) was displaying it in the new art of "cubism." Not that every thinker of the twentieth century was a relativist, of course. Some fought bitterly against relativism: Edmund Husserl (1859–1938) and Alfred North Whitehead (1861–1947), for instance. But if the perennial struggle had been primarily between the this-worldly and the otherworldly, the new tension in philosophy was between relativism and one or another form of absolutism, whether it was the residue absolutism of religion (as in contemporary America) or by way of fascism, which gained a frightening foothold in Europe midcentury. At the beginning of the twenty-first century, this struggle has by no means been resolved. If anything, it has intensified, as absolutism takes the form of religious fundamentalism and relativism finds new stylistic expression in the writings and sometimes the ravings of the postmodernists.

But this broad-brush sketch leaves out most of the world. As noble as the philosophical traditions of the West may be, they should be humble in comparison to the much longer-standing traditions of Asia. The first philosophical scriptures were the Vedas, produced in India some thirty-five hundred years ago. Indian philosophy progressed through scholarly commentary and argument by way of Vedanta and the great literature of the Mahabharata and through the breakaway philosophies of Buddhism and Jainism. Buddhism migrated north and east through Tibet and southeast Asia to China, where it joined with the indigenous Chinese philosophies of Daoism and Confucianism, and on to Japan where it transformed the local spirit-worship called Shintoism and gave rise to the dramatic philosophy of Zen, captivating the Samurai class who ruled the country. But the fate of philosophy in Asia displayed some dramatic differences from the fate of philosophy in the West. In Asia there was never so much of an opposition between philosophy and religion, nor for that matter were the various philosophy-religions so antagonistic. Buddhism, Daoism, Confucianism, and Hinduism had more of a mix-and-match relation to each other, and they were treated more as a spiritual smorgasbord than as competing occasions for a "leap of faith." Beneath the Eastern emphasis on spirituality is that thread familiar to us from the ancient Greeks, the ultimate ideal of living a good life, philosophically. And, ironically, the Asians pursued this ideal in what is supposed to be the prototypical American fashion—pragmatically.

Contemporary Philosophy

Philosophy from its inception has always been all-embracing and thus lends itself to both a learned eclecticism as well as dilettantism. Ironically, then, philosophy has also always tended to encourage a certain sense of superiority as well as

schoolishness, even cultishness. The schools of the ancient world—Skeptics, Stoics, Cynics, and Academics—and the schools of medieval Scholasticism were paralleled (unknowingly) by the many competing schools of Confucianism, Daoism, Legalism, Buddhism, Zen, and neo-Confucianism in Asia. In the "professional" philosophy of the twentieth century, especially in American universities, the tendency to overspecialization can be partly explained by philosophers' efforts to distinguish philosophy from all of those other disciplines that it originally spawned from its womb. But it is also the very nature of philosophy itself, which while striving for the all-embracing universal has always tended to be laughably parochial. Thus contemporary philosophy has predictably become Balkanized, not quite to say cult-like. In particular, there is the well-known opposition between "analytic" and "continental" philosophy, although it should be said from the first that the distinction itself is problematic as well as destructive. To begin with, the contrast is a false one. "Analysis" refers to a method that, superficially at least, concentrates on the use of language and is mainly concerned with logic and conceptual analysis. "Continental" refers to a place, namely, Continental Europe. Apart from the fact that "the Continent" so referred to usually includes only Germany and France and the fact that "analytic philosophy" includes a fair number of contrasting and competing methodologies, there are many twisted and interwoven schools, methods, and styles of philosophy that are not distinguished by such a narrow body of water as the English Channel.

Analytic philosophy is often defined in terms of its interest in logic and language, but that interest emerges first in Germany (with Gottlob Frege [1848–1925], in particular) and is fully shared by the progenitor of this century's "Continental" movements, Edmund Husserl. The most influential philosopher of the century, Ludwig Wittgenstein (1889–1951), who was twice the definitive philosopher of the "analytic" tradition, came to England from Austria, never leaving his "Continental" roots behind him. He was particularly interested in the limits of language, but so are such contemporary poststructuralists as Jacques Derrida (1930–), the nemesis of most analytic philosophers. There are analytic philosophers who, like their peers on the Continent, talk and write about sex, gender, death, and the meaning of life. And despite the more polemical pronouncements of some of its practitioners, analytic philosophy is not just logic, devoid of concern for content. Though it still prides itself on being "scientific," analytic philosophy is not wholly devoid of interest in history, context, empirical content, and etymology. If Bertrand Russell (1872–1970) misrepresented the analysts' case against the Hegelians at Cambridge in his day, he was, nevertheless, the very model of an engaged and popular philosopher, with a great deal to say to ordinary people about immensely important issues. At the start of the twenty-first century, too, there are philosophers at the barricades, which means on television, talking about the vital issues of the day. One of the areas of contemporary interest in philosophy is "cognitive science," which brings together the empirical research of neurologists, evolutionary biologists, computer specialists, psychologists, and linguists with the conceptual demands and arguments of the philosophers. At its best, contemporary philosophy breaks through its traditional provincialism—as it always has in those golden epochs of the past—and synthesizes as well as analyzes the knowledge of the world. In this endeavor, analytic and continental philosophers work best when they work together, when they try to overcome their respective mind-numbing technical devices and jargon and grapple with what Husserl kept referring to as "the things themselves," the distinctive content of human experience and the Big Questions of philosophy that get us all started down the philosophical road to begin with.

The ancient quest for the good life has all too often tended to get lost, or at any rate eclipsed, by the contemporary squabbling over the name "philosophy." (Is philosophy, indeed, nothing but logic and conceptual analysis? Or is it worry about matters of "ultimate concern"? Or is it a bottomless spiral of self-reference that ultimately leads to nothing at all?) The perennial quest for the good life, shared by philosophers and non-philosophers alike, ensures that everyone is a philosopher, not just a few thousand university-trained specialists. (French philosopher Maurice Riseling has commented, "sooner or later, life makes philosophers of us all.") This explains, in the face of increasingly specialized and inaccessible academic philosophy, why there continues to be widespread fascination with Eastern philosophy, often repackaged as "New Age" philosophy. If philosophy abandons what has always been its noble aim, to teach us how to live well, other alternatives will always be attractive. But this particular fascination with the East only began in the nineteenth century (Arthur Schopenhauer's flirtation with Buddhism was particularly significant), when the first wave of professionalized academic philosophy swept over Germany in the wake of Immanuel Kant. (Before that, most of the great philosophers were "independent scholars," except perhaps for Plato and Aristotle, who owned their own academies.) The importance of the East and cosmopolitan philosophy has only become more intense as the distortions of the Cold War on geopolitics came to an abrupt end, as global markets open up, and now that Islam has made a new forceful entrance into the world of ideas. But despite its disdained "popular" appeal and the intricacies of ideology and ideas, the fascination with non-Western and comparative philosophies is one of the most exciting late developments of the twentieth and now the twenty-first century.

To contrast "Eastern" with "Western" philosophy is not to suggest that false stereotype too long accepted among Western philosophers, namely, that Eastern philosophy is all religion and mysticism devoid of concern about knowledge and science. Buddhist philosophy, in particular, has a long rich history of logic and brilliant logicians. But the theme of living a good life is pervasive, and it is this, perhaps, that explains the appeal of the generic "East" in the West. There is also the obvious concern with spirituality that pervades so much of Eastern philosophy. Spirituality should not be confused with mysticism, nor should it be conflated with mindlessness. (It is instructive than one of the favorite terms in New Age philosophy today is "mindfulness.") Spirituality is, as the present author has written, "the thoughtful love of life." But in the pursuit of a rigorously "scientific" philosophy, Western philosophy since the Enlightenment has tended to dump all mention of spirituality as just so much "superstition" and sentimentality. Thus it is often said that there is a widespread "spiritual hunger" that is not satisfied by either philosophy or traditional organized religion. But if scientific philosophy has thrown out the baby with the bath water, traditional organized religion has violated philosophy's new insistence on pluralism (relativism), even if orthodox (absolutist) pretensions still remain. Much of Eastern philosophy, not burdened with the antagonism between philosophy and religion, has less trouble capturing both spirituality and truth in the same intellectual package, even where the main conclusion is that neither spirituality nor truth can be captured intellectually.

Conclusion

What is happening in philosophy at the start of the twenty-first century? Philosophy is as vibrant as ever, an opinion that is shared by the various Balkanized citizens of the philosophical profession, although from dramatically different perspectives on what that vibrancy consists of. Analytic philosophers will puff with pride about the technical abilities that are so much in evidence among the newly minted philosophers among them. Poststructuralist philosophers will point with pride to the number of art and literature departments, especially, that have been converted to their ways of thinking. Comparative philosophers with an eye on the East (and, to a lesser extent, on the southern hemisphere) will make sure to mention the number of courses and the extensive interest in ideas from beyond the ever more narrow borders of Anglo-American and European philosophy. Philosophers who do "cognitive science" will beam with satisfaction at the progress being made in understanding the human brain and its manifestations. And more practical ("applied") philosophers will tell you about the number of philosophers employed by business schools, law schools, medical schools, and hospitals. But the truth is that philosophy continues as always, stimulating wonder and argument and spawning intelligent if not always loving attention to the world and to the myriad of human activities that, on reflection, become philosophical.

See also **Analytical Philosophy; Continental Philosophy; Philosophy and Religion in Western Thought; Philosophy of Religion; Structuralism and Poststructuralism.**

BIBLIOGRAPHY

Copelston, Frederick. *The History of Philosophy.* 9 vols. Rev. ed. Westminster, Md.: Newman Bookshop, 1946–1975.

Durant, Will. *The Story of Philosophy: The Lives and Opinions of the Great Philosophers of the Western World.* 9 vols. New York: Simon and Schuster, 1933. Reprint, 1983.

Kenny, Anthony. *A Brief History of Western Philosophy.* Malden, Mass.: Blackwell, 1998.

Russell, Bertrand. *A History of Western Philosophy.* Simon and Schuster, 1945.

———. *The Problems of Philosophy.* 2nd ed. Oxford and New York: Oxford University Press, 1998.

Skorupski, John. *English-Language Philosophy 1750–1945.* Oxford and New York: Oxford University Press, 1992.

Solomon, Robert C. *The Joy of Philosophy: Thinking Thin Versus the Passionate Life.* New York: Oxford University Press, 1999.

———. *Spirituality for the Skeptic: The Thoughtful Love of Life.* Oxford and New York: Oxford University Press, 2002.

Solomon, Robert C., and Kathleen M. Higgins. *A Short History of Philosophy*. New York: Oxford University Press, 1996.

Spiegelberg, Herbert. *The Phenomenological Movement: A Historical Introduction*. The Hague: Nijhoff, 1960.

Weitz, Morris, ed. *Twentieth-Century Philosophy: The Analytic Tradition*. New York: Free Press, 1966.

Whitehead, Alfred North. *Adventures of Ideas*. New York: Macmillan, 1933.

Robert C. Solomon

RELATIONS TO OTHER INTELLECTUAL REALMS

According to an ancient tradition deriving from Heraclides of Pontus (388–310 B.C.E.), a disciple of Plato (c. 428–348 or 347 B.C.E.), Pythagoras of Samos (c. 580–c. 500 B.C.E.) was the first to describe himself as a philosopher. Three types of person, he is alleged to have said, attend the festal games: those who seek fame by taking part in them; those who seek financial gain by selling their trade goods there; and those ("the best people") who are content to be spectators (Diogenes Laertius, *De vita et moribus philosophorum,* I, XII). Philosophers or "lovers of wisdom" resemble persons of this third class: spurning both fame and profit, they seek to arrive at the truth by means of contemplation. Pythagoras distinguished the wisdom (*sophia*) sought by the philosopher—knowledge of the truth—from the mercantile skills of the merchant and the physical prowess of the athlete. Whether or not these distinctions derived from an actual utterance of Pythagoras, they can most certainly be found in the works of other ancient thinkers such as Plato, who was much preoccupied with the question of what philosophy is and how it differs from other forms of intellectual inquiry. Many of Plato's contemporaries had thought his teacher Socrates (c. 470–399 B.C.E.) a sage; some considered him a Sophist, while others believed him to be a cosmologist. In Plato's eyes and in the judgment of posterity, Socrates was none of these things; he was first and foremost a *philosopher.* But what made him different from a sage or Sophist? What made him recognizable as a seeker after wisdom and truth? In attempting to find answers to these questions, it is possible to learn something of the manner in which philosophers have traditionally characterized their métier, and how their different views on the scope and point of philosophical practice has led them to speculate on the relations between philosophy and other forms of intellectual labor.

Many ancient savants believed Socrates to be inimitable for the reason stated by Marcus Tullius Cicero (106–43 B.C.E.): he "first called philosophy down from the heavens" and thereby made the study of nature instrumental to human happiness (*Tusculan Disputations,* 5.X–XI; cf. Diogenes Laertius, *De vita et moribus philosophorum,* II. 16, 45). In other words, Socrates' life as a philosopher was devoted not to the scientific description of the universe in the manner earlier advanced by Ionian cosmologists, but to the pursuit of wisdom in order to secure genuine human happiness. For this reason a philosopher, according to Socrates, could not devote himself simply to the study of the requisite arts and sciences, but had to have his mind attuned to the requirements of wisdom in the context of striving to live the best possible life. Such a life *had* to be

lived, even if it entailed the bitter fate of drinking a draft of hemlock.

For Plato, the first characteristic of philosophical wisdom is that it meet the needs of rational inquiry. As he suggests at *Apology* 22, this criterion precludes all types of quotidian knowledge and other homespun verities in favor of genuine philosophical insight. Neither the statesman, the artisan, nor the poet can explain *why* he is doing what is he doing, for none of them has formulated a clear, tractable, and explicit method of self-reflexive reasoning. That some members of humanity may act wisely on occasion does not prove that they possess genuine wisdom, for to be wise such persons must be able to offer explanatory and justificatory reasons for their deeds that will stand up to dispassionate scrutiny. The philosopher has this ability, and by means of dialectic, he can make progress in the quality of his self-understanding by criticizing received opinions. Philosophy thus liberates the space of reasons and never imposes itself upon the human mind by means of arbitrary techniques or conflated methods. Even mathematics, which for Plato is the most developed and admirable of the sciences, is subject to philosophical criticism. Philosophy is the highest form of speculative thought because it alone involves no presuppositions and is predicated on gratuitous reflection.

Unlike other branches of human learning and industry, philosophy has direct access to a "true reality" as distinct from the phenomenal world of ever-changing things. Having access to such a world, philosophy can offer pertinent and definitive criticisms of received opinions about the nature of meaning, beauty, and goodness. And since it concerns itself with the relationship between eternal and unchanging entities and verities, philosophy can validate its claim to possess certain knowledge of what actually exists rather than what seems to exist. At *Phaedo* 98–99, Plato suggests that the Ionian cosmologists did not possess true philosophical learning because they could not explain the purpose and nature of things. Being ignorant of the reality that upholds and sustains the universe and its objects, the cosmologists could not explain anything of real value concerning the nature of the world.

Lastly, and on account of a philosopher's certain knowledge of an eternal and unchanging reality, he can know how people ought to live. For Plato, this entails that the speculative excellence of philosophical thought can be applied to the variable conditions of action, thereby reforming the moral quality of human life. Echoing the earlier pronouncements of Socrates, Plato readily castigated the proud claim of the Sophists to teach their charges the art of immediate worldly gain by means of quick wit and self-serving judgment. Such "fruits" of sophistical learning can never amount to genuine knowledge, since the mere exertion of intelligence is not comparable to the exercise of wisdom. Though the philosopher might look forlorn and foolish next to those who claim to teach the most efficacious route to fame and fortune, he is privileged by being in receipt of a form of understanding whose enduring qualities stand in stark contrast to the fleeting glories and superficialities of the world. For Plato, any attempt to explain and interpret the nature of the universe and human beings must involve philosophy. That is why the ideal ruler must be a philosopher, and those who would claim to be wise must be imbued, like Socrates, with a spirit of critical reflection.

What can be learned from Plato's specification of the differences that separate philosophy from other branches of human learning is the idea that philosophy is quite unlike anything else. It is not reducible to another art or science, and its subject matter as well as its point and scope are not circumscribed by considerations that are external to its method of enquiry. Philosophy, then, belongs at the very summit of human knowledge. If prosecuted appropriately, it bequeaths to the individual mind a form of sagacity and judgment that will enable any human being to live well. Like Socrates, the philosopher stands apart from the world while seeking to make sense of it; philosophy is a *sui generis* activity.

After Plato

These ideas found repeated expression, albeit in different forms, throughout the course of ancient philosophy. Aristotle, although he made enduring contributions to most forms of human knowledge (especially the natural sciences), was mindful of the differences between more rarefied forms of intellectual speculation, such as metaphysics and theology, and prosaic methods of taxonomy and description that belonged to the sciences of physics and what we could now term biology. Aristotle can be said to preserve the spirit if not the letter of Platonic teaching, especially in his insistence that the goal of human life is gratuitous contemplation of the divine.

In the schools of the Hellenistic period and late antiquity, the writings of adherents to Stoicism, Epicureanism, Cynicism, and Skepticism demonstrate a similar commitment to preserve a conception of philosophy as an autonomous discipline that can authenticate a reflective way of life. While individual members of these schools all emphasized the need to preface philosophical study by securing a sound knowledge of other fields of human enquiry, they held firm to the belief that the study of subjects such as physics, mathematics, or rhetoric is but a preface to the more challenging regime of philosophy. Even in certain Neoplatonic schools, where the view that theology is the goal of any genuine intellectual quest had gained momentum, there is little evidence to suggest that philosophers were prepared to characterize their subject, or at least to specify its difference from other branches of intellectual enquiry, in a manner that radically departed from the views of Socrates and Plato. Seen thus, an important aspect of the intellectual legacy of the ancients was the idea that philosophy stands apart from all other abstract and cerebral pursuits. Philosophy is not a physical science concerned with the description of natural phenomena; it is not a form of poetical discourse or artistic endeavor; it is not civic religion; philosophy is about critical reflection on the nature and conditions of human life leading to the development and practice of wisdom.

Although the idea that philosophy enjoyed a unique position in the scheme of human knowledge and was thereby unanswerable to anything but itself did not go unchallenged in antiquity, when ancient philosophy came into contact with biblically-based monotheistic religions of the Judeo-Christian tradition, it met with a thorough reappraisal of its claim to

dominance. While Jewish and Christian thinkers such as the Alexandrians, Philo Judaeus (20 B.C.E.–45 C.E.), St. Clement of Alexandria (c. 150–between 211 and 215), and Origen of Alexandria (185?– ?254), all endeavored to make sense of doctrinal issues by appropriating philosophical insights, a growing and increasingly vocal constituency, especially in Christian circles, argued that philosophy ought to be subservient to the claims of revealed religious teaching.

From the advent of the common era, a discussion was set in place that aimed to clarify the exact relations between philosophy and theology or sacred teaching (*sacra doctrina*). At its simplest, this debate sought to posit clear lines of demarcation that would distinguish the nature of philosophy and remit it from the province of theology. The debate sought to arrive at a view of how philosophy might or might not contribute to the path of individual salvation as that idea had been set down by Jewish, Christian, and from the seventh century onwards, Islamic teaching. The debate between "Athens and Jerusalem," so famously instituted by Tertullian (c. 160–c. 220), was in part a discussion as to how ancient philosophy might or might not be arrogated by the theological doctrines of a biblically-grounded monotheism. A by-product of this discussion would be its detailed consideration of the relationship of philosophy to other fields of intellectual activity.

In their distinctive ways, Christian thinkers as dissimilar as the Cappadocian Fathers, St. Augustine of Hippo (354–430), Boethius (c. 480–c. 524), and Gregory I (c. 540–604); early medieval thinkers such as John Scotus Erigena (c. 810–c. 877), Peter Abelard (1079–?1144), and St. Anselm of Canterbury (1033 or 1034–1109); and the scholastics of the thirteenth and fourteenth centuries all attempted to clarify the relationship of philosophy to theology. For these thinkers, the subject of "philosophy" amounted to the scientific teaching and ethical wisdom of the ancients (specifically Aristotelian learning conjoined to aspects of the Neoplatonic tradition and trace elements of Stoicism), while prevailing ideas of "theology" were distilled from ongoing attempts to codify the requirements of revealed teaching by means of ideas of tradition and authority. In different guises and with very different exigencies, these efforts were replicated by thinkers in the Jewish and Islamic traditions. One of the more pressing questions confronted by all who attempted to gauge the relationship between philosophy and theology was the issue of *duplex veritatis* or "double truth," a problem that was debated in earnest from the thirteenth century onwards following the reintroduction of the *corpus Aristotelicum* to the Latin West.

Medieval and Renaissance

Given the authority assigned to Aristotle's arguments on a wide variety of philosophical and scientific questions, it became apparent to many that what he had to say about such pressing topics as the origins of the world, the nature of the soul, and the final end of human life were at variance with the strictures of revealed biblical teaching. Some thirteenth-century theologians such as Albertus Magnus (c. 1200–1280), St. Thomas Aquinas (c. 1224–1274), and St. Bonaventure (1217–1274) advocated the use of aspects of Aristotelian philosophy, supplemented and corrected by the "higher truths" of revelation.

Other thinkers, though—especially members of the Arts Faculty of the University of Paris, the so-called Latin Averroists—attempted to balance Aristotelian philosophy in its own right over against Christian revelation by arguing that a distinction could be enunciated between philosophical teaching and theological truth. In short, they proposed a theory that looked to their opponents and generations of more impartial scholars as a theory of "double truth," according to which something might be true in philosophy, such as Aristotle's well-known cosmological theory of the eternity of the world, yet false in theology and vice versa.

As medieval scholarship has long pointed out, the Latin Averroists, most notably Siger de Brabant (1240–between 1281 and 1284) and Boethius, did not themselves argue for a theory of double truth; rather, they reserved the term *truth* in an ultimate sense for revealed doctrine and never claimed the possibility that there could ever be two equally true contradictory truths specific to the competing requirements of theological and philosophical discourse. Nonetheless, they did recognize that reason rightly used could reach conclusions that did not agree with revealed doctrine, or else placed the veracity of certain biblical statements in question. Such was the hostility to their views in theological circles that Bishop of Paris Stephen Tempier issued condemnations of propositions associated with their work in 1270 and 1277.

In the later Middle Ages, yet another element was added to the general debate about the relationship of philosophy to theology by the nominalists and Scotists, followers of John Duns Scotus (c. 1266–1308): they contended that rationally deducible concepts and theological systems do not necessarily stand in any pertinent relationship to one another. The issue here is not one of *duplex veritatis* but rather one of a radical diastasis between philosophical or, in a Scotist dispensation, specifically metaphysical argument and the claims and requirements of theology. Some scholars have argued that this late medieval perspective underlies a good deal of the early Reformers' rejection of philosophy in their initial attempts to codify their emerging theological positions. The problem set in motion by late medieval Scotism was further complicated by a shared proclivity among many Lutheran and Reformed theologians to embrace an Augustinian view of how the effects of original sin corrupt and deprave an individual's powers of reasoning and the exercise of will.

The issue of double truth also appears in sixteenth-century philosophy in the writings of the Renaissance thinker Pietro Pomponazzi (1462–1525). He turned the medieval discussion on its head by arguing for the superiority of philosophical over theological truth. As an Aristotelian philosopher whose principal work was the exposition and analysis of the pages of Aristotle for the sake of developing a modern Peripatetic philosophy, Pomponazzi addressed the issue of the immortality of the soul and argued that the question could only be clarified and resolved philosophically. His conclusion was that the soul was indeed capable of discovering knowledge of higher things, especially the eternal truths of the universe, but he also indicated that such knowledge was restricted temporally to the life of the individual. The mind cannot survive the death of the body and cannot exist in a disembodied state. All of this Pomponazzi argued from the perspective of (Aristotelian) philosophy, while at the same time acknowledging that Scripture is without error and the doctrine of the immortality of the soul can be proved from it. More so than the much-maligned Siger de Brabant and Boethius of Dacia, Pomponazzi began to trespass into the territory of *duplex veritatis,* and can be said to have reasserted the traditional claim of philosophy to be the final tribunal in any dispute of reason.

One consequence of the protracted and sophisticated medieval debate on the relationship of philosophy to theology—a discussion that can be said to have continued in different guises, albeit with slightly altered terms of references, in the polemical disputations of the Renaissance and Reformation—was to initiate by the end of the sixteenth century a willingness on the part of philosophers to assert their independence from the theologians. In the time of the ancients, philosophers had enjoyed preeminence among the cognoscenti, yet with the advent of biblical monotheism and the rapid expansion of Islamic and Christian civilization, the place of philosophy had been relegated in importance next to theology. In addition to this, the developing system of university education that was established in Western Europe supported subjects such as medicine and law, each of which claimed their own unique intellectual status and professional structure. For the medieval tradition, philosophy (which included logic and the natural sciences) was at best the handmaid of theology, a valuable intellectual training that prepared the able minded for the dizzy heights of speculation on the truths of the bible and the mystery of the Godhead. While many of the most important and enduring achievements of high scholastic theology are framed within philosophical terms of reference (e.g., the use of the language of Aristotelian metaphysics to describe issues concerning the Trinity, the Incarnation, and the Eucharist), for the authors of these works these discussions were theological, pertaining to *sacra doctrina,* and not philosophy.

Early Modern
With the dissolution of the medieval outlook in the sixteenth and seventeenth centuries, philosophers set about the long enterprise of recasting their subject so as to ensure its independence from theology but also to align it with new developments in scientific thinking. These tendencies can be observed in the writings of influential figures in the history of early-modern thought ranging from Galileo Galilei (1564–1642), Francis Bacon (1561–1626), Thomas Hobbes (1588–1679), and René Descartes (1596–1650). That said, what in the early twenty-first century tends to be thought of as philosophy—a broad but relatively precise discipline distinct from the humanities, sciences, and religion and characterized by certain kinds of difficult and even irresoluble questions—would have struck an early modern thinker as a definition all too parsimonious in scope. The term *philosophy* in the seventeenth century included a great deal more than it does in the twenty-first, and this complicates any attempt to clarify the relationship of philosophy to other forms of human leaning in the early modern period. Philosophical learning would include the physical and biological sciences, as much as the logical structure of argument,

conceptions of the good life, as well as questions about being and the existence and nature of God. Thus, a natural scientist in the seventeenth century would consider himself a "natural philosopher," and though preoccupied with issues in mathematics and physics, would attempt to relate his understanding of these questions to more general areas of philosophical concern. Here one thinks of the very different writings of Marin Mersenne (1588–1648), Pierre Gassendi (1592–1655), Johann Clauberg (1622–1665), Robert Boyle (1627–1691), and Sir Isaac Newton (1642–1727). Similarly, it would be wrong to detach figures who are believed to be purely "philosophical" (as that term is currently understood) from those who were "theologians," "biblical exegetes," "political theorists," and "jurists." Authors such as John Locke (1632–1704), Ralph Cudworth (1617–1688), Gottfried Wilhelm von Leibniz (1646–1716), Nicholas Malebranche (1638–1715), Antoine Arnauld (1616–1694), Baruch Spinoza (1632–1677), Blaise Pascal (1623–1662), and Hugo Grotius (1583–1645) all displayed expertise in these disciplines. The range and generality of so many seventeenth-century philosophical questions, and the continuing disputes concerning the appropriate characterization of the world of nature accompanied by several thorny theological problems concerning divine grace and predestination, provides evidence that philosophy was connected to most fields in the arts and sciences, and enjoyed a close association with theology. The synoptic enterprise of seventeenth century philosophy would have to include not only the well-known canonical figures but also confessional apologists, corpuscularian scientists, alchemists and chemists, Jansenist polemists, Jesuit moralists, activists advancing toleration, country clergy, urban rabbis, city intellectuals, and a panorama of intellectually gifted royalty and nobles.

From the seventeenth century to the Enlightenment, a new intellectual entity known as "culture," an enterprise that connoted more than simple custom but less than learning, began to occupy the middle ground between knowledge and ignorance. Most philosophes of the salons conceived their métier quite differently from the preceding generation of seventeenth-century thinkers who had attempted, with some optimism, to translate the fruits of scientific knowledge into an accessible idiom open to all educated persons. Not all the protagonists of the European Enlightenment upheld belief in the incremental democratization of human learning; rather, they held to the view that an encyclopedic understanding of all branches of knowledge would enhance the cause of civilization and harmony among nations.

Such ideas helped to facilitate a very different understanding of philosophy and its re lationship to the arts and sciences. Enlightenment thinkers and their successors no longer embraced a model of the subject that was directly influenced by the ancients. Aristotle's teaching was believed to have been made obsolete by the intellectual developments of the seventeenth century, and while the deeds and opinions of ancient thinkers like Socrates, Plato, the Stoics, and the Epicureans were widely respected and valorized, post-Enlightenment thinkers looked more to the "novelties of the moderns" than the "wisdom of the ancients" for essential instruction about the nature of the world and the purpose of human life. In addition, the increasing secularization of European thought and the general advancement of science in society, industry, and learning became increasingly opposed to the earlier models of philosophical practice that had encouraged the gratuitous pursuit of wisdom or the importance of a metaphysics leading to theology. Such views of philosophy were deemed to be out of keeping with the intellectual, cultural, and mercantile needs of the age. Perhaps more than at any other time in its illustrious history, the proud boast of the ancients that philosophy should stand at the top of the hierarchy of knowledge was now forcefully challenged by thinkers who remained unconvinced that philosophy was any different than other reputable branches of learning.

Modern Times

What one might term the conversion of philosophy from the quest for wisdom to the more prosaic pursuit of conceptual analysis, or the abstract clarification of the claims of more important scientific theories, is a marked feature of the philosophical thought since the turn of the nineteenth century. Since Immanuel Kant (1724–1804), philosophers have become more limited in their intellectual ambitions and, at times, have dispensed with the pretensions of their subject to be a synoptic discipline, or else to propose something of enduring value or pertinence on the subjects of God, ethics, and beauty. For good or ill, modern philosophy has preferred to restrict its purview to those matters that can be demonstrated to be legitimate objects of discourse and has eschewed ways of talking about issues that are deemed to lie outside the boundaries of sense meaning.

The prominence of such views, especially in the English-speaking world, eventually led to a recasting of the relationship of philosophy to other subjects of intellectual concern. In those quarters where the influence of scientism has been unyielding, there has been widespread support for the view that philosophy can never pretend to emulate the accuracy, reliability, and verisimilitude of valid scientific theories. Going on from there, some thinkers have taken the further step and argued that there are no perennial philosophical questions, and that traditional philosophical puzzles concerning the nature of the mind, the structure of the world, and the moral qualities of human beings have either been resolved or else superceded by advancements in physics, biology, and psychology. For these thinkers, there is nothing special about philosophy, and there is nothing to privilege it over and above other branches of intellectual inquiry. A well-known position associated with the work of the American thinker Richard Rorty (b. 1931) has even suggested that philosophy has expired through exhaustion. Now that science has demystified the world and resolved the perennial mysteries, what else is there for philosophy to do? Given the end of philosophy, Rorty has suggested that scholars turn to subjects such as literature in order to make sense of the seeming intractabilities of human worldly existence.

Yet Rorty's position, though it is based on a set of metaphysical commitments that are widely shared by contemporary philosophers, is by no means universal, and despite the blandishments of fashion and novelty, the daily grind of philosophical speculation still goes on. Few are persuaded that the subject first commissioned by father Thales (c. 625–c. 547 B.C.E.) and so suggestively ameliorated by Socrates and his successors is really at an end. What is perhaps significant about this phenomenon is the fact that the very practice of philosophy, whether it be in dialogical or in written form, helps to ensure the impression among practitioners of the subject that the discipline is really quite different from every branch of the humanities, sciences, and theology. Why is this so? It really comes down to the type of question, the supporting framework of reference, and the variety of answer that it invites that identify and individuate a question as a *philosophical* question. Socrates understood this and the Sophists did not. That each generation of his successors has attempted to honor the special nature of the discipline he did so much to create stands as testimony to the fact that philosophy will always enjoy a vicarious relationship to other branches of human learning.

See also **Interdisciplinarity; Knowledge; Logic; Philosophy, History of; Truth.**

BIBLIOGRAPHY

Boys-Stones, George. *Post-Hellenistic Philosophy: A Study of its Development from the Stoics to Origen.* Oxford: Oxford University Press, 2001.

Copenhaver, Brian, and Charles Schmitt. *Renaissance Philosophy.* Oxford: Oxford University Press, 1992.

Funkenstein, Amos. *Theology and the Scientific Imagination from the Middle Ages to the Seventeenth Century.* Princeton, N.J.: Princeton University Press, 1986.

Grant, Edward. *God and Reason in the Middle Ages.* Cambridge, U.K.: Cambridge University Press, 2001.

Hadot, Pierre. *Exercices Spirituels et Philosophie Antique.* 2nd ed. Paris: Études Augustiniennes, 1987.

Jordan, William. *Ancient Concepts of Philosophy.* London: Routledge, 1990.

Oberman, Heiko Augustinius. *The Harvest of Medieval Theology: Gabriel Biel and Late Medieval Nominalism.* Cambridge, Mass.: Harvard University Press, 1963.

Rorty, Richard. *Philosophy and the Mirror of Nature.* Princeton, N.J.: Princeton University Press, 1980.

Sorell, Tom, ed. *The Rise of Modern Philosophy: The Tension Between the New and Traditional Philosophies from Machiavelli to Leibniz.* Oxford: Clarendon, 1993.

Stone, M.W.F. and Jonathan Wolf, eds. *The Proper Ambition of Science.* London: Routledge, 2000.

M. W. F. Stone

PHILOSOPHY, HISTORY OF. A respected Princeton philosopher keeps a sign on his office door forbidding the discussion therein of any philosophy more than ten years old. At this late stage in his career the restriction includes a good deal of his own work. This may well be the limit case of the antihistorical attitude that prevailed throughout much academic philosophy of the twentieth century, motivated by the view that philosophy, as an academic discipline, need have no more connection to its past than does any other positive domain of inquiry. A physicist, for example, may be interested to know how exactly Newton came upon his discovery of the laws of gravity.

But this interest is, as it were, extracurricular, not a necessary part of the specialized knowledge of a competent physicist. It will be enough that the physicist learn the relevant laws in a textbook; Newton's name need not appear at all, much less the details of his distinctly seventeenth-century concerns.

Can philosophy be understood in the same way? At the other end of the spectrum from our Princeton philosopher, we find some maintaining that philosophy is entirely constituted by its history, that the study of philosophy can never be anything but the study of the history of philosophy. Between these two extremes, there are a vast number of intermediate positions concerning the value of philosophy's history to its present practice. Among those who accept that this history is in some degree valuable, moreover, there are vastly different conceptions of the nature of this value. What follows is a review, with the help of some slightly cumbersome "-isms," of some of the possible perspectives on the history of philosophy from within philosophy at the beginning of the twenty-first century, with an eye toward the deeper understanding of the nature of philosophy itself that informs these perspectives.

Indifferentism

Indifferentism is plainly summed up in the message on the Princeton office door. But this label does not tell all, for indifferentism's vociferous defenders are anything but indifferent about what philosophy (as an ahistorical discipline) is, and about what philosophers ought to be doing. Most likely, the indifferentist would like to see philosophy come forward as a science, to adapt a phrase of Immanuel Kant's (1724–1804), and believes that it can do so by simply focusing on an appropriate, rather narrow set of questions. In the twentieth century, these were questions arising in the analysis of language and the methodology of science, and so it has been with some justice that indifferentism has commonly been associated with analytic philosophy.

Around the turn of the twenty-first century, though, most philosophers working in this tradition had come to recognize the usefulness to their own work of the history of philosophy, and particularly of the history of analytic philosophy itself. It has become rare that a philosopher of science or language who does not also have some competence in the history of these subdisciplines will find a job. Some of the best contemporary analytic philosophers choose to congregate at meetings of the History of the Philosophy of Science group to discuss, among other things, the revision of our understanding of the very notion of "analysis" as it was understood in early analytic philosophy by, for example, Rudolph Carnap (1891–1970) or Otto Neurath (1882–1945). What is sometimes described as "post-analytic philosophy," then, might better be thought of as analytic philosophy after its historical turn, and is in any case a sure sign that strict indifferentism is on its way out.

Indifferentists tend to believe that philosophy, like any other discipline, has seen some progress over the past few millennia. One standard example is the resolution of the paradoxes of Zeno of Citium (c. 335–c. 263 B.C.E.) with mathematical tools that had to wait until the nineteenth century to see the light of day. On another understanding, though, what happens when a philosophical question is "solved" is that it ipso facto ceases to be a philosophical question at all and becomes a mathematical or scientific one. Thus, any philosophical question is by definition unanswerable, and the history of philosophy becomes but the prehistory of science, the initial recognition that a problem exists without any clue as to how to render it scientifically tractable. It may be impossible to say which perspective is right; but those who believe that the mathematization of Zeno's paradoxes was an instance of philosophical progress will likely think that there is no reason to dwell too much in the past. Why waste our time on those who hadn't yet figured out as much as we have? We may be grateful to past philosophers for having discerned the problem and taken some initial stabs at solving it, as a twenty-first century astronomer might appreciate Claudius Ptolemy (c. 100–c. 170), but there is no pressing need to figure out the details of their theories and how they came up with them.

Those who believe philosophy is cumulative and progressive, then, will likely incline toward indifferentism in some degree. Others, though, believe that what makes philosophy unique is that it never really gets anywhere. There may be personal progress that comes from studying it and learning how complex the problems it addresses are, but the discipline as a whole witnesses no real progress over the course of centuries. On this view, history will be of tremendous value, because it is only through the study of philosophy's history, the way it keeps circling back around the same challenges, always coming up with solutions from within a limited range of options, that one can experience personal progress out of an adolescent optimism, or even arrogance, about these problems' facile solvability.

Appropriationism

Appropriationism may describe any approach to the history of philosophy that seeks to take from it tools that may be of service to one's ahistorical philosophical task. An appropriationist asks of the history of philosophy: What can it do for me? Representatives of different strains of appropriationism will have different answers to this question.

Reconstructionism.
This breed of appropriationism searches philosophy's past for arguments that have stood the test of time and can still be of service in defense of some philosophical position advocated by the appropriator. For instance, a reconstructionist who believes that no better account of personal identity has been offered since the late seventeenth century than that presented by John Locke (1632–1704)—who roots it in continuity of memory—will cite Locke's argument for this theory in support of his or her own, similar one. The same reconstructionist, though, will not feel obligated to adopt, or even take an interest in, Locke's support of, say, a cosmological argument for the existence of God. Reconstructionists take piecemeal from philosophy's past what is useful for their own projects, and will generally not feel obligated to consider whether the argument borrowed from a past figure was *really* offered in response to concerns similar to theirs. As Jonathan Bennett approvingly describes this approach to history, dead philosophers should be approached as colleagues, with the one minor but not insurmountable difference that they are, well,

dead. In this spirit, twentieth-century scholars of the philosophy of René Descartes (1596–1650) have been able to portray him as engaged, to use Bernard Williams' phrase, in a "project of pure enquiry," without acknowledging that he was also engaged in a project of empirical physiology, and other areas of seventeenth-century philosophy that have since been outsourced to the appropriate science departments.

Neo-x-ism.
An absolutely dogmatic Marxist would be an entirely uninteresting character, not because Karl Marx (1818–1883) was wrong, but because a follower who adheres utterly to every aspect of his predecessor's thought is in essence only a relay station for that thought's dissemination, not a thinker in his own right. Any noteworthy Marxist thinker, other than Marx himself, will be in his or her unique way a *neo*-Marxist, even if the prefix remains only implicit. Thus V. I. Lenin (1870–1924), a Marxist if there ever was one, nonetheless modified some of Marx's central doctrines concerning the essential class-rootedness of conflict to account for the new phenomena of imperialism and the growing antagonism between the colonizing and the colonized parts of the world that at least the early Marx could not possibly have foreseen. Similarly, Jacques Lacan (1901–1981) adopts the basic categories developed by Sigmund Freud (1856–1939) for the analysis of the psyche but explicates them in terms of a poststructuralist philosophy of language. Lenin and Lacan are not reconstructionists; they do not pretend that Marx and Freud were concerned with the same problems they themselves face or even that their predecessors would approve of the way they are tackling these problems. But they are appropriationists of a different stripe, mastering and defending the ideas of a predecessor, while showing how these ideas can be of use in application to new and unforeseen problems.

Neo-x-ists will speak of working within a "broadly x-ian framework" while dealing with questions that admittedly did not concern x. Conversely, a reconstructionist will find and extract passages in which some predecessor x dealt with the same questions that interest him or her today, without, in performing this extraction, feeling obligated to confess to any broadly x-ian framework or world-view.

Contextualism

A contextualist will, to the extent possible, let philosophical predecessors speak for themselves through the texts they have left behind. If a great thinker from some bygone era turns out to have believed in ghosts or astrology, then so be it; these features of his or her thought need to be acknowledged and understood just as much as those that have stood the test of time. Facing up to these odd and sundry concerns of our predecessors, a contextualist thinks, has more than just the virtue of shocking our shockingly narrow colleagues. Contextualism, in its honesty about the distance between our concerns and those of our predecessors, reminds us that past philosophers were not just early models of ourselves, but were concerned with a largely different set of problems and saw their role and responsibility as thinkers very differently. In this way, contextualism can help overcome the tendency to see the past as a mere prelude to the present. And this benefit may be of more philosophical significance than it first appears.

Contextualism, understood as the "merely" historical study of the history of philosophy, helps history to be something more than history of the present, in the same way that the study of natural selection in now-extinct evolutionary lines can help to drive home the important point that evolution is not a teleological process that has as its end its crowning accomplishment, *homo sapiens.* The present state of philosophy is not the end toward which the past has been striving, just as human beings are not the end toward which evolution has been striving. Against this view, it might be pointed out that the tradition of philosophy has been a common project, whereas evolution has been a blind and stumbling affair. But the contextualist will remind us that, even if we might recruit the dead to help us with our philosophical tasks, this does not mean that they would recognize as much commonality with us as we claim with them if *per impossibile* they could have been given advance warning about their posthumous affiliations. Among the contextualists, we may mention, by way of example, the names of Dan Garber, Roger Ariew, Lloyd Gerson, and Michael Frede, each of whom seeks, to a greater or lesser extent, to reveal the circumstances of time and place that help to shine light on the philosophical thought of that time and place.

Constitutivism

A constitutivist tends to believe that philosophy just is a particular tradition, fundamentally rooted in history and comprehensible only synchronically. For the constitutivist, it is our primary task today to investigate how we came to inherit the philosophical concerns we have, rather than to continue to seek answers to questions as though they were timelessly meaningful. Thus for Marx, each era's philosophy is one of the superstructural reflections, along with other outcroppings of culture, of the class relations that fundamentally define that era; for Michel Foucault (1926–1984), philosophy as the contemplation of timeless questions is in need of replacement by a genealogy of the concepts that came to predominate, mostly in only very recent history, in philosophical discourse. There is an air of subject-changing in these accounts of the history of philosophy: they want to reveal the true nature of philosophical discourse, rather than to continue to participate in it. For instance, when Frederic Jameson describes Daniel Dennett's *Consciousness Explained* (1991) as an allegory of late capitalism—as outlined by Slavoj Žižek in the *London Review of Books* ("Bring Me My Phillips Mental Jacket," 22 May 2003)—he is not engaging with Dennett's arguments in a way that could even permit the author to respond. He is explaining Dennett's concerns, his very conception of philosophy, as the product of a history of which Dennett need not be at all aware. Dennett may say this is unfair (though more likely he will not say anything at all); Jameson, for his part, could respond, true to his Marxist constitutivist convictions, that the deepest and most fundamental account of the philosophy of any era, including recent analytic philosophy, will be one that roots it in its time and place. Any account that does not do this will fail to grasp what the theory it is studying is really "all about." And any constitutivist would insist that such a failure is a philosophical failure, perhaps the cardinal one.

Conclusion

Most scholars working in the history of philosophy will combine in varying degrees some or all of these various approaches. Many scholars believe that, qua *historian* of philosophy, one is required to accomplish some serious historical research, preferably involving archives and manuscripts, in order to claim any expertise on the subject studied. A real *historian* must know at least a few languages, understand the basics of historiographical method, and know at least a bit about the social and political background of the era in question. But, qua *philosopher,* at the end of the day one must also prove able to do what other philosophers demand of their colleagues: namely, offer some insight into the essences of things, or show that what was thought to have an essence lacks one, or show, as the American philosopher Wilrid Sellars says, how things hang together in the broadest sense. This may be done simply through the discussion of what some past thinker thought on these topics, but the crucial thing is that essences, hangings-together, and other such philosophical staples be tackled directly or through the mediation of one who has gone before, rather than resting content with, say, a tally of the dates and recipients of some seventeenth-century philosopher's letters.

Some historians of philosophy might not be exactly sure what they're doing. While many of us know of no other way to talk or write about the history of philosophy than by purporting to explain what the philosopher in question *actually meant,* we are too sophisticated to believe that this is what we are really doing. We claim to be setting the record straight, but sense that at least to some extent we are pushing our own agendas. These need not be mutually exclusive tasks, however. A feminist historian of philosophy may wish to push her worthy agenda, for example, by setting the record straight concerning the great number of largely ignored women active in the central philosophical debates of the seventeenth century, such as Anne Conway (1631–1679) and Damaris Masham (1658–1708). And yet, even after this correction to the record is made and women gain their rightful place in the canon, it would be naïve to think that the record has been set straight once and for all. A future generation will undoubtedly discover something else that has remained sub-rosa in earlier generations' reception of our shared past. There are ever new and previously undetected angles from which to consider philosophy's past. So long as it interests us, we will never cease to find new ones. The ones we find, moreover, will always be at least partially a reflection of our own interests, even if we hold out just letting the texts speak for themselves as the soundest methodology. We might worry that this is to allow rather too much "as if" to enter into our understanding of our own projects: know that you can never do more than reflect your time and place in your reception of the past, but approach the past as if you had the power of discernment to say once and for all what it was all about. This and similar worries, far from indicating professional incompetence, might be better understood as proof that the study of the history of philosophy is a quintessentially philosophical endeavor, and carries with it all the aggravation and perplexity one might expect from any endeavor deserving of this label.

See also **Historiography; Ideas, History of; Philosophy.**

BIBLIOGRAPHY

Bennett, Jonathan. *Learning from Six Great Philosophers: Descartes, Spinoza, Leibniz, Locke, Berkeley, Hume.* 2 vols. New York: Oxford University Press, 2001.

Collingwood, R. G. *The Idea of History.* Oxford: Clarendon, 1946. Reprint, edited by Jan Van Der Dussen, Oxford: Clarendon, 1993.

Foucault, Michel. *The Order of Things: An Archaeology of the Human Sciences.* London: Tavistock, 1970.

Gracia, Jorge J. E. *Philosophy and Its History: Issues in Philosophical Historiography.* Albany: State University of New York Press, 1992.

Hutton, Sarah. *Anne Conway: A Woman Philosopher.* New York: Cambridge University Press, 2004.

Rorty, Richard. *Philosophy and the Mirror of Nature.* Princeton, N.J.: Princeton University Press, 1979.

Rorty, Richard, Jerome B. Schneewind, and Quentin Skinner, eds. *Philosophy in History: Essays in the Historiography of Philosophy.* Cambridge, U.K.: Cambridge University Press, 1984.

Tully, James, ed. *Meaning and Context: Quentin Skinner and His Critics.* Princeton, N.J.: Princeton University Press, 1988.

Williams, Bernard. *Descartes: The Project of Pure Enquiry.* Atlantic Highlands, N.J.: Humanities Press, 1978.

Justin E. H. Smith

PHILOSOPHY, MORAL.

This entry includes four subentries:

Africa
Ancient
Medieval and Renaissance
Modern

AFRICA

Morality consists of two parts: first, morality in the strict sense; and second, morality as custom or mores. The defining principle of the first is the golden rule, that of the second, local utility, idiosyncrasy, or even accident. The first is known to be universal to all human cultures. This has to be so of a necessity, in view of what the rule entails. The golden rule, to follow Harry Gensler, enjoins that one ought not to endeavor to do something to somebody without conceding that it would be acceptable for that person to do the same thing to one in an imagined, exactly reversed situation. From this, specific imperatives of honesty, fairness, and respect are derivable without which human community is inconceivable.

To take an example reminiscent of Immanuel Kant (1724–1804), suppose a particular individual's project is to make a promise to someone that he or she has not the slightest intention of keeping. If that person pauses for a moment to consider whether he or she is prepared grant that it would be all right for the other person, in an exactly reversed situation, to do the same, the person making the promise will see that this is not possible. Moreover, if one has basic intelligence, one will see that the general avowal among all people of the reverse of the injunction against false promises would bring human community to an end.

The working of the golden rule in the shape of specific rules, such as this last, is manifest in moral conduct and discourse all over the world, irrespective of differences of culture or even of individual thought habits. Thus, for example, if Christians are at least theoretically dedicated to the counsels of the golden rule, so also have Chinese Confucians have also been so since pre-Christian antiquity. Nor, similarly, is it difficult to find formulations of the golden rule in the repertoire of didactic epigrams in the oral traditions of Africa. The Yoruba say, "Whenever a person breaks a stick in the forest, let him consider what it would feel like if it were himself [who was thus broken]" (Idowu, p. 166). And defining the quintessence of moral insensitivity by way of the inverse of the golden rule, the Akans remonstrate, "Sticking into another person's flesh, it might just as well be sticking into a piece of wood" (Wiredu, 1992, p. 198). To be moral, accordingly, is to evince empathetic impartiality in one's actions on the model of the golden rule.

Notwithstanding this universality in the living of the moral life, the theorizing of it, that is, its philosophy, gives rise to great diversities of persuasion not only among cultures but also within them. Famously, Western philosophers, sharing basically the same moral values, have been in earnest conflict about the nature of moral ideas and the ultimate principles of moral judgment. So among other "isms," there are subjectivism and objectivism, on the first front, and consequentialism and deontology, on the second. In contemporary African philosophy, too, unanimity does not reign. But the bone of contention lies in the interpretation of the traditional communal philosophy of morals.

Morality Based on Religion in African Thought

By one account, African life and thought is religious through and through, and ethics is only a special case of this orientation: everything in morality, as regards both meaning and principle, comes from God. A most eloquent articulation of this view is found in Bolaji Idowu's *Odumare: God in Yoruba Belief.* After rejecting any suggestion that morality derives from society's need for self-preservation or that morality is "the product of commonsense" (Idowu, p. 144), he asserts "Our own view is that morality is basically the fruit of religion and that, to begin with, it was dependent upon it. Man's concept of deity has everything to do with what is taken to be the norm of morality" (p. 145). More specifically, "The sense of right and wrong, *by the decree of God,* has always been part of human nature" (p. 146, italics added). Again, "With the Yoruba, morality is the fruit of religion" (p. 146). See also, in support of this standpoint, M. Akin Makinde's *African Philosophy, Culture, and Traditional Medicine* (1988).

There is a general objection to a view of this sort that is well known in Western philosophy. If something is good irrespective of its intrinsic character simply because it is decreed by God, then if God were to decree something like slavery, it would have to be accepted it as moral. But surely, one might retort, God would never decree so radical an affront to human dignity as slavery! Exactly this is the point. One is inconsistently proceeding with a criterion of moral goodness that is logically antecedent to God's decrees, on the basis of which one already esteems God as morally good (in the highest). Note further that if moral goodness were defined in terms of the decrees of God, then to say that God is good would amount to just saying that God decrees what he decrees. In African philosophy, however, it is not these objections but rather a consideration linked to a deep feature of African culture that has militated against any kind of divine-decree view of morals.

The feature in question is, actually, the lack of a feature familiar to students of the "world religions." These religions—almost all of them—are *dogmatic* religions, and the dogma relevant here is that of revelation: God is supposed to reveal directly to a select few what the rules of right conduct are. This is necessary because if right conduct is by definition what is decreed by God, there is an urgent need to know what those decrees are. Obviously this is too important to be left to fallible individual speculation. On the other hand, in African traditional religions, as far as one can see from the literature and from one's experience, direct revelation from God is unheard of. Alleged "specialists" do indeed claim direct knowledge from extrahuman sources, frequently hyperbolically described as "gods." But these are mundane sources, and the information volunteered by them is empirical and open to falsification. In fact, in the traditional scheme of things, repeated falsification of the messages of such "gods" can lead to their demise by reason of the accumulated contempt of their erstwhile devotees.

It is of a piece with these last considerations that there are no prophets of God in African traditional religion and, in particular, none with any pretenses to moral or any kind of revelation. J. B. Danquah, speaking of the Akans, has declared with good reason that "Never in the history of the Akan people, so far as we know, have we had what is known as a revealed religion, a revelation to, or by, a prophet, of duty to a Supreme or Lord" (p. 3). Naturally, therefore, the Akans and, it would seem, Africans south of the Sahara generally do not seek the rationale of morality in the decrees of God but in the exigencies of social existence (see Wiredu, 1991). The Akan philosopher Kwame Gyekye has argued to the same conclusion (Gyekye, 1995, chap. 8). Regarding the Yoruba, Segun Gbadegesin also maintains that they "are very pragmatic in their approach to morality, and although religion may serve them as a motivating force, it is not the ultimate appeal in moral matters" (p. 82).

The remaining impediment to a just conception of the African approach to the foundation of morals is the notion that African morality is determined by the decrees of the ancestors. Two things may be meant here. First, the suggestion may be that the conduct of Africans is decisively influenced by considerations as to the likes and dislikes of the ancestors. If so, some validity may be conceded to it. It is true that in "family" (or, more strictly, lineage) matters the ancestors are believed to reward rectitude on the part of the living and punish its opposite in their own extrahuman manner. But the principles supposed to be used in their evaluations are the moral and in some cases customary principles by which the ancestors themselves lived when they were alive in this world, and these, as suggested above, have a this-worldly rationale. Besides, those in African society who are moved to action or forbearance by the thought of ancestral rewards or reprisals are those of a weak moral fiber. Those of a more solid moral aptitude adjust their conduct by a direct cognizance of the principles themselves. The same applies to moral action or inaction enforced by the "fear" of God or motivated by any sort of religious causes. Second, the notion under consideration may mean that for Africans, moral rightness or goodness is defined in terms of the will (or wills?) of the ancestors. If so, the considerations already adduced concerning the relativization of morality to the decrees of God should be more than enough to lay this to rest too.

What then, more specifically, is the foundation of morality in African thought? It is morality in the strict sense that is being considered here, that is, as defined by the golden rule. This rule, indeed, defines morality, but it does not motivate it. Why is this rule needed at all? It is because of the following. Human individuals have their own interests that they pursue or desire to pursue. But they live in society, and in that setting, the efforts of individuals in pursuit of their interests not infrequently threaten to conflict or actually conflict with varying degrees of severity, not excluding the deadly. Only the most basic ability to reflect is needed to see that in this situation it is in the interests of all concerned that a way be found for harmonizing those interests. Any principle for pursuing such a harmony of interests will inevitably involve the occasional pruning down of the interests of an individual in deference to the interests of others. But this restraint must apply to individuals impartially. The golden rule is exactly that principle.

These thoughts on the rationale of morality, strictly so called, are encapsulated in an Akan art motif depicting a freak crocodile with one stomach and two heads locked up in a fight over food. The profundity of this art construct is typical of the way in which art is used in Africa to express ethical and more generally philosophical conceptions. Its meaning will not be exhausted here, but it is crucial to note that the two heads symbolize the reality and diversity of the interests of individuals, while the common stomach represents the common interests of all and sundry. The teaching is that the conflict can be resolved only by the realization of this second-order commonality of interests. And the resolution will have to be one in which the targeted resource is shared in a manner impartially sensitive to the original interests of all the parties, that is, in accordance with the golden rule. This reflection also suggests a succinct characterization of the rationale or foundation of morals as the evenhanded pursuit of human interests, where the evenhandedness is thanks to the golden rule. The reader might like to note the rational bent of this conception of morality.

The golden rule had a similar centrality in the moral system of the seventeenth-century Ethiopian philosopher Zara Yacob (1592–1692). He was a contemporary of René Descartes who, independently of Descartes, developed a rationalistic philosophy that was if anything more radical in its insistence on reason than that of Descartes (see Sumner, p. 224 ff.). Although he laid much stress on the will of God, he self-consciously construed it as that which is in conformity with reason: "God does not order absurdities" (Sumner, 1994, p. 238).

Morality as Custom

The foregoing has been about morality as determined by the golden rule. But there are, as hinted in the opening paragraph, countless behavioral as well as institutional options that are neither prescribed nor proscribed by the golden rule. This brings us to the sphere of custom, broadly conceived. Customs are multifarious, both in nature and origin, in Africa and everywhere else. Some precipitate philosophical questions; others do not. It is in terms of custom that cultures are differentiated. And one of the most important criteria of differentiation lies in the contrast between individualism and communitarianism. It is a contrast that is also, philosophically, quite challenging.

There is a veritable consensus among students of African societies south of the Sahara that traditional African culture is communitarian. A communitarian society is one in which individuality is regarded as a construct out of community, and an individualistic society, one in which community is regarded as a construct out of individuality. The apparent sharpness of the contrast, however, is illusory. It is a matter of degree, for without individuals there is no community, and without a community there are no *human* individuals. Still, a lively concern in moral philosophy among contemporary African philosophers is to clarify and evaluate the claims of individuality in the context of African communitarianism. Kwame Gyekye, for example, stresses the importance of individuality and entitles his version of communitarianism "moderate communitarianism" (Gyekye 1997, chap. 2). Dismas Masolo (pp. 495f.) also suggests that African communitarianism, properly considered, is hospitable to individuality. The enterprise of reassessment naturally spills over into social and political philosophy (Gyekye 1995, chaps. 8, 10; Masolo).

See also **Communitarianism in African Thought; Personhood in African Thought; Philosophies: African**

BIBLIOGRAPHY
Danquah, J. B. "Obligation in Akan Society." *West African Affairs* Series, no. 8. London: Bureau of Current Affairs, 1952.
Gbadegesin, Segun. *African Philosophy: Traditional Yoruba Philosophy and Contemporary African Realities.* New York: Peter Lang, 1991.
Gensler, Harry J. *Symbolic Logic: Classical and Advanced Systems.* Englewood Cliffs, N.J.: Prentice-Hall, 1990.
Gyekye, Kwame. *An Essay on African Philosophical Thought: The Akan Conceptual Scheme.* Rev. ed. Philadelphia: Temple University Press, 1995.
———. *Tradition and Modernity: Philosophical Reflections on the African Experience.* New York: Oxford University Press, 1997.
Idowu, Bolaji E. *Olódùmarè: God in Yoruba Belief.* London: Longmans, 1962.
Kant, Immanuel. *Foundations of the Metaphysics of Morals, and What is Enlightenment?* Translated with an introduction by Lewis White Beck. New York: Liberal Arts Press, 1959.
Makinde, M. Akin. *African Philosophy, Culture, and Traditional Medicine.* Athens: Ohio University Center for International Studies, 1988.
Masolo, Dismas. "African Communalism and Western Communitarianism: A Comparison." In *A Companion to African Philosophy,* edited by Kwasi Wiredu. Malden, U.K.: Blackwell, 2004.
Sumner, Claude. *Classical Ethiopian Philosophy.* Los Angeles: Adey, 1994.
Wiredu, Kwasi. *Cultural Universals and Particulars: An African Perspective.* Bloomington: Indiana University Press, 1996.
———. "Moral Foundations of an African Culture." In *Person and Community: Ghanaian Philosophical Studies,* edited by Kwasi Wiredu and Kwame Gyekye. Vol. 1. Washington, D.C.: Council for Research in Values and Philosophy, 1992.
———. "Morality and Religion in Akan Thought." In *African-American Humanism: An Anthology,* edited by Norm R. Allen Jr. Buffalo, N.Y.: Prometheus Books, 1991.

Kwasi Wiredu

ANCIENT

Ancient Greek moral theories are concerned in the first instance with the good life for human beings, or, in a word, happiness—what it is and how we might attain it—and with the role of the virtues of character—for example, temperance, courage, and especially justice—in achieving it. Serious critical inquiry into these questions began in Athens in the fifth century B.C.E. with Socrates (469–399), peaked twice in the theories of Plato (427?–347) and Aristotle (384–322), and came to rest in the Hellenistic period (323–30) with the calmer and more austere theories of the Epicureans and Stoics.

Socrates

Our picture of Socrates derives mainly from several short, inconclusive dialogues by his disciple Plato. In these, Socrates, believing that "the unexamined life is not worth living," typically challenges the conventional beliefs of his fellows, both ordinary people and more sophisticated thinkers, with questions about how human life should be lived. When his interlocutors prove unable to defend their opinions on such questions, Socrates offers his own, radical, positive agenda in their place. We are happy, he thought, when our souls are in the best condition—when, as he believed, we have the virtues of character, especially justice. Since we all want to be happy, we will inevitably do what is virtuous if we know what it is. Hence happiness is achieved by removing ignorance and vice from our souls and replacing them with knowledge and virtue. Socrates' moral seriousness and courage, in discussion and in life, won favor not only with posterity but also with many of his contemporaries—but not all of them: in 399 he was tried and convicted on a charge of impiety, and put to death.

Plato

Socratic ethics insists that we will do what makes us happy if we know what that is. Often enough, however, when we (think we) know what will make us happy, we would rather do something else instead, and sometimes we do that something else. Also, Socratic ethics does not say enough about the soul to establish that justice and the other virtues bring the soul into its best condition or that we are happy when our souls are in their best condition.

In response to these concerns, Plato in the *Republic* (360 B.C.E.) distinguishes between the "rational," "emotional," and "appetitive" parts of the soul.

Each part is defined by desires: reason, by desires for what is best for us; emotion, by desires for honor, achievement, power, domination of others, and so on; and appetite, by desires for various kinds of physical pleasure. Plato also associates each part of the soul with goals: reason he associates with seeking after knowledge or understanding and emotion, and appetite with the various forms of emotional and physical gratification. Given these distinctions, Plato goes on to argue that our souls will be in better condition to the extent that our lives are structured and our practical activities are motivated by goals associated with reason, not goals associated with emotion and appetite.

Plato's metaphysics provides us with his account of the proper objects of understanding. According to his "theory of forms," the world that we are familiar with and the items populating it are merely "shadows" or "reflections" of a separate world of eternal and unchanging "forms," or "ideas," such as Number, Man, and Justice. By "sharing in" or "participating in" these most fundamental realities, ordinary objects are what they are and have the features they do. The desire to attain understanding of these entities should dominate our lives. Apprehending and appreciating formal reality, Plato thinks, makes us happy and makes our lives worth living.

It also makes us moral. Formal reality, Plato thinks, is so appealing—so riveting—as to cause us to lose interest altogether in emotional and physical forms of gratification. In consequence we will behave decently toward our fellows. Justice is thus the natural expression in the field of human relationships of a properly lived human life.

Aristotle

Aristotle in the *Nicomachean Ethics* (350 B.C.E.), like Plato in the *Republic,* makes knowledge or understanding central to his conception of what is good for us as human beings. He also sees the virtues as expressing knowledge or understanding in action and in a life. But the kind of knowledge he takes to be involved in the virtues and how exactly he sees the virtues give expression to them are very different from what Plato thought.

Happiness for Aristotle consists primarily in the contemplation of the eternal truths of mathematics, physics, and theology. But practical wisdom, which is deployed in living a life well, is a separate intellectual virtue for Aristotle, and the virtues of character are closely connected with it. In the case of justice, Plato thinks that I will not take what is yours because, given my compelling interest in intellectual activities, I am no longer interested in what is yours. Arguably, this is not to take you and your rights as a person seriously. Aristotle's account of justice is a useful corrective. To be just requires not that I am uninterested in what is yours, but that I am disinterested or impartial; I see what is yours as yours and what is mine as mine.

I can achieve this perspective in matters of justice, Aristotle thinks, if I assume the perspective of a judge who sees us as free and equal citizens, each with his own interests and entitlements, and decides matters between us accordingly. And if I achieve this perspective, I will behave justly toward you. Thus being just requires that I understand what it is to be a citizen on a par with other citizens and to act from that

perspective. So too with the other virtues: each involves correctly understanding the area of human reality appropriate to it and embodying that understanding in our actions and passions.

Hellenistic Theories

The most important ethical theories of the Hellenistic period are Epicureanism and Stoicism. According to the Epicureans, we are happy to the extent that we achieve a state of mind called "peace of mind" or "lack of disturbance." Disturbance is pain, and its absence is pleasure. To achieve peace of mind, we need to recognize that any fear of death or of the gods is baseless and that wronging others or pursuing physical pleasures beyond what is necessary will produce more pain than pleasure in the end. Thus knowledge as well as virtues such as justice and temperance do have value for the Epicureans, but they are valued only as means to peace of mind, not for themselves as they are for Socrates, Plato, and Aristotle.

The Stoics identified happiness with a state of mind called "absence of passion" or "spiritual peace." We can achieve this by coming to understand and identify with the impartial moral order of the universe and living "according to nature." This means living in ways that express our nature as rational beings. Crucial to such a life are the virtues, since they are all forms of knowledge; for example, justice is knowledge of what we owe to other people. Such knowledge is of a piece and is all or nothing; if we attain it, we will become calm and indifferent to such ills as poverty, pain, and even enslavement and death. Thus, although the Stoics' conception of happiness resembles that of the Epicureans, their view of virtue and its relation to happiness is closer to the views of Socrates, Plato, and Aristotle.

See also **Philosophy, Moral: Medieval and Renaissance; Philosophy, Moral: Modern; Virtue Ethics.**

BIBLIOGRAPHY

Barnes, Jonathan, ed. *The Complete Works of Aristotle: The Revised Oxford Translation.* Princeton, N.J.: Princeton University Press, 1984. A two-volume revision of the Oxford Translation that includes all of Aristotle's works mentioned earlier, as well as a number of works attributed to Aristotle but of doubtful authenticity; various fragments, including parts of two poems; and Aristotle's will.

Bekker, Immanuel, ed. *Aristotelis Opera.* 5 vols. Berlin: G. Reimerum, 1831–1870. The complete Greek text of Aristotle's writings but for the *Constitution of Athens.*

Burnet, John, ed. *Platonis Opera.* 5 vols. Oxford: Clarendon, 1900–1907. A complete Greek text of Plato's writings.

Cooper, J., ed. *Plato: Complete Works.* Indianapolis and Cambridge, U.K.: Hackett, 1997. A one-volume translation by various hands of all of Plato's writings, including works attributed to Plato that he may not have written.

Hamilton, Edith, and Huntington Cairns, eds. *The Collected Dialogues of Plato, Including the Letters.* Translated by Lane Cooper and others. New York: Pantheon, 1961.

Inwood, Brad, and L. P. Gerson, trans. *Hellenistic Philosophy: Introductory Readings,* 2nd ed. Indianapolis: Hackett, 1998. A one-volume selection of materials.

Long, A. A., and D. N. Sedley, eds. *The Hellenistic Philosophers.* 2 vols. Cambridge, U.K., and New York: Cambridge University Press, 1987. Greek and Latin texts of the principal sources for Hellenistic philosophy, with notes, translations, and commentary.

McKeon, Richard, ed. *The Basic Works of Aristotle.* New York: Random House, 1941. A one-volume abridgment of the Oxford Translation.

Ross, W. D., and J. A. Smith, eds. *The Works of Aristotle Translated into English.* Oxford: Clarendon, 1910–1952. The standard English version of Aristotle's writings, referred to as the "Oxford Translation."

Charles M. Young

MEDIEVAL AND RENAISSANCE

Moral philosophy in the medieval West derived from two main sources: Christianity and classical ethics. The attempt to reconcile these different traditions and develop a viable synthesis of the two was a central concern of moral philosophy throughout the period.

Christianity and Classical Ethics in the Medieval West

Starting with the early church fathers, Christian thinkers took differing views of the proper relationship between their moral system and that of the pagan philosophers of antiquity. On the one hand, St. Ambrose (c. 340–397), in *De officiis ministrorum* (On the duties of the ministry), was prepared to adapt the Stoic-inspired account of virtue set out in Cicero's (106–43 B.C.E.) *De officiis* (On duties) to the needs of Christians seeking eternal bliss in the afterlife. On the other hand, St. Augustine (354–430), another doctor of the church, denied that Christians could learn anything from pagans about either virtue in the present life or happiness in the next, both of which were gifts of God's grace.

Ambrose's conviction that the ancient framework of ethical theory could be extended and modified to accommodate Christianity found wide resonance in thinkers from the Iberian bishop St. Martin of Braga (c. 520–580), who wrote influential moral tracts closely based on the writings of the Roman Stoic Seneca (4 B.C.E.?–65 C.E.), to the Cistercian abbot Ailred of Rievaulx (1109–1166), whose treatise *De spirituali amicitia* (On spiritual friendship) is modeled on Cicero's *De amicitia* (On friendship).

The uncompromising position of Augustine was echoed by monastic moralists such as Abbot Rupert of Deutz (c. 1076–c. 1129), who rejected pagan philosophers out of hand on the ground that they had no knowledge of spiritual or heavenly values. The first medieval philosopher to put forward a serious challenge to Augustine's characterization of virtues as gifts of divine grace was Peter Abelard (1079–1142). Drawing on Cicero and on Boethius's (c. 480–c. 524) commentary on Aristotle's (384–322 B.C.E.) *Categories,* he defined natural virtues as fixed dispositions that were acquired by the exercise of human powers and that could be transformed into Christian virtues by being directed toward God. Abelard was nevertheless acutely aware that while Seneca, the pagan philosopher he most admired, held that virtue must be sought for its own

sake, Christians believed that virtue should be pursued in the hope of a greater reward: happiness in the future life.

It was precisely this issue that made Aristotelian ethics, with its this-worldly orientation, particularly problematic for medieval Christians. In the *Nicomachean Ethics,* which began to be available in Latin translation at the end of the twelfth century, Aristotle declared that humankind's supreme good was a happiness that consisted of philosophical contemplation in the present life—a view that was clearly incompatible with the Christian belief that humanity's highest and ultimate goal was everlasting bliss in the afterlife. A solution to the problem was found in the mid-thirteenth century by scholastic philosophers at the University of Paris. Building on a distinction originally made by the French theologian William of Auxerre (d. 1231), they maintained that the subject of Aristotle's treatise was imperfect happiness, a natural state attainable in the present life by human powers, while perfect happiness or beatitude, a supernatural state attainable in the next life through grace, was the subject of theological, not philosophical, inquiry.

This position was further developed by the Dominican theologian and philosopher Thomas Aquinas (c. 1225–1274), who carved out a legitimate area of investigation for moral philosophy: the examination of the limited happiness that can be achieved by man through the naturally acquired virtues described by Aristotle, whereas theology was concerned with the unlimited heavenly beatitude produced by divinely infused virtues. This formulation, which established that Aristotelian moral philosophy, though vastly inferior to Christian theology, was nonetheless fundamentally in agreement with it, made it possible for university professors from the late Middle Ages to the end of the Renaissance and beyond to base the teaching of ethics firmly on the doctrines of Aristotle.

Islam, Judaism, and Classical Ethics

As in the Christian West, medieval Islamic and Jewish moral philosophy devoted considerable effort to reconciling scriptural precepts and values with those deriving from the classical ethics inherited from Greece. Muslim moral philosophers, rather than drawing a clear distinction between the imperfect happiness of the present life and the perfect beatitude of the hereafter in the manner of their Christian counterparts, emphasized the harmony between religion and philosophy (or *falsafah* from the Greek term *philosophia*) by pointing out that both were based on a proper understanding of the universe and mankind's place within it. Ethics was linked to theoretical knowledge, acquired by rational means, which led individuals toward the ultimate goal of attaining happiness in this life or the next. The Spanish Muslim philosopher Ibn Rushd (1126–1198), who produced comprehensive commentaries on the Aristotelian corpus that circulated widely in the West under his Latinized name Averroës, held that the path to happiness was an intellectual ascent to the contemplation of ever higher beings, culminating in the contemplation of the first cause and temporary union with the source of intellectual understanding. This account of happiness, which had no need for divine revelation or life after death, apparently gained adherents among Latin Averroists at the University of Paris in the late thirteenth century, since the doctrine "that happiness is to be had in this life and not in another" was among the 219 propositions condemned by the bishop of Paris in 1277.

Jewish moral philosophy was also concerned with establishing the proper relationship between religious and philosophical ethics. Moses Maimonides (1135–1204), the most influential of medieval Jewish philosophers, held that faith and reason were not in conflict and therefore, attempted to ground the basic principles of Aristotelian ethics in Jewish tradition, modifying them according to its needs. Maimonides, like Islamic moral philosophers, had a highly intellectualist conception of ethical perfection, in relation to which moral perfection played a merely subsidiary and preparatory role. A different trend in ethics, however, arose in conjunction with Kabbalah, a form of Jewish mysticism. Kabbalists such as Moses ben Jacob Cordovero (1522–1570) regarded moral perfection as the road to mystical union with aspects of the deity and believed that the moral behavior of individuals had an impact on the cosmic struggle between good and evil.

The Renaissance Recovery of Ancient Moral Philosophy

Although Aristotelianism dominated ethics in the West well into the seventeenth century, the Renaissance witnessed the recovery of other ancient traditions of moral philosophy. As had happened with Aristotle's ethical thought in the Middle Ages, the acceptability of these revived philosophies was largely conditioned by their compatibility with Christianity. The Florentine priest and philosopher Marsilio Ficino (1433–1499), who played the key role in the fifteenth-century revival of Platonism, stressed the extent to which the doctrines of Plato, unlike those of his student Aristotle, were in accord with Christianity. Ficino demonstrated this agreement most successfully in relation to moral philosophy through his influential theory of Platonic love, in which Plato's intellectual ascent from physical beauty to the realm of Ideas was interpreted as a spiritual journey whose final destination was God.

Stoic ethics inspired admiration from many Renaissance thinkers on account of its high-minded principle that virtue alone was sufficient for the good life. Yet its stern moral demands, which included a complete eradication of the emotions, provoked an equal amount of criticism for requiring a superhuman strength that surpassed even the powers of Christ, who had given way to both anger and sorrow. This ambivalent attitude toward Stoic moral philosophy was not overcome until the late sixteenth century, when a new brand of Stoicism, more accommodated to Christianity, was promoted by the Flemish humanist Justus Lipsius (1547–1606). The Spaniard Francisco de Quevedo (1580–1645) attempted to carry forward Lipsius's program of Christianizing Stoicism by claiming that the ultimate source of the philosophy of patient resignation recommended by the Greek Stoic Epictetus (c. 55–135) was the Book of Job. The recovery of Stoic moral philosophy, with its belief that human beings through their reason can comprehend and participate in the rational order of nature, contributed to renewed interest in natural-law theory.

Compared to Platonism and Stoicism, Epicurean moral philosophy made very few inroads into Renaissance thought.

Epicurus's doctrine that pleasure was the supreme good, misinterpreted since antiquity as an endorsement of sensual indulgence, combined with his rejection of divine providence and immortality, rendered his philosophy unacceptable to Christians. Not surprisingly, serious attempts to adapt Epicureanism to Christianity were rare. When the Italian humanist Lorenzo Valla (1407–1457) transferred the earthly pleasures of Epicurus to the heavenly ones enjoyed by the virtuous in the next life, his aim was less to rehabilitate the ancient philosophy than to reassess Christian theology. Similarly, the Dutch humanist Desiderius Erasmus (1466?–1536), by maintaining that Christ was the true Epicurean, since his disciples led the most pleasurable life, sought to highlight the ethical dimension of Christian piety.

The first Renaissance thinker to tap the ethical potential of Pyrrhonian skepticism, which held that it was impossible to attain certain knowledge, was the French essayist Michel de Montaigne (1533–1592). Adopting the motto *Que sais-je?* (What do I know?), he deployed skeptical arguments to undermine any claims to moral knowledge, in the hope of deflating human presumption, which he regarded as the root of all evil. The recovery of skepticism was part and parcel of the Renaissance movement to revive ancient philosophical traditions. Yet it presented epistemological challenges that in the following era would turn moral philosophy from a discipline based on classical and Christian authority to one founded on principles that had been rationally deduced from self-evident axioms.

See also **Aristotelianism; Natural Law; Neoplatonism; Skepticism; Stoicism.**

BIBLIOGRAPHY

PRIMARY SOURCES

Abelard, Peter. *Peter Abelard's Ethics.* Edited and translated by D. E. Luscombe. Oxford: Clarendon, 1971.

Aquinas, Thomas. *Selected Writings.* Edited and translated by Ralph McInerny. London and New York: Penguin, 1998.

Kraye, Jill, ed. *Cambridge Translations of Renaissance Philosophical Texts.* Vol. 1: *Moral Philosophy.* Cambridge, U.K., and New York: Cambridge University Press, 1997.

Montaigne, Michel de. *The Complete Essays.* Edited and translated by M. A. Screech. London and New York: Penguin, 1993.

SECONDARY SOURCES

Becker, Lawrence C., and Charlotte Becker, eds. *A History of Western Ethics.* 2nd ed. New York and London: Routledge, 2003. See especially chapters 5–7 for early medieval, late medieval, and Renaissance ethics.

Butterworth, Charles E. "Ethics in Medieval Islamic Philosophy." *Journal of Religious Ethics* 11 (1983): 224–239.

Dan, Joseph. *Jewish Mysticism and Jewish Ethics.* Seattle: University of Washington Press, 1986.

Hovannisian, Richard G., ed. *Ethics in Islam.* Malibu, Calif.: Undena Publications, 1985.

Kraye, Jill. *Classical Traditions in Renaissance Philosophy.* Aldershot, U.K.: Ashgate, 2002. See especially the section "Classical Ethics in the Renaissance."

Lagerlund, Henrik, and Mikko Yrjönsuuri, eds. *Emotions and Choice from Boethius to Descartes.* Dordrecht, Netherlands, and Boston: Kluwer, 2002.

Lines, David A. *Aristotle's "Ethics" in the Italian Renaissance (ca. 1300–1650): The Universities and the Problem of Moral Education.* Leiden, Netherlands, and Boston: Brill, 2002.

McGrade, A. S., ed. *The Cambridge Companion to Medieval Philosophy.* Cambridge, U.K., and New York: Cambridge University Press, 2003. Chapters 10 and 11 deal with moral philosophy.

Weiss, Raymond L. *Maimonides' Ethics: The Encounter of Philosophic and Religious Morality.* Chicago: University of Chicago Press, 1991.

Wieland, Georg. "The Reception and Interpretation of Aristotle's *Ethics*" and "Happiness: The Perfection of Man." In *The Cambridge History of Later Medieval Philosophy: From the Rediscovery of Aristotle to the Disintegration of Scholasticism, 1100–1600,* edited by Norman Kretzmann, Anthony Kenny, and Jan Pinborg; associate editor, Eleonore Stump. Cambridge, U.K., and New York: Cambridge University Press, 1982.

Jill Kraye

MODERN

The moral philosophy of the modern period traditionally included ethics as well as natural-law theories of rights and the normative foundations of state authority. Nowadays, the term *moral philosophy* tends to be used mainly with reference to ethics proper, while modern natural-law theories and their history are often treated under the headings of political philosophy and philosophy of law. In keeping with this convention, the following summaries concentrate mainly on developments in ethics since 1600.

Seventeenth Century

Modern Western philosophy emerged in conjunction with the religious, political, and social upheavals that characterized the Reformation period and the first half of the seventeenth century. Early modern moral philosophy reflected the need to reassess the ways that European thinkers had viewed moral knowledge, the human good and the nature of moral value, and the relation between God's will and the principles of human conduct. The extent to which seventeenth-century moral thought represents a break with late medieval and Renaissance views is controversial. But by the early 1600s modern conceptions of the character and goals of the theory of morals differed significantly from their historical antecedents. Hugo Grotius (1583–1645) provided an alternative to Scholastic natural-law theory as well as a response to the skeptical views on moral knowledge put forward by sixteenth-century thinkers like Michel de Montaigne (1533–1592). Grotius took a broadly empirical approach to the question of universal natural law by considering the features of human nature that make law-governed cooperation between individuals both possible and necessary. When presenting the basic precepts of human conduct, Grotius tended to focus on the self-interested individual. While Grotius accepted that humans are naturally sociable, he did not ground his natural jurisprudence in a rich, substantive conception of the good life or the chief good for human beings. Rather, he offered key elements of a theory of natural rights. Grotius regarded natural rights as subjective qualities of the human individual that must be respected by morally viable forms of human association. Subsequent

modern natural-law theories were generally in keeping with Grotius's minimalist conception of the good as well as with the Grotian idea of rights.

Thomas Hobbes (1588–1679) combined a denial of natural sociability with an egoistic view of human motives. His works on moral philosophy were interpreted as providing a naturalistic account of obligation, an account based on the fundamental good (the self-preservation) of the separate agent. An important problem linked to Grotius's and Hobbes's moral thought was the relationship between the laws of nature and God. Samuel von Pufendorf (1632–1694) made the will of God the ultimate source of such laws, and made God's power to punish and reward the ultimate ground of our obligation to obey them. This voluntarist view of morality as obedience to the will of a superior generated the systematic theory of duties and rights found in Pufendorf's immensely influential works. A similar view underlies the treatment of moral ideas given by John Locke (1632–1704). Locke combined a hedonistic explanation of the origins of our ideas of moral good and evil with a voluntarist conception of the relationship between law and the sanctioning power of a superior.

The voluntarist view of morality was a primary target of early modern perfectionist philosophers. Baruch Spinoza (1632–1677) held that the world is not the separate creation of God but a natural whole completely determined by eternal truths and laws knowable by reason. The philosophically informed agent's moral task is not to *obey* God's commands. Rather, the task is to understand divine law as the expression of eternal truths and thus to grasp the object of law as the supreme good. The true knowledge and love of God represents the highest state of human perfection. Striving to know this good through reason, the agent transcends selfish motivation and narrow self-interest. Nicolas Malebranche (1638–1715) viewed the world as having causal order through continual divine intervention. According to Malebranche, we are wholly dependent on God, and morality is obedience to God. This obedience, however, does not involve blind or even self-interested acceptance of divine commandments. Obedience requires that we understand God's order, and our intellectual apprehension of this order moves us to act from love in accordance with God's will. Repudiating the central tenets of voluntarist morality, Gottfried Wilhelm von Leibniz (1646–1716) based his moral system on the supposition that all actions must have a sufficient reason, a supposition linked to the notions of divine omniscience and metaphysical perfection. While many possible worlds are conceivable, God's perfection and infallibility guarantee that he chose optimally, thus creating the best of all possible worlds. Humans act morally when they act from the habit of loving or willing the good; and they act in this way when they learn to act on their knowledge of the world's perfection. The ethics of Christian von Wolff (1679–1754) were generally in keeping with the Leibnizian perfectionist view, although Wolff modified Leibniz's metaphysical tenets in a variety of ways.

Eighteenth Century

A characteristic component of eighteenth-century sentimentalist ethics was the rejection of the rationalist accounts of moral knowledge and motivation that supported theoretical views like those just summarized. Sentimentalist thinkers held that our awareness of moral good and evil, our ability to judge actions and character traits, and our motives for action depend on our capacity to be affected by feelings that are common to all human beings. The notion of a moral sense thus often figured prominently in the sentimentalists' portrayals of the source of our feelings of moral approval and disapproval. Contrary to the theorists of natural law discussed above, these theorists of moral sensibility tended not to regard concepts of law, obligation, and duty as primary ethical notions. Anthony Ashley Cooper, better known as the earl of Shaftesbury (1671–1713), understood virtue in terms of actions that give rise to feelings of approbation, actions that in turn show evidence of an agent's self-ordered affective harmony with respect to the feelings that move him to act. According to Francis Hutcheson (1694–1746), human moral sensibility is naturally structured in such a way that we approve of actions and character traits to the extent that they exhibit benevolent inclination as their motivating condition. Hutcheson formulated a theory of virtue in which universally benevolent inclination features as the morally best of motives. While David Hume (1711–1776) did not follow Hutcheson in maintaining that benevolent inclination supplied the only genuinely moral basis for action, he advanced a secular science of morality founded on the analysis of the moral sentiments and the human capacity for sympathy. Making use of the systematic superstructure of modern natural-law accounts of duties and rights, Hume constructed a comprehensive theory of the virtues revolving around the distinction between the "natural" virtues (such as compassion and generosity) and convention-dependent "artificial" virtues (such as justice). Jean-Jacques Rousseau (1712–1778) and Adam Smith (1723–1790) published highly influential treatises that further articulated the view that human morality has its grounds in the sensuous dimension of our nature.

A further type of approach was furnished by ethical theories that assumed egoistic explanations of moral motivation, typically in conjunction with hedonistic accounts of the good and proto-utilitarian principles requiring the maximal promotion of human happiness. These theories were often rooted in the Augustinian view of the sinfulness and corruption of human nature that was presupposed not only by Lutheran and Calvinist moral theology but also by French Jansenist ethical thought. Interweaving the Augustinian view with themes drawn from Hobbes's anthropology, Pierre Nicole (1625–1695) maintained that, although virtuous action is at bottom the result of self-interested passion, such selfish action has beneficial consequences for society as a whole. Bernard de Mandeville (1670–1733), writing in English, radicalized this line of thinking to the point of rupture with traditional religious conceptions of vice and sinfulness. While Mandeville's theory of morals scandalized his immediate contemporaries, the connection between selfish motivation and general utility came to be regarded with increasing favor during the eighteenth century. That connection provides a crucial element of the moral philosophies of Claude-Adrien Helvétius (1715–1771) and Paul-Henri-Dietrich d'Holbach (1723–1789), both of whom were important influences on the full-fledged utilitarian ethics of Jeremy Bentham (1748–1832). Bentham argued that the

general happiness, to be promoted through actions and governmental policies, must be understood quantitatively in terms of the favorable balance of pleasure over pain, as experienced by separate individuals in the pursuit of their particular ends.

Immanuel Kant (1724–1804) sought the grounds of morality in concepts and principles of practical reason that could be established independently of facts about the sensuous dimension of human nature. Kant's major works on moral philosophy aimed to give an account of the fundamental moral law as a supreme formal principle of duty, which he called the categorical imperative. Kant thought of the categorical imperative as an objectively valid principle by which an agent can determine the moral content of subjective practical principles called maxims. Maxims conforming to the universality requirements expressed by the categorical imperative supply laws of practical reason that specify particular duties. The categorical imperative, however, is much more than just an abstract and legalistic formal principle of duty. For it requires the individual agent to make it *her* maxim to act in such a way that the maxims of her actions can be willed as universal laws, thus making the principle of duty itself the sufficient incentive for action, independently of inclination and sentiment. The rationally legislating human agent gives laws of duty to herself in conformity with the idea that every human will *can* be a will that legislates universally through all its maxims. Such is the Kantian idea of rational self-legislation as autonomy of the will. In keeping with this idea, Kant asserted that morality is "the relation of actions to the autonomy of the will, that is, to a possible giving of universal law through its maxims."

Nineteenth Century

Kant's theory of autonomy and his treatments of the universal principles of rational willing were of determinative significance for the idealist philosophy of Georg Wilhelm Friedrich Hegel (1770–1831). Yet Hegel considered the Kantian method of grounding ethics strictly in the analysis of the formal aspects of rational self-legislation to be fundamentally incomplete. According to Hegel, that method could not overcome its "empty formalism" because it was unable to take proper account of the human agent's embeddedness in historically conditioned societal settings. Hegel's work on moral philosophy reflects the concern to understand both the form and the content of modern morality in its systematic connections with, on the one side, abstract principles of property law, contractual relations, and legal wrongdoing and, on the other side, the concrete norms governing the historically given institutional structures of the bourgeois family, civil society, and the political state.

An important characteristic of nineteenth-century British ethics is the opposition between utilitarian and intuitionist theories. Intuitionists maintained that we have the rational capacity to apprehend self-evident moral principles and that we can be moved to act by virtue of our intuitive grasp of these principles. Intuitionist accounts of morality were formulated on terrain already well prepared by thinkers like Samuel Clarke (1675–1729), Joseph Butler (1692–1752), Richard Price (1723–1791), and Thomas Reid (1710–1796). William Whewell (1794–1866) may be taken as the representative figure for nineteenth-century intuitionism in Britain. John Stuart Mill (1806–1873) defended utilitarianism against its intuitionist detractors. His theory of happiness, however, rejects Bentham's purely quantitative version of hedonism. Mill emphasized the distinction between higher and lower pleasures, and he argued that higher pleasures are better than the lower ones. Henry Sidgwick (1838–1900) investigated egoism, intuitionism, and hedonistic utilitarianism in relation to the principles that underlie intuitive commonsense morality. While Sidgwick took a utilitarian position, he concluded that the standardly accepted antithesis between utilitarianism and intuitionism was spurious since self-evident moral principles are required in order to provide a rational foundation for utilitarian ethics.

Friedrich Nietzsche (1844–1900), who was to have a decisive impact above all on Continental European ethical thought during the twentieth century, devoted much of his writing to a frontal criticism of Western moral philosophy. Rejecting the universality claims of modern thinkers like Kant, Nietzsche focused on historically existing moralities and treated them naturalistically as the outcome of society's development. He was concerned to uncover the psychological underpinnings of our attributions of value and to articulate a "genealogy" of morals that supports a fundamental revaluation of values. Nietzsche regarded modern morality as the result of the creation and imposition of value by the weak, by those who have always struggled against the "master" morality of the strong and noble. Nietzsche emphasized the necessity of overcoming the roots of modern morality, hence the life-affirming will to go "beyond good and evil."

Twentieth Century

Offering an alternative to neo-Kantian ethics and prevalent strains of utilitarian ethics, the emergence of systematic value theory represented an important trend in German and Austrian academic philosophy during the late nineteenth century and the early decades of the twentieth century. The pivotal thinkers in this regard, Franz Brentano (1838–1917) and Max Scheler (1874–1928), held that ethics must be based on the investigation of objective and intrinsic values that are apprehended through the emotions. Brentano's theory of the intrinsically good and bad focused on the implications of the analogical relationship between the intellectual operations of judgment and our emotive attitudes (such as love and hate) toward intentional objects. Stressing the objectivity of values as intentional objects of feeling, Scheler investigated the a priori structures of emotive experience. Scheler devoted much of his work to the detailed phenomenological description of particular emotions such as resentment, love, and sympathy, often in opposition to Nietzsche's moral psychological claims.

Influenced by Brentano, and disavowing the Kantian and neo-Hegelian proclivities of many of his contemporaries, George Edward Moore (1873–1958) held that the fundamental object of ethics was the "good," understood as an intuitively apprehensible, simple, and indefinable property. Moore criticized theories that conceive of the good as something specifiable in terms of natural properties (such as pleasure). Moore held that such theories commit the "naturalistic

fallacy," and his criticism of naturalism in ethics fed into the rise of an analytic tradition that was prevalent in Anglo-American philosophy throughout the twentieth century. Analytic ethical theorists characteristically concentrated on "metaethical" issues such as the meaning of moral terms and the justification of moral judgments. They generally kept these issues separate from the examination of substantive proposals concerning ethical values and the norms of conduct and character. Normative ethics, as distinguished from metaethics, was predominantly utilitarian until the later decades of the 1900s. This situation changed dramatically with John Rawls (1921–2002). Drawing on aspects of modern natural-law theory, but also on Kantian as well as on certain features of intuitionist ethics, Rawls's contractarian theory of justice furnished a clear alternative to the various types of utilitarian approach taken by twentieth-century thinkers. The publication of Rawls's theory of justice represents, in effect, the beginning of the international renaissance of normative ethics that has characterized moral philosophy since the 1970s.

The revival of virtue ethics has been an important factor in Anglo-American philosophy since the 1970s. Criticizing especially Kantian and utilitarian moral thought, virtue ethicists have often located the sources of their theoretical projects in Aristotle and Thomas Aquinas. But eighteenth-century sentimentalist thinkers have also had significant impact on recent virtue ethics. Reflecting the demand that ethics should have relevance beyond the confines of academia, the late twentieth century also witnessed the proliferation of fields in professional and applied ethics as philosophers became increasingly concerned with social and political issues such as the environment, war, medical and business practices, and questions of race and gender. Feminist ethics, which benefited from the expanded scope of practical ethical inquiry, has become a central area of contemporary research. Feminist philosophers have aimed to reconstruct traditional moral philosophy by insisting that ethics should finally take proper account of women's experience and the historically given structures of female subordination. The emancipatory impetus of North American feminist ethics has often been supported by the reception of Continental thought, especially by work stemming from the phenomenological and existentialist tradition, from broadly Marxist schools of social criticism, and from structuralist and poststructuralist philosophy.

See also **Existentialism; Good; Law; Moral Sense; Natural Law; Utilitarianism.**

BIBLIOGRAPHY

Becker Lawrence C., and Charlotte B. Becker, eds. *Encyclopedia of Ethics.* 2nd ed. 3 vols. New York: Routledge, 2001.

Darwall, Stephen, Allan Gibbard, and Peter Railton, eds. *Moral Discourse and Practice.* Oxford: Oxford University Press, 1997.

Haakonssen, Knud. *Natural Law and Moral Philosophy: From Grotius to the Scottish Enlightenment.* Cambridge, U.K.: Cambridge University Press, 1996.

Keohane, Nannerl O. *Philosophy and the State in France: The Renaissance to the Enlightenment.* Princeton, N.J.: Princeton University Press, 1980.

Schneewind, J. B. *The Invention of Autonomy: A History of Modern Moral Philosophy.* Cambridge, U.K.: Cambridge University Press, 1998.

———. *Sidgwick's Ethics and Victorian Moral Philosophy*. Oxford: Oxford University Press, 2000.

———, ed. *Moral Philosophy from Montaigne to Kant*. Cambridge, U.K.: Cambridge University Press, 2003.

Schneiders, Werner. *Naturrecht und Liebesethik*. Hildesheim: Georg Olms, 1971.

Singer, Peter, ed. *A Companion to Ethics*. Oxford: Blackwell, 1991.

Tuck, Richard. *Philosophy and Government, 1572–1651*. Cambridge, U.K.: Cambridge University Press, 1993.

Jeffrey Edwards
Michael Hughes

PHILOSOPHY AND RELIGION IN WESTERN THOUGHT.

Before Socrates, speculative thinkers addressed in several ways what would be identified as religious matters in the twenty-first century. Some of them criticized what they deemed to be implausible features of conventional religion: thus Xenophanes of Colophon (c. 560–c. 478 B.C.E.) attacked both the immorality and the anthropomorphism of the poets' depiction of the gods, while Democritus of Abdera (fifth century B.C.E.) provided explanations of the causes of events that were opposed to ideas of divine intention or arguments from design. Several early philosophers further advanced an understanding of the concept of divinity in terms that were opposed to ordinary religious experience. Their efforts were often caricatured by the public imagination as instances of impiety. It is revealing that Aristophanes (c. 450–c. 388 B.C.E.) in his play *The Clouds* depicted philosophers as promoters of irreligion, and Socrates (c. 470–399 B.C.E.) at his trial was accused of being "completely godless" (*to parapan atheos*).

With the work of Plato (c. 428–348 or 347 B.C.E.) and Aristotle (384–322 B.C.E.), these strategies for addressing the claims of religion were consolidated in ways that did much to determine future discussion. Plato's Socrates defends traditional mythology and participates in civic rituals. He recounts to Phaedrus the myth about Boreas and Orithyia and admonishes those who seek to explain its point naturalistically, and his famous last words to Crito request that a ritual sacrifice be made on his behalf. More formally, however, Plato's dialogues repeatedly turn on a rejection of doubts about the divine (see *Laws*, book 10), and he provides several arguments against those who deny the existence, nature, or providence of the gods. His most enduring representation of divine action is the account in the *Timaeus* of the Demiurge who creates the universe out of a benevolent motive.

In the works of Aristotle, criticisms of popular misconceptions of divinity and genuine moments of piety are combined. More important for later thinking about theology, however, are Aristotle's arguments for the existence of a divine prime mover of the universe and his account of that entity. At the end of *Physics* (book 8) and in *Metaphysics* (book 12), he argues that the impossibility of an infinite regress in motion requires that there be a fully actualized entity who causes all other motions by being the universal object of desire. In the *Metaphysics*, Aristotle describes the life of this being as one of "thinking of thinking" (*noesis noeseos*). Beyond this highly suggestive passage and a few allusions elsewhere, the Aristotelian corpus affords researchers no explicit description of a divine agent.

After the deaths of Plato and Aristotle, their followers widely disseminated their theologies throughout the ancient world and engaged in dialogue with some of the teachings of Stoicism. The Stoic analysis of pain and misadventure was facilitated by a doctrine of divine providence. The Stoics were also very capable natural scientists, and this led to their promulgation of many theories about the origin of the universe. Such physical processes, however, were held to be orchestrated by a divine mind, a mind that could find expression in the civic gods of traditional religion. These three schools—the Platonic, the Aristotelian, and the Stoic—all disputed at great length with the Epicureans, for whom the gods' interventions in human affairs were nothing but a series of malicious fictions. What "gods" the Epicureans did permit were always characterized in terms that made them fully physical and natural, subject to the same laws of generation and corruption, pleasure and tranquility, that conditioned human life. An illustration of the dialectic between these competing views, as well as a resistance to Epicurean doctrines, can be found in Cicero's (106–43 B.C.E.) *On the Nature of the Gods* (book 1).

The Early Christian and Medieval Periods

The course of ancient speculation about divine matters was dramatically altered as early as the first century of the common era by the pagan world's contact with Judaism and subsequently Christianity. The intellectual directions of these faiths were also shaped as a result of coming into contact with ancient philosophy. In pagan thought, the contact produced a renewed interest in the representation of the divine nature. In Judaism and Christianity, it produced an energetic effort to present the claims of revelation in philosophically coherent ways. The renewed interest among the pagans is most evident in Neoplatonism, a school that included Plotinus (205–270), Porphyry (c. 234–c. 305), Iamblichus (c. 250–c. 330), and Proclus (410?–485). The new effort of speculation about divine matters can be seen, albeit in a different guise, in Jewish thinkers such as Philo Judaeus of Alexandria (first century C.E.) and among Christian thinkers such as Clement of Alexandria (150–between 211 and 215) and Origen (185?–254?). It led not only to philosophical explorations of Scripture but also to the development of a view within Christian circles that the "best" philosophy was to be found in Scripture.

After 400, philosophy became fully subsumed within the three monotheistic religions—Judaism, Christianity, and then Islam. Throughout the thousand years from the fifth to the fifteenth century, the largest part of speculative talent in the West was devoted to considering questions about the God of the Scriptures or revelation. Very few philosophers neglected the issues raised by the confrontation of ancient philosophy with the monotheistic religions, as can be observed in the writings of Arab thinkers such as al-Kindi (fl. ninth century), Avicenna (Ibn Sina; 980–1037), and Averroës (Ibn Rushd; 1126–1198).

In many Latin works the conversion or ascent of philosophy to faith is the central theme, as can be witnessed in the *Confessions* of St. Augustine of Hippo (354–430). For other late antique and early medieval thinkers, philosophy served as a prolegomenon to faith grasped and expressed as sacred doctrine (*sacra doctrina*). In Boethius's (c. 480–524) *Consolation of Philosophy*, the figure of philosophy reminds Boethius of verities without which his faith cannot be restored. One of the more enduring models of reflection on divine matters was presented by Anselm of Canterbury (1033 or 1034–1109) in his *Proslogion*. Building on the intellectual heritage of Augustine, he uses the phrase *fides quaerens intellectum*—faith seeking understanding. This strategy can clearly be seen at work in Anselm's so-called "ontological argument" in the *Proslogion* 2 and 54. It can be argued that one does much better justice to Anselm's intentions if one views the argument not as a demonstration of the existence of God but as a systematic investigation into God's mode of existence. As a person seeking understanding *(fidelis quaerens intellectum),* Anselm begins from a faith that provides the conceptual parameters of his philosophical reflection and then attempts to win his way through to a better understanding of the divine nature.

In terms loosely contiguous with Anselm's project, other medieval authors clarified the relation between philosophy and theology by insisting that philosophy must be studied thoroughly before proceeding to theology. Different examples of this tendency can be found in thinkers as diverse as the Christian Bonaventure (c. 1217–1274), in his *Itinerarium,* and the Jewish polymath Moses ben Maimon (Maimonides; 1135–1204). In a similar spirit, the Oxford philosopher and natural scientist Roger Bacon (c. 1220–1292) argued that nothing could be known about God without a prior study of languages, mathematics, optics, experiential science, and moral philosophy.

When arriving at the zenith of Scholastic speculation on God in the last quarter of the thirteenth and the first half of the fourteenth century, one finds a profound illustration of the range and diversity of the engagement of Christian theologians with the Aristotelian inheritance in the works of Thomas Aquinas (c. 1224–1274), John Duns Scotus (c. 1266–1308), and William of Ockham (c. 1285–?1349). For Aquinas, theology (*theologia*) employs, improves, and then perfects the best of ancient philosophy. He extended great deference to pagan philosophers, especially Aristotle, but whenever he spoke in his own voice he systematically transformed most of the Aristotelian doctrines he discussed, often in directions quite opposed to Aristotle's original intentions. Duns Scotus, on the other hand, began by candidly refusing to accommodate Aristotle, but what is called his "Augustinianism" is nothing but a mélange of the theological legacy from Augustine, the philosophical deposit of Neoplatonism, Scotus's reaction to the work of his contemporaries (in particular Henry of Ghent [c. 1217–1293]), and a model of Aristotelianism derived from reading Aristotle refracted through the glass of Latin Averroism. William of Ockham saw fit to repudiate some of the central features of the Aristotelianism espoused by his forebears, but he repeatedly sought to use Aristotle's work to support his own philosophical views and aspired to be perceived as a faithful Aristotelian.

The Early Modern Period

The medieval requirement of *fides quaerens intellectum* carried forward into the early modern period. Yet its legacy was complicated in three distinct ways. First, the Christian reform movements of the Reformation were often sharply critical of the use of philosophy in any discussion of God and his creation. This criticism varied in intensity from one reforming group to another and often coexisted with humanist learning and philosophical erudition. For example, both Martin Luther (1483–1546) and John Calvin (1509–1564) frequently mocked Aristotle, and by implication much of the Scholastic tradition of philosophical theology. But more commonly, their criticisms of philosophy arose from claims about the opposition of philosophy to the Gospels, or from a vivid conviction of the impotence of "sinful" human reason, or from a confidence that God would teach what was needed in human affairs by "inspiration" and would do so not only for the prince, philosopher, and prelate but also for the common ploughboy. That said, it is telling that in the years immediately after the schism with Rome, the speculative theology of Lutheran and Reformed traditions is characterized by a return to the resources of the Aristotelian metaphysics and Scholastic argument in order to make sense of their distinctive theological claims. This can be observed in the writings of Philipp Melanchthon (1497–1560) and Théodore de Bèze (1519–1605).

The second complication in the relations of philosophy to theological issues arose from fierce disputes over the conclusions of the *nova scientia,* or "new science." The condemnation of Galileo Galilei (1564–1642) is one well-known example. Opposition to the metaphysical implications of the new science in certain religious quarters made many philosophers cautious in expressing their views. It thus becomes tricky to construe the exact nature of their theological allegiances. On the surface, the work of René Descartes (1596–1650), for example, appears to display a scrupulous Catholic orthodoxy accompanied by frequent protestations of obedience to the *magisterium* (or "teaching authority") of the Roman Church. But Descartes was also extremely reticent and somewhat guarded about many of his cosmological views, and he continually did his very best to ensure that his publications would not provoke theological controversy. Likewise, Baruch Spinoza (1632–1677) littered his *Tractatus theologico-politicus* (anonymously published in 1670) with misdirections in order to increase the likelihood that the reader would miss his heterodox interpretation of Scripture.

The final complication arose from a more pronounced ambivalence concerning the status or even utility of advancing rational arguments for the existence of God. Thinkers such as Blaise Pascal (1623–1662) argued that the universe is characterized by a fundamental ambiguity and that arguments for the existence of God were inconclusive. On this basis, he argued that individuals ought instead to ground their religious practices in a volitional choice by which they would make themselves firmly assent to the teaching and doctrines of the church. Without such a decision, he argued, one's faith would be without foundation. This tendency, however, was opposed by a strong support for a posteriori arguments in support of "natural religion," the claim being that it is only by means of impartial human reason that the truths of revelation can be authenticated and defended. The consequence of this move was to usher in the view that religious belief was irrational unless buttressed by a prior philosophical justification. Of course, this left open the distinct possibility that reason might in the end disprove belief in God.

By themselves, these complications could not undo the ancient engagement of philosophy with speculation about divine matters, nor could they sever the ancient dependence of religious thought upon established modes of philosophical discourse. The overwhelming majority of early modern philosophers affirmed the existence and activity of a God, and most aligned themselves with one Christian denomination or another. John Locke (1632–1704) and George Berkeley (1685–1753) were both Anglicans. Nicolas Malebranche (1638–1715), Antoine Arnauld (1612–1694), and Pascal all published works that reflected their own distinctive brands of Roman Catholicism. Gottfried Wilhelm von Leibniz (1646–1716), while a Lutheran, distinguished himself in a period woefully characterized by religious conflict by advancing for ecumenicalism. Jonathan Edwards (1703–1758) forcefully expounded the Puritan notion of the utter dependence of all things on God. Of all the philosophers of the period, only Thomas Hobbes (1588–1679) appears a heterodox theist.

The Eighteenth and Nineteenth Centuries

If many of the central figures of the European Enlightenment were trenchant critics of established religion, they often enough professed views about a divine origin or general governance of the created order. This is true of Denis Diderot (1713–1784), Voltaire (1694–1778), and Jean-Jacques Rousseau (1712–1778). The most important works of this time regarding religion are David Hume's (1711–1776) *Natural History of Religion* (1757) and *Dialogues concerning Natural Religion* (1779, but first written in the 1750s). The former deals with the causes of religion, as it originates in human nature and society, while the latter examines the reasons or putative grounds for believing in a God or gods. The force of Hume's work resided in his claim that the culminative arguments of natural religion do not establish the existence of any deity that could be the proper object of religious belief. If revelation cannot be authenticated by reason, it might seem that the only answer that can be given to the question "Why does anyone believe in God or gods?" is that such practices have a natural origin. An investigation of these causes is the subject of the *Natural History of Religion*. Central to Hume's argument there is the provocative contention that the source of a belief in deities is to be found in numerous human pathologies that derive from a fear of the unknown.

It was not only Hume who fired a successful broadside at the theistic tradition of Western philosophy. Immanuel Kant (1724–1804) sought to refute the questionable metaphysical assumptions he believed inherent in the traditional "speculative proofs" for the existence of God, by demonstrating the incoherence of the ontological argument, the cosmological proof, and the argument from design. The effect of Kant's onslaught was to undermine not only the substance of these arguments but also trust in their philosophical efficacy. After him, philosophers such as Georg Wilhelm Friedrich Hegel (1770–1831) chose to construct a metaphysico-religious view of "Absolute Spirit," a highly suggestive concept that draws on pantheistic ideas of the identity of the universe and God, together with theistic ideas concerning the necessary "self-consciousness" of God. The peculiarity of Hegel's view lies in his notion that the mind of God becomes actual only via the minds of his creatures.

While Kant and Hegel by no means excluded religious topics or even religious sentiments from their work, many of their subsequent readers appropriated only the negative conclusion that could be distilled from their critique of traditional theism. Thus it is unsurprising that they were followed either by fideistic thinkers such as Søren Kierkegaard (1813–1855) or else resolutely antitheistic thinkers, of whom Ludwig Feuerbach (1804–1872), Arthur Schopenhauer (1788–1860), Karl Marx (1818–1883), Friedrich Nietzsche (1844–1900), and Sigmund Freud (1856–1939) were the most influential. This atheistic legacy was prosecuted still further in the twentieth century by luminaries of the Continental tradition such as Martin Heidegger (1889–1976) and Jean-Paul Sartre (1905–1980), whose philosophical systems leave no room for God.

The Twentieth Century

Only in the twentieth century did it become commonplace for philosophers in the West to engage with the central concerns of their subject without so much as raising questions about God. A collective penchant for empiricism in both Britain and America prompted Rudolph Carnap (1891–1970) and A. J. Ayer (1910–1989) to argue that all religious claims are meaningless. Other influential philosophers such as Willard Van Orman Quine (1908–2000) essayed a metaphysics and epistemology that disqualified many of the assumptions on which a theistic philosophy could be based. It was only with the move away from strict verificationism and the development of a greater pluralism in so-called "analytic philosophy" that religious topics reappeared in philosophical thought. The work of Ludwig Wittgenstein (1889–1951), while by no means concordant with earlier traditions of metaphysics, was believed by many of his followers to have a broadly theological outlook whereby religious practices and belief could be shown to have dignity and purpose, as well as a discursive integrity that insulated them from the critiques of Hume and Kant.

In the final decades of the twentieth century, philosophers such as Alvin Plantinga in the United States and Richard Swinburne in Great Britain set about the task of applying the rigorous standards of analytic philosophy to the discussion of traditional theological subjects. The effect of their work was to increase the institutional profile of the subject known in the early 2000s as "the philosophy of religion" in professional philosophy. In many senses, this subdiscipline provides the main conceptual forum in which philosophers can debate the claims of the Western theistic tradition.

Notwithstanding the reemergence of the philosophy of religion, it is important to stress that philosophy has become a secular discipline in most Western countries. Yet the fact that it is practiced by philosophers with little or no faith or indeed historical understanding of religion does not negate the fact that throughout the ages philosophy has been closely connected to religion and speculative theology. While the impulse to philosophize and to reflect on ourselves and the world around us may or may not have its origins in a protoreligious sentiment or disposition, the very nature of philosophical reflection will always dispose itself to intrude upon matters connected with religion and concepts of divinity. Even in this godless age, it is to be expected that the uneasy and, at times, vicarious relationship between philosophy and religion will continue.

See also **Aristotelianism; Christianity: Overview; Deism; Enlightenment; Epicureanism; Monism; Neoplatonism; Philosophy, History of; Philosophy: Relations to Other Intellectual Realms; Religion and Science; Scholasticism; Skepticism; Stoicism.**

BIBLIOGRAPHY
Davidson, Herbert A. *Proofs for Eternity, Creation, and the Existence of God in Medieval Islamic and Jewish Philosophy.* New York: Oxford University Press, 1987.
Frank, Günter. *Die Vernunft des Gottesgedankens: Religionsphilosophische Studien zur frühen Neuzeit.* Stuttgart, Germany: Frommann-Holzboog, 2003.
Funkenstein, Amos. *Theology and the Scientific Imagination from the Middle Ages to the Seventeenth Century.* Princeton, N.J.: Princeton University Press, 1986.
Gerson, Lloyd P. *God and Greek Philosophy.* London: Routledge, 1990.
Grant, Edward. *God and Reason in the Middle Ages.* Cambridge, U.K.: Cambridge University Press, 2001.
Israel, Jonathan I. *Radical Enlightenment: Philosophy and the Making of Modernity, 1650–1750.* Oxford: Oxford University Press, 2001.
Marrone, Steven P. *The Light of Thy Countenance: Science and Knowledge of God in the Thirteenth Century.* 2 vols. Leiden, Netherlands: Brill, 2001.
Oberman, Heiko. *The Harvest of Medieval Theology.* Rev. ed. Grand Rapids, Mich.: Baker, 2000.
Popkin, Richard H., and Arjo Vanderjagt, eds. *Scepticism and Irreligion in the Seventeenth and Eighteenth Centuries.* Leiden, Netherlands: Brill, 1993.
Webb, Clement C. J. *Studies in the History of Natural Theology.* Oxford: Clarendon, 1915.
Wolfson, Harry A. *Philosophy of the Church Fathers.* 3rd rev. ed. Cambridge, Mass.: Harvard University Press, 1970.

M. W. F. Stone

PHILOSOPHY OF LANGUAGE. *See* **Language, Philosophy of.**

PHILOSOPHY OF MIND.

This entry includes two subentries:

Overview
Ancient and Medieval

OVERVIEW

Issues related to the mind are an important component in contemporary philosophy. While colleagues in psychology, neuroscience, and cognitive ethology do empirical scientific studies of the mind, philosophers tend to focus on more general questions: What is the nature of mind, such as it may be found in *any* creature or thing? Philosophers tend to concentrate on questions such as: How is mind related to body? and How are we to understand the nature of such operations of mind as believing, knowing, perceiving, thinking, willing, understanding, and the like? Philosophers ask as well about the nature of self, of consciousness, and of the relation of these to the capacity for language.

Early Ideas
It is generally agreed that the question What is mind?—with all its modern connotations—is not found in ancient texts. The question first emerges clearly in the philosophical work of René Descartes (1596–1650). For centuries, psychological and philosophical inquiry proceeded together. The term *psychology* has its roots in the Greek term *psyche,* which has come to be translated as *soul.* In very early texts *psyche* is associated with breath, the loss of which is thought to result either in unconsciousness or death. In the work of Plato (c. 428–348 or 347 B.C.E.), the soul is taken to be simple and immortal. It is the soul—and in particular that rational part of soul, *nous*—that apprehends the Forms, and, in life, controls the body's passions. It is with Aristotle (384–322 B.C.E.) and his more biological orientation that the study of *psychology* is launched (although it is not until the late nineteenth century that the discipline is fully defined). In Aristotle we find the idea of the soul as the form of a living body, a form that has different aspects in plants, in nonrational animals, and in human animals.

Descartes's Legacy
The contemporary study of mind was given its shape by the seventeenth century philosopher René Descartes. In his *Meditations on First Philosophy,* Descartes begins with questions about what he can know. He carefully peels away from all that he has taken to be true anything that can be doubted. Descartes claims to reach the limits of doubt when he considers that, although he can doubt the existence of his body, he cannot doubt the existence of his mind. Descartes interestingly (and importantly) conducts the entire of his *Meditations* in the first person singular. He then presents the conclusion of his doubt thus: "*I am, I exist,* is necessarily true whenever it is put forward by me or conceived in my mind." (In another of his works, he formulates the conclusion thus: "I think, therefore I am.") This conclusion then launches him onto an examination of what he (this *I*) is. He considers, and rejects, the suggestion that he is a body (he can, after all, doubt the belief that his body exists). Thinking, however, is "inseparable from me." Descartes concludes that he is a thinking thing, "a thing that doubts, understands, affirms, denies, is willing, is unwilling, and also imagines and has sense perception." Descartes interestingly considers sense perception and points out that, although the objects of sight and sound may not exist, it is still indubitable that one has certain visual and auditory perceptions—that one *seems* to see and *seems* to hear. By the end of the *Meditations,* Descartes has set the stage in the philosophy of mind for the ensuing generations: Mind and body are distinct, each with a different essential nature. The world

can seem exactly as it is to a mind, while the bodies to which we take them to correspond may not exist; our world could be the result of the machinations of an evil demon. This is the metaphysical and epistemological position that Descartes bequeathed to future generations of philosophers.

This Cartesian philosophy of mind contains several key aspects. First, it establishes the position known as Cartesian, or substantial, dualism (mind and body are distinct substances). Second, it sets up the possibility of various kinds of skepticism concerning not only the external world, but also the existence of other minds. Third, it sets forth the mind as an arena that is private to the thinker, and—as far as what one *seems* to perceive—an arena whose contents are infallible and incorrigible. Fourth, it includes in the term *thought* (Latin *cogitatio*) not only understanding, willing, imagination, and the like, but also feeling. Fifth, it represents a deliberate rejection of the ancient way of thinking about the soul. Descartes holds that mind is not part of the soul but the "thinking soul in its entirety." The result of this shift is significant. Whereas the ancients allowed souls to all living organisms, with mind restricted to human animals, Descartes holds that the soul or mind is to be found only in human animals. All nonhuman living creatures are, accordingly, mere mechanisms. Interestingly, Descartes views the human body as a mere machine, albeit one to which God has endowed a mind or soul.

Philosophy and Psychology

The study of mind, from these Cartesian roots, can be seen to take two identifiable paths (although these paths were not clearly distinguished for some considerable time). One path is through philosophy, where questions concerning mind remain closely connected with other philosophical issues such as the nature of the self, the mind's knowledge of the world, and the nature of perception, belief, memory, and the emotions. The other path leads from philosophy to the development of psychology. The work of the British empiricists (John Locke [1632–1704], George Berkeley [1685–1753], David Hume [1711–1776])— in particular their sensationalism and associationism—was taken up in the eighteenth and nineteenth century and developed into a more empirical study of mind. This new study of mind gained momentum both in Great Britain (with associationalists such as David Hartley [1705–1757], James Mill [1773–1836] and John Stuart Mill [1806–1873], and Alexander Bain [1818–1903], as well as with the more Darwinian-inspired work of Sir Francis Galton [1822–1911], James Ward [1843–1925], and G. F. Stout [1806–1944]), in France (with the work of Etienne Bonnot de Condillac [1715–1780] and Claude-Adrien Helvétius [1715–1771]), and in Germany (with the work of Ernst Heinrich Weber [1795–1878], Gustav Theodor Fechner [1801–1887], Friedrich Beneke [1798–1854], Hermann von Helmholz [1821–1894], Wilhelm Wundt [1832–1920], and others).

This study transferred to the United States in the very early twentieth century, where it gave rise (by way of revolt against associationalism) to the highly influential school of behaviorism under the direction of J. B. Watson (1878–1958) and B.F. Skinner (1904–1990). Behaviorism was a rejection of much of Descartes's legacy—of his dualism, as well as of his use of an introspective method in the study of mind. Behaviorists favored a physicalism rooted in the study of responses to stimuli in the environment. Behaviorist doctrines are to be found in both psychological and philosophical studies of the mind at this time. From around the middle of the twentieth century, behaviorist doctrine came under heavy attack. The American linguist Noam Chomsky published an influential review of Skinner's work in which he pointed out that it is not possible to come up with a reduction of, say, a belief in terms of behavior without mentioning other mental states such as desire. The elements of the mind work *together* to produce behavior. The hope of finding a behaviorist reduction of mind seemed doomed.

With the demise of behaviorism came a renewed interest in mentalist causes and the rise of cognitive psychology. An interaction between philosophy and cognitive psychology emerged in the mid- to late twentieth century in the form of the philosophy of psychology, the study of conceptual issues in psychology using many of the methodological tools of the philosopher. The philosophy of psychology is firmly grounded in empirical studies of the mind. Questions concerning the nature of mental representation, mental imagery, what it is to have a concept, and whether there are innate ideas figure high on the agenda of these philosophers of psychology. Also around this time, there developed a multidisciplinary approach to the study of mind, *cognitive science,* encompassing philosophy, cognitive psychology, neuroscience, linguistics, and computer science. What these practitioners from different areas of study share is a belief that the workings of the mind can be modeled on the workings of a computer—that the mind is an information processing system and a representational devise. Cognitive science incorporates work that stretches from artificial intelligence (AI) to parallel distributed processing (PDP or connectionist networks). It has been fueled by work such as Chomsky's on generative grammar in linguistics, the work of the American philosopher Jerry Fodor on the language of thought in philosophy and psychology, and the work of the psychologist David Marr on visual processing. The American philosopher John Searle, with a thought experiment called "the Chinese Room," has played the gadfly to much of the work in cognitive science. What Searle questions is the very idea that a computer program, a mere syntactic engine, can be identical to a mind, a semantic engine. In effect, we are back trying to understand the relationship of mind to body.

Identity Theory, Eliminativism, Functionalism, and Anomalous Monism

Attempts to get a grip on mind and to understand its relationship to body proliferated in the twentieth century. In the 1950s, J. J. C. Smart and U. T. Place advocated a form of identity theory. As these physicalists (or materialists) put it, consciousness is a brain process just as lightening is electrical discharge or water is H_2O. This identity was famously challenge by the American philosopher Saul Kripke who, with his "Cartesian intuitions," argued that such an identity could only be maintained if it could be explained why it seemed to one that there could be a brain process in the absence of experience and experience in the absence of the brain process.

Alternative accounts of mind were proposed. One highly influential account, functionalism, took its cue from the development of information processing and computer technology, with its important distinction between the level of implemented software and that of implementing hardware. According to functionalism, mental states are the upshot of various causal impacts from the world, and they, in their turn, typically cause certain behavior as well as other mental states. Functionalism was hailed as an advance on both behaviorism and physicalism. Unlike behaviorism, functionalism is committed to internal, causal states. Unlike physicalism, functionalism is defined as a relation among states, thus leaving open the possibility that what realizes this function may vary from individual to individual. In the words of one early exponent, the American philosopher Hilary Putnam, our brains could be made up of gray matter or Swiss cheese; what matters is the functional organization of the system. Another important proposal for the understanding of mind came from the work of another American philosopher, Donald Davidson, who aimed to reconcile the irreducibility of mind with a commitment to monism. Davidson's anomalous monism draws a distinction between type and token identity theories. Earlier identity theorists—for example, Place and Smart—aimed to identify types of mental states with types of physical states (e.g., pain with c-fiber firing); Davidson insisted that only token mental states could be identified with token physical states (e.g., my pain at noon on 3 January 2004 with a state of my brain on that date at that time). Ontological monism (all that there is, is physical) can now be combined with conceptual dualism (mental concepts are distinct from, and cannot be reduced to, physical concepts). The principle of rationality governs the mental realm, but not the physical. With this distinction Davidson hoped to reconcile our culture of materialism/physicalism with an understanding of those characteristics of mind that make us free and moral agents.

By the turn of the twentieth century, it had become clear that talk of "the mind" is too broad and that there may be issues to do with experience and sensation that are distinct from those that arise in connection with such mental states as believing, desiring, and the like (the so-called propositional attitudes). It was thought that, while functionalism, for example, might provide a plausible account of belief, it encountered real difficulties when it came to accounting for experience. This thought was reinforced with the work of the American philosopher Thomas Nagel, who pointed out that human beings—as well as other animals such as bats—enjoy conscious experiences: there is something it is like to *be* that organism, something it is like *for* that organism. Nagel labels this the "subjective character of experience" and he argues that it is hard to see how this subjectivity could be captured in an objective science of the brain. Nagel, like Descartes before him, wants to understand just how the working of the grey matter that constitutes our brain could possibly explain the way the world seems to us—explain the dazzle of fireworks or the taste of chocolate. The philosopher Colin McGinn has argued that there is a very simple explanation here, but it is not one our human minds will ever be able to comprehend. Those working in the scientific study of mind have vigorously rejected this mysterianism. One empirically oriented American philosopher, Daniel

Dennett, claims to be able to reconcile our view of ourselves as rational, free, and conscious agents with a belief in the completeness of science by arguing that the former constitutes an ineliminable level of description of our behavior. Others, like the American philosophers Paul and Patricia Churchland, argue that psychological concepts such as belief, desires, and so on produce no definable brain activity and therefore these concepts should form no part of a completed science of mind.

The study of mind extends from philosophy to psychology and has expanded more recently to include neurophysiology, as well as cognitive ethology. The race is on to look ever more closely at the workings of the brain and at the behavior of all animals. On the one hand there is the age-old fascination with the idea of man as a machine, while on the other there is the hope that by understanding the fine-tuning of behavior we will find evidence that we share mentality with non-human animals.

Ludwig Wittgenstein

The Cartesian legacy is strong and everywhere apparent in discussions of the mind. It received a penetrating critique in the early part of the twentieth century, however, in the later work of Ludwig Wittgenstein (1889–1951), such as his *Philosophical Investigations.* Wittgenstein can be taken to have rejected the introspective method as well as the dualism of Cartesianism, and for this reason is sometimes said to be a behaviorist of sorts. It is, however, best to avoid this comparison. What Wittgenstein urges is that when we study the mind, we need to accept and understand the fact that the mind has both a first and a third person aspect; that is, each one of us knows the mind both from the "inside" as a subject and from the "outside" as the observer of other subjects. For Wittgenstein, the study of mind needs to be taken to be the study of the concept of mind, a concept that has application to oneself as well as to others. Wittgenstein's private language argument is interpreted as a critique of the very idea that one can make sense of the application of mental states to oneself in the absence of the acquisition of a concept—an acquisition that takes place through the use of language and in a social setting. Through the interaction with others, the child comes to understand that pain, for instance, is something that happens when, for example, one encounters sharp objects and reacts with a cry. The child's nature is such as to respond to its environment in certain ways; this nature and this response form the basis of the child's use of language and contribute to the development of the child's concepts. In this way the child develops concepts that have application both to the child and to others. With its constant reminder of the role that others play in the way we understand the mind, Wittgenstein's work offers a fundamental alternative to Cartesian individualism.

Conclusion

The study of mind in the early 2000s has been invigorated through the study of disorders of the mind. Appreciating the ways in which mind can break down can add to our understanding of what it is that we are studying. The mind is at once most intimately familiar to each of us and at the same time most mysterious and elusive to our understanding. While the human mind retains its preeminence, it is a real question whether it represents something continuous or discontinuous with what we find in other animals, and in machines. While materialism is the dominant culture, we must not forget the observations of Descartes and others that make it difficult to understand just how a mere body can produce the various activities we associate with mind. The history of mind is the history of our attempt to explain how our experiences, perceptions, thoughts, emotions, and the like can be fully understood in relation to the world of flesh and blood.

See also **Behaviorism; Cartesianism; Consciousness; Mind; Psychoanalysis; Psychology and Psychiatry.**

BIBLIOGRAPHY

Chomsky, Noam. "Review of B. F. Skinner's *Verbal Behavior.*" In *Readings in Philosophy of Psychology,* edited by Ned Block. 2 vols. Cambridge, Mass.: Harvard University Press, 1980.

Churchland, Paul. *Matter and Consciousness: A Contemporary Introduction to the Philosophy of Mind.* Cambridge, Mass.: M.I.T. Press, 1984.

Davidson, Donald. *Essays on Actions and Events.* Oxford: Clarendon, 1980.

Dennett, Daniel. *Consciousness Explained.* Boston: Little, Brown, 1991.

Descartes, René. *The Philosophical Writings of Descartes.* Translated by John Cottingham, Robert Stoothoff, and Dugald Murdoch. 2 vols. Cambridge, U.K.: Cambridge University Press, 1984.

Kripke, Saul. *Naming and Necessity.* Cambridge, Mass.: Harvard University Press, 1980.

McGinn, Colin. *Problems in Philosophy: The Limits of Inquiry.* Oxford: Blackwell, 1993.

Nagel, Thomas. *Mortal Questions.* Cambridge, U.K.: Cambridge University Press, 1979.

Putnam, Hilary. *Mind, Language and Reality.* Cambridge, U.K.: Cambridge University Press, 1975.

Wittgenstein, Ludwig. *Philosophical Investigations.* Translated by G. E. M. Anscombe. Oxford: Blackwell, 1953.

Anita Avramides

ANCIENT AND MEDIEVAL

The mind is a modern notion. But like many modern notions, it did not emerge from nowhere. What contemporary philosophers mean when they talk about the mind is part of a long tradition, stretching back through the Middle Ages to Greek and Roman antiquity.

The mind in its modern sense is best understood in opposition to the body, the extended, flesh-and-blood entity that it seems to inhabit and move at will. It was René Descartes (1596–1650) who popularized the idea that humans are two things, mind and body, and who argued further that the mind is a completely separable and immaterial substance capable of surviving the death of the body. The influence of Cartesian dualism can be seen in the fact that even in the twenty-first century, competing viewpoints tend to be defined in terms of it.

Although dualism in its strongest form originated with Descartes, there are some similarities with earlier accounts.

Descartes might even have been inspired by them. Unfortunately, this has proved to be a stumbling block for many modern scholars, who, because their thinking has been shaped by the Cartesian paradigm, cannot help but see earlier philosophers as proto-Cartesians or read their works as contributing to the solution of Cartesian problems. While this makes for interesting reading, it does a disservice to ancient and medieval authors because it refuses to understand what they were trying to do on its own terms. But Descartes's agenda differs from Plato's, which is different again from that of Aristotle, Epicurus, Chrysippus, Plotinus, Augustine, Thomas Aquinas, and John Buridan.

Ancient Greek and Roman Views

The main precursor of the modern concept of mind is the ancient Greek notion of soul (*psyche*), which was originally used to mark the difference between things that are alive and things that are dead. Conceptually, it was related to breath (*pneuma*), and was thought to come in degrees corresponding to different states of consciousness. Thus, a dead man was said to have lost his *psyche* entirely, whereas a sleeping or fainting man has lost enough of it to lose consciousness, though that too would bring him a step closer to death. The soul is composed of extremely light and tenuous matter, variously identified with pure and "breathable" elements such as air (as by the philosophers Thales [c. 625–c. 547 B.C.E.] and Anaximenes [570?–500? B.C.E.]) or fire (by Heraclitus [c. 540–480 B.C.E.]). Most pre-Socratic thinkers would have understood the expression "he breathed his last" literally, and seen the dying gasps of a Homeric warrior, say, as the exhalation of his soul. If *psyche* could exist in a disembodied state—and it is doubtful whether most early Greek philosophers thought that it could—it would have been as a shadowy or ephemeral form, like the denizens of Hades.

With Plato (c. 428–348 or 347 B.C.E.), philosophers began to ask more sophisticated questions about how one can feel, think, possess knowledge, and choose rightly. Plato's strategy here was to divide the soul in terms of its capacities, producing the first faculty psychology in the western tradition.

In his earlier writings, Plato came closer than any other ancient or medieval philosopher to advancing a dualist account like that of Descartes. In the *Phaedo,* he took immortality to be an essential feature of the soul, so that "mortal soul" is a contradiction in terms. Thus, "when death comes to a man, the mortal part of him dies, but the immortal part retires at the approach of death and escapes unharmed and indestructible" (106e). But a soul immortal by definition has more in common with what is cosmic and divine than with anything in the visible realm—such as its own body, for example—which is why Plato shows little interest in exploring its everyday operations. The soul's union with the body is not its natural state; in fact, the whole point of philosophy is to prepare the soul for its release from the "prison" of the body (80c–84b).

Plato is more forthcoming in his later works, where the concept of the soul plays a major role in his explanation of moral conflict and human action. From the fact that one can be affected by two or more desires simultaneously, he infers that the soul cannot be unitary, since it is impossible for the same thing to act in opposite ways at the same time (there are obvious affinities here with the logical principle of non-contradiction, which Plato learned from Socrates [c. 470–399 B.C.E.]). Accordingly, in the *Republic* he identifies three distinct parts of the soul—reason (*nous*), passion (*thumos*), and appetite (*epithumia*)—and posits these as the source of conflicting desires (IV, 439d–e). Reason rules over the soul with wisdom, but opposed to it is appetite, the irrational part of the soul "with which it loves, hungers, thirsts, and feels the flutter and titillation of other desires" (439d). Reason and appetite would remain in unending combat but for the intervention of passion, the "spirited" part of the soul that helps reason subdue appetite. Plato has in mind here the experience of steeling our resolve, when we angrily force ourselves to do something we don't want to do because reason has judged it to be the best course of action. What is important about this model, however, is the elevation of rationality to the dominant position in the soul, and conversely, the denigration of appetite as an irrational force that threatens to destroy our well-being. In the *Phaedrus*, Plato likens reason to a charioteer trying to control two horses: a good horse (passion), who "needs no whip" because he is driven by the command of reason alone, and a bad horse (appetite), who is hard to control and who would run the chariot into the ditch if left unchecked (253d–254e). Plato saw no redeeming value for the emotions in human moral life, though anger, at least, could sometimes be placed in the service of reason.

Aristotle (384–322 B.C.E.) took the study of the soul in a less speculative direction. He wrote an entire treatise on the soul—*Peri psyche,* or *De anima* in its Latin translation—that views the soul as a natural phenomenon. The soul is defined as "an actuality of the first kind of a natural organized body" (412b4): that which makes the body alive and capable of performing its characteristic functions. Aristotle divides these into vegetative powers, concerned with nutrition and growth; sensory powers (that is, vision, hearing, taste, smell, and touch, as well as the internal senses of imagination and memory); and intellectual powers (understanding, assertion, and discursive thinking). In his broader taxonomy of life forms, these correspond to the souls of plants, brute animals, and human beings, respectively, with the higher forms subsuming the powers of those lower in the hierarchy (so brute animals are capable of nutrition and sensation but not understanding, whereas human beings exhibit all three capacities). Only the third capacity is relevant to the modern conception of mind, though it should be noted that this is far from being a dualist conception. Aristotle's intellect is a perfection of the organic unity of body and soul, and although he concedes that the activity of thinking is "separable, impassible, and unmixed" (430a17), thinking cannot occur without sensory images.

The Hellenistic period was a time of great philosophical activity, but unfortunately, most of the primary sources have been lost. Thankfully, scholars have managed to piece together some of what was said from fragments of texts and reports in the work of other philosophers. Three figures and their representative schools were especially important. Epicurus (341–270 B.C.E.) revitalized the materialist doctrine of earlier atomists such as

Democritus (470–360 B.C.E.), arguing that the soul is composed of extremely light and mobile atoms (thereby accounting for the spontaneity of sensation), whose unpredictable "swerves" are the source of human free choice. Particular features of living things result from the blending of soul atoms, of which there are four different types, each with its own psychological effect: fiery (bodily heat), air-like (rest), wind-like (movement), and a fourth, nameless atom responsible for sensation. The soul is also quickly dispersed at death, its atoms moving on to rain invisibly through the cosmos until joining together with other atoms to make new things. This led Epicurus to argue that "that most frightful of evils, death, is nothing to us, seeing that when we exist death is not present, and when death is present we do not exist" (*Letter to Menoeceus,* 124-25; Long and Sedley, 24A). Death is literally nothing to an Epicurean, though whether this is sufficient to dispel the fear of death remains an open question.

The Stoics were another Hellenistic school with a materialistic conception of the soul, though their theory was highly nuanced and more teleologically sophisticated than even Aristotle's. Rejecting the tripartite accounts of Plato and Aristotle, they held that the soul is unitary. As Chrysippus of Soli (c. 280–206 B.C.E.), one of the leading Stoics, explained, the soul is a mixture of air and fire (*pneuma*) whose "parts flow from their seat in the heart, as if from the source of a spring, and spread through the whole body. They continually fill all the limbs with vital breath, and rule and control them with countless different powers—nutrition, growth, locomotion, sensation, impulse to action" (Calcidius, *Commentary on Plato's Timaeus,* 220; Long and Sedley, 53G). Because their *pneuma* exists in a certain tension, animal souls can register sense impressions and initiate impulses (*hormē*), or move towards what they desire. Humans are higher still because they are capable of assenting to (or rejecting) these impressions. Assent is just rational impulse, "a movement of thought towards something in the sphere of action" (Stobaeus, 2.86, 17–87, 6; Long and Sedley, 53Q). Thus, words are sounds arising through our vocal apparatus from impulses in the heart, so that on the Stoic view, "language is sent out imprinted, and stamped as it were, by the conceptions present in thought" (Galen, *On Hippocrates' and Plato's Doctrines,* 2.5, 9–13; Long and Sedley, 53U).

Plato's teachings were refined throughout the Hellenistic period, culminating in the movement that later came to be known as Neoplatonism. Its foremost practitioner was Plotinus (205–270 C.E.), who offered an original synthesis of the Platonic and Aristotelian perspectives, advancing the former as the model of intelligible reality and the latter of sensible reality. There are three principles in his metaphysical system: the One, the utterly transcendent and unknowable source of everything in the universe; Intelligence or Mind (*nous*), which is where all eternal and necessary truths are actively thought; and Soul, which is the discursive manifestation of Mind's activity in lesser beings throughout the cosmos. Intellectual thinking is a quasi-mystical act through which we move beyond ourselves and our particular bodily circumstances to grasp eternal principles: "We are not separated from the One, not distant from it, even though bodily nature has closed about us and drawn us to itself" (*Enneads,* VI, 9.ix). From the Stoics,

Plotinus borrows the concept of "seminal reasons," or patterns implanted in Soul by Mind, which Soul then uses to produce the sensible world. This idea was later picked up by Christian thinkers such as St. Augustine of Hippo (354–430), who explains providence in terms of seminal reasons existing eternally in the mind of God.

Medieval Views

Two main factors shaped medieval thinking about the mind or soul. The first is religious doctrine. The idea that God freely created the world from nothing is absent from ancient Greek philosophy, but more or less definitive of medieval philosophy in all three monotheistic traditions: Christian, Islamic, and Jewish. In the Western or Christian tradition, it was expressed in terms of providence, the idea that creation is a product of God's wisdom and goodness, and that this is manifested in the orderly structure of the universe all the way down to its smallest details. Needless to say, it would have struck an ancient Greek philosopher as absurd that something could be made from nothing, or that a divinity—especially an omnipotent divinity—would care what happens to beings less powerful than it. But such doctrines changed the way the mind was understood, granting pride of place to the human soul and human modes of cognition. Since humans are made in God's image (Gen. 1:26), their own nature must in some way reflect the divine.

The second factor is simply physical access to ancient texts, which became more and more difficult in the West until direct knowledge of most Greek sources was lost for nearly six centuries. Philosophical psychology was especially hard hit, as none of the works mentioned above was available after the sixth century, and eventually only Aristotle's *De anima* was recovered in a form that could have any direct influence. This meant that medieval thinkers had to learn about ancient theories indirectly, via textbook summaries and discussions by early Church fathers who were trained in or otherwise influenced by pagan schools of philosophy. Platonic, Epicurean, Stoic, and Neo-Platonist doctrines went underground, as it were, and sometimes came to be defended by philosophers who were unaware of their true origins.

Augustine is the most important medieval philosopher in the sense that his teachings set the agenda in Western thought for the next millennium, including the kinds of questions that were asked about the soul. For Augustine, the human mind is the foremost expression of the truth of *Genesis* 1:26, and the doctrine of the Trinity provides the mode of resemblance. Just as God is three persons (Father, Son, and Spirit) in one being, so the mind is three aspects or activities in one substance: "Since then these three, memory, understanding, will, are not three lives but one life, nor three minds but one mind, it follows certainly that neither are they three substances but one substance" (*De trinitate* X, 11.18). It is possible that Descartes was influenced by Augustine's use of the Latin term *mens* or "mind" here (*anima* was used for the souls of living things more generally), except that Augustinian *mens* always has a dense layer of Neo-Platonic and Christian associations attached to it that would have certainly made Descartes cringe. Augustine also thought that because it is immediately present to itself, the mind knows itself and that in knowing itself, it knows God as well. There are remarkable similarities between Augustine's argument that a man who knows he is alive cannot be deceived about this fact (from *De trinitate* XV, 12.21), and Descartes's more famous anti-skeptical argument, the "I think; therefore, I am," of his *Meditations* II.

Some seven centuries after Augustine, philosophical psychology was transformed again by the reintroduction of Aristotle's *De anima* and the commentary tradition that surrounded it. Philosophers and theologians struggled to assimilate this new authority with Christian teaching on the soul, which by now had acquired its own authority in Augustine. St. Thomas Aquinas (c. 1224–1274) was perhaps the most successful at synthesizing pagan and Christian philosophical learning, especially in his magisterial *Summa theologiae,* a beautifully ordered compendium of theological teachings prepared for Dominican novices. The first part contains a series of fifteen "Questions" on human nature in which he defends the Aristotelian account of the soul as the first principle of the human body, and explains the soul's various powers and modes of operation. But he parts company with Aristotle on the question of the human soul's immortality (recall that Aristotle was willing to treat only the active part of the capacity of thinking as immortal). To allow for disembodied existence, Aquinas argues that the soul is a special kind of form because it is also a substance, and that it can therefore continue to exist after the death of the body. In fact, he claims that "a separated soul is in a way more free to use the intellect, insofar as the weight and distraction of the body keeps it from the pure operation of intellect" (*Summa theologiae* Ia, q.89, a.3). Much of his account of disembodied thinking is indebted to Augustine and Christian Neoplatonism. But Aquinas also subscribed to the Christian doctrine of the resurrection, according to which everyone's separated souls will be reunited with their (glorified and incorruptible) bodies at the Last Judgment. This forces him into the awkward position of arguing that despite its capacity to exist on its own in a purer and presumably higher state, it is somehow more natural for the soul to be united to the body.

After Aquinas, philosophers tended to be less optimistic about the prospects of uniting Athens and Jerusalem. Theories about the nature of the soul were trimmed almost to the vanishing point in favor of discussions of what the soul does, on the grounds that only the latter is naturally or empirically evident to us. Thus, John Buridan (1300–1358) argues that there is no philosophical knowledge of the soul, if by that one means the soul's essential nature, although one can know its faculties and operations. The notion that the human soul, something that is by definition immaterial and unextended, could inhere in a divisible and extended body, amazed him—he declared it "a miracle" (*mirabile*) (*Questions on Aristotle's* De anima II.9). That is, he believed it, but he did not regard it as knowledge. In this, of course, Buridan is well on the way to modernity, and to the modern distinction between faith and reason.

See also **Aristotelianism; Neoplatonism; Person, Idea of the; Platonism.**

BIBLIOGRAPHY

PRIMARY SOURCES

Aristotle. *The Complete Works of Aristotle: The Revised Oxford Translation.* Edited by Jonathan Barnes. Princeton, N.J.: Princeton University Press, 1984.

Augustine, St. *The Essential Augustine.* Edited by Vernon J. Bourke,. New York: New American Publishing, 1964.

Long, A. A., and D. N. Sedley. *The Hellenistic Philosophers.* 2 vols. New York: Cambridge University Press, 1987.

Plato. *The Collected Dialogues of Plato.* Edited by Edith Hamilton and Huntington Cairns. New York: Pantheon, 1961.

Plotinus. *The Enneads.* Translated by Stephen MacKenna and abridged by John Dillon. London: Penguin, 1991.

SECONDARY SOURCES

Des Chene, Dennis. *Life's Form: Late Aristotelian Conceptions of the Soul.* Ithaca, N.Y.: Cornell University Press, 2000.

Fitzgerald, Allan D., ed. *Augustine through the Ages: An Encyclopedia.* Grand Rapids, Mich.: Eerdmans, 1999.

Pasnau, Robert. *Thomas Aquinas on Human Nature: A Philosophical Study of* Summa theologiae Ia, 75-89. Cambridge, U.K.: Cambridge University Press, 2002.

Sorabji, Richard. *Emotion and Peace of Mind: From Stoic Agitation to Christian Temptation.* Oxford: Oxford University Press, 2000.

Zupko, Jack. *John Buridan: Portrait of a Fourteenth-Century Arts Master.* Notre Dame, Ind.: University of Notre Dame Press, 2003.

Jack Zupko

PHILOSOPHY OF RELIGION. A well-established discipline in early-twenty-first-century Western philosophy, the subject known as "the philosophy of religion" has not always been easily demarcated with respect to its nature and scope. The reason for this is historical. The long engagement of philosophy with the claims of religion has manifested itself from antiquity to the early twenty-first century in a wide variety of intellectual enquiries. Thus, early-twenty-first-century philosophers of religion address topics and analyze arguments that were earlier conceived as belonging to very different areas of philosophical thought. These topics and arguments once fell under the heads of what ancient Greek philosophers simply called philosophy (*philosophia*), of what patristic and medieval thinkers referred to as revealed teaching or theology (*sacra doctrina* and *theologia*), and of what philosophers in the modern period characterized as natural theology or "natural religion." Many of the questions of early-twenty-first-century philosophy of religion also fall within the traditional purview of subjects such as metaphysics and ethics. In themselves, these titles indicate very different views about how to address the questions that arise from the engagement of philosophy with religion and theology. For this reason it is difficult to sustain the idea that the "philosophy of religion" has always been a recognizable discipline with an unvarying subject matter that has spanned the course of Western philosophical history.

Changing Conceptions

The actual term "philosophy of religion" is itself a modern addition to the philosophical lexicon, being used sparingly in early modern times. One of the first occurrences in the English language can be found in the work of the Cambridge Platonist Ralph Cudworth (1617–1688), while toward the end of the eighteenth century the term *Religionsphilosophie* became part of an accepted terminology used by German-speaking philosophers. At this time, many thinkers sought to replace the previous idea of a "natural religion" with a "philosophy of religion," since the latter notion was deemed to bequeath a much more rigorous method of discovering truths about the nature and origin of religion. This conception of the subject received lucid exposition in Immanuel Kant's (1724–1804) *Religion within the Limits of Reason Alone* (1793). Building on his earlier demolition of the traditional proofs for the existence of God in the *Critique of Pure Reason* (1781, revised in 1787), Kant argues in this work that religion is not a matter of theoretical cognition but of moral disposition. Hence religion is to be understood as a moral outlook to observe all duties as divine commands.

By the early decades of the nineteenth century, however, the term had already changed its meaning. In Georg Wilhelm Friedrich Hegel's (1770–1831) famous *Lectures on the Philosophy of Religion* (1821–1831) the subject is defined as the study of the manner and ways in which God is represented in religious consciousness. What is interesting about the respective projects of Kant and Hegel is the gulf that separated their respective accounts of philosophical theology from more orthodox religious doctrines. Indeed such was the extent of these differences that, despite their very best intentions, many of their theories eventually lent themselves to forms of antitheistic skepticism. Given this, it is unsurprising that Kant and Hegel are followed by resolutely atheistic thinkers of whom Arthur Schopenhauer (1788–1860), Ludwig Feuerbach (1804–1872), Karl Marx (1818–1883), Friedrich Nietzsche (1844–1900), and Sigmund Freud (1856–1939) are the most prominent. Although the general drift toward atheism in Continental thought might be said to have been countered by the writings of thinkers such as Friedrich Schleiermacher (1768–1834) and Søren Kierkegaard (1813–1855), the inheritance of nontheistic philosophers who followed in the wake of Kant and Hegel was subsequently refined and extended in the twentieth century by figures such as Jean-Paul Sartre (1905–1980) and Martin Heidegger (1889–1976), whose own work yet further entrenched philosophical atheism in many areas of French- and German-speaking thought. In many ways, early-twenty-first-century philosophers of religion who look to these various traditions of so-called Continental philosophy can be said to explore and clarify questions about the nature and meaning of religion that go back to the very different legacies of Kant, Hegel, Nietzsche, and Freud.

Early-twenty-first-century English-speaking philosophers of religion, however, be they of theistic, agnostic, or atheistic orientation, can be said to adopt a quite different outlook on their subject. In opposition to Continental thought, they tend to characterize philosophy of religion as the critical analysis of certain concepts and issues deemed central to the study of monotheistic Western religions. An important stimulus to their work can be found in the trenchant critique of religion advanced by David Hume (1711–1776), specifically in his *Natural History of Religion* (1757) and *Dialogues Concerning*

Natural Religion (1779, but first written in the 1750s). For Hume the arguments of what he terms "natural religion" do not establish the existence of any deity that could be the proper object of religious belief. If revelation cannot be authenticated in any way conducive to reason, then religious beliefs can be deemed to have natural causes. Central to Hume's argument in the *Natural History of Religion* is the contention that the very origin of religious belief is to be found in numerous human pathologies that derive from a fear of the unknown. Hume's views have been typically regarded as providing a dialectical framework for modern English-speaking philosophy of religion. Accordingly, those who adhere to the claims of natural theology and traditional religion are supposed to address his intricate critique of their position, while those enamored of atheism invariably look to Hume's works as providing a paradigm for how to demonstrate that the claims of the theistic tradition are but a set of philosophical fictions.

Modern Conceptions

The modern subject of "philosophy of religion" continues to debate the legacy of Hume's broadside against theology. English-speaking philosophers of different persuasions still address a posteriori proofs for the existence of God such as cosmological arguments and arguments from design, while interest in the ontological argument—a specific object of Kant's wrath—shows no signs of fading. For much of the twentieth century many forces conspired to thwart the progress of those enamored of the project of responding to Kant's and Hume's critique. Predominant among these was the influence and legacy of logical positivism in both Great Britain and North America. The strict empiricism that was the hallmark of positivism launched a wide-ranging critique of traditional metaphysics by insisting that the subject matter of philosophy ought to be addressed by scientifically conditioned methods of inquiry. The collective penchant for empiricism in both Britain and America prompted philosophers like Rudolph Carnap (1891–1970) and Sir Alfred Jules Ayer (1910–1989) to argue that all religious claims are meaningless. In keeping with these tendencies, many philosophers of religion either sought to apply the methods of logical empiricism to their own discipline with the consequence that the subject became almost solely preoccupied with the topic of meaning in religious language, or else to fight a rearguard action to expose the inadequacies of the positivist position. Both of these strategies met with paltry success, as they failed to bring the philosophy of religion back within the mainstream of English-speaking philosophy.

With the move away from verificationism and the development of a greater pluralism in Anglophone philosophy, however, philosophers like Alvin Plantinga in the United States and Richard Swinburne in Britain set about the task of applying the rigorous standards of analytic philosophy to the discussion of traditional theological subjects. The effect of their work, particularly when combined with the historical studies of Anthony Kenny and Norman Kretzmann, was to increase the institutional profile of the subject in professional philosophy. However, the tremendous growth of the philosophy of religion in the English-speaking world is a phenomenon of the late twentieth century and is due in part to the establishment

of new journals and confessionally minded societies dedicated to the study of the discipline.

Much of the best late-twentieth- and early-twenty-first-century work in philosophy of religion has taken place in the subdivision of the subject then specified as "philosophical theology" and "religious epistemology." The first, which claims a distinguished ancestry in ancient and medieval philosophy, can be said to concern itself with issues focusing on the nature and coherence of our concept of God, and especially the manner in which God's attributes (omnipotence, omniscience, simplicity, eternity, and the like), can be defined so as to escape confusion and paradox. The second is concerned with the nature and justification of religious belief. Topics here have to do with whether or not it is ever reasonable to conclude that religious belief must always be justified by external evidence, or whether it is best to argue that religious belief is sui generis and quite different in form and structure from our more prosaic beliefs about the world. In this sphere many philosophers, following the lead of Plantinga, have argued that religious belief need not be beholden to canons of external evidence and have thereby debunked Hume's putative challenge to any rational justification of theistic belief. The effect of their writings has been to shift the focus of philosophy of religion away from natural theology, such as a strict attention to the a posteriori proofs for the existence of God, to a more general epistemological concern with the justification of religious belief. An important by-product of this change in emphasis has been the rehabilitation of the subject of religious experience as an area of pressing philosophical concern. The American philosopher William Alston, whose own approach to philosophy of religion can be said to steer a middle course between the work of Swinburne and Plantinga, can be credited with bringing this subject to the foreground of recent debate.

Alongside these important developments there has been a growing interest in religious pluralism and a greater philosophical attention to the claims of nonwestern religious traditions. As part of this general revival of the philosophy of religion, a number of philosophers whose main work lies in other areas have been attracted to the discipline. Thus, complex arguments about substance, space and time, free will, and determinism, which might be thought more properly at home in metaphysics, epistemology, philosophical logic, philosophy of mind, and philosophy of science, have all been explored with reference to the idea of God. At the turn of the twenty-first century, there are efforts to explore cross-cultural philosophies of religion, to articulate feminist challenges to traditional religions, and to consider many political, moral, and social problems from the standpoint of a religiously motivated ethics or political theory. Further to this, specific issues that are internal to religious traditions, such as monotheistic faiths like Judaism, Christianity, and Islam, are also receiving some coverage with increased philosophical effort being given to speculation on heaven, hell, atonement, the sacraments, and the meaning of prophesy and Scripture.

Philosophy of religion, then, might be said to have its place in English-speaking and Continental philosophy not only in the domain of the history of philosophy but also in areas of genuine and earnest philosophical debate. It is for this reason that the subject presents to the individual already acquainted with the traditional core of Western philosophy, namely logic, metaphysics, epistemology, and ethics, an opportunity to apply their philosophical learning to a set of important questions. Since "philosophy of religion," as its history testifies, is nothing more than a rich deposit of questions that have always belonged to the central core of subjects that have characterized the concerns of philosophers from antiquity onward, it could be said that to engage with it is to acquaint oneself with the basic questions of Western philosophy itself. In contrast with its dire fortunes at the outset of the twentieth century, philosophy of religion reveals itself, one hundred years later, to be a confident and sophisticated area of philosophy at ease with itself and its place within the philosophical curriculum.

See also **Continental Philosophy; Epistemology; Logic; Metaphysics; Philosophy and Religion in Western Thought; Philosophy of Mind; Religion.**

BIBLIOGRAPHY

Alston, William P. *Perceiving God: The Epistemology of Religious Experience.* Ithaca, N.Y.: Cornell University Press, 1991. Seminal treatment of religious experience by a leading epistemologist.

Kenny, Anthony. *The God of the Philosophers.* Oxford: Clarendon, 1979. A helpful guide to the medieval origins of many debates in contemporary philosophical theology.

Kretzmann, Norman. *The Metaphysics of Theism: Aquinas's Natural Theology in Summa contra gentiles I.* Oxford: Clarendon, 1997. An influential statement of the power and force of natural theology based on the work of Thomas Aquinas.

———. *The Metaphysics of Creation: Aquinas's Natural Theology in Summa contra gentiles II.* Oxford: Oxford University Press, 1999. The second installment of a planned trilogy left incomplete at Kretzmann's death.

Plantinga, Alvin. *Warranted Christian Belief.* New York and Oxford: Oxford University Press, 2000. Plantinga's definitive statement of his theory that theistic belief, specifically Christian belief, can enjoy warrant.

Plantinga, Alvin, and Nicholas Wolterstorff, eds. *Faith and Rationality: Reason and Belief in God.* Notre Dame, Ind.: University of Notre Dame Press, 1983. Influential anthology that initiated a move away from natural theology to questions of religious epistemology.

Swinburne, Richard. *The Coherence of Theism.* Oxford: Clarendon, 1977. The first installment of Swinburne's trilogy, which takes issue with the claim that religious discourse is meaningless.

———. *The Existence of God.* Oxford: Clarendon, 1979. The second volume, which uses the methods of Bayesian probability theory to advance a culminative case argument for the existence of God.

———. *Faith and Reason.* Oxford: Clarendon, 1981. The final volume of the trilogy that seeks to reinvigorate the traditional teaching about the compatibility of faith and reason by means of the arguments of analytic philosophy.

Westphal, Merold. *Overcoming Onto-Theology: Toward a Postmodern Christian Faith.* New York: Fordham University Press, 2001. An accessible guide to recent developments in "continental" philosophy of religion.

Martin Stone

PHRENOLOGY. Phrenology, a science popular from the early to the mid-nineteenth century, was dedicated to the discernment of one's character or traits of personality from reading—that is, feeling the shape and size of—the bumps on one's skull. As formulated by the German physician and anatomist Franz Josef Gall (1758–1828) and as popularized by his student and follower Johann Gaspar Spurzheim (1776–1832), phrenology was based on five main tenets: (1) the brain is the organ of the mind—mental activity is produced by the structure and function of the brain, not through some spiritual or immaterial process; (2) the brain is not unitary but a congeries, or collection, of separate faculties; (3) these faculties are localized in different regions of the brain; (4) the activity of a mental faculty determines the size of the brain organ that represents it; and (5) the skull ossifies over the brain during infant development, so that an external examination of the size and shape of the bumps on the skull will reveal the size of the underlying brain organs. A staunchly materialistic doctrine, phrenology held that each mental faculty, envisioned by Gall as an innate instinct, produced a striking behavior or characteristic. Each innate mental faculty was in turn produced by its underlying brain organ, whose size depended on its activity and which could be revealed by its corresponding cranial bump.

Origins and Development

Gall was born in Baden, Germany, and studied medicine in Strasbourg and Vienna, where he established a successful medical practice and became renowned as a comparative anatomist. In the 1790s he began to develop the principles of phrenology out of his observations of his fellow students—those with protuberant eyes, he noted, had particularly good memories—and of animals, as well as from dissection of human and animal brains. He also amassed a large collection of skulls, both human and animal, and busts, to support his theory. His method, however, depended on anecdote and striking confirmation rather than rigorous experimental testing of his theory. In Vienna, Gall lectured on phrenology as a "craniologist," but by 1805, joined by Spurzheim, he traveled around Europe to spread his ideas, eventually settling in Paris. There, between 1810 and 1819, he and Spurzheim published the four volumes and atlas of 100 engraved plates of *Anatomy and Physiology of the Nervous System . . . with Observations on the Possibility of Identifying Many Intellectual and Moral Dispositions of Men and Animals by the Configuration of Their Heads.* In addition to propounding the principles of phrenology, the work constituted a major contribution to cerebral anatomy.

Gall identified twenty-seven basic mental faculties, each correlated with a brain organ: faculties such as veneration, wonder, wit, tune, memory, language, cautiousness, secretiveness, and philoprogenitiveness (love of children). He rejected the notion that the mind was a tabula rasa—a blank slate—and emphasized that each of these mental faculties was inherited as an innate instinct. He and the phrenologists who followed him tended to be interested in differences between individuals as well as between groups. Men and women, for example, were thought to possess different types of faculties.

Spurzheim, however, parted ways with his mentor, changing the content and focus of Gall's science in several

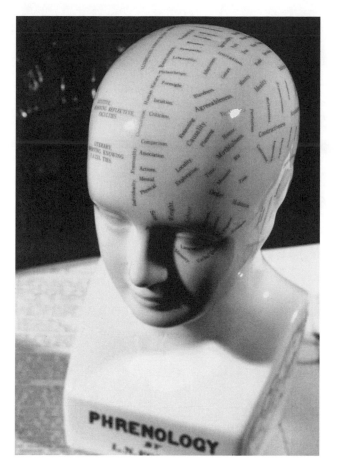

Phrenological bust for mapping areas of the skull. The science of phrenology reached its apex during the early 1830s and began its eventual decline approximately a decade later. Adherents were still numerous in the late nineteenth century, especially in the United States and Britain. PHOTO RESEARCHERS, INC.

important ways. First, Spurzheim actually coined the term *phrenology,* distinguishing it from physiognomy (reading character from the face) and craniology (measurement of the skull), thereby establishing its claim as a new science. Second, Spurzheim shifted the emphasis of phrenology from anatomy, which was Gall's main interest, to the religious, moral, and philosophical aspects of the science and to its political and social applications and consequences, a move that laid the groundwork for its popularity. He added new mental faculties to Gall's original twenty-seven and grouped the faculties into two major categories: feelings, including propensities and sentiments, and intellectual faculties, of perceptive and reflective kinds. Finally, Spurzheim abandoned Gall's emphasis on the innateness of the faculties and promulgated phrenology as a doctrine of self-help instead of determinism. In Spurzheim's formulation, education and exercise were the means to build up, train, or control the mental faculties and brain organs, and it was this more optimistic view that became part and parcel of popular phrenology. Leaving aside Gall's notion that human beings possessed such evil faculties as murder, Spurzheim promulgated the notion that people were intrinsically good and could be perfected through the practice of phrenology, altering their mental faculties through exercise.

To spread phrenological doctrine, Spurzheim traveled to Britain, where he met George Combe (1788–1858), a lawyer and moral philosopher in Edinburgh. Spurzheim's teachings converted Combe to phrenology, and he helped to popularize the science in Britain and North America. In 1828 Combe published *The Constitution of Man Considered in Relation to External Objects,* a work that formed the basis for orthodox phrenology and that developed Spurzheim's connection between phrenology, self-help, and social reform. At the height of phrenology's popularity in the early 1830s, there were more than two dozen phrenological societies in Britain alone. Numerous books, lecture series, and journals were devoted to the science, including the *Phrenological Journal,* which Combe edited in Edinburgh from 1832 to 1847. Thousands of serious believers espoused the doctrine, from the eminent doctors and scientists of the day to famous literary and cultural figures. Phrenology became central to the sociology and psychology of Herbert Spencer, the evolutionary science of Robert Chambers and Alfred Russel Wallace, and the anthropology of James Hunt and Paul Broca. Because of its associations with social and political reform, phrenology surged in popularity among the less educated classes as well.

Decline

As it became increasingly popularized and vulgarized, phrenology fell into disrepute and by the 1840s was discredited by most physiologists. The increasing demand for phrenologists' services in assessment of character allowed charlatans to flourish as head readers, undermining the scientific integrity of the doctrine. Disunity and splits within the movement itself, antagonism from the religious establishment on account of its perceived materialism, and new discoveries about brain function in neuroanatomy and physiology all helped to push phrenology to the margins of science. In the second half of the nineteenth century, however, its popularity remained strong, especially in Britain and the United States. In America, for example, the entrepreneurial Fowler brothers, Lorenzo and Orson, established a successful business in character advice based on phrenological principles and sold china busts, models of the head marked with the divisions of the various phrenological faculties, that became popular among collectors. Phrenology also became associated with other popular psychological movements: in the combination of phrenology and mesmerism known as phreno-mesmerism, when the practitioner touched various parts of the subject's head, the subject evinced the traits supposedly connected to the underlying brain organs. Such continuing popular uses for phrenology show that it maintained its place in drawing room and parlor throughout the nineteenth century, even if it had lost scientific sanction.

Phrenology was relegated to the status of pseudoscience for political and social reasons as well as scientific ones. As medicine and the sciences of anatomy and physiology diversified and professionalized in the late nineteenth century, there was no longer any room in them for the kind of informally trained practitioner that many a popular phrenologist represented.

Meanwhile, the work in localization of function in the brain, associated with Broca and with the German researchers Gustav Fritsch and Eduard Hitzig, while seemingly returning to Gall's principles, actually disputed them by localizing not complex mental faculties but much simpler sensory and motor functions. But debate over the extent and type of localization of brain function—a debate that phrenology can be understood to have started—continued throughout the twentieth century and is still not entirely settled.

See also **Anthropology; Philosophy of Mind; Pseudoscience.**

BIBLIOGRAPHY

Combe, George. *The Constitution of Man Considered in Relation to External Objects.* Edinburgh: Anderson, 1828.

Cooter, Roger. *The Cultural Meaning of Popular Science: Phrenology and the Organization of Consent in Nineteenth-Century Britain.* New York: Cambridge University Press, 1984.

————. *Phrenology in the British Isles: An Annotated Historical Bibliography and Index.* Metuchen, N.J.: Scarecrow Press, 1989.

De Giustino, David. *Conquest of Mind: Phrenology and Victorian Social Thought.* London: Croom, Helm; and Totowa, N.J.: Rowman and Littlefield, 1975.

Gall, Franz Josef. *On the Functions of the Brain and Each of Its Parts.* Translated by Winslow Lewis Jr. Boston: Marsh, Capen, and Lyon, 1835.

Shapin, Steven. "Homo Phrenologicus: Anthropological Perspectives." In *Natural Order: Historical Studies of Scientific Culture,* edited by Barry Barnes and Steven Shapin. Beverly Hills, Calif.: Sage, 1979.

Spurzheim, Johann Gaspar. *Phrenology, or the Doctrine of the Mental Phenomena.* Boston: Marsh, Capen, and Lyon, 1833.

Young, Robert M. *Mind, Brain, and Adaptation in the Nineteenth Century: Cerebral Localization and Its Biological Context from Gall to Ferrier.* Oxford: Clarendon, 1970.

Nadine Weidman